R. Gupta's®

POPULAR MASTER GUIDE

DSSSB

Delhi Subordinate Services Selection Board

Nursing Officer
Staff Nurse
Nurse Grade-A

Recruitment Exam

by

RPH Editorial Board

2027
EDITION

RAMESH PUBLISHING HOUSE, NEW DELHI

Published by
O.P. Gupta *for* Ramesh Publishing House

Admin. Office
12-H, New Daryaganj Road, Opp. Officers' Mess,
New Delhi-110002 ✆ 23275224, 23245124

E-mail: info@rameshpublishinghouse.com
For Online Shopping: www.rameshpublishinghouse.com

Showroom
• Balaji Market, Nai Sarak, Delhi-110006 ✆ 23282525 📱 9354373464
• 4457, Nai Sarak, Delhi-110006

Book Code: R-1208

ISBN: 978-93-87918-41-2

Price: ₹ 560

Printed at: Rajdhani Offset, Delhi

CONTENTS

SELECTION PROCESS

There will be Tier-I Examination comprising 200 Objective Multiple Choice Questions (MCQs) in two sections:

SECTION-A

It will comprise 100 MCQs of one mark each from the following:

S. No.	Subject	Marks
1.	General Awareness	20
2.	General Intelligence & Reasoning Ability	20
3.	Arithmetical & Numerical Ability	20
4.	Test of Hindi Language & Comprehension	20
5.	Test of English Language & Comprehension	20
	Total Marks	**100**

SECTION-B

It will comprise 100 MCQs of one mark each from the subject concerned (Nursing)	**100**

NOTE: Negative Marking will be applicable and deduction of 0.25 mark will be made for each wrong MCQ answer.

Previous Years' Paper

Delhi Subordinate Services Selection Board (DSSSB)

Nursing Officer Exam 2025

(Exam held on 04-07-2025)

General Intelligence and Reasoning Ability

1. K is the husband of L. M is the daughter of K. N is the sister of M. O is the brother of L. How is O related to N?

1. Brother
2. Mother's father
3. Mother's brother
4. Husband

2. Read the given statements and conclusions carefully. Assuming that the information given in the statements is true, even if it appears to be at variance with commonly known facts, decide which of the given conclusion(s) logically follow(s) from the statements.

Statements:

All lions are tigers.

Some tigers are bears.

No bear is a deer.

Conclusions:

I. No lion is a deer.

II. Some bears are lions.

1. Neither conclusion (I) nor (II) follows.
2. Both conclusions (I) and (II) follow.
3. Only conclusion (II) follows.
4. Only conclusion (I) follows.

3. In a certain code language, 'LORD' is coded as '2618' and 'ROAD' is coded as '6287'. What is the code for 'L' in the given code language?

1. 8
2. 7
3. 2
4. 1

4. Refer to the following number and symbol series and answer the question that follows. Counting to be done from left to right only.

(Left) * * 1 3 2 £ & $ 6 $ 2 5 1 5 6 7 1 € * 1 @ 5 (Right)

How many such symbols are there that are immediately preceded by a number and also immediately followed by a symbol?

1. 2
2. 3
3. 1
4. 4

5. Select the triad that follows the same pattern as that followed by the two triads given below. Both triads follow the same pattern.

(NOTE: Operations should be performed on the whole numbers, without breaking down the numbers into their constituent digits. E.g. 13 – Operations on 13 such as adding/subtracting/multiplying to 13 can be performed. Breaking down 13 into 1 and 3 and then performing mathematical operations on 1 and 3 is not allowed.)

11 - 3 - 14

4 - 6 - 10

1. 55 - 4 - 60
2. 67 - 3 - 71
3. 9 - 4 - 12
4. 40 - 50 - 90

6. E, F, G, H, I, and J live on six different floors of the same building. The lowermost floor in the building is numbered 1, the floor above it, number 2 and so on till the topmost floor is numbered 6. Only four people live between F and E. J lives immediately below G. H lives on an even numbered floor but not on floor number 6. I lives on an odd numbered floor. F lives on the uppermost floor. G lives on floor 5, J lives on floor 4. Who lives on floor number 3?

1. E   2. I
3. H   4. F

7. In a certain code language, 'BORN' is coded as '3628' and 'BONE' is coded as '6318'. What is the code for 'R' in the given code language?

1. 6   2. 1
3. 2   4. 3

8. If the water source is placed along X-Y, as shown in the figure, which of the given options will be the water reflection of the given figure.

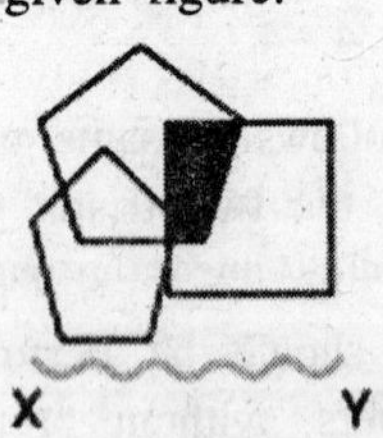

1. 
2. 
3. 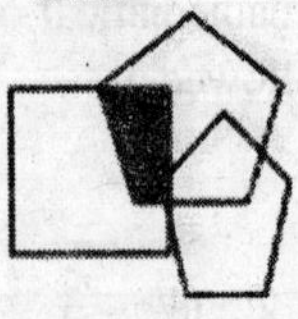
4. 

9. Each of D, E, F, I, J, K and S has an exam on a different day of a week starting from Monday and ending on Sunday of the same week. Only two people have an exam after F. Only two people have an exam between D and F. Only four people have an exam between J and D. K has an exam immediately after I. S does not have an exam on Monday. How many people have an exam before S and after E?

1. Three   2. One
3. Two   4. Four

10. Three of the following four numbers are alike in a certain way and thus form a group. Which is the one that does NOT belong to that group?

(Note: Operations should be performed on the whole numbers, without breaking down the numbers into their constituent digits. E.g. 13 – Operations on 13 such as adding/subtracting/multiplying to 13 can be performed. Breaking down 13 into 1 and 3 and then performing mathematical operations on 1 and 3 is not allowed.)

14 - 5 - 19
23 - 20 - 43

1. 15 - 9 - 26   2. 5 - 10 - 20
3. 6 - 2 - 8   4. 14 - 7 - 22

11. Based on the English alphabetical order, three of the following four letter-cluster pairs are alike in a certain way and thus form a group. Which letter-cluster pair DOES NOT belong to that group?

(Note: The odd one out is not based on the number of consonants/vowels or their position in the letter-cluster.)

1. JI-ZS   2. WX-MK
3. NO-DB   4. YZ-OM

12. What should come in place of the question mark (?) in the given series?

4 7 20 43 76 ?

1. 99   2. 119
3. 123   4. 109

13. If 'A' stands for '÷', 'B' stands for '×', 'C' stands for '+' and 'D' stands for '−', then what will come in place of the question mark (?) in the following equation?

365 B 3 D 525 A 5 C 172 = ?

1. 1425   2. 1162
3. 1812   4. 1536

14. Based on the English alphabetical order, three of the following four letter-cluster pairs are alike in a certain way and thus form a group. Which letter-cluster pair DOES NOT belong to that group?

(Note: The odd one out is not based on the number of consonants/vowels or their position in the letter-cluster.)

1. MJ - KH 2. FI - HG
3. WT - UR 4. RO - PM

15. What should come in place of the question mark (?) in the given series?

14 16 28 50 ? 124

1. 82 2. 88
3. 64 4. 94

16. Select the triad that follows the same pattern as that followed by the two triads given below. Both triads follow the same pattern.

EI-FJ-HK
MQ-NR-PS

1. QX-RV-TU 2. SV-YZ-TU
3. QU-RV-TW 4. SX-WV-TU

17. In the following triads, each group of letters is related to the subsequent one following a certain logic. Select from the given options, the one which follows the same logic.

TAPE – APTE – ETAP
HUNT - UNHT TIIUN

1. RATE – TERA – TREA
2. SINK – INKS – KISN
3. CAMP – AMCP – CAPM
4. POND – ONPD – DPON

18. What will come in the place of the question mark (?) in the following equation, if '+' and '−' are interchanged and '×' and '÷' are interchanged?

$180 \times 4 - 3 + 3 \div 9 = ?$

1. 30 2. 21
3. 33 4. 18

19. Refer to the following letter series and answer the question that follows.

(Left) V J D G B A U X E S Q C H M F W N L Z O P (Right)

How many letters are there in the English alphabetical series between the letter which is second from the right end and second from the left end of the series?

1. Six 2. Five
3. Four 4. Seven

20. Seven people J, K, L, M, P, Q, and R are sitting in a straight line facing north. Only R sits to the right of L. Only two people sit between J and P. Only two people sit between P and R. K sits at some place to the right of M but at some place to the left of Q. How many people sit between M and Q?

1. Three 2. One
3. Four 4. Two

General Awareness

21. When was the Dogri language added in the Eighth Schedule of the Constitution of India?

1. 2015 2. 2001
3. 2004 4. 1998

22. What does the concept of opportunity cost refer to in the context of production?

1. The financial expenses incurred in production
2. The cost of the next best alternative foregone
3. The total cost of materials used in production
4. The cost of labour only

23. Which of the following options best defines profit in the context of business?

1. The total income generated from selling goods or services

2. The total value of assets owned by a business
3. The total expenses incurred by a business
4. The difference between total revenue and total expenses

24. Which of the following cricketers is the author of the book 'I Have the Streets: A Kutti Cricket Story'?

1. R Ashwin 2. Anil Kumble
3. VVS Laxman 4. MS Dhoni

25. Allicin is present in:

1. potato 2. ginger
3. tomato 4. garlic

26. For how many days is the Pitru Paksha observed in India, which is dedicated to departed souls?

1. 13 2. 5
3. 9 4. 16

27. Which of the following Chinese travellers visited the Gupta Kingdom and gave an account of the life of the people living there?

1 Mao-Chuang 2. Huen-Tsang
3. Fa-Hsien 4. I-Tsing

28. What is the primary objective of the Amrit Sarovar initiative launched by the Government of India?

1. To develop smart cities with water-efficient infrastructure
2. To create inland water transport corridors for freight
3. To construct/renovate at least 75 ponds in each district to improve water availability
4. To build 75 water theme parks in urban areas

29. Writ Jurisdiction of the High Courts is mentioned in which of the following Articles of the Indian Constitution?

1. Article 75 2. Article 229
3. Article 226 4. Article 78

30. Who among the following founded the revolutionary organisation 'Mitra Mela' in Nashik?

1. Mahadeva Vinayak Ranade
2. Balkrishna Hari Chapekar
3. Vasudev Balwant Phadke
4. Vinayak Damodar Savarkar

31. As of March 2025, what type of engine is ISRO developing that uses liquid oxygen and kerosene as propellants?

1. Solid rocket engine
2. Ion propulsion engine
3. Hybrid engine
4. Semicryogenic engine

32. Which of the following pairs of the physiographic divisions of India and related features is INCORRECT?

1. The Himalaya – Kamet Peak
2. The Coastal Plains – Nallamala Hills
3. The Peninsular Plateau – Ajanta Range
4. The Northern Plain – Tarai Region

33. On the basis of provisions of the Government of India Act, 1919, and the recommendations of the Lee Commission in 1924, the Public Service Commission was established in the year _____.

1 1926 2. 1925
3. 1929 4. 1930

34. The _______ people from the Kalahandi district in Odisha celebrate 'Chhatar Jatra' by worshipping their family Goddess, Maa Manikeswari.

1. Bhumia 2. Koya
3. Khond 4. Bonda

35. Which of the following places in India experiences a cold desert climate?

1. Kolkata 2. Ladakh
3. Mumbai 4. Chennai

36. Who among the following is authorised by the Constitution to suspend the Fundamental Rights?

1. Governor 2. President of India
3. Law Minister 4. Prime Minister

37. The Jal Shakti ministry, along with the ______ ministry, approved an action plan for river rejuvenation in 145 cities, located along different rivers across the country, in April 2025.

1. Ministry of Environment, Forest and Climate Change
2. Ministry of Housing and Urban Affairs
3. Ministry of Rural Development
4. Ministry of Agriculture & Farmers Welfare

38. According to Census 2011, what is the child sex ratio of India?

1. 941 2. 919
3. 963 4. 939

39. Which of the following animals is classified under the class Reptilia?

1. Fish 2. Sea horse
3. Frog 4. Snake

40. Hiuen Tsang visited India during the reign of:

1. Mahendravarman-I
2. King Harshavardhana
3. King Prabhakar Vardhana
4. King Pushyabhuti

Arithmetical and Numerical Ability

41. Find the simple interest (in ₹) on ₹ 2,000 at 5.25% per annum rate of interest for the period from 6 February 2023 to 20 April 2023.

1. 21 2. 20
3. 22 4. 19

42. The price of a television increases by 40% and after one month decreases by 20%. What is the net percentage change in the price?

1. 12% increase 2. 10% increase
3. 12% decrease 4. 10% decrease

43. A and B can do a piece of work in 5 days and 20 days, respectively. The number of days required to complete the work if both A and B work together is:

1. 4 2. 3
3. 5 4. 2

44. If the mean proportional of P and 81 is 54, then find the value of P.

1. 36 2. 35
3. 33 4. 37

45. A shopkeeper purchases a PC for ₹ 34,000 and sells it for ₹ 38,200. What is the percentage profit? (Rounded off to two decimal places.)

1. 16.55% 2. 10.35%
3. 14.55% 4. 12.35%

46. If p is an integer, and when $(8p + 8)^2$ is divided by 64, the remainder is:

1. 12 2. 13
3. 4 4. 0

47. The radius of the base and the slant height of a right circular cone are in the ratio of 9 : 14. If the curved surface area of the cone is 1584 cm^2, find the radius of the base of the cone. (Use $\pi = 22/7$)

1. 18 cm
2. 36 cm
3. 27 cm
4. 9 cm

48. Sachin buys a mobile phone for ₹ 24,000 and sells it two years later for ₹ 20,000. What is the percentage loss? (Round up to two decimal places.)

1. 16.67% 2. 18.34%
3. 19.34% 4. 17.67%

49. Find the area of a regular hexagon whose longest diagonal is 4 m.

1. $4\sqrt{3}\ m^2$ 2. $5\sqrt{3}\ m^2$
3. $6\sqrt{3}\ m^2$ 4. $7\sqrt{3}\ m^2$

50. If a student scores 86 on a test that carries a weight of 40% and 72 on another test that carries a weight of 60%, what is his weighted average score?

1. 77.6 2. 81.6
3. 78.6 4. 78.4

51. Rohit deposited a certain amount of money in a bank. He received ₹ 208 as compound interest, compounded annually in the second year, at the rate of 4% per annum. What is the amount he deposited?

1. ₹ 6,000 2. ₹ 8,000
3. ₹ 5,000 4. ₹ 10,000

52. The following table shows the number of candidates who appeared (A) and qualified (Q) in an examination from States P, N, R, and S from 2016 to 2019. Study the table and answer the question:

States	Years							
	2016		2017		2018		2019	
	A	Q	A	Q	A	Q	A	Q
P	250	157	340	285	405	224	332	315
N	260	180	150	120	369	250	420	381
R	490	320	280	200	446	348	567	444
S	570	460	370	358	320	306	391	348

The total number of candidates who qualified from all the states together in 2016 and 2018 is what percentage (rounded off to one decimal place) of the total number of candidates who appeared from all the states together in 2017 and 2019?

1. 55.9% 2. 78.8%
3. 87.6% 4. 62.7%

53. The population of a country grows by 1.2% during the first year and by 1.6% during the second year. What is the total percentage increase (rounded off to two decimal places) in the population after two years?

1. 2.82% 2. 2.92%
3. 2.98% 4. 2.89%

54. A pipe can fill a tank in 8 hours, but there is a leakage that can empty the tank in 12 hours. If both the pipe and leakage are functioning simultaneously, how long will it take to fill the tank?

1. 16 hours 2. 12 hours
3. 20 hours 4. 24 hours

55. A laptop is marked at ₹ 61,500. Two successive discount of 10% and 20% are given. What is the final selling price of laptop?

1. ₹ 44,820 2. ₹ 44,208
3. ₹ 44,802 4. ₹ 44,280

56. A man travels from point A to B at a speed of 52 km/hr and returns to A through the same route by increasing his speed by 60% of his earlier speed. His average speed (in km/hr) for the whole journey is:

1. 69 2. 61
3. 64 4. 62

57. The average of 8 numbers is 12. If one of the numbers is removed, and the new average is 11, what is the value of the removed number?

1. 20 2. 22
3. 19 4. 21

58. The decimal 5.2333... is equal to which of the following vulgar fractions?

1. $\frac{157}{31}$ 2. $\frac{177}{30}$
3. $\frac{157}{30}$ 4. $\frac{457}{90}$

59. Two trains are moving in opposite directions at speeds of 50 km/hr and 90 km/hr. The length of one train is 500 m. The time taken by them to cross each other is 17 seconds. The length (in m) of the other train, correct to 2 decimal places, is:

1. 159.87 2. 161.11
3. 161.36 4. 160.92

60. ₹ 60,800 was divided among A, B and C such that 8 times of A = 6 times of B = 3 times of C. Find the share of A.

1. ₹ 12,028 2. ₹ 12,160
3. ₹ 12,183 4. ₹ 12,359

English Language and Comprehension

61. Select the most appropriate adverb to fill the blank in the given sentence.

Even though they spoke _____, nervousness stayed in the room.

1. clumsily
2. sarcastically
3. awkwardly
4. calmly

62. Sentences of a paragraph are given below in jumbled order. Arrange the sentences in the correct order to form a meaningful and coherent paragraph.

P. Faced with uncertainty, a decisive leader evaluates options and commits to a course of action, even when the path is unclear.

Q. Ultimately, a leader's success is not just measured by individual achievements but by the collective growth and success of their team.

R. This vision involves not only setting ambitious goals but also inspiring and motivating team members to collectively pursue them.

S. Effective leadership, at its core, hinges on the ability to cultivate a clear and compelling vision for the future.

1. PQRS
2. RPSQ
3. SRPQ
4. QPSR

63. Select the INCORRECTLY spelt word.

1. Ephimeral
2. Cacophony
3. Diaphanous
4. Ameliorate

64. Select the most appropriate one-word substitute for the given group of words.

A person who is devoted to the pursuit of pleasure and self-indulgence.

1. Ascetic
2. Hedonist
3. Puritan
4. Stoic

65. Select the most appropriate ANTONYM of the given word.

Deceptive

1. Straightforward
2. Precise
3. Persuasive
4. Enthusiastic

66. Select the most appropriate ANTONYM of the given word.

Beguile

1. Enchant
2. Guide
3. Bore
4. Mislead

67. Select the most appropriate adjective to fill in the blank.

She had a _____ voice, due to which she was often misunderstood.

1. loud
2. loudest
3. louder
4. loudly

68. Select the most appropriate option to fill in the blank.

You may attend the seminar, _____ you submit your registration by Friday.

1. since
2. provided that
3. although
4. unless

69. Select the most appropriate meaning of the given idiom.

Off the hook

1. Get out of trouble
2. Get punished
3. Get a responsibility
4. Get trapped

70. Sentences of a paragraph are given below in jumbled order. Arrange the sentences in the correct order to form a meaningful and coherent paragraph.

A. In chasing perfection, he had built walls so high that not even the people who cared most about him could peer over them.

B. For years, he believed that excellence required isolation — a fortress where vulnerability was banished in the name of discipline.

C. But somewhere along the way, silence became suffocating, and the echo of his own thoughts began to sound less like wisdom and more like loneliness.

D. Now, staring at the empty seat beside him, he realized that success had never asked for solitude — that perhaps, it was he who misinterpreted the cost.

1. D → B → A → C
2. B → C → A → D
3. B → A → C → D
4. A → B → D → C

71. Identify the MISSPELT word in the given sentence.

It is a punishable offense to enter the station premises without a valid ticket or at least a plateform ticket.

1. Offense 2. Premises
3. Plateform 4. Punishable

72. Select the most appropriate option to fill in the blank.

She _____ to improve her performance by attending additional training sessions.

1. striving 2. striven
3. strives 4. strive

73. Select the option that can be used as a one-word substitute for the underlined group of words/phrase in the sentence below.

I can't leave him alone in his apartment. He has <u>a fear of being alone</u>.

1. xenophobia 2. agoraphobia
3. aquaphobia 4. monophobia

74. Select the most appropriate option to fill in the blank. Select 'No article required' if no article is required in the blank.

The musician cherished _____ violin that once belonged to his late grandfather.

1. the
2. a
3. No article required
4. an

75. Select the most appropriate option to fill in the blanks.

He gave me _____ honest review of my book, which came as _____ surprise considering our last interaction.

1. a, an 2. an, a
3. an, an 4. a, a

Directions (Qs. No. 76 to 80): *Read the given passage and answer the questions that follow.*

Brights Zoo in Limestone, Tennessee is celebrating the birth of a very unusual baby giraffe. What makes this giraffe special is that it doesn't have any spots. The zoo is asking for help from the public to name the unique animal.

Tall, long-necked giraffes are famous for their spots. The spots are believed to help the animals hide from their enemies. The skin beneath the spots may also help giraffes stay at the right temperature. Just like no two humans have the same fingerprints, each giraffe has its own special pattern of spots.

Unless, of course, it doesn't have any spots. On 31 July, a baby giraffe was born at Brights Zoo with no spots at all. Instead, its fur is a light brown. The giraffe is a reticulated giraffe, which is one of the four different kinds of giraffes. It was born perfectly healthy. It just doesn't have any spots.

76. Based on the passage, why are giraffes' spots important?

1. They are used to attract mate.
2. They help giraffes see in the dark.
3. They determine the giraffe's species.
4. They help giraffes blend in and regulate their body temperature.

77. What would be the most appropriate title for this passage?

1. A Rare Spotless Giraffe Born at Brights Zoo
2. Reticulated Giraffes: The Most Common Species

3. The Struggles of Newborn Giraffes
4. Giraffes and Their Spot Patterns

78. Where was the spotless giraffe born?
1. Brights Zoo, Tennessee
2. San Diego Zoo, California
3. Bronx Zoo, New York
4. Miami Zoo, Florida

79. What is the closest synonym of the word 'unique' as used in the passage?
1. Ordinary
2. Common
3. Unusual
4. Average

80. What is the colour of the baby giraffe's fur?
1. Dark brown with spots
2. Golden with patches
3. Light brown
4. Grey and white

हिन्दी भाषा और बोध

81. निम्न में से सर्वोचित अपूर्ण क्रिया शब्द से वाक्य का रिक्त स्थान पूर्ण करें:

सुरेश गीत गा ______ जबकि गीता सो रही थी।

1. रहा था 2. चुका था
3. चुकेगा 4. रहा है

82. 'दाँतों तले उँगली दबाना' लोकोक्ति का अर्थ क्या है?
1. बदनामी करना
2. एक जैसा स्वभाव होना
3. आश्चर्यचकित रह जाना
4. समय का दुरुपयोग करना

83. निम्नलिखित में से 'व्याल' का पर्यायवाची शब्द कौन-सा है?
1. साँप 2. मेंढ़क
3. मछली 4. पक्षी

84. निम्नलिखित शब्दों तथा वाक्यांशों को क्रमानुसार व्यवस्थित कर एक सार्थक वाक्य बनाने वाले विकल्प का चयन कीजिए:
1. दूसरी कुंजी 2. से नहीं खुलता
3. यह ताला 4. किसी

1. 1, 2, 4, 3 2. 4, 1, 2, 3
3. 3, 4, 1, 2 4. 4, 1, 3, 2

85. तुम आजकाल कहाँ रहते हो?

उपरोक्त दिए गए वाक्य के किस भाग में वर्तनी संबंधी अशुद्धि है?

1. आजकाल 2. कहाँ
3. रहते हो 4. तुम

86. वाक्य विन्यास की दृष्टि से निम्न में से शुद्ध वाक्य का चयन करें।
1. मुझे टमाटर का गर्म सूप पीना अच्छा लगता है।
2. मुझे टमाटर का सूप गर्म पीना अच्छा लगता है।
3. मुझे टमाटर का गर्म सूप पीना लगता है अच्छा।
4. टमाटर का गर्म सूप पीना अच्छा लगता है मुझे।

87. 'जो सबको समान भाव से समझता देखता हो'

उपरोक्त दिए गए वाक्यांश के लिए एक सार्थक शब्द का चुनाव करें:
1. समदर्शी
2. समर्थित
3. समानार्थी
4. समर्पित

88. दिए गए विकल्पों में से तद्भव शब्द की पहचान करें:
1. गौरी 2. मयूर
3. हाथी 4. हस्ती

89. निम्नलिखित वाक्य में उचित विशेषण का प्रयोग कर वाक्य पूर्ण करें:

'लड़के खेल रहे हैं'

1. आगामी 2. वर्तमान
3. प्राचीन 4. कुछ

90. दिए गये वाक्यों में से शुद्ध वर्तनी वाले वाक्य का चयन कीजिए।

1. इस सभा के पदाधिकारियों का चुनाव है।
2. इस सभा के पधाधिकारियों का चुनाव है।
3. इस सभा के पदाधिकारियों का चुनाब है।
4. इस सभा के पदधिकारियों का चुनाव है।

91. 'किसी देश के मंत्रियों में सबसे बड़ा'

उपरोक्त दिए गए वाक्यांश के लिए एक सार्थक शब्द का चुनाव करें:

1. मंत्रीगण
2. प्रमुख
3. प्रमेय
4. प्रधानमंत्री

92. 'अड्डे पर चहकना' मुहावरे का सही अर्थ क्या है?

1. बहुत गुस्सा करना
2. अपने घर पर रोब दिखाना
3. पीछे पड़ना
4. तुरंत भाग जाना

93. नीचे दिए गए चार विकल्पों में से कोई एक उचित कारक का चुनाव कर वाक्य पूर्ण करें।

दौड़ कर जाओ और कुछ खाने ______ ले आओ।

1. पर
2. ने
3. के लिए
4. भे

94. 'हंस' शब्द के अनेक अर्थों में से निम्न में से एक अर्थ है:

1. पक्षी
2. यमराज
3. अंश
4. जीवात्मा

95. 'तरिणी' शब्द का अर्थ है:

1. नदी
2. तम्बू
3. ताल
4. नौका

निर्देशः (प्र.सं. 96 से 100 तक): *दिए गए गद्यांश को ध्यानपूर्वक पढ़कर पूछे गए प्रश्नों के सर्वाधिक उपयुक्त उत्तर वाले विकल्प चुनकर लिखिए:*

मानव जीवन के आदिकाल में अनुशासन की कोई संकल्पना नहीं थी और न आज की भाँति बड़े-बड़े नगर या राज्य ही थे। मानव जंगल में रहता था, 'जिसकी लाठी उसकी भैंस' वाली कहावत उसके जीवन पर पूर्णतः चरितार्थ होती थी, व्यक्ति पर किसी भी नियम का बंधन या किसी प्रकार के कर्तव्यों का दायित्व नहीं था, किन्तु इतना स्वतंत्र और <u>निरंकुश</u> होते हुए भी मानव प्रसन्न नहीं था। आपसी टकराव होते थे, अधिकारों-कर्तव्यों में संघर्ष होता था और नियमों की कमी उसे खलती थी। धीरे-धीरे उसकी अपनी ही आवश्यकताओं की पूर्ति के लिए समाज और राज्य का उद्भव और विकास हुआ। अपने उद्देश्य की सिद्धि एवं आवश्यकताओं की पूर्ति के लिए मानव ने अंततः कुछ नियमों का निर्माण किया। उनमें से कुछ नियमों के पालन करवाने का अधिकार राज्य को और कुछ का अधिकार समाज को दे दिया गया। व्यक्ति के बहुमुखी विकास में सहायक होने वाले इन नियमों का पालन ही अनुशासन कहलाता है। अनुभव सबसे बड़ा शिक्षक होता है। समाज ने प्रारम्भ में अपने अनुभवों से ही अनुशासन के इन नियमों को सीखा, विकसित किया और सुव्यवस्थित किया होगा।

96. आदिकाल में मानव प्रसन्न नहीं था, क्योंकि:

1. उसका जीवन और रहन-सहन सरल न था
2. उसकी जीवन-आवश्यकताओं की पूर्ति नहीं हो पाती थी
3. वह नगरों में न रहकर जंगलों में रहता था
4. उस काल में सामाजिक नियमों का निर्धारण नहीं हुआ था

97. गद्यांश में रेखांकित शब्द से आशय ऐसे व्यक्ति से है:

1. जो निरपराध एवं निरभिमान हो
2. जिसके मन में घमंड भरा हो
3. जिसका व्यवहार कुश जैसा न हो
4. जो किसी व्यवस्था को न माने

98. गद्यांश का भाव पहचानें:

1. सामाजिक नियमों का पालन करना चाहिए
2. स्वतंत्र और निरंकुश होना चाहिए
3. आवश्यकताओं की पूर्ति के लिए पशु बल का प्रयोग करना चाहिए
4. अधिकारों के लिए संघर्ष करना चाहिए

99. 'अनुशासन' से अभिप्रेत है:
1. शासन द्वारा निर्धारित नियमों की पहचान और परख
2. प्रजा पर शासक का पूर्णरूप से नियंत्रण जिससे राजव्यवस्था सुचारु बन सके
3. शासित द्वारा शासक के आदेशों का सम्यक् रूप से पालन
4. व्यक्ति द्वारा अपने बहुमुखी विकास के लिए बनाये गये सामाजिक नियमों का पालन

100. इस गद्यांश का सर्वाधिक उपयुक्त शीर्षक हो सकता है:
1. आवश्यकता आविष्कार की जननी है
2. जिसकी लाठी उसकी भैंस
3. अनुशासन की संकल्पना
4. जीवन का उद्देश्य

Post Specific Subject-Related Questions

101. The percentage of protein in a balanced diet is:
1. 10-35%   2. About 55%
3. 35-70%   4. 5-7%

102. Which of the following is a diagnostic test to detect chromosomal abnormality?
1. Positron emission tomography
2. Chorionic villus sampling
3. Karyotyping
4. Amylase test

103. _____ is an abnormal curvature of the lens that interferes with the light path, causing blurred vision.
1. Myopia
2. Hyperopia
3. Presbyopia
4. Astigmatism

104. Which of the following disinfectants is used to clean contaminated Mackintoshes?
1. 0.12 % chlorhexidine
2. 0.2 % chlorhexidine
3. 0.5% sodium hypochlorite
4. 10 % sodium hypochlorite

105. A patient with a known history of poisoning and frequent vomiting for the past 8 hours will lead to:
1. respiratory alkalosis
2. metabolic alkalosis
3. metabolic acidosis
4. respiratory acidosis

106. _____ are the sounds that a nurse listens for when they are measuring blood pressure using a non-invasive procedure.
1. Korotkoff sounds
2. Crepitus
3. Ronchi
4. Murmurs

107. A 50-year-old male patient with a history of smoking presents with chronic cough and sputum production. His ABG shows: pH 7.38, $PaCO_2$ 45 mmHg, and PaO_2 75 mmHg. What does the PaO_2 value indicate in this patient?
1. Hypoxemia
2. Alkalosis
3. Normal oxygenation
4. Hyperoxia

108. A nurse educates a patient to consume more of green leafy vegetables, cucumbers and drumstick leaves to prevent which of the following conditions?
1. Constipation   2. Weakness
3. Muscle wasting   4. Haemorrhage

109. Which of the following intramuscular sites is a recommended site for infants?
1. Dorsogluteal   2. Ventrogluteal
3. Deltoid   4. Vastus lateralis

110. Which of the following is a colourless, odourless and tasteless poisonous gas?
1. Carbonated gas   2. Carbon monoxide
3. Carbon trioxide   4. Carbon dioxide

111. _____ is an act of emptying the bladder involuntarily with sudden increase in abdominal pressure.

1. Stress incontinence
2. Functional incontinence
3. Urge incontinence
4. Reflex incontinence

112. Celia, the nurse in charge, used a series of cards in a portable index file to organise the data collected from the patient during admission. Which of the following methods did she follow?

1. Progress notes 2. Kardex
3. Flow sheets 4. Critical pathway

113. In ABCD Nutritional Assessment, what does 'A' stand for?

1. Appropriateness 2. Advice
3. Anthropometry 4. Assessment

114. Which of the following methods of sterilisation is done by steam under pressure?

1. Hot air oven
2. Fumigation
3. Ultraviolet light sterilisation
4. Autoclaving

115. A cycle of decreasing rate and depth with a pause in respiration is called:

1. cheyne-strokes 2. tachypnoea
3. bradypnoea 4. apnoea

116. Following are the structures within the prostrate, EXCEPT:

1. prostatic utricles
2. two ejaculatory ducts
3. urethra
4. ureter

117. Which of the following substances triggers cell degranulation?

1. Prostaglandin 2. Heparin
3. Histamine 4. Serotonin

118. In a respiratory emergency, the first action to be performed by the first aider is to:

1. check the victim's pulse
2. start chest compressions
3. call for emergency help
4. open the airway and check for breathing

119. Which of the following is a measure to relieve the congestion of pelvic organs?

1. Cold sponge bath
2. Sitz bath
3. Cold compress
4. Hot compress

120. Which of the following is the immediate nursing action performed on a patient with infiltration?

1. Hot application
2. Stopping IV infusion
3. Informing the doctor
4. Cold application

121. The ABG values of pH 7.6, $PaCO_2$ 30 mmHg, HCO_3 24 mEq and normal PaO_2 suggest:

1. metabolic alkalosis
2. respiratory acidosis
3. metabolic acidosis
4. respiratory alkalosis

122. What is the primary difference between mitosis and meiosis in terms of their outcomes?

1. Mitosis is involved in sexual reproduction, while meiosis is involved in asexual reproduction.
2. Mitosis results in a reduction of chromosome number, while meiosis maintains the chromosome number.
3. Mitosis results in the formation of four genetically identical daughter cells, while meiosis results in two genetically diverse daughter cells.
4. Mitosis results in two diploid daughter cells, while meiosis results in four haploid daughter cells.

123. The trachea is supported by a series of C-shaped cartilaginous rings. What is the primary function of these cartilaginous rings?
1. To maintain an open airway and prevent collapse during respiration
2. To anchor the trachea to the surrounding oesophagus
3. To facilitate the production of mucus in the trachea
4. To allow for expansion and contraction of the trachea during swallowing

124. Osmoreceptors, which monitors water content of the blood, is located in the:
1. adrenal gland 2. nephron
3. renal pelvis 4. hypothalamus

125. Which of the following is the principal immunoglobulin present in secretions such as milk, saliva, tears, sweat, nasal fluids and colostrum, and in the secretions of respiratory, intestinal and genital systems?
1. Immunoglobulin M
2. Immunoglobulin G
3. Immunoglobulin A
4. Immunoglobulin E

126. Insufficient oxygen supply to the tissue is termed as:
1. dyspnea 2. cyanosis
3. hypoxia 4. asphyxia

127. Antibody-mediated cytotoxic hypersensitivity is otherwise known as what type of hypersensitivity?
1. Type I hypersensitivity
2. Type III hypersensitivity
3. Type IV hypersensitivity
4. Type II hypersensitivity

128. Chyle, the creamy white-coloured lymph is drained from the _____.
1. small intestine 2. large intestine
3. stomach 4. liver

129. Which of the following structures is formed by the inward projection of the inner layer of the cerebral dura mater between the cerebral hemispheres?
1. Transverse sinus
2. Straight sinus
3. Tentorium cerebelli
4. Falx cerebri

130. A patient in septic shock in the intensive care unit has the following ABG results: pH = 7.25, PCO_2 = 34, PaO_2 = 90 and bicarbonate = 10 with a lactate of 4.2 mmol/L. How can this ABG be corrected?
1. Increase the patient's respiratory rate
2. Administer diuretics to reduce bicarbonate levels
3. Administer 1 ampule of sodium bicarbonate
4. Improve tissue perfusion and oxygenation

131. Which of the following respiratory muscles lift the ribcage upwards and outwards in inspiration?
1. Accessary muscles of forced expiration
2. Internal intercostal muscles
3. External intercostal muscles
4. Diaphragmatic muscle

132. Which of the following is an example of a ball and socket joint?
1. Shoulder joint 2. Wrist joint
3. Elbow joint 4. Knee joint

133. Which of the following are the connective tissues with a fluid matrix?
1. Bone and muscle
2. Meninges and muscle
3. Blood and lymph
4. Tendon and ligament

134. Which of the following accessory inspiratory muscles does the upper back and neck muscle help to stabilise the scapula and assist in elevating the ribs?
1. Serratus Anterior
2. Sternocleidomastoid
3. Scalenes
4. Vastus

135. In the postnatal period, puerperal infection is caused by _____ bacteria.

1. Group-A streptococcus
2. staphylococcus
3. Group-B streptococcus
4. spirochetes

136. Which of the following structures of a bacteria helps in motility?

1. Flagella 2. Episome
3. Spore 4. Fimbriae

137. Which of the following is the nursing management for a patient with syndrome of inappropriate antidiuretic hormone?

1. Avoiding range of motion exercise
2. 10-degree elevation of head bed
3. Observation for signs of hypernatremia
4. Fluid > 1000 ml/day

138. Nurse explains the life cycle of malaria parasite. Which of the following are considered as the male gametocytes?

1. Megagametocytes
2. Misogametocytes
3. Macrogametocytes
4. Microgametocytes

139. _____ protects humans through a product that is injected into him.

1. Innate immunity
2. Permanent immunity
3. Active immunity
4. Passive immunity

140. Oral Candidiasis occurs due to prolonged usage of:

1. antiemetics 2. corticosteroids
3. analgesics 4. antacids

141. The inability to recognise objects by touch is known as:

1. astereognosis 2. apraxia
3. agnosia 4. akinesia

142. 'Steatorrhea' in obstructed bile flow is due to the:

1. lack of vitamin K
2. deposition of bile salts in skin tissues
3. absence of bile salt in duodenum
4. presence of soluble bilirubin in urine

143. When explaining microorganisms, for which type of microorganisms is it important to keep in mind that the type of nucleic acid (DNA or RNA) and molecular weight are major characteristics used to classify that type?

1. Fungi 2. Parasite
3. Virus 4. Bacteria

144. The flow of pancreatic juice into the duodenum is controlled by:

1. pyloric antrum
2. duct of Wirsung
3. sphincter of Oddi
4. ampulla of Vater

145. A woman experiences postpartum blues on the 3rd postnatal day. The recommended management of this condition is:

1. separation from the newborn
2. reassurance and psychological support
3. administration of antidepressants
4. electroconvulsive therapy

146. Which type of renal calculi is more common in women than men?

1. Uric acid 2. Cystine
3. Calcium oxalate 4. Struvite

147. Chyme is formed in the:

1. duodenum 2. esophagus
3. stomach 4. jejunum

148. Which feature of a compound microscope has the ability to separate the details of the specimen being studied?

1. Mirror 2. Magnification
3. Eyepiece 4. Resolution

149. Central nervous system stimulants are prescribed to patients with _____.

1. anxiety
2. mania
3. Attention Deficit Hyperactivity Disorder (ADHD)
4. phobia

150. Which of the following nutrients is required for the production of RBC?

1. Vitamin E 2. Vitamin A
3. Vitamin C 4. Vitamin B12

151. Which of the conditions needs to be monitored by a nurse in response to thyroid replacement therapy among patients with severe myxedema coma?

1. Thyroid failure
2. Acute pancreatitis
3. Myocardial ischemia
4. Acute kidney injury

152. Anosmia refers to the loss of:

1. smell 2. taste
3. vision 4. touch

153. The nurse is caring for a patient with acute kidney injury. While assessing the patient, which of the following factors may lead to reduced blood supply and cause poor kidney function?

1. Hyperaemia 2. Hyperhidrosis
3. Hyperthermia 4. Hypovolaemia

154. The following are the responsibilities of nurses in pain management, EXCEPT:

1. identifying goals for pain management
2. prescribing pain relieving medications
3. performing pain assessment
4. providing patient teaching

155. The Johari window model can be used to resolve conflicts by:

1. avoiding confrontation
2. placing all the blame on others
3. improving communication
4. ignoring the problem

156. A postnatal mother has puerperal sepsis. Which of the following clinical features indicate(s) extrauterine spread of infection?

1. Uterus is subinvoluted and tender
2. Slight rise of temperature and generalised malaise
3. Pus in pouch of Douglas with swinging temperature and diarrhea
4. Lochial discharge is offensive and copious

157. Which of the following should the nurse NOT include in the teachings for a patient on anticoagulant therapy?

1. Do not take NSAIDs
2. Limit alcohol intake
3. No dietary restriction
4. Avoid vigorous brushing

158. Following delivery of the baby, the mother is encouraged to pass urine as soon as possible, to prevent _____.

1. cystitis
2. vaginitis
3. urinary tract infection
4. rupture of bladder

159. Arrhythmia with sawtooth-shaped waves is:

1. paroxysmal supraventricular tachycardia
2. atrial fibrillation
3. premature atrial contraction
4. atrial flutter

160. Psychomotor retardation is common in patients with _____.

1. dementia 2. anxiety
3. depression 4. phobia

161. The Denver developmental screening test (DDST) is appropriate to use for children of the age group of:

1. 0-6 years 2. 0-4 years
3. 0-8 years 4. 0-2 years

162. The Thematic Apperception Test (TAT) is primarily used to assess an individual's _____.

1. attitude 2. personality
3. aptitude 4. intelligence

163. A systematic formal written report of a therapeutic conversation between a nurse and patient is called:

1. nursing process 2. documentation
3. nurses' notes 4. process recording

164. If a physician ordered fluid D5w1200 ml in 24 hours using an IV drip set with drop factor 60, what will be the IV infusion rate (in drops/min)?

1. 35 2. 50
3. 45 4. 25

165. Isoniazid is the drug of choice to treat which of the following?

1. Diptheria 2. Tetanus
3. Tuberculosis 4. Poliomyelitis

166. The anatomical change seen in cardiovascular system due to gravid uterus is:

1. a decreased CVP
2. shifting of apex beat
3. increased heartbeats
4. a decreased cardiac output

167. School-age children perceive hospitalisation as:

1. God's anger 2. a way to relax
3. parents' anger 4. punishment

168. The CSF analysis report of a child admitted with fever and nuchal rigidity shows decreased glucose and elevated protein. The nurse will suspect:

1. fungal meningitis 2. bacterial meningitis
3. viral meningitis 4. protozoa meningitis

169. Which of the following pieces of advice by a nurse related to breast feeding for a postnatal mother is INCORRECT?

1. Stress on exclusive breastfeeding and demand feeding
2. Emphasise to give prelacteal feeds
3. Advise to feed from both breasts during a feed
4. Initiate breastfeeding within one hour of the birth

170. During the postnatal period, the genital organs revert approximately to the state before pregnancy through the process of _______.

1. involution 2. puerperation
3. regeneration 4. degeneration

171. The increased synthesis of which of these vasoconstrictors is known to cause preeclampsia?

1. Thromboxane 2. Prostacyclin
3. Prostaglandin E2 4. Nitric oxide

172. The feeling of being detached from oneself is called:

1. depersonalisation 2. derealisation
3. disorientation 4. deja vu

173. In which month is the head circumference of a newborn equal to its chest circumference?

1. 9th month 2. 6th month
3. 12th month 4. 24th month

174. Vitamin A supplementation helps in the prevention of:

1. rubella 2. mumps
3. measles 4. pertussis

175. An ultrasound is advised for a pregnant woman of 10 weeks' gestation. The midwife explains the purpose of the scan as:

1. assessing the viability
2. assessing the growth restriction
3. detecting the placental maturation
4. identifying the amniotic fluid index

176. Maternal perception of foetal movement is decreased during the following conditions, EXCEPT:

1. chronic smoking
2. maternal obesity
3. foetal CNS anomalies
4. maternal hypoglycaemia

177. A woman who has delivered in a sub-centre develops signs of Postpartum hemorrhage. The nurse administers which of the following agents before transferring her to a higher centre?

1. Misoprostol 800 mcg sublingually
2. Misoprostol 600 mcg orally
3. Intramuscular Methergine 0.2 mg
4. Intravenous Oxytocin bolus 10 IU

178. The process whereby a secondary oocyte is released from the ovary following rupture of a mature Graafian follicle is:

1. ovulation 2. menstruation
3. fertilisation 4. gastrulation

179. Hirschberg test is otherwise known as:

1. visual acuity test
2. colour vision test
3. peripheral vision test
4. corneal light reflex test

180. In the foetal skull, the fontanel is formed by sagittal suture anteriorly and lambdoid suture on either side is:

1. lateral fontanel 2. inferior fontanel
3. anterior fontanel 4. posterior fontanel

181. The concept of education is to:

1. earn status
2. earn money
3. create safe society
4. discipline the mind

182. Which of the following is an example of an internal recruitment method, where employees are moved from one department to another within the organisation?

1. Deputation 2. Demotion
3. Transfer 4. Promotion

183. Who among the following is the ex-officio secretary of the Panchayat Samiti?

1. District health officer
2. Chief medical officer
3. Sarpanch
4. Block development officer

184. According to the ecological concept, health is viewed as a/an:

1. genetic predisposition to diseases
2. perfect adaptation to modern health services
3. absence of disease
4. dynamic equilibrium between man and environment

185. An organisation has a plan to fully computerise and automate in 10 years through a phased approach to hospital functioning. What is this type of planning called?

1. Operational 2. Corporate
3. Strategic 4. Functional

186. A nurse is assessing a newborn for DDH. Which manoeuver will they use to detect hip instability in the infant?

1. Ortolani manoeuver
2. Gowers's manoeuver
3. Valsalva manoeuver
4. Heimlich manoeuver

187. Which of the following is an individual method of performance appraisal?

1. Ranking method
2. Paired comparison method
3. Management by objective
4. 360 degree feedback

188. What does the term 'induction' denote in nursing service manpower management?

1. Supporting new nurses to adjust to the new job and organisation
2. Helping new nurses to analyse individual capacities and skills
3. Reinforcing rules and regulations for existing nurses working in the unit
4. Assessing the personal qualities of new nurses

189. Which of the following methods can be used for post-coital contraception?

1. Copper IUD within 10 days
2. Levonorgestrel 0.75 mg tablet within 72 hours and a second tablet 24 hours later
3. Four oral contraceptive pills containing 50 mcg of ethinyl estradiol within 72 hours and 4 tablets after 12 hours
4. Mifepristone 10 mg once within 72 hours

190. What does the term 'secular trend' refer to in epidemiology?

1. Changes over a long period with consistent tendency in one direction
2. Short-term fluctuations in disease prevalence
3. Epidemic outbreaks in developed countries
4. Seasonal variations in disease patterns

191. In a rural community, where the rate of smoking among teenagers is rising, which strategy best exemplifies primordial prevention?

1. Providing smoking cessation programmes for adults with a smoking habit
2. Incorporating anti-smoking education into the school curriculum for middle and high school students
3. Offering tax breaks for businesses that implement smoke-free policies
4. Implementing a campaign to raise awareness about the dangers of smoking among adults with a smoking habit

192. Which of the following is NOT part of the Panchayati Raj system at the village level?

1. Zilla Parishad
2. Nyaya Panchayat
3. Gram Sabha
4. Gram Panchayat

193. Which of the following is an important component of mental health services in the community to provide effective mental health care?

1. Assuming mental illness is self-limiting
2. After-care services
3. Isolation of the mentally ill person
4. Encouraging immediate treatment

194. Which family coping index describes maturity and integrity within family members?

1. Health Conditions
2. Emotional Competence
3. Family Living
4. Health Attitudes

195. The risk of cardiovascular disease in men is more apparent when the waist circumference is _____.

1. 88-92 cms
2. less than 88 cms
3. more than 102 cms
4. 92-102 cms

196. Which neurological sign constitutes the primary somatoneurological manifestation in approximately 90% of stroke patients?

1. Coma
2. Monoplegia
3. Paraplegia
4. Hemiplegia

197. The labour law imposes a specific number of working hours for the nurses in an organisation. The source of this law is an example of which of the following policies?

1. Originated policy
2. Implicit policy
3. Appealed policy
4. Imposed policy

198. Which of the following should be AVOIDED when providing first aid for burns?

1. Ensuring your own safety first
2. Wrapping the patient in a clean cloth for transport
3. Using cool running water to reduce burn temperature
4. Applying ice to reduce the depth of the injury

199. What type of vaccine should NOT be given to a child with HIV infection?

1. Live vaccine
2. Killed vaccine
3. Toxoids
4. Immunoglobulins

200. In which of the following leadership styles are leaders proactive and inspire and empower the followers?

1. Charismatic leader
2. People-oriented leader
3. Transformational leader
4. Transactional leader

ANSWERS

1	2	3	4	5	6	7	8	9	10
3	1	4	1	4	2	3	2	4	3
11	**12**	**13**	**14**	**15**	**16**	**17**	**18**	**19**	**20**
1	2	2	2	1	3	4	2	3	4
21	**22**	**23**	**24**	**25**	**26**	**27**	**28**	**29**	**30**
3	2	4	1	4	4	3	3	3	4
31	**32**	**33**	**34**	**35**	**36**	**37**	**38**	**39**	**40**
4	2	1	3	2	2	2	2	4	2
41	**42**	**43**	**44**	**45**	**46**	**47**	**48**	**49**	**50**
1	1	1	1	4	4	1	1	3	1
51	**52**	**53**	**54**	**55**	**56**	**57**	**58**	**59**	**60**
3	2	1	4	4	3	3	3	2	2
61	**62**	**63**	**64**	**65**	**66**	**67**	**68**	**69**	**70**
4	3	1	2	1	3	1	2	1	3
71	**72**	**73**	**74**	**75**	**76**	**77**	**78**	**79**	**80**
3	3	4	1	2	4	1	1	3	3
81	**82**	**83**	**84**	**85**	**86**	**87**	**88**	**89**	**90**
1	3	1	3	1	1	1	3	4	1
91	**92**	**93**	**94**	**95**	**96**	**97**	**98**	**99**	**100**
4	2	3	4	4	4	4	1	4	3
101	**102**	**103**	**104**	**105**	**106**	**107**	**108**	**109**	**110**
1	3	4	3	2	1	1	1	4	2
111	**112**	**113**	**114**	**115**	**116**	**117**	**118**	**119**	**120**
1	2	3	4	1	4	3	4	2	2
121	**122**	**123**	**124**	**125**	**126**	**127**	**128**	**129**	**130**
4	4	1	4	3	3	4	1	4	4
131	**132**	**133**	**134**	**135**	**136**	**137**	**138**	**139**	**140**
3	1	3	1	1	1	2	4	4	2
141	**142**	**143**	**144**	**145**	**146**	**147**	**148**	**149**	**150**
1	3	3	3	2	4	3	4	3	4
151	**152**	**153**	**154**	**155**	**156**	**157**	**158**	**159**	**160**
3	1	4	2	3	3	3	1	4	3
161	**162**	**163**	**164**	**165**	**166**	**167**	**168**	**169**	**170**
1	2	4	2	3	2	4	2	2	1
171	**172**	**173**	**174**	**175**	**176**	**177**	**178**	**179**	**180**
1	1	3	3	1	4	1	1	4	4
181	**182**	**183**	**184**	**185**	**186**	**187**	**188**	**189**	**190**
4	3	4	4	3	1	3	1	4	1
191	**192**	**193**	**194**	**195**	**196**	**197**	**198**	**199**	**200**
2	1	2	2	3	4	4	4	1	3

EXPLANATORY ANSWERS

1. K is the husband of L, so L is K's wife. M is the daughter of K, so L is also the mother of M. N is the sister of M, so N is also the child of K and L (i.e., L is N's mother). O is the brother of L, so O is the brother of N's mother ⇒ O is N's mother's brother (maternal uncle).

2. From "All lions are tigers," we only know Lions $\subseteq$ Tigers. From "Some tigers are bears," we know there exists at least one animal that is both a tiger and a bear. From "No bear is a deer," Bears $\cap$ Deer $= \varnothing$. Conclusion I ("No lion is a deer") does not follow because we have no direct relation given between tigers (or lions) and deer; lions could still be deer in some possible case without violating any statement. Conclusion II ("Some bears are lions") also does not follow because "Some tigers are bears" does not force those bears to be lions, and "All lions are tigers" does not force any lion to be a bear. Hence neither conclusion follows.

3. "LORD" → 2618 and "ROAD" → 6287. The common letters in both words are R, O, D, and the common digits in both codes are 6, 2, 8, so R/O/D correspond to {6,2,8} in some order. The remaining letter in "LORD" is L and the remaining digit in 2618 (not in 6287) is 1, so L → 1.

4. We need symbols that are immediately preceded by a number and immediately followed by a symbol. In the series, "£" is preceded by 2 and followed by "&" (counts). "€" is preceded by 1 and followed by "*" (counts). No other symbol satisfies both conditions. Therefore, the count is 2.

5. In both given triads, the pattern is first number + second number = third number: 11 + 3 = 14 and 4 + 6 = 10.
Checking options: 40 + 50 = 90 matches the same rule, so this triad follows the pattern.

6. 6 floors are numbered 1 (lowest) to 6 (top). F lives on the uppermost floor ⇒ F = floor 6. "Only four people live between F and E" means the floors of F and E differ by 5 (because 4 floors in between) ⇒ E must be on floor 1. Given G lives on floor 5 and J lives on floor 4, and also J lives immediately below G, this condition is satisfied (4 is immediately below 5). H lives on an even-numbered floor but not on 6 ⇒ H can be on 2 or 4; but floor 4 is already J ⇒ H = floor 2. I lives on an odd-numbered floor ⇒ possible odd floors are 1, 3, 5; but floor 1 is E and floor 5 is G ⇒ I = floor 3. Therefore, the person on floor number 3 is I.

7. 'BORN' → 3628 and 'BONE' → 6318. The common letters in both words are B, O, N and the common digits in both codes are 3, 6, 8, so B/O/N correspond to {3,6,8} in some order. The remaining letter in 'BORN' is R, and the remaining digit in 3628 (not present in 6318) is 2. Hence, R is coded as 2.

8. The water source is placed along the X–Y line, which represents a horizontal reflecting surface. In water reflection, the image formed is an exact vertical inversion of the original figure while maintaining the left-to-right arrangement of all components. Accordingly, the square remains on the right side, but the relative vertical positions of the pentagon and the shaded region are reversed with respect to the X–Y line. In Option 2, the entire figure appears as a correct vertical mirror image of the original: the pentagonal shape is reflected downward, the square stays on the right without lateral displacement, and the black shaded portion is inverted vertically while preserving its shape and relative alignment. Thus, the correct water reflection of the given figure is shown in Option 2.

9. Days are Monday(1) to Sunday(7). Only two people have an exam after F, so F must be on day 5. Only two people have an exam between D and F, so with F on day 5, D must be on day 2. Only four people have an exam between J and D, so with D on day 2, J must be on day 7. K has an exam immediately after I, and the only consecutive vacant days available are days 3 and 4, so I is on day 3 and K on day 4. The remaining days are 1 and 6 for E and S. Since S does not have an exam on Monday,

S is on day 6 and E on day 1. People who have an exam after E (day 1) and before S (day 6) are on days 2, 3, 4, and 5, which are four people.

10. The logical pattern shown by the given examples is that the third number is obtained by adding the first and the second numbers, that is, A + B = C. In the examples, 14 + 5 = 19 and 23 + 20 = 43, so both clearly follow this rule. Checking the options, 15 + 9 = 24 ≠ 26, 5 + 10 = 15 ≠ 20, and 14 + 7 = 21 ≠ 22, so these do not satisfy the same condition. Only in option 3, 6 + 2 = 8, the third number is exactly the sum of the first two numbers. Therefore, option 3 is the distinct group based on the established logic.

11. In all first clusters, the letters are consecutive in reverse order (JI, WX, NO, YZ). In options 2, 3 and 4, the second cluster letters have a constant gap of 2 in reverse order: MK (13 → 11), DB (4 → 2), OM (15 → 13). Only in option 1, ZS has a gap of 7 (26 → 19), so it does not follow the same pattern.

12.
$$7 - 4 = 3$$
$$20 - 7 = 13$$
$$43 - 20 = 23$$
$$76 - 43 = 33$$

The differences increase by +10 each time, so next difference = 33 + 10 = 43.

Next term = 76 + 43 = 119.

13. Given: A = ÷, B = ×, C = +, D = −

So, 365 × 3 − 525 ÷ 5 + 172
$$365 \times 3 = 1095$$
$$525 \div 5 = 105$$
$$1095 - 105 + 172 = 990 + 172 = 1162.$$

14. In options 1, 3 and 4, each letter of the first cluster is shifted 2 letters backward to get the second cluster:

MJ → KH (M → K, J → H)

WT → UR (W → U, T → R)

RO → PM (R → P, O → M)

But FI → HG does not follow "both letters −2" (F would go to D, not H), so it is the odd one out.

15.
$$16 - 14 = 2$$
$$28 - 16 = 12$$
$$50 - 28 = 22$$

Differences increase by +10, so next differences are 32 and 42.

Missing term = 50 + 32 = 82, and 82 + 42 = 124 matches the last term.

16. In each triad, the 2nd cluster is formed by shifting both letters of the 1st cluster by +1 (EI → FJ, MQ → NR), and the 3rd cluster is formed by shifting the 1st letter of the 2nd cluster by +2 and the 2nd letter by +1 (FJ → HK, NR → PS). In option 3, QU → RV (both +1) and RV → TW (R → T is +2, V → W is +1), so it matches the same pattern.

17. The pattern is: 2nd term = 2nd, 3rd, 1st, 4th letters; 3rd term = 4th, 1st, 2nd, 3rd letters. For POND (P O N D), ONPD = O N P D and DPON = D P O N, so option 4 follows exactly.

18. After interchanging operators, 180 × 4 − 3 + 3 ÷ 9 becomes 180 ÷ 4 + 3 − 3 × 9; 180 ÷ 4 = 45, 3 × 9 = 27; so 45 + 3 − 27 = 48 − 27 = 21.

19. Second from the left is J and second from the right is O. In the alphabet, letters between J and O are K, L, M, N, which are 4 letters.

20. "Only R sits to the right of L" ⇒ L is 6th and R is 7th. "Only two people between P and R" ⇒ P is 4th. "Only two people between J and P" ⇒ J is 1st. Remaining seats (2, 3, 5) are for M, K, Q with M < K < Q ⇒ M = 2nd, K = 3rd, Q = 5th. Between M (2nd) and Q (5th) are positions 3 and 4, i.e., 2 people.

21. The Dogri language was added to the Eighth Schedule of the Constitution of India through the Constitution (Ninety-second Amendment) Act, 2003. Although the amendment Act is titled as 2003, it received the assent of the President of India on 7 January 2004 and came into force on the same date, with its official notification published in the Gazette of India on 8 January 2004. Hence, the effective year of inclusion of Dogri in the Eighth Schedule is 2004, making option 3 the correct answer.

22. In production, opportunity cost refers to the value of the next best alternative that is sacrificed when a particular choice is made. Since resources are limited, choosing one option automatically means giving up the benefits of another feasible option.

23. In business economics, profit is defined as what remains after all costs and expenses are deducted from total revenue. It reflects the net gain earned by a business from its operations.

24. *The book I Have the Streets: A Kutti Cricket Story* is authored by Ravichandran Ashwin. The book narrates a fictional story inspired by street cricket culture and is aimed primarily at young readers.

25. Allicin is a sulphur-containing compound found in garlic. It is released when garlic cloves are crushed or chopped and is known for its antimicrobial and medicinal properties.

26. Pitru Paksha is a lunar period dedicated to the worship of ancestors and is observed for 16 lunar days during the Krishna Paksha of the Hindu month of Bhadrapada (or Ashwin, depending on the lunar calendar). It begins on the full moon day (Purnima) and ends on the new moon day (Amavasya), which is known as Sarva Pitru Amavasya.

27. Fa-Hsien visited India during the reign of the Gupta emperor Chandragupta II (around the early 5th century CE). He provided detailed accounts of the social life, religious practices, administration, and general prosperity of the Gupta Kingdom, making him the most important Chinese traveller associated with the Gupta period.

28. The Amrit Sarovar initiative was launched with the objective of creating or rejuvenating 75 water bodies in every district of India. The aim is to enhance water conservation, groundwater recharge, and community participation as part of the Azadi Ka Amrit Mahotsav celebrations.

29. Article 226 of the Indian Constitution empowers High Courts to issue writs such as Habeas Corpus, Mandamus, Prohibition, Certiorari, and Quo Warranto for the enforcement of Fundamental Rights as well as for "any other purpose," giving High Courts a wider writ jurisdiction than the Supreme Court.

30. The revolutionary organisation Mitra Mela was founded in Nashik by Vinayak Damodar Savarkar in 1904. The organisation later evolved into the more radical Abhinav Bharat Society and played a significant role in revolutionary activities against British rule.

31. As of March 2025, Indian Space Research Organisation (ISRO) is developing a semi-cryogenic engine that uses liquid oxygen (LOX) as the oxidiser and kerosene as the fuel. This engine, commonly referred to as the SCE-200, is intended to enhance the payload capacity and performance of future Indian launch vehicles.

32. The Nallamala Hills are part of the Eastern Ghats and belong to the Peninsular Plateau, not the Coastal Plains. The other pairs are correctly matched with their respective physiographic divisions, making option 2 the incorrect pair.

33. Based on the provisions of the Government of India Act, 1919, and the recommendations of the Lee Commission (1924), the Public Service Commission was established in 1926, which later evolved into the Federal Public Service Commission.

34. The Khond (Kandh/Kondh) people of the Kalahandi district in Odisha celebrate Chhatar Jatra by worshipping their family and regional deity, Maa Manikeswari, who is regarded as the presiding Goddess of the Kalahandi royal house. The festival is a major cultural and religious event, celebrated mainly on Maha Ashtami during Durga Puja. A ceremonial umbrella (Chhatar) symbolising the Goddess is taken in a grand procession from Jenakhal to her main temple at Bhawanipatna. The Khond tribe has deep historical and ritual associations with the festival; traditionally, a Khond tribal head (Pat Majhi) played a key role in royal coronation rituals. Tribal cultural elements such as Ghumura dance, traditional drums, and long-preserved sacrificial rites form an integral part of the Chhatar Jatra.

35. Ladakh experiences a cold desert climate, characterised by extremely low temperatures, scanty rainfall, sparse vegetation, and high altitude conditions, unlike the other options which have humid or tropical climates.

36. The Constitution of India authorises the President of India to suspend the enforcement of Fundamental Rights during the proclamation of a National Emergency under Article 352. Specifically, Article 359 empowers the President to suspend the right to move any court for the enforcement of Fundamental Rights (except Articles 20 and 21). Neither the Governor, Law Minister, nor the Prime Minister has such constitutional authority.

37. In April 2025, the Jal Shakti Ministry, in coordination with the Ministry of Housing and Urban Affairs, approved an action plan for river rejuvenation in 145 cities situated along various rivers across India. The initiative focuses on urban river management, sewage treatment, pollution control, and integrating river rejuvenation with urban planning under missions such as AMRUT and Swachh Bharat.

38. According to Census 2011, the child sex ratio of India (number of girls per 1000 boys in the 0–6 age group) is 919. This figure reflected a decline from the 2001 Census and highlighted serious concerns regarding gender imbalance in the country.

39. A snake belongs to the class Reptilia, which includes cold-blooded vertebrates characterised by scales, lungs for respiration, and egg-laying (or ovoviviparity). Fish belong to Pisces, sea horse is a fish, and frog belongs to Amphibia, leaving snake as the correct reptilian example.

40. Hiuen Tsang visited India during the reign of King Harshavardhana in the 7th century CE. He spent several years travelling across the subcontinent and provided valuable accounts of Indian society, administration, education, and Buddhism, particularly praising Harsha's rule and patronage of learning and religion.

41. Principal P = 2000

Rate R = 5.25% per annum

Time period:

From 6 Feb to 28 Feb = 22 days

March = 31 days

1 April to 20 April = 20 days

Total time = 22 + 31 + 20 = 73 days

$$SI = \frac{P \times R \times T}{100}$$

$$= \frac{2000 \times 5.25 \times 73}{100 \times 365}$$

$$= \frac{105 \times 73}{365} = \frac{105}{5} = 21.$$

42. Let original price = 100

After 40% increase = 140

After 20% decrease = $140 \times \frac{80}{100}$ = 112

Net change = 112 - 100

= 12% increase.

43. Work done by A in 1 day = $\frac{1}{5}$

Work done by B in 1 day = $\frac{1}{20}$

Combined work per day = $\frac{1}{5} + \frac{1}{20} = \frac{5}{20} = \frac{1}{4}$

Total days = 4.

44. Mean proportional formula:

$\sqrt{P \times 81}$ = 54

P × 81 = 54^2 = 2916

$P = \frac{2916}{81} = 36.$

45. Cost Price = 34000

Selling Price = 38200

Profit = 38200 - 34000 = 4200

Profit % = $\frac{4200}{34000} \times 100$

= 12.3529% ≈ 12.35%.

46. $(8p + 8)^2 = (8(p + 1))^2 = 64(p + 1)^2$

$64(p + 1)^2 \div 64 \Rightarrow$ quotient = $(p + 1)^2$, remainder = 0.

So, the remainder is 0.

47. Given, $r : l = 9 : 14 \Rightarrow l = \frac{14}{9}r$

Curved surface area of cone:

CSA = πrl = 1584

$$\frac{22}{7} \times r \times \frac{14}{9} r = 1584$$

$$\frac{22 \times 14}{7 \times 9} r^2 = 1584$$

$$\Rightarrow \frac{44}{9} r^2 = 1584$$

$$r^2 = 1584 \times \frac{9}{44}$$

$$\frac{1584}{44} = 36 \Rightarrow r^2 = 36 \times 9 = 324$$

$$r = \sqrt{324} = 18$$

So, radius = 18 cm.

48. Cost price = 24000
Selling price = 20000
Loss = 24000 – 20000 = 4000

$$\text{Loss \%} = \frac{4000}{24000} \times 100$$

$$= \frac{1}{6} \times 100$$

$$= 16.666... \approx 16.67\%.$$

49. In a regular hexagon, the longest diagonal is equal to twice the side length.
Given longest diagonal = 4 m,

$2a = 4 \Rightarrow a = 2$ m

Area of a regular hexagon:

$$\text{Area} = \frac{3\sqrt{3}}{2} a^2$$

Substituting $a = 2$:

$$\text{Area} = \frac{3\sqrt{3}}{2} \times 2^2 = \frac{3\sqrt{3}}{2} \times 4 = 6\sqrt{3}$$

So, the area of the regular hexagon is $6\sqrt{3}$ m^2.

50. Weighted average:

$$= 86 \times \frac{40}{100} + 72 \times \frac{60}{100}$$

$$= 86 \times 0.4 + 72 \times 0.6$$
$$= 34.4 + 43.2 = 77.6.$$

51. Let the principal deposited = P. Rate of interest = 4% per annum. Compound interest of the second year only is given as 208.
Amount after 1st year

$$= P \times \left(1 + \frac{4}{100}\right) = 1.04P$$

Inerest of 2nd year

$$= 4\% \text{ of } 1.04\text{ P}$$

$$= \frac{4}{100} \times 1.04P = 0.0416P$$

Given,

$$0.0416P = 208$$

$$P = \frac{208}{0.0416} = 5000.$$

52. Qualified candidates: 2016

P = 157, N = 180,
R = 320, S = 460

Total_{2016} = 157 + 180 + 320 + 460
= 1117

2018

P = 224, N = 250, R = 348, S = 306

Total_{2018} = 224 + 250 + 348 + 306
= 1128

Total qualified (2016 + 2018):
1117 + 1128 = 2245

Appeared candidates: 2017
340 + 150 + 280 + 370 = 1140
2019
332 + 420 + 567 + 391 = 1710
Total appeared (2017 + 2019):
1140 + 1710 = 2850

Percentage

$$= \frac{2245}{2850} \times 100$$

$$= 78.7719\% \approx 78.8\%.$$

53. Let initial population = 100.
After 1st year
100 × 1.012 = 101.2
After 2nd year
101.2 × 1.016 = 102.8192
Total increase = 102.8192 – 100
= 2.8192% ≈ 2.82%.

54.
$$\text{Filling rate} = \frac{1}{8} \text{ tank/hour}$$

$$\text{Leakage emptying rate} = \frac{1}{12} \text{ tank/hour}$$

$$\text{Net rate} = \frac{1}{8} - \frac{1}{12} = \frac{3-2}{24} = \frac{1}{24}$$

$$\text{Time required} = \frac{1}{1/24} = 24 \text{ hours.}$$

55. Marked price = 61500

After first discount (10%)

$$61500 \times \frac{90}{100} = 55350$$

After second discount (20%)

$$55350 \times \frac{80}{100} = 44280$$

Final selling price = ₹ 44,280.

56.
$$v_1 = 52$$
$$v_2 = 52 + \frac{60}{100} \times 52$$
$$= 52 \times 1.6 = 83.2$$
$$v_{avg} = \frac{2v_1v_2}{v_1 + v_2} = \frac{2 \times 52 \times 83.2}{52 + 83.2}$$
$$= \frac{8652.8}{135.2} = 64.$$

57. Sum of 8 numbers = 8 × 12 = 96

Sum of remaining 7 numbers = 7 × 11 = 77

Removed number = 96 − 77 = 19.

58. Let, $x = 5.2333...$

Separate the integer and decimal part:

$$x = 5 + 0.2333...$$

Let, $y = 0.2333...$

Multiply by 10:

$$10y = 2.333...$$

Subtract:

$$10y - y = 2.333... - 0.2333...$$
$$9y = 2.1$$
$$y = \frac{2.1}{9} = \frac{21}{90} = \frac{7}{30}$$

Now,

$$x = 5 + \frac{7}{30} = \frac{150 + 7}{30} = \frac{157}{30}$$

So, the correct vulgar fraction is $\frac{157}{30}$.

59. Speed of first train = 50 km/hr

Speed of second train = 90 km/hr

Relative speed (opposite directions):

$$50 + 90 = 140 \text{ km/hr}$$

Convert into m/s:

$$140 \times \frac{1000}{3600} = \frac{350}{9} = 38.888... \text{ m/s}$$

Total distance crossed in 17 seconds:

$$\frac{350}{9} \times 17 = \frac{5950}{9} = 661.11 \text{ m}$$

Length of one train = 500 m

Length of other train:

$$661.11 - 500 = 161.11 \text{ m.}$$

60. Given,

$$8A = 6B = 3C = k$$
$$A = \frac{k}{8}, B = \frac{k}{6}, C = \frac{k}{3}$$

Toatl money: $\frac{k}{8} + \frac{k}{6} + \frac{k}{3}$

LCM = 24:

$$\frac{3k + 4k + 8k}{24} = \frac{15k}{24} = \frac{5k}{8}$$

Given total = 60800:

$$\frac{5k}{8} = 60800$$
$$k = \frac{60800 \times 8}{5} = 97280$$

Share of A:

$$A = \frac{k}{8} = \frac{97280}{8} = 12160$$

So, the share of A is ₹ 12,160.

61. The sentence contrasts outward behaviour with inner atmosphere. Even though they spoke calmly, nervousness stayed in the room, which correctly reflects calm speech not removing tension. Other options do not logically fit this contrast.

62. Sentence **S** introduces the central idea of leadership and vision. **R** logically follows by explaining what that vision involves. **P** then adds how a leader acts when facing uncertainty while pursuing that vision. **Q** concludes by defining how leadership success is ultimately measured, making **SRPQ** the most coherent order.

63. The correct spelling is Ephemeral. The given word "Ephimeral" is incorrectly spelt, while the other options are correctly spelled English words.

64. A hedonist is a person who is devoted to pleasure and self-indulgence. The other options describe restraint, moral strictness, or emotional control, which are opposite in meaning.

65. The antonym of deceptive is straightforward, as it implies honesty and lack of deceit. The other options do not express the opposite meaning of deception.

66. Beguile means to charm or attract someone pleasantly, sometimes deceptively. Bore is the opposite, as it means to make someone feel weary or uninterested. The other options are either similar in meaning (enchant, mislead) or not true opposites.

67. The blank requires an adjective to describe the noun "voice." Loud is the correct adjective. Loudest and louder are comparative/superlative forms, and loudly is an adverb, so they are grammatically incorrect here.

68. The sentence expresses a condition under which attending the seminar is allowed. Provided that correctly introduces a condition. The other options do not fit the intended conditional meaning.

69. The idiom *off the hook* means being freed from blame, responsibility, or punishment, that is, to get out of trouble. The other options convey opposite or unrelated meanings.

70. Sentence **B** introduces his long-held belief about isolation and excellence. **A** logically follows by describing the consequences of that belief. **C** shows the emotional turning point where isolation becomes unbearable. **D** concludes with realization and reflection, making this the most coherent and meaningful order.

71. The word plateform is misspelt. The correct spelling is platform. All other words–offense, premises, and punishable–are correctly spelt.

72. The subject "She" is third person singular, so the verb must be in the present simple form with -s. Hence, strives is grammatically correct. The other options do not fit the sentence structure.

73. Monophobia means fear of being alone. The sentence clearly describes fear of solitude, making this the correct one-word substitute. The other options refer to fear of foreigners, open spaces, and water, respectively.

74. The noun violin is specific and identifiable because it "once belonged to his late grandfather." Therefore, the definite article the is required.

75. Honest begins with a silent 'h' sound, so an is used. Surprise begins with a consonant sound, so a is correct. Hence, the correct pair is an, a.

76. The passage explains that giraffes' spots help them hide from enemies (camouflage) and that the skin beneath the spots may help them maintain the right body temperature.

77. The central focus of the passage is the birth of an unusual giraffe without spots at Brights Zoo, making this title the most accurate and comprehensive.

78. The passage clearly states that the baby giraffe was born at Brights Zoo in Limestone, Tennessee.

79. In the passage, the word unique is used to describe how rare and different the giraffe is because it has no spots. Unusual is the closest synonym in this context.

80. The passage specifies that instead of having spots, the baby giraffe's fur is light brown.

81. वाक्य में भूतकाल में दो कार्य एक साथ चल रहे हैं–सुरेश का गाना और गीता का सोना। ऐसी स्थिति में अपूर्ण भूतकाल का सही प्रयोग "रहा था" होता है।

82. 'दाँतों तले उँगली दबाना' लोकोक्ति का अर्थ किसी घटना पर अत्यधिक आश्चर्य व्यक्त करना होता है।

83. 'व्याल' शब्द का प्रयोग प्रायः बड़े या भयानक साँप के लिए किया जाता है, अतः इसका सही पर्यायवाची साँप है।

84. सही क्रम से वाक्य बनेगा–"यह ताला किसी दूसरी कुंजी से नहीं खुलता", जो व्याकरण और अर्थ दोनों की दृष्टि से सही है।

85. सही वर्तनी "आजकल" होती है। वाक्य में "आजकाल" लिखना वर्तनी की अशुद्धि है।

86. हिंदी व्याकरण और वाक्य-विन्यास के अनुसार विशेषण उस संज्ञा से पहले आता है जिसकी वह विशेषता बताता है। यहाँ गर्म विशेषण सूप की विशेषता बता रहा है, इसलिए "गर्म सूप" का प्रयोग व्याकरणसम्मत है। वाक्य की संरचना भी मानक क्रम में है– मुझे (कर्ता/अनुभवकर्ता) + टमाटर का गर्म सूप (कर्म) + पीना अच्छा लगता है (क्रिया)। अन्य विकल्पों में या तो विशेषण का स्थान अस्वाभाविक है या पदक्रम मानक हिंदी के अनुरूप नहीं है।

87. 'जो सबको समान भाव से समझता-देखता हो' के लिए समदर्शी शब्द सर्वाधिक उपयुक्त है, क्योंकि इसका अर्थ सभी को समान दृष्टि से देखने वाला व्यक्ति होता है।

88. हाथी तद्भव शब्द है, जो संस्कृत शब्द हस्ती से विकसित हुआ है। अन्य विकल्प तत्सम शब्द हैं।

89. वाक्य 'कुछ लड़के खेल रहे हैं' में कुछ शब्द लड़कों की संख्या बताने वाला उचित विशेषण है और वाक्य को अर्थपूर्ण बनाता है।

90. इस वाक्य में सभी शब्दों की वर्तनी शुद्ध है। अन्य विकल्पों में 'पदाधिकारी' या 'चुनाव' शब्द की वर्तनी गलत है।

91. 'किसी देश के मंत्रियों में सबसे बड़ा' पद प्रधानमंत्री को दर्शाता है, क्योंकि वही मंत्रिपरिषद् का प्रमुख होता है।

92. 'अड्डे पर चहकना' मुहावरे का अर्थ अपने ही क्षेत्र या स्थान पर प्रभाव/रोब दिखाना होता है।

93. वाक्य में उद्देश्य सूचक कारक की आवश्यकता है– "कुछ खाने के लिए ले आओ" वाक्य व्याकरण की दृष्टि से सही है।

94. 'हंस' शब्द के अनेक अर्थों में दर्शनशास्त्र में जीवात्मा का अर्थ भी प्रचलित है (परमहंस, हंस-तत्त्व आदि संदर्भों में)।

95. 'तरिणी' शब्द का अर्थ पार लगाने वाली वस्तु अर्थात नौका होता है।

96. गद्यांश में स्पष्ट है कि आदिकाल में व्यक्ति पर किसी भी नियम का बंधन नहीं था, अधिकार-कर्तव्यों में संघर्ष होता था और नियमों की कमी उसे खलती थी। इसी कारण मानव प्रसन्न नहीं था।

97. गद्यांश में रेखांकित शब्द 'निरंकुश' ऐसे व्यक्ति के लिए प्रयुक्त है जो किसी नियम, बंधन या व्यवस्था को स्वीकार नहीं करता।

98. पूरे गद्यांश का केंद्रीय भाव यह है कि मानव ने अपनी आवश्यकताओं की पूर्ति और विकास के लिए नियम बनाए और उन्हीं नियमों का पालन अनुशासन कहलाता है। इसलिए सामाजिक नियमों के पालन पर बल दिया गया है।

99. गद्यांश के अनुसार व्यक्ति के बहुमुखी विकास में सहायक नियमों का पालन ही अनुशासन है, न कि केवल शासक या शासन से जुड़ा नियंत्रण।

100. गद्यांश का मुख्य विषय मानव जीवन में अनुशासन का उद्भव, उसका महत्व और विकास है, इसलिए इसका सर्वाधिक उपयुक्त शीर्षक 'अनुशासन की संकल्पना' है।

101. In a balanced diet, protein should contribute about 10–35% of the total daily energy intake. This range is considered appropriate for maintaining body functions, growth, and tissue repair.

102. Karyotyping is a diagnostic test used to study the number and structure of chromosomes. It helps in detecting chromosomal abnormalities such as Down syndrome. Chorionic villus sampling is a sampling technique, not the diagnostic analysis itself.

103. Astigmatism is a condition caused by abnormal curvature of the lens or cornea, which interferes with the proper focusing of light on the retina, resulting in blurred vision.

104. 0.5% sodium hypochlorite is used as a disinfectant to clean contaminated Mackintoshes because it is effective against a wide range of microorganisms.

105. Prolonged vomiting leads to loss of gastric hydrochloric acid from the body. This increases blood alkalinity and results in metabolic alkalosis.

106. Korotkoff sounds are the characteristic sounds heard through a stethoscope when measuring blood pressure using a non-invasive method. They indicate the systolic and diastolic pressures as blood flow changes in the artery.

107. A normal PaO_2 value is about 80–100 mmHg. The given PaO_2 of 75 mmHg is below normal, indicating reduced oxygen levels in arterial blood, which is termed hypoxemia, commonly seen in chronic smokers with lung disease.

108. Green leafy vegetables, cucumbers, and drumstick leaves are rich in dietary fiber. Increased fiber intake improves bowel movement and helps prevent constipation.

109. The vastus lateralis muscle is the recommended intramuscular injection site for infants because it is well developed, easily accessible, and has minimal risk of nerve or vascular injury.

110. Carbon monoxide is a colourless, odourless, and tasteless poisonous gas. It binds strongly with haemoglobin, reducing oxygen delivery to tissues and making it highly dangerous.

111. Stress incontinence refers to the involuntary leakage of urine that occurs when there is a sudden increase in intra-abdominal pressure, such as during coughing, sneezing, laughing, or lifting heavy objects.

112. A Kardex is a portable card-based index system used by nurses to organise and quickly access essential patient information collected during admission, such as care plans, medications, and treatments.

113. In ABCD Nutritional Assessment, the letter 'A' stands for Anthropometry, which involves the measurement of body parameters like height, weight, BMI, and skinfold thickness to assess nutritional status.

114. Autoclaving is a method of sterilisation that uses steam under pressure to destroy microorganisms, including spores, and is commonly used for sterilising surgical instruments and medical equipment.

115. Cheyne-Stokes respiration is characterised by a gradual decrease in the rate and depth of breathing followed by a temporary pause (apnoea), commonly seen in certain neurological and cardiac conditions.

116. The prostate gland contains the prostatic utricle, two ejaculatory ducts, and the prostatic urethra. The ureter does not pass through the prostate; it carries urine from the kidneys to the bladder.

117. Cell degranulation refers to the release of preformed mediators from mast cells or basophils. Histamine is a major mediator stored in these granules and is released during degranulation. In addition, histamine can act as a regulator and, under certain conditions, further induce or promote mast cell degranulation, especially in IgE-mediated allergic reactions. Prostaglandins are synthesized after activation, while heparin and serotonin are mainly released products rather than primary triggers. Hence, histamine is the most appropriate answer.

118. In a respiratory emergency, the priority is to ensure airway patency and breathing. Opening the airway and checking for breathing follows the basic life support principle of Airway first.

119. A sitz bath (warm water bath covering the hips and buttocks) helps improve blood circulation and relieves congestion of pelvic organs, commonly used in conditions like hemorrhoids and pelvic discomfort.

120. In case of infiltration, the immediate nursing action is to stop the IV infusion to prevent further fluid leakage into surrounding tissues. Other interventions follow after stopping the infusion.

121. The pH is elevated (7.6), indicating alkalosis. $PaCO_2$ is decreased (30 mmHg), while HCO_3^- is normal (24 mEq), showing that the alkalosis is due to excessive loss of carbon dioxide from the lungs. Hence, this ABG pattern suggests respiratory alkalosis.

122. Mitosis produces two genetically identical diploid cells for growth and repair, whereas meiosis produces four genetically different haploid cells for sexual reproduction.

123. The C-shaped cartilaginous rings of the trachea keep the airway open at all times, preventing its collapse during breathing, especially during inspiration.

124. Osmoreceptors that monitor the water content and osmolarity of the blood are located in the hypothalamus, which plays a key role in regulating thirst and antidiuretic hormone (ADH) secretion.

125. Immunoglobulin A (IgA) is the principal antibody found in body secretions such as milk, saliva, tears, sweat, nasal fluids, colostrum, and secretions of the respiratory, intestinal, and genital tracts, providing mucosal immunity.

126. Hypoxia refers to insufficient oxygen supply to body tissues. Dyspnea is difficulty in breathing, cyanosis is bluish discoloration due to low oxygen saturation, and asphyxia is severe oxygen deprivation often due to airway obstruction.

127. Antibody-mediated cytotoxic hypersensitivity is classified as Type II hypersensitivity, in which IgG or IgM antibodies bind to antigens on cell surfaces, leading to cell damage or destruction.

128. Chyle is a milky white lymph rich in absorbed fats, formed during digestion and absorbed from the small intestine via lacteals.

129. The falx cerebri is formed by an inward projection of the inner layer of the cerebral dura mater between the two cerebral hemispheres.

130. The ABG shows metabolic acidosis (low pH, low bicarbonate) with elevated lactate due to septic shock. The correct management is to treat the underlying cause by improving tissue perfusion and oxygenation, not by routine bicarbonate administration, which does not correct lactic acidosis at its source.

131. The external intercostal muscles elevate the ribs upwards and outwards during inspiration, thereby increasing the transverse diameter of the thoracic cavity and aiding inhalation.

132. The shoulder joint is a classic ball and socket joint, allowing movement in all directions. Wrist, elbow, and knee joints are examples of gliding or hinge joints.

133. Blood and lymph are connective tissues with a fluid matrix. Their matrix is plasma in blood and lymphatic fluid in lymph, unlike solid connective tissues such as bone or tendon.

134. The serratus anterior muscle helps stabilise the scapula and assists in elevating the ribs during forced inspiration, making it an accessory inspiratory muscle of the upper back and chest.

135. Puerperal infection in the postnatal period is classically caused by Group-A streptococcus, which is historically associated with puerperal sepsis and severe postpartum infections.

136. Flagella are long, whip-like appendages that provide motility to bacteria. Episomes are genetic elements, spores are for survival, and fimbriae are mainly for attachment.

137. In SIADH, fluid retention leads to dilutional hyponatremia. Slight head-end elevation helps reduce cerebral edema and intracranial pressure. Patients require fluid restriction, not excess fluids, and monitoring is for hyponatremia, not hypernatremia.

138. In the life cycle of the malaria parasite, microgametocytes develop into male gametes, while macrogametocytes are female.

139. Passive immunity protects humans through the administration of ready-made antibodies via injection, such as immunoglobulins or antiserum. The body does not actively produce antibodies in this type.

140. Prolonged use of corticosteroids suppresses immunity and alters oral flora, predisposing individuals to oral candidiasis.

141. Astereognosis refers to the inability to recognise objects by touch despite intact sensory function. Apraxia is inability to perform learned movements, agnosia is inability to recognise objects by sight/sound, and akinesia is absence or loss of voluntary movement.

142. Steatorrhea (fatty stools) occurs in obstructed bile flow because bile salts do not reach the duodenum. Bile salts are essential for emulsification and absorption of fats; their absence leads to fat malabsorption.

143. Viruses are classified based on the type of nucleic acid (DNA or RNA), molecular weight, and structure. These features are central to viral classification systems, unlike fungi, parasites, or bacteria.

144. The sphincter of Oddi regulates the flow of pancreatic juice and bile into the duodenum by controlling the opening at the hepatopancreatic ampulla.

145. Postpartum blues typically occur within a few days after delivery and are self-limiting. The recommended management is reassurance, emotional support, and counseling rather than medications or invasive treatments.

146. Struvite renal calculi are more common in women because they are frequently associated with urinary tract infections caused by urease-producing bacteria, which occur more often in females.

147. Chyme is the semi-fluid mixture of partially digested food and gastric juices that is formed in the stomach before passing into the duodenum.

148. Resolution is the ability of a compound microscope to distinguish two closely placed points as separate, allowing clear separation of fine details of the specimen.

149. Central nervous system stimulants are prescribed in ADHD to improve attention span, concentration, and impulse control by enhancing neurotransmitter activity in the brain.

150. Vitamin B12 is essential for red blood cell production and DNA synthesis. Deficiency leads to impaired RBC formation and megaloblastic anemia.

151. In patients with severe myxedema coma, thyroid hormone replacement increases metabolic rate and myocardial oxygen demand. Therefore, nurses must closely monitor for myocardial ischemia, especially in elderly patients or those with underlying cardiac disease.

152. Anosmia is the medical term for the loss of the sense of smell. Loss of taste is ageusia, vision is amaurosis, and touch is hypoesthesia/anesthesia.

153. Hypovolaemia leads to reduced circulating blood volume, resulting in decreased renal perfusion and poor kidney function, which can precipitate or worsen acute kidney injury.

154. Prescribing medications is the responsibility of a physician or authorised prescriber. Nurses are responsible for pain assessment, setting goals, and providing patient education, but not prescribing analgesics.

155. The Johari Window model helps resolve conflicts by enhancing self-awareness and improving communication, thereby increasing mutual understanding and reducing interpersonal barriers.

156. Extrauterine spread of puerperal infection is indicated by pelvic or peritoneal involvement, evidenced by pus in the pouch of Douglas along with systemic signs like swinging fever and gastrointestinal symptoms.

157. Patients on anticoagulant therapy (e.g., warfarin) require dietary regulation, especially consistent vitamin K intake. Advising "no dietary restriction" is incorrect; the other options are appropriate precautions.

158. Early voiding after delivery helps prevent bladder overdistension and urinary stasis, which can predispose to cystitis.

159. Atrial flutter is characterized on ECG by sawtooth-shaped flutter (F) waves, distinguishing it from atrial fibrillation and other arrhythmias.

160. Psychomotor retardation—slowed speech, thought, and movement—is a common feature of depressive disorders, rather than anxiety, phobia, or dementia.

161. The Denver Developmental Screening Test (DDST) is designed to assess developmental milestones in children from birth up to 6 years of age, covering gross motor, fine motor, language, and personal-social domains.

162. The Thematic Apperception Test (TAT) is a projective psychological test primarily used to assess an individual's personality, including underlying motives, conflicts, and interpersonal relationships.

163. A process recording is a systematic, formal written report of a therapeutic conversation between a nurse and a patient. It is used mainly in psychiatric nursing to analyze communication and nurse–patient interaction.

164. Total fluid = 1200 ml

$$\text{Time} = 24 \text{ hours}$$
$$= 24 \times 60 = 1440 \text{ minutes}$$
$$\text{Drop factor} = 60 \text{ drops/ml}$$
$$\text{Flow rate} = \frac{1200 \times 60}{1440}$$
$$= \frac{72000}{1440} = 50 \text{ drops/min.}$$

165. Isoniazid (INH) is a first-line antitubercular drug and is the drug of choice for the treatment and prophylaxis of tuberculosis.

166. During pregnancy, the enlarging gravid uterus elevates the diaphragm and displaces the heart upward and to the left, leading to a shift in the apex beat. The other options describe functional or hemodynamic changes rather than a direct anatomical change.

167. School-age children often view hospitalisation as a punishment for some wrongdoing. This perception is related to their developing sense of morality and cause-and-effect thinking.

168. In bacterial meningitis, CSF analysis typically shows decreased glucose (due to bacterial consumption) and elevated protein (due to increased permeability of the blood–brain barrier), along with fever and nuchal rigidity.

169. Advising prelacteal feeds is incorrect because they interfere with exclusive breastfeeding and increase the risk of infection. Exclusive breastfeeding, early initiation, and feeding from both breasts are correct practices.

170. During the postnatal period, the genital organs gradually return to their pre-pregnancy size and state through the physiological process known as involution.

171. Increased synthesis of thromboxane, a potent vasoconstrictor and platelet aggregator, leads to vasospasm and endothelial dysfunction, which are key mechanisms in the development of preeclampsia. Prostacyclin and nitric oxide are vasodilators.

172. Depersonalisation is the feeling of being detached from oneself, as if observing one's own thoughts or body from outside. Derealisation refers to detachment from the environment.

173. At birth, head circumference is greater than chest circumference. By around the 12th month, the head and chest circumferences become approximately equal.

174. Vitamin A supplementation helps reduce the severity, complications, and mortality associated with measles, especially in children.

175. At 10 weeks of gestation, ultrasound is primarily done to confirm and assess fetal viability, including presence of fetal heartbeat and accurate dating.

176. Maternal perception of fetal movements is reduced in conditions like chronic smoking, maternal obesity, and fetal CNS anomalies. Maternal hypoglycaemia does not typically reduce maternal perception of fetal movements and is therefore the exception.

177. In a sub-centre where injectable uterotonics may not be feasible, misoprostol 800 mcg sublingually is recommended as an immediate measure for postpartum hemorrhage before referral to a higher centre.

178. Ovulation is the process by which a secondary oocyte is released from the ovary following rupture of a mature Graafian follicle.

179. The Hirschberg test is also known as the corneal light reflex test, used to detect strabismus by observing the reflection of light on the cornea.

180. The fontanel formed by the sagittal suture anteriorly and the lambdoid sutures on either side is the posterior fontanel.

181. The fundamental concept of education is the discipline and development of the mind, enabling individuals to think rationally, act ethically, and contribute meaningfully to society. Earning money or status are outcomes, not the core purpose.

182. Transfer is an internal recruitment method in which an employee is shifted from one department to another at the same level within the organisation, without change in rank or pay.

183. The Block Development Officer (BDO) functions as the ex-officio secretary of the Panchayat Samiti, coordinating administration and implementing development programmes at the block level.

184. According to the ecological concept, health is viewed as a dynamic balance between human beings and their environment, emphasizing adaptation and interaction rather than mere absence of disease.

185. A long-term, future-oriented plan spanning 10 years with phased implementation for computerisation and automation is known as strategic planning, which sets overall direction and goals for the organisation.

186. The Ortolani manoeuver is used in newborns to detect hip instability and developmental dysplasia of the hip (DDH) by attempting to relocate a dislocated femoral head into the acetabulum. Other manoeuvers listed are unrelated to hip assessment.

187. Management by Objective (MBO) is an individual method of performance appraisal, where performance is evaluated against clearly defined, mutually agreed objectives. Ranking and paired comparison are comparative methods, while 360-degree feedback is a multi-source method.

188. In nursing manpower management, induction refers to the process of orienting and helping newly appointed nurses adjust to their roles, responsibilities, work environment, and organisational culture.

189. Mifepristone 10 mg, taken as a single dose within 72 hours of unprotected intercourse, is an accepted method of post-coital (emergency) contraception. The other options contain incorrect doses or timings.

190. In epidemiology, secular trend refers to long-term changes in disease frequency or health indicators that show a consistent upward or downward pattern over many years, distinct from seasonal or short-term variations.

191. Primordial prevention focuses on preventing the emergence of risk factors themselves. Educating adolescents before smoking habits develop directly prevents initiation, making this the best example.

192. Zilla Parishad functions at the district level, not the village level. Gram Sabha, Gram Panchayat, and Nyaya Panchayat operate at or are associated with the village level.

193. Effective community mental health care includes after-care services to ensure continuity of treatment, rehabilitation, relapse prevention, and social reintegration of persons with mental illness.

194. Emotional competence in the family coping index reflects maturity, integrity, emotional stability, and the ability of family members to manage stress and relationships effectively.

195. In men, a waist circumference greater than 102 cm is associated with a significantly increased risk of cardiovascular disease due to central (abdominal) obesity.

196. About 90% of stroke patients present with hemiplegia, which is paralysis of one side of the body due to involvement of the motor pathways in the brain.

197. Laws regulating working hours are externally enforced by the government, not framed by the organisation itself; hence they are examples of imposed policies.

198. Ice application can worsen tissue damage by causing vasoconstriction and frost injury. Cooling with cool running water is recommended, not ice.

199. Live vaccines are contraindicated in children with HIV infection due to the risk of causing disease in an immunocompromised host. Killed vaccines, toxoids, and immunoglobulins are generally safe.

200. Transformational leadership is characterised by proactive leadership that inspires, motivates, and empowers followers, fostering change and higher levels of performance.

Previous Years' Paper

DSSSB—Nursing Officer Exam 2024

(Exam held on 14-08-2024)

SECTION-A

General Intelligence and Reasoning Ability

1. Seven boxes A, B, C, D, R, S and T are kept one over the other but not necessarily in the same order.

Only three boxes are kept below B. Only two boxes are kept between B and S. Only A is kept above C. R is kept at some place below D and at some place above T.

Which box is kept at the second position from the bottom?

1. D
2. T
3. C
4. A

2. Read the given statements and conclusions carefully. Assuming that the information given in the statements is true, even if it appears to be at variance with commonly known facts, decide which of the given conclusions logically follow(s) from the statements.

Statements:

Some mountains are ants.

All elephants are ants.

Conclusions:

I. Some elephants are mountains.

II. Some ants are not mountains.

1. Neither conclusion (I) nor (II) follows.
2. Only conclusion (I) follows.
3. Only conclusion (II) follows.
4. Both conclusions (I) and (II) follow.

3. Identify the figure given in the options which when put in place of '?' will logically complete the series.

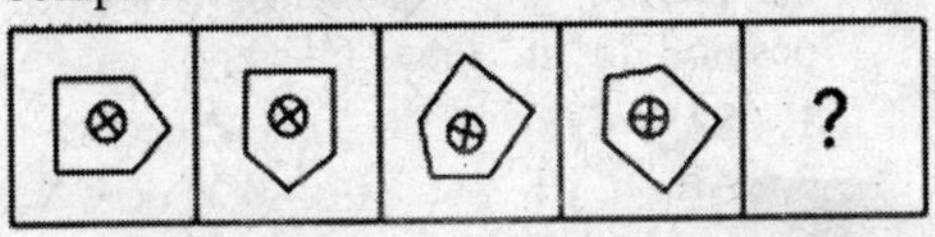

1. 

2. 

3. 

4. 

1. 2	**2.** 1	**3.** 3

4. If the water source is placed along A-B, as shown in the figure, which of the given options will be the water reflection of the given figure?

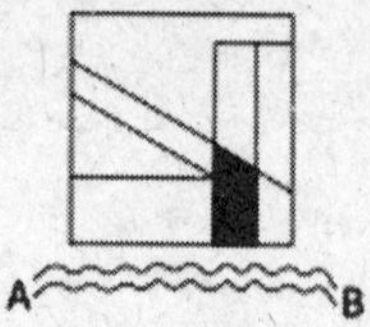

1. 
2. 
3. 
4. 

5. Based on the English alphabetical order, three of the following four letter-cluster pairs are alike in a certain way and thus form a group. Which letter-cluster pair DOES NOT belong to that group?

(Note: The odd one out is not based on the number of consonants/vowels or their position in the letter-cluster.)

1. SZ – QB 2. HZ – EB
3. AR – YT 4. WV – UX

6. In a certain code language, 'time to study' is coded as 'mh cy sp' and 'study the case' is coded as 'bg km cy'. How is 'study' coded in that language?

1. cy 2. km
3. sp 4. mh

7. Ehmran ranked 62nd from the bottom and 11th from the top in his class. How many students are there in his class?

1. 72 2. 60
3. 59 4. 68

8. A, B, C, D, Q and R live on six different floors of the same building. The lowermost floor in the building is numbered 1, the floor above it is numbered 2 and so on till the topmost floor, which is numbered 6. Only A lives above B. D lives immediately below B. Only R lives below Q. Who lives on floor number 3?

1. A 2. D
3. C 4. R

9. Select the set in which the numbers are related in the same way as are the numbers of the following sets.

(NOTE: Operations should be performed on the whole numbers, without breaking down the numbers into their constituent digits. E.g. 13 – Operations on 13 such as adding/subtracting/multiplying to 13 can be performed. Breaking down 13 into 1 and 3 and then performing mathematical operations on 1 and 3 is not allowed.)

(18, 44, 21)
(32, 65, 28)

1. (44, 53, 89) 2. (29, 93, 13)
3. (25, 67, 11) 4. (41, 63, 17)

10. What should come in place of '?' in the given series?

18 39 67 102 144 ?

1. 181 2. 185
3. 189 4. 193

11. Select the triad that follows the same pattern as that followed by the two triads given below. Both triads follow the same pattern.

LO-JR-MP
MP-KS-NQ

1. QT-OW-RV 2. PS-NV-QT
3. OR-MU-PT 4. NQ-LT-OS

12. Six teachers are sitting around a circular table facing the centre. Kerkar is an immediate neighbour of both Anika and Natasha. Kavita is sitting second to the left of Anika. Poonam is an immediate neighbour of Natasha and Kavita. Sasha is sitting second to the left of Kerkar. Who is sitting third to the left of Poonam?

1. Kavita 2. Anika
3. Sasha 4. Kerkar

4. 3	**5.** 2	**6.** 1	**7.** 1	**8.** 3	**9.** 4	**10.** 4	**11.** 2	**12.** 2

13. Identify the figure given in the options which when put in place of the question mark (?) will logically complete the series.

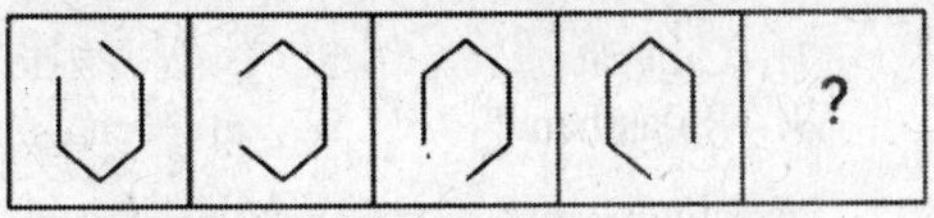

1. 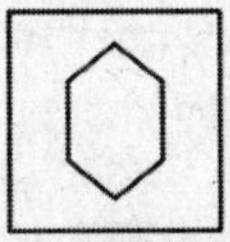
2. 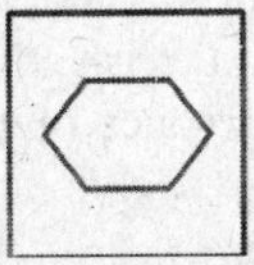
3. 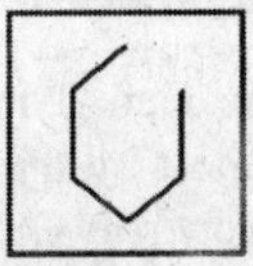
4. 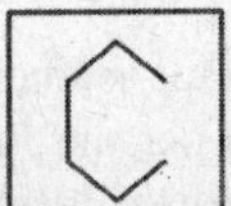

14. Refer to the following letter and symbol series and answer the question that follows. Counting to be done from left to right only.

(Left) G C & R Ω Y # E S * £ B U C & % D @ U $ P % Q & E (Right)

How many such symbols are there each of which is immediately preceded by a vowel but not immediately followed by a vowel?

1. Three
2. One
3. None
4. Two

15. W is the sister of N's mother P. F is the husband of P. R is the brother of F. How is W related to R?

1. Brother's wife's mother
2. Brother's mother
3. Brother's sister
4. Brother's wife's sister

16. Based on the English alphabetical order, three of the following four letter-clusters are alike in a certain way and thus form a group. Which letter-cluster DOES NOT belong to that group?
(Note: The odd one out is not based on the number of consonants/vowels or their position in the letter-cluster.)

1. DZX
2. LHF
3. UQN
4. GCA

17. What will come in place of the question mark (?) in the following equation, if '+' and '−' are interchanged and '×' and '÷' are interchanged?
$363 \div 3 + 1148 \times 4 - 269 = ?$

1. 1022
2. 1071
3. 1036
4. 1098

18. Select the set in which the numbers are related in the same way as are the numbers of the following sets.

(NOTE: Operations should be performed on the whole numbers, without breaking down the numbers into its constituent digits. E.g. 13 – Operations on 13 such as adding/subtracting/multiplying etc. to 13 can be performed. Breaking down 13 into 1 and 3 and then performing mathematical operations on 1 and 3 is not allowed)

(10, 80, 8)
(6, 96, 16)

1. (13, 117, 8)
2. (15, 117, 8)
3. (11, 88, 7)
4. (9, 108, 12)

19. If 'A' stands for '÷', 'B' stands for '×', 'C' stands for '+' and 'D' stands for '−', what will come in place of the question mark (?) in the following equation?
27 A 9 D 35 C 11 B 6 = ?

1. 38
2. 34
3. 28
4. 36

20. Refer to the following number and symbol series and answer the question that follows. Counting to be done from left to right only.

(Left) 2 & 6 @ 8 $ 7 & 4 Ω 9 # 1 * 8 @ Ω 9 1 (Right)

How many such symbols are there each of which is immediately preceded by an odd number but not immediately followed by an even number?

1. One
2. Three
3. Two
4. None

13. 4	**14.** 2	**15.** 4	**16.** 3	**17.** 2	**18.** 4	**19.** 2	**20.** 1

General Awareness

21. Aravind Adiga was given the Booker Prize in 2008 for which of the following books?

1. The White Tiger
2. The God of Small Things
3. Fasting, Feasting
4. The Inheritance of Loss

22. Which season in India experiences the highest temperatures?

1. Monsoon 2. Summer
3. Winter 4. Pre-monsoon

23. Who among the following unveiled 'Ethanol 100', an automotive fuel aimed at reducing emissions and promoting sustainability?

1. Narendra Modi
2. Hardeep Singh Puri
3. Rajnath Singh
4. Amit Shah

24. According to Article 51A of the Indian Constitution, which of the following Fundamental Duties requires citizens to uphold and protect the sovereignty, unity and integrity of India?

1. Second Fundamental Duty
2. Fourth Fundamental Duty
3. Third Fundamental Duty
4. Seventh Fundamental Duty

25. Which of the following is an advantage of Functional Organisation?

1. Increases coordination
2. Promotes flexibility
3. Encourages specialisation
4. Reduces conflicts

26. According to the Census 2011 of India, which of the following states has the lowest literacy rate?

1. Gujarat 2. Uttar Pradesh
3. Rajasthan 4. Arunachal Pradesh

27. In which year did Julius von Sachs' study establish that starch is the first visible product of photosynthesis?

1. 1890 2. 1854
3. 1840 4. 1875

28. What is India's rank in GenAI innovations as per the July 2024 report by the UN body World Intellectual Property Organisation (WIPO)?

1. Third 2. Seventh
3. First 4. Fifth

29. Who among the following announced his retirement from the head coach position of the Indian cricket team after team India won the T20 Cricket World Cup in July 2024?

1. Rahul Dravid 2. Sanjay Bangar
3. Ravi Shastri 4. Gautam Gambhir

30. Which of the following Articles of the Indian Constitution deals with the establishment and constitution of the Supreme Court?

1. Article 124 2. Article 44
3. Article 214 4. Article 370

31. Crop yields can decrease due to biotic and abiotic stresses in various conditions. Which of the following factors is/are classified as abiotic stress?

1. Insects 2. Frost
3. Nematodes 4. Diseases

32. At which place did Ishwar Chandra Vidyasagar set up a school for girls in India for the first time?

1. Madras 2. Calcutta
3. Delhi 4. Poona

21. 1	**22.** 2	**23.** 2	**24.** 3	**25.** 3	**26.** 4
27. 2	**28.** 4	**29.** 1	**30.** 1	**31.** 2	**32.** 2

33. Which of the following programmes has the Indian government started to support minority communities regarding women's rights?
1. Swachh Bharat Abhiyan
2. Pradhan Mantri Jan Dhan Yojana
3. Nai Roshni
4. Atal Pension Yojana

34. Which cytoskeletal element has a diameter of about 10 nanometres?
1. Centrioles
2. Microfilaments
3. Microtubules
4. Intermediate filaments

35. The Law of Variable Proportions assumes that:
1. all inputs are variable in the long run
2. one input is variable while others are fixed in short run
3. all inputs are fixed in the long run
4. all inputs are fixed in the short run

36. Tamil was the first language in India to be accorded Classical Language status in ____.
1. 1954 2. 1997
3. 2004 4. 2000

37. Magha Saptam Mela is celebrated in which of the following months?
1. January
2. April
3. February
4. March

38. In which year did Punjab National Bank start operating its business?
1. 1895 2. 1885
3. 1875 4. 1865

39. In which year was the Presidential and Vice-Presidential Elections Act passed?
1. 1952 2. 1953
3. 1950 4. 1951

40. What does IMD stand for in the context of weather forecasting in India?
1. Indian Meteorology Division
2. Indian Meteorological Department
3. Indian Monsoon Department
4. Indian Monsoon Directorate

Arithmetical and Numerical Ability

41. A and B can do a job in 24 days and 13 days, respectively. A works alone for 19 days and leaves. The number of days required by B to complete the remaining job is:
1. $2\frac{20}{24}$ 2. $2\frac{17}{24}$
3. $2\frac{15}{24}$ 4. $2\frac{14}{24}$

42. The volume (in m^3) of a cuboidal tank, whose dimensions are given as 16 m × 36 m × 14 m, is:
1. 8078
2. 8064
3. 8017
4. 8034

43. Find the value of q.

$$(q-2)^2 = \left[(19-8) \div 11 + \left(\frac{1}{2} \times 48\right)\right]$$

1. 5
2. 2
3. 7
4. 9

33. 3	**34.** 4	**35.** 2	**36.** 3	**37.** 3	**38.** 1
39. 1	**40.** 2	**41.** 2	**42.** 2	**43.** 3	

44. A train goes from A to B at a speed of 12 km/h and returns from B to A by the same route at 24 km/h. The average speed (in km/h) of the train during the two-way journey is:

1. 13 2. 18
3. 16 4. 14

45. Preetam bought an article for ₹ 344 and sold it to Preeti at a loss of 20%. With this amount, Preetam bought another article and sold it at a gain of 56%. What is Preetam's overall gain percentage?

1. 0.271 2. 0.248
3. 0.281 4. 0.274

46. A fruit seller had some Guavas. He sells 80% Guavas and still has 900 Guavas. Originally, number of Guavas, he had:

1. 6750 2. 1125
3. 4050 4. 4500

47. An amount of ₹ 903 is divided among three persons in the ratio of 6 : 2 : 7. The difference (in ₹) between the largest and the smallest shares in the distribution is:

1. 341 2. 301
3. 249 4. 367

48. A number divided by 56 gives the quotient 147 and remainder as 10. If the same number is divided by 55, the remainder is:

1. 47 2. 49
3. 54 4. 52

49. The internal surface area (in m^2) of an open cuboidal tank whose internal length, internal breadth, and internal height are given as 31 m, 20 m, and 22 m, respectively, is:

1. 2864 2. 2900
3. 2827 4. 2899

50. One-third of a journey is covered at a speed of 21 km/h, the next one-third of the journey is covered at a speed of 63 km/h and the remaining journey is covered at a speed of 86 km/h. The average speed (in km/h, rounded off to 1 decimal place) for the entire journey is:

1. 41.6 2. 38.6
3. 39.9 4. 43.4

51. Simplify: $2\frac{3}{5}+3\frac{1}{2}-\frac{3}{5}$.

1. $7\frac{1}{2}$ 2. $5\frac{1}{2}$
3. $6\frac{1}{2}$ 4. $8\frac{1}{2}$

52. A fruit seller had some Oranges. He sells 80% Oranges and still has 720 Oranges. Originally, number of Oranges, he had:

1. 3240
2. 3600
3. 5400
4. 900

53. A person saves 60% of his income. If his expenditure is ₹ 400, then his income (in ₹) is:

1. 840 2. 1040
3. 1000 4. 700

54. What sum (in ₹) will earn a simple interest of ₹ 480 in 3 years at 20% per year rate of interest?

1. 800 2. 400
3. 1600 4. 1200

55. The average of 13 numbers is 14. If each number is multiplied by 4, then what will the new average be:

1. 14 2. 56
3. 13 4. 4

44. 3	**45.** 2	**46.** 4	**47.** 2	**48.** 1	**49.** 1
50. 3	**51.** 2	**52.** 2	**53.** 3	**54.** 1	**55.** 2

56. Virat invested ₹ 52500 at 8% p.a. for 1 year at compound interest, compounded half-yearly. The amount received by him is:

1. ₹ 56784 2. ₹ 55909
3. ₹ 56480 4. ₹ 56992

57. A started a business with a capital of ₹ 922000. After 2 months, B joined him with a certain amount of capital. At the end of a year of A's starting the business, the profit was shared in the ratio 6 : 5. How much (in ₹) did B invest?

1. 922000 2. 937300
3. 910300 4. 933200

58. The sum of 6 numbers is 372. Find their average.

1. 60 2. 61
3. 63 4. 62

59. The list price of an article is ₹ 2000 and a discount of 10% is offered on the list price. What additional discount per cent on the already discounted price must be offered to a customer to bring the net selling price to ₹ 828?

1. 56 2. 50
3. 54 4. 57

60. Akash can complete a piece of work alone in 8 days and Prakash can complete the same piece of work alone in 14 days. They started the work together, but Akash had to leave 4 days before the completion of the work. In how many days will the work complete?

1. $7\frac{10}{11}$ days 2. $7\frac{12}{11}$ days
3. $7\frac{7}{11}$ days 4. $7\frac{8}{11}$ days

English Language and Comprehension

61. Select the most appropriate idiom that can substitute the underlined words in the given sentence.

The new policy will <u>start immediately</u>.

1. pull the wool over your eyes
2. hit the nail over the head
3. hit the ground running
4. cry over spilt milk

62. Select the option that can be used as a one-word substitute for the given phrase.

A person who pretends to have more knowledge or skill than they actually possess.

1. Drifter 2. Wanderer
3. Charlatan 4. Nihilist

63. Select the most appropriate option to fill in the blank.

She runs _____ athlete in her team.

1. faster than any other
2. fast than any
3. fastest than
4. more fast than any other

64. Select the most appropriate ANTONYM of the given word.

Profuse

1. Compliant
2. Sparse
3. Abundant
4. Depressed

65. Select the most appropriate synonym of the underlined word.

Ms. Apoorva's <u>enthusiasm</u> for the project was contagious.

1. Eagerness 2. Reluctance
3. Fear 4. Indifference

56. 1	**57.** 1	**58.** 4	**59.** 3	**60.** 3	**61.** 3	**62.** 3	**63.** 1	**64.** 2	**65.** 1

66. Select the most appropriate articles to fill in the blanks.

She saw _____ eagle flying over _____ mountains.

1. an; a
2. a; a
3. the; a
4. an; the

67. Select the most appropriate article to fill in the blank.

We visited _____ Louvre when we were in Paris.

1. a
2. the
3. an
4. No article required

68. Sentences of a paragraph are given below in jumbled order. Arrange the sentences in the correct order to form a meaningful and coherent paragraph.

P. Biotechnology and genetic engineering are at the forefront of scientific innovation.
Q. They offer solutions for medicine, agriculture and environmental sustainability.
R. They enable the improvement of crop resilience and development of biofuels.
S. They pave the way for gene therapy in which faulty genes are replaced with healthy ones.

1. PQRS
2. SQPR
3. RSQP
4. QRSP

69. Select the most appropriate idiom that can substitute the underlined words in the given sentence.

She completed the project <u>unaware of the situation</u>.

1. out of the woods
2. in the loop
3. in the dark
4. out of the blue

70. Select the most appropriate option to fill in the blank.

She has _____ experience in the field of aeronautics.

1. many
2. much
3. few
4. several

71. Select the most appropriate option to fill in the blank.

The politician's speech was filled with _____ promises that failed to address the real concerns of the people.

1. tangible
2. empty
3. meaningful
4. repugnant

72. Sentences of a paragraph are given below in jumbled order. Arrange the sentences in the correct order to form a meaningful and coherent paragraph.

A. The modern game of golf originated in 15th-century Scotland.
B. It is played on a course with a series of holes, usually 18, though recreational courses can have fewer holes.
C. The object of the game is to use as few strokes as possible to get a ball into each hole.
D. Golf is a club-and-ball sport in which players use various clubs to hit balls into a series of holes on a course.

1. DBCA
2. ABDC
3. DABC
4. ADBC

73. Select the INCORRECTLY spelt word.

1. Supercede
2. Commitment
3. Resilience
4. Frustration

74. Select the most appropriate ANTONYM of the given word.

Expensive

1. Valuable
2. Cheap
3. Costly
4. Pricey

75. Select the most appropriate option to fill in the blank.

There are only _____ apples left.

1. any
2. little
3. less
4. a few

66. 4	**67.** 2	**68.** 1	**69.** 3	**70.** 2	**71.** 2	**72.** 3	**73.** 1	**74.** 2	**75.** 4

Directions (Qs. No. 76 to 80): *Read the given passage and answer the questions that follow.*

In the heart of the bustling city, there lies a quaint bookstore that has stood the test of time. The shop, known as 'The Book Nook,' is a haven for book lovers of all ages. Its shelves are lined with a vast array of genres, from classic literature to modern science fiction. The owner, Mr. Thompson, is a bibliophile with an encyclopaedic knowledge of books. He often hosts reading clubs and author signings, fostering a sense of community among the city's literary enthusiasts. Despite the rise of digital media, The Book Nook continues to thrive, offering a serene escape from the fast-paced city life.

76. What can be inferred about Mr. Thompson's role in the community?

1. He is a key figure in fostering a love for reading.
2. He is indifferent to books.
3. He discourages social gatherings.
4. He only sells digital books.

77. Which real-world trend is contrary to the success of The Book Nook?

1. The increasing popularity of audiobooks
2. The growth of urban farming
3. The decline of digital media
4. The revival of independent bookstores

78. What is the name of the bookstore mentioned in the passage?

1. The Book Nook
2. The Reading Room
3. The Literary Lounge
4. The Novel Corner

79. Which of the following titles best fits the passage?

1. The Book Nook
2. A Digital World
3. Modern Science Fiction
4. The Bustling City

80. What is the antonym of the word "thrive" as used in the passage?

1. Prosper 2. Flourish
3. Decline 4. Succeed

हिन्दी भाषा और बोध

81. निम्नलिखित वाक्यों में से शुद्ध वाक्य का चयन कीजिए:

1. कालिदास का नाम किसने नहीं सुना?
2. कलिदाश का नाम किसने नहीं सुना?
3. कालिदाश का नाम किसने नहीं सुना?
4. कालीदास का नाम किसने नहीं सुना?

82. मक्खन का पर्यायवाची शब्द क्या है?

1. पावक 2. नवनीत
3. रसाल 4. कुमकुम

83. निम्नलिखित वाक्यों में उनके प्रथम तथा अन्तिम अंश संख्या 1 और 6 के अंतर्गत दिए गए हैं। बीच वाले चार अंश (य), (र), (ल), (व) के अंतर्गत बिना क्रम के हैं। चारों अंशों को उचित क्रमानुसार व्यवस्थित कर सही विकल्प चुनें:

1. सब जानते हैं कि हिन्दी

(य) सिद्ध होगी ही, अंग्रेजी सह राजभाषा पद

(र) देर-सवेर भारत की एकमात्र राजभाषा

(ल) से हटेगी ही, तो उस स्थिति

(व) के अनुकूल अपने को बना लेने के लिए

6. हम हिन्दी का अध्ययन कर रहे हैं।

1. र व ल य
2. ल र व य
3. र य ल व
4. ल य र व

76. 1	77. 1	78. 1	79. 1	80. 3	81. 1	82. 2	83. 3

84. 'कोयल आम की डाल ______ कूक रही है' वाक्य के रिक्त स्थान के लिए सर्वाधिक उपयुक्त कारक चिह्न है:

1. पर 2. से
3. में 4. के कारण

85. 'जिसकी थाह का पता न हो' वाक्यांश के लिए सार्थक शब्द है:

1. आहुत 2. अथाह
3. अथक 4. थाह

86. निम्नलिखित में से एक 'थामना' का अनेकार्थी नहीं है:

1. रोकना 2. पकड़ना
3. सहारा देना 4. भाग्य
1. 3 2. 2
3. 4 4. 1

87. 'मैं आया हूँ दर्शन करने'– उपर्युक्त वाक्य का उचित क्रम क्या है?

1. करने मैं दर्शन आया हूँ
2. मैं दर्शन करने हूँ आया
3. मैं दर्शन करने आया हूँ
4. करने आया मैं दर्शन हूँ
1. 1 2. 4
3. 2 4. 3

88. चर्म का तद्भव शब्द क्या है?

1. चुना 2. चना
3. चमड़ा 4. चंदा

89. निम्नलिखित कौन-सा शब्द 'स्त्री' का उपयुक्त पर्यायवाची नहीं है:

1. कांता 2. भार्या
3. वनिता 4. रमणी

90. निश्चित रूप से होने वाला। वाक्यांश के लिए सही शब्द क्या होगा?

1. अवश्यंभावी 2. भविष्य
3. अनिश्चित 4. अतीत

91. 'गाल बजाना' मुहावरे का सही अर्थ है:

1. व्यर्थ की बातें करना
2. चिल्लाना
3. अवसरवादी होना
4. सावधानी बरतना

92. मालिक सेवक को वेतन देता है। वाक्य में कारक है:

1. अधिकरण कारक 2. संप्रदान कारक
3. अपादान कारक 4. संबोधन कारक

93. अहिल्या गौतम ऋषि की पत्नी थी। वर्तनी के आधार पर शुद्ध रूप क्या है?

1. एहिल्या गौतम ऋषि की पत्नी थी।
2. अहिलिया गौतम ऋषि की पत्नी थी।
3. अहल्या गौतम ऋषि की पत्नी थी।
4. आहिल्या गौतम ऋषि की पत्नी थी।

94. निम्न में कौन-सा मुहावरा अपने अर्थ से असुमेलित है:

1. अँधेरे में रखना – कैद में रखना
2. अंधेर नगरी – जहाँ धाँधली हो
3. अंधेरखाता – अन्याय
4. अंधेरे घर का उजाला – इकलौता बेटा

95. सही विकल्प चुनकर वाक्य पूरा कीजिए:
वह ______ अलग रहता है।

1. तुझे 2. तुम
3. तेरे को 4. मुझसे

निर्देश (प्र.सं. 96-100 तक): *दिए गए गद्यांश के आधार पर पूछे गए प्रश्न का उत्तर दीजिए।*

न्याय हासिल करने के लिए हिंसात्मक और संवैधानिक दो रास्ते रहे हैं यह भी माना गया है कि हिंसा की राह से कुछ तात्कालिक स्वार्थ सिद्ध हो सकते हैं, न्याय हासिल नहीं

84. 1	**85.** 2	**86.** 3	**87.** 4	**88.** 3	**89.** 2
90. 1	**91.** 1	**92.** 2	**93.** 3	**94.** 1	**95.** 4

हो सकता, न्याय सिर्फ अपराधी को दंड देना नहीं है, उसे सुधारना तथा सच्चाई और ईमानदारी का एक समग्र वातावरण पैदा करना है ताकि अपराध न हो। एक उदारवादी समाज, गैर फौजी संस्कृति, पर्यावरण सचेतना, वैश्विक साझेदारी, टिकाऊ आर्थिक विकास, सामाजिक न्याय, गरीबों का आर्थिक सशक्तिकरण, बुद्धि सम्मत राष्ट्रवाद, धार्मिक सहिष्णुता, प्रेम और व्यवहार में संवेदनशीलता आदि को नए युग में न्याय के कदमों के रूप में देखा जाता है। यह भी कहा जा सकता है कि जहाँ भ्रष्टाचार का बढ़ा-चढ़ा रूप है, वहाँ न्याय बालू से तेल निकालना है।

96. प्रस्तुत गद्यांश के लिए उचित शीर्षक क्या है?

1. न्याय 2. अन्याय
3. विकासमान 4. उतार-चढ़ाव

1. 4 2. 3
3. 2 4. 1

97. न्याय हासिल करने के लिए कितने रास्ते होते हैं?

1. एक 2. दो
3. तीन 4. दस

1. 4 2. 3
3. 2 4. 1

98. 'बालू से तेल निकालना' मुहावरे का अर्थ क्या है?

1. निरंतर गतिशील होना।
2. समझदार होना।
3. प्रगतिशील होना।
4. असंभव को संभव कर दिखाना।

1. 3 2. 2
3. 4 4. 1

99. प्रस्तुत गद्यांश का वास्तविक जीवन से संबंध क्या है?

1. तात्कालिक स्वार्थ।
2. न्याय का मानव जीवन में उपयोग।
3. व्यवहार में संवेदनशीलता।
4. ईमानदारी का वातावरण पैदा करना।

1. 1 2. 4
3. 3 4. 2

100. उपर्युक्त गद्यांश के आधार पर एक का संबंध 'अपराध' से नहीं है?

1. अभियोग 2. गुनाह
3. मुजिर 4. भूल

1. 4 2. 3
3. 1 4. 2

SECTION-B

Post Specific Subject-Related Questions

101. Which of the following is an example of a Hinge joint?

1. Shoulder joint
2. Hip joint
3. Atlantoaxial joint
4. Elbow joint

102. Serotonin is produced by the _____.

1. beta cells 2. raphe nuclei
3. alpha cells 4. substantia nigra

103. The calcitonin hormone is produced by the _____.

1. parathyroid gland
2. thyroid gland
3. adrenal medulla
4. adrenal cortex

104. Which of the following is an abnormal breathing pattern characterised by deep, gasping inspiration with a pause at full inspiration followed by a brief, insufficient release?

1. Apneustic respiration
2. Paradoxical respiration
3. Kussmaul's respiration
4. Cheyne stokes respiration

96. 4	97. 3	98. 3	99. 4	100. 1	101. 4	102. 2	103. 2	104. 1

105. Which of the following diets is preferred in patients with gout?

1. Low purine diet
2. High sodium diet
3. High fat diet
4. High purine diet

106. What is the meaning of PRN order in medicine administration?

1. Post meal, before sleep
2. Administered immediately
3. When required
4. Single administration

107. The term procidentia means:

1. first-degree uterine prolapse
2. zero-degree uterine prolapse
3. second-degree uterine prolapse
4. third-degree uterine prolapse

108. Which of the following statements is FALSE about systemic circulation?

1. It starts in the right ventricle.
2. It is greater-pressure circulation.
3. It ends in the right atrium.
4. It starts in the left ventricle.

109. The nurse was performing a cardiovascular assessment of an adult male patient. Where will she find the aortic area?

1. The fourth intercostal space in the left sternal border
2. The second intercostal space in the left sternal border
3. The fifth intercostal space in the midclavicular line
4. The second intercostal space in the right sternal border

110. _____ is the fluid in the posterior chamber of the eye.

1. Aqueous humor 2. Perilymph
3. Vitreous humor 4. Endolymph

111. The nurse working in a preoperative unit was caring for a patient with a cataract and observed an order of the eye drops Atropine OS, every hour. What do you mean by OS?

1. Right eye 2. Both eye
3. Left eye 4. Unaffected eye

112. All of the following are the branches of the thoracic aorta, EXCEPT:

1. Bronchial Artery
2. Pericardial Artery
3. Coronary Artery
4. Superior Phrenic Artery

113. Which of the following is the primary site for T-lymphocyte differentiation?

1. Thalamus 2. Epithalamus
3. Hypothalamus 4. Thymus

114. The external cephalic version is commonly used to manage:

1. anencephaly
2. breech presentation
3. placenta previa
4. hydrocephalus

115. Which of the following vitamin deficiencies in pregnancy leads to spina bifida in the foetus?

1. Tocopherol 2. Niacin
3. Folate 4. Riboflavin

116. Negri bodies in the brain commonly occur in:

1. measles 2. polio
3. rabies 4. tetanus

117. The disease that is also known as darling's disease is:

1. oral thrush 2. histoplasmosis
3. candidiasis 4. mucormycosis

105. 1	**106.** 3	**107.** 4	**108.** 1	**109.** 4	**110.** 1	**111.** 3
112. 3	**113.** 4	**114.** 2	**115.** 3	**116.** 3	**117.** 2	

118. Ziehl-Neelsen acid-fast staining method is commonly used to demonstrate:

1. *Mycobacterium tuberculosis*
2. *Klebsiella pneumonia*
3. *Escherichia coli*
4. *Coryne bacterium diphtheriae*

119. Which of the following is the sensory speech area?

1. Parietal area 2. Wernicke's area
3. Occipital area 4. Broca's area

120. All of the following are the proximate principles of food, EXCEPT:

1. vitamins 2. carbohydrates
3. fats 4. proteins

121. At what age is night-time control of the bladder and bowel normally attained?

1. 3 years 2. 6 years
3. 1 year 4. 2 years

122. What is the drug of choice for leprosy?

1. Chloroquine 2. Primaquine
3. Dapsone 4. Rifampicin

123. IDSP stands for:

1. Integrated Death Surveillance Project
2. Integrated Diarrhoea Surveillance Project
3. Integrated Disease Surveillance Programme
4. Integrated Diarrhoea Screening Programme

124. Which of the following diseases can be prevented by avoiding the touch of fresh water that may be contaminated with animal urine?

1. Japanese encephalitis
2. Hansen's Disease
3. Lymphatic filariasis
4. Leptospirosis

125. Wolff-Parkinson-White Syndrome is characterised by all of the following, EXCEPT:

1. wide QRS complex
2. delta wave
3. Salvador Dali sagging
4. short PR interval

126. Which of the following diseases can be classified by using Stanford criteria?

1. Transposition of great arteries
2. Takayasu arteritis
3. Brugada syndrome
4. Aortic dissection

127. The Nadas criteria are used to assess:

1. epispadias in children
2. congenital heart disease in children
3. spina bifida in children
4. gastroschisis in children

128. Which of the following stages of psychosexual development is commonly characterised by the Oedipus complex?

1. Phallic stage 2. Genital stage
3. Anal stage 4. Oral stage

129. The neurotransmitter abnormality commonly associated with epilepsy is:

1. low level of epinephrine
2. high level of epinephrine
3. low level of GABA
4. high level of GABA

130. Net-EN contraceptive injections contain:

1. norepinephrine ease nonoxynol
2. norepinephrine enantiomer
3. norethisterone enanthate
4. nono-estradiol edetate

131. The disease cycle which represents the height of the disease and characterised by clear-cut signs and symptoms is:

1. convalescence 2. defervescence
3. fastigium 4. defection

118. 1	**119.** 2	**120.** 1	**121.** 1	**122.** 3	**123.** 3	**124.** 4
125. 3	**126.** 4	**127.** 2	**128.** 1	**129.** 3	**130.** 3	**131.** 3

132. All of the following are the principles of primary care, EXCEPT:
1. Inter-sectoral Coordination
2. Eliminating Technology
3. Community Participation
4. Equitable Distribution

133. The nurse working in the emergency department is assessing the lung sounds of a patient with asthma. Which of the following sounds is the nurse most likely to hear?
1. Murmurs 2. Korotkoff sounds
3. Wheezing 4. Pleural friction rub

134. What is the antidote for dopamine?
1. Dobutamine 2. Phentolamine
3. Epinephrine 4. Norepinephrine

135. Which of the following pairs is INCORRECTLY matched?
1. Trisomy 13 - Patau syndrome
2. Trisomy 15 - Turner syndrome
3. Trisomy 21 - Down syndrome
4. Trisomy 18 - Edward syndrome

136. What is cryptorchidism?
1. A trapping of the penis foreskin behind the glans penis
2. A failure of the descent of testicles into the scrotum
3. A failure of the closure of the abdominal wall
4. The inability to retract the foreskin or prepuce

137. What are simian creases?
1. The transverse ridge and creases in the nail
2. Single transverse palmar creases
3. Creases between the first and second toes of the feet
4. Longitudinal creases in the scalp

138. The following ECG represents:

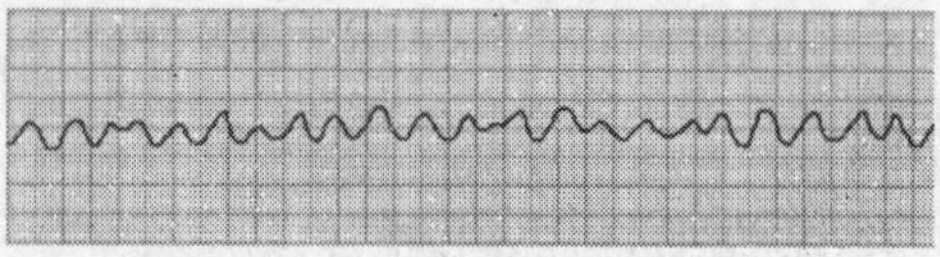

1. ventricular fibrillation
2. ventricular tachycardia
3. atrial flutter
4. atrial fibrillation

139. In which indirect speech does the individual digress to give unnecessary and often irrelevant details before arriving at the main point?
1. Neologism
2. Circumstantiality
3. Confabulation
4. Tangentiality

140. Which of the following is NOT a LMWH?
1. Enoxaparin 2. Dalteparin
3. Warfarin 4. Reviparin

141. Which of the following is an eye disease affecting prematurely born babies due to excess oxygen therapy?
1. Nyctalopia
2. Erythroblastosis fetalis
3. Amblyopia
4. Retrolental fibroplasia

142. Pain on deep inspiration, when an inflamed gallbladder is palpated by pressing the fingers under the rib cage is known as:
1. Rovsing's sign 2. Psoa's sign
3. Mcburney's sign 4. Murphy's sign

143. All of the following are the common manifestations of neonatal tetanus, EXCEPT:
1. trismus
2. dysphagia
3. hypotonia
4. opisthotonus

132. 2	**133.** 3	**134.** 2	**135.** 2	**136.** 2	**137.** 2
138. 1	**139.** 2	**140.** 3	**141.** 4	**142.** 4	**143.** 3

144. A nurse working in an ICU is performing surgical hand hygiene. After hand washing, they must keep their hands:

1. in a comfortable position
2. below the elbows
3. below waist level
4. above elbow level

145. A person moves away and assumes a new identity, forgetting their old identity; this is a feature of:

1. dissociative amnesia
2. derealisation
3. dissociative fugue
4. depersonalisation

146. What was the theme of the International Nurses Day 2024?

1. Nurses: A Voice to Lead - Nursing the world to health
2. Our Nurses. Our Future. The economic power of care
3. A Voice to Lead - Invest in nursing and respect the rights to secure global health
4. Nurses: A Voice to Lead - A vision for future healthcare

147. Which of the following is NOT a feature of type 2 diabetes mellitus?

1. The most common type of DM
2. Insulin-dependent diabetes mellitus
3. Adult-onset diabetes mellitus
4. Endogenous insulin production is present

148. The extreme limit of human noise tolerance is:

1. 210 decibels
2. 70 decibels
3. 140 decibels
4. 35 decibels

149. All of the following statements are true regarding the Rockefeller Foundation, EXCEPT:

1. the Rockefeller Foundation began its activities in 1913
2. the philosophy is that freedom and progress of Asia's emerging nations can be best achieved through economic, social and cultural cooperation with industrial nations
3. its purpose is to promote the well-being of mankind throughout the world.
4. the All-India Institute of Hygiene and Public Health at Calcutta and the Virus Research Institute at Poona were established with aid from the foundation

150. All of the following are included in the CLABSI bundle, EXCEPT:

1. use a maximal sterile barrier when the insertion
2. always try to insert a central line at the femoral vein
3. scrub the hub before and after each use
4. wash hands before all procedures

151. Which of the following involves recurrent, intense sexual arousal from cross-dressing?

1. Transvestism
2. Frottage
3. Bestiality
4. Sodomy

152. BUN used for kidney function tests stands for:

1. blood uric acid nitrogen
2. blood uracil nitrogen
3. blood urea nitrogen
4. blood urine nitrogen

153. The term 'evisceration' means:

1. the separation of wound edges
2. the protrusion of organs through an opening in wound edges
3. pus formation in wound layers
4. the healing of a surgical wound and incision

144. 4	**145.** 3	**146.** 2	**147.** 2	**148.** 3	**149.** 2	**150.** 2	**151.** 1	**152.** 3	**153.** 2

154. According to the National Immunization Schedule, the first, second and third doses of the pentavalent vaccine are administered at what ages, respectively?

1. At 2, 4 and 6 weeks
2. At 6, 10 and 14 months
3. At 6, 10 and 14 weeks
4. At 2, 4 and 6 months

155. Which of the following health committees recommended creating a band of para-professionals and semi-professional health workers from within the community?

1. Chadha Committee
2. Shrivatsav Committee
3. Bhore Committee
4. Mudaliar Committee

156. A method of operative treatment for habitual abortions in the second trimester of pregnancy is called:

1. Nissen's fundoplication
2. Waterson's operation
3. Potts shunt operation
4. Shirodkar cperation

157. For implantation, the zygote is propelled into the uterus normally after:

1. 14-21 days after ovulation
2. 8-14 days after ovulation
3. 6-7 days after ovulation
4. 1-2 days after ovulation

158. Which is a rare genetic malformation syndrome characterised by the partial or complete absence of the corpus callosum?

1. Allport syndrome
2. Aicardi syndrome
3. Leopard syndrome
4. Felty syndrome

159. According to WHO, breastfeeding should be continued with appropriate foods till the age of:

1. 6 months 2. 4 years
3. 2 years 4. 1 year

160. Which of the following is a rare disease in which tumours cause the stomach to produce too much acid, resulting in peptic ulcers?

1. Boerhaave syndrome
2. Zollinger–Ellison syndrome
3. Mallory-Weiss syndrome
4. Abdominal compartment syndrome

161. Which of the following is true regarding placenta formation?

1. Placenta formation usually begins in the 6th week and is completed by the 12th week.
2. Placenta formation usually begins in the 12th week and is completed by the 28th week.
3. Placenta formation usually begins in the 10th week and is completed by the 36th week.
4. Placenta formation usually begins in the 4th week and is completed by the 6th week.

162. What is the process through which the government and financial institutions put forward invitation bids for large projects?

1. Tendering 2. Requisition
3. Procurement 4. Cost analysis

163. Loosing or detachment of the nails from the nail bed is known as:

1. onychomycosis 2. koilonychia
3. paronychia 4. onycholysis

164. In which leadership style leaders rely on rewards and punishments to achieve maximum and optimal job performance from their subordinates?

1. Transformational leadership
2. Transactional leadership
3. Democratic leadership
4. Laissez-faire leadership

154. 3	**155.** 2	**156.** 4	**157.** 3	**158.** 2	**159.** 3
160. 2	**161.** 1	**162.** 1	**163.** 4	**164.** 2	

165. The instrument used to grasp and hold the uterus or cervix during vaginal examinations, intrauterine devices placement or removal, and cervical dilatation is called:
1. Magill forceps
2. Babcock forceps
3. Vulsellum forceps
4. Kocher artery forceps

166. The National Tuberculosis Control Programme (NTP) has been in operation since:
1. 1982 2. 1962
3. 1952 4. 1972

167. All of the following are three-dimensional AV aids, EXCEPT:
1. Models 2. Puppets
3. Charts 4. Specimens

168. All of the following statements are true regarding Item C in ABC analysis, EXCEPT:
1. these items have tight control
2. it accounts for 40-50% of all inventory items
3. these items are managed by the low-level manager
4. it needs 5-10% of total inventory cost

169. Farsightedness is corrected by using:
1. cylindrical lens 2. bifocal lens
3. concave lens 4. convex lens

170. The modification of behaviour by study participants in response to their knowledge that they are being observed or singled out for special treatment is known as:
1. Reactive effect 2. Hawthorne effect
3. Novelty effect 4. Experimental effect

171. Which of the following signs is positive if a postnatal woman has DVT?
1. Fleischner sign 2. Romberg's sign
3. Spalding sign 4. Homan's sign

172. Calculate the mean from the following sample of data.

2, 4, 4, 6, 6, 8, 8, 8, 17
1. 9 2. 7
3. 6 4. 8

173. In which phase of the therapeutic nurse-patient relationship are the patient problems noted, and coping skills identified?
1. Introductory phase
2. Working phase
3. Termination phase
4. Pre-introductory phase

174. How many blood vessels are present in the umbilical cord? How many blood vessels are present in the umbilical cord?
1. Two veins and one artery
2. Two arteries and one vein
3. Two arteries and two veins
4. One artery and one vein

175. While doing CVP calibration, zeroing of the manometer should be done at which of the following levels?
1. Erb's point
2. Koch's point
3. Kauffman's point
4. Phlebostatic axis

176. Who defined nursing as utilising the patient's environment to improve their conditions and assist in their recovery?
1. Martha Roger
2. Florence Nightingale
3. Dorothy Johnson
4. Virginia Henderson

177. Which of the following diseases is characterised by Charcot's triad?
1. Multiple sclerosis
2. Parkinson's disease
3. Gullain barre syndrome
4. Myasthenia gravis

165. 3	**166.** 2	**167.** 3	**168.** 1	**169.** 4	**170.** 2	**171.** 4
172. 2	**173.** 2	**174.** 2	**175.** 4	**176.** 2	**177.** 1	

178. What are the possible foetal positions in the breech presentation?

1. LOA and LOP
2. ROA and ROP
3. LSA and LSP
4. RMS and LMA

179. Quickening usually occurs at:

1. 8-12 weeks
2. 12-16 weeks
3. 24-28 weeks
4. 16-20 weeks

180. Which educational philosophy combines and draws upon ideas and principles from various philosophical traditions and perspectives?

1. Idealism
2. Naturalism
3. Pragmatism
4. Eclecticism

181. Which of the following sequences is correct regarding Maslow's hierarchy of needs?

1. Physiological → Safety → Love and belonging needs → Esteem → Self-actualisation
2. Esteem → Self-actualisation → Physiological → Safety → Love and belonging needs
3. Self-actualisation → Physiological → Love and belonging needs → Esteem → Safety
4. Love and belonging needs → Physiological → Safety → Esteem → Self-actualisation

182. Which of the following is the action of Diltiazem?

1. Stimulants
2. Calcium channel blockers
3. Beta-blockers
4. Sedatives and hypnotics

183. Which test is used to identify the presence of occult blood in stool?

1. Benzidine test
2. Duke's test
3. Ivy test
4. Benedict test

184. Johari window is mainly used to assess which of the following?

1. Self-awareness
2. Semantic memory
3. Intelligence
4. Attitude

185. Which kit is shown in the given image?

1. TPN kit
2. Gastric gavage kit
3. Ryle's tube-feeding kit
4. Gastric lavage kit

186. A positive drop arm test indicates:

1. Potts fracture
2. Golfer's elbow
3. Colles's fracture
4. Rotator cuff injury

187. Which of the following is a methylxanthine group of bronchodilators?

1. Terbutaline
2. Aminophylline
3. Salmeterol
4. Ipratropium

188. Waste collected under the yellow category should be treated by:

1. autoclaving
2. hydroclaving
3. microwaving
4. incineration

189. The most common fracture in children is:

1. comminuted fracture
2. stress fracture
3. compression fracture
4. greenstick fracture

190. All of the following are antipsychotics, EXCEPT:

1. quetiapine
2. risperidone
3. ziprasidone
4. bromocriptine

178. 3	**179.** 4	**180.** 4	**181.** 1	**182.** 2	**183.** 1	**184.** 1
185. 1	**186.** 4	**187.** 2	**188.** 4	**189.** 4	**190.** 4	

191. Uric acid crystal deposits under the skin in gout are known as:

1. Heberden's node
2. Erythema nodosum
3. Tophi
4. Erythema marginatum

192. What is the article shown in the following image?

1. Infant feeding tube
2. Foley's urinary catheter
3. Malecot catheter
4. Silicon urinary catheter

193. All of the following are the diseases commonly transmitted by lice, EXCEPT:

1. epidemic typhus 2. giardiasis
3. relapsing fever 4. trench fever

194. What is ambitendency?

1. Obeying every command irrespective of their nature
2. Two contradictory feelings towards something
3. A conflict to do or not to do
4. Repetition of actions observed

195. According to Emile Durkheim, when or why does an egoistic suicide occur?

1. It occurs when a man becomes socially isolated or feels that he has no place in society and thus destroys himself.
2. It occurs due to overregulation in society, when a servant or slave commits suicide or when a barren woman commits suicide.
3. It occurs due to a break in social equilibrium, such as after bankruptcy or after winning a lottery, or in a situation that has cropped up suddenly.
4. It occurs when individuals and the group are too close and intimate and results from over-integration of the individual into social proof.

196. The act of purging or purification or elimination of a complex by bringing it to consciousness and affording to expression is:

1. catharsis 2. aversion therapy
3. flooding 4. systematic analysis

197. Select the stage of the pressure ulcer shown in the given image.

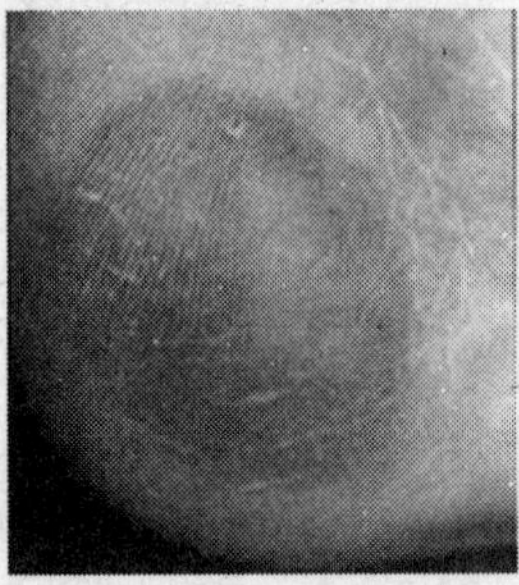

1. Stage 4 2. Stage 2
3. Stage 3 4. Stage 1

198. The most appropriate nursing intervention for a patient during acute intoxication is:

1. encourage the use of positive coping skills
2. decrease in environmental stimuli
3. educate family members on how to control alcohol behaviour
4. educate on the ill effects of alcoholism

199. Which of the following drugs is an alpha-blocker?

1. Propranolol 2. Nifedipine
3. Verapamil 4. Prazosin

200. Which of the following drugs is mainly used in the management of glaucoma?

1. Penicillin 2. Acetazolamide
3. Atropine 4. Tropicamide

191. 3	**192.** 3	**193.** 2	**194.** 3	**195.** 1	**196.** 1	**197.** 4	**198.** 2	**199.** 4	**200.** 2

EXPLANATORY ANSWERS

1. (2): Given, seven boxes are kept one over the other.

Boxes
A
C
D
B
R
T
S

Here, box T is kept at the second position from the bottom.

2. (1): From given statements:

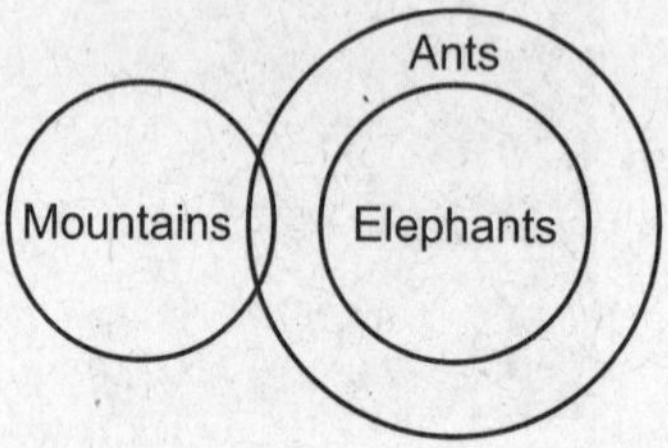

Conclusions:

I. Some elephants are mountains. (False)

II. Some ants are not mountains. (False)

Here, Neither conclusion (I) nor (II) follows.

5. (2):

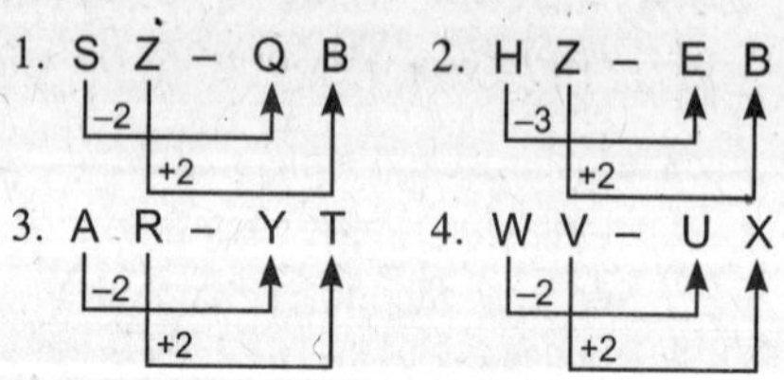

Here, Option (2) letter-cluster pair DOES NOT belong to the group.

6. (1): Given,

'time to study' = 'my cy sp' ...(*i*)

and 'study the case' = 'bg km cy' ...(*ii*)

from (i) and (ii), we get

'study' = 'cy'

∴ Study is coded as 'cy'.

7. (1): Number of students in his class

$= 62 + 11 - 1 = 72.$

8. (3): Given A, B, C, D, Q and R live on six different floors of the same building.

Floor
6 – A
5 – B
4 – D
3 – C
2 – Q
1 – R

Here, C lives on floor number 3.

9. (4): Given, set

(18, 44, 21)

$\Rightarrow 18 + 21 + 5 = 39 + 5 = 44$

(32, 65, 28)

$\Rightarrow 32 + 28 + 5 = 60 + 5 = 65$

Similarly,

(41, 63, 17)

$\Rightarrow 41 + 17 + 5 = 58 + 5 = 63$

∴ Option (4) is related in the same way as are the numbers of the given sets.

10. (4): 18, 39, 67, 102, 144, 193

+21 +28 +35 +42 +49

+7 +7 +7 +7

∴ 193 should come in place of '?' in the given series.

11. (2): Given,

L O – J R – M P

+3 +8 +3

M P – K S – N Q

+3 +8 +3

Similarly,

P S – N V – Q T

+3 +8 +3

∴ Option (2) follows the same pattern as given in two triads.

12. (2): Given, Six teachers are sitting around a circular table facing the centre.

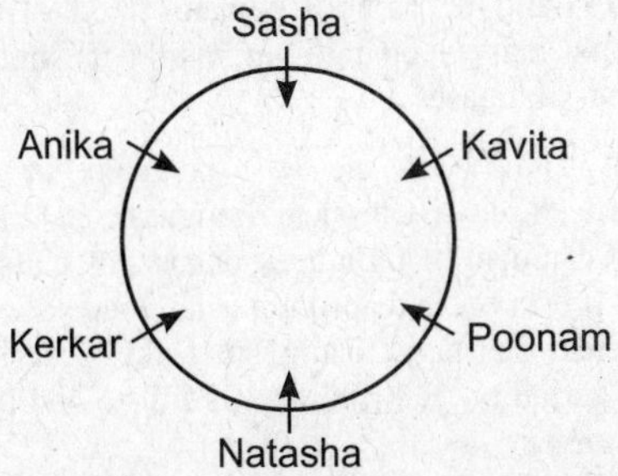

Here, Anika is sitting third to the left of Poonam.

14. (2): From given letter and symbol series: There is only one symbol (U $ P) in the series which is immediately preceded by a vowel but not immediately followed by a vowel.

15. (4):

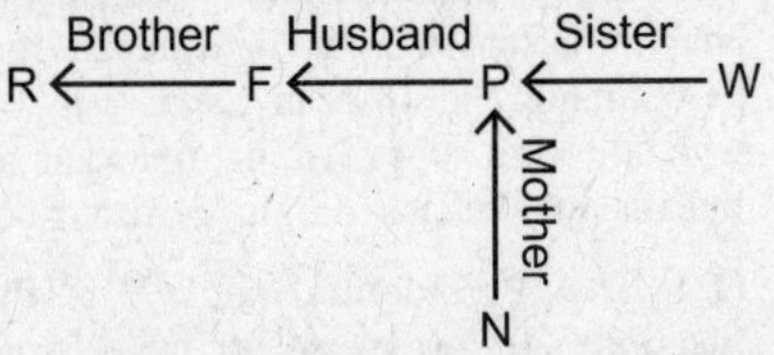

Here, W is Brother's wife's sister of R.

16. (3):

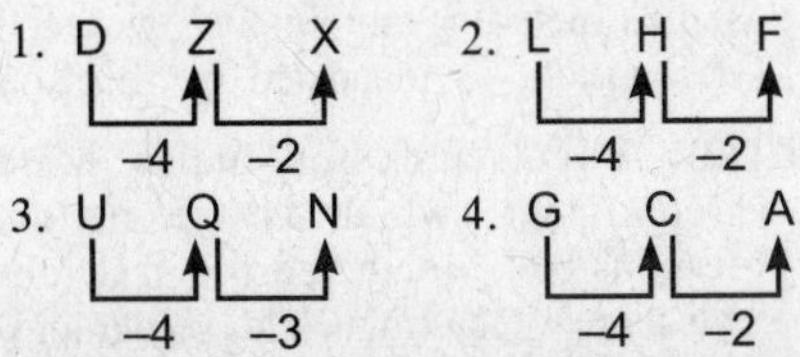

Here, Option (3) letter-cluster DOES NOT belong to the group.

17. (2): Given, + = – and × = ÷

$\therefore$ 363 ÷ 3 + 1148 × 4 – 269 = ?

$\Rightarrow$ 363 × 3 – 1148 ÷ 4 + 269 = ?

$\Rightarrow$ 363 × 3 – 287 + 269 = ?

$\Rightarrow$ 1089 – 287 + 269 = ?

$\Rightarrow$ 1358 – 287 = ?

$\Rightarrow$? = 1071.

18. (4): Given, set

(10, 80, 8) $\Rightarrow$ 10 × 8 = 80,

(6, 96, 16) $\Rightarrow$ 6 × 16 = 96

Similarly,

(9, 108, 12) $\Rightarrow$ 9 × 12 = 108

$\therefore$ Option (4) is related in the same way as are the numbers of the given sets.

19. (2): Given, A = ÷, B = ×,

C = +, D = –

$\Rightarrow$ 27 A 9 D 35 C 11 B 6 = ?

$\Rightarrow$ 27 ÷ 9 – 35 + 11 × 6 = ?

$\Rightarrow$ 3 – 35 + 11 × 6 = ?

$\Rightarrow$ 3 – 35 + 66 = ?

$\Rightarrow$ 69 – 35 = ?

$\Rightarrow$? = 34.

20. (1): From given number and symbol series: There is only one symbol (9 # 1) in the series which is immediately preceded by an odd number but not immediately followed by an even number.

21. (1): Aravind Adiga was awarded the Man Booker Prize in 2008 for his debut novel *The White Tiger*. This novel provides a darkly humorous perspective on class struggle in India and explores the journey of a poor villager who becomes a successful entrepreneur, exposing corruption and inequality in the process.

22. (2): The highest temperatures in India are experienced during the summer season, particularly in May and early June. Regions in North and Central India often record temperatures above 45°C during this period, just before the onset of the monsoon.

23. (2): Union Minister Hardeep Singh Puri unveiled 'Ethanol 100' as part of India's initiative to promote clean fuel alternatives. Ethanol 100 is a biofuel aimed at reducing carbon emissions and enhancing sustainability in transportation.

24. (3): As per Article 51A(c) of the Indian Constitution, the third Fundamental Duty is "to uphold and protect the sovereignty, unity and integrity of India." This duty emphasizes the citizen's role in preserving the nation's core values.

25. (3): In a Functional Organisation, work is divided based on specialized functions such as marketing, finance, HR, etc. This encourages employees to develop deep expertise in their area, leading to efficiency and skill development.

26. (4): As per Census 2011, Arunachal Pradesh had the lowest literacy rate among the options given, with approximately 65.38%. Although Bihar had the overall lowest among all states, from the provided choices, Arunachal Pradesh ranks lowest.

27. (2): Julius von Sachs' significant work on photosynthesis began in the mid-19th century, but it was in 1854 that his experiments began shaping the foundational understanding that starch is the first visible product formed during photosynthesis. His later work in the 1860s and 1870s further refined these conclusions, but 1854 marks the early phase of this discovery.

28. (4): As per the July 2024 report by the World Intellectual Property Organisation (WIPO), India ranked fifth globally in Generative AI (GenAI) innovations. The ranking was based on the number of patent filings, AI research outputs, and technology development, following countries like the US, China, UK, and South Korea.

29. (1): Rahul Dravid officially announced his retirement as the head coach of the Indian cricket team after India won the ICC T20 World Cup in July 2024. His tenure ended on a high note with India's memorable victory.

30. (1): Article 124 of the Indian Constitution provides for the establishment and constitution of the Supreme Court of India. It outlines the appointment, qualifications, and tenure of judges, including the Chief Justice.

31. (2): Abiotic stresses are non-living environmental factors that affect plant growth and yield. Frost is an abiotic stress caused by low temperatures, which can damage crops. In contrast, insects, nematodes, and diseases are biotic stresses since they involve living organisms.

32. (2): Ishwar Chandra Vidyasagar was a pioneer of women's education in India. He established the first girls' school in Calcutta (now Kolkata) in the 19th century and worked extensively to promote education for women, breaking social taboos of the time.

33. (3): 'Nai Roshni' is a scheme launched by the Government of India to empower minority women through leadership development training. It aims to educate and motivate them on rights, health, and economic independence.

34. (4): Among cytoskeletal elements, intermediate filaments have a diameter of about 10 nanometres. They provide mechanical strength to cells. In contrast, microfilaments are ~7 nm and microtubules are ~25 nm in diameter.

35. (2): The Law of Variable Proportions applies only in the short run and assumes that one input (typically labour) is variable while all others (like land or capital) remain fixed. This setup helps analyze changes in output as the variable input increases.

36. (3): Tamil was the first language in India to be declared a Classical Language in 2004. The Government of India introduced this classification to preserve and promote languages with rich ancient heritage. Tamil met the criteria based on antiquity, rich literary tradition, and historical continuity.

37. (3): Magha Saptami Mela is celebrated in the Hindu month of Magha, which usually falls in February. It is observed especially in Odisha at Konark Sun Temple, where devotees take a holy dip and worship the Sun God at sunrise.

38. (1): Punjab National Bank (PNB), the first Indian bank to be started solely with Indian capital, began its operations in 1895 in Lahore. It was founded with the goal of providing financial services by Indians for Indians during British rule.

39. (1): The Presidential and Vice-Presidential Elections Act was enacted in 1952 to regulate the procedures for conducting these elections in India, including nomination, voting, and result declaration, as mandated by the Constitution.

40. (2): IMD stands for Indian Meteorological Department, which is the national agency responsible for meteorological observations, weather forecasting, and seismology in India. It was established in 1875 and functions under the Ministry of Earth Sciences.

41. (2): A's day's job $= \frac{1}{24}$

and B's 1 day's job $= \frac{1}{13}$

$\therefore$ A's 19 day's work $= \frac{19}{24}$

$\therefore$ Remaining work $= 1 - \frac{19}{24} = \frac{5}{24}$

$\therefore$ The number of days required by B to complete the remaining job is

$$\frac{\frac{5}{24}}{\frac{1}{13}} = \frac{65}{24} = 2\frac{17}{24} \text{ days.}$$

42. (2): The volume of a cuboidal tank

$= l \times b \times h$

$= 16 \text{ m} \times 36 \text{ m} \times 14 \text{ m}$

$= 8064 \text{ m}^3$.

44. (3): The average speed of train $= \dfrac{2xy}{x+y}$

$= \dfrac{2 \times 12 \times 24}{12 + 24}$

$= \dfrac{2 \times 12 \times 24}{36} = 16$ km/h.

45. (2): Given, C.P. of an article = ₹ 344

$\therefore$ S.P. of an article $= 344 \times \dfrac{100 - 20}{100}$

$=$ ₹ $344 \times \dfrac{4}{5}$

Now, C.P. of another article $= 344 \times \dfrac{4}{5}$

$\therefore$ S.P. of another article $= 344 \times \dfrac{4}{5} \times \dfrac{156}{100}$

$= 344 \times \dfrac{4}{5} \times 1.56$

$= 68.8 \times 4 \times 1.56$

$= 429.312$

$\therefore$ Profit = S.P. − C.P.

$= 429.312 - 344$

$=$ ₹ 85.312

$\therefore$ Overall gain = 83.312

$\therefore$ Overall gain % $= \dfrac{85.312 \times 100}{344}$

$= \dfrac{8531.2}{344} = 24.8\% = 0.248.$

46. (4): Let originally, number of Guavas be x

Then, $x \times \dfrac{(100 - 80)}{100} = 900$

$\Rightarrow \quad x \times \dfrac{1}{5} = 900$

$\Rightarrow \quad x = 4500.$

47. (2): Given, Amount = ₹ 903

Let the shares of three persons be $6x$, $2x$ and $7x$

Then, $6x + 2x + 7x = 903$

$\Rightarrow \quad 15x = 903$

$\Rightarrow \quad x = \dfrac{903}{15} = \dfrac{301}{5}$

$\therefore$ The difference between the largest and the smallest shares in the distribution

$= 7x - 2x = 5x = 5 \times \dfrac{301}{5}$

$=$ ₹ 301.

48. (1): Number $= 56 \times 147 + 10$

$= 8232 + 10$

$= 8242$

Now, $8242 = 55 \times 149 + 47$

So, When the same number (8242) is divided by 55, it gives the remainder 47.

49. (1): Given, $l = 31$ m, $b = 20$ m

and $h = 22$ m

$\therefore$ The internal surface area of an open cuboidal tank $= lb + 2(bh + lh)$

$= 31 \times 20 + 2(20 \times 22 + 31 \times 22)$

$= 620 + 2(440 + 682)$

$= 620 + 2(1122) = 620 + 2244$

$= 2864 \text{ m}^2$.

50. (3): The average speed for the entire journey.

$= \dfrac{3xyz}{xy + yz + xz}$

$= \dfrac{3 \times 21 \times 63 \times 86}{21 \times 63 + 63 \times 86 + 21 \times 86}$

$= \dfrac{3 \times 21 \times 63 \times 86}{21 \times 63 + 3 \times 21 \times 86 + 21 \times 86}$

$= \dfrac{3 \times 63 \times 86}{63 + 3 \times 86 + 86} = \dfrac{16254}{63 + 258 + 86}$

$= \dfrac{16254}{407} = 39.9$ km/h.

51. (2): $2\dfrac{3}{5} + 3\dfrac{1}{2} - \dfrac{3}{5}$

$= \dfrac{13}{5} + \dfrac{7}{2} - \dfrac{3}{5} = \dfrac{26 + 35 - 6}{10}$

$= \dfrac{61 - 6}{10} = \dfrac{55}{10} = \dfrac{11}{2} = 5\dfrac{1}{2}.$

52. (2): Let, Originally, number of oranges be x.

Then, $x \times \frac{(100-80)}{100} = 720$

$\Rightarrow \quad x \times \frac{20}{100} = 720$

$\Rightarrow \quad x \times \frac{1}{5} = 720$

$\Rightarrow \quad x = 3600.$

53. (3): Let person's income = ₹ x

Then, $x \times \frac{(100-60)}{100} = 400$

$\Rightarrow \quad x \times \frac{40}{100} = 400$

$\Rightarrow \quad x \times \frac{2}{5} = 400$

$\Rightarrow \quad x = 1000.$

54. (1): $\text{P} = \text{Sum} = \frac{\text{S.I.} \times 100}{t \times r}$

$= \frac{480 \times 100}{3 \times 20}$

$= 8 \times 100 =$ ₹ 800.

55. (2): Given, the average of 13 number is 14

$\because$ Each number is multiplied by 4

$\therefore$ The new average $= 14 \times 4 = 56.$

56. (1): Given, P = ₹ 52500, $r = 8\%$ p.a., $t = 1$ year

Compunded half-yearly

$\therefore \quad r = 4\%, \; n = 2$

$\because \quad \text{A} = \text{P}\left(1 + \frac{r}{100}\right)^n$

$= 52500\left(1 + \frac{4}{100}\right)^2$

$= 52500\left(\frac{26}{25}\right)^2$

$= 52500 \times \frac{26}{25} \times \frac{26}{25}$

$= 84 \times 26 \times 26$

= ₹ 56784.

57. (1): Ratio of profit of A and B

₹ $922000 \times 12 : x \times (12 - 2) = 6 : 5$

$\Rightarrow 922000 \times 12 : x \times 10 = 6 : 5$

$\Rightarrow x \times 10 \times 6 = 922000 \times 12 \times 5$

$\Rightarrow \quad x = 92200 \times 2 \times 5$

$\Rightarrow \quad x =$ ₹ 922000

$\therefore$ B's investment was ₹ 922000.

58. (4): Their average $= \frac{372}{6} = 62.$

59. (3): Let the additional discount be $x\%$

Then, $2000 \times \frac{(100-10)}{100} \times \frac{(100-x)}{100} =$ ₹ 828

$\Rightarrow 20 \times 90 \times \frac{(100-x)}{100} = 828$

$\Rightarrow \quad 18(100 - x) = 828$

$\Rightarrow \quad 100 - x = \frac{828}{18} = 46$

$\Rightarrow \quad x = 100 - 46 = 54$

$\therefore$ Additional discount = 54%.

60. (3): Akash's 1 day's work $= \frac{1}{8}$

and Prakash's 1 day's work $= \frac{1}{14}$

Let they will complete work in x days

Then, $\frac{x-4}{8} + \frac{x}{14} = 1$

$\Rightarrow \quad \frac{7(x-4) + 4x}{56} = 1$

$\Rightarrow \quad 11x - 28 = 56$

$\Rightarrow \quad 11x = 28 + 56$

$\Rightarrow \quad 11x = 84$

$\Rightarrow \quad x = \frac{84}{11}$

$\Rightarrow \quad x = 7\frac{7}{11}$ days.

61. (3): The idiom "hit the ground running" means to start a task or project immediately and with full energy or enthusiasm. It fits perfectly with the phrase "start immediately" in the sentence.

62. (3): A "charlatan" is someone who pretends to have knowledge, skills, or qualifications they do not possess—especially in order to deceive others. It is the correct one-word substitute.

63. (1): The grammatically correct and meaningful sentence is: "She runs faster than any other athlete in her team." The phrase ensures proper comparison with the rest of the group, excluding the subject herself.

64. (2): "Profuse" means abundant or excessive, so the opposite (antonym) would be sparse, which means scanty or limited in quantity.

65. (1): The synonym for "enthusiasm" is eagerness, which reflects strong interest and excitement about something, aligning with the meaning used in the sentence.

66. (4): The sentence is "She saw an eagle flying over the mountains."

"An" is used before vowel sounds like "eagle," and "the" is used before specific or known things like "the mountains."

67. (2): The correct sentence is "We visited the Louvre when we were in Paris."

Famous monuments, museums, and institutions usually take the definite article "the."

68. (1): The paragraph should start with the broad topic (P), followed by its benefits (Q), and then examples (R and S).

So the correct order is: P (introduction), Q (scope), R (application in agriculture), S (application in medicine).

69. (3): The idiom "in the dark" means unaware of the facts or situation, which fits the context of someone working without full knowledge.

70. (2): "Experience" is an uncountable noun, so the correct quantifier is "much." The sentence should read: "She has much experience in the field of aeronautics."

71. (2): The correct sentence is: "The politician's speech was filled with empty promises..."

"Empty promises" means statements that are made but not intended to be fulfilled, which fits perfectly in the context of political speeches ignoring real concerns.

72. (3): The correct order is:

D. (defines the sport of golf),

A. (mentions its historical origin),

B. (explains where it is played),

C. (states the objective of the game).

This order forms a logical and coherent paragraph.

73. (1): The correct spelling is supersede, not supercede.

All other words — commitment, resilience, and frustration — are correctly spelled.

74. (2): The antonym of expensive is cheap, meaning something that costs little money.

Other options like costly, pricey, and valuable are either synonyms or near-synonyms.

75. (4): The correct sentence is: "There are only a few apples left."

"Apples" is a countable noun, and "a few" is used for small quantities of countables.

76. (1): Mr. Thompson hosts reading clubs and author signings, actively building a literary community, which clearly shows his role in encouraging reading and interaction among book lovers.

77. (1): The success of The Book Nook, a physical bookstore, goes against the trend of rising audiobook and digital media usage. This contrast highlights the store's uniqueness and resilience.

78. (1): The passage clearly names the bookstore as 'The Book Nook', describing it as a serene haven in the bustling city.

79. (1): Since the passage revolves entirely around the bookstore, its history, atmosphere, and role in the community, "The Book Nook" is the most appropriate and fitting title.

80. (3): "Thrive" means to grow, prosper, or flourish. Its antonym is "decline", which means to deteriorate or fall into a worse condition.

81. (1): यह वाक्य व्याकरण की दृष्टि से शुद्ध है। इसमें 'कालिदास' का सही रूप तथा वाक्य संरचना ठीक है। अन्य विकल्पों में 'कालिदास', 'कलिदाश', 'कालीदास' जैसे अशुद्ध रूप हैं।

82. (2): 'नवनीत' मक्खन का उपयुक्त पर्यायवाची शब्द है। यह संस्कृत शब्द है जिसका अर्थ होता है– दूध से निकला हुआ ताजा मक्खन।

83. (3): वाक्य का सही क्रम है:

1. सब जानते हैं कि हिन्दी

(र) देर-सवेर भारत की एकमात्र राजभाषा

(य) सिद्ध होगी ही, अंग्रेजी सह राजभाषा पद

(ल) से हटेगी ही, तो उस स्थिति

(व) के अनुकूल अपने को बना लेने के लिए

6. हम हिन्दी का अध्ययन कर रहे हैं।

84. (1): सही वाक्य होगा: ''कोयल आम की डाल पर कूक रही है।''
'पर' स्थान सूचक (अधिकरण कारक) है और यहाँ उपयुक्त है क्योंकि क्रिया 'कूक रही है' डाल के ऊपर की स्थिति को दर्शाती है।

85. (2): 'जिसकी थाह का पता न हो' के लिए उपयुक्त शब्द है: अथाह, जिसका अर्थ है– जिसकी गहराई या सीमा न जानी जा सके, जैसे कि समुद्र।

86. (3): 'थामना' के कई अर्थ होते हैं जैसे: रोकना, पकड़ना, सहारा देना, लेकिन 'भाग्य' इसका अर्थ नहीं होता। इसलिए 'भाग्य' इसका अनेकार्थी नहीं है।

87. (4): यह वाक्य शुद्ध और अर्थपूर्ण क्रम में है। इसमें कर्ता (मैं), उद्देश्य (दर्शन करने) और क्रिया (आया हूँ) का क्रम व्याकरणिक दृष्टि से सही है।

88. (3): 'चर्म' का तद्भव शब्द है चमड़ा, जो दैनिक बोलचाल में इस्तेमाल होता है। 'चर्म' संस्कृत शब्द है जिसका अर्थ भी चमड़ा ही है।

89. (2): 'भार्या' शब्द विशिष्ट रूप से पत्नी के लिए प्रयुक्त होता है, जबकि प्रश्न में 'स्त्री' के सामान्य पर्यायवाची शब्द की बात की गई है। 'कांता', 'वनिता' और 'रमणी' जैसे शब्द स्त्री के अधिक व्यापक अर्थ में प्रयुक्त होते हैं, जो किसी भी महिला का संकेत कर सकते हैं– चाहे वह विवाहित हो या नहीं। इसके विपरीत, 'भार्या' केवल विवाहित स्त्री (wife) के संदर्भ में आता है, अतः यह 'स्त्री' का व्यापक और उपयुक्त पर्यायवाची नहीं माना जाएगा। इसलिए, विकल्प (2) 'भार्या' इस प्रश्न के लिए सबसे कम उपयुक्त है।

90. (1): 'निश्चित रूप से होने वाला' के लिए सही शब्द है अवश्यंभावी, जिसका अर्थ है– जो निश्चित ही घटेगा।

91. (1): 'गाल बजाना' मुहावरे का अर्थ है– बिना मतलब की बातें करना, यानि फिजूल की बकवास करना। यह उस व्यक्ति के लिए कहा जाता है जो सिर्फ बोलता है पर काम कुछ नहीं करता।

92. (2): वाक्य: ''मालिक सेवक को वेतन देता है'' – इसमें 'सेवक को' का संबंध संप्रदान कारक से है, जो क्रिया का लाभ पाने वाले को दर्शाता है। यहां वेतन प्राप्त करने वाला सेवक है, इसलिए यह संप्रदान कारक है।

93. (3): शुद्ध वर्तनी में 'अहिल्या' को अहल्या लिखा जाता है। यह संस्कृतनिष्ठ और पारंपरिक रूप है जो प्राचीन ग्रंथों तथा पौराणिक संदर्भों में मिलता है। अन्य विकल्पों – एहिल्या, अहिलिया, आहिल्या – में या तो अनावश्यक स्वर हैं या वर्णविन्यास अशुद्ध है। अतः सही वाक्य है: ''अहल्या गौतम ऋषि की पत्नी थी।''

94. (1): यह अर्थ गलत है।
'अँधेरे में रखना' का सही अर्थ है – सूचना न देना या अनभिज्ञ बनाए रखना।
'कैद में रखना' इसका उपयुक्त अर्थ नहीं हैं। इसलिए यह विकल्प असुमेलित है।

95. (4): वाक्य: ''वह मुझसे अलग रहता है।''
यह सही व्याकरणिक और अर्थपूर्ण रूप है। 'मुझसे' संबंध दर्शाने वाला शब्द है, और यहां विषय 'वह' और 'मैं' के बीच दूरी को दर्शाता है।

96. (4): इस गद्यांश में न्याय के विभिन्न आयामों – संवैधानिक मार्ग, सामाजिक सुधार, सहिष्णुता, ईमानदारी और पर्यावरणीय संतुलन आदि – पर चर्चा की गई है। इसलिए इस गद्यांश के लिए सबसे उपयुक्त शीर्षक है: न्याय।

97. (3): गद्यांश के अनुसार, न्याय प्राप्त करने के दो रास्ते बताए गए हैं– हिंसात्मक और सवैधानिक। अतः सही उत्तर है: दो।

98. (3): 'बालू से तेल निकालना' एक प्रसिद्ध मुहावरा है, जिसका अर्थ होता है – असंभव कार्य को करने की चेष्टा करना या असंभव को संभव कर दिखाना। अतः यही इसका अर्थ है।

99. (4): गद्यांश न्याय की अवधारणा को सामाजिक, आर्थिक, सांस्कृतिक और मानवीय पहलुओं से जोड़ता है। यह बताता है कि न्याय केवल दंड नहीं, बल्कि समाज में सकारात्मक और सुधारात्मक बातावरण बनाना है। इसलिए इसका वास्तविक जीवन से संबंध है – न्याय का मानव जीवन में उपयोग।

100. (1): 'अभियोग', 'गुनाह' और 'मुजिर' – तीनों शब्द अपराध या दंडात्मक प्रक्रिया से जुड़े हैं। जबकि 'भूल' का अर्थ है अनजाने में की गई त्रुटि, जो अपराध नहीं होता। अतः 'भूल' का संबंध अपराध से नहीं है।

101. (4): The elbow joint is a classic example of a hinge joint, which allows movement in one plane — flexion and extension — like the motion of a door hinge.

102. (2): Serotonin is primarily produced in the raphe nuclei of the brainstem. These nuclei are a group of neurons involved in regulating mood, sleep, and pain.

103. (2): Calcitonin is secreted by the parafollicular cells (C-cells) of the thyroid gland. It helps in lowering blood calcium levels.

104. (1): Apneustic respiration is characterized by prolonged, deep inspirations followed by inadequate expirations. It indicates damage to the pons in the brainstem.

105. (1): Patients with gout are advised a low purine diet to reduce uric acid production, as purines are broken down into uric acid which precipitates in joints causing inflammation.

106. (3): PRN is a Latin abbreviation for "pro re nata", meaning "as needed" or "when required", commonly used in prescriptions.

107. (4): Procidentia refers to a third-degree uterine prolapse, where the uterus protrudes entirely outside the vaginal opening.

108. (1): This is FALSE. Systemic circulation begins in the left ventricle and ends in the right atrium. The right ventricle starts pulmonary circulation.

109. (4): The aortic area for auscultation is located at the second intercostal space, right sternal border — this is where the aortic valve is best heard.

110. (1): The aqueous humor is the fluid found in the posterior and anterior chambers of the eye. It nourishes the cornea and lens and maintains intraocular pressure.

111. (3): OS is a Latin abbreviation "oculus sinister", which means the left eye. OD = right eye, OU = both eyes.

112. (3): The coronary arteries arise from the ascending aorta, not the thoracic aorta. The thoracic aorta gives rise to bronchial, pericardial, esophageal, mediastinal, and superior phrenic arteries, but not the coronary arteries.

113. (4): The thymus is the primary site for T-lymphocyte differentiation and maturation, especially active during childhood. The brain structures listed (thalamus, hypothalamus, etc.) are unrelated to this immune function.

114. (2): External cephalic version (ECV) is a manual procedure used to turn a baby from a breech position to a head-down (cephalic) position before labour, usually around 36–37 weeks of gestation.

115. (3): Folic acid (folate) deficiency during early pregnancy is associated with neural tube defects, such as spina bifida in the fetus. That's why folic acid supplementation is recommended in early pregnancy.

116. (3): Negri bodies are intracytoplasmic inclusion bodies seen in the neurons of individuals infected with rabies. They are pathognomonic of the disease.

117. (2): Histoplasmosis is also called Darling's disease. It is a fungal infection caused by Histoplasma capsulatum, often found in bird or bat droppings.

118. (1): The Ziehl-Neelsen stain is an acid-fast staining technique used to detect Mycobacterium tuberculosis due to its waxy, lipid-rich cell wall that retains the red dye.

119. (2): Wernicke's area is the sensory speech area, involved in language comprehension. Broca's area, in contrast, controls speech production.

120. (1): The proximate principles of food include carbohydrates, proteins, and fats, which provide energy. Vitamins are micronutrients, not part of the proximate principles, hence the correct exception.

121. (1): Most children achieve night-time bladder and bowel control by around 3 years of age. However, minor delays may occur and are considered normal up to age 5.

122. (3): Dapsone is the first-line drug used in multidrug therapy (MDT) for leprosy due to its bacteriostatic effect against *Mycobacterium leprae*. It is often combined with rifampicin and clofazimine.

123. (3): IDSP is a health program launched in India for early detection and response to disease outbreaks, aimed at strengthening surveillance systems at the district and state levels.

124. **(4):** Leptospirosis is a bacterial infection transmitted through contact with water contaminated by animal urine, especially from rodents. Avoiding such water can help prevent infection.

125. **(3):** Wolff-Parkinson-White (WPW) Syndrome shows a short PR interval, delta wave, and wide QRS complex on ECG. "Salvador Dali sagging" is not a clinical or diagnostic feature.

126. **(4):** The Stanford criteria are a widely used classification system for aortic dissection, dividing the condition into Type A (involving the ascending aorta) and Type B (not involving it). This classification is essential for guiding treatment: Type A usually requires surgical intervention, while Type B may be managed medically.

127. **(2):** Nadas criteria are a set of clinical findings used to help identify congenital heart disease in pediatric patients, particularly based on murmurs and other heart sounds.

128. **(1):** According to Freud's psychosexual theory, the Oedipus complex occurs during the phallic stage (3–6 years), when children develop unconscious desires for the opposite-sex parent.

129. **(3):** Epilepsy is often associated with low levels of GABA, an inhibitory neurotransmitter that normally helps suppress excessive neuronal firing. Its deficiency leads to hyperexcitability.

130. **(3):** Net-EN is a contraceptive injection that contains norethisterone enanthate, a progestin used for long-acting birth control, typically given intramuscularly every 2 months.

131. **(3):** The fastigium stage in the disease cycle is when the illness reaches its peak severity, and signs and symptoms are clearly evident. It's the height of the disease process, preceding recovery.

132. **(2):** Eliminating technology is not a principle of primary health care. The core principles include equitable distribution, community participation, inter-sectoral coordination, and appropriate technology — not eliminating it.

133. **(3):** In asthma, wheezing is the most characteristic lung sound. It is a high-pitched whistling sound heard during expiration due to narrowed airways from bronchospasm and inflammation.

134. **(2):** Phentolamine is an antidote used to treat extravasation of dopamine, a potent vasoconstrictor. It works by causing local vaso**dilation, minimizing tissue damage.**

135. **(2):** This is incorrectly matched. Turner syndrome is not caused by trisomy 15, but by monosomy X (45,X). The other options are correctly matched chromosomal disorders.

136. **(2):** Cryptorchidism is the condition where one or both testes fail to descend into the scrotum. It is commonly observed in premature male infants.

137. **(2):** Simian crease is a single, deep transverse crease across the palm, often associated with Down syndrome and other chromosomal abnormalities.

138. **(1):** Ventricular fibrillation (VF) is identified on ECG by chaotic, irregular, and disorganized electrical activity without identifiable P waves or QRS complexes — a medical emergency.

139. **(2):** Circumstantiality is a thought pattern where the person gives excessive, unnecessary detail but eventually returns to the point. It's common in some psychiatric conditions.

140. **(3):** Warfarin is not a low molecular weight heparin (LMWH); it is an oral vitamin K antagonist. Enoxaparin, dalteparin, and reviparin are LMWHs used for anticoagulation.

141. **(4):** Retrolental fibroplasia, now known as retinopathy of prematurity (ROP), is an eye disease that affects premature infants exposed to excess oxygen therapy, leading to abnormal blood vessel growth in the retina and potential blindness.

142. **(4):** Murphy's sign is positive when a patient experiences pain and halts inspiration as the inflamed gallbladder is palpated under the right costal margin. It is a key sign of cholecystitis.

143. **(3):** Neonatal tetanus typically presents with trismus (lockjaw), dysphagia, and opisthotonus (arched back due to muscle rigidity). Hypotonia (low muscle tone) is not a typical feature; rather, tetanus causes hypertonia and spasms.

144. **(4):** After surgical hand washing, nurses must keep their hands above the elbows to prevent water and contaminants from the arms running back onto the clean hands, maintaining asepsis.

145. **(3):** Dissociative fugue is characterized by sudden travel away from home, with inability to recall one's identity, often accompanied by adoption of a new identity. It is a type of dissociative disorder.

146. **(2):** The theme of International Nurses Day 2024 was:
"Our Nurses. Our Future. The economic power of care", highlighting the financial and societal value of nurses' contributions.

147. **(2):** Type 2 diabetes mellitus is usually non-insulin-dependent in early stages. This term applies more to Type 1 diabetes. Therefore, this statement is not true for Type 2 DM.

148. **(3):** The maximum human tolerance to sound is around 140 decibels. Prolonged exposure to sounds at or above this level can cause permanent hearing damage or pain.

149. **(2):** This statement is not related to the actual philosophy of the Rockefeller Foundation. Its mission focuses on global health, education, and social upliftment, not geopolitical or national cooperation ideologies.

150. **(2):** Femoral vein insertion is avoided unless necessary, due to higher infection risk. The CLABSI bundle promotes using subclavian or internal jugular sites, sterile technique, hand hygiene, and scrubbing the hub.

151. **(1):** Transvestism is a paraphilic disorder involving recurrent, intense sexual arousal from cross-dressing. It is typically seen in heterosexual males and classified under paraphilic disorders.

152. **(3):** BUN (Blood Urea Nitrogen) is a test used to assess kidney function, measuring the amount of nitrogen in the blood that comes from the waste product urea.

153. **(2):** Evisceration is a surgical emergency where internal organs protrude through a dehisced wound, often in the abdominal area after surgery.

154. **(3):** As per the National Immunization Schedule (India), the pentavalent vaccine is administered in three doses at 6, 10, and 14 weeks of age to protect against five diseases including diphtheria, pertussis, and hepatitis B.

155. **(2):** The Shrivastav Committee (1975) recommended the creation of a band of para-professional and semi-professional health workers selected from within the community to strengthen primary health care.

156. **(4):** The Shirodkar operation is a surgical method used to prevent habitual second-trimester abortions by reinforcing the cervix through cervical cerclage.

157. **(3):** The zygote normally reaches the uterus and implants around 6–7 days after ovulation, aligning with the time required for blastocyst formation and travel through the fallopian tube.

158. **(2):** Aicardi syndrome is a rare genetic disorder that primarily affects females and is characterized by partial or complete absence of the corpus callosum, seizures, and retinal abnormalities.

159. **(3):** According to the World Health Organization (WHO), breastfeeding should be continued up to 2 years of age or beyond, along with appropriate complementary foods from 6 months onward.

160. **(2):** Zollinger–Ellison syndrome is a rare condition where gastrin-secreting tumors (gastrinomas) cause the stomach to produce excess acid, leading to multiple and recurrent peptic ulcers.

161. **(1):** Placenta formation begins around the end of the 2nd to 3rd week, but it is functionally well-developed by the 12th week of gestation. The initial structural development starts by the 6th week, and by the end of the first trimester, it is fully formed.

162. **(1):** Tendering is the process through which government or organizations invite bids from contractors or suppliers for large-scale projects or procurement. It's a transparent, competitive method to select the best vendor.

163. **(4):** Onycholysis refers to the painless separation of the nail from the nail bed. It is often caused by trauma, infections, or systemic conditions such as hyperthyroidism or psoriasis.

164. **(2):** In transactional leadership, leaders motivate subordinates through rewards and punishments to meet performance goals. It is goal-focused and works well for routine, structured tasks.

165. (3): Vulsellum forceps are used to grasp the cervix or uterus during gynecological procedures like IUD insertion, cervical dilation, or biopsy due to their toothed jaws providing a firm grip.

166. (2): The National Tuberculosis Control Programme (NTP) was officially launched in India in 1962 to combat the growing burden of tuberculosis. Initially focused on BCG vaccination and treatment through district TB centers, it was later found to be ineffective in achieving its goals. The program was subsequently reviewed in 1992, and based on WHO recommendations, it was revamped as the Revised National Tuberculosis Control Programme (RNTCP) in 1997. In 2020, it further evolved into the National Tuberculosis Elimination Programme (NTEP) with a target to eliminate TB in India by 2025.

167. (3): Charts are two-dimensional visual aids. The question asks for three-dimensional AV aids, which include models, puppets, and specimens. Hence, charts are the exception.

168. (1): In ABC analysis, Item C represents low-value items, which require least control. Only Item A requires tight control. Therefore, saying that Item C has "tight control" is incorrect.

169. (4): Farsightedness (hypermetropia) is corrected using convex lenses, which converge the incoming light rays so that they focus correctly on the retina.

170. (2): The Hawthorne effect refers to participants modifying their behaviour because they are aware they are being observed. It was first observed during worker productivity studies at the Hawthorne Works.

171. (4): Homan's sign is a clinical indicator of deep vein thrombosis (DVT). It is considered positive when dorsiflexion of the foot causes pain in the calf, especially in postnatal women at increased thrombotic risk.

172. (2): To find the mean of the data set: 2, 4, 4, 6, 6, 8, 8, 8, 17

First, add all the values:

$$2 + 4 + 4 + 6 + 6 + 8 + 8 + 8 + 17 = 63$$

Now divide the total by the number of values:

$$63 \div 9 = 7$$

Hence, the correct mean is: 7.

173. (2): In the working phase of the therapeutic nurse-patient relationship, problems are identified, and coping mechanisms are developed. It is the active, goal-oriented part of the relationship.

174. (2): The umbilical cord typically contains three blood vessels — two arteries that carry deoxygenated blood from the fetus and one vein that carries oxygenated blood from the placenta.

175. (4): Zeroing the manometer for central venous pressure (CVP) measurement is done at the phlebostatic axis, which is located at the level of the 4th intercostal space at the mid-axillary line, approximating the right atrium.

176. (2): Florence Nightingale defined nursing as "the act of utilizing the patient's environment to assist in recovery," emphasizing hygiene, fresh air, and proper nutrition for healing.

177. (1): Charcot's triad in multiple sclerosis includes:

- Nystagmus,
- Intentional tremor,
- Scanning speech.

It reflects lesions in the central nervous system affecting coordination and speech.

178. (3): In breech presentations, the fetal sacrum is the denominator. Thus, the common positions are Left Sacro-Anterior (LSA) and Left Sacro-Posterior (LSP).

179. (4): Quickening, the first perception of fetal movement by the mother, usually occurs around 16 to 20 weeks of gestation in primigravida and may be slightly earlier in multigravida.

180. (4): Eclecticism in education refers to combining ideas from multiple philosophies (like idealism, realism, pragmatism) to create a flexible, balanced teaching approach suited to varied learners.

181. (1): Maslow's hierarchy of needs is a five-level model arranged in order from basic to higher needs:

Physiological (food, water) → Safety (security) → Love and belonging (relationships) → Esteem (respect) → Self-actualisation (realizing potential).

182. (2): Diltiazem is a calcium channel blocker that works by relaxing the muscles of the heart and blood vessels, commonly used to treat hypertension, angina, and some arrhythmias.

183. (1): The Benzidine test is a chemical test used to detect occult (hidden) blood in stool, helping diagnose conditions like gastrointestinal bleeding.

184. (1): The Johari Window is a model used to enhance self-awareness and interpersonal relationships by dividing knowledge about oneself into four quadrants: open, blind, hidden, and unknown areas.

185. (1): On careful observation of the image, the setup includes a large parenteral nutrition bag with tubing, IV infusion set, and associated sterile accessories. These components are typical of a Total Parenteral Nutrition (TPN) kit, which is used to deliver essential nutrients directly into the bloodstream when the gastrointestinal tract cannot be used.

186. (4): A positive drop arm test indicates a rotator cuff tear, particularly involving the supraspinatus muscle, where the patient is unable to slowly lower the arm from abduction.

187. (2): Aminophylline belongs to the methylxanthine class of bronchodilators. It works by relaxing bronchial muscles and is used in asthma and COPD treatment.

188. (4): Yellow category biomedical waste (like human tissues, organs, soiled waste) should be treated by incineration, which ensures safe and complete destruction of infectious materials.

189. (4): Greenstick fractures are the most common in children due to their more flexible bones. The bone bends and cracks partially rather than breaking completely.

190. (4): Bromocriptine is not an antipsychotic; it is a dopamine agonist used in conditions like Parkinson's disease, hyperprolactinemia, and sometimes diabetes. The other drugs listed are atypical antipsychotics.

191. (3): Tophi are deposits of uric acid crystals that accumulate under the skin in patients with chronic gout, often seen around joints, the ear, or soft tissues in advanced stages of the disease.

192. (3): The article shown in the image is a Malecot catheter, identifiable by its winged or flower-shaped expanded tip which allows secure placement, typically used for drainage of thick fluids or in suprapubic cystostomy.

193. (2): Giardiasis is transmitted through contaminated food or water, not by lice. In contrast, lice transmit diseases like epidemic typhus, relapsing fever, and trench fever through their bites or feces.

194. (3): Ambitendency refers to a psychological state of opposing impulses — the patient experiences simultaneous urges to act and not act, leading to hesitation or indecisiveness.

195. (1): Egoistic suicide, according to Emile Durkheim, results from a lack of social integration. It occurs when individuals feel alienated or isolated from the group or society.

196. (1): Catharsis is a psychological process of releasing repressed emotions by bringing them to consciousness, often leading to emotional relief. It is widely used in psychoanalytic therapy.

197. (4): The image shows non-blanchable redness of intact skin, which is characteristic of a Stage 1 pressure ulcer. At this stage, the skin is not broken, and the affected area may feel warmer, firmer, or softer than surrounding tissue. No open wound is visible, which rules out Stages 2–4.

198. (2): During acute intoxication, it is critical to reduce environmental stimuli such as noise and light to promote calmness, minimize agitation, and ensure patient safety.

199. (4): Prazosin is an alpha-1 adrenergic blocker used primarily in treating hypertension and PTSD-related nightmares. The other drugs listed are beta-blockers or calcium channel blockers.

200. (2): Acetazolamide is a carbonic anhydrase inhibitor that reduces aqueous humor production and is commonly used in the management of glaucoma to lower intraocular pressure.

YOUR SPACE

Previous Paper (Solved)

DSSSB Nursing Officer Exam 2019*

SECTION-A

General Intelligence & Reasoning Ability

1. Which two symbols should be interchanged to make the equation given below mathematically correct?

$14 - 2 \times 3 \div 1 + 3 = 23$

A. +, − B. −, ×
C. +, ÷ D. −, ÷

2. If blue is red, red is orange, orange is green, green is yellow, then what is the colour of blood?

A. Green
B. Yellow
C. Orange
D. Red

3. Select the option which is related to the third term in the same way as the first term is related to the second term.

APV : DSY : : RWB : ?

A. UZE B. VBG
C. VAG D. UXF

4. Which of the following answer figure completes the series of question figure?

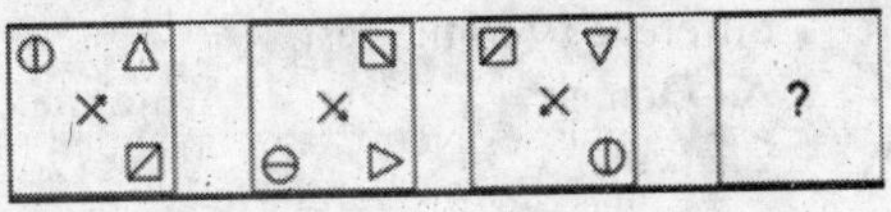

A. 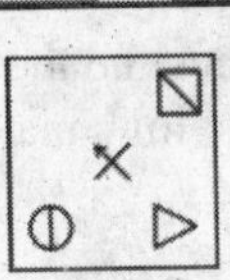

B. 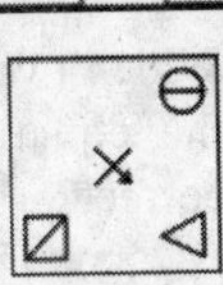

C. 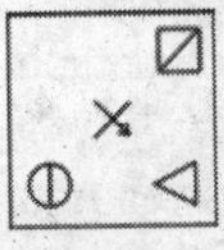

D. 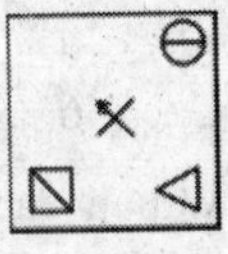

5. If you are in 13th position on either side of a line, how many people are standing in that line?

A. 25 B. 13
C. 21 D. 26

6. Find the missing number in the following number series.

−54, 63, −72, ______, −90

A. 84 B. −84
C. −81 D. 81

7. Which answer figure will complete the pattern in the question figure?

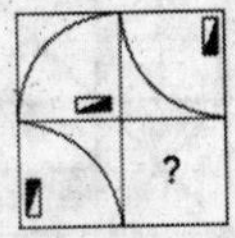

A. 

B. 

C. 

D. 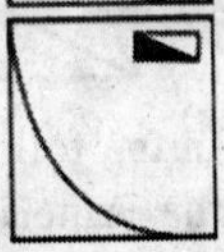

8. Read the given statement and conclusions carefully. Assuming that the information given in the statement is true, even if they appear to be at variance with commonly known facts, select the conclusion that logically follows that statement beyond reasonable doubt.

Statements : I. All cats are dogs.
II. No horse is dog.

Conclusions : I. Some cats are horses.
II. No dog is horse.

* Online exam held on 29/08/2019.

A. No conclusion follows.
B. Only conclusion I follows.
C. Only conclusion II follows.
D. Both conclusion I and II follow

9. Aman and Shailesh were two men riding bicycles from the same starting point. Aman goes 6 km north, then turns to the left and walks 5 km, then he turns to his right and walks 3 km further. Shailesh walks 8 km west, then turns to the right and walks 9 km further, then turns to his left and walks 5 km further. How far and in which direction is Shailesh from the present point of Aman?

A. 5 km West B. 8 km West
C. 8 km East D. 5 km East

10. From the given answer figures, select the one which contains the question figure.

A. 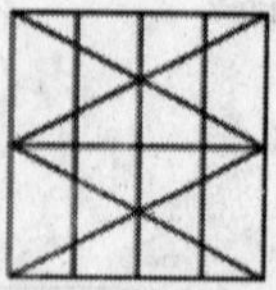

B. 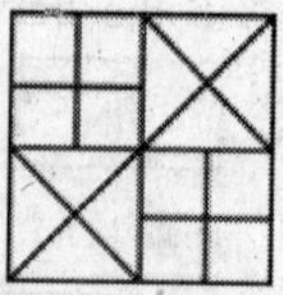

C. 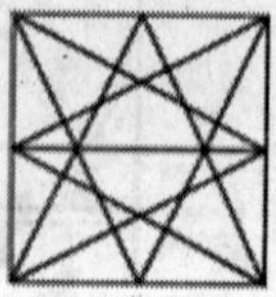

D. 

11. In the following figure, the square represents the Americans, the triangle represents the astronomers, the circle represents the doctors, and the rectangle represents the men. Which set of letters represents men who are doctors?

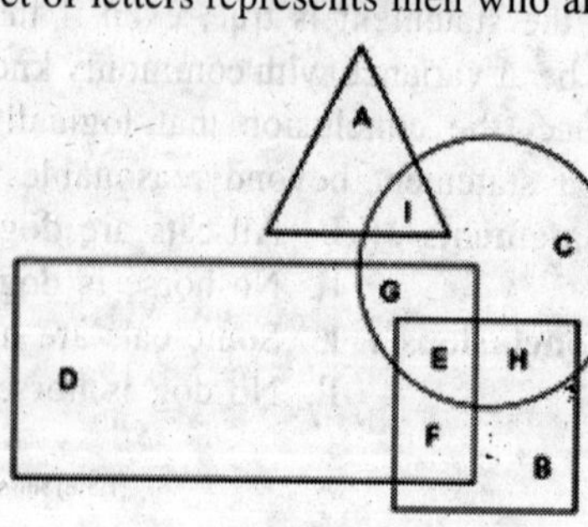

A. I B. EH
C. GE D. FE

12. Select the option that is related to the third number in the same way as the second number is related to the first number.

343 : 49 : : 729 : ?

A. 81 B. 9
C. 243 D. 312

13. Some letters are given 1, 2, 3, 4, 5 and 6 numbers. In the options, four possible arrangements of these numbers are given. Select that option in which the letters become a meaningful word.

P A M S I H

1 2 3 4 5 6

A. 321654 B. 623451
C. 354621 D. 523641

14. If FAITH is coded as IDLWK, then how will GLOBE be coded?

A. INRFH B. JOSDH
C. JOREH D. INQDG

15. Three of the given options are identical in a certain way. However, one option is not like the other three. Select the option that is different from the rest.

A. 144 B. 343
C. 512 D. 729

16. Three of the given options are identical in a certain way. However, one option is not like the other three. Select the option that is different from the rest.

A. Orange B. Watermelon
C. Banana D. Apple

17. Which two numbers must be moved to make the equation given below mathematically correct?

$(15 \times 2) \div 4 \times 6 - 10 = 10$

A. 2, 6 B. 6, 10
C. 4, 6 D. 15, 4

18. Which cube in the answer figure cannot be formed on the basis of the cube appearing in the question figure?

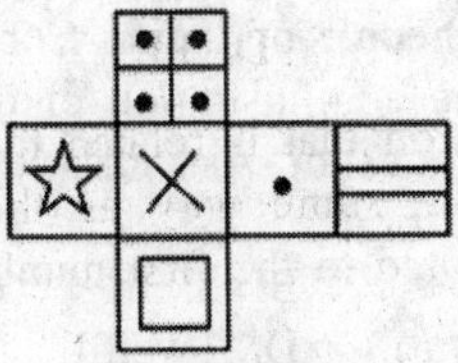

A.  B. 

C.  D. 

19. The average age of a group of 6 people is 48 years. If one member of the group is excluded, the average becomes 45 years. What is the age of the member who was excluded?
A. 52 years
B. 62 years
C. 63 years
D. 50 years

20. Three of the given options are identical in a certain way. However, one option is not like the other three. Select the option that is different from the rest.
A. JNR B. LPS
C. WAE D. TXB

General Awareness

21. Which of the following women player has won the maximum French Open singles titles?
A. Martina Navratilova
B. Serena Williams
C. Steffi Graf
D. Chris Evert

22. With which of the following states Mand folk music is associated?
A. Rajasthan B. Arunachal Pradesh
B. Uttarakhand D. Goa

23. With which of the following state Shigmo festival, held in Falgun month, is associated?
A. Maharashtra B. Goa
C. Haryana D. Tripura

24. What is SI unit of force?
A. Darcy B. Galileo
C. Newton D. Ampere

25. The concept of 'cabinet system' of the Indian Constitution has been adopted from the ________ Constitution.
A. Britain B. Ireland
C. Australia D. Canada

26. Which of the following teams was the first team to win the FIFA World Cup?
A. Uruguay B. Belgium
C. France D. Germany

27. Who was the founder of Nanda Dynasty?
A. Panduka
B. Ghananand
C. Mahapadma Nanda
D. Kaivart Nand

28. Where is the World Trade Organization (WTO) located?
A. Australia B. New York
C. China D. Switzerland

29. Thoraci is part of ______ .
A. Skull B. Chest
C. Spinal cord D. Arm

30. When was the Indian Freedom League established?
A. 1935 B. 1921
C. 1925 D. 1928

31. Which of the following is a tax imposed on all foreign currency transactions?
A. Excise duty B. Tobin tax
C. Corporate tax D. Pigovian tax

32. With which of the following state Duffmuttu dance is associated?
A. Rajasthan
B. Assam
C. Kerala
D. Himachal Pradesh

33. Which of the following mountain ranges is located in Africa?

A. Andes B. The rockies
C. Drakensberg D. Alps

34. Which of the following is the third highest civilian award of the Indian Republic?

A. Padma Bhushan
B. Padma Vibhushan
C. Bharat Ratna
D. Padma Shri

35. When was the Export-Import Bank of India established?

A. 1 May, 1983 B. 28 April, 1985
C. 1 January, 1982 D. 15 March, 1980

36. In which of the following states Kadra Dam is located?

A. Maharashtra B. Assam
C. Karnatak D. Gujarat

37. The ______ schedule of Indian Constitution provides for the administration of the tribal areas of the states of Assam, Meghalaya, Tripura and Mizoram.

A. Tenth B. Sixth
C. Fifth D. Twelfth

38. Which of the following river has a tributary named 'Tungabhadra'?

A. Bhima B. Krishna
C. Narmada D. Mahanadi

39. Which was the only amendment adopted unanimously by Parliament?

A. 71 B. 52
C. 61 D. 92

40. The famous Shalimar Bagh of Srinagar was built during the reign of ______.

A. Azam Shah B. Akbar
C. Humayun D. Jahangir

Arithmetical and Numerical Ability

41. The following table (000s) shows the expenditure incurred by a company in various departments over the years. What is the ratio of total expenditure incurred by IT department and Operations department over the years?

Year	IT	Operations	Marketing	Human Resource
2015	220	250	200	120
2016	320	350	300	250
2017	410	500	400	320
2018	450	500	450	410

A. 9 : 8 B. 2 : 5
C. 3 : 2 D. 7 : 8

42. A can finish a job in 32 days. B can do that work in 20 days. After working alone for 15 days, B left that work. In how many days A can complete the remaining work?

A. 12 B. 16
C. 20 D. 8

43. A 2 mm wire is drawn from a copper wire of 110 cubic centimetre diameter. What is the length of the wire?

A. 255 m B. 17.5 m
C. 140 m D. 70 m

44. A bag contains 25 paise, 1 rupee and 2 rupee coins in the ratio 8 : 5 : 3. There is a total of 78 rupees, how many coins of 25 paise are there?

A. 24 B. 32
C. 45 D. 48

45. The following rectangle shows the revenue of the services sector (in billions) over different years. What is the percentage increase in service sector revenue from 2017-2018 to 2019-2020?

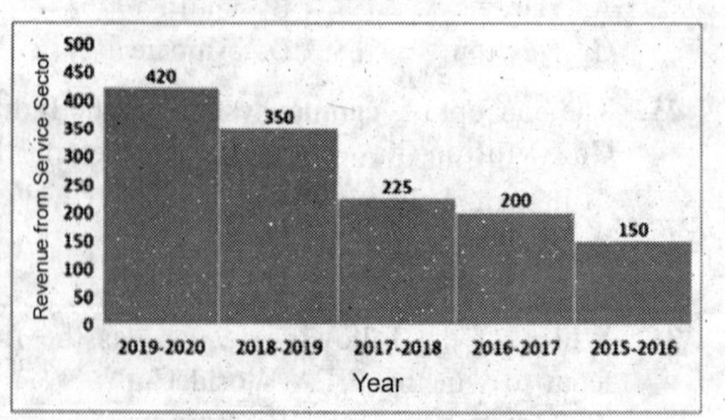

A. 82.2% B. 75.21%
C. 86.67% D. 90.05%

46. A man has 320 rupees, in coins of 1 rupee, 5 rupees and 10 rupees. The number of coins of each denomination is equal. How many coins does he have?

A. 45 B. 15
C. 60 D. 30

47. The length of a rectangular plot is 20 meters more than its breadth. The cost of fencing the plot is ₹ 2200 at the rate of ₹ 5 per meter. What is the length of the plot?

A. 110 m B. 120 m
C. 100 m D. 140 m

48. A worker covered a distance of 138 km in 15 hours. He travelled at a speed of 6 km/h, partly on foot and partly on bicycle at 12 km/h. What is the walking distance?

A. 36 B. 30
C. 42 D. 48

49. If ₹ 1410 is to be divided into three parts in the ratio of 1/3 : 1/4 : 1/5, what is the value of the first part?

A. ₹ 450 B. ₹ 720
C. ₹ 420 D. ₹ 600

50. In an election between 2 candidates, one got 37.5% of the total valid votes, 20% of the total votes were invalid. If the total number of votes was 50000, how many valid votes did the other candidate get?

A. 27500 B. 25000
C. 30000 D. 32500

51. 120 fruits are bought for ₹ 1200 and sold at the rate of ₹ 180 per dozen. What is the profit or loss percentage?

A. 25% profit B. 50% profit
C. 25% loss D. 50% loss

52. An item is marked up to 50% above the price, how many maximum discounts can be allowed so that there is neither profit nor loss?

A. 50% B. 33.33%
C. 37.5% D. 40%

53. A man covering a distance of 18 km in 3 hours, 7.2 km in 2 hours and 15 km in 5 hours. What is the average distance travelled by him per hour?

A. 3.62 km B. 4.22 km
C. 3.82 km D. 4.02 km

54. Two students appeared in an examination. One of them scored 20 marks more than the other and his marks were 60% of the sum of his marks. What were the total marks obtained by both of them?

A. 100% B. 120%
C. 125% D. 110%

55. Two numbers are in the ratio of 3 : 4, 5 is subtracted from each of the number as a result of which the ratio becomes 5 : 7. Find the smallest number of them.

A. 30 B. 27
C. 36 D. 33

56. A sum of money has increased by 45% over 9 years at simple interest. What will be the compound interest of ₹ 12,000 after 3 years at the same rate?

A. ₹ 1760 B. ₹ 1820
C. ₹ 1891.5 D. ₹ 1854.25

57. The population of a town increased from 12,0000 to 16,5000 in a decade. What is the average increase of population per year?

A. 0.035 B. 0.045
C. 0.0375 D. 0.0425

58. What is the largest 4 digit number which is divisible by 12, 30, 60, and 72?

A. 9600 B. 9960
C. 9840 D. 9720

59. A can finish a job in 24 days. B, he can work in 18 days. After working together for 12 days, B left that work. In how many days can A complete the remaining work?

A. 6 B. 12
C. 8 D. 24

60. What will be the last remaining balance in an account after depositing ₹ 820.47 and withdrawaling of ₹ 726.91, if there is a balance of ₹ 610.27 in that?

A. ₹ 620.83
B. ₹ 685.83
C. ₹ 703.83
D. ₹ 650.82

Language : English

61. Four words are given, out of which only one word is spelt correctly. Choose the correctly spelt word.

A. Surreptitious
B. Surpetious
C. Sureptious
D. Surreptious

62. In the following statement, one part of the sentence may have an error. Find out which part of the sentence has an error and click the button corresponding to it. If the sentence is free from error, select the "No error" option.

(A) There is no question / (B) of Radha's failing / (C) in the examination. / (D) No error

A. D
B. B
C. C
D. A

63. Four words are given, out of which only one word is spelt correctly. Choose the correctly spelt word.

A. Ventraloqust
B. Ventriloquist
C. Ventraloquist
D. Ventreloquist

64. In the following question, out of four alternatives, select the alternative which is the best substitute of the words/sentences.

A person who is pretending to be someone he is not

A. Sycophant
B. Philogynist
C. Statesman
D. Impostor

65. In the following question, out of four alternatives, select the alternative which is the best substitute of the words/sentences.

A poem or speech at the end of the play.

A. Euphony
B. Lecture
C. Monologue
D. Epilogue

66. What does the following idiom mean?

Ivory tower

A. A state of involvement in everybody's personal problems.
B. A state where an individual is going through hardships in life.
C. A state of seculation from the hardships of practical problems of real life.
D. A state of strong mindset like a tower of steel.

67. Out of the four alternatives, choose the word which best expresses the meaning of the given word.

Censure

A. Condemn
B. Approval
C. Seize
D. Appreciation

68. In the following statement, one part of the sentence may have an error. Find out which part of the sentence has an error and click the button corresponding to it. If the sentence is free from error, select the "No error" option.

(A) Ankit wrote her / (B) a very long message/ (C) but she didn't read it. / (D) No error

A. D
B. B
C. A
D. C

69. Fill in the blanks with the appropriate word.

Don't step _____ the broken glass.

A. on
B. at
C. in
D. of

70. What does the following idiom mean?

End in smoke

A. To end a fight with someone.
B. To not produce concrete or positive results.
C. To start a fight with someone.
D. To say negative things about someone else.

71. Out of the four alternatives, choose the word which is OPPOSITE in meaning to the given word.

Stringent

A. Artificial
B. Rigid
C. Firm
D. Lenient

72. Replace the words in the bracket from the set of options given.

Ashima hasn't eaten (from) breakfast and she is very hungry.

A. since
B. to
C. with
D. before

73. Four words are given, out of which only one word is spelt correctly. Choose the correctly spelt word.

A. Millennium B. Millineum
C. Milleniuum D. Milenium

74. Replace the words in the bracket from the set of options given.

The floor of his room was (covered upon) marble.

A. covered with B. covered by
C. covered in D. covered at

75. The questions below consist of a set of labelled parts of a sentence. Out of four options given, select the most logical order of the parts which form a coherent sentence.

Adolf Hitler said
P : would be hanged
Q : who do not obey
R : those persons
S : his commands

A. RSPQ B. PSQR
C. RQSP D. QPRS

Directions (Qs. No. 76-80): *Read the passage carefully and answer the given questions:*

In 1772, when Warren Hastings was appointed the first Governor General of the Company's Indian territories, one of his first undertakings was the rapid expansion of the Company's army. Since the available soldiers, or Sepoys, from Bengal many of whom had fought against the British in the Battle of Plassey (23 June, 1757), were now suspect in British eyes. Hastings recruited the soldiers from the high castle rural Rajputs and Brahmans of Oudh and Bihar, a practice that continued for the next 75 years. However, in order to forestall any social friction, the Company also took pains to adapt its military practices to the requirement of their religious rituals. Consequently, these soldiers dined in separate facilities; in addition, overseas service, considered polluting to their caste, was not required of them, and the army soon came to officially recognize Hindu festivals.

76. When was the first Governor General of the Company's Indian territories appointed?

A. 1775 B. 1772
C. 1757 D. 1778

77. Who were the suspects in the British eyes?

A. The Rajputs and Brahmans
B. Those residing in Oudh and Bihar
C. Warren Hastings
D. Soldiers from Bengal

78. When was the Battle of Plassey fought?

A. 1757 B. 1772
C. 1775 D. 1760

79. From where did Hastings recruit the soldiers?

A. From the people who participated in the Battle of Plassey.
B. From other countries
C. From the Bengal
D. From the rural Rajputs and Brahmans of Oudh and Bihar.

80. Who was the first Governor General of the Company's Indian territories?

A. Lord Cornwall
B. Lord Mountbatten
C. Warren Hastings
D. John Shore

हिन्दी भाषा

81. निम्नलिखित प्रश्न में, चार विकल्पों में से, उस सही विकल्प का चयन करें जो वाक्यांशों के लिए एक शब्द का विकल्प हो।

जिसका कोई उद्देश्य न हो।

A. निर्दोष B. निरुत्तर
C. निरुद्देश्य D. निराकार

82. निम्नलिखित प्रश्न में, चार विकल्पों में से, रिक्त स्थान के लिए निर्देशानुसार उचित विकल्प का चयन करें।

रोहन ________ साइकिल चलाई जाती है। (कर्मवाच्य)

A. द्वारा B. पर
C. ने D. से द्वारा

83. निम्नलिखित प्रश्न में, चार विकल्पों में से, उस विकल्प का चयन करें जो उपसर्ग से बना है।

A. सोकर B. घबराहट
C. निर्माण D. नकली

84. निम्नलिखित प्रश्न में, चार विकल्पों में से, उस विकल्प का चयन करें जो दिए गए वाक्य के लिए पक्ष के भेद का सबसे अच्छा विकल्प है।

बाजार में सब्जियों के दाम लगातार बढ़ते जा रहे हैं।

A. सातप्यबोधक B. नित्यताद्योतक
C. आरंभद्योतक D. प्रगतिद्योतक

85. निम्नलिखित प्रश्न में, चार विकल्पों में से, उस विकल्प का चयन करें जो समानार्थी शब्द का सही विकल्प नहीं है।

गुफा

A. विवर B. गेह
C. गव्हर D. गुहा

86. निम्नलिखित प्रश्न में, चार विकल्पों में से, उस विकल्प का चयन करें जो दिए गए वाक्य के लिए पक्ष के भेद का सबसे अच्छा विकल्प है।

बच्चे अब काफी पढ़ चुके हैं।

A. आरंभद्योतक B. प्रगतिद्योतक
C. सातप्यबोधक D. पूर्णताद्योतक

87. निम्नलिखित प्रश्न में, चार विकल्पों में से, उस विकल्प का चयन करें जो विशेषण के भेद वाला विकल्प हो।

एक दर्जन में बारह केले होते हैं।

A. परिमाणवाचक B. गुणवाचक
C. संख्यावाचक D. सर्वनामक

88. निम्नलिखित प्रश्न में, चार विकल्पों में से, उस विकल्प का चयन करें जो दिए गए वाक्य के लिए पक्ष के भेद का सबसे अच्छा विकल्प है।

उमा कितना अच्छा खाना बना रही है।

A. आरंभद्योतक B. नित्यताद्योतक
C. सातप्यबोधक D. अभ्यासद्योतक

89. निम्नलिखित प्रश्न में, चार विकल्पों में से, उस सही विकल्प का चयन करें जो प्रत्यय से बना शब्द है।

A. विक्रेता B. आनंदित
C. स्वागत D. बदबू

90. निम्नलिखित प्रश्न में, चार विकल्पों में से, उस विकल्प का चयन करें जो दिए गए मुहावरे का सही अर्थ वाला विकल्प है।

पापड़ बेलना।

A. काम करना। B. मेहनत करना।
C. खाना बनाना। D. संघर्ष करना।

91. निम्नलिखित प्रश्न में, चार विकल्पों में से, रिक्त स्थान के लिए निर्देशानुसार उचित विकल्प का चयन करें।

स्वामीजी ने शिकागो जाने का ______ किया।

A. समझा B. निश्चय
C. भला D. प्रगति

92. निम्नलिखित प्रश्न में, चार विकल्पों में से, उस विकल्प का चयन करें जो विराम चिह्न युक्त वाक्य का सही विकल्प हो।

A. सरदार! सारे डाकू मारे गए?
B. सरदार-सारे डाकू मारे गए।
C. सरदार, 'सारे डाकू मारे गए।'
D. सरदार! सारे डाकू मारे गए।

93. निम्नलिखित प्रश्न में, चार विकल्पों में से, उस विकल्प का चयन करें जो दिए गए मुहावरे का सही अर्थ वाला विकल्प है।

उलटा तवा

A. काम खत्म B. कोई काम न करना
C. कुछ न मिलना D. बहुत काला

94. निम्नलिखित प्रश्न में, चार विकल्पों में से, उस विकल्प का चयन करें जो विलोम शब्द का सबसे अच्छा विकल्प है।

ऋजु

A. कुटिल B. सरल
C. सीधा D. शालीन

95. निम्नलिखित प्रश्न में, चार विकल्पों में से, रिक्त स्थान के लिए निर्देशानुसार उचित विकल्प का चयन करें।

एक नौकरी ______ उसने सारा काम कर दिया। (साधनवाचक)

A. के पश्चात् B. के बगैर
C. के ऊपर D. के सहारे

निर्देश (प्र.सं. 96 से 100 तक): *इस गद्यांश को ध्यानपूर्वक पढ़ें और चार विकल्पों में से प्रत्येक प्रश्न का सर्वोत्तम उत्तर चुनें।*

मनुष्य को जितनी जरूरत हवा, पानी और अन्न की होती है, उतनी व्यायाम की भी होती है। हाँ, कसरत के बिना मनुष्य जिन्दा तो रह सकता है लेकिन निरोगी नहीं। कसरत का अर्थ केवल हॉकी, टेनिस, फुटबॉल, क्रिकेट और घूमना ही नहीं है। कसरत का अर्थ है शारीरिक और मानसिक कार्य। जिस प्रकार भोजन शरीर के लिए ही नहीं मन के लिए भी आवश्यक है, वैसे ही कसरत शरीर के साथ-साथ मन के लिए भी जरूरी है। एक कहावत है कि निरोगी वही है, जिसके निरोगी शरीर में स्वस्थ मन का निवास है।

96. इनमें से कौन-सा निरोगी का पर्यायवाची नहीं है?
A. रोगहीन B. रोगमुक्त
C. दोषमुक्त D. अवध

97. दिए गए विकल्पों में से मानसिक कार्य क्या है?
A. बोझा ढोना B. मजदूरी करना
C. दौड़ लगाना D. पढ़ाई करना

98. दिए गए विकल्पों में से शारीरिक कार्य क्या है?
A. गाना सुनना B. गीत लिखना
C. पुस्तक पढ़ना D. भोजन पकाना

99. इस अनुच्छेद का कोई उपयुक्त शीर्षक :
A. कसरत का अर्थ B. स्वास्थ्य और हम
C. शारीरिक जीवन D. निरोगी शरीर

100. अनुच्छेद के अनुसार मनुष्य को व्यायाम की आवश्यकता क्यों होती है?
A. जिन्दा रहने के लिए
B. प्रसन्न रहने के लिए
C. प्रशंसा के लिए
D. रोगमुक्त रहने के लिए

SECTION-B

Post Specific Subject Related Questions

101. Wilson's disease is associated with:
A. ceruloplasmin B. amylase
C. creatine kinase D. lipase

102. The amount of air exhaled from lungs as water vapour is about:
A. 1000 ml B. 500 ml
C. 1500 ml D. 100 ml

103. An eating disorder in which binge eating is followed by depression and guilt, self-induced vomiting and purging is:
A. bulimia nervosa
B. dysphagia
C. anorexia nervosa
D. binge eating disorder

104. pH is the negative logarithm of the concentration of:
A. hydrogen ions B. magnesium ions
C. potassium ions D. calcium ions

105. Identify the type of reinforcement that increases the possibility of a response by presenting a pleasurable stimulus after a desired response:
A. negative reinforcement
B. partial reinforcement
C. positive reinforcement
D. continuous reinforcement

106. Sleep walking in medical terms is:
A. insomnia B. somnolent
C. somnambulism D. hypersomnia

107. Prone position is:
A. lying face upwards
B. lying face downwards
C. turning upwards
D. lying face sideways

108. The term infant is used for a child of age:
A. 0-2 months B. 1-4 years
C. 1-10 years D. 2 months-1 year

109. The presence of bilirubin in urine indicates:
A. raised blood glucose levels
B. renal stones
C. indicate biliary disease
D. malignancy

110. A method of self-observation of an individual of their own mental status directly and by use of their memory is called:
A. observation B. introspection
C. experimental D. clinical

111. Vitamin B12 and folic acid deficiency causes:
A. iron deficiency anaemia
B. thalassemia
C. megaloblastic anaemia
D. sickle cell anaemia

112. A child grasps fingers when palm touch occurs at the age of:
A. 4 months B. 6 months
C. 9 months D. 4 weeks

113. Haemorrhage in a new-born is caused by the deficiency of:
A. Vitamin A B. Vitamin K
C. Vitamin E D. Vitamin D

114. BMI is calculated by using the formula:
A. weight (kg) × height $(m)^2$
B. height $(m)^2$ / weight (kg)
C. weight (lb) + height $(m)^2$
D. weight (kg) / height $(m)^2$

115. A system which provides support with a variety of joints that enable a wide range of movements is:
A. the central nervous system
B. the skeleton
C. the spine and discs
D. the peripheral nervous system

116. A bluish appearance of the skin and mucous membranes caused by inadequate oxygenation is called:
A. hypercapnia B. dyspnoea
C. bradypnoea D. cyanosis

117. The carrier for acyl groups are:
A. pantothenic acid B. niacin
C. retinol D. tocopherol

118. A deposit of food and bacteria on the teeth, which may produce tartar and dental caries is called:
A. stomatitis B. tenting
C. plaque D. oral hygiene

119. Name the drive that becomes active when the physiological balance within our body, called homeostasis, is disturbed:
A. social drive
B. physiological drive
C. unconscious drive
D. personal drive

120. Which of the following clinical signs is NOT related to confirming the death status of the patient?
A. No evidence of pulse
B. Movements of limbs
C. Pupils fixed and dilated
D. No evidence of respirations or blood pressure

121. This phase is so named because it is when the follicles in the ovary grow and form a mature egg. Name the phase:
A. luteal phase B. follicular phase
C. menstruation D. ovulation

122. A wide range of recurrent symptoms that occur during the luteal phase or last half of the menstrual cycle and resolve with the onset of menstruation is known as:
A. dysfunctional uterine bleeding
B. amenorrhea
C. premenstrual syndrome
D. dysmenorrhea

123. When a child weights below 3rd or 5th centile, failure to gain weight over a period of time or a change in the rate of growth that has crossed two major centiles is referred to as:
A. failure to thrive
B. skeletal dysplasia
C. small to gestational age
D. constitutional growth delay

124. The expulsion of an embryo or foetus before it is viable is called:
A. medical abortion B. miscarriage
C. surgical abortion D. abortion

125. A generic term that means inflammation and infection of the vagina is:
A. endometriosis B. pruritus
C. vaginitis D. candidiasis

126. Clients with a diagnosis of HIV or another sexually transmitted infection should be screened for:
A. chlamydia B. syphilis
C. gonorrhoea D. hepatitis

127. The procedure for women, that is performed postpartum, after an abortion, or as an interval procedure unrelated to pregnancy is called:
A. sterilisation B. tubal ligation
C. abortion D. vasectomy

128. The abbreviation ASHA, stands for:
A. Anganwadi Social Health Advisor
B. Auxiliary Social Health Advisor
C. Accredited Social Heatlh Activist
D. Affiliated Social Health Activist

129. Vasectomy is done with a surgical procedure, what is that procedure called?
A. Sterilization B. Tubal ligation
C. Abortion D. Vasectomy

130. Painful menstruation is termed as:
A. premenstrual syndrome
B. dysmenorrhea
C. dysfunctional uterine bleeding
D. amenorrhea

131. Coitus interruptus is also known as:
A. standard days method
B. withdrawal
C. cervical mucus ovulation method
D. symptothermal method

132. An inflammatory state of the upper female genital tract and nearby structures is called:
A. gonorrhoea
B. syphilis
C. pelvic inflammatory disease
D. hepatitis

133. Name the test where secretion is mixed with a drop of 10% potassium hydroxide on a slide, producting a characteristic stale fishy odour.
A. Treponemal tests
B. Whiff test
C. Nontreponemal tests
D. Rapid plasma reagin

134. Name the phase in the endometrial cycle that begins as the spiral arteries rupture secondary to ischemia, releasing blood into the uterus, and the sloughing of the endometrial lining begins.
A. Ischemic phase B. Proliferative phase
C. Secretory phase D. Menstrual phase

135. The Universal Immunization Program was started in 1985. How many diseases focused on vaccination at that time?
A. One B. Six
C. Five D. Two

136. A method to identify missing out cases is known as:
A. sentinel surveillance
B. screening
C. notification
D. testing

137. A barrier method in which a soft latex dome surrounded by a metal spring is used, is called:
A. cervical cap B. condom
C. contraceptive cap D. diaphragm

138. The inability to conceive a child after 1 year of regular sexual intercourse unprotected by contraception, or the inability to carry a pregnancy to term is known as:
A. infertility B. dysmenorrhea
C. amenorrhea D. endometriosis

139. A defence mechanism in which original goals or desires are substituted by others is called:
A. substitution B. sublimation
C. projection D. displacement

140. Women experiencing physical changes associated with decreasing oestrogen levels, which may include irregular menstrual cycles, sleep disruptions, mood disturbances, decreased vaginal lubrication, fatigue, vaginal arophy, and depression is seen during:
A. labour B. menarche
C. maternity D. menopause

141. Pain at Mcburney's point is seen in:
A. arthritis B. gastritis
C. appendicitis D. cholecystitis

142. In gout, there is an accumulation of crystals in the joints, which are made of:
A. calcium B. magnesium
C. uric acid D. ammonia

143. Which of the following is NOT a sign of dehydration?
A. Dry skin
B. Increased skin turgor
C. Hypotension
D. Decreased urine output

144. Which of the following is an example of gram negative bacteria?
A. Clostridium B. Streptococcus
C. Salmonella D. Staphylococcus

145. Fluid accumulation in tissues is called:
A. oedema B. carcinoma
C. pleural effusion D. ascites

146. Alpha 1 antitrypsin deficiency leads to:
A. bronchiectasis
B. emphysema
C. pulmonary oedema
D. bronchitis

147. Difficulty in breathing is called:
A. bradypnoea B. apnoea
C. dyspnea D. tachypnoea

148. Which of the following is NOT indicated by increased pulmonary blood flow that is left to right shunting?
A. Atrial septal defect (ASD)
B. Ventricular septal defect (VSD)
C. Patent ductus arteriosus (PDA)
D. Tetralogy of Fallot (TOF)

149. Name the condition in which, bleeding usually originates in the subependymal germinal matrix region of the brain, with extension into the ventricular system.
A. Retinopathy of prematurity
B. Leukomalacia
C. Necrotising enterocolitis
D. Periventricular haemorrhage

150. Gaseous exchange takes place in the:
A. alveoli B. trachea
C. nose D. bronchus

151. Bronchopulmonary dysplasia is currently referred to as:
A. bronchitis
B. bronchiectasis
C. chronic lung disease
D. acute lung disease

152. Normal blood pressure is considered :
A. 120/80 mm Hg
B. 150/100 mm Hg
C. 160/90 mm Hg
D. 50/40 mm Hg

153. The phenomenon where a newborn has an excessive birthweight of more than 4,000 g is called:
A. microsomia B. macrosomia
C. macrocephaly D. microcephaly

154. The premature fusion of one or more cranial sutures, either major or minor is called:
A. hydrocephalus B. craniosynostosis
C. microcephaly D. macrocephaly

155. The organ of adhesion is:
A. fimbriae B. mitochondria
C. nucleus D. flagella

156. A breathing disorder resulting from lung immaturity and lack of alveolar surfactant is known as:
A. ischemic hypoxia
B. cyanosis
C. respiratory distress syndrome
D. transient tachypnea of the newborn

157. By assessment, one can assign development quotient (DQ) for any developmental sphere. It is calculated as the:
A. average age at attainment by obtained age at attainment
B. average age at attainment + obtained age at attainment × 100
C. average age at attainment by obtained age at attainment × 100
D. average age at attainment – obtained age at attainment × 100

158. Foetal growth below the 10th percentile in terms of weight, length or head circumference based on standardised gestational rates is called:
A. dwarfism
B. short stature
C. delayed development
D. intrauterine growth restriction

159. The cell wall deficient bacteria is:
A. spirochetes B. vibrios
C. mycoplasma D. actinomycetes

160. The condition that occurs, when oxygen delivery is insufficient to meet metabolic demands is called:
A. prolapse B. acidosis
C. compression D. asphyxia

161. Colonoscopy is done to view the:
A. pancreas B. lungs
C. stomach D. large intestine

162. Which of the following is NOT a vital indicator for health?
A. Disability indicators
B. Mortality indicators
C. Health policy indicators
D. Morbidity indicators

163. The dissemination of microbial aerosols to a suitable portal of entry, usually the respiratory tract, is called:
A. vector-borne
B. vehicle-borne
C. air-borne
D. water-borne

164. Which of the following one is an example for ground water?
A. Rain water
B. River and streams
C. Springs
D. Ponds and tanks

165. An example of hormonal methods of contraception is:
A. depot formulations
B. abortion
C. tubectomy
D. condom

166. Which of the following statements is correct?
A. Sociology is a natural science
B. Sociology is a social science
C. Sociology is a biological science
D. Sociology is an applied science

167. Hypothyroidism in adults is called:
A. Addison's disease
B. Grave's disease
C. Cretinism
D. Myxedema

168. What causes Plasmodium vivax?
A. Filariasis
B. Dengue
C. Chikungunya fever
D. Malaria

169. Which of the following, is NOT a determinant in epidemiological triad:
A. host B. environment
C. agent D. time

170. What happens in case of antidiuretic hormone deficiency?
A. Diabetes insipidus
B. Diabetes mellitus
C. Ketoacidosis
D. Pellagra

171. Name the term that is concerned with good and evil:
A. law B. morality
C. religion D. culture

172. A cystometrogram is done to assess the function of the:
A. prostate B. lungs
C. urinary bladder D. gall bladder

173. Disability limitation and rehabilitation comes under:
A. specific protection
B. secondary prevention
C. tertiary prevention
D. primary prevention

174. Progesterone antagonist is:
A. regesterone
B. prostaglandins
C. misoprostol
D. mifepristone

175. In the case of burns, the involvement of the epidermis only comes under:
A. first degree B. second degree
C. third degree D. fourth degree

176. The other name of Hansen's disease is:
A. gonorrhoea B. tuberculosis
C. syphilis D. leprosy

177. The disease known as plague was transmitted to humans by:
A. bugs B. flies
C. mosquitoes D. rat fleas

178. Which of the following diseases is caused by bacterial infections?
A. Meningococcal meningitis
B. Measles
C. German measles
D. Influenza

179. Which of the following falls under experimental study?
A. Clinical trial
B. Case report and case series
C. Correlation/ecological study
D. Cross-sectional study

180. If socio-economic status is measured using the modified Kuppuswamy scale (if a family is called a high middle-class family), the score must be in the _______ range.
A. 26-29 B. 16-25
C. 30-32 D. 11-15

181. The change that does NOT occur during pregnancy is:
A. low haematocrit
B. increase in tone in the lower oesophageal sphincter
C. haemodilution
D. increase in plasma volume

182. The Likert scale is otherwise called the:
A. cumulative scale B. summated scale
C. differential scale D. arbitrary scale

183. The time taken for the involution of the uterus after delivery is:
A. 6 weeks B. 1 week
C. 2 weeks D. 4 weeks

184. The attitudes, values, interests and appreciations are concerned with:
A. psychomotor domain
B. affective domain
C. cognitive domain
D. both psychomotor and cognitive domains

185. If a curriculum exists in the heart and mind of educators but seldom exists in reality, it is called:
A. null curriculum
B. hidden curriculum
C. legitimate curriculum
D. illegitimate curriculum

186. Salpingectomy is the surgical removal of the:
A. kidney B. uterus
C. fallopian tubes D. ovary

187. In a research process, the first and foremost step happens to be that of selecting and properly defining a:
A. statistical analysis
B. hypothesis testing
C. research methods
D. research question

188. Among the following methods, which one is a learner centred method?
A. demonstration B. lecture
C. role play D. bedside clinic

189. Meta communication was classified under which of the following types of communication?
A. None of the above types
B. Both verbal and Non-verbal communication
C. Non-verbal communication
D. Verbal communication

190. In labour, the separation and explusion of the placenta comes under the:
A. fourth stage B. first stage
C. third stage D. second stage

191. The characteristic feature of true labour is:
A. contractions continue irrespective of posture
B. irregular contractions
C. pain felt in front of the abdomen
D. contractions not getting stronger

192. Vaginal discharge that occurs after the birth of a baby is called:
A. spinnbarkeit B. colostrum
C. fern pattern D. lochia

193. A history of three or four consecutive spontaneous abortion is called:
A. habitual abortion
B. incomplete abortion
C. missed abortion
D. threatened abortion

194. According to the situational theory of leadership, a person becomes a leader in spite of himself. He does not seek the role, it is thrusted upon him by the group and by the tide of events, this type of a leader is called a:
A. natural leader B. consensus leader
C. rational leader D. charismatic leader

195. The earlier biochemical marker of pregnancy is:
A. oestrogen
B. prolactin
C. human chorionic gonadotropin
D. progesterone

196. Morula is a stage stage of _______ .
A. 16 cell B. 24 cell
C. 32 cell D. 20 cell

197. A treponemal test is done to diagnose:
A. syphilis B. chlamydiasis
C. AIDS D. gonorrhoea

198. In a hierarchical line of command, which is responsible for making non-program decisions in every organization, is called:
A. Staff nurse
B. Chief nursing officer
C. Sub nursing officer
D. Assistant nursing officer

199. Fevering tenacity, disturbed sleep and disturbances of mood are seen during the period of _______ .
A. Menopause B. Gestation
C. Ovulation D. Hyperemesis

200. What is called a fetal head when the vagina opens during labor?
A. Chadwick sign
B. Hegar sign
C. Crowning
D. Hyperemesis

ANSWERS

1	2	3	4	5	6	7	8	9	10
D	C	A	D	A	D	A	C	B	A
11	**12**	**13**	**14**	**15**	**16**	**17**	**18**	**19**	**20**
C	A	C	C	A	C	C	D	C	B
21	**22**	**23**	**24**	**25**	**26**	**27**	**28**	**29**	**30**
D	A	B	C	A	A	C	D	C	D
31	**32**	**33**	**34**	**35**	**36**	**37**	**38**	**39**	**40**
B	C	C	A	C	C	B	B	B	D
41	**42**	**43**	**44**	**45**	**46**	**47**	**48**	**49**	**50**
D	D	A	D	C	C	B	C	D	B
51	**52**	**53**	**54**	**55**	**56**	**57**	**58**	**59**	**60**
B	B	D	A	A	C	C	D	C	C
61	**62**	**63**	**64**	**65**	**66**	**67**	**68**	**69**	**70**
A	B	B	D	D	C	A	A	A	B

71	72	73	74	75	76	77	78	79	80
D	A	A	A	C	B	D	A	D	C
81	**82**	**83**	**84**	**85**	**86**	**87**	**88**	**89**	**90**
C	A	C	D	B	D	C	C	B	D
91	**92**	**93**	**94**	**95**	**96**	**97**	**98**	**99**	**100**
B	D	D	A	D	D	D	D	B	D
101	**102**	**103**	**104**	**105**	**106**	**107**	**108**	**109**	**110**
A	B	A	A	C	C	B	D	C	B
111	**112**	**113**	**114**	**115**	**116**	**117**	**118**	**119**	**120**
C	D	B	D	B	D	A	C	B	B
121	**122**	**123**	**124**	**125**	**126**	**127**	**128**	**129**	**130**
B	C	A	D	C	B	A	C	D	B
131	**132**	**133**	**134**	**135**	**136**	**137**	**138**	**139**	**140**
B	C	B	D	B	B	D	A	A	D
141	**142**	**143**	**144**	**145**	**146**	**147**	**148**	**149**	**150**
C	C	B	C	A	B	C	D	D	A
151	**152**	**153**	**154**	**155**	**156**	**157**	**158**	**159**	**160**
C	A	B	B	A	C	C	D	C	D
161	**162**	**163**	**164**	**165**	**166**	**167**	**168**	**169**	**170**
D	C	C	C	A	B	D	D	D	A
171	**172**	**173**	**174**	**175**	**176**	**177**	**178**	**179**	**180**
B	C	C	D	A	D	D	A	A	B
181	**182**	**183**	**184**	**185**	**186**	**187**	**188**	**189**	**190**
B	B	A	B	A	C	D	C	B	C
191	**192**	**193**	**194**	**195**	**196**	**197**	**198**	**199**	**200**
A	D	A	A	C	A	A	B	D	C

Previous Paper (Solved)

DSSSB Staff Nurse Exam 2017*

SECTION-A

General Awareness

1. Kamakhya Temple is a famous pilgrim centre of .... state.
A. Assam B. Himachal Pradesh
C. Andhra Pradesh D. West Bengal

2. 'Upanishad' is philosophical treatise, which is part of ....
A. Vedas
B. Puranas
C. Nyay Shastras
D. Bauddh Pali Granthas

3. .... is called common keyboard layout of computer.
A. ABCDEF B. ASDFGH
C. QWERTY D. ZXCVBN

4. Which of the city has equatorial type of climate?
A. New Delhi B. Singapore
C. Tokyo D. Beijing

5. Which was the French colony in India?
A. Goa B. Diu
C. Puducherry D. Lakshadweep

6. Which one of the pair is not correct?
A. Satish Gujrat — Crafts
B. Nikhil Banerjee — Sitar
C. Allah Rakha Khan — Santoor
D. Jamini Roy — Paintings

7. What happen when a ship enters from sea into river?
A. He slightly down
B. He slightly uplift
C. He maintains the previous level
D. Depends on metal by which ship made

8. Diamond shines by the phenomenon, which is called ....
A. Interference
B. Total Internal Reflection
C. Diffusion
D. Diffraction

9. 'Nilgiri mountain' which is situated in Tamil Nadu, is a example of ....
A. Fold mountains B. Block mountains
C. Plateaus D. Volcanic mountains

10. Who is the founder and editor of national dialogue magazine 'Kesari' during independence movement?
A. Mahatma Gandhi
B. Ras Bihari Bose
C. Aurobindo Ghosh
D. Lokmanya Tilak

11. Recently who is appointed as Chief Election Commissioner?
A. Nasim Zaidi
B. Achal Kumar Jyoti
C. Rajiv Mehrishi
D. Kewal Kumar Sharma

12. Which component of petroleum is used as aviation fuel in Jet planes?
A. CNG B. Petrol
C. Kerosine D. Diesel

13. Which famous traveller travelling in India during the Muhammad bin Tughluq period?
A. Sheikh Saadi B. Harun al-Yusuf
C. Amir-ul-Mulk D. Ibn battuta

14. Which temple is related to Gupta Dyanasty?
A. Khajuraho
B. Ellora
C. Konark Sun Temple
D. Mahabalipuram

* Held on 13/08/2017

15. GST is a ....
A. Direct Tax
B. Indirect Tax
C. Components of Direct and Indirect Tax
D. Direct or Indirect tax on the basis of tax levied on that item

16. Development of 'Yoga' related with which ministry?
A. Ayush Mantralaya
B. Ministry of health and family welfare
C. Ministry of sports and youth affairs
D. Ministry of culture

17. Dola Benerjee is associated with which sport?
A. Archery B. Gymnastics
C. Pistol shooting D. Boxing

18. On 3rd May, 2017 which film is awarded as 64th best film award?
A. Bahubali B. Kasab
C. Neerja D. Pink

19. If one item is missed from union list, state list and concurrent list of the constitution, then who is entitled to made law on that item?
A. Only Parliament
B. Only Legislative Assemblies
C. Both of them
D. Only ordinance enforced on that item

20. Recently, the issue related to Kulbhushan Jadhav arises before 'International Court of Justice'. This court is situated at:
A. Copenhagen B. The Hague
C. Vienna D. Jeneva

General Intelligence & Reasoning Ability

21. In a certain code language SIKKIM is written as THLJJL. In the same code language EXAMINATION can be written as:
A. FWBLJMBSJNO B. FYBNJOBUJPO
C. DWZLHMZSHNM D. FZCMILATKMN

22. Select the word, which is present in the word RECREATION and not prepared by using only one time.
A. REFER B. RATION
C. CREATE D. TORN

23. What will be the next figure in the following series?

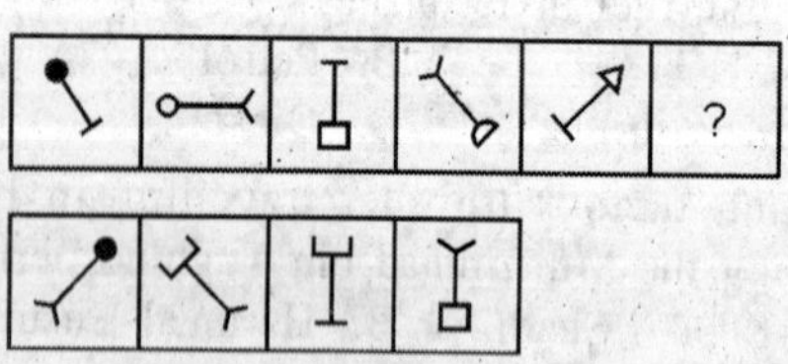

A B C D

24. How many rectangles are in it?

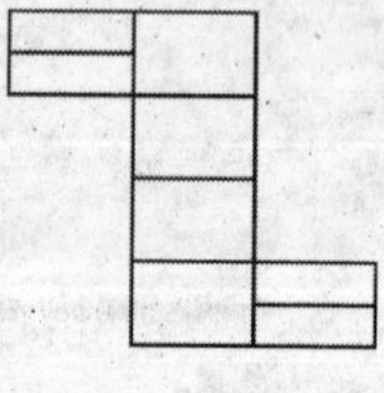

A. 16 B. 14
C. 18 D. 20

25. Happy : Dark : : ?
A. Sad : Pleasure B. Sadness : Sad
C. Sadness : Bright D. Pleasure : Sadness

26. 327 : 464 : : ? : 6216
A. 5125 B. 595
C. 5000 D. 505

Directions (Qs. No. 27 and 28): *Select the odd one from it:*

27. A. January B. June
B. August D. October

28. A. Thermometer B. Barometer
B. Anemometer D. Odometer

Directions (Qs. No. 29-31): *Some questions and some statements are given below, read them and calculate that whether the statement given under the question is sufficient to answer the question and then choose an option from the given options.*

A. If only statement I is sufficient to answer the question but statement II alone is not sufficient to answer the question
B. If only statement I is not sufficient to answer the question and only statement II is sufficient to answer the question

C. If both the statements I and II are essential to answer the question
D. If both the statements I and II are not sufficient to answer the question

29. Which is the smallest river?
I. Five rivers are A, B, C, D and E, and C is the longest river and river 'D' is smaller than 'B' and slightly longer than 'A'.
II. River A is smaller than river B, but longer than river E.

30. What is quantity of mangoes exporting from India?
I. India exports 50000 tonnes mangoes to Europe and it is 25% import of total mangoes of Europe.
II. Total amount of Indian mangoes is 2.5 million tonne, which is 10% of total production of mango.

31. What is the total profit of publisher ABC from book XYZ?
I. 12000 books are sold to company PQR and total sale of this book is 10%.
II. Selling price of the book is ₹ 500.

32. Which diagram best shows the relationship among singer, Gitar player and artist?

A. 
B. 
C. 
D. 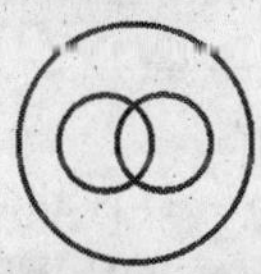

Directions (Qs. No. 33 and 34): *There is a special relation between figure 1 & 2. From the given options, choose the option which is related to figure 3 is the same manner as figure 2 is related to figure 1.*

33.
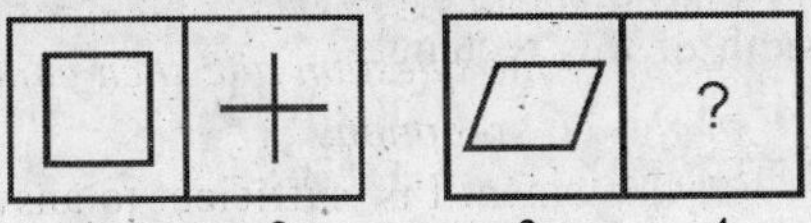

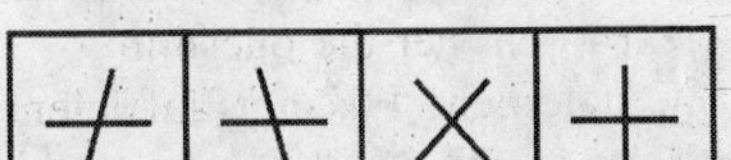

34.
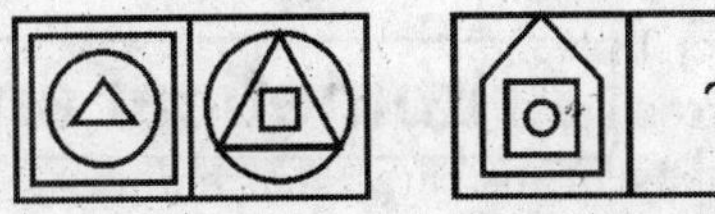

35. Find the missing figure.

36. Principal : Lecture : : Doctor : ?
A. Illness
B. Medicine
C. Hospital
D. Patient

37. Arrange the following in logical order.
1. Painting
2. Weaving
3. Seweing
4. Agriculture of cotton
5. Spinning
A. 1, 4, 2, 3, 5
B. 4, 5, 2, 1, 3
C. 5, 2, 3, 1, 4
D. 1, 2, 3, 4, 5

Directions (Qs. No. 38-40): *Find out the missing number of this series.*

38. 2, 3, 4, 9, 6, 27, 8, 81, ?
A. 93
B. 127
C. 10
D. 17

39. ACF, CEH, EGJ, ?, IKN
A. FHK
B. IJN
C. GIL
D. GIK

40. $\frac{4}{5}, \frac{6}{7}, \frac{10}{11}, \frac{12}{13}, \frac{16}{17}, ?$
A. $\frac{18}{19}$
B. $\frac{22}{23}$
C. $\frac{24}{25}$
D. $\frac{26}{27}$

Arithmetical and Numerical Ability

41. If 3A = 5B and 4B = 6C, then A : C is equal to ....

A. 2 : 5 B. 3 : 7
C. 5 : 2 D. 4 : 5

42. The ratio of boys and girls in a class is 3 : 2, then what will be the total expected number of students of that class?

A. 25 B. 26
C. 28 D. 42

43. What is the simple interest ₹ 100 for 6 months at the rate of 20 paise per rupees per month?

A. ₹ 1.20 B. ₹ 20
C. ₹ 12 D. ₹ 4.80

44. The length of a rectangle is L and its breadth is $\frac{1}{4}$th part of its length, then what will be the are of that rectangle?

A. $\frac{L}{4}$ B. $\frac{1}{2}L^2$
C. $4L^2$ D. $\frac{1}{4}L^2$

45. It the average of 5 observations x, $x + 2$, $x + 4$, $x + 6$ and $x + 8$ is 11, then what will be the average of the last 3 observations?

A. 15 B. 13
C. 11 D. 9

Directions (Qs. No. 46-48): *Statement I and II are given under the questions, Read questions and statements and to answer the given questions, determine whether the statement is sufficient or not.*

Choose the option:

A. If only statement I is sufficient to answer the question but only statement II is not sufficient to answer the question
B. If only statement II is sufficient to answer the question but only statement I is not sufficient to answer the question
C. If both statement I and statement II are essential to answer the question
D. If both statement I and statement II are not sufficient to answer the question

46. How many marks does Rakesh obtain?

I. The marks obtained by Rakesh is an average marks obtained by Ravi and Ashok.
II. Ashok has obtained 72 marks, which is 10% more than the obtained marks of Ravi.

47. How many people have internet connection in the town?

I. 70% people have mobile in town.
II. 90% mobile holders have internet data pack in town.

48. The value of $p : q$ ratio is ....

I. $3p = 4q$
II. $4p - q = 7$

49. If N is divided by 4 then it gives remainder 3, then what is the remainder when 2N is divided by 4?

A. 6 B. 3
C. 2 D. 1

50. What will be the result when –2 is subtracted from +2 ?

A. 0 B. – 4
C. 4 D. None of these

51. What is the value of smallest natural number N where 2N + 1 is not a prime number?

A. 2 B. 5
C. 3 D. 4

52. If $(n - 1)$ is an odd number, then what are its nearest next two odd numbers?

A. $(n - 3), (n + 1)$ B. $(n - 2), (n + 2)$
C. $(n - 5), (n + 1)$ D. $(n - 2), (n + 3)$

53. Ratio of perimeter and length of a rectangle is 3 : 1. What will be the ratio of length and breadth of this rectangle?

A. 1 : 1 B. 1 : 2
C. 2 : 1 D. 3 : 1

54. What is the area of a square whose perimeter is 48 cm?

A. 48 cm²
B. 144 cm²
C. 240 cm²
D. can not be determined

55. If the angles of a triangle are in the ratio 2 : 3 : 4, then what is the value of the greatest angle?

A. 90° B. 80°
C. 75° D. 60°

56. If the ratio of cost price and selling price of an object is 10 : 12, then what is the profit per cent of this object?

A. 12% B. 10%
C. 12.5% D. 20%

57. Find the product of 0.08 and 0.007?

A. 0.56000 B. 0.00056
C. 0.00560 D. 0.000056

58. What is the value of $\frac{3+4\div2\times3}{4+3\times2\div3}=?$

A. $\frac{9}{23}$ B. $\frac{3}{2}$
C. $\frac{9}{4}$ D. $\frac{11}{19}$

59. For emptied of a full tank water required 25 buckets. How many small buckets ($\frac{2}{5}$ of this bucket) required for emptied of this tank?

A. 70 B. 62.5
C. 87.5 D. None of these

60. If $y = 5$, then find the value of $10y\sqrt{y^3-y^2}=?$

A. $100\sqrt{2}$ B. 5000
C. 500 D. $2\sqrt{150}$

Language : Hindi

निर्देशः *अनुच्छेद को ध्यान से पढ़िए और उस पर पूछे गए प्रश्नों के उत्तर लिखिए। प्रत्येक प्रश्न के लिए चार सम्भावित उत्तर हैं जिन्हें A, B, C और D क्रम दिया गया है। आपको सही उत्तर चुनना है।*

अनुच्छेद

हम अनेक प्रकार का भोजन करते हैं। सामान्य भोजन के अलावा हम कुछ चीजें उनके स्वाद के लिए खाते हैं। उनमें से कुछ हैं : आइसक्रीम, चॉकलेट, ब्रेड, चीज़ आदि। चॉकलेट बच्चों को बहुत प्रिय होती है। यह कोई दावत नहीं रही। विश्व के प्रायः प्रत्येक देश में इसकी खपत होती है। संयुक्त राज्य अमेरिका इसका सबसे बड़ा उपभोक्ता है। चॉकलेट का स्वाद अच्छा होता है और यह हमें शक्ति भी देती है। चॉकलेट की कहानी बड़ी रोचक है। सैकड़ों वर्ष पूर्व चॉकलेट नाम के एक पेय का रहस्य मैक्सिको से स्पेन भेजा गया। मैक्सिको के लोग इस पेय को पसंद करते थे। इस चॉकलेट को बनाने के लिए वे कोकोआ की फलियों को तोड़कर पानी में उबालते थे, इस मिश्रण को वे वैनिला और किसी अन्य मसाले से सुगंधित बना देते थे। स्पेन के लोगों को पेय का तीखापन पसंद नहीं आया। शक्कर मिला देने के बाद उन्हें यह अधिक अच्छा लगा। यह चॉकलेट बनाने की शुरुआत थी।

61. किस देश को चॉकलेट का तीखा स्वाद पसंद नहीं आया?

A. भारत B. स्पेन
C. मैक्सिको D. संयुक्त राज्य अमेरिका

62. मैक्सिको के लोगों की पसंदीदा सुगंध क्या थी?

A. वैनिला B. पाइनएपल
C. स्ट्रॉबेरी D. गुलाब

63. निम्नलिखित में से कौन-सी चीज बच्चों को अधिक प्रिय है?

A. आइसक्रीम B. चॉकलेट
C. ब्रेड D. मक्खन

64. किस देश में चॉकलेट अधिक खाई जाती है?

A. मैक्सिको B. स्पेन
C. संयुक्त राज्य अमेरिका D. रूस

65. चॉकलेट में शक्कर मिलाने की शुरुआत किस देश ने की?

A. मैक्सिको B. स्पेन
C. फ्रांस D. भारत

निर्देशः *निम्नलिखित वाक्यों में रेखांकित शब्दों के पद-परिचय के लिए दिए गए विकल्पों में से सही विकल्प चुनकर लिखिए।*

66. मैं पुस्तक पढ़ता हूँ।

A. व्यक्तिवाचक संज्ञा, एकवचन, पुल्लिंग
B. जातिवाचक संज्ञा, एकवचन, स्त्रीलिंग

C. व्यक्तिवाचक संज्ञा, एकवचन, स्त्रीलिंग
D. जातिवाचक संज्ञा, एकवचन, पुल्लिंग

67. उसने ऊँचा महल देखा।
A. विशेषण, गुणवाचक, पुल्लिंग, एकवचन
B. विशेषण, परिमाणवाचक, स्त्रीलिंग, एकवचन
C. विशेषण, संख्यावाचक, पुल्लिंग, एकवचन
D. विशेषण, सार्वनामिक, स्त्रीलिंग, एकवचन

68. कौन आया है?
A. सर्वनाम, प्रश्नवाचक, पुल्लिंग, एकवचन
B. सर्वनाम, पुरुषवाचक, पुल्लिंग, एकवचन
C. सर्वनाम, निश्चयवाचक, स्त्रीलिंग, एकवचन
D. सर्वनाम, संबंधवाचक, पुल्लिंग, एकवचन

69. मैं अवश्य पहुँचूँगा।
A. क्रियाविशेषण, रीतिवाचक, 'पहुँचूँगा' का विशेषण
B. क्रियाविशेषण, स्थानवाचक, 'पहुँचूँगा' का विशेषण
C. क्रियाविशेषण, कालवाचक, 'पहुँचूँगा' का विशेषण
D. क्रियाविशेषण, परिमाणवाचक, 'पहुँचूँगा' का विशेषण

70. जिस वाक्य में एक सरल वाक्य के अलावा अन्य उपवाक्य आश्रित होकर आएँ कहते हैं:
A. संयुक्त वाक्य B. साधारण वाक्य
C. मिश्र वाक्य D. सरल वाक्य

निर्देश (प्र.सं. 71-73): *रिक्त स्थानों को उपयुक्त शब्दों से भरें।*

71. बहुत-सी पत्रिकाओं का .... बन्द हो गया है।
A. चलन B. प्रकाशन
C. प्रचलन D. क्रयन

72. कल दशहरे की वजह से .... है।
A. बन्द B. छुट्टी
C. अवतरण D. अवकाश

73. कविता पठन से हृदय का .... धुल जाता है।
A. प्रकाश B. मलिन
C. कलुष D. शोक

निर्देश (प्र.सं. 74 एवं 75): *मुहावरों के सही अर्थ का चयन करें।*

74. घी के दिए जलाना
A. खूब खर्च करना B. खुशियाँ मनाना
C. उद्घाटन करना D. त्योहार मनाना

75. गागर में सागर भरना
A. धन संचय करना B. कंजूस होना
C. थोड़े में बहुत कहना D. बहुत कम बोलना

निर्देश (प्र.सं. 76 एवं 77): *निम्नलिखित प्रश्नों में तीन वाक्य त्रुटिपूर्ण हैं। सही वाक्य का चयन करें।*

76. A. एक कहानियों की पुस्तक ला दो।
B. कहानी की पुस्तक एक ला दो।
C. कहानियों की एक पुस्तक ला दो।
D. एक कहानी की पुस्तक ला दो।

77. A. मैं पूरी रात भर जागता रह गया।
B. सारी रात भर में मैं जागता रह गया।
C. मैं सारी रात भर जागता रह गया।
D. मैं सारी-रात जागता रहा।

निर्देश (प्र.सं. 78-80): *निम्नलिखित शब्दों के विलोम शब्द चुनें।*

78. याचना
A. मांगना B. खरीदना
C. देना D. क्षमा मांगना

79. रजनी
A. दिन B. सूर्य
C. रात D. पुष्प

80. भोगी
A. कामी B. त्यागी
C. संन्यासी D. भिक्षु

Language : English

81. 'A piece of cake' is an idiomatic expression which means:
A. A piece of cake
B. Something very edible
C. Something that can be accomplished very easily
D. A bribe

82. Do not .... He can be very dangerous if provoked beyond a point.
A. drive him
B. drive him to hell
C. drive him to the cart
D. drive him to the wall

Directions (Qs. No. 83-85): *Fill in the blanks with appropriate word(s).*

83. One power supply was .... for several hours yesterday.

A. cut out B. cut up
C. cut off D. cut in

84. The .... of prawns has increased after the Blue Revolution.

A. price B. production
C. size D. significance

85. It is a great .... to represent one's nation .... the Olympics.

A. prize, in B. significance, on
C. respect, in D. honour, at

Directions (Qs. No. 86-88): *Select the word which is most similar in meaning to the given word.*

86. Inebriated

A. Weakened B. Drunk
C. Rebellious D. Irritated

87. Sundry

A. Dried in the sun B. Connected
C. Assorted D. Brave

88. Dissimilar

A. Divergent B. Together
C. Separated D. Matched

Directions (Qs. No. 89-91): *Select the word which is most opposite in meaning to the given word.*

89. Boundless

A. Unboundless B. Unbounded
C. Limited D. Prisoner

90. Prudent

A. Careful B. Miserly
C. Spendthrift D. Reckless

91. Verbose

A. Wordy B. Terse
C. Diffused D. Expanded

92. One who despises persons of lower social position is called:

A. Prim B. Prissy
C. Snob D. Tyrant

93. Person who brings an action at law is called:

A. Lawyer B. Plaintiff
C. Litigant D. Defendent

Directions (Qs. No. 94 and 95): *Select the option which will improve the underlined part of the sentence.*

94. The drug store <u>hadn't hardly any of those kinds of medicines.</u>

A. had hardly any of those kind
B. had scarcely any of those kind
C. had hardly not any of those kinds
D. had hardly any of those kinds

95. <u>Can't you never</u> understand how to work properly?

A. Can't you rather B. Can't you ever
C. Can't you will D. No improvement

96. Choose the correct spelling.

A. Amature B. Permanant
C. Diction D. Examption

97. Select the wrong spelling.

A. Exterminate B. Analytical
C. Grammatical D. Convarsation

Directions (Qs. No. 98-100): *A Sentence has been divided into three parts out of which one part may contain error(s). If there is an error, select that option. If there is no error, select (D).*

98. A. The reason why
B. he was selected
C. was because of his father's influence
D. No error

99. A. Passengers are prohibited
B. to smoke in
C. the delhi Metro
D. No error

100. A. Ram and Shyam always help
B. one another
C. in times of need
D. No error

SECTION-B

Post Specific Subject Related Questions

101. The international Council of Nurses (ICN) is headquartered in

A. New York B. London
C. Geneva D. Toronto

102. Isotonic exercises such as walking are intended to

A. Increase muscle tone
B. Increase endurance

C. Increase muscle size
D. Deplete muscle oxygen

103. An individual who is addicted to heroin is likely to experience which of the following symptoms of withdrawal?
A. Increased heart rate and blood pressure
B. Tremors, insomnia and seizures
C. Lack of co-ordination and unsteady gait
D. Nausea and vomiting, diarrhoea and diaphoresis

104. NANDA is
A. International nursing diagnosis glossary of terms
B. Diagnostics company
C. North American nursing diagnosis association
D. Nursing diagnosis list

105. The objective of BLS include
A. CAB B. ABC
C. BAC D. BCA

106. A client is admitted to the hospital and has edematous ankles. What should you instruct the student to do to reduce edema to lower extremities?
A. Restrict fluids
B. Elevate the legs
C. Apply elastic adhesive bandages
D. do ROM exercise

107. A client with GERD complains about having difficulty sleeping at night. What should the nurse instructs the client to do?
A. Sleep on several pillows
B. Eliminate carbohydrate from diet
C. Suggest glass of milk before sleep
D. Take antacids

108. Before cholecystectomy, the physician orders vitamin K. The nurse understands that this is administered because it is used in the formation of
A. Bilirubin B. Prothrombin
C. Thromboplastin D. Cholecystokinin

109. Which explanation is accurate regarding intussusception?
A. Kinking of bowel into itself
B. Band of connective tissue compressing the bowel
C. Telescoping of proximal loop to distal loop
D. Protrusion of an organ through wall that contains it

110. When evaluating fluid loss in a burned client, the nurse understands that the relationship between surface area and fluid loss is
A. Equal
B. Unrelated
C. Inversely related
D. Directly proportional

111. How long you will instruct the students to wait before checking the oral temperature, if the client has just consumed hot or cold or smoked?
A. 5 minutes B. 10 minutes
C. 20 minutes D. 30 minutes

112. If the first method of data collection is to conduct an interview, what is the second method?
A. Evaluation
B. Laboratory work
C. Performance of a physical examination
D. Diagnostic tests

113. Which of the following is not a physician prescribed intervention?
A. Performing wound test
B. Ordering diagnostic test
C. Elevating a edematous limb
D. Drug administration

114. Clear precise description of a problem is termed as
A. Diagnosis B. Etiology
C. Intervention D. Definition

115. A common framework that helps to guide the priotization of nursing tasks during the process of planning is
A. Maslow's hierarchy
B. Erickson's psychosocial development
C. Glasgow coma scale
D. Bern celli principle

116. How should you instruct the student nurse to modify the examination for a 7 year old child?
A. Ask the parents to leave the room before the examination
B. Demonstrate the equipment before using it

C. Allow the child to help with the examination
D. Perform invasive procedures last

117. All are motor nerves except:
A. Accessory B. Abducent
C. Trochlear D. Trigeminal

118. Substances that do not cross the placental barrier is:
A. IgG B. IgA
C. IgM D. IgE

119. In spinal cord myelin sheath is formed by:
A. Schwann cells B. Oligodendrocytes
C. Osteocytes D. Microglia

120. TNAI was formed in the year:
A. 1922 B. 1947
C. 1908 D. 1888

121. Antibodies are produced by:
A. Plasma cells B. Erythrocytes
C. Monocytes D. Basophils

122. Inability to speak or understand the spoken word is called as:
A. Apraxia B. Aphasia
C. Agnosia D. Insomnia

123. The hormone which is responsible for the ejection of milk is:
A. Prolactin B. Oxytocin
C. Estrogen D. ADH

124. The preferred site for IM injections in infants is:
A. Dorsogluteal B. Vastus lateralis
C. Rectus femoris D. Ventrogluteal

125. The size of IV cannula used for neonates is:
A. 24 gauge B. 22 gauge
C. 20 gauge D. 16 gauge

126. At 24 weeks of gestation, the fundal height is:
A. Between umbilicus and symphysis pubis
B. 4 cm below the umbilicus
C. At the level of umbilicus
D. 4 finger above umbilicus

127. Discolouration of anterior vaginal wall due to vascular congestion is called:
A. Chadwick's signs B. Osiander's sign
C. Goodell's sign D. Homan's sign

128. Mothers last LMP is December 7th. Calculate her EDD.
A. September 14th B. November 14th
C. September 27th D. August 23rd

129. Apgar score includes assessment of:
A. Reflex, grasp and pulse
B. Reflex, sleep and behaviour
C. Sleep, activity, colour
D. Colour, behaviour, respiration

130. Normal head circumference of new born at birth ranges from:
A. 31 – 33 cm B. 30 – 33 cm
C. 35 – 38 cm D. 33 – 37 cm

131. In working with the patient, when is the best time to prepare the patient for the termination phase?
A. Pre interaction phase
B. Orientation
C. Working
D. Termination phase

132. In schizophrenia, the term anhedonia refers to:
A. An inability to enjoy food
B. An inability to express empathy
C. An inability to react to enjoyable or pleasurable events
D. An inability to react appropriately to social cues

133. Anxiety is caused by:
A. An objective threat
B. A subjectively perceived threat
C. Hostility turned to self
D. Masked depression

134. The client on haloperidol has pill rolling tremors and muscle rigidity. He is likely manifesting:
A. Tardive dyskinesia
B. Pseudoparkinsonism
C. Akinesia
D. Dystonia

135. Which of the following is not a live vaccine?
A. Typhoid B. HIB vaccine
C. OPV D. BCG

136. An essential tool in patient education is:
A. Case study B. Health education
C. Counselling D. Handouts

137. The Government of India announced the first National Health Policy in the year:
A. 1951 B. 1983
C. 1977 D. 1991

138. Which of the following is an Indian Health Care Accrediting Agency?
A. JCI B. JCAHO
C. NABH D. INC

139. Bhore Committee is also known as:
A. Health Survey and Development Committee
B. Health Survey and Planning Committee
C. Hospital Review
D. Mudhaliar Committee

140. A written statement of policies and principles that guides the behaviour of all employees is called:
A. Code of ethics B. Work of ethics
C. Ethical dilemma D. None of the above

141. Kernig's sign is associated with:
A. Meningitis'
B. Spinal cord injury
C. Cerebral aneurysm
D. Seizures

142. Broca's area is in the:
A. Frontal lobe B. Parietal lobe
C. Occipital lobe D. Temporal lobe

143. To enhance absorption of calcium, which vitamin is needed?
A. Vitamin K B. Vitamin E
C. Vitamin D D. Vitamin A

144. Fertilization occurs in which area?
A. Ovary
B. Ampulla of fallopian tube
C. Uterus
D. Vagina

145. Blind spot is known as:
A. Macula lutea B. Optic disc
C. Fovea centralis D. None of the above

146. The category of drug that acts to prevent blood from clotting is:
A. Analgesic B. Antibiotic
C. Anticoagulant D. Antidiuretic

147. Which is not an essential standard precaution used in the care of patients irrespective of the diagnosis?
A. Hand hygiene
B. Improper sharps and waste disposal
C. Personal protective equipment
D. Aseptic techniques

148. The nurse is to administer an iron injection to an adult. How should this be administered?
A. SC in the arm
B. Intra dermal in forearm
C. IM in deltoid
D. Z tract IM in the gluteus

149. Changes that occurs in the musculoskeletal system due to immobility is:
A. Muscle endurance, strength and mass
B. Change in calcium metabolism
C. Alteration in fluid and electrolyte
D. None of the above

150. Which is not an non-verbal message in a mode of communication?
A. Tone and pitch of voice
B. Facial expression
C. Gesture
D. Touch

151. The student prepares to administer buccal medication : The medication should be placed:
A. On the client's skin
B. Between the client's cheeks and gums
C. Under the client's tongue
D. On the client's conjunctiva

152. It is transparent membrane that focuses the light that enters the eyes to the retina:
A. Lens B. Sclera
C. Cornea D. Pupils

153. Another name for knee-chest position is:
A. Genu-dorsal B. Genu-pectoral
C. Lithotomy D. Sim's

154. Which of the following is included in Orem's theory?
A. Maintenance of a sufficient intake of air
B. Self-perception
C. Love and belongingness
D. Physiologic need

155. One tsp is equal to how many drops?
A. 15 B. 60
C. 10 D. 30

156. An inborn error of metabolism that causes premature destruction of RBC is
A. G6PD B. Homocystinuria
C. Phenylketonuria D. Celiac disease

157. The 12 year old boy has fractured his arm. After the injury is casted, the nurse has to

perform all of the following assessments except:
A. Capillary refill B. Radial ulnar pulse
C. Finger movement D. Skin integrity

158. The causative organism for peptic ulcer is:
A. Helicobacter pylori
B. Staphylococci
C. Eschericia coli
D. Streptococci

159. Colour coding for Nitrous oxide cylinder is:
A. Black
B. Black with white shoulders
C. Light blue
D. Gray

160. False sensory perceptions with no basis in reality is known as:
A. Hallucinations
B. Delusions
C. Loose associations
D. Neologisms

161. Which of the following procedure always requires surgical asepsis?
A. Vaginal irrigation
B. Urinary catheterization
C. Nasogastric tube insertion
D. Colostomy irrigation

162. The most appropriate time for the nurse to obtain a sputum specimen for culture is:
A. Early in the morning
B. After the patient eats a light breakfast
C. After aerosol therapy
D. After chest physiotherapy

163. Mania is a:
A. Anxiety related disorder
B. Dissociative disorder
C. Mood disorder
D. Thought disorder

164. Kaposi's sarcoma is associated with:
A. Human papilloma virus
B. Human T cell lymphotropic virus type I (HTLV-I)
C. Human immunodeficiency virus
D. Epstein-Barr virus

165. Which of the following is heart shaped pelvis?
A. Anthropoid B. Platypelloid
C. Android D. Gynaecoid

166. Peripheral vision is assessed by:
A. Snellen chart
B. Ishihara chart
C. Slit lamp examination
D. Confrontation test

167. Sudden gush of blood or lengthening of the umbilical cord after the delivery of the infant indicates:
A. Placenta accreta
B. Retained placenta
C. Abruptio placenta
D. Placental separation

168. The two pubic bones meet anteriorly to form:
A. Coccyx
B. Symphysis pubis
C. Sacrococcygeal ligament
D. Sacrolliac joint

169. Which is a primary sign of labour?
A. Uterine contraction
B. Pushing by the mother
C. Intrathoracic pressure
D. Abdominal contraction

170. A 24 yrs old primigravida weight 57 kg, hemoglobin 11 gm/dl visits an antenatal clinic during second trimester of pregnancy seeking advice of dietary intake. She should be adviced to take:
A. Additional intake of 300 kcal
B. Additional intake of 500 kcal
C. Additional intake of 650 kcal
D. No extra kcal

171. A primary health centre covers a population in tribal area of
A. 50000 B. 30000
C. 20000 D. 5000

172. Which of the nutritional programme launched by the Government of India is to enhance admission, retain students in school and improve health?
A. Special Nutrition Programme
B. ICDS
C. Mid-day Meal Programme
D. Vitamin

173. WHO theme for the year 2017 is:
A. International health security
B. Small bites big threat

C. Make hospital safe in emergencies
D. Depression – let's talk

174. The peripheral worker of ICDS scheme is:
A. Trained dai
B. Anganwadi worker
C. Health guide
D. Health assistant female

175. In the occurrence of SARS and other pandemics, which of the following is the most important role of a nurse in epidemiology?
A. Health promotion
B. Disease prevention
C. Surveillance
D. Case finding

176. Maximum participation of students is possible in teaching through:
A. Lecture method
B. Discussion method
C. Textbook method
D. A.V. Aids

177. Which of the following belongs to a projected aid?
A. Blackboard B. Diorama
C. Epidiascope D. Globe

178. In the grief process, statements such as "no this cannot be true, this is not possible" are indicative of:
A. Denial stage B. Acceptance stage
C. Anger D. Bargaining

179. The first therapeutic use of electricity induced seizures in the treatment of mental disorders is related to:
A. Bini and Cereletti B. D. Goldman
C. Harold A. Sackeim D. Sigmund Freud

180. Handy–Dandy this is my work and want shop apple pie–custard pie, this is:
A. Neologism B. Word salad
C. Flight of ideas D. Clang association

181. Questionnaries is a:
A. Research method
B. Measurement technique
C. Tool for data collection
D. Data analysis

182. "I don't care", attitude of a student demonstrates his/her:
A. Aggression B. Defence
C. Denial D. Regression

183. The problem solving process begins with:
A. Clarification of the situation
B. Establishment of alternatives
C. Identification of the difficulty
D. Isolation of the cause

184. Success of each organization is depending upon the performance of:
A. Employer B. Management
C. Vendor D. Employee

185. The method which consists of series of cards which are flashed one after another while teaching is:
A. Flannel graph B. Flash card
C. Puppet show D. Charts

186. Incubation period of mumps is:
A. 18 days B. 5 days
C. 14 days D. 10 days

187. A very useful principle of learning is that a new response is strengthened by:
A. Punishment B. Reinforcement
C. Biofeedback D. Stimulus

188. Punishment is effective only when it weakens:
A. Undersirable response
B. Desirable response
C. Positive response
D. Negative response

189. Early diagnosis and prompt treatment is emphasized in:
A. Primary prevention
B. Secondary prevention
C. Tertiary prevention
D. Rehabilitation

190. The centre symbol of under five clinics represents:
A. Health education
B. Family planning
C. Immunization
D. Adequate nutrition

191. Hormone secreted by islets of Langerhans of pancreas is:
A. Progesterone B. Testosterone
C. Insulin D. Haemoglobin

192. It is to describe as a collection of people who share some attributes of their lives:

A. Family B. Illness
C. Community D. Nursing

193. Five teaspoon is equivalent to how many milliliters (ml)?
A. 30 ml B. 25 ml
C. 12 ml D. 22 ml

194. How will you instruct the students to record the clients pulse rate that is found above normal?
A. Tachypnea B. Hyperpyrexia
C. Arrhythmia D. Tachycardia

195. Resonance is best described as:
A. Sounds created by air filled lungs
B. Short, high pitch and threading
C. Moderately loud and musical quality
D. Drum like

196. In this method of teaching, the presence of patient is not necessary:
A. Bed side clinic
B. Nursing care conference
C. Nursing rounds
D. Case study method

197. An effective teaching means all of the following except:
A. A teacher teaches with enthusiasm
B. A teacher finds fault in his students
C. A teacher puts emphasis more on teaching than on class control
D. A teacher is interested in making the subject matter understand rather than completing the course

198. Learning which involves motor organs is called:
A. Sensory learning
B. Motor learning
C. Verbal learning
D. Sensory-motor learning

199. When developing a plan of care for a male adolescent, the nurse considers the Child's psychosocial needs during adolescents; psychosocial development focuses on:
A. Becoming industrious
B. Establishing an identity
C. Achieving intimacy
D. Developing initiatives

200. Which of the following organisms is responsible for the development of rheumatic fever?
A. Streptococcal pneumonia
B. Haemophilus influenzae
C. Group A beta hemolytic streptococcus
D. Staphylococcus aureus

ANSWERS

1	2	3	4	5	6	7	8	9	10
A	A	C	B	C	C	A	B	B	D
11	**12**	**13**	**14**	**15**	**16**	**17**	**18**	**19**	**20**
B	D	D	B	B	A	A	B	A	B
21	**22**	**23**	**24**	**25**	**26**	**27**	**28**	**29**	**30**
A	A	A	C	A	A	B	D	C	B
31	**32**	**33**	**34**	**35**	**36**	**37**	**38**	**39**	**40**
D	D	A	B	A	A	B	C	C	A
41	**42**	**43**	**44**	**45**	**46**	**47**	**48**	**49**	**50**
C	A	A	D	B	C	C	A	C	C
51	**52**	**53**	**54**	**55**	**56**	**57**	**58**	**59**	**60**
D	A	C	B	B	D	B	B	B	C
61	**62**	**63**	**64**	**65**	**66**	**67**	**68**	**69**	**70**
B	A	B	C	B	B	A	A	A	C

71	72	73	74	75	76	77	78	79	80
B	D	C	B	C	C	D	C	A	C
81	**82**	**83**	**84**	**85**	**86**	**87**	**88**	**89**	**90**
C	D	C	B	D	B	C	A	C	D
91	**92**	**93**	**94**	**95**	**96**	**97**	**98**	**99**	**100**
B	C	B	A	B	C	D	C	C	B
101	**102**	**103**	**104**	**105**	**106**	**107**	**108**	**109**	**110**
C	A	D	A	A	B	A	B	C	D
111	**112**	**113**	**114**	**115**	**116**	**117**	**118**	**119**	**120**
D	C	C	D	A	B	D	C	B	A
121	**122**	**123**	**124**	**125**	**126**	**127**	**128**	**129**	**130**
A	B	B	B	A	D	A	A	D	D
131	**132**	**133**	**134**	**135**	**136**	**137**	**138**	**139**	**140**
D	C	B	B	A	C	B	C	A	A
141	**142**	**143**	**144**	**145**	**146**	**147**	**148**	**149**	**150**
A	A	C	B	B	C	B	D	A	A
151	**152**	**153**	**154**	**155**	**156**	**157**	**158**	**159**	**160**
B	C	B	A	B	A	D	A	C	A
161	**162**	**163**	**164**	**165**	**166**	**167**	**168**	**169**	**170**
B	A	C	C	C	D	D	B	A	A
171	**172**	**173**	**174**	**175**	**176**	**177**	**178**	**179**	**180**
C	C	D	D	C	B	C	A	A	B
181	**182**	**183**	**184**	**185**	**186**	**187**	**188**	**189**	**190**
C	C	C	D	B	A	B	A	B	B
191	**192**	**193**	**194**	**195**	**196**	**197**	**198**	**199**	**200**
C	C	B	D	A	B	C	B	B	C

Explanatory Answers

21. In a certain language

S I K K I M is written as
+1↓ −1↓ +1↓ −1↓ +1↓ −1↓
T H L J J L

Similarly,

E X A M I N A T I O N
+1↓−1↓+1↓−1↓+1↓−1↓+1↓−1↓+1↓−1↓+1↓
F W B L J M B S J N O

will be written as.

22. The letter F is not in the given word RECREATION. Hence, the word REFER can not be make from the given word.

26.

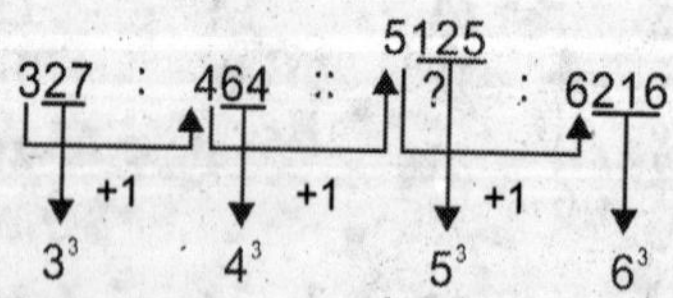

Hence 5125 will come at the place of question mark.

27. There are 31 days in January, August and October while in June 30 days. Hence, June is odd.

28. Temperature is measured by thermometer. Pressure of air is measured by others. Hence, thermometer is odd.

37. First of all Agriculture of cotton then, spinning, weaving, painting and in the last seweing.

Hence, option (B) 4, 5, 2, 1, 3 is true order.

38.

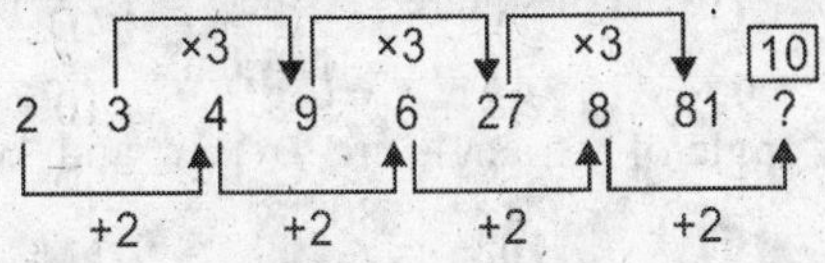

Hence, 10 will come at the place of question mark.

39.

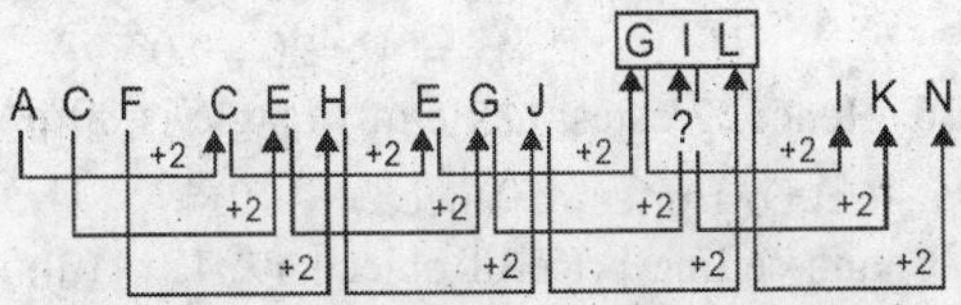

Hence, GIL will come at the place of question mark.

40.

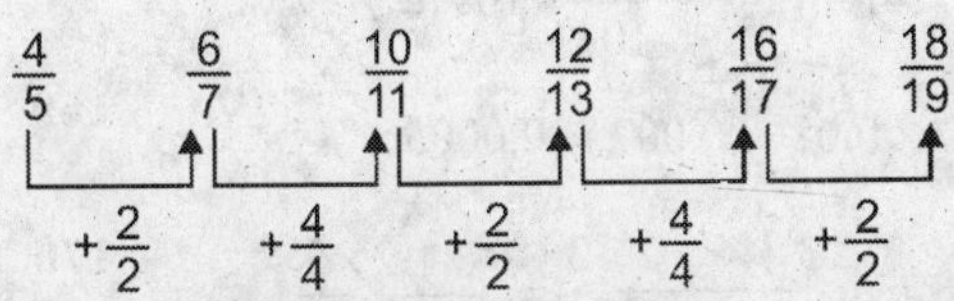

Hence, $\frac{18}{19}$ will come at the place of question mark.

41. $\because \quad 3A = 5B$

$$\Rightarrow \quad A = \frac{5B}{3}$$

and $\quad 4B = 6C$

$$\Rightarrow \quad C = \frac{4B}{6}$$

$$\frac{A}{C} = \frac{\frac{5B}{3}}{\frac{4B}{6}} = \frac{5B}{3} \times \frac{6}{4B} = \frac{5}{2}$$

Hence, A : C = 5 : 2.

42. Let number of boys $3x$ and no. of girls $2x$ in the class.

Number of students in the class = $3x + 2x = 5x$

According to the question,

$5x = 25 \Rightarrow x = 5$

$\therefore$ No. of boys = 15

No. of girls = 10

Hence, no. of students 25 is correct option.

43.
$$\text{S.I.} = \frac{P \times R \times T}{100}$$
$$= \frac{100 \times 20 \times 6}{100}$$
= 120 Paise = ₹ 1.20.

44. $\because$ Length of rectangle be l

$$\therefore \text{ Breadth} = \frac{1}{4}l = \frac{l}{4}$$

Area of rectangle = length × breadth

$$= l \times \frac{l}{4} = \frac{1}{4}l^2.$$

45. Sum of 5 observations = 11 × 5

$x + x + 2 + x + 4 + x + 6 + x + 8 = 55$

$\Rightarrow 5x + 20 = 55$

$\Rightarrow 5x = 35 \Rightarrow x = 7$

Sum of last three observations

= 11 + 13 + 15 = 39

Average of last three observations = $\frac{39}{3}$ = 13.

46. Let Ravi got x marks

$$x + \frac{10}{100} \times x = 72 \Rightarrow \frac{11x}{10} = 72$$

$$\Rightarrow \quad x = \frac{720}{11} = 65.45$$

Hence, Ravi got 65.45 marks

$$\text{Rakesh got} = \frac{72 + 65.45}{2} = \frac{137.45}{2}$$

= 68.725 = 68.73 marks

Statement I and II both are essential to answer the question. Hence, option (C) is correct.

47. Statement I: 70% people have mobiles.

Statement II: 90% mobile holders have internate data pack.

Hence, 63% people have internate connection.

Statements I and II both are essential to answer the question. Hence, option (C) is correct.

48. From statement I, $3p = 4q$

Dividing both side by 'q'

$$\frac{3p}{q} = \frac{4q}{q}$$

$$\Rightarrow \quad 3\frac{p}{q} = 4 \Rightarrow \frac{p}{q} = \frac{4}{3}$$

$$\therefore \quad p : q = 4 : 3$$

Hence, Statement I is sufficient alone to answer the question. But statement II is not sufficient to answer the question. Hence, option (A) is correct.

49. $\because$ Dividend = Quotient × Divisor + Remainder

$$N = (\text{Quotient} \times 4) + 3$$

Now, $2N = 2[(\text{Quotient} \times 4) + 3]$

$$= 2 \text{ Quotient } + 6$$

$$= 3 \text{ Quotient } + 2$$

Hence, when 2N is divided by 4, then remainder = 2.

50. $+2 - (-2) = +2 + 2 = 4$

When (–2) is subtracted from +2, then result will be 4.

51. $\because$ 2N + 1 is not a prime number

Put N = 1, 2, 3, ... 9

2(1) + 1 = 3 which is prime number

2(2) + 1 = 5 which is prime number

2(3) + 1 = 7 which is prime number

2(4) + 1 = 9 which is not prime number

Hence, smallest natural number N = 4.

52. $\because$ $(n - 1)$ is an odd number then its nearest other two odd numbers are $(n - 3)$, $(n + 1)$.

53. 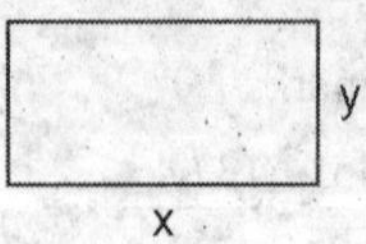

Let length of rectangle = x and breadth = y

$$\text{Perimeter} = 2(x + y)$$

According to the question,

$$\frac{2(x+y)}{x} = \frac{3}{1}$$

$$\Rightarrow \quad 3x = 2x + 2y \Rightarrow x = 2y$$

$$\therefore \quad \frac{x}{y} = \frac{2}{1} \Rightarrow x : y = 2 : 1.$$

54. 

$\because$ Perimeter of square = 4 × side

$$\Rightarrow \quad 48 = 4 \times \text{side}$$

$$\therefore \quad \text{Side} = \frac{48}{4} = 12 \text{ cm}$$

$$\text{Area of square} = (\text{side})^2 = 12 \times 12$$

$$= 144 \text{ cm}^2.$$

55. Let angle of a triangle are $2x°$, $3x°$ and $4x°$

$$\therefore \quad 2x + 3x + 4x = 180°$$

$$\Rightarrow \quad 9x = 180° \Rightarrow x = 20°$$

$$2x = 2 \times 20 = 40°$$

$$3x = 3 \times 20 = 60°$$

$$4x = 4 \times 20 = 80°$$

Hence, greatest angle of triangle is 80°.

56. Let cost price of object = ₹ $10x$

and selling price of object = ₹ $12x$

Profit = $12x - 10x = 2x$

$$\text{Profit\%} = \frac{2x}{10x} \times 100 = 20\%.$$

57. $0.08 \times 0.007 = 0.00056.$

58.
$$\frac{3+4\div 2\times 3}{4+3\times 2\div 3} = \frac{3+2\times 3}{4+3\times\frac{2}{3}}$$

$$= \frac{3+6}{4+2} = \frac{9}{6} = \frac{3}{2}.$$

59. Let no. of x buckets required to emptied the tank.

According to the quetion,

$$25 = \frac{2}{5}x$$

$$\Rightarrow \quad 2x = 125 \Rightarrow x = \frac{125}{2} = 62.5.$$

60. $\because \quad y = 5$

$$\therefore \quad 10y\sqrt{y^3 - y^2}$$

$$= 10 \times 5\sqrt{5^3 - 5^2}$$

$$= 50\sqrt{125 - 25}$$

$$= 50\sqrt{100}$$

$$= 50 \times 10 = 500.$$

Previous Paper (Solved)

Nurse Recruitment Exam, 2015*

SECTION-A

GENERAL AWARENESS

1. Which Airline on 17-12-2014 cancelled its 150 flights due to oil companies refusal to supply fuel and thus thousands of fliers were left stranded?
   A. Indigo B. Jet Airways
   C. Spice Jet D. Go Air
2. In which city of Pakistan, Taliban gunmen stormed an army run school and killed 132 children and staffers on 16-12-2014?
   A. Lahore B. Peshawar
   C. Islamabad D. Karachi
3. In the small car segment, Tata Motors came out recently with which car comprising Electronic Power Assisted system with 'Active Return' function and speed sensitive power steering?
   A. Zest B. Indica
   C. Bolt D. Nano
4. Expand CBI
   A. Criminal Branch of Investigation
   B. Criminal Bureau of Investigation
   C. Central Branch of Investigation
   D. Central Bureau of Investigation
5. Name the Indian-American who has recently become the youngest ever US Surgeon General at the age of 37
   A. Vivek Murthy B. Vikram Murthy
   C. Ami Bera D. None of these
6. Kidambi Srikanth is a famous
   A. Shooter B. Boxer
   C. Shuttler D. Weight Lifter
7. Who among the following introduced local self government in India?
   A. Lord Canning
   B. Lord Rippon
   C. Raja Rammohan Roy
   D. Lord Mountbatten
8. The statue of Gomateshwara at Shravanabelagola was built by
   A. Chandragupta Maurya
   B. Kharavela
   C. Amoghavarsha
   D. Chavundaraya
9. Which of the following is not a metal?
   A. Ammonia B. Sodium
   C. Radium D. Plutonium
10. Antigen is a substance which
    A. Lowers body temperature
    B. Destroys harmful bacteria
    C. Triggers the Immune system
    D. Is used as an antidote to poison
11. Where is Golconda Fort?
    A. Jaipur B. Delhi
    C. Hyderabad D. Aurangabad
12. Kuchipudi is a dance form of
    A. Tamil Nadu B. Andhra Pradesh
    C. Kerala D. Karnataka
13. Four 1.5 V cells are connected in parallel. The output voltage is
    A. 1.5 V B. 6 V
    C. 0.375 V D. None of these
14. Light year is the unit of
    A. Time
    B. Distance
    C. Light
    D. Intensity of light

* Held on 26/04/2015

15. Which Article of our Constitution has abolished untouchability?
A. Article 14 B. Article 15
C. Article 16 D. Article 17

16. Which day is observed as United Nations Day?
A. May 8 B. April 7
C. October 24 D. October 2

17. Among the following who represents Theatre Artists in Rajya Sabha?
A. Sachin Tendulkar
B. Oscar Fernandes
C. Jayashree
D. Dr. Manmohan Singh

18. Among the following, which is an input device?
A. Key Board
B. Printer
C. Visual Display Unit
D. Graph Plotter

19. Who directed the film "Dweepa" (Kannada-Colour-2001) which won the Swarna Kamal for best film and national award for best cinematography?
A. Girish Karnad B. Girish Kasaravalli
C. Nagabharana D. Puttanna Kanagal

20. Who was crowned Miss World 2014 on 14-12-2014 in the Miss World Pageant held in London?
A. Koyal Rana
B. Kathryn Bigelow
C. Rolene Strauss
D. Whitney Houston

GENERAL INTELLIGENCE AND REASONING ABILITY

21. Choose the one that does not belong to the group of the other three.
A. 12 B. 18
C. 21 D. 28

22. If A is substituted by 2, B by 3, C by 4, D by 2, E by 3, F by 4 and so on, then what will be total of the numerical values of the letters of the word LINE?
A. 14 B. 12
C. 16 D. 15

23. KN NL QJ TH ?
A. WE B. WF
C. XF D. XE

Directions (Qs. 24 to 26): *A, B, C, D, E and F are sitting along a circle facing the centre. B is an immediate neighbour of D. C is an immediate neighbour of A but is not an immediate neighbour of F. A is to the immediate left of B.*

24. Who is the second to the right of E?
A. B B. A
C. D D. F

25. Who are the neighbours of F?
A. D and B B. D and A
C. D and E D. B and C

26. Who is to the immediate right of A?
A. B B. C
C. D D. E

Directions (Qs. 27 to 29): *These questions are based on the following 6 numbers. 283, 347, 518, 829, 748, 827.*

27. If the first and the second digits of each number are interchanged, which number will be the second lowest?
A. 827 B. 829
C. 518 D. 748

28. If the second and third digits of each number are interchanged, which number will be the third highest?
A. 347 B. 748
C. 829 D. 827

29. If the first and the third digits of each number are interchanged, which number will be the third lowest?
A. 347 B. 827
C. 283 D. 748

30. If A is denoted by 4, L by 7, J by 2, R by 8, E by 1 and I by 3, then what will be the numeric form of the word JAILER when written in the reverse order?

A. 813742 B. 243718
C. 871342 D. 817342

31. If 283 is written as 328, 347 as 734 and so on, then which of the following two numbers will have least difference between them?
A. 347 and 518 B. 283 and 748
C. 827 and 347 D. 748 and 518

32. In a certain code 'GENIOUS' is written as 'EGINSOU'. How will 'GARNISH' be written in the code?
A. AGNRHIS B. AGNRHSI
C. NGRHISA D. NGARHSI

33. In a certain code INKER is written as KPLCP and GLIDE is written as INJBC. How ill JINKS be written in that code?
A. LJOIQ B. MKOIQ
C. LKOIQ D. LKOLT

Directions (Qs. 34 to 36): *These questions are based on the following arrangement of symbols, letters and numbers.*

£ L 2 = ? P C 7 $ E H @ ÷ 8 K & M 5 T V 3 *

34. How many such symbols are there in the arrangement, each of which is immediately preceded by a letter?
A. Four B. Two
C. One D. Three

35. How many such numbers are there in the arrangement each of which is immediately followed by a letter?
A. Three B. One
C. Nil D. Two

36. If all the symbols are deleted from the arrangement which element will be the 5th to the right of the 12th element from the right end?
A. K B. H
C. 8 D. M

37. P is the brother of Q. R is the sister of S. Q is the mother of S. How is P related to R?
A. Uncle B. Brother-in-law
C. Brother D. Father-in-law

38. N is to West of M, P is to the East of N, R is to the North of P. What is R's position with respect to M?
A. To the North-West
B. To the North-East
C. To the North
D. Cannot be decided

39. Choose the alternative that does not belong to the group of the other three.
A. Jawaharlal Nehru
B. S. Radhakrishnan
C. Lal Bahadur Shastry
D. Narendra Modi

40. Karnataka : Bengaluru : : Tamil Nadu : ?
A. Erode B. Chennai
C. Palani D. Madhurai

ARITHMETICAL AND NUMERICAL ABILITY

41. What is the least number to be added to 3333 to make it a perfect square?
A. 31 B. 84
C. 78 D. 57

42. $13^3 - 13^2 = ?$
A. 13 B. 2028
C. 1369 D. 1

43. The difference between 89% of a number and 72% of the same number is 391. What is 48% of that number?
A. 986 B. 1098
C. 1104 D. 1212

44. If $\sqrt{2} = 1.414$, $\sqrt{50} = ?$
A. 35.35 B. 14.14
C. 8.484 D. 7.070

45. $\dfrac{98.5^2 - 1.5^2}{98.5 - 1.5} = ?$
A. 97.0 B. 100
C. 121 D. None of these

46. What would be the compound interest obtained on an amount of Rs. 11,000 at 10% p.a. for 3 years?

A. Rs. 3,541 B. Rs. 3,641
C. Rs. 4,361 D. Rs. 3,461

47. A car covers a distance of 816 kms in 720 minutes. What is the speed of the car in kms/hour?
A. 64 kms/hour B. 62 kms/hour
C. 68 kms/hour D. 60 kms/hour

48. The average of 4 consecutive even numbers A, B, C and D is 99. What is the product of B and D?
A. 9996 B. 9800
C. 9792 D. 9408

49. If log 2 = 0.1310, log 5 = 0.2130, log 10 = ?
A. 0.0279 B. 0.3440
C. 1.0650 D. 0.6550

50. If $3a = 4b$, $2b = 5c$, $a : b : c = ?$
A. 15 : 20 : 6 B. 6 : 15 : 20
C. 15 : 6 : 20 D. 20 : 15 : 6

51. When an article is sold for Rs. 62, there is a profit of 24%. What should be the selling price to make a profit of 30%?
A. Rs. 64 B. Rs. 66
C. Rs. 65 D. Rs. 67

52. The market value of a share of Rs. 10 is Rs. 13. How many such shares can be bought by investing Rs. 26,000?
A. 2000 B. 200
C. 2600 D. 260

53. If $x+\frac{1}{x}=5$, $x^2+\frac{1}{x^2}=?$
A. 25 B. 23
C. 22 D. 26

54. 8 men can dig a field in 14 days by working 6 hours a day. In how many days can 7 men dig the same field working 8 hours a day?
A. 14 days B. 13 days
C. 15 days D. 12 days

55. Jeevan goes from station A to station B at a speed of 40 km/h and returns from B to A at a speed of 60 km/h. Find the average speed of his total journey.
A. 50 km/h B. 49 km/h
C. 48 km/h D. 52 km/h

56. A man is 24 yeas older than his son, 12 years ago, he was five times as old as his son. Find the present age of the father.
A. 40 years B. 42 years
C. 50 years D. 45 years

57. There are three circles with centers A, B and C with radii 5 cm, 3 cm and 2 cm respectively. Circles with centres B and C touch each other externally but both touch circle with centre A internally. Find the perimeter of ΔABC.
A. 10 cm B. 12 cm
C. 14 cm D. 20 cm

58. The area of a rhombus is 24 cm^2. If its one diagonal is of 8 cm length, find the length of its other diagonal.
A. 7 cm B. 9 cm
C. 8 cm D. 6 cm

59. The ratio of the areas of two circles is 9 : 16. Find the ratio of their perimeters.
A. 7 : 8 B. 8 : 5
C. 3 : 4 D. 4 : 5

60. The perimeter of the base of a cone is 44 cm. Its slant height is 12 cm. Find its curved surface area.
A. 264 cm^2 B. 246 cm^2
C. 212 cm^2 D. 260 cm^2

LANGUAGE : ENGLISH

Directions (Qs. 61 to 64): *Read the passage given below and answer the questions based on it.*

Cynthia was a shy girl. She believed that she was plain and untalented. One day her teacher ordered the entire class to show up for audition for the school play. Cynthia nearly died of fright when she was told that she would have to stand on stage in front of the entire class and deliver dialogues. The mere thought of it made her feel sick. But a remarkable transformation occured during the audition. A thin, shy girl, her knees quaking, her stomach churning in terror, began to stun everyone with her excellent performance. Her bored classmates suddenly stopped their noisy chat to stare at her slender figure on the stage. At the end of her audition, the entire room erupted in thunderous applause.

61. Cynthia was afraid to stand on stage because
A. She felt her classmates may laugh at her
B. Her stomach was churning
C. She lacked self-confidence
D. She did not like school plays

62. Cynthia's classmates were chatting because
A. It was their turn to act next
B. They were bored of the performances
C. Cynthia did not act at all
D. The teacher had no control over them

63. The transformation that occurred during the audition refers to
A. The nervousness of Cynthia
B. The eruption of the entire room in thunderous applause
C. The surprise on the faces of her classmates
D. The stunning performance of Cynthia

64. Cynthia's knees were quaking because
A. She felt nervous and shy
B. The teacher scolded her
C. She was very thin and weak
D. She was afraid of her classmates

Directions (Qs. 65 to 66): *Choose the word which is most opposite in meaning to the given word.*

65. Reveal
A. Disclose B. Proclaim
C. Hide D. Publish

66. Inaudible
A. Suppressed B. Low
C. Murmuring D. Loud

Directions (Qs. 67 to 68): *Choose the word which is most similar in meaning to the given word.*

67. Design
A. plan B. wild
C. delete D. desert

68. Anticipation
A. Surprise B. Unexpectedness
C. Expectation D. Apology

Directions (Qs. 69 to 71): *Find out in which part of the sentence (A), (B) or (C) there is an error. If there is no error, your answer is (D)*

69. (A) One of the important lesson/(B) he taught me was to save at least/(C) thirty per cent of my gross income./(D) No error.

70. (A) Most of the tribals in the region/(B) are depended on the forest/(C) to earn their livelihoods./(D) No error.

71. (A) Senior citizens prefer banks /(B) which branches are located/(C) near their homes./(D) No error.

Directions (Qs. 72 to 75): *Fill in the blank with the appropriate alternative.*

72. Where ______ in a village near pune.
A. lives your uncle?
B. does your uncle live?
C. your uncle lives?
D. does live your uncle?

73. Why _____ angry with me yesterday?
A. were you B. was you
C. you were D. have you been

74. How long _____ English? "Six months".
A. do you learn
B. are you learning
C. you are learning
D. have you been learning

75. I saw Naveen at the station when I was going to work this morning but he ______ me.
A. didn't see B. don't see
C. hasn't seen D. didn't saw

76. Usually I go to work ______ bus.
A. in B. on
C. by D. from

77. We arrived ______ the airport in time.
A. on B. at
C. to D. by

78. He had finished his work.
The tense of the verb in the above sentence is:
A. Past continuous B. Present perfect
C. Past perfect D. Future

79. The plural of brother-in-law is:
A. Brother-in-laws
B. Brothers-in-law
C. Brothers-in-laws
D. None of these

80. He is looking *at* me.
Name the part of speech of 'at' in the above sentence.
A. Pronoun B. Verb
C. Conjunction D. Preposition

SECTION-B

POST SPECIFIC SUBJECT-RELATED QUESTIONS

81. The Blood group referred as 'Universal Donor' is
A. O B. B
C. AB D. A

82. The longest bone of our body is
A. Skull B. Radius
C. Humerus D. Femur

83. The functional unit of kidney is
A. Neuron B. Nephron
C. Alveoli D. Pleura

84. The regulation of blood glucose is maintained by the hormone
A. Insulin B. Prolactin
C. Oxytocin D. Testosterone

85. The colour of the RBC's is given by
A. Actin B. Globin
C. Chyme D. Haeme

86. Total number of bones in our body is
A. 208 B. 206
C. 204 D. 200

87. Total number of chromosomes in our body is
A. 47 B. 44
C. 46 D. 45

88. The normal Hemoglobin level is
A. 18-23 g/dl B. 14-16 g/dl
C. 8-10 g/dl D. 16-20 g/dl

89. The normal blood glucose level of an average adult is
A. 80-110 mg/dl
B. 60-100 mg/dl
C. 180-210 mg/dl
D. 150-180 mg/dl

90. The covering of the heart is
A. Peritoneum B. Pleura
C. Pericardium D. Myocardium

91. The volume of blood pumped from the Left Ventricle is termed as
A. Circulatory Volume
B. Stroke Volume
C. Cardiac Output
D. Cardiac Input

92. Vitamin C is also known as
A. Nicotinic Acid B. Riboflavin
C. Calciferol D. Ascorbic Acid

93. Goitre occurs due to the deficiency of
A. Iodine B. Calcium
C. Potassium D. Chloride

94. Xerophthalmia is a deficiency due to which Vitamin?
A. D B. A
C. K D. E

95. The blood pressure of a normal healthy person is
A. 120/60 mm of Hg
B. 120/80 mm of Hg
C. 90/60 mm of Hg
D. 140/60 mm of Hg

96. Bradycardia refers to heart rate below
A. 60 beats/min B. 70 beats/min
C. 80 beats/min D. 100 beats/min

97. Blusih discoloration of the skin is referred as
A. Hypoxia B. Dyspnea
C. Apnea D. Cyanosis

98. Prolonged bed ridden patients have the risk of developing
A. Decubitus Ulcer
B. Cellulitis
C. Scabies
D. Psoriasis

99. The most preferred site for giving IM injection of an average adult is
A. Deltoid B. Umbilicus
C. Gluteal Region D. Forearm

100. Analgesic drugs reduce
A. Sugar level B. Fever
C. Secretions D. Pain

101. The break in the continuity of bone is referred as
A. Wound B. Arthritis
C. Fracture D. Inflammation

102. ICDS programme initiated in India by
A. 1965 B. 1975
C. 1985 D. 1981

103. The national health programs related to mother and child is
A. Maternal and Child Health Program
B. Child Survival and Safe Motherhood Program (CSSM)
C. Reproductive and Child Health Program
D. All of the above

104. The normal supplement of IFA during antenatal period is for
A. One tablet throughout period
B. Only one tablet for 100 days
C. 2 tablets for 100 days
D. 3 tablets for 90 days

105. IFA tablet is given when
A. Hb below 10 g% of a mother
B. Hb below 10 g% of a child
C. Both A and B
D. None of the above

106. The Ovarian cycle is initiated by
A. FSH
B. Estrogen
C. LH
D. Progesterone

107. In 40 days of menstruation cycle the ovulation occurs at
A. 14th day B. 20th day
C. 26th day D. 30th day

108. Bluish discoloration of the vagina is called as
A. Heger's sign B. Goodell's sign
C. Chadwick's sign D. McDonald's sign

109. Regular rhythmic contraction that can be felt during bimanual examination is called as
A. Palmer's sign B. Heger's sign
C. Uterine suffle D. Rovsign's sign

110. The normal heart of the infant, after birth may range between
A. 100 to 180 B. 130 to 170
C. 120 to 160 D. 100 to 130

111. Morning sickness usually disappears by the end of
A. 1 month B. 2 months
C. 3 months D. 4 months

112. Which formula is used for calculating EDD?
A. Naegele's Rule B. Infant Formula
C. Labor Rule D. Rule of Nine

113. Which of the following is recognised as teratogenic?
A. Scarlett fever
B. Rubella
C. Fever
D. Coronary Heart Disease

114. Which of the following is not present in bottle formula for new born?
A. Amino Acid
B. Complex carbohydrate
C. Electrolytes
D. Immuno globulin

115. Endometriosis is common in
A. Nullipara
B. Multipara
C. Perimenopausal age
D. Virgins

116. During Pregnancy the client will have an increased need for
A. Potassium B. Sodium
C. Iron D. Cabohydrate

117. A possible complicaton of an infant delivered by Caesarean section is
A. Respiratory distress
B. Hypothermia
C. Hyperthermia
D. Anemia

118. Immunity transferred to fetus from mother through placenta is
A. Active natural immunity
B. Passive artificial immunity
C. Passive natural immunity
D. Active artificial immunity

119. First trimester morning sickness can be overcome by
A. Eating nothing until nausea subsides
B. Eating Fat before sleep
C. Taking heavy food at bed time
D. Eating protein before sleep

120. The drug of choice for eclampsia is
A. $MgSO_4$
B. Prostodin
C. Timolol
D. Beta Adrenergic Blocker

121. Which of the following is used in colposcopy?
A. Povidone Iodine
B. Acetic Acid
C. Methylene blue
D. Gentian violet

122. The commonest cause of postpartum hemorrhage is
A. Instrumental Trauma
B. Postmature Pregnancy
C. Premature Pregnancy
D. Atonic Uterus

123. The commonest type of episiotomy
A. J shaped episiotomy
B. Mediolateral episiotomy
C. Lateral episiotomy
D. Left Lateral episiotomy

124. Drug of choice for induction of abortion is
A. Prostaglandin
B. Ergometrine
C. Methtrexate
D. Clomiphene Citrate

125. Klinefelter syndrome is indicated by
A. Chromosome 47XXY
B. Chromosome 23XY
C. Chromosome 47 X
D. Chromosome 46XY

126. The complaint of Oligomenorrhea, obesity and Hirsutism in a 20 year old lady indicates
A. PCOD
B. Cancer of Endometrium
C. Prolactenoma
D. Pregnancy

127. Birth trauma is a risk factor for
A. Uterine Prolapse
B. Endometriosis
C. PID
D. Abortions

128. Total calorie requirement for a pregnant women is
A. 1000 to 1500 kcal
B. 2000 to 2500 kcal
C. 2500 to 2700 kcal
D. 2700 to 3000 kcal

129. First fetal movement felt by the mother is called as
A. Ballotment
B. Quickening
C. Lightening
D. Kicking

130. Pearly white or silvery bright lines, headed after delivery are called as
A. Linea Albicantes
B. Linea Nigra
C. Striae Gravidarum
D. Striae Nigra

131. Meconium mixed with liquor amnil indicates
A. Congenital anomalies
B. Chromosomal anomalies
C. Fetal Distress
D. Chorea

132. Presence of complete ring of bubbles at the meniscus in shake test indicates
A. Maturity of fetal brain
B. Septal defect
C. Maturity of fetal lungs
D. Fetal cyanosis

133. Less than how many number of kicks in 12 hours indicates the failure of Placental Function?

A. 2 B. 5

C. 10 D. 20

154. Total weight gain of mother in pregnancy is

A. 10 to 12 kg B. 18 to 20 kg

C. 12 to 14 kg D. 9 to 10 kg

135. Normal labor is called as

A. Spurious Labor B. Dystocia

C. Eutocia D. False Labor

136. 'Show' is the sign of

A. True labor pain

B. False labor pain

C. Sign of Abnormal labor

D. Sign of Placenta Previa

137. What is the total time period for the 3rd stage of labor primi and multi?

A. 15 minutes B. 30 minutes

C. 45 minutes D. 1 hour

138. After deliver the immediate care given to the baby is

A. To clear the airway

B. To clamp the cord

C. Clean the cord

D. Initiate the feeding

139. Overlapping of the paritel bone during birth is called as

A. Caput B. Moulding

C. Hematoma D. Fixation

140. Which of the following drug is given to increase uterine contraction?

A. Methargine B. Oxytocin

C. Pethedine D. Phenergan

141. The process of giving birth is called as

A. Parturition B. Postpartum

C. Lightening D. Labor

142. What is the normal dilatation of cervix?

A. 20 cm B. 50 cm

C. 7 cm D. 10 cm

143. The duration of puerperal period is

A. From delivery to 1 week

B. Delivery to 4 weeks

C. Delivery to 6 weeks

D. Delivery to 10 weeks

144. The vaginal discharge during the first fortnight of puerperium is known as

A. Show B. Lochia

C. Effacement D. Leucorrhea

145. What are the indications of Caesarean section?

A. Fetal distress

B. Central Placenta Praevia

C. Obstructed Labor

D. All of the above

146. The hormone responsible for lactation is

A. Growth Hormone

B. FSH

C. Prolactin

D. Corpus Luteum

147. A fetus have fine downy hair which is called as

A. Vernix caseosa B. Amnion

C. Chorion D. Lanugo

148. The main objective of nursing care in asphyxia baby is

A. Initiate early breathing

B. Administer oxygen

C. Gentle Handling of the Baby

D. Maintain clear Airway

149. Cyanosis in preterm baby is due to

A. Jaundice

B. Cleft Palate

C. Respiratory distress syndrome

D. Intra cranial injury

150. In fully flexed cephalic presentation we feel

A. Occiput of fetus

B. Sinciput of the fetus

C. Eyebrow of the fetus

D. Oral cavity of the fetus

151. Noenate is resuscitated if pulse rate is below

A. 40 beats/min

B. 60 beats/min

C. 80 beats/min

D. 20 beats/min

152. Which of the following is tertiary level of prevention?

A. Health Promotion
B. Specific Protection
C. Early Diagnosis and Treatment
D. Disability Limitation

153. Only human beings are reservoir for
A. Smallpox
B. Influenza
C. Salmonella
D. Rabies

154. As per the latest WHO guidelines which dehydration status requires ORS
A. Mild dehydration
B. Moderate dehydration
C. Severe dehydration
D. Any form of dehydration

155. Maximum maternal mortality is seen from
A. Hepatitis B B. Hepatitis E
C. Hepatitis A D. Hepatitis C

156. Which vaccine is contra-indicated in pregnancy?
A. Rubella B. OPV
C. BCG D. Hepatitis

157. In Polio transmission, easy block can be applied by acting on
A. Reservoir B. Susceptible Host
C. Faeco-oral route D. Agent

158. Vaccine which is given at the earliest
A. BCG B. MMR
C. DT D. DPT

159. BCG Vaccine is administered to children
A. Intradermally B. Subcutaneously
C. Intramuscularly D. Orally

160. Tuberculin test is read after
A. 48 hours B. 72 hours
C. 96 hours D. 24 hours

161. Incubation period for mumps is
A. 18 days B. 14 days
C. 10 days D. 5 days

162. Which of the following gives lifelong immunity after an attack?
A. Typhoid B. Mumps
C. Tetanus D. Diphtheria

163. Communication period of chickenpox is
A. till last scab falls off
B. 4-5 days after rash
C. only during incubation period
D. only upto fever lasts

164. Sharp instruments may be sterlized with
A. Radiation B. Lysol
C. Hot air D. Any of the above

165. Which of the following is powerful disinfectant?
A. Phenol
B. Lysol
C. Dettol
D. Potassium Permanganate

166. Keratomalacia is associated with
A. Measles B. Mumps
C. Rubella D. Chickenpox

167. For disposable items, the best method for sterilization is
A. Dry heat B. Incineration
C. Gamma radiation D. Boiling heat

168. Vertical Transmission is by
A. Mosquito B. Direct contact
C. Droplet D. Placenta

169. Which is most difficult to block spreading of?
A. Vector B. Man to man
C. Airborne D. Waterborne

170. The period after entry of the organism to produce maximum infection is known as
A. Incubation Period
B. Generation time
C. Serial interval period
D. Lead time

171. The drug used by Health workers in the management of Acute respiratory illness is
A. Clotrimoxazole
B. Chloramphenicol
C. Benzyl Pencillin
D. Gentamycin

172. Prevalence of tuberculosis infection is measured by
A. Chest X-ray
B. Sputum AFB
C. Tuberculin Test
D. Sputum Culture

173. Malaria is transmitted to man by which mosquito?
A. Culin
B. Culex
C. Aedes
D. Female Anopheles

174. Identify the water borne disorder.
A. Dengue B. Malaria
C. Cholera D. Polio

175. The procedure of removal and ligation of Fallopian tube is referred as
A. Mastectomy B. Vasectomy
C. Appendectomy D. Tubectomy

176. The best time for IUD insertion is between which days of Menstruation cycle?
A. within 2 days B. 3 to 7 days
C. 8 to 10 days D. 11 to 14 days

177. The metal which is commonly used for family planning is
A. Iron B. Aluminium
C. Copper D. Silver

178. Mala D is an example of
A. Pill form
B. Injectable contraceptive
C. Vaginal diaphragm
D. Foam tablet

179. The Multi-Purpose Worker in general serves a rural population of
A. < 500 B. 1000
C. 3000 D. 5000

180. The system of storing and transporting vaccines is termed as
A. Cold Chain B. Freezer Chain
C. Cool Chain D. Vaccination

ANSWERS

1	**2**	**3**	**4**	**5**	**6**	**7**	**8**	**9**	**10**
C	B	C	D	A	C	B	D	A	C
11	**12**	**13**	**14**	**15**	**16**	**17**	**18**	**19**	**20**
C	B	A	B	D	C	C	A	B	C
21	**22**	**23**	**24**	**25**	**26**	**27**	**28**	**29**	**30**
D	A	B	B	C	A	A	B	A	D
31	**32**	**33**	**34**	**35**	**36**	**37**	**38**	**39**	**40**
C	A	C	B	D	C	A	D	B	B
41	**42**	**43**	**44**	**45**	**46**	**47**	**48**	**49**	**50**
A	B	C	D	B	B	C	A	B	D
51	**52**	**53**	**54**	**55**	**56**	**57**	**58**	**59**	**60**
C	A	B	D	C	B	A	D	C	A
61	**62**	**63**	**64**	**65**	**66**	**67**	**68**	**69**	**70**
C	A	D	A	C	D	A	C	A	B
71	**72**	**73**	**74**	**75**	**76**	**77**	**78**	**79**	**80**
B	B	A	D	A	C	B	C	B	D
81	**82**	**83**	**84**	**85**	**86**	**87**	**88**	**89**	**90**
A	D	B	A	D	B	C	B	A	C
91	**92**	**93**	**94**	**95**	**96**	**97**	**98**	**99**	**100**
B	C	A	B	B	A	D	A	C	D
101	**102**	**103**	**104**	**105**	**106**	**107**	**108**	**109**	**110**
C	B	D	B	C	A	C	C	A	C

111	112	113	114	115	116	117	118	119	120
C	A	B	D	A	C	A	C	D	A
121	**122**	**123**	**124**	**125**	**126**	**127**	**128**	**129**	**130**
B	D	B	A	A	A	A	C	B	A
131	**132**	**133**	**134**	**135**	**136**	**137**	**138**	**139**	**140**
C	C	C	A	C	A	B	A	B	B
141	**142**	**143**	**144**	**145**	**146**	**147**	**148**	**149**	**150**
A	D	C	B	D	C	D	B	C	A
151	**152**	**153**	**154**	**155**	**156**	**157**	**158**	**159**	**160**
A	A	C	D	B	A	D	A	A	B
161	**162**	**163**	**164**	**165**	**166**	**167**	**168**	**169**	**170**
A	B	B	D	B	C	C	D	C	B
171	**172**	**173**	**174**	**175**	**176**	**177**	**178**	**179**	**180**
A	C	D	C	D	B	C	A	D	A

SOME SELECTED EXPLANATORY ANSWERS

21. 12, 18 and 21 are divisible by 3, whereas 28 is not.

22. Based on the given pattern numerical values of letter 'L' = 4; 'I' = 4, 'N' = 3 and 'E' = 3.
So, Numerical value of 'LINE'
= 4 + 4 + 3 + 3 = 14.

23. 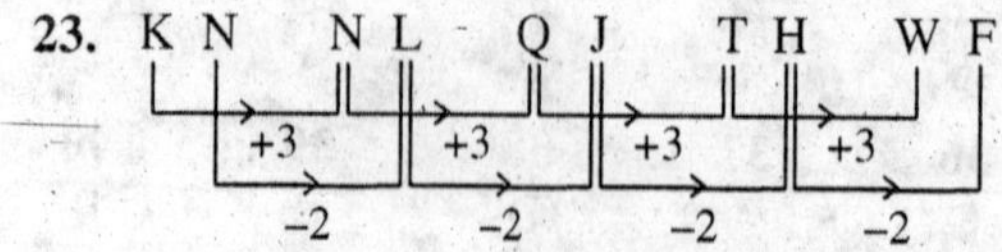

Qs. 24 – 26 : Based on given data the sitting arrangement along the circle is like this.

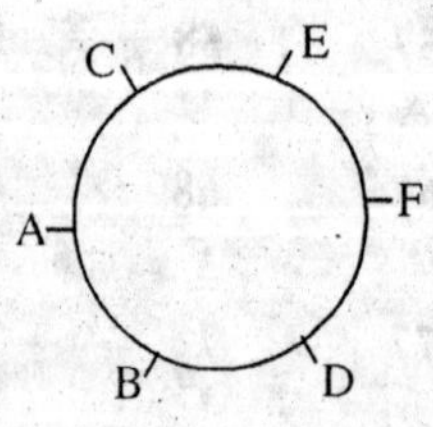

Qs. 27 – 29 :

27. Ascending order arrangement of the number after interchanging first and second digits:

158 287 289 437 478 823
↑
Second Lowest

Hence, second lowest number '287' is obtained from '827'.

28. Arrangement (in ascending order) after interchanging second and third digits:

238 374 581 784 872 892
↑
Third highest

Hence, third highest number '784' is obtained from '748'.

29. Arrangement (In ascending order) after interchanging first and third digits:

382 728 743 815 847 928
↑
Third Lowest

Hence, third lowest number '743' is obtained from '347'.

30. Reverse order of J A I L E R → R E L I A J
| | | | | |
8 1 7 3 4 2

31. Based on given pattern, number difference.
A. 734 – 851 = –117
B. 328 – 874 = –546
C. 782 – 734 = 48
D. 874 – 851 = 23
Hence, correct option is B

32. 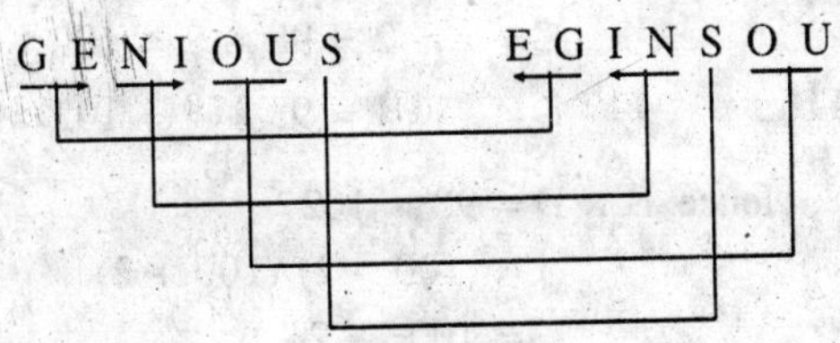

Similarly,

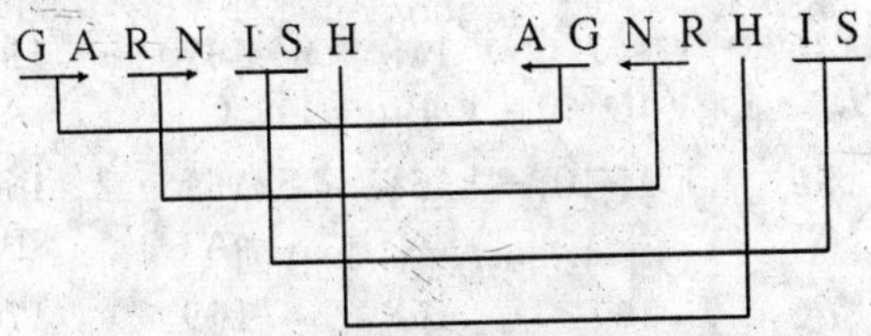

33. 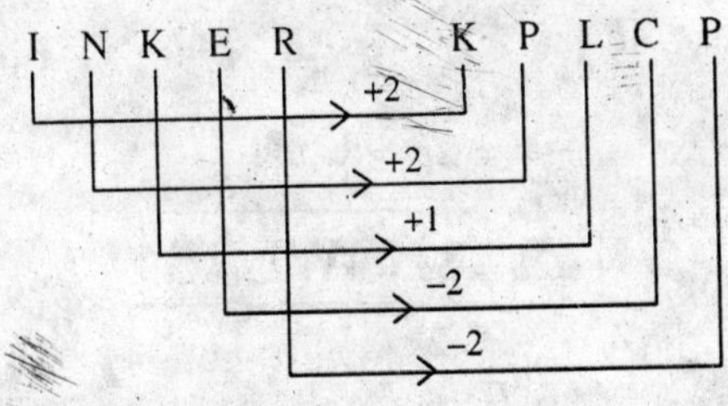

and

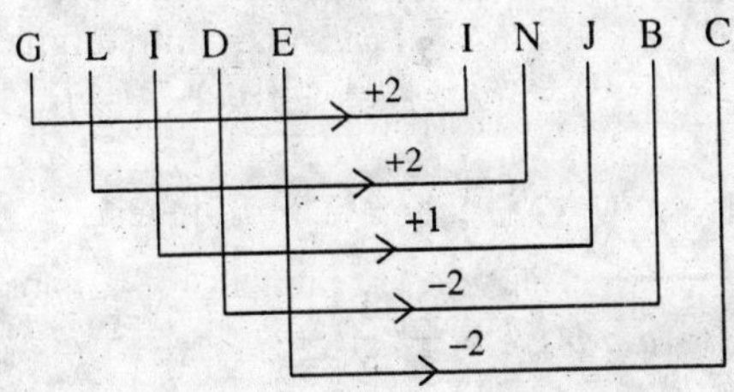

Similarly,

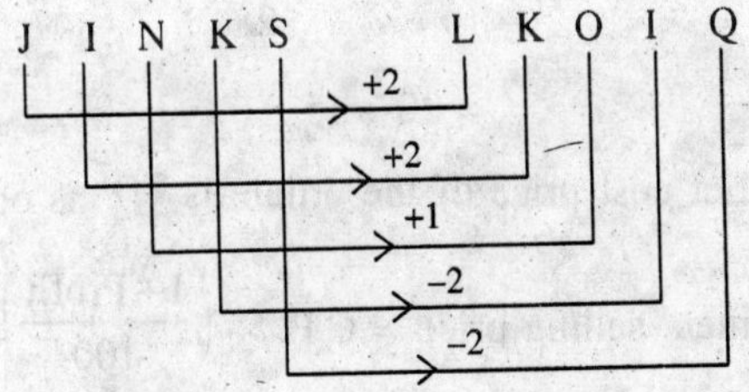

37. 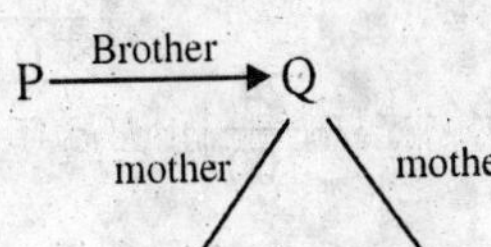

So, P is the uncle (maternal) of R.

39. S. Radhakrishnan was a former President of India, whereas other three are/were Prime Ministers.

40. 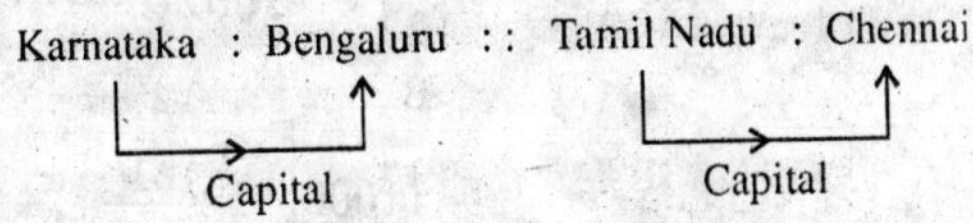

41. Two square numbers between which '3333' lies are 3249 and 3364.

$3249 < 3333 < 3364$

So, number to be added $= 3364 - 3333$

$= 31.$

42. $13^3 - 13^2 = 13^2(13 - 1)$

$= 169\ (12)$

$= 2028.$

43. Let, the required number is P.

then, $P \times \frac{89}{100} - P \times \frac{72}{100} = 391$

$P\left(\frac{89-72}{100}\right) = 391$

$P\left(\frac{17}{100}\right) = 391$

$P = \frac{391 \times 100}{17}$

$= 2300$

Now, $P \times \frac{48}{100} = 2300 \times \frac{48}{100}$

$= 1104.$

44. $\sqrt{50} = \sqrt{5 \times 5 \times 2} = 5\sqrt{2}$

$= 5 \times 1.414 = 7.07$

45. $\frac{98.5^2 - 1.5^2}{98.5 - 1.5} = \frac{(98.5-1.5)(98.5+1.5)}{(98.5-1.5)}$

$= (98.5 + 1.5)$

$= 100.$

46. Compound Interest (C.I.)

$$= P\left[\left(1+\frac{r}{100}\right)^{t}-1\right]$$

$$= 11000\left[\left(1+\frac{10}{100}\right)^{3}-1\right]$$

$$= 11000\times\left[\left(\frac{110}{100}\right)^{3}-1\right]$$

$$= 11000\times\left[\left(\frac{11}{10}\right)^{3}-1\right]$$

$$= 11000\times\left(\frac{1331-1000}{1000}\right)$$

$$= \frac{11000\times 331}{1000} = ₹\ 3641.$$

47. 720 minutes $= \frac{720}{60}$ hours $= 12$ hours

$$\text{Speed}\left(\frac{\text{km}}{\text{hr}}\right)\text{ of Car} = \frac{\text{Distance Travelled (km)}}{\text{Time Taken (hr.)}}$$

$$= \frac{816}{12} = 68 \text{ km/hr.}$$

48. Let four consecutive even numbers are

$x-2$, x, $x+2$ and $x+4$.

$$\text{Average} = \frac{x-2+x+x+2+x+4}{4} = 99$$

$$= \frac{4x+4}{4} = 99$$

$x + 1 = 99$

$\Rightarrow$ $x = 98$

$\therefore$Four even numbers are

A $= x - 2 = 98 - 2 = 96$

B $= x = 98$

C $= x + 2 = 98 + 2 = 100$

D $= x + 4 = 98 + 4 = 102$

Hence, B $\times$ D $= 98 \times 102$

$= (100 - 2)(100 + 2)$

$= 100^2 - 2^2$

$= 10000 - 4$

$= 9996.$

49. $\log(a \times b) = \log a + \log b$

$\log(10) = \log(2 \times 5) = \log 2 + \log 5$

$= 0.131 + 0.213$

$= 0.344$

50. $3a = 4b$

$$\Rightarrow \quad \frac{3}{2}a = 2b = k$$

$$2b = 5c = k$$

$$\therefore \quad a = \frac{2k}{3},$$

$$b = \frac{k}{2},$$

$$c = \frac{k}{5}$$

$$a : b : c = \frac{2}{3} : \frac{1}{2} : \frac{1}{5}$$

$$= \frac{30\times 2}{3} : \frac{30}{2} : \frac{30}{5}$$

$$= 20 : 15 : 6$$

51. Let cost price of the article is ₹ P.

$$\text{then, selling price} = \text{C.P.} \times \left(\frac{1+\text{Profit}}{100}\right)$$

$$62 = P \times \left(1+\frac{24}{100}\right)$$

$$62 = \left(1+\frac{24}{100}\right)$$

$$62 = P \times \frac{124}{100}$$

$$\Rightarrow \quad P = \frac{62 \times 100}{124}$$

$$P = 50$$

$\therefore$Required Selling Price

$$= 50 \times \left(1 + \frac{30}{100}\right)$$

$$= 50 \times \frac{130}{100}$$

$$= ₹\ 65$$

53. $x + \frac{1}{x} = 5$

Squaring both sides, we have

$$\left(x + \frac{1}{x}\right)^2 = 5^2$$

$$x^2 + \frac{1}{x^2} + 2 \cdot x \cdot \frac{1}{x} = 25$$

$$x^2 + \frac{1}{x^2} + 2 = 25$$

$$\therefore \quad x^2 + \frac{1}{x^2} = 25 - 2 = 23.$$

54. From Question,

$$M_1T_1D_1 = M_2T_2D_2$$

Here, $M_1 = 8$ men, $M_2 = 7$ men

$T_1 = 6$ hours, $T_2 = 8$ hours

$D_1 = 14$ days, $D_2 = ?$

$$\therefore \quad D_2 = \frac{M_1T_1D_1}{M_2T_2} = \frac{8 \times 6 \times 14}{7 \times 8}$$

$$= 12 \text{ days.}$$

55. Let, distance between station A and B is d km.

then, time required to go from A to B

$$t_1 = \frac{d}{40}$$

Time required to come from B to A

$$t_2 = \frac{d}{60}$$

Total distance travelled in both courses

$$d + d = 2d$$

Total time taken $= t_1 + t_2$

$$\therefore \text{ Average Speed} = \frac{2d}{t_1 + t_2}$$

$$= \frac{2d}{\frac{d}{40} + \frac{d}{60}} = \frac{2d}{\frac{d(60+40)}{60 \times 40}}$$

$$= \frac{2 \times 60 \times 40}{100}$$

$$= 48 \text{ km/hr.}$$

56. Let, present age of the father = = x years

then his son's age = $(x - 24)$ years

from question,

$$(x - 12) = 5(x - 24 - 12)$$

$$x - 12 = 5(x - 36)$$

$$x - 12 = 5x - 180$$

$$5x - x = 180 - 12$$

$$4x = 168$$

$$x = 42$$

Hence, present age of the father = 42 years.

57. Distance BC = Sum of the radii of two circles with centres B and C = 3 + 2 = 5 cm

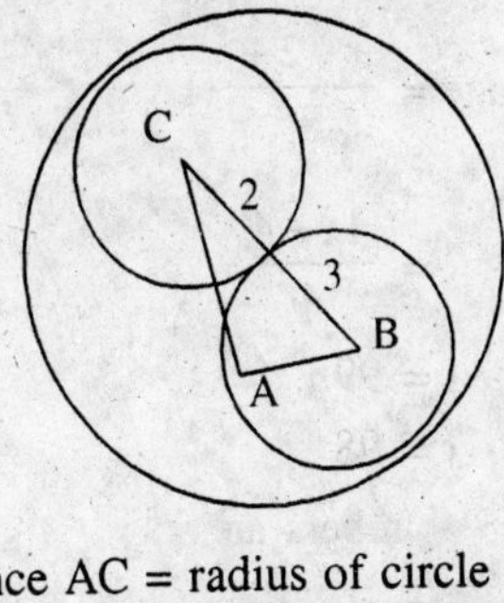

Distance AC = radius of circle with centre A – radius of circle wih centre C

= 5 – 2 = 3 cm

Distance AB = radius of circle with centre A
– radius of circle with centre B
= 5 – 3 = 2 cm

∴ Perimeter of Δ ABC
= AB + BC + AC
= 2 + 5 + 3 = 10 cm.

58. Area of rhombus

$$= \frac{1}{2} \times \text{Product of its diagonals}$$

$$24 = \frac{1}{2} \times 8 \times d$$

$$\therefore \text{diagonal (d)} = \frac{24 \times 2}{8} = 6 \text{ cm.}$$

59. Ratio of Areas of two circles with radius r_1 and r_2

$$\frac{A_1}{A_2} = \frac{\pi r_1^2}{\pi r_2^2}$$

$$\Rightarrow \quad \frac{r_1}{r_2} = \sqrt{\frac{A_1}{A_2}}$$

$$\Rightarrow \quad = \sqrt{\frac{9}{16}}$$

Now, ratio of perimeter of the two circles $= \frac{3}{4}$

$$\frac{P_1}{P_2} = \frac{2\pi r_1}{2\pi r_2} = \frac{r_1}{r_2} = \frac{3}{4}.$$

60. Radius of the base of the cone

$$r_1 = \frac{44 \times 7}{2 \times 22} = 7 \text{ cm}$$

Curved surface area = πrl

$$= \frac{22}{7} \times 7 \times 12 = 264 \text{ cm}^2.$$

Previous Paper (Solved)

DSSSB Staff Nurse Exam, 2013*

SECTION-A

GENERAL AWARENESS

1. "The Servants of India Society" was founded by
A. Annie Besant
B. Gopalakrishna Gokhale
C. Bal Gangadhar Tilak
D. Dadabhai Naoroji

2. "Dandia" is a popular dance of
A. Punjab B. Gujarat
C. Tamil Nadu D. Maharashtra

3. The words "Satyameva Jayate" inscribed below the base plate of the emblem of India are taken from
A. Rigveda
B. Satpath Brahmana
C. Mundak Upanishad
D. Ramayana

4. In the form of which Constitution Amendment Bill Anti-Defection Bill was by the Indian Parliament on 30th January 1985?
A. 42 B. 52
C. 61 D. 44

5. The Prakrit text "Gatasaptasati" is attributed to the Satavahana King
A. Vasishtiputra Pulumavi
B. Hala
C. Gautamiputra Satkarni
D. Amaru

6. The intersecting lines drawn on maps and globes are
A. latitudes B. longitudes
C. geographic grids D. None of the above

7. The hot and cold deserts together occupy nearly .... land area of the world.
A. 1/2 B. 1/4th
C. 1/3rd D. 3/4th

8. Who wrote the famous book: 'We the People'?
A. T.N. Kaul B. J.R.D Tata
C. Khushwant Singh D. Nani Palkhivala

9. The original name of Mahabharatha was
A. Brihit Katha B. Sahastra Samhita
C. Jaya Samhita D. Rajatha Rangini

10. Jainism differed from Buddhism in which of the following aspects?
A. Faith in Karma B. Doctrine of Ahimsa
C. Belief in Fasting D. Rejection of Yagna

11. Entomology is the science that studies
A. Behaviour of human beings
B. Insects
C. The origin and history of technical and scientific terms
D. The formation of rocks

12. Film and TV Institute of India is located at
A. Pune (Maharashtra)
B. Rajkot (Gujarat)
C. Pimpri (Maharashtra)
D. Perambur (Tamil Nadu)

13. The language spoken in Lakshadweep Island is
A. Malayalam B. Marathi
C. Tamil D. Gujarati

14. In the estimation of expenditure charged on the Consolidated Fund of India, the Parliament has
A. No power to discuss
B. Full power to discuss
C. Full power to discuss during emergency
D. None of the above

* Held on 09/06/2013

15. The members of the Rajya Sabha are elected by
A. The people
B. Lok Sabha
C. Elected members of the Legislative Assembly
D. Elected members of the Legislative Council

16. Under Akbar, the Mir Bakshi was required to look after
A. military affairs
B. the state treasury
C. the royal household
D. the land revenue system

17. Which of the following states lie partly on the north of the Himalayas?
A. Himachal Pradesh
B. Arunachal Pradesh
C. Jammu and Kashmir
D. Sikkim

18. B.C. Roy Award is given in the field of
A. Music B. Journalism
C. Medicine D. Environment

19. Gandhi Peace Prize for the year 2000 was awarded to the former President of South Africa along with
A. Sathish Dhawan
B. C. Subramanian
C. Grameen Bank of Bangladesh
D. World Health Organisation

20. The Primitive tribes of Andaman are descendents of
A. Negroids B. Australoids
C. Mongoloids D. Caucasoids

GENERAL INTELLIGENCE AND REASONING ABILITY

Directions (Qs. 21-23): *There is some relationship between the two words on one side. The same relationship obtains between the other two words, one of which is missing and given as an alternative below the question. Find the correct alternative.*

21. Bud : Flower : : ? : Fruit
A. Seed B. Flower
C. Taste D. Twig

22. Leader : Follower : : Captain : ?
A. Soldiers B. Game
C. Ships D. Army

23. Angry : ? : : Night : Day
A. Kind B. Helpful
C. Pleased D. Loving

Direction (Qs. 24): *Select the option which shows similar relationship.*

24. AA 23 : CC 25   PP 61 : RR 63
TT 52 : ?
A. UV 54 B. UU 54
C. VV 51 D. VV 54

25. If "+" means 'multiplied by', "−" means 'divided by', '×' means 'plus', '÷' means minus, then
(18 + 10 × 20) − 8 ÷ 6 = ?
A. 35 B. 92
C. 26 D. 19

Directions (Qs. 26-28): *Two statements are given followed by two conclusions numbered (x) and (y). You have to take the given statements to be true even if they seem to be false or contradictory to the commonly known facts. Decide logically which of the answer choices is correct.*
A. Only (*x*) follows
B. Only (*y*) follows
C. Both (*x*) and (*y*) follow
D. Either (*x*) or (*y*) follows

26. Statements: All cakes are ice-creams.
All ice-creams are toffees.
Conclusions: (*x*) All cakes are toffees.
(*y*) All toffees are ice-creams.

27. Statements: All players are tall.
Mohan is tall.
Conclusions: (*x*) Mohan is a player.
(*y*) Mohan is not a player.

28. Statements: India got her independence at midnight.
Getting independence is a very great event for a nation and call for celebration.

Conclusions: (*x*) Most of the people were sleeping as it was the midnight hour.

(*y*) The celebrations started right at midnight.

29. John ranks twenty-first in a class of fifty-one. What is his rank from the last?

A. 31 B. 30
C. 17 D. 21

30. 'b' is in 'doubt' in the same way as 'h' is in ....

A. enhance B. inhibit
C. house D. honest

31. In a certain code, PRAMOD is written as RTCOQF. How is BUSTLE written in that code?

A. URGENT B. DWUVNG
C. RTLEIN D. DUWNVG

32. Step is related to staircase, in the same way as soldier is related to ....

A. Army B. Rifle
C. War D. Bravery

Direction (Qs. 33): *Choose the pair which shows similar relationship that the given pair shows.*

33. AB 123 : CD 456

A. PQ 234 : ST 567
B. JK 345 : LM 678
C. EF 345 : GH 687
D. PQ 456 : SR 789

34. How many 6's are there in the following number series which are preceded by 5 but not followed by 7?

5 6 7 6 5 6 4 9 2 7 6 7 4 3 5 6 8 6 4 9 5 6 7

A. Two B. Three
C. Four D. One

35. R is the sister of Q, S is the sister of R, P is the brother of Q. How is Q related to S?

A. brother B. sister
C. brother or sister D. son

36. Four years ago Ashoka was six years older than Ravi. What is the difference of their ages now?

A. Four years B. Six years
C. Eight years D. Two years

37. Which of the following will come next in the series below?

shg, rif, qje, pkd, ?

A. ome B. olb
C. ole D. None of these

38. Six students are sitting in a row. K is sitting between V and R, V is sitting next to M. M is sitting next to B who is sitting on the extreme left and Q is sitting next to R. Who are sitting adjacent to V?

A. M and K B. Q and K
C. B and M D. V and R

39. Three of the following are alike in a certain way and so form a group. Which is the one that does not belong to that group?

A. Biology B. Geometry
C. Trigonometry D. Algebra

40. Srikanth is shorter than Nilima. Prathima is taller than Srikanth. Subhash is taller than Nilima but shorter than Heramb. Nilima is taller than Prathima. Who will be in the middle if they stand in a row according to height?

A. Srikanth B. Prathima
C. Nilima D. Subhash

ARITHMETICAL AND NUMERICAL ABILITY

41. The average weight of 20 children is 35 kg. While calculating the average, a boy's weight was taken as 25 kg instead of 45 kg. What is the correct average weight?

A. 45 kg B. 42 kg
C. 36 kg D. 40 kg

42. The area of a right angled triangle is 10 cm^2, if one of the sides which form the right angle is 5 cm, find the other

A. 4 cm B. 2 cm
C. 5 cm D. 3 cm

43. The ratio of the perimeters of two circles is 3 : 4. What is the ratio of their areas?

A. 6 : 8 B. 4 : 5
C. $\sqrt{3}:2$ D. 9 : 16

44. After John gave ₹ 12 to Hari and Hari gave ₹ 4 to John, both had equal amounts with them. Who had smaller amount initially and by how much?

A. Hari by ₹ 8 B. John by ₹ 4
C. Hari by ₹ 16 D. John by ₹ 8

45. P and Q started a business by investing ₹ 5 lakhs and ₹ 7 lakhs respectively. After 8 months R joined their business with an investment of ₹ 9 lakhs. At the end of the year they made a profit of ₹ 3 lakhs. What is the share of R in the total profit ?

A. ₹ 60,000 B. ₹ 50,000
C. ₹ 70,000 D. ₹ 30,000

46. A person gets simple interest of ₹ 500 for one month for his deposit of ₹ 60,000. Find the rate of interest.

A. 15% B. 10%
C. 12% D. 11%

47. 10 workers complete a work in 15 days by working 8 hours/day. How many days 15 workers take to complete the same work by working 5 hours/day?

A. 15 B. 20
C. 10 D. 16

48. The three angles of a triangle are in Arithmetic progression. The smallest angle is 50°. Find the other angles.

A. 60°, 70° B. 70°, 90°
C. 50°, 80° D. 40°, 90°

49. A 250 metres long train speeds past a pole in 12 seconds. What is its speed in kilometres per hour?

A. 7.5 B. 50
C. 75 D. 25

50. Girish has $\frac{2}{3}$ as much money as Guru has and Guru has $\frac{3}{5}$ as much money as Raju has, if Raju has ₹ 800, how many rupees Girish has?

A. 320 B. 480
C. 720 D. 420

51. $\frac{1}{2}+\frac{1}{2}\times\frac{1}{2}=?$

A. $\frac{1}{2}$ B. $1\frac{1}{2}$
C. $\frac{1}{8}$ D. $\frac{3}{4}$

52. By selling a pen for ₹ 10, Raju gets a profit of ₹ 2. By selling the same pen for ₹ 20, how much profit does he get?

A. ₹ 4 B. ₹ 12
C. ₹ 8 D. ₹ 10

53. Face value of a share is ₹ 100. It is sold at a premium of ₹ 20. Brokerage is 1%. How many of these shares can be purchased by investing ₹ 24,200?

A. 180 B. 200
C. 220 D. 400

54. A purchases a pre-owned car for ₹ 2,00,000 which includes ₹ 10,000 given to the broker. He spends ₹ 30,000 for its repair. He sells it through a broker for ₹ 2,44,800 and gives ₹ 10,000 to the broker. Find the percentage of profit or loss in this transaction.

A. Profit of 6% B. Loss of 6%
C. Profit of 5% D. None of these

55. Find the sum of all the first 15 odd natural numbers.

A. 200 B. 215
C. 225 D. 235

56. There are 9 teachers including the Head Master. How many committees of 4 teachers can be made with the Head Master as the Chairman?

A. 50 B. 66
C. 76 D. 56

57. $\frac{56}{13}+\frac{7}{39}\times\frac{103}{8}=?$

A. $\frac{192}{103}$ B. $\frac{127}{8}$
C. 2742 D. 309

58. 75% of 200 = 15 × ?

A. 26 B. 11
C. 110 D. 165

59. $\frac{?}{\sqrt{.81}} = 450$

A. 4u5 B. 4050
C. 364.5 D. 40.50

60. P : Q = 3 : 2, Q : R = 3 : 5, P : Q : R = ?

A. 3 : 2 : 5 B. 2 : 3 : 5
C. 9 : 3 : 10 D. 9 : 6 : 10

LANGUAGE : HINDI

निर्देशः *नीचे दिये गये प्रकरण को पढ़िए। इस पर पाँच प्रश्न हैं। उसके चार-चार उत्तरं दिये गये हैं। उनमें से सही उत्तर चुनकर लिखिये।*

विक्रम के प्रिय विषय गणित और विज्ञान थे। उनकी भौतिकशास्त्र में विशेष अभिरुचि थी। उन्होंने बीस वर्ष की उम्र में कैंब्रिज विश्वविद्यालय लंदन से भौतिकी में त्रिपोस परीक्षा उत्तीर्ण कर ली थी। द्वितीय विश्व युद्ध के प्रारंभ में वे भारत लौट आये। यहाँ एक ओर उनका संपर्क सर सी.वी. रमण जैसे प्रसिद्ध वैज्ञानिकों से हुआ, वहीं दूसरी ओर राष्ट्रीय स्वतंत्रता आंदोलन ने भी उन्हें एक नवीन चेतना प्रदान की। उन्होंने अंतरिक्ष की गहराइयों से आनेवाली रहस्यमयी कॉस्मिक किरणों पर अनुसंधान करके कैंब्रिज विश्वविद्यालय से सन् 1947 में पी.एच.डी. की उपाधि अर्जित की थी।

61. किस विषय में विक्रम की विशेष अभिरुचि थी?

A. गणित शास्त्र B. भाषा शास्त्र
C. भौतिकशास्त्र D. जीवशास्त्र

62. वे लंदन से भारत कब लौट आये?

A. प्रथम विश्व युद्ध के प्रारंभ में
B. द्वितीय विश्व युद्ध के प्रारंभ में
C. भारत-चीन युद्ध के समय
D. भारत-पाक युद्ध के समय

63. भारत में विक्रमजी को किससे संपर्क हुआ?

A. विश्वेश्वरैया B. गाँधीजी
C. सर सी.वी. रमण D. नेहरुजी

64. विक्रमजी को एक नवीन चेतना देने वाला विषय क्या था?

A. नाटक क्षेत्र B. स्वतंत्रता आंदोलन
C. धार्मिक विचार D. राजकीय क्षेत्र

65. कैंब्रिज विश्वविद्यालय से उन्होंने कौन-सी उपाधि प्राप्त की?

A. पी.एच.डी. B. एम. फिल
C. एम. टेक D. डी. लिट

सूचनाः *नीचे दिये गये हर एक प्रश्न के चार उत्तर दिये गये हैं, उनमें से सही उत्तर चुनकर लिखिए:*

66. 'हिक्मत' शब्द का समानार्थक रूप है

A. हुकूमत B. हिम्मत
C. उपाय D. अभिप्राय

67. 'नायक' इस पद का अन्यलिंग रूप है

A. नायकानी B. नायिका
C. नयकी D. नायके

68. 'व्यवस्था' पद का अर्थ है

A. व्यस्थ B. अव्यवस्था
C. इंतजाम D. अवस्था

69. भारत देश के ज्यादा लोगों की मातृभाषा है

A. अंग्रेजी B. हिन्दी
C. पाली D. संस्कृत

70. 'गरीब' पद का विरुद्ध पद है

A. दौलत B. अगरीब
C. अमीर D. दरिद्र

71. श्रीमती इन्दिरा गाँधी हमारे देश की ....

A. राष्ट्रपति थीं B. रानी थीं
C. मुख्यमंत्री थीं D. प्रधानमंत्री थीं

72. 'पत्रिका' पद का बहुवचन रूप है

A. पत्रिकाएँ B. पत्रे
C. पत्रिके D. पत्र

73. 'खुशबू' पद का विरुद्धार्थक पद है

A. सुवासना B. दुर्वासना
C. बदबू D. वासना

74. 'धंधा' इस पद का बहुवचन रूप है

A. धंधी B. धंधे
C. धंधाएँ D. धंधों

75. 'कारकाना' इस पद का शुद्ध रूप है

A. कारकाने B. खारकाना
C. खारखाना D. कारखाना

76. 'बालक' इस पद का अन्यलिंग रूप है

A. बालिका
B. बालकी
C. बाला
D. बाले

77. 'हाथ पर हाथ रखकर बैठना' इस मुहावरे का अर्थ है

A. नमस्कार करना
B. ताली बजाना
C. खाली बैठे रहना
D. योजना में मग्न होना

78. 'निगरानी' पद का मतलब है

A. मारना
B. देखरेख
C. मर जाना
D. पानी में डूब जाना

79. 'लिखना' शब्द का भाववाचक संज्ञा है

A. लिखाना
B. लिखापट
C. लिखावट
D. लिखा हुआ

80. 'आत्मीयता' इस पद का विशेषण रूप है

A. आत्मीय
B. आत्मा
C. आत्मी
D. आत्म

LANGUAGE : ENGLISH

81. The word or phrase which is opposite in meaning to the word "charitable" is ....

A. generous
B. selfish
C. merciful to others
D. benevolent

Direction (Qs. 82): *Find out which part of the below given sentence has an error. If there is no error, mark your answer as (D).*

82. I was about to start my car (A)/when I found (B)/that there is no petrol in it. (C)/No error (D)

83. One word which can substitute. "One who believes in God" is ....

A. secularist
B. agnostic
C. theist
D. atheist

84. Out of these four words the correctly spell word is ....

A. foreigner
B. foreiner
C. forienor
D. foriegner

85. Few could understand Vimala's mental .... when her husband died.

A. health
B. feelings
C. thought
D. balance

86. Plural form of radius is ....

A. roudies
B. radios
C. radii
D. radiuses

87. Past tense of the verb 'strike' is ....

A. striked
B. struck
C. stroke
D. struk

88. The thieves were caught by the police as they were trying to get away with the looted money. The alternative which best expresses the meaning of the idiom underlined in the above sentence is ....

A. to dispose of
B. to bury
C. to play foul
D. to escape

Directions (Qs. 89-92): *Fill in the blank with the appropriate alternative given below each question.*

89. As the driver swerved violently at the turning, the wheel came off as it was already ....

A. luse
B. lose
C. loose
D. loos

90. I congratulated him .... his success.

A. for
B. on
C. to
D. by

91. The meaning of domicile is ....

A. dwelling place
B. bicycle
C. domination
D. delete

92. The violence has succeeded in .... our attention to the demands of employees.

A. taking
B. inviting
C. dividing
D. drawing

Directions (Qs. 93-96): *Read the following passage carefully and choose the best answer to each question from the four alternatives given.*

The cockroach has learnt more about survival than any other creature. He can live anywhere from the middle of the Sahara desert to the kitchens in freezing Labrador. The cockroaches ability to survive comes from his ability to eat anything. His tastes in food include everything from flower buds to shoes. He eats his own cast-off skin, and if there is nothing else, dines on eggs of his own species. He can live for a month without any food or water. Cockroaches have wings and six powerful short legs. With the help of its two antennae cockroach feels his way in the dark.

93. If a cockroach cannot get anything to eat, he even eats ....
A. flower buds
B. the eggs of the cockroach
C. shoes
D. cast-off skin

94. Cockroach feels its way in the dark with the help of ....
A. its wings B. its powerful legs
C. its eyes D. its antennae

95. How many powerful short legs has a cockroach?
A. six B. four
C. two D. eight

96. How long can a cockroach live without any food or water?
A. one year B. one week
C. one month D. one fortnight

97. A light breeze .... the forest fire and made it more dangerous.
A. blew B. ignited
C. hit D. fanned

98. I speak English, but .... French.
A. I speak not B. I don't speak
C. I'm not speaking D. I doesn't speak

99. "How long .... learning English?" "Six months."
A. have you been B. you are
C. are you D. do you

100. Don't take that newspaper away, ... it.
A. I read
B. I'll read
C. I am going to read
D. I'll not read

SECTION-B

POST SPECIFIC SUBJECT-RELATED QUESTIONS

101. Antidote for heparin is
A. Vitamin K
B. Protamine sulphate
C. Aminocarpoic acid
D. Aminodorone

102. A patient in the second stage of labour is given which of the following injections to improve uterine contractions?
A. Oxytocin B. Methergin
C. Phenergan D. Diazopam

103. Acute pancreatitis is manifested by an elevated
A. Serum Bilirubin
B. Serum Amylase
C. Serum Alkaline Phosphatase
D. Serum Creatinine

104. Which of the following antituberculosis drugs can damage the 8th cranial nerve?
A. Isoniazid (INH)
B. Paraoaminosalicylic acid (PAS)
C. Ethambutol hydrochloride (myambutol)
D. Streptomycin

105. Which of the following is used in the management of hyperkalemia?
A. Insulin with glucose
B. Sodium bicarbonate
C. Potassium chloride
D. Magnesium sulphate

106. Distended abdomen and absence of bowel sounds after abdominal surgery indicates
A. Intussusception B. Paralytic ileus
C. Hemorrhage D. Ruptured colon

107. The normal intraocular pressure is
A. 8-21 mmHg B. 16-25 mmHg
C. 20-35 mmHg D. 19-38 mmHg

108. Which of the following ECG findings indicate the presence of hypokalemia?

A. Tall, peak T wave
B. ST segment depression
C. Widening of QRS complex
D. Prolonged PR interval

109. Which of the following need to be performed before radial arterial cannulation to evaluate radial and ulnar arterial patency?
A. Allen's test B. Anglography
C. Buerger's test D. Capillary refill test

110. Common risk of severe depression is
A. Fatigability B. Hallucinations
C. Thought block D. Suicide

111. Dumping syndrome is a complication of
A. Colectomy
B. Subtotal gastrectomy
C. Nephrectomy
D. Histrectomy

112. Which of the following is used as an antidote for organophosphorous poisoning?
A. Atropine B. Adrenaline
C. Avil D. Aminodorone

113. Lactulose is prescribed for patients with hepatic ancephalopathy to
A. decrease the bilirubin level
B. decrease the serum ammonia level
C. increase the protein level
D. increase the glucose level

114. Apical pulse is assessed by placing the diaphragm of the stethoscope at the area of
A. Aortic area B. Pulmonic area
C. Mitral area D. Tricuspid area

115. Abnormal proliferation of uterine endometrial tissue outside the uterus is known as
A. Cystic fibrosis B. Endometriosis
C. Metrorrhagia D. Menorrhagia

116. The size of the intravenous cannula used for neonates is
A. 18 B. 20
C. 22 D. 24

117. Normal serum potassium level in meq/L is
A. 2.5 to 3.5 B. 3.5 to 5
C. 5.5 to 6.5 D. 6.5 to 7.5

118. Bleeding from the nose is known as
A. Epistaxis B. Hemoptysis
C. Hematemesis D. Hematuria

119. Which of the following is used to assess the level of consciousness?
A. Apgar score
B. Braden scale
C. Glasgow coma scale
D. Snellen's chart

120. Physician prescribed to administer Tablet, Digoxin 0.125 mg OD orally. Tablet Digoxin is available in 0.25 mg. The nurse should administer
A. 1/4 tablet B. 1/2 tablet
C. 2 tablets D. 4 tablets

121. Prescription is inj. Dopamine 200 mg in 250 cc D_5W to infuse at 5 mcg/kg/min. The patient's weight is 50 kg. How many cc/hour would this be on an infusion pump?
A. 19 B. 22
C. 28 D. 30

122. Which of the following is most important to prevent the progress of disease in thromboangiitis obliterans (Buerger's disease)?
A. Controlling blood pressure
B. Controlling diabetes
C. Weight reduction
D. Smoking cessation

123. While giving NG tube feeding, which of the following nursing actions prevents complications?
A. Advance tube 2 cm
B. Flush with 20 mL of air
C. Provide high Fowler's position
D. Plug the air vent during feeding

124. A patient who is on Sengstaken-Blakemore tube, suddenly experiences difficulty in breathing. Which of the following actions should the nurse take first?
A. Administer oxygen with a nasal cannula
B. Elevate the head of the bed
C. Cut and remove the tube
D. Listen to the client's lungs

125. Which among the following is an indication of portal hypertension?
A. Asterixis
B. Hematemesis
C. Elevated blood pressure
D. Confusion

126. A patient's GRBS is 40 mg%. The immediate management is to administer

A. 5% dextrose
B. 50% dextrose
C. 10 units Human Actrapid insulin
D. Normal saline

127. Buck's extension traction is

A. Applied as cervical head halter
B. Skin traction to the lower leg
C. Skeletal traction to the lower leg
D. Tongs applied to the head

128. Gonlometer is used to assess

A. Auditory acuity
B. Muscle strength
C. Range of motion of joints
D. Visual acuity

129. The surgical procedure done to relieve pressure in compartment syndrome is

A. Open Reduction with Internal Fixation (ORIF)
B. Meniscectomy
C. Fasciotomy
D. Arthroplasty

130. Fractures of the distal radius is called

A. Hume fracture
B. Monteggia fracture
C. Galeazzi fracture
D. Colles' fracture

131. The causative organism for peptic ulcer is

A. Helicobacter pylori
B. Staphylococci
C. Eschericia coli
D. Streptococci

132. Color coding for Nitrous oxide cylinder is

A. Black
B. Black with white shoulders
C. Light blue
D. Gray

133. False sensory perceptions with no basis in reality is known as

A. Hallucinations
B. Delusions
C. Loose associations
D. Neologisms

134. Which of the following procedure always requires surgical asepsis?

A. Vaginal irrigation
B. Urinary catheterization
C. Nasogastric tube insertion
D. Colostomy irrigation

135. The most appropriate time for the nurse to obtain a sputum specimen for culture is

A. Early in the morning
B. After the patient eats a light breakfast
C. After aerosol therapy
D. After chest physiotherapy

136. Mania is a

A. Anxiety related disorder
B. Dissociative disorder
C. Mood disorder
D. Thought disorder

137. Kaposi's sarcoma is associated with

A. Human papilloma virus
B. Human T cell lymphotropic virus type I (HTLV-I)
C. Human immunodeficiency virus
D. Epstein-Barr virus

138. Ondansetron, 8 mg IV given before chemotherapy is to prevent

A. Alopecia B. Fatigue
C. Vomiting D. Pain

139. All of the following are side effects of phenytoin, EXCEPT

A. Ataxia B. Hirsuitism
C. Hypoglycemia D. Gum hypertrophy

140. Lateral curvature of the spine is called as

A. Kyphosis B. Lordosis
C. Scoliosis D. Pectus excavatum

141. Sensitivity and reaction is tested by administering the drug

A. Intradermally B. Intramuscularly
C. Intravenously D. Subcutaneously

142. Which of the following is used for assessing the pain in children?

A. Brief pain inventory
B. Numerical rating scale
C. Visual analogue scale
D. Wong-Baker faces pain rating scale

143. Medications used for nausea and vomiting is known as
A. Analgesics B. Antipyretics
C. Antiemetics D. Antibiotics

144. The equipment used in the examination of ear is
A. Laryngoscope B. Ophthalmoscope
C. Otoscope D. Proctoscope

145. Removal of an entire lung is called as
A. Lobectomy
B. Pneumonectomy
C. Segmental resection
D. Wedge resection

146. Which of the following is the medication of choice for patient with an open contaminated injury and no recent history of tetanus immunization?
A. DPT vaccine
B. Tetanus toxoid
C. Tetanus antitoxin
D. Tetanus immunoglobulin

147. A patient who is receiving antibiotic therapy complaints of ringing in the ears. This ototoxicity is damage to
A. 4th CN B. 8th CN
C. 7th CN D. 9th CN

148. Which of the following cannot be corrected by dialysis?
A. Hypernatremia
B. Hyperkalemia
C. Elevated creatinine
D. Decreased hemoglobin

149. The normal mean pulmonary artery pressure is
A. 10-15 mm Hg B. 15-20 mm Hg
C. 20-25 mm Hg D. 25-30 mm Hg

150. ECG change in myocardial infarction is
A. ST segment elevation
B. Wide QRS complex
C. Presence of U wave
D. Prolonged PR interval

151. The normal cholesterol level is
A. 100-150 mg/dl B. 150-200 mg/dl
C. 200-250 mg/dl D. 250-300 mg/dl

152. Inflammation of tissues surrounding the nail is known as
A. Clubbing B. Koilonychia
C. Paronychia D. Onycholysis

153. Which of the following is an indicator of AIDS?
A. CD4 count lower than 200 cells/mm^3
B. CD4 count more than 400 cells/mm^3
C. CD4 count lower than 600 cells/mm^3
D. CD4 count lower than 1000 cells/mm^3

154. Medical management for increased intracranial pressure (ICP) include
A. Administer Mannitol
B. Administer half strength saline
C. Administer plasma volume expanders
D. Reduce the number of breaths in the ventilator

155. Fever, headache and nuchal rigidity are classic symptoms seen in
A. Parkinson's disease
B. Alzheimer's disease
C. Brain abscess
D. Meningitis

156. The appropriate needle size for insulin injection is
A. 18G, 1½" long B. 22G, 1" long
C. 22G, 1½" long D. 25G, 5/8" long

157. All of the following nursing interventions are correct when using the Z-track method of injection EXCEPT
A. Prepare the injection site with alcohol
B. Use a needle that's a least 1" long
C. Aspirate for blood before injection
D. Rub the site vigorously after the injection

158. Deficiency of vitamin D causes
A. Night blindness B. Beriberi
C. Rickets D. Anemia

159. While performing tracheostomy suctioning, suction time should not be more than
A. 10 seconds B. 20 seconds
C. 30 seconds D. 45 seconds

160. Which of the following condition is manifested by increased intraocular pressure?
A. Cataract B. Conjunctivitis
C. Dacryocystitis D. Glaucoma

161. Bradenscale is used for assessing the risk of
A. Decubitus ulcer
B. Diabetes mellitus
C. Hypertension
D. Urinary tract infection

162. Which of the following is a manifestation of pyloricstenosis?
A. Projectile vomiting
B. Regurgitation
C. Steatorrhea
D. Tenesmus

163. The percentage and the flow of oxygen in a red colour venturi mask is
A. 31% and 6 lit/minute
B. 35% and 8 lit/minute
C. 40% and 10 lit/minute
D. 60% and 15 lit/minute

164. Failure to pass meconium within the first 24 hours after birth may indicate
A. Abdominal wall defect
B. Celiac disease
C. Hirschsprung disease
D. Intussusception

165. The primigravida reports that her last menstrual period started on January 15 and ended on January 20. Using Nagele's rule, the EDD will be
A. September 22 B. October 22
C. November 8 D. December 28

166. Severe allergic reaction to a drug is known as
A. Anaphylactic B. Interaction
C. Adverse D. Toxicity

167. One of the major cause for cirrhosis of liver is
A. Alcohol abuse B. Drug abuse
C. Smoking D. Viral hepatitis

168. Which of the following is NOT a clinical manifestation of diabetes mellitus?
A. Glycosuria B. Polyphagia
C. Hyperglycemia D. Hypernatremia

169. Distant vision is assessed by using
A. Confrontation test
B. Hirschbergs test
C. Jaeger card
D. Snellen chart

170. Inflammation of the tongue is known as
A. Gingivitis B. Glossitis
C. Parotitis D. Stomatitis

171. Diabetes insipidus is due to the deficiency of
A. Anti diuretic hormone
B. Insulin
C. Glucose
D. Glucagon

172. The size of the intravenous cannula (in gauge) used for neonates is
A. 28 B. 24
C. 22 D. 20

173. Lead poisoning is known as
A. Asterixis
B. Plumbism
C. Plummer Virison syndrome
D. Parder Willi syndrome

174. The drug of choice in pre eclamsia is
A. Dopamine
B. Magnesium sulphate
C. Sodium bicarbonate
D. Sodium nitropruside

175. Which of the following medication is administered sublingually for managing angina pectoris?
A. Asprin B. Betaloc
C. Nitroglycerin D. Warfarin

176. Which of the following is a complication of splenectomy?
A. Cholecystitis B. Pancreatitis
C. Appendicitis D. Gastritis

177. Parkinson's disease is caused by
A. Hereditary factors
B. Death of brain cells due to old age
C. Impairment of dopamine producing cells in the brain
D. Demyelination of the nerve cells

178. Inability to speak or understand the spoken words is called as
A. Insomnia B. Aphraxia
C. Agnosia D. Aphasia

179. Which of the following intervention can best prevent bed sore?
A. Massage reddened areas with lotion or oils

B. Change the position every 1 hour
C. Use special water mattress
D. Keep skin clean and dry

180. Pre-operative preparation for appendectomy include all of the following except
A. Consent
B. Enema STAT
C. Skin preparation
D. Remove the jewelries

181. Which of the following is a specific investigation to detect seizures?
A. CT scan B. MRI scan
C. EEG D. X-ray

182. Which of the following listed drug is a proton pump inhibitor?
A. Pantoprazole B. Ranitidine
C. Sucraifate D. Famotidine

183. Ineffectual straining at stool is known as
A. Borborygmi B. Constipation
C. Steatorrhoea D. Tenesmus

184. Which of the following position is given to a patient with severe breathing difficulty?
A. Dorsal recumbent
B. Fowlers
C. Supine
D. Trendlenberg

185. Which of the following is used to assess the function of brain stem?
A. Cold caloric test
B. Glasgow coma scale
C. Braden scale
D. Intracranial pressure

186. Which of the following can lead to greenish discoloration of the amniotic fluid?
A. Lanugo B. Hydramnios
C. Meconium D. Vernix

187. Purple-blue tinge of the cervix is
A. Braxton-Hicks sign
B. Chadwick's sign
C. Goodell's sign
D. McDonald's sign

188. Premature separation of a normally implanted placenta during the second half of pregnancy, usually with severe hemorrhage is known as
A. Placenta previa
B. Ectopic pregnancy
C. Incompetent cervix
D. Abruptio placentae

189. Post-partum hemorrhage is loss of blood which is more than
A. 200 ml B. 300 ml
C. 400 ml D. 500 ml

190. Classic symptoms of deep vein thrombosis include all of the following EXCEPT
A. Muscle pain B. Homans sign
C. Swelling D. Redness

191. While instilling ear drops, the ear canal of an adult is straightened by pulling the pinna
A. Down and back
B. Up and back
C. Straight down
D. Straight back

192. Which of the following drug is withheld if the patient's pulse is less than 60/minute?
A. Digoxin B. Dopamine
C. Dobulamine D. Phenytoin

193. Which of the following position is used while administering enema?
A. Dorsal recumbent
B. Lithotomy
C. Left lateral
D. Right lateral

194. Which of the following drug is contraindicated in pancreatitis?
A. Morphine B. Meperidine
C. Diclofenac D. Spasmoproxyvon

195. The solution used to disinfect the bed linen of HIV positive patient is
A. Dettol
B. Lysol
C. Savlon
D. Sodium hypochlorite

196. While measuring central venous pressure the Zero point of the manometer is adjusted to
A. Anterior axillary line
B. Midaxillary line
C. Posterior axillary line
D. Shoulder level

197. Which of the following is the preferred site for intramuscular injection in infants?
A. Deltoid B. Rectus femoris
C. Vastus lateralis D. Ventrogluteal

198. If 500 ml of ringer lactate is to be administered in four hours, how many drops per minute it would be (drop factor = 20 drops/ml)?
A. 20 B. 42
C. 35 D. 60

199. Which of the following medication order is immediately and once only administration?
A. prn order B. stat order
C. single order D. standing order

200. Nursing assessment for neurovascular status of the extremity with a cast include the following EXCEPT
A. Pallor B. Range of motion
C. Paresthesia D. Pain

ANSWERS

1	2	3	4	5	6	7	8	9	10
B	B	C	B	B	C	C	D	C	C
11	12	13	14	15	16	17	18	19	20
B	A	A	B	C	A	C	C	C	A
21	22	23	24	25	26	27	28	29	30
D	A	C	D	D	A	A	B	A	D
31	32	33	34	35	36	37	38	39	40
B	A	B	A	C	B	D	A	A	C
41	42	43	44	45	46	47	48	49	50
C	A	D	C	A	B	D	A	C	A
51	52	53	54	55	56	57	58	59	60
D	B	B	D	C	D	D	B	A	D
61	62	63	64	65	66	67	68	69	70
C	B	C	B	A	C	B	C	B	C
71	72	73	74	75	76	77	78	79	80
D	A	C	B	D	A	C	B	C	A
81	82	83	84	85	86	87	88	89	90
B	C	C	A	B	C	B	D	C	B
91	92	93	94	95	96	97	98	99	100
A	D	B	D	A	C	D	B	A	C
101	102	103	104	105	106	107	108	109	110
B	A	B	D	A	B	A	B	A	D
111	112	113	114	115	116	117	118	119	120
B	A	B	C	B	D	B	A	C	B
121	122	123	124	125	126	127	128	129	130
A	D	C	C	B	B	B	C	C	D
131	132	133	134	135	136	137	138	139	140
A	C	A	B	A	C	C	C	C	C
141	142	143	144	145	146	147	148	149	150
A	D	C	C	B	B	B	D	B	A

151	152	153	154	155	156	157	158	159	160
B	C	A	A	D	D	D	C	A	D
161	162	163	164	165	166	167	168	169	170
A	A	C	C	B	A	A	D	D	B
171	172	173	174	175	176	177	178	179	180
A	B	B	B	C	B	C	D	B	B
181	182	183	184	185	186	187	188	189	190
C	A	D	B	A	C	B	D	D	D
191	192	193	194	195	196	197	198	199	200
B	A	C	A	D	B	C	B	B	B

SOME SELECTED EXPLANATORY ANSWERS

24. (AA 23 : CC 25) (PP 61 : RR 63)

TT 52 : VV54

Because, given alphabets are increased by two position. And similar trends followed by given number.

25. + means ×

− means ÷

× means +

÷ means −

then, (18 + 10 × 20) − 8 ÷ 6

= (18 × 10 + 20) ÷ 8 − 6

= (180 + 20) ÷ 8 − 6

= 200 ÷ 8 − 6 = 25 − 6 = 19.

29. 1, 2, 3 .... 21 51

⟶ | ⟵

Rank from the last = 51 − 20 = 31.

30. *b* is in doubt in the same way as *h* is in honest (because *b* and *h* are silent).

31. ∵ PRAMOD is written as RTCOQF

∴ BUSTLE is written as DWUVNG because every letter is increased by two position right.

35. ∵ R is the sister of Q, S is the sister of R, P is the brother of Q

∴ Q is related to S as brother or sister.

36. Let four years ago Ravi's age = x years

Four years ago Ashoka's are = $(x + 6)$ years

Present age of Ravi = $(x + 4)$ years

Present age of Ashoka = $(x + 6 + 4)$ years

∴ Differenc of their ages = $x + 10 - x - 4$ = 6 years.

37. shg, rif, qje, pkd

∴ Next will come olc

because, c, d, e, f, g (last letter each)

opqrs (starting letter each)

hijkl (middle letter each)

38. B M V K R Q are sitting in a row

B is sitting on the extreme left

M and K are sitting adjacent to V.

39. Geometry, Trigonometry and Algebra are chapters of Maths book but Biology is not in that group.

41. Total weight of 20 children = 35 × 20 = 700 kg

Increased weight = 45 − 25 = 20

Now total weight = 700 + 20 = 720

$$\text{Correct average} = \frac{720}{20} = 36 \text{ kg.}$$

42. Area of right triangle = $\frac{1}{2} \times b \times h$

$\Rightarrow$ $10 = \frac{1}{2} \times 5 \times x$

$\Rightarrow$ $5x = 20 \Rightarrow x = 4$

∴ Other side = 4 cm.

43. $\frac{2\pi r}{2\pi R} = \frac{3}{4} \Rightarrow \frac{r}{R} = \frac{3}{4}$

$$\therefore \frac{\pi r^2}{\pi R^2} = \left(\frac{r}{R}\right)^2 = \left(\frac{3}{4}\right)^2 = \frac{9}{16} = 9 : 16.$$

44. Let Hari has ₹6 and John has ₹22

John   Hari

22   6

22–12 = 10   12   12 + 6 = ₹18

10 + 4 = ₹14   4   18 – 4 = ₹14

Also, 22 – 6 = 16

Hence, Hari had smaller amount difference by ₹ 16.

45. Investment by P = ₹ 5 lakhs for 12 months

∴ Capital of P = 12 × 5 = 60 lakhs for 1 month

Investment by Q = ₹ 7 lakhs for 12 months

∴ Capital of Q = 12 × 7 = 84 lakhs for 1 month

Investment by R = ₹ 9 lakhs for 4 months

∴ Capital of R = 9 × 4 = 36 lakhs for 1 month

Ratio of their capitals

P : Q : R = 60 : 84 : 36

= 5 : 7 : 3

Sum of proportional = 5 + 7 + 3 = 15

Total profit = 3 lakhs

∴ Share of R = $\frac{3}{15} \times 300000$ = ₹ 60,000

46. $SI = \frac{p \times r \times t}{100}$

$\Rightarrow 500 = \frac{60000 \times r \times 1}{12 \times 100} = 50r$

$\Rightarrow r = \frac{500}{50} = 10\%$

47. 10 workers working 8 hrs/day in 15 days

1 worker working 1 hr/day in 15 × 10 × 8 days

15 workers working 5 hrs/day in

$\frac{15 \times 10 \times 8}{15 \times 5} = 16$ days

48. ∵ Smallest angle of a triangle is 50° and they are in A.P.

Let common difference = d

$50° + 50° + d + 50 + 2d = 180°$

$\Rightarrow 3d = 180° - 150° = 30°$

$\Rightarrow d = 10°$

Hence, angles are 50°, 60° and 70°.

49. Distance = 250 m = $\frac{250}{1000}$ km

time = 12 seconds = $\frac{12}{3600}$ hrs.

$\therefore \text{speed} = \frac{\text{distance}}{\text{time}} = \frac{\frac{250}{1000}}{\frac{12}{3600}}$

$= \frac{250}{1000} \times \frac{3600}{12} = 75$ km/hr

51. $\frac{1}{2} + \frac{1}{2} \times \frac{1}{2} = \frac{1}{2} + \frac{1}{4} = \frac{2+1}{4} = \frac{3}{4}$

52. SP = ₹ 10

Profit = ₹ 2

CP = SP – profit = ₹ 10 – ₹ 2 = ₹ 8

If SP = ₹ 20

then profit = SP – CP = ₹ 20 – ₹ 8 = ₹ 12

55. Sum of first-n odd natural numbers = n^2

∴ Sum of first 15 odd numbers

$= (15)^2 = 225$

57. $\frac{56}{13} \times \frac{39}{7} \times \frac{103}{8} = 3 \times 103 = 309$

58. $\frac{75}{100} \times 220 = 15 \times x$

$\Rightarrow x = 11$

59. $\frac{x}{\sqrt{.81}} = 450 \Rightarrow \frac{x}{.9} = 450$

$\Rightarrow x = 405$

60. P : Q = 3 : 2, Q : R = 3 : 5

P : Q = (3 : 2) × 3 = 9 : 6

Q : R = $\left(\frac{3}{5}\right) \times 2$ = 6 : 10

∴ P : Q : R = 9 : 6 : 10

GENERAL INTELLIGENCE & REASONING

1. LETTER SERIES

In letter series, the letters follow a definite order. The given series of letters can be in natural order or in reverse order or combination of both. The letters may be skipped or repeated or consecutive. The given series may be single or may even comprise of two different series merged at alternate positions. While attempting questions on letter series one should note the pattern of alphabet series.

Alphabets in natural series are :

A B C D E F G H I J K L M N O P Q R S T U V W X Y Z

A ↓ 1st, E ↓ 5th, J ↓ 10th, O ↓ 15th, T ↓ 20th, Y ↓ 25th

Alphabets in reverse series are :

Z Y X W V U T S R Q P O N M L K J I H G F E D C B A

Z ↓ 1st, V ↓ 5th, Q ↓ 10th, L ↓ 15th, G ↓ 20th, B ↓ 25th

Note : On reaching Z, the series restarts from A and on reaching A, it restarts from Z.

EXERCISE

Directions : *In each of the following series determine the order of the letters. Then from the given options select the one which will complete the given series.*

1. B Y C X D W E ?
(*a*) S (*b*) T
(*c*) U (*d*) V

2. B A F E J I P O ? U
(*a*) V (*b*) T
(*c*) S (*d*) Q

3. B A D C ? H G J I
(*a*) EF (*b*) FE
(*c*) FG (*d*) DF

4. ADG, XVT, BEH, WUS, ?
(*a*) VTR (*b*) CFI
(*c*) DFJ (*d*) STU

5. GMSY, IOUA, KQWC, ?
(*a*) MSYE (*b*) NSYE
(*c*) MTYE (*d*) MSYF

6. ADG, GJM, ?, SVY
(*a*) MPS (*b*) MQR
(*c*) MQS (*d*) SPM

7. XYZ, UVW, ?, OPQ
(*a*) RST (*b*) STU
(*c*) QRS (*d*) TUV

8. JOBS, KMEO, LKHK, ?, NGNC
(*a*) MJLH (*b*) LIKG
(*c*) MIKG (*d*) MNGM

9. AZ, GT, MN, ?, YB
(*a*) KF (*b*) TS
(*c*) RX (*d*) SH

10. BMY, DNW, FOU, ?
(*a*) HPT (*b*) HPS
(*c*) HQS (*d*) GPS

11. AZ, CX, EV, ?
(*a*) HU (*b*) GS
(*c*) GT (*d*) HT

12. DMP, FLN, HKL, JJJ, ?
(*a*) MIH (*b*) III
(*c*) LIH (*d*) MII

13. ECA, JHF, OMK, ?, YWU
(*a*) TRP (*b*) LNP
(*c*) QPN (*d*) RPT

14. ABP, CDQ, EFR, ?
(*a*) GHS (*b*) HGS
(*c*) GHR (*d*) GHT

15. BEH, KNQ, TWZ, ?
(*a*) IJL (*b*) BDF
(*c*) CFI (*d*) ADG

EXPLANATORY ANSWERS

1. (*d*) : There are two alternate series.

+1 +1 +1
B Y C X D W E V
−1 −1 −1

Series I : BCDE (natural order)
Series II : YXWV (reverse order)

2. (*a*) : Each vowel (AEIOU) is preceded by the letter that comes next to it in the natural alphabetical series.

B A F E J I P O V U

3. (*b*) : The letters in natural series are divided into sections of two letters each. The letters in each section are written backward.
BA DC FE HG JI

4. (*b*) : There are two alternate series.

ADG XVT BEH WUS CFI

Series I : ADG BEH CFI
+1 +1
+1 +1
+1 +1

Series II : XVT WUS
−1
−1
−1

5. (*a*) : The series is formed by moving each letter two steps forward from one group to the next.

GMSY IOUA KQWC MSYE
+2 +2 +2
+2 +2 +2
+2 +2 +2
+2 +2 +2

(The series restarts from A on reaching Z)

6. (*a*) : In each group of three letters the alphabet is in the succession of +3. The next group begins with the last alphabet of the previous group.

A D G G J M M P S S V Y
+3 +3 +3 +3 +3 +3 +3 +3

7. (*a*) : The alphabet from one group to the next are in recession of −3, *i.e.*,

XYZ UVW RST OPQ
−3 −3 −3
−3 −3 −3
−3 −3 −3

8. (*c*) : The alphabets in each group follow the pattern +1, −2, +3 and −4 respectively from one group to the next group.

JOBS KMEO LKHK MIKG NGNC
+1 +1 +1 +1
−2 −2 −2 −2
+3 +3 +3 +3
−4 −4 −4 −4

9. (*d*) : The letters in one group correspond to the letters in the next group in the manner +6, −6 respectively, *i.e.*,

AZ GT MN SH YB
+6 +6 +6 +6
−6 −6 −6 −6

10. (*b*) : The letters in one group correspond to the letters in the next group in the manner +2, +1, -2 respectively, *i.e.*,

BMY DNW FOU HPS
+2 +2 +2
+1 +1 +1
−2 −2 −2

11. (*c*) : The letters in each group correspond to the letters in the next group in the manner +2, –2 respectively, *i.e.,*

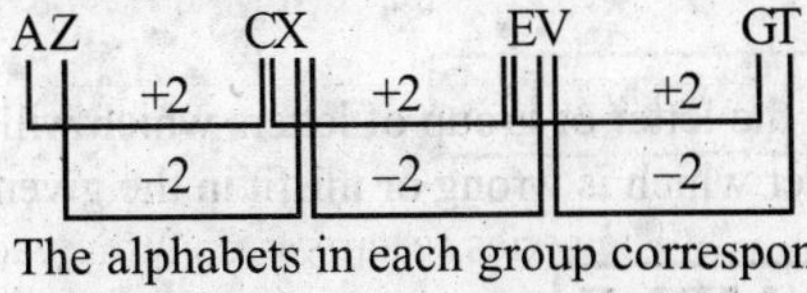

12. (*c*) : The alphabets in each group correspond to the alphabets in the next group in the manner +2, –1, –2 respectively, *i.e.,*

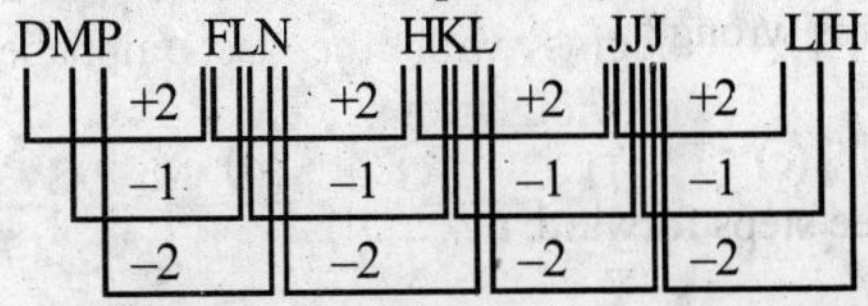

13. (*a*) : The alphabets in each group are moved five steps forward, *i.e.,*

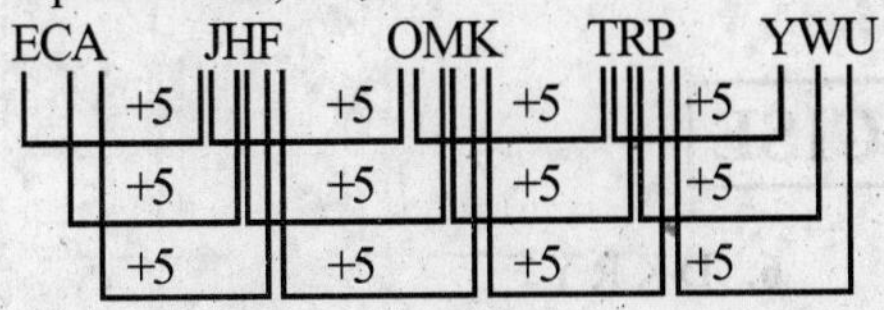

14. (*a*) : The letters in one group correspond to the letters in the next group in the manner +2, +2, +1 respectively, *i.e.,*

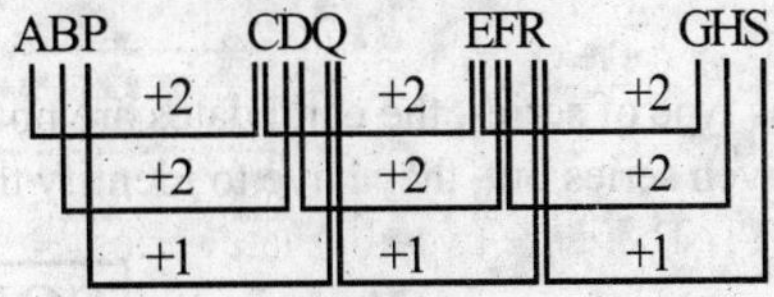

15. (*c*) : All the letters in each group are moved nine steps forward.

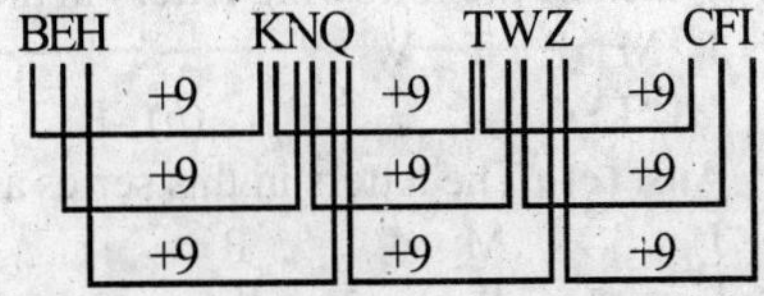

2. WRONG LETTER SERIES

In this type of series, the candidates are not required to find the letter or group of letters which will complete the given series but, they have to identify the letter or number which is wrong or misfit in the given series.

SOLVED EXAMPLE

1. Which of the following letters in the given series is wrong?

J M P T V Y

(*a*) J (*b*) P (*c*) T (*d*) Y

Ans. (*c*) : The letters in this series are moved three steps forward, *i.e.*,

J M P S V Y

+3 +3 +3 +3 +3

Letter 'T' should have been 'S'.

EXERCISE

Directions : *Which letter(s) in each of the following series is wrong or is misfit in the series?*

1. A E H O U

(*a*) U (*b*) O
(*c*) H (*d*) E

2. C H M S W B

(*a*) C (*b*) S
(*c*) B (*d*) W

3. X S N I C Y

(*a*) Y (*b*) C
(*c*) S (*d*) I

4. Z A W B X C

(*a*) D (*b*) C
(*c*) X (*d*) W

5. M L O N Q P R

(*a*) R (*b*) O
(*c*) Q (*d*) L

6. D K R Y F L

(*a*) L (*b*) D
(*c*) R (*d*) Y

7. L N Q T W Z C F

(*a*) C (*b*) Q
(*c*) L (*d*) F

8. XW, DC, CB, NM, PQ

(*a*) NM (*b*) CB
(*c*) PQ (*d*) XW

9. B E I N S A I

(*a*) A (*b*) E
(*c*) S (*d*) I

10. Z T P K H F

(*a*) Z (*b*) P
(*c*) T (*d*) F

EXPLANATORY ANSWERS

1. (*c*) : The series is made with vowels only. AEIOU. I should be in place of H.

2. (*b*) : The letters in the series are moved five steps forward.

C H M R W B

+5 +5 +5 +5 +5

R should be in place of S

(The series restarts from A on reaching Z)

3. (*b*) : The pattern in the series is –5, *i.e.*,

X S N I D Y

–5 –5 –5 –5 –5

D should be in place of C.

4. (*d*) : There are two alternate series

+1 +1

Z A Y B X C

–1 –1

Series I : ZYX (reverse series)

Series II : ABC (natural series)

Y should be in place of W.

5. (*a*) : Two consecutive letters are written backwards.

ML ON QP SR

S should be in place of R.

6. (*a*) : The pattern in this series in moving the letters seven steps forward.

D K R Y F M

+7 +7 +7 +7 +7

M should be in place of L.

7. (*c*) : The pattern in the series is +3

K N Q T W Z C F

+3 +3 +3 +3 +3 +3 +3

K should be in place of L.

8. (*c*) : The series is made with any two consecutive letters written backwards.

XW DC CB NM QP

← ← ← ← ←

Q should come before P in the series.

9. (*c*) : The difference between the letters is increased by one at each step.

B E I N T A I

+3 +4 +5 +6 +7 +8

T should be in place of S.

10. (*b*) : The difference between the letters is decreased by one at each step.

Z T O K H F

–6 –5 –4 –3 –2

O should be in place of P.

3. REPEAT SERIES

In this type of series, small letters of the alphabet are used to make a set of letters which are repeated. The candidate has to find the set of letters which will fit the blanks left in the given series in such a manner that one section of the series is further repeated in the same manner.

SOLVED EXAMPLE

1. Which of the following groups of letters will complete the given series?
ba-b-aab-a-b
(*a*) baab (*b*) abba (*c*) abaa (*d*) babb
Ans. (*b*) : The series is baab, baab, baab. Here the section 'baab' is repeated in the series.

***Solving steps* :** The candidate has to look for clues to solve such series pattern. 'aab' in the Series indicates that 'b' in this series is preceded by two 'a' so, the first blank and the last blank will be filled by 'a'. Now the first set is formed, *i.e.*, 'baab' in the beginning. This set is repeated, so the second and third blanks will have 'b' filling them. Now, solve the exercise given below to know the different ways in which these series are formed.

EXERCISE

Directions : *Which of the following groups of letters will complete the given series?*

1. ab---b-bbaa-
(*a*) babba (*b*) abaab
(*c*) abbab (*d*) baaab

2. aa-ab--aaa-a
(*a*) baaa (*b*) abab
(*c*) aaab (*d*) aabb

3. -baa-aab-a-a
(*a*) baab (*b*) abab
(*c*) aaba (*d*) aabb

4. -a cca-ccca-acccc-aaa
(*a*) ccaa (*b*) acca
(*c*) caac (*d*) caaa

5. c-bbb--abbbb-abbb-
(*a*) abccb (*b*) bacbb
(*c*) aabcb (*d*) abacb

6. ac-cab-baca-aba-acac
(*a*) bcbb (*b*) aacb
(*c*) babb (*d*) acbc

7. --aba--ba-ab
(*a*) abbab (*b*) bbaba
(*c*) baabb (*d*) abbba

8. --babbba-a--
(*a*) bbaba (*b*) babbb
(*c*) baaab (*d*) ababb

9. k-mk-lmkkl-kk-mk
(*a*) lklm (*b*) lkmk
(*c*) lkmm (*d*) lkml

10. abc-d-bc-d-b-dd
(*a*) decdb (*b*) dadac
(*c*) cdabe (*d*) bacde

11. b-abbc-bbca-bcabb-ab
(*a*) acba (*b*) acaa
(*c*) cacc (*d*) cabc

12. aca-ac--a-ac
(*a*) babc (*b*) aaac
(*c*) cacc (*d*) caca

13. ba-cb-b-bab-?
(*a*) acbb (*b*) bcaa
(*c*) cabb (*d*) bacc

14. ab-aa-caab-aab-a
(*a*) bcbc (*b*) bbca
(*c*) cbcc (*d*) caba

15. -bbcaa-bcaa-bc-a-bca
(*a*) bacab (*b*) abbab
(*c*) abcba (*d*) bcaab

16. a-bccb-ca-cca-baab-c
(*a*) accab (*b*) abcaa
(*c*) bacaa (*d*) ababc

17. b-dabbcd-b-c-ab
(*a*) cabd (*b*) bcad
(*c*) dcba (*d*) acbd

18. a-ba-caacb-bc-
(*a*) acbb (*b*) cbab
(*c*) cbaa (*d*) cbba

19. c-baa-aca-cacab-acac-bca
(*a*) acbaa (*b*) cbaac
(*c*) bccab (*d*) bbcaa

20. -bcc-ac-aabb-ab-cc
(*a*) bacab (*b*) abaca
(*c*) aabca (*d*) bcaca

21. ab-ccca-bccc-bbcc-
(*a*) abbc (*b*) bbac
(*c*) bbca (*d*) cabc

22. -cbc-a-bcaac-ca
(*a*) aaba (*b*) caab
(*c*) bcab (*d*) aacb

23. ab-ba--ba-
(*a*) abba (*b*) baab
(*c*) baba (*d*) abab

24. yx-yx-yxz-xzy-zyxz
(*a*) zzyx (*b*) xxzy
(*c*) yyzx (*d*) yzxz

25. xxxy-y-xxy-yxx-
(*a*) xyxy (*b*) yxyx
(*c*) yyxx (*d*) xxyy

EXPLANATORY ANSWERS

1. (*d*) : The series is abbaab, abbaab.
2. (*c*) : The series is aaaaba, aaaaba.
3. (*b*) : The series is aba, aba, aba, aba.
4. (*d*) : The series is c,a,cc,aa, ccc, aaa, cccc, aaaa.
5. (*a*) : The series is cabbbb, cabbbb, cabbbb.
6. (*b*) : The series is acac, abab, acac, abab, acac.
7. (*a*) : The series is ab, ab, ab, ab, ab, ab.
8. (*b*) : The series is bababb, bababb.
9. (*d*) : The series is klmk, klmk, klmk, klmk.
10. (*b*) : The series is abcdd, abcdd, abcdd.
11. (*d*) : The series is bcab, bcab, bcab, bcab, bcab.
12. (*c*) : The series is ac, ac, ac, ac, ac, ac.
13. (*d*) : The series is babc, babc, babc.
14. (*c*) : The series is abca, abca, abca, abca.
15. (*b*) : The series is abbca, abbca, abbca, abbca.
16. (*d*) : The series is aabcc, bbcaa, ccabb, aabcc.
17. (*a*) : The series is bcdab, bcdab, bcdab.
18. (*c*) : The series is acbabca, acbabca.
19. (*a*) : The series is cabaac, acabca, cabaac, acabca.
20. (*a*) : The series is bbccaa, ccaabb, aabbcc.
21. (*b*) : The series is abbccc abbccc.
22. (*d*) : The series is acbca acbca acbca.
23. (*d*) : The series is ab ab ab ab ab.
24. (*a*) : The series is yxz yxz yxz yxz yxz yxz.
25. (*b*) : The series is xxx yyy xxx yyy xxx.

4. NUMBER SERIES

In this type of series, the set of given numbers in a series are related to one another in a particular pattern or manner. The relationship between the numbers may be (i) consecutive odd/even numbers; (ii) consecutive prime numbers; (iii) squares/cubes of some numbers with/without variation of addition or subtraction of some number; (iv) sum/product/difference of preceding numbers; (v) addition/subtraction/multiplication/division by some number; and (vi) many more combinations of the relationships given above.

EXERCISE

Directions : *In the following questions, select the number(s) from the given options for completing the given series.*

1. 7776, 1296, 216, 36, 6, ?
(*a*) 6 (*b*) 0
(*c*) 3 (*d*) 1

2. 29282, 2662, 242, 22, ?
(*a*) 1 (*b*) 2
(*c*) 0 (*d*) 11

3. 1, 2, 2, 4, 16, ?, 65536
(*a*) 276 (*b*) 64
(*c*) 256 (*d*) 198

4. 3, 5, 9, 15, 23, ?, 45
(*a*) 37 (*b*) 35
(*c*) 31 (*d*) 33

5. 7, 21, 35, 49, 63, ?
(*a*) 70 (*b*) 77
(*c*) 81 (*d*) 108

6. 10, 14, 23, 39, 64, ?, 149
(*a*) 78 (*b*) 128
(*c*) 103 (*d*) 100

7. 6, 24, 29, 116, 121, ?, 489
(*a*) 468 (*b*) 484
(*c*) 243 (*d*) 363

8. 5, 50, 45, 450, 445, ?, 4445
(*a*) 4450 (*b*) 4600
(*c*) 4550 (*d*) 4500

9. 6.25, 9, 12.25, 16, 20.25, 25, 30.25?
(*a*) 36 (*b*) 32
(*c*) 28.25 (*d*) 40.25

10. 243, 5, 81, 15, 27, 45, 9, ?
(*a*) 5 (*b*) 15
(*c*) 135 (*d*) 27

11. 2, 7, 14, 23, ?, 47
(*a*) 31 (*b*) 38
(*c*) 28 (*d*) 34

12. 0, 1, 8, 27, 64, ?
(*a*) 125 (*b*) 128
(*c*) 256 (*d*) 121

13. 37, 47, 58, ?, 79, 95
(*a*) 71 (*b*) 69
(*c*) 68 (*d*) 67

14. 4, –8, 14, –22, 32, ?
(*a*) –44 (*b*) 42
(*c*) –42 (*d*) 44

15. 6, 7, 9, 11, 15, 15, 24, 19, ?
(*a*) 32 (*b*) 34
(*c*) 36 (*d*) 37

EXPLANATORY ANSWERS

1. (*d*) : The numbers in this sequence are divided by 6 each time.

2. (*b*) : The numbers in the series are divided by 11 at each step.

3. (*c*) : The number in the series is product of all the numbers preceding it.

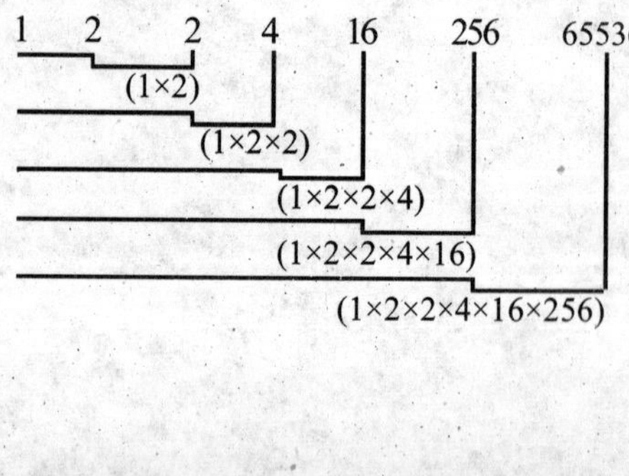

4. *(d)* : The difference between consecutive numbers increases by 2 at each step.

3 5 9 15 23 33 45

+2 +4 +6 +8 +10 +12

5. *(b)* : The series is multiplication of 7 by odd numbers starting from 3.

7 21 35 49 63 77

× 3

× 5

× 7

× 9

× 11

6. *(d)* : The number plus the square of numbers in natural order starting from 2 gives the next number in the series.

10 14 23 39 64 100 149

$+2^2$ $+3^2$ $+4^2$ $+5^2$ $+6^2$ $+7^2$

7. *(b)* : The sequence in the series is ×4, +5, which is repeated.

8. *(a)* : The sequence in the series is ×10, –5, which is repeated.

9. *(a)* : There are two alternate series :

+6 +8 +10

6.25 9 12.25 16 20.25 25 30.25 36

+7 +9 +11

Series I : 6.25, 12.25, 20.25, 30.25 (sequence is +6, +8, +10)

Series II : 9, 16, 25, 36 (sequence is +7, +9, +11)

10. *(c)* : There are two alternate series :

÷3 ÷3 ÷3

243 5 81 15 27 45 9 135

×3 ×3 ×3

Series I : 243, 81, 27, 9 (division by 3)

Series II : 5, 15, 45, 135 (multiplication by 3)

11. *(d)* : The difference between two consecutive numbers is increasing by 2 starting from 5.

2 7 14 23 34 47

+5 +7 +9 +11 +13

12. *(a)* : The numbers are cubes of numbers in natural order.

13. *(a)* : The sum of the digits of the number is added to the number to obtain the next number in the series.

37 47 58 71 79 95

+(3+7) +(4+7) +(5+8) +(7+1) +(7+9)

14. *(a)* : Alternate numbers are marked positive and negative, but the difference between their magnitude increases by 2 at each step.

4 – 8 14 – 22 32 – 44

4 6 8 10 12

15. *(c)* : There are two alternate series :

+3 +6 +9 +12

6 7 9 11 15 15 24 19 36

+4 +4 +4

Series I: 6, 9, 15, 24, 36 (sequence is +3, +6, +9, +12)

Series II : 7, 11, 15, 19 (addition of 4 at each step)

5. WRONG NUMBER SERIES

In this type of series, the given series may be complete but what needs to be identified is the number in the given completed series which is disturbing the sequential pattern of that series and does not fit in with the relationship shared between the other numbers.

EXERCISE

Directions : *In the given series find the number which is wrong.*

1. 5, 25, 120, 625, 3125, 15625
(*a*) 15625 (*b*) 625
(*c*) 120 (*d*) 5

2. 4, 8, 11, 22, 18, 36, 24, 50
(*a*) 8 (*b*) 22
(*c*) 36 (*d*) 24

3. 2, 4, 12, 24, 72, 142, 432
(*a*) 432 (*b*) 12
(*c*) 142 (*d*) 72

4. 2, 3, 4, 4, 6, 8, 9, 12, 16
(*a*) 3 (*b*) 9
(*c*) 6 (*d*) 12

5. 97, 91, 86, 83, 79, 77, 76, 76
(*a*) 86 (*b*) 76
(*c*) 91 (*d*) 83

6. 7, 11, 11, 9, 15, 7, 19, 5, 23, 1
(*a*) 5 (*b*) 7
(*c*) 1 (*d*) 9

7. 3, 7, 12, 28, 48, 118, 192, 448
(*a*) 12 (*b*) 118
(*c*) 28 (*d*) 7

8. 10, 100, 1100, 11000, 111000, 1210000
(*a*) 1210000 (*b*) 11000
(*c*) 100 (*d*) 111000

9. 24576, 6144, 1536, 386, 96, 24
(*a*) 386 (*b*) 6144
(*c*) 96 (*d*) 1536

10. 11, 13, 15, 17, 19, 23, 29, 31, 37
(*a*) 13 (*b*) 23
(*c*) 15 (*d*) 31

11. 36, 43, 49, 54, 60, 61, 63, 64
(*a*) 60 (*b*) 63
(*c*) 54 (*d*) 43

12. 3, 10, 41, 206, 1236, 8660
(*a*) 10 (*b*) 41
(*c*) 206 (*d*) 1236

13. 17, 25, 37, 50, 65, 82, 101
(*a*) 25 (*b*) 17
(*c*) 101 (*d*) 65

14. 12, 20, 38, 42, 56, 72
(*a*) 20 (*b*) 38
(*c*) 56 (*d*) 72

15. 5, 6, 11, 22, 42, 88, 176
(*a*) 5 (*b*) 42
(*c*) 176 (*d*) 11

EXPLANATORY ANSWERS

1. (*c*) : The numbers in the series are multiplied by 5 to get the next number.
∴ 125 should be in place of 120.

2. (*d*) : Two numbers form a pair. The first number increases by 7 for the next pair and the second number is the double of first number.

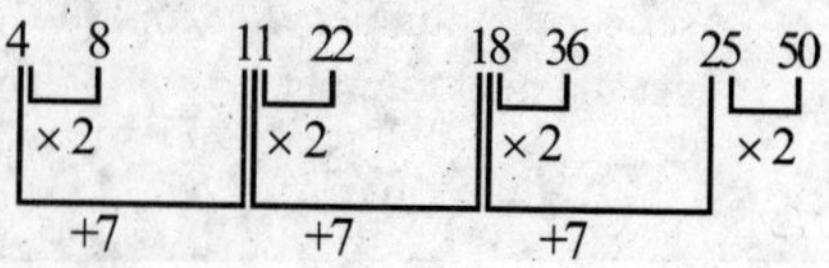

∴ 25 should be in place of 24.

3. (c) : There are two alternate series and in each series, the numbers are multiplied by 6 to get the next number.

×6 ×6 ×6

2 4 12 24 72 144 432

×6 ×6

$\therefore$ 144 should be in place of 142.

4. (b) : There are three alternate series and in each series, the numbers are multiplied by 2 to get the next number.

×2 ×2

2 3 4 4 6 8 8 12 16

×2 ×2

×2 ×2

Series I : 2, 4, 8 *Series II* : 3, 6, 12

Series III : 4, 8, 16

$\therefore$ 8 should be in place of 9.

5. (d) : The difference between the consecutive numbers in the series decreases by 1 at each step.

97 91 86 82 79 77 76 76

−6 −5 −4 −3 −2 −1 −0

$\therefore$ 82 should be in place of 83.

6. (c) : There are two alternate series :

+4 +4 +4 +4

7 11 11 9 15 7 19 5 21 3

−2 −2 −2 −2

Series I : 7, 11, 15, 19, 23 (addition of 4)

Series II : 11, 9, 7, 5, 3 (subtraction of 2)

$\therefore$ 3 should be in place of 1.

7. (b) : There are two alternate series and in each series, the numbers are multiplied by 4 to get the next number.

×4 ×4 ×4

3 7 12 28 48 112 192 448

×4 ×4 ×4

$\therefore$ 112 should be in place of 118.

8. (d) : The numbers in this series are multiplied by 10 and 11 alternately is, *i.e.*, × 10, × 11.

10 100 1100 11000 121000 1210000

×10 ×11 ×10 ×11 ×10

$\therefore$ 121000 should be in place of 111000.

9. (a) : The numbers in this series are divided by 4 to get the next number.

24576 6144 1536 384 96 24

÷4 ÷4 ÷4 ÷4 ÷4

$\therefore$ 384 should be in place of 386.

10. (c) : The series comprises of prime numbers in increasing order. Only 15 is an exception.

11. (a) : The difference between two consecutive numbers is decreasing by 1 at each step.

36 43 49 54 58 61 63 64

+7 +6 +5 +4 +3 +2 +1

$\therefore$ 58 should be in place of 60.

12. (d) : The sequence followed in this series is :

$3 \times 3 + 1 = 10$, $10 \times 4 + 1 = 41$

$41 \times 5 + 1 = 206$, $206 \times 6 + 1 = 1237$; and

$1237 \times 7 + 1 = 8660$

$\therefore$ 1237 should be in place of 1236.

13. (a) : The numbers in the series are 1 plus the squares of numbers in natural order starting from 4.

17 26 37 50 65 82 101

↓ ↓ ↓ ↓ ↓ ↓ ↓

4^2+1 5^2+1 6^2+1 7^2+1 8^2+1 9^2+1 10^2+1

$\therefore$ 26 should be in place of 25.

14. (b) : The sequence followed in this series is :

$3 \times 4 = 12$, $4 \times 5 = 20$, $5 \times 6 = 30$,

$6 \times 7 = 42$, $7 \times 8 = 56$, $8 \times 9 = 72$

$\therefore$ 30 should be in place of 38.

15. (b) : The numbers in the series are the sum of all the numbers preceding them.

5 6 11 22 44 88 176

(5+6)

(5+6+11)

(5+6+11+22)

(5+6+11+22+44)

(5+6+11+22+44+88)

$\therefore$ 44 should be in place of 42.

6. WORD ANALOGY

In Analogy Tests, the relationship between two given words is established and then applied to the other words. The type of relationship may vary, so while attempting such questions the first step is to identify the type of relationship, which can be any one of the following.

EXERCISE

Directions : *In the questions given below one term is missing. Based on the relationship of the two given words find the missing term from the given options.*

1. HUNGER : FOOD : : THIRST : ?
(*a*) Water (*b*) Drink
(*c*) Tea (*d*) Coffee

2. HUNTER : GUN : : WRITER : ?
(*a*) Book (*b*) Pen
(*c*) Poem (*d*) Page

3. WOOL : SHEEP : : SILK : ?
(*a*) Saree (*b*) String
(*c*) Silkworm (*d*) Moth

4. FOOD : STOMACH : : FUEL : ?
(*a*) Engine (*b*) Automobile
(*c*) Rail (*d*) Aeroplane

5. WATER : SAND : : OCEAN : ?
(*a*) Island (*b*) River
(*c*) Desert (*d*) Waves

6. ADULT : BABY : : FLOWER : ?
(*a*) Seed (*b*) Bud
(*c*) Fruit (*d*) Butterfly

7. WRITER : READER : : PRODUCER : ?
(*a*) Creator (*b*) Contractor
(*c*) Creature (*d*) Consumer

8. ENTRANCE : EXIT : : LOYALTY : ?
(*a*) Treachery (*b*) Patriotism
(*c*) Fidelity (*d*) Reward

9. MOTHER : MATERNAL : : FATHER : ?
(*a*) Eternal (*b*) Detrimental
(*c*) Paternal (*d*) Formidable

10. PEARL : NECKLACE : : FLOWER : ?
(*a*) Plant (*b*) Garden
(*c*) Petal (*d*) Bouquet

11. ALPHABET : WORD : : WORD : ?
(*a*) Sound (*b*) Music
(*c*) Sentence (*d*) Dictionary

12. LIFE : DEATH : : HOPE : ?
(*a*) Cry (*b*) Pain
(*c*) Despair (*d*) Sad

13. GOOD : BAD : : VIRTUE : ?
(*a*) Blame (*b*) Sin
(*c*) Despair (*d*) Vice

14. BIRD : FLY : : SNAKE : ?
(*a*) Timid (*b*) Clatter
(*c*) Crawl (*d*) Hole

15. CAT : MOUSE : : BIRD : ?
(*a*) Cage (*b*) Trap
(*c*) Eagle (*d*) Worm

16. STATE : EXILE
(*a*) Police : Arrest
(*b*) Judge : Convict
(*c*) Constitution : Amendment
(*d*) Church : Excommunicate

17. CAPRICIOUSNESS : RELIABILITY
(*a*) Extemporaneous : Predictability
(*b*) Unreliable : Inhuman
(*c*) Tenacious : Practicality
(*d*) Arbitrary : Whimsical

18. LOATH : COERCION
(*a*) Detest : Caressing
(*b*) Irritate : Caressing
(*c*) Irate : Antagonism
(*d*) Reluctant : Persuasion

19. SCALES : FISH
(*a*) Lady : Dress (*b*) Tree : Leaves
(*c*) Bird : Feather (*d*) Skin : Man

20. TREE : SAPLING
(*a*) Hut : Mansion
(*b*) Giant : Dwarf
(*c*) Horse : Foal
(*d*) Ant : Elephant

21. CHALK : BLACKBOARD
(*a*) Door : Handle
(*b*) Table : Chair
(*c*) Ink : Paper
(*d*) Type : Paint

22. PRIMEVAL : MEDIEVAL
(*a*) Dinosaur : Dragon
(*b*) Gorilla : Soldier
(*c*) Evolution : Revelation
(*d*) Thorn : Rose

23. TRILOGY : NOVEL
(*a*) Rice : Husk
(*b*) Milk : Cream
(*c*) Fabric : Weaving
(*d*) Serial : Episode

24. PEDANT : ERUDITION
(*a*) Prude : Modesty
(*b*) Blunt : Politician
(*c*) Diplomats : Tactless
(*d*) Enemy : Friendly

25. FURY : IRE
(*a*) Convulsion : Spasm
(*b*) Amusement : Happiness
(*c*) Joke : Laugh
(*d*) Dispassion : Emotion

EXPLANATORY ANSWERS

1. *(a)* : Hunger is satiated by food, thirst by water.

2. *(b)* : Weapon of a hunter is a gun, weapon of a writer is a pen.

3. *(c)* : Wool is obtained from sheep, silk is obtained from silkworm.

4. *(a)* : Food is consumed in stomach, fuel is consumed in engine.

5. *(c)* : The related words are near opposites.

6. *(b)* : The youngone of an adult is a baby and that of a flower is a bud.

7. *(d)* : A writer aims to please the readers by his writings, a producer aims to please the consumers by his products.

8. *(a)* : The related words are opposites.

9. *(c)* : Relations on the mother's side are maternal and on the father's side paternal.

10. *(d)* : Many pearls make a necklace, many flowers make a bouquet.

11. *(c)* : More than one alphabet make a word, more than one word make a sentence.

12. *(c)* : The related words are opposites.

13. *(d)* : The related words are opposites.

14. *(c)* : Birds fly, snakes crawl.

15. *(d)* : Cat chases the mouse, bird chases the worm.

16. *(d)* : Punishment of leaving the State is exile, punishment of leaving the Church is excommunication.

17. *(c)* : The related words are antonyms.

18. *(d)* : Loathing is the result of constant coersion, reluctance is the result of constant persuasion.

19. *(d)* : Covering of the fish is scales, covering of man is skin.

20. *(c)* : Young tree is a sapling, young horse is a foal.

21. *(c)* : Chalk is used to write on blackboard, ink is used to write on paper.

22. *(a)* : The related words represent almost the same time period and answer option represents almost the same sized creatures.

23. *(d)* : Trilogy is section of a novel, episode is a section of a serial.

24. *(a)* : The related words are synonyms.

25. *(b)* : Fury causes ire, amusement causes happiness.

7. NUMBER ANALOGY

In number analogy also, the relationship between the given numbers is detected and then applied to the second part to find the missing numbers. This relationship between the numbers can be based on any of the following patterns : *(i)* numbers can be odd/even/prime numbers; *(ii)* numbers can be multiples of one number; *(iii)* numbers can be squares/cubes of different numbers; *(iv)* some numbers can be added to/ subtracted from/multiplied to/divided into the first number to get the second number; *(v)* the second number can be the sum/product/difference of the digits of first number; and *(vi)* combinations of any mathematical calculations given above can apply to the relationship between the two given numbers.

EXERCISE

Directions : *In the following questions, select the number from the given options which follows the same relationship as shared between the first two numbers.*

1. 1 : 11 : : 2 : ?

(*a*) 20 (*b*) 22
(*c*) 24 (*d*) 44

2. $\frac{1}{7} : \frac{1}{14} :: \frac{1}{9} : ?$

(*a*) $\frac{1}{88}$ (*b*) $\frac{1}{80}$
(*c*) $\frac{1}{81}$ (*d*) $\frac{1}{18}$

3. 0.16 : 0.0016 : : 1.02 : ?

(*a*) 10.20 (*b*) 0.102
(*c*) 0.0102 (*d*) 1.020

4. 663 : 884 : : 221 : ?

(*a*) 332 (*b*) 554
(*c*) 773 (*d*) 442

5. 16 : 0.16 : : ?

(*a*) 2 : 0.02 (*b*) 7 : 0.007
(*c*) 1.3 : 0.13 (*d*) 0.01 : 0.001

6. $3 : \frac{1}{3} :: ?$

(*a*) 6 : 12 (*b*) 5 : 2/15
(*c*) 8 : 1/8 (*d*) 9 : 27

7. 65 : 13 : : 180 : ?

(*a*) 93 (*b*) 36
(*c*) 133 (*d*) 102

8. 125 : 27 : : 343 : ?

(*a*) 729 (*b*) 64
(*c*) 216 (*d*) 512

9. 357 : 73 : : ?

(*a*) 429 : 94
(*b*) 201 : 21
(*c*) 138 : 38
(*d*) 93 : 39

10. 731 : 902 : : 655 : ?

(*a*) 646 (*b*) 800
(*c*) 793 (*d*) 556

11. 162 : 9 : : 310 : ?

(*a*) 33 (*b*) 27
(*c*) 16 (*d*) 4

12. 13 : 17 : : 15 : ?

(*a*) 19 (*b*) 11
(*c*) 21 (*d*) 16

13. 225 : 15 : : 256 : ?

(*a*) 26 (*b*) 16
(*c*) 20 (*d*) 28

14. 46 : 48 : : 54 : ?

(*a*) 59 (*b*) 40
(*c*) 67 (*d*) 62

15. 33 : 36 : : 21 : ?

(*a*) 9 (*b*) 18
(*c*) 25 (*d*) 32

EXPLANATORY ANSWERS

1. (b) : The first number is repeated to obtain the second number.

2. (d) : The first fraction is multiplied by half to obtain the second fraction.

$\frac{1}{7} : \frac{1}{14} :: \frac{1}{9} : \frac{1}{18}$ ($\times\frac{1}{2}$, $\times\frac{1}{2}$)

3. (c) : The decimals are divided by 100.

0.16 : 0.0016 :: 1.02 : 0.0102 ($\div 100$, $\div 100$)

4. (d) : The digits at tens and hundreds place is same but the digit at the units place is half the other identical digits.

663 : 884 :: 221 : 442

5. (a) : Of the two related numbers, the second number is the result of first number divided by 100.

16 : 0.16 :: 2 : 0.02 ($\div 100$, $\div 100$)

6. (c) : Of the two related numbers, the second number is the part fraction of the first number, *i.e.* 3 is related to one-third $\left(\frac{1}{3}\right)$. Similarly, 8 will be related to one-eighth $\left(\frac{1}{8}\right)$.

7. (b) : The first number is divided by 5 to get the second number.

65 : 13 :: 180 : 36 ($\div 5$, $\div 5$)

8. (a) : The numbers are cubes of different odd numbers.

125 : 27 :: 343 : 729

5^3 3^3 7^3 9^3

9. (a) : The central digit of the first number is left out and the corner digits written in reverse order to get the second number.

357 : 73 :: 429 : 94

10. (a) : The sum of the digits of both the numbers is same.

$731 : 902 \rightarrow 7+3+1$

$= 9+0+2$ *i.e.* $11 = 11$

$655 : 646 \rightarrow 6+5+5$

$= 6+4+6$ *i.e.* $16 = 16$

11. (d) : The sum of the digits of the first number is the second number.

162 : 9 :: 310 : 4 ($1+6+2$, $3+1+0$)

12. (a) : First number plus 4 gives the second number.

13 : 17 :: 15 : 19 ($+4$, $+4$)

13. (b) : The root of first number is the second number.

225 : 15 :: 256 : 16 ($\sqrt{225}$, $\sqrt{256}$)

14. (b) : The product of the digits of first number is multiplied by 2 to get the second number.

46 : 48 :: 54 : 40 ($(4\times6)\,2$, $(5\times4)\,2$)

15. (a) : The square of the sum of the digits of the first number is the second number.

33 : 36 :: 21 : 9 ($(3+3)^2$, $(2+1)^2$)

8. ODD ONE OUT

In this type of classification, four words are given out of which three are almost same in matter or meaning and only one word is different from the common three. One has to find out the word which is different from the rest.

EXERCISE

Directions : *In each of the following questions, three words are alike in some manner. Spot the odd one out.*

1. (*a*) Green (*b*) Red (*c*) Colour (*d*) Orange

2. (*a*) Stable (*b*) Hole (*c*) Canoe (*d*) Sty

3. (*a*) Nose (*b*) Eyes (*c*) Skin (*d*) Teeth

4. (*a*) Venus (*b*) Moon (*c*) Pluto (*d*) Mars

5. (*a*) Happy (*b*) Gloomy (*c*) Lively (*d*) Cheerful

Directions : *Three of the following four in each question are alike in a certain way and so form a group. Select the group of letters that does not belong to that group.*

6. (*a*) ACE (*b*) LOR (*c*) GIK (*d*) VXZ

7. (*a*) TSR (*b*) LKJ (*c*) PQO (*d*) HGF

8. (*a*) EF LM (*b*) KJ SR (*c*) XW HG (*d*) ED YX

9. (*a*) JOPK (*b*) BOPC (*c*) QOPR (*d*) TOPS

10. (*a*) DfH (*b*) MoQ (*c*) UwY (*d*) lnO

Directions : *In each of the following questions, there are four options. Three numbers, in these options, are alike in certain manner. Only one number does not fit in. Choose the one which is different from the rest.*

11. (*a*) 1948 (*b*) 2401 (*c*) 966 (*d*) 1449

12. (*a*) 182 (*b*) 169 (*c*) 130 (*d*) 158

13. (*a*) 129 (*b*) 130 (*c*) 131 (*d*) 132

14. (*a*) 3215 (*b*) 9309 (*c*) 4721 (*d*) 2850

15. (*a*) 1776 (*b*) 2364 (*c*) 1976 (*d*) 3776

Directions : *In the following questions select the pair which is different from the other three.*

16. (*a*) Chair - Furniture
(*b*) Shirt - Garment
(*c*) Necklace - Jewellery
(*d*) Bogie - Engine

17. (*a*) Crayon - Paper
(*b*) Pencil - Lead
(*c*) Pen - Ink
(*d*) Brush - Paint

18. (*a*) War - Peace
(*b*) Real - Natural
(*c*) Premiere - First
(*d*) Wrath - Anger

19. (*a*) Finger - Thimble
(*b*) Head - Cap
(*c*) Waist - Tiara
(*d*) Foot - Shoe

20. (*a*) Day - Night
(*b*) Clever - Foolish
(*c*) Clear - Blurred
(*d*) Arrive - Come

Directions : *In the following questions, which of the following pair of letters is different from the other three?*

21. (*a*) FGH - HIJ (*b*) PQR - RST (*c*) MNO - OPQ (*d*) CDE - DEF

22. (*a*) JuM - jUm (*b*) iLo - Ilo (*c*) PSa - psA (*d*) ZeX - zEx

23. (*a*) NQT - JMP (*b*) CFI - RUX (*c*) ADG - FGH (*d*) SVY - ORU

24. (*a*) DXD - XDX (*b*) KUK - UKU (*c*) FHF - EHE (*d*) RSR - SRS

25. (*a*) AYT - BZU (*b*) FNG - EMF (*c*) RWO - QVN (*d*) HJD - GIC

EXPLANATORY ANSWERS

1. (*c*) : All others are types of colour.

2. (*c*) : Canoe is a boat. Others are resting places of birds/animals.

3. (*d*) : All others are sense organs.

4. (*b*) : All others are planets.

5. (*b*) : All others are expressions of joy.

6. (*b*) : The sequence in each group is +2. Only option (*b*) has sequence in +3, *i.e.*,

ABCDE: +2 +2 ; LMNOPQR: +3 +3
GHIJK: +2 +2 ; VWXYZ: +2 +2

7. (*c*) : The sequence of alphabet in each group is in reverse order. Only option (*c*) has sequence in disturbed order.

8. (*a*) : Two consecutive alphabet in each group are in reverse sequence (–1), *i.e.*,

KJ SR; XW HG; ED YX
–1 –1 –1 –1 –1 –1

Only in option (*a*) the sequence is in natural order (+1), *i.e.*,

E F: +1 ; L M: +1

9. (*d*) : In each group, letters 'OP' are common. The two corner alphabet are in natural order (+1); *i.e.*,

JOPK ; BOPC ; QOPR
+1 +1 +1

Only in option (*d*) they are in reverse order (–1); *i.e.*,

TOPS
–1

10. (*d*) : In other groups, only the alphabet in the centre is of lower case. In this option letter 'L' on the left is also in lower case.

11. (*a*) : Other numbers are divisible by 7.

12. (*d*) : Other numbers are multiples of 13.

13. (*c*) : 131 is a prime number.

14. (*b*) : In other numbers, no digit is repeated.

15. (*b*) : In other numbers, the last two digits are same.

16. (*d*) : Bogie is a part of train which is a type of conveyance. Chair, Shirt and Necklace are types of furniture, garment and jewellery respectively.

17. (*a*) : The medium used for writing with pencil is lead, with pen it is ink and with brush, it is paint. With crayon it should be wax.

18. (*a*) : The pair of words are opposite. Other pairs are synonyms.

19. (*c*) : Tiara is worn on the head.

20. (*d*) : Other words are opposite to each other.

21. (*d*) : In all other groups, the letters are in natural series and the last letter of first part is the first letter of the second part.

22. (*b*) : In all other groups, only the vowel is in lower case in the first part and in second part the case is reversed.

23. (*c*) : In all other groups, the letters jump two letters in between them.

24. (*c*) : In all other groups, the single letter in first part is repeated in the second and vice versa.

25. (*a*) : In all other groups, the letters in the first part are one step forward than the corresponding letters in the second part.

9. CODING AND DECODING

Coding is a secretive language which is used to change the representation of the actual term/word/value. This coded language can be framed by *(i)* moving the letters one or more steps forward or backward; *(ii)* substituting numbers for letters and vice–versa; *(iii)* writing the letters of the given word in reverse order in part or in whole; and *(iv)* replacing the letters in their natural series by the same positioned letters in their reverse series.

There is variety in ways of coding. Coding language is not only for words and numbers but also for hiding a group of words, statements or even sentences. This form of coding pattern may appear to be confusing but after solving only a few questions it is very easy to understand. Questions based on this coding pattern require no moving of steps or straining efforts of calculations, but only quick tallying or comparing ability. The codes can be letters or numbers.

EXERCISE

Directions : *In the following questions select the right option which indicates the correct code for the word or letter given in the question.*

1. If MUSK is coded as 146816, then ZERO will be coded as :

(*a*) 113811 (*b*) 122912
(*c*) 15915 (*d*) 2651815

2. If BAD is coded as 7, HIS as 9, LOW will be coded as :

(*a*) 50 (*b*) 8
(*c*) 23 (*d*) 5

3. In a certain code LIBERATE is written as 56403170, TRIBAL will be written in the same code as :

(*a*) 734615 (*b*) 736415
(*c*) 136475 (*d*) 034615

4. In certain military code, SYSTEM is written as SYSMET, and NEARER as AENRER, what will be the code for FRACTION?

(*a*) CRAFNOIT (*b*) FRCAITNO
(*c*) CARFNOIT (*d*) FRACNOIT

5. If CRUDE is written as BSTED, then MOIST will be coded as :

(*a*) NNJRU (*b*) LNHRS
(*c*) NPJTU (*d*) LPHTS

6. In a certain code ALPACA is written as ACAPLA. How will ANIMAL be written in that code?

(*a*) LAMINA (*b*) ALAMIN
(*c*) LAMNIA (*d*) AAMLIN

7. In a certain code FINGER is written as DGLECP. What will be the code for KIDNEY?

(*a*) IGBLCW (*b*) IGCLBW
(*c*) IBCGLE (*d*) IGBKCV

8. In a certain code QUESTION is written as NXBVQLLQ. How will REPLY be coded?

(*a*) YHMOV (*b*) OBMVI
(*c*) VHSOB (*d*) OHMOV

9. If in a certain code SKEW is coded as PNCY, then what will JXQV will stand for?

(*a*) MUTS (*b*) MUST
(*c*) MTSU (*d*) STUM

10. In a certain code LONDON is written as MPOEPO. What will IVOHSZ mean in the same code?

(*a*) HUNGRY (*b*) HUNDRY
(*c*) GRUNHY (*d*) HONDUS

11. In a certain code language 8514 is a code for HEAD, 3945 for RIDE and 057 for BEG. What will be the code for GRADE?

(*a*) 71345 (*b*) 73415
(*c*) 74135 (*d*) 73145

12. If MOTHERLAND is coded as 9501623748, how will DREAM be coded?
(*a*) 82697 (*b*) 86297
(*c*) 82769 (*d*) 82679

13. If OATH is coded in a certain language as TEYL, then how will WORD be coded?
(*a*) BWRH (*b*) HRWB
(*c*) BSWH (*d*) CSXI

14. If FINANCE is coded as GKQESIL, then how will BANK be coded in the same manner?
(*a*) CBOL (*b*) CDRP
(*c*) CCQO (*d*) CCPN

15. PLANNING is coded in a certain language as UFFHSCSA. How will AUTHORITY be coded in the same language?
(*a*) FOYBTLNND
(*b*) FYOTBNNLT
(*c*) FBOYTLNTN
(*d*) FBOYTNLTN

EXPLANATORY ANSWERS

1. (*b*) : The coded number signifies the position of the alphabet in its reverse order of the alphabetical series (ZYXW...)

M U S K → MUSK
↓ ↓ ↓ ↓
14th 6th 8th 16th → 146816

Similarly,

Z E R O → ZERO
↓ ↓ ↓ ↓
1st 22nd 9th 12th → 122912

2. (*d*) : The coded number is the sum of number digits signifying the position of the alphabet in the natural order.

B A D
↓ ↓ ↓
2nd 1st 4th *i.e.,* 2 + 1 + 4 = 7

Similarly,

H I S
↓ ↓ ↓
8th 9th 19th *i.e.,* 8 + 9 + 19 = 36
further, 3 + 6 = 9

Also,

L O W
↓ ↓ ↓
12th 15th 23rd *i.e.,* 12 + 15 + 23 = 50
further, 5 + 0 = 0

3. (*b*) : The letters of the word TRIBAL are picked from LIBERATE. So will be the coded numbers.

L I B E R A T E → given word
5 6 4 0 3 1 7 0 → codes

Similarly,

T R I B A L → word to be coded
7 3 6 4 1 5 → answer codes

4. (*c*) : The word is divided into two equal parts and the letters of each part are written in reverse order.

Similarly,

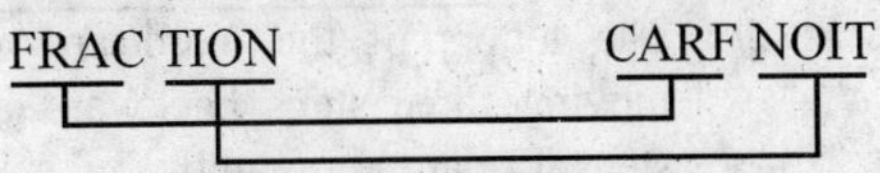

5. (*d*) : The code is formed by moving the letters one step backwards and one step forward alternately.

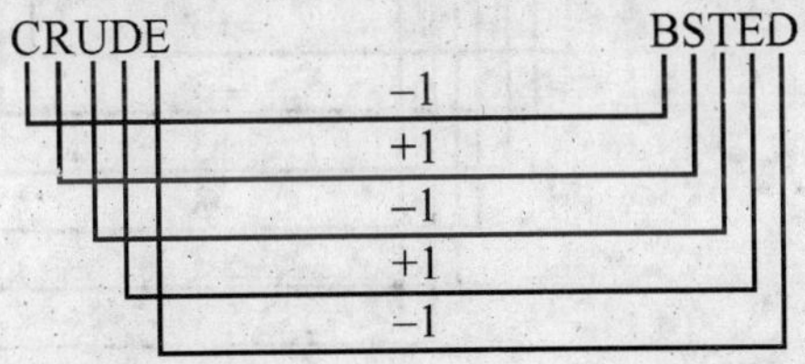

Similarly,

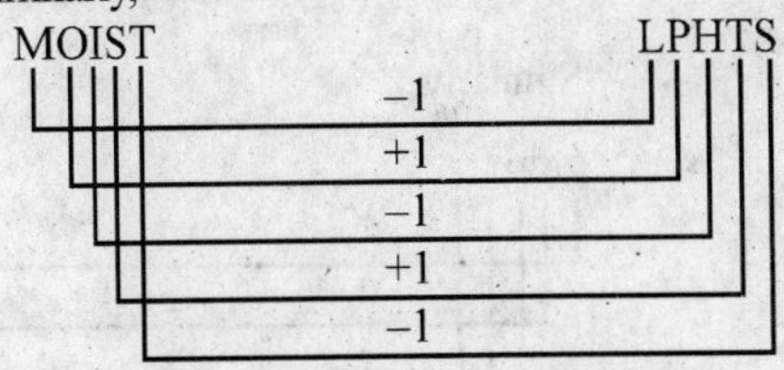

6. (*a*) : The letters of the word are written backwards.

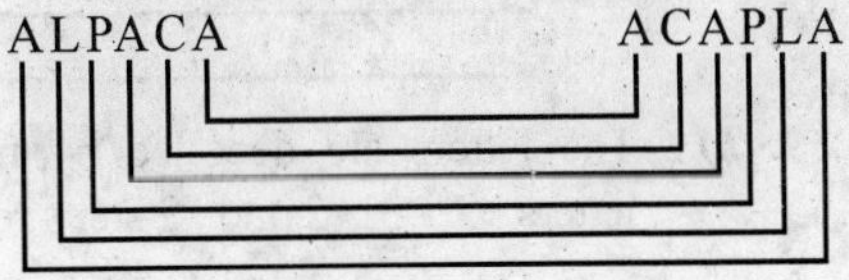

Similarly,

ANIMAL LAMINA

7. *(a)*: The word is coded by moving the letters two steps backwards.

FINGER DGLECP

–2
–2
–2
–2
–2
–2

Similarly,

KIDNEY IGBLCW

–2
–2
–2
–2
–2
–2

8. *(d)*: The letters of the word are coded by moving three steps backward and three steps forward alternately.

QUESTION NXBVQLLQ

–3
+3
–3
+3
–3
+3
–3
+3

Similarly,

REPLY OHMOV

–3
+3
–3
+3
–3

9. *(b)*: The letters are decoded by moving the letters +3, –3, +2 and –2 steps respectively.

PNCY SKEW

+3
–3
+2
–2

Similarly,

JXQV MUST

+3
–3
+2
–2

10. *(a)*: The letters of the coded word are moved one step backward.

MPOEPO LONDON

–1
–1
–1
–1
–1
–1

Similarly,

I V O H S Z H U N G R Y

–1
–1
–1
–1
–1
–1

11. *(d)*: The word GRADE is framed by letters in the given words. So, in order to find the code for GRADE select the respective number codes.

H E A D R I D E B E G → letters
8 5 1 4 3 9 4 5 0 5 7 → codes

So,

G R A D E →letters
7 3 1 4 5 →answer codes

12. *(d)*: The letters of the word are coded by numbers. So to find the code for DREAM select the respective numbers.

M O T H E R L A N D → letters
9 5 0 1 6 2 3 7 4 8 → codes

So, D R E A M → letters
8 2 6 7 9 → answer codes

13. *(c)* : The letters are coded by moving five and four steps forward alternately.

OATH TEYL

+5
+4
+5
+4

Similarly,

WORD BSWH

+5
+4
+5
+4

14. *(c)* : The letters of the word are coded by moving one step ahead and increasing the difference by one.

FINANCE GKQESIL

+1
+2
+3
+4
+5
+6
+7

Similarly,

BANK CCQO

+1
+2
+3
+4

15. *(a)* : The letters of the word are coded by moving five steps forward and six steps backward alternately.

PLANNING UFFHSCSA

+5
–6
+5
–6
+5
–6
+5
–6

Similarly,

AUTHORITY FOYBTLNND

+5
–6
+5
–6
+5
–6
+5
–6
+5

10. STATEMENT ANALYSIS

In these type of questions, a few statements are given. Certain facts are broken up and mentioned in these statements. What is required is to analyse the statements, arrange and sort out the given facts and then answer the questions related to the given statements.

EXERCISE

1. Among five friends, A is heavier than B; C is lighter than D; B is lighter than D but heavier than E. Who among them is the heaviest?

(*a*) B (*b*) C
(*c*) A (*d*) Can't say

2. Pune is bigger than Jhansi, Sitapur is bigger than Chittor. Raigarh is not as big as Jhansi, but is bigger than Sitapur. Chittor is not as big as Sitapur. Which is the smallest?

(*a*) Jhansi (*b*) Pune
(*c*) Chittor (*d*) Sitapur

3. Ajay works more than Ram. Alok works as much as Raju. Pankaj works less than Alok. Ram works more than Alok. Who works the most of all?

(*a*) Ajay (*b*) Ram
(*c*) Alok (*d*) Raju

4. Among five friends P, Q, R, S and T, who is the youngest? To arrive at the answer which of the following information given in the statements (A) and (B) is sufficient?

(A) R is younger than P and T.
(B) S is younger than Q.

(*a*) Only A alone is sufficient
(*b*) Either A or B is sufficient
(*c*) Both A and B together are needed
(*d*) Both A and B together are not sufficient

5. A is elder to B while C and D are elder to E who lies between A and B. If C be elder to B, which one of the following statements is necessarily true?

(*a*) E is elder to B
(*b*) A is elder to C
(*c*) C is elder to D
(*d*) D is elder to C

6. Suresh is as much older than Kamal as he is younger than Prabodh. Navin is as old as Kamal. Which of the following statements is wrong?

(*a*) Suresh is older than Navin
(*b*) Kamal is younger than Suresh
(*c*) Prabodh is not the oldest
(*d*) Navin is younger than Prabodh

Directions (Qs. 7 to 9) : *Ram, Sohan and Mohan play football, hockey and cricket. Ram, Ramesh and Mohan play hockey, cricket and basketball. Ram, Sohan, Rahim and Mohan play football and cricket. Now answer the following questions based on the above statements :*

7. Which game is played by all the boys?

(*a*) Football (*b*) Hockey
(*c*) Cricket (*d*) Basketball

8. Which two boys play all the games?

(*a*) Ram, Sohan (*b*) Ram, Ramesh
(*c*) Sohan, Mohan (*d*) Ram, Mohan

9. Who does not play football?

(*a*) Ramesh (*b*) Sohan
(*c*) Rahim (*d*) Mohan

Directions (Qs. 10 to 12) : *Read the following directions and answer the questions given below :*

There are five persons in a group. Out of these two are men. Only three persons know swimming, of which one is a man. There is a couple, of which the husband knows swimming. A is the younger sister of D and B is the husband of E. C is a swimming champion.

10. Who is the other man in the group?
(*a*) C (*b*) B
(*c*) A (*d*) D

11. The two women who know how to swim are:
(*a*) A and C (*b*) C and D
(*c*) D and E (*d*) A and E

12. The two persons who do not know how to swim are :
(*a*) B and D (*b*) D and E
(*c*) A and E (*d*) A and D

Directions (Qs. 13 to 15) : *Read the following statements and answer the questions given below :*

Rajat, Sushil and Nagesh play football, hockey and cricket. Rajat, Ramu and Nagesh play hockey, cricket and basketball. Rajat, Sushil, Mayank and Nagesh play football and cricket.

13. Which game is played by all the boys?
(*a*) Hockey (*b*) Basketball
(*c*) Football (*d*) Cricket

14. Who does not play football?
(*a*) Rajat (*b*) Nagesh
(*c*) Sushil (*d*) Ramu

15. Which of the following two boys play all the games?
(*a*) Nagesh, Rajat (*b*) Mayank, Ramu
(*c*) Ramu, Nagesh (*d*) Sushil, Mayank

EXPLANATORY ANSWERS

1. (*d*) : The five friends in descending order of weight are : A/D, B/C, E or A/D, B, C/E. Either A or D is the heaviest.

2. (*c*) : The order of cities in descending order of size is : Pune, Jhansi, Raigarh, Sitapur, Chittor.

3. (*a*) : On the basis of doing work, the descending order will be : Ajay, Ram, Alok/Raju, Pankaj.

4. (*d*) : Statements are not inter-related.

5. (*a*) : The order in descending seniority will be : A/C/D, E, B.

6. (*c*) : On the basis of age the descending order will be : Prabodh, Suresh, Kamal/Navin.

Chart for Answers 7 to 9

Boy	*Games Played*
Ram	Football, Hocky, Cricket, Basketball
Sohan	Football, Hockey, Cricket
Mohan	Football, Hockey, Cricket, Basketball
Ramesh	Hockey, Cricket, Basketball
Rahim	Football, Cricket.

7. (*c*) **8. (*d*)** **9. (*a*)**

For Answers 10 to 12 the information chart will be :

A. Woman ((younger sister of D); knows swimming.

B. Man (husband of E); knows swimming

C. Woman; Swimming champion

D. Man (brother of A)

E. Woman (wife of B)

From the couple B & E, B (husband) knows swimming. C is a swimming champion. Three persons know how to swim of which only B is a man. So, the two women who know how to swim are C and A (the younger sister of D). There are two men in the group of five. One is B and the other will be D.

10. (*d*) **11. (*a*)** **12. (*b*)**

Chart for Answers 13 to 15

Boy	*Games Played*
Rajat	— Football, Hockey, Cricket, Basketball
Sushil	— Football, Hockey, Cricket, Basketball
Nagesh	— Football, Hockey, Cricket, Basketball
Ramu	— Hockey, Cricket, Basketball
Mayank	— Football, Cricket

13. (*d*) **14. (*d*)** **15. (*a*)**

11. PLACE ARRANGEMENT

Place arrangement generally refers to the positioning of persons or objects in a manner indicated by set of information given. One has to understand the order of placement and then attempt questions following the given information.

EXERCISE

Directions : *In the following questions, understand the arrangement pattern and then select the right answer from the given options :*

1. Five boys are sitting in a row. Raghu is not adjacent to Shyam or Amit. Ajay is not adjacent to Shyam. Raghu is adjacent to Mayank. If Mayank is at the middle in the row, then Ajay is adjacent to whom out of the following?

(*a*) Amit (*b*) Raghu
(*c*) Mayank (*d*) Shyam

2. Mini is to the right of Rajni but to the left of Ananta. Saya is to the right of Mini but to the left of Jaya. Who is on the extreme left if all the girls are facing North?

(*a*) Jaya (*b*) Mini
(*c*) Rajni (*d*) Saya

3. O, P, Q, R, S and T are standing on a bench according to their height. P is taller than O but shorter than S. Only S is taller than T. R is shorter than P but taller than Q. Who is the shortest?

(*a*) O (*b*) Q
(*c*) P (*d*) Cannot be said

4. Five personalities are living in a multistoried building. Mr. Effortless lives in a flat above Mr. Active, Mr. Charge lives in a flat below Mr. Diligent, Mr. Active lives in a flat above Mr. Diligent and Mr. Behaved lives in a flat below Mr. Charge. Who lives in the topmost flat?

(*a*) Mr. Charge (*b*) Mr. Diligent
(*c*) Mr. Effortless (*d*) Mr. Behaved

5. Six friends are sitting in a circle and playing cards. Kenny is to the left of Danny. Michael is in-between Bob and John. Roger is in between Kenny and Bob. Who is sitting to the right of Michael?

(*a*) Danny (*b*) John
(*c*) Kenny (*d*) Bob

6. Four girls A, B, C and D are sitting in a circle. B and C are facing each other. Which of the following is definitely true?

(*a*) A is to the left of C
(*b*) D is to the left of C
(*c*) A and D are facing each other
(*d*) A is not between B and C

7. Brijesh, Jayesh, Amar and Praveer are playing a game of cards. Amar is to the right of Jayesh who is to the right of Brijesh. Who is to the right of Amar?

(*a*) Brijesh
(*b*) Praveer
(*c*) Brijesh or Praveer
(*d*) Jayesh

8. In a pile of 10 books there are 3 of History, 3 of Hindi, 2 of Maths, and 2 of English. Taking from above there is an English book between a History and Maths book, a History book between a Maths and an English book, a Hindi book between an English and a Maths book, a Maths book between two Hindi books, and two Hindi books between a Maths and a History book. Book of which subject is at the sixth position from the top?

(*a*) English (*b*) Hindi
(*c*) History (*d*) Maths

9. Five persons A, B, C, D and E are sitting in a row facing you such that D is on the left of C and B is on the right of E. A is on the right of C and B is on the left of D. If E occupies a corner position, then who is sitting in the centre?

(*a*) A (*b*) B
(*c*) C (*d*) D

10. Six friends A, B, C, D, E and F are standing in a circle. B is between F and C; A is between E and D; F is to the left of D. Who is between A and F?

(*a*) C (*b*) B
(*c*) D (*d*) E

EXPLANATORY ANSWERS

1. *(b)* : The order of sitting is :
Amit, Shyam, Mayank, Ajay, Raghu
or
Ajay, Raghu, Mayank, Amit, Shyam

2. *(c)* : The order in which the girls are positioned is :
Rajni, Mini, Ananta, Saya, Jaya
or
Saya, Jaya, Ananta
or
Saya, Ananta, Jaya

3. *(d)* : In descending order of height, the standing positions are :

S		S
T		T
P	*or*	P
R		R
O		Q
Q		O

Either O or Q is the shortest. The informa-tion given is not enough to clarify the answer.

4. *(c)* : The personalities living in flats in multi-storied building are in order given below :
Mr. Effortless
Mr. Active
Mr. Diligent
Mr. Charge
Mr. Behaved

5. *(d)* : The order in which the friends are sitting is :

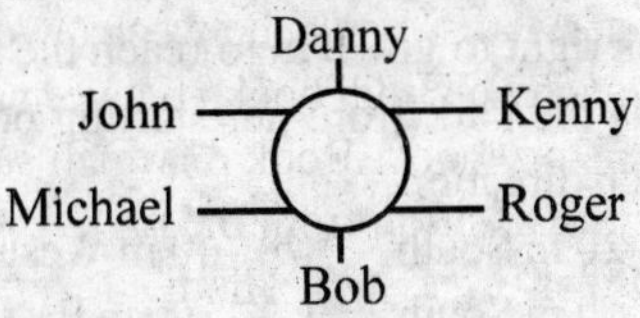

6. *(c)* : The sitting positions are :

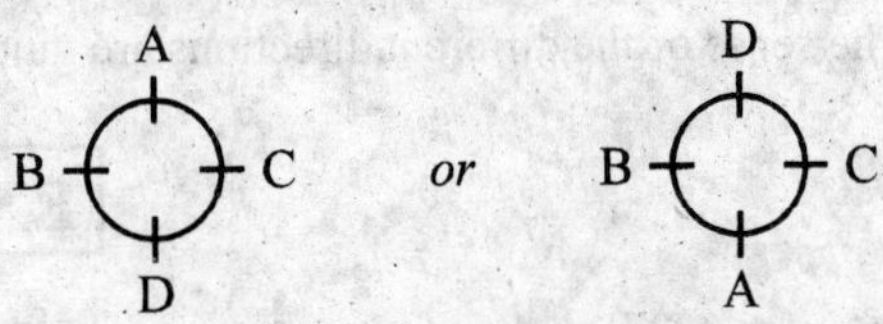

7. *(b)* : The order from left to right is :
Brijesh, Jayesh, Amar, Praveer

8. *(b)* : The pile of books is in the order :
1st — History
English
Maths
History
English
6th — Hindi
Maths
Hindi
Hindi
10th — History

9. *(d)* : Sitting order while facing us is :
A, C, D, B, E

10. *(c)* : The pattern of standing is :

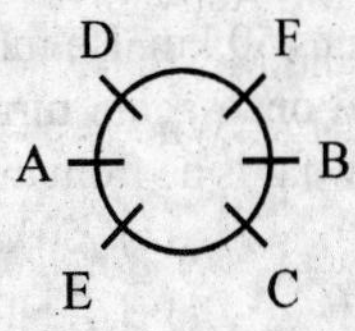

12. DIRECTION SENSE

In these type of tests, the directions in questions needs to be perceived. Such questions are based on the direction chart.

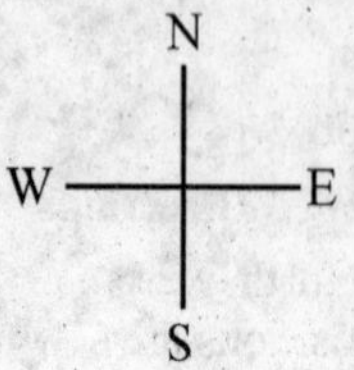

N = North S = South E = East W = West

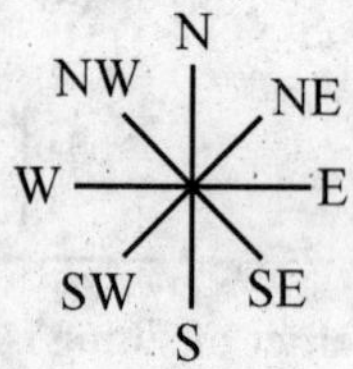

The sense of the different directions are guided by the left and right turns or angular turns.

EXERCISE

Directions : *In the following questions, select the right answer from the given options to depict the correct direction/distance.*

1. Kittu walks towards East and then towards South. After walking some distance he turns towards West and then turns to his left. In which direction is he walking now?

(*a*) North (*b*) South
(*c*) East (*d*) West

2. A person is driving towards West. What sequence of directions should he follow so that he is driving towards South?

(*a*) left, right, right
(*b*) right, right, left
(*c*) left, left, left
(*d*) right, right, right

3. Richa drives 8 km to the South, turns left and drives 5 km. Again, she turns left and drives 8 km. How far is she from her starting point?

(*a*) 3 km (*b*) 5 km
(*c*) 8 km (*d*) 13 km

4. Dingi runs 40 km towards North then turns right and runs 50 km. He turns right and runs 30 km, and once again turns right and runs 50 km. How far is he from his starting point?

(*a*) 90 km (*b*) 50 km
(*c*) 10 km (*d*) 5 km

5. If North is called North-West, North-West is called West, West is called South-West and so on. What will South-East be called?

(*a*) East (*b*) West
(*c*) North-East (*d*) South-East

6. A man travels 100 km towards South. From there he turns right and travels 100 km and again turns right to travel 50 km. Which direction is he in from his starting point?

(*a*) North (*b*) North-East
(*c*) East (*d*) South-West

7. A train runs 120 km in West direction, 30 km in South direction and then 80 km in east direction before reaching the station. In which direction is the station from the train's starting point?

(*a*) South-West (*b*) North-West
(*c*) South-East (*d*) South

8. Facing the West direction, Priya jogs for 20 m, turns left and goes further 40 m. She turns left again and jogs for 20 m. Then she turns right to go 20 m to reach the park. How far is the park from her starting point and in which direction?

(*a*) 20 m South (*b*) 40 m West
(*c*) 60 m South (*d*) 100 m East

9. If all the directions are rotated, *i.e.*, if North is changed to West and East to North and so on, then what will come in place of North-West?

(*a*) South-West (*b*) North-East
(*c*) East-North (*d*) East-West

10. A and B start together from one point. They walk 10 km towards North. A turns left and covers 5 km whereas B turns right and covers 3 km. A turns left again and covers 15 km whereas B turns right and covers his 15 km. How far is A from B?

(*a*) 18 km (*b*) 10 km
(*c*) 5 km (*d*) 8 km

EXPLANATORY ANSWERS

1. (*b*) :

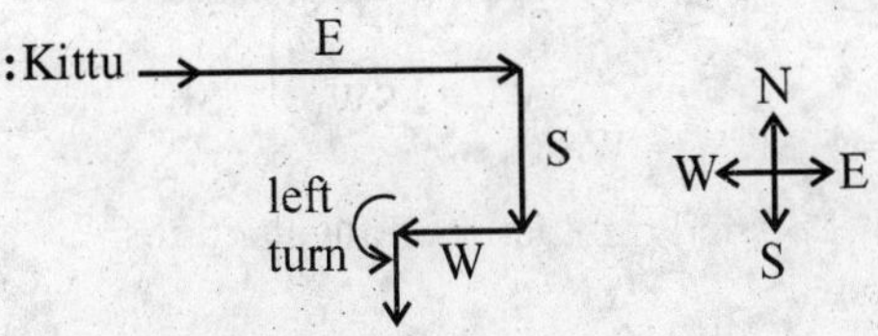

2. (*d*) :

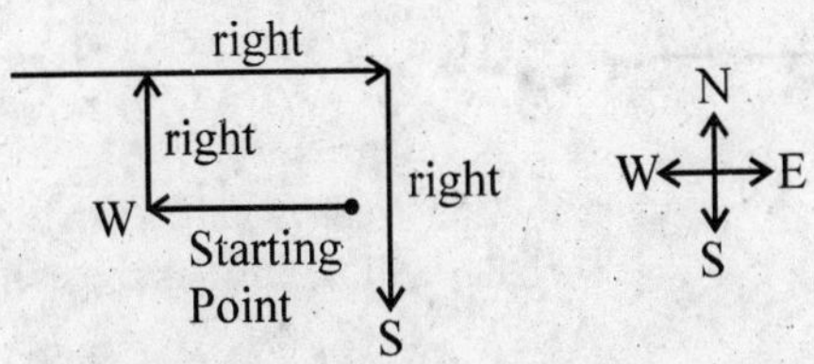

3. (*b*) :

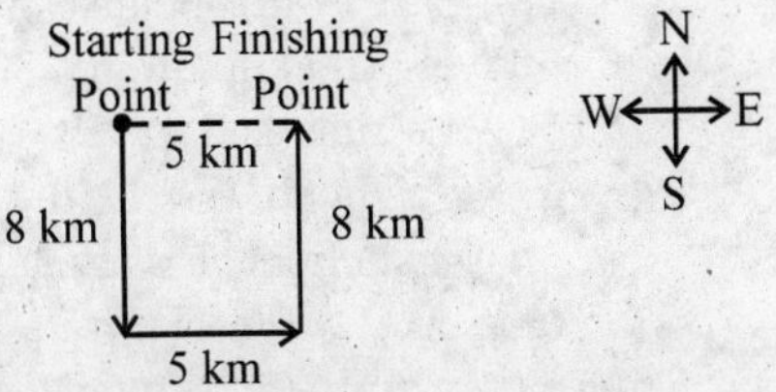

4. (*c*) :

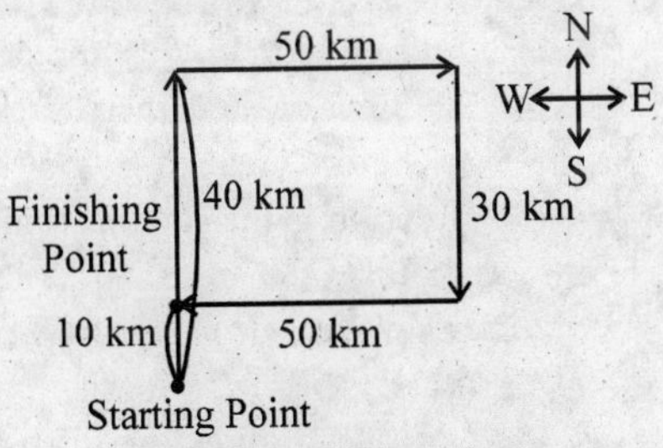

5. (*a*) :

Original Directions

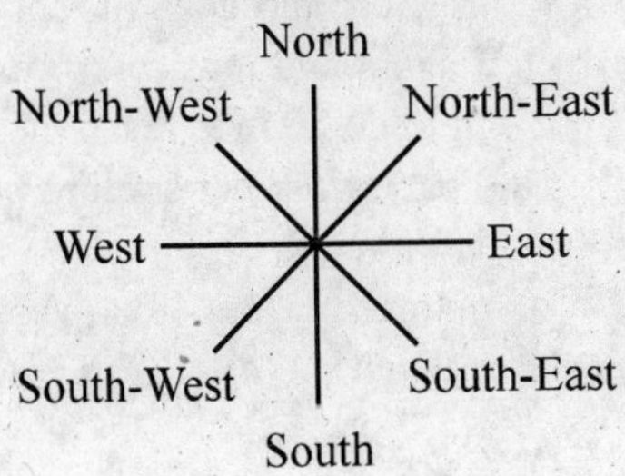

Changed Directions

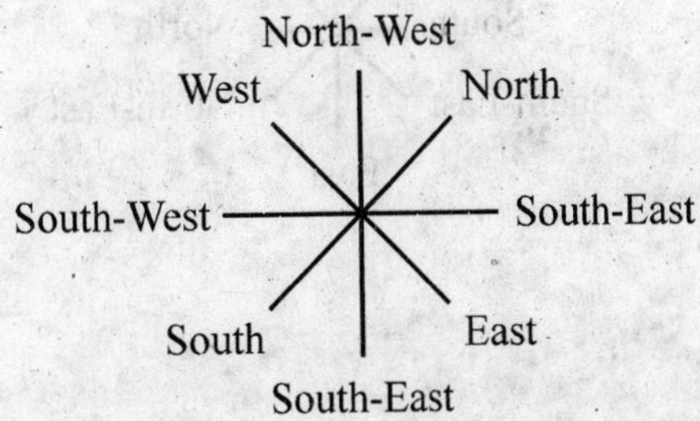

6. (*d*) :

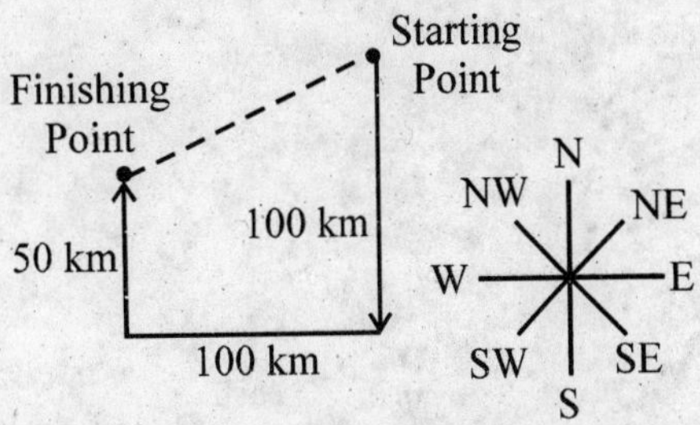

7. (*a*) :

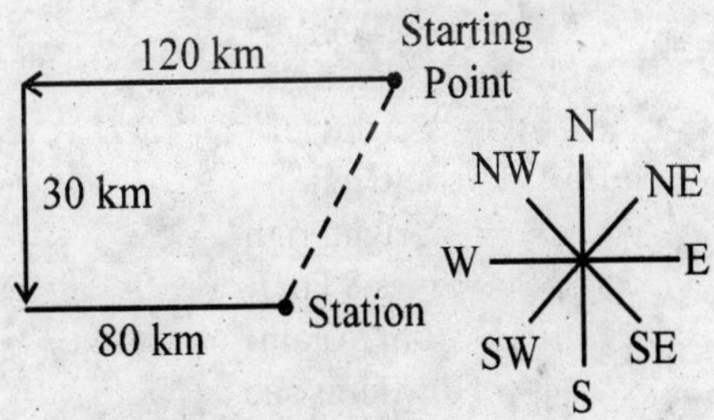

8. (*c*) : (40 + 20) = 60 metres South

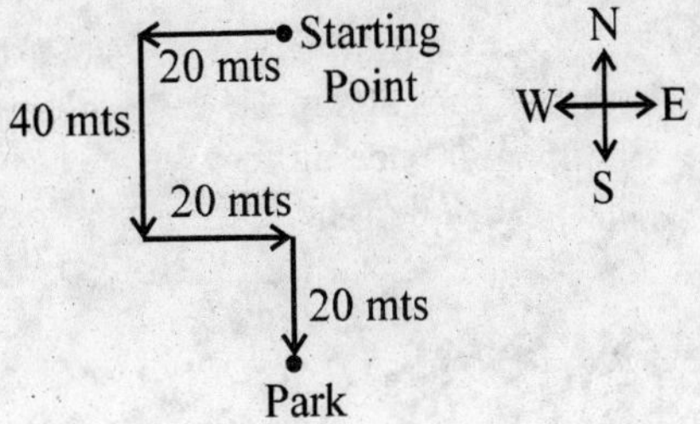

9. ***(a)*** **: Original Directions**

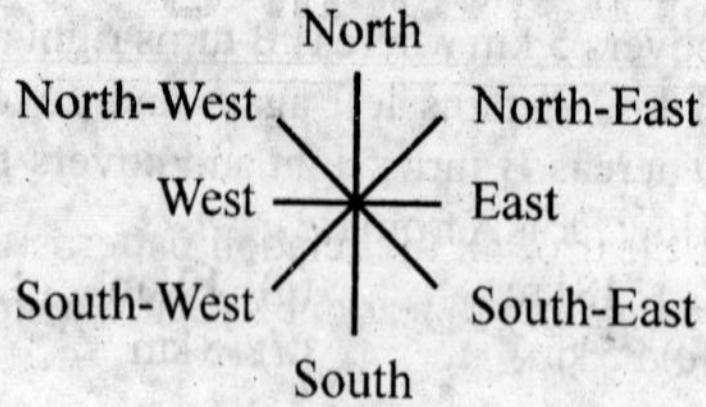

Changed Directions

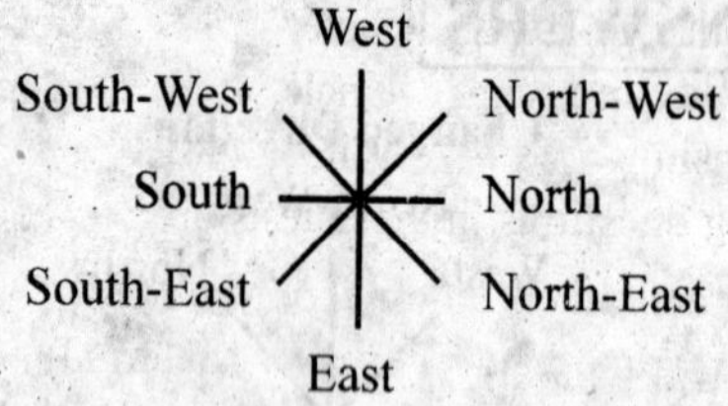

10. ***(d)*** **:**

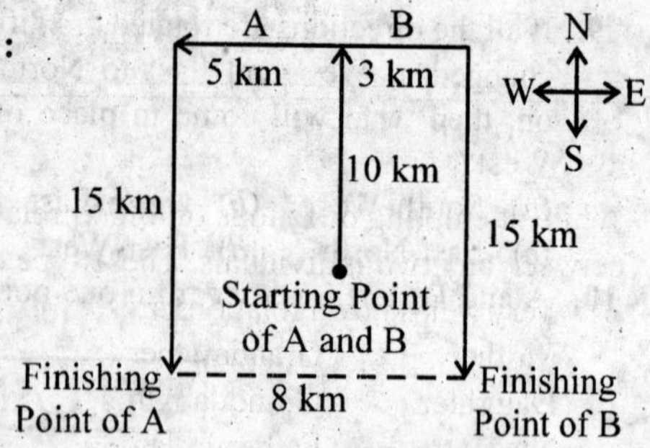

13. BLOOD RELATIONSHIPS

While attempting questions on blood relations, one should be clear of all the relation patterns that can exist between any two individuals. These type of questions are given mainly to test one's relationship ability.

Very well-known relations are :

Mother	Grandmother	Father	Grandfather	Son	Grandson
Daughter	Granddaughter	Brother	Brother-in-law	Sister	Sister-in-law
Niece	Father-in-law	Nephew	Mother-in-law	Uncle	Son-in-law
Aunt	Daughter-in-law	Husband	Cousin	Wife	

The patterns of some relationships which help in solving questions in these tests are :

Father's *or* Mother's Father	—	Grandfather (Paternal *or* Maternal)
Father's *or* Mother's Mother	—	Grandmother (Paternal *or* Maternal)
Father's *or* Mother's Son	—	Brother
Father's *or* Mother's Daughter	—	Sister
Father's Brother	—	Paternal Uncle
Father's Sister	—	Paternal Aunt
Mother's Brother	—	Maternal Uncle
Mother's Sister	—	Maternal Aunt
Uncle *or* Aunt's Son *or* Daughter	—	Cousin
Son's Wife	—	Daughter-in-law
Daughter's Husband	—	Son-in-law
Husband's *or* Wife's Brother	—	Brother-in-law
Husband's *or* Wife's Sister	—	Sister-in-law
Brother's Wife	—	Sister-in-law
Sister's Husband	—	Brother-in-law
Brother's Son	—	Nephew
Brother's Daughter	—	Niece

EXERCISE

Directions : *In each of the following questions keenly study the relationship mentioned between the persons, and then from the given options select the right relationship as the answer.*

1. A lady said, "The person standing there is my grandfather's only son's daughter". How is the lady related to the standing person?

(*a*) Sister (*b*) Mother
(*c*) Aunt (*d*) Cousin

2. Ajay is the brother of Vijay. Mili is the sister of Ajay. Sanjay is the brother of Rahul and Mehul is the daughter of Vijay. Who is Sanjay's Uncle?

(*a*) Rahul (*b*) Ajay
(*c*) Mehul (*d*) Data inadequate

3. A man introduced the boy coming with him as "He is son of the father of my wife's daughter". What relation did the boy bear to the man?

(*a*) Son-in-law (*b*) Son
(*c*) Brother (*d*) Father

4. If Amit's father is Billoo's father's only son and Billoo has neither a brother nor a daughter, what is the relationship between Amit and Billoo?

(*a*) Uncle — Nephew
(*b*) Father — Daughter
(*c*) Father — Son
(*d*) Cousins

5. Pointing to a woman in the photograph a man said, "She is the daughter of my grand-mother's only son." How is the woman related to the man?

(*a*) Mother (*b*) Daughter
(*c*) Sister-in-law (*d*) Sister

6. Pointing to a photograph, a woman said, "She is the only daughter of my mother's father." How is the woman related to the person in the photograph?

(*a*) Mother
(*b*) Grandmother
(*c*) Daughter
(*d*) Cannot be determined

7. Ram is the brother of Shyam and Mahesh is the father of Ram. Jagat is the brother of Priya and Priya is daughter of Shyam. Who is the uncle of Jagat ?

(*a*) Shyam (*b*) Mahesh
(*c*) Ram (*d*) Data insufficient

8. Introducing a man, a woman said, "His wife is the only daughter of my father". How is the man related to the woman?

(*a*) Husband (*b*) Father
(*c*) Father-in-law (*d*) Brother

9. If Maya is the only daughter of Richa's grandmother's brother, how is Maya's daughter related to Richa?

(*a*) Niece (*b*) Cousin
(*c*) Aunt (*d*) Mother

10. Pointing to a woman, a man said, "Her husband's mother is the wife of my father's only son". How is the man related to the woman?

(*a*) Son (*b*) Brother-in-law
(*c*) Uncle (*d*) Father-in-law

EXPLANATORY ANSWERS

1. (*a*) :

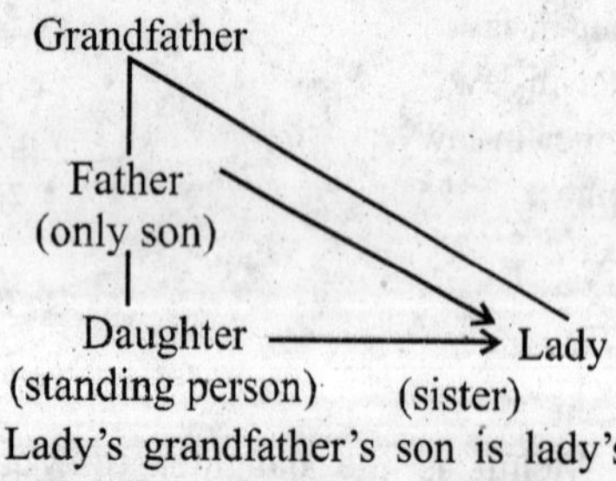

Lady's grandfather's son is lady's father and father's daughter will only be lady's sister.

2. (*d*) : 1. Mili →(sister) Ajay →(brother) Vijay ↓ Mehul (daughter)

2. Sanjay →(brother) Rahul

There are two sets of relationship. Information given is incomplete and no relation can be established between the two sets.

3. (*b*) : The relationship chart based on problem is :

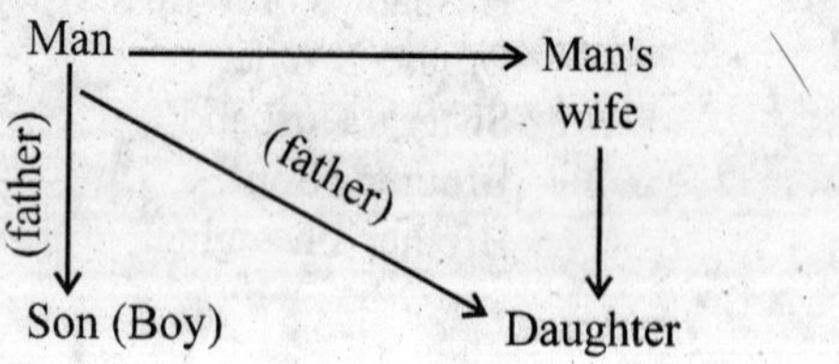

'Father of the man's wife's daughter' is the man himself and the boy in question is the man's son.

4. (*c*) : The relationship chart based on problem is :

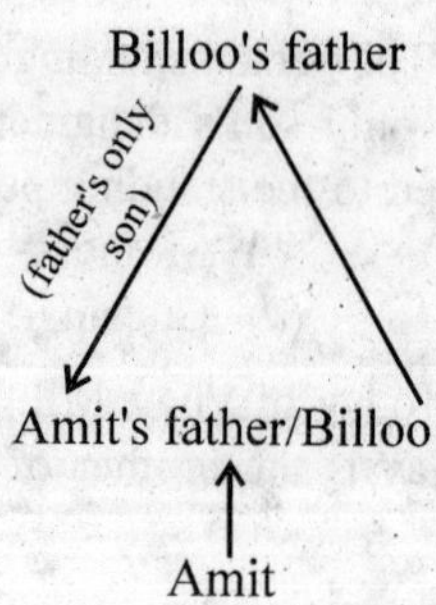

Amit's father is Billoo's father's only son means Billoo is the only son in question also, he is the father of Amit. It must be noted that Billoo has no brother which means he is single and also, when he has no daughter, Amit is his only son.

5. (***d***) **:**

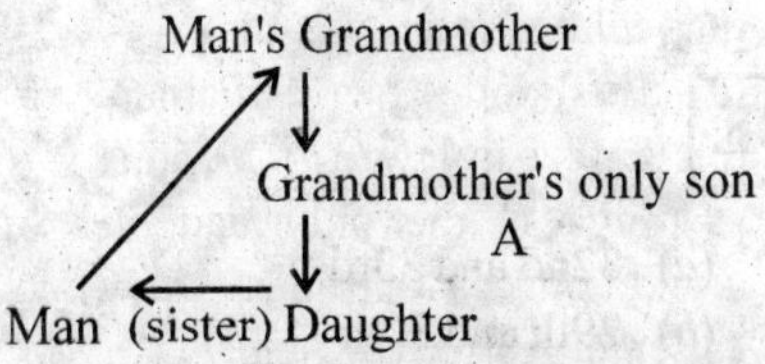

'My grandmother's only son' is the father of the man, and 'daughter of my grandmother's only son' is the sister of the man.

6. (***c***) **:**

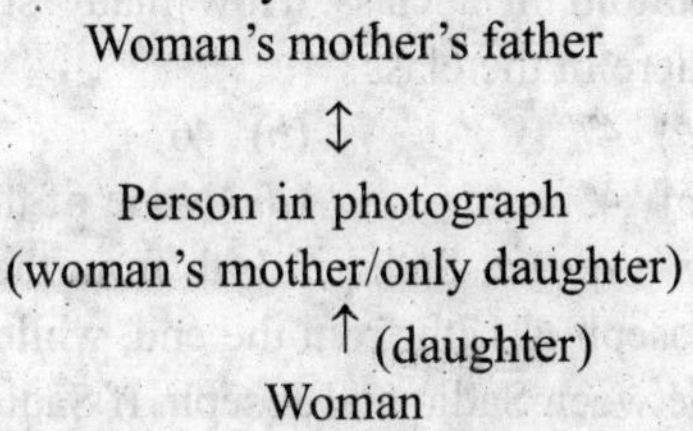

'Only daughter of my mother's father' is the person in the photograph and she is also the mother of the woman. So, the woman is the daughter of the person in the photograph.

7. (***c***) **:**

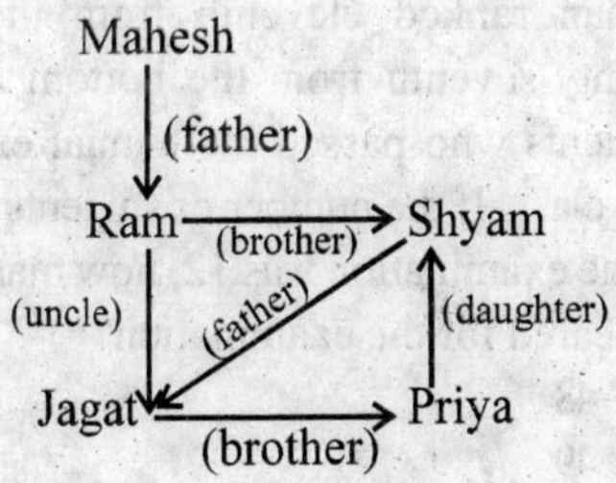

Jagat is brother of Priya and Priya is daughter of Shyam. So Shyam is also the father of Jagat. Ram is the brother of Shyam. So, Jagat's father's brother Ram is the uncle of Jagat.

8. (***a***) **:**

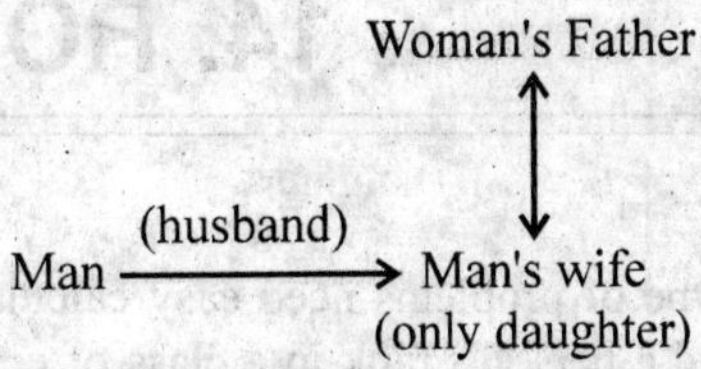

'Only daughter of my father' is the woman herself and the man is her husband.

9. (***b***) **:**

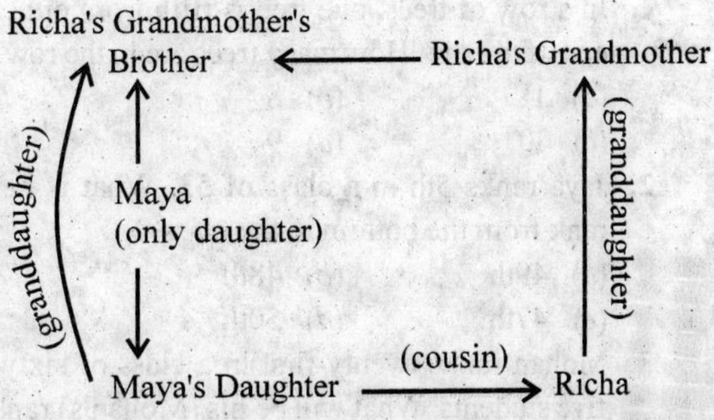

Both Maya's Daughter and Richa are granddaughters of a brother and a sister respectively. So Maya's daughter is the cousin of Richa.

10. (***d***) **:**

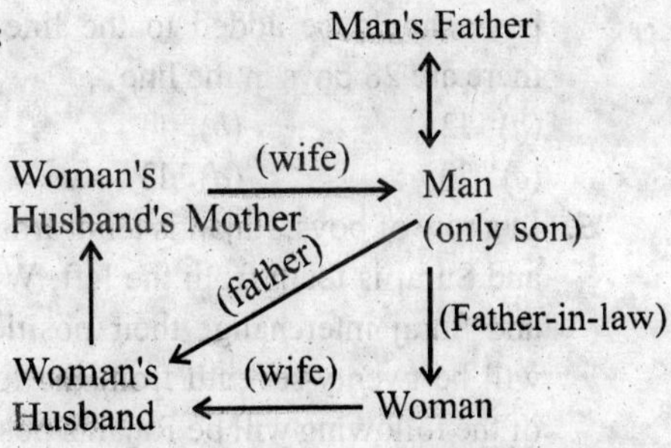

'My father's only son' is the man himself. 'Her husband's mother' is the wife of the man and so the man is the father of the woman's husband. As the woman is the wife of man's son, the man is the father-in-law of the woman.

14. ROWS AND RANKS

These type of problems need easy calculations to find out the number of objects in a row, lane or queue or to find a person's rank in a class of certain number of students; or to find the total number of students.

EXERCISE

1. In a row of trees, one tree is fifth from either end of the row. How many trees are in the row?

(*a*) 11 (*b*) 8
(*c*) 10 (*d*) 9

2. Jaya ranks 5th in a class of 53. What is her rank from the bottom in the class?

(*a*) 49th (*b*) 48th
(*c*) 47th (*d*) 50th

3. Mohan ranks twenty-first in a class of sixty-five students. What will be his (Mohan's) rank if the lowest candidate is assigned rank 1?

(*a*) 44th (*b*) 45th
(*c*) 46th (*d*) Data inadequate

4. If Rahul finds that he is 12th from the right in a line of boys and 4th from the left, how many boys should be added to the line such that there are 28 boys in the line?

(*a*) 12 (*b*) 14
(*c*) 20 (*d*) 13

5. In a row of boys, Rajan is tenth from the right and Suraj is tenth from the left. When Rajan and Suraj interchange their positions, Suraj will be twenty-seventh from the left. Which of the following will be Rajan's position from the right?

(*a*) Tenth
(*b*) Twenty-sixth
(*c*) Twenty-ninth
(*d*) None of these

6. Mahesh and Suresh are ranked 11th and 12th respectively from the top in a class of 41 students. What will be their respective ranks from the bottom?

(*a*) 32nd and 33rd
(*b*) 29th and 30th
(*c*) 30th and 31st
(*d*) 31st and 30th

7. Uma ranked 8th from the top and 37th from bottom in a class. How many students are there in the class?

(*a*) 47 (*b*) 46
(*c*) 45 (*d*) None of these

8. In a queue, Sadiq is 14th from the front and Joseph is 17th from the end, while Jane is in between Sadiq and Joseph. If Sadiq be ahead of Joseph and there be 48 persons in the queue, how many persons are there between Sadiq and Jane?

(*a*) 5 (*b*) 6
(*c*) 7 (*d*) 8

9. Rohan ranked eleventh from the top and twenty-seventh from the bottom among the students who passed the annual examination in a class. If the number of students who failed in the examination was 12, how many students appeared for the examination?

(*a*) 48
(*b*) 49
(*c*) 50
(*d*) Cannot be determined

10. Some boys are sitting in a row. P is sitting fourteenth from the left and Q is seventh from the right. If there are four boys between P and Q, how many boys are there in the row?

(*a*) 19 (*b*) 21
(*c*) 25 (*d*) 23

EXPLANATORY ANSWERS

1. (*d*):

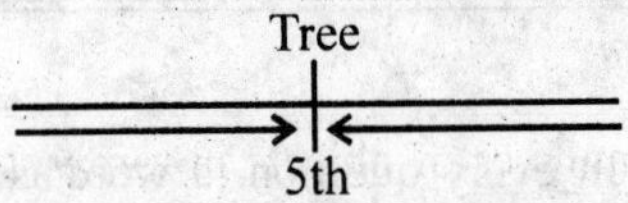

Total number of trees in the row are : $(5+5)-1=9$.

2. (*a*) :

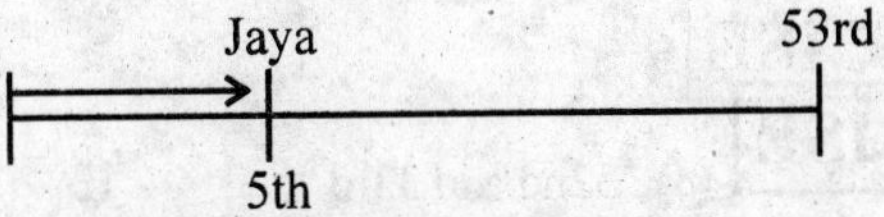

Jaya's rank from the bottom is : $(53-5)+1=49$th.

3. (*b*) :

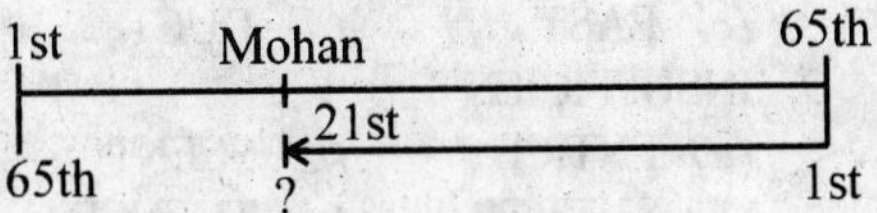

Note : Mohan's rank from the last or the question asked means the same.

Mohan's rank is $(65-21)+1=45$th.

4. (*d*) :

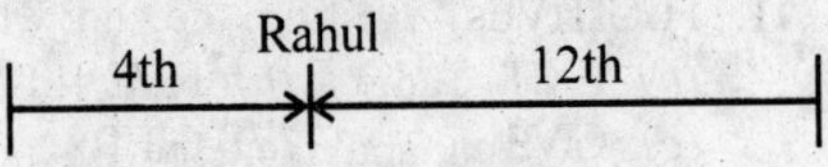

The number of boys in the line are : $(4+12)-1=15$

To make a line of 28 boys, $(28-15)$ *i.e.* 13 more boys are needed.

5. (*d*) :

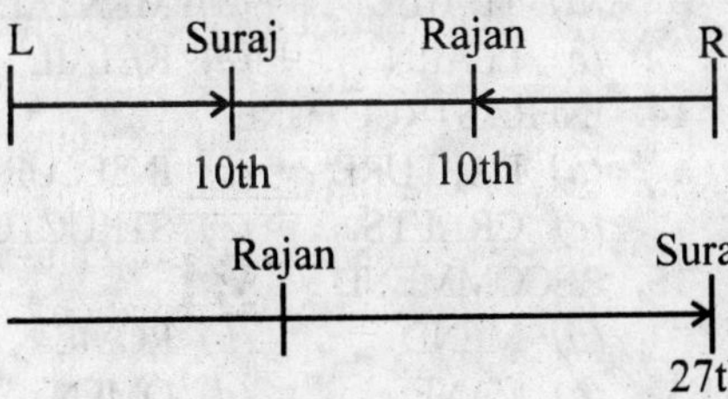

As the position of boys is equal from both ends, Rajan will also be 27th from the right after changing positions.

6. (*d*) :

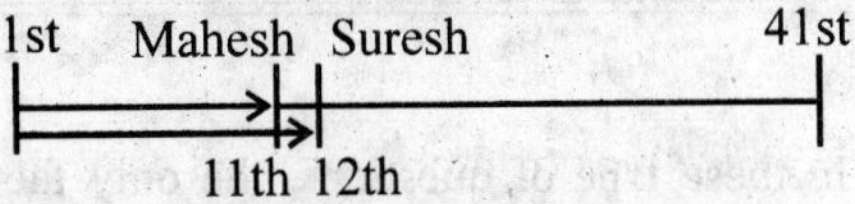

Mahesh's position from bottom is : $(41-11)+1=31$st

Suresh's position from bottom is : $(41-12)+1=30$th.

7. (*d*) :

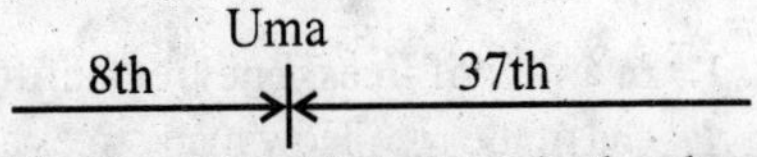

Total number of students in the class are : $(8+37)-1=44$.

8. (*d*) :

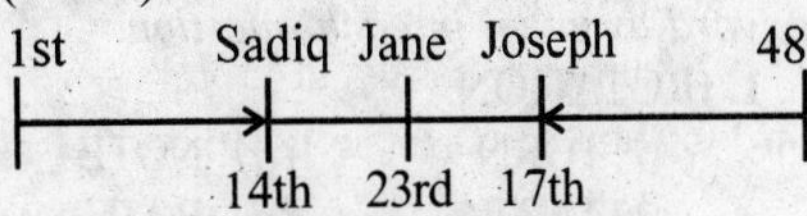

Sadiq's position from front : 14th

Joseph's position from last : 17th or $48-17+1=32$nd from front.

Middle postion between Sadiq & Joseph

$$=\frac{(32-14)}{2}+14=23\text{ rd.}$$

Hence, Jane position is 23rd from front

Person between Sadiq & Jane $=23-14-1=8$.

9. (*b*) :

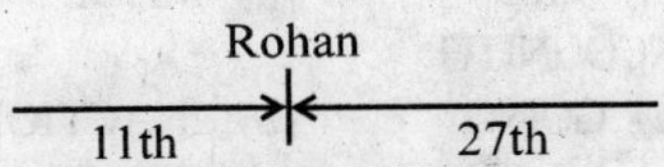

Number of students who passed the examination $(11+27)-1=37$

Those who failed = 12

Total number of students who appeared in the examination $=37+12=49$.

10. (*c*) :

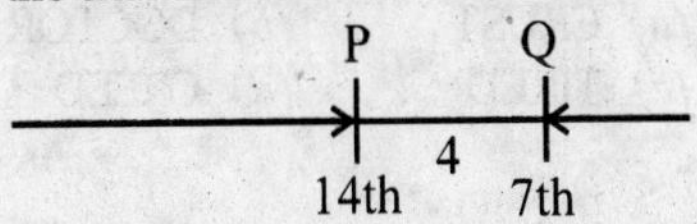

The number of boys in the row are : $(14+4+7)=25$.

15. PERMUTATIONS AND COMBINATIONS

In these type of questions, the only factor essential is alertness. In every question, a word is given. By using the letters of this given word the options are formed. The candidates are required to find from the given options the word *(i)* which cannot be formed by using the letters of the given word or *(ii)* which can be formed by using the letters of the given word.

EXERCISE

Directions : *Find out the one word among the options which cannot be formed by using the letters of the word as given in each question.*

1. ROTATION
(a) TORN *(b)* NOTE
(c) TART *(d)* RAIN

2. PHILOSOPHY
(a) SOIL *(b)* SHIP
(c) SOLO *(d)* SPIN

3. SLAVATION
(a) SNORT *(b)* LATVIA
(c) SALIVA *(d)* AVAIL

4. ACADEMY
(a) DEMY *(b)* MACE
(c) DIRE *(d)* MADE

5. INCOGNITO
(a) GOING *(b)* INACTION
(c) IGNITION *(d)* TONGO

6. JUDICIARY
(a) INJURY *(b)* CADDY
(c) DICY *(d)* ACRID

7. DOCTRINE
(a) CRUST *(b)* DOCTOR
(c) TIRED *(d)* CREED

8. EDUCATED
(a) DATE *(b)* CUTE
(c) EAST *(d)* DUCT

9. INSUFFICIENT
(a) ENTICE *(b)* SCENT
(c) SUFFICE *(d)* THENCE

10. DECEMBER
(a) REDEEM *(b)* DECREE
(c) BRACED *(d)* MEMBER

11. FUGITIVE
(a) EXIT *(b)* FIVE
(c) GIVE *(d)* GIFT

12. CATASTROPHE
(a) TASTE *(b)* CHEAP
(c) POUCH *(d)* STARE

13. TORRENTIAL
(a) TRAIL *(b)* MENTAL
(c) LEARN *(d)* RETAIL

14. INFRASTRUCTURE
(a) RAPTURE *(b)* INSECURE
(c) CRAFTS *(d)* STRUCTURE

15. RECOMMEND
(a) MEND *(b)* ROME
(c) CANE *(d)* OMEN

ANSWERS

1	2	3	4	5	6	7	8	9	10
(b)	*(d)*	*(a)*	*(c)*	*(b)*	*(a)*	*(a)*	*(c)*	*(d)*	*(c)*
11	**12**	**13**	**14**	**15**					
(a)	*(c)*	*(b)*	*(a)*	*(c)*					

16. SYMBOL SUBSTITUTION

Questions in these category are easy to attempt. Candidates must be quick in substituting symbols and calculations. The common pattern of questions asked are given below.

EXERCISE

1. If "+" means "–"; "–" means "×"; "×"means "÷" and "÷" means "+", then $15 \times 5 \div 10 + 5 - 3 = ?$
   (a) 9.5 (b) 0
   (c) – 2 (d) 24
2. If "+" means "×"; "–" means "÷"; "÷"means "+" and "×" means "–", then what will be the value of $20 \div 40 - 4 \times 5 + 6 = ?$
   (a) 60 (b) 1.67
   (c) 150 (d) 0
3. If × stands for addition, < for subtraction, + stands for division, > for multiplication, – stands for equal to, ÷ for greater than, and = stands for less than, state which of the following is true?
   (a) $5 \times 3 < 7 \div 8 + 4 \times 1$
   (b) $3 \times 4 > 2 - 9 + 3 < 3$
   (c) $5 > 2 + 2 = 10 < 4 \times 8$
   (d) $3 \times 2 < 4 \div 16 > 2 + 4$
4. If → stands for subract, ← stands for add, •↑↑ stands for multiply, ↓↓ stands for divide, ↔ for greater than, ⟷ stands for equal to, then which of the following alternatives is true?
   (a) 4 ← 6 ↑↑ 2 ⟷ 3 → 12 ← 12
   (b) 10 ↓↓ 5 ↑↑ 5 ⟷ 9 → 3 ← 4
   (c) 15 ↑↑ 2 → 5 ⟷ 12 ↓↓ 4 ← 3
   (d) 13 ↓↓ 13 ← 1 ↔ 20 → 5 ↑↑ 2
5. If Δ denotes =; + denotes >, – denotes <, □ denotes ≠, × denotes > and ÷ denotes < then a + b – c denotes
   (a) b Δ c □ a
   (b) b □ a ÷ c
   (c) a ÷ b × c
   (d) b – a + c
6. If '✱' denotes '×', 'Δ' denotes '÷', '□' denotes '–', '●' denotes '+', 'α' denotes '=' and 'β' denotes ≠, then which of the following euations is correct?
   (a) 2 □ 10 ✱ 4 Δ 5 α 5 ● 12 Δ 6
   (b) 27 Δ 9 ● 6 β 3 ✱ 6 □ 9
   (c) 4 Δ 2 ✱ 0 α 7 Δ 1 ✱ 0
   (d) 5 ● 6 Δ 3 □ 2 α 8 Δ 4 ✱ 3
7. If ↓ stands for '÷', ↑ stands for '×', → stands for '+' and ← stands for '–', then 25 ↓ 5 → 3 ↑ 6 ← 8 = ?
   (a) 9 (b) 12
   (c) 16 (d) 15
8. If the + and × signs of the following equations are interchanged, which will be the correct equation?
   (a) $7 \times 5 + 3 = 20$
   (b) $4 + 9 \times 1 = 42$
   (c) $6 \times 5 + 8 = 46$
   (d) $2 + 11 \times 4 = 28$
9. If '+' stands for multiplication, '×' stands for addition, '÷' stands for subtraction and '–' stands for division, then what will be the result of the following equation?
   $7 \times 4 \div 10 \times 2 + 5 = ?$
   (a) 7 (b) 0
   (c) 11 (d) 15
10. If 'A' means '÷', 'B' means '+', 'C' means '×' and 'D' means '–', then 12 C 4 A 24 D 10 B 1 = ?
   (a) $11\frac{1}{3}$ (b) 23
   (c) – 7 (d) $16\frac{4}{5}$

EXPLANATORY ANSWERS

1. *(c)* : $15 \div 5 + 10 - 5 \times 3$
$3 + 10 - 15 = -2$

2. *(d)* : $20 + 40 \div 4 - 5 \times 6$
$20 + 10 - 30 = 0$

3. *(c)* : *(a)* $5 + 3 - 7 > 8 \div 4 + 1$
$1 > 3$
(b) $3 + 4 \times 2 = 9 \div 3 - 3$
$11 = 0$
(c) $5 \times 2 \div 2 < 10 - 4 + 8$
$5 < 14$
(d) $3 + 2 - 4 > 16 \times 2 \div 4$
$1 > 8$

4. *(b)* : *(a)* $4 + 6 \times 2 = 3 - 12 + 12$
$16 = 3$
(b) $10 \div 5 \times 5 = 9 - 3 + 4$
$10 = 10$
(c) $15 \times 2 - 5 = 12 \div 4 + 3$
$25 = 6$
(d) $13 \div 13 + 1 > 20 - 5 \times 2$
$2 > 10$

5. *(d)* : What is given is $a > b < c$
The equations are :
(a) $b = c \neq a$ which is wrong
(b) $b \neq a < c$ which is wrong
(c) $a < b > c$ which is wrong
(d) $b < a > c$ which is correct
Therefore, *(d)* is the answer.

6. *(c)* : The solved equations will be :
(a) $2 - 10 \times 4 \div 5 = 5 + 12 \div 6$
$2 - 8 = 5 + 2$
$-6 = 7$ which is wrong
(b) $27 \div 9 + 6 \neq 3 \times 6 - 9$
$3 + 6 \neq 18 - 9$
$9 \neq 9$ which is wrong
(c) $4 \div 2 \times 0 = 7 \div 1 \times 0$
$2 \times 0 = 7 \times 0$
$0 = 0$ which is correct
(d) $5 + 6 \div 3 - 2 = 8 \div 4 \times 3$
$5 = 6$ which is wrong

7. *(d)* : $25 \div 5 + 3 \times 6 - 8$
$5 + 18 - 8 = 15$

8. *(c)* : After interchanging the signs the equations are :
(a) $7 + 5 \times 3 = 22$ which is wrong
(b) $4 \times 9 + 1 = 37$ which is wrong
(c) $6 + 5 \times 8 = 46$ which is correct
(d) $2 \times 11 + 4 = 26$ which is wrong

9. *(c)* : $7 + 4 - 10 + 2 \times 5$
$7 + 4 - 10 + 10 = 11$

10. *(c)* : $12 \times 4 \div 24 - 10 + 1$
$2 - 10 + 1 = -7$

17. MISSING NUMBERS

Playing with numbers and mathematical skills are needed to attempt these type of tests. The candidates have to work out the right combination of arithmetical symbols to arrive at the answer options which will take the place of the interrogation sign in the given questions.

EXERCISE

Directions: *In each question given below which one number can be placed at the sign of interrogation?*

1.

(*a*) 693 (*b*) 939
(*c*) 981 (*d*) 993

2.

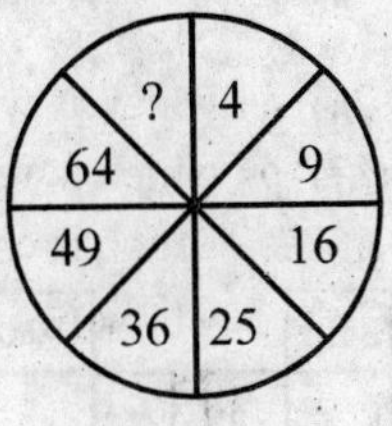

(*a*) 68 (*b*) 100
(*c*) 72 (*d*) 81

3.

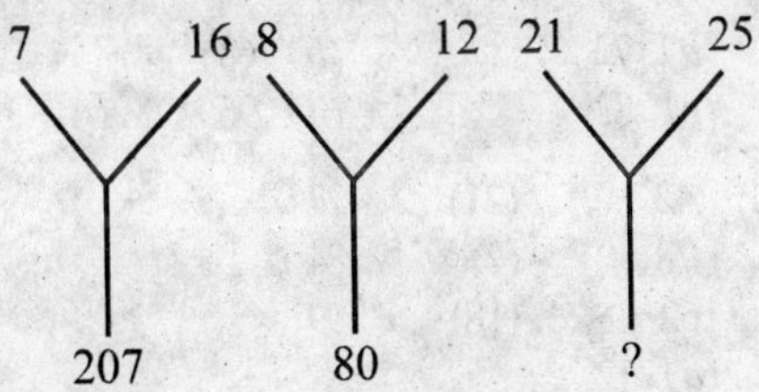

(*a*) 425 (*b*) 184
(*c*) 241 (*d*) 210

4.

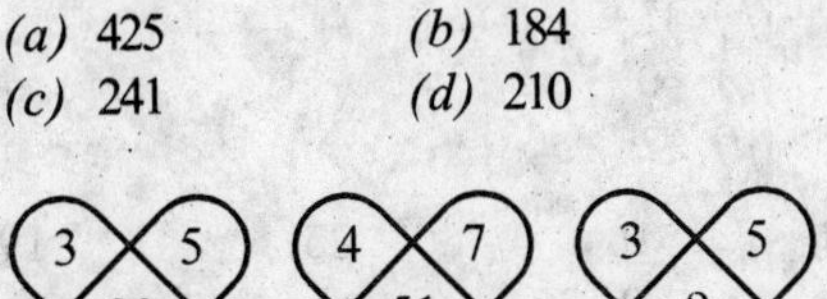

(*a*) 35 (*b*) 37
(*c*) 45 (*d*) 48

5.

(*a*) 4 (*b*) 8
(*c*) 20 (*d*) 14

6.

14	9	4
12	7	2
10	5	0
16	11	?

(*a*) 9 (*b*) 6
(*c*) 3 (*d*) 7

7.

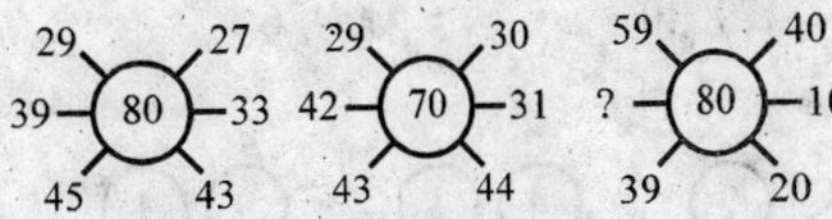

(*a*) 69 (*b*) 49
(*c*) 50 (*d*) 60

8.

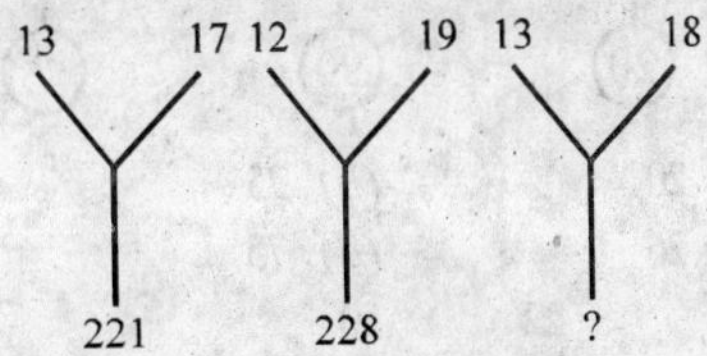

(*a*) 31 (*b*) 229
(*c*) 234 (*d*) 312

9.

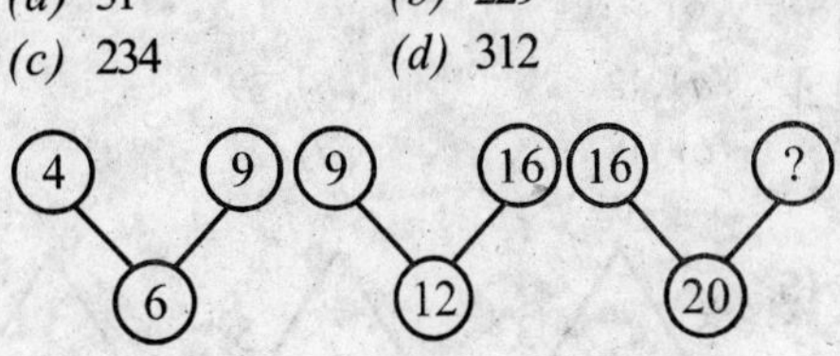

(*a*) 21 (*b*) 25
(*c*) 50 (*d*) 60

10. 51 (11) 61
64 (30) 32
35 (?) 43

(a) 25 *(b)* 27
(c) 32 *(d)* 37

11. 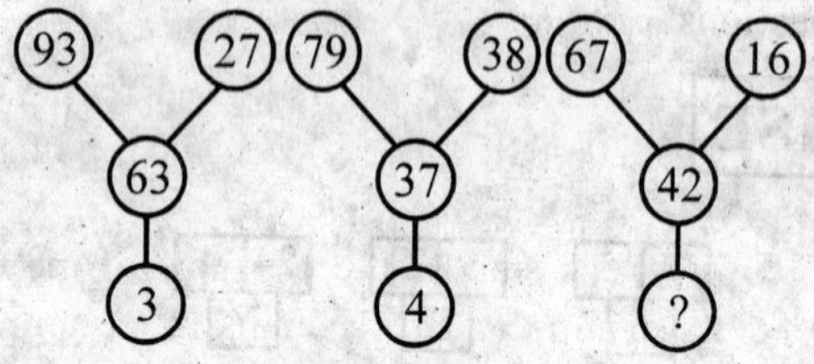

(a) 5 *(b)* 6
(c) 8 *(d)* 9

12. 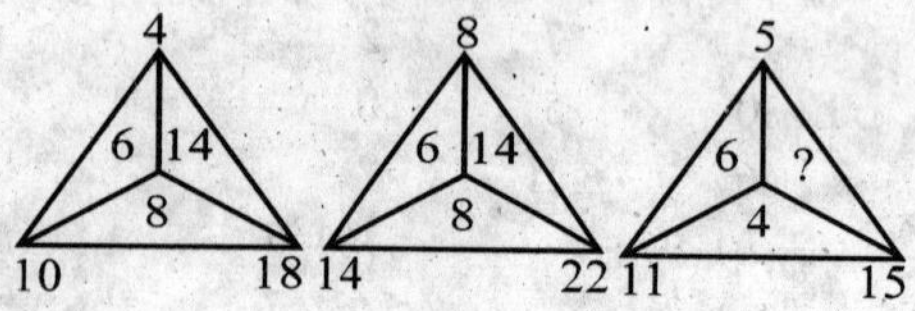

(a) 8 *(b)* 14
(c) 10 *(d)* 6

13. 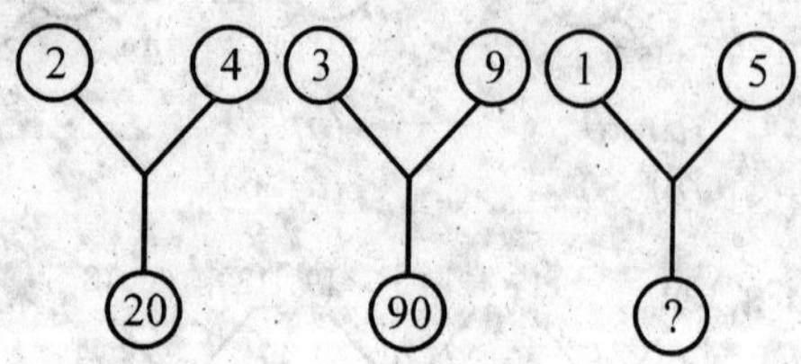

(a) 20 *(b)* 25
(c) 26 *(d)* 75

14. 27 22 50
13 12 26
9 2 ?

(a) 12 *(b)* 39
(c) 18 *(d)* 24

15. 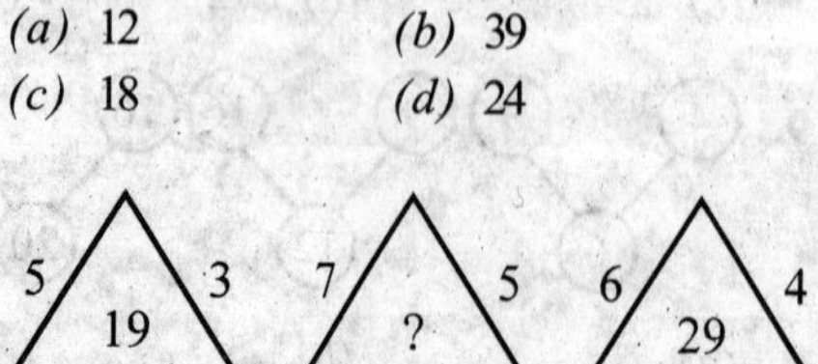

(a) 25 *(b)* 47
(c) 37 *(d)* 41

16. 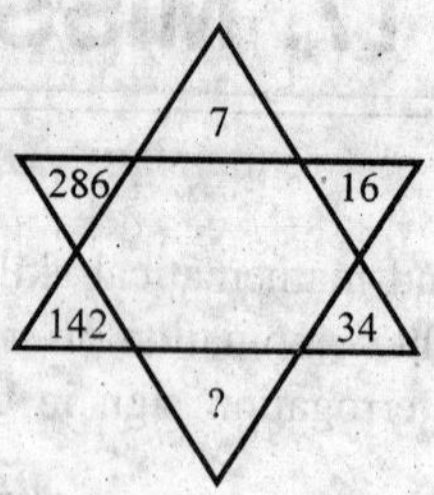

(a) 70
(b) 68
(c) 56
(d) 92

17. 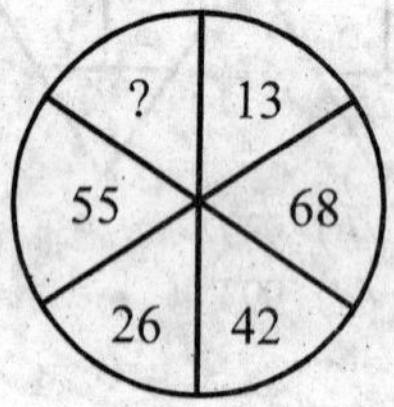

(a) 41 *(b)* 37
(c) 29 *(d)* 25

18. 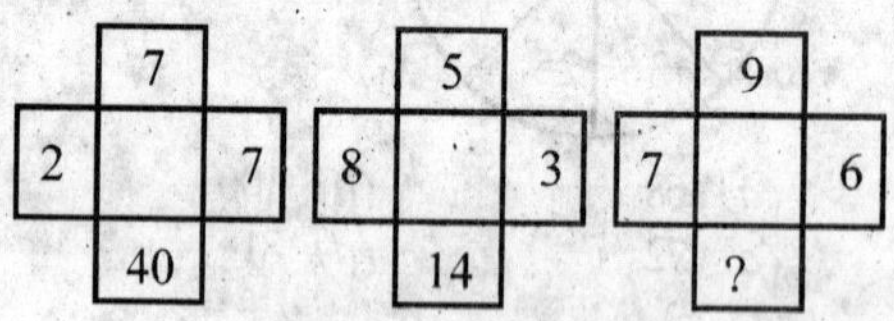

(a) 72 *(b)* 68
(c) 82 *(d)* 96

19. 42 (21) 22
78 (?) 84
162 (18) 99

(a) 12
(b) 13
(c) 60
(d) 72

20. 

(a) 68 *(b)* 93
(c) 175 *(d)* 217

EXPLANATORY ANSWERS

1. (c) : The squares of two numbers on the top placed side by side gives the number inside the bottom triangle, *i.e.*,
6^2 and $3^2 = 369$
2^2 and $5^2 = 425$, similarly
3^2 and $9^2 = 981$.

2. (d) : Starting from number 4 the numbers are the squares of numbers in natural order *i.e.*, $2^2 = 4, 3^2 = 9, 4^2 = 16 \ldots\ldots 9^2 = 81$.

3. (b) : The number at the bottom is the difference of the squares of two numbers at the top, *i.e.*,
$16^2 - 7^2 = 256 - 49 = 207$
$12^2 - 8^2 = 144 - 64 = 80$, similarly
$25^2 - 21^2 = 625 - 441 = 184$.

4. (b) : The number in the centre is the sum of the products of diagonal numbers, *i.e.*,
$(3 \times 3) + (5 \times 6) = 39$
$(4 \times 4) + (7 \times 5) = 51$, similarly
$(3 \times 4) + (5 \times 5) = 37$.

5. (d) : Sum of two numbers on the top divided by 2 gives the third number, *i.e.*,
$(7 + 5) \div 2 = 6$
$(5 + 21) \div 2 = 13$, similarly
$(24 + 4) \div 2 = 14$.

6. (b) : The numbers in 2nd and 3rd columns are 5 less than the nunbers in 1st and 2nd columns respectively, *i.e.*,
$14 - 5 = 9$ and $9 - 5 = 4$
$12 - 5 = 7$ and $7 - 5 = 2, \ldots$ similarly
$16 - 5 = 11$ and $11 - 5 = 6$.

7. (a) : The sum of 3 numbers in each line in one figure is same, *i.e.*,
$29 + 80 + 43$ or $39 + 80 + 33$ or $45 + 80 + 27 = 152$
$29 + 70 + 44$ or $42 + 70 + 31$ or $43 + 70 + 30 = 143$,
similarly $59 + 80 + 20$ or $39 + 80 + 40 = 159$.
The missing number is :
$159 - (80 + 10) = 69$.

8. (c) : The number at the bottom is the product of two numbers at the top, *i.e.*,
$13 \times 17 = 221$
$12 \times 19 = 228$, similarly
$13 \times 18 = 234$.

9. (b) : Square of number at the bottom is equal to the product of two numbers at the top, *i.e.*,
$6^2 = 4 \times 9$, *i.e.*, 36
$12^2 = 9 \times 16$, *i.e.*, 144, similarly
$20^2 = 16 \times ?$, *i.e.*, 400. The missing number is $400 \div 16 = 25$.

10. (b) : The sum of the products of the digits of numbers in 1st and 3rd columns is the number in the 2nd column, *i.e.*,
$(5 \times 1) + (6 \times 1) = 11$
$(6 \times 4) + (3 \times 2) = 30$, similarly
$(3 \times 5) + (4 \times 3) = 27$.

11. (d) : The sum of numbers on right and centre subtracted from the number on the left gives the number at the bottom, *i.e.*,
$93 - (27 + 63) = 3$
$79 - (38 + 37) = 4$, similarly
$67 - (16 + 42) = 9$.

12. (c) : The number inside each triangle is the difference of the numbers at its base *i.e.*
$10 - 4 = 6, 18 - 4 = 14$ and $18 - 10 = 8$
$14 - 8 = 6, 22 - 8 = 14$ and $22 - 14 = 8$, similarly
$11 - 5 = 6, 15 - 5 = 10$ and $15 - 11 = 4$.

13. (c) : The sum of squares of two numbers at the top gives the third number below, *i.e.*,
$2^2 + 4^2 = 20$
$3^2 + 9^2 = 90$, similarly
$1^2 + 5^2 = 26$.

14. (a) : The sum of numbers in 1st and 2nd column plus 1 is the number in the 3rd column, *i.e.*,
$27 + 22 + 1 = 50$
$13 + 12 + 1 = 26$, similarly
$9 + 2 + 1 = 12$.

15. (d) : The product of numbers on either side of the triangle plus the number at the base is the number inside the triangle, *i.e.*,
$(5 \times 3) + 4 = 19$
$(6 \times 4) + 5 = 29$, similarly
$(7 \times 5) + 6 = 41$.

16. *(a)* : Clockwise starting from number 7, the next number is obtained by doubling the number and adding 2, *i.e.,*

$(7 \times 2) + 2 = 16$

$(16 \times 2) + 2 = 34 \ldots$, similarly

$(34 \times 2) + 2 = 70$

$(70 \times 2) + 2 = 142$

$(142 \times 2) + 2 = 286$.

17. *(c)* : The difference between the numbers in opposite sectors is 13, *i.e.,*

$26 - 13 = 13$

$68 - 55 = 13$, similarly

The missing number is $42 - 13 = 29$

($42 + 13 = 55$ is not given as option).

18. *(b)* : The number at the bottom is obtained by subtracting the sum of two numbers in the centre grid line from the square of the number at the top, *i.e.,*

$7^2 - (2 + 7) = 40$

$5^2 - (8 + 3) = 14$, similarly

$9^2 - (7 + 6) = 68$.

19. *(b)* : The number inside the brackets is obtained by multiplying the number on the left by 2 and then dividing the product by the sum of digits of number on the right, *i.e.,*

$(42 \times 2) \div (2 + 2) = 21$

$(162 \times 2) \div (9 + 9) = 18$, similarly

$(78 \times 2) \div (8 + 4) = 13$.

20. *(a)* : Subtracting the sum of squares of two numbers at the base from the square of number at the apex gives the number inside the triangle, *i.e.,*

$16^2 - (7^2 + 10^2) = 107$

$25^2 - (20^2 + 4^2) = 209$, similarly

$19^2 - (2^2 + 17^2) = 68$.

18. ALPHABET PROBLEMS

Alphabet problems are fun to attempt. They are based on alphabetical series in natural as well as reverse order.

Natural Order

A B C D E F G H I J K L M N O P Q R S T U V W X Y Z

Reverse Order

Z Y X W V U T S R Q P O N M L K J I H G F E D C B A

Note : The series starts from A on reaching Z and from Z on reaching A. Of these A E I O U are vowels and the rest are consonants.

EXERCISE

1. Which letter should be ninth letter to the left of ninth letter from the right if the first half of the alphabet is reversed?

(a) I *(b)* D
(c) F *(d)* E

2. Starting from the fifth letter from the left, if twelve letters are written in reverse order, then which letter will be the seventh to the left of the fourteenth letter from the right?

(a) N *(b)* H
(c) L *(d)* O

3. What letter will come in the centre of sixth letter from the right and thirteenth letter from the left?

(a) Q *(b)* R
(c) P *(d)* S

4. If in the word "DISTURBANCE", the first letter is interchanged with the last letter, the second letter is interchanged with the tenth letter and so on, which letter would come after the letter "T" in the newly formed word?

(a) I *(b)* U
(c) N *(d)* S

5. If it is possible to make a meaningful word with the third, the fifth, the seventh and the tenth letters of the word PROJECTION. If no such word can be made, give 'O' as the answer. If more than one such word can be made, give 'M' as the answer.

(a) T *(b)* N
(c) O *(d)* M

6. A meaningful word is made if we take the first, fourth, fifth, seventh, tenth, eleventh and the twelfth letters of the word "FELICITATIONS". Which of the following will be the fifth letter of that word from the right end of that word?

(a) T *(b)* C
(c) N *(d)* I

7. On rearranging the jumbled spelling of the word SKARTINS, a language is obtained. What is the fifth letter from the right of the rearranged word?

(a) N *(b)* K
(c) R *(d)* S

8. If the 1st, 3rd, 5th, 7th, 10th and 13th letters of the word "ENTERTAINMENT" are used to make a meaningful word, then what two letters will come in the centre?

(a) AM *(b)* TT
(c) RE *(d)* NA

9. On rearranging the jumbled spelling of the word GRUBY a sport is obtained. What is the letter in the centre?

(a) R *(b)* B
(c) G *(d)* U

10. If the letters 'ERVSECI' can be rearranged to form a meaningful word what will be the fifth letter from the right?

(a) R *(b)* V

(c) E *(d)* None of these

11. From the word HASTEN how many independent meaningful English words can be made without changing the order of the letters and using each letter only once?

(a) 1 *(b)* 2

(c) 3 *(d)* 4

EXPLANATORY ANSWERS

1. *(d)* : MLKJIGHFEDCBANOPQRSTUVWXYZ

9th 9th

2. *(d)* : ABCDPONMLKJIHGFEQRSTUVWXYZ

7th 14th

3. *(a)* :

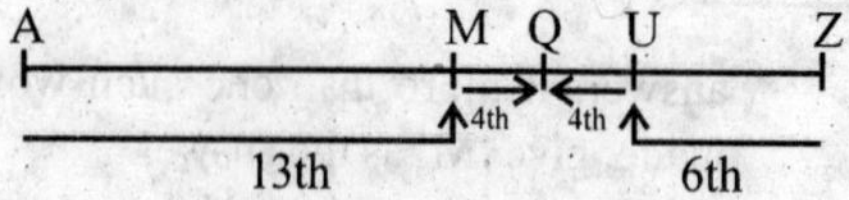

13th letter from left is 'M' and 6th letter from right is 'U'. The letter in the centre of 'M' and 'U' is 'Q'.

4. *(d)* : E C N A B R U T S I D

5. *(d)* : P R O J E C T I O N

The 3rd, 5th, 7th and 10th letters are OETN.

The words formed are TONE and NOTE.

6. *(b)* : F E L I C I T A T I O N S

The 1st, 4th, 5th, 7th, 10th, 11th and 12th lettes are FICTION.

The word is FICTION and 5th letter from right is 'C'.

7. *(d)* : The word is SANSKRIT and 5th letter from right is 'S'.

8. *(b)* : E N T E R T A I N M E N T

The 1st, 3rd, 5th 7th, 10th and 13th letters are ETRAMT.

The word formed is MATTER.

9. *(c)* : The sport is RUGBY. The letter in the centre is 'G'.

10. *(a)* : The word is SERVICE and fifth letter from right is 'R'.

11. *(b)* : The words formed are : HAS, TEN.

19. LOGICAL DIAGRAM

In these type of questions, a set of five different figures is given as options. Each figure represents a logical pattern of certain groups of related words wherein each word represents a class. One has to identify the most appropriate logical figure for the set of words given. Some of the relationships represented by these diagrams are given below. Understand the relationship patterns and then attempt the exercise following the explanation.

EXERCISE

Directions : *From the five logical Diagrams, select one which best illustrates the relationship among three given classes in the questions 1 to 10.*

(a)

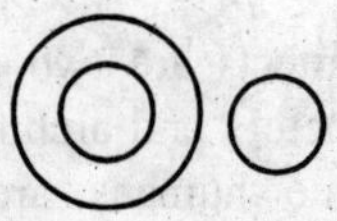

(b)

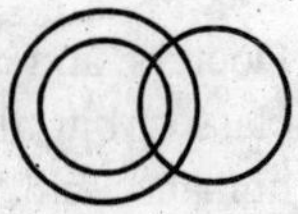

(c)

(d)

(e)

1. Birds, fruits, mangoes
2. Criminals, lawyers, bandits
3. Swimmers, bachelors, men
4. Smart, engineers, women
5. Vegetables, potatoes, brinjals
6. Grapes, sweet, fruit
7. Doctors, architects, humans
8. Scholars, people, Indians
9. Children, naughty, studious
10. Pens, pencils, stationery

Directions : *From the five logical diagrams select one which best illustrates the relationship among three given classes in questions 11 to 20.*

(a)

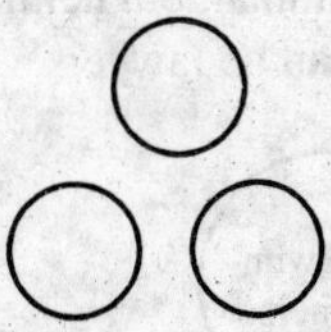

(b)

(c)

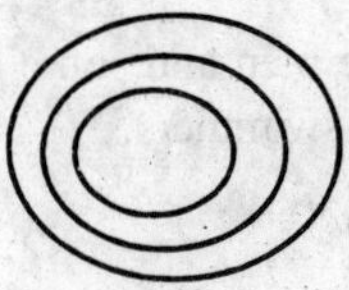

(d)

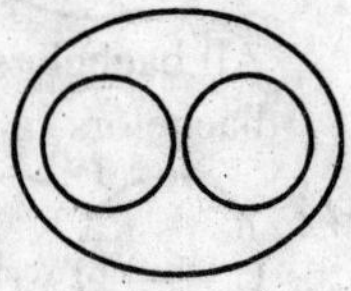

(e)

11. Ink, crayons, red
12. Canines, dogs, pups
13. Table, chair, stool
14. Ripe, mangoes, basket
15. Scholars, studious, illiterates
16. Cars, ships, means of conveyance
17. Age, number, thirteen
18. Country, state, continent
19. Father, parent, mother
20. Iron, metal, mercury

EXPLANATORY ANSWERS

1. *(a)* :

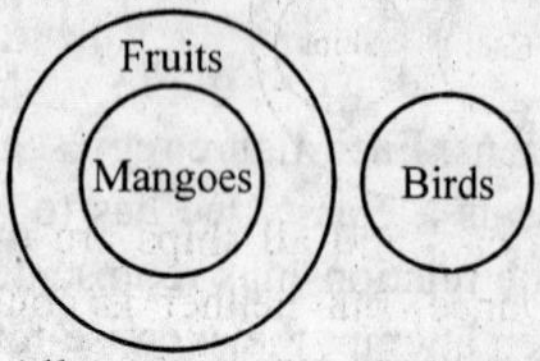

All mangoes are fruits, but neither fruits, nor mangoes can be birds.

2. *(a)* :

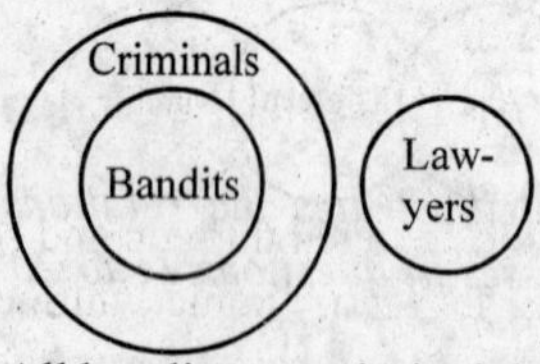

All bandits are criminal, but neither criminals nor bandits can be lawyers.

3. *(b)* :

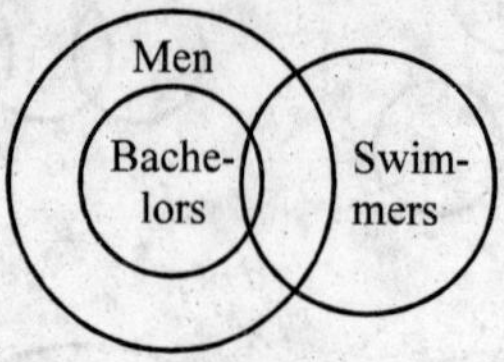

All bachelors are men and some men and bachelors can be swimmers.

4. *(c)* :

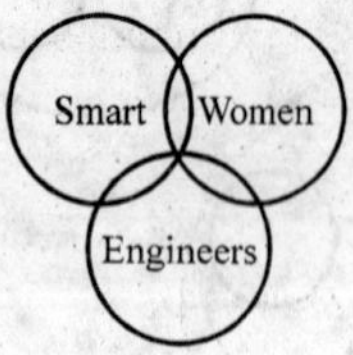

Some women can be smart and some women can be engineers and vice–versa. Some engineers can be women and some engineers can be smart and vice–versa.

5. *(d)* :

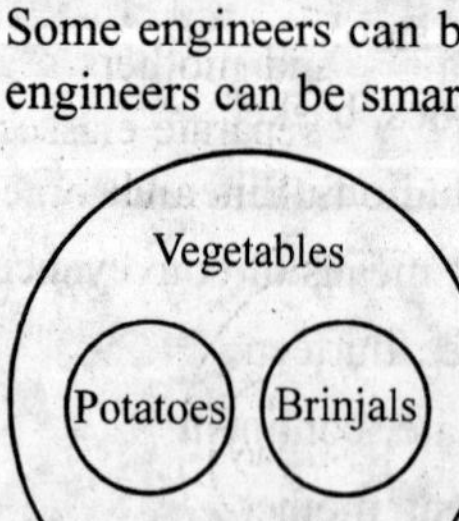

Potatoes and brinjals are vegetables but they have nothing in common. Some vegetables are potatoes and some are brinjals.

6. *(b)* :

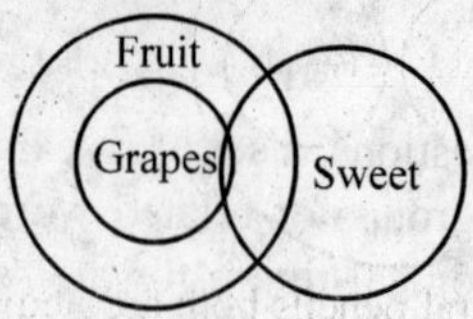

Some grapes are sweet and all grapes are fruit. But not all that is sweet is fruit.

7. *(d)* :

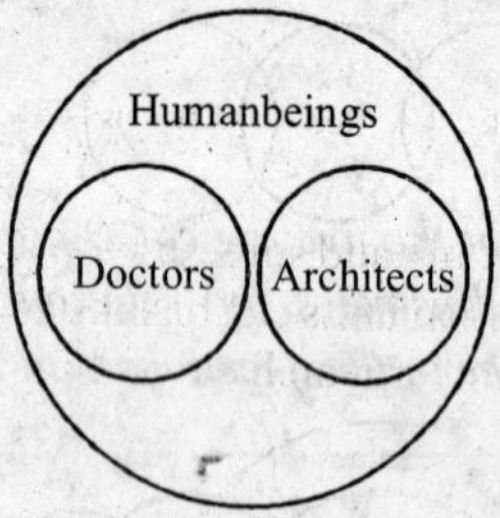

Doctors and architects are two separate classes, but all doctors and architects are humans and some humans are either doctors or architects.

8. *(e)* :

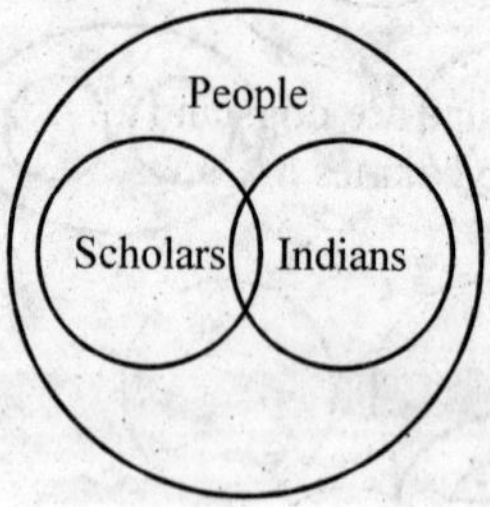

Some Indians can be scholars and some scholars can be Indians. All scholars and Indians are people.

9. *(c)* :

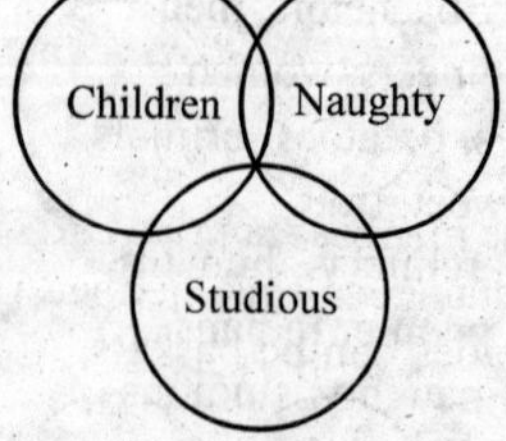

Some children can be naughty and some can be studious, some studious can be children and some naughty. Some naughty can be studious and some children.

10. ***(d)*** **:**

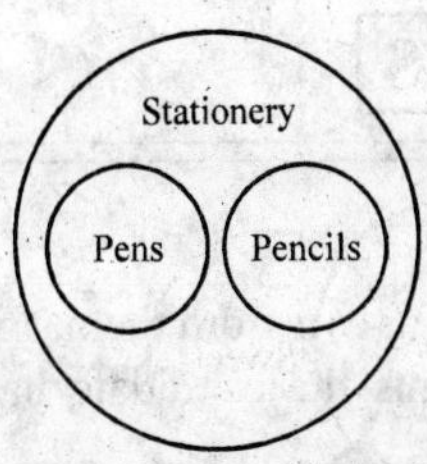

Pens and pencils both are items of stationery and some stationery is pens and pencils, but pens and pencils are two separate classes.

11. ***(b)*** **:**

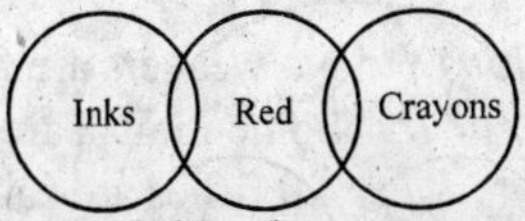

Some ink and some crayons can be red and some red units can be inks and crayons, but ink and crayon have nothing in common.

12. ***(c)*** **:**

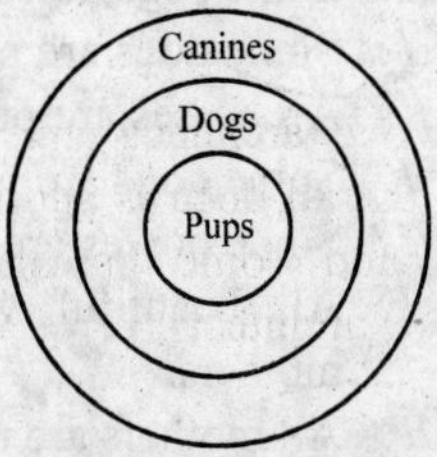

All pups are dogs and all dogs are canines. Some canines are dogs, of which some are pups.

13. ***(a)*** **:**

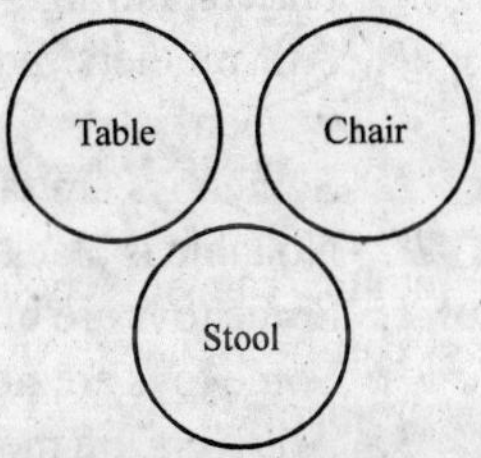

All three are different classes.

14. ***(e)*** **:**

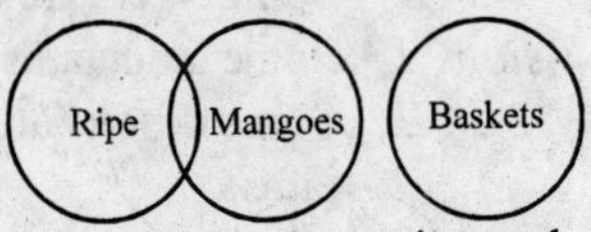

Some mangoes are ripe and some ripe units are mangoes, but neither ripe units nor mangoes can be baskets.

15. ***(e)*** **:**

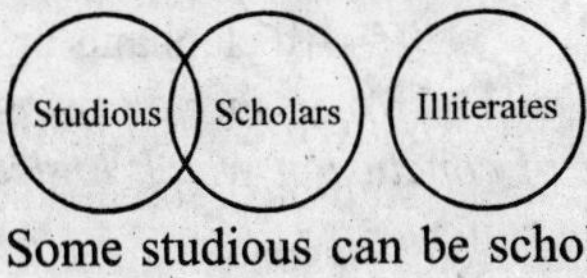

Some studious can be scholars and some scholars can be studious, but neither studious nor scholars can be illiterates.

16. ***(d)*** **:**

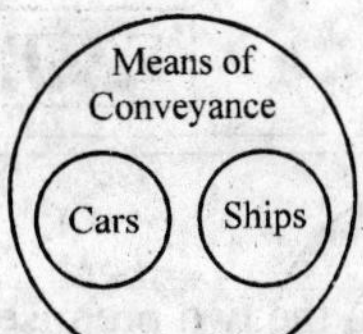

All cars and all ships are means of conveyance, but neither is contained in the other. Some means of conveyance are cars and some ships.

17. ***(b)*** **:**

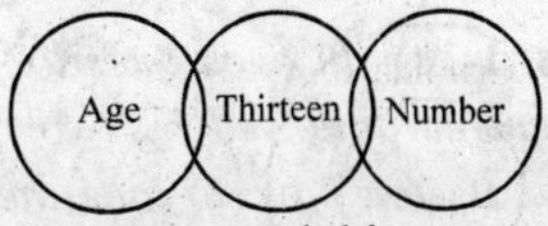

Some are aged thirteen and some numbers are thirteen. Some thirteen units are numbers and some ages. Age and number have nothing in common.

18. ***(c)*** **:**

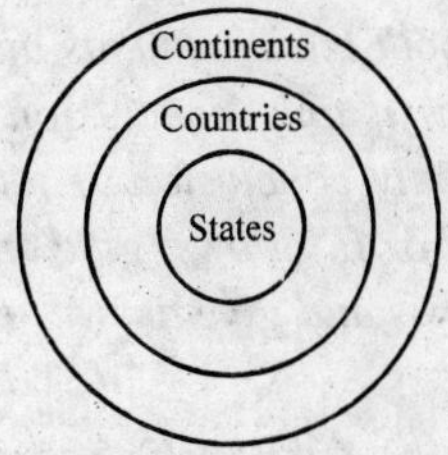

All continents contain countries within it and each country contains states within it.

19. ***(d)*** **:**

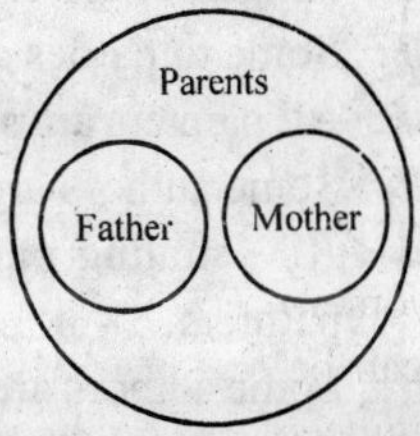

All fathers and mothers are parents, but they are two separate classes. Some of the parents are fathers and some are mothers.

20. ***(d)*** **:**

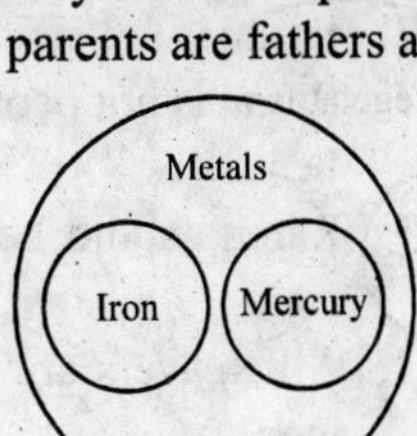

Iron and mercury are metals, but they have nothing in common. Some metals are iron and some mercury.

20. SYLLOGISM

In this reasoning pattern, the two premises are followed by two conclusions drawn from them. Five options *(a)*, *(b)*, *(c)*, *(d)* and *(e)* are given as answers. Based on the two statements the candidate has to select the right option as answer.

EXERCISE

Directions (Qs. 1-10): *In each question below are given two statements followed by two conclusions numbered I and II. You have to take the two given statements to be true even if they seem to be at variance from commonly known facts and then decide which of the given conclusions logically follows from the two given statements, disregarding commonly known facts. Read both the statements and—*

Give answer (a) if only conclusion I follows; give answer (b) if only conclusion II follows; give answer (c) if either I or II follows; give answer (d) if neither I nor II follows and give answer (e) if both I and II follows.

1. *Statements* *I*: All tomatoes are red.
II: All grapes are tomatoes.
Conclusions *I*: All grapes are red.
II: Some tomatoes are grapes.

2. *Statements* *I*: All painters are smilling.
II: Some authors are painters.
Conclusions *I*: All smiling authors are painters.
II: Some authors are smiling.

3. *Statements* *I*: All peons in this office are efficient.
II: Ramu is not efficient.
Conclusions *I*: Ramu is not peon in this office.
II: Ramu should be more efficient.

4. *Statements* *I*: All weavers are hard working.
II: No hard working men are foolish.
Conclusions *I*: No weavers are foolish.
II: Some foolish are weavers.

5: *Statements* *I*: All fishes are cars.
II: All cars are vegetables.
Conclusions *I*: Some vegetables are cars.
II: Some vegetables are fishes.

6. *Statements* *I*: Some dogs are pups.
II: All horses are pups.
Conclusions *I*: Some dogs are horses.
II: Some horses are dogs.

7. *Statements* *I*: All beautiful women are mothers.
II: All mothers are understanding.
Conclusions *I*: All beautiful women are understanding.
II: All mothers are beautiful women.

8. *Statements* *I*: Some toys are tables.
II: No table is black.
Conclusions *I*: Some toys are black.
II: Some toys are not black.

9. *Statements* *I*: All rivers are mountains.
II: Some rivers are deserts.
Conclusions *I*: Some mountains are deserts.
II: Some deserts are not mountains.

10. *Statements* *I*: All men are horses.
II: All horses are elephants.
Conclusions *I*: All men are elephants.
II: All elephants are men.

Directions (Qs. 11-15): *In the following questions, select the set of conclusion which logically follows from the given statements.*

11. *Statements* *I* : All foxes are plates.
II : All plates are trees.
Conclusions *I* : All foxes are trees.
II : All trees are foxes.
III : Some trees are foxes.
IV : Some trees are plates.

(*a*) All conclusions are correct.
(*b*) Only conclusions I, III, and IV follow.
(*c*) Only conclusions II, III, and IV follow.
(*d*) Only conclusions I and IV follow.
(*e*) None of the above.

12. *Statements* *I* : Some cubes are squares.
II : All squares are circles.
Conclusions *I* : All cubes are circles.
II : Some circles are cubes.
III : Some circles are squares.
IV : All squares are cubes.

(*a*) Only conclusion I follows.
(*b*) Only conclusion I, II and III follow.
(*c*) All conclusions are correct.
(*d*) Only conclusions II and III follow.
(*e*) None of the above.

13. *Statements* *I* : All cups are goats.
II : All goats are tins.
Conclusions *I* : All goats are cups.
II : All tins are goats.
III : No cups are tins.
IV : No tins are cups.

(*a*) Only conclusions III and IV follow.
(*b*) Only conclusios I and II follow.
(*c*) Only conclusions I, II and III follow.
(*d*) All conclusions are correct.
(*e*) None of the above.

14. *Statements* *I* : All bombs are bags.
II : Some bags are jets.
Conclusions *I* : All bombs are jets.
II : All jets are bombs.
III : Some jets are bombs.
IV : Some bombs are jets.

(*a*) Only conclusion III follows.
(*b*) Only conclusions I and II follow.
(*c*) All conclusions are correct.
(*d*) Only conclusions III and IV follow.
(*e*) None of these.

15. *Statements* *I* : Some thorns are jackets.
II : Some jackets are boats.
Conclusions *I* : No thorns are boats.
II : All jackets are boats.
III : Some boats are thorns.
IV : No jackets are thorns.

(*a*) Either conclusion I or IV follows.
(*b*) Either conclusion I or II follows.
(*c*) Either conclusion I or III follows.
(*d*) No conclusion is correct.
(*e*) All conclusions are correct.

EXPLANATORY ANSWERS

1. (*e*) : When all tomatoes are red and all grapes are tomatoes, then all grapes are also red. When all grapes are tomatoes, then some tomatoes must be grapes. Therefore, both conclusions I and II are correct.

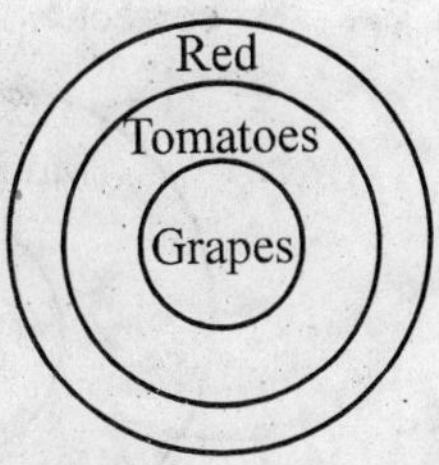

2. (*b*) : When all painters are smiling and some authors are painters, then some authors are smiling. Therefore, only conclusion II is correct.

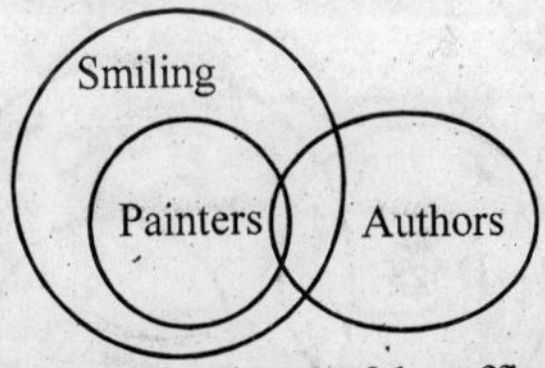

3. (*a*) : When all the peons of the office are efficient, then Ramu cannot be a peon in this office. Therefore, only conclusion I is correct.

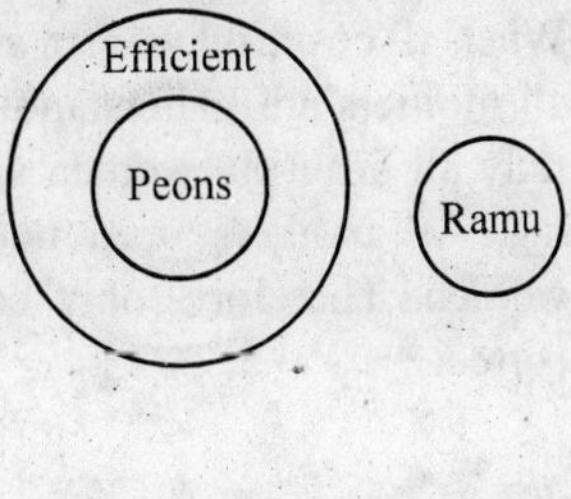

4. *(a)* : When all weavers are hardworking and no hardworking men are foolish, then no weavers are foolish. Therefore, only conclusion I is correct.

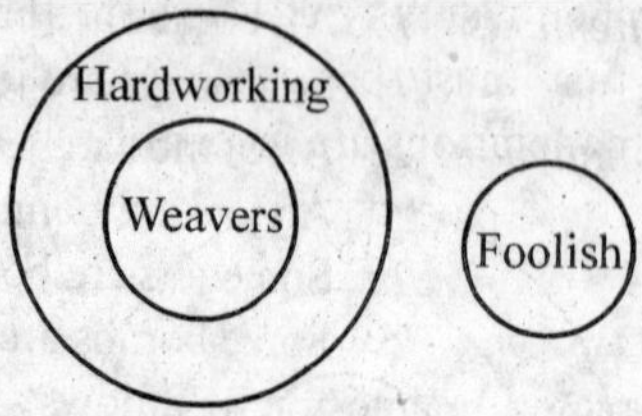

5. *(e)* : When all fishes are cars and all cars are vegetables, then all fishes will naturally be vegetables. This means that some vegetables are fishes. And when all cars are vegetables, then some vegetables will be cars naturally. Therefore, both the conclusions I and II are correct.

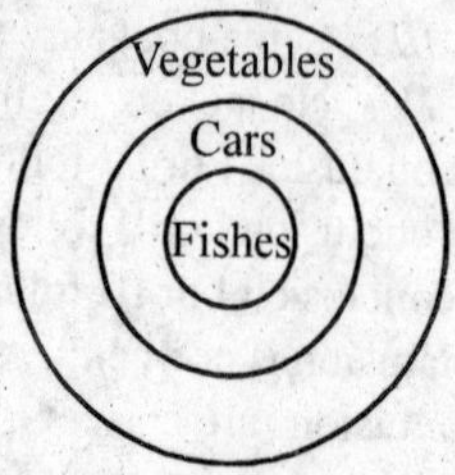

6. *(d)* : No relationship can be established between the two statements. Therefore, neither conclusion I nor conclusion II is correct.

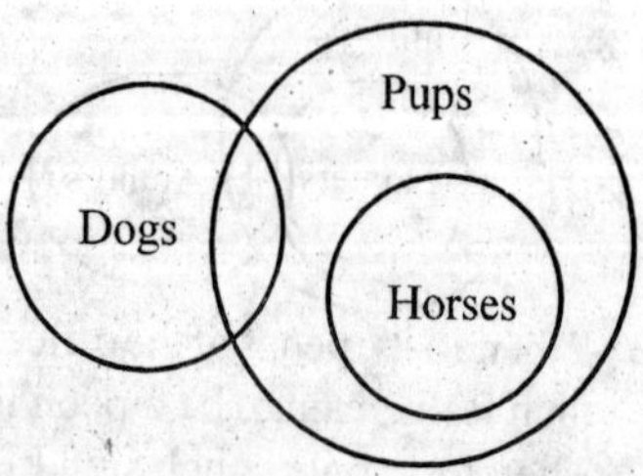

7. *(a)* : When all beautiful women are mothers and all mothers are understanding, then naturally all beautiful women are understanding. All mothers need not be beautiful women. Therefore, only conclusion I is correct.

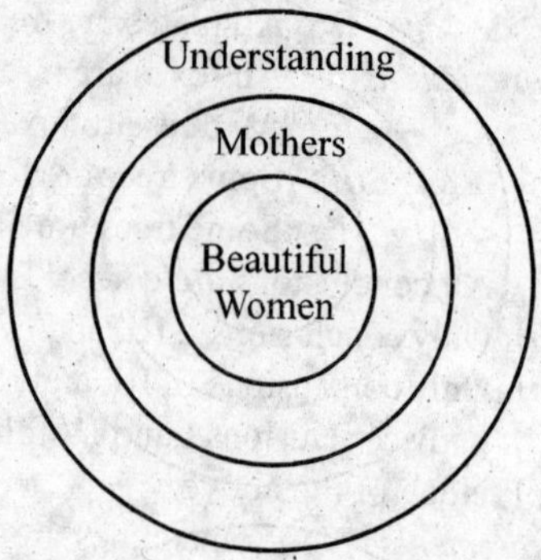

8. *(c)* : When some toys are tables and no table is black, then it is indicated that some toys can be black, as all toys are not tables. On the other hand, some toys may not be black. Therefore, there is a possibility that some toys may or may not be black. As such, either conclusion I or conclusion II can be correct.

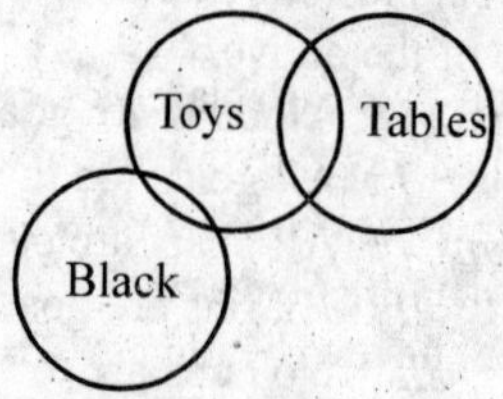

9. *(e)* : When all rivers are mountains and some rivers are deserts, then some deserts cannot be mountains and also, some mountains need not be deserts. Therefore, both conclusion I and conclusion II are correct.

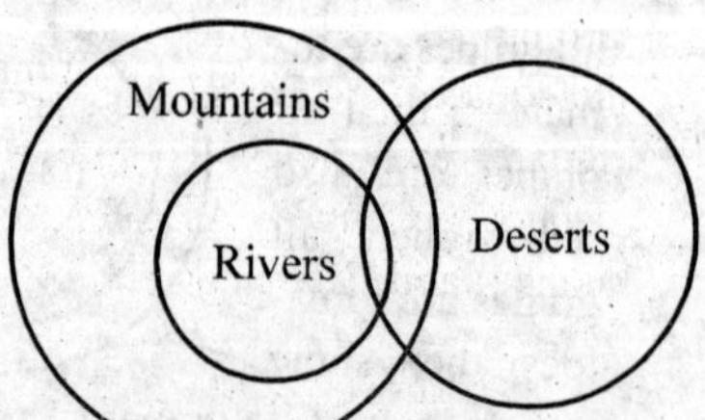

10. *(a)* : When all men are horses and all horses are elephants then, naturally all men are elephants, but all elephants need not be men. Therefore, only conclusion I is correct.

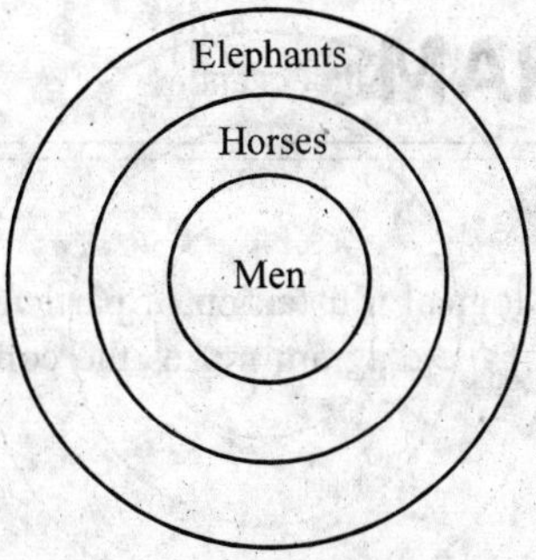

11. ***(b)*** **:**

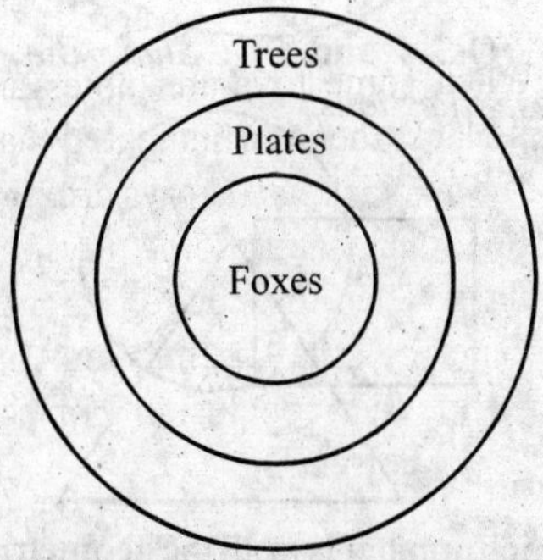

When all foxes are plates and all plates are trees, then naturally all foxes will be trees and some trees will then have to be foxes. And when all plates are trees then some trees will have to be plates. Therefore, only conclusions I, III and IV are correct.

12. ***(d)*** **:** When it is given that some cubes are squares and all squares are circles, then some cubes will naturally be circles, though all cubes cannot be circles. When some cubes are circles, then some circles will have to be cubes. And when all squares are circles, then some circles will have to be squares. As per given statement II, all squares are circles. Therefore all squares cannot be cubes. As such only conclusions II and III are correct.

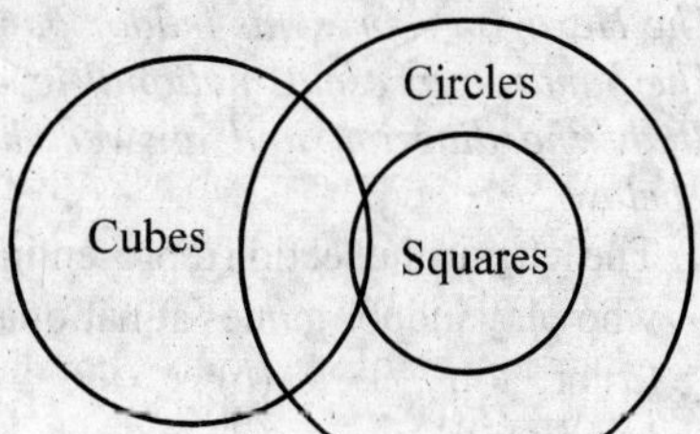

13. ***(e)*** **:** When all cups are goats, then only some goats can be cups. When all goats are tins, then only some tins can be goats. When all cups are goats and all goats are tins, then naturally all cups are tins and some tins must be cups. Therefore, all the conclusions are incorrect.

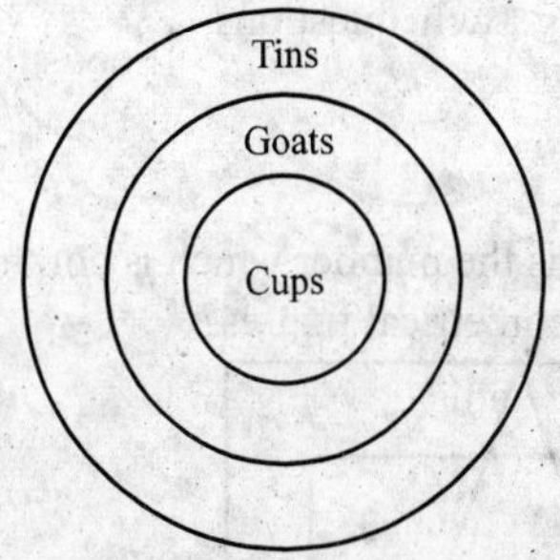

14. ***(e)*** **:** When all bombs are bags and some bags are jets then all bombs cannot be jets. 'Some bags' indicate that there is no chance of some bombs being jets, or some jets being bombs. Further all jets cannot be bombs. Therefore, all conclusions are incorrect.

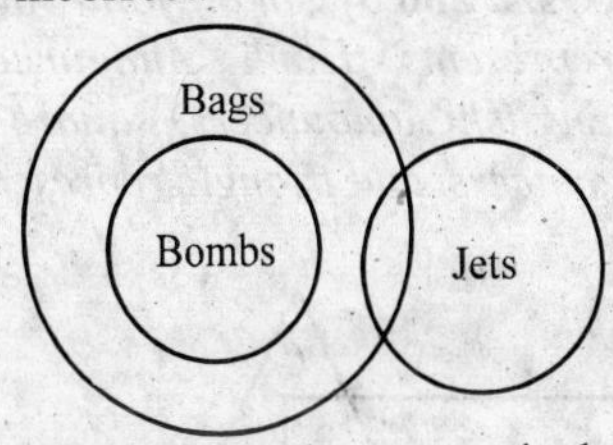

15. ***(d)*** **:** When some thorns are jackets and some jackets are boats, then some thorns may be boats but some boats cannot be thorns. As per Statement I, some thorns are jackets, some jackets need to be thorns. When Statement II conveys that some jackets are boats, then it is clear that all jackets cannot be boats. Therefore, no particular given conclusion can be drawn from the given statements.

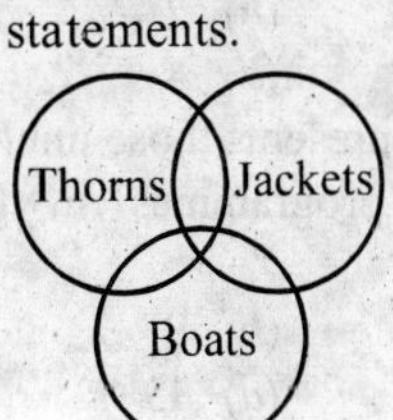

21. VENN DIAGRAMS

In these type of questions, diagrammatic representation presents a logical illustration of particular class or statements based on which the questions are asked. A clear view of the diagram makes the concepts clear for attempting such questions.

EXERCISE

1. What is the number which is common to only two geometrical figures?

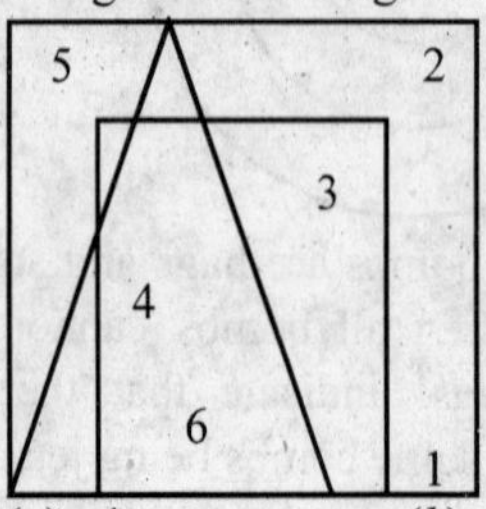

(*a*) 4 (*b*) 3
(*c*) 5 (*d*) 2

Directions (Qs. 2 and 3) : *In the following diagram, rectangle represents Hindi Announcers, circle represents English Announcers, square represents French Announcers, and triangle represents German Announcers.*

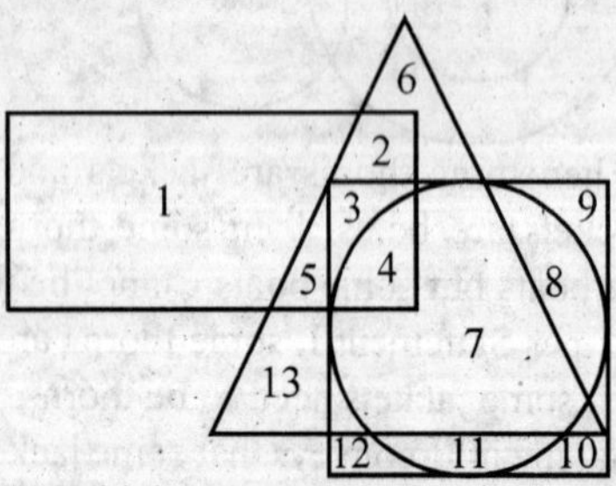

2. Which area represents those announcers who can present programmes in Hindi, French and German only?

(*a*) 1 (*b*) 2
(*c*) 3 (*d*) 4

3 Which area represents those announcers who can present programmes in French and English only?

(*a*) 7 (*b*) 9
(*c*) 11 (*d*) 13

Directions (Qs. 4 and 5) : *Study the diagram to answer these questions.*

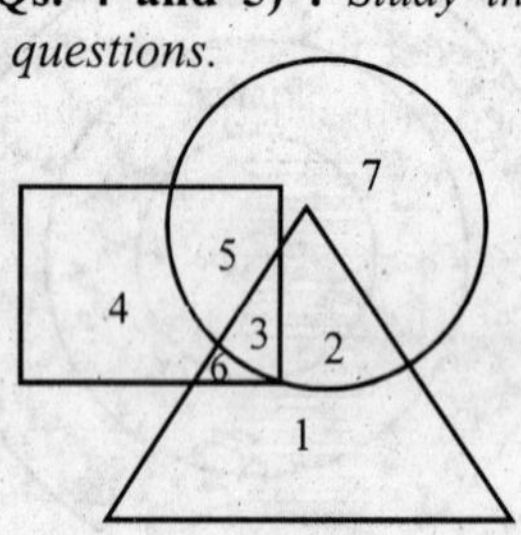

4. Which number is in all the geometrical figures?

(*a*) 5 (*b*) 6
(*c*) 2 (*d*) 3

5. Number 6 is in :

(*a*) Rectangle and triangle
(*b*) Circle and traingle
(*c*) Rectangle and circle
(*d*) Rectangle only

Directions (Qs. 6 to 9) : *In the following diagram*

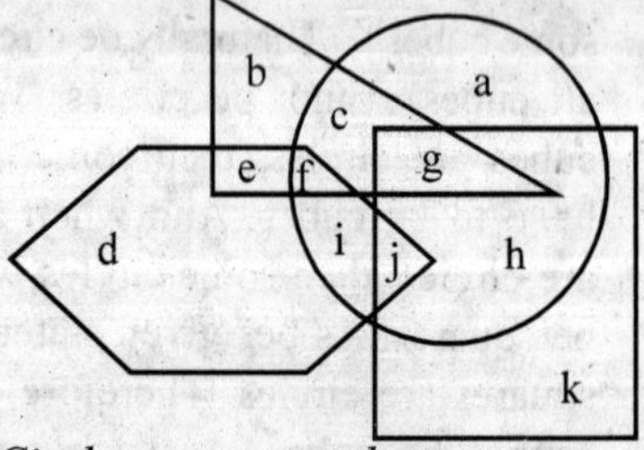

The Circle represents players
The Triangle represents outdoor games
The Hexagon represents indoor games and
The Square represents national level players
Study the diagram and answer the questions given below :

6. The letter in the section representing the players who play indoor games at national level is :

(*a*) f (*b*) i
(*c*) j (*d*) g

7. The letter representing the section of outdoor as well as indoor game players who do not play at the national level is :
(*a*) c (*b*) f
(*c*) e (*d*) i

8. The section representing national level players who do not play either outdoor or indoor games but still come under the category of players is :
(*a*) k (*b*) g
(*c*) c (*d*) h

9. Persons who play outdoor games but do not come under the category of players are represented in the section marked :
(*a*) b (*b*) c
(*c*) a (*d*) d

Direction (Qs. 10) : *Study the diagram given below.*

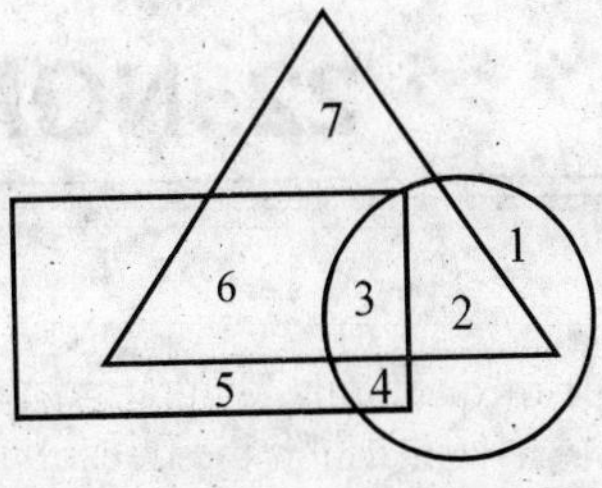

A college provides three different activities, students union represented by triangle, literary society represented by rectangle and social service league represented by circle.

10. Those who take part in both literary society and social service league but not in students union are represented by :
(*a*) 3 & 4 (*b*) 5 & 6
(*c*) 5 & 1 (*d*) 4

EXPLANATORY ANSWERS

1. (*b*) :

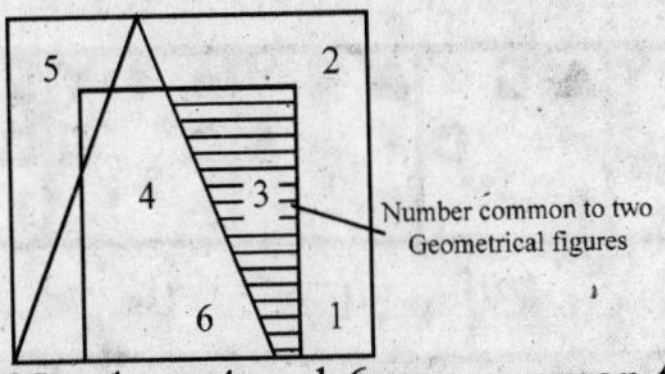

Note : Numbers 4 and 6 are common to all three geometrical figures.

2. (*c*), 3. (*c*) :

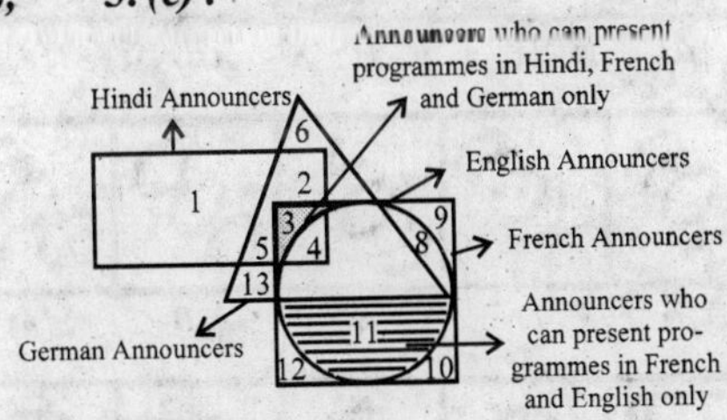

4. (*d*), 5. (*a*) :

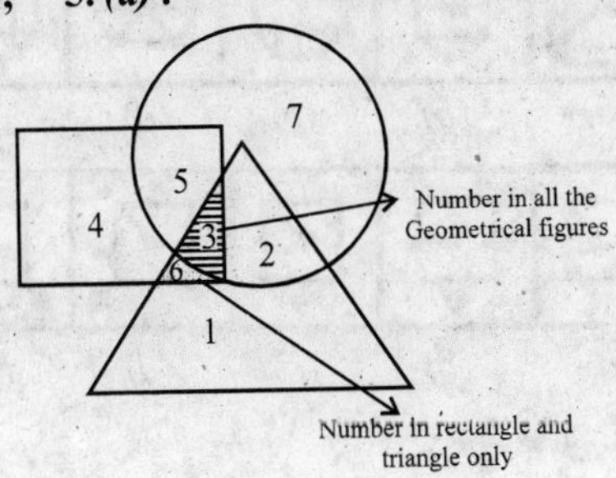

6. (*c*), 7. (*b*), 8. (*d*), 9. (*a*) :

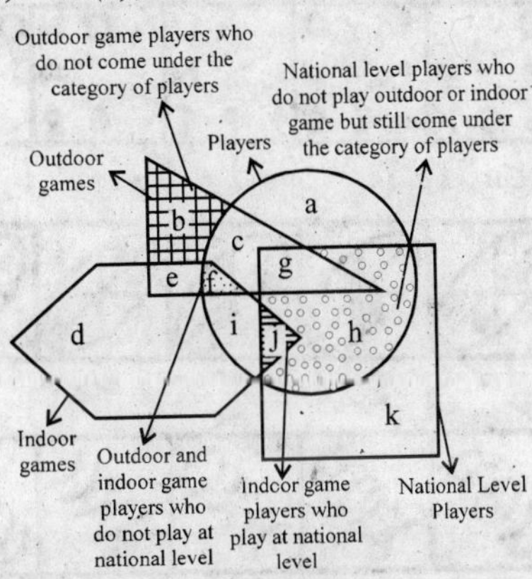

10. (*d*)

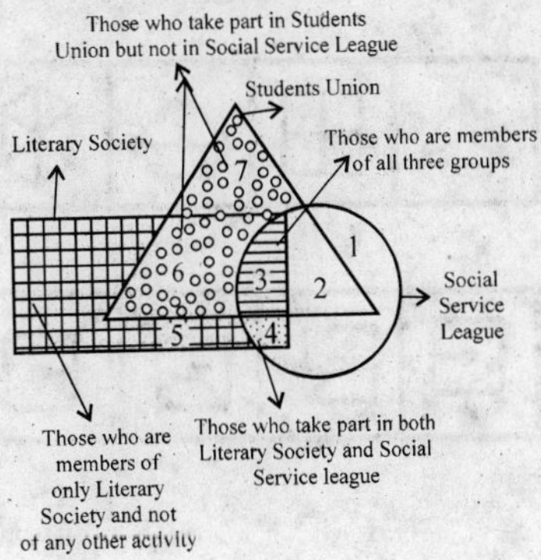

22. NON-VERBAL SERIES

EXERCISE

Directions (Q. 1–10) : *In each of the following questions which one of the five answer figures given below should come after the problem figures if the sequence are continued?*

Problem Figures | **Answer Figures**

1. 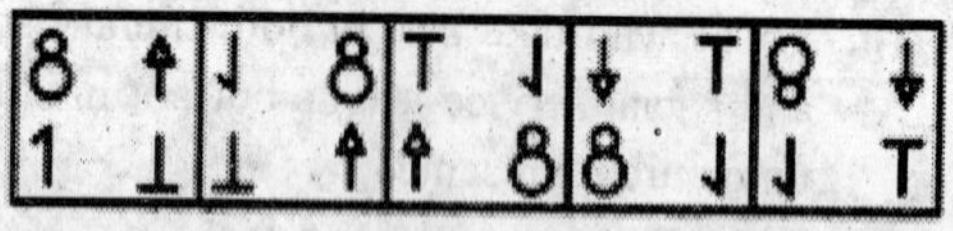 

(a) *(b)* *(c)* *(d)* *(e)*

2. 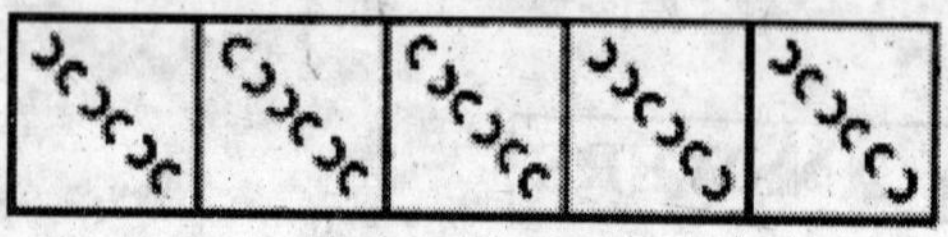 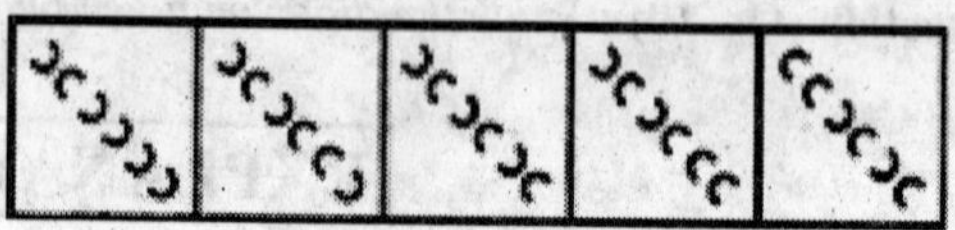

(a) *(b)* *(c)* *(d)* *(e)*

3. 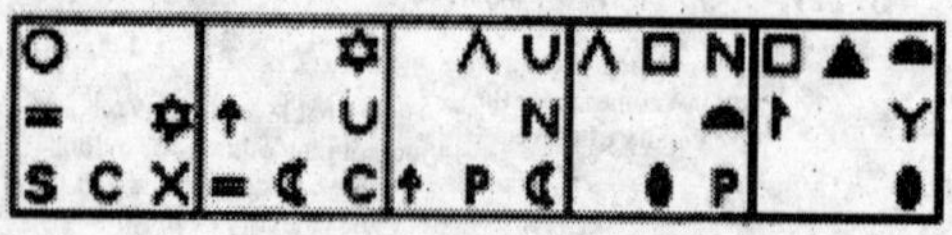 

(a) *(b)* *(c)* *(d)* *(e)*

4.  

(a) *(b)* *(c)* *(d)* *(e)*

5. 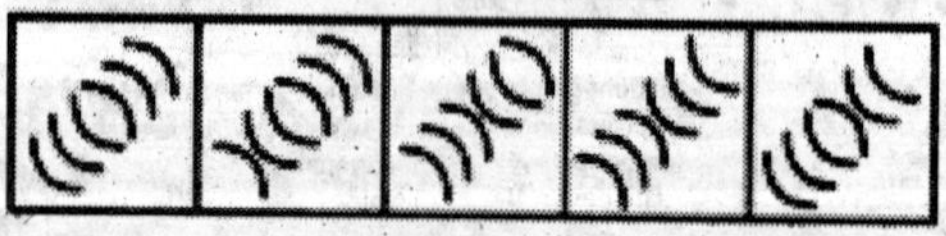 

(a) *(b)* *(c)* *(d)* *(e)*

6.  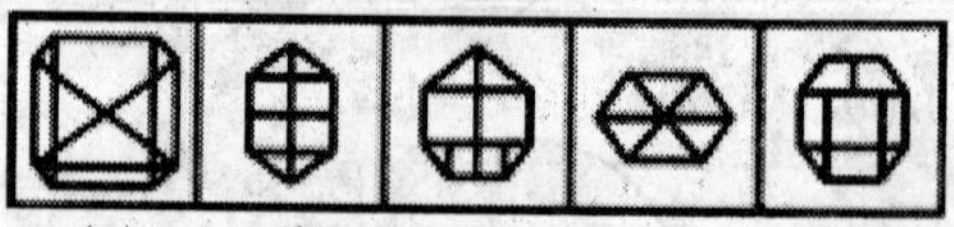

(a) *(b)* *(c)* *(d)* *(e)*

7. 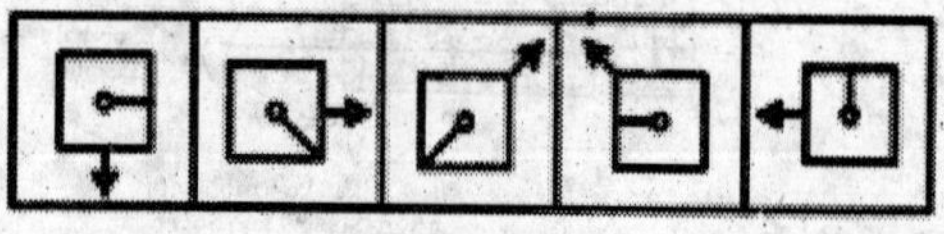 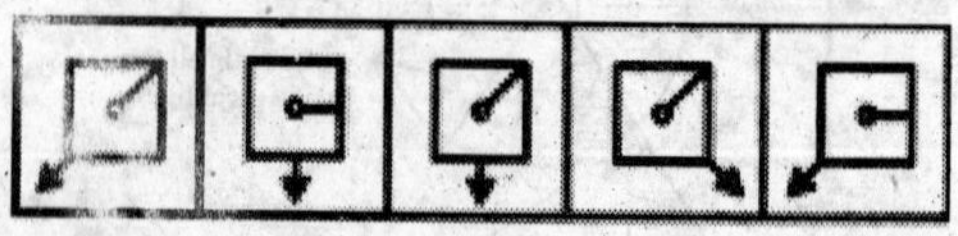

(a) *(b)* *(c)* *(d)* *(e)*

Problem Figures **Answer Figures**

8. 

(a) (b) (c) (d) (e)

9. 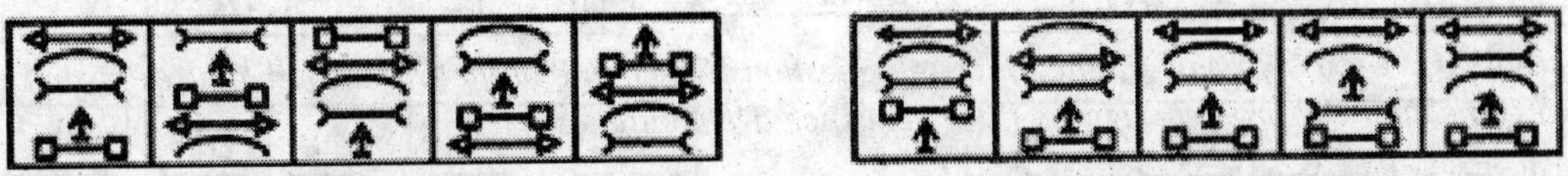

(a) (b) (c) (d) (e)

10. 

(a) (b) (c) (d) (e)

Directions (Q. 11-20) : *In each of these questions, a series begins with an unmarked figure on the extreme left in the row of figures. One and only one of the five lettered figures in the series does not fit into the series. The two unmarked figures, one on the extreme left and the other on the extreme right fit into the series. Take as many aspects into account as possible of the figures in the series and find out the one and only of the five marked figures which does not fit into the series. The letter of that figure is the answer.*

11. 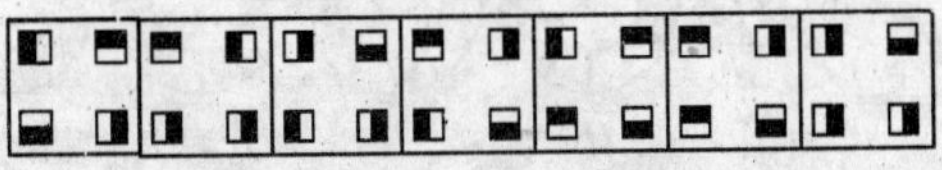

(a) (b) (c) (d) (e)

12. 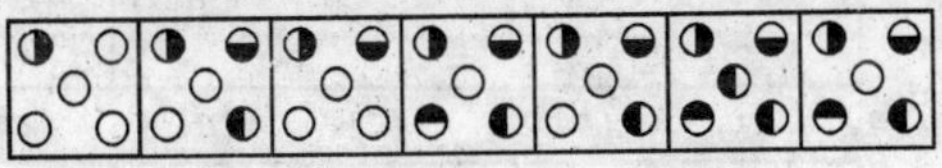

(a) (b) (c) (d) (e)

13. 

(a) (b) (c) (d) (e)

14. 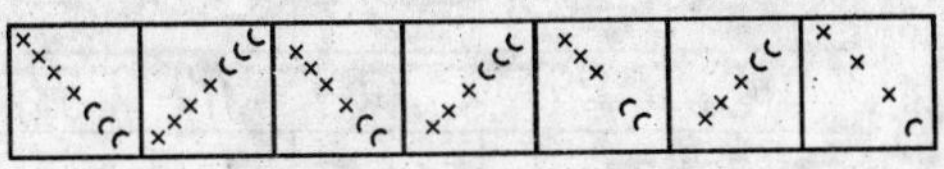

(a) (b) (c) (d) (e)

15. 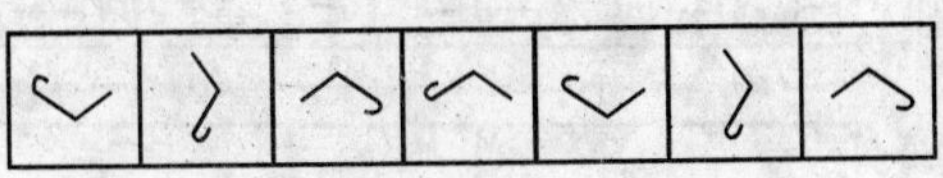

(a) (b) (c) (d) (e)

16. 

(a) (b) (c) (d) (e)

17. 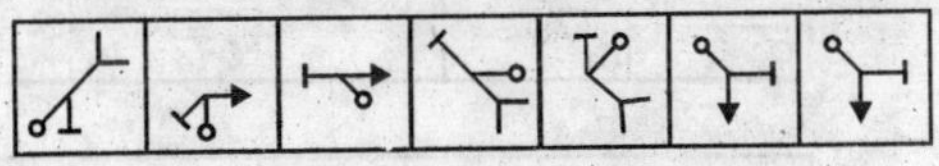

(a) (b) (c) (d) (e)

18. 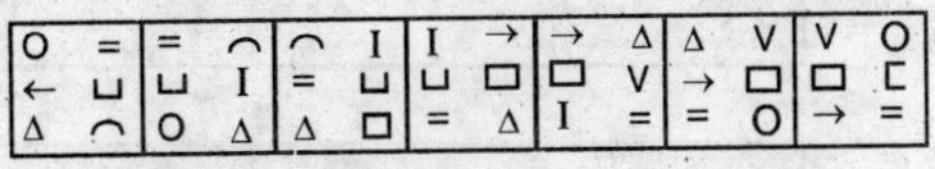

(a) (b) (c) (d) (e)

19. 

(a) (b) (c) (d) (e)

20. 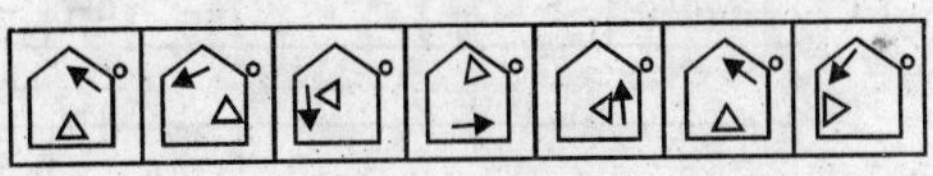

(a) (b) (c) (d) (e)

Directions (Q. 21–30) : *Each of the following questions consist of problem figures followed by answer figures. Select a figure from amongst the answer figures which will continue the same series or pattern as established by the problem figures.*

Problem Figures | **Answer Figures**

21. 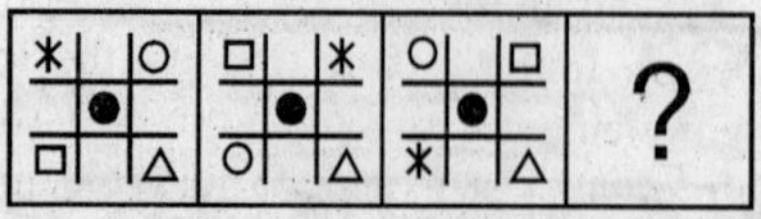 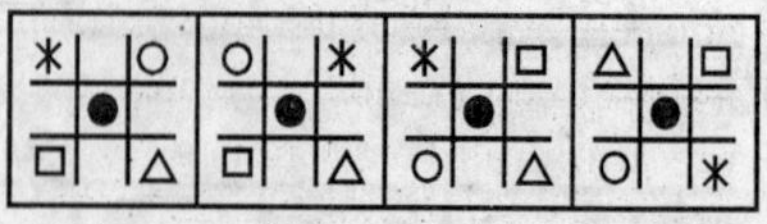

(a) (b) (c) (d)

22. 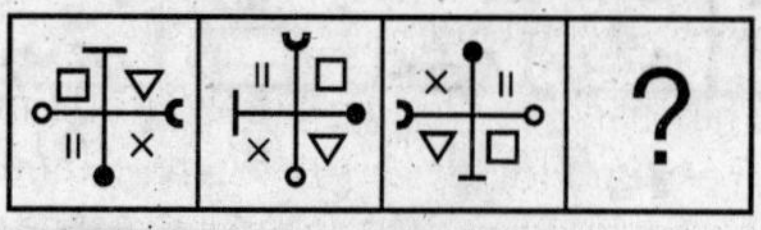 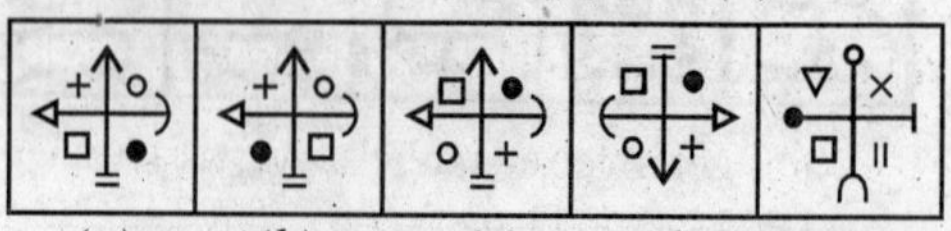

(a) (b) (c) (d) (e)

23. 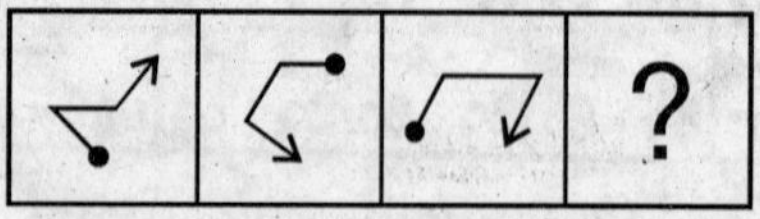 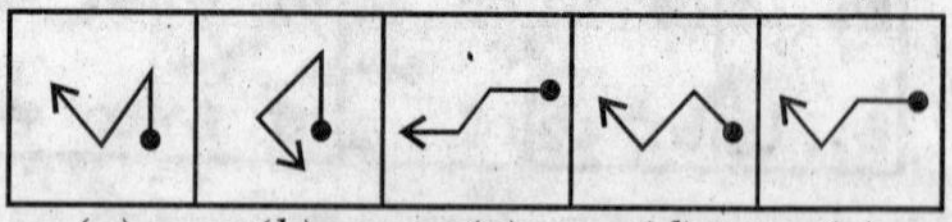

(a) (b) (c) (d) (e)

24. 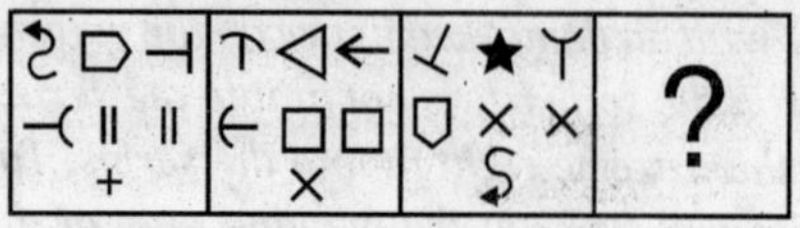 

(a) (b) (c) (d) (e)

25. 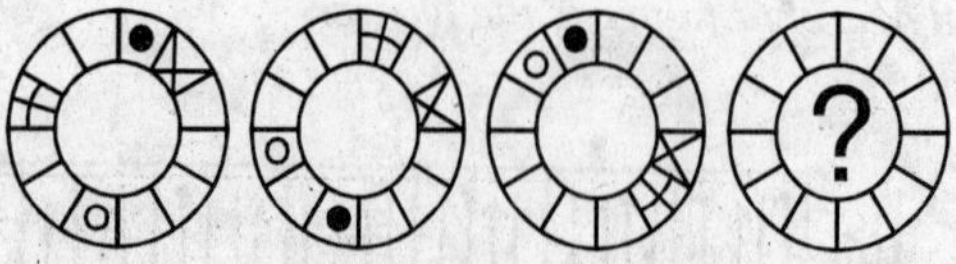 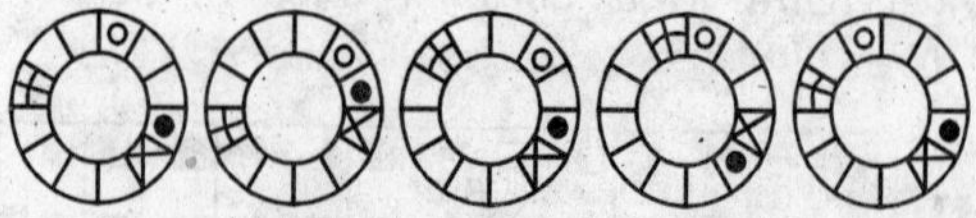

(a) (b) (c) (d) (e)

26. 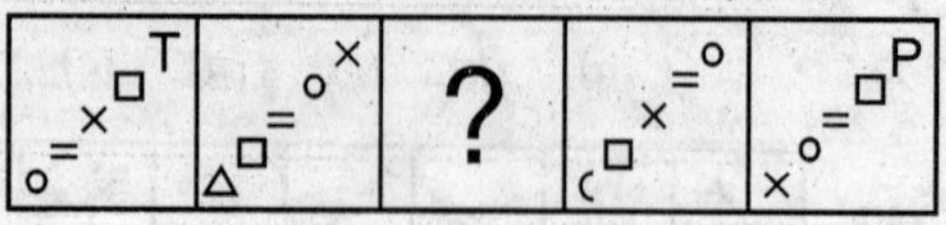 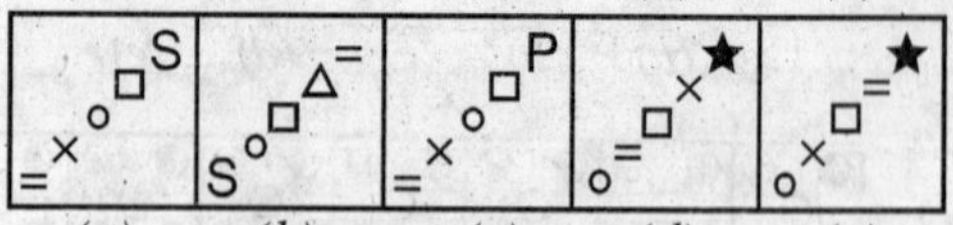

(a) (b) (c) (d) (e)

27. 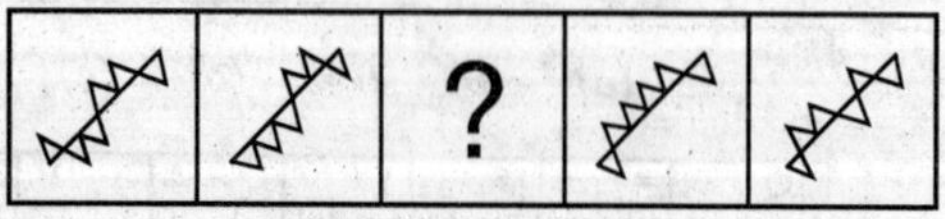 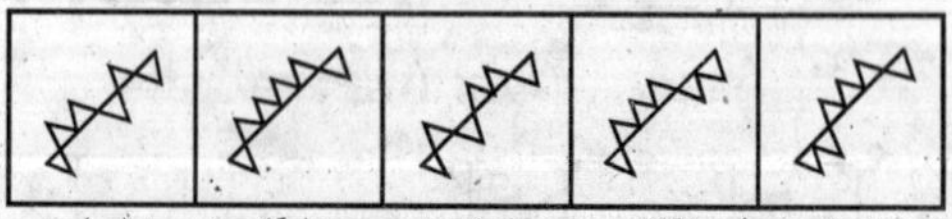

(a) (b) (c) (d) (e)

28. 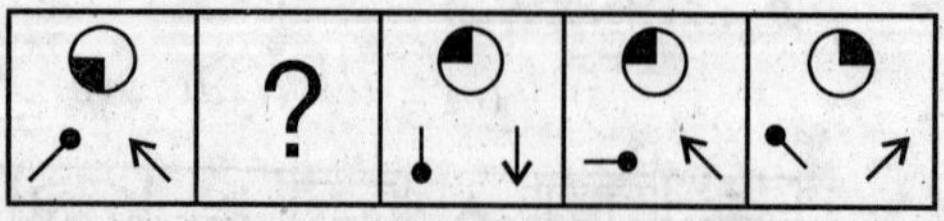 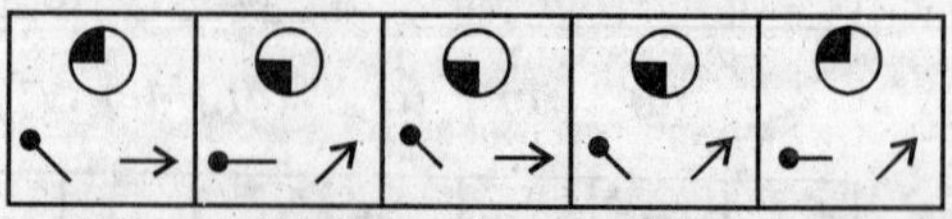

(a) (b) (c) (d) (e)

29.  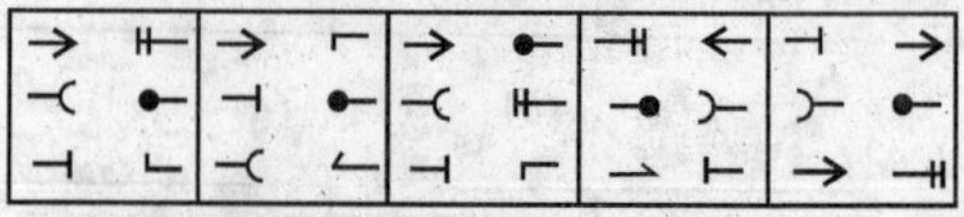

(a) (b) (c) (d) (e)

30. 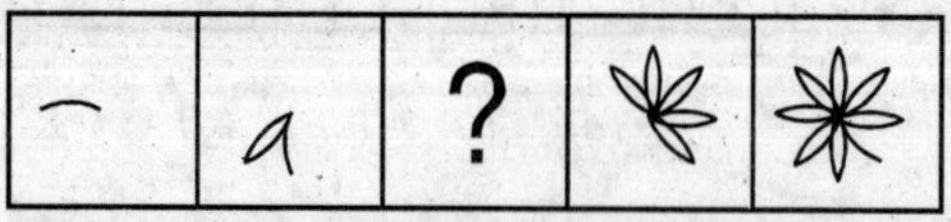 

(a) (b) (c) (d) (e)

EXPLANATORY ANSWERS

1. (d) : In each step, all the elements move to the adjacent corner (of the square boundary) in a CW direction and the element that reaches the upper-left corner gets vertically inverted.

2. (c) : We can label the arcs as shown . The arcs get inverted in the sequence (1 & 2), (3, 4 & 5), (6 & 1), (2, 3 & 4), (5 & 6), ...

3. (d) : All the elements move half-a-side of the square boundary in ACW direction in each step. Also, first, third and fifth elements are replaced by new elements in one step and second, fourth and sixth elements are replaced by new elements in the next step. The two steps are repeated alternately.

4. (a) : In each step, the dot moves one space CW and the arrow moves two spaces CW.

5. (c) : One arc and four arcs get inverted alternately.

6. (e) : The number of parts increases by one along with the number of sides in the figure.

7. (c) : The pin rotates 45°CW and 90°CW alternately and moves one space (each space is equal to half-a-side of the square) and two spaces CW alternately. The arrow rotates 90°ACW and 45°ACW alternately and moves two spaces and one space.

8. (e) : In one step, the two elements interchange positions and the smaller element gets enlarged while the larger element gets reduced in size. In the next step, the smaller element is replaced by a new small element and the larger element is replaced by a new large element.

9. (c) : In each step, the elements move in the order

10. (b) : The upper-left element gets laterally inverted in first, third, fifth. .... steps; the upper-right element gets rotated through 180° is first, fourth, seventh,.... steps; the lower-left element gets laterally inverted in second, fourth, sixth, ... steps; the lower-right element gets rotated through 180° in third, sixth,... steps and the pin at the middle-right position gets laterally inverted in every second step.

11. (a) : The shade in the top left square is moved one step clockwise till figure B and then reversed, the process is repeated. The shade in the top right square is moved one step anticlockwise till figure D and then reversed. The shade in the bottom left square is moved one step clockwise in alternate figures and the shade in bottom right square is moved one step clockwise after two figures. In figure 'A' the rule is isolated by the shade in the bottom left square.

12. (e) : In alternate figures a new circle is shaded clockwise. The pattern of the shade is also moved clockwise. In figure 'E' right half of the circle in the centre should have been shaded.

13. (a) : The three elements are placed either horizontally or vertically. In option 'A' neither of the placements can be applied.

14. (c) : The placement of elements is same in alternate figures. The number and type of elements is same in two subsequent figures. In this manner, figure 'C' should have four crosses and two C shapes.

15. (c) : The element is moved one step anticlockwise and the arc at one end is turned outside and inside alternately. In figure 'C' the element should be on the right side with the arc turned outside on the top side.

16. (e) : The left most element, line segment with the dot is moved one step towards right till figure C where it reaches the extreme right position. This process is repeated from figure D where the element on the extreme left, line segment with a circle, is moved. In figure 'E' the placement of the elements does not follow the rule of the series.

17. *(e)* : The 'T' line is rotated 45° clockwise and the line with the circle 45° anticlockwise. The 'Y' shape and the arrow are repeated twice after two figures. In option E, the 'T' shape and the line with the circle are rotated by 90°.

18. *(e)* : First the elements in the four corners are moved one step anticlockwise, next the four elements from the top are moved one step anticlockwise and then the four elements from the bottom are moved one step anticlockwise. Of the remaining two elements, the one on the left is made new each time and then their places are interchanged. This process is repeated from figure D. In option 'E' open square should have been in place of circle to continue the series.

19. *(a)* : At each step the outermost figure is removed and a new figure is placed right in the centre of other two figures. In option 'A' the triangle is turned upside down, which violates the rule of the series.

20. *(a)* : The arrow is moved one step anticlockwise and the triangle one step clockwise. In figure 'A' the triangle should have been on the left side of the figure.

21. *(a)* : The places of star, circle and square are moved one step clockwise at each step.

22. *(e)* : The elements in the four quadrants are moved one step clockwise and the elements at the ends of the cross are moved one step anticlockwise in this series.

23. *(a)* : In alternate figures, the line with the dot is turned 90° clockwise and the arrow 180° clockwise.

24. *(e)* : In alternate figures, the element in the top left position is horizontally inverted and moved one and half steps anticlockwise, the top middle element is turned 90° clockwise and moved one step anticlockwise, the top right element is turned 135° clockwise and moved one step anticlockwise, the element at the bottom is replaced by a new element and moved to the top middle position, and the two identical elements are replaced by two new identical elements.

25. *(a)* : The cross and the circle move one and two steps clockwise respectively (at each step), the plus moves 3, 4 and 5 steps clockwise, and the dot 6, 5 and 4 steps clockwise.

26. *(a)* : At first step, the fifth or the bottom most element is moved to the second place from top, the second element moved to the fourth place, the fourth element is moved to the third place, the third element is moved to the first or the topmost place and the element on the top, which is made new, is moved to the last or the fifth place. At second step i.e., from second problem figure to third problem figure the above process is reversed. The bottom most element is the first and the top most element is the last or fifth. Hereafter, the process is repeated from the beginning. Option 'A' is the right answer.

27. *(c)* : Starting from the bottom, one triangle is moved to the opposite side at each step in upward order. Option 'C' fits into the question marked space.

28. *(c)* : The shade inside the circle is rotated clockwise in alternate figures; the line segment with a dot is rotated 135° clockwise in alternate figures and the arrow is rotated 135° anticlockwise in alternate figures. By this process answer figure 'C' completes the series.

29. *(a)* : At each step the elements are moved diagonally upward and then laterally inverted, and the top two elements are made new and placed at the bottom line. By this process, option figure 'A' completes the series.

30. *(a)* : The number of arcs making the petals of the flower are increased by one, one and half, two, two and half respectively at each step. Also, the flower is turned 45° anticlockwise. By this process, option 'A' is the right answer.

23. NON-VERBAL ANALOGY

EXERCISE

TYPE-I

Directions (Q. 1-15): *The second figure in the first unit of the Problem Figures bears a certain relationship to the first figure. Similarly, one of the figures in the Answer Figures bears the same relationship to the first figures in the second unit of the Problem Figures. Locate the figure which would fit the questions marks.*

Problem Figures **Answer Figures**

1.

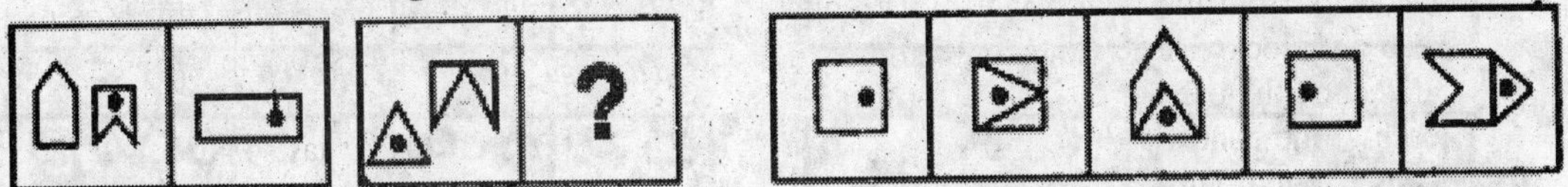

1 2 3 4 (a) (b) (c) (d) (e)

2.

1 2 3 4 (a) (b) (c) (d) (e)

3.

1 2 3 4 (a) (b) (c) (d) (e)

4.

1 2 3 4 (a) (b) (c) (d) (e)

5.

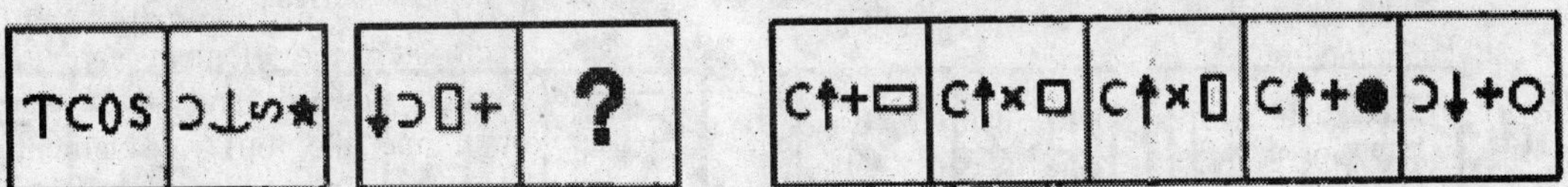

1 2 3 4 (a) (b) (c) (d) (e)

6.

1 2 3 4 (a) (b) (c) (d) (e)

Problem Figures **Answer Figures**

7. 

1 2 3 4 (a) (b) (c) (d) (e)

8. 

1 2 3 4 (a) (b) (c) (d) (e)

9. 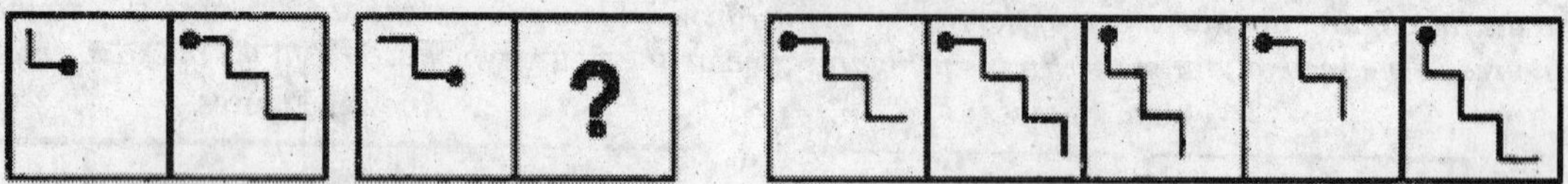

1 2 3 4 (a) (b) (c) (d) (e)

10. 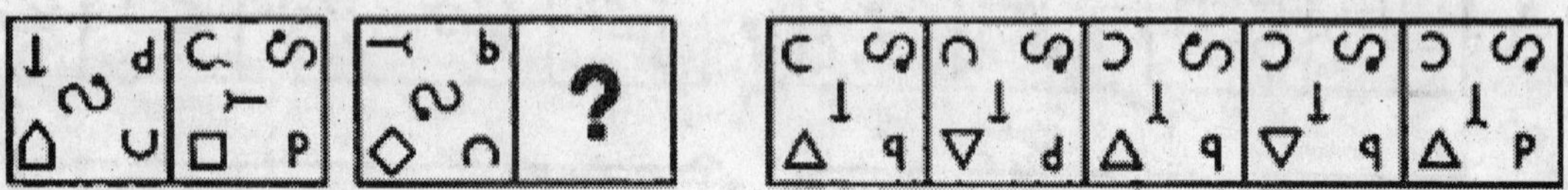

1 2 3 4 (a) (b) (c) (d) (e)

11. 

1 2 3 4 (a) (b) (c) (d) (e)

12. 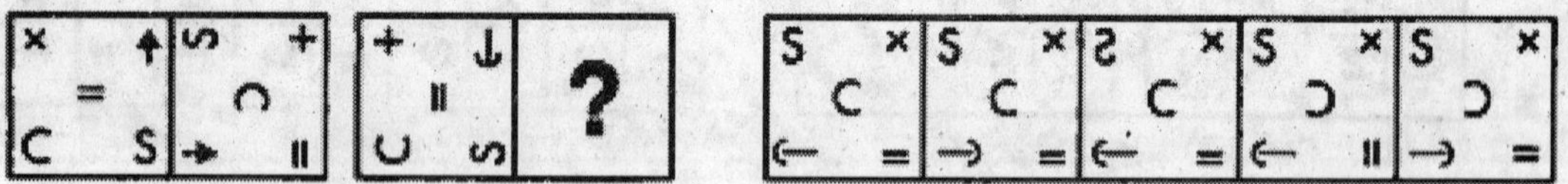

1 2 3 4 (a) (b) (c) (d) (e)

13. 

1 2 3 4 (a) (b) (c) (d) (e)

14. 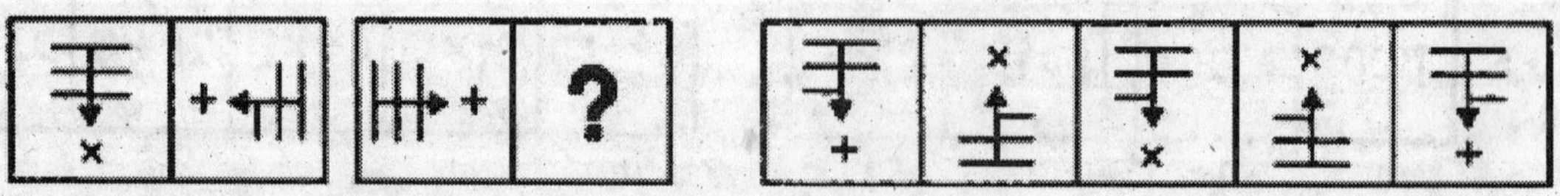

1 2 3 4 (a) (b) (c) (d) (e)

15. 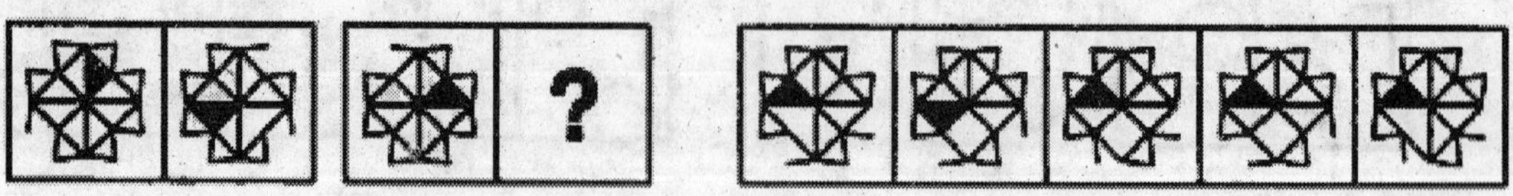

1 2 3 4 (a) (b) (c) (d) (e)

TYPE-II

Directions (Q. 16–30): *In each of the following questions, a related pair of figures is followed by five numbered pairs of figures. Select the pair that has a relationship* **similar** *to that in the unnumbered pair.*

Problem Figure **Answer Figures**

16.
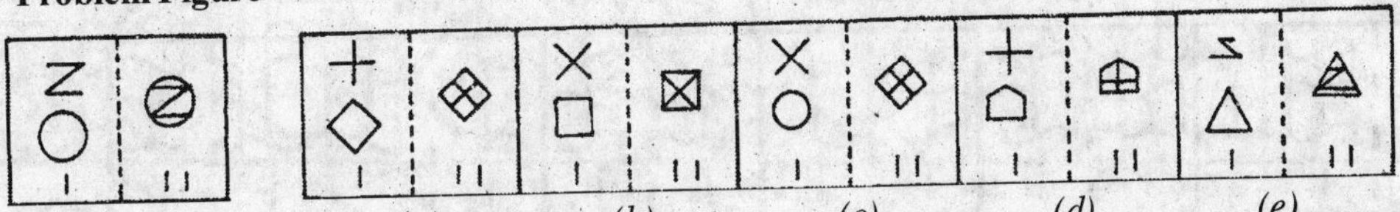
(a) (b) (c) (d) (e)

17.
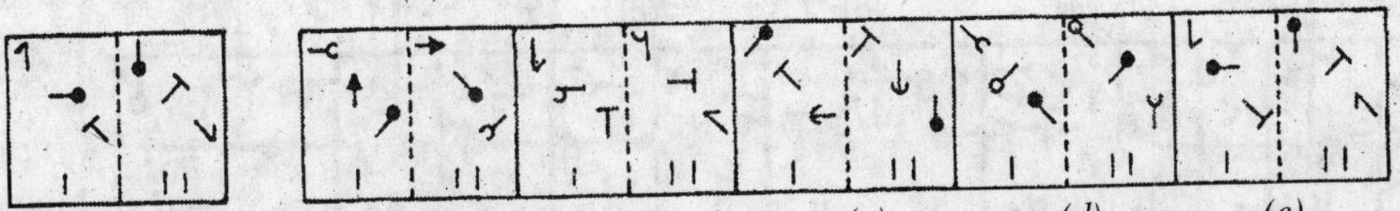
(a) (b) (c) (d) (e)

18.
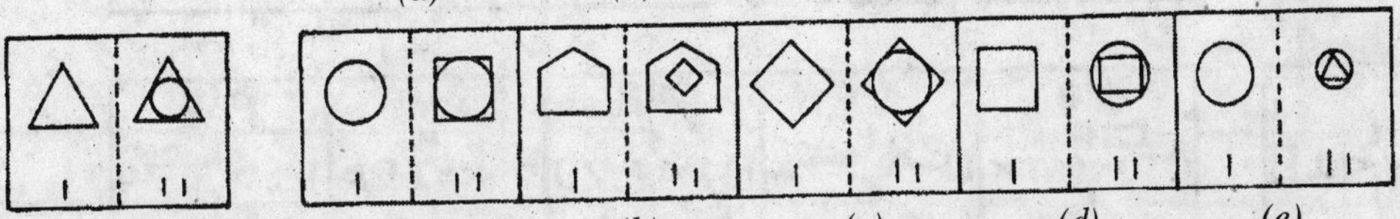
(a) (b) (c) (d) (e)

19.
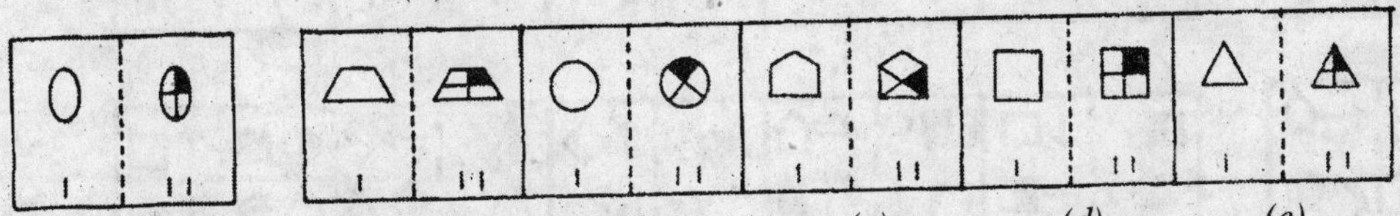
(a) (b) (c) (d) (e)

20.
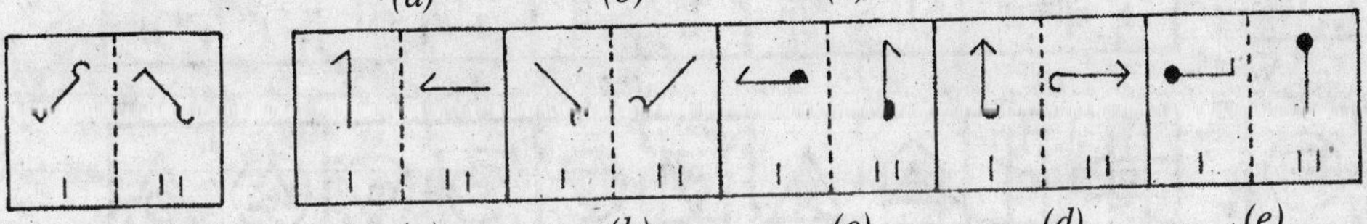
(a) (b) (c) (d) (e)

21.
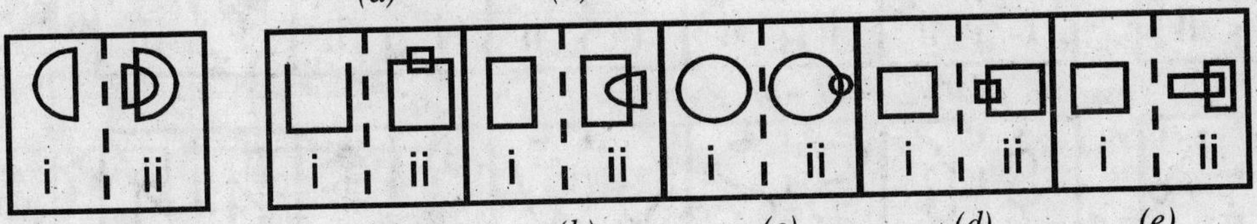
(a) (b) (c) (d) (e)

22.
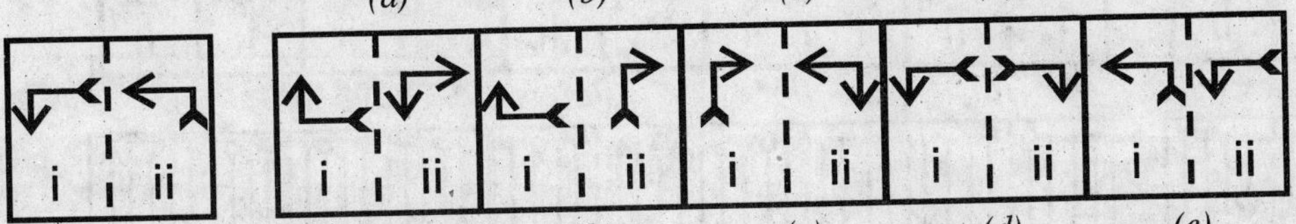
(a) (b) (c) (d) (e)

Problem Figure **Answer Figures**

23. 

(a) (b) (c) (d) (e)

24. 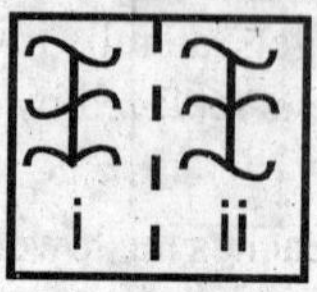

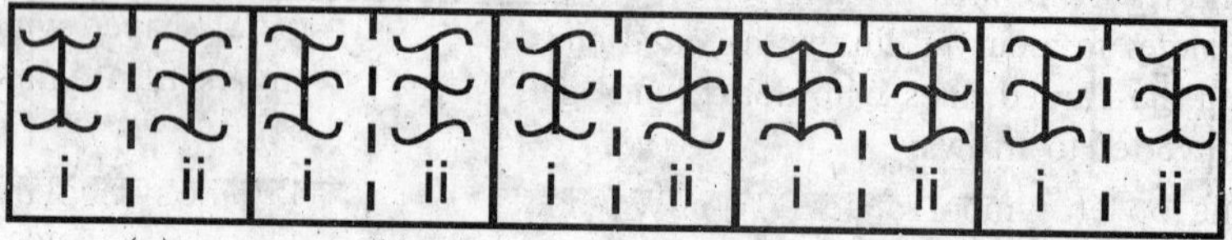

(a) (b) (c) (d) (e)

25. 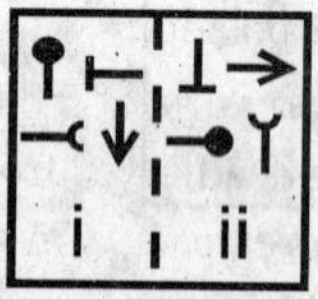

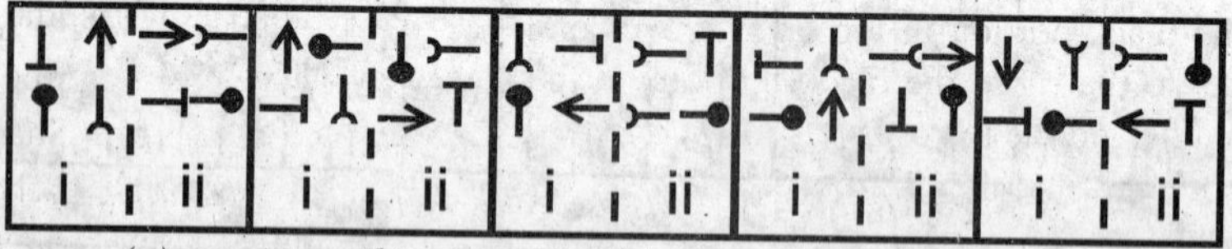

(a) (b) (c) (d) (e)

26. 

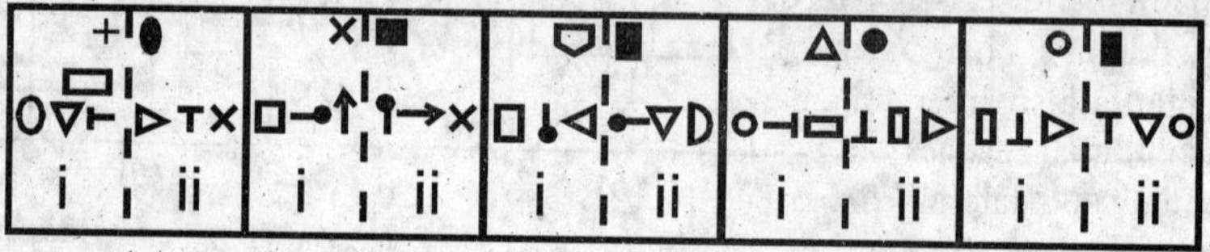

(a) (b) (c) (d) (e)

27. 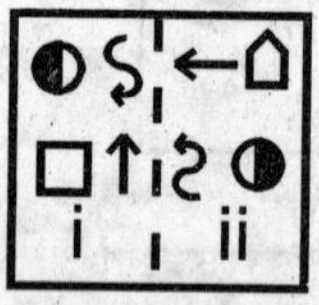

(a) (b) (c) (d) (e)

28. 

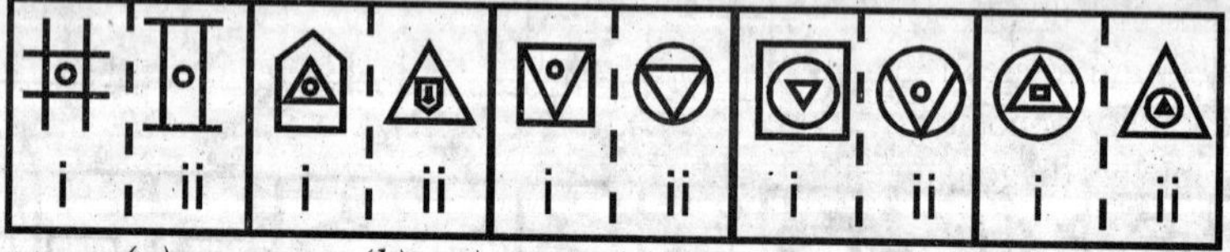

(a) (b) (c) (d) (e)

29. 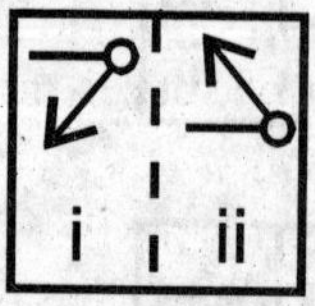

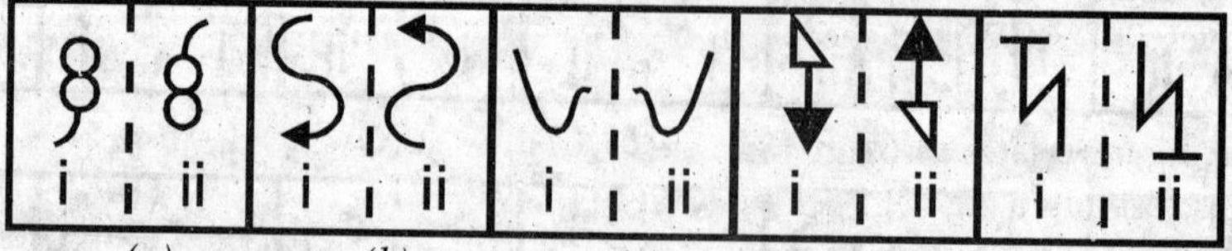

(a) (b) (c) (d) (e)

30. 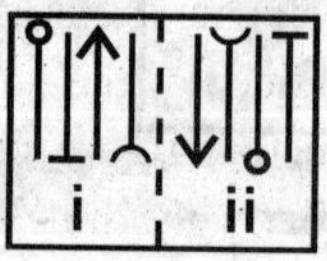

(a) (b) (c) (d) (e)

EXPLANATORY ANSWERS

1. (b) : The R.H.S. figure is fitted into the L.H.S. figure and the resulting figure is rotated 90° CW.

2. (b) : The figure rotates 45° ACW, the arrow changes to a curved line with dotted ends and the curved lines with dotted ends get converted to arrows.

3. (d) : The top left symbol rotates 90° ACW while all other symbols rotate 90° CW.

4. (e) : The black portion in top layer moves one step to the right; the black portions in the middle and the lower layers move one step to the left and the dot moves one step upwards.

5. (d) : The first and second symbols from the left interchange positions and the other two symbols also interchange positions. The symbol that reaches the first position from the left gets laterally inverted; the symbol that reaches the second position gets inverted, the third symbol rotates 90° CW and the fourth symbol gets replaced by a new one.

6. (d) : The single figure is replaced by a figure similar to the double figures and the double figures are replaced by figures similar to the single figure.

7. (e) : The figure rotates 135° ACW; a 'T' appears diagonally opposite to the black leaf and a 'Y' appears diagonally opposite to the white leaf.

8. (c) : The square rotates through 45°. The arrow moves 90° ACW and the pin moves 45° ACW.

9. (b) : The figure rotates through 180° and three lines forming a zig-zag, get attached to its lower end.

10. (d) : The symbols move in the order

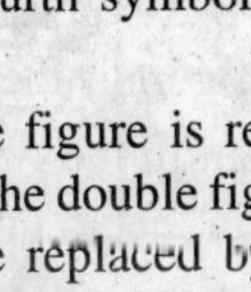

The symbol that reaches the central position rotates 90° CW and its arc gets inverted; the 'P' shaped symbol rotates through 180°; the 'C' shaped symbol rotates 90° CW; the 'S' Shaped symbol gets laterally inverted and the fifth symbol gets replaced by a new one.

45°, the symbol that reaches the lower right corner rotates 90° ACW and a new symbol appears in middle-left position.

11. (e) : The upper and the lower parts of the figure get separated. Shading is removed from the upper part and the lower part is inverted. The two parts are then placed side by side.

12. (a) : The symbols move in the order

The symbol that reaches the top-left corner rotates 90° ACW; the symbol in the top-right corner rotates through 45°; the symbols in the lower-left corner and in the central positions rotates 90° CW and the symbol that reaches the lower-right corner rotates through 90°.

13. (e) : The figure gets laterally inverted. The dot on the larger arc, the pin and the small arc rotate 90° ACW. Also, the pin gets inverted.

14. (c) : The figure rotates 90° CW. One half of one of the lines on the arrow is lost. The figure in front of the arrowhead rotates through 45°.

15. (d) : The missing line segment in the first figure is replaced in second. Then moving ACW, the third line segment is removed along the two next consecutive sides of the square. Shaded portion in the first figure moves three steps ACW. Similarly, the third figure gives figure (D).

16. *(b)* : The uppermost design enters into innerside side of the lower design from Ist figure to the IInd figure.

17. *(a)* : In element I to II upper left design comes at lower right rotating 135° C.W. Middle design goes to upper left and rotates 90° CW. While lower right design goes to middle and it also rotates 90° C.W. The same changes occur in option A.

18. *(e)* : In element I to II and ellipse is put in the triangle. Similarly in option E a triangle is put in the ellipse.

19. *(d)* : From first figure to IInd figure, design is divided into four equal parts and right side of the upper portion becomes shaded.

20. *(e)* : From Ist figure to IInd figure, design is reversed after moving 90° anticlockwise direction.

21. *(d)* : The figure in the first part is laterally inverted and a similar but smaller design is placed on its left side in the second part.

22. *(e)* : The element in first part is moved by 90° and the places of short and long line segments are interchanged.

23. *(c)* : The number of sides making the top left figure is increased by one and a new figure is made, shaded and moved to the top right position. The element in the centre is turned 90° anticlockwise and the small line on the other side is turned by 180°. The element in the bottom right is turned upside down and moved to the bottom left position.

24. *(a)* : The direction of both arcs on the top, are on the middle right and arc on the bottom left in first part are turned to the other side in the second part.

25. *(b)* : From part one to part two, the element in the top left is turned 90° clockwise and the other three 90° anticlockwise, also the elements are moved one step anticlockwise.

26. *(b)* : From part one to part two, the top right element is turned by 90° and moved down, the lower right and middle elements are turned 90° clockwise and 90° anticlockwise respectively and moved to the left and the lower left element is shaded and moved up.

27. *(a)* : All the four elements exchange place diagonally and in doing so the top left element is laterally inverted, the top right element is horizontally inverted, the bottom right element is turned 90° anticlockwise and the number of lines making the element in bottom left is increased by one.

28. *(e)* : The innermost figure is removed and the new innermost figure also encloses the other two figures. The innermost and smallest figure is then shaded.

29. *(b)* : The design in the first part is horizontally inverted in the second.

30. *(b)* : All the elements in the first part are turned upside down and then 1st, 2nd, 3rd and 4th positioned elements become 3rd, 4th, 1st and 2nd elements in the second part.

24. ODD MAN OUT

In this type of reasoning a statement is followed by inferences drawn from it. From these inferences only one definitely follows which is the hidden proposition of the sentence and it is the right answer to the question.

EXERCISE

Directions (Q. 1–10) : *In each question below five figures are given. Four are similar in a certain way and so form a group. The question is— which one of the figures* **does not** *belong to that group?*

1.

(a) (b) (c) (d) (e)

2.

(a) (b) (c) (d) (e)

3.

(a) (b) (c) (d) (e)

4.

(a) (b) (c) (d) (e)

5.

(a) (b) (c) (d) (e)

6.

(a) (b) (c) (d) (e)

7.

(a) (b) (c) (d) (e)

8.

(a) (b) (c) (d) (e)

9.

(a) (b) (c) (d) (e)

10.

(a) (b) (c) (d) (e)

Directions (Q. 11–20) : *In each of the following questions, in four out of the five figures, element I is related to element II in the same particular way. Find out the figure in which the element I is* **not** *so related to element II.*

11.

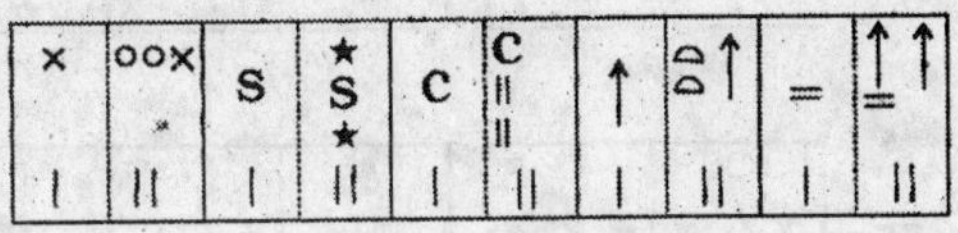

(a) (b) (c) (d) (e)

12.

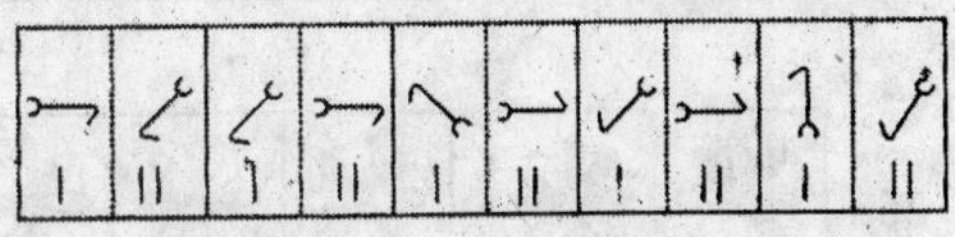

(a) (b) (c) (d) (e)

13. 

(a) (b) (c) (d) (e)

14. 

(a) (b) (c) (d) (e)

15. 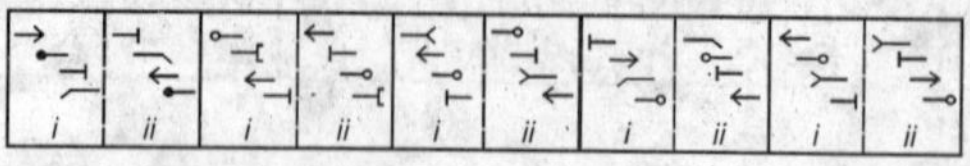

(a) (b) (c) (d) (e)

16. 

(a) (b) (c) (d) (e)

17. 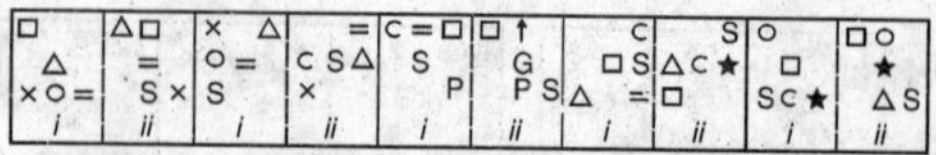

(a) (b) (c) (d) (e)

18. 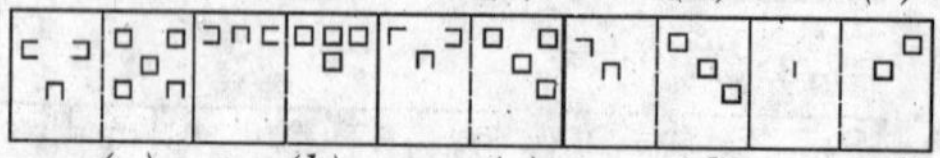

(a) (b) (c) (d) (e)

19. 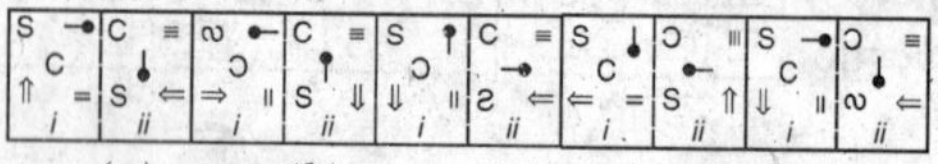

(a) (b) (c) (d) (e)

20. 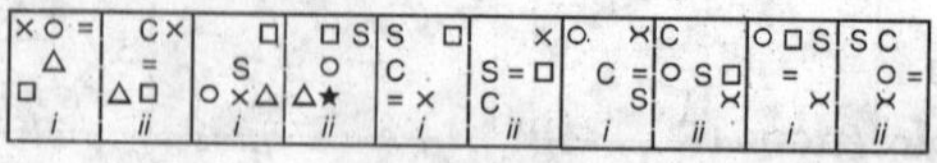

(a) (b) (c) (d) (e)

Directions (Q. 21–30) : *In each of the following questions, a related pair of figures (unnumbered) is followed by five numbered pairs of figures. Out of these five, four have relationship similar to that in the unnumbered pair. Only one pair of figures does not have similar relationship. Select that pair of figures which does not have a similar relationship to that in the unnumbered pair. Number of that pair is your answer.*

21. 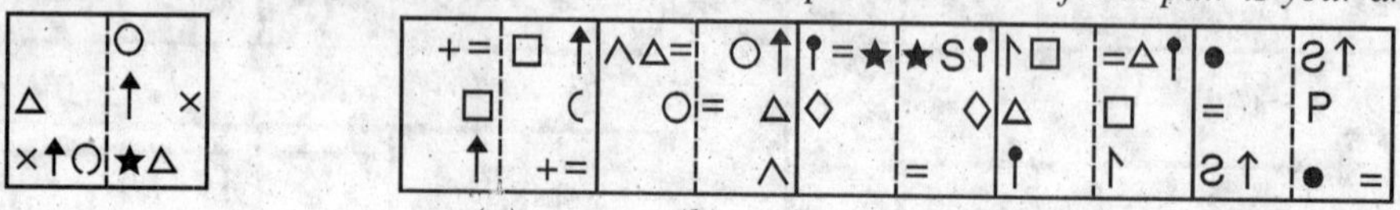

(a) (b) (c) (d) (e)

22. 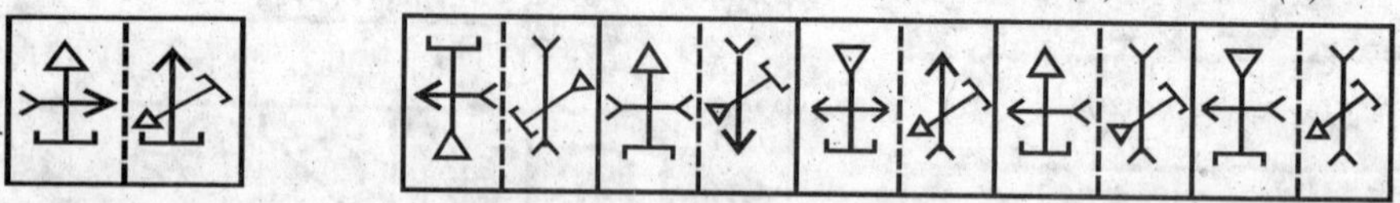

(a) (b) (c) (d) (e)

23. 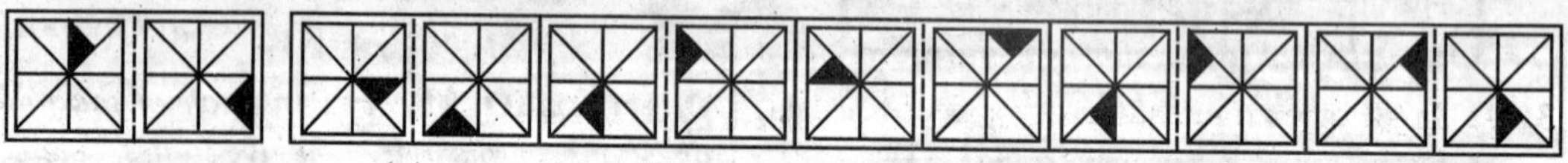

(a) (b) (c) (d) (e)

24. 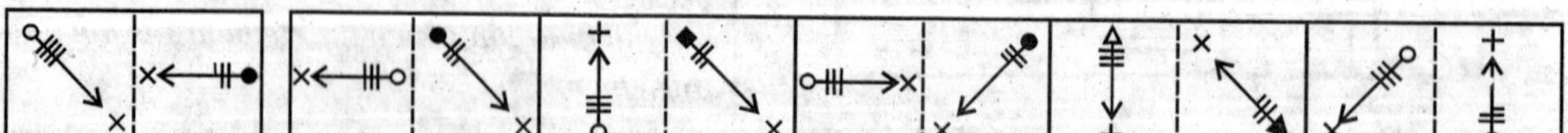

(a) (b) (c) (d) (e)

25. 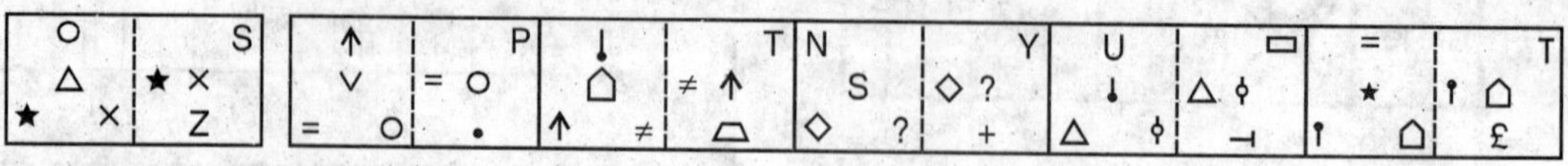

(a) (b) (c) (d) (e)

26. 

(a) (b) (c) (d) (e)

27. 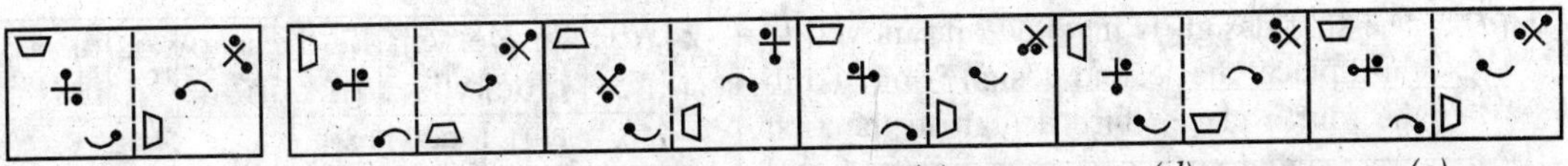

(a) (b) (c) (d) (e)

28. 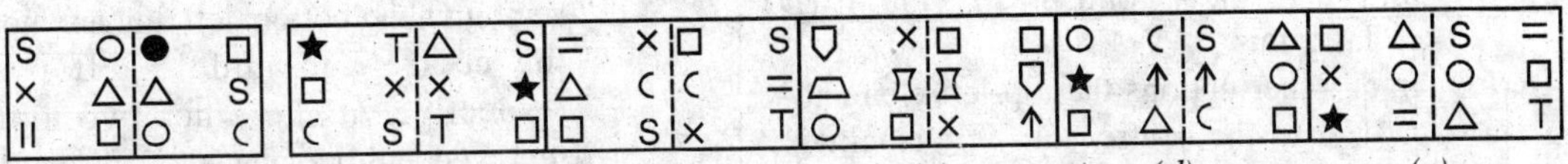

(a) (b) (c) (d) (e)

29. 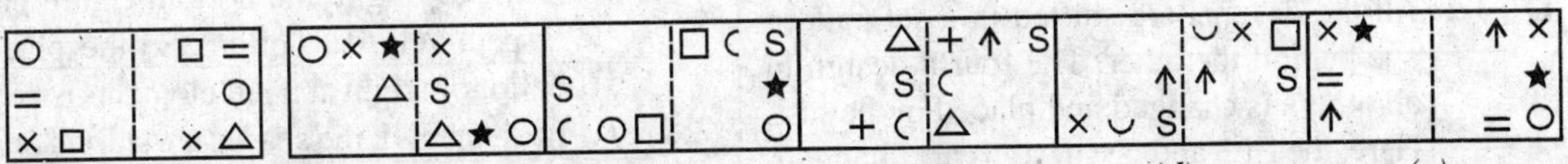

(a) (b) (c) (d) (e)

30. 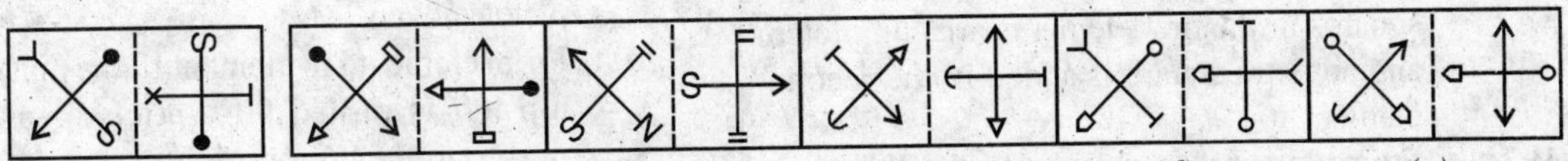

(a) (b) (c) (d) (e)

EXPLANATORY ANSWERS

1. *(d)* : In all other figures, the arrow and the + sign lie towards the black end of the main figure.

2.*(a)* : The pins, equal in number of sides in the main figure are attached to the midpoint of a side of the main figure in case of figures (B), (C), (D) and (E). In figure (A), these pins are attached to a vertex of the main figure.

3.*(c)* : In all other figures, the dot appears in the angle formed between the arrow and the pin.

4.*(a)* : All other figures can be rotated into each other. (In each figure except figure (A), the middle element is obtained by rotating the outer element through 90° CW and the inner element is obtained by rotating the middle element through 90° CW).

5.*(c)* : All other figures have at least one line of symmetry.

6.*(c)* : All other figures can be rotated into each other.

7.*(e)* : In each one of the other four figures, four arcs are curved towards the left and four other arcs are curved towards the right.

8.*(c)* : All other figures can be rotated into each other.

9.*(d)* : In all other figures, the number of dots outside the main figure is one more than the number of dots inside the main figure.

10.*(a)* : In all other figures, one of the dots lies outside the triangle as well as the circle.

11.*(e)* : Except in figure (B), in all other figures, from element I to II two new designs are added in one side of the main design.

12.*(c)* : In each figure from element I to II the main design rotates through 135° clockwise or anticlockwise. Except in figure (C), in all other figures, the smaller line segment moves to other side from element I to II.

13.*(a)* : In all other figures the element II can be obtained by the lateral inversion of the element I. In figure (A), the lower design has not been inverted.

14.*(b)* : In figure (B), the small segment is on the same side as that of the half shaded circle in both the elements.

15.(*d*) : The first design is inverted and moved to third place, the second design is moved to the fourth place, third design to the first place and fourth design is inverted and moved to the second place. Option (D) violates this.

16.(*b*) : In all other options the top-left element is moved to the centre with 90° clockwise rotation. Here, it is rotated anticlockwise.

17.(*d*) : All the designs are shifted in a set pattern one behind the other. The fourth design in all others is changed and placed in the last. Here, the fifth and last designs are changed.

18.(*a*) : In all other pair of figures, all incomplete squares in the first elements are completed and an extra square is added in the second element.

19.(*a*) : From element I to element II, the 'S' shape is turned 90° clockwise and moved down, the double arrow shape '⇒' is turned 90° clockwise and moved to the right, the two parallel lines one turned by 90°; one parallel line is added and all three lines are moved up, the line with a dot is turned 90° clockwise and moved to the centre and the 'C' shape in the centre is turned by 180° and moved to top left position. Here, the double arrow is turned anticlockwise.

20.(*c*) : Starting from one unit, all units are moved in a set pattern, the places of last two units moved are interchanged and the last unit is then made new. Here, no changes are made in the last two units.

21.(*d*) : From element I to element II clockwise the first unit is moved 2 steps forward, the second unit 1 step forward, the third unit 2½ steps forward and the fourth unit 3 steps forward. In option 'D' the third unit violates the rule.

22.(*e*) : From element I to element II, the horizontal bar is turned 135° anticlockwise and the unit at the lower end is turned by 180°. The vertical bar is turned 90° anticlockwise and the unit at the lower end is turned by 180°. In option 'E' one more unit at the top is turned by 180°.

23.(*e*) : In element II, the shade is moved two sections clockwise and shifted from the centre to the base. In option 'E' it is not so.

24.(*a*) : In element II, the arrow is turned 135° clockwise. In option 'A' it is turned anticlockwise.

25.(*b*) : From element I to element II, the bottom right unit and bottom left unit are moved to the centre and middle left position respectively. The other two units are removed and two new elements are placed in the top right and bottom centre position respectively. In option 'B' the placement of bottom right and left elements is not right.

26.(*c*) : In element II, the shades are shifted one petal clockwise. In option 'C' one of the shades is not moved.

27.(*b*) : From element I to element II, the unit on the top left is turned 90° anticlockwise and moved to the bottom right corner position, the unit in the centre is turned 135° anticlockwise and moved to the top right position, and the unit in the bottom right is turned by 180° and moved to the centre. In option 'B', the middle unit is turned 135° clockwise.

28.(*a*) : From element I to element II, a new unit is placed in the top left position, the top left unit is moved to the middle right position, the middle right unit is moved to the left position, the middle left unit is replaced by a new unit and placed in bottom right position, the bottom right unit is moved to the top right position, and the top right unit is moved diagonally to replace the bottom left unit. In option 'A', the middle left unit is not changed when moved to the bottom right position.

29.(*e*) : From element I to element II starting anticlockwise, the first and second units are moved 1½ steps clockwise respectively, the third unit ½ step anticlockwise, the fourth unit 2 steps clockwise, and a new unit is placed ahead of the first unit. Option 'E' violates the rules.

30.(*e*) : In element II, the cross is turned 135° clockwise and then the positions of left and top units on the cross are interchanged. In option 'E' it is not so.

ARITHMETIC

1. NUMBERS

The development of the number system started with natural numbers. These are generally known as counting numbers.

Natural Numbers

Numbers which start from 1 are known as natural numbers. It is denoted by N. The smallest natural number is 1. It is written as,

$$N = \{1, 2, 3, ..., \infty\}$$

Whole Numbers

A number which starts from zero (0) is known as whole number. It is denoted by W. It is written as,

$$W = \{0, 1, 2, 3, ..., \infty\}$$

Integers

Natural numbers along with 0 and their negatives are known as integers. It is denoted by I. It is written as,

$$I = \{..., -4, -3, -2, -1, 0, 1, 2, 3, 4, ...\}$$

Even Numbers

A number which is divisible by 2 is known as even numbers.

Such as, 2, 4, 6, 10, 12, 128, 432 etc.

Odd Numbers

A number which is not divisible by 2 is known as odd numbers:

Such as, 1, 3, 5, 7, 9, 11, 13, 21, 29, 123 etc.

Prime Numbers

A number which is divided by itself is known as prime numbers. The smallest prime number is 2.

Such as, 2, 3, 5, 7, 11, 13, 17, 19, 23, ... etc.

Composite Numbers

A number which is divided by itself and others also is known as composite numbers. The smallest composite number is 4.

Such as, 4, 6, 8, 9, 10, 12, 14, 15, 16, 18, ... etc.

There are 25 prime numbers between 1 to 100.

Such as, 2, 3, 5, 7, 11, 13, 17, 19, 23, 29, 31, 37, 41, 43, 47, 53, 59, 61, 67, 71, 73, 79, 83, 89, 97.

Test, whether a given number is prime or composite: If we want to test any number more than 100, whether it is prime or not, take an integer larger than the approximate square root of that number. Let it be *x*. Test the divisibility of the given number by every prime number less than *x*. If it is not divisible by any of them, then it is prime; otherwise it is composite number.

EXAMPLE: Which of the following numbers are prime numbers?

(*i*) 421 (*ii*) 671

SOLUTION:

(*i*) The square root of 421 is nearly 21.
Prime numbers less than 21 are 2, 3, 5, 7, 11, 13, 17, 19. Clearly, 421 is not divisible by any of them. So, 421 is a prime number.

(*ii*) The square root of 671 is nearly 26.
Prime numbers less than 26 are 2, 3, 5, 7, 11, 13, 17, 19, 23. Out of these, 671 is divisible by 11. So, 671 is not a prime number. Hence it is composite number.

The formulae given below are quite useful for quick multiplication:

(*i*) $(a+b)^2 = a^2 + 2ab + b^2$

(*ii*) $(a-b)^2 = a^2 - 2ab + b^2$

(*iii*) $a^2 - b^2 = (a+b)(a-b)$
(*iv*) $a^2 + b^2 = (a+b)^2 - 2ab$
(*v*) $(a+b)^3 = a^3 + b^3 + 3ab(a+b)$
(*vi*) $(a-b)^3 = a^3 - b^3 - 3ab(a-b)$
(*vii*) $a^3 + b^3 = (a+b)(a^2 - ab + b^2)$
(*viii*) $a^3 - b^3 = (a-b)(a^2 + ab + b^2)$

EXAMPLE: Simplify the following.

(*i*) $\dfrac{348 \times 348 \times 348 + 252 \times 252 \times 252}{348 \times 348 - 348 \times 252 + 252 \times 252}$

(*ii*) $\dfrac{261 \times 261 \times 261 - 77 \times 77 \times 77}{261 \times 261 + 261 \times 77 + 77 \times 77}$

SOLUTION:

(*i*) $\dfrac{348 \times 348 \times 348 + 252 \times 252 \times 252}{348 \times 348 - 348 \times 252 + 252 \times 252}$

Let $348 = a$
and $252 = b$

$\therefore$ Given expression is written as

$$\frac{a \times a \times a + b \times b \times b}{a \times a - a \times b + b \times b} = \frac{a^3 + b^3}{a^2 - ab + b^2}$$

$$= \frac{(a+b)(a^2 - ab + b^2)}{(a^2 - ab + b^2)} = a + b$$

$= 348 + 252 = 600.$

(*ii*) $\dfrac{261 \times 261 \times 261 - 77 \times 77 \times 77}{261 \times 261 + 261 \times 77 + 77 \times 77}$

Let $261 = a$
and $77 = b$

$$\therefore \frac{a^3 - b^3}{a^2 + ab + b^2} = \frac{(a-b)(a^2 + ab + b^2)}{(a^2 + ab + b^2)} = a - b$$

$\therefore 261 - 77 = 184.$

If we divide a given number by another number, then

Dividend = (Divisor × Quotient) + Remainder

EXAMPLE: On dividing 18254 by a certain number, the quotient is 289 and the remainder is 47. Find the divisor.

SOLUTION: Here, Dividend = 18254
quotient = 289
remainder = 47

$$\therefore \text{Divisor} = \frac{\text{Dividend} - \text{Remainder}}{\text{Quotient}}$$

$$= \frac{18254 - 47}{289} = \frac{18207}{289} = 63$$

Hence, divisor = 63.

EXAMPLE: What least number must be subtracted from 862 to get a number exactly divisible by 31?

SOLUTION: On dividing 862 by 31, the remainder obtained is 25.

Hence, the required number = 25.

MULTIPLE CHOICE QUESTIONS

1. The face value of 8 in the numeral 458926 is:
A. 8000 B. 8
C. 1000 D. 458000

2. $106 \times 106 + 94 \times 94 = x$, the value of x is:
A. 21032 B. 20032
C. 23032 D. 20072

3. If $m \times 48 = 173 \times 240$ then the value of m is:
A. 545 B. 685
C. 865 D. 495

4. $\left(1-\frac{1}{3}\right)\left(1-\frac{1}{4}\right)\left(1-\frac{1}{5}\right)\ldots\left(1-\frac{1}{n}\right) = x$

then the value of x is:

A. $\dfrac{1}{n}$ B. $\dfrac{2}{n}$

C. $\dfrac{2(n-1)}{n}$ D. $\dfrac{2}{n(n+1)}$

5. When simplified the product

$\left(2-\frac{1}{3}\right)\left(2-\frac{3}{5}\right)\left(2-\frac{5}{7}\right)\ldots\left(2-\frac{997}{999}\right)$ is equal to:

A. $\dfrac{5}{999}$ B. $\dfrac{1001}{999}$

C. $\dfrac{1001}{3}$ D. None of these

6. Which number should replace both the asterisks in $\left(\frac{*}{21}\right) \times \left(\frac{*}{189}\right) = 1$?

A. 21　　B. 63
C. 3969　　D. 147

7. In a division sum, the divisor is 12 times the quotient and 5 times the remainder. If the remainder be 48, then the dividend is:

A. 240　　B. 576
C. 4800　　D. 4848

8. What least number must be subtracted from 1294 so that the remainder when divided by 9, 11, 13 will leave in each case the same remainder 6?

A. 0　　B. 1
C. 2　　D. 3

9. If $\sqrt{\left(1+\frac{27}{169}\right)} = \left(1+\frac{x}{13}\right)$, then the value of x is:

A. 1　　B. 3
C. 5　　D. 7

10. If $\frac{x}{y} = \frac{3}{4}$, then the value of $\left(\frac{6}{7}+\frac{y-x}{y+x}\right)$ equals:

A. $\frac{5}{7}$　　B. $1\frac{1}{7}$
C. 1　　D. 2

11. The largest natural number by which the product of three consecutive even natural numbers is always divisible, is:

A. 16　　B. 24
C. 48　　D. 96

12. The least number of five digits which is exactly divisible by 12, 15 and 18 is:

A. 10080　　B. 10800
C. 18000　　D. 81000

13. The least number which when divided by 8, 9, 12, 16 and 20 leaves the same remainder 1 in each case is:

A. 712　　B. 271
C. 721　　D. 720

14. The value of 0.8693 + 0.092 + 0.87 + 0.4 equals:

A. 2.3213　　B. 2.2331
C. 3.2313　　D. 2.2313

15. The prime numbers between 1 to 50 are:

A. 8　　B. 12
C. 15　　D. 10

ANSWERS

1	2	3	4	5	6	7	8	9	10
B	D	C	B	C	B	D	B	A	C
11	**12**	**13**	**14**	**15**					
C	A	C	D	C					

EXPLANATORY ANSWERS

1. The face value of 8 in the numeral 458926 is 8.

2. $106 \times 106 + 94 \times 94 = x$

$\Rightarrow \quad (106)^2 + (94)^2 = x$

$\Rightarrow \quad (100 + 6)^2 + (100 - 6)^2 = x$

$\Rightarrow 10000 + 1200 + 36 + 10000 - 1200 + 36 = x$

$\Rightarrow \quad 20072 = x$

$\Rightarrow \quad x = 20072.$

3. $\because m = \frac{173 \times 240}{48} = 865.$

4. $\left(1-\frac{1}{3}\right)\left(1-\frac{1}{4}\right)\left(1-\frac{1}{5}\right)...\left(1-\frac{1}{n}\right) = x$

$\because \quad 1-\frac{1}{3} = \frac{3-1}{3} = \frac{2}{3}$

$$1-\frac{1}{4}=\frac{4-1}{4}=\frac{3}{4}$$

$$1-\frac{1}{5}=\frac{5-1}{5}=\frac{4}{5}$$

$$\vdots$$

$$1-\frac{1}{n}=\frac{n-1}{n}$$

$$\therefore \frac{2}{3}\times\frac{3}{4}\times\frac{4}{5}\times\ldots\times\frac{n-2}{n-1}\times\frac{n-1}{n}=\frac{2}{n}$$

5. $\left(2-\frac{1}{3}\right)\left(2-\frac{3}{5}\right)\left(2-\frac{5}{7}\right)\ldots\left(2-\frac{997}{999}\right)$

$$2-\frac{1}{3}=\frac{6-1}{3}=\frac{5}{3}$$

$$2-\frac{3}{5}=\frac{10-3}{5}=\frac{7}{5}$$

$$2-\frac{5}{7}=\frac{14-5}{7}=\frac{9}{7}$$

$$2-\frac{997}{999}=\frac{1998-997}{999}=\frac{1001}{999}$$

$$\therefore \frac{5}{3}\times\frac{7}{5}\times\frac{9}{7}\times\ldots\times\frac{999}{997}\times\frac{1001}{999}=\frac{1001}{3}$$

6. $\frac{*}{21}\times\frac{*}{189}=1$

$$\frac{x^2}{21\times189}=1$$

$\Rightarrow$ $x^2=21\times189=21\times21\times9$

$\Rightarrow$ $x^2=21\times21\times3\times3$

$\Rightarrow$ $x=21\times3=63$

7. Let quotient = Q and remainder = R

Then, divisor = 12Q = 5R

Now, R = 48

$\Rightarrow$ 12Q = 5 × 48 $\Rightarrow$ Q = 20

$\therefore$ Dividend = (20 × 240 + 48) = 4848

8. The number when divided by 9, 11, 13 leaving remainder 6 = (LCM of 9, 11, 13) + 6 = 1293

$\therefore$ Required number = (1294 – 1293) = 1

9. $\sqrt{\left(1+\frac{27}{169}\right)}=\left(1+\frac{x}{13}\right)$

$\Rightarrow$ $\sqrt{\frac{169+27}{169}}=\frac{13+x}{13}$

$\Rightarrow$ $\sqrt{\frac{196}{169}}=\frac{x+13}{13}$

$\Rightarrow$ $\frac{14}{13}=\frac{x+13}{13}$

$\Rightarrow$ $x+13=14$

$\Rightarrow$ $x=1$

10. $\because \frac{x}{y}=\frac{3}{4}$ then,

$$\frac{6}{7}+\frac{y-x}{y+x}=\frac{6}{7}+\frac{\frac{y}{y}-\frac{x}{y}}{\frac{y}{y}+\frac{x}{y}}$$

[Divide numerator and denominator by y.]

$$=\frac{6}{7}+\frac{1-\frac{3}{4}}{1+\frac{3}{4}}=\frac{6}{7}+\frac{\frac{1}{4}}{\frac{7}{4}}=\frac{6}{7}+\frac{1}{7}=\frac{7}{7}=1$$

11. It is 2 × 4 × 6 = 48

12. Least number of 5 digits is 10000.

LCM of 12, 15, 18 is 180.

On dividing 10000 by 180, the remainder is 100.

$\therefore$ The least number = 10000 + (180 – 100)
= 10080.

13. Least number = (LCM of 8, 9, 12, 16, 20) + 1

2	8,	9,	12,	16,	20
2	4,	9,	6,	8,	10
2	2,	9,	3,	4,	5
3	1,	9,	3,	2,	5
	1,	3,	1,	2,	5

$\therefore$ LCM = $2^4\times3^2\times5=720$

Hence, least number = (720 + 1) = 721.

14.
```
   0.8693
   0.092
   0.87
+  0.4
   2.2313
```

$\therefore$ The value of 0.8693 + 0.092 + 0.87 + 0.4
= 2.2313.

15. The prime numbers between 1 to 50 are 2, 3, 5, 7, 11, 13, 17, 19, 23, 29, 31, 37, 41, 43, 47.

Hence, there are 15 prime numbers between 1 to 50.

2. HCF AND LCM

FACTORS

The numbers are said to be factors of a given number when they exactly divide that number.

Example: Factors of 15 are 1, 3, 5 and 15 because each of these completely divides 15.

Highest Common Factor

The HCF of two or more than two numbers is the greatest number that divides each of them exactly. The highest common factor is also known as Greatest Common Divisor or Greatest Common Measure.

EXAMPLE: Let us consider two numbers 24 and 36. All possible factors of 24 are 1, 2, 3, 4, 6, 8, 12 and 24. All possible factors of 36 are 1, 2, 3, 4, 6, 9, 12, 18 and 36. The common factors of 24 and 36 are 1, 2, 3, 4, 6, 12. The greatest factor among these common factors is 12.

Hence, 12 is the HCF of 24 and 36.

EXAMPLE: Let us consider two numbers 18 and 30.

Now, $18 = 2 \times 3 \times 3$

and $30 = 2 \times 3 \times 5$

The factors common to the two numbers are 2 and 3. Hence the required HCF $= 2 \times 3 = 6$.

There are two methods of determining the HCF of two or more numbers.

(*i*) HCF by Factorization method

(*ii*) HCF by Division method.

HCF by Factorization Method

Express each one of the given number as the product of prime factors. Now choose common factors and take the product of these factors to obtain the required HCF.

EXAMPLE: Find the HCF of 126, 396 and 5400.

SOLUTION:
$$126 = 2 \times 3 \times 3 \times 7$$
$$396 = 2 \times 2 \times 3 \times 3 \times 11$$
$$5400 = 2 \times 2 \times 2 \times 3 \times 3 \times 3 \times 5 \times 5$$

Common factors are 2, 3 and 3.

Hence, the HCF $= 2 \times 3 \times 3 = 18$.

EXAMPLE: Find the HCF of 1056, 1584 and 2178.

SOLUTION:
$$1056 = 2^5 \times 3 \times 11$$
$$1584 = 2^4 \times 3^2 \times 11$$
and $2178 = 2 \times 3^2 \times 11^2$

Hence, HCF $= (2 \times 3 \times 11) = 66$.

HCF by Division Method

Suppose we have to find the HCF of two given numbers. Divide the larger number by the smaller one. Now, divide the divisor by the remainder. Repeat the process of dividing the preceding divisor by the remainder last obtained till zero is obtained as remainder. The last divisor is the required HCF.

Suppose we have to find the HCF of three numbers. Then HCF of [(HCF of any two numbers) and (the third number)] gives the HCF of three given numbers. Similarly, the HCF of more than three numbers may be obtained.

EXAMPLE: Find the HCF of 48, 168 and 324.

SOLUTION: Firstly, we find the HCF of 48 and 168.

```
48) 1 6 8 (3
  - 1 4 4
    -----
      2 4) 4 8 (2
           4 8
          -----
            0
          -----
```

Thus, HCF of 48 and 168 = 24.

Now, we find the HCF of 24 and 324.

```
24) 3 2 4 (13
  - 2 4
    8 4
  - 7 2
    1 2) 2 4 (2
         2 4
           0
```

Thus, the HCF of 48, 168 and 324 is 12.

Lowest Common Multiple

The LCM of two or more numbers is the lowest or least number which is exactly divisible by each of them. In other words, it is the lowest number which contains each of them as a factor.

LCM by Factorization

Resolve each one of the given numbers into a product of prime factors. Then LCM is the product of highest powers of all the factors.

EXAMPLE: Find the LCM of 72, 189 and 1026.

SOLUTION: $72 = 2^3 \times 3^2$

$189 = 3^3 \times 7$

and $1026 = 2 \times 3^3 \times 19$

$\therefore$ $\text{LCM} = 2^3 \times 3^3 \times 7 \times 19$

$= 8 \times 27 \times 7 \times 19 = 28728$

EXAMPLE: Find the LCM of 12, 15, 20 and 54 by short cut method.

SOLUTION:

2	12,	15,	20,	54
2	6,	15,	10,	27
3	3,	15,	5,	27
5	1,	5,	5,	9
	1,	1,	1,	9

$\therefore$ LCM $= 2 \times 2 \times 3 \times 5 \times 9 = 540$

FORMULA

Product of two numbers = HCF × LCM.

$$\text{LCM} = \frac{\text{Product of numbers}}{\text{HCF}}$$

$$\text{HCF} = \frac{\text{Product of numbers}}{\text{LCM}}$$

$$\text{First number} = \frac{\text{LCM} \times \text{HCF}}{\text{2nd number}}$$

$$\text{2nd number} = \frac{\text{LCM} \times \text{HCF}}{\text{First number}}$$

HCF and LCM of Fractions

(*i*) $\text{HCF} = \dfrac{\text{HCF of numerators}}{\text{LCM of denominators}}$

(*ii*) $\text{LCM} = \dfrac{\text{LCM of numerators}}{\text{HCF of denominators}}$

EXAMPLE: Find the HCF and LCM of $\frac{3}{4}, \frac{6}{8}, \frac{15}{64}$ and $\frac{12}{32}$.

SOLUTION: $\text{HCF} = \dfrac{\text{HCF of 3, 6, 15, 12}}{\text{LCM of 4, 8, 64, 32}} = \dfrac{3}{64}$

$\text{LCM} = \dfrac{\text{LCM of 3, 6, 15, 12}}{\text{HCF of 4, 8, 64, 32}} = \dfrac{60}{4}$.

MULTIPLE CHOICE QUESTIONS

1. HCF of 1485 and 4356 is:

A. 189 B. 89
C. 99 D. 83

2. LCM of 18, 24, 42, 63 is:

A. 302 B. 604
C. 504 D. 404

3. Which of the following fractions is the greatest of all?

$\frac{7}{8}, \frac{6}{7}, \frac{4}{5}, \frac{5}{6}$

A. $\frac{6}{7}$ B. $\frac{4}{5}$
C. $\frac{5}{6}$ D. $\frac{7}{8}$

4. Which of the following is in ascending order?

A. $\frac{5}{7}, \frac{7}{8}, \frac{9}{11}$ B. $\frac{5}{7}, \frac{9}{11}, \frac{7}{8}$
C. $\frac{7}{8}, \frac{5}{7}, \frac{9}{11}$ D. $\frac{9}{11}, \frac{7}{8}, \frac{5}{7}$

5. HCF of three numbers is 12. If they be in the ratio 1 : 2 : 3, the numbers are:
A. 12, 24, 36 B. 10, 20, 30
C. 5, 10, 15 D. 4, 8, 12

6. The largest natural number which exactly divides the product of any four consecutive natural numbers is:
A. 6 B. 12
C. 24 D. 120

7. The traffic lights at three different road crossings change after every 48 seconds, 72 seconds and 108 seconds respectively. If they all change simultaneously at 8 : 20 : 00 hrs; then they will again change simultaneously at:
A. 8 : 27 : 12 hrs B. 8 : 27 : 24 hrs
C. 8 : 27 : 36 hrs D. 8 : 27 : 48 hrs

8. The HCF of two numbers is 16 and their LCM is 160. If one of the number is 32, then the other number is:
A. 48 B. 80
C. 96 D. 112

9. The HCF of two numbers is 12 and their difference is also 12. The numbers are:
A. 66, 78 B. 70, 82
C. 94, 106 D. 84, 96

10. The largest number which exactly divides 210, 315, 147 and 161 is:
A. 3 B. 7
C. 21 D. 4410

11. The least perfect square number which is divisible by 3, 4, 5, 6 and 8 is:
A. 900 B. 1200
C. 2500 D. 3600

12. The smallest number which is divisible by 12, 15, 20 and is a perfect square, is:
A. 400 B. 900
C. 1600 D. 3600

13. The sum of two numbers is 216 and their HCF is 27. The numbers are:
A. 54, 162 B. 108, 108
C. 27, 189 D. None of these

14. The HCF and LCM of two numbers are 44 and 264 respectively. If the first number is divided by 2, the quotient is 44. The other number is:
A. 33 B. 66
C. 132 D. 264

15. The number of prime factors in $2^{222} \times 3^{333} \times 5^{555}$ is:
A. 3 B. 1107
C. 1110 D. 1272

16. The number of prime factors in the expression $(6)^{10} \times (7)^{17} \times (11)^{27}$ is:
A. 54 B. 64
C. 71 D. 81

17. Three measuring rods are 64 cm, 80 cm and 96 cm in length. The least length of cloth that can be measured exact number of times using any one of the above rod is:
A. 0.96 m B. 19.20 m
C. 9.60 m D. 96.00 m

18. The product of two numbers is 1600 and their HCF is 5. The LCM of the numbers is:
A. 320 B. 1605
C. 1595 D. 8000

19. About the number of pairs which have 16 as their HCF and 136 as their LCM, we can definitely say that:
A. Only one such pair exists
B. Only two such pairs exist
C. Many such pairs exist
D. No such pair exist

20. The total number of prime factors of the product $(8)^{20} \times (15)^{24} \times (7)^{15}$ is:
A. 59 B. 98
C. 123 D. 138

ANSWERS

1	2	3	4	5	6	7	8	9	10
C	C	D	B	A	C	A	B	D	B
11	**12**	**13**	**14**	**15**	**16**	**17**	**18**	**19**	**20**
D	D	C	C	C	B	C	A	D	C

EXPLANATORY ANSWERS

1.
```
1485) 4 3 5 6 (2
      2 9 7 0
      -------
      1 3 8 6) 1 4 8 5 (1
               1 3 8 6
               -------
                  9 9) 1 3 8 6 (14
                         9 9
                         -----
                         3 9 6
                         3 9 6
                         -----
                           0
```
$\therefore$ HCF of 1485 and 4356 is 99.

2.

2	18, 24, 42, 63
3	9, 12, 21, 63
3	3, 4, 7, 21
7	1, 4, 7, 7
	1, 4, 1, 1

LCM of 18, 24, 42, 63 = $2 \times 3^2 \times 7 \times 4 = 504$.

3. $\frac{7}{8} = 0.875$, $\frac{6}{7} = 0.857$, $\frac{4}{5} = 0.8$

$\frac{5}{6} = 0.833$

Clearly, 0.875 is the greatest of all.

Hence, $\frac{7}{8}$ is the greatest of all.

4. $\frac{5}{7} = 0.714$, $\frac{7}{8} = 0.875$, $\frac{9}{11} = 0.818$

Now, $0.714 < 0.818 < 0.875$

Hence, $\frac{5}{7} < \frac{9}{11} < \frac{7}{8}$.

5. Let the numbers be x, $2x$ and $3x$.

Then, their HCF = x

According to the question, $x = 12$

$\therefore$ The numbers are 12, 24, 36.

6. $1 \times 2 \times 3 \times 4 = 24$

$\therefore$ Required number = 24.

7. LCM of 48, 72, 108 = 432

432 seconds = 7 min 12 seconds.

So, the next simultaneous change will take place at 8 : 27 : 12 hrs.

8. Other number = $\frac{\text{LCM} \times \text{HCF}}{\text{One number}} = \frac{160 \times 16}{32} = 80$

Hence, other number = 80.

9. 12 is not the HCF of given options A, B and C. Hence, D is correct answer.

In 84, 96, 12 is HCF of 84 and 96

Difference of 96 − 84 = 12

So, required numbers are 84 and 96.

10. HCF of 210, 315, 147 and 161 = 7

Hence, the required number = 7.

11.

2	3, 4, 5, 6, 8
2	3, 2, 5, 3, 4
3	3, 1, 5, 3, 2
	1, 1, 5, 1, 2

LCM of 3, 4, 5, 6, 8 = $2 \times 2 \times 3 \times 5 \times 2$

Required number

$= (2 \times 2 \times 3 \times 3 \times 5 \times 5 \times 2 \times 2) = 3600$

12. LCM of 12, 15 and 20 = 60

Hence, required number = $60 \times 60 = 3600$.

13. HCF of 54, 162 = 54

HCF of 108, 108 = 108

HCF of 27, 189 = 27

Hence, required numbers are 27 and 189.

14. According to the question,

First number = $2 \times 44 = 88$

Other number

$= \frac{\text{LCM} \times \text{HCF}}{\text{First number}} = \frac{264 \times 44}{88} = 132$

15. The number of prime factors in the given product = $(222 + 333 + 555) = 1110$

16. 2, 3, 7, 11 are prime numbers in the given expression. The number of prime factors in the given expression $(10 + 10 + 17 + 27) = 64$

17. Required length = (LCM of 64, 80, 96) cm = 960 cm = 9.60 m.

18. LCM = $\frac{\text{Product of numbers}}{\text{HCF}} = \frac{1600}{5} = 320$

19. HCF is always a factor of LCM. So no two numbers exist with HCF = 16 and LCM = 136.

20. Since 2, 3, 5, 7 are prime numbers and the given expression is $(2^3)^{20} \times (3 \times 5)^{24} \times (7)^{15}$ *i.e.* $2^{60} \times 3^{24} \times 5^{24} \times 7^{15}$, so the number of prime factors in the given expression

$= (60 + 24 + 24 + 15) = 123$

3. SIMPLIFICATION

Simplification means expressing in a simpler form. In order to simplify an expression we use the operations in the following order which is easily remembered as "BODMAS".

(*i*) Bracket (*ii*) Of (*iii*) Division (*iv*) Multiplication (*v*) Addition (*vi*) Subtraction.

'Of' means multiplication but it is operated even before division.

While removing brackets, first of all bar bracket '—' and after that small bracket '( )' is removed. Thereafter curley bracket '{ }' and at last square bracket '[ ]' is removed.

EXAMPLE: Simplify: $100 \div 25 \times 6 + 16 - 32$

SOLUTION: $100 \div 25 \times 6 + 16 - 32$

$= 4 \times 6 + 16 - 32$

$= 24 + 16 - 32$

$= 40 - 32 = 8$

EXAMPLE: Simplify: $54 + 24 \div 4 - 8 \times 5 + 4 \times 3$

SOLUTION: $54 + 24 \div 4 - 8 \times 5 + 4 \times 3$

$= 54 + 6 - 40 + 12$

$= 72 - 40 = 32$

EXAMPLE: Simplify: $10 - \left[6 - \left\{7 - \left(6 - \overline{8 - 5}\right)\right\}\right]$

SOLUTION: $10 - \left[6 - \left\{7 - (6 - 3)\right\}\right]$

$= 10 - [6 - \{7 - 3\}]$

$= 10 - [6 - 4] = 10 - 2 = 8.$

EXAMPLE: Simplify: $\dfrac{12 \times 12 \times 12 - 1 \times 1 \times 1}{12 \times 12 + 12 \times 1 + 1 \times 1}$

SOLUTION: Let $a = 12$ and $b = 1$

$$\therefore \quad \frac{a \times a \times a - b \times b \times b}{a \times a + a \times b + b \times b} = \frac{a^3 - b^3}{a^2 + ab + b^2}$$

$$= \frac{(a - b)(a^2 + ab + b^2)}{(a^2 + ab + b^2)}$$

$$= a - b = 12 - 1 = 11$$

EXAMPLE: Simplify:

$$\frac{2.33 \times 2.33 \times 2.33 + 7.67 \times 7.67 \times 7.67}{2.33 \times 2.33 - 2.33 \times 7.67 + 7.67 \times 7.67}$$

SOLUTION: Let $a = 2.33$ and $b = 7.67$

$$\frac{a^3 + b^3}{a^2 - ab + b^2} = \frac{(a + b)(a^2 - ab + b^2)}{(a^2 - ab + b^2)} = (a + b)$$

$$= 2.33 + 7.67 = 10$$

MULTIPLE CHOICE QUESTIONS

1. $\dfrac{48 - 12 \times 3 + 9}{12 - 9 \div 3}$ equals:

A. 3 B. 21

C. $\dfrac{7}{3}$ D. $\dfrac{1}{3}$

2. $\dfrac{69 - 14 \times 3 + 2}{9 \times 5 - (5)^2}$ equals:

A. 1.45 B. 2.75

C. 26.5 D. 265

3. If $\dfrac{17.28 \div x}{3.6 \times 0.2} = 2$ then, the value of x is:

A. 120 B. 1.20
C. 12 D. 0.12

4. $171 \div 19 \times 9$ equals:

A. 0 B. 1
C. 18 D. 81

5. $3120 \div 26 + 13 \times 30$ equals:

A. 2400 B. 3900
C. 536 D. None of these

6. $\dfrac{31}{10} \times \dfrac{3}{10} + \dfrac{7}{5} \div 20$ equals:

A. 0 B. 1
C. 100 D. $\dfrac{107}{200}$

7. The simplification of $1 + \dfrac{1}{2 + \dfrac{1}{1 - \dfrac{1}{3}}}$ yields the result:

A. $\dfrac{2}{7}$ B. $\dfrac{7}{9}$
C. $\dfrac{9}{7}$ D. $\dfrac{13}{7}$

8. The value of $1 + \dfrac{1}{4 \times 3} + \dfrac{1}{4 \times 3^2} + \dfrac{1}{4 \times 3^3}$ up to four places of decimals is:

A. 1.1202 B. 1.1203
C. 1.1204 D. None of these

9. $\dfrac{\dfrac{1}{2} \div 4 + 20}{\dfrac{1}{2} \times 4 + 20}$ equals:

A. $\dfrac{81}{88}$ B. $2\dfrac{3}{11}$
C. $\dfrac{161}{176}$ D. 1

10. $3 \div \left[(8-5) \div \left\{(4-2) \div \left(2 + \dfrac{8}{13}\right)\right\}\right]$ equals:

A. $\dfrac{13}{17}$ B. $\dfrac{68}{13}$
C. $\dfrac{17}{13}$ D. $\dfrac{13}{68}$

11. $10 - [9 - \{8 - (7 - 6)\}] - 5$ is equal to:

A. –5 B. 1
C. 3 D. 9

12. $\dfrac{\dfrac{1}{5} \div \dfrac{1}{5} \text{ of } \dfrac{1}{5}}{\dfrac{1}{5} \text{ of } \dfrac{1}{5} \div \dfrac{1}{5}}$ is equal to:

A. 1 B. 5
C. $\dfrac{1}{5}$ D. 25

13. The value of $1 + \dfrac{1}{1 + \dfrac{1}{1 + \dfrac{1}{9}}}$ is:

A. $\dfrac{29}{19}$ B. $\dfrac{10}{19}$
C. $\dfrac{29}{10}$ D. $\dfrac{10}{9}$

14. $\dfrac{3}{48}$ is what part of $\dfrac{1}{12}$?

A. $\dfrac{3}{7}$ B. $\dfrac{1}{12}$
C. $\dfrac{4}{3}$ D. None of these

15. How many $\dfrac{1}{8}$ s are there in $37\dfrac{1}{2}$?

A. 300 B. 400
C. 500 D. None of these

ANSWERS

1	2	3	4	5	6	7	8	9	10
C	A	C	D	D	B	C	B	C	A
11	**12**	**13**	**14**	**15**					
C	D	A	D	A					

EXPLANATORY ANSWERS

1. $\dfrac{48-12\times3+9}{12-9\div3}=\dfrac{48-36+9}{12-3}$

$=\dfrac{57-36}{9}=\dfrac{21}{9}=\dfrac{7}{3}.$

2. $\dfrac{69-14\times3+2}{9\times5-5^2}=\dfrac{69-42+2}{45-25}$

$=\dfrac{71-42}{20}=\dfrac{29}{20}=1.45.$

3. $17.28\div x=2\times3.6\times0.2$

$\Rightarrow \dfrac{17.28}{x}=1.44\Rightarrow 1.44\,x=17.28$

$\Rightarrow \quad x=\dfrac{17.28}{1.44}=\dfrac{1728}{144}=12.$

4. $171\div19\times9=9\times9=81.$

5. $3120\div26+13\times30=120+390=510.$

6. $\dfrac{31}{10}\times\dfrac{3}{10}+\dfrac{7}{5}\div20=\dfrac{31}{10}\times\dfrac{3}{10}+\dfrac{7}{5}\times\dfrac{1}{20}$

$=\dfrac{93}{100}+\dfrac{7}{100}=\dfrac{93+7}{100}=\dfrac{100}{100}=1$

7. $1+\dfrac{1}{2+\dfrac{1}{1-\dfrac{1}{3}}}=1+\dfrac{1}{2+\dfrac{1}{\dfrac{3-1}{3}}}$

$=1+\dfrac{1}{2+\dfrac{1}{\dfrac{2}{3}}}=1+\dfrac{1}{2+\dfrac{3}{2}}=1+\dfrac{1}{\dfrac{7}{2}}=1+\dfrac{2}{7}=$

8. $1+\dfrac{1}{4\times3}+\dfrac{1}{4\times3^2}+\dfrac{1}{4\times3^3}$

$=1+\dfrac{1}{12}+\dfrac{1}{36}+\dfrac{1}{108}=\dfrac{108+9+3+1}{108}$

$=\dfrac{121}{108}=1.1203$

9. $\dfrac{\dfrac{1}{2}\div4+20}{\dfrac{1}{2}\times4+20}=\dfrac{\dfrac{1}{8}+20}{2+20}=\dfrac{\dfrac{1+160}{8}}{22}$

$=\dfrac{161}{8\times22}=\dfrac{161}{176}$

10. $3\div\left[(8-5)\div\left\{(4-2)\div\left(2+\dfrac{8}{13}\right)\right\}\right]$

$=3\div\left[3\div\left\{2\div\dfrac{34}{13}\right\}\right]$

$=3\div\left[3\div\left\{2\times\dfrac{13}{34}\right\}\right]=3\div\left[3\div\dfrac{13}{17}\right]$

$=3\div\left[3\times\dfrac{17}{13}\right]=3\div\dfrac{51}{13}=3\times\dfrac{13}{51}=\dfrac{13}{17}$

11. $10-[9-\{8-(7-6)\}]-5$

$=10-[9-\{8-1\}]-5$

$=10-[9-7]-5=10-2-5=10-7=3$

12. $\dfrac{\dfrac{1}{5}\div\dfrac{1}{5}\text{ of }\dfrac{1}{5}}{\dfrac{1}{5}\text{ of }\dfrac{1}{5}\div\dfrac{1}{5}}=\dfrac{\dfrac{1}{5}\div\dfrac{1}{25}}{\dfrac{1}{25}\div\dfrac{1}{5}}=\dfrac{\dfrac{1}{5}\times\dfrac{25}{1}}{\dfrac{1}{25}\times\dfrac{5}{1}}=\dfrac{\dfrac{5}{1}}{\dfrac{1}{5}}$

$=\dfrac{5}{1}\times\dfrac{5}{1}=25$

13. $1+\dfrac{1}{1+\dfrac{1}{1+\dfrac{1}{9}}}=1+\dfrac{1}{1+\dfrac{1}{\dfrac{10}{9}}}=1+\dfrac{1}{1+\dfrac{9}{10}}$

$=1+\dfrac{1}{\dfrac{19}{10}}=1+\dfrac{10}{19}=\dfrac{29}{19}$

14. Let x of $\dfrac{1}{12}=\dfrac{3}{48}$

$\Rightarrow \quad \dfrac{x}{12}=\dfrac{3}{48}\Rightarrow 48x=36$

$\Rightarrow \quad x=\dfrac{36}{48}=\dfrac{3}{4}.$

15. Let n times $\dfrac{1}{8}=37\dfrac{1}{2}$

$\Rightarrow \quad \dfrac{n}{8}=\dfrac{75}{2}\Rightarrow 2n=8\times75$

$\Rightarrow \quad n=\dfrac{8\times75}{2}=4\times75=300.$

4. SURDS AND INDICES

SURDS

If 'a' is a rational number and n is a positive integer such that nth root of 'a', *i.e.*, $a^{1/n}$ or $\sqrt[n]{a}$ is an irrational number, then $a^{1/n}$ is called a surd or radical.

In other words, an irrational root of a rational number is called a surd. The symbol '√' is known as surd sign or radical.

For example, $\sqrt{2} = 2^{1/2}$ = Square root of 2

$\sqrt[3]{5} = 5^{1/3}$ = Cube root of 5

Pure and Mixed Surds

Pure Surd: A surd which has unity only as rational factor, the other factor being irrational, is called a pure surd.

For example, $\sqrt{2}$, $\sqrt[3]{3}$, $\sqrt[5]{3}$ are pure surds.

Mixed Surd: A surd which has a rational factor other than unity, the other factor being irrational, is called a mixed surds.

For example, $2\sqrt{5}$ $3\sqrt[4]{7}$, $5\sqrt[3]{11}$ are mixed surds.

Rationalising Factor: When the product of two surds is a rational number, then each of them is called the rationalising factor (R.F.) of the other.

For example, $3\sqrt{5} \times \sqrt{5} = 3 \times 5 = 15$

$\therefore$ $\sqrt{5}$ is a rationalising factor of $3\sqrt{5}$.

Important Formulae Based on Surds

$\sqrt[n]{a} = a^{1/n}$ and it is called a surd of order n.

(*i*) $\sqrt[n]{a^n} = a$

(*ii*) $\sqrt[n]{ab} = \sqrt[n]{a}\,\sqrt[n]{b}$

(*iii*) $\sqrt{a} \times \sqrt{a} = a$

(*iv*) $\sqrt{a} \times \sqrt{b} = \sqrt{ab}$

(*v*) $\sqrt{a^2 b} = a\sqrt{b}$

(*vi*) $\left(\sqrt{a} + \sqrt{b}\right)^2 = a + b + 2\sqrt{ab}$

(*vii*) $\left(\sqrt{a} - \sqrt{b}\right)^2 = a + b - 2\sqrt{ab}$

(*viii*) $\left(\sqrt{a} + \sqrt{b}\right)\left(\sqrt{a} - \sqrt{b}\right) = a - b$ where a and b are positive rational numbers.

INDICES

Let n be a positive integer and 'a' be a real number. The continued product of n factors each equal to a *e.g.*, $a \times a \times a \times \ldots \times n$ times is written as a^n and is called "n^{th} power of a" or "a raised to the power n".

The expression a^n is termed as power function or simply power, a is called the base and n is called index or exponent of the power a^n.

For example, 2^2 = square of 2, 2^3 = cube of 2, etc.

Laws of Indices

(*i*) $a^m \times a^n = a^{m+n}$

(*ii*) $a^m \times a^n \times a^p \times \ldots = a^{m+n+p+\ldots}$

(*iii*) $\dfrac{a^m}{a^n} = a^{m-n}$, if $m > n$

(*iv*) $\dfrac{a^m}{a^n} = \dfrac{1}{a^{n-m}}$, if $m < n$

(*v*) $(a^m)^n = a^{mn}$

(*vi*) $(ab)^n = a^n b^n$

(*vii*) $a^0 = 1$

(*viii*) If $a^m = a^n$ then $m = n$

(*ix*) If $a^m = b^m$ then $a = b$

(*x*) $\dfrac{a^m}{a^m} = a^{m-m} = a^0 = 1$

MULTIPLE CHOICE QUESTIONS

1. If the infinite series is $x = \sqrt{6+\sqrt{6+\sqrt{6+...}}}$ then the value of x is:

A. 2.5 B. 3
C. 6 D. 8

2. If $\dfrac{9^n \cdot 3^2 \cdot 3^n - (27)^n}{3^{3m} \cdot 2^3} = \dfrac{1}{27}$, then the value of $(m - n)$ is:

A. 1 B. 2
C. $\sqrt{3}$ D. $\sqrt{\dfrac{2}{3}}$

3. If $x = \dfrac{\sqrt{5}+\sqrt{3}}{\sqrt{5}-\sqrt{3}}$ and $y = \dfrac{\sqrt{5}-\sqrt{3}}{\sqrt{5}+\sqrt{3}}$, then $(x + y)$ is equal to:

A. 8 B. 6
C. $2\sqrt{15}$ D. $2\left(\sqrt{5}+\sqrt{3}\right)$

4. $2^{x+1} + 2^{x+3} = 2560$, then x is equal to:

A. 12 B. 11
C. 8 D. 6

5. If $\dfrac{5+2\sqrt{3}}{7+4\sqrt{3}} = a + b\sqrt{3}$, then b is equal to:

A. –6 B. 6
C. –11 D. 11

6. If $\dfrac{(21)^{5.36}}{(21)^{3.47}} = (21)^x$, then the value of x is:

A. 8.88 B. 1.54
C. 9.32 D. 1.89

7. $\sqrt{24}+\sqrt{12}$ equal to:

A. $\sqrt{36}$ B. $2\sqrt{6}+2\sqrt{3}$
C. $6\sqrt{2}$ D. $\sqrt{288}$

8. If $a^b = 64$, where a and b are positive integers then $(a - b)^{a+b-4}$ is:

A. 0 B. 1
C. 2 D. $\dfrac{1}{2}$

9. The value of $\dfrac{5^{10+n} \cdot 25^{3n-4}}{5^{7n}}$ is:

A. 5 B. 8
C. 25 D. 16

10. $3^x - 3^{x-1} = 18$, then the value of x^x is:

A. 3 B. 8
C. 27 D. 216

11. If $x = \sqrt{10+\sqrt{25+\sqrt{121}}}$, then x is equal to:

A. –2 only B. 2 only
C. ± 4 D. 4 only

12. If $a^x = b^y = c^z$ and $b^2 = ac$, then y is equal to:

A. $\dfrac{xz}{x+z}$ B. $\dfrac{xz}{2(x-z)}$
C. $\dfrac{xz}{2(z-x)}$ D. $\dfrac{2xz}{x+z}$

13. $\dfrac{5^{n+3} - 6 \times 5^{n+1}}{9 \times 5^n - 5^n \times 2^2}$ is equal to:

A. 5 B. 19
C. 25 D. 95

14. The value of $\left(\dfrac{x^a}{x^b}\right)^{(a+b)} \times \left(\dfrac{x^b}{x^c}\right)^{(b+c)} \times \left(\dfrac{x^c}{x^a}\right)^{(c+a)}$ is equal to:

A. 0 B. 2
C. 1 D. 3

15. If $\sqrt{3^n} = 729$, then the value of n is:

A. 12 B. 8
C. 10 D. 6

ANSWERS

1	2	3	4	5	6	7	8	9	10
B	A	A	C	A	D	B	B	C	C
11	**12**	**13**	**14**	**15**					
D	D	B	C	A					

EXPLANATORY ANSWERS

1. $x = \sqrt{6+x}$

Squaring both sides

$$x^2 = 6 + x$$
$$\Rightarrow \quad x^2 - x - 6 = 0$$
$$\Rightarrow \quad x^2 - 3x + 2x - 6 = 0$$
$$\Rightarrow \quad x(x-3) + 2(x-3) = 0$$
$$\Rightarrow \quad (x-3)(x+2) = 0$$
$$\Rightarrow \quad x = 3 \text{ or } x = -2$$

But x cannot be –2.

Hence, the required value of x is 3.

2. $$\frac{9^n \cdot 3^2 \cdot 3^n - (27)^n}{3^{3m} \cdot 2^3} = \frac{1}{27}$$

$$\Rightarrow \quad \frac{3^{2n} \times 9 \times 3^n - 3^{3n}}{8 \times 3^{3m}} = \frac{1}{3^3}$$

$$\Rightarrow \quad \frac{3^{3n}(9-1)}{8\ 3^{3m}} = 3^{-3}$$

$$\Rightarrow \quad 3^{3n-3m} = (3)^{-3}$$
$$\Rightarrow \quad 3m - 3n = 3$$
$$\Rightarrow \quad 3(m-n) = 3$$
$$\Rightarrow \quad m - n = \frac{3}{3} = 1$$

3. $$x = \frac{\sqrt{5}+\sqrt{3}}{\sqrt{5}-\sqrt{3}} \times \frac{\sqrt{5}+\sqrt{3}}{\sqrt{5}+\sqrt{3}} = \frac{\left(\sqrt{5}+\sqrt{3}\right)^2}{5-3}$$

$$\Rightarrow x = \frac{5+3+2\sqrt{15}}{2} = \frac{8+2\sqrt{15}}{2} = \frac{2\left(4+\sqrt{15}\right)}{2}$$

$$\therefore \quad x = 4 + \sqrt{15}$$

Again, $$y = \frac{\sqrt{5}-\sqrt{3}}{\sqrt{5}+\sqrt{3}} \times \frac{\sqrt{5}-\sqrt{3}}{\sqrt{5}-\sqrt{3}}$$

$$= \frac{\left(\sqrt{5}-\sqrt{3}\right)^2}{5-3}$$

$$\Rightarrow \quad y = \frac{5+3-2\sqrt{15}}{2}$$

$$= \frac{8-2\sqrt{15}}{2} = \frac{2\left(4-\sqrt{15}\right)}{2}$$

$$\Rightarrow \quad y = 4 - \sqrt{15}$$

$$\therefore \quad x + y = 4 + \sqrt{15} + 4 - \sqrt{15} = 8$$

4. $$2^{x+1} + 2^{x+3} = 2560$$
$$\Rightarrow \quad 2^x \times 2 + 2^x \times 2^3 = 2560$$
$$\Rightarrow \quad 2 \times 2^x + 8 \times 2^x = 2560$$
$$\Rightarrow \quad 2^x(2+8) = 2560$$
$$\Rightarrow \quad 2^x = 256 = 2^8$$
$$\Rightarrow \quad x = 8$$

5. $$\because \quad \frac{5+2\sqrt{3}}{7+4\sqrt{3}} = a + b\sqrt{3}$$

$$\frac{5+2\sqrt{3}}{7+4\sqrt{3}} \times \frac{7-4\sqrt{3}}{7-4\sqrt{3}} = \frac{35-20\sqrt{3}+14\sqrt{3}-24}{49-48}$$

$$= \frac{11-6\sqrt{3}}{1}$$

Comparing then we get,

$a = 11, b = -6$

Hence, $b = -6$.

6. $$\frac{(21)^{5.36}}{(21)^{3.47}} = (21)^x$$

$$\Rightarrow \quad (21)^{5.36-3.47} = (21)^x$$
$$\Rightarrow \quad x = 1.89$$

7. $\sqrt{24} + \sqrt{12} = 2\sqrt{6} + 2\sqrt{3}$

8. $a^b = 64 = (4)^3 \Rightarrow a = 4, b = 3$

$\therefore (a-b)^{a+b-4} = (4-3)^{4+3-4} = (1)^3 = 1$

9. $$\frac{5^{10+n} \cdot 25^{3n-4}}{5^{7n}} = \frac{5^{10} \times 5^n \times (5^2)^{3n-4}}{5^{7n}}$$

$$= \frac{5^{10} \times 5^n \times 5^{6n} \times 5^{-8}}{5^{7n}}$$

$$= \frac{5^{10-8} \times 5^{7n}}{5^{7n}} = 5^2 \times 5^{7n-7n}$$

$$= 25 \times 5^0 = 25 \times 1 = 25$$

10. $$3^x - 3^{x-1} = 18$$
$$\Rightarrow \quad 3^x - 3^x \times 3^{-1} = 18$$
$$\Rightarrow \quad 3^x\left(1 - \frac{1}{3}\right) = 18$$
$$\Rightarrow \quad 3^x\left(\frac{2}{3}\right) = 18$$

$\Rightarrow \quad 3^x = \frac{18 \times 3}{2} = 27$

$\Rightarrow \quad 3^x = (3)^3 \Rightarrow x = 3$

$\therefore \quad x^x = (3)^3 = 27$

11. $x = \sqrt{10 + \sqrt{25 + \sqrt{121}}}$

$\Rightarrow \quad x = \sqrt{10 + \sqrt{25 + 11}}$

$\Rightarrow \quad x = \sqrt{10 + \sqrt{36}}$

$\Rightarrow \quad x = \sqrt{10 + 6} = \sqrt{16}$

$\Rightarrow \quad x = 4$

12. Let $a^x = b^y = c^z = k$

then $a = k^{\frac{1}{x}}$, $b = k^{\frac{1}{y}}$, $c = k^{\frac{1}{z}}$

Now, $\quad b^2 = ac$

$\Rightarrow \quad \left(k^{\frac{1}{y}}\right)^2 = k^{\frac{1}{x}} \cdot k^{\frac{1}{z}}$

$\Rightarrow \quad k^{\frac{2}{y}} = k^{\frac{1}{x}+\frac{1}{z}}$

$\Rightarrow \quad \frac{2}{y} = \frac{z + x}{xz}$

$\Rightarrow \quad 2xz = y(x + z)$

$\Rightarrow \quad y = \frac{2xz}{x + z}$

13. $\frac{5^{n+3} - 6 \times 5^{n+1}}{9 \times 5^n - 5^n \times 2^2} = \frac{5^n \times 5^3 - 6 \times 5^n \times 5}{9 \times 5^n - 4 \times 5^n}$

$= \frac{5^n(125 - 30)}{5^n(9 - 4)} = 5^0 \times \frac{95}{5}$

$= 1 \times 19 = 19.$

14. $\left(\frac{x^a}{x^b}\right)^{(a+b)} \times \left(\frac{x^b}{x^c}\right)^{(b+c)} \times \left(\frac{x^c}{x^a}\right)^{(c+a)}$

$= \left(x^{a-b}\right)^{(a+b)} \times \left(x^{b-c}\right)^{(b+c)} \times \left(x^{c-a}\right)^{c+a}$

$= x^{a^2-b^2} \times x^{b^2-c^2} \times x^{c^2-a^2}$

$= x^{a^2-b^2+b^2-c^2+c^2-a^2}$

$= x^0 = 1$

15. $\sqrt{3^n} = 729 \Rightarrow 3^{n/2} = 3^6$

$\Rightarrow \quad \frac{n}{2} = 6$

$\Rightarrow \quad n = 12.$

5. RATIO AND PROPORTION

RATIO

When comparison is made by dividing one quantity by another of the same kind, the result is called ratio. If a and b are two numbers, ratio of a to b is denoted by $a : b$ or $\frac{a}{b}$. Here a is called first term and b is called the second term. The first term is also called antecedent and the second term is also called consequent.

Example: The ratio 3 : 10 represents $\frac{3}{10}$ with antecedent 3 and consequent 10.

The multiplication or division of each term of a ratio by a same non-zero number does not effect the ratio.

PROPORTION

Equality of two ratios is called proportion. If $a : b = c : d$, then a, b, c, d are called in proportion. In a proportion $a : b : : c : d$, then a and d are called extremes and b and c are called means.

Product of extremes = Product of means

Comparison of Ratio: Suppose $\frac{a}{b} > \frac{c}{d}$ then we say that $a : b > c : d$.

Compounded Ratio: The compound ratio of the ratios $a : b$, $c : d$ and $e : f$ is $ace : bdf$.

Duplicate Ratio: The duplicate ratio of $a : b$ is $a^2 : b^2$.

Triplicate Ratio: The triplicate ratio of $a : b$ is $a^3 : b^3$.

Sub-duplicate and Sub-triplicate ratios

The sub-duplicate and Sub-triplicate ratios of ratio $a : b$ are $a^{1/2} : b^{1/2}$ and $a^{1/3} : b^{1/3}$ respectively.

Mean Proportional: Mean proportional between a and b is $\sqrt{ab}$.

Third Proportional: The third proportional to a, b is the fourth proportional to a, b, b.

Fourth Proportional: If $a : b : : c : d$ is a proportion, then d is called the fourth proportional to a, b, c.

Example: If A : B = 3 : 4 and B : C = 8 : 9 then find A : C.

Solution: $A : B = 3 : 4 \Rightarrow \frac{A}{B} = \frac{3}{4}$

$$B : C = 8 : 9 \Rightarrow \frac{B}{C} = \frac{8}{9}$$

$$\frac{A}{C} = \frac{A}{B} \times \frac{B}{C} = \frac{3}{4} \times \frac{8}{9} = \frac{2}{3}$$

$$\Rightarrow \quad A : C = 2 : 3$$

Example: If 15% of A is the same as 20% of B, then find A : B.

Solution: Given : 15% of A = 20% of B

$$\Rightarrow \quad \frac{15}{100} \times A = \frac{20}{100} \times B$$

$$\Rightarrow \quad 3A = 4B$$

$$\Rightarrow \quad \frac{A}{B} = \frac{4}{3}$$

$$\Rightarrow \quad A : B = 4 : 3$$

Example: A stick 1.4 m long casts a shadow 1.3 m long at the same time when a pole casts a shadow 5.2 m long. Find the length of the pole.

Solution: Clearly, more is the length of shadow, more is the length of the object.

Let the length of the pole be x metres.

Then, $1.3 : 5.2 :: 1.4 : x$

$$\Rightarrow \quad \frac{1.3}{5.2} = \frac{1.4}{x}$$

$$\Rightarrow \quad \frac{1}{4} = \frac{1.4}{x}$$

$$\Rightarrow \quad x = 1.4 \times 4 = 5.6$$

Hence, the length of the pole is 5.6 m.

MULTIPLE CHOICE QUESTIONS

1. If A : B = 2 : 3 and B : C = 4 : 5, then C : A is equal to:

A. 15 : 8 B. 12 : 10
C. 8 : 5 D. 8 : 15

2. If 10% of x is the same as 20% of y, then $x : y$ is equal to:

A. 1 : 2 B. 2 : 1
C. 5 : 1 D. 10 : 1

3. The mean proportional to $6+\sqrt{27}$ and $6-\sqrt{27}$ is:

A. 3 B. 9
C. 10 D. $\sqrt{10}$

4. If $x : y = 9 : 11$, the value of $\dfrac{5x+3y}{3x+5y}$ is:

A. 45 : 55 B. 18 : 22
C. 37 : 41 D. 39 : 41

5. If $a+b : b+c : c+a = 6 : 7 : 8$ and $a + b + c = 14$, then the value of c is:

A. 14 B. 7
C. 8 D. 6

6. Two numbers are in the ratio 2 : 3. If 5 is added to each number, the ratio becomes 5 : 7. The bigger number is:

A. 30 B. 40
C. 60 D. 20

7. What should be added to each of the numbers 12, 30, 40 and 86, so that they are in proportion?

A. 6 B. 4
C. –6 D. –4

8. The ratio of males and females of a village is 5 : 3. If there are 800 males in the village, females are:

A. 240 B. 480
C. 840 D. 488

9. In a mixture of 60 litres, the ratio of ethanol to ether is 4 : 1. How much ether must be added to the mixture to make this ratio 2 : 1?

A. 10 litres B. 12 litres
C. 18 litres D. 24 litres

10. The proportion of zinc and copper in a brass piece is 4 : 5. How much zinc will be there in 180 kg of such a piece?

A. 40 kg B. 80 kg
C. 100 kg D. 120 kg

11. The prices of a scooter and a television set are in the ratio 3 : 2. If a scooter costs ₹ 6000 more than the television set, the price of the television set is:

A. ₹ 18000 B. ₹ 12000
C. ₹ 10000 D. ₹ 6000

12. The weight of a 13 metres long iron rod be 23.4 kg. The weight of 6 metres long of such rod will be:

A. 7.2 kg B. 12.4 kg
C. 10.8 kg D. 18 kg

13. The ratio between the ages of Gayatri and Savitri is 6 : 5 and the sum of their ages is 44 years. The ratio of their ages after 8 years will be:

A. 5 : 6 B. 7 : 8
C. 8 : 7 D. 14 : 13

14. Two numbers are such that the ratio between them is 3 : 5 but if each is increased by 10, the ratio between them becomes 5 : 7. The numbers are:

A. 3, 5 B. 7, 9
C. 13, 22 D. 15, 25

15. In a factory the ratio of male workers to female workers was 5 : 3. If the number of female workers was less by 40, the total number of workers in the factory was:

A. 100
B. 500
C. 160
D. 200

ANSWERS

1	2	3	4	5	6	7	8	9	10
A	B	A	D	D	A	A	B	B	B
11	**12**	**13**	**14**	**15**					
B	C	C	D	C					

EXPLANATORY ANSWERS

1. $\frac{A}{B} = \frac{2}{3}$ and $\frac{B}{C} = \frac{4}{5}$

$\Rightarrow \quad \frac{A}{B} \times \frac{B}{C} = \frac{2}{3} \times \frac{4}{5} \Rightarrow \frac{A}{C} = \frac{8}{15}$

$\Rightarrow \quad \frac{C}{A} = \frac{15}{8}$

Hence, $\quad$ C : A = 15 : 8.

2. 10% of x = 20% of y

$\Rightarrow \quad \frac{10}{100}x = \frac{20}{100}y \quad \Rightarrow \quad \frac{x}{10} = \frac{y}{5}$

$\Rightarrow \quad \frac{x}{y} = \frac{10}{5} \quad \Rightarrow \quad x : y = 2 : 1$

3. Mean proportional = $\sqrt{(6+\sqrt{27})(6-\sqrt{27})}$

$= \sqrt{36-27} = \sqrt{9} = 3$

4. $\because \quad \frac{x}{y} = \frac{9}{11}$

$$\frac{5x+3y}{3x+5y} = \frac{\frac{5x}{y}+\frac{3y}{y}}{\frac{3x}{y}+\frac{5y}{y}} = \frac{5\left(\frac{x}{y}\right)+3}{3\left(\frac{x}{y}\right)+5}$$

$$= \frac{5\times\frac{9}{11}+3}{3\times\frac{9}{11}+5} = \frac{\frac{45+33}{11}}{\frac{27+55}{11}} = \frac{78}{82} = \frac{39}{41}$$

Hence, the value of $\frac{5x+3y}{3x+5y} = \frac{39}{41}$.

5. Given : $\quad a + b = 6x,\ b + c = 7x$

and $\quad c + a = 8x \quad$ ...(*i*)

and $\quad a + b + c = 14 \quad$ ...(*ii*)

Adding Eq. (*i*)

$a + b + b + c + c + a = 6x + 7x + 8x$

$\Rightarrow \quad 2(a + b + c) = 21x$

$\Rightarrow \quad 2 \times 14 = 21x \quad$ [from Eq. (*ii*)]

$\Rightarrow \quad x = \frac{28}{21} = \frac{4}{3}$

$\therefore \quad a + b = 6x = 6 \times \frac{4}{3} = 8$

$\because \quad a + b + c = 14 \Rightarrow c = 14 - 8 = 6$

6. Let the two numbers are a and b

According to the question,

$\frac{a}{b} = \frac{2}{3} \Rightarrow 3a = 2b \Rightarrow b = \frac{3a}{2}$

Now, $\quad \frac{a+5}{b+5} = \frac{5}{7} \Rightarrow 7a + 35 = 5b + 25$

$\Rightarrow \quad 7a - 5b = -10$

$\Rightarrow \quad 7a - 5\left(\frac{3a}{2}\right) = -10$

$\Rightarrow \quad 14a - 15a = -20 \Rightarrow -a = -20$

$\Rightarrow \quad a = 20,\ b = 3 \times \frac{20}{2} = 30$

Hence, the bigger number is 30.

7. Let x be added to each of the numbers.

Then, $(12 + x) : (30 + x) :: (40 + x) : (86 + x)$

$\Rightarrow \quad \frac{12+x}{30+x} = \frac{40+x}{86+x}$

$\Rightarrow (12 + x)(86 + x) = (30 + x)(40 + x)$

$\Rightarrow 12 \times 86 + 12x + 86x + x^2$

$\quad = 30 \times 40 + 30x + 40x + x^2$

$\Rightarrow \quad 1032 + 98x = 1200 + 70x$

$\Rightarrow \quad 28x = 168 \Rightarrow x = 6$

8. Ratio of Males : Females = 5 : 3

$\Rightarrow \quad \frac{800}{x} = \frac{5}{3} \Rightarrow 5x = 3 \times 800$

$\Rightarrow \quad x = \frac{3 \times 800}{5} = 3 \times 160 = 480$

Hence, number of females = 480.

9. Let ethanol = $4x$ and ether = $1x$

$4x + 1x = 60 \Rightarrow 5x = 60 \Rightarrow x = 12$

Quantity of ethanol = $12 \times 4 = 48$ litres

Quantity of ether = $1 \times 12 = 12$ litres

Let m litres of ether be added to mixture to get the desired ratio. Then,

$$\frac{48}{12+m} = \frac{2}{1} \Rightarrow 24 + 2m = 48$$

$$\Rightarrow \quad 2m = 24 \Rightarrow m = 12$$

Hence, 12 litres of ether is to be added.

10. In 9 kg of brass, zinc = 4 kg

$\therefore$ In 180 kg of brass, zinc = $\frac{4}{9} \times 180 = 80$ kg.

11. Let the prices of a scooter and a television be ₹ $3x$ and $2x$ respectively.

According to the question,

$3x - 2x = 6000 \Rightarrow x = 6000$

$\therefore$ Price of a television = 2×6000 = ₹ 12000.

12. Weight of 13 m long iron rod = 23.4 kg

Weight of 6 m long iron rod

$= \frac{23.4}{13} \times 6$ kg $= 1.8 \times 6 = 10.8$ kg.

13. Let present age of Gayatri = $6x$ years and present age of Savitri = $5x$ years.

According to the question,

$$6x + 5x = 44 \Rightarrow 11x = 44 \Rightarrow x = 4$$

Gayatri's age = $6 \times 4 = 24$ years

Savitri's age = $5 \times 4 = 20$ years

After 8 years their ages will be 32 years and 28 years.

Ratio of their ages after 8 years = $\frac{32}{28} = 8 : 7$.

14. Let numbers are x and y

$$\frac{x}{y} = \frac{3}{5}$$

$$\Rightarrow \quad 5x = 3y \Rightarrow x = \frac{3y}{5}$$

According to the question,

$$\frac{x+10}{y+10} = \frac{5}{7} \Rightarrow 7x + 70 = 5y + 50$$

$$\Rightarrow \quad 7x - 5y = -20$$

$$\Rightarrow \quad 7\left(\frac{3y}{5}\right) - 5y = -20$$

$$\Rightarrow \quad 21y - 25y = -100$$

$$\Rightarrow \quad 4y = 100 \Rightarrow y = 25$$

$$\therefore \quad x = \frac{3 \times 25}{5} = 15$$

Hence, numbers are 15 and 25.

15. Let the number of male and female workers be $5x$ and $3x$ respectively.

According to the question,

$5x - 3x = 40 \Rightarrow 2x = 40 \Rightarrow x = 20$.

$\therefore$ Number of male = $5 \times 20 = 100$

and number of female = $3 \times 20 = 60$

Hence, total number of workers = $100 + 60 = 160$.

6. PARTNERSHIP

Partnership is a form of association of two or more persons who contribute resources like money together in order to carry on a business. It may be of simple or compound type.

Simple partnership is one in which the capitals of the partners are invested for the same time. The profits or losses are divided among the partners in the ratio of their investments.

Compound partnership is one in which the capitals of the partners are invested for different periods. In such cases, equivalent capitals are calculated for each partner by multiplying their capital contributions with time. The profits or losses are then divided in the ratio of these equivalent capitals. Thus, the ratio of profits is directly proportional to both capital invested as well as time.

The partner who invests the money in the business as well as takes part in its management, is known as **Working partner**.

The partner who only invests the money in the business and does not work, is known as **Sleeping partner**.

A working partner gets either monthly payment or a share in the profit for his contribution in the management of the business. This payment is deducted from the total profit before its distribution.

EXAMPLE: A, B and C invest ₹ 15000, ₹ 20000 and ₹ 25000 respectively in a business. The profit earned is ₹ 1200. Find the share of each in the profit.

SOLUTION: This is a case of simple partnership

Ratio of investments, A : B : C

= 15000 : 20000 : 25000

= 3 : 4 : 5

Sum of the ratios = 3 + 4 + 5 = 12

Share in the profit

$$\text{For A} = \frac{3}{12} \times 1200 = ₹\,300$$

$$\text{For B} = \frac{4}{12} \times 1200 = ₹\,400$$

$$\text{For C} = \frac{5}{12} \times 1200 = ₹\,500$$

EXAMPLE: A and B are partners in a firm. A invests ₹ 15000 and B ₹ 25000. A is the working partner and gets 20% of the profit for his contribution in the management of the firm. B is the sleeping partner. If the profit is ₹ 475, find the share of each.

SOLUTION: First we have to deduct the payment to be made to A from the total profit for his contribution in the management of the firm.

20% of ₹ 475 = ₹ 95

Balance profit = 475 – 95 = ₹ 380

This has to be divided between A and B in the ratio of their investments *i.e.*, ₹ 15000 : ₹ 25000 = 3 : 5

$$\text{A's share} = ₹\,380 \times \frac{3}{8} = ₹\,142.5$$

$$\text{B's share} = ₹\,380 \times \frac{5}{8} = ₹\,237.5$$

Finally, A gets a total of (95 + 142.5) = ₹ 237.5 and B gets = ₹ 237.5

EXAMPLE: In a business A and B gained some amount in a certain ratio. B and C received the profit in the ratio as that of A and B. If B received ₹ 6400 and C received ₹ 10,000 then find the amount invested by B.

SOLUTION: Let the ratio of A's and B's profit be $\frac{a}{b}$.

Hence, the ratio of B's and C's profit = $\frac{a}{b}$

Thus, $A : B : C = a : b : \frac{b^2}{a}$

when A's profit, $a = ₹\ 6400$

and C's profit, $\frac{b^2}{a} = ₹\ 10,000$

$\Rightarrow \quad b^2 = 10,000 \times 6400 = 100 \times 100 \times 80 \times 80$

$\Rightarrow \quad b = 100 \times 80 = 8000$

Hence, the amount invested by B = ₹ 8000.

MULTIPLE CHOICE QUESTIONS

1. A, B and C share the profit in the ratio of 3 : 5 : 7. If the gain is ₹ 2040, then C's share is:
   A. ₹ 360 B. ₹ 600
   C. ₹ 952 D. ₹ 120
2. A, B and C started a business with ₹ 47000. A puts in ₹ 5000 more than B and B ₹ 3000 more than C. The share of A out of the profit of ₹ 14100 will be:
   A. ₹ 3600 B. ₹ 4500
   C. ₹ 6000 D. ₹ 6300
3. A starts a business with ₹ 5000. After 4 months B joins him with a sum of ₹ 4000. In the end of the year there is a profit of ₹ 8970. The share of A in the profit will be:
   A. ₹ 3120 B. ₹ 4020
   C. ₹ 5850 D. ₹ 6360
4. A, B, C are three partners in a business. The profit share of A is $\frac{3}{16}$ of the profit and B's share is $\frac{1}{4}$ of the profit. If C receives ₹ 243, then the amount received by B will be:
   A. ₹ 90 B. ₹ 96
   C. ₹ 108 D. ₹ 120
5. A, B and C share the profit in the ratio 2 : 3 : 7. If the average gain is ₹ 8000, then B's share is:
   A. ₹ 2000 B. ₹ 1000
   C. ₹ 1500 D. ₹ 3000
6. Ashok started a business investing ₹ 90,000. After 3 months Shabir joined him with a capital of ₹ 1,20,000. If at the end of one year the total profit made by them was ₹ 96,000, what will be the difference between their shares?
   A. ₹ 24000 B. ₹ 8000
   C. ₹ 20000 D. None of these
7. Mahesh received ₹ 6000 as his share out of the total profit of ₹ 9000 which he and Ram entered at the end of one year. If Mahesh invested ₹ 20,000 for 6 months, whereas Ram invested his amount for the whole year, what was the amount invested by Ram?
   A. ₹ 4000 B. ₹ 5000
   C. ₹ 3000 D. ₹ 6000
8. A and B started a business jointly. A's investment was thrice the investment of B and the period of his investment was two times the period of investment of B. If B received ₹ 40,000 as profit, then their total profit is:
   A. ₹ 2,40,000 B. ₹ 28000
   C. ₹ 24000 D. ₹ 2,80,000
9. Anil started a business investing ₹ 70,000. After 8 months Vimal joined him with a capital of ₹ 1,80,000. In what ratio should Anil and Vimal share the profit after two years?
   A. 8 : 7 B. 7 : 5
   C. 7 : 6 D. None of these
10. A, B and C starts a business. A invests ₹ 3,20,000 for four months. B invests ₹ 5,10,000 for three months and C invests ₹ 2,70,000 for five months. If at the end of year there is a profit of ₹ 1,24,800, then share of B is:
    A. ₹ 79000 B. ₹ 49200
    C. ₹ 50000 D. ₹ 45900
11. A, B and C contract a work for ₹ 550. Together A and B are to do $\frac{7}{11}$ of the work. The share of C should be:
    A. ₹ 400 B. ₹ 300
    C. ₹ 200 D. ₹ $183\frac{1}{3}$
12. Jagmohan, Rooplal and Pankaj rented a video cassette for one week at a rent of ₹ 350. If they use it for 6 hrs, 10 hrs and 12 hrs respectively, the rent to be paid by Pankaj is:
    A. ₹ 75 B. ₹ 125
    C. ₹ 35 D. ₹ 150

13. Manoj got ₹ 6000 as his share out of the total profit of ₹ 9000 which he and Ramesh earned at the end of one year. If Manoj invested ₹ 20,000 for 6 months, whereas Ramesh invested his amount for the whole year, the amount invested by Ramesh was:

A. ₹ 60,000 B. ₹ 10,000
C. ₹ 4000 D. ₹ 5000

14. A, B and C invest ₹ 2000, ₹ 3000 and ₹ 4000 in a business. After one year A removed his money, B and C continued the business for one more year. If the net profit after 2 years be ₹ 3200, then A's share in the profit is:

A. ₹ 1000 B. ₹ 600
C. ₹ 800 D. ₹ 400

15. A and B enter into partnership investing ₹ 12000 and ₹ 16000 respectively. After 8 months, C also joins the business with a capital of ₹ 15000. The share of C in a profit of ₹ 46500 after 2 years will be:

A. ₹ 12000 B. ₹ 14400
C. ₹ 19200 D. ₹ 21200

ANSWERS

1	2	3	4	5	6	7	8	9	10
C	C	C	C	A	D	B	D	D	D
11	**12**	**13**	**14**	**15**					
C	D	D	D	A					

EXPLANATORY ANSWERS

1. C's share $= \frac{7}{15} \times 2040 = ₹\, 952.$

2. Let C's capital be ₹ x

Then B's capital = ₹ $(x + 3000)$

and A's capital = ₹ $(x + 3000 + 5000) = x + 8000$

$\Rightarrow \quad x + (x + 3000) + (x + 8000) = 47000$

$\Rightarrow \quad 3x + 11000 = 47000$

$\Rightarrow \quad 3x = 47000 - 11000$

$= 36000$

$\Rightarrow \quad x = 12000$

Thus, capital of A, B and C are ₹ 20000, ₹ 15000 and ₹ 12000 respectively.

∴ Profit sharing ratio = 20 : 15 : 12

∴ Profit of A $= \frac{20}{47} \times 14100 = ₹\, 6000$

3. ₹ 5000 × 12 = ₹ 60,000 for A

₹ 4000 × (12 – 4) = 4000 × 8 = ₹ 32000 for B

Ratio of profit sharing = 60000 : 32000

= 60 : 32 = 15 : 8

∴ Share of A in the profit $= \frac{15}{23} \times 8970$

= 15 × 390 = ₹ 5850

4. Let the profit be ₹ 1. Then,

$$A : B : C = \frac{3}{16} : \frac{1}{4} : \left[1 - \left(\frac{3}{16} + \frac{1}{4}\right)\right]$$

$$= \frac{3}{16} : \frac{1}{4} : \frac{9}{16}$$

$$= \frac{3}{16} : \frac{4}{16} : \frac{9}{16} \quad i.e.,\ 3 : 4 : 9$$

when C's share is ₹ 9, then B's share = ₹ 4

when C's share is ₹ 243, then B's share

$$= \frac{4 \times 243}{9} = ₹\, 108$$

5. B's share $= \frac{3}{2+3+7} \times 8000$

$= \frac{3 \times 8000}{12} = ₹\, 2000$

6. The ratio of their investment

$= 12 \times 90000 : (12 - 3) \times 120000$

$= 12 \times 9 : 9 \times 12 = 1 : 1$

Ashok's share $= \frac{1}{1+1} \times 96000 = ₹\, 48000$

Shabir's share $= \frac{1}{1+1} \times 96000 = ₹\, 48000$

Difference between their shares

$= ₹\ 48000 - ₹\ 48000 = 0.$

7. The ratio of their profit

$= ₹\ 6000 : ₹\ (9000 - 6000)$

$= ₹\ 6000 : ₹\ 3000 = 2 : 1$

Let ₹ x be the amount invested by Ram.

The ratio of their profit = The ratio of their investment

$\Rightarrow \quad 2 : 1 = 6 \times 20000 : 12 \times x$

$\Rightarrow \quad \frac{2}{1} = \frac{6 \times 20000}{12 \times x} \Rightarrow 2x = 10000$

$\Rightarrow \quad x = 5000$

$\therefore$ The investment of Ram is ₹ 5000.

8. Let ₹ x be the investment of B and n years be the period of investment of B.

Given : A's investment $= 3 \times ₹\ x = ₹\ 3x$

and period of investment of A $= 2n$ years

$\therefore$ The ratio of investment of A and B

$= 2n \times 3x : n \times x$

$= 6nx : nx = 6 : 1$

Let the total profit be ₹ y

Given B's share in profit = ₹ 40,000

$\Rightarrow \frac{1}{6+1} \times y = ₹\ 40{,}000 \Rightarrow y = ₹\ 2{,}80{,}000$

$\therefore$ Total profit is ₹ 2,80,000.

9. The ratio of Anil's and Vimal's share in the profit

= Ratio of their investments

$= 24 \times 70000 : 16 \times 180000$

$= 24 \times 7 : 16 \times 18 = 7 : 12$

10. The ratio of investments of A, B and C

$= 4 \times 320000 : 3 \times 510000 : 5 \times 270000$

$= 4 \times 32 : 3 \times 51 : 5 \times 27$

$= 128 : 153 : 135$

Total profit after 1 year = ₹ 124800

Share of B $= ₹\ \frac{153}{128 + 153 + 135} \times 124800$

$= ₹\ \frac{153}{416} \times 124800 = ₹\ 45900$

11. C's share $= ₹\left(550 \times \frac{4}{11}\right) = ₹\ 200$

12. Ratio of rents $= 6 : 10 : 12 = 3 : 5 : 6$

$\therefore$ Pankaj's share of rent $= ₹\left(350 \times \frac{6}{14}\right) = ₹\ 150$

13. Let amount invested by Ramesh be ₹ x

$\therefore 20000 \times 6 : 12x = 6000 : 3000$

i.e., $\frac{12x}{120000} = \frac{3000}{6000}$ or $x = ₹\ 5000$

14. Ratio of investments

$= (2000 \times 1) : (3000 \times 2) : (4000 \times 2)$

$= 1 : 3 : 4$

$\therefore$ A's share $= ₹\left(3200 \times \frac{1}{8}\right) = ₹\ 400.$

15. Ratio of investments

$= (12000 \times 24) : (16000 \times 24) : (15000 \times 16)$

$= 6 : 8 : 5$

C's share of profit $= ₹\left(45600 \times \frac{5}{19}\right) = ₹\ 12000$

7. AVERAGE

The sum of all the quantities of same kind divided by their number is called average (or mean) of those quantities.

FORMULAE

1. $\text{Average} = \left(\dfrac{\text{Sum of observations}}{\text{Number of observations}}\right)$
2. Sum of the first n natural numbers
$$= 1 + 2 + 3 + ... + n = \frac{n(n+1)}{2}$$
3. Sum of the squares of the first n natural numbers
$$= 1^2 + 2^2 + ... + n^2 = \frac{n(n+1)(2n+1)}{6}$$
4. Sum of the cubes of the first n natural numbers
$$= 1^3 + 2^3 + ... + n^3 = \left\{\frac{n(n+1)}{2}\right\}^2$$
5. Sum of the first n odd numbers
$= 1 + 3 + 5 + ... + (2n - 1) = n^2$
6. Distance between two stations P and Q is x km. A person covers the journey from P to Q at 'a' km/hr and returns back to P with a uniform speed of 'b' km/hr. Then the average speed of the person during the whole journey
$$= \frac{2ab}{a+b} \text{ km/hr.}$$

Different kinds of mean or average:

(*a*) Arithmetic mean

(*b*) Geometric mean

(*c*) Harmonic mean

(*a*) **Arithmetic Mean:** It is most popularly used of all the averages. For example, average income, average profit, average mileage etc. As defined earlier, it is the sum total of all values of items divided by the total number of items. For detailed discussion we will confine ourselves to Arithmetic Mean only because this is the most relevant of all the average for us.

Let $x_1, x_2, x_3, ..., x_n$ be the n values of x.
Their average is denoted by $\bar{x}$ and given by

$$\bar{x} = \frac{\text{Sum of observations}}{\text{Total number of observations}}$$

or
$$\bar{x} = \frac{x_1 + x_2 + x_3 + ... + x_n}{n}$$

(*b*) **Geometric Mean :** For observations $x_1, x_2, x_3, ..., x_n$ the geometric mean denoted by G.M. is defined as:

$$\text{G.M.} = (x_1 . x_2 . x_3 ... x_n)^{1/n}$$

It is useful in calculating averages of ratios such as average population, growth rate, average percentage increase etc.

(*c*) **Harmonic Mean:** It is defined as

$$\text{H.M.} = \frac{n}{\dfrac{1}{x_1} + \dfrac{1}{x_2} + ... + \dfrac{1}{x_n}}.$$

EXAMPLE: Find the average of first ten prime numbers.

SOLUTION: First ten prime numbers are 2, 3, 5, 7, 11, 13, 17, 19, 23 and 29.

$$\therefore \text{Average} = \frac{2+3+5+7+11+13+17+19+23+29}{10}$$

$$= \frac{129}{10} = 12.9$$

EXAMPLE: If x_1, x_2, x_3, x_4, x_5 are five consecutive odd numbers then find the average of these numbers.

SOLUTION: Since x_1 is the first odd number.

$$\therefore \quad x_2 = x_1 + 2$$
$$x_3 = x_2 + 2 = x_1 + 4$$
$$x_4 = x_3 + 2 = x_1 + 6$$
$$x_5 = x_4 + 2 = x_1 + 8$$

$$\therefore \text{ Average} = \frac{x_1 + x_1 + 2 + x_1 + 4 + x_1 + 6 + x_1 + 8}{5}$$

$$= \frac{5x_1 + 20}{5} = \frac{5(x_1 + 4)}{5} = x_1 + 4$$

EXAMPLE: If the average of four consecutive even numbers is 27, then find the largest of these numbers.

SOLUTION: Let x be the first even number in the series of four consecutive even numbers.

$\therefore$ 2nd even number $= x + 2$

3rd even number $= x + 4$

4th even number $= x + 6$

$$\text{Average} = \frac{x + x + 2 + x + 4 + x + 6}{4}$$

$$\Rightarrow \quad 27 = \frac{4x + 12}{4}$$

$$\Rightarrow \quad 4x + 12 = 27 \times 4 = 108$$

$$\Rightarrow \quad 4x = 96$$

$$\Rightarrow \quad x = 24$$

Largest number in this series is $x + 6$

i.e., $24 + 6 = 30$

EXAMPLE: The average of eight numbers is 14. The average of six of these numbers is 16. What is the average of the remaining two numbers?

SOLUTION: Sum of the eight numbers $= 14 \times 8 = 112$

Sum of six of these eight numbers $= 16 \times 6 = 96$

$\therefore$ Sum of the remaining two numbers $= 112 - 96 = 16$

$\therefore$ Average of the remaining two numbers $= \frac{16}{2} = 8$

EXAMPLE: What is the average of first 30 multiples of 7?

SOLUTION: Required Average

$$= \frac{7 + 14 + 21 + ... + 210}{30}$$

$$= \frac{7(1 + 2 + 3 + ... + 30)}{30}$$

$$= \frac{7 \times 30(30 + 1)}{2 \times 30}$$

$$= \frac{7 \times 31}{2} = \frac{217}{2} = 108.5$$

EXAMPLE: The average of 11 results is 50. If the average of first six results is 49 and that of last six is 52, find the sixth result.

SOLUTION: Sum of 11 results $= 11 \times 50 = 550$

Sum of first 6 results $6 \times 49 = 294$

Sum of last 6 results $= 6 \times 52 = 312$

$\therefore$ 6th result $= 294 + 312 - 550$

$= 56$

EXAMPLE: The average age of three boys is 15 years. If their ages are in the ratio 3 : 5 : 7. What is the age of the youngest boy?

SOLUTION: Let the ages of the three boys be $3x$, $5x$ and $7x$.

$$\text{Average age} = \frac{3x + 5x + 7x}{3} = 5x$$

and $\quad 5x = 15 \Rightarrow x = 3$

The age of the youngest boy $= 3x = 3 \times 3 = 9$ years.

EXAMPLE: The average of 100 observations is 45. It was later found that two observations 19 and 31 were incorrectly recorded as 91 and 13. Find the correct average.

SOLUTION: Sum of 100 observations

$= 100 \times 45 = 4500$

New sum of 100 observations

$= 4500 + (19 + 31) - (91 + 13)$

$= 4500 + 50 - 104 = 4446$

$$\text{Correct average} = \frac{4446}{100} = 44.46$$

MULTIPLE CHOICE QUESTIONS

1. The average of first five multiples of 3 is:
   A. 3 B. 9
   C. 12 D. 15
2. The average of 25 results is 18, that of first 12 is 14 and of the last 12 is 17. Thirteenth result is:
   A. 78 B. 85
   C. 28 D. 72
3. Out of three numbers, the first is twice the second and is half of the third. If the average of the three numbers is 56, the three numbers in order are:
   A. 48, 96, 24 B. 48, 24, 96
   C. 96, 24, 48 D. 96, 48, 24
4. The sum of three numbers is 98. If the ratio between first and second be 2 : 3 and that between second and third be 5 : 8, then the second number is:
   A. 30 B. 20
   C. 58 D. 48
5. The average age of a committee of seven trustees is the same as it was 5 years ago; a young man having been substituted for one of them. The new man compared to the replaced old man, is younger in age by:
   A. 5 years B. 7 years
   C. 12 years D. 35 years
6. The average expenditure of a man for the first five months is ₹ 120 and for the next seven months is ₹ 130. His monthly average income if he saves ₹ 290 in that year, is:
   A. ₹ 160 B. ₹ 170
   C. ₹ 150 D. ₹ 140
7. The average salary of 20 workers in an office is ₹ 1900 per month. If the manager's salary is added, the average becomes ₹ 2000 per month. The manager's salary is:
   A. ₹ 24000 B. ₹ 25200
   C. ₹ 45600 D. None of these
8. The average temperature of first 3 days is 27°C and of the next 3 days is 29°C. If the average of the whole week is 28.5°C, the temperature of the last day is:
   A. 31.5°C B. 10.5°C
   C. 21°C D. 42°C
9. A cricketer scored 180 runs in the first test and 258 runs in the second. How many runs should he score in the third test so that his average score in the three tests would be 230 runs?
   A. 219 B. 242
   C. 334 D. None of these
10. The average of first five prime numbers is:
    A. 5.0 B. 5.2
    C. 5.6 D. 6.0
11. The average weight of 3 men A, B and C is 84 kg. Another man D joins the group and the average now becomes 80 kg. If another man E, whose weight is 3 kg more than that of D, replaces A, then average weight of B, C, D and E becomes 79 kg. The weight of A is:
    A. 70 kg B. 72 kg
    C. 75 kg D. 80 kg
12. The average age of A, B, C, D 5 years ago was 45 years. By including x, the present average of all the five is 49 years. The present age of x is:
    A. 64 years B. 48 years
    C. 45 years D. 40 years
13. The average height of 30 boys, out of a class of 50, is 160 cm. If the average height of the remaining boys is 165 cm, the average height of the whole class (in cm) is:
    A. 161 B. 162
    C. 163 D. 164
14. The average age of an adult class is 40 years. 12 new students with an average age of 32 years join the class, thereby decreasing the average of the class by 4 years. The original strength of the class was:
    A. 10 B. 11
    C. 12 D. 15
15. If a, b, c, d, e are five consecutive odd numbers, their average is:
    A. $5(a+4)$ B. $\frac{abcde}{5}$
    C. $5(a+b+c+d+e)$ D. None of these
16. Of the three numbers, second is twice the first and is also thrice the third. If the average of the three numbers is 44, the largest number is:
    A. 24 B. 36
    C. 72 D. 108

17. The average of 50 numbers is 38. If two numbers namely, 45 and 55 are discarded, the average of remaining number is:

A. 36.50 B. 37.00
C. 37.50 D. 37.52

18. The average height of 30 girls out of a class of 40 is 160 cm and that of the remaining girls is 156 cm. The average height of the whole class is:

A. 158 cm B. 158.5 cm
C. 159 cm D. 159.5 cm

19. The average of n numbers is x. If 36 is subtracted from any two numbers each, then new average is $(x - 8)$. The value of n is:

A. 6 B. 8
C. 9 D. 72

20. The average salary of male employees in a firm is ₹ 520 and that of female employees is ₹ 420. The mean salary of all the employees is ₹ 500. The percentage of female employees is:

A. 40% B. 30%
C. 25% D. 20%

ANSWERS

1	2	3	4	5	6	7	8	9	10
B	A	B	A	D	C	D	A	D	C
11	**12**	**13**	**14**	**15**	**16**	**17**	**18**	**19**	**20**
C	C	B	C	D	C	C	C	C	D

EXPLANATORY ANSWERS

1. $$\text{Average} = \frac{3(1+2+3+4+5)}{5} = \frac{(3\times15)}{5} = 9$$

2. Thirteenth result

$= [(25 \times 18) - (12 \times 14 + 12 \times 17)]$
$= [450 - (168 + 204)]$
$= 450 - 372 = 78.$

3. Let the numbers be $2x$, x and $4x$.

$$\text{Average} = \frac{2x+x+4x}{3} = \frac{7x}{3}$$

According to the question,

$$\frac{7x}{3} = 56$$

$\Rightarrow$ $7x = 3 \times 56$

$\Rightarrow$ $x = \frac{3\times56}{7} = 24$

Hence, the numbers in order are 48, 24 and 96.

4. Let the numbers be x, y, z, then

$x + y + z = 98$

$\frac{x}{y} = \frac{2}{3}$ and $\frac{y}{z} = \frac{5}{8}$

$\therefore$ $x = \frac{2y}{3}$ and $z = \frac{8y}{5}$

So, $\frac{2y}{3} + y + \frac{8y}{5} = 98$

$\Rightarrow$ $\frac{10y+15y+24y}{15} = 98$

$\Rightarrow$ $49y = 15 \times 98$

$\Rightarrow$ $y = \frac{15\times98}{49} = 30$

5. During these five years, the total age would have increased by $(7 \times 5) = 35$ years. But, it remains the same as it was 5 years ago.
$\therefore$ The new man is younger than the replaced old man by 35 years.

6. Total income for 12 months

$= ₹\ (120 \times 5 + 130 \times 7 + 290)$
$= ₹\ 1800$

Average monthly income $= ₹\frac{1800}{12} = ₹150$

7. Total salary of 20 workers

$= 20 \times 1900 = ₹\ 38000$

Total salary of 20 workers and manager

$= 21 \times 2000 = ₹\ 42000$

Monthly salary of the manager

$= 42000 - 38000 = ₹\ 4000.$

8. Total temperature of first 3 days

$= 27 \times 3 = 81°C$

Total temperature of next 3 days

$= 29 \times 3 = 87°C$

Total temperature of 7 days

$= 28.5 \times 7 = 199.5°C$

Temperature of the last day

$= 199.5 - (81 + 87)$

$= 199.5 - 168 = 31.5°C$

9. Let runs he should score in third test be x :

Then, $\frac{180+258+x}{3} = 230$

$\Rightarrow \quad x = 690 - 438 = 252.$

10. Average $= \frac{2+3+5+7+11}{5} = \frac{28}{5} = 5.6.$

11. Weight of D = $(80 \times 4 - 84 \times 3)$ kg = 68 kg

Weight of E = $(68 + 3)$ kg = 71 kg

(B + C + D + E)'s weight = (79×4) kg = 316 kg

$\therefore$ (B + C)'s weight

= [316 − (68 + 71)] kg = 177 kg

Hence, A's weight

= [(84 × 3) − 177]kg = 75 kg

12. Total age of A, B, C and D 5 years ago

= (45 × 4) years = 180 years.

Total present age of A, B, C, D and x

= (49 × 5) years = 245 years.

Present age of A, B, C and D

= (180 + 5 × 4) years = 200 years.

$\therefore$ Present age of x = 45 years.

13. Total height of 30 boys = 30 × 160 = 4800

Total height of 20 boys = 20 × 165 = 3300

Total height of 50 boys = 8100

Average height of 50 boys $= \frac{8100}{50} = 162.$

14. $40x + 12 \times 32 = (12 + x) \times 36$

$\Rightarrow \quad 40x + 384 = 432 + 36x$

$\Rightarrow \quad 4x = 432 - 384 = 48$

$\Rightarrow \quad x = \frac{48}{4} = 12$

Hence, the original strength of the class was 12.

15. Average $= \frac{a+a+2+a+4+a+6+a+8}{5}$

$= \frac{5a+20}{5} = \frac{5(a+4)}{5} = a+4$

16. Let the numbers be x, $2x$ and $\frac{2x}{3}$.

Average $= \frac{x+2x+\frac{2x}{3}}{3}$

$\Rightarrow \quad \frac{11x}{9} = 44$

$\Rightarrow \quad x = \frac{44 \times 9}{11} = 36$

So, the numbers are 36, 72 and 24.

Hence, the largest one is 72.

17. Total of 50 numbers = 50 × 38 = 1900

Average of 48 numbers $= \frac{1900-(45+55)}{48}$

$= \frac{1800}{48} = 37.50$

18. The average of the whole class

$= \frac{(30 \times 160 + 10 \times 156)}{40} = \frac{4800+1560}{40}$

$= \frac{6360}{40} = 159$ cm

19. $\frac{nx-36-36}{n} = x - 8$

$\Rightarrow \quad nx - 72 = nx - 8n$

$\Rightarrow \quad 8n = 72$

$\Rightarrow \quad n = 9$

20. Let the total employees be 100.

n_1 = number of females = x

n_2 = number of males = $100 - x$

$\bar{x} = \frac{n_1\bar{x}_1 + n_2\bar{x}_2}{n_1 + n_2}$

$\Rightarrow \quad 500 = \frac{x \times 420 + (100 - x) \times 520}{100}$

$\Rightarrow \quad 500 = \frac{42x + 5200 - 52x}{10}$

$\Rightarrow \quad 5000 = 5200 - 10x$

$\Rightarrow \quad 10x = 200$

$\Rightarrow \quad x = 20$ *i.e.*, 20%.

8. PROFIT AND LOSS

Cost Price (CP)

The price at which an article is purchased is called the cost price of the article.

Selling Price (SP)

The price at which an article is sold is called the selling price of the article.

Profit or Gain

If SP is greater than the CP, the seller is said to have a profit or gain.

Clearly, $\text{Gain} = \text{SP} - \text{CP}$

Loss

If SP is less than CP, the seller is said to have a loss.

Clearly, $\text{Loss} = \text{CP} - \text{SP}$

Profit or loss per cent is calculated on cost price.

$$\text{Profit \%} = \frac{\text{Profit}}{\text{CP}} \times 100$$

$$\text{Loss \%} = \frac{\text{Loss}}{\text{CP}} \times 100$$

$$\text{SP} = \frac{\text{CP} \times (100 + \text{Profit\%})}{100}, \text{ if there is gain}$$

$$\text{SP} = \frac{\text{CP} \times (100 - \text{Loss\%})}{100}, \text{ if there is loss}$$

$$\text{CP} = \text{SP} \times \left(\frac{100}{100 + \text{Profit\%}}\right), \text{ if there is gain}$$

$$\text{CP} = \text{SP} \times \left(\frac{100}{100 - \text{Loss\%}}\right), \text{ if there is loss}$$

If an article is sold at a gain of 20%,

then, $\text{SP} = (120\% \text{ of CP})$

If an article is sold at a loss of 20%,

then, $\text{SP} = (80\% \text{ of CP})$

Overheads

The expenses incurred on transportation, rent, personnel salary, maintenance, packaging, advertisements and the like are included under the general heading of overheads. These overhead and the profit when added to the cost price determine the selling price. If the overheads are not separately mentioned in the problem, we assume it to be zero or else these have been included in the cost price itself.

Discount

It is an offer made by the seller to the buyer for reduction in price to be paid. There are several cases where discounts are allowed. For instance, to dispose off old goods, to increase its market share when the customer is ready to pay the whole amount in cash instead of instalment and so on. It is subtracted from the original price and is usually expressed as per cent or a fraction of the marked price. The price obtained after deducting the discount from the original price is the selling price which the customer has to pay.

EXAMPLE: If an article is purchased for ₹ 570 and sold for ₹ 518.70, find the lost per cent.

SOLUTION: CP = ₹ 570

SP = ₹ 518.70

∴ Loss = CP – SP

= 570 – 518.70 = ₹ 51.30

$$\text{Loss \%} = \frac{\text{Loss}}{\text{CP}} \times 100 = \frac{51.30}{570} \times 100$$

$$= \frac{5130}{570} = \frac{513}{57} = 9\%$$

EXAMPLE: A man buys a TV for ₹ 16,000. After two years he sells it for ₹ 12800. Find his loss per cent.

SOLUTION: $\text{Loss \%} = \frac{\text{Loss}}{\text{CP}} \times 100$

$$= \frac{16000 - 12800}{16000} \times 100$$

$$= \frac{3200}{16000} \times 100 = 20\%$$

EXAMPLE: Mohan sells his watch at a loss of ₹ 500 for ₹ 1000. Find the cost price and loss per cent.

SOLUTION: $\text{CP} = \text{SP} + \text{Loss}$

$$= 1000 + 500 = ₹\ 1500$$

$$\text{Loss \%} = \frac{\text{Loss}}{\text{CP}} \times 100 = \frac{500}{1500} \times 100$$

$$= \frac{100}{3} = 33\frac{1}{3}\%$$

EXAMPLE: Ravi buys an article for ₹ 5000 and sells it at 20% gain. Find it selling price.

SOLUTION: $\text{Profit} = 20\% \text{ of CP} = \frac{20}{100} \times 5000$

$\Rightarrow$ Profit = ₹ 1000

SP = CP + Profit

= 5000 + 1000

= ₹ 6000

EXAMPLE: A man sells an article at 20% gain for ₹ 3600. Find its cost price.

SOLUTION: Let CP = ₹ 100

then SP = 100 + 20 = ₹ 120

When SP ₹ 120 then CP = ₹ 100

When SP ₹ 3600 then $\text{CP} = \frac{100}{120} \times 3600$

Hence CP = ₹ 3000

EXAMPLE: The cost price of 6 pens is equal to the selling price of 4 pens. Find the profit per cent.

SOLUTION: SP of 4 pens = CP of 6 pens

SP of 2 pens = CP of $\frac{6}{4} \times 2 = 3$ pens

Profit = CP of 3 pens

investment = CP of 6 pens

$$\text{Profit \%} = \frac{3}{6} \times 100 = 50\%$$

Alternatively:

Let the CP of 1 pen be ₹ x.

$\therefore$ CP of 6 pens = ₹ $6x$

Also, SP of 4 pens = ₹ $6x$

$\therefore$ SP of 6 pens = $\frac{6x}{4} \times 6 = ₹\ 9x$

Profit = SP – CP = $9x - 6x = 3x$

$$\text{Profit \%} = \frac{3x}{6x} \times 100 = 50\%$$

EXAMPLE: If CP of 20 tables is equal to the SP of 25 tables. Find the loss percent.

SOLUTION: Let the CP of 1 table be ₹ x.

$\therefore$ CP of 20 tables = ₹ $20x$

Also, SP of 25 tables = ₹ $20x$

$\therefore$ SP of 20 tables = ₹ $\frac{20x}{25} \times 20 = ₹\ 16x$

Loss = $20x - 16x = 4x$

$$\text{Loss \%} = \frac{\text{Loss}}{\text{CP}} \times 100$$

$$= \frac{4x}{20x} \times 100 = 20\%$$

EXAMPLE: Ram sold a book at a profit of 6%. Had he sold it for ₹ 2 more he would have gained 10%. Find the cost price of the book.

SOLUTION: (10% – 6%) of CP = 4% of CP = ₹ 2

$\Rightarrow$ $\frac{4}{100} \times \text{CP} = 2$

$\Rightarrow$ $\text{CP} = \frac{200}{4} = ₹\ 50$

EXAMPLE: An article is sold for ₹ 4600 at a gain of 15%. What would be the profit or loss per cent if it is sold for ₹ 3600?

SOLUTION: $\text{CP} = 4600 \times \frac{100}{115} = ₹\ 4000$

$$\text{Loss \%} = \frac{4000 - 3600}{4000} \times 100 = 10\%$$

MULTIPLE CHOICE QUESTIONS

1. A loss of 5% was suffered by selling a plot for ₹ 4085. The cost price of the plot was:
A. ₹ 4350 B. ₹ 4259.25
C. ₹ 4200 D. ₹ 4300
2. On selling an article for ₹ 240, a trader loses 4%. In order to gain 10%, he must sell that article for:
A. ₹ 264.00 B. ₹ 273.20
C. ₹ 275.00 D. ₹ 280.00
3. A man purchased a watch for ₹ 400 and sold it at a gain of 20% of the selling price. The selling price of the watch is:
A. ₹ 300 B. ₹ 320
C. ₹ 440 D. ₹ 500
4. If 5% more is gained by selling an article for ₹ 350 than by selling it for ₹ 340, the cost of the article is:
A. ₹ 50 B. ₹ 160
C. ₹ 200 D. ₹ 225
5. Profit after selling a commodity for ₹ 425 is same as loss after selling it for ₹ 355. The cost of the commodity is:
A. ₹ 385 B. ₹ 390
C. ₹ 395 D. ₹ 400
6. The cost price of an article, which on being sold at a gain of 12% yields ₹ 6 more than when it is sold at a loss of 12%, is:
A. ₹ 30 B. ₹ 25
C. ₹ 20 D. ₹ 24
7. The CP of an article which is sold at a loss of 25% for ₹150, is:
A. ₹ 125 B. ₹ 175
C. ₹ 200 D. ₹ 225
8. When the price of pressure cooker was increased by 15%, its sale fell down by 15%. The effect on the money receipt was:
A. no effect B. 15% decrease
C. 7.5% increase D. 2.25% decrease
9. A man sells 320 mangoes at the cost price of 400 mangoes. His gain per cent is:
A. 10% B. 25%
C. 15% D. 20%
10. By selling 12 oranges for one rupee a man loses 20%. How many for a rupee should he sell to get a gain of 20%?
A. 5 B. 8
C. 10 D. 15
11. A man sells a car to his friend at 10% loss. If the friend sells it for ₹ 54000 and gains 20%, the original CP of the car was:
A. ₹ 25000 B. ₹ 37500
C. ₹ 50000 D. ₹ 60000
12. The loss incurred on selling an article for ₹ 270 is as much as the profit made after selling it at 10% profit. The CP of the article is:
A. ₹ 90 B. ₹ 110
C. ₹ 363 D. ₹ 300
13. An item costing ₹ 200 is being sold at 10% loss. If the price is further reduced by 5%, the selling price will be:
A. ₹ 179 B. ₹ 175
C. ₹ 171 D. ₹ 170
14. A trader lists his articles 20% above CP and allows a discount of 10% on cash payment. His gain per cent is:
A. 10% B. 6%
C. 8% D. 5%
15. A discount series of 10%, 20% and 40% is equal to a single discount of:
A. 50% B. 56.80%
C. 70% D. 70.28%

ANSWERS

1	2	3	4	5	6	7	8	9	10
D	C	D	C	B	B	C	D	B	B
11	**12**	**13**	**14**	**15**					
C	D	C	C	B					

EXPLANATORY ANSWERS

1. Loss = 5%, SP = ₹ 4085

Let CP = ₹ 100

∴ SP = ₹ 100 – 5 = ₹ 95

When SP ₹ 95 then CP = ₹ 100

When SP ₹ 4085 then CP = $\frac{100}{95} \times 4085$

$= 4300$

Hence, the cost price of the plot was ₹ 4300.

2. Loss = 4%, SP = ₹ 240

Let CP = ₹ 100

∴ SP = 100 – 4 = 96

When SP ₹ 96 then CP = ₹ 100

When SP ₹ 240 then CP = $\frac{100}{96} \times 240$ = ₹ 250

Again 100 + 10 = 110

When CP 100 then SP = ₹ 110

When CP 250 then SP = $\frac{110}{100} \times 250$ = ₹ 275

3. Let SP = ₹ x

then, profit = $\frac{20}{100} \times x$ = ₹ $\frac{x}{5}$

CP = SP – profit = $x - \frac{x}{5}$ = ₹ $\frac{4x}{5}$

According to the question,

$$\frac{4x}{5} = 400 \Rightarrow 4x = 2000$$

$$\Rightarrow x = 500$$

Hence, selling price of the watch = ₹ 500.

4. Let CP = ₹ x

Then, if SP = ₹350

Profit = SP – CP = ₹ $(350 - x)$

if SP = ₹ 340 then, profit = ₹ $(340 - x)$

$$\therefore (350 - x) - (340 - x) = \frac{5}{100}x$$

$$\Rightarrow 10 = \frac{5}{100}x \quad \Rightarrow x = 200$$

Hence, the cost of the article = ₹ 200.

5. Let CP = ₹ x,

then, $425 - x = x - 355 \Rightarrow 2x = 780$

$\Rightarrow x = 390$

Hence, the cost of commodity is ₹ 390.

6. Let CP of the article = ₹ x

Then, SP when profit is 12%

$$= \left(\frac{12x}{100} + x\right) = \frac{112x}{100}$$

$$\therefore \frac{112x}{100} - \frac{88x}{100} = 6$$

$$\Rightarrow 24x = 600$$

$$\Rightarrow x = \frac{600}{24} = 25$$

∴ CP of the article is ₹ 25.

7. 100 – 25 = 75

When SP 75 then CP = ₹ 100

When SP 150 then CP = ₹ $\frac{100}{75} \times 150$ = ₹ 200

8. Let the original cost of each cooker be ₹ 1 and let the number sold originally be 100.

Total sale proceed = ₹ (100 × 1) = ₹ 100

New rate = (115% of ₹ 1) = ₹ 1.15

Number sold now = 85

∴ Sale proceed now = ₹(1.15 × 85) = ₹ 97.75

So, there is a decrease of 2.25% in the money receipt.

9. Let CP of each mango be ₹ 1.

Then, CP of 400 mangoes = ₹ 400

∴ CP of 320 mangoes = ₹ 320

SP of 320 mangoes = ₹ 400

Profit = 400 – 320 = ₹ 80

$$\text{Profit\%} = \frac{80}{320} \times 100 = 25\%$$

10. SP = ₹ 1, Loss = 20%

$\Rightarrow$ CP = $\left(\frac{100}{80} \times 1\right) \Rightarrow$ CP = ₹ $\frac{5}{4}$

Now, CP = ₹ $\frac{5}{4}$, gain, 20%

$\Rightarrow$ SP = $\frac{120}{100} \times \frac{5}{4}$ = ₹ $\frac{3}{2}$

For ₹$\frac{3}{2}$, he must sell 12 oranges

For ₹ 1, he must sell $\left(12 \times \frac{2}{3}\right)$ = 8 oranges.

11. SP = ₹ 54000 and gain earned = 20%

CP = ₹$\left(\frac{100}{120} \times 54000\right)$ = ₹ 45000

Now, SP = ₹ 45000 and Loss = 10%

∴ CP = ₹$\left(\frac{100}{90} \times 45000\right)$ = ₹ 50000

12. Let CP be ₹ x. Then,

$$x - 270 = 10\% \text{ of } x = \frac{x}{10}$$

$$\Rightarrow \quad x - \frac{x}{10} = 270$$

$$\Rightarrow \quad 9x = 10 \times 270$$

$$\Rightarrow \quad x = \frac{10 \times 270}{9}$$

$$\Rightarrow \quad x = 300$$

∴ CP of the article is ₹ 300.

13. SP = 90% of ₹ 200 = ₹ 180

Further, SP = (95% of ₹180) = ₹ 171

14. Let CP = ₹ 100. Then, MP = ₹ 120.

SP = 90% of ₹ 120 = $\frac{90}{100} \times 120$ = ₹ 108

Profit = SP − CP = 108 − 100 = ₹ 8

Profit % = $\frac{\text{Profit}}{\text{CP}} \times 100 = \frac{8}{100} \times 100 = 8\%$

15. Let original price = ₹ 100

Price after 1st discount = ₹ 90

Price after 2nd discount

= ₹$\left(\frac{80}{100} \times 90\right)$ = ₹ 72

Price after 3rd discount

= ₹$\left(\frac{60}{100} \times 72\right)$ = ₹ 43.20

∴ Single discount = 100 − 43.20 = 56.8%.

9. SIMPLE AND COMPOUND INTEREST

In any money transaction there is a **lender** who gives money, and a **borrower** who receives money. The amount of loan borrowed, is called the principal (P). The borrower pays a certain amount for the use of this money. This is called **Interest (I)**. Interest is always calculated on the principal borrowed. The borrowing is for a specified **Time (t)** and on specified terms. The specified term is expressed as per cent of the principal and is called rate of interest.

The sum of the principal and the interest is called the **Amount (A)**. In general, the rate of interest may be yearly, half yearly, quarterly or monthly as mutually agreed upon by both parties at the time of transaction. Depending upon the period of rate of interest, time is expressed in multiples of this period.

Interest is of two kinds—**Simple Interest and compound Interest**. If the interest is calculated only, on a certain sum borrowed it is called Simple Interest.

The simple interest (SI) on a principal P at R% per annum for T years is given by:

$$SI = \frac{P \times R \times T}{100}$$

$$\therefore \quad P = \frac{SI \times 100}{R \times T}$$

$$\therefore \quad R = \frac{SI \times 100}{P \times T}$$

$$\therefore \quad T = \frac{SI \times 100}{P \times R}$$

Compound Interest differs from Simple Interest that in CI the interest for the future period is calculated not only on the principal but also on the interest earned until the previous period. Thus, the total interest earned in case of CI is not uniformly distributed over time units whereas in Simple Interest it is uniformly distributed. The interest due at the end of the first unit of time is added to the principal and the amount so obtained becomes the principal for the second unit. Similarly, the amount after the 2nd unit of time becomes the principal for the third unit of time and continues till the last unit of time.

The difference between the final amount (A) obtained at the last unit of time and the original principal is called the **Compound Interest**.

Important Relations

Principal = ₹ P (in rupees)

Rate = R % (in per cent per annum)

Time period = T years (in years)

Amount = ₹ A (in rupees)

I. When interest is compounded annually,

$$A = P\left[1 + \frac{R}{100}\right]^{T}$$

II. When interest is compounded half-yearly,

$$A = P\left[1 + \frac{R/2}{100}\right]^{2T} = P\left[1 + \frac{R}{200}\right]^{2T}$$

[R is divided by 2 and T is multiplied by 2.]

III. When interest is compounded quarterly,

$$A = P\left[1+\frac{R/4}{100}\right]^{4T} = P\left[1+\frac{R}{400}\right]^{4T}$$

[R is divided by 4 and T is multiplied by 4.]

IV. When interest is $R_1\%$ for first year, $R_2\%$ for 2nd year and $R_3\%$ for third year;

$$A = P\left[1+\frac{R_1}{100}\right]\left[1+\frac{R_2}{100}\right]\left[1+\frac{R_3}{100}\right]$$

V. CI = A – P

Example: Find the simple interest on ₹ 1000 for 3 years at 10% p.a.

Solution: $SI = \frac{P\times R\times T}{100} = \frac{1000\times 10\times 3}{100} = ₹\,300$

Example: Find the amount of ₹ 600 in 4 years at 3% p.a.

Solution: $SI = \frac{P\times R\times T}{100} = \frac{600\times 3\times 4}{100} = ₹\,72$

$\therefore$ Amount = P + SI = 600 + 72 = ₹ 672

Example: In what time will ₹ 7000 give ₹ 3675 as interest at the rate of 7% p.a. simple interest?

Solution: $T = \frac{SI\times 100}{P\times R} = \frac{3675\times 100}{7000\times 7}$

$$= \frac{15}{2} = 7\frac{1}{2} \text{ years.}$$

Example: At what rate per annum will a sum of ₹ 5000 amount to ₹ 6000 in 4 years?

Solution: SI = A – P = 6000 – 5000 = ₹ 1000

$$R = \frac{SI\times 100}{P\times T} = \frac{1000\times 100}{5000\times 4} = 5\%$$

Example: In how many years will a sum of money double itself at 5% rate of interest?

Solution: A sum doubles itself when amount of interest becomes equal to the principal

SI = P, R = 5%

$$\therefore \quad T = \frac{100\times P}{P\times 5} = 20 \text{ years}$$

Example: A certain sum amounts to ₹ 115200 in 2 years and to ₹ 165888 in 4 years. Find the sum and rate per cent.

Solution: Here, amount on ₹ 115200 for 2 years at CI is ₹ 165888

$$\therefore \quad 115200\left(1+\frac{R}{100}\right)^2 = 165888$$

$$\left(1+\frac{R}{100}\right)^2 = \frac{165888}{115200} = 1.44$$

$$\therefore \quad 1+\frac{R}{100} = 1.2$$

$$\frac{R}{100} = 1.2-1 = 0.2$$

$$\Rightarrow \quad R = 0.2\times 100 = 20\%$$

Amount after 2 years is ₹ 115200

$$\therefore \quad P\left(1+\frac{20}{100}\right)^2 = 115200$$

$$\Rightarrow \quad P = \frac{115200}{\left(1+\frac{20}{100}\right)^2} = \frac{115200}{1.44} = 80000$$

$\therefore$ Principal = ₹ 80000

Example: A sum of money doubles itself at CI in 15 years. In how many years will it become eight times?

Solution: $P\left(1+\frac{R}{100}\right)^{15} = 2P$

$$\Rightarrow \quad \left(1+\frac{R}{100}\right)^{15} = 2$$

Let T be the required number of years that makes the principal 8 times of it.

$$\therefore \quad P\left(1+\frac{R}{100}\right)^T = 8P$$

$$\Rightarrow \quad \left(1+\frac{R}{100}\right)^T = 8 = (2)^3$$

$$\Rightarrow \quad \left(1+\frac{R}{100}\right)^T = \left[\left(1+\frac{R}{100}\right)^{15}\right]^3$$

$$\Rightarrow \quad \left(1+\frac{R}{100}\right)^T = \left(1+\frac{R}{100}\right)^{45}$$

$$\Rightarrow \quad T = 45 \text{ years}$$

Hence, required number of years is 45 years.

EXAMPLE: The difference between simple and compound interest on a sum of money at 5% p.a. for 2 years is ₹ 25. Find the sum.

SOLUTION: Let P = ₹ 100

$$SI = \frac{P \times R \times T}{100} = \frac{100 \times 5 \times 2}{100} = ₹\,10$$

$$A = P\left(1 + \frac{R}{100}\right)^T = 100\left(1 + \frac{5}{100}\right)^2$$

$$= \frac{100 \times 21 \times 21}{400} = ₹\frac{441}{4}$$

$$CI = A - P = \frac{441}{4} - 100 = ₹\frac{41}{4}$$

$$CI - SI = \frac{41}{4} - 10 = \frac{41-40}{4} = ₹\frac{1}{4}$$

When difference ₹$\frac{1}{4}$ then P = ₹ 100

When difference ₹ 25 then P = 100 × 4 × 25

= ₹ 10000

Hence, sum = ₹ 10000.

MULTIPLE CHOICE QUESTIONS

1. The simple interest on ₹ 500 for 6 years at 5% p.a. is:
A. ₹ 250 B. ₹ 150
C. ₹ 140 D. ₹ 120

2. A certain sum of money at SI amounts to ₹ 1012 in $2\frac{1}{2}$ years and to ₹ 1067.20 in 4 years. The rate of interest per annum is:
A. 2.5% B. 3%
C. 4% D. 5%

3. ₹ 1200 amounts to ₹ 1632 in 4 years at a certain rate of simple interest. If the rate of interest is increased by 1%, it would amount to how much?
A. ₹ 1635 B. ₹ 1644
C. ₹ 1670 D. ₹ 1680

4. A man will get ₹ 87 as simple interest on ₹ 725 at 4% per annum in:
A. 3 years B. 3½ years
C. 4 years D. 5 years

5. At simple interest, a sum doubles after 20 years. The rate of interest per annum is:
A. 5% B. 10%
C. 20% D. Data inadequate

6. A lent ₹ 600 to B for 2 years and ₹ 150 to C for 4 years and received altogether from both ₹ 90 as simple interest. The rate of interest is:
A. 12% B. 10%
C. 5% D. 4%

7. Interest on a certain sum of money for $2\frac{1}{3}$ years at $3\frac{3}{4}$% per annum is ₹ 210. The sum is:
A. ₹ 2800 B. ₹ 1580
C. ₹ 2400 D. None of these

8. A certain sum of money at simple interest amounts to ₹ 1260 in 2 years and to ₹ 1350 in 5 years. The rate per cent per annum is:
A. 2.5% B. 3.75%
C. 5% D. 7.5%

9. A sum of money doubles itself in 5 years. It will become 4 times itself in:
A. 10 years B. 12 years
C. 15 years D. 20 years

10. The simple interest on a sum of money will be ₹ 600 after 10 years. If the principal is trebled after 5 years, the total interest at the end of 10 years will be:
A. ₹ 600 B. ₹ 900
C. ₹ 1200 D. Data inadequate

11. ₹ 800 amounts to ₹ 920 in 3 years at simple interest. If the interest rate is increased by 3%, it would amount to how much?
A. ₹ 1056 B. ₹ 1112
C. ₹ 1182 D. ₹ 992

12. A sum of money at simple interest amounts to ₹ 2240 in 2 years and ₹ 2600 in 5 years. The sum is:
A. ₹ 1880 B. ₹ 2000
C. ₹ 2120 D. Data inadequate

13. If ₹ 7500 are borrowed at CI at the rate of 4% per annum, then after 2 years the amount to be paid is:
A. ₹ 8082 B. ₹ 7800
C. ₹ 8100 D. ₹ 8112

14. Simple interest on a sum at 4% per annum is ₹ 80 in 2 years. The compound interest on the same sum for the same period is:
A. ₹ 81.60 B. ₹ 160
C. ₹ 1081.60 D. None of these

15. ₹ 800 at 5% per annum compound interest will amount to ₹ 882 in:
A. 1 year B. 2 years
C. 3 years D. 4 years

ANSWERS

1	2	3	4	5	6	7	8	9	10
B	C	D	A	A	C	C	A	C	C
11	**12**	**13**	**14**	**15**					
D	B	D	A	B					

EXPLANATORY ANSWERS

1. $SI = \frac{P \times R \times T}{100} = \frac{500 \times 5 \times 6}{100} = ₹ 150$

2. SI for $1\frac{1}{2}$ years $= 1067.20 - 1012 = ₹ 55.20$

SI for $2\frac{1}{2}$ years $= 55.20 \times \frac{2}{3} \times \frac{5}{2} = ₹ 92$

$\therefore$ Principal $= ₹ (1012 - 92) = ₹ 920$

$R = \frac{SI \times 100}{P \times T} = \frac{92 \times 100 \times 2}{920 \times 5} = 4\%$

3. $R = \frac{SI \times 100}{P \times T} = \frac{432 \times 100}{1200 \times 4} = 9\%$

New rate $= (9 + 1)\% = 10\%$

$SI = \frac{P \times R \times T}{100} = \frac{1200 \times 10 \times 4}{100} = ₹ 480$

Amount $= P + SI = 1200 + 480 = ₹ 1680$

4. $T = \frac{SI \times 100}{P \times R} = \frac{87 \times 100}{725 \times 4} = 3$ years

5. Let P be ₹ x then A = ₹ $2x$

$SI = A - P = 2x - x = ₹\, x$

$R = \frac{SI \times 100}{P \times T} = \frac{x \times 100}{x \times 20} = 5\%$

6. $SI = \frac{P \times R \times T}{100} = \frac{600 \times R \times 2}{100} = 12R$

Again $SI = \frac{P \times R \times T}{100} = \frac{150 \times R \times 4}{100} = 6R$

Total SI = 12R + 6R = 18R

According to the question,

$18R = 90 \Rightarrow R = \frac{90}{18} = 5\%$

7. $T = 2\frac{1}{3} = \frac{7}{3}$ years,

$R = 3\frac{3}{4}\% = \frac{15}{4}\%$

$P = \frac{SI \times 100}{P \times T} = \frac{210 \times 100}{\frac{15}{4} \times \frac{7}{3}}$

$= \frac{210 \times 100 \times 4 \times 3}{15 \times 7} = ₹ 2400$

8. SI for 3 years = ₹ 1350 – ₹ 1260 = ₹ 90

SI for 1 year $= \frac{90}{3} = ₹ 30$

SI for 2 years = ₹ 30 × 2 = ₹ 60

P = A – SI = 1260 – 60 = ₹ 1200

$R = \frac{SI \times 100}{P \times T} = \frac{60 \times 100}{1200 \times 2} = \frac{5}{2} = 2.5\%$

9. Let P be ₹ x, A = ₹ $2x$,
SI = $2x - x$ = ₹ x

$$R = \frac{SI \times 100}{P \times T} = \frac{x \times 100}{x \times 5} = 20\%$$

Again, P = ₹ x, A = $4x$,
SI = $4x - x = 3x$

$$T = \frac{SI \times 100}{P \times R} = \frac{3x \times 100}{x \times 20} = 15 \text{ years}$$

10. Let P be ₹ x
SI = ₹ 600, T = 10 years.

$$R = \frac{SI \times 100}{P \times T} = \frac{600 \times 100}{x \times 10} = \frac{6000}{x}\%$$

$$\text{SI for first 5 years} = \frac{x \times 5 \times 6000}{100 \times x} = ₹\ 300$$

$$\text{SI for last 5 years} = \frac{3x \times 5 \times 6000}{100 \times x} = ₹\ 900$$

Total interest at the end of 10 years
= 900 + 300 = ₹ 1200.

11. P = ₹ 800, SI = 920 – 800 = ₹ 120
T = 3 years

$$R = \frac{SI \times 100}{P \times T} = \frac{120 \times 100}{800 \times 3} = 5\%$$

New rate = 8% (increase 3%)

$$SI = \frac{P \times R \times T}{100} = \frac{800 \times 8 \times 3}{100} = ₹\ 192$$

$\therefore$ A = P + SI = 800 + 192 = ₹ 992.

12. SI for 3 years = 2600 – 2240 = ₹ 360

$$\text{SI for 2 years} = \frac{360}{3} \times 2 = ₹\ 240$$

$\therefore$ Sum = 2240 – 240 = ₹ 2000

13.
$$A = P\left(1 + \frac{R}{100}\right)^T = 7500\left(1 + \frac{4}{100}\right)^2$$

$$= 7500 \times \frac{26}{25} \times \frac{26}{25} = ₹\ 8112$$

14.
$$P = \frac{SI \times 100}{T \times R} = \frac{80 \times 100}{4 \times 2} = ₹\ 1000$$

$$A = P\left(1 + \frac{R}{100}\right)^T = 1000\left(1 + \frac{4}{100}\right)^2$$

$$= 1000 \times \frac{26}{25} \times \frac{26}{25} = 1081.60$$

CI = A – P = 1081.60 – 1000 = ₹ 81.60

15. Let time = x years

$$A = P\left(1 + \frac{R}{100}\right)^T$$

$$882 = 800\left(1 + \frac{5}{100}\right)^x$$

$$\Rightarrow \frac{882}{800} = \left(\frac{21}{20}\right)^x$$

$$\Rightarrow \left(\frac{21}{20}\right)^2 = \left(\frac{21}{20}\right)^x \Rightarrow x = 2$$

$\therefore$ Time = 2 years

10. TIME AND WORK

Performing or doing work of any amount involves efforts of person (S) over a period of time. Therefore, the number of persons (P), the quantity of work (W) and the period of time (T) are important variables in problems related to "Time and Work". Moreover time (T) taken to do a work depends not only on how many persons are employed to do it but also on how efficient they are. Efficiency here means rate of doing same work. This aspect comes into picture when the problem involves comparison of work done by different categories of persons. For instance, efficiencies of man, woman, boy, girl in general are different. Even efficiency of one man may not be same as that of other; but unless otherwise specifically stated in the problem, all men or women working in a group are assumed to do work with equal efficiency.

The problems on Time and Work can be solved by following two methods:

(*i*) Ratio and proportion method

(*ii*) Unitary method

(*i*) Ratio and Proportion Method: Since problems concerning to Time and Work have proportional relation, these can be solved by this method. We have tried to solve questions based on Time and Work in the chapter mentioned.

(*ii*) Unitary Method: This is a very simple and useful method. The term 'Unitary' is self-evident. In this method, we first proceed to reduce the problem to either work done by one person or work done in 1 day and so on as per the requirement of the problem. Let us try to understand it.

(*a*) If a man can do a piece of work in 10 days he will do $\frac{1}{10}$ of the work in 1 day. Conversely, if a man can do $\frac{1}{10}$ of the work in 1 day, he will do the work in 10 days.

(*b*) If the number of men engaged to do a piece of work be changed in the ratio 5 : 4, the time required for the work will be changed in the ratio 4 : 5.

(*c*) If A is x times as good a workman as B, then A will take $\frac{1}{x}$ of the time that B takes to do a certain work.

All the above points can be summarised into one and can be written in the following form:

If M_1 persons can do W_1 works in D_1 days and M_2 persons can do W_2 works in D_2 days then we have a very general formula in the relationship of

$$M_1 D_1 W_2 = M_2 D_2 W_1$$

The above relationship can be taken as a very basic and all-in-one formula we also derive:

(*i*) More men less days and conversely more days less men.

(*ii*) More men more work and conversely more work more men.

(*iii*) More days more work and conversely more work more days.

$$M_1 D_1 T_1 W_2 = M_2 D_2 T_2 W_1$$

EXAMPLE: 5 men can prepare 10 toys in 6 days working 6 hrs a day. How many days can 12 men prepare 16 toys working 8 hrs a day?

SOLUTION: $M_1 D_1 T_1 W_2 = M_2 D_2 T_2 W_1$

$$5 \times 6 \times 6 \times 16 = 12 \times D_2 \times 8 \times 10$$

$$D_2 = \frac{5 \times 6 \times 6 \times 16}{12 \times 8 \times 10} = 3 \text{ days.}$$

EXAMPLE: A can reap a field in 8 days, which B alone can reap in 12 days. In how many days, both together, can reap this field?

SOLUTION: A's 1 day's work $= \frac{1}{8}$

B's 1 day's work $= \frac{1}{12}$

(A + B)'s 1 day's work $= \left(\frac{1}{8}+\frac{1}{12}\right)$

$= \frac{3+2}{24} = \frac{5}{24}$

$\therefore$ Both together can reap the field in $\frac{24}{5}$ days

$= 4\frac{4}{5}$ days.

EXAMPLE: A and B together can do a piece of work in 12 days, B alone can finish it in 30 days. In how many days can A alone finish the work?

SOLUTION: (A + B)'s 1 day's work $= \frac{1}{12}$

B's 1 day's work $= \frac{1}{30}$

$\therefore$ A's 1 day's work $= \frac{1}{12}-\frac{1}{30}$

$= \frac{5-2}{60} = \frac{3}{60} = \frac{1}{20}$

Hence, A alone can finish the work in 20 days.

EXAMPLE: A and B can do a piece of work in 12 days, C and A in 20 days and B and C in 15 days. In how many days will they finish it together and separately?

SOLUTION: (A + B)'s 1 day's work $= \frac{1}{12}$

(B + C)'s 1 day's work $= \frac{1}{15}$

(C + A)'s 1 day's work $= \frac{1}{20}$

Adding, 2(A + B + C)'s 1 day's work

$= \left(\frac{1}{12}+\frac{1}{15}+\frac{1}{20}\right) = \frac{5+4+3}{60}$

$= \frac{12}{60} = \frac{1}{5}$

or (A + B + C)'s 1 day's work $= \frac{1}{10}$

$\therefore$ A, B, C together can finish the work in 10 days.

Now, C's 1 day's work $= \frac{1}{10}-\frac{1}{12} = \frac{1}{60}$

$\therefore$ C alone can finish the work in 60 days.

Similarly B's 1 day's work $= \frac{1}{10}-\frac{1}{20} = \frac{1}{20}$

$\therefore$ B alone can finish the work in 20 days.

A's 1 day's work $= \frac{1}{10}-\frac{1}{15} = \frac{1}{30}$

$\therefore$ A alone can finish the work in 30 days.

EXAMPLE: A can do a piece of work in 25 days and B can finish it in 20 days. They work together for 5 days and then A goes away. In how many days will B finish the work?

SOLUTION: (A + B)'s 5 days work $= 5\left(\frac{1}{25}+\frac{1}{20}\right) = \frac{9}{20}$

Remaining work $= 1-\frac{9}{20} = \frac{11}{20}$

Now, $\frac{1}{20}$ work is finished by B in 1 day

$\therefore$ $\frac{11}{20}$ work will be finished by B in $\left(\frac{20\times 11}{20}\right)$

= 11 days.

EXAMPLE: A is thrice as good a workman as B and is therefore able to finish a piece of work in 60 days less than B. Find the time in which they can do it, working together.

SOLUTION: Ratio of work done by A and B in the same time = 3 : 1

Ratio of time taken by A and B = 1 : 3

Suppose B takes x days to finish a work

then, A takes $(x - 60)$ days

$\therefore$ $\frac{x-60}{x} = \frac{1}{3}$ or $3(x-60) = x \Rightarrow x = 90$

$\therefore$ B can finish the work in 90 days.

A can finish the work in (90 – 60) = 30 days

Both finish the work $= \left[\frac{1}{30}+\frac{1}{90} = \frac{2}{45}\right]$

$= \frac{45}{2} = 22\frac{1}{2}$ days.

EXAMPLE: A certain number of men complete a piece of work in 60 days. If there were 8 men more, the work could be finished in 10 days less. How many men were originally there?

SOLUTION: Let the original number of men be x.

Now, x men can finish the work in 60 days

and $(x+8)$ men can finish it in $(60-10)$ *i.e.*, 50 days.

$\therefore \quad x+8 : x :: 60 : 50$

$\Rightarrow \quad \frac{x+8}{x} = \frac{60}{50} = \frac{6}{5}$

$\Rightarrow \quad 6x = 5x + 40 \Rightarrow x = 40$

Hence, the original number of men = 40.

EXAMPLE: If 4 men or 6 boys can finish a piece of work in 20 days, in how many days can 6 men and 11 boys finish it?

SOLUTION: 4 men = 6 boys

$\therefore \quad 6 \text{ men} = \frac{6}{4} \times 6 = \frac{36}{4} = 9 \text{ boys}$

6 men + 11 boys = 9 + 11 = 20 boys

Now, 6 boys can finish a work in 20 days.

1 boy can finish the same work in 6×20 days.

20 boys can finish the same work in $\frac{6 \times 20}{20}$

$= 6$ days.

EXAMPLE: If 12 men can build a wall 360 m long in 54 days, how many days will it take to build a similar wall 160 m long, if 16 men working on it?

SOLUTION: 12 men can build 360 m long wall in 54 days.

1 man can build 360 m long wall in 54×12 days.

1 man can build 1 m long wall in $\frac{54 \times 12}{360}$ days

16 men can build 1 m long wall in $\frac{54 \times 12}{360 \times 16}$ days

16 men can build 160 m long wall in $\frac{54 \times 12 \times 160}{360 \times 16}$ days

$= 18$ days.

EXAMPLE: If 3 persons weave 168 carpets in 7 days, how many carpets will 8 persons weave in 5 days?

SOLUTION: 3 persons can weave in 7 days 168 carpets

1 person can weave in 7 days $= \frac{168}{3}$ carpets

1 person can weave in 1 day $= \frac{168}{3 \times 7}$ carpets

8 persons can weave in 1 day $= \frac{168 \times 8}{3 \times 7}$ carpets

8 persons can weave in 5 days $= \frac{168 \times 8 \times 5}{3 \times 7}$ carpets

$= 320$ carpets

EXAMPLE: Mukesh can do a job in 12 days while Manoj can do the same job in 15 days. They undertake to complete the job for ₹ 5400. What will be the share of each in the income?

SOLUTION: Mukesh's 1 day's work $= \frac{1}{12}$

Manoj's 1 day's work $= \frac{1}{15}$

Ratio of their 1 day's work $= \frac{1}{12} : \frac{1}{15} = 5 : 4$

$\therefore$ Mukesh's share = ₹ $\frac{5}{9} \times 5400$ = ₹ 3000

Manoj's share = ₹ $\frac{4}{9} \times 5400$ = ₹ 2400

MULTIPLE CHOICE QUESTIONS

1. A and B can together do a piece of work in 15 days. B alone can do it in 20 days. In how many days can A alone do it?

A. 30 days B. 40 days
C. 45 days D. 60 days

2. A can do a piece of work in 30 days while B can do it in 40 days. A and B working together can do it in:

A. 70 days B. $42\frac{3}{4}$ days
C. $27\frac{1}{7}$ days D. $17\frac{1}{7}$ days

3. A can do $\frac{1}{3}$ of the work in 5 days and B can do $\frac{2}{5}$ of the work in 10 days. In how many days both A and B together can do the work?

A. $7\frac{3}{4}$ days B. $8\frac{4}{5}$ days

C. $9\frac{3}{8}$ days D. 10 days

4. A, B and C can do a piece of work in 6, 12 and 24 days respectively. They altogether will complete the work in:

A. $3\frac{3}{7}$ days B. $\frac{7}{24}$ days

C. $4\frac{4}{5}$ days D. $\frac{5}{24}$ days

5. A, B and C contract a work for ₹ 550. Together A and B are to do $\frac{7}{11}$ of the work. The share of C should be:

A. ₹ $183\frac{1}{3}$ B. ₹ 200

C. ₹ 300 D. ₹ 400

6. A and B finish a job in 12 days while A, B and C can finish it in 8 days. C alone will finish the job in:

A. 20 days B. 14 days

C. 24 days D. 16 days

7. 12 men can complete a work in 8 days. Three days after they started the work, 3 more men joined them. In how many days will all of them together complete the remaining work?

A. 2 B. 4

C. 5 D. 6

8. Mahesh and Umesh can complete a work in 10 and 15 days respectively. Umesh starts the work and after 5 days Mahesh joins him. In all, the work would be completed in:

A. 9 days B. 7 days

C. 11 days D. None of these

9. Sunil completes a work in 4 days whereas Dinesh completes the work in 6 days. Ramesh works $1\frac{1}{2}$ times as fast as Sunil. How many days it will take for the three together to complete the work?

A. $\frac{7}{12}$ B. $1\frac{5}{12}$

C. $1\frac{5}{7}$ D. None of these

10. A can complete a work in 6 days and B in 5 days. They work together, finish the job and receive ₹ 220 as wages. B's share should be:

A. ₹ 120 B. ₹ 110

C. ₹ 100 D. ₹ 90

11. 12 men and 8 children can finish a piece of work in 9 days. If each child takes twice the time taken by a man to finish the work, in how many days will 12 men finish the same work?

A. 8 days B. 15 days

C. 9 days D. 12 days

12. A, B and C together earn ₹ 150 per day while A and C together earn ₹ 94 and B and C together earn ₹ 76. The daily earning of C is:

A. ₹ 75 B. ₹ 56

C. ₹ 34 D. ₹ 20

13. If 5 men or 9 women can finish a piece of work in 19 days, 3 men and 6 women will do the same work in:

A. 10 days B. 12 days

C. 13 days D. 15 days

14. A can do a piece of work in 12 days. B is 60% more efficient than A. The number of days, it takes B to do the same piece of work, is:

A. $7\frac{1}{2}$ days B. $6\frac{1}{4}$ days

C. 8 days D. 6 days

15. A and B can do a piece of work in 45 and 40 days respectively. They began the work together, but A leaves after some days and B finished the remaining work in 23 days. After how many days did A leave?

A. 6 days B. 8 days

C. 9 days D. 12 days

ANSWERS

1	2	3	4	5	6	7	8	9	10
D	D	C	A	B	C	B	A	D	A
11	**12**	**13**	**14**	**15**					
D	D	D	A	C					

EXPLANATORY ANSWERS

1. $(A+B)$'s 1 day's work $= \frac{1}{15}$

B's 1 day's work $= \frac{1}{20}$

A's 1 day's work $= \frac{1}{15} - \frac{1}{20} = \frac{4-3}{60} = \frac{1}{60}$

$\therefore$ A can do this work alone in 60 days.

2. A's 1 day's work $= \frac{1}{30}$

B's 1 day's work $= \frac{1}{40}$

$(A+B)$'s 1 day's work

$= \frac{1}{30} + \frac{1}{40} = \frac{4+3}{120} = \frac{7}{120}$

$\therefore$ Both together will finish the work in $\frac{120}{7}$

$= 17\frac{1}{7}$ days.

3. $\frac{1}{3}$ of the work is done by A in 5 days.

$\therefore$ Whole work will be done by A in 3×5

$= 15$ days

$\frac{2}{5}$ of the work is done by B in 10 days.

Whole work will be done by B in $\left(10 \times \frac{5}{2}\right)$

$= 25$ days

$(A+B)$'s 1 day's work $= \frac{1}{15} + \frac{1}{25} = \frac{5+3}{75} = \frac{8}{75}$

$\therefore$ Both together can finish it in $\frac{75}{8} = 9\frac{3}{8}$ days.

4. A's 1 day's work $= \frac{1}{6}$

B's 1 day's work $= \frac{1}{12}$

C's 1 day's work $= \frac{1}{24}$

$(A+B+C)$'s 1 day's work $= \frac{1}{6} + \frac{1}{12} + \frac{1}{24}$

$= \frac{4+2+1}{24} = \frac{7}{24}$

$\therefore$ They all together will complete the work in

$\frac{24}{7}$ days $= 3\frac{3}{7}$ days

5. Work to be done by $C = \left(1 - \frac{7}{11}\right) = \frac{4}{11}$

$\therefore (A+B) : C = \frac{7}{11} : \frac{4}{11} = 7 : 4$

$\therefore$ C's share $=$ ₹$\frac{4}{11} \times 550 =$ ₹ 200

6. $(A+B)$'s 1 day's work $= \frac{1}{12}$

$(A+B+C)$'s 1 day's work $= \frac{1}{8}$

C's 1 day's work $= \frac{1}{8} - \frac{1}{12} = \frac{3-2}{24} = \frac{1}{24}$

Hence, C will complete the work in 24 days.

7. 1 man's 1 day's work $= \frac{1}{96}$

12 men's 3 day's work $= \frac{12}{96} \times 3 = \frac{3}{8}$

Remaining work = $\left(1-\frac{3}{8}\right) = \frac{5}{8}$

15 men's 1 day's work = $\frac{15}{96}$

Now, $\frac{15}{96}$ work is done by them in 1 day

$\therefore$ $\frac{5}{8}$ work will be done by them in $\frac{96}{15}\times\frac{5}{8}$

$= 4$ days

8. Umesh's 5 day's work = $\frac{5}{15} = \frac{1}{3}$

Remaining work = $\left(1-\frac{1}{3}\right) = \frac{2}{3}$

Now, $\left(\frac{1}{10}+\frac{1}{15}\right)$ work is done by A and B in 1 day.

$\therefore$ $\frac{2}{3}$ work will be done by A and B in $6\times\frac{2}{3}$

$= 4$ days.

So, the work would be completed in $(5 + 4)$

$= 9$ days.

9. Time taken by Ramesh alone = $\frac{2}{3}\times 4 = \frac{8}{3}$ days

$\therefore$ Their 1 day's work = $\left(\frac{1}{4}+\frac{1}{6}+\frac{3}{8}\right)$

$= \frac{6+4+9}{24} = \frac{19}{24}$

So, together they can finish the work in $\frac{24}{19}$ days

$= 1\frac{5}{19}$ days.

10. Ratio of time taken by A and B = 6 : 5

Ratio of work done in same time = 5 : 6

So, the money is to be divided among A and B in the ratio 5 : 6.

$\therefore$ B's share = ₹$\frac{6}{11}\times 220$ = ₹ 120

11. 2 children = 1 man

$\therefore$ 8 children + 12 men = 4 + 12 = 16 men

Now, less men, more days

$12 : 16 :: 9 : x \Rightarrow \frac{12}{16} = \frac{9}{x} \Rightarrow x = 12$ days

12. B's daily earning = ₹ (150 – 94) = ₹ 56

A's daily earning = ₹ (150 – 76) = ₹ 74

C's daily earning = ₹ [150 – (56 + 74)] = ₹ 20

13. 5 men = 9 women $\Rightarrow$ 1 man = $\frac{9}{5}$ women

$\therefore$ 3 men + 6 women = $\left(3\times\frac{9}{5}+6\right) = \frac{57}{5}$ women

Now, 9 women can do the work in 19 days

$\therefore$ $\frac{57}{5}$ women can do it in $\frac{9\times 19\times 5}{57} = 15$ days

14. A's 1 day's work = $\frac{1}{12}$

B's 1 day's work = $\frac{1}{12}$ + 60% of $\frac{1}{12} = \frac{2}{15}$

Hence, B can do the whole work in $\frac{15}{2}$

$= 7\frac{1}{2}$ days.

15. B's 23 day's work = $\frac{23}{40}$

Remaining work = $\left(1-\frac{23}{40}\right) = \frac{17}{40}$

Now, (A + B)'s 1 day's work = $\left(\frac{1}{45}+\frac{1}{40}\right) = \frac{17}{360}$

$\frac{17}{360}$ work is done by A and B in 1 day

$\frac{17}{40}$ work is done by A and B in $\frac{360}{17}\times\frac{17}{40}$

$= 9$ days.

Hence, A left after 9 days.

11. AREA AND PERIMETER

The area of any figure is the amount of surface enclosed within its boundary lines. It is measured by the number of square metres or square centimetres or square inches (or some other units of square measure) it contains.

Perimeter

Perimeter of a geometrical figure is the total length of the sides enclosing the figure.

Triangle

A triangle is a plane figure bounded by three sides. It includes three angles. It is denoted by the symbol Δ. The sum of angles of a triangle is 180°.

(i) **Equilateral Triangle:** A triangle in which all sides are equal is called an equilateral triangle.

(ii) **Isosceles Triangle:** A triangle in which two sides are equal is called an isosceles triangle.

(iii) **Scalene Triangle:** A triangle in which all sides are different or unequal is called scalene triangle.

(iv) **Right Angled Triangle:** A triangle having one of the angles equal to 90° is called a right angled triangle. The side opposite to the right angle of a triangle is called its hypotenuse.

Quadrilateral

A plane figure bounded by four straight lines is called a quadrilateral.

Various Types of Quadrilaterals:

(i) **Rectangle:** A quadrilateral whose opposite sides are equal and all angles are at right angles. The diagonals of a rectangle are equal.

(ii) **Square:** A rectangle having all sides are equal is called a square.

(iii) **Parallelogram:** A quadrilateral whose opposite sides are equal and parallel is called parallelogram.

(iv) **Rhombus:** A parallelogram having all the sides equal is called a rhombus. Diagonals of a rhombus are not equal and they bisect each other at right angles.

(v) **Trapezium:** A quadrilateral having one pair of opposite sides parallel, is called a trapezium.

Circle

The path traced by a point which moves in such a way that its distance from a fixed point is always same, is called a circle. The fixed point is called its centre and fixed distance is called its radius. The length of the whole path of a circle is called its circumference.

(i) **Arc:** Any part of the circumference of a circle is called an arc.

(ii) **Chord:** The straight line joining the ends of an arc of a circle is called a chord.

(iii) **Diameter:** The chord passing through the centre of a circle is called its diameter.

The diameter of a circle divides the circle into two equal parts, each one of which is called a semi-circle.

(iv) **Segment:** The area enclosed by an arc and a chord is called a segment.

(v) **Sector:** The area bounded by an arc and two radii is called a sector.

Formulae for Area of Various Figures:

(i) **Rectangle:**

Area of rectangle = $l \times b$

Perimeter of rectangle = $2(l + b)$.

(ii) Square:

Area of square = $(\text{side})^2$

Perimeter of square = $4 \times$ side

Area of room = $l \times b$

Area of 4 walls of a room = $2(l + b) \times h$

(iii) Parallelogram:

Area of $||^{gm} = b \times h$

Area of rhombus = $\frac{1}{2} \times d_1 \times d_2$.

(iv) Trapezium:

Area of trapezium = $\frac{1}{2}$(sum of parallel sides) × (distance between them)

(v) Triangle:

(*a*) Area of right triangle = $\frac{1}{2} \times b \times h$

(*b*) Area of equilateral triangle = $\frac{\sqrt{3}}{4} \times (\text{side})^2$

(*c*) Area of scalene triangle

$$= \sqrt{s(s-a)(s-b)(s-c)}$$

where, $s = \frac{a+b+c}{2}$

(vi) Circle:

(*a*) Area of circle = πr^2

(*b*) Circumference of a circle = $2\pi r$

(*c*) Length of arc = $\frac{\theta}{360} \times 2\pi r$

(*d*) Area of sector = $\frac{\theta}{360} \times \pi r^2$

Polygon

A polygon is plane figure bounded by multiple number of sides. Normally, it is used for figures enclosed by more than four sides: *e.g.*, pentagon, hexagon, octagon etc.

Regular Polygon

It is a polygon whose all sides are equal.

For a regular polygon of n equal sides, its vertex angle θ is given by

$$\theta = \left(\frac{n-2}{n}\right) \times 180°$$

EXAMPLE: Find the area and perimeter of a rectangle whose length is 25 m and breadth is 15 m.

SOLUTION: Area of rectangle $= l \times b$

$= 25 \times 15 = 375 \text{ m}^2$

Perimeter of rectangle $= 2(l + b)$

$= 2(25 + 15) = 80 \text{ m}$

EXAMPLE: Find the area of a rectangle whose one side is 6 m and the diagonal is 10 m.

SOLUTION: Another side of rectangle $= \sqrt{(10)^2 - (6)^2}$

$= \sqrt{100 - 36} = \sqrt{64} = 8 \text{ m}$

Area of rectangle $= l \times b = 8 \times 6 = 48 \text{ m}^2$

EXAMPLE: Find area and perimeter of a square whose each side is 12 cm.

SOLUTION: Area of square = $(\text{side})^2 = (12)^2 = 144 \text{ cm}^2$

Perimeter of square = $4 \times \text{side} = 4 \times 12 = 48$ cm

EXAMPLE: Find the area of a parallelogram whose base is 35 m and altitude 18 m.

SOLUTION: Area of parallelogram $= b \times h$

$= 35 \times 18 = 630 \text{ m}^2$

EXAMPLE: Find the area of a rhombus one side of which measures 20 cm and one diagonal 24 cm.

SOLUTION: Since the diagonals of a rhombus bisect at right angles, so one side and half of each of the diagonals form a right angled triangle. In this right angled triangle,

One side = 20 cm, another side = $\frac{24}{2} = 12$ cm

Third side $= \sqrt{(20)^2 - (12)^2} = \sqrt{400 - 144}$

$= \sqrt{256} = 16$ cm

Hence other diagonal $= 16 \times 2 = 32$ cm

Area of rhombus $= \frac{1}{2} \times d_1 \times d_2$

$= \frac{1}{2} \times 24 \times 32 = 12 \times 32$

$= 384 \text{ cm}^2$

EXAMPLE: Find the area of an equilateral triangle each of whose sides measures 12 cm.

SOLUTION: Area of equilateral triangle

$= \frac{\sqrt{3}}{4}(\text{side})^2 = \frac{\sqrt{3}}{4} \times (12)^2$

$$= \frac{\sqrt{3}}{4} \times 144 = 36\sqrt{3}\ \text{cm}^2$$

$$= 36 \times 1.73 = 62.28\ \text{cm}^2$$

EXAMPLE: Find the area of a triangle whose sides are 40 cm, 41 cm and 9 cm respectively.

SOLUTION: $s = \frac{a+b+c}{2} = \frac{9+40+41}{2}$

$$= \frac{90}{2} = 45\ \text{cm}$$

Area of triangle $= \sqrt{s(s-a)(s-b)(s-c)}$

$$= \sqrt{45(45-9)(45-40)(45-41)}$$

$$= \sqrt{45 \times 36 \times 5 \times 4}$$

$$= \sqrt{225 \times 144}$$

$$= 15 \times 12 = 180\ \text{cm}^2$$

EXAMPLE: Find the circumference and the area of a circle of radius 3.5 cm.

SOLUTION: Circumference $= 2\pi r$

$$= 2 \times \frac{22}{7} \times 3.5 = 22\ \text{cm}$$

Area of circle $= \pi r^2 = \frac{22}{7} \times 3.5 \times 3.5$

$$= 38.5\ \text{cm}^2$$

EXAMPLE: In a circle of radius 35 cm, an arc subtends an angle of 72° at the centre. Find the length of the arc and the area of the sector.

SOLUTION: Length of arc $= \frac{\theta}{360} \times 2\pi r$

$$= \frac{72}{360} \times 2 \times \frac{22}{7} \times 35$$

$$= 44\ \text{cm}$$

Area of the sector $= \frac{\theta}{360} \times \pi r^2$

$$= \frac{72}{360} \times \frac{22}{7} \times 35 \times 35$$

$$= 770\ \text{cm}^2$$

EXAMPLE: Find the area of a trapezium whose parallel sides are 77 cm, 60 cm and the other sides are 25 cm and 26 cm.

SOLUTION:

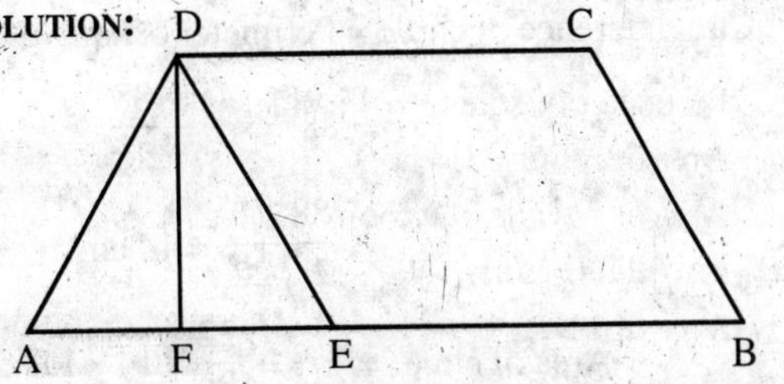

Let ABCD be the given trapezium in which AB = 77 cm, CD = 60 cm, BC = 25 cm, AD = 26 cm.

Draw DE || BC and DF ⊥ AB

Now, DE = BC = 25 cm

AE = AB – EB = AB – CD

= 77 – 60 = 17 cm

In ΔDAE, $s = \frac{17+25+26}{2} = \frac{68}{2} = 34\ \text{cm}$

Area of ΔDAE $= \sqrt{34(34-17)(34-25)(34-26)}$

$$= \sqrt{34 \times 17 \times 9 \times 8} = 204\ \text{cm}^2$$

Again area of ΔDAE $= \frac{1}{2} \times \text{AE} \times \text{DF}$

$$204 = \frac{1}{2} \times 17 \times \text{DF}$$

$$\Rightarrow \quad \text{DF} = \frac{2 \times 204}{17} = 24\ \text{cm}$$

∴ Area of trapezium ABCD $= \frac{1}{2}(\text{AB} + \text{CD}) \times \text{DF}$

$$= \frac{1}{2}(77+60) \times 24$$

$$= \frac{1}{2} \times 137 \times 24$$

$$= 1644\ \text{cm}^2$$

EXAMPLE: A copper wire when bent in the form of a square, encloses an area of 484 cm². If the same wire is bent in the form of circle, find the area enclosed by it.

SOLUTION: Area of the square = 484 cm²

Side $= \sqrt{484} = 22$ cm

Length of wire = Perimeter of square

= 4 × side = 4 × 22

= 88 cm

Let r be the radius of the circle.

$\therefore$ Circumference of circle = Perimeter of square

$$\therefore \quad 2\pi r = 88 \Rightarrow r = \frac{88}{2\pi}$$

$$= \frac{88 \times 7}{2 \times 22} = 14 \text{ cm}$$

$$\text{Area of circle} = \pi r^2 = \frac{22}{7} \times 14 \times 14$$

$$= 616 \text{ cm}^2$$

EXAMPLE: A bicycle wheel makes 5000 revolutions in moving 11 km. Find the diameter of the wheel.

SOLUTION: Distance covered by the wheel in 1 revolution

$$= \frac{\text{Distance covered}}{\text{Number of revolutions}} = \frac{11}{5000} \text{ km}$$

$$= \frac{11 \times 1000 \times 100}{5000} \text{ cm} = 220 \text{ cm}$$

$\therefore$ Circumference of the wheel = 220 cm

$$2\pi r = 220 \Rightarrow 2 \times \frac{22}{7} \times r = 220$$

$$\Rightarrow \quad r = \frac{220 \times 7}{44} = 35 \text{ cm}$$

Hence, diameter of the wheel = 35 × 2 = 70 cm

EXAMPLE: The perimeter of a square is 44 cm and circumference of a circle is 44 cm. Which area is greater and by how much?

SOLUTION: Side of square $= \frac{44}{4} = 11$ cm

$$\text{Area of square} = (11)^2 = 121 \text{ cm}^2$$

Circumference of a circle $= 2\pi r$

$$\Rightarrow \quad 44 = 2 \times \frac{22}{7} \times r$$

$$\Rightarrow \quad r = \frac{44 \times 7}{44} = 7 \text{ cm}$$

$$\text{Area of circle} = \pi r^2$$

$$= \frac{22}{7} \times 7 \times 7 = 154 \text{ cm}^2$$

Clearly, area of circle > area of square

Difference = 154 – 121 = 33 cm^2.

EXAMPLE: A sheet of paper is in the form of a rectangle ABCD in which AB = 40 cm and AD = 28 cm. A semi-circular portion with BC as diameter is cut off. Find the area of the remaining paper.

SOLUTION:

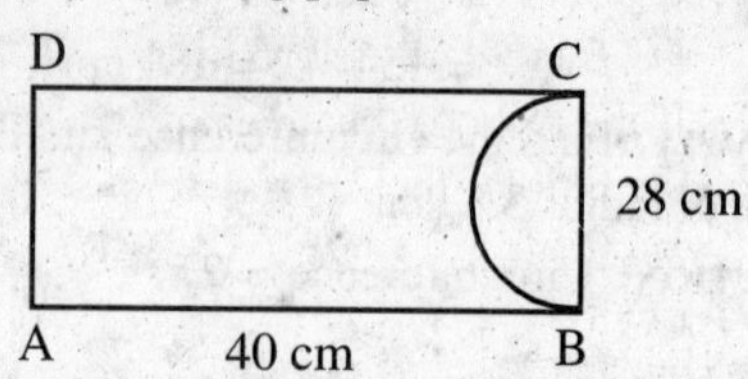

$$\text{Area of ABCD} = 40 \times 28 = 1120 \text{ cm}^2$$

$$\text{Area of semicircle} = \frac{1}{2}\pi r^2$$

$$= \frac{1}{2} \times \frac{22}{7} \times 14 \times 14$$

$$= 22 \times 14 = 308 \text{ cm}^2$$

Area of the remaining paper = 1120 – 308 = 812 cm^2

MULTIPLE CHOICE QUESTIONS

1. The length of a plot is four times its breadth. A playground measuring 1200 square metres occupies a third of the total area of the plot. What is the length of the plot, in metres?

A. 20 B. 30
C. 60 D. None of these

2. The width of a rectangular hall is $\frac{3}{4}$ of its length. If the area of the hall is 300 m^2, then the difference between its length and width is:

A. 3 m B. 4 m
C. 5 m D. 15 m

3. The length and breadth of a rectangular piece of land are in ratio of 5 : 3. The owner spent ₹ 3000 for surrounding it from all the sides at ₹ 7.50 per metre. The difference between its length and breadth is:

A. 50 m
B. 100 m
C. 150 m
D. 200 m

4. A room 8 m × 6 m is to be carpeted by a carpet 2 m wide. The length of carpet required is:
A. 12 m B. 36 m
C. 24 m D. 48 m

5. The length of a rectangle is increased by 60%. By what per cent would the width have to be decreased to maintain the same area?
A. $37\frac{1}{2}\%$ B. 60%
C. 75% D. 120%

6. A man walked 20 m to cross a rectangular field diagonally. If the length of the field is 16 m, the breadth of the rectangle is:
A. 4 m
B. 16 m
C. 12 m
D. Cannot be determined

7. If the ratio of the areas of two squares is 9 : 1, the ratio of their perimeters is:
A. 9 : 1 B. 3 : 1
C. 3 : 4 D. 1 : 3

8. The perimeter of both, a square and a rectangle are each equal to 48 m and the difference between their areas is 4 m^2. The breadth of the rectangle is:
A. 10 m B. 12 m
C. 14 m D. None of these

9. Area of a square with side x is equal to the area of a triangle with base x. The altitude of the triangle is:
A. $\frac{x}{2}$ B. x
C. $2x$ D. $4x$

10. If only the length of the rectangular plot is reduced to $\frac{2}{3}$rd of its original length, the ratio of original area to reduced area is:
A. 2 : 3 B. 3 : 2
C. 1 : 2 D. None of these

11. If the radius of a circle be reduced by 50%, its area is reduced by:
A. 25% B. 50%
C. 75% D. 100%

12. The perimeter of a rhombus is 52 m while its longer diagonal is 24 m. Its other diagonal is:
A. 5 m B. 10 m
C. 20 m D. 28 m

13. The circumference of a circle is 352 m, then its area in m^2 is:
A. 9856 B. 8956
C. 6589 D. 5986

ANSWERS

1	2	3	4	5	6	7	8	9	10
D	C	A	C	A	C	B	A	C	B
11	**12**	**13**							
C	B	A							

EXPLANATORY ANSWERS

1. Area of the plot = 3 × 1200 = 3600 m^2
Let breadth be x m. Then length = $4x$ m
According to the question,
$4x \times x = 3600 \Rightarrow x^2 = 900 \Rightarrow x = 30$
Hence, length of the plot = 4 × 30 = 120 m.

2. Let length be x m, then breadth = $\frac{3x}{4}$ m

Area of the hall = $x \times \frac{3x}{4} = \frac{3x^2}{4}$

According to the question,

$\frac{3x^2}{4} = 300 \Rightarrow x^2 = 400 \Rightarrow x = 20$

Length = 20 m and breadth = $\frac{3}{4} \times 20$ = 15 m

Difference = 20 – 15 = 5 m

3. Let length = $5x$ m and breadth = $3x$ m
Perimeter of rectangle = $2(5x + 3x) = 16x$ m

But perimeter = $\frac{\text{Total cost}}{\text{Rate}} = \frac{3000}{7.50}$ = 400 m

Now, $16x = 400 \Rightarrow x = 25$

length $= 5x = 5 \times 25 = 125$ m

breadth $= 3x = 25 \times 3 = 75$ m

Difference $= 125 - 75 = 50$ m

4. Length of the carpet $= \dfrac{8 \times 6}{2} = 24$ m.

5. Initially, let length $= x$ and breadth $= y$

Let new breadth $= z$.

Then new length $= \dfrac{160x}{100} = \dfrac{8x}{5}$

$\therefore \quad \dfrac{8x}{5} \times z = xy \Rightarrow z = \dfrac{5y}{8}$

Decrease in breadth $= \left(y - \dfrac{5y}{8}\right) = \dfrac{3y}{8}$

$\therefore$ Decrease per cent $= \dfrac{3y}{8} \times \dfrac{1}{y} \times 100$

$= \dfrac{75}{2} = 37.5\% =$

6. Breadth $= \sqrt{(20)^2 - (16)^2}$

$= \sqrt{400 - 256} = \sqrt{144} = 12$ m.

7. Let the areas of the squares be $(9x^2)$ m^2 and (x^2) m^2

Then, their sides are $3x$ m and x m respectively

Ratio of their perimeters $= \dfrac{12x}{4x} = 3 : 1$

8. Let length of rectangle $= x$ m

and breadth of rectangle $= y$ m

Also, let the side of the square be z m

According to the question,

$2(x + y) = 4z = 48$

$x + y = 24$ and $z = 12$

Also, $z^2 - xy = 4$

$\Rightarrow \quad (12)^2 - 4 = xy$

$\Rightarrow \quad xy = 140$

$\because \quad x + y = 24$ and $xy = 140$

$(x - y)^2 = (x + y)^2 - 4xy$

$\Rightarrow \quad (x - y)^2 = (24)^2 - 4(140)$

$\Rightarrow \quad (x - y)^2 = 576 - 560 = 16$

$\Rightarrow \quad x - y = 4$

Now, $x + y = 24$

$x - y = 4$

Solving and get $x = 14$, $y = 10$

Hence, breadth of rectangle $= 10$ m.

9. According to the question,

$x^2 = \dfrac{1}{2} \times x \times h$

$\Rightarrow \quad h = \dfrac{2x^2}{x} = 2x$

10. Let length $= x$ and breadth $= y$

New length $= \dfrac{2}{3}x$

$\therefore \quad \dfrac{\text{Original area}}{\text{Reduced area}} = \dfrac{xy}{\frac{2}{3}xy} = \dfrac{3}{2} = 3 : 2$

11. Original area $= \pi r^2$, New area $= \pi\left(\dfrac{r}{2}\right)^2 = \dfrac{\pi r^2}{4}$

Reduction in area $= \pi r^2 - \dfrac{\pi r^2}{4} = \dfrac{3\pi r^2}{4}$

Reduction per cent $= \dfrac{3\pi r^2}{4} \times \dfrac{1}{\pi r^2} \times 100 = 75\%$

12. Side of rhombus $= \dfrac{52}{4} = 13$ m

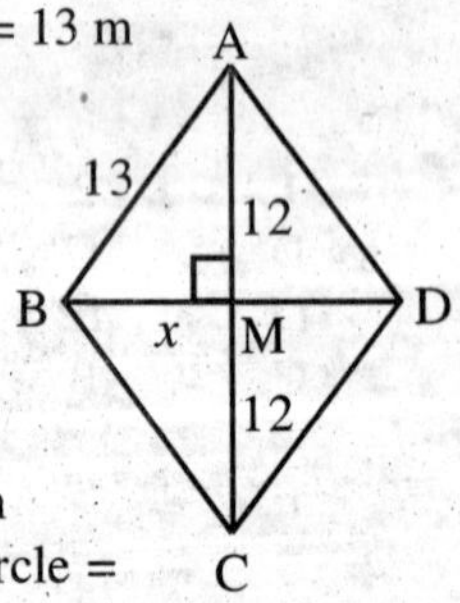

In ΔABM,

$x^2 = (13)^2 - (12)^2$

$x^2 = 169 - 144$

$x^2 = 25$

$\Rightarrow \quad x = 5$ m

$\therefore$ Another diagonal

$= 2 \times 5 = 10$ m

13. Circumference of a circle $= 2\pi r$

$\Rightarrow \quad 352 = 2 \times \dfrac{22}{7} \times r$

$\Rightarrow \quad r = \dfrac{352 \times 7}{44} = 56$ m

Area of circle $= \pi r^2 = \dfrac{22}{7} \times 56 \times 56$

$= 9856$ m^2

12. VOLUME AND SURFACE AREA

We know that every real object occupies some space. It is usually specified by its three dimensions—length, breadth and depth (or height or thickness). It may be a solid or a hollow object. In case of circular, cylindrical and spherical object the specifying dimensions may change to radius, angle etc. The amount of space occupied by the object is called its volume. Its unit of measurement is m^3, cm^3, $(inches)^3$ etc. The area of the surfaces (plane/curved) of the object is called its surface area.

A Cuboid and A Cube

The solid like wooden boxes, tea containers, match box etc. which have six faces, each of which is a rectangle, are called cuboids. It has 12 edges.

A cuboid in which every face is a square is called a cube. Length of each face of a cube is called its edge.

Prism

A right prism is a solid in which the two ends are congruent parallel figures and the side faces are rectangles. The total area of side faces of a prism is called the lateral surface of the prism.

Cylinder

The solid generated by the revolution of a rectangle about one of its sides as axis is called a cylinder.

Pyramid

A solid whose base is a plane rectilinear figure having the side faces as triangles meeting at a common vertex is called a pyramid. When the base of a pyramid is a triangle, the pyramid is called a tetrahedron.

Cone

The solid generated by the revolution of a right angled triangle about one of the sides containing the right angle as the axis is called a right circular cone.

The perpendicular distance from the vertex to the base is called the height of the cone and the length of slant face from vertex to the base is called the slant height of the cone.

Frustum

If a cone is cut by a plane parallel to the base so as to divide the cone into two parts, then the lower part is called the frustum of the cone.

Sphere

When a semicircle moves about its diameter, the solid generated is called a sphere.

Formulae

Cuboid:

Volume of cuboid = $l \times b \times h$ cubic units

Whole surface area = $2(lb + bh + hl)$ square units

Diagonal of cuboid = $\sqrt{l^2 + b^2 + h^2}$ units

Area of 4 walls of a room = $2(l + b) \times h$ square units

Cube:

Volume of cube = a^3 cubic units

Side of cube = $\sqrt[3]{\text{Volume}}$

Lateral surface area = $4a^2$ square units

Total surface area = $6a^2$ square units

Diagonal of the cube = $\left(\sqrt{3}\,a\right)$ units

Cylinder:

Volume of cylinder = $\pi r^2 h$ cubic units

Lateral surface area = $2\pi rh$ square units

Total surface area = $2\pi r(h + r)$ square units

Cone:

Volume of cone = $\frac{1}{3}\pi r^2 h$ cubic units

Lateral surface area = πrl square units

Total surface area = $\pi r(l + r)$ square units

Slant height (l) = $\sqrt{r^2 + h^2}$

Sphere:

Volume of sphere = $\frac{4}{3}\pi r^3$ cubic units

Surface area = $4\pi r^2$ square units

Hemisphere:

Volume = $\frac{2}{3}\pi r^3$ cubic units

Lateral surface area = $2\pi r^2$ square units

Total surface area = $3\pi r^2$ square units

Frustum:

Volume = $\frac{1}{3}\pi h(r_1^2 + r_1 r_2 + r_2^2)$ cubic units

Curved surface area = $\pi(r_1 + r_2) \times l$ square units

Total surface area = $\pi\left[r_1^2 + r_2^2 + (r_1 + r_2)l\right]$ square units

Pyramid:

Volume = $\frac{1}{2} \times$ (area of base) $\times$ height cubic units

EXAMPLE: The dimensions of a metallic cuboid are 100 cm × 80 cm × 64 cm. It is melted and recast into cube. Find the total surface area of the cube.

SOLUTION: Volume of cuboid = $l \times b \times h$

$= 100 \times 80 \times 64$

$= 512000 \text{ cm}^3$

Volume of cube = a^3

According to the question,

$a^3 = 512000$

$\Rightarrow \quad a^3 = 8 \times 8 \times 8 \times 10 \times 10 \times 10$

$\Rightarrow \quad a = 8 \times 10 = 80 \text{ cm}$

Total surface area of cube = $6a^2 = 6 \times 80 \times 80 = 38400$

Hence, total surface area of cube is 38400 cm^2.

EXAMPLE: Three cubes whose edges measure 3 cm, 4 cm and 5 cm respectively form a single cube. Find the total surface area of the new cube.

SOLUTION: Let the edge of new cube = x cm

$x^3 = 3^3 + 4^3 + 5^3$

$= 27 + 64 + 125 = 216 \text{ cm}^3$

$\Rightarrow \quad x^3 = 6 \times 6 \times 6 \Rightarrow x = 6 \text{ cm}$

Total surface area of cube = $6(x)^2 = 6 \times 6 \times 6 = 216 \text{ cm}^2$

Hence, total surface area of new cube = 216 cm^2.

EXAMPLE: The capacity of a cylindrical tank is 6160 m^3. If the radius of its base is 14 m, find the depth of the tank.

SOLUTION: Volume of cylinder = $\pi r^2 h$

$\pi r^2 h = 6160$

$\Rightarrow \quad \frac{22}{7} \times 14 \times 14 \times h = 6160$

$\Rightarrow \quad h = \frac{6160}{44 \times 14} = 10 \text{ m}$

Hence, depth of the tank is 10 m.

EXAMPLE: How many bullets can be made out of a lead cylinder 28 cm high and 6 cm radius, each bullet being 1.5 cm in diameter?

SOLUTION: Number of bullets

$$= \frac{\text{Volume of cylinder}}{\text{Volume of 1 bullet}}$$

$$= \frac{\pi \times 6 \times 6 \times 28}{\frac{4}{3} \times \pi \times 0.75 \times 0.75 \times 0.75}$$

$$= \frac{6 \times 6 \times 28 \times 3}{4 \times \frac{3}{4} \times \frac{3}{4} \times \frac{3}{4}} = \frac{6 \times 6 \times 28 \times 4 \times 4 \times 3}{3 \times 3 \times 3}$$

$= 1792$

EXAMPLE: A metal sphere of diameter 42 cm is dropped into a cylindrical vessel, which is partly filled with water. The diameter of the vessel is 1.68 metres. If the sphere is completely submerged, find by how much the surface of water will rise.

SOLUTION: Radius of the sphere = 21 cm

Volume of sphere = $\frac{4}{3}\pi r^3$

$= \frac{4}{3} \times \frac{22}{7} \times 21 \times 21 \times 21$

$= 38808 \text{ cm}^3$

Volume of water displaced by sphere = 38808 cm^3
Let water rise by h cm.

Volume of cylinder = $\pi r^2 h$

$$\frac{22}{7} \times 84 \times 84 \times h = 38808$$

$$\Rightarrow \quad h = \frac{38808 \times 7}{22 \times 84 \times 84} = \frac{7}{4} = 1.75 \text{ cm}$$

EXAMPLE: A tent is in the form of a right circular cylinder surmounted by a cone. The diameter of cylinder is 24 m. The height of the cylindrical portion is 11 m while the vertex of the cone is 16 m above the ground. Find the area of the canvas required for the tent.

SOLUTION: Lateral surface area of cylinder = $2\pi rh$

$$= 2 \times \frac{22}{7} \times 12 \times 11 = \frac{5808}{7} \text{ m}^2$$

Height of cone = 16 – 11 = 5 m
Radius of cone = 12 m

$$\text{Slant height } l = \sqrt{r^2 + h^2} = \sqrt{12^2 + 5^2}$$

$$= \sqrt{169} = 13 \text{ m}$$

Lateral surface area of cone = πrl

$$= \frac{22}{7} \times 12 \times 13 = \frac{3432}{7} \text{ m}^2$$

$$\text{Area of canvas} = \frac{5808}{7} + \frac{3432}{7}$$

$$= \frac{9240}{7} = 1320 \text{ m}^2$$

EXAMPLE: The slant height of the frustum of a cone is 20 cm and the height of the frustum is 16 cm. The radius of the smaller circle is 8 cm. Find the volume and total surface area of the frustum.

SOLUTION: $l = \sqrt{h^2 + (R - r)^2} = \sqrt{16^2 + (R - 8)^2}$

$$\Rightarrow \quad 20 = \sqrt{256 + R^2 - 16R + 64}$$

$$= \sqrt{R^2 - 16R + 320}$$

$\Rightarrow R^2 - 16R + 320 = 400$

$\Rightarrow R^2 - 16R - 80 = 0 \Rightarrow R = 20$ cm

$$\text{Volume of frustum} = \frac{1}{3}\pi h(R^2 + r^2 + Rr)$$

$$= \frac{1}{3} \times \frac{22}{7} \times 16(400 + 64 + 160)$$

$$= \frac{73216}{7} \text{ cm}^3$$

Total surface area = $\pi(R^2 + r^2 + Rl + rl)$

$$= \frac{22}{7}(400 + 64 + 400 + 160)$$

$$= \frac{22}{7} \times 1024 = \frac{22528}{7}$$

$$= 3218.28 \text{ cm}^2$$

EXAMPLE: The length of a garden roller is 2 m and diameter is 1.4 m. How much area will it cover in 10 revolutions?

SOLUTION: Area covered

= Curved surface × no. of revolutions

= $2\pi rh \times 10$

$$= 2 \times \frac{22}{7} \times 0.7 \times 2 \times 10 = 88 \text{ m}^2$$

EXAMPLE: A cylinder is made by lead whose radius is 4 cm and height is 10 cm. By melting it how many spheres of radius 2 cm can be made?

SOLUTION: Given, radius of the cylinder = 4 cm
and height of the cylinder = 10 cm

$\therefore$ Volume of the cylinder = $\pi r^2 h = \pi(4)^2 \times 10$
= 160π cm^3

$$\text{Volume of sphere} = \frac{4}{3}\pi r^3 = \frac{4}{3}\pi(2)^3$$

$$= \frac{32}{3}\pi \text{ cm}^3$$

$$\therefore \quad \text{Number of spheres} = \frac{\text{Volume of cylinder}}{\text{Volume of one sphere}}$$

$$= \frac{160\pi}{\frac{32}{3}\pi} = \frac{160 \times 3}{32} = 15$$

Hence, number of spheres that can be made are 15.

MULTIPLE CHOICE QUESTIONS

1. The surface area of a cube is 726 m^2. The volume of cube is:
   A. 1300 m^3 B. 1331 m^3
   C. 1452 m^3 D. 1542 m^3
2. Sum of the length, width and depth of a cuboid is s and its diagonal is d. Its surface area is:
   A. s^2 B. d^2
   C. $s^2 - d^2$ D. $s^2 + d^2$
3. A wooden box of dimensions 8 m × 7 m × 6 m is to carry rectangular boxes of dimensions 8 cm × 7 cm × 6 cm. The maximum number of boxes that can be carried in 1 wooden box is:
   A. 1200000 B. 1000000
   C. 9800000 D. 7500000
4. The length of the longest rod that can be placed in a room 30 m long, 24 m broad and 18 m high is:
   A. 30 m B. $15\sqrt{2}$ m
   C. 60 m D. $30\sqrt{2}$ m
5. If the volume of two cubes are in the ratio 8 : 1, the ratio of their edges is:
   A. 8 : 1 B. $2\sqrt{2} : 1$
   C. 2 : 1 D. None of these
6. A metal sheet 27 cm long 8 cm broad and 1 cm thick is melted into a cube. The difference between the surface areas of two solids will be:
   A. 284 cm^2 B. 296 cm^2
   C. 286 cm^2 D. 300 cm^2
7. If each edge of a cube is increased by 50%, the percentage increase in surface area is:
   A. 50% B. 75%
   C. 100% D. 125%
8. If a right circular cone of vertical height 24 cm has a volume of 1232 cm^3, then the area of its curved surface in cm^2 is:
   A. 1254 B. 704
   C. 550 D. 154
9. Two cubes have volumes in the ratio 1 : 27. The ratio of their surface areas is:
   A. 1 : 3 B. 1 : 8
   C. 1 : 9 D. 1 : 18
10. If the volumes of two cones are in the ratio 1 : 4 and their diameters are in the ratio 4 : 5, then the ratio of their heights is:
    A. 1 : 5 B. 5 : 4
    C. 5 : 16 D. 25 : 64
11. The radius of a wire is decreased to one-third. If volumes remains the same, length will increase:
    A. 1 time B. 3 times
    C. 6 times D. 9 times
12. A cylindrical piece of metal of radius 2 cm and height 6 cm is shaped into a cone of same radius. The height of cone is:
    A. 18 cm B. 14 cm
    C. 12 cm D. 8 cm
13. If 1 cubic cm of cast iron weight 21 g then the weight of a cast iron pipe of length 1 m with a bore of 3 cm and in which the thickness of the metal is 1 cm, is:
    A. 21 kg B. 24.2 kg
    C. 26.4 kg D. 18.6 kg
14. The number of solid spheres, each of diameter 6 cm, that could be moulded to form a solid metal cylinder of height 45 cm and diameter 4 cms, is:
    A. 3 B. 4
    C. 5 D. 6
15. A right cylinder and a right circular cone have the same radius and the same volume. The ratio of the height of the cylinder to that of the cone is:
    A. 3 : 5 B. 2 : 5
    C. 3 : 1 D. 1 : 3

ANSWERS

1	2	3	4	5	6	7	8	9	10
B	C	B	D	C	C	D	C	C	D
11	**12**	**13**	**14**	**15**					
D	A	C	C	D					

EXPLANATORY ANSWERS

1. Surface area of cube = $6a^2$

$6a^2 = 726 \Rightarrow a^2 = \frac{726}{6} = 121 \Rightarrow a = 11$ m

Volume of cube = $a^3 = 11 \times 11 \times 11 = 1331$ m^3

2. $l + b + h = s$

and $\sqrt{l^2 + b^2 + h^2} = d \Rightarrow l^2 + b^2 + h^2 = d^2$

$(l + b + h)^2 = s^2$

$\Rightarrow l^2 + b^2 + h^2 + 2(lb + bh + hl) = s^2$

$\Rightarrow d^2 + 2(lb + bh + hl) = s^2$

$\Rightarrow 2(lb + bh + hl) = s^2 - d^2$

$\therefore$ Surface area $= (s^2 - d^2)$.

3. Number of boxes $= \frac{800 \times 700 \times 600}{8 \times 7 \times 6} = 1000000$

4. Diagonal of cuboid $= \sqrt{l^2 + b^2 + h^2}$

$\therefore$ Length of longest rod $= \sqrt{30^2 + 24^2 + 18^2}$

$= \sqrt{900 + 576 + 324} = \sqrt{1800}$

$= \sqrt{30 \times 30 \times 2} = 30\sqrt{2}$ m

5. Let their volumes be $8x^3$ and x^3.
Then, their sides are $2x$ and x
$\therefore$ Ratio of their edges = 2 : 1

6. Volume of sheet = $27 \times 8 \times 1 = 216$ cm^3
Volume of cube formed = 216 cm^3

Side of cube $= \sqrt[3]{216} = 6$ cm
Surface area of cuboid $= 2(lb + bh + hl)$
$= 2(27 \times 8 + 8 \times 1 + 1 \times 27) = 502$ cm^2
Surface area of cube $= 6(\text{side})^2 = 6 \times 36 = 216$ cm^2
Difference in areas $= 502 - 216 = 286$ cm^2

7. Let original length of cube = x
then, its surface area = $6x^2$

New edge $= \left(\frac{150}{100}x\right) = \frac{3}{2}x$

New surface area $= 6 \times \left(\frac{3}{2}x\right)^2$

$= 6 \times \frac{9}{4}x^2 = \frac{27}{2}x^2$

Increase in surface area $= \left(\frac{27}{2} - 6\right)x^2 = \frac{15}{2}x^2$

$\therefore$ Increase % $= \frac{15x^2/2}{6x^2} \times 100$

$= \frac{15x^2}{12x^2} \times 100 = 125\%$

8. Volume of cone = 1232

$\Rightarrow \frac{1}{3}\pi r^2 h = 1232$

$\Rightarrow \frac{1}{3} \times \frac{22}{7} \times r^2 \times 24 = 1232$

$\Rightarrow r^2 = \frac{3 \times 7 \times 1232}{22 \times 24} = 49 \Rightarrow r = 7$ cm

$\Rightarrow l = \sqrt{r^2 + h^2} = \sqrt{7^2 + 24^2} = \sqrt{625} = 25$ cm

Lateral surface area of cone = πrl

$= \frac{22}{7} \times 7 \times 25 = 22 \times 25 = 550$ cm^2

9. Let their volumes are x^3 and $27x^3$.
Then, their sides are x and $3x$.

Ratio of their surface areas $= \frac{6x^2}{6(3x)^2} = \frac{x^2}{9x^2}$

$= 1 : 9$

10. Let the diameters of the bases of the cones be $4r$ and $5r$. Let their heights be h and H.

then, $\frac{\frac{1}{3}\pi \times \left(\frac{4r}{2}\right)^2 \times h}{\frac{1}{3}\pi\left(\frac{5r}{2}\right)^2 \times H} = \frac{1}{4}$

$\Rightarrow \frac{16}{25} \times \frac{h}{H} = \frac{1}{4}$

$\Rightarrow \frac{h}{H} = \frac{25}{64}$

11. Let original radius = r

and original length = h

$$\text{New radius} = \frac{1}{3}r$$

Let new length = H

then, $$\pi r^2 h = \pi\left(\frac{1}{3}r\right)^2 \times \text{H} = \frac{\pi r^2 \text{H}}{9}$$

$\therefore$ $$\text{H} = 9h$$

Thus length becomes 9 times.

12. Volume of cone = Volume of cylinder

$$\frac{1}{3}\pi r^2 h = \pi r^2 h$$

$$\Rightarrow \frac{1}{3}\times\frac{22}{7}\times 2\times 2\times h = \frac{22}{7}\times 2\times 2\times 6$$

$$\Rightarrow \frac{h}{3} = 6 \Rightarrow h = 18 \text{ cm}$$

$\therefore$ Height of cone = 18 cm

13. Diameter = 3 cm, h = 1 m = 100 cm

$\therefore$ Radius = $\frac{3}{2}$ cm = 1.5 cm

thickness = 1 cm

$\therefore$ R = 1.5 + 1 = 2.5 cm

r = 1.5 cm

$$\text{Volume of metal} = \pi(\text{R}^2 - r^2)\times h$$
$$= \pi[(2.5)^2 - (1.5)^2]\times 100$$
$$= \pi[4]\times 100 = \pi\times 400 \text{ cm}^3$$

$\because$ $1 \text{ cm}^3 = 21$ g

$\therefore$ $\pi\times 400 \text{ cm}^3 = 21\times\pi\times 400$ g

$$= 21\times\frac{22}{7}\times\frac{400}{1000}\text{ kg}$$
$$= 26.4 \text{ kg}$$

14. $$\text{Number of spheres} = \frac{\text{Volume of cylinder}}{\text{Volume of sphere}}$$

$$= \frac{\pi\times 2\times 2\times 45}{\frac{4}{3}\pi\times(3)^3} = \frac{4\times 45\times 3}{4\times 27} = 5$$

15. Volume of cylinder = Volume of cone

$$\pi r^2 h = \frac{1}{3}\pi r^2 \text{H}$$

$$\Rightarrow 3h = \text{H} \Rightarrow \frac{h}{\text{H}} = \frac{1}{3}$$

13. DATA INTERPRETATION

The collection of figures and facts in every field is called the statistical data. There are three types of statistical data.

(*a*) **Primary data:** The data collected by the investigator or the statistician to be used or integrated himself are called primary data. It is more reliable and relevant because it is collected by the investigator himself for the first time for his study.

(*b*) **Secondary data:** The data which are collected originally by someone else and used and interpreted by others for statistical analysis are called secondary data.

(*c*) **Grouped data:** When primary data is arranged in classes or groups to bring out certain sailent feature of the data is called grouped data.

Graphical Representation of Data

A graph is a visual form for presentation of data, highlighting their basic facts and relationship.

The word graph, chart and diagram are used interchangeably for the pictorial representation of data. However, the visual form made by using rectangular coordinate system is called a graph. In general, the other pictorial representation in which the coordinate system is not used are called diagrams or charts.

Variate: The quantity that we measure from observation-to-observation is called a variate.

Class-Interval: Every data is generally divided into small group using some interval is said to be in class-interval, *e.g.*, 0–5, 5–10, 10–15 etc.

Class-Size: The difference between the true upper limit and true lower limit of a class gives the size of a class-interval, *e.g.*, class-size of the class-interval 0–5 is 5.

Mid Value: The variable value which is mid-way between the lower and upper limit of a class is called its mid-value, *e.g.*, mid-value of class-interval 0–5 is $\frac{0+5}{2} = 2.5$.

Frequency: The number of observations corresponding to particular class is said to be the frequency of that class, *e.g.*, frequency of the interval 5–10 is 6. It means 6 persons have got 5 or more articles but less than 10.

Cumulative Frequency: The sum of the preceding frequencies is called cumulative frequency. Last frequency of cumulative frequency column is equal to the sum of the frequencies.

Class Limit: Every interval has two limits. Lower number of the interval is called lower limit while upper number of the interval is called upper limit, *e.g.*, in class-interval 0–5, 0 is lower limit while 5 is the upper limit.

Histogram

A statistical graph that represents by the height of a rectangular column the number of times that each class of result occurs in a sample or experiment, *e.g.*, the following table represents the number of matured persons in age group (15–20) in a city.

Age Group	Number of persons
15–20	200
20–25	350
25–30	475
30–35	600
35–40	750
40–45	900
45–50	100

Then the histogram of the data is given below:

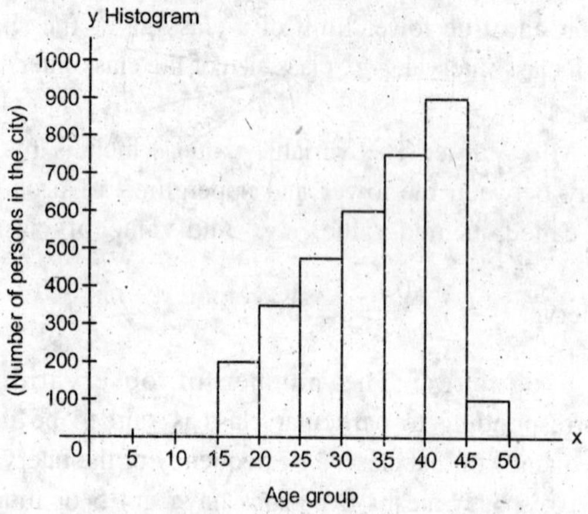

Bar Chart

A graph consisting of bars whose lengths are proportional to quantities in a set of data. It can be used when one axis cannot have a numerical scale, *e.g.*, to show how many different columns of flowers grow from a packet of mixed seeds, *e.g.*,

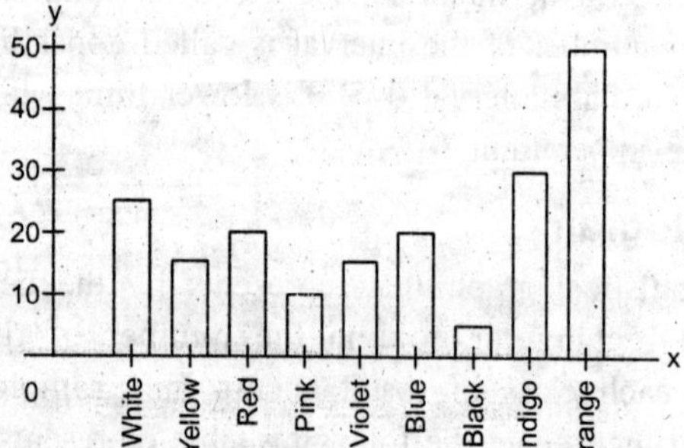

Pie Chart

A diagram in which proportions are illustrated as sectors of a circle. The relative area of the sectors representing the different proportions, *e.g.*, if out of 100 military personnels 25 personnels use tank, 30 personnels use warship, 40 personnels use aircraft and rest of them use rifles. Then pie-chart of the above data is

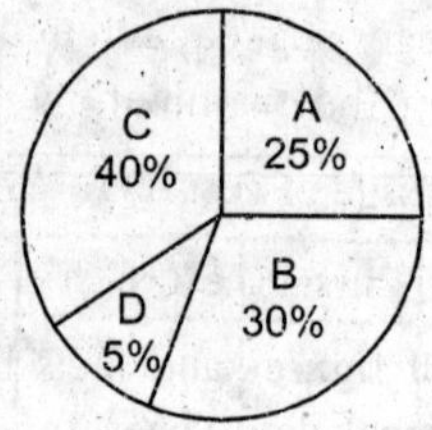

$$\text{A uses tank} = \frac{25}{100} \times 360 = 90^\circ$$

$$\text{B uses warship} = \frac{30}{100} \times 360 = 108^\circ$$

$$\text{C uses aircraft} = \frac{40}{100} \times 360 = 144^\circ$$

$$\text{D uses rifles} = \frac{5}{100} \times 360 = 18^\circ$$

EXAMPLE: Find out the marks obtained in different subjects from the following pie-diagram, if the total marks be 540.

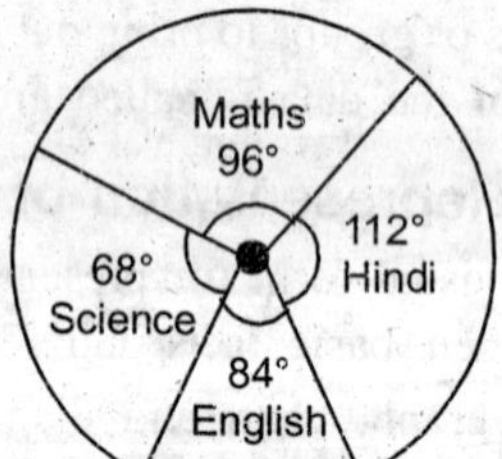

SOLUTION: Sum of the angles at the centre of circle $= 360^\circ$

$$\text{Total marks} = 540$$

$$\therefore \text{ Marks obtained in Hindi} = \frac{112}{360} \times 540 = 168$$

$$\text{Marks obtained in English} = \frac{84}{360} \times 540 = 126$$

$$\text{Marks obtained in Science} = \frac{68}{360} \times 540 = 102$$

$$\text{Marks obtained in Maths} = \frac{96}{360} \times 540 = 144$$

MULTIPLE CHOICE QUESTIONS

Directions (Qs. 1 to 5): *Answers the questions on the basis of the following table:*

Assume all colleges sent equal number of candidates in all subjects for the examination.

Percentage of results for Subjects

College	Maths	Physics	Chemistry	Zoology	Botany
A	52	65	62	47	40
B	47	62	52	35	38
C	53	70	46	54	39
D	35	72	58	62	57

1. Taking all the colleges into account which subject has shown highest percentage result?

A. Chemistry
B. Maths
C. Zoology
D. Physics

2. Taking the performance in all the subjects into account which college has shown highest level of percentage results?

A. D   B. A
C. B   D. C

3. Seeing the performance of all the four colleges together which combination of groups has shown lowest level of percentage results?

A. Zoology and Botany
B. Physics and Chemistry
C. Maths and Physics
D. Chemistry and Botany

4. Taking all the colleges into account which subject has shown lowest percentage result?

A. Maths
B. Physics
C. Chemistry
D. Botany

5. Taking the performance in all subjects into account which college has shown lowest level?

A. A   B. B
C. C   D. D

Directions (Qs. 6 to 10): *These questions refer to the following circle graph showing the expenditure distribution of a certain family. The family spends ₹6500 per month.*

Expenditure Distribution of a Certain Family

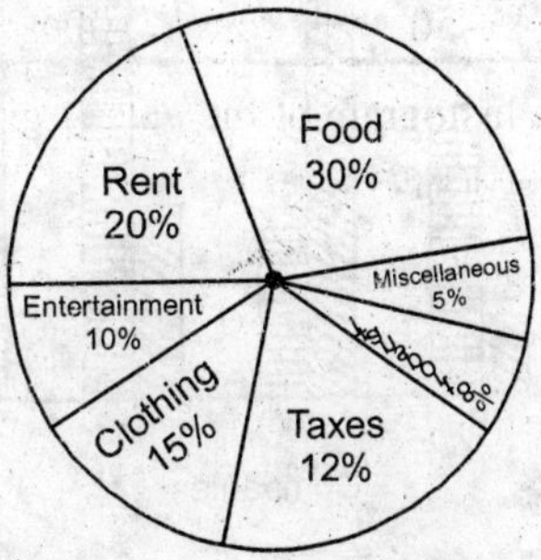

6. How much it spends on food per month?

A. ₹ 1950
B. ₹ 2950
C. ₹ 4850
D. ₹ 850

7. How much are its annual taxes?

A. ₹ 6500   B. ₹ 9360
C. ₹ 8900   D. ₹ 9500

8. How many degrees should there be in the central angle showing clothing, taxes and transportation combined?

A. 100   B. 115
C. 118   D. 126

9. How much more money per month is spent by the family on food as compared to the rent?

A. ₹ 650   B. ₹ 750
C. ₹ 550   D. ₹ 850

10. If the expenditure budget of the family is raised to ₹ 8000 per month and distribution on various items remain the same, then the monthly expenses on both, the entertainment and the transport, will be:

A. ₹ 1700
B. ₹ 1650
C. ₹ 1440
D. ₹ 1320

Directions (Qs. 11 to 15): *Study the following graph carefully and answer the following questions.*

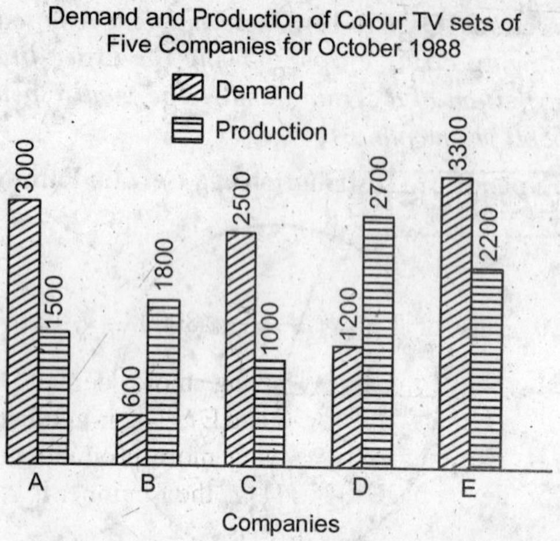

11. What is the ratio of companies having more demand than production of those having more production than demand?

A. 2 : 3 B. 4 : 1
C. 2 : 2 D. 3 : 2

12. What is the difference between average demand and average production of the five companies taken together?

A. 1400 B. 400
C. 280 D. 138

13. The production of Company 'D' is approximately how many times that of the production of the Company A?

A. 1.8 B. 4.5
C. 2.5 D. 4.9

14. The demand for Company 'B' is approximately what per cent of the demand for Company 'C'?

A. 4% B. 24%
C. 20% D. 60%

15. If Company A desires to meet the demand by purchasing surplus TV sets from a single company, which one of the following companies can meet the need adequately?

A. B B. C
C. D D. None of these

Directions (Qs. 16 to 20): *Study the following graph to answer the given questions.*

Per cent profit earned by two companies over the given years

$$\% \text{ Profit} = \frac{\text{Income} - \text{Expenditure}}{\text{Expenditure}} \times 100$$

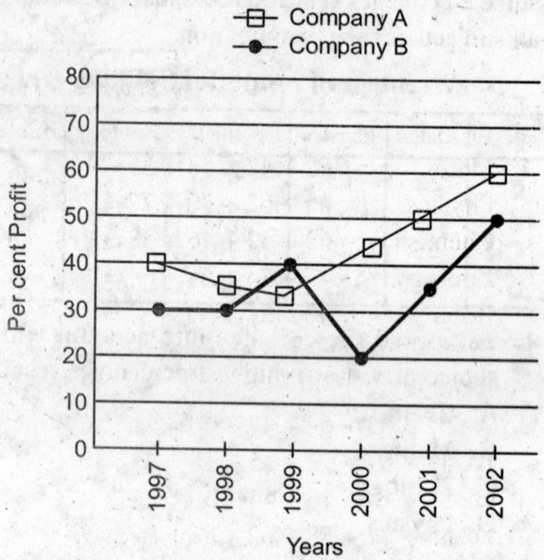

16. If the expenditure of Company B in 2000 was ₹ 200 crores, what was its income?

A. ₹ 240 crores B. ₹ 220 crores
C. ₹ 160 crores D. ₹ 180 crores

17. If the income of Company A in 2002 was ₹ 600 crores, what was its expenditure?

A. ₹ 360 crores B. ₹ 480 crores
C. ₹ 375 crores D. ₹ 320 crores

18. If the income of Company B in 1998 was ₹ 200 crores, what was its profit in 1999?

A. ₹ 21.5 crores
B. ₹ 153 crores
C. ₹ 46.15 crores
D. Cannot be determined

19. If the incomes of the two companies in 1998 were equal, what was the ratio of their expenditure?

A. 1 : 2 B. 26 : 27
C. 4 : 5 D. 100 : 67

20. What is the per cent increase in per cent profit for Company B from year 2000 to 2001?

A. 75 B. 175
C. 160 D. 150

ANSWERS

1	2	3	4	5	6	7	8	9	10
D	A	A	D	B	A	B	D	A	C
11	**12**	**13**	**14**	**15**	**16**	**17**	**18**	**19**	**20**
D	C	A	B	C	A	C	D	B	A

EXPLANATORY ANSWERS

1. Maths : $52 + 47 + 53 + 35 = 187$
Physics : $65 + 62 + 70 + 72 = 269$
Chemistry : $62 + 52 + 46 + 58 = 218$
Zoology : $47 + 35 + 54 + 62 = 198$
Botany : $40 + 38 + 39 + 57 = 174$
Clearly, Physics has shown highest percentage result.

2. A : $52 + 65 + 62 + 47 + 40 = 266$
B : $47 + 62 + 52 + 35 + 38 = 234$
C : $53 + 70 + 46 + 54 + 39 = 262$
D : $35 + 72 + 58 + 62 + 57 = 284$
Clearly, college D has shown highest level of percentage result.

3. Zoology and Botany of groups has shown lowest level of percentage result.

4. Total marks of Botany = 174 which shows lowest percentage result.

5. College B has shown lowest level because its total percentage result in all five subjects is 234 which is lowest.

6. Food 30% of ₹ 6500 = $\frac{30}{100} \times 6500$ = ₹ 1950

7. Taxes = 12% of ₹ 6500

$= \frac{12}{100} \times 6500$ = ₹ 780/month

= ₹ 780 × 12 = ₹ 9360/year

$\therefore$ Annual taxes = ₹ 9360

8. Clothing, taxes and transportation combined are 35%.

Now, $100\% = 360°$

$35\% = \frac{360°}{100} \times 35 = 126°$

9. 10% of ₹ 6500 = $\frac{10}{100} \times 6500$ = ₹ 650/month

10. 18% of ₹ 8000 = $\frac{18}{100} \times 8000$ = ₹ 1440

11. The companies having more demand than production are A, C and E *i.e.* their number is 3. The companies having more production than demand are B and D *i.e.* their number is 2. So, the required ratio is 3 : 2.

12. Average demand

$= \frac{1}{5}(3000 + 600 + 2500 + 1200 + 3300)$

$= \frac{10600}{5} = 2120$

Average production

$= \frac{1500 + 1800 + 1000 + 2700 + 2200}{5}$

$= \frac{9200}{5} = 1840$

$\therefore$ Difference between average demand and average production = 2120 – 1840 = 280

13. Let $K(1500) = 2700$

$\Rightarrow \quad K = \frac{2700}{1500} = \frac{9}{5} = 1.8.$

14. Let x% of (demand for C) = (demand for B)

$\Rightarrow \quad \frac{x}{100} \times 2500 = 600$

$\Rightarrow \quad x = \frac{600 \times 100}{2500} = 24\%$

15. Since Company D produces highest number of TV sets and Company A desires to meet the demand by purchasing surplus TV sets from a single Company.
Clearly, D can meet the demand of A.
$\therefore$ Correct answer is C.

16. Let the income be ₹ x crores

$$\therefore \quad 20 = \frac{x-200}{200} \times 100$$

$$\Rightarrow \quad 40 = x - 200$$

$$\Rightarrow \quad x = 240$$

$\therefore$ Income = ₹ 240 crores

17. The income of Company A in 2002

= ₹ 600 crores

% Profit = 60

Let the expenditure be ₹ x crores.

$$\therefore \quad 60 = \frac{600-x}{x} \times 100$$

$$\Rightarrow \quad x = \frac{600-x}{60} \times 100$$

$$\Rightarrow \quad x = \frac{(600-x)5}{3}$$

$$\Rightarrow \quad 3x = 3000 - 5x$$

$$\Rightarrow \quad 8x = 3000$$

$$\Rightarrow \quad x = \frac{3000}{8} = 375$$

Hence, expenditure = ₹ 375 crores.

18. It cannot be determined as Income and Expenditure of respective year is not known.

19. Let their equal incomes be ₹ 1 crore. Also, let expenditure of Company A be ₹ E_1 crores and that of Company B be ₹ E_2 crores.

Now, $$35 = \frac{1-E_1}{E_1} \times 100$$

$$35\,E_1 = 100 - 100\,E_1$$

$$135\,E_1 = 100 \quad \text{...}(i)$$

Similarly $$30 = \frac{1-E_2}{E_2} \times 100$$

$$130\,E_2 = 100 \quad \text{...}(ii)$$

From (i) and (ii)

$$135\,E_1 = 130\,E_2$$

$$\Rightarrow \quad \frac{E_1}{E_2} = \frac{130}{135} = \frac{26}{27}$$

$$\therefore \quad E_1 : E_2 = 26 : 27$$

20. Required percentage $= \frac{35-20}{20} \times 100$

$$= \frac{15}{20} \times 100 = 75.$$

सामान्य हिंदी

व्याकरण

व्याकरण वह शास्त्र है जिसके द्वारा किसी भी भाषा के शब्दों और वाक्यों के शुद्ध स्वरूपों एवं शुद्ध प्रयोगों का ज्ञान कराया जाता है।

व्याकरण के चार अंग हैं : (i) वर्ण विचार (ii) शब्द विचार (iii) पद विचार और (iv) वाक्य विचार

भाषा : भाषा अभिव्यक्ति का एक ऐसा साधन है जिसके द्वारा मनुष्य अपने विचारों को दूसरों पर प्रकट कर सकता है और दूसरों के विचार जान सकता है। भाषा के दो रूप हैं–(i) मौखिक और (ii) लिखित।

बोली : भाषा का क्षेत्रीय रूप बोली कहलाता है।

लिपि : किसी भी भाषा के लिखने की विधि को लिपि कहते हैं।

वर्ण : हिन्दी भाषा में प्रयुक्त सबसे छोटी ध्वनि वर्ण कहलाती है। जैसे–अ, आ, ई, क्, ख्, आदि

वर्णमाला : वर्णों के समुदाय को वर्णमाला कहते हैं। हिन्दी वर्णमाला में 44 वर्ण हैं। जिनमें 11 स्वर तथा 33 व्यंजन हैं।

स्वरवर्ण : उन वर्णों को कहते हैं, जिनका उच्चारण बिना किसी दूसरे वर्ण की सहायता से होता है। हिन्दी में 11 स्वर हैं–अ, आ, इ, ई, उ, ऊ, ए, ऐ, ओ, औ, ऋ।

व्यंजन वर्ण : उन वर्णों को कहते हैं, जिनका उच्चारण स्वर वर्णों की सहायता के बिना नहीं हो सकता है। इनकी संख्या 33 है–

क ख ग घ ड़ च
छ ज झ ञ ट् ठ
ड ढ़ ण त थ द
ध न प फ ब भ
म य र ल व श
ष स ह।

वर्ण : एक या अधिक वर्णों से बनी हुई स्वतन्त्र सार्थक ध्वनि शब्द कहलाती है।

शब्दों को तत्सम, तद्भव, देशज और विदेशी भागों में बाँटा जाता है।

तत्सम : जो शब्द संस्कृत भाषा से हिन्दी में बिना किसी परिवर्तन के लिए जाते हैं वे तत्सम कहलाते हैं, जैसे– अग्नि, क्षेत्र, मित्र, नासिका आदि।

तद्भव : उन शब्दों को कहते हैं, जो संस्कृत से ही लिए गए हैं, परन्तु हिन्दी में आने पर जिनका रूप बदल गया है। जैसे–आग, खेत, रात आदि।

देशज : उन शब्दों को कहते हैं, जो बोलचाल तथा देश की अन्य भाषाओं से लिए गए हैं। जैसे–कटोरा, झंझत, डिबिया, लोटा आदि।

विदेशज या विदेशी : उन शब्दों को कहते हैं, जो किसी विदेशी भाषा से आए हैं।

जैसे–स्कूल, कार, कमरा, खुदा, जोश, सरकार आदि।

शब्द सम्पदा

तत्सम शब्दों के तद्भव रूप

तत्सम	तद्भव	तत्सम	तद्भव
अग्नि	आग	अद्य	आज
अष्ट	आठ	अक्षि	आँख
अर्ध	आधा	अस्थि	हड्डी
अश्रु	आँसू	आम्र	आम

तत्सम	तद्भव	तत्सम	तद्भव
ग्राम	गाँव	गर्दभ	गधा
गृघ्र	गीध	गौर	गोरा
गृह	घर	घट	घड़ा
धातु	धात	धृत	घी

तत्सम	तद्भव	तत्सम	तद्भव
लक्ष	लाख	सप्त	सात
त्वम्	तुम	दुग्ध	दूध
रत्न	रतन	वर्ष	बरस
भक्त	भगत	मर्कट	बन्दर
रात्रि	रात	उलूक	उल्लू
अन्धकार	अन्धेरा	क्षीर	खीर
निद्रा	नींद	पृष्ठ	पीठ
ज्येष्ठ	जेठ	स्वर्ण	सोना
श्वास	साँस	काक	काग
कार्य	काज	कर्ण	कान
पाद	पाँव	हस्त	हाथ
नासिका	नाक	कंटक	काँटा
दश	दस	दधि	दही
दीप	दीया	निद्रा	नींद
नव	नौ	पत्र	पत्ता

विराम चिह्न

विराम का अर्थ रुकना। अपने विचारों को ठीक ढंग से प्रकट करने के पढ़ते अथवा लिखते समय हमें कुछ रुकना पड़ता है। इस प्रकार के रुकने को विराम कहते हैं। प्रत्येक-विराम के लिए अलग-अलग चिह्न हैं–

पूर्ण विराम	[।]
अल्प विराम	[,]
अर्ध विराम	[;]
प्रश्न बोधक	[?]
विस्मयादि बोधक	[!]
योजक	[–]
उद्धरण	[" "]

तत्सम	तद्भव	तत्सम	तद्भव
प्रस्तर	पत्थर	जिह्वा	जीभ
हस्ती	हाथी	दन्त	दाँत
क्षेत्र	खेत	नृत्य	नाच
सूचिका	सूई	स्वर्णकार	सुनार
लोक	लोग	पर्यङ्क	पलंग
स्वप्न	सपना	कातर	कायर
पुत्र	पूत	मानव	मनुष्य
शत	सौ	पुष्प	फूल
पक्व	पक्का	कृषक	किसान
कर्म	कार्य	आम्र	आम
कर्ण	कान	अष्ट	आठ
घंटिका	घंटी	चन्द्र	चन्द
यव	जौ	धूम्र	धुआँ
भ्रमर	भँवर		

कारक

कारक शब्द उस रूप को कहते हैं, जिससे संज्ञा या सर्वनाम वाक्य के साथ सम्बन्ध जाना जाता है।

जैसे–शीला कलम **से** लिखती है।

यह सीमा **की** पुस्तक है।

कारक के भेद विभक्ति चिह्नों सहित

कारक	विभक्ति
कर्त्ता	ने
कर्म	को
करण	से
सम्प्रदान	के लिए
अपादान	से
सम्बन्ध	का, के, की
अधिकरण	में, पर
सम्बोधन	हे, अरे!

पर्यायवाची शब्द

जिन शब्दों से एक समान अर्थ का बोध होता है, उन्हें पर्यायवाची या समानार्थी शब्द कहते हैं।

कुछ पर्यायवाची शब्दों के उदाहरण निम्नलिखित हैं–

आग – अग्नि, अनल, पावक, हुताशन, ज्वाला।

आकाश – नभ, आसमान, गगन, लोभ।

असुर – राक्षस, दानव, निशाचर, दैत्य।

अमृत – अभिय, पीयूष, सुधा, सोम।

अन्धकार – अन्धेरा, तिमिर, तम, तमिस्त्र।

आँख – नेत्र, नयन, लोचन, चक्षु, दृग।

कमल – जलज, पंकज, नीरज, राजीव।

इन्द्र – सुरपति, देवेन्द्र, सुरेन्द्र, देवेश।
ईश्वर – प्रभु, भगवान, जगदीश, दीनबन्धु।
पक्षी – खग, विहग, चिड़िया, नभचर।
बादल – घन, जलधर, वारिद, नीरद।
गंगा – सुरसरि, जाह्नवी, त्रिपथगा, देवनदी, विष्णुपदी।
चन्द्रमा – शशि, मयंक, निशाकर, सुधाकर, सुधांशु, सोम हिमांशु, राकेश।
जल – पानी, नीर, लोभ, अम्बु, सलिल, क्षीर, वारि।
फूल – पुष्प, कुसुम, सुमन, प्रसून, सारंग।
पृथ्वी – भू, भूमि, धरा, वसुन्धरा, वसुधा, धरती क्षमा, लोक।
कपड़ा – पट, वस्त्र, चीर, अम्बर, दुकूल।
घर – गृह, गेह, निकेतन, आलय, निलय, भवन, शाला, धाम, सदन।
जंगल – वन, कानन, अरण्य, विपिन।
तालाब – सरोवर, ताल, जलाशय, तड़ाग।
दिन – दिवस, वासर, वार।
पहाड़ – गिरि, पर्वत, गूधर, नग, महीधर, मेरू।
पत्थर – पहाड़, प्रस्तर, पाहन।
पवन – वायु, समीर, हवा, मारुत, अनिल।
पुत्र – सुत, तनय, पूत, आत्मज।
बिजली – तड़ित, चपला, दामिनी।
वृक्ष – तरू, रूख, विटप, पेड़।
मनुष्य – नर, मानव, मनुज, आदमी।
हाथी – करि, हस्ती, गज।
मित्र – सखा, मीत, सहचर, दोस्त।
राजा – नरेश, नृप, महीप, भूप।
समुद्र – सागर, सिन्धु, जलधि, नीरधि।
सरस्वती – शारदा, वागेश्वरी, भारती, महाश्वेता।
साँप – पन्नग, सर्प, विषधर, अहि, व्याल।
सूर्य – दिनकर, दिवाकर, रवि, भानु, भास्कर।
स्त्री – नारी, महिला, दारा, वामा।
शरीर – देह, तन, काया, गात, बदन।
गणेश – गजानन, गणपति, विनायक, एकदन्त, गजवदन लम्बोदर, विघ्न नाशक।
घोड़ा – तुरंग, बाजि, हय, अश्व, घोटक।
युद्ध – समर, रण, संग्राम।
सिंह – केसरी, मृगराज, केहरी।
शत्रु – अरि, रिपु, बैरी।
विष्णु – हरि, कमलेश, रमापति, चक्रपाणि, केशव, माधव, पीताम्बर।
कोष – खजाना, भण्डार, निधि।
धन – दौलत, द्रव्य, मुद्रा।
तलवार – कृपाण, असि, खड्ग।
अंग – भाग, हिस्सा, अवयव।
चोर – तस्कर, दस्यु, रजनीचर।
पत्नी – भार्या, दारा, गृहिणी।
पुत्र – तनय, सुत, लड़का, बेटा।
पुत्री – तनया, सुता, लड़की, बेटी।
माता – जननी, अम्बा, अम्बिका, अम्मा, माँ, धात्री।
मोर – शिखी, नीलकण्ठ, मयूर।
मृत्यु – मौत, काल, देहान्त।
रक्त – रुधिर, शोणित, खून, लहू।
विष – जहर, हलाहल, गरल।
सोना – कंचन, स्वर्ण, कनक।
हृदय – उर, छाती, वक्ष, वक्षस्थल, हिय, हिया।
सभा – अधिवेशन, परिषद्, बैठक, महासभा, समागम, समिति, सम्मेलन।
यमुना – कालिन्दी, कृष्णा, जमुना, रविसुता तरणि-तनुजा।

विलोम-शब्द

शब्दों के अपने निश्चित अर्थ होते हैं। उन अर्थों के विपरीत अर्थ देने वाले शब्द को विलोम-शब्द कहते हैं।

शब्द	विलोम	शब्द	विलोम	शब्द	विलोम	शब्द	विलोम
अमृत	विष	उदार	संकीर्ण	आदि	अन्त	उत्थान	पतन
अनुकूल	प्रतिकूल	अनुराग	विराग	इच्छा	अनिच्छा	उचित	अनुचित

शब्द	विलोम	शब्द	विलोम
अल्पायु	दीर्घायु	अनुज	अग्रज
उन्नति	अवनति	आकाश	पाताल
अधिक	न्यून	आयात	निर्यात
एक	अनेक	अन्धकार	प्रकाश
अर्थ	अनर्थ	उदय	अस्त
परकीया	स्वकीया	जड़	चेतन
जय	पराजय	अनिवार्य	वैकल्पिक
नकद	उधार	अपेक्षा	उपेक्षा
उपस्थित	अनुपस्थित	आदर	अनादर
अन्धेरा	उजाला	अपना	पराया
उत्तम	अधम	आय	व्यय
सुपुत्र	कुपुत्र	स्वाधीन	पराधीन
आहार	निराहार	कठोर	कोमल
दाता	याचक	दोषी	निर्दोषि
खेद	प्रसन्नता	धनी	निर्धन
निकट	दूर	चर	अचर
देव	दानव	खरा	खोटा
गरीब	अमीर	प्रेम	घृणा
जीवन	मृत्यु	बुरा	भला
सजीव	निर्जीव	मित्र	शत्रु
सुगन्ध	दुर्गन्ध	मौखिक	लिखित
संक्षेप	विस्तार	कटु	मधुर
आरम्भ	अन्त	कड़वा	मीठा
कृतज्ञ	कृतघ्न	दिन	रात
साक्षर	निरक्षर	पवित्र	अपवित्र
पाप	पुण्य	जल	थल
धीर	अधीर	निर्मल	मलिन
गुण	अवगुण	नश्वर	अनश्वर
निन्दा	स्तुति	भारी	हल्का
मनुष्यता	पशुता	सरस	नीरस
मान	अपमान	क्रय	विक्रय

शब्द	विलोम	शब्द	विलोम
धर्म	अधर्म	गहरा	उथला
गुरु	शिष्य	पक्ष	विपक्ष
जन्म	मृत्यु	बन्धन	मुक्ति
यश	अपयश	ज्ञान	अज्ञान
आदर	अनादर	पूर्ण	अपूर्ण
सफल	असफल	शान्त	अशान्त
कीर्ति	अपकीर्ति	वादी	प्रतिवादी
आस्तिक	नास्तिक	स्वदेश	परदेश
सज्जन	दुर्जन	राग	द्वेष
ऊसर	उर्वर	उदार	कृपण
अगला	पिछला	अगम	सुगम
अग्नि	जल	अति	अल्प
अर्थ	अनर्थ	अतल	वितल
अत्यधिक	स्वल्प	अधः	उपरि
अधिकतम	न्यूनतम	अतिवृष्टि	अनावृष्टि
अनाथ	सनाथ	ईश्वर	जीव
अनुलोम	विलोम	अर्पण	ग्रहण
अवनि	अम्बर	अस्त	उदय
आकर्षण	विकर्षण	आगे	पीछे
आजाद	गुलाम	आदान	प्रदान
आधुनिक	प्राचीन	आना	जाना
आय	व्यय	आयात	निर्यात
आवश्यक	अनावश्यक	आशा	निराशा
आस्था	अनास्था	इहलोक	परलोक
उच्च	निम्न	उत्थान	पतन
उपकार	अपकार	उपयोग	दुरुपयोग
एकता	अनेकता	कल	आज
कृत्रिम	प्राकृत	कृष्ण	शुक्ल
कपूत	सपूत	कोमल	कठोर
गगन	धरा	ज्ञान	अज्ञान
झूठ	सच		

लिंग

लिंग का अर्थ है 'चिह्न'। लिंग शब्द उस चिह्न को कहते हैं जिससे वस्तु के पुरुष या स्त्री होने की कल्पना हो। लिंग दो प्रकार के होते हैं—(1) पुल्लिंग (2) स्त्रीलिंग

पुल्लिंग—पुल्लिंग संज्ञा के उस रूप को कहते हैं जिससे उसके पुरुष होने का ज्ञान होता है। जैसे—राम, श्याम, घोड़ा, हाथी, कुत्ता आदि। **स्त्रीलिंग**—स्त्रीलिंग संज्ञा के उस रूप को

कहते हैं जिससे उसके स्त्री होने का ज्ञान हो। जैसे—भैंस, गाय, बकरी, सीता, रमा इत्यादि।

पुल्लिंग	स्त्रीलिंग	पुल्लिंग	स्त्रीलिंग
इन्द्र	इन्द्राणी	मेहतर	मेहतरानी
नौकर	नौकरानी	जेठ	जेठानी
देवर	देवरानी	सेठ	सेठानी
पण्डित	पण्डिताइन	ओझा	ओझाइन
बनिया	बनियाइन	दुबे	दुबाइन
हलवाई	हलवाइन	चौबे	चौबाइन
गुरु	गुरुआइन	लड़का	लड़की
दास	दासी	कबूतर	कबूतरी
हिरण	हिरणी	क्षत्रिय	क्षत्राणी
मुगल	मुगलानी	हिन्दू	हिन्दुआनी
चौधरी	चौधरानी	भव	भवानी
लाला	ललाइन	पण्डा	पण्डाइन
ठाकुर	ठकुराइन	बाबू	बबुआइन
घोड़ा	घोड़ी	गूँगा	गूँगी
बच्चा	बच्ची	चाचा	चाची
बकरा	बकरी	मामा	मामी
मुर्गा	मुर्गी	साला	साली
चींटा	चींटी	रस्सा	रस्सी
देव	देवी	ब्राह्मण	ब्राह्मणी
बेटा	बेटी	बूढ़ा	बुढ़िया
चूहा	चुहिया	डिब्बा	डिबिया
गुड्डा	गुड़िया	कुम्हार	कुम्हारिन
सुनार	सुनारिन	नाती	नातिन
जुलाहा	जुलाहिन	दर्जी	दर्जिन
पापी	पापिन	हाथी	हथिनी
पिता	माता	बैल	गाय
कवि	कवयित्री	विधुर	विधवा
बाप	माँ	बादशाह	बेगम

पुल्लिंग	स्त्रीलिंग	पुल्लिंग	स्त्रीलिंग
नर	मादा	मर्द	औरत
युवक	युवती	वर	वधू
सम्राट्	सम्राज्ञी	साढ़ू	साली
फूफा	बुआ	पुत्र	पुत्री
पहाड़	पहाड़ी	गोप	गोपी
गधा	गधी	तरुण	तरुणी
नर्तक	नर्तकी	बेटा	बिटिया
बछड़ा	बछिया	चिड़ा	चिड़िया
बन्दर	बन्दरिया	कुत्ता	कुतिया
नाई	नाइन	धोबी	धोबिन
ग्वाला	ग्वालिन	भंगी	भंगिन
स्वामी	स्वामिनी	विद्वान्	विदुषी
साधु	साध्वी	पुरुष	स्त्री
पति	पत्नी	वीर	वीरांगना
साहब	मेम	सास	ससुर
मियाँ	बीबी	राजा	रानी
बिलाड़	बिल्ली	अनुज	अनुजा
छात्र	छात्रा	महोदय	महोदया
प्रिय	प्रिया	मामा	मामी
लोटा	लुटिया	मोर	मोरनी
शेर	शेरनी	जाट	जाटिन
डाक्टर	डाक्टरनी	मालिक	मालकिन
माली	मालिन	बाघ	बाघिन
हाथी	हथिनी	स्वामी	स्वामिनी
बालक	बालिका	धनवान	धनवती
धावक	धाविका	नेता	नेत्री
गुणवान	गुणवती	नर	मादा
अभिनेता	अभिनेत्री	प्राचार्य	प्राचार्या
प्रबन्धकर्ता	प्रबन्धकर्ती	दाता	दात्री
ननदोई	ननद	अध्यापक	अध्यापिका

वचन

शब्द के जिस रूप से उसके एक अथवा अनेक होने का बोध हो, उसे वचन कहते हैं।

हिन्दी में दो वचन होते हैं—

(1) एकवचन और (2) बहुवचन

एकवचन—शब्द के जिस रूप से एक ही वस्तु का बोध हो, उसे एकवचन कहते हैं। जैसे—लड़का, गाय, बकरी, घोड़ा, राम, सीता आदि।

बहुवचन—शब्द के जिस रूप से अनेकता का बोध हो उसे बहुवचन कहते हैं। जैसे—लड़के, कपड़े, गायें आदि।

एकवचन	बहुवचन	एकवचन	बहुवचन
लड़का	लड़के	कौवा	कौवे
बेटा	बेटे	कमरा	कमरे
कपड़ा	कपड़े	बहन	बहनें
चीज	चीजें	गधा	गधे
रुपया	रुपये	घोड़ा	घोड़े
नहर	नहरें	रात	रातें
बात	बातें	सड़क	सड़कें
दाना	दाने	लोटा	लोटे
पैसा	पैसे	पुस्तक	पुस्तकें
कन्या	कन्याएँ	वधू	वधुएँ
नारी	नारियाँ	लड़की	लड़कियाँ
मुर्गा	मुर्गे	घण्टा	घण्टे
गद्दा	गद्दे	हीरा	हीरे
बच्चा	बच्चे	प्याला	प्याले
छाता	छाते	गाय	गायें
कथा	कथाएँ	कविता	कविताएँ
बहू	बहुएँ	टोपी	टोपियाँ
नाली	नालियाँ	बेटा	बेटे
ताला	ताले	जूता	जूते

एकवचन	बहुवचन	एकवचन	बहुवचन
डिबिया	डिबियाँ	नाक	नाकें
पूँछ	पूँछें	मूँछ	मूँछें
चिड़िया	चिड़ियाँ	सरिता	सरिताएँ
बालिका	बालिकाएँ	चाभी	चाभियाँ
कहानी	कहानियाँ	दरवाजा	दरवाजे
कलम	कलमें	कुटिया	कुटियाँ
रानी	रानियाँ	नाई	नाइयों
माता	माताएँ	बाल	बालों
हाथ	हाथों	मुख	मुख
कोट	कोट	दाँत	दाँतों
नाखून	नाखूनों	पैर	पैरों
बैल	बैलों	माली	मालियों
राजा	राजाओं	पिता	पिता
चन्द्रमा	चन्द्रमा	कवि	कवियों
मुनि	मुनियों	कौआ	कौए
छात्रा	छात्राएँ	सेना	सेनाएँ
दिशा	दिशाएँ	गुड़िया	गुड़ियाँ
मेज	मेजें	भैंस	भैंसें
अंगूर	अंगूरों	समुद्र	समुद्र
केला	केले	पत्ता	पत्ते

अनेक शब्दों के लिए एक शब्द

जिसकी कोई उपमा न हो : **अनुपम**
तेज बुद्धि वाला : **कुशाग्रबुद्धि**
कल्पना से परे हो : **कल्पनातीत**
जो उपकार नहीं मानता है : **कृतघ्न**
जो उपकार मानता है : **कृतज्ञ**
किसी की हँसी उड़ाना : **उपहास**
ऊपर कहा हुआ : **उपर्युक्त**
ऊपर लिखा हुआ : **उपरलिखित**
जिस पर उपकार किया गया हो : **उपकृत**
इतिहास का ज्ञाता : **इतिहासज्ञ**
आलोचना करने वाला : **आलोचक**
ईश्वर में आस्था रखने वाला : **आस्तिक**
बिना वेतन का : **अवैतनिक**
जो कहा न जा सके : **अकथनीय**
जो गिना न जा सके : **अगणित**
जिसका कोई शत्रु ही न जन्मा हो : **अजातशत्रु**
जिसके समान कोई दूसरा न हो : **अद्वितीय**
जो परिचित न हो : **अपरिचित**
आकाश में उड़ने वाला : **नभचर**
जो टुकड़े-टुकड़े हो गया हो : **खण्डित**
मछली की तरह आँखों वाली : **मीनाक्षी**
मयूर की तरह आँखों वाली : **मयूराक्षी**
बच्चों के लिए काम की वस्तु : **बालोपयोगी**
जिसकी बहुत अधिक चर्चा हो : **बहुचर्चित**
जिस स्त्री को कभी सन्तान न हुई हो : **बन्ध्या (बाँझ)**
फेन से भरा हुआ : **फेनिल**
प्रिय बोलने वाली स्त्री : **प्रियम्वदा**
जिसकी उपमा न हो : **निरुपम**
जो थोड़ी देर पहले पैदा हुआ हो : **नवजात**
जिसका कोई आधार न हो : **निराधार**

नगर में वास करने वाला : **नागरिक**
रात में घूमने वाला : **निशाचर**
ईश्वर में विश्वास न रखने वाला : **नास्तिक**
माँस न खाने वाला : **निरामिष**
बिल्कुल बर्बाद हो गया : **ध्वस्त**
जिसकी धर्म में निष्ठा हो : **धर्मनिष्ठ**
देखने योग्य : **दर्शनीय**
बहुत तेज चलने वाला : **द्रुतगामी**
जो किसी पक्ष में न रहे : **तटस्थ**
तत्त्व को जानने वाला : **तत्त्वज्ञ**
तप करने वाला : **तपस्वी**
जिसे देखकर डर लगे : **डरावना**
जो जन्म से अन्ध हो : **जन्मान्ध**
जीने की प्रबल इच्छा : **जिजीविषा**
जिसने इन्द्रियों को जीत लिया हो : **जितेन्द्रिय**
चिन्ता में डूबा हुआ : **चिन्तित**
जो बहुत समय तक ठहरे : **चिरस्थायी**
जिसकी चार भुजाएँ हों : **चतुर्भुज**
जिसके हाथ में चक्र हों : **चक्रपाणि**
जिससे घृणा की जाए : **घृणित**
जिसे गुप्त रखा जाए : **गोपनीय**
गणित ज्ञाता : **गणितज्ञ**
आकाश को चूमने वाला : **गगनचुम्बी**
जिसका आदि न हो : **अनादि**
जो कुछ न जानता हो : **अज्ञ**
जो अनुकरण करने योग्य हो : **अनुकरणीय**
जिसका अन्त न हो : **अनन्त**
जो कभी न मरे : **अमर**
जो कम बोलता हो : **अल्पभाषी**
जिसका इलाज न हो : **लाइलाज**
जिसका कोई नाथ न हो : **अनाथ**
कम जानने वाला : **अल्पज्ञ**
जहाँ जाना सम्भव न हो : **अगम**
बड़ा भाई : **अग्रज**
कम खाने वाला : **अल्पाहारी**
जो बात पहले कभी न हुई हो : **अभूतपूर्व**
दूसरों के पीछे चलने वाला : **अनुचर**
जो पहले न पढ़ा हो : **अपठित**

जिसके आर-पार दिखाई देता हो : **पारदर्शी**
आज्ञा पालन करने वाला : **आज्ञाकारी**
काम से जी चुराने वाला : **कामचोर**
प्रतिदिन होने वाला : **दैनिक**
जिसका कोई अर्थ न हो : **निरर्थक**
हाथ से लिखा हुआ : **हस्तलिखित**
आँखों के सामने होने वाला : **प्रत्यक्ष**
जिसका आचरण अच्छा हो : **सदाचारी**
वह पुरुष जिसकी पत्नी मर गई हो : **विधुर**
वह स्त्री जिसका पति मर गया हो : **विधवा**
जिसका रूप अच्छा न हो : **कुरूप**
सदा सत्य बोलने वाला : **सत्यवादी**
बड़ी इमारत के टूटे-फूटे भाग : **खण्डहर**
प्रशंसा के योग्य : **प्रशंसनीय**
जहाँ अनाथ रहते हों : **अनाथालय**
प्रत्येक मास होने वाला : **मासिक**
जहाँ पानी के जहाज आकर रुकते हैं : **बन्दरगाह**
प्रत्येक सप्ताह होने वाला : **साप्ताहिक**
प्रत्येक वर्ष होने वाला : **वार्षिक**
जो कठिनाई से मिले : **दुर्लभ**
जिसका आकार हो : **साकार**
जिसका आकार न हो : **निराकार**
जो कभी बूढ़ा न हो : **अजर**
बहुत बोलने वाला : **वाचाल**
पृथ्वी पर रहने वाला : **थलचर**
जल में रहने वाला : **जलचर**
नभ में विचरण करने वाला : **नभचर**
जल-थल दोनों में रहने वाला : **उभयचर**
जिसमें रस न हो : **नीरस**
पढ़ने वाला : **पाठक**
जो भाषण देता हो : **वक्ता**
जो साथ में पढ़ता हो : **सहपाठी**
जिसके नीचे रेखा खींची हो : **रेखांकित**
जानने की इच्छा रखने वाला : **जिज्ञासु**
जिसकी कोई सन्तान न हो : **निःसन्तान**
जिसका कोई मूल्य न हो : **अमूल्य**
जो वन में घूमता हो : **वनचर**
जो इस लोक के बाहर की बात हो : **अलौकिक**

जो इस लोक की बात हो	: **लौकिक**
जिसका सम्बन्ध पश्चिम से हो	: **पाश्चात्य**
जो स्थिर रहे	: **स्थावर**
दुःखान्त नाटक	: **त्रासदी**
ज्ञान देने वाली	: **ज्ञानदा**
भूत, वर्तमान भविष्य को देखने वाला	: **त्रिकालदर्शी**
जो क्षमा के योग्य हो	: **क्षम्य**
हिंसा करने वाला	: **हिंसक**
हित चाहने वाला	: **हितैषी**
सब कुछ जानने वाला	: **सर्वज्ञ**
जो स्वयं पैदा हुआ हो	: **स्वयंभू**
जो शरण में आया हो	: **शरणागत**
जिसका वर्णन न किया जा सके	: **वर्णनातीत**
व्याकरण जानने वाला	: **वैयाकरण**
रचना करने वाला	: **रचयिता**
खून से रंगा हुआ	: **रक्तरंजित**
अत्यन्त सुन्दर स्त्री	: **रूपसी**
कीर्तिमान पुरुष	: **यशस्वी**

महत्त्वपूर्ण शब्दों की भाववाचक संज्ञा

शब्द	भाववाचक संज्ञा	शब्द	भाववाचक संज्ञा
दास	दासता	क्षत्रिय	क्षत्रियत्व
पशु	पशुता	बालक	बालकपन
बन्धु	बन्धुत्व	मित्र	मित्रता
बूढ़ा	बुढ़ापा	सती	सतीत्व
सेवक	सेवा	शिशु	शैशव
अपना	अपनत्व	पराया	परायापन
सर्व	सर्वस्व	मम	ममत्व
पण्डित	पाण्डित्य	पुरुष	पुरुषत्व
ब्राह्मण	ब्राह्मणत्व	बच्चा	बचपन
प्रभु	प्रभुता	नारी	नारीत्व
देव	देवत्व	लड़का	लड़कपन
मनुष्य	मनुष्यता	दानव	दानवता
निज	निजता	स्व	स्वत्व

शब्द	भाववाचक संज्ञा	शब्द	भाववाचक संज्ञा
अहं	अहंकार	अपना	अपनापन
व्यक्ति	व्यक्तित्व	मीठा	मिठास
गरीब	गरीबी	सफल	सफलता
बुरा	बुराई	स्वस्थ	स्वास्थ्य
सरल	सरलता	कंजुस	कंजुसी
कमजोर	कमजोरी	हरा	हरियाली
गर्म	गर्मी	मोटा	मोटाई
चालाक	चालाकी	गम्भीर	गम्भीरता
पढ़ना	पढ़ाई	लिखना	लिखाई
थकना	थकावट	लिखना	लिखावट
लूटना	लूट	लड़ना	लड़ाई
हँसना	हँसी	आप	अपनत्व

महत्त्वपूर्ण शब्दों के विशेषण

शब्द	विशेषण	शब्द	विशेषण
अंक	अंकित	अर्थ	आर्थिक
इतिहास	ऐतिहासिक	उदासी	उदास
कलंक	कलंकित	कुसुम	कुसुमित
जटा	जटिल	भार	भारी
बनारस	बनारसी	बाजार	बाजारू
प्यास	प्यासा	पुराण	पौराणिक
पंक	पंकित	पक्ष	पाक्षिक
धन	धनी	दो	दूसरा

शब्द	विशेषण	शब्द	विशेषण
तीन	तीसरा	झगड़ा	झगड़ालू
ठण्ड	ठण्डा	जाति	जातीय
काँटा	कँटीला	विदेश	विदेशी
रोज	रोजाना	भूगोल	भौगोलिक
पीड़ा	पीड़ित	पुत्र	पुत्रवान
आलस्य	आलसी	अंतर	आंतरिक
ईर्ष्या	ईर्ष्यालु	कर्म	कर्मठ
करुणा	कारुणिक	कृपा	कृपालु

शब्द	विशेषण	शब्द	विशेषण	शब्द	विशेषण	शब्द	विशेषण
गुण	गुणी	जल	जलमय	फ्रांस	फ्रांसीसी	बाहर	बाहरी
जीव	जैविक	तट	तटस्थ	भय	भयभीत	मधु	मधुर
तर्क	तार्किक	धर्म	धार्मिक	मौन	मौनी	मन	मानसिक
नमक	नमकीन	पत्थर	पथरीला	मानव	मानवीय	रक्षा	रक्षक
पल्लव	पल्लवित	पान	पनवाड़ी	रघु	राघव	रोग	रोगी
मुख	मुखर	मिठास	मीठा	वर्ष	वार्षिक	शक्ति	शक्तिशाली
मास	मासिक	मद	मादक	श्रम	श्रमिक	अंत	अंतिम
रक्त	रक्तिम	रस	रसीला	कागज	कागजी	मर्म	मार्मिक
वन	वन्य	विष्णु	वैष्णव	शब्द	शाब्दिक	अज्ञान	अज्ञानी
शहर	शहरी	तप	तपस्वी	गुलाब	गुलाबी	प्रकृति	प्राकृतिक
जापान	जापानी	तेज	तेजस्वी	परिचय	परिचित	पूजा	पुजारी
तत्त्व	तात्त्विक	दया	दयालु	रोग	रोगी	ग्राम	ग्रामीण
देव	दैविक	निंदा	निंदक	सुगंध	सुगंधित	मैं	मेरा
नव	नवीन	पोषण	पोषक	जो	जैसा	आप	आप-सा
पेट	पेटू	पाप	पापी	तुम	तुम्हारा	कौन	कैसा
पूजा	पूज्य	भूख	भूखा	वह	वैसा	पढ़ना	पढ़ाकू
फेन	फेनिल	भारत	भारतीय	गाना	गायक	बेचना	बिकाऊ
माया	मायावी	रंग	रंगीन	भागना	भगोड़ा	वन्द	वन्दनीय
विष	विषैला	श्री	श्रीमान	चलना	चलती	घूमना	घुमक्कड़
सुर	सुरीला	विवाह	वैवाहिक	चलना	चालू	मरना	मरियल
आदर	आदरणीय	ऋण	ऋणी	भूलना	भुलक्कड़	पीछे	पिछला
किताब	किताबी	क्रम	क्रमिक	भीतर	भीतरी	नीचे	निम्न
ग्राम	ग्रामीण	घर	घरेलू	अणु	आणविक	अधिकार	आधिकारिक
चतुर	चतुरता	जहर	जहरीला	अनुभव	अनुभवी	अन्याय	अन्यायी
सप्ताह	साप्ताहिक	अनुभव	अनुभवी	अपमान	अपमानित	अभ्यास	अभ्यासी
ओज	ओजस्वी	कल्पना	काल्पनिक	अवश्य	आवश्यक	आदि	आदिम
कुल	कुलीन	गाँव	गँवार	आयु	आयुष्मान्	उदय	उदित
चमक	चमकीला	चाचा	चचेरा	उपज	उपजाऊ	एकता	एक
दीन	दीनता	नगर	नागरिक	अंत	अंतिम	कुल	कुलीन
नागपुर	नागपुरी	परिवार	पारिवारिक	खर्च	खर्चीला	खून	खूनी
पुष्प	पुष्पित	पिता	पैतृक	गुण	गुणी		

श्रुतिसम भिन्नार्थक शब्द

शब्द	अर्थ	शब्द	अर्थ	शब्द	अर्थ	शब्द	अर्थ
आदि	आरम्भ	आदी	अभ्यस्त	अरि	शत्रु	अरी	सम्बोधन
कुल	वंश	कूल	किनारा	अगम	दुर्गम	आगम	शास्त्र

शब्द	अर्थ	शब्द	अर्थ
अयंश	अपकीर्ति	अयस्क	लोहा
अपेक्षा	चाहना, तुलना में	उपेक्षा	निरादर
अनिल	हवा	अनल	आग
अवधि	काल, समय	अवधी	अवध की भाषा
आयात	बाहर से आना	आयत	एक आकृति
चिर	पुराना	चीर	कपड़ा
तनु	पतला	तनू	पुत्र, गाय
तरंग	लहर	तुरंग	घोड़ा
दारा	स्त्री	द्वार	दरवाजा
दूत	संदेशवाहक	द्यूत	जुआ
जलद	बादल	जलज	कमल
प्रदीप	दीपक	प्रतीप	उल्टा
प्रसाद	कृपा	प्रासाद	महल
पास	निकट	पाश	बन्धन
द्विप	हाथी	द्वीप	टापू
देव	देवता	दैव	भाग्य
नीर	जल	नीड़	घोंसला
पवन	वायु	पावन	पवित्र
बन्द	खुला नहीं	बद	बुरा
पथ	रास्ता	पथ्य	रोगी का भोजन

शब्द	अर्थ	शब्द	अर्थ
पुर	नगर	पूर	बाढ़
भवन	महल	भुवन	संसार
लक्ष्य	उद्देश्य	लक्ष	लाख
सर	तालाब	शर	बाण
सर्ग	अध्याय	स्वर्ग	एक लोक
कर्म	कार्य	क्रम	सिलसिला
चिता	शव जलाने के लिए लकड़ियों का ढेर	चीता	बाघ
शव	लाश	शब	रात
शस्त्र	हथियार	शास्त्र	ग्रन्थ
श्रवण	सुनना	श्रमण	बौद्ध संन्यासी
मत	विचार	मत्त	मस्त
शोक	दुःख	शौक	चाव
ग्रह	नक्षत्र	गृह	घर
कपट	धोखा	कपाट	दरवाजा
उपयुक्त	ठीक	उपर्युक्त	ऊपर कहा गया
सुत	बेटा	सूत	धागा
शूर	वीर	सूर	अंधा
श्याम	कृष्ण	शाम	संध्या
दिन	वार	दीन	गरीब
कटिबद्ध	तैयार रहना	करबद्ध	हाथ जोड़ना

अनेकार्थक शब्द

शब्द	विभिन्न अर्थ
अंक	संख्या, गोद
अक्षर	वर्ण, ईश्वर
पानी	जल, प्रतिष्ठा
अचल	पवर्त, स्थिर
आम	फल, सामान्य
अंबर	वस्त्र, आकाश
अवस्था	आयु, दशा
उत्तर	दिशा, जबाव
विधि	तरीका, भाग्य
कर	हाथ, टैक्स
कनक	सोना, धतुरा
गुरु	श्रेष्ठ, शिक्षक
हान	भारी हथौड़ा, बादल
जड़	मूर्ख, मूल
कल	मशीन, आनेवाला कल, चैन
सुर	देवता, स्वर
द्विज	पक्षी, ब्राह्मण
तीर	किनारा, बाण
प्रकृति	स्वभाव, कुदरत
पत्र	चिट्ठी, पत्र
पद	पैर, उपाधि
फल	परिणाम, फल
तनु	पतला, कोमल
वर्ण	रंग, जाति
हल	समाधान, खेत जोतने का साधन
अशोक	राजा, वृक्ष

शब्द	विभिन्न अर्थ
आभीर	अहीर, एक राग
एकाक्ष	काना, कौआ
खल	दुष्ट, खलिहान

शब्द	विभिन्न अर्थ
घट	घड़ा, हृदय
जलज	कमल, मछली
हेम	सोना, जल

सामान्य अशुद्धियाँ

अशुद्ध	शुद्ध	अशुद्ध	शुद्ध
दुनियां	दुनिया	श्रीमति	श्रीमती
सामिग्री	सामग्री	वापिस	वापस
प्रदर्शिनी	प्रदर्शनी	द्वारिका	द्वारका
ऊत्थान	उत्थान	दुसरा	दूसरा
प्रशाद	प्रसाद	अमावश्या	अमावस्या
बसंत	वसंत	बर्ष	वर्ष
विना	बिना	बन	वन
दाइत्व	दायित्व	सम्वाद	संवाद
कुन्डली	कुण्डली	मॉसिक	मानसिक
कन्ठ	कण्ठ	अगामी	आगामी
सप्ताहिक	साप्ताहिक	संसारिक	सांसारिक
आधीन	अधीन	हस्ताक्षेप	हस्तक्षेप
बरात	बारात	क्षत्रीय	क्षत्रिय
तिथी	तिथि	कालीदास	कालिदास
पुर्ती	पूर्ति	अतिथी	अतिथि
नीती	नीति	ग्रहणी	गृहिणी
क्यूँ	क्यों	साधू	साधु
वधु	वधू	रेणू	रेणु
नुपुर	नूपुर	निर्वान	निर्वाण
जादु	जादू	द्रश्य	दृश्य
अनुग्रहीत	अनुगृहीत	बृज	ब्रज
बनस्पति	वनस्पति	श्राप	शाप
सैना	सेना	सेनिक	सैनिक
इतिहासिक	ऐतिहासिक	प्रथक	पृथक
सम्पति	सम्पत्ति	कृतघन	कृतघ्न
बिमारी	बीमारी	व्यक्तिक	वैयक्तिक
वितीत	व्यतीत	निस्वार्थ	निःस्वार्थ
परिस्थित	परिस्थिति	रचियता	रचयिता
मैथिलिशरण	मैथिलीशरण	आर्शिवाद	आशीर्वाद
निरिक्षण	निरीक्षण	पत्नि	पत्नी

अशुद्ध	शुद्ध	अशुद्ध	शुद्ध
शताब्दि	शताब्दी	लड़ायी	लड़ाई
स्थाई	स्थायी	लिखायी	लिखाई
अलोकिक	अलौकिक	कृप्या	कृपया
गंवार	गँवार	असोक	अशोक
दुस्कर	दुष्कर	मूल्यावान	मूल्यवान्
नवम्	नवम	क्षात्र	छात्र
छमा	क्षमा	प्रन्तु	परन्तु
प्रीक्षा	परीक्षा	मरयादा	मर्यादा
दुदर्शा	दुर्दशा	विषेश	विशेष
उज्वल	उज्ज्वल	आल्हाद	आहलाद्
महत्व	महत्त्व	उपलक्ष	उपलक्ष्य
लीये	लिये	पिओ	पियो
हुये	हुए	कवित्री	कवयित्री
प्रमात्मा	परमात्मा	घनिष्ट	घनिष्ठ
यथेष्ठ	यथेष्ट	पियास	प्यास.
व्यस्क	वयस्क	त्यौहार	त्योहार
मुसलिम	मुस्लिम	ऐनक	ऐनक
नोकरी	नौकरी	कल्यान	कल्याण
पाणी	पानी	आसा	आशा
हुदय	हृदय	ग्रणा	घृणा
श्रंगार	शृंगार	हिन्दुस्थान	हिन्दुस्तान
प्रशन	प्रश्न	ग्यान	ज्ञान
अन्धेरा	अँधेरा	पेड	पेड़
महयान्हन	मध्यान्ह	मेंहदी	मेहंदी
शमशान	श्मशान	चिन्ह	चिह्न
कुंज	कुञ्ज	ग्रहस्थ	गृहस्थ
अजोध्या	अयोध्या	अनधिकार	अनाधिकार
अनिष्ठा	अनिष्ट	अनुकुल	अनुकूल
अनुसंगिक	आनुषंगिक	अनुशरण	अनुसरण
अभिसेक	अभिषेक	अरमाण	अरमान

अशुद्ध	शुद्ध	अशुद्ध	शुद्ध	अशुद्ध	शुद्ध	अशुद्ध	शुद्ध
अहिल्या	अहल्या	आदरनीय	आदरणीय	सम्राज	साम्राज्य	सविनयपूर्वक	सविनय
आविस्कार	आविष्कार	उँचाई	ऊँचाई	सिंदुर	सिंदूर	स्त्रवण	श्रवण
उत्तरदाई	उत्तरदायी	उपर	ऊपर	हरीश्चन्द्र	हरिश्चन्द्र	हिन्दु	हिन्दू
उपरोक्त	उपर्युक्त	उश्रृंखल	उच्छृंखल	हिन्दूस्तान	हिन्दुस्तान	बुद्धिवान	बुद्धिमान्
कलस	कलश	कल्यान	कल्याण	भाग्यमान	भाग्यवान	विद्वान	विद्वान्
गनित	गणित	जबाब	जवाब	श्रीमान	श्रीमान्	आंख	आँख
तत्व	तत्त्व	तलाब	तालाब	ऊंट	ऊँट	कंगना	कँगना
तिरष्कार	तिरस्कार	त्रिवार्षिक	त्रैवार्षिक	गँगा	गंगा	गांधी	गाँधी
दिपिका	दीपिका	देहिक	दैहिक	जांच	जाँच	तांगा	ताँगा
द्वन्द	द्वन्द्व	नरायन	नारायण	दांत	दाँत	महंगा	महँगा
निरव	नीरव	निरोग	नीरोग	मांस	माँस	मुंह	मुँह
पुष्टी	पुष्टि	पुस्प	पुष्प	सांप	साँप	सांस	साँस
पेत्रिक	पैतृक	प्रनय	प्रणय	हुँकार	हुंकार	निर्पेक्ष	निरपेक्ष
प्रनाम	प्रणाम	प्रयाप्त	पर्याप्त	भाष्कर	भास्कर	सन्मुख	सम्मुख
प्रसंशा	प्रशंसा	प्रांगन	प्रांगण	माताहीन	मातृहीन	विद्यार्थि	विद्यार्थी
प्रान	प्राण	पृष्ट	पृष्ठ	गुणि	गुणी	द्वैवाषिक	द्विवार्षिक
ब्रत	व्रत	भगीरथी	भागीरथी	पूज्यनीय	पूजनीय	अकाश	आकाश
भरथ	भरत	भष्म	भस्म	इद	ईद	इसलाम	इस्लाम
मंत्रीमंडल	मंत्रिमण्डल	रसायण	रसायन	ऐैसा	ऐसा	दोसरा	दूसरा
राज्यमहल	राजमहल	रामायन	रामायण	पुत्रि	पुत्री	प्रस्तूत	प्रस्तुत
वनोवास	वनवास	वानी	वाणी	हरयाली	हरियाली	दिवाली	दीवाली
वाल्मीकी	वाल्मीकि	वास्प	वाष्प	राष्ट्रिय	राष्ट्रीय	एकहरा	इकहरा
व्योहार	व्यवहार	सन्यासी	संन्यासी	एतबार	इतबार		

वाक्यगत अशुद्धियाँ

अशुद्ध	शुद्ध	अशुद्ध	शुद्ध
हम अच्छी भाषण दिए थे।	हमने अच्छा भाषण दिया था।	राम और सीता आयी थी।	राम और सीता आए थे।
आप खाए कि नहीं?	आपने खाया कि नहीं?	भाई-बहन जा रही हैं।	भाई-बहन जा रहे हैं।
वह मुझे देखा तो घबरा गया।	उसने मुझे देखा तो घबरा गया।	वह लड़की को बुलाओ।	उस लड़की को बुलाओ।
मैं किताब पढ़ा हूँ।	मैंने किताब पढ़ी है।	मेरे लिए पढ़ता हूँ।	अपने लिए पढ़ता हूँ।
मैं सारी पुस्तक पढ़ डाली।	मैंने सारी पुस्तक पढ़ डाली।	सीता राम की आज्ञाकारी पत्नी थी।	सीता राम की आज्ञाकारिणी पत्नी थीं।
सीता भात खायी।	सीता ने भात खाया।		
राम रोटी खाया।	राम ने रोटी खायी।	देरी न करना।	देर न करना।
लड़की ने दही गिरा दी।	लड़की ने दही गिरा दिया।	उसे मृत्युदण्ड की सजा मिली।	उसे मृत्युदण्ड मिला।
शुद्ध गाय की घी दो।	गाय का शुद्ध घी दो।	हमारे शिक्षक प्रश्न पूछते हैं।	हमारे शिक्षक प्रश्न करते हैं।
तुम, मैं और वह चलेगा।	तुम, वह और मैं चलूँगा।	कै बजे? तीन बजा।	कितना बजा? तीन बजे।

अशुद्ध	शुद्ध
उसका प्राण उड़ गया।	उसके प्राण उड़ गये।
मैंने आँख से देखा।	मैंने आँखों से देखा।
अपन को पढ़ना है।	मुझे पढ़ना है।
पुस्तक फट गया।	पुस्तक फट गई है।
घोड़ी तेज दौड़ता है।	घोड़ी तेज दौड़ती है।
मेरा प्रणम स्वीकार करो।	मेरा प्रणाम स्वीकार करो।
दो बालक खेलता है।	दो बालक खेलते हैं।
ये सब मेरा पुस्तक है।	ये सब मेरी पुस्तकें हैं।
सूरज पूरब में उगते हैं।	सूरज पूर्व में उगता है।
वह लौट आए।	वे लौट आए।
वहाँ अनेकों लोग थे।	वहाँ अनेक लोग थे।

अशुद्ध	शुद्ध
मेरे को मत मारो।	मुझे मत मारो।
मोहन ने पत्र को पढ़ा।	मोहन ने पत्र पढ़ा।
पुस्तक पर नहीं लिखो।	पुस्तक पर मत लिखो।
वह सज्जन पुरुष है।	वह सज्जन है।
आप हमारे घर आओ।	आप हमारे घर आइए।
हम आपसे कुछ कहे थे।	हमने आपसे कुछ कहा था।
मकान की दायीं ओर सड़क है।	मकान के दायीं ओर सड़क है।
पिताजी घर नहीं हैं।	पिताजी घर पर नहीं हैं।
घर पर सब कुशल हैं।	घर में सब कुशल हैं।
उसे भारी दुःख हुआ।	उसे बहुत दुःख हुआ।
सड़क में मत खेलो।	सड़क पर मत खेलो।

मुहावरे तथा लोकोक्तियाँ

- अँगूठी का नगीना–अत्यन्त महत्त्वपूर्ण।
- अंधा दरबार–न्यायहीन स्थान।
- अंधेर नगरी–न्याय का अभाव।
- अक्ल का दुश्मन–मूर्ख।
- अक्ल का दुम–मूर्ख।
- आँख का तारा–अतिप्रिय।
- ईद का चाँद–बहुत दिनों के बाद दिखाई देना।
- कछुआ चाल–धीमी गति।
- काला नाग–दुष्ट आदमी।
- किताबी कीड़ा–सदैव कुछ-न-कुछ पढ़ना।
- किस्मत का मारा–भाग्य का मन्द।
- कोल्हू का बैल–बहुत कठिन परिश्रम करनेवाला।
- कोड़ी का तीन–तुच्छ।
- खाली हाथ–पैसे का अभाव।
- गाजर-मूली–अशक्त।
- गुलर का फूल–दुर्लभ वस्तु।
- गोबर-गणेश–निरामूर्ख।
- घर का उजाला–कुल-दीपक।
- घड़ियाली आँसू–बनावटी शोक।
- चलता-पुरजा–चालाक।
- चाँद का टुकड़ा–परम सुन्दर वस्तु या व्यक्ति।
- चाँदी का जूता–रिश्वत।
- चार दिन की चाँदनी–थोड़े समय का सुख।
- जलती आँख–क्रोधाभिभूत।
- जीभ का पतला–लालची।
- टेढ़ी खीर–विकट काम।
- ठिकाने की बात–न्यायसंगत बात।
- अढ़ाई दिन की हुकूमत–थोड़े समय का ऐश्वर्य।
- तकदीर का सिकन्दर–भाग्य का बलवान्।
- थाली का बैंगन–मत बदलते रहना।
- दाँत कटी रोटी–घनिष्ठता।
- दाहिना हाथ–सहायक।
- दिल का बादशाह–बहुत बड़ा उदार।
- दूध का दूध और पानी का पानी–उचित न्याय।
- दूध का धोआ–निर्दोष।
- दो दिन का मेहमान–बहुत थोड़े समय ठहरने वाला।
- धरती का फूल–ऐसा व्यक्ति जो हाल में अमीर हुआ है।
- धोबी का कुत्ता–निकम्मा।
- नसीब का मारा–बुरे दिन देखनेवाला।
- निन्यानबे का फेरा–धन बढ़ाने की चिन्ता।
- पत्थर का कलेजा–हर दुःख सहने की शक्ति।
- पत्थर की लकीर–चिरस्थायी सदा सत्य।
- फूलों की सेज–आनन्ददायक कार्य।
- बगुला-भगत–कपटी व्यक्ति।
- बच्चों का खेल–साधारण काम।
- बलि का बकरा–निःसहाय व्यक्ति।

- बरसाती बादल–अस्थायी।
- बात का पक्का–सत्यवादी।
- बायें हाथ का खेल–सरल काम।
- बिन बादल बरसात–असमय लाभ।
- बे-पेंदी का लोटा–बे ठिकाने का आदमी।
- भागीरथ प्रयत्न–अत्यधिक परिश्रम।
- भीष्म प्रतिज्ञा–दृढ़ संकल्प।
- मक्खी चूस–कंजूस।
- मिट्टी के मोल–बहुत सस्ता।
- मोटा असामी–मूर्ख मालदार।
- राम कहानी–आत्मवृतान्त।
- लँगोटिया यार– बचपन का मित्र।
- हवाई महल–कोरी कल्पना।
- आँख लगना–नींद आना।
- आँख खुलना–होश में आना।
- आँखें दिखाना–क्रोध से घूरना।
- आँसू पोंछना–धैर्य बँधाना।
- अन्धे की लकड़ी–एकमात्र सहारा।
- कान भरना–चुगली करना।
- कान पर जूँ न रेंगना–कोई असर न होना।
- नाक कटना–प्रतिष्ठा खत्म होना।
- नाक रगड़ना–दीनता दिखाना।
- नाकों चने चबवाना–खूब सताना।
- मुँह की खाना–बुरी तरह हारना।
- आस्तीन का साँप–विश्वासघाती मित्र।
- कन्धे से कन्धा मिलाना–पूरा सहयोग करना।
- ईंट से ईंट बजाना–पूरी तरह नष्ट कर देना।
- नौ दो ग्यारह होना–भाग जाना।
- दाँत खट्टे करना–बुरी तरह हराना।
- हाथ मलना–पछताना।
- खून का प्यासा–जानी दुश्मन।
- घी के दिए जलाना–खुशी मनाना।
- चार चाँद लगाना–प्रतिष्ठा बढ़ाना।
- तीन तेरह होना–अलग-अलग होना।
- पानी फेर देना–नाश कर देना।
- गाल बजाना–डींगे मारना।
- जान से हाथ धो बैठना–मारा जाना।
- पानी-पानी होना–बहुत लज्जित होना।
- फूला न समाना–बहुत प्रसन्न होना।
- अपना उल्लू सीधा करना–अपना मतलब निकालना।
- आँखें चुरा लेना–अनदेखा कर देना।
- अन्धे की लाठी–एकमात्र सहारा।
- आसमान पर चढ़ना–बहुत अभिमान करना।
- आँखें खुलना–होश आना।
- चोरी और सीना जोरी–दोषी होकर धमकाना।
- आग में घी डालना–क्रोध को भड़काना।
- अँगुली पर नचाना– अच्छी तरह वश में करना।
- एक आँख से देखना–समान दृष्टि से देखना।
- एक ही थैले के चट्टे-बट्टे–एक जैसे।
- ओखली में सिर देना–जान-बूझकर आपत्ति मोल लेना।
- कलेजा मुँह को आना–बहुत दुःखी होना।
- कफन बाँधकर चलना–मौत से न घबराना।
- काँटे बिछाना–बाधा डालना।
- कलेजा ठण्डा होना–सन्तोष होना।
- कमर कसना–तैयार होना।
- खून खौलना–जोश में आना।
- खाक छानना–मारे-मारे फिरना।
- गागर में सागर भरना–थोड़े शब्दों में बहुत कुछ कह देना।
- घाव पर नमक छिड़कना–दुखी को अधिक दुखी करना।
- घी के दिए जलाना–खुशी मनाना।
- घोड़े बेचकर सोना–गहरी नींद में सोना।
- चल बसना–परलोक सिधारना।
- छठी का दूध याद आना–भारी संकट में पड़ना।
- छाती पर साँप लोटना–बहुत ईर्ष्या होना।
- जमीन पर पैर न रखना–अधिक घमण्ड होना।
- झक मारना–व्यर्थ समय खोना।
- टेढ़ी खीर–कठिन काम।
- डींग मारना–अपनी झूठी प्रशंसा करना।
- डूब मरना–बहुत लज्जित होना।
- तलवे चाटना–चापलूसी करना।
- ताक में रहना–मौका ढूँढ़ते रहना।
- दंग रह जाना–आश्चर्य में पड़ जाना।
- दाल न गलना–वश न चलना।
- दाल में काला होना–संदेह होना।
- पीठ दिखाना–हारकर भागना।
- मुँह तोड़ उत्तर देना–खरा उत्तर देना।

वस्तुनिष्ठ प्रश्न

अभ्यास-1

निर्देशः *नीचे प्रत्येक शुद्ध शब्द की वर्तनी के लिए चार विकल्प दिए गए हैं। आपको सही विकल्प का चयन करना है।*

1. A. ऋषि B. ऋषी C. रिषी D. ऋसि

2. A. विषेसन B. विशेषण C. विसेशन D. विशेशन

3. A. दुशासन B. दुसाशन C. दूशाषण D. दुःशासन

4. A. संस्कृति B. संसकृति C. संष्कृति D. संस्कृती

5. A. दूनियां B. दुनियां C. दुनिया D. दूनिआ

6. A. टिपनी B. टिप्पणि C. टिप्पणी D. टिप्पनी

7. A. शाषण B. साशन C. शासन D. शाशन

8. A. किसमस B. किरसमस C. क्रिसमूस D. कृसमस

9. A. अनुग्रहित B. अनुग्रहीत C. अनुगृहीत D. अनुग्रहित

10. A. पराकम B. प्राक्रम C. पराक्रम D. प्राकर्म

11. A. नायका B. नाइका C. नाइक D. नायिका

12. A. समरिधी B. समद्धी C. समृद्धि D. समरिद्धि

13. A. युधिष्ठर B. यूधिष्ठर C. युधिष्ठिर D. युधिष्टर

14. A. वाल्मीकि B. बाल्मीकि C. बालमीकि D. बाल्मिक

15. A. परलोकिक B. प्रलौकिक C. पारलौकिक D. परलौकिक

16. A. त्रितीय B. तर्तीय C. तृतीय D. तिरतीय

17. A. व्योहार B. व्यौहार C. व्यवहार D. ब्यवहार

18. A. अहिल्या B. अहल्या C. अहिलया D. अहीलया

19. A. आदरनीय B. आदरणीय C. आदरनीया D. आदरणीया

20. A. आर्द B. आद्र C. आर्द्र D. आर्दृ

21. A. आधीन B. अधिन C. अधीन D. अधीम

22. A. आविस्कार B. आविष्कार C. आवीस्कार D. आविश्कार

23. A. आसा B. आषा C. आशा D. अशा

24. A. उज्वल B. उजज्वल C. उजज्वल D. उज्ज्वल

25. A. उन्नती B. उन्नित C. उन्नति D. उन्नती

26. A. कलस B. कलष C. कलश D. कलशा

27. A. गनीत B. गनित C. गणीत D. गणित

28. A. तलाव B. तालाव C. तलाब D. तालाब

29. A. दुष्ट B. दूष्ट C. दुस्त D. दुश्त

30. A. निरोग B. निररोग C. नीरोग D. नीरोगी

उत्तरमाला

1. A	2. B	3. D	4. A	5. C
6. C	7. C	8. C	9. C	10. C
11. D	12. C	13. C	14. A	15. C
16. C	17. C	18. B	19. B	20. C
21. C	22. B	23. C	24. D	25. C
26. C	27. D	28. D	29. A	30. C

अभ्यास-2

निर्देशः *नीचे कुछ शब्द दिए गए हैं। प्रत्येक के पर्यायवाची के चार विकल्प दिए गए हैं। इनमें से एक विकल्प सही पर्यायवाची है, उसका चयन कीजिए :*

1. अग्नि
A. अनिल B. अनल
C. गर्म D. ताप

2. अमृत
A. पीयूष B. गरल
C. सरस D. जीवनदायनी

3. आँख
A. लोचन B. आस्थि
C. वदन D. जलज

4. आकाश
A. अनन्त B. पाताल
C. वितल D. तल

5. कपड़ा
A. परिधान B. पटिका
C. पीताम्बर D. लँहगा

6. कमल
A. सरोज B. सरोवर
C. पंक D. पुष्प

7. गंगा
A. पाताल नदी B. हिमनदी
C. भागीरथ D. त्रिपथगा

8. चाँद
A. मयंक B. भानु
C. दिनकर D. रवि

9. नदी
A. सरिता B. प्रवाह
C. धारा D. जलधर

10. पर्वत
A. पत्थर B. चट्टान
C. शिखर D. मेरू

11. पवन
A. अनिल B. अनल
C. अग D. विहग

12. पति
A. साजन B. प्रिया
C. भार्या D. दारा

13. पानी
A. मही B. मेदिनी
C. अम्बु D. तरणी

14. पुत्र
A. आत्मज B. तनया
C. सुता D. आत्मजा

15. पुत्री
A. सुता B. सुत
C. आत्मज D. नन्दन

16. फूल
A. बहार B. मधु
C. माधव D. सुमन

17. वृक्ष
A. विटप B. अम्र
C. प्रसून D. रसा

18. बादल
A. अज B. व्यामोह
C. नीरद D. मधुप

19. बिजली
A. चंचला B. खटका
C. त्रास D. संत्रास

20. माता
A. धात्री B. धरणी
C. धरित्री D. श्यामा

21. घोषणा
A. आवाज B. पुकारना
C. ऐलान D. ललकारना

22. उत्कर्ष
A. आकर्षण B. विकर्षण
C. उन्नति D. निष्कर्ष

23. उदय
A. अन्त B. विकास
C. प्रगट D. व्यस्त

24. दक्ष
A. निपुण B. समर्थ
C. कर्मठ D. मेहनती

25. संवाद
A. विवाद B. झगड़ा
C. सम्बोधन D. वार्तालाप

उत्तरमाला

1. B	**2.** A	**3.** A	**4.** A	**5.** A
6. A	**7.** D	**8.** A	**9.** A	**10.** D
11. A	**12.** A	**13.** C	**14.** A	**15.** A
16. D	**17.** A	**18.** C	**19.** A	**20.** A
21. C	**22.** C	**23.** C	**24.** A	**25.** D

अभ्यास-3

निर्देशः *नीचे चार-चार शब्दों के समूह दिए गए हैं। प्रत्येक समूह में एक शब्द बेमेल है तथा शेष तीन शब्द पर्यायवाची हैं, आपको उस शब्द का चयन करना है, जो बेमेल है :*

1. A. तम B. अंधकार
C. तिमिर D. अंश

2. A. अनल B. आग
C. दहन D. तमिस्त्रा

3. A. अतुल B. अद्वितीय
C. अनुपम D. शुष्मा

4. A. अहं B. अहंकार
C. दर्प D. निराला

5. A. पता B. खोज
C. जाँच D. शोध

6. A. गरल B. पीयूष
C. सुधा D. सोम

7. A. कानन B. जंगल
C. पादप D. वन

8. A. अश्व B. गज
C. घोड़ा D. तुरंग

9. A. दानव B. मानव
C. दैत्य D. राक्षस

10. A. आँख B. चक्षु
C. नयन D. मुख

11. A. अन्तरिक्ष B. वसुन्धरा
C. आसमान D. गगन

12. A. इच्छा B. अभिलाषा
C. कामना D. प्रयोजन

13. A. कपड़ा B. चीर
C. वसन D. पोशाक

14. A. अब्ज B. कमल
C. राजीव D. आम्र

15. A. कोयल B. पिक
C. काग D. वनप्रिय

16. A. गंगा B. देवनदी
C. गोदावरी D. भागीरथी

17. A. गणेश B. एकदन्त
C. देवराज D. गणपति

18. A. घर B. निलय
C. निकेतन D. झोपड़ी

19. A. चाँद B. हिमांशु
C. विनायक D. सुधांशु

20. A. नदी B. तरणी
C. तटिनी D. सरिता

21. A. पक्षी B. चिड़िया
C. सुमन D. विहग

22. A. पवन B. अचला
C. वात D. वायु

23. A. समीर B. पृथ्वी
C. भू D. भूमि

24. A. पानी B. समीर
C. अम्बु D. जल

25. A. पुत्र B. तनया
C. तनय D. सुत

26. A. पुत्र B. तनया
C. सुता D. कन्या

27. A. गृहिणी B. आदमी
C. पुरुष D. नर

28. A. मधु B. फूल
C. पुष्प D. सुमन

29. A. माधव B. तरु
C. पेड़ D. वृक्ष

30. A. माता B. अम्बु
C. अम्मा D. जननी

उत्तरमाला

1. D	**2.** D	**3.** D	**4.** D	**5.** A
6. A	**7.** C	**8.** B	**9.** B	**10.** D
11. B	**12.** D	**13.** D	**14.** D	**15.** C
16. C	**17.** C	**18.** D	**19.** C	**20.** B
21. C	**22.** B	**23.** A	**24.** B	**25.** B
26. A	**27.** A	**28.** A	**29.** A	**30.** B

अभ्यास-4

निर्देशः ***गहरे काले शब्द*** *के विलोम शब्द का चयन कीजिएः*

1. उसे हर काम में **सफ़लता** मिल रही है।
A. असफलता B. सफल
C. कुशलता D. निपुणता

2. कभी किसी की **निन्दा** नहीं करनी चाहिए।
A. गुणगान B. स्तुति
C. प्रशंसा D. यशोगान

3. आलस्य व्यक्ति का सबसे बड़ा **दुश्मन** है।
A. शत्रु B. घातक
C. मित्र D. सहायक

4. वे बुढ़ापे से **दुखी** हैं।
A. अप्रसन्न B. सुखी
C. खुश D. नाराज

5. यहाँ उसकी **चतुराई** नहीं चली।
A. चालाकी B. बहादुरी
C. निपुणता D. मूर्खता

6. शहद की **मिठास** कम नहीं होती।
A. मीठा B. तीखा
C. कड़ुवा D. खहा

7. साहसी के **साहस** को देखकर मैं चकित रह गया।
A. हिम्मत B. बहादुरी
C. निडर D. भय

8. फिल्मोत्सव में सर्वश्रेष्ठ **अभिनेता** को पुरस्कार प्रदान किया गया।
A. हीरोइन B. नेत्री
C. मीनाक्षी D. अभिनेत्री

9. नाटक में नायक और **नायिका** की भूमिका महत्वपूर्ण होती हैः
A. हीरो B. नायक
C. नेत्र D. नेता

10. कवि-सम्मेलन में एक कवि और एक **कवयित्री** को आमंत्रित किया गया था।
A. लेखक B. सम्पादक
C. नेता D. कवि

11. विद्यालय के वार्षिकोत्सव के लिए नेता और एक **नेत्री** को आमंत्रित किया गया।
A. अभिनेता B. विद्वान्
C. विदुषी D. नेता

12. मोहन बहुत **चतुर** है।
A. निपुण B. तेज
C. सुस्त D. मूर्ख

13. सोहन अब पूर्ण **स्वस्थ** है।
A. प्रसन्न B. खुश
C. अंस्वस्थ D. अप्रसन्न

14. पक्षी **आकाश** में उड़ते हैं :
A. गगन B. नम
C. धरती D. पाताल

15. वह विद्यालय में देर से आया और **अनुपस्थित** हो गया।
A. पूर्व B. उपस्थित
C. प्रवेश D. समयपूर्व

16. **बालक** चाँद की ओर देख रहा है।
A. बालिका B. लड़का
C. बच्चा D. बच्ची

17. मैं उसके विचार से बिल्कुल **सहमत** नहीं हूँ।
A. समर्थन B. सहमति
C. असहमत D. प्रशंसक

18. उसकी हालत **अधिक** खराब है।
A. बहुत B. कम
C. ठीक D. कुशल

19. **धर्म** की सर्वत्र विजय **होती** हैः
A. अधर्म **B.** ज्ञान
C. भक्ति D. ईमानदारी

20. अच्छे चरित्र के बिना जीवन **निरर्थक** हैः
A. व्यर्थ B. अर्थपूर्ण
C. सार्थक D. कुशल

21. **ईमानदारी** बड़ी दुर्लभ वस्तु है:

A. सच्चाई B. भलाई
C. बेइमानी D. परोपकारी

22. एवरेस्ट संसार का सबसे **ऊँचा** पर्वत है:

A. नीचा B. वितल
C. पाताल D. मध्यम

23. वह विश्वास के **योग्य** नहीं है:

A. काबिल B. विश्वासी
C. अयोग्य D. बेकार

24. क्या वह इतना **मूर्ख** है?

A. चालाक B. विद्वान्
C. बुद्धिमान D. धूर्त

25. कितना सुहावना **दृश्य** है!

A. अदृश्य B. दर्शनीय
C. सुन्दर D. व्यर्थ

उत्तरमाला

1. A	**2.** C	**3.** C	**4.** B	**5.** D
6. C	**7.** D	**8.** D	**9.** B	**10.** D
11. D	**12.** D	**13.** C	**14.** D	**15.** B
16. A	**17.** C	**18.** B	**19.** A	**20.** C
21. C	**22.** A	**23.** C	**24.** C	**25.** A

अभ्यास-5

निर्देशः नीचे प्रत्येक **काले गहरे शब्द** के चार विलोम दिए गए हैं। इनमें सही विलोम का चयन कीजिए :

1. अग्नि

A. आग B. अनल
C. दहन D. जल

2. अग्रज

A. अनुज B. भ्राता
C. भाई D. अम्बा

3. अच्छा

A. बुरा B. खराब
C. गंदा D. भ्रष्ट

4. अंत

A. प्रारम्भ B. समाप्त
C. शेष D. अल्प

5. अचल

A. विचल B. वितल
C. सजल D. चल

6. अति

A. अधिक B. बहुत
C. अल्प D. कम

7. अत्यधिक

A. अल्प B. अधिक
C. स्वल्प D. न्यूनतम

8. अंधकार

A. अंधेरा B. प्रकाश
C. रात्रि D. दिन

9. अतिवृष्टि

A. अनावृष्टि B. वृष्टि
C. वर्षा D. वर्षण

10. अनाथ

A. नाथ B. स्वामी
C. मासिक D. सनाथ

11. अनुकूल

A. मनोकूल B. प्रतिकूल
C. अनुकरण D. मनस्वी

12. अनुराग

A. राग B. विराग
C. विग्रह D. स्नेह

13. अन्त

A. श्री गणेश B. आदि
C. शुरुआत D. समाप्त

14. अपना

A. अपनत्व B. पराया
C. मित्र D. शत्रु

15. अपमान

A. मान B. सम्मान
C. वर्तमान D. स्वाभिमान

16. अपेक्षा

A. इच्छा B. स्वेच्छा
C. प्रविच्छा D. उपेक्षा

17. अमर

A. मर्त्य B. मृत्यु
C. सुधा D. गरल

18. अल्पायु
A. चिरायु B. उमरदराज
C. नश्वर D. सनातन

19. अस्त
A. उदय B. विकास
C. निर्माण D. सृष्टि

20. आकर्षण
A. प्रतिकर्षण B. विकर्षण
C. सम्मोहन D. विरत

21. आकाश
A. गगन B. नभ
C. वसुन्धरा D. पाताल

22. आगे
A. पीछे B. पूर्व
C. पृष्ट D. पृष्ठ

23. आजाद
A. स्वतंत्र B. स्वतंत्रतता
C. परतंत्र D. गुलाम

24. आदान
A. आयात B. निर्यात
C. प्रदान D. निदान

25. आधुनिक
A. अर्वाचीन B. नूतन
C. प्राचीन D. वर्तमान

उत्तरमाला

1. D	**2.** A	**3.** A	**4.** A	**5.** D
6. D	**7.** C	**8.** B	**9.** A	**10.** D
11. B	**12.** B	**13.** A	**14.** B	**15.** B
16. D	**17.** A	**18.** A	**19.** A	**20.** B
21. D	**22.** A	**23.** D	**24.** C	**25.** C

अभ्यास-6

निर्देशः *नीचे कुछ शब्द दिए गए हैं प्रत्येक शब्द के चार वैकल्पिक अर्थ दिए गए हैं। सही अर्थ का चयन कीजिए :*

1. सुरक्षित
A. कुशल B. घटना
C. दुर्घटना D. बचाव

2. प्रतिभाशाली
A. सज्जन B. कुशाग्र
C. विद्वान् D. वैभवशाली

3. आत्मसमर्पण
A. अपने आप को सौंपना B. समर्पण
C. अर्पण D. त्यागज

4. सिद्धहस्त
A. निपुण B. कर्मठ
C. मेहनती D. परिश्रमी

5. सुशोभित
A. मजेदार B. सुस्वागतम्
C. अच्छा D. शोभा पाना

6. स्वादिष्ट
A. मजेदार B. बेकार
C. मीठा D. तीखा

7. स्वावलम्बी
A. निर्भर B. परालंबी
C. आत्मनिर्भर D. अतिथि

8. उपकरण
A. साधन B. युक्ति
C. यंत्र D. मशीन

9. कीमत
A. क्रय B. विक्रय
C. मूल्य D. बिक्री

10. संगठन
A. एकता B. अनेकता
C. समूह D. संस्था

11. विपत्ति
A. दुख B. विपदा
C. मुसीबत D. सुख

12. तृण
A. तिनका B. धूल
C. धूप D. लकड़ी

13. आश्चर्य
A. निरीक्षण B. दृष्टिगोचर
C. हैरानी D. थकावट

14. हार्दिक
A. हृदय से B. शरीर से
C. मन से D. मस्तिष्क से

15. नियति

A. भाग्य B. किनारा
C. समय D. पवित्र

16. सुगन्धित

A. दुर्गन्ध B. खुशबू वाला
C. फूल D. कमल

17. उत्साह

A. होश B. हवास
C. जोश D. हिम्मत

18. सहयोग

A. मिलन सार B. मेहनती
C. परोपकारी D. आपसी सहायता

19. मुसीबत

A. विपत्ति B. सुशोभित
C. सहायता D. मदद

20. निरक्षर

A. साक्षर B. दर्शनीय
C. पठनीय D. अनपढ़

21. उपवन

A. वन B. तीर
C. जंगल D. बाग

22. मेघ

A. बादल B. पंकज
C. राजीव D. मेघनाद

23. आधुनिक

A. प्राचीन B. पुरातन
C. भूतकाल D. आज का

24. तीर

A. वाण B. धनुष
C. किनारा D. नदी

25. परीक्षण

A. जाँच B. पड़ताल
C. परीक्षा D. इम्तहान

26. अभिवादन

A. नमस्ते B. प्रणाम
C. बधाई D. शुभकामना

27. सर्वत्र

A. नश्वर B. सजीव
C. ईश्वर D. सभी जगह

28. हलवाहा

A. चरवाहा B. किसान
C. मजदूर D. हल चलाने वाला

29. शिखर

A. पर्वत B. पहाड़
C. टीला D. चोटी

30. भयानक

A. डरावना B. भयभीत
C. डरना D. खूँखार

उत्तरमाला

1. D	**2.** B	**3.** A	**4.** A	**5.** D
6. A	**7.** C	**8.** C	**9.** C	**10.** A
11. C	**12.** A	**13.** C	**14.** A	**15.** A
16. B	**17.** C	**18.** D	**19.** A	**20.** D
21. D	**22.** A	**23.** D	**24.** A	**25.** A
26. B	**27.** D	**28.** D	**29.** D	**30.** A

अभ्यास-7

निर्देशः *नीचे कुछ शब्द दिए जा रहे हैं। प्रत्येक शब्द के* **उपसर्ग** *के सन्दर्भ में चार विकल्प दिए गए हैं। आपको सही विकल्प का चयन करना है :*

1. अलबत्ता

A. अ B. अल
C. लंब D. त्ता

2. अलगरज

A. अल B. लग
C. गर D. रज

3. कमसिन

A. क B. कम
C. सि D. सिन

4. अनमोल

A. अ B. अन
C. मो D. मोल

5. अनजान

A. अ B. अन
C. जा D. जान

6. अनपढ़

A. अ B. पढ़
C. प D. अन

7. अधखिला
A. अ B. अध
C. ला D. खिला

8. अधजला
A. अ B. ज
C. अध D. ला

9. अधपका
A. अ B. अध
C. पका D. का

10. अघखिला
A. अ B. अघ
C. खिला D. ला

11. उन्नीस
A. उन B. उन्
C. नीस D. स

12. उनसठ
A. उ B. उन
C. सठ D. ठ

13. दुकाल
A. द B. दुक
C. दु D. काल

14. दुबला
A. दब B. दुब
C. ला D. दु

15. निकम्मा
A. नि B. निक
C. कम्मा D. मा

16. निर्लज्ज
A. निर B. निल
C. नि D. लज्ज

17. बिनब्याहा
A. बि B. बिन
C. ब्याहा D. हा

18. भरपेट
A. भर B. पेट
C. पे D. ट

19. भरपाई
A. भ B. र
C. पा D. भर

20. कुपात्र
A. कु B. कुप
C. पा D. पात्र

21. सुजान
A. सु B. सुज
C. सुजा D. जान

22. गैर कानूनी
A. गै B. गैर
C. कानु D. नुनी

23. गैरसरकारी
A. गैर B. सर
C. का D. कारी

24. अपमान
A. अ B. अप
C. मा D. मान

25. अनुशासन
A. अ B. शासन
C. सन D. अनु

26. अविनीत
A. अवि B. अ
C. नी D. नीत

27. अभिमान
A. अभि B. अ
C. मा D. मान

28. अभियान
A. अ B. मान
C. यान D. अभि

29. अध्ययन
A. अध् B. अधि
C. यन D. न

30. निश्चल
A. नि B. निर
C. निस D. चल

उत्तरमाला

1. B	**2.** A	**3.** B	**4.** B	**5.** B
6. D	**7.** B	**8.** C	**9.** B	**10.** B
11. A	**12.** B	**13.** C	**14.** D	**15.** B
16. A	**17.** B	**18.** A	**19.** D	**20.** A

21. A **22.** B **23.** A **24.** B **25.** D
26. B **27.** A **28.** D **29.** B **30.** A

अभ्यास-8

निर्देशः *निम्नलिखित शब्दों में प्रयुक्त प्रत्यय सम्बन्धी चार विकल्प दिए गए हैं, सही विकल्प का चयन कीजिए :*

1. भलाई
A. ई B. लाई
C. आई D. भला

2. चतुराई
A. चतु B. रा
C. ई D. आई

3. भूखा
A. भू B. भूख
C. खा D. आ

4. भिड़न्त
A. भिड् B. भि
C. न्त D. अन्त

5. प्यासा
A. आस B. सा
C. आसा D. सा

6. बिकाऊ
A. बिक B. काऊ
C. आऊ D. ऊ

7. तैराक
A. तै B. तैर
C. राक D. आक

8. सन्नाटा
A. सन् B. सन्ना
C. नाटा D. आटा

9. लोहार
A. लोह B. आरा
C. आरी D. आर

10. मिलान
A. आना B. आने
C. आनी D. आन

11. चढ़ाव
A. चढ़ B. चढ़ा
C. आव D. व

12. लगाव
A. लग B. अव
C. आव D. गाव

13. लिखावट
A. लिख B. लिखा
C. वट D. आवट

14. मिलावट
A. मिल B. वट
C. आवट D. ट

15. मिठास
A. मिठ B. ठास
C. आस D. स

16. चिकनाहट
A. चिक B. नाह्ट
C. हट D. आहट

17. सड़ियल
A. सड़ B. यल
C. ड़ियल D. इयल

18. मरियल
A. मर B. यल
C. मरि D. इयल

19. गड़रिया
A. गड़ B. इया
C. रिया D. या

20. सजीला
A. ईला B. इला
C. ला D. स

21. लुटेरा
A. लुट B. एरा
C. ऐरा D. रा

22. लठैत
A. ए B. ऐ
C. ऐत D. त

23. भगोड़ा
A. ओ B. ओड़ा
C. ड़ा D. भगो

24. खपत
A. ख B. प
C. त D. पत

25. जीवट

A. व B. अट

C. जीव D. जी

उत्तरमाला

1. C	**2.** D	**3.** D	**4.** D	**5.** D
6. C	**7.** D	**8.** D	**9.** D	**10.** D
11. C	**12.** C	**13.** D	**14.** C	**15.** C
16. D	**17.** D	**18.** D	**19.** B	**20.** A
21. B	**22.** C	**23.** B	**24.** C	**25.** B

अभ्यास-9

निर्देशः *नीचे कुछ मुहावरे दिए गए हैं। प्रत्येक के अर्थ के लिए चार विकल्प दिए गए हैं। आपको सही विकल्प का चयन करना है :*

1. अक्ल पर पत्थर पड़ना

A. बुद्धि काम न करना B. दुविधा होना

C. संकट में होना D. परेशान होना

2. अपना उल्लू सीधा करना

A. अवसर देखना B. काम निकालना

C. मतलब साधना D. मूर्ख बनाना

3. अपने मुँह मियाँ-मिट्ठू बनना

A. मिठाई खाना

B. प्रशंसा करना

C. निंदा करना

D. अपनी प्रशंसा स्वयं करना

4. अपने पाँव पर आप कुल्हाड़ी मारना

A. हानि पहुँचाना B. खेद होना

C. अपना पैर काटना D. अपनी हानि स्वयं करना

5. आँखें चुरा लेना

A. भाग जाना B. छिप जाना

C. अनदेखा करना D. मिल जाना

6. अक्ल का दुश्मन

A. मित्र होना B. शत्रु होना

C. महामूर्ख D. महाविद्वान्

7. अंधे की लाठी

A. एक मात्र सहारा B. मित्र होना

C. शत्रु होना D. दुख पहुँचाना

8. आकाश-पाताल एक करना

A. भाग-दौड़ करना B. परेशान होना

C. थक जाना D. कठिन परिश्रम करना

9. घड़ों पानी पड़ना

A. लज्जित होना B. तुच्छ समझना

C. लाभ होना D. थकावट

10. अगर-मगर करना

A. नुकसान करना B. बहाने बनाना

C. बदनाम करना D. कपट करना

11. मुँह की खाना

A. गिर जाना B. हार जाना

C. भाग जाना D. व्यर्थ होना

12. आस्तीन का साँप होना

A. शत्रु B. मित्र

C. कपटी मित्र D. दयालु

13. एक आँख से देखना

A. बुरा व्यवहार B. समान व्यवहार

C. कपट करना D. लज्जित होना

14. बाल-बाँका न होना

A. घायल होना B. साफ बच जाना

C. क्रोधित होना D. स्वस्थ होना

15. दाँतों तले उँगली दबाना

A. उँगली काटना B. चिंतित हो जाना

C. चकित रह जाना D. प्रसन्न हो जाना

16. जान के लाले पड़ना

A. मरने का खतरा होना B. भाग जाना

C. हार जाना D. मुश्किल में पड़ना

17. बोली मारना

A. ताना देना B. सताना

C. मजाक करना D. याद दिलाना

18. अंधों में काना राजा

A. मूर्खों में अल्पज्ञ को विद्वान् माना जाना

B. सबको मूर्ख समझना

C. अत्यधिक महत्त्वपूर्ण

D. काना राजा

19. अक्ल के घोड़े दौड़ाना

A. बुद्धि लड़ाना

B. कल्पना करना

C. तरह-तरह के उपाय सोचना

D. ज्ञान-प्राप्त करना

20. पानी उतर जाना
A. शर्म करना B. लज्जित न होना
C. भाग जाना D. इज्जत करना

21. तीन-पाँच करना
A. तितर-बितर करना
B. वचन देकर फिर जाना
C. घुमा-फिरा कर बातें करना
D. परेशान करना

22. हथियार डाल देना
A. हार जाना B. जीत जाना
C. धोखा देना D. विजय होना

23. आँख खुलना
A. होश में आना B. अत्यन्त प्यार होना
C. उल्टा काम करना D. क्रोध करना

24. कमर सीधी करना
A. थक जाना B. थकावट दूर करना
C. काम करना D. परिश्रम करना

25. पगड़ी रखना
A. चैन की सांस लेना
B. अपमान करना
C. दया की भीख माँगना
D. अपमान होना

26. लोहा मानना
A. संघर्ष करना
B. विजय होना
C. श्रेष्ठता स्वीकार करना
D. खुशामद करना

27. काठ मार जाना
A. दुःखी होना B. चुप होना
C. सफल होना D. मर जाना

28. चाँद पर थूकना
A. अपमान करना
B. बढ़कर बातें करना
C. महान पुरुष पर लांछन लगाना
D. महत्त्वाकांक्षी होना

29. उगल देना
A. अपराध स्वीकार कर लेना
B. सच बोलना
C. उल्टी करना
D. अनपच होना

30. हाथ मलना
A. पश्चाताप करना B. सर्दी मिटाना
C. दुख करना D. तैयार होना

उत्तरमाला

1. A	**2.** C	**3.** D	**4.** D	**5.** C
6. C	**7.** A	**8.** D	**9.** A	**10.** B
11. B	**12.** C	**13.** B	**14.** B	**15.** C
16. D	**17.** A	**18.** A	**19.** A	**20.** B
21. C	**22.** A	**23.** A	**24.** B	**25.** C
26. C	**27.** B	**28.** C	**29.** A	**30.** A

अभ्यास-10

निर्देशः *नीचे कुछ वाक्य खण्ड दिए गए हैं, पूरे वाक्य खण्ड के लिए एक शब्द का चयन कीजिए।*

1. जिसका आदि न हो
A. अनंत B. अमर
C. शाश्वत D. अनादि

2. जो कुछ न जानता हो
A. मूर्ख B. महामूर्ख
C. ज्ञानी D. अज्ञ

3. जो अनुकरण करने योग्य हो
A. अनुकरणीय B. अद्वितीय
C. आदरणीय D. अगम

4. जिसका अंत न हो
A. अनंत B. अनादि
C. आदि D. परलोक

5. जो कभी न मरे
A. मर्त्य B. मुर्त्त
C. अर्मुत्त D. अमर

6. जिसके समान दूसरा न हो
A. अनुकूल B. प्रतिकूल
C. कृतज्ञ D. अद्वितीय

7. जो कम बोलता हो
A. मृदुभाषी B. वाचाल
C. अल्पभाषी D. अल्पज्ञ

8. जिसका इलाज न हो

A. मरणशील B. अमरत्व

C. बिमारी D. लाइलाज

9. जिस का विश्वास न किया जा सके

A. विश्वसनीय B. अविश्वसनीय

C. विश्वासी D. धूर्त्त

10. जिसका कोई नाथ न हो

A. सनाथ B. स्वामी

C. नाथ D. अनाथ

11. कम जानने वाला

A. अल्पज्ञ B. अज्ञ

C. विद् D. विद्वान

12. जहाँ जाना संभव न हो

A. दुर्गम B. अगम

C. तल D. वितल

13. कम खाने वाला

A. बहुभोजी B. पेटु

C. कंजूस D. अल्पाहारी

14. जो बात पहले कभी न हुई हो

A. भूतपूर्व B. अभूतपूर्व

C. प्राचीन D. अर्वाचीन

15. जिस स्त्री के सन्तान न हों

A. बाँझ B. कुलटा

C. पतिता D. विधवा

16. जो कहा न जा सके

A. अकथनीय B. अकथ्य

C. करणीय D. सम्भव

17. एहसान न मानने वाला

A. कृतज्ञ B. कृतघ्न

C. आस्तिक D. विश्वासी

18. जिसने देश के साथ विश्वासघात किया हो

A. विश्वासघाती B. द्रोही

C. आतंकवादी D. देश द्रोही

19. जिसने राष्ट्र के हित में अपना जीवन बलिदान कर दिया हो

A. देशभक्त B. शहीद

C. राष्ट्रभूत D. भारतपुत्र

20. वह जमीन जिसमें कुछ भी पैदा न हो

A. ऊसर B. बंजर

C. उर्वर D. पथरीला

21. वह वस्तु जिसकी चाह हो

A. श्रेष्ठ B. आवश्यक

C. इच्छित D. अभीष्ट

22. दूसरों के पीछे चलने वाला

A. अनुयायी B. अनुज

C. अनुचर D. अनुकरणीय

23. जो पहले न पढ़ा हो

A. पठित B. अपठित

C. पठनीय D. अपठनीय

24. जिसके आर-पार दिखाई देता हो

A. अपारदर्शी B. गम्य

C. अगम्य D. पारदर्शी

25. आज्ञा पालन करने वाला

A. शिष्य B. शिष्या

C. अनुचर D. आज्ञाकारी

26. काम से जी चुराने वाला

A. कामचोर B. आलसी

C. कर्मठ D. परिश्रमी

27. प्रतिदिन होने वाला

A. दैनिक B. शाश्वत

C. सनातन D. अमर

28. जिसका कोई अर्थ न हो

A. सार्थक B. निरर्थक

C. आर्थिक D. अनार्थिक

29. उपकार मानने वाला

A. कृतज्ञ B. कृतघ्न

C. विश्वासी D. अनुयायी

30. हाथ से लिखा हुआ

A. पठनीय B. अपठनीय

C. स्पष्ट D. हस्तलिखित

उत्तरमाला

1. D	**2.** D	**3.** A	**4.** A	**5.** D
6. D	**7.** C	**8.** D	**9.** B	**10.** D
11. A	**12.** A	**13.** D	**14.** B	**15.** A
16. A	**17.** B	**18.** D	**19.** B	**20.** A
21. C	**22.** C	**23.** B	**24.** D	**25.** D
26. A	**27.** A	**28.** B	**29.** A	**30.** D

अभ्यास-11

निर्देशः *नीचे कुछ संज्ञा शब्द दिए जा रहे हैं। प्रत्येक के संज्ञा-भेद के लिए चार विकल्प दिए गये है। सही विकल्प का चयन कीजिए :*

1. तुलसीदास
A. जातिवाचक B. भाववाचक
C. व्यक्तिवाचक D. समूहवाचक

2. यमुना
A. व्यक्तिवाचक B. जातिवाचक
C. समूहवाचक D. भाववाचक

3. बच्चा
A. जातिवाचक B. समूहवाचक
C. भाववाचक D. व्यक्तिवाचक

4. मानवता
A. भाववाचक B. जातिवाचक
C. द्रव्यवाचक D. समूहवाचक

5. हिमालय
A. व्यक्तिवाचक B. जातिवाचक
C. भाववाचक D. समूहवाचक

6. भारत
A. जातिवाचक B. भाववाचक
C. व्यक्तिवाचक D. समूहवाचक

7. एशिया
A. व्यक्तिवाचक B. भाववाचक
C. द्रव्यवाचक D. समूहवाचक

8. महाराष्ट्र
A. जातिवाचक B. व्यक्तिवाचक
C. समूहवाचक D. द्रव्यवाचक

9. सूर सागर
A. व्यक्तिवाचक B. भाववाचक
C. द्रव्यवाचक D. समूहवाचक

10. सोमवार
A. जातिवाचक B. व्यक्तिवाचक
C. द्रव्यवाचक D. समूहवाचक

11. खटमल
A. जातिवाचक B. व्यक्तिवाचक
C. द्रव्यवाचक D. समूहवाचक

12. मैना
A. जातिवाचक B. व्यक्तिवाचक
C. द्रव्यवाचक D. समूहवाचक

13. चाँदी
A. द्रव्यवाचक B. समूहवाचक
C. भाववाचक D. व्यक्तिवाचक

14. अच्छाई
A. भाववाचक B. समूहवाचक
C. जातिवाचक D. व्यक्तिवाचक

15. पीतल
A. द्रव्यवाचक B. भाववाचक
C. व्यक्तिवाचक D. जातिवाचक

16. वीरता
A. भाववाचक B. जातिवाचक
C. द्रव्यवाचक D. समूहवाचक

17. रूस
A. जातिवाचक B. व्यक्तिवाचक
C. भाववाचक D. द्रव्यवाचक

18. लम्बाई
A. भाववाचक B. समूहवाचक
C. द्रव्यवाचक D. व्यक्तिवाचक

19. दल
A. जातिवाचक B. व्यक्तिवाचक
C. समूहवाचक D. द्रव्यवाचक

20. मार्च
A. समूहवाचक B. व्यक्तिवाचक
C. द्रव्यवाचक D. जातिवाचक

21. झुण्ड
A. समूहवाचक B. जातिवाचक
C. व्यक्तिवाचक D. द्रव्यवाचक

22. टोली
A. जातिवाचक B. व्यक्तिवाचक
C. समूहवाचक D. द्रव्यवाचक

23. सुभाष चौक
A. जातिवाचक B. समूहवाचक
C. व्यक्तिवाचक D. भाववाचक

24. संघ
A. जातिवाचक B. द्रव्यवाचक
C. समूहवाचक D. भाववाचक

25. गिरोह
A. समूहवाचक B. द्रव्यवाचक
C. जातिवाचक D. भाववाचक

उत्तरमाला

1. C	**2.** A	**3.** A	**4.** A	**5.** A
6. C	**7.** A	**8.** B	**9.** A	**10.** B
11. A	**12.** A	**13.** A	**14.** A	**15.** A
16. A	**17.** B	**18.** A	**19.** C	**20.** B
21. A	**22.** C	**23.** C	**24.** C	**25.** A

अभ्यास-12

निर्देशः *नीचे दिए गए वाक्य में रिक्त स्थान है। प्रत्येक वाक्य के नीचे कारक चिह्न दिए गए हैं। रिक्त स्थान की पूर्ति के लिए उपयुक्त कारक चिह्न का चयन कीजिए :*

1. निम्नलिखित शब्दों........अर्थ बताइए
A. का B. के
C. से D. पर

2. सरकार मुझे नौकरी........मत निकालिए
A. पर B. में
C. से D. को

3. इस कथन........पुष्टि कीजिए
A. को B. से
C. की D. ने

4. छात्र-छात्राएँ राष्ट्र........सम्पत्ति और उसके भावी कर्णधार होते हैं
A. के B. की
C. को D. में

5. प्रत्येक प्रश्न........चार सम्भावित उत्तर दिए गए हैं
A. के लिए B. में
C. के D. से

6. माता बच्चे........पढ़ाती है
A. को B. के
C. की D. से

7. गुरुजी........सबसे छोटे लड़के को एक नारंगी दी
A. ने B. को
C. से D. के लिए

8. मोहन सोहन से मिलने........गया है
A. से B. के
C. को D. के लिए

9. उसने कलम........लिखा
A. के B. में
C. पर D. से

10. मैं ड्राइवर........गाड़ी चलवाता हूँ
A. के B. पर
C. में D. से

11. शिक्षक छात्रों........पुस्तक पढ़वाते हैं
A. के लिए B. मैं
C. पर D. से

12. मैंने दाढ़ी........उसे मुसलमान समझ लिया
A. से B. के
C. को D. के लिए

13. श्याम अपने भाई हरि........आम लाया है
A. के B. के लिए
C. का D. पर

14. मोहन घर........आता है
A. में B. पर
C. से D. का

15. उसे पाँच दिनों........मूर्च्छा आया करती है
A. पर B. से
C. के D. को

16. मेधावी छात्र परीक्षा........चोरी नहीं करते
A. में B. पर
C. से D. के लिए

17. अच्छे आदमी........पहचान क्या है?
A. के B. का
C. की D. के लिए

18. परिश्रम........सफलता निश्चित है
A. से B. के
C. को D. के लिए

19. शूर्पणखा........नाक और कान काटे गए
A. का B. की
C. के D. से

20. युद ने राधा........तीन संतरे दिए
A. से B. के
C. के लिए D. को

उत्तरमाला

1. A	**2.** C	**3.** C	**4.** B	**5.** C
6. A	**7.** A	**8.** D	**9.** D	**10.** D
11. D	**12.** A	**13.** B	**14.** C	**15.** B
16. D	**17.** C	**18.** A	**19.** B	**20.** D

गद्यांश (अपठित-बोध)

गद्यांश 1

यदि हम निरन्तर प्रयत्न करेंगे तो निश्चय ही अपने सभी लक्ष्यों को प्राप्त कर लेंगे, किन्तु प्रायः देखा जाता है कि अधिक आशावादी लोग थोड़ा सा प्रयत्न करके अधिक फल की कामना करने लगते हैं और मनोवांछित फल प्राप्त न होने पर निराश हो जाते हैं। अतः जीवन में सफलता प्राप्त करने के लिए परिस्थितियों के समक्ष घुटने न टेकें, बल्कि दृढ़ता से उनका मुकाबला करें। याद रखें, जितना कठोर हमारा परिश्रम होगा उसका फल भी उतना ही मीठा होगा।

उपर्युक्त गद्यांश को ध्यानपूर्वक पढ़ें और निम्न प्रश्नों के उत्तर के लिए सही विकल्प को चुनें:

1. फल न मिलने पर कौन निराश हो जाते हैं?

A. आशावादी लोग B. कम आशावादी लोग
C. अधिक आशावादी लोग D. निराशावादी लोग

2. लक्ष्य प्राप्ति के लिए क्या किया जाना चाहिए?

A. फल की कामना
B. हिम्मत से मुकाबला
C. निरन्तर प्रयत्न
D. परिस्थितियों से मुकाबला

3. आशावादी शब्द का विलोम शब्द है:

A. निराश B. निराशावादी
B. दुखी D. अप्रसन्न

4. मनोवांछित शब्द का क्या अर्थ है?

A. इच्छित B. परीक्षित
C. लाभदायक D. मन को खुश करने वाले

5. परिश्रम शब्द का अर्थ है:

A. साहस B. हिम्मत
C. काम D. कठिन मेहनत

गद्यांश 2

पन्द्रह अगस्त 1947 को हमारा देश स्वतंत्र हुआ। स्वतन्त्रता प्राप्ति के बाद विश्व के दूसरे देशों के साथ भारत के राजनयिक एवं सांस्कृतिक सम्बन्ध जुड़े। पर्यटकों के साथ-साथ राजनीतिज्ञों और साहित्यकारों को भी विदेश यात्रा के पर्याप्त अवसर मिले। विभिन्न प्रकार की छात्रवृत्तियों के माध्यम से बहुत से लोग विदेशों में पढ़ने गए। बहुत से लोगों ने विदेशों में उपलब्ध आजीविका के अवसरों का लाभ उठाया। इन सबके परिणामस्वरूप प्रचुर मात्रा में यात्रावृत्तांत लिखे गए। विदेश-विषयक यात्रावृतांत्तों में रूस और स्वदेश-विषयक यात्रावृतांत्तों में लेखकों की दृष्टि कश्मीर से कन्याकुमारी तक व्याप्त हुई।

उपर्युक्त गद्यांश को ध्यानपूर्वक पढ़ें और निम्नलिखित प्रश्नों के उत्तर के लिए सही विकल्प को चुनें:

1. भारत कब स्वतंत्र हुआ?

A. 15 अगस्त 1947
B. 15 अगस्त 1946
C. 15 अगस्त 1948
D. 15 अगस्त 1949

2. स्वतंत्र भारत के अन्य देशों के साथ किस प्रकार के संबंध जुड़े?

A. राजनीतिक
B. राजनयिक
C. धार्मिक
D. राजनयिक एवं सांस्कृतिक

3. आजीविका का क्या अर्थ है?

A. उपार्जन B. वेतन
C. मेहनत D. रोजगार

4. यात्रा-वृत्तांत का क्या अर्थ है?

A. भ्रमण B. पर्यटन
C. सफरनामा D. विदेशभ्रमण

5. स्वतंत्र का विलोम शब्द है:

A. परतंत्र B. आजाद
C. गुलामी D. मुक्ति

गद्यांश 3

युवा वर्ग का मस्तिष्क नई-नई बातों की ओर ज्यादा तेज दौड़ता है। उसमें अन्य वर्ग के व्यक्तियों से अधिक आवेश और शक्ति होती है। इस अवस्था में यदि सही शिक्षा और

उचित मार्ग-दर्शन न मिले तो यही शक्ति प्रेरणा और निर्माण के स्थान पर विनाश की ओर ले जाती है। बिगड़ने और बनने की यही आयु होती है। दुर्भाग्य से हमारे देश में शिक्षा पद्धति केवल उपाधि बाँटने का काम ही करती है। एक सम्पूर्ण व्यक्तित्वपूर्ण मनुष्य बनाना आज की शिक्षा पद्धति के लिए मुश्किल है।

उपर्युक्त गद्यांश को ध्यानपूर्वक पढ़ें और निम्नलिखित प्रश्नों के उत्तर के लिए सही विकल्प को चुनें।

1. निर्माण का विलोम शब्द क्या हैं?

A. रचना B. बनावट
C. विनाश D. सृजन

2. मार्ग-दर्शन का क्या अर्थ है?

A. उपाधि B. रास्ता
C. उद्देश्य D. रास्ता दिखलाना

3. शक्ति विनाश की ओर कब अग्रसर होती है?

A. अधिक आवेश और शक्ति के अभाव में
B. सही शिक्षा और उचित मार्ग दर्शन के अभाव में
C. दुर्भाग्यपूर्ण शिक्षा पद्धति के कारण
D. इनमें से कोई नहीं

4. हमारे देश की शिक्षा पद्धति क्या कार्य करती है?

A. मार्ग-दर्शन B. शक्ति प्रेरणा
C. उपाधि देना D. उपर्युक्त सभी

5. दुर्भाग्य का विपरीत शब्द है:

A. भाग्य B. सौभाग्य
C. भाग्यशाली D. भाग्यवान

गद्यांश 4

भिखारी की भाँति गिड़गिड़ाना प्रेम की भाषा नहीं है। यहाँ तक कि मुक्ति के लिए भगवान् की उपासना करना भी अधम उपासना में गिना जाता है। प्रेम कोई पुरस्कार नहीं चाहता। प्रेम सर्वथा प्रेम के लिए ही होता है। भक्त इसलिए प्रेम करता है कि बिना प्रेम किए वह रह ही नहीं सकता। जब तुम किसी मनोहर प्राकृतिक दृश्य को देखकर उस पर मोहित हो जाते हो तो तुम किसी फल की याचना नहीं करते और न वह दृश्य ही तुमसे कुछ माँगता है। फिर भी उस दृश्य का दर्शन तुम्हारे मन को आनंद से भर देता है।

उपर्युक्त गद्यांश को ध्यानपूर्वक पढ़ें और निम्नलिखित प्रश्नों के उत्तर के लिए सही विकल्प का चयन करें:

1. प्रेम का उद्देश्य क्या होता है?

A. मुक्ति B. उपासना
C. भक्ति D. प्रेम

2. मुक्ति का अर्थ है:

A. आजादी B. स्वतंत्रता
C. परतंत्र D. निर्वाण

3. कैसी उपासना अधम मानी गई है?

A. प्रेम की उपासना
B. भगवान की उपासना
C. मुक्ति की उपासना
D. भक्ति की उपासना

4. मनोहर शब्द हैं:

A. विशेषण B. संज्ञा
C. सर्वनाम D. अव्यव

5. प्राकृतिक शब्द का अर्थ है:

A. ईश्वरीय B. मानव संबंधी
C. प्रकृति संबंधी D. प्रेम संबंधी

गद्यांश 5

कुछ लोग भाग्यवादी होते हैं और सब-कुछ भाग्य के सहारे छोड़कर कर्म से विरत हो जाते हैं। ऐसे लोग समाज के लिए बोझ हैं। वे कभी कोई बड़ा काम नहीं कर पाते। बड़ी-बड़ी खोज, बड़े-बड़े आविष्कार और बड़े-बड़े निर्माण कार्य कर्मशील लोगों के द्वारा ही संभव हो सके हैं। हम अपनी बुद्धि और प्रतिभा तथा कार्य-क्षमता के बल पर सही मार्ग पर चल सकते हैं, किन्तु बिना कठिन श्रम के अपने लक्ष्य तक नहीं पहुँच सकते। कठिन परिश्रम करने के बाद पाई गई सफलता हमारे मन को अलौकिक आनंद से भर देती है। यदि हम अपने कार्य में अपेक्षित श्रम नहीं करते तो हमारा मन ग्लानि का अनुभव करता है।

उपर्युक्त गद्यांश को ध्यानपूर्वक पढ़ें और निम्नलिखित प्रश्नों के उत्तर के लिए सही विकल्प चुनें:

1. "आविष्कार" शब्द का अर्थ है :

A. अनुसंधान B. खोज
C. निर्माण D. विनाश

2. **अलौकिक** शब्द का क्या अर्थ है?
A. संसारिक B. भौतिक
C. अमानुषी D. प्राकृतिक

3. सफलता का विलोम क्या है?
A. सफल B. असफल
C. सफलतापूर्वक D. असफलता

4. परिश्रम करने और न करने से हमारे जीवन पर क्या प्रभाव पड़ता है?
A. लोग भाग्यवादी बन जाते हैं
B. कर्म से विरत हो जाते हैं
C. मन में ग्लानि का अनुभव होता है
D. इनमें से कोई नहीं

5. किस प्रकार के लोग समाज के लिए बोझ हैं?
A. भाग्यवादी B. कर्मठ
C. परिश्रमी D. प्रतिभाशाली

गद्यांश 6

वैदिक काल से हिमालय के पहाड़ बहुत पवित्र माने जाते हैं। इसमें कोई सन्देह नहीं कि हिमालय के पहाड़ों का दृश्य अति सुन्दर है। उसकी विशालता को देखकर मन में आनन्द और कृतज्ञता की लहर उठती है। ऐसा लगता है कि यह विशाल सृष्टि प्रभु की अनुपम देन है। सारी सृष्टि के प्रति समभाव जाग्रत होता है। वस्तुतः यह दृष्टि कोरी कल्पनात्मक या आध्यात्मिक नहीं है। देखा जाए तो सारे भारत की जलवायु का समतोल करने वाले यह हिमालय के पहाड़ हैं, विशेषकर उत्तरी भारत को वर्षा और पानी देने वाले ये ही हैं। गंगोत्री, यमुनोत्री, बद्री, केदार को तीर्थ माना जाता है, जो व्यर्थ कल्पना नहीं है। उन स्थानों से निकलने वाली पवित्र नदियाँ ही वास्तव में हमारी प्राणदात्री रही हैं।

उपर्युक्त गद्यांश को ध्यानपूर्वक पढ़ें और निम्नलिखित प्रश्नों के उत्तर के लिए सही विकल्प चुनें :

1. हिमालय के पर्वत बहुत पवित्र कब से माने जाते हैं?
A. पाषाण काल से B. वैदिक काल से
C. प्राचीन काल से D. आधुनिक काल से

2. विशालता शब्द है :
A. जातिवाचक B. भाववाचक
C. विशेषण D. सर्वनाम

3. भारत की जलवायु को समतोल कौन करता है?
A. गंगोत्री B. यमुनोत्री
C. केदार D. हिमालय

4. सृष्टि का समानार्थक शब्द है :
A. सृजन B. रचना
C. प्रकृति D. संसार

5. प्राणदात्री का क्या अर्थ है?
A. गंगोत्री
B. यमुनोत्री
C. प्राणसंचार करने वाली
D. समभाव जाग्रत करने वाली

गद्यांश 7

सच्चा मित्र एक शिक्षक की भाँति होता है। जिस प्रकार शिक्षक अपने छात्र को सन्मार्ग की ही ओर अग्रसर करता है, उसी प्रकार एक सच्चा मित्र अपने मित्र को पाप के गर्त में गिरने से बचाता है। मानव-जीवन अधिक रहस्यपूर्ण है। कभी-कभी जीवन में ऐसे अवसर उपस्थित हो जाते हैं, जब मनुष्य की धर्मबुद्धि नष्ट हो जाती है और उसका मन द्रुत गति से पाप की ओर दौड़ता है। ऐसे समय में मित्र का ही उपदेश अधिक कल्याणकारी सिद्ध होता है। मित्र के उपदेश का जितना प्रभाव हृदय पर पड़ता है, उतना और किसी का नहीं पड़ता है।

उपर्युक्त गद्यांश को ध्यानपूर्वक पढ़ें और निम्नलिखित प्रश्नों के उत्तर के लिए सही विकल्प चुनें :

1. सच्चा मित्र किस प्रकार का होता है?
A. विपत्ति में सहायता देने वाला
B. गलत मार्ग पर चलने से रोकने वाला
C. शिक्षक के भाँति
D. धार्मिक गुरु की तरह

2. सन्मार्ग शब्द का विपरीत शब्द है :
A. अग्रसर B. कुमार्ग
C. सुमार्ग D. मार्गदर्शक

3. व्यक्ति को पाप के गर्त्त में गिरने से कौन बचाता है?
A. शिक्षक B. भाई
C. पिता D. सच्चा मित्र

4. मानव पाप की ओर कब दौड़ता है?
   A. जब स्वार्थी बन जाता है
   B. जब धर्म-बुद्धि नष्ट हो जाती है
   C. जब सच्चामित्र साथ छोड़ देता है
   D. जब धनवान बन जाता है
5. उपदेश में कौन-सा उपसर्ग है?
   A. उ B. उप
   C. दे D. देश

गद्यांश 8

सब तरह के भावों को प्रकट करने की योग्यता रखने वाली और निर्दोष होने पर भी यदि कोई भाषा अपना निज का साहित्य नहीं रखती, तो वह रूपवती भिखारिन की तरह कदापि आदरणीय नहीं हो सकती। उनकी शोभा, उसकी बड़ी सम्पन्नता, उसकी मान-मर्यादा उसके साहित्य पर ही अवलम्बित रहती है। उसके विचारों और राजनैतिक स्थितियों का प्रतिबिम्ब देखने को यदि कहीं मिल सकता है, तो उसके ग्रन्थ साहित्य में मिल सकता है। सामाजिक शक्ति या सजीवता, सामाजिक अशक्ति या निर्जीवता और सामाजिक सभ्यता तथा असभ्यता का निर्णायक एकमात्र साहित्य है।

उपर्युक्त गद्यांश को ध्यानपूर्वक पढ़ें और निम्नलिखित प्रश्नों के उत्तर के लिए सही विकल्प चुनें :

1. साहित्य विहीन भाषा किस प्रकार की होती है?
   A. आदरणीय B. भिखारिन
   C. रूपवती D. रूपवती भिखारिन
2. रूपवती का पुल्लिंग रूप है:
   A. रूपवान B. सुन्दर
   C. सुन्दरी D. रूपवत
3. भाषा की मान मर्यादा किस पर निर्भर करती है?
   A. लिपि पर B. साहित्यकार पर
   C. भक्ति पर D. साहित्य पर
4. "सम्पन्नता" शब्द का विपरीत शब्द है:
   A. गरीबी B. विपन्न
   C. अमीर D. विपन्नता
5. राजनैतिक, सामाजिक शक्ति का दर्शन हमें किसमें मिलता है?
   A. समाज B. राज्य
   C. नेता D. साहित्य

गद्यांश 9

स्वतंत्र भारत का सम्पूर्ण दायित्व आज विद्यार्थियों के ही ऊपर है, क्योंकि आज जो विद्यार्थी हैं, वे ही कल स्वतंत्र भारत के नागरिक होंगे। भारत की उन्नति, उसका उत्थान उन्हीं की उन्नति और उत्थान पर निर्भर करता है। अतः विद्यार्थियों को चाहिए कि वे अपने भावी जीवन का निर्माण बड़ी सतर्कता और सावधानी के साथ करें। उन्हें प्रत्येक क्षण अपने राष्ट्र, अपने समाज, अपने धर्म, अपनी संस्कृति को अपनी आँखों के सामने रखना चाहिए, जिससे उनके जीवन से राष्ट्र को कुछ बल प्राप्त हो सके। जो विद्यार्थी राष्ट्रीय दृष्टिकोण से अपने जीवन का निर्माण नहीं करते, वे राष्ट्र और समाज के लिए भार-स्वरूप हैं।

उपर्युक्त गद्यांश को ध्यानपूर्वक पढ़ें और निम्नलिखित प्रश्नों के उत्तर के लिए सही विकल्प चुनें :

1. भारत की उन्नति किस पर निर्भर करती है?
   A. युवाओं पर B. नेताओं पर
   C. साहित्यकारों पर D. विद्यार्थियों पर
2. **उन्नति** का समानार्थक शब्द है :
   A. पतन B. उत्थान
   C. विकास D. उदय
3. **उत्थान** का विपरीत शब्द है :
   A. उदय B. पतन
   C. पराजय D. हार
4. किसे अपने जीवन का निर्माण सतर्कता और सावधानी से करना चाहिए?
   A. युवाओं को B. नेताओं को
   C. बच्चों को D. विद्यार्थियों को
5. धर्म, संस्कृति तथा समाज का रक्षक कौन है?
   A. नागरिक B. ग्रामीण
   C. विद्यार्थी D. युवा

गद्यांश 10

हास्य एक ऐसा माध्यम है, जो नीरस-जीवन को भी सुखद बना देता है। हास्य का जादू इतना प्रभावशाली होता है कि वह छूत के रोग की तरह चारों ओर फैल जाता है। जिसने कभी हँसना नहीं सीखा, सचमुच उसने जीना नहीं सीखा। सामान्यतः मनुष्य को जीवन में इतनी मुसीबतें झेलनी

पड़ती हैं कि वह अपने जीवन को पहाड़ समझने लगता है। ऐसे दूभर जीवन को यदि जीने योग्य बनाना हो तो उसके लिए आवश्यक है कि जीवन में हँसने की गुंजाइश हो। हँसी के सहारे मनुष्य अपने कष्टों को भुलाने का प्रयत्न करता है। संघर्ष, तनाव, व्यस्तता, घुटन यदि आज के जीवन की सहज देन हैं, तो इनसे बचने के लिए यह आवश्यक है कि हम हँसना सीखें।

उपर्युक्त गद्यांश को ध्यानपूर्वक पढ़ें और निम्नलिखित प्रश्नों के उत्तर के लिए सही विकल्प चुनें :

1. नीरस जीवन को कौन सुखद बना देता है?

A. संगीत B. गीत
C. आमोद प्रमोद D. हास्य

2. **नीरस** का संधि विच्छेद है :

A. नी + रस B. नि + रस
C. निः + रस D. नीः + रस

3. किसका जीवन व्यर्थ है?

A. जिसने रोना नहीं सीखा
B. जिसने हँसना नहीं सीखा
C. जिसने गाना नहीं सीखा
D. इनमें से कोई नहीं

4. **हँसना** शब्द है :

A. संज्ञा B. विशेषण
C. क्रिया विशेषण D. क्रिया

5. तनाव और घुटन से बचने के लिए क्या करना चाहिए?

A. रोना चाहिए B. गाना चाहिए
C. हँसना चाहिए D. काम करना चाहिए

गद्यांश 11

किसी पुस्तक को पढ़ने में जल्दी नहीं करनी चाहिए, जो कुछ लेखक कहता है, उसे समझने की चेष्टा करनी चाहिए। प्रत्येक शब्द का अर्थ समझने की चेष्टा करनी चाहिए। यदि लेखक योग्य है, तो दूसरी बार वह पुस्तक और अधिक आनन्द देगी और तीसरी बार और अधिक। प्रत्येक बार अध्ययन करने पर आपको नवीन सुन्दर और नए विचार मिलेंगे और उसे आप जितना ही पढ़ेंगे, उतना ही स्नेह करने लगेंगे। सहस्रों व्यक्तियों ने गीता और रामायण तथा कुरान और बाइबिल को बार-बार पढ़ा है। उनका अनुभव है कि प्रत्येक बार उन्हें नई सूझ और नए विचार मिलते गए। कुछ लोग तो इस बात पर गर्व करते हैं कि उन्होंने अमुक पुस्तक को अनेक बार पढ़ा है, उन्हें कंठस्थ हो गई है।

उपर्युक्त गद्यांश को ध्यानपूर्वक पढ़ें और निम्नलिखित प्रश्नों के उत्तर के लिए सही विकल्प चुनें :

1. किसे समझने की चेष्टा करनी चाहिए?

A. पुस्तक B. रामायण
C. महाभारत D. गीता

2. पुस्तक की सजीवता किस पर निर्भर करती है?

A. लेखक B. प्रकाशक
C. पाठक D. चिन्तक

3. **आनन्द** का विपरीत शब्द है :

A. शोक B. दुख
C. संताप D. खुशी

4. नवीन, सुन्दर और नए विचार हमें कहाँ से प्राप्त होता हैं?

A. पुस्तक को बार-बार पढ़कर
B. सुनकर
C. भाषण से
D. अच्छे व्यक्तियों से मिलने पर

5. **कंठस्थ** शब्द का शब्दार्थ है :

A. कंठ में स्थित B. सुंदर कंठ
C. जबानी याद D. पंडित जी

गद्यांश 12

अहिंसा परम धर्म है और हिंसा आपद् धर्म। मनुष्य बराबर अहिंसा की ओर चलना चाहता है, किन्तु परिस्थितियाँ उससे हिंसा कराती है, अर्थात् परमधर्म की रक्षा के लिए आदमी बराबर आपद्धर्म से काम लेता रहा है। भारत अपनी सेनाओं को विघटित कर दे, तब भी उसका अपमान उससे अधिक होने वाला नहीं, जितना नेफा में हुआ। किन्तु परमधर्म पर टिकने की सामर्थ्य अगर भारत में नहीं है, तो आपद्धर्म पर उसे आना चाहिए। व्यवहारतः आपद्धर्म परमधर्म का विरोधी नहीं, उसका रक्षक है।

उपर्युक्त गद्यांश को ध्यानपूर्वक पढ़ें और निम्नलिखित प्रश्नों के उत्तर के लिए सही विकल्प चुनें :

1. **परमधर्म** का विपरीत शब्द है :
A. महान धर्म B. आपद्धर्म
C. सच्चाधर्म D. इनमें से कोई नहीं

2. आपद्धर्म किसे कहा जाता है?
A. अहिंसा B. सत्याग्रह
C. विपत्ति D. हिंसा

3. मानव से हिंसा कौन करवाती है?
A. लोभ B. स्वार्थ
C. द्वेष D. परिस्थितियाँ

4. **सामर्थ्य** का शब्दार्थ है :
A. संघर्ष B. परिश्रम
C. शक्ति D. पराक्रम

5. **परमधर्म** की रक्षा कौन करता है?
A. अहिंसा B. हिंसा
C. आपदधर्म D. युद्ध

गद्यांश 13

वर्तमान काल विज्ञापन का युग माना जाता है। समाचार-पत्रों के अतिरिक्त रेडियो और टेलीविजन भी विज्ञापन के सफल साधन हैं। विज्ञापन का मूल उद्देश्य उत्पादक और भोक्ता में सीधा सम्पर्क स्थापित करना होता है। जितना अधिक विज्ञापन किसी पदार्थ का होगा, उतनी ही उसकी लोकप्रियता बढ़ेगी। इन विज्ञापनों पर धन तो अधिक व्यय होता है, पर इनसे बिक्री बढ़ जाती है। ग्राहक जब इन आकर्षक विज्ञापनों को देखता है तो वह उस वस्तु-विशेष के प्रति आकृष्ट होकर उसे खरीदने को बाध्य हो जाता है।

उपर्युक्त गद्यांश को ध्यानपूर्वक पढ़ें और निम्नलिखित प्रश्नों के उत्तर के लिए सही विकल्प चुनें :

1. वर्तमान को किसका युग माना जाता है?
A. फैशन B. विज्ञापन
C. संगीत D. धन

2. उत्पादक तथा भोक्ता के बीच कौन संबंध स्थापित करता है?
A. टेलीविजन B. समाचार-पत्र
C. रेडियो D. विज्ञापन

3. **वर्तमान** शब्द का विपरीत शब्द है :
A. अर्वाचीन B. आधुनिक
C. आजकल D. प्राचीन

4. **आकर्षक** का शब्दार्थ है :
A. विकर्षक B. सुन्दर
C. मनमोहक D. आश्चर्यजनक

5. भोक्ता किस कारण वस्तुओं को खरीदने के लिए बाध्य हो जाता है?
A. विज्ञापन
B. आकर्षक विज्ञापन
C. लोकप्रियता के कारण
D. आसानी से उपलब्ध होना

गद्यांश 14

लगभग दो सौ वर्ष की गुलामी ने भारत के राष्ट्रीय स्वाभिमान को पैरों से रौंद डाला, हमारी संस्कृति को समाप्त कर दिया, हमारे विश्वासों को हिला दिया और हमारे आत्मविश्वास को चकनाचूर कर दिया, किन्तु अपने इस बूढ़े देश से प्यार करने वाले, इसके एक सामान्य संकेत पर प्राण न्यौछावर करने वाले दीवानों का अभाव न था। एक आवाज उठी और देखते ही देखते राष्ट्र का दबा हुआ आत्माभिमान उन्मत्त हो उठा। इतिहास साक्षी है जाने और अनजाने सहस्त्रों देशभक्त स्वतंत्रता की अनमोल निधि को पाने के लिए शहीद हो गए।

उपर्युक्त गद्यांश को ध्यानपूर्वक पढ़ें और निम्नलिखित प्रश्नों के उत्तर के लिए सही विकल्प चुनें :

1. **स्वाभिमान** का संधि विच्छेद है:
A. स्वा + भिमान B. स्वः + अभिमान
C. स्व + अभिमान D. स्वा + अभिमान

2. भारत का राष्ट्रीय स्वाभिमान किस कारण समाप्त हो गया था?
A. लम्बे गुलामी से B. निरंकुश शासक से
C. स्वार्थी मानव से D. धर्म के विनाश से

3. **आत्मविश्वास** का शब्दार्थ है
A. घमण्ड B. गर्व
C. अपने पर विश्वास D. अभिमान

4. भारत की अनमोल निधि को पाने के लिए कौन शहीद हो गए?
A. देशभक्त B. नेता
C. युवा D. युवती

5. **अनमोल निधि** का शब्दार्थ है:

A. अनन्त खजाना B. अमूल्य खजाना

C. बहुमूल्य D. स्वतंत्रता

गद्यांश 15

दुनिया के विभिन्न देशों के विकास पर विहंगम दृष्टि डालने से यह स्पष्ट हो जाता है कि आज जिस देश ने वैज्ञानिक उपलब्धियों के सहारे अपना औद्योगीकरण कर लिया, उसी को उन्नत देश कहा जाता है। जिस देश में औद्योगीकरण का स्तर नीचा है, वह पिछड़ा हुआ देश कहा जाता है। वैज्ञानिक आविष्कारों और औद्योगीकरण के आधार पर ही किसी देश की प्रगति को आँका जाता रहा है। विज्ञान ने मानव को पूरी तरह बदल दिया है।

उपर्युक्त गद्यांश को ध्यानपूर्वक पढ़ें और निम्नलिखित प्रश्नों के उत्तर के लिए सही विकल्प चुनें :

1. **विहंगम दृष्टि** का क्या अर्थ है?

A. एक झलक B. गहन दृष्टि

C. गहन चिन्तन D. इनमें से कोई नहीं

2. **विकास** का विपरीत शब्द है :

A. उत्थान B. उदय

C. पतन D. विनाश

3. **वैज्ञानिक** शब्द में कौन-सा प्रत्यय हैं?

A. निक B. वै

C. ईक D. इक

4. मानव जीवन को किसने बदल दिया है :

A. विकास B. वैज्ञानिक

C. विज्ञान D. उद्योग

5. किसी भी देश की स्तर को किससे नापा जाता है?

A. उपलब्धियों पर

B. औद्योगीकरण से

C. वैज्ञानिकों से

D. आविष्कारों से

गद्यांश 16

विश्व का वर्तमान उन्नत रूप मानव-श्रम की ही कहानी कह रहा है। गगन चुंबी अट्टालिकाएँ, लंबी-चौड़ी सड़कें, बड़े-बड़े विशाल नगर आकाश में उड़ते वायुयान तथा मानव-जीवन को सुखी और समृद्ध बनाने में योगदान करने वाले ज्ञान-विज्ञान के अनन्त रूप-ये सभी मनुष्य के श्रम का जयघोष करते हैं। स्पष्ट है कि मनुष्य और उसका शरीर विधाता की अनुपम रचना है जो निश्चय ही महान उद्देश्यों की संपूर्ति के लिए दिया गया है। इस दुर्लभ तन को यदि हम आलस्य, प्रसाद अथवा घटिया कामों में गँवा देते हैं तो उस विधाता के प्रति अन्याय करते हैं।

उपर्युक्त गद्यांश को ध्यानपूर्वक पढ़ें और निम्नलिखित प्रश्नों के उत्तर के लिए सही विकल्प चुनें :

1. विश्व का वर्तमान रूप किसका उद्योतक है?

A. चिन्तक का B. नेता का

C. वैज्ञानिक का D. मानव श्रम

2. **गगन चुंबी अट्टालिकाएँ** का अर्थ है :

A. आकाश में उड़ने वाला

B. आकाश को छूने वाला

C. बहुमंजिली इमारत

D. इनमें से कोई नहीं

3. आकाश का समानार्थक शब्द है :

A. वसुन्धरा B. धरा

C. पयोद D. गगन

4. **सुखी** का विपरीत शब्द है :

A. प्रसन्न B. अप्रसन्न

C. दुखी D. उदासी

5. विधाता की अनुपम रचना क्या है?

A. मानव शरीर B. समुद्र

C. वन D. पृथ्वी

गद्यांश 17

हमारे देश में एक ऐसा भी युग था जब नैतिक और आध्यात्मिक विकास ही जीवन का वास्तविक लक्ष्य माना जाता था। अहिंसा की भावना सर्वोपरि थी। आज पूरा जीवन दर्शन ही बदल गया है। सर्वत्र पैसे की हाय-हाय तथा धन का उपार्जन ही मुख्य ध्येय हो गया है, भले ही धन-उपार्जन के तरीके गलत ही क्यों न हों? इन सबका असर मनुष्य के प्रतिदिन के जीवन पर पड़ रहा है। समाज का वातावरण दूषित हो गया है-

बाह्य वातावरण तो दूषित है ही, आज सब जानते हैं पर्यावरण की समस्याएँ कितनी चिन्तनीय हो उठी है। इन

सबके कारण मानसिक और शारीरिक तनाव-खिंचाव और व्याधियाँ पैदा हो रही हैं।

उपर्युक्त गद्यांश को ध्यानपूर्वक पढ़ें और निम्नलिखित प्रश्नों के उत्तर के लिए सही विकल्प चुनें :

1. भारत का प्राचीन आदर्श था :

A. सत्य और अहिंसा

B. नैतिक और आध्यात्मिक विकास

C. धन उपार्जन

D. इनमें से कोई नहीं

2. **अहिंसा** का विपरीत शब्द है :

A. हिंसा B. सत्याग्रह

C. विनम्रता D. नैतिकता

3. जीवन दर्शन क्यों बदल गया है?

A. हिंसा के कारण

B. अहिंसा के कारण

C. धन लिप्सा के कारण

D. आध्यात्मिक विकास के कारण

4. समाज का वातावरण दूषित क्यों हो गया है?

A. शारीरिक तनाव

B. मानसिक व्याधियाँ

C. पर्यावरण की समस्याएँ

D. धन उपार्जन के गलत तरीके

5. **पर्यावरण** का शब्दार्थ है:

A. जलमंडल B. स्थलमंडल

C. वायुमंडल D. वातावरण

गद्यांश 18

राजा राम मोहन राय में ''होनहार बिरवान के होत चीकने पांत'' वाली कहावत पूरी तरह चरितार्थ हुई। बाल्यकाल में उनकी बुद्धि कितनी कुशाग्र थी, इसकी अनेक कहानियाँ सुनी जाती हैं। उनके पिता ने उनकी पढ़ाई का समुचित प्रबन्ध किया। गाँव की पाठशाला में उन्होंने बंगला सीखी। उन दिनों कचहरियों में फारसी का बोलबाला था। अतः उन्होंने घर पर ही मौलवी से फारसी पढ़ी। नौ वर्ष की उम्र में वे अरबी की उच्च शिक्षा के लिए पटना भेजे गये। पटना उस समय भारतवर्ष में इस्लामी संस्कृति का केन्द्र था। पटना में वे तीन वर्ष तक रहे। उन्होंने कुरान का मूल अरबी में अध्ययन किया। चार वर्ष तक काशी में संस्कृत का अध्ययन किया। उपनिषदों के अद्वैतवाद का उनपर पूरा प्रभाव पड़ा। फलतः उन्हें निराकार ईश्वर पर विश्वास हुआ।

उपर्युक्त गद्यांश को ध्यानपूर्वक पढ़ें और निम्नलिखित प्रश्नों के उत्तर के लिए सही विकल्प चुनें :

1. राजा राममोहन राय ने बंगला कहाँ सीखी?

A. पटना B. काशी

C. कलकत्ता D. गाँव की पाठशाला

2. अरबी की शिक्षा उन्होंने कहाँ पाई?

A. काशी B. पटना

C. ईरान D. ईराक

3. संस्कृत साहित्य का अध्ययन उन्होंने कहाँ किया?

A. पटना B. काशी

C. इलाहाबाद D. कलकत्ता

4. **कुशाग्र** शब्द का अर्थ है :

A. तेज B. बुद्धिमान

C. होनहार D. विद्वान्

5. निराकार शब्द का विलोम है :

A. साकार B. आकार

C. विशाल D. मूर्ति

गद्यांश 19

मोती राजा साहब की सवारी का खास हाथी था। यों तो वह बहुत सीधा और समझदार था, पर कभी-कभी उसका मिजाज गर्म हो जाता था। एक बार पागलपन में उसने अपने महावत को मार डाला। राजा साहब ने यह खबर सुनी, तो उन्हें बहुत क्रोध आया, मोती की पदवी छिन गई। उसे राजा साहब की सवारी से निकाल दिया गया। कुलियों की तरह उसे लकड़ियाँ ढ़ोनी पड़ती, पत्थर लादने पड़ते और शाम को वह पीपल के नीचे मोटी जंजीरों से बाँध दिया जाता।

उपर्युक्त गद्यांश को ध्यानपूर्वक पढ़ें और निम्नलिखित प्रश्नों के उत्तर के लिए सही विकल्प चुनें :

1. राजा साहब की सवारी के हाथी का क्या नाम था?

A. सोना B. मोती

C. हीरा D. ऐरावत

2. किसने महावत को मार डाला था?

A. राजा B. हाथी

C. मोती D. दरबारी

3. **मिजाज** शब्द का शब्दार्थ है :

A. विचार B. ध्यान
C. मन D. दिल

4. किसकी पदवी छिन गई थी?

A. महावत की B. राजा की
C. मोती की D. हाथी की

5. समझदार और सीधा कौन था?

A. राजा साहब B. महावत
C. मोती D. इनमें से कोई नहीं

गद्यांश 20

मनुष्य का यह दावा है कि वह सक्षम है, समर्थ है। हिमालय की तराई में घने जंगलों के बीच में बना एक छोटा-सा स्टेशन, जो दोपहर के बाद वाली ढ़लती धूप में भी बुरी तरह जल रहा था, मानो मनुष्य के इस दावे का प्रमाण था। प्रकृति इस मनुष्य के वश में है, वह इस प्रकृति को मनचाहा नवीन रूप देता है। वह इस प्रकृति के साथ न जाने कितने खिलवाड़ करता है। तराई का वह जंगल भी तो उसी प्रकृति का एक भाग था।

उपर्युक्त गद्यांश को ध्यानपूर्वक पढ़ें और निम्नलिखित प्रश्नों के उत्तर के लिए सही विकल्प चुनें :

1. **सक्षम** शब्द समानार्थक शब्द है :

A. समर्थ B. शक्तिशाली
C. कायर D. निर्माता

2. सक्षम और समर्थ होने का दावा कौन करता है?

A. प्रकृति B. मानव
C. दानव D. पशु

3. छोटा-सा स्टेशन कहाँ स्थित है?

A. घने जंगलों में B. हिमालय की तराई में
C. नदी के किनारे D. नगर में

4. प्रकृति के साथ कौन खिलवाड़ करता है?

A. मानव B. वैज्ञानिक
C. नेता D. युवा

5. **नवीन** का विपरीत शब्द है :

A. पुराना B. नूतन
C. नवनीत D. अतीत

गद्यांश 21

पता नहीं जंगल में भी प्राण होते हैं या नहीं। वैसे जन्म लेना, मरना, शैशव, युवावस्था और वृद्धावस्था, जीवन के सब चिह्न जंगल में होते हैं। न जाने कितने पशु-पक्षी इन जंगलों की गोद में आश्रय लिए हुए हैं। कभी भयानक रूप से क्रुद्ध और उबलते हुए और कभी निष्प्राण से सुखे हुए नदी-नाले। ये सब जंगल के भाग हैं और जंगल के अन्दर इन अनगिनत प्राणियों में जीवन-मरण का संघर्ष चला करता है। रोज ही जन्म होते हैं, रोज ही मृत्यु के फेरे लगते हैं। जीवन-मरण की सीमाओं में बद्ध जो प्रकृति का क्रम है। वह तो चलता ही रहता है।

उपर्युक्त गद्यांश को ध्यानपूर्वक पढ़ें और निम्नलिखित प्रश्नों के उत्तर के लिए सही विकल्प चुनें :

1. जीवन के सब चिह्न किसमें होते है?

A. जंगल में
B. मानव में
C. पशु में
D. पादप में

2. **शैशव** का शब्दार्थ है :

A. युवा B. बुढ़ापा
C. बचपन D. नश्वर

3. जंगलों में कौन आश्रय लेता है :

A. पशु-पक्षी B. जन्तु
C. पादप D. मानव

4. **निष्प्राण** का समानार्थक शब्द है :

A. सजीव B. निर्जीव
C. शाश्वत D. नश्वर

5. **जीवन** का विपरीत शब्द है :

A. मरण B. अमर
C. प्राण D. नश्वर

गद्यांश 22

यह आदान-प्रदान ही मानव-सभ्यता का मूल स्रोत है; इस आदान-प्रदान के लिए ही मुनष्य ने पहाड़ों को लाँघकर और सागरों को पार करके दुनिया के हर-एक कोने का पता लगाया। इस आदान-प्रदान की क्रिया-प्रतिक्रिया के रूप में न जाने कितने युद्ध लड़े गए, न जाने कितने देश बरबाद किए गए, न जाने कितनी सभ्यताएँ नष्ट की गई और यह आदान-प्रदान चल रहा है।

उपर्युक्त गद्यांश को ध्यानपूर्वक पढ़ें और निम्नलिखित प्रश्नों के उत्तर के लिए सही विकल्प चुनें :

1. मानव-सभ्यता का मूल स्रोत क्या है?
   A. आदान B. प्रदान
   C. आदान-प्रदान D. इनमें से कोई नहीं
2. **मानव** का विपरीत शब्द है :
   A. नर B. मनुष्य
   C. दानव D. दुष्ट
3. दुनिया के हर एक भाग का पता किसने किया है?
   A. मानव B. खोजकर्ता
   C. आविष्कारक D. दानव
4. युद्ध क्यों लड़े गए थे :
   A. क्रिया-प्रतिक्रिया के कारण
   B. आदान-प्रदान के कारण
   C. स्वार्थ के कारण
   D. धन उपार्जन के कारण
5. **आदान-प्रदान** शब्द है :
   A. विपरीत शब्द
   B. क्रिया विशेषण
   C. पर्यायवाची शब्द
   D. सहचर-शब्द

उत्तरमाला

गद्यांश 1

1. C **2.** D **3.** B **4.** A **5.** D

गद्यांश 2

1. A **2.** D **3.** D **4.** C **5.** A

गद्यांश 3

1. C **2.** D **3.** B **4.** C **5.** B

गद्यांश 4

1. D **2.** D **3.** C **4.** A **5.** C

गद्यांश 5

1. B **2.** D **3.** D **4.** C **5.** A

गद्यांश 6

1. B **2.** B **3.** D **4.** A **5.** C

गद्यांश 7

1. C **2.** B **3.** D **4.** B **5.** B

गद्यांश 8

1. D **2.** A **3.** D **4.** D **5.** D

गद्यांश 9

1. D **2.** B **3.** B **4.** D **5.** C

गद्यांश 10

1. D **2.** C **3.** B **4.** D **5.** C

गद्यांश 11

1. A **2.** A **3.** A **4.** A **5.** C

गद्यांश 12

1. B **2.** D **3.** D **4.** C **5.** C

गद्यांश 13

1. B **2.** D **3.** D **4.** C **5.** B

गद्यांश 14

1. C **2.** A **3.** C **4.** A **5.** B

गद्यांश 15

1. A **2.** D **3.** C **4.** C **5.** B

गद्यांश 16

1. D **2.** C **3.** D **4.** C **5.** A

गद्यांश 17

1. B **2.** A **3.** C **4.** D **5.** D

गद्यांश 18

1. D **2.** B **3.** B **4.** A **5.** A

गद्यांश 19

1. B **2.** C **3.** C **4.** C **5.** C

गद्यांश 20

1. A **2.** B **3.** B **4.** A **5.** A

गद्यांश 21

1. C **2.** C **3.** A **4.** B **5.** A

गद्यांश 22

1. C **2.** C **3.** A **4.** B **5.** D

❑❑❑

ENGLISH LANGUAGE

1. COMPREHENSION PASSAGES

In the English language paper, questions on comprehension test are very important for the examinees appearing in the competitive examinations.

Comprehension means the act of comprehending or the capacity of the mind to understand. In the examination papers, questions on comprehension test are included to judge the ability of the examinees to understand the given passage.

Therefore, they should understand how to solve these questions. Practice of solving these questions will greatly help them in the examination.

Directions: *Read the following passages carefully and answer the questions given after each passage. Out of the four alternatives, choose the correct answer according to the context of the passage.*

PASSAGE-1

This is the age of the Machine, Machines are everywhere, in the fields, in the factory, at home, in the street, in the city, in the country, every where. To fly, it is not necessary to have wings; there are machines. The swim under the sea, it is not necessary to have gills; there are machines. To kill our fellowmen in over-whelming numbers, there are machines. Petrol machines alone provide ten times more power than all human beings in the world. In the busiest countries, each individual has six hundred human slaves in his machines.

What are the consequences of this abnormal power? Before the War, it looked as though it might be possible, for the first time in history to provide food and clothing and shelter for the teeming population of the world—every man, woman and child. This would have been the greatest triumphs of science. And yet, if you remember, we saw the world crammed, full of food and people hungry. Today, the larders are bare and millions, starving. That's the war, you would say. When the machines of peace once more begin to ....

1. According to the passage, which of the following is not necessary to fly?
   A. Wings B. Arms
   C. Feet D. Machines
2. Petrol machinery is used to provide:
   A. ten times more power than human beings in the world
   B. less power than human beings in the world
   C. as much power as human beings in the world
   D. none of the above is correct
3. What could be one of the greatest triumphs of science?
   A. to provide food, clothing and shelter to everyone
   B. none would get food, clothing and shelter
   C. only rich people would get food, clothing and shelter
   D. people would get only clothing
4. This is the age of the:
   A. machine B. animal husbandry
   C. agriculture D. wars
5. The machine age produces:
   A. goods
   B. food
   C. goods but avoids the consequences
   D. none of the above

Answers

1	2	3	4	5
A	A	A	A	C

PASSAGE-2

What are the good parts of our civilization? First and foremost there are order and safety. If today I have a quarrel with another man, I do not get beaten merely because I am physically weaker and he can knock me down. I go to law and the law will decide as fairly as it can between the two of us. Thus in disputes between man and man. Right has taken the place of might. Moreover, the law protects me from robbery and violence. Nobody may come and break into my house, steal my books or run off with my children. Of course, there are burglars, but they are very rare and the law punishes them whenever, it catches them.

It is difficult for us to realize how much this safety means. Without safety those higher activities of mankind which make up civilization could not go on. The inventor could not invent, the scientist find out or the artist make beautiful things. Hence, order and safety, although they are not themselves civilization, are things without which civilization could be impossible. They are as necessary to our civilization as the air we breathe is to us; and we have-grown so used to them that we do not notice them any more than we notice the air.

1. The first and foremost good parts of civilization are:
A. order and insecurity
B. only insecurity
C. order and safety
D. insecurity and lawlessness.

2. In disputes between man and man:
A. right has taken the place of might
B. might has taken the place of right
C. might is right
D. none of the above

3. According to the passage, the burglars are:
A. many B. rare
C. found nowhere D. not punished

4. An artist can create beautiful things only if:
A. there is disorder
B. there is no safety
C. there is safety
D. there is neither safety nor order

5. According to the writer, man does not notice order and safety as:
A. he does not notice the air he breathes
B. he does not notice the food he eats
C. he does not notice the shelter he needs
D. none of the above is correct

Answers

1	2	3	4	5
C	A	B	C	A

PASSAGE-3

The purpose of education is to make the student an expert in his subject. This must be clearly understood, and mere muddling through lessons and lectures and books and passing examination are relegated to secondary importance as means to the end—which is excellence in the field choosen.

But there are so many fields, and no man can become an expert in all the fields. It is necessary to decide which fields are the important ones that a man should know well.

It is clear that one's own work is the most important. This has been realised and modern civilization has accordingly provided vocational education. It is now possible to acquire high professional skill in the various fields, medicine, engineering production, commerce and so on—but with good and bad mixed together, and no standard for guidance.

1. The purpose of education is to make the student:
A. an expert in all fields
B. an expert in his subject
C. only capable of earning
D. confident only

2. What, according to the writer, is the end?
A. excellence in the field choosen
B. passing the examination
C. earning more and more money
D. cramming lectures and books

3. According to the passage, can a man become an expert in all fields?
A. Yes B. Partially yes
C. Sometimes D. No

4. According to the writer, which of the following is the most important work?
A. someone else's work
B. one's own work
C. nobody's work
D. everyone's work

5. The modern civilization has provided
   A. vocational education
   B. art of conversation
   C. adult education
   D. higher education

Answers

1	2	3	4	5
B	A	D	B	A

PASSAGE-4

English education, which was introduced in India in the earlier part of the nineteenth century, established her cultural contact with the West. Prior to this, India had for centuries remained in a state of isolation, although in very early times she had sent out cultural missions to the other Asiatic countries. India really began to borrow from the West and assimilate new ideas on an extensive scale only after the British had taken up the direction of her educational policy.

It is true that Western education at first exerted an unsettling: influence on young men and led to errors in life and conduct. They hated everything Indian, aped western manners and modes of life, and forgot their glorious past. There were scholars who ignored modern Indian languages, avoided classical Indian literature, and made a fetish of speaking and writing English.

1. When was English education introduced in India?
   A. in the twentieth century
   B. in the later part of the nineteenth century
   C. in the earlier part of the nineteenth century
   D. in the eighteenth century
2. When did India begin to borrow from the West?
   A. after the British had taken up the direction of her educational policy
   B. before the British had taken up the direction of her educational policy
   C. in the twentieth century
   D. none of the above is correct
3. What did India send out to other Asiatic countries?
   A. economic mission B. military forces
   C. cultural missions D. none of these
4. Western education exerted an unsettling influence on:
   A. old men B. young men
   C. old women D. children
5. Young men forgot their:
   A. glorious past B. present
   C. future D. originality

Answers

1	2	3	4	5
C	A	C	B	A

PASSAGE-5

Each nation has its own peculiar character which distinguishes it from others. But the peoples of the world have more points in which they are all like each other than points in which they are different. One type of person that is common in every country is the one who always tries to do as little as he possibly can and to get as much in return as he can. His opposite, the man who is in the habit of doing more than is strictly necessary and is ready to accept what is offered in return, is rare everywhere.

Both these types are usually unconscious of their character. The man who avoids effort is always talking about his 'rights'; he appears to think that society owes him a pleasant easy life. The man who is always doing more than his sheer talks of 'duties' feels that the individual is in debt to society, and not society to the individual. As a result of their view, neither of these men thinks that he behaves at all strangely.

1. What type of person is common in every nation?
   A. A person who wants to do little and get more
   B. A person who wants to do more and get little
   C. Each person is different
   D. There is no such type of person that is common in every country
2. A person doing more and getting little:
   A. is rare everywhere
   B. is found in our country
   C. is common in all countries
   D. is found nowhere

3. The man who talks about his 'rights':
   A. avoids meeting other people
   B. avoids hard work
   C. knows his duties well
   D. believes in hard work
4. The man who talks of 'duties':
   A. is always hard working
   B. avoids hard work
   C. does not know his duties well
   D. always thinks of his 'right' first
5. Which one of the following thinks that the individual is in debt to the society?
   A. a person who talks of his 'rights only'
   B. a person who is always doing more than his sheer talks of 'duties'
   C. every citizen of the country
   D. a person who talks of his 'duties' only

Answers

1	2	3	4	5
A	A	B	A	C

PASSAGE-6

The history of civilization shows how man always has to choose between making the right and wrong use of the discoveries of science. This has never been more true than in our own age. In a brief period amazing discoveries have been made and applied to practical purpose.

It would be ungrateful not to recognize how immense are the boons, which science has given to mankind. It has brought within the reach of multitudes benefits and advantages which only a short time ago were the privilege of the few. It has shown how malnutrition, hunger and disease can be overcome. It has not only lengthened life but it has deepened its quality. Fields of knowledge, experience and recration open in the past only a few, have been thrown open to millions. Through the work of science the ordinary man today has been given the opportunity of a longer and fuller life then was over possible to his grandparents.

1. Amazing discoveries of science have been made:
   A. in a brief period
   B. in a long period
   C. in our orefather's age
   D. in centuries
2. The boons of science are:
   A. few
   B. found nowhere
   C. immense
   D. very few
3. Which of the following can be overcome with the help of science?
   A. Malnutrition
   B. Disease
   C. Hunger
   D. All of these
4. Science provides a chance of:
   A. shorter and fuller life
   B. longer and fuller life
   C. longer and dull life
   D. none of these
5. What on the whole, has science done to mankind?
   A. It has reduced the quality of our life
   B. It has shortened our life
   C. It has deepened the quality of life
   D. It has done a great harm to mankind

Answers

1	2	3	4	5
A	C	D	B	C

PASSAGE-7

It is said that wars are fought for the sake of peace. Many a politician justifies wars as being the means of bringing about stability in the international relations. So far as the aim of those who are always busy in society is concerned, their motive is not always to achieve freedom from work. Their ultimate purpose is not to be idle. To be busy is a mode of life or habit. Those who are busy in society, say, businessmen, or people in authority, politicians or statesmen, officials or employees, are all part of the continuous machine which keeps the society going.

People are busy so that different activities of a society are carried out and the wherewithals which mankind badly needs are provided. No society, however, prosperous and endowed with bounties of nature, can afford to have the objective of being idle in the long run. No doubt, advanced countries ensured minimum facilities of living and amenities of work for their workmen; they even fix their working hours so that after their busy day's life they can have some leisure at their disposal for self development or peace of mind. Yet, with the passage of time a busy society has the tendency to become busier. Even with the best computers and automations at the disposal of the modern technocrats manpower continues to remain busy, as one phase of achievement leads automatically to the second phase of work. War may have the intention of peace but business is undending so long as a society has the objective of progress and does not become stationary or stagnant or decadent.

1. According to the passage, busy people:
   A. want freedom work
   B. want to be idle
   C. do not like rest
   D. are part of a machine which runs society
2. Why are people busy?
   A. to carry out different activities of society
   B. to provide needs of mankind
   C. both A and B
   D. none of the above
3. Author says that:
   A. no society can be idle
   B. developed countries can be idle
   C. underdeveloped countries can be idle
   D. all of the above
4. Computers and automations:
   A. have made man idle
   B. could not relieve man from busy life
   C. both of the above
   D. none of the above
5. With the passage of time man is becoming busier because
   A. he likes to be busy
   B. he is born to be busy
   C. to be busy is mode of life or habit
   D. all of the above

Answers

1	2	3	4	5
D	C	A	B	C

PASSAGE-8

Every genius that comes to the world, achieves greatness through the capacity of taking trouble. All great men of the world who have achieved impossible things in their life time have undergone hardships, sacrifices, trials and tribulations. There is no easy victory over failure. No hard achievement is smooth and easy. History of great men reminds us that with strong determination man can achieve any thing he may set his mind upon, however impossible it may seem apparently.

A man with determination and iron will can defeat all hurdles in the way of his mission. Even the most intelligent people suffer in life if they cannot cope with their circumstances and labour hard to achieve the goal of their life. A genius who is fired with real zeal and determination to achieve his ideal comes to possess the necessary capacity to bear the hardships, cross the hurdles and achieve the final victory. Genius and hard work go together to bring the desired results. The stage of greatness comes after many stages of frustration and disappointment. The weaker man gives way to those frustrations but the genius perseveres and holds on to their mission until they achieve the object of their life.

1. The writer feels that victory over failure:
   A. is not possible B. is not good
   C. is absolute D. is not easy
2. According to the passage genius implies:
   A. failing again and again
   B. capacity of taking trouble and hardship
   C. stages of frustration and disappointment
   D. escape from hardship
3. Which of the following is correct?
   A. Only dull people should work hard
   B. Intelligent people need not labour hard
   C. Even intelligent people have to cope with circumstances
   D. None of the above
4. It can be inferred that:
   A. genius and hard work go together
   B. genius and hard work are opposed to each other
   C. genius and hard work end in frustration
   D. all of the above
5. A man can defeat all hurdles by:
   A. coping with all situations
   B. strong determination and iron will
   C. becoming strong
   D. becoming tall

Answers

1	2	3	4	5
D	B	C	A	B

PASSAGE-9

Life is a struggle. "We live in deeds and not in years." If we rest, we rust. If we work we shine like jewels. Adventures are the essence of life but action also entails contemplation. Proper action needs the proper initiative. Napoleon took the wrong initiative and brought the downfall of France. Proper action is always taken by the wise persons. The wise persons always foreshadow the hardships for executing a policy. They become passive when they forecast that their efforts are at stake. All great leaders and diplomats take the steps keeping in view their reputation.

We should strike when the iron is hot. Some persons take the steps haphazardly with the result that they lose the opportunity and thus they are treated as fools. Angels are wise people and very particular about their action. It has been the aim of all philosophers to understand the world. After understanding, they move very gradually and not like fools who plunge into the situation without contemplation. Mr. Ayub Khan under Bhutto's influence plunged into war with India inflicting destruction to humanity. Our ex-prime Minister Lal Bahadur Shastri gauged the situation. He responded to the challenge of Pakistan and won the battle. Fools always meddle with the situation without bringing about any change but wise persons penetrate into the matter and take the appropriate action.

1. According to the writer:
A. Napoleon acted wisely
B. we may rust like iron
C. we may shine like metals
D. leaders and diplomats act keeping in view their reputation

2. Some people are treated as fools because
A. they act haphazardly
B. they strike when the iron is hot
C. they act like philosophers
D. all of the above

3. Mr. Ayub Khan was
A. wise to decalre was against India
B. foolish to disobey Bhutto
C. not wise in declaring war against India
D. none of the above

4. What is the aim of the philosopher?
A. To act like angels
B. To act like Ayub Khan
C. To act like Bhutto
D. To understand the world

5. The passage implies that
A. one should act quickly
B. understanding should precede action
C. fools penetrate into the matter
D. none of the above

Answers

1	2	3	4	5
D	A	C	D	B

PASSAGE-10

With human beings the world ever ensnared by the performance of mechanical tasks and the pursuit of equally mechanical distractions, the time is not distant when nothing but the most abominable entertainments will succeed in steering them. If it happens so, the present civilisation will emerge as a mere imitation of the Roman in which the Romans desired more gladiators, tightrope walking elephants and fantastically rare animals to be slaughtered. This is one danger which is likely to cut at the roots of the modern civilisation because it threatens the existence of mental activities.

I would prefer to be bored by an eight hour job in an office or writing streams of words of journalism rather than be amused by the monotony of modern pleasures. It is the lack of participation which is the most damaging aspect of modern pleasures. This organised distraction combines within itself the performance of movies, gramophones, radios and the press which go a long way in killing the residue of initiative or sense of participation. Even in the case of newspapers, no mental effort is required on the part of the readers as the contents are presented in such a cut and dried manner that one need not undergo the fatigue of a single thought.

Consequently for years together men continue scanning newspapers and magazines by merely moving their eyes.

If idealists failed to stem the rot, in future, pleasures will take on incredibly monostrous shape.

1. The writer feels that human activities and distractions are:

A. logical B. interesting
C. intellectual D. mechanical

2. According to the passage entertainments

A. relieve a man
B. are badly needed
C. threaten the existence of mental activities
D. are useless

3. The writer prefers

A. modern pleasures to office work
B. modern pleasures to journalism
C. neither journalism nor office work
D. journalism and office work to modern pleasures

4. Modern pleasures, according to the writer

A. are indispensable
B. are useless because they don't amuse men
C. cripple the sense of participation
D. do not make men take the initiative

5. Which of the following is correct?

A. The author says that reading newspapers is bad
B. Mental effort is not required in reading newspapers
C. We should imitate Romans
D. We should slaughter animals

Answers

1	2	3	4	5
D	C	D	C	B

PASSAGE-11

Courage is not only the basis of all virtue; it is its expression. Faith, hope, charity and all the rest don't become virtues until it takes courage to exercise them. There are roughly two types of courage. The first, an emotional state which urges a man to risk injury or death, is physical courage. The second, a more reasoning attitude which enables him to take coolly his career, happiness, his whole future, or his judgement of what he thinks either right or worthwhile, is moral courage.

I have known many men, who had marked physical courage, but lacked moral courage. Some of them were in high places, but they failed to be great in themselves because they lacked moral courage. On the other hand, I have seen men who undoubtedly possessed moral courage but were very cautious about taking physical risks. But I have never met a man with moral courage who couldn't, when it was really necessary, face a situation boldly.

1. All virtues become meaningful because of

A. faith B. charity
C. courage D. hope

2. Physical courage is an expression of

A. emotions B. deliberation
C. uncertainty D. defiance

3. People with physical courage often lack

A. mental balance
B. capacity for reasoning
C. emotional stability
D. will to fight

4. A man with moral courage can

A. defy his enemies
B. overcome all difficulties
C. face a situation boldly
D. be very pragmatic

5. A man of courage is

A. cunning B. intelligent
C. curious D. careful

Answers

1	2	3	4	5
C	A	B	C	D

2. Cloze Test

A cloze test is a procedure in which an examinee is asked to supply words that have been removed from a passage as a test of his ability to comprehend text. Practise it regularly to score well.

TEST 1

Today most Indian businessmen are very worried. To begin with, they are not used to competition. In the past, they sold whatever ..... (1) ..... produced at whatever prices thay chose. But ..... (2) ..... increasing competition, customers began to ..... (3) ..... and choose. Imports suddenly became ..... (4) ..... available and that too at cheaper ..... (5) .....

1. A. it B. he
   C. they D. we
2. A. with B. by
   C. after D. from
3. A. buy B. take
   C. pick D. want
4. A. hardly B. easily
   C. frequently D. conveniently
5. A. costs B. returns
   C. dividend D. prices

TEST 2

As a rule of thumb, a manned mission costs from fifty to a hundred times more than a comparable unamanned mission. Thus, for scientific exploration alone, ... (1) ..... missions, employing machine intelligence, are ..... (2) ..... However, there may well be ..... (3) ..... other than scientific for exploring ..... (4) ..... social, economic, political, cultural or ..... (5) .....

1. A. manned B. unmanned
   C. space D. lunar
2. A. liked B. wanted
   C. used D. preferred
3. A. reasons B. causes
   C. clues D. objects
4. A. moon B. sun
   C. space D. mission
5. A. casual B. historic
   C. historical D. histrionic

TEST 3

The principal advantage in having a clear-cut objective of business is that it does not derail; the enterprise does not stray ..... (1) ..... the direct route that it has set for ..... (2) ..... Enterprises with well-defined objectives can conveniently undertake ..... (3) ..... and follow long-range development policies. Recognition of objectives ..... (4) ..... the temptation to compromise long-range ..... (5) ..... for short-term gains and improves coordination in work and consistency in policy.

1. A. from B. on
   C. along D. towards
2. A. others B. industry
   C. itself D. government
3. A. production B. research
   C. audit D. appraisal
4. A. invites B. defers
   C. shifts D. removes
5. A. objectives B. losses
   C. interests D. profits

TEST 4

Let children learn to judge their own work. A child ..... (1) ..... to talk does not learn ..... (2) ..... being corrected all the time ..... (3) ..... corrected too much, he will ..... (4) ..... talking. He notices a thousand times a day the difference between the ..... (5) ..... he uses and the language those around him use.

1. A. endeavouring B. learning
   C. experimenting D. experiencing
2. A. in B. on
   C. by D. to
3. A. unless B. being
   C. until D. if
4. A. stop B. halt
   C. avoid D. shun
5. A. speech B. language
   C. talk D. skill

TEST 5

His talk used to be full of wit and humours. He liked reading. He was a ..... **(1)** ..... reader and would pore over books ..... **(2)** ..... a wide range of interest as ..... **(3)** ..... he got them. He had ..... **(4)** ..... a standing order to two bookshops ..... **(5)** ..... city.

1. A. voracious B. fervent
   C. anxious D. enthusiastic
2. A. covering B. barring
   C. including D. containing
3. A. firmly B. quickly
   C. soon D. urgently
4. A. offered B. proclaimed
   C. intimated D. given
5. A. at B. in
   C. within D. inside

TEST 6

An old scholar ..... **(1)** ..... that Truth was in the country. He ..... **(2)** ..... to find her, as he had devoted his life to studying her in all her ..... **(3)** ..... . He came upon the cottage in the ..... **(4)** ..... where Truth lived. He ..... **(5)** ..... on the door. Truth ..... **(6)** ..... what he wanted. The scholar ..... **(7)** ..... who she was. He added that he had ..... **(8)** ..... a thousand times ..... **(9)** ..... she really was ..... **(10)** .....

1. A. hard B. herd
   C. heard D. hired
2. A. decide B. decides
   C. decided D. decision
3. A. firms B. forms
   C. farms D. ferns
4. A. maintain B. fountain
   C. mountain D. plantain
5. A. locked B. shocked
   C. knocked D. pocked
6. A. told B. said
   C. asked D. advised
7. A. explored B. exhorted
   C. explained D. exported
8. A. wandered B. wondered
   C. wondrous D. wounded
9. A. which B. what
   C. whom D. whose
10. A. like B. lake
    C. lick D. lack

TEST 7

Each species has its special place or habitat. An ..... **(1)** ..... bird-watcher can look at ..... **(2)** ..... forest, meadow, lake, swamp or field and ..... **(3)** ..... almost exactly what birds he ..... **(4)** ..... find there ..... **(5)** ..... birds are found all over the world; others ..... **(6)** ..... themselves to certain areas. Still ..... **(7)** ..... migrate from one country to another in ..... **(8)** ..... in search of warmth and ..... **(9)** ..... and then return in spring, ... **(10)** ..... the season is more favourable.

1. A. expert B. experienced
   C. advanced D. active
2. A. the B. some
   C. a D. certain
3. A. predict B. suggest
   C. prophesy D. calculate
4. A. should B. must
   C. might D. will
5. A. more B. some
   C. most D. all
6. A. keep B. entrust
   C. confine D. involve
7. A. some B. others
   C. few D. all
8. A. winter B. summer
   C. spring D. autumn
9. A. seeds B. crops
   C. fruit D. food
10. A. while B. until
    C. after D. when

TEST 8

In the large shops ..... **(1)** ..... for Diwali are begun ..... **(2)** ..... or six weeks before ..... **(3)** ..... actual day. Shop owners ..... **(4)** ..... Diwali because lots of ..... **(5)**

..... are given, which means ..... **(6)** ..... goods are bought than ..... **(7)** ..... any other time of ..... **(8)** ..... year. The main shops ..... **(9)** ..... decorated many weeks before ..... **(10)** ..... to tempt people to buy things.

1. A. preparations B. shopping
C. purchases D. preparing
2. A. two B. five
C. few D. couple
3. A. a B. an
C. the D. which
4. A. hate B. anticipate
C. recommend D. like
5. A. purchases B. prizes
C. presents D. presentation
6. A. many B. more
C. few D. less
7. A. at B. in
C. on D. for
8. A. any B. a
C. the D. this
9. A. were B. are
C. have been D. will be
10. A. occasion B. festival
C. festivities D. Diwali

TEST 9

Many parents greet their children's teenage years with needless dread. While teens ..... **(1)** ..... assault us with heavy-metal music ..... **(2)** ..... outlandish clothes and spend all ..... **(3)** ..... time with friends, such behaviour ..... **(4)** ..... adds up to full-scale revolt. Teenage ..... **(5)** ..... according to psychologist Laurence Steinberg, has been ..... **(6)** ..... exaggerated. Sociologist Sanford Dornbusch agrees. "The ..... **(7)** ..... that teenagers inevitably rebel is a ..... **(8)** ..... that has the potential for great family ..... **(9)**," say Dornbusch. He believes the notion can ..... **(10)** ..... communication during this critical time for parents to influence youngsters.

1. A. should B. may
C. must D. can
2. A. put B. show
C. dress D. flaunt
3. A. our B. their
C. his D. her
4. A. infrequently B. sporadically
C. scarcely D. always
5. A. revolution B. mania
C. subversion D. rebellion
6. A. greatly B. hardly
C. never D. always
7. A. surmise B. idea
C. complaint D. accusation
8. A. story B. reality
C. fact D. myth
9. A. ruin B. harm
C. defeat D. downfall
10. A. damage B. destroy
C. injure D. suffocate

TEST 10

Well, it was done and the debt was paid. But I began to feel ..... **(1)** ..... sorry for myself that I could not ..... **(2)** ..... it. I made up my mind never to steal ..... **(3)** ..... I also made up my mind to tell ..... **(4)** ..... to my father. But I did not have the ..... **(5)** ..... to speak to him. It was not that ..... **(6)** ..... was afraid that my father would beat me. I ..... **(7)** ..... not remember any time when he beat ..... **(8)** ..... of us. I was afraid that my confession ..... **(9)** ..... cause him great pain. But I ..... **(10)** ..... felt that I had to take this risk. I would never be happy again unless I told everything to my father.

1. A. so B. as
C. very D. too
2. A. accept B. like
C. bear D. understand
3. A. also B. again
C. still D. ever
4. A. anything B. something
C. nothing D. everything
5. A. bravery B. courage
C. fortitude D. gallantry
6. A. I B. he
C. she D. me
7. A. would B. should
C. do D. did
8. A. all B. some
C. any D. none
9. A. shall B. can
C. will D. would
10. A. soon B. again
C. once D. since

TEST 11

It is difficult to find a person who would put in a good word for the kind of bureaucracy we have in India. Incidentally, things may now be seen as coming to a head. ..... **(1)** ..... the attainment of Independence, India ..... **(2)** from time to time several ..... **(3)** ..... power Committees or Commissions to ..... **(4)** ..... administration. In spite of all this, the impression ..... **(5)** ..... that the Indian variety of bureaucracy has been slow and slothful. Fact is that the ..... **(6)** ..... of bureaucracy happens to be ..... **(7)** ..... the same all over the world. Even in the U.S.A. Presidents have ..... **(8)** ..... a great deal of concern ..... **(9)** ..... the manner in which bureaucracy has been functioning at various levels. In spite of all this, not much change can be ..... **(10)** ..... in the near future. One may feel like hanging one's head the despair unless one believes in some super-human power that looks after our universe.

1. A. From B. With C. Till D. Since

2. A. arranged B. appointed C. framed D. selected

3. A. great B. super C. high D. multiple

4. A. perform B. reform C. revive D. transform

5. A. insists B. subsists C. consists D. persists

6. A. structure B. function C. growth D. behaviour

7. A. practically B. structurally C. precisely D. strictly

8. A. asserted B. declared C. voiced D. waged

9. A. on B. at C. with D. from

10. A. accepted B. expected C. affected D. admitted

ANSWERS

Test 1

1	2	3	4	5
C	A	C	B	D

Test 2

1	2	3	4	5
B	D	A	C	C

Test 3

1	2	3	4	5
A	C	A	D	A

Test 4

1	2	3	4	5
B	C	D	C	B

Test 5

1	2	3	4	5
A	A	C	D	B

Test 6

1	2	3	4	5
C	C	B	C	C
6	**7**	**8**	**9**	**10**
C	B	B	B	A

Test 7

1	2	3	4	5
A	C	D	B	B
6	**7**	**8**	**9**	**10**
C	A	A	D	D

Test 8

1	2	3	4	5
A	B	C	D	C
6	**7**	**8**	**9**	**10**
B	A	C	B	D

Test 9

1	2	3	4	5
B	D	B	D	D
6	**7**	**8**	**9**	**10**
B	B	B	A	D

Test 10

1	2	3	4	5
A	C	B	D	B
6	**7**	**8**	**9**	**10**
A	D	C	D	A

Test 11

1	2	3	4	5
D	B	C	B	D
6	**7**	**8**	**9**	**10**
B	A	C	B	B

3. Spot the Error

The most common errors in English are of spellings, grammar and usage of words. By regular practice, the errors can be easily spotted and minimised.

COMMON ERRORS WITH NOUNS AND NOUN-PHRASES

Incorrect	Correct
1. I have bought new *furnitures.*	I have bought new *furniture.*
2. The wages of sin *are* death.	The wages of sin *is* death.
3. She told these *news* to her mother.	She told her mother this *news.*
4. He took *troubles* to do his work.	He took *trouble* (or pains) over his work.
5. The *cattles* were grazing.	The *cattle* were grazing.
6. He showered *many abuses* on me.	He showered *much abuse* on me.
7. I spent the holidays with my *family members.*	I spent the holidays with my *family.*
8. There is no *place* in this compartment.	There is no *room* in this compartment.
9. Write this new *poetry* in your *copy.*	Write this new *poem* in your *note-book.*
10. He took *insult* at this.	He took *offence* at this.
11. Put your *sign* here.	Put your *signatures* here.
12. She is my *cousin sister.*	She is my *cousin.*
13. *Sunil's* my *neighbour's* house was burgled.	*Sunil* my *neighbour's* house was burgled.
14. I lost a *ten-rupees* note.	I lost *a ten-rupee* note.
15. Road closed for *repair.*	Road closed for *repairs.*
16. His house is out of *repairs.*	His house is out of *repair.*
17. What is the *reason* of an earthquake?	What is the *cause* of an earthquake?
18. This building is made of *stones.*	This building is made of *stone.*
19. I disapprove of *these kinds* of games.	I disapprove of *this kind* of games.
20. Veena's and Sheela's father is ill.	Veena and Sheela's father is ill.
21. His *son-in-laws* are doctors.	His *sons-in-law* are doctors.
22. *Alms* is given to the *poor.*	*Alms* are given to the poor.
23. He always keeps his words.	He always keeps his *word.*
24. I carried the *luggages.*	I carried the *luggage.*
25. *Two-third* of the work is left.	*Two-thirds* of the work is left.

COMMON ERRORS WITH PRONOUNS

	Incorrect	Correct
1.	Both did not go.	Neither went.
2.	We all did not go.	None of us went.
3.	Each of these boys play.	Each of these boys plays.
4.	Whoever does best he will get a prize.	Whoever does best will get a prize.
5.	One should not waste his time.	A man should not waste his time.
6.	I and she are sisters.	She and I are sisters.
7.	He is wiser than me.	He is wiser than I.
8.	Between you and I, Anil is not to be trusted.	Between you and me, Anil is not to be trusted.
9.	Nobody was there but I.	Nobody was there but me.
10.	Who is there ? It is me.	Who is there ? It is I.
11.	Only he and me can use this card.	Only he and I can use this card.
12.	Let you and I go now.	Let you and me go now.
13.	Everyone got one's pay.	Everyone got his pay.
14.	Everyone is frightened when they see a tiger.	Everyone is frightened when he sees a tiger.
15.	These two friends are fond of one another.	These two friends are fond of each other.
16.	I did not like him coming at that hour.	I did not like his coming at that hour.
17.	Who do you think I met?	Whom do you think I met?
18.	You should avail this opportunity.	You should avail yourself this opportunity.
19.	When you have read these books, please return the same to me.	When you have read the books, please return them to me.
20.	They that are humble need fear no fall.	Those that are humble need fear no fail.

COMMON ERRORS WITH ADJECTIVES

	Incorrect	Correct
1.	These all oranges are good.	All these oranges are good.
2.	He held the book in the both hands.	He held the book in both hands.
3.	Both men have not come.	Neither man has come.
4.	That man should do some or other work.	That man should do some work or other
5.	He is elder than I.	He is older than I.
6.	Shakespeare is greater than any other poets.	Shakespeare is greater than any other poet.
7.	He is a coward man.	He is a cowardly man.
8.	Many villagers cannot write his own name.	Many villagers cannot write their own name.
9.	Each of us loves our home.	Each of us loves his home.
10.	Much efforts bring their reward.	Much effort brings its reward.
11.	He found hundred rupees.	He found a hundred rupees.
12.	He had leave of four days.	He had four days leave.

Incorrect	Correct
13. This is a worth seeing sight.	This is a sight worth seeing.
14. He will spend his future life here.	He will spend the rest of his life here.
15. There is a best teacher in that class.	There is a very good teacher in that class.
16. Of the two plans this is the best.	Of the two plans this is the better.
17. He is becoming strong every day.	He is becoming stronger every day.
18. He is worst than I.	He is worse than I.
19. Jaipur is hot than Delhi.	Jaipur is hotter than Delhi.
20 In our library the number of books is less.	In our library the number of books is small.
21. From the three he is more clever.	He is the cleverest of the three.
22. India is the first peace-loving country in the world.	India is the foremost peace-loving country in the world.
23. Verbal instruction will not do.	Oral instruction will not do.
24. Her command over French is most excellent.	Her command over French is excellent.
25. He has not some money with him.	He has not any money with him.
26. I have visited Bombay many a times.	I have visited Bombay many a time.
27. Death is more preferable to dishonour.	Death is preferable to dishonour.
28. I gave him a few books I had.	I gave him the few books I had.
29. If he wants farther help send him to me.	If he wants further help, send him to me.
30. She is so cunning as a fox.	She is as cunning as a fox.

COMMON ERRORS WITH VERBS

Incorrect	Correct
1. He asked had we taken our luggage.	He asked if we had taken our luggage.
2. She asked what are you doing.	She asked what we were doing.
3. Rama asked to Anil why he is angry.	Rama asked Anil why he was angry.
4. He does not care for his money.	He does not take care of his money.
5. He does not care for his work.	He takes no care over his work.
6. No one cared for him after his mother died.	No one took care of him after his mother died.
7. He got angry before I said a word.	He got angry before I had said a word.
8. I met a man who was my tutor 20 years ago.	I met a man who had been my tutor twenty years ago.
9. I had been for walking yesterday.	I went for a walk yesterday.
10 If I shall do this I shall be wrong.	If I do this I shall be wrong.
11. I have left trekking.	I have given up trekking.
12. I came to know as to how he did this.	I learnt how he did this.
13. I came to know why he was sad.	I found out why he was sad.
14. He knows to swim.	He knows how to swim.
15. The criminal's head was cut.	The criminal's head was cut off.

Incorrect	Correct
16. I said to him to go.	I told him to go.
17. I told the teacher to excuse me.	I asked the teacher to excuse me.
18. He is troubling me.	He is giving me trouble.
19. I have got a hurt on my leg.	I have hurt my leg.
20. She gave a speech.	She made a speech.
21. He has given his examination.	He has sat for his examination.
22. He took out his shoes.	He took off his shoes.
23. I have ordered for a new car.	I have ordered a new car.
24. He would not hear me.	He would not listen to me.
25. I struck a blow on his face.	I struck him in the face.
26. He denied to come.	He refused to come.
27. He lived there for a day.	He stayed there for a day.
28. The book is not found.	The book is lost.
29. Shut the light.	Turn off the light.
30. I must revenge my brother.	I must avenge my brother.

COMMON ERRORS IN SUBJECT-VERB AGREEMENT

Incorrect	Correct
1. The owners of this factory *is* very rich.	The owners of this factory *are* very rich.
2. The pleasures of nature that one can experience at Shimla *is* beyond description.	The pleasures of nature that one can experience at Shimla *are* beyond description.
3. There *is* no street lights in our colony.	There *are* no street lights in our colony.
4. He and I *am* entrusted with the job.	He and I *are* entrusted with the job.
5. Rice and curry *are* his favourite dish.	Rice and curry *is* his favourite dish.
6. The honour and glory of our country *are* at stake.	The honour and glory of our country *is* at stake.
7. Time and tide *waits* for none.	Time and tide *wait* for none.
8. All the passengers with the driver *was* killed.	All the passengers, with the driver, *were* killed.
9. The teacher, with her students, *were* going out.	The teacher, with her students, *was* going out.
10. I as well as they *am* tired.	I as well as they *are* tired.
11. Not only the soldiers but their captain also *were* captured.	Not only the soldiers but their captain also *was* captured.
12. Neither you nor I *were* selected.	Neither you nor I *was* selected.
13. Either of these two applicants *are* fit for the job but neither want to accept it.	Either of these two applicants *is* fit for the job but neither wants to accept it.
14. One of these students are sure to stand first.	One of these students *is* sure to stand first.
15. Everyone of these workers want a raise.	Everyone of these workers wants a raise.
16. None of these letters has been answered so far.	None of these letters *have* been answered so far.

	Incorrect	Correct
17.	None of the girls were present at the party.	None of the girls *was* present at the party.
18.	Many a battle were fought on Indian soil.	Many a battle *was* fought on Indian soil.
19.	A lot of work remain to be done.	A lot of work *remains* to be done.
20.	The majority of these girls likes music.	The majority of these girls *like* music.
21.	The number of admissions are encouraging.	The number of admissions *is* encouraging.
22.	A large number of boys was present.	A large number of boys *were* present.
23.	A variety of books was on display.	A variety of books *were* on display.
24.	Variety are the spice of life.	Variety *is* the spice of life.
25.	If my estimates are correct. I will need another hundred rupees.	If my estimate is correct, I will need another hun dred rupees.
26.	Mathematics *are* my favourite subject.	Mathematics *is* my favourite subject.
27.	'Gulliver's Travels' *are* written by Swift.	'Gulliver's Travels' *is* written by Swift.
28.	Ten miles *are* a long distance to cover on foot.	Ten miles *is* a long distance to cover on foot.
29.	A new pair of shoes *are* to be purchased.	A new pair of shoes *is* to be purchased.
30.	The Committee *have* issued its report.	The Committee *has* issued its report.
31.	I, who am your friend, *has* always been on your side,	I, who am your friend, *have* always been on your side.
32.	I am the person who *have* always stood by you.	I am the person who *has* always stood by you.
33.	This is one of the best novels that *has* been published this year.	This is one of the best novels that *have* been published this year.
34.	Less than half the amount *have* been wasted.	Less than half the amount *has* been wasted.
35.	A lot of people *has* turned up for the show.	A lot of people *have* turned up for the show.
36.	Much of their honour *are* un-deserved.	Much of their honour *is* un-deserved.
37.	More than a decade *have* passed since this house was built.	More than a decade *has* passed since this house was built.
38.	Either she or he *are* mistaken.	Either she or he *is* mistaken.
39.	Plenty of information *are* available on the subject.	Plenty of information *is* available on the subject.
40.	Plenty of pamphlets *is* available on the subject.	Plenty of pamphlets *are* available on the subject.

COMMON ERRORS IN USE OF WILL, SHALL, WOULD, SHOULD, MAY, MIGHT, MUST

	Incorrect	Correct
1.	When I shall see him I shall tell him this.	When I *see* him, I shall tell him this.
2.	If I should do wrong, he would punish me.	If I *did* wrong, he would punish me.
3.	Until he will have confessed his fault, he will be kept in prison,	Until he *has* confessed his fault, he will be kept in prison.
4.	She will obey me.	She *shall* obey me.
5.	You would work hard.	You *should* work hard.
6.	You shall find him in the garden.	You *will* find him in the garden.

	Incorrect	Correct
7.	He must have died of exposure, but we cannot be certain.	He *might* have died of exposure, but we cannot be certain.
8.	You might not show disrespect to your elders.	You *must* not show disrespect to your elders.
9.	You may take exercise in order to maintain good health,	You *must* take exercise in order to maintain good health.
10.	He must be a crook for all we know.	He *may* be a crook for all we know.

COMMON ERRORS IN THE USE OF ADVERBS

(Very, Much, Too, Enough, Quite, Hardly, Scarcely, Before, Ago, Since, Yet, Still, etc.)

	Incorrect	Correct
1.	He is very much angry.	He is *very* angry.
2.	She was very good enough to help me.	She was *good enough* to help me.
3.	She runs much fast.	She runs *very* fast.
4.	She runs very faster than Seema.	She runs *much* faster than Seema.
5.	It is bitter cold today.	It is *bitterly* cold today.
6.	He is a much learned man.	He is a very learned man.
7	She is thinking very hardly.	She is thinking very hard.
8.	To tell in brief the film was boring.	*In short* the film was boring.
9.	He told the story in details.	He told the story *in detail.*
10.	I did it anyhow.	I *managed to do* it somehow.
11.	Aeroplanes reach Europe soon.	Aeroplanes reach Europe quickly.
12.	Before long there were dinosaurs on the earth.	*Long ago,* there were dinosaurs on the earth.
13.	This book is too interesting.	This book is *very* interesting.
14.	He lives miserly.	He lives in *a miserly* way.
15.	Just I had gone when she came.	I had just gone when she came.
16.	He sings good.	He sings *well.*
17.	He sings good than I.	He sings *better* than I.
18.	Really speaking it is cold.	*As a matter of fact* it is cold.
19.	He is enough tall to reach the ceiling.	He is *tall enough* to reach the ceiling.
20.	He went directly to his college.	He went *direct* to his college.
21.	He is presently at Delhi	He is at Delhi *at present.*
22.	Last night she returned lately.	Last night she *returned late.*
23.	He was even blamed by his friends.	He was *blamed even* by his friends.
24.	I only employed him for a week.	I employed him for a week only.
25.	I met him four months before.	I met him four *months ago.*

	Incorrect	Correct
26.	Anil seldom ever goes to school.	Anil *seldom goes* to school.
27.	I will wait here until you do not go.	I will wait here until *you go.*
28.	I never remember having met her before.	I *do not remember* having met her before.
29.	She has not been here too long to have many friends,	She has not *been here long* enough to have many friends.
30.	Hardly I have had any rest since one week.	Hardly have *I had* any rest for a week.
31.	Scarcely the water crossed the danger level, the warning signals were sounded.	Scarcely *had the* water *crossed the* danger level, when the warning signals were sounded.
32.	She is neat but fairly slow.	She is *neat* but rather slow.
33.	It is a rather good film.	It is a *fairly good* film.
34.	We yet have time to catch the bus.	We *still have* time to catch the bus.
35.	She has not still spent all her money.	She has *not yet* spent all her money.

COMMON ERRORS IN THE USE OF CONJUNCTIONS

	Incorrect	Correct
1.	As he is fat so he runs slowly.	As he is fat *he* runs slowly.
2.	If he is fat then he will run slowly.	If he is fat, he will run slowly.
3.	Though he is fat still he runs fast.	Though he is fat, *he runs* fast.
4.	*As* I pulled the trigger at the sametime he shook my arm.	As I pulled the trigger, he shook my arm.
5.	No sooner I had spoken than he left.	No sooner *had* I spoken than he left.
6.	Not only he will go, but also he will stay there.	Not only *will he* go, but he *will also* stay there.
7.	Neither he comes nor he writes.	Neither *does he* come nor *does he* write.
8.	Scarcely he entered the room than the telephone rang.	Scarcely *had* he entered the room *when the* telephone rang.
9.	Hardly she had left the house than it began to rain.	Hardly *had she* left the house *when* it began to rain.
10.	He is the fastest runner and he comes last.	He is the fastest runner *but* he comes last.
11.	She is as innocent as if she looks.	She is as innocent as she looks.
12.	Until he does not try he must be punished.	He must be punished unless he tries.
13.	I want to know as to why you are late.	I want to know why you are late.
14.	I am fond of Chinese food as for example sweet and sour prawns.	I am fond of Chinese food, for example, sweet and sour prawns.
15.	He was angry therefore I ran away.	He was angry so I ran away.
16.	I was trying to work, at that time he was disturbing me.	While I was trying to work, he was disturbing me.
17.	Supposing if he is late, what will happen?	Supposing he is late (or if he is late) what will happen?
18.	He asked me that why I was late.	He asked me why I was late.

Incorrect	Correct
19. Let us catch a taxi lest we should not get late.	Let us catch a taxi lest we should get late.
20. She dresses herself like the teacher does.	She dresses herself as the teacher does.
21 Wait while I come.	Wait *until* (or *till)* I come.
22. Until, there is corruption in India, there can be little progress.	*As long* as there is corruption in India there can be little progress.
23. I have never told a lie nor cheated anybody.	I have never told a lie *nor have I* cheated anybody.
24. Both Mohan as well as Arun are responsible for this action.	Both Mohan *and* Arun are responsible for this action.
25. Hindus and Muslims both are to blame for the riots.	*Both Hindus* and Muslims are to blame for the riots.
26. I have bought paintings, books, records, and etc.	I have bought paintings, books *and records etc.*
27. He as well as you is a fool.	He as well as you *are* a fool.
28. He is so poor and he cannot save anything.	He is so *poor that* he cannot save anything.
29. Such a' book that you want is not available.	Such a book *as* you want is not available.
30. Such was her condition as everyone was moved to pity.	Such was her condition that everyone was moved to pity.

COMMON ERRORS IN THE USE OF PREPOSITIONS

Incorrect	Correct
1. I will not listen him.	I will not listen *to* him.
2. Copy this word by word.	Copy this word *for* word.
3. He enquired from her where she lived.	He enquired *of* her where she lived.
4. Sign here with ink.	Sign here *in* ink.
5. Has she come in train or by foot?	Has she come *by* train or *on* foot?
6. She said this at his face.	She said this *to* his face.
7. Open the book on page one	Open the book *at* page one.
8. I was invited for lunch.	I was *invited to* lunch.
9. I am ill since three months.	I have been *ill for* three months.
10. This paper is inferior than that.	This paper is inferior *to* that.
11. This resembles to that.	This *resembles* that.
12. My brother is superior than you in strength.	My brother is superior *to* you in strength.
13. He wrote me	He wrote *to* me.
14. I shall explain them this.	I shall explain this *to* them.
15. Send this letter on my address.	Send this letter *to* my address.
16. He suggested me this.	He suggested this *to* me.
17. He goes *on his* work.	He goes *to his* work.
18. He *reached to* Nagpur.	He *reached* Nagpur.
19. He told *to me* to go.	He told *me* to go.

Incorrect	Correct
20 The term begins *from* July 1st.	The term begins *on* July 1st.
21. There are many advantages *from* this.	The advantages *of* this are many.
22. We waste much time *in* trifles.	We waste much time *on* (or *over)* trifles.
23. He sat *on* a tree.	He sat *in* a tree.
24. This is a comfortable house to *live.*	This is a comfortable house to *live in.*
25. This is the road to *go.*	This is the road to *go by.*
26. He married *with* an Indian lady.	He *married an Indian* lady.
27. He accompanied *with* his friend.	He *accompanied his* friend.
28. He went *for doing some* business.	He went away *on* business.
29. He went for *riding.*	He went *for a ride.*
30. I *pitied on* him.	I *pitied* him.
31. When this was searched it was found.	When this was searched *for* it was found.
32. I shall inform them *this.*	I shall inform them *of* this.
33. *Due to illness* I cannot go to school.	*Owing* to illness I cannot go to school.
34. He went *to the back side* of the house.	He went *behind* (or to the back of) the house.
35. I must go; there is no *help.*	I must go; there is no help *for it.*
36. I *met with your* friend there.	I *met your* friend there.
37. The First World War was fought *during* 1914-1918.	The First World War was fought *between* 1914-1918.
38. England grew prosperous *between* Queen Victoria's reign.	England grew prosperous *during* Queen Victoria's reign.
39. He asked a holiday.	He asked *for* a holiday.
40. I am obliged of you for this good turn.	I am obliged *to* you for this good turn.
41. There is no harm to try.	There is no harm *in trying.*

MISCELLANEOUS ERRORS

(Including Ambiguities and Indianisms)

Incorrect	Correct
1. Many *homes* are lying vacant.	Many *houses* are lying vacant.
2. It is cool in the *shadow* of the tree.	It is cool in the *shade* of the tree.
3. She *keeps* good health.	She *enjoys* good health.
4. My leg is *paining.*	*I am feeling pain* in my leg.
5. *See* this word in the dictionary.	*Look up* this word in the dictionary.
6. The train will arrive *just now*	The train will arrive *shortly.*
7. They are *pulling* on well.	They are *getting* on well.
8. The river has *over flown* its bank.	The river has *over flown* its banks.
9. He was appointed *on* the post.	He was appointed *to* the post.
10. Last but not *the least,* we have to discuss the problem of over population.	Last but not *least,* we have to discuss the problem of over population.

Incorrect	Correct
11. *Cities* after *cities* fell.	*City* after *city* fell.
12. What is the use Munir going there?	What is the use of Munir going there?
13. He *did many mischief.*	He *made much mischief.*
14. It is exact five *in* my watch.	It is exact five *by* my watch.
15. I will dine with them on *next Sunday.*	I will dine with them *Sunday next.*
16. Misfortunes when faced bravely and *manly* become less troublesome.	Misfortunes when faced bravely and *manfully* become less troublesome.
17. I am *laid down* with fever.	I am *laid up* with fever.
18. He is habituated to smoking.	He is *addicted* to smoking.
19. *According to my opinion* he is right.	*In my opinion* (or according *to me)* he is right.
20. Could you please *open* this knot?	Could you please *untie* this knot?

MULTIPLE CHOICE QUESTIONS

Directions: *In the following questions some of the sentences have errors and some are correct. Find out which part of a sentence has an error, the number of that part is your answer. If a sentence is free from errors, then your answer is D i.e., No error.*

1. (A) Either Ram or/(B) you is responsible/(C) for this action./(D) No error.

2. (A) The student flatly denied/(B) that he had copied/(C) in the examination hall./(D) No error.

3. (A) By the time you arrive tomorrow/(B) I have finished/(C) my work./(D) No error.

4. (A) The captain with the members of his team/(B) are returning/(C) after a fortnight./(D) No error.

5. (A) After returning from/(B) an all-India tour/(C) I had to describe about it./(D) No error.

6. (A) The teacher asked his students/(B) if they had gone through/(C) either of the three chapters included in the prescribed text./(D) No error.

7. (A) Do you know/(B) how old were you/(C) when you came here?/(D) No error.

8. (A) Beware of/(B) a fair-weather friend/(C) who is neither a friend in need nor a friend indeed./(D) No error.

9. (A) Copernicus proved/(B) that Earth/(C) moves round the Sun./(D) No error.

10. (A) The property/(B) was divided/(C) among the two brothers./(D) No error.

11. (A) I am quite certain/(B) that the lady is not only greedy/(C) but miserly./(D) No error.

12. (A) The brilliant success in the examination/(B) as well as his record in sports/(C) deserves high praise./(D) No error.

13. (A) I cannot find/(B) where has he gone/(C) though I have tried may best./(D) No error.

14. (A) If I was/(B) the Prime Minister of India/(C) I would work wonders/(D) No error.

15. (A) If it weren't/(B) for you,/(C) I wouldn't be alive today./(D) No error.

16. (A) He looked like a lion/(B) baulked from/(C) its prey./(D) No error.

17. (A) Widespread flooding/(B) is affecting/(C) large areas of the villages./(D) No error.

18. (A) If we really set to/(B) we can get the whole house/(C) cleaned in an afternoon./(D) No error.

19. (A) It's arrogant for you/(B) to assume you'll/(C)win every time./(D) No error.

20. (A) The two books are the same/(B) except for the fact that this/(C) has an answer in the back./(D) No error.

21. (A) Your husband doesn't/(B) believe that you are older/(C) than I./(D) No error.

22. (A) I could not/(B) answer to/(C) the question./ (D) No error.

23. (A) Two years passed/(B) since/(C) my cousin died./(D) No error.

24. (A) I am learning English/(B) for ten years/(C) without much effect./(D) No error.

25. (A) Ramesh has agreed/(B) to marry with the girl/(C) of his parent's choice./ (D) No error.

26. (A) When he was arriving./(B) the party was/ (C) in full swing./(D) No error.

27. (A) The most studious boy/(B) in the class/ (C) was made as the captain./(D) No error.

28. (A) I am participating/(B) in the two-miles race/(C) tomorrow morning./(D) No error.

29. (A) When the boy committed a mistake/(B) the teacher made him to do/(C) the sum again./(D) No error.

30. (A) Whenever a person lost anything/(B) the poor folk around/(C) are suspected./(D) No error.

ANSWERS

1. **(B):** Replace 'is' by 'are'
2. **(D):** No error
3. **(B):** Replace 'have' by 'would have'
4. **(B):** Replace 'are' by 'its'
5. **(C):** Replace 'had to describe' by 'described'
6. **(C):** Replace 'either' by 'any'
7. **(D):** No error
8. **(D):** No error
9. **(B):** Omit 'that'
10. **(C):** Replace 'among' by 'between'
11. **(C):** Add 'also'
12. **(D):** No error
13. **(B):** Replace 'has he' by 'he has'
14. **(A):** Replace 'was' by 'were'
15. **(C):** Replace 'wouldn't be' by 'would not have been'
16. **(C):** Replace 'its' by 'his'
17. **(C):** Replace 'areas' by 'area'
18. **(A):** Replace 'set to' by 'set on'
19. **(A):** Replace 'for' by 'of'
20. **(C):** Replace 'in' by 'on'
21. **(C):** Replace 'I' by 'me'
22. **(B):** Omit 'to'
23. **(A):** Replace 'passed' by 'have passed'
24. **(A):** Replace 'am' by 'have been'
25. **(B):** Omit 'with'
26. **(A):** Replace 'was arriving' by 'arrived'
27. **(C):** Omit 'as'
28. **(B):** Replace 'in' by 'at'
29. **(B):** Omit 'to'
30. **(A):** Replace 'lost' by 'loses'

4. SENTENCE IMPROVEMENT

One may use the same words in many ways but the best way is only one that makes the perfect usage of the words and conveys the proper meaning of the expression. Try it yourself in this exercise.

MULTIPLE CHOICE QUESTIONS

Directions: *In these questions, a part of the sentence is **bold**. Below are given alternatives to the **bold** part at A, B and C which may improve the sentence. Choose the correct alternative to edit and improve the sentence. In case no improvement is needed, your answer is D.*

1. For most people who exercise **at the** morning, there is no getting around the question: Eat and run? Or run and eat later?
   A. in the B. in
   C. at the time of D. No Improvement
2. Are ad agencies even attempting to peer into the keyhole of this indulgence sanctum to garner consumer insights **ahead of** the curve?
   A. above B. over
   C. within D. No Improvement
3. Too many people rush into the world of credit and don't stop to think about how **their actions could affect their** credit score and ability to qualify for credit in the future.
   A. their actions may affect their
   B. their actions might affect their
   C. their actions will affect their
   D. No Improvement
4. According to the report, **number of deal with** vaccines were energized by concerns around avian flu, SARS, and biodefense products, while looming patent expirations led to more deals in generics.
   A. number of deals in
   B. number of deal in
   C. number of deals with
   D. No Improvement
5. This is how the Bombay High Court responded to the state government's purported **moral stand which** dance bars were causing grave harm to society.
   A. moral stand in B. moral stand at
   C. moral stand that D. No Improvement
6. If you have a high credit limit, use **at least a** third of it.
   A. atleast a B. at last a
   C. utmost a D. No Improvement
7. Fitness experts will say that **first eating provides** fuel for a proper workout.
   A. eating in the beginning provides
   B. first eat provides
   C. eating first provides
   D. No Improvement
8. One study that examined the claim directly in 2012 found that a group of people did **burned much calories from fat on days** when they exercised on an empty stomach than on days when they had a small breakfast first.
   A. burn more calories from fat on days
   B. burn more calorie from fat on days
   C. burnt more calories from fat on days
   D. No Improvement
9. Carefree children spent their afternoons **to run about barefoot**, their clothes dusty, and telltale twigs of the neighbour's mango tree in their hair.
   A. running barefoot in the sun
   B. run about barefoot in the sun
   C. running about barefoot in the sun
   D. No Improvement

10. A year ago, a 13-year-old girl attempted suicide because her mother **refuses to pay his** mobile bills.

A. refuses to pay her B. refused to pay her
C. refused to pay his D. No Improvement

11. Discreet salience **is extremely important** to create that 'irresistible-yet-unattainable' image for brands that want to take India seriously

A. was extremely important
B. is mainly important
C. was important extremely
D. No Improvement

12. This, over a designer outfit that he wanted for a friend's party and **that his sensitive** parents refused him.

A. which his sensitive
B. which his insensitive
C. that his insensitive
D. No Improvement

13. Goa was full of non-Goa property hunters **rushing about buying up the place** like tomorrow was an expired lease.

A. rushing in buying up the place
B. rushed about buying up the place
C. rushing about to buy up the place
D. No Improvement

14. Property hunting is a **tired and hungry** making business.

A. is a tiresome and hungry
B. is a tiring and hungry
C. is a tiring and waste
D. No Improvement

15. Cultural differences aside, **till luxury need speaks** in a manner that befits.

A. luxury still needs to speak
B. luxury still need to speak
C. luxury till need to speak
D. No Improvement

16. Indian food – the culinary avatar of the subcontinent's social history presented on a platter – **is without doubt the best food** in the world.

A. is undoubtly the greatest food
B. is without doubt greatest food
C. is best food without doubt
D. No Improvement

17. It must retain the language of poetry. **It needed to create** stories, and not statements.

A. It needed creating B. It needs creating
C. It needs to create D. No Improvement

18. In 2012, Asia-Pacific has become the first region **to reach aggregate profiting** in biotech.

A. to reach aggregated profi-tability
B. to reach aggregate profi-tability
C. to reach aggregate of profit
D. No Improvement

19. India is deviating to embrace the West. If Western luxury brands deviate a little, **albeit selectively**, they will find rich Indian arms open far and wide.

A. though selectively
B. however selectively
C. albeit selectedly
D. No Improvement

20. China and India continued to attract attention and deals, motivated by the desire to increase access to these **largest and growing** drug markets and by the need to lower the costs of drug development.

A. larger and growing B. large and growing
C. larger and grown D. No Improvement

21. Luxury brands are **still above of the** clover curve here, with their elite (small) audiences.

A. still ahead of the B. still in the
C. still far of the D. No Improvement

22. Agencies **hence needed to be** sure of returns before investing, say ad men.

A. hence needs to be B. so needs to be
C. hence need to be D. No Improvement

23. India is still a nascent market and that's the spirit everyone's **looking at it**.

A. looking for it B. looking in it
C. looking with it D. No Improvement

24. Questioning the state's move to allow women to serve liquor but not dance in bars **of the ground that** dancing aroused physical lust

A. on the grounds that
B. of the grounds that
C. over the grounds that
D. No Improvement

25. For England the positives from their crushing series lose come in the shape of James Anderson and Kevin Pietersen, **both of which** have made significant strides up the rankings

A. both of which B. both of whom
C. both of who D. No Improvement

26. International campaigns can work well for luxury here, **but context cannot be** ignored.

A. so context cannot be
B. but context cannot
C. but context couldn't
D. No Improvement

27. For one, the Indian luxury context, **while evolved rapidly**, still has its own meaning, and its own implications.

A. while evolved rapid
B. which evolving rapidly
C. while evolving rapidly
D. No Improvement

28. But too much of availability can compromise a luxury brand or **made it lose** its lustre.

A. make her lose B. make him lose
C. make it lose D. No Improvement

29. Still, it's under-the-upper **layers themselves who** are aspiring for slivers of luxury

A. layers themselves which
B. layer itself who
C. layers themself which
D. No Improvement

30. It is like saying Hindi movies, with skimpily dressed dancers, would **effect public** order

A. effect your B. affect public
C. affected public D. No Improvement

31. The court held that a few women being involved in prostitution was no **justice to deny other** bar girls the right to livelihood

A. justification to declare other
B. justification to deny other
C. justice to let other
D. No Improvement

32. All-rounder Irfan Pathan has also made some progress **over the** player rankings.

A. above the B. at the
C. up the D. No Improvement

33. Former PM on Sunday **joined hands** with suspended Lok Sabha members to float a new political outfit.

A. folded hands
B. walked hand in hand
C. shaked hands
D. No Improvement

34. Pakistan's former PMs will meet in London on Monday **to ask** a strategy to return home from exile.

A. to chalk out B. to negotiate
C. to create D. No Improvement

35. It's a family potboiler, medical thriller and political drama **all in one** – except that it's all too real and all too grim.

A. all 3 in one
B. all coupled into one
C. all rolled into one
D. No Improvement

ANSWERS

1	2	3	4	5	6	7	8	9	10
A	D	C	A	C	D	C	A	C	B
11	**12**	**13**	**14**	**15**	**16**	**17**	**18**	**19**	**20**
D	C	D	B	A	D	C	C	D	B
21	**22**	**23**	**24**	**25**	**26**	**27**	**28**	**29**	**30**
C	C	D	A	C	D	C	C	C	B
31	**32**	**33**	**34**	**35**					
B	C	C	A	C					

5. REORDERING WORDS

The words form a sentence and convey their meaning only when they are arranged in a proper order. One must study and practise it regularly.

MULTIPLE CHOICE QUESTIONS

Directions: *In the following questions, some parts of the sentence have been jumbled up. You are required to rearrange these parts which are labelled P, Q, R and S to produce the correct sentence. Choose the option with proper sequence.*

1. We are doing
P : to the people
Q : to give relief
R : all we can
S : but more funds are needed
The correct sequence should be
A. P Q R S B. R Q P S
C. Q P R S D. S P Q R

2. The man
P : when he was
Q : in the office last evening
R : could not finish
S : all his work
The correct sequence should be
A. P Q R S B. Q R S P
C. R Q P S D. R S P Q

3. The people decided
P : they were going
Q : how much
R : to spend
S : on the construction of the school building
The correct sequence should be
A. Q P R S B. P Q R S
C. P R Q S D. S Q P R

4. The man said that
P : those workers
Q : would be given a raise
R : who did not go on
S : strike last month
The correct sequence should be
A. P Q R S B. P R S Q
C. Q P R S D. R S P Q

5. I think
P : the members
Q : are basically in agreement
R : of the group
S : on the following points.
The correct sequence should be
A. R Q P S B. S Q R P
C. P R Q S D. P Q S R

6. While it was true that
P : I had
Q : to invest in industry
R : some lands and houses
S : I did not have ready cash
The correct sequence should be
A. P Q R S B. P R S Q
C. S Q P R D. Q P R S

7. P : But your help
Q : to finish this work
R : it would not have been possible
S : in time
The correct sequence should be
A. P R Q S B. S P Q R
C. R P Q S D. P Q R S

8. The boy
P : in the competition
Q : who was wearing spectacles
R : won many prizes
S : held in our college

The correct sequence should be
A. P Q R S B. R P S Q
C. Q R P S D. Q P S R

9. About 200 years ago,
P : in the south of India
Q : an old king
R : ruled over a kingdom
S : called Rajavarman.
The correct sequence should be
A. Q S R P B. P Q R S
C. Q P S R D. Q S P R

10. P : his land
Q : a wooden plough
R : the Indian peasant still uses
S : to cultivate.
The correct sequence should be
A. R Q P S B. Q P S R
C. S R Q P D. R Q S P

11. He was a man,
P : even if he had to starve
Q : who would not beg
R : borrow or steal
S : from anyone.
The correct sequence should be
A. P Q R S B. P R Q S
C. Q R S P D. Q P R S

12. P : in the progress of
Q : universities play a crucial role
R : our civilization
S : in the present age.
The correct sequence should be
A. S Q P R B. Q R S P
C. Q R P S D. S Q R P

13. P : far out into the sea
Q : for the next two weeks there were further explosions
R : which hurled
S : ashes and debris.
The correct sequence should be
A. Q R P S B. R S P Q
C. Q R S P D. S R P Q

14. William Shakespeare,
P : in his lifetime
Q : the great English dramatist
R : wrote thirty five plays
S : and several poems.
The correct sequence should be
A. P Q R S B. R S P Q
C. Q S R P D. Q R S P

15. Whenever I am,
P : with an old friend of mine
Q : in New Delhi
R : to have dinner
S : I always try.
The correct sequence should be
A. S Q P R B. Q S R P
C. R P S Q D. P R Q S

16. P : I don't know
Q : must have thought
R : what people sitting next to me
S : but I came away.
The correct sequence should be
A. R S Q P B. R Q S P
C. P Q R S D. P R Q S

17. P : in estimating the size of the earth
Q : but they were hampered by the lack of instruments of precision
R : ancient astronomers
S : used methods which were theoretically valid
The correct sequence should be
A. R P Q S B. P R Q S
C. R S Q P D. R P S Q

18. P : It is a pity that
Q : by offering a handsome dowry
R : a number of parents think that
S : they will be able to ensure the happiness of their daughters
The correct sequence should be
A. S Q R P B. P R S Q
C. P S R Q D. P R Q S

19. The common man
P : in nurturing
Q : a more active role
R : communal harmony
S : should play
The correct sequence should be
A. P R S Q B. S Q P R
C. S Q R P D. P R Q S

20. The doctor
P : able to find out
Q : what has caused

R : the food poisoning
S : has not been
The correct sequence should be
A. S P R Q B. P R Q S
C. P R S Q D. S P Q R

21. P : was suspended
Q : the officer being corrupt
R : before his dismissal
S : from service
The correct sequence should be
A. Q P S R B. Q P R S
C. R S Q P D. R S P Q

22. With an unsteady hand
P : on my desk
Q : from his pocket
R : he took an envelope
S : and threw it
The correct sequence should be
A. Q R P S B. Q R S P
C. R Q P S D. R Q S P

23. P : she gave her old coat
Q : to a beggar
R : the one with the brown fur on it
S : shivering with cold
The correct sequence should be
A. S Q R P B. S P R Q
C. P R Q S D. P S Q R

24. It is a privilege
P : to pay tax
Q : of every citizen
R : as well as the duty
S : as well as the duty who is well-placed
The correct sequence should be
A. R P S Q B. S P R Q
C. R Q S P D. S Q R P

25. It is not good
P : of the wicked persons
Q : to overthrow
R : to accept the help
S : the righteous persons
The correct sequence should be
A. R S Q P B. Q S R P
C. R P Q S D. Q P R S

26. Life is judged
P : and not by
Q : of work done
R : the longevity of years
S : by the quality
The correct sequence should be
A. Q S P R B. S Q R P
C. Q S R P D. S Q P R

27. P : When he learns that
Q : you have passed the examination
R : in the first division
S : your father will be delighted
The correct sequence should be
A. Q P S R B. S P Q R
C. Q R S P D. S R Q P

28. P : The journalist
Q : saw
R : countless number of the dead
S : driving across the field of battle
The correct sequence should be
A. P Q S R B. P Q R S
C. P S Q R D. S R Q P

29. P : Jane planned
Q : some stamps
R : to buy
S : this afternoon
The correct sequence should be
A. P R Q S B. P S Q R
C. Q R P S D. Q S P R

30. Her mother
P : when she was
Q : hardly four years old
R : began to teach Neha
S : English
The correct sequence should be
A. R S Q P B. S R P Q
C. R S P Q D. S R Q P

31. It was
P : in keeping with my mood
Q : a soft summer evening
R : as I walked sedately
S : in the direction of the new house
The proper sequence should be:
A. S R P Q B. Q R P S
C. Q P R S D. S Q P R

32. With her body
P : dragging her unwilling feet
Q : weak and infirm

R : doubled with age
S : she persisted in her mission
The proper sequence should be:
A. P Q R S B. Q P R S
C. R Q P S D. S R P Q

33. A.P.J. Abdul Kalam
P : is popularly know as
Q : from 2002 and 2007 and
R : was the 11th president of the country
S : 'Misile Man' of India
The proper sequence should be:
A. P Q R S B. Q P R S
C. S R P Q D. R Q P S

34. When he
P : did not know
Q : he was nervous and
R : heard the hue and cry at midnight
S : what to do
The proper sequence should be:
A. R Q P S B. Q S P R
C. S Q P R D. P Q R S

35. A French woman
P : committed suicide
Q : where she had put up
R : who had come to Calcutta
S : by jumping from the first floor balcony of the hotel
The proper sequence should be:
A. P R Q S B. Q S R P
C. R P S Q D. S R Q P

36. He has
P : while having a reverie
Q : found the book
R : at the bus-stop
S : he lost
The proper sequence should be:
A. Q R S P B. P R Q S
C. Q S R P D. P Q S R

37. Then the women
P : lamenting their evil desire
Q : that had brought
R : wept loudly
S : this sorrow upon them
The proper sequence should be:
A. R P Q S B. R Q P S
C. P Q S R D. P R Q S

38. It is easy to excuse
P : but it is hard
Q : in a boy of fourteen
R : the mischief of early childhood
S : to tolerate even unavoidable faults
The proper sequence should be:
A. R P Q S B. Q R S P
C. Q R P S D. R P S Q

39. I don't remember
P : I saw a man dying in front of a hospital
Q : but when I left Lucknow in 1984
R : hit apparently by a fast moving car
S : the exact date
The proper sequence should be:
A. S Q R P B. S Q P R
C. Q R P S D. S P R Q

40. Since the beginning of history
P : have managed to catch
Q : the Eskimos and Red Indians
R : by a very difficult method
S : a few specimens of this acquatic mammal
The proper sequence should be:
A. Q P R S B. S Q P R
C. S Q R P D. Q P S R

ANSWERS

1	2	3	4	5	6	7	8	9	10
B	D	A	B	C	C	A	C	A	D
11	**12**	**13**	**14**	**15**	**16**	**17**	**18**	**19**	**20**
C	A	C	D	B	D	C	B	B	D
21	**22**	**23**	**24**	**25**	**26**	**27**	**28**	**29**	**30**
B	D	C	C	B	D	B	C	A	C
31	**32**	**33**	**34**	**35**	**36**	**37**	**38**	**39**	**40**
C	C	D	A	C	C	A	D	B	D

6. ORDERING OF SENTENCES

A Paragraph is formed from sentences, it will convey its true meaning and purpose only when the sentences are arranged in a proper manner. Try and practise it in this exercise.

MULTIPLE CHOICE QUESTIONS

Directions: *A number of sentences are given below which when properly sequenced form a coherent paragraph. Each sentence is labelled as abcdef...... Choose the most logical order of sentences from among the given choices to construct a coherent paragraph:*

1. (a) The leopard was discovered in the servant quarters of a farmhouse.

(b) The injuries appeared to have been caused by the paws of the leopard, and were not teeth wounds.

(c) It took the wild life officials, Delhi Police and Delhi zoo vets eight hours to capture the leopard that had wandered into a factory in south Delhi.

(d) The leopard then jumped into the factory where the workers managed to lock it in a small generator room before calling in the police.

(e) Before its capture, the leopard attacked two women and a man in the farmhouse.

A. aebdc B. bdaec
C. eadbc D. adbec

2. (a) The project has already started on an experimental basis in the west district.

(b) A website is soon going to be launched where application forms can be downloaded and submitted.

(c) Standing in a queue at a government office to submit application form will be a thing of the past.

(d) A unique code will be alloted while submitting the form which will help in finding the status of the application.

A. abcd B. dabc
C. cbda D. badc

3. (a) Police suspect a carpenter working at John's house as he has not reported for work since the day the boy went missing.

(b) John did not return home in the afternoon.

(c) John's mother had herself put the boy on the vehicle in the morning.

(d) John smiled at him and was last seen walking up to him.

(e) His parents called the school and were told John had not been to school at all and had been marked absent.

(f) He was about to enter the school when someone called out his name.

A. cfdbea B. debfca
C. bfdaec D. abcdef

4. (a) A state champion from the past four years, Tushar began swimming at the age of six.

(b) But he has no plans of making swimming a career.

(c) Tushar's passion for swimming is unshakable.

(d) Something that began as a hobby rewarded him with all the fame he has achieved.

(e) His day begins at 4.30 am for a dip at Talkatora Stadium.

(f) He is determined to make a mark in the world of swimming.

A. dbaecf B. bcadef
C. edfbac D. cefadb

5. (a) However, the mayhem over the last few months is deeply shocking.

(b) Yet I do not agree with the prophets of doom who see nothing but disaster ahead.
(c) When I came back to my motherland India after a stay in Switzerland, I felt I was trading a hotbed of intense religious and political violence for peace and quiet.
(d) I think our nation is searching for an identity.
(e) And a new vision of the future will emerge from this.
A. abcde B. cabde
C. cebad D. bedca

6. (a) The universities in a democracy can no longer be content with the limited goal of scholarship.
(b) They are to respond to changed conditions and to new demands.
(c) Universities in the modern world are called upon to play a crucial role in the progress of our civilization.
(d) They have to devise new programmes and take into account the needs of society.
(e) They must not merely display their traditional resourcefulness but also must have the capacity for effective growth.
A. cbdae B. cbead
C. cadbe D. dbaec

7. (a) He decided to enter a new line by investing in some new equipments.
(b) Some of the old machines were to be sold to raise the money.
(c) Ram's business was not prospering.
(d) For this more money had to be found.
(e) He was still short of money and had to borrow some.
A. cadbe B. adebc
C. ebdac D. cbdae

8. (a) Parts of northern region were pounded by heavy rains today,
(b) Vehicular traffic came to a near halt.
(c) As mid and high altitude areas of Himachal Pradesh were in grip of severe cold wave with snow lashing the tribal areas and mid ranges receiving showers.
(d) As the sky remained heavily overcast with dark clouds reducing the visibility considerably.
(e) A large number of tourists were forced to buy heavy woollens and stay indoors due to inclement weather.
A. ecabd B. adecb
C. edabc D. acbde

9. (a) Clearly, age is not a deterrent in one's choice of learning.
(b) Perhaps, it was because of her childhood desire.
(c) When Rachna came to Delhi eight years back, she had not anticipated a career in the field of art.
(d) She has been successful in the various exhibitions that she has been part of in terms of business.
(e) She had got into expressing her thoughts with the help of a brush and colours only because her daughter refused to get initiated into it.
(f) She feels that her use of colour appeals to people.
A. aedcbf B. cdefba
C. cebadf D. acdebf

10. (a) The idea is that students should be able to find employment for themselves after the course.
(b) The Central Board of Secondary Education is planning a revamp of its vocational courses.
(c) For this it is necessary to tie up with the industry as well as mobilise schools for their support.
(d) While others will be made less academic and more in tune with the needs of the industry.
(e) A number of courses have been identified as 'deadwood' and will be done away with.
A. bedac B. abcde
C. acebd D. baced

11. (a) An integrated and combined approach was required to reveal the mystery of the brain – its structure, composition and function.
(b) Since the early 80's, scientists were clear that the brain would be the final frontier to conquer.
(c) The initiative was flagged off and came to be known as the Human Brain Project.

(d) But that wasn't easy because understanding the brain involved completely integrating information from the level of the gene to the level of behaviour.
(e) To fulfill this requirement a group of American scientists from various diciplines decided to work together.

A. acbed B. bdaec
C. abdec D. badec

12. (a) The rehabilitation record has been dismal.
(b) It has been two years years since the earthquake rudely rattled the people of Gujrat.
(c) And since then, life has been a constant struggle.
(d) The quake set Gujrat's clock back by 10 years.
(e) Things changed forever.

A. bedca B. bcade
C. dbace D. edcba

13. (a) In fact, success in exams depended on rote learning from old notes.
(b) when he was studying civil engineering in a college in Gujrat.
(c) He was detained for lack of attendance.
(d) Lectures were soporific, classes rarely worth attending and 80 per cent attendance compulsory.
(e) The college became a trap he hated.
(f) His is a plight many engineers across India would identify with.
(g) He found the going tough.

A. abcdgef B. bgdacef
C. fabcdge D. abcdefg

14. (a) In a country that has close to 600 recognised engineering colleges, there are only seven IITs.
(b) Barring a few exeptions, the academic atmosphere in these is moribund.
(c) The very best students usually get there.
(d) many waste themselves in frustration.
(e) Most of those who get into engineering are good students.
(f) but about 1.25 lakh others and up in the remaining colleges.

A. aecfbd B. abecdf
C. abcdef D. acfbed

15. (a) Whatever the job market, common wisdom says that IIT graduates will find jobs where others have failed.
(b) The IIT brand name is a ticket to success.
(c) When recruiters go headhunting, the IITs are still top of their list.
(d) Its possessor is understood to have an excellent academic record and the will to succeed.
(e) In the job market, that counts.

A. bdeac B. abcde
C. abdce D. dbace

16. (a) It will pave the way ....
(b) signalling a new beginning in strategic ties......
(c) for a tangible Indian economic presence in Iran and Central Asia.
(d) Iran has offered India valuable road linkages to central Asia ......
(e) aimed at promoting peace and economic cooperation in the region.

A. dbeac B. debca
C. acebd D. abced

17. (a) A good college is essential for a successful career and admissions are based on marks.
(b) The marks-based system followed by all the boards in the country recognises only a small percentage of students as successful.
(c) The marks one scores in the crucial board exams dictate the path his life takes.
(d) Anyone scoring below a certain percentage is automatically branded a 'failure'.
(d) So if you cannot make it into the best college, your career is over even before it has started.

A. abcde B. bcdea
C. bdcae D. abdec

18. (a) the pride of their batch.
(b) they're not too far off from taking charge of India's future.
(c) They were the toppers of their class
(d) they may have won accolades, made their schools and families proud, but
(e) Yesterday's toppers have their hands full.
(f) these confident go-getters have had their share of failure too.

A. eacfbd B. eadbfc
C. eadbcf D. cabedf

19. (a) Mistakes or errors should be treated as teacher.
(b) When you make mistake, you should neither feel ashamed nor desperate.
(c) Everybody makes mistakes.
(d) You should be bold enough to accept your mistakes before anybody.
(e) But the only sensible course is to study and analyse why you made that mistake.
(f) Only then you can learn not to make mistakes in future.
A. abfced B. acefbd
C. adbcfe D. cdfbea

20. (a) Our lessons in love and respect make us a tolerant people.
(b) I love Indian culture.
(c) I feel I have to repay my country whatever way I can.
(d) In no other country have I seen so much love and respect.
(e) I was born and brought up in this country and feel I owe everything to it.
A. bcade B. dcbea
C. acdeb D. ecbda

21. (a) To curb bio-terroriom is a difficult task.
(b) To check these attacks and lessen their impact, we need an impartial team of sincere, strong and dedicated men.
(c) The media can play a strong role in stopping this unnecessary spread of panic.
(d) Since Bio-terrorism is not visible or easily detectable, it can be used often.
(e) Men who honour the lives of their fellow countrymen before their own.
A. abcde B. dabce
C. adbec D. acbed

22. (a) He was dying.
(b) No one was ready to touch him as even shifting him from one place to another would lead to profuse bleeding.
(c) He was a five-day old infant, premature and bleeding profusely.
(d) Even if injected one small needle, blood would ooze out and continue to flow for an hour at a stretch.
(e) This small being had haematoma, a thick blood clot in his brain.
A. edbca B. cabde
C. eacdb D. cedba

23. (a) The day I don't treat a patient, I feel ......
(b) I have enough to eat, I crave for blessings now.
(c) But if a financially weak patient gives me only ₹ 50, I don't mind.
(d) Each month I do three to four operations free of cost.
(e) I have lost something in life.
(f) My consultation fee is ₹ 300.
A. fcdeab B. dfcbae
C. fcabde D. bdfcea

24. (a) When he was rushed to the nearby Primary Health Centre after his fall, the doctor referred him to a hospital.
(b) This worsened his injury.
(c) Had a little precaution been exercised after the accident, Tarun would have continued with his gymnastic classes.
(d) He was paralysed from waist downwards when he fell from the vaulting horse while doing gymnastics.
(e) However, the doctor forgot to tell Tarun's parents to take him on a stretcher as he had suffered spinal injuries.
(f) Tarun is wheelchair bound for two years.
A. fdeabc B. abcdef
C. fdcaeb D. fdbcae

25. (a) As the temperature rises, staying hydrated can become a greater challenge for people exercising both indoors and out.
(b) Several things can influence this process, including age, gender, physical conditioning. humidity and a lack of sufficient fluids.
(c) In hot weather, individuals can lose as much as two quarts of sweat per hour.
(d) As we age, we have a lower perceived level of thirst in response to fluid loss and early stages of dehydration.
(e) If not replenished, this can lead to dehydration, heat exhaustion and even heatstroke.
A. abcde B. dbcae
C. cbdca D. acebd

26. (a) Students become passive listeners in the class-room.
(b) Mostly lecturing method is preferred to cover the syllabus.
(c) I feel that there is a lacunae in the teaching techniques adopted by the lecturers in engineering colleges.
(d) Unless the teachers are exposed to different teaching techniques, they will not succeed in imparting knowledge.
(e) Lack of training in teaching can be ascribed to this sorry state of affairs.
A. dbeca B. cadbe
C. chaed D. dceab

27. (a) A product is something that is made in a factory, a brand is something that is bought by a consumer.
(b) The trick therefore, lies in the brand positioning.
(c) For a counsumer, the satisfaction of becoming associated with a name that is the 'best' and the 'leader' is far more important and at times makes him ignore the price factor.
(d) Brands come and go.
(e) Still there are those who manage to stay and develop an affinity with consumers.
A. aebcd B. debac
C. decab D. aecdb

28. (a) Many people fail simply because they make too many wrong decisions.
(b) Over a period of time you make a series of decisions, each seemingly of little consequence.
(c) So do people's lives.
(d) It has been said that history turns on small hinges.
(e) Yet the total of these decisions finally determines the outcome of your life.
(f) A successful life depends upon developing a higher percentage of wisdom than error.
A. acbedf B. adcbef
C. fedcba D. abcdef

29. (a) The younger you are when you discover this mighty power, the more likely you are to live successfully and happily.
(b) Everything you do has some effect upon others, as do their actions upon you.
(c) You are influenced by other people's acts and wishes, by law and custom, by your duties and your responsibilities.
(d) You live in a world filled with outside influences which impinge upon you.
(e) And yet you must find out how to live your own life.
A. abcde B. adebc
C. dcbea D. baedc

30. (a) She had wanted to go to Mars.
(b) Lots of young people talk about how they dream of this or that.
(c) Kalpana Chawla had wanted to make at least one more trip to space.
(d) She is one person who got to live out her dreams.
(e) She had also said that when it was time for her to die, she would like to die in space.
A. bcade B. bdeac
C. caebd D. cbead

ANSWERS

1	2	3	4	5	6	7	8	9	10
A	C	A	D	B	B	A	D	C	A
11	**12**	**13**	**14**	**15**	**16**	**17**	**18**	**19**	**20**
B	B	B	D	A	A	C	D	B	D
21	**22**	**23**	**24**	**25**	**26**	**27**	**28**	**29**	**30**
C	D	B	C	D	C	B	B	C	C

7. Sentence Completion

A sentence conveys its meaning effectively only when it is completed in a proper way. Try and practise it in this exercise.

Directions: *In each question, an incomplete statement (Stem) followed by four fillers is given. Pick out the best one which can complete the incomplete stem correctly and meaningfully.*

1. He is so lazy that he .....
A. cannot depend on others for getting his work done.
B. cannot delay the schedule of completing the work.
C. can seldom complete his work on time.
D. dislike to postpone the work that he undertakes to do.

2. He always stammers in public meetings, but his today's speech .....
A. was fairly audible to everyone present in the hall.
B. was not received satisfactorily.
C. could not be understood properly.
D. was free from that defect.

3. In order to raise the company's profit, the employees .....
A. demanded two additional increments.
B. decided to go on paid holidays.
C. requested the management to implement new welfare schemes.
D. offered to work overtime without any compensation.

4. Although, he is reputed for making very candid statements, ...
A. his today's speech was not fairly audible.
B. his promises had always been realistic.
C. his speech was very interesting.
D. his today's statements were very ambiguous.

5. I felt somewhat more relaxed .....
A. but tense as compared to earlier.
B. and tense as compared to earlier.
C. as there was already no tension at all.
D. and tension-free as compared to earlier.

6. With great efforts his son succeeded in convincing him not to donate his entire wealth to an orphanage .....
A. and lead the life of a wealthy merchant.
B. but to a home for the forsaken children.
C. and make an orphan of himself.
D. as the orphange needed a lot of donations.

7. Even though it is a very large house, ...
A. there is a lot of space available in it for children.
B. there is hardly any space available for children.
C. there is no dearth of space for children.
D. the servants take a long time to clean it.

8. Practically, very little work could be completed in the last week as it was .....
A. full of working days.
B. a very hectic week.
C. full of holidays.
D. a very busy week.

9. He tames animals because he .....
A. is fond of them.
B. hates them.
C. is afraid of them
D. wants to set them free

10. He has no money now .....
A. although he was very poor once.
B. as he has given up all his wealth.
C. because he was very rich once.
D. because he has received huge donation.

11. The employer appeared to be in such an affable mood that Rohit .....
A. decided to ask for a raise in his salary.
B. was scared to talk to him about his leave.
C. felt very guilty for his inadvertent slip.
D. promised him that he would not commit mistake again.

12. Since people cannot learn through legitimate channels all that they are anxious to learn .....
A. they resort to ways and means without any ethical or moral considerations.
B. they join academics in order to quench their thirst for learning.
C. they adopt formal ways and means to achieve what they want to.
D. these social service organisations provide them the required input of knowledge.

13. It was an extremely pleasant surprise for the hutment-dweller when the Government officials told him that .....
A. he had to vacate hutment which he had been unauthorisedly occupying
B. he had been gifted with a furnished apartment in a multi-storeyed building.
C. he would be arrested for wrongfully encroaching on the pavement outside his dwelling.
D. they would not accede to his request.

14. Despite his best efforts to conceal his anger .....
A. we could detect that he was very happy.
B. he failed to give us an impression of his agony.
C. he succeeded in camouflaging his emotions.
D. people came to know that he was annoyed.

15. His appearance is unsmiling but .....
A. his heart is full of compassion for others.
B. he looks very serious on most occasions.
C. people are afraid of him.
D. he is uncompromising on matters of task performance.

16. The weather outside was extremely pleasant and hence we decided to .....
A. utilise our time in watching the television.
B. refrain from going out for a morning walk.
C. enjoy a morning ride in the open.
D. employ this rare opportunity for writing letters.

17. The officer who had neglected to file his income tax returns had to .....
A. return the files. B. pay a fine.
C. be rewarded. D. play mischief.

18. In order to help the company attain its goal of enhancing profit, all the employees .....
A. urged the management to grant paid leave.
B. appealed the management to implement new welfare schemes.
C. voluntarily offered to work overtime with lucrative compensation.
D. voluntarily offered to render additional services in lieu of nothing.

19. His behaviour is so unpredictable that he .....
A. never depends upon others for getting his work done.
B. is seldom trusted by others.
C. always finds it difficult to keep his word.
D. always insists on getting the work completed on time.

20. Since it is already midnight, we .....
A. had better leaving.
B. ought to have leave.
C. should take our leave.
D. might as well as leave.

21. It is not easy to remain tranquil when those around you .....
A. behave in a socially acceptable manner.
B. exhibit pleasant mannerism.
C. are losing their heads.
D. agree to whatever you say.

22. Although initial investigations pointed towards him, ...
A. the preceding events corroborated his involvement in the crime.
B. the additional information confirmed his guilt.
C. the subsequent events established that he was guilty.
D. the subsequent events proved that he was innocent.

23. Because he believes in democratic principles, he always .....
A. decides all the matters himself.
B. listens to others' views and enforces his own.
C. shown respect to others' opinions if they match his own.
D. reconciles with the majority's views and gives us his own.

24. Owing to the acute power shortage, the people of our locality have decided to .....
A. dispense with other non-conventional energy sources.
B. resort to abundant use of electricity for illumination.
C. off-switch the electrical appliance while not in use.
D. resort to use of electricity only when it is inevitable.

25. She never visits any zoo because she is a strong opponent of the idea of .....
A. setting the animals free into the forest.
B. feeding the animals while others are watching.
C. watching the animals in their natural abode.
D. holding the animals in captivity for our joy.

26. Unless you work harder you will fail, means .....
A. if you fail you will work harder.
B. you must at least plan well than you will not fail.
C. hardly you will fail if you do not desire so.
D. if you do not put more efforts, then you will fail.

27. Even if it rains I shall come, means .....
A. if I come it will not rain.
B. if it rains I shall not come.
C. I will certainly come whether it rains or not.
D. whenever there is rain I shall come.

28. Dinesh is as stupid as he is lazy means .....
A. Dinesh is stupid because he is lazy.
B. Dinesh is lazy because he is stupid.
C. Dinesh is either stupid or lazy.
D. Dinesh is equally stupid and lazy.

29. Mahesh needn't have purchased the bag, means .....
A. it was not necessary for Mahesh to purchase the bag but he has purchased it.
B. it was necessary for Mahesh to purchase the bag and he has not purchased it.
C. it was not necessary for Mahesh to purchase the bag and he has not purchased it.
D. it was necessary for Mahesh to purchase the bag but he has not purchased it.

30. The Manager would like you to help Dhiraj, means .....
A. the Manager would like you if you help Dhiraj.
B. the Manager desires you to help Dhiraj.
C. the Manager likes you because you help Dhiraj.
D. Dhiraj expects the Manager to tell you to help him.

ANSWERS

1	2	3	4	5	6	7	8	9	10
C	D	D	D	D	C	B	C	A	B
11	12	13	14	15	16	17	18	19	20
A	A	B	D	A	C	B	D	B	D
21	22	23	24	25	26	27	28	29	30
C	D	D	D	D	D	C	D	A	B

8. Nouns, Numbers & Pronouns

NOUN

A word which denotes a place, a thing, an animal or a person is said to be a noun.

1. Note the plurals of the following nouns:

Singular	*Plural*	*Singular*	*Plural*
copy	copies	cry	cries
baby	babies	duty	duties
body	bodies	country	countries
family	families	diary	diaries
fly	flies	fairy	fairies
city	cities	spy	spies
army	armies	storey	storeys
bay	bays	monkey	monkeys

2. The following nouns do not undergo any change in plural form, in general.

Singular	*Plural*	*Singular*	*Plural*
deer	deer	sheep	sheep
thousand	thousand	pair	pair
hundred	hundred	score	score
dozen	dozen	gross	gross

Note: We can write—

(*a*) thousands of men; (*b*) two pairs of shoes; (*c*) dozens of mangoes; (*d*) scores of people. etc. But—

(*a*) two thousand rupees; (*b*) three hundred men; (*c*) five dozen eggs, etc.

3. The following nouns are usually used in plural forms. They take a plural verb after them—

eatables	fetters	surroundings
riches	alms	spectacles
trousers	pants	scissors
premises	thanks	annals
congratulations	goods	shorts
tongs	pains	arms
breeches	(for troubles)	

4. The following are the nouns which are plural in appearance but are usually used in singular number. They are followed by a singular verb—

news	politics	physics
mathematics	economics	ethics
politics	classics	gallows
statistics	athletics	innings
mechanics	swnmons	mumps

5. Collective nouns often used as plurals—

public	police	cattle
audience	clergy	folk
people	poultry	nation
elite	gentry	glitterati

6. The nouns that are usually used in singular forms—

advice	hair	rice
fuel	alphabet	machinery
offspring	issue	furniture
mischief	stationery	luggage
bedding	information	abuse

7. Material nouns are always used in singular number—

gold	copper	milk
water	silk	wool

Note: They may be used in plural with a different meaning.

copper coins (coppers), chains or fetters (irons), cans made of tin (tins).

Formation of Feminine Gender from Masculine Gender

(*a*) By adding 'ess'/ 'trix'/ 'a' / 'sne' etc.
e.g., lion into lioness

(*b*) Placement of a word before or after noun
e.g., Servant into Maid-Servant; Milkman into Milkmaid

(*c*) A masculine noun containing vowel *e.g.*, Actor Avoid vowel and add 'ess' *i.e.*, Actress

(*d*) No specific note will be applied in some nouns (while changing into feminine gender) *e.g.*, Monk into Nun, Drone into Bee, Drake into Duck, Dog into Bitch.

THE PRONOUN

A pronoun is a word which is used in place of noun.

Kinds of Pronouns

(i) **Personal Pronoun:** I, we, my, mine, our, ours, you, he, she, they, him, her etc.

(ii) **Reflexive Pronoun:** Herself, himself, myself, yourself, themselves etc.

(iii) **Emphatic Pronoun:** I myself, we ourselves.

(iv) **Demonstrative Pronoun:** This, that, there, those etc.

(v) **Indefinite Pronoun:** Somebody, nobody, many, none, someone, few etc.

(vi) **Interrogative Pronoun:** What, who, whose, which, whom etc.

(vii) **Distributive Pronoun:** Neither, each, either, every, none, both etc.

(viii) **Relative Pronoun:** Who, which, whom etc.

MULTIPLE CHOICE QUESTIONS

Directions: *In the following questions choose the correct options to fill the blanks.*

1. The place was so dirty that ..... wished to run away from there.

A. everbody B. anybody
C. few D. some

2. ..... was there to help me.

A. Something B. Anything
C. Anybody D. Nobody

3. Is there .... to eat?

A. some B. something
C. any D. few

4. ..... of the students were making a great noise.

A. Anyone B. Somebody
C. Many D. Nobody

5. ..... of the students can solve this sum.

A. Someone B. Anybody
C. Somebody D. None

6. ...... of us should try our best to make India a heaven.

A. Any B. Somebody
C. Anybody D. All

7. ...... of us do not know the real meaning of our lives.

A. Any B. Something
C. Several D. Many

8. She presented me a .... of flowers.

A. troup B. galaxy
C. bouquet D. cluster

9. There was a .... of eggs floating on the dirty water of the ditch.

A. clump B. shoal
C. clutch D. pile

10. A .... of dancers was dancing on the stage.

A. troupe B. galaxy
C. herd D. clump

11. To save the drowning man, a .... of sailors came out on the boats.

A. troop B. crew
C. band D. gang

12. A .... (of stars) consists of millions of stars.

A. group B. herd
C. stack D. galaxy

13. Mr. Peter Cash was arranging a .... of bricks near his house.

A. group B. band
C. herd D. stack

14. A ...... of geese was swimming in the water.

A. group B. gaggle
C. troupe D. bunch

15. There was a .... of mosquitoes hovering over the slum area.

A. swarm B. group
C. gang D. herd

16. Last night a .... of burglars broke into my house.
A. group B. cluster
C. clump D. gang

17. Devika lost her .... of keys.
A. bunch B. branch
C. band D. gang

18. I have some .... for you to do.
A. working B. worker
C. work D. works

19. They highly admire the .... of Kashmir.
A. scenery B. sceneries
C. scene D. scenes

20. I can easily read and write the English ....
A. alphabets B. alphabetic
C. alphabet D. alphabetical

21. I have met her many a ....
A. times B. timing
C. time D. timings

22. She has written many ... .
A. poetry B. poetries
C. poem D. poems

23. One is supposed to do ....
A. our duty B. their duty
C. one's duty D. his duty

24. He is .... faithful partner.
A. Yours B. You
C. Your D. Your's

25. Ajay is more smart than ....
A. her B. hers
C. herself D. she

26. The ..... of the Minister's statement cannot be verified by people who have no access to official records.
A. veracity B. verbosity
C. ambiguity D. validity

27. Life is to death as pleasure is to ......
A. poverty B. suffering
C. anguish D. pain

28. 'Please' and 'Thank you' are the little courtesies by which we keep the ..... of life oiled and running smoothly.
A. path B. machine
C. garden D. river

29. Catching the earlier train will give us the ..... to do some shopping.
A. chance B. luck
C. possibility D. occasion

30. Leave a two-inch ..... on each page for the teacher's remarks.
A. border B. margin
C. blank D. gap

31. What is the ..... for an airletter?
A. fare B. value
C. postage D. stamp

32. The manner in which bombs exploded in five trains within a short span of time suggests that it is a part of a .....
A. game B. conspiracy
C. villainy D. sabotage

33. Some regions of our country still remain ..... to the average man.
A. inaccessible B. impossible
C. impermeable D. impenetrable

34. The old 'Nature Versus .....' debate regarding crime continues even today.
A. Man B. Universe
C. Culture D. Nurture

ANSWERS

1	2	3	4	5	6	7	8	9	10
A	D	B	C	D	D	D	C	C	A
11	**12**	**13**	**14**	**15**	**16**	**17**	**18**	**19**	**20**
B	D	D	B	A	D	A	C	A	C
21	**22**	**23**	**24**	**25**	**26**	**27**	**28**	**29**	**30**
C	D	C	C	D	A	D	B	A	B
31	**32**	**33**	**34**						
C	B	A	A						

9. PREPOSITIONS

A Preposition is a word which comes before a Pronoun or a Noun and expresses the relationship between Noun or Pronoun and some part of the remaining sentence.

(*a*) He is busy **with** his work.
(*b*) The boy jumped **into** the river.
(*c*) The birds are chirping *in* the trees.

In these sentences the words **with**, **into** and **in** show the relationship between the verbs **busy**, **jumped** and **chirping** with the nouns **work**, **river** and **trees** respectively.

Position of the Preposition

1. A Preposition usually precedes its object.
   (*i*) He laughs **at** the poor.
   (*ii*) He is angry **with** you.
   (*iii*) She agrees **with** me.
2. In the case of Relative Pronouns it comes after the subject.
   (*i*) This is the boy whom I was looking **for**.
   (*ii*) That is the pen whose mention I was making **of**.
3. In the following cases, the Preposition comes after its object.
   (*i*) Where is the boy you were complaining **against**?
   (*ii*) What things are there you are looking **for**?
   (*iii*) Who is there, you are waiting **for**?

Omission of the Preposition

In many cases when the sentences contain Nouns of Time or Place, the Prepositions **from**, **in** and **for** are often omitted.

(*i*) He walked many kilometres.
(*ii*) He came to see me last year.
(*iii*) As I could not find my puppy anywhere. I looked here and there.

Prepositions are small words that show the relationship between one word and another. Prepositions in the following sentences show the position of the paper in relation to the desk, the book, his hand and the door.

The paper is **on** the desk.
The paper is **under** the book.
The paper is **in** his hand.
The paper is **by** the door.

Common Prepositions

about	at	by
in	onto	toward
above	before	concerning
inside	out	under
across	behind	despite
into	over	until
after	below	down
like	since	up
against	beneath	during
near	through	upon
along	beside	except
of	throughout	with
amid	between	for
off	till	within
among	beyond	from
on	to	without

MULTIPLE CHOICE QUESTIONS

Directions: *Tick the correct Preposition for the blank in each of the following sentences.*

1. He applied ...... the manager.
A. for B. to
C. with D. by

2. Trust ...... God and do the right.
A. in B. for
C. to D. with

3. She is worthy ...... a prize.
A. with B. for
C. to D. of

4. Mr. Gomes has no taste ...... music.
A. of B. for
C. with D. to

5. You are hard ...... hearing.
A. at B. of
C. with D. for

6. He is sure ...... his success
A. for B. with
C. on D. of

7. Preeti was warned ...... the danger ahead.
A. for B. at
C. of D. about

8. I am thankful ...... you for a good advice.
A. for B. with
C. to D. from

9. Deepak would not surrender ...... the police.
A. with B. to
C. for D. on

10. The small plant in your lawn is very sensitive ...... touch.
A. on B. with
C. to D. for

11. Divya was sure to succeed ..... the examination.
A. for B. in
C. to D. with

12. Geeta was jealous ...... Ravina's beauty.
A. to B. with
C. for D. of

13. He was ignorant ..... what was happening there.
A. for B. of
C. to D. with

14. Your pen is inferior ...... mine.
A. than B. with
C. from D. to

15. Reenu is no match ...... Meenu.
A. to B. for
C. with D. upon

16. It is necessary ...... you to apply for this job.
A. on B. with
C. for D. to

17. Be loyal ...... your country.
A. for B. to
C. on D. with

18. Mukesh is junior ...... me.
A. than B. to
C. from D. of

19. Deepika was innocent ...... the crime.
A. of B. with
C. from D. to

20. I am desirous.... joining the Indian cricket team.
A. for B. of
C. to D. on

21. Pradeep is not eligible ...... the post.
A. to B. on
C. upon D. for

22. Does she believe ...... God?
A. to B. for
C. in D. over

23. Mr. Posh was charged..... the murder of his aunt.
A. for B. with
C. on D. to

24. Tagore is famous (or popular) ...... Indians.
A. for B. with
C. to D. towards

25. Kalidasa is famous ...... his drama the *Shakuntalam*.
A. for B. with
C. on D. about

26. He applied ...... the post of a teacher.
A. to B. on
C. for D. at

27. I differ ...... you in this matter.
A. from B. with
C. for D. above

28. My pen differs ...... yours.
A. with B. from
C. for D. upon

29. The air escaped out ...... the balloon.
A. from B. of
C. to D. under

30. I am confident ...... success.
A. of B. to
C. from D. about

31. He was deprived ...... his share and property.
A. of B. with
C. from D. about

32. He complains ...... headache.
A. about B. to
C. of D. in

33. My father deals ...... sugar.
A. with B. to
C. in D. about

34. His services were dispensed ......
A. for B. to
C. with D. of

35. Mohinder was born ...... a noble famly.
A. with B. about
C. towards D. in

36. He was born ...... poor parents.
A. of B. to
C. in D. on

37. A son was born ...... him.
A. to B. for
C. in D. upon

38. I was aware ...... the matter.
A. to B. of
C. in D. upon

39. He was absorbed ...... study.
A. in B. into
C. of D. under

40. The boy jumped ...... the river.
A. in B. under
C. below D. into

41. I agree ...... you.
A. upon B. to
C. with D. None of these

42. Wolves abound ...... this forest.
A. for B. in
C. with D. to

43. She did not agree ...... your proposal.
A. with B. in
C. to D. None of these

44. I was angry ...... his misconduct.
A. with B. to
C. at D. on

45. He is bent ...... mischief.
A. on B. of
C. to D. for

ANSWERS

1	2	3	4	5	6	7	8	9	10
B	A	D	B	B	D	C	C	B	D
11	**12**	**13**	**14**	**15**	**16**	**17**	**18**	**19**	**20**
B	D	B	D	B	C	B	B	A	B
21	**22**	**23**	**24**	**25**	**26**	**27**	**28**	**29**	**30**
D	C	B	B	A	C	B	B	A	A
31	**32**	**33**	**34**	**35**	**36**	**37**	**38**	**39**	**40**
A	C	C	C	D	A	A	B	A	D
41	**42**	**43**	**44**	**45**					
C	B	C	C	A					

10. Adjectives, Adverbs & Degree of Comparison

Some words tell more about another word they are called *modifiers*. There are two main kinds of modifiers: *adjectives* and *adverbs*.

Adjectives

An *adjective* modifies—tells more about—a noun or pronoun. It tells *what kind, how many,* or *which one*.

Example: *beautiful* music, *blue* sky, *large* room.

Adjectives are usually found right before a noun, right after a noun, or after a linking verb.

Note: Some adjectives, such as articles, numbers, and possessive adjectives, usually come before the noun.

Adverb

An *adverb* modifies—tells more about—a verb, adjective, or another adverb. It tells *how, when, where,* or *to what extent.*

Comparison and Adjectives

Adjectives and adverbs have three forms that show a greater or lesser degree of the characteristic of the basic word: the positive, the comparative, and the superlatives.

Use the comparative to compare two things:

1. Mary is the more lazy of the two.
2. I've tasted creamier cheese than this.
3. James is the shorter of the two boys.

Use the superlative to compare more than two things:

1. Mary is the laziest girl I know.
2. This is the creamiest cheese I've ever tasted.
3. James is the shortest boy in the class.

There are some words to which comparison does not apply, since they already indicate the highest degree of a quality.

Here are some examples:

Immediately	Superlative	First
Last	very	unique
Uniquely	universally	perfect
Perfectly	exact	complete
Correct	dead	deadly
Preferable	round	perpendicularly
Square	third	supreme
Totally	infinitely	immortal

Errors to Avoid in Comparison

Do not combine two superlatives:

Incorrect: That was the most bravest thing he ever did.

Correct: That was the bravest thing he ever did.

Incorrect: He grew up to be the most handsomest boy in the town.

Correct: He grew up to be the most handsome boy in the town.

Do not combine two comparatives:

Incorrect: Mary was more friendlier than Susan.

Correct: Mary was friendlier than Susan.

Incorrect: The puppy was more timider last week.

Correct: The puppy was more timid last week.

MULTIPLE CHOICE QUESTIONS

Directions: *In the following questions choose the correct option to fill the blank.*

1. The girl whom you met is the .... sister of Ravi.
A. eldest B. elder
C. older D. oldest

2. The historical place is ....
A. seeing worth B. worthy of seeing
C. worth seeing D. worthy seeing

3. These flowers smell ....
A. sweet B. sweetly
C. more sweetly D. most sweetly

4. .... aspirant can not pass the UPSC examination.
A. Each B. Every
C. All D. No

5. Harivansh Rai .... second Shakespeare.
A. is a B. is
C. is the D. is another

6. .... student in the class got prizes.
A. Each and every B. Every and each
C. Every D. Never

7. It is .... picture than the one we saw last Monday.
A. interesting B. much interesting
C. more interesting D. most interesting

8. She is clever ....
A. that her mother B. as her mother
C. so her mother D. than her mother

9. They will get ....
A. Red, green and black paper
B. Red, green black paper
C. Red and green and black paper
D. Either B or C

10. Health is .... wealth.
A. preferable to
B. more preferable than
C. more preferable to
D. most preferable then

11. .... water that was in the jug evaporated.
A. Little B. The little
C. Small D. A small

12. He has not sung .... songs.
A. much B. most
C. more D. many

13. Srishti has searched .... office.
A. whole the B. the whole
C. a whole D. some whole

14. K.R. Dhiraj was .... best and .... famous writer.
A. a, the most B. the, a most
C. the, more D. the, the most

15. Willam Shakespeare is famous as ....
A. a poet and a dramatist
B. a poet and dramatist
C. the poet and the dramatist
D. the poet and a dramatist

16. What does .... leader suggest?
A. other B. another
C. others D. anothers

17. He .... money
A. has few B. have few
C. has little D. have little

18. The .... boys are rewarded.
A. first two B. two first
C. firsts two D. two's first

19. He is .... brave.
A. strong B. stronger
C. more strong D. strong and

20. No sooner said ....
A. so done B. and done
C. than done D. but done

ANSWERS

1	2	3	4	5	6	7	8	9	10
A	C	A	B	C	C	C	D	A	A
11	**12**	**13**	**14**	**15**	**16**	**17**	**18**	**19**	**20**
B	D	B	D	B	A	C	A	D	C

11. Determiners & Articles

Determiners are actually Adjectives. They are always followed by nouns.

Determiners are of the following kinds:

(A) Demonstrative Determiners
this, that, these, those etc.

(B) Possessive Determiners
my, our, your, his, her, its, their etc.

(C) Quantitative Determiners
some, any, much, enough, sufficient, whole, a little, the little, little, all, both etc.

(D) Numerical Determiners
a few, some, few, the few, any, several, many, no, etc.

One, two, three .... (Cardinals)

First, second, third .... (Ordinals)

(E) Distributive Determiners
either, neither etc.

(F) Articles
Indefinite: a, an
Definite: the

MULTIPLE CHOICE QUESTIONS

Directions: *In the following questions choose the correct options to fill the blanks.*

1. Give me .... rice.
   A. some B. few
   C. a few D. any
2. .... sheep grazing on the slope of the hill had gone away.
   A. Any B. The few
   C. This D. Much
3. Have you got .... magazines to read?
   A. all B. much
   C. some D. little
4. I have .... money that I want to spend on shares.
   A. any B. much
   C. less D. some
5. There is .... owl on the branch of the tree.
   A. a B. the
   C. an D. some
6. My brother is .... MBA.
   A. a B. an
   C. the D. any
7. Have you got .... cheese?
   A. some B. many
   C. a few D. few
8. No, I haven't got .... cheese.
   A. many B. few
   C. any D. some
9. There is only .... milk left in the bottle.
   A. enough B. few
   C. much D. a little
10. There is .... hope of his recovery.
    A. any B. little
    C. many D. few
11. .... dogs were barking at the strangers.
    A. some B. any
    C. much D. less
12. The girl bought her father .... juice.
    A. few B. some
    C. any D. many
13. You should take .... honey everyday.
    A. any B. many
    C. a little D. a few

14. .... boy was punished by the teacher.
A. Either B. All
C. Any D. Many

15. .... girl was asked to join the army.
A. None B. Neither
C. All D. Any

16. .... water in the jug has been drunk by Mohan.
A. The little B. The few
C. A few D. Few

17. I shall play .... piano at the party.
A. some B. any
C. the D. few

18. .... labourers were found dead in the mine.
A. Any B. Fewer
C. Many D. Less

19. Could I borrow .... umbrella?
A. our B. your
C. yours D. my

20. My brother is standing in the .... row.
A. any B. many
C. some D. first

21. Do you want .... tea?
A. any B. more
C. much D. few

22. He can fly .... aeroplane.
A. a B. an
C. some D. many

23. .... students were asked to bring their birth certificates.
A. Many B. Any
C. Much D. Less

24. .... gun needs oiling.
A. It B. This
C. These D. Those

25. .... shirts are mine.
A. These B. This
C. It D. That

26. .... child was allowed to enter the kitchen.
A. The B. All
C. Many D. A few

27. I have been waiting for you for .... hour.
A. a B. an
C. the D. a few

28. You must pay .... visit to your brothers.
A. the B. an
C. a few D. a

29. Why are you making .... noise?
A. your B. enough
C. a D. whole

30. He is .... honourable man.
A. a B. the
C. an D. much

31. .... cup is chipped.
A. These B. That
C. Those D. It

32. .... glasses belong to Mr. Jack.
A. This B. That
C. Those D. It

33. .... birds have colourful wings.
A. That B. These
C. This D. It

34. I want a car. I'll get ....one.
A. these B. this
C. those D. it

35. I need a camera. I'll get .... now.
A. it B. these
C. this D. those

ANSWERS

1	2	3	4	5	6	7	8	9	10
A	B	C	D	C	B	A	C	D	B
11	**12**	**13**	**14**	**15**	**16**	**17**	**18**	**19**	**20**
A	B	C	A	B	A	C	C	B	D
21	**22**	**23**	**24**	**25**	**26**	**27**	**28**	**29**	**30**
B	B	A	B	A	A	B	D	C	C
31	**32**	**33**	**34**	**35**					
B	C	B	B	A					

12. CONJUNCTIONS

A word which joins either two or more than two words/sentences is known as conjunction. e.g.,

Neither .... nor (in negative sense)
Either .... or (in affirmative sense)
Both .... and
Hardly .... when/before
No sooner .... than
Scarcely .... when/before
Though .... yet

Some illustrations based on above guidelines
Illustration:

(i) Yashwant is [neither] good [nor] bad.

(ii) It is [both] cheap [and] good.

(iii) [No sooner] did Ashok see the police [than] he ran away.

MULTIPLE CHOICE QUESTIONS

Directions: *In the following questions choose the correct options to fill the blanks.*

1. Neither he .... his friend is good.
   A. or B. and
   C. but D. nor
2. The officer asked the peon .... why he was late.
   A. that B. if
   C. but D. No word
3. Both Ajay .... Vijay are intelligent.
   A. or B. nor
   C. and D. No word
4. No sooner did the thief see the public .... he ran away.
   A. then B. and
   C. but D. than
5. Abhinav .... his brothers was going to Mumbai.
   A. but B. yet
   C. no word D. together
6. He behaves .... he were the captain of the team.
   A. as if B. as
   C. no word D. that
7. Either Rupali .... Sonali is going to attend the meeting.
   A. and B. but
   C. nor D. or
8. Neither Nirmal .... Ashwinee is going to listen the speech of the minister.
   A. and B. but
   C. nor D. or

9. Ravi .... Prakash are going to Kolkata.
A. or B. nor
C. but D. and

10. Rice .... curry is my usual breakfast.
A. and B. but
C. then D. than

11. Hardly had he left .... his brother came.
A. then B. than
C. when D. that

12. I would rather have a copy .... a book.
A. then B. than
C. when D. that

13. He is no other .... my friend.
A. then B. than
C. when D. but

14. He saw a snake ....he awoke.
A. then B. when
C. than D. No word

15. Ten years have passed .... my grandmother died.
A. since B. when
C. then D. than

16. She is .... good .... bad.
A. either, not B. neither, or
C. neither, nor D. neither, than

17. The cellphone is both cheap .... best.
A. than B. and
C. then D. or

18. No sooner did the thief see the police .... he ran away.
A. then B. than
C. so D. because

19. Srishti will go .... Sanju goes.
A. if B. than
C. then D. although

20. She is wise .... timid.
A. and B. yet
C. but D. however

21. Make hay .... the sun shines.
A. though B. while
C. after D. before

22. He is so weak .... he cannot walk.
A. but B. that
C. then D. so

23. Although he is rich, ... he is unhappy.
A. but B. yet
C. so D. still

24. Wait here .... I come back.
A. till B. until
C. before D. after

25. He is my friend .... I shall help him.
A. so B. hence
C. that is why D. therefore

26. He must go away .... he will be beaten.
A. otherwise B. and
C. or D. else

27. God loves good men .... good men love God.
A. and B. or
C. that D. those

28. He was late .... he was not punished.
A. but B. yet
C. still D. therefore

29. Walk slowly ...., you may fall.
A. and B. or
C. so D. otherwise

30. Work hard, ... you will fail.
A. and B. or
C. otherwise D. else

ANSWERS

1	2	3	4	5	6	7	8	9	10
D	D	C	D	D	A	D	C	D	A
11	12	13	14	15	16	17	18	19	20
C	B	B	B	A	C	B	B	A	C
21	22	23	24	25	26	27	28	29	30
B	B	B	A	B	C	A	C	D	D

13. Tenses & Verbs

1. Tense indicates a point in time or period of time in the past, present, or future tense.
2. The verb may consist of a single word, or a main verb and one or more auxiliary words. The key point is that tense is related to the form of verb. There are normally three forms of the verb, say, V_1, V_2, V_3 and for convenience a fourth form V_4 as verb+ing may be assumed.

A Comparative Chart Regarding Tenses and Verbs

Simple Present	**Simple Past**	**Simple Future**
V_1	V_2	shall/will + V_1
Present Continuous	**Past Continuous**	**Future Continuous**
is/am/are + V_4	was/were + V_4	shall/will + be + V_4
Present Perfect	**Past Perfect**	**Future Perfect**
has/have + V_3	had + V_3	shall/will + have + V_3
Present Perfect Cont.	**Past Perfect Cont.**	**Future Perfect Cont.**
has/have + been + V_4	had + been + V_4	shall/will + have been + V_4

SIMPLE PRESENT:

A. A present state of affairs. — A. My sister lives in Nagpur.
B. A general fact. — B. The sun rises in the east.
C. Habitual actions. — C. I listen to the radio in the mornings.
D. Future time-tables. — D. My flight leaves at 10:00.

PRESENT CONTINUOUS:

A. A specific action that is occurring. — A. Arvind is watching TV (right now).
B. A general activity that takes. — B. These days, I'm taking it easy.
C. Future arrangements. — C. I'm inviting Hari to the party on Friday.

SIMPLE PAST:

A. An action that began and ended at a particular time in the past. — A. The mail came early this Morning.
B. An action that occurred over a period of time but was completed in the past. — B. Dad worked in advertising in the past.
C. An activity that took place regularly in the past. — C. We jogged every morning before class.

PAST CONTINUOUS:

A. Interrupted Actions. — A. I was sewing when the telephone rang.

B. A continuous state over a period of time but was completed in the past.
C. Events planned in the past.

D. Expressing a future intent.
E. Predicting an event.

B. She was looking very ill. I was meeting lots of people at that time.
C. Neetu was leaving for Kolkata but had to make a last minute change
D. Jyoti is going to bring her sister tonight.
E. You are going to pass the test. Don't worry.

SIMPLE FUTURE:

A. Making a future decision.
B. Predicting a future event.
C. Indicating willingness to do something.

A. I will call you after lunch.
B. You will pass the test. Don't worry.
C. If I don't feel better soon, I will go to to the doctor.

FUTURE CONTINUOUS:

A. An action that will be going at a particular time in the future.
B. Future actions which have already been decided.

A. At noon tomorrow, I will be taking the children to their piano lessons.
B. I will be wearing my black dress to the dinner.

PRESENT PERFECT:

A. An action that happened at an unspecified time.
B. An action that has recently occurred.
C. An action that began in the past and continues up to the present (often used with "for" or "since").
D. An action that happened repeatedly before now.

A. She has never climbed a mountain. I'm sorry. I have forgotten your Name.
B. He's just gone to sleep.
C. Jack has lived in Chennai all his life. I have been here since Monday. He has known her for two weeks.
D. We have flown across the Pacific four times. I've failed my driver's test twice.

PRESENT PERFECT CONTINUOUS:

A. An action that began in the past and has just recently ended.
B. An action that began in the past and continues in the present.
C. An action repeated over a period of time in the past and continuing in present.

A. Have you been ringing the Bell?
B. Lokesh has been studying for two hours.
C. Suresh has been smoking since he was fifteen.

PAST PERFECT:

A. An action that occurred before another past action.
B. An action that was expected to occur in the past.

A. Tarun had left hours before we got there.
B. I had hoped to know about the job before now.

PAST PERFECT CONTINUOUS:

A. An action that occurred before another past action.
B. An action that was expected to occur in the past.

A. His eyes hurt because he had been Reading for eight hours.
B. I had been expecting a change in his attitude.

FUTURE PERFECT:

A. An action that will be completed before a particular time in the future.

A. By next July, my parents will have been married for fifty years.

FUTURE PERFECT CONTINUOUS:

A. Emphasizing the length of time that has occurred before a specific time in the future.

A. By May, my father will have been working at the same job for thirty years.

AGREEMENT OF THE VERB WITH THE SUBJECT

It is very important that the verb in a sentence should obey the subject, otherwise the sentence will be considered wrong.

I. When the Subject is a Singular Noun

A singular noun takes a singular verb.

(i) Mohit **makes** a noise in the class.

(ii) The child is **crying** for a cake.

II. When two singular nouns are joined with 'and'

When two singular nouns are joined with 'and' and they refer to two different persons, the plural verb should be used, *e.g.*,

(i) The novelist and the poet **were** honoured by the government.

(ii) The black and the white dogs **bark** at the strangers.

Note: Article 'the' is used with both the subjects. If article is used only once, the singular verb should be used.

(i) The painter and singer is going abroad.

(ii) The white and black dog has a bushy tail.

III. When the subjects together give a single idea, singular verb is used:

(i) Slow and steady wins the race.

(ii) Rice and curry is my favourite dish.

IV. A collective noun takes a singular verb when it acts as a whole, but it takes a plural verb when the individual, of which it is composed are considered separately.

(i) The committee was unanimous on imposing the new law.

(ii) The committee have given their separate opinions in the matter.

V. When the subjects are joined by neither . . . nor, either . . . or, and 'or', the verb should obey the last subject.

(i) Rakesh or his friends have been selected for the match.

(ii) His friends or Rakesh has been selected for the match.

(iii) Neither Rohit nor his brothers are going abroad.

(iv) Neither his brothers nor Rohit is going abroad.

(v) Either Sohan or his sisters were dancing at the function.

(vi) Either his sisters or Sohan was dancing at the function.

VI. Either, neither, either of, neither of, takes singular verb.

(i) Either boy was honest.

(ii) Neither girl was allowed to leave the premises.

(iii) Either of the boys was ready to help the old man.

(iv) Neither of the girls was asked to join the extra classes.

VII. Some nouns are always used as plurals so, they take plural verbs.

(i) Where are your glasses?

(ii) His pants are attractive.

(iii) Cattle are grazing in the field.

(iv) Whose scissors are these?

VIII. Some nouns are always used as singulars, so, they take singular verbs.

(i) What is the latest news?

(ii) The furniture in the house is of a poor quality.

(iii) Mumps is not a fatal disease.

(vi) Physics is a tough subject.

IX. Nouns formed by alongwith, as well as, together with, accompanied by, etc., take verb according to the first subject.

(i) I as well as you am to blame.
(ii) You as well as I are going to see a movie.
(iii) John accompanied by his parents is going to visit the Taj.
(iv) His parents accompanied by John are going to visit the Taj.
(v) His brothers together with Vivek are ready to whitewash the fence.

X. To indicate something hypothetical or not factually true, plural verb 'were' with *as if* is used.

(i) He talks as if he were a king.
(ii) She dresses herself as if she were a princess.

MULTIPLE CHOICE QUESTIONS

Directions: *Find the correct word(s) that correctly completes the sentence.*

1. A woman came in with a baby who, she said, ... a safety pin.
A. was just swallowing
B. swallowed
C. had just swallowed
D. just swallowed

2. The telephone ..... several times before I answered it.
A. was ringing B. has rung
C. had rung D. would ring

3. An employment advertisement should ..... the number of vacancies.
A. provide B. specify
C. contain D. declare

4. A crescendo of metallic thuds arose from the market, where the iron-smiths were ..... the pieces of metals.
A. flattening B. striking
C. hammering D. thrashing

5. Ambition is one of those ..... which are never satisfied.
A. ideas B. fancies
C. passions D. needs

6. The new education policy provides a useful ..... for the planners to remove illiteracy.
A. breakup B. breakthrough
C. breakaway D. break-in

7. The family gave father a gold watch on the ..... of his fiftieth birthday.
A. time B. event
C. occasion D. celebration

8. The passengers were afraid but the captain ..... them that there was no danger.
A. promised B. assured
C. advised D. counselled

9. It's very kind of you to ..... to speak at the meeting.
A. accept B. agree
C. comply D. concur

10. The miser gazed ..... at the pile of gold coins in front of him.
A. avidly B. admiringly
C. thoughtfully D. earnestly

11. The pilot had been warned about the storm before he .....
A. took away B. took up
C. took over D. took off

12. On account of the dearth of grass on the arid plains the cattle became .....
A. flippant B. jubilant
C. agitated D. emaciated

13. I saw a ..... of cows in the field.
A. group B. herd
C. swarm D. flock

14. He was sent to the prison for his .....
A. sin B. vice
C. crime D. guilt

15. ..... of old paintings is a job for the experts.
A. Resurrection B. Retrieval
C. Restoration D. Resumption

16. Once he has signed the agreement, he won't be able to .....
A. back up B. back in
C. back at D. back out

17. She ..... a brief appearance at the end of the party.
A. put on B. put in
C. put across D. put up

18. The battalion operating from the mountain was able to ..... three enemy divisions.
A. tie up B. tie down
C. tie on D. tie with

19. Do you know ..... ?
A. where she comes from
B. where does she come from
C. where from she comes
D. from where does she come

20. ..... works of reference are so valuable as the Encyclopaedia Britannica.
A. A few B. Few
C. The few D. Fewer

21. The paths of glory lead ..... to the grave.
A. straight B. but
C. in D. directly

22. Walking at three o'clock, I heard the ..... of thunder.
A. crackle B. rumble
C. ripple D. clank

23. The thief ..... all the money.
A. made up B. made off with
C. made do with D. made good

24. Either Surendra or his friends ..... asked to pay a visit to the university.
A. has been B. have been
C. has D. have

25. Where ..... your spectacles?
A. is B. are
C. were D. have

26. Measles ..... not a fatal disease.
A. is B. are
C. has D. have

27. He walks as if he ..... a prince.
A. was B. were
C. have been D. has been

28. The captain alongwith his team mates ..... reached the ground.
A. have B. has
C. is D. are

29. The jury ..... given its opinion.
A. has B. have
C. is D. are

30. Slow and steady ..... the race.
A. win B. wins
C. has wins D. have win

31. The poet and the novelist ..... invited by the PM.
A. is B. are
C. has D. have

32. Mathematics ..... a tough subject.
A. is B. are
C. has D. have

33. Either girl ..... in a sad mood.
A. was B. were
C. has D. have

34. You should not avoid ...... him.
A. for meeting B. in meeting
C. to meet D. meeting

35. Are you ...... you lessons?
A. busy for preparing
B. busy preparing
C. busy to prepare
D. busy of preparing

ANSWERS

1	2	3	4	5	6	7	8	9	10
C	C	B	C	C	B	C	B	B	A
11	**12**	**13**	**14**	**15**	**16**	**17**	**18**	**19**	**20**
D	D	B	C	C	D	B	B	A	B
21	**22**	**23**	**24**	**25**	**26**	**27**	**28**	**29**	**30**
B	B	B	B	B	A	B	B	A	B
31	**32**	**33**	**34**	**35**					
B	A	A	D	B					

14. NARRATION

The words spoken by a speaker are in Direct Speech.

The words spoken by somebody and expressed by someone else with some modification are known as Indirect Speech. *e.g.*,

(*a*) Rohit says to me, "You do not understand me." (Direct speech)

(*b*) Rohit tells me that I do not understand him. (Indirect speech)

MULTIPLE CHOICE QUESTIONS

Directions: *Each sentence in this assignment is followed by four options, only one is correct. Spot the correct answer.*

1. She said to me, "Keep quite and listen to my words".
   - A. She requested me to keep quite and listen to her words.
   - B. She ordered me to keep quite and listen to her words.
   - C. She entreated me to keep quite and listen to her words.
   - D. She told me to keep quite and listen to her words.

2. My brother said to me, "What are you doing here?"
   - A. My brother asked me that what I was doing there.
   - B. My brother asked me what I was doing there.
   - C. My brother asked me that what was I doing there.
   - D. My brother asked me what I was doing here.

3. Ravi said, "My father lived in this city two years ago."
   - A. Ravi said that his father had lived in that city two years before.
   - B. Ravi said that his father had lived in that city two years ago.
   - C. Ravi told that his father had lived in that city ago two years.
   - D. Ravi asked that his father had lived in that city before two years.

4. My brother said to me, "When I was young, I used to play cricket".
   - A. My brother told me that when I was young, I used to play cricket.
   - B. My brother told me that when I was young, I used to play cricket.
   - C. My brother told me that when he was young, I used to play cricket.
   - D. My brother told me that when he was young, he used to play cricket.

5. The student said, "Sir, I am not guilty".
   - A. The student said with respect that he was not guilty.
   - B. The student pleaded that he was not guilty.
   - C. The student pleaded with respect that he was not guilty.
   - D. The student said respectfully that he was not guilty.

6. She said, "I am an early-riser".
   - A. She regretted that she was an early-riser.
   - B. She said that she is an early-riser.
   - C. She said that she was an early-riser.
   - D. She regretted that she is an early-riser.

7. The police officer said to the criminal, "Speak as I tell you".
   - A. The police officer directed the criminal to speak as he told him.
   - B. The police officer told the criminal to speak as he told him.
   - C. The police officer advised the criminal to speak as he told him.

D. The police officer requested the criminal to speak as he told him.

8. The preacher said to me, "May God help you!"
A. The preacher prayed that God might help me.
B. The preacher prayed that God might help him.
C. The preacher requested that God might help me.
D. The preacher requested the God might help them.

9. She said to me, "Happy Diwali!"
A. She blessed me a happy Diwali.
B. She wished me a happy Diwali.
C. She prayed a happy Diwali.
D. She said to me a very happy Diwali.

10. He said, "Shall I open the gate?"
A. He asked that he should open the gate.
B. He asked if he should open the gate.
C. He ordered that he should open the gate.
D. He requested that he should open the gate.

11. I told Ravi, "Do have a cup of tea".
A. I ordered Ravi to have a cup of tea.
B. I advised Ravi to had a cup of tea.
C. I requested Ravi to have a cup of tea.
D. I said Ravi to have a cup of cold tea.

12. He told me, "Shall I go to the picture?"
A. He asked that he should go to the picture.
B. He asked me if he shall go to the picture.
C. He asked me if he should go to the picture.
D. He requested me to go to the picture.

13. The teacher says, "Two and two makes four".
A. The teacher says that two and two made four.
B. The teacher wishes that two and two makes four.
C. The teacher advises that two and two makes four.
D. The teacher says that two and two makes four.

14. Baby said, "I will go".
A. Baby said that she will go.
B. Baby said that she could go.
C. Baby say that she will go.
D. Baby said that she would go.

15. I said to my sister, "Please, give me more money".
A. I requested my sister to give me more money.
B. I ordered my sister to give me more money.
C. I advised my sister to gave me more money.
D. I requested my sister to give her more money.

16. He said, "Bring a chair at once".
A. He ordered to bring a chair at once.
B. He requested to bring a chair at once.
C. He told to bring a chair at once.
D. He says to bring a chair at once.

17. The teacher said, "Don't make a noise".
A. The teacher says to us not to make a noise.
B. The teacher asked us not to make a noise.
C. The teacher requested us not to make a noise.
D. The teacher asked us not to made a noise.

18. My father said, "The earth is round".
A. My father said that the earth was round.
B. My father says that the earth is round.
C. My father said that the earth is round
D. My father ordered that the earth is round.

19. We said, "What a place it is!"
A. We said that it was a very fine place.
B. We said that is a very fine place.
C. We said that the place is fine.
D. We exclaimed with joy that the place was very fine.

20. She said, "Shall I thread the needle?"
A. She asked if she should thread the needle
B. She asked if she shall thread the needle.
C. She requested if she should thread the needle.
D. She says that if she would thread the needle.

ANSWERS

1	2	3	4	5	6	7	8	9	10
B	B	A	D	C	C	A	A	B	B
11	**12**	**13**	**14**	**15**	**16**	**17**	**18**	**19**	**20**
C	C	D	D	A	A	B	C	D	A

15. Active & Passive Voice

An active sentence focuses on the person or thing doing the action. A passive sentence focuses on the person or thing affected by the action.

e.g., The tower was built. (Active voice)

Someone built the tower. (Passive voice)

Transformation of Voice

i.e., Active voice to Passive voice & vice versa.

- Voice and Tense are closely associated with each other.
- Tense plays an important role while transforming the voice.

MULTIPLE CHOICE QUESTIONS

Directions: *In these questions, the sentences have been given in Active/Passive voice. From the given options, choose the one which best expresses the given sentence in Passive/Active voice.*

1. Help the poor.
A. The poor should be helped.
B. The poor would be helped.
C. The poor must be helped.
D. The poor will be helped.

2. Bring a glass of water.
A. A glass of water will be brought.
B. A glass of water should be brought.
C. Let a glass of water be brought.
D. Let a glass of water will be brought.

3. He gave me a beautiful flower pot.
A. A beautiful flower pot was given to me by him.
B. A beautiful flower pot had given to me by him.
C. A beautiful flower pot had been giving by him.
D. I was giving him a beautiful flower pot.

4. Is he answering the question?
A. The question is answered by him.
B. The question is being answered by him.
C. Is the question being answered by him?
D. Is the question being answering by him?

5. Who gave you this letter?
A. This letter was given to you by whom?
B. This letter had given to you by whom?
C. Was this letter given to you?
D. By whom was this letter given to you?

6. The professor teaches students.
A. Students are being taught by the professor.
B. Students are taught by the professor.
C. The professor is being taught by students.
D. Students being taught by the professor.

7. M.S. Dhoni has created a world record.
A. A world record has been created by M.S. Dhoni.
B. A world record has created by M.S. Dhoni.
C. A world record is created by M.S. Dhoni.
D. A world record is being created by M.S. Dhoni.

8. Srishti sings a lovely song.
A. A lovely song had sung by Srishti.
B. A lovely song was sung by Srishti.
C. A lovely song is sung by Srishti.
D. A lovely song is sang by Srishti.

9. He was drawing a picture.
A. A picture was drawn by him.
B. A picture was being drawn by him.
C. A picture was drawing by him.
D. A picture was drew by him.

10. We made him leader.
A. He was made leader by us.

B. He was maded leader.
C. He made leader by us.
D. He was made leader.

11. There is no time to waste.
A. There is no time to be wasted.
B. No time to be wasted there.
C. No time to be wasted by there.
D. No time is to be wasted.

12. Take medicine in time.
A. In time medicine to be taken.
B. Medicine should be taken in time.
C. Medicine in time will be taken.
D. Medicine has to be in time taken.

13. He reads a novel.
A. A novel was read by him.
B. A novel has read by him.
C. A novel is being read by him.
D. A novel is read by him.

14. They had cleared the dues.
A. The dues had been cleared by them.
B. The dues had cleared by them.
C. The dues are being cleared.
D. The dues is cleared.

15. I invite you on the dinner.
A. On the dinner you have been invited.
B. On the dinner you are inviting.
C. You are inviting by me on the dinner.
D. You are invited by me on the dinner.

16. We chose him our leader.
A. He was chosen our leader.
B. He has been chosen our leader.
C. He had chosen our leader.
D. He have been chosen our leader.

17. Who made a maiden century?
A. By whose was a maiden century made?
B. By whom was a maiden century make?
C. By whom was a maiden century made?
D. By whom had a maiden century made?

18. I may help her in her project.
A. She might be helped by me in her project.
B. She may be helped by me in her project.
C. She might be helped in her project by me.
D. In her project, she may be help by me.

19. Take medicine in time.
A. Medicine should be taken in time.
B. Medicine will be taken in time.
C. Medicine will be took in time.
D. Medicine shall take in time.

20. I am solving the questions.
A. The questions are being solved by me.
B. The questions have been solved by me.
C. The questions are to be solved by me.
D. The question are solved by me.

21. May I take this pen?
A. May this pen will be taken by me?
B. May this pen shall be taken by me?
C. May this pen should be taken by me?
D. May this pen be taken by me?

22. Can we send it by air?
A. Can this be sent by air?
B. Can it be sent by air?
C. Can it go by air?
D. Can it be send by air?

23. Who wrote this book?
A. By whom was this book written?
B. By whom is this book written?
C. By whom was this book being written?
D. By whom is this book being written?

24. What did you buy?
A. What is bought by you?
B. What is being bought by you?
C. What was bought by you?
D. What was being bought by you?

25. Whom do you want?
A. Who is wanted by you?
B. Who is being wanted by you?
C. You are wanted by whom?
D. You are being wanted by whom?

ANSWERS

1	2	3	4	5	6	7	8	9	10
A	C	A	C	D	B	A	C	B	A
11	**12**	**13**	**14**	**15**	**16**	**17**	**18**	**19**	**20**
A	B	D	A	D	A	C	B	A	A
21	**22**	**23**	**24**	**25**					
D	B	A	C	A					

16. SYNONYMS, ANTONYMS & HOMONYMS

Synonym: A word or phrase that means the same as another word or phrase.
Antonym: A word or phrase that means the opposite of another word or phrase.
Homonyms: Two or more words having the same spelling or pronunciation but different meanings.

MULTIPLE CHOICE QUESTIONS

Directions: *In the following questions choose the word which best expresses the meaning of the given word.*

1. INDICT
   A. Condemn B. Reprimand
   C. Accuse D. Allege
2. SCINTILLATING
   A. Smouldering B. Gilittering
   C. Touching D. Warming
3. REFECTORY
   A. Restaurant B. Parlour
   C. Living Room D. Dining Room
4. DISTINCTION
   A. Diffusion B. Disagreement
   C. Different D. Degree
5. IMPROVEMENT
   A. Advancement B. Betterment
   C. Promotion D. Preference
6. ADVERSITY
   A. Failure B. Helplessness
   C. Misfortune D. Crisis
7. TURN UP
   A. Land up B. Show up
   C. Crop up D. Come up
8. DEIFY
   A. Flatter B. Challenge
   C. Worship D. Face
9. ERROR
   A. Misadventure B. Misgiving
   C. Ambiguity D. Blunder
10. SHALLOW
    A. Artificial B. Superficial
    C. Foolish D. Worthless
11. MASSACRE
    A. Murder B. Stab
    C. Assassinate D. Slaughter
12. COMBAT
    A. Conflict B. Quarrel
    C. Feud D. Fight
13. VORACIOUS
    A. Wild B. Hungry
    C. Angry D. Quick
14. IMPROMPTU
    A. Offhand B. Unimportant
    C. Unreal D. Effective
15. RABBLE
    A. Mob B. Noise
    C. Roar D. Rubbish
16. TEPID
    A. Hot B. Warm
    C. Cold D. Boiling
17. MAYHEM
    A. Jubilation B. Havoc
    C. Excitement D. Defeat
18. TIMID
    A. Fast B. Slow
    C. Medium D. Shy
19. CANTANKEROUS
    A. Quarrelsome B. Rash
    C. Disrepectful D. Noisy

20. PRECARIOUS
A. Cautious B. Critical
C. Perilous D. Brittle

Directions: *In the following questions choose the word which best expresses the opposite of the given word.*

21. DEAR
A. Priceless B. Free
C. Worthless D. Cheap

22. FLAGITIOUS
A. Innocent B. Vapid
C. Ignorant D. Frivolous

23. LIABILITY
A. Property B. Assets
C. Debt D. Treasure

24. VIRTUOUS
A. Wicked B. Corrupt
C. Vicious D. Scandalous

25. ENCOURAGE
A. Dampen B. Disapprove
C. Discourage D. Warn

26. MORTAL
A. Divine B. Immortal
C. Spiritual D. Eternal

27. LEND
A. Borrow B. Cheat
C. Pawn D. Hire

28. COMIC
A. Emotional B. Tragic
C. Fearful D. Painful

29. ADDITION
A. Division B. Enumeration
C. Subtraction D. Multiplication

30. MINOR
A. Big B. Major
C. Tall D. Heavy

31. REPEL
A. Attend B. Concentrate
C. Continue D. Attract

32. ARTIFICIAL
A. Red B. Natural
C. Truthful D. Solid

33. CAPACIOUS
A. Limited B. Caring
C. Foolish D. Changeable

34. PROVOCATION
A. Vocation B. Pacification
C. Peace D. Destruction

35. METICULOUS
A. Mutual B. Shaggy
C. Meretricious D. Slovenly

36. Choose the correct homonym for the word 'been'.
A. done B. being
C. bean D. covered

37. Choose the correct homonym for the word 'dose'?
A. doze B. does
C. douse D. dyes

38. Choose the correct homonym for the word 'would':
A. could B. weed
C. wood D. hold

39. Choose the correct homonym for the word 'load':
A. loud B. laud
C. lead D. lode

40. Choose the correct homonym for the word 'loan':
A. lawn B. lean
C. lone D. long

ANSWERS

1	2	3	4	5	6	7	8	9	10
C	B	D	C	B	C	B	C	D	B
11	12	13	14	15	16	17	18	19	20
D	D	B	A	A	B	B	D	A	B
21	22	23	24	25	26	27	28	29	30
D	A	B	C	C	B	A	B	C	B
31	32	33	34	35	36	37	38	39	40
D	B	A	B	D	C	A	C	D	C

17. ONE WORD SUBSTITUTION

There are many words in English language which can be perfectly used for a number of words. These words help in expressing ideas in a short and correct manner for the right occasion. Such words not only increase the vocabulary but also enable you to economise in the use of words to a great extent.

MULTIPLE CHOICE QUESTIONS

Directions: *In questions given below out of the four alternatives choose the one which can be substituted for the given words/sentence.*

1. Something that relates to everyone in the world
A. General B. Common
C. Usual D. Universal

2. An expression of mild disapproval
A. Warning B. Denigration
C. Impertinence D. Reproof

3. One who is not easily pleased by anything
A. Maiden B. Medieval
C. Precarious D. Fastidious

4. Murder of a king
A. Infanticide B. Matricide
C. Genocide D. Regicide

5. A remedy for all diseases
A. Stoic B. Marvel
C. Panacea D. Recompense

6. A dramatic performance
A. Mask B. Mosque
C. Masque D. Mascot

7. Study of birds
A. Orology B. Optology
C. Ophthalmology D. Ornithology

8. Ready to believe
A. Credulous B. Credible
C. Creditable D. Incredible

9. Incapable of being seen through
A. Ductile B. Opaque
C. Obsolete D. Potable

10. One who eats everything
A. Omnivorous B. Omniscient
C. Irresistible D. Insolvent

11. A place where bees are kept is called
A. An apiary B. A mole
C. A hive D. A sanctuary

12. One who cannot be corrected
A. Incurable B. Incorrigible
C. Hardened D. Invulnerable

13. One who is in charge of a museum
A. Curator B. Supervisor
C. Caretaker D. Warden

14. Continuing fight between parties, families, clans, etc.
A. Enmity B. Feud
C. Quarrel D. Skirmish

15. A voice loud enough to be heard
A. Audible B. Applaudable
C. Laudable D. Oral

16. A paper written by hand
A. Handicraft B. Manuscript
C. Handiwork D. Thesis

17. Habitually silent or talking little
A. Serville B. Unequivocal
C. Taciturn D. Synoptic

18. To slap with a flat object
A. Chop B. Hew
C. Gnaw D. Swat

19. A person who speaks many languages
A. Linguist B. Monolingual
C. Polyglot D. Bilingual

20. A light sailing-boat built specially for racing
A. Canoe B. Yacht
C. Frigate D. Dinghy

21. A fixed orbit in space in relation to earth
A. Geological B. Geo-synchronous
C. Geo-centric D. Geo-stationary

22. A style in which a writer makes a display of his knowledge
A. Pedantic B. Verbose
C. Pompous D. Ornate

23. A religious discourse
A. Preach B. Stanza
C. Sanctorum D. Sermon

24. A place that provides refuge
A. Asylum B. Sanatorium
C. Shelter D. Orphanage

25. Detailed plan of a journey
A. Travelogue B. Travelkit
C. Schedule D. Itinerary

26. A person who insists on something
A. Disciplinarian B. Stickler
C. Instantaneous D. Boaster

27. A drawing on transparent paper
A. Red print B. Blue print
C. Negative D. Transparency

28. One who believes that all things and events in life are predetermined is a
A. Fatalist B. Puritan
C. Egoist D. Tyrant

29. A school boy who cuts classes frequently is a
A. Defeatist B. Sycophant
C. Truant D. Martinet

30. The act of violating the sanctity of the church is
A. Blasphemy B. Heresy
C. Sacrilege D. Desecration

31. A place where monks live as a secluded community
A. Cathedral B. Diocese
C. Convent D. Monastery

32. One who is fond of fighting
A. Bellicose B. Aggressive
C. Belligerent D. Militant

33. Tending to move away from the centre or axis
A. Centrifugal B. Centripetal
C. Axiomatic D. Awry

34. A person of good understanding, knowledge and reasoning power
A. Expert B. Intellectual
C. Snob D. Literate

35. One absorbed in his own thoughts and feelings rather than in things outside
A. Scholar B. Recluse
C. Introvert D. Intellectual

36. One who does not marry, especially as a religious obligation
A. Bachelor B. Celibate
C. Virgin D. Recluse

37. A person who tries to deceive people by claiming to be able to do wonderful things.
A. Trickster B. Impostor
C. Magician D. Mountebank

38. To take secretly in small quantities
A. Robbery B. Pilferage
C. Theft D. Defalcation

39. Policemen riding on motorcycles as guards to a VIP.
A. Outriders B. Servants
C. Commandos D. Attendants

40. The part of a government which is concerned with making of rules.
A. Court B. Tribunal
C. Bar D. Legislature

ANSWERS

1	2	3	4	5	6	7	8	9	10
D	D	D	D	C	C	D	A	B	A
11	**12**	**13**	**14**	**15**	**16**	**17**	**18**	**19**	**20**
A	B	A	B	A	B	C	D	A	B
21	**22**	**23**	**24**	**25**	**26**	**27**	**28**	**29**	**30**
D	A	D	A	D	B	D	A	C	C
31	**32**	**33**	**34**	**35**	**36**	**37**	**38**	**39**	**40**
D	A	A	B	C	B	A	B	A	D

18. Idioms, Phrases & Proverbs

An idiom is a group of words established by usage as having a meaning different from the individual words.
A phrase is a small group of words standing together as an idiomatic expression.
A proverb is a short pithy saying in general use, stating a general truth or piece of advice.

MULTIPLE CHOICE QUESTIONS

Directions: *Some idioms/phrases are given below with their meanings. Choose their correct meanings.*

1. To beg the question
A. To refer to
B. To take for granted
C. To raise objections
D. To be discussed

2. To drive home
A. To find one's roots
B. To return to place of rest
C. Back to original position
D. To emphasise

3. To hit the right nail on the head
A. To do the right thing
B. To destroy one's reputation
C. To announce one's fixed views
D. To teach someone a lesson

4. To pick holes
A. To find some reason to quarrel
B. To destory something
C. To criticise someone
D. To cut some part of an item

5. To smell a rat
A. To see signs of plague epidemic
B. To get bad smell of a dead rat
C. To suspect foul dealings
D. To be in a bad mood

6. A black sheep
A. An unlucky person
B. A negro
C. An ugly person
D. A disgraced member

7. To catch a tarter
A. To trap wanted criminal with great difficulty
B. To catch a dangerous person
C. To meet with disaster
D. To deal with a person who is more than one's watch.

8. To be above board
A. To have a good height
B. To be honest in any business deal
C. To have no debts
D. To try to be beautiful

9. To keep one's temper
A. To become angry
B. To be in good mood
C. To preserve one's energy
D. To be aloof from

10. To have an axe to grind
A. A private end to serve
B. To fail to arouse interest
C. To have no result
D. To work for both sides

11. To cry wolf
A. To listen eagerly
B. To give false alarm
C. To turn pale
D. To keep off starvation

12. A man of straw
A. A man of no substance
B. A very active person
C. A worthy fellow
D. An unreasonable person

13. To make clean breast of
A. To gain prominence
B. To praise oneself
C. To confess without reserve
D. To destroy before it blooms

14. To end in smoke
A. To make completely understand
B. To ruin oneself
C. To excite great applause
D. To produce no result

15. To leave someone in the lurch
A. To come to compromise with someone
B. Constant source of annoyance to someone
C. To put someone at ease
D. To desert someone in his difficulties

16. To play second fiddle
A. To be happy, cheerful and healthy
B. To reduce importance of one's senior
C. To support the role and view of another person
D. To do back seat driving

17. To set one's face against
A. To oppose with determination
B. To judge by appearance
C. To get out of difficulty
D. To look at one steadily

18. To put one's hand to the plough
A. To take up agricultural farming
B. To take a difficult task
C. To get entangled into unnecessary things
D. Take interest in technical work

19. To join issue with
A. To cooperate with others for a cause
B. To join any voluntary organisation for good purpose
C. To resolve dispute and restore peace
D. To enter into argument over any issue

20. To do oneself justice
A. To dispense justice on our own
B. To treat others with due respect
C. To defend one's point of view
D. To perform and be able

21. Once in a blue moon
A. Once in a while
B. Often
C. At a short interval
D. At a particular time

22. Necessity is the mother of invention
A. The mother of a girl named 'Necessity' made an invention.
B. She who can make some invention should be called 'mother'.
C. Your mother will feel happy if you make some invention.
D. A difficult problem compels people to think about its solution.

23. No pain, no gain
A. It is useless to suffer so much pain just for a little gain.
B. If you want to achieve something, you have to suffer to some extent.
C. Unless you have pain in your body, no doctor will care for you.
D. If you get injured in a competition, you will be allowed to get the prize.

24. Beauty is only skin deep
A. The real beauty of a person lies in his character and not in his outer appearance.
B. Only the quality of skin makes a person really beautiful.
C. If you want to be beautiful, give attention to your skin.
D. Rub cosmetics below the skin to get really beautiful.

25. Beggars cannot be choosers
A. Beggars are not allowed at all places.
B. Begging is prohibited by law.
C. It is not easy even to become a beggar.
D. Beggars have to accept (without choice) whatever is given to them.

ANSWERS

1	2	3	4	5	6	7	8	9	10
C	D	A	C	C	D	B	B	B	A
11	**12**	**13**	**14**	**15**	**16**	**17**	**18**	**19**	**20**
B	A	C	D	D	C	A	B	D	D
21	**22**	**23**	**24**	**25**					
A	D	B	A	D					

19. Modals & Auxiliaries

AUXILIARY VERBS

Modals are actually helping verbs. They help the finite verbs in framing sentences:

She was cooking food.

I **shall** guide you.

Kinds of Auxiliary Verbs

Auxiliary verbs are of two kinds:

A. Primary Auxiliaries (Modals)

B. Modal Auxiliaries (Auxiliary Modals)

A. Primary Modals

Primary modals work both as Helping Verbs and Finite Verbs.

Be = is, am, are, was, were, being, been

Have = has, have, had, having

Do = do, does, did, done, doing

(*a*) **Usage of be/have/do as Helping verbs:**

She **is** making a cane basket.

I **have** finished my homework.

She **does** know French.

(*b*) **Usage of be/have/do as Finite verbs:**

She **was** happy.

I **have** an expensive pen.

She **is doing** her homework.

B. Modal Auxiliaries

Shall, should, will, would, can, could, may, might, must, ought to, used to, have to, had to, dare, daren't, need needn't, mustn't are modal Auxiliaries.

Shall

'Shall' is used in the following ways:

(*a*) **With first Person Pronouns (I/we)**

I shall lend you my book.

We shall go to school together.

(*b*) **to express a suggestion**

Shall we go out for a walk?

Shall we meet the officer tomorrow?

Sometimes 'Shall' is used with Second and Third Person Pronouns as under:

(*a*) **to express a command**

You shall not tell a lie.

You shall not disturb us.

(*b*) **to express prohibition**

You shall not smoke here.

You shall not drink here.

(*c*) **to express a legal obligation**

You shall submit your sales tax return before the end of this month.

Should

'Should' is used in the following ways:

(*a*) **As Past Tense of 'shall'**

She said that she **should** settle in America.

(*b*) **to express duty and obligation**

You should do your duty honestly.

(*c*) **to express advice**

You should reach the station before time.

(*d*) **to express guess**

It should be 9 o'clock now.

(*e*) 'Should' is used with lest to express purpose.

Walk fast lest you should miss the train.

Will

'Will' is used in the following ways:

(*a*) **With Second and Third person Pronouns:**

You will dance at the party.

He will sing a song.

(*b*) **to express (Invitation/offer)**

Will you dine with me tonight?

(*c*) **to express an order**

Will you shut your big mouth?

(*d*) **to express probability**

He will come to see me tomorrow.

Sometimes 'Will' is used with 'I'

(*a*) **Determination**

I will win the first position.

(*b*) **A threat**

I will punish you.

(*c*) **A promise**

I will lend you Rs. 500/- tomorrow.

Would

'Would' is used in the following ways:

(*a*) **As Past Tense of 'will'**

He said that they would be attending the meeting the next day.

(*b*) **to express a desire or wish**

Would that I were a king!

(*c*) **to express a polite invitation**

Would you like some biscuits?

(*d*) **The usage of would in conditional sentences**

You would get good marks if you worked hard.

You would have won the race if you had run fast.

(*e*) **to express a piece of advice**

I would not meet him if I were you.

Can

'Can' is used in the following ways:

(*a*) **to express ability**

He can speak English fluently.

(*b*) **to grant permission**

You can go now.

(*c*) **to express impossibility**

Who can defeat his fate?

(*d*) **to make a request**

Can I use your motorbike?

Could

'Could' is used in the following ways:

(*a*) **As Past Tense of 'can'**

She said that she could see the sun rising.

(*b*) **to express past ability**

I could sing and dance when I was young.

(*c*) **to express a request**

Could I use your phone?

May

'May' is used in the following ways:

(*a*) **to express a request**

May I use your bicycle?

(*b*) **to seek and allow permission**

May I come in, sir?

Yes, you may.

(*c*) **to express possibility**

It may rain tonight.

(*d*) **In optative sentences**

May you live long!

Might

'Might' is used in the following ways:

(*a*) **As past tense of 'may'**

She said that her brother might come back home.

(*b*) **to express less possibility**

It might rain tonight.

(*c*) **to give and seek permission**

Might I come in, sir?

You might go home now.

Must

'Must' is used in the following ways:

(*a*) **to express duty**

You must serve your motherland.

(*b*) **to express obligation**

We must obey our elders.

(*c*) **to express advice**

You must take an umbrella before going to office.

(*d*) **to express probability**

'Must' expresses a stronger probability than may.

It must rain tonight.

Ought to

'Ought to' is used in the following ways:

(*a*) **to express obligation**

We ought to respect our teachers.

(*b*) **to express advice**

You ought to help the poor.

Used to

'Used to' is used in the following ways:

(*a*) **to express past habits**
He used to smoke.

(*b*) **to express past existence of something**
There used to be a five star hotel in this city.

Have to

'Have to' expresses compulsion in the present tense.
You have to sign the documents.

Had to

'Had to' expresses compulsion in the past time.
She had to join the office again.

Dare

'Dare' is used as a Modal only in Interrogative sentences.
How dare you touch my bag?

Dare not (Daren't)

'Dare not (Daren't)' is used in negative sentences.
She daren't complain against me.

Need

'Need' expresses an obligation/compulsion. It is used in Interrogative Sentences.
Need I say more?

Need not (Needn't)

'Need not (Needn't)' is used in negative sentences.
You needn't come here again.

Must not (Mustn't)

'Must not (Mustn't)' is the negative form of must.
You mustn't follow us.

MULTIPLE CHOICE QUESTIONS

Directions: *In the following questions choose the correct options to fill in the blanks:*

1. Work hard lest you .... fail.
A. should B. may
C. can D. must

2. .... I come in, madam?
A. Can B. May
C. Will D. Must

3. It ...... rain tonight.
A. shall B. will
C. may D. can

4. You ...... love your countrymen.
A. need to B. have to
C. had to D. ought to

5. .... you like some pastries?
A. Should B. Would
C. Could D. Will

6. ...... that I were an actor!
A. Would B. Should
C. Could D. Will

7. Had you made one more effort you ...... have won the race.
A. will B. may
C. would D. shall

8. I ...... solve any sum.
A. may B. am
C. must D. can

9. ...... I smoke here?
A. Can B. Will
C. Could D. Must

10. The passengers .... keep watch on their luggage.
A. has B. have
C. should D. had

11. You .... submit your file to the authorities within a week.
A. have B. had
C. should D. would

12. ...... I use your phone?
A. Have B. Could
C. Would D. Had

13. ..... you give me your pen?
A. May B. Can
C. Must D. Dare

14. There ...... be an hospital at this place.
A. have to B. may
C. used to D. might

15. He ...... read and write when he was young.
A. would B. could
C. should D. can

16. He said that he ...... sing a song at the party.
A. should B. would
C. can D. will

17. She asked if he ...... help her.
A. should B. can
C. must D. would

18. We .... respect our elders.
A. need to B. have to
C. ought to D. had to

19. Nothing .... be done under such circumstances.
A. can B. used to
C. must D. have to

20. She ..... not ask about it.
A. has B. have
C. had D. dare

21. You .... not bring the child here.
A. have B. had
C. need D. would

22. ..... you live long!
A. Will B. May
C. Shall D. Can

23. ..... God help you!
A. Can B. Will
C. May D. Shall

24. ..... that I were a leader!
A. Would B. Should
C. Could D. Will

25. It ...... be ten o'clock now.
A. could B. would
C. should D. will

26. He ..... have reached the station by now.
A. shall B. will
C. would D. should

27. Being a receptionist, she will .... type a letter.
A. has to B. have to
C. need to D. must

28. The birds ...... fly high in the sky.
A. may B. should
C. can D. would

29. ...... I open the main gate?
A. Should B. Would
C. Could D. Must

30. If you played well, we ...... win the match.
A. would B. should
C. must D. need

31. If I were you I ... not attend the meeting.
A. can B. would
C. could D. should

32. She ...... smoke in those days.
A. used to B. could
C. would D. had to

33. You ...... take the child to an intelligent doctor.
A. shall B. will
C. ought to D. would

34. ..... I sit here for some time?
A. Can B. Shall
C. Will D. Must

35. I think you .... not mind my reciting the poem loudly.
A. should B. could
C. may D. would

ANSWERS

1	2	3	4	5	6	7	8	9	10
A	B	C	D	B	A	C	D	A	C
11	**12**	**13**	**14**	**15**	**16**	**17**	**18**	**19**	**20**
C	B	B	C	B	B	D	C	A	D
21	**22**	**23**	**24**	**25**	**26**	**27**	**28**	**29**	**30**
C	B	C	A	C	C	B	C	A	A
31	**32**	**33**	**34**	**35**					
B	A	C	A	D					

20. NON FINITES

Read the following sentences:

1. She has decided to resign.
2. I see a thief running.
3. She insists on my sitting beside her.

In the above sentences, the underlined words are non-finites because they are not changed with the change of the subject, *e.g.,*

They have decided to resign.

She sees a thief running.

You insist on my sitting beside you.

Non-finites are of three kinds:

1. The Infinitives (to + v_1)
2. The Participles (v_1 + ing)
3. The Gerund (v_1 + ing)

1. THE INFINITIVE

To plus first form of the verb is called an Infinitive. It is often used as a Noun.

Uses of the Infinitive

(*a*) Subject of a sentence.
To laugh loudly is good for health.
To steal is bad.

(*b*) After a transitive verb.
He loves **to eat** sweets.
She likes **to play** tennis.

(*c*) After a preposition.
They are about **to leave.**

(*d*) As a complement after the verb 'be'.
Her ambition is **to be** a teacher.
His immediate aim is **to help** her.

(*e*) As an object.
He made me **weep.**
I saw him **go.**

(*f*) After an adjective.
Honey is sweet **to taste.**
He was ashamed **to talk** to his criminal friend.

(*g*) After a noun. (often in passive)
Here is a book **to be** read carefully.

Bare Infinitive

Some Infinitives are used without 'to' and are called Bare Infinitives.

You had better **go** home.
I saw him **go.**
I heard him **sing.**
He would rather **rest** than **play.**
I can **solve** this sum.
I watched him **steal** your purse.
I watched him **open** the safe.
Let him **come** in.
You had sooner **read** your book than **play.**

Note: Bare Infinitives are usually used after 'causal' (or 'causative') verbs and 'modals'.

2. THE PARTICIPLE

Participles serve the purpose of Adjectives.

I heard him **singing.**
I saw him **going.**

Kinds of Participles

Participles are of the following kinds:

I. Present Participle

I watched the boy **stealing** your purse.
I saw him **climbing** the hill.
She smelt something **burning.**
Don't let me catch you **smoking.**

II. Past Participle

I got the house **painted** last week.
I had my hair **cut.**
The rose has **faded.**

He had **written** five letters.

I want the office **built** in a month.

III. Perfect Participle

Having finished cooking,,she started reading a novel.

Having dusted the room, the maid began to wash the dishes.

Having written a letter to her mother, she walked out of the room.

Joining of Sentences by using Participles

(I) By using Present Participles

1. Look at the boy. He is climbing the tree.
   Look at the boy climbing the tree.
2. He was dusting the room. He found a coin.
   While dusting the room, he found a coin.
3. The child opened the box. He found a toy.
   Opening the box, the child found a toy.

3. THE GERUND

A. (verb + ing) is usually used as a Gerund. Like a Noun, it is used as under.

(*a*) As a subject of the verb.
Killing birds is not good.
Smoking is injurious to health.

(*b*) As an object of the verb.
I like **singing.**
She loves **dancing.**

(*c*) As a complement of the verb 'be'.
What I hate the most is **drinking.**
What I love the most is **playing.**

(*d*) As an object of a preposition.
I am fond of **eating.**
She was punished for **telling** a lie.

B. In some cases, instead of Gerunds Infinitives can be used.

Subject + Verb	Gerund or Infinitive
I love	singing or to sing.
He hates	smoking or to smoke.
I like	dancing or to dance.
He prefers	reading novels/to read novels.
Your bike needs	oiling or to be oiled.

C. It + be + Adjective + Gerund (Phrase).

Subject + be	Adjective/ Noun	Gerund (Phrase)
It is	wrong	making so much noise.
It is	good	drinking juice in the evening.
It is	nice	walking in the moon light.

D. Subject + be + Adjective or Past Participle + Preposition + Gerund.

Subject + be	Adjective/ Past Participle	Preposition	Gerund (Phrase)
He is	fond	of	swimming.
She was	annoyed	at	his talking so loudly.
He is	capable	of	solving all the sums.

MULTIPLE CHOICE QUESTIONS

Directions: *In the following questions choose the correct options to replace the words given in brackets.*

1. He came (run) to his aunt.
A. run B. running
C. to run D. in run

2. She dislikes (eat) meat.
A. eat to B. to eat
C. eating D. to eating

3. He likes (sing).
A. sing to B. singing
C. to sing D. to singing

4. We are ready (play) the match.
A. play to B. to playing
C. playing D. to play

5. (Smoke) is injurious to health.
A. Smoking B. To smoke
C. To smoking D. Smoke to

6. He loves (eat) raw vegetables.
A. eaten B. eating
C. to eating D. eat to

7. He seemed (have) finished his homework.
A. have to B. to have
C. having D. to having

8. It is not easy (achieve) this target.
A. achieve to B. achieving to
C. to achieve D. to achieving

9. It is always difficult (climb) a mountain.
A. climb to B. to climb
C. climbing to D. to climbing

10. She avoided (argue) with him.
A. argue to B. arguing
C. to arguing D. argues

11. I saw him (go).
A. to go B. to going
C. going D. gone

12. I heard him (sing).
A. to sing B. singing
C. to singing D. sung

13. She smelt something (burn).
A. burning B. to burn
C. to burning D. burn to

14. He claimed (be) the best player of hockey.
A. being to B. to be
C. been D. has been

15. We eat (live).
A. living B. to living
C. to live D. lively

16. He wanted (go) across the world.
A. go to B. to going
C. to go D. going to

17. I cannot bear (kill) birds.
A. killing B. to killing
C. to kill D. kill to

18. He wished (be) there inside the hotel.
A. being to B. to be
C. been D. been to

19. It is time (drink) some juice.
A. drinking B. to drinking
C. drink to D. to drink

20. He is too busy (take) care of his kids.
A. taking to B. to take
C. to taking D. take to

21. I forbore myself (slap) him on the face.
A. to slap B. slap to
C. slapping D. slapping to

22. She tried (open) the safe.
A. open to B. opening
C. to open D. to opening

23. It is no use (cry) over spilt milk.
A. cry to B. in crying
C. crying D. crying to

24. They enjoyed (fly) kites.
A. to fly B. fly to
C. flying D. flying to

25. It is your responsibility (keep) the accounts of every happening here.
A. keep to B. keeping to
C. to keep D. keeping

26. Please give me a pair of scissors (cut) cloth.
A. cut to B. cutting to
C. cutting D. to cut

27. She prefers (play) chess to sitting idly.
A. to playing B. playing
C. play to D. playing to

28. I prefer (talk) to the officer alone.
A. talk to B. talking to
C. to talk D. to talking

29. Would you mind your (bring) some cake for me?
A. to bring B. bring to
C. bringing to D. bringing

30. (Err) is human.
A. Err to B. Erring to
C. To erring D. To err

31. (Steal) is not good.
A. Stealing B. To steel
C. To stealing D. Stealing to

32. She heard the lion (roar).
A. to roar B. roaring
C. roar to D. to roaring

33. He is reported (be) dead.
A. be to B. to be
C. to being D. to been

34. You are ordered (bring) the file number 100.
A. bringing B. to bringing
C. bring to D. to bring

35. You are advised (take) part in sports.
A. taking to B. to taking
C. to take D. take to

36. He appeared (have) cast his vote in favour of us.
A. having B. to having
C. to have D. have to

37. His ambition is (become) a doctor.
A. becoming B. to becoming
C. to become D. become to

38. We are asked (be) there in the main hall.
A. being B. been
C. to be D. be to

39. Our immediate aim is (provide) financial help to the needy.
A. provide to B. providing to
C. to providing D. to provide

40. We read and write (become) civilized.
A. becoming B. becoming to
C. to become D. become to

41. You need (improve) your health.
A. improving B. improvinto to
C. to improve D. improve to

42. You are allowed (paint) this door.
A. painting B. painting to
C. to paint D. paint to

43. Remind me (post) this letter.
A. posting B. posting to
C. to post D. post to

44. The teacher forgot (bring) the roll call register.
A. bringing B. to bringing
C. bring to D. to bring

45. He was appointed (keep) a check on the accounts.
A. keep to B. keeping to
C. to keep D. keeping

46. Your activities are (be) noticed.
A. being B. been
C. to be D. be to

47. Stop (talk), please.
A. talk to B. talking
C. to talk D. to talking

48. He does not bother (listen to) anybody.
A. listen to B. to listen to
C. listening D. listening to

49. He is not accustomed to (have) soup before meal.
A. have to B. to have
C. having D. to having

50. She is glad (be) in the company of children.
A. being B. been
C. to be D. be to

ANSWERS

1	2	3	4	5	6	7	8	9	10
B	C	B	D	A	B	B	C	B	B
11	**12**	**13**	**14**	**15**	**16**	**17**	**18**	**19**	**20**
C	B	A	B	C	C	A	B	D	B
21	**22**	**23**	**24**	**25**	**26**	**27**	**28**	**29**	**30**
C	C	C	C	C	D	B	C	D	D
31	**32**	**33**	**34**	**35**	**36**	**37**	**38**	**39**	**40**
A	B	B	D	C	C	C	C	D	C
41	**42**	**43**	**44**	**45**	**46**	**47**	**48**	**49**	**50**
C	C	C	D	C	A	B	B	C	C

21. Commonly Confusing Words

There are many words in English which may look or sound similar but there is lot of difference in their meanings and usage. Learn more about such words in this exercise.

MULTIPLE CHOICE QUESTIONS

Directions: *In the following questions choose the correct word to fill the blank. Two words at A and B are provided for choice. If either of the words can be filled, mark C and if none of the word can be filled then mark D as your choice.*

1. She comes of a .... family.
A. respectable B. respectful
C. Any one of these D. None of these

2. It began to .... as I reached my office.
A. reign B. rain
C. Any one of these D. None of these

3. The teacher told the students to be ....
A. quiet B. quite
C. Any one of these D. None of these

4. The .... has gone to attend the meeting.
A. principle B. principal
C. Any one of these D. None of these

5. .... makes a man perfect.
A. Practice B. Practise
C. Any one of these D. None of these

6. Uttar Pradesh is the most .... state of India.
A. popular B. populous
C. Any one of these D. None of these

7. The bird had a .... of bread with beak.
A. piece B. peace
C. Any one of these D. None of these

8. As she read the letter, her face turned ....
A. pail B. pale
C. Any one of these D. None of these

9. Man is the maker of his own ....
A. destination B. destiny
C. Any one of these D. None of these

10. Try this medicine, it will prove ....
A. effectual B. effective
C. Any one of these D. None of these

11. Maninder has employed an .... boy for his office works.
A. errand B. errant
C. Any one of these D. None of these

12. The soldiers wanted to .... over their victory in the battle.
A. exalt B. exult
C. Any one of these D. None of these

13. When I asked him to accompany us, he .... illness.
A. fained B. feigned
C. Any one of these D. None of these

14. The books are lying on the .... piece.
A. mantal B. mantle
C. Any one of these D. None of these

15. Sohan lives a .... life.
A. luxurious B. luxuriant
C. Any one of these D. None of these

16. She is a lady of .... birth.
A. lowly B. low
C. Any one of these D. None of these

17. We should not be ....of other's wealth.
A. jealous B. zealous
C. Any one of these D. None of these

18. It is two days .... from Delhi to Kerala by train.
A. journey B. voyage
C. Any one of these D. None of these

19. My father makes a .... selection of books before buying.
A. judicial B. judicious
C. Any one of these D. None of these

20. Marconi had an .... mind.
A. ingenious B. ingenuous
C. Any one of these D. None of these

21. It is .... to spend more than what you earn.
A. impudent B. unprudent
C. Any one of these D. None of these

22. Orders for his arrest were issued by the .... court.
A. imperial B. imperious
C. Any one of these D. None of these

23. During the voyage she suffered from sea ....
A. sickness B. illness
C. Any one of these D. None of these

24. Akbar was a .... ruler.
A. human B. humane
C. Any one of these D. None of these

25. Gandhiji was a .... leader.
A. notorious B. famous
C. Any one of these D. None of these

26. The boys broke the window .... of the class room.
A. pain B. pane
C. Any one of these D. None of these

27. My new trousers are very ....
A. lose B. loose
C. Any one of these D. None of these

28. She has learnt her ....
A. lesson B. lessen
C. Any one of these D. None of these

29. Brutus is an .... man.
A. honorary B. honourable
C. Any one of these D. None of these

30. I have to replace the .... of my shoe.
A. heal B. heel
C. Any one of these D. None of these

31. Dara Singh .... from Punjab.
A. hales B. hails
C. Any one of these D. None of these

32. Constant worry .... his health.
A. affected B. effected
C. Any one of these D. None of these

33. John refused to .... his decision.
A. altar B. alter
C. Any one of these D. None of these

34. Vivek is a .... young man.
A. handsome B. beautiful
C. Any one of these D. None of these

35. He competed in the race .... footed.
A. bear B. bare
C. Any one of these D. None of these

36. She has given .... to a son.
A. birth B. berth
C. Any one of these D. None of these

37. Stalin was .... of poor parents.
A. borne B. born
C. Any one of these D. None of these

38. Please check your ....
A. brakes B. breaks
C. Any one of these D. None of these

39. The princess ordered for a new .... dress.
A. bridle B. bridal
C. Any one of these D. None of these

40. The .... of Plassey was fought in 1757.
A. War B. Battle
C. Any one of these D. None of these

ANSWERS

1	2	3	4	5	6	7	8	9	10
A	B	A	B	A	B	A	B	B	B
11	**12**	**13**	**14**	**15**	**16**	**17**	**18**	**19**	**20**
B	B	B	B	A	B	A	A	B	A
21	**22**	**23**	**24**	**25**	**26**	**27**	**28**	**29**	**30**
A	A	A	B	B	B	B	A	B	B
31	**32**	**33**	**34**	**35**	**36**	**37**	**38**	**39**	**40**
B	A	B	A	B	A	B	A	B	B

22. Spelling Errors

There are thousands of words in English language. It is difficult to remember the spellings and meanings of all at once. Try to learn as many as you can. Use a dictionary regularly.

MULTIPLE CHOICE QUESTIONS

Directions: *Find the correctly spelt words.*

1. A. Damage B. Dammage
C. Damaige D. Dammege

2. A. Efficiant B. Effecient
C. Efficient D. Eficient

3. A. Schedule B. Schdule
C. Schedale D. Schedeule

4. A. Occurad B. Occurred
C. Ocurred D. Occured

5. A. Grieff B. Grief
C. Grieef D. Grrief

6. A. Guarantee B. Garuntee
C. Guaruntee D. Gaurantee

7. A. Meddicine B. Medicine
C. Medicene D. Medicinne

8. A. Benefeted B. Benefitted
C. Benifited D. Benefited

9. A. Acommodation B. Acomodation
C. Accomodation D. Accommodation

10. A. Querrelsome B. Quarrelsame
C. Quarrelsome D. Querralsome

11. A. Sympathetic B. Smypathetic
C. Sympothetic D. Sympethetic

12. A. Prograssive B. Progressive
C. Progresive D. Prograsive

13. A. Uncivilized B. Uncevilized
C. Uncivillized D. Uncevelized

14. A. Extravagant B. Extreragent
C. Extreregant D. Extravegent

15. A. Missunderstood B. Miesunderstood
C. Misunderstood D. Misunderstod

16. A. Belligerent B. Beligirent
C. Belligarant D. Belligerrent

17. A. Astonished B. Astronished
C. Astoneshed D. Asstonished

18. A. Sincerely B. Sencerely
C. Sincerelly D. Sincerrely

19. A. Rigourous B. Rigerous
C. Rigorous D. Regerous

20. A. Satellite B. Sattellite
C. Satelite D. Sattelite

21. A. Pesanger B. Passenger
C. Pessenger D. Pasanger

22. A. Humurous B. Humorous
C. Humoreus D. Humorrous

23. A. Exeggerate B. Exaggerate
C. Exadgerate D. Exagerate

24. A. Fariegn B. Forein
C. Foriegn D. Foreign

25. A. Excesive B. Excessive
C. Exccessive D. Exccesive

26. A. Forcaust B. Forcast
C. Forecast D. Forecaste

27. A. Paralleled B. Paralelled
C. Parralleled D. Parallelled

28. A. Ocasion B. Occassion
C. Occasion D. Ocassion

29. A. Boquet B. Bouquet
C. Bouquete D. Bouquette

30. A. Chettering B. Chaterring
C. Chattering D. Chatering

31. A. Discourage B. Disscourage
C. Discourege D. Discaurage

32. A. Curageous B. Courageous
C. Courrageous D. Couregeous

33. A. Abandon B. Abanddon
C. Abendon D. Abbandon

34. A. Embarassment B. Emberrassement
C. Embarrassment D. Embbaresment

35. A. Eccintric B. Eccentrie
C. Eccentric D. Eccintrie

36. A. Occasional B. Occassional
C. Occesional D. Occessional

37. A. Querrel B. Querral
C. Quarrel D. Quarel

38. A. Contrebution B. Contribution
C. Contributtion D. Conterbution

39. A. Desgrace B. Disgrece
C. Disgrice D. Disgrace

40. A. Harassment B. Herassment
C. Harasment D. Harassmient

41. A. Imaginative B. Imeginative
C. Imagenative D. Imaginetive

42. A. Suficient B. Suficiant
C. Sufficient D. Sufficiant

43. A. Adequate B. Edequate
C. Adaquete D. Edaquete

44. A. Exparienced B. Experianced
C. Experienced D. Experrienced

45. A. Flatering B. Fletering
C. Flattering D. Fletaring

46. A. Cuttiveted B. Culltrivated
C. Cultivated D. Caltivated

47. A. Praiceworthy B. Peiseworthy
C. Praiseworthy D. Praisaworthy

48. A. Profesional B. Professionel
C. Professional D. Profissional

49. A. Ameteur B. Amateur
C. Amataur D. Amateor

50. A. Unfevourable B. Unfevaurable
C. Unfavourable D. Unfivourable

ANSWERS

1	2	3	4	5	6	7	8	9	10
A	C	A	B	B	A	B	D	D	C
11	12	13	14	15	16	17	18	19	20
A	B	A	A	C	A	A	A	C	A
21	22	23	24	25	26	27	28	29	30
B	B	B	D	B	C	A	C	B	C
31	32	33	34	35	36	37	38	39	40
A	B	A	C	C	A	C	B	D	A
41	42	43	44	45	46	47	48	49	50
A	C	A	C	C	C	C	C	B	C

23. PUNCTUATION

Punctuation marks help us to make grammatically correct sentences.

The following pairs of sentences will bring home to you the importance of punctuation marks:

(*a*) Jack, my neighbour, is going abroad.

(*b*) Jack, my neighbour is going abroad.

The sentence (*a*) means 'Jack' is my neighbour and he is going abroad. The sentence (*b*) means that I'm telling Jack that my neighbour is going abroad.

Learn and practise the correct usage of punctuation marks.

The following are some most commonly used punctuation marks:

(*i*)	Full Stop	(.)
(*ii*)	Note of Interrogation	(?)
(*iii*)	Note of Exclamation	(!)
(*iv*)	Comma	(,)
(*v*)	Inverted commas	(" ")
(*vi*)	Apostrophe	(')
(*vii*)	Capital Letters	(A)
(*viii*)	Colon	(:)
(*ix*)	Semicolon	(;)
(*x*)	Dash	(–)
(*xi*)	Oblique	(/)
(*xii*)	Parentheses	( )
(*xiii*)	Hyphen	(-)

MULTIPLE CHOICE QUESTIONS

Directions: *In the questions given below, which one alternative out of four has been applied with correct punctuation marks?*

1. When mankind passed through the grunt-and-groan stage and language had been invented everyone was happy

A. When mankind passed through the grunt-and-groan stage, and language had been invented, everyone was happy.

B. When, mankind passed through the grunt-and-groan stage, and language had been invented everyone was happy.

C. When mankind passed, through the grunt-and-groan stage and language had been invented everyone was happy.

D. When mankind, passed through the grunt-and-groan stage and language had been invented everyone was happy.

2. Communication has been established they said and now we can understand each other

A. Communication has been established, they said and now, we can understand each other.

B. ''Communication has been established,'' they said, ''and now we can understand each other.''

C. Communication has been established, they said, "and now we can understand, each other."

D. "Communication has been established" they said and now we can understand each other.

3. Then writing was developed so that words could be given some durability

A. Then, writing was developed so that words could be given some durability.

B. Then writing was developed, so that words could be given some durability.

C. Then writing was developed so that words could be given some durability.
D. Then writing was developed, so that words could be given, some durability.

4. How wonderful everyone exclaimed now we can read and write
A. How wonderful! everyone exclaimed, now we can read and write.
B. How wonderful everyone exclaimed! now we can read and write.
C. "How wonderful everyone exclaimed!" now we can read and write.
D. ''How wonderful!'' everyone exclaimed, ''Now we can read and write.''

5. But then they began to have difficulty understanding what was written down because everything seemed to run together
A. But then they began to have difficulty understanding what was written down, because everything seemed to run together.
B. But, then they began to have difficulty understanding, what was written down? because everything seemed to run together.
C. But then, they began to have difficulty understanding–what was written down? because everything seemed to run together.
D. But then they began to have difficulty, understanding what was written down because, everything seemed to run together.

6. How confusing they complained
A. "How confusing, they complained!"
B. "How confusing!" they complained.
C. "How confusing" they complained.
D. "How confusing?" they complained.

7. So they invented sentences phrases clauses and punctuation
A. So, they invented sentences phrases clauses and punctuation.
B. So they, invented sentences phrases clauses and punctuation.
C. So they invented sentences, phrases, clauses and punctuation.
D. So they invented, sentences, phrases, clauses and punctuation.

8. Now they stated gleefully we can set our thoughts down read them and understand just what is meant
A. Now, they stated gleefully, "we can set our thoughts down, read them and understand just what is meant.
B. Now, they stated, "gleefully we can set our thoughts down read them and understand just what is meant."
C. Now they stated gleefully, "we can set our thoughts down read them and understand," just what is meant.
D. ''Now,'' they stated gleefully, ''we can set our thoughts down, read them and understand just what is meant.''

9. Will you lend me ten rupees said sarla yes i will promila replied
A. "Will you lend me ten rupees?" said Sarla. "Yes, i will," promila replied.
B. "Will you lend me ten rupees," said Sarla. 'Yes, I will' Promila replied.
C. 'Will you lend me ten rupees?' said Sarla 'Yes, I will,' Promila replied.
D. "Will you lend me ten rupees?" said Sarla. "Yes, I will," Promila replied.

10. You are a thief policeman said the thief you asked for a bribe
A. "You are a thief!" policeman said, the thief, "You asked for a bribe."
B. "You are a thief policeman!" said the thief, You asked for a bribe.
C. "You are a thief policeman!" said, the thief, 'you asked for a bribe.'
D. "You are a thief, policeman!" said the thief, "You asked for a bribe."

ANSWERS

1	2	3	4	5	6	7	8	9	10
A	B	C	D	A	B	C	D	D	D

Professional Knowledge Study Material

LATIN ABBREVIATIONS

Abbreviation	Derivation (Latin)	Meaning
a.c.	Ante cibum	Before meal
a.e.d. (T.D.S.)	Ter die sumendus	Three times a day
a.i.d	quarter in die	Four times a day
a.m.	Ante meridiem	Before noon
alt. die	Alternus diebus	Alternate days
b.d. (b.i.d.)	bis die	Two times a day
c.m.	cras mane	Tomorrow morning
h.	Hora	Hour per hour
h.n.	Hac nocte	Today night
h.s.	Hora somni	Bed time
o.d.	Omni die	Once a day
o.m.	Omni mane	Every morning
o.n.	Omni nocte	Every night
p.c.	Post cibum	After meal
p.m.	Post meridiem	After noon
p.r.n.	Pro-re-nata	As per required
q.	quaque	Each
rep	repetatur	Repeat again
s.o.s.	Si opus sit	As per required in emergency
stat	statim	At once

ABBREVIATIONS

ABG	Artial Blood Gas
AFB	Acid Fast Bacilli
AFP	Alfa Fetoprotein
AHF	Antihemophilic Factor
AHG	Antihemophilic Globulin
AIDS	Acquired Immune Deficiency Syndrome
ASD	Atrial Septal Defect
ASD	Atrial Septal Defect
ASOT	Antistreptolysin O titer
AST	Aspartate Aminotransferase
ATTK	Anti Tubercular Treatment Kits
BBB	Bundle Branch Block
BMI	Body Mass Index
BMR	Basal Metabolic Rate
BMT	Bone Marrow Transplantation
CABG	Coronary Artery bypass Graft
CAG	Coronary Angiography
CAT/CT	Computerised Axial Tomography/Computerised Tomography
CHD	Congenital Heart Disease
CHF	Congestive Heart Failure
CPK	Creatine Phsophokinase
CSOM	Chronic Suppurative Otitis Media
CSP	Cerebro Spinal Fluid

CSSD	Centrise Sterile Supply Department
CSSM	Child Servival and Safe Motherhood
DES	Deithyle Stilbestrol
DPT	Diphtheria Pertussis Tetanus
DVT	Deep Veins Thrombosis
ECG	Electrocardiogram
ECT	Electroconvulsive Therapy
EEG	Electroencephalogram
ELISA	Enzyme Linked Immuno Sorbent Assay
EPS	Extrapyramidal Syndroms
ERCP	Endoscopic Retrograde Cholangio Pancreatography
ESRD	End stage Renal disease
ESWL	Extracorporeal Shock Wave Lithotripsy
ESWL	Extracorporeal Shock Wave Lithotripsy
ETT	Endotracheal Tube
FBS	Fasting Blood Sugar
GTT	Glucose Tolerance Test
HCG	Human Chorionic Gonadotrapic
IABP	Intra Aortic Ballon Pump
ICDS	Integrated Child Development Service
ICP	Intracranial Pressure
ICU	Intensive Care Unit
IHD	Ischemic Heart Disease
IOP	Intraocular Pressure
IPPB	Intermitted Positive Pressure Breathing
IQ	Intelligence Quotients
IVP	Intra Venous Pyelogram
IVU	Intravenous Urogram
KUB	Kidney Uterus Bladder
MAOI	Monoamine Oxidase Inhibitor
MMR	Measles Mumps Rubella
MOPP	Mechlorethamine Oncovin Procarbazine Prednisone
MRI	Magnetic Resonance Imaging
NACO	National Aids Control Organisation
NFCP	National Filaria Control Programme
NSAIDS	Nonsteroidal Anti Inflammatory Drug
OCD	Obessive Compulsive Disorder
ORS	Oral Rehydration Solution
PDA	Patent Ductus Arteriosus
PET	Positron Emission Tomography
PID	Pelvic Inflammatory Disease
PID	Prolapsed Intravertibrae Disk
PND	Paroxysmal Noetural Dyspnea
PR	Per Rectum
PSA	Prostate Specific Antigen
PTCA	Percutaneous Transluminal Coronay Angioplasty
PVT	Proxysmal Ventricular Trachycardia
RBS	Random Blood Sugar
RCH	Reproduction and Child Health
RDS	Respiratory Distress Syndrome
REM	Rapid Eye Movement
ROM	Range of Motion
RPLND	Retroperitoneal Lymph Node Dissection
SGOT	Serum Glutamic Oxalocetic Transaminase
SGPT	Serum Glutamic Pyruvic Transaminase
SMR	Submuscous Resection
SVPB	Supraventricular Premature Beat
SVT	Supraventricular Trachycardia
TAO	Thrombo Angitis Obliterans
TCA	Tricyclic Antidepressants
TPN	Total Parental Nutrition
TURP	Trans Urethral Resection of Prostate
UNICEF	United Nations International Children's Emergency Fund (United Nations Children's Funds)
VVF	Vesicovaginal Fustula

1

Health and Diseases

INTRODUCTION

Health is a common theme in most cultures. In fact, all communities have their concept of health, as part of their culture. Probably the oldest definitions still used, is that health is the "absence of disease". In some cultures, health and harmony are considered equivalent, harmony being defined as "being at peace with the self, the community, god and cosmos". The ancient Indians and Greeks shared this concept and attributed disease to disturbances in bodily equilibrium of what they called "humors".

"Health" is one of these terms which most people find it difficult to define although they are confident of its meaning. Therefore, many definitions of health have been offered from time to time, including the following:

"A state of relative equilibrium of body form and function which result from its successful dynamic adjusment to forces tending to disturb it. It is not passive interplay between body substance and forces impinging upon it but an active response of body forces working toward readjustment" (*Perkins*) .

VARIABLES OF HEALTH

Health has multifactorial influence. The factors which influence health lie both within the individual and externally in the society in which he or she lives. These factors interact among themselves may be health–promoting or deleterious. Thus conceptionally, the health of individuals and whole communities may be considered to be the result of many interactions.

Some of the most important determinats or variables are given below:

1. Heredity
2. Environment
3. Life-Style
4. Socio-economic conditions
5. Health and family Welfare Services
6. Other factors

1. Heredity

The physical and mental status of every human being are to some extent determined by the nature of his genes at the moment of conception. The genetic make-up is unique in that it cannot be altered after conceptions. A number of diseases are now know to be of genetic origin due to, chromosomal anomalies, mutation etc. The state of health, therefore depends partially on the genetic constitution of man.

2. Environment

It was Hipppocrates who first related disease to environment, *e.g.*, climate, water, air, *etc.* Centuries later, Pettenkofer in Germany revived the concept of disease environment association.

Environment is classified as "internal" and "external". The internal environment of man pertains to "each and every component part, every tissue, organ and organ-system and their harmonious functioning within the system." Internal environment is the domain of internal medicine. The external or macro-environment consists of those things to which man is exposed. It is defined as "all that which is external to the individual human."

3. Life-Style

The term "lifestyle" is rather a diffuse concept often used to denote "the way people live", reflecting a whole range of social values, altitude and activities. It is composed of cultural and behavioural patterns and lifelong personal habits (*e.g.*, smoking, alcoholism) that have developed through processes of socialization. Lifestyle are learnt through social interaction with parents, peer groups, friends and siblings and through school and mass media.

4. Socio-Economic Conditions

Socio-economic conditions have long been known to influence human health. For the majority of the world's people, health status is determined primarily by their level of Socio-economic development, *e.g.,* per capita G.N.P., education nutrition, employment, housing, the political system of the country, *etc.*

5. Health Services

The term health and family welfare services cover a wide spectrum of personal and community services for treatment of disease, prevention of illness and promotion of health. The purpose of health services is to improve the health status of population. For example, immunization of children can influence the incidence/prevalence of particular disease. Provision of safe water can prevent mortality and morbidity from water-borne diseases. In case of pregnant women and children would contribute to the reduction of maternal and child morbidity and mortality. To be effective, the health services must reach the social periphery equitably distributed, accessible at a cost the country and community can afford and Socially acceptable. All these are ingredients of what is now termed "primary health care", which is seen as the way to better health.

Health services can also be seen as essential for social and economic development. It is well to remind ourselves that "health care does not produce good health". Whereas, there is a strong co-relation between GNP and expectation of life at birth, there is no significant cor-relation between medical density and expectation of life at birth. The most we can expect from an effective health service is good care. The epidemiological perspective emphasizes that health services, no matter how technically elegant or cost-effective, are ultimately pertinent only if they improve health.

6. Other Factors

Other contributions to the health of a population is derive from systems outside the formal health care system, or health related system (*e.g.*, food and agriculture, education, industry, social welfare, rural development) as well as adoption of policies in the economic and social fields that would assist in raising the standards of living. This would include employment opportunities, increased wages, prepaid medical programmes and family support systems.

INDICATORS OF HEALTH

Indicators are required not only to measure the health status of a community, but also to compare the health status of one country with that of another; for assessment of health care needs, for allocation of health resources; and for monitoring and evaluation of health services, activities and programmes. Indicators help to measure the extent to which the objectives and targets of a programme are being attained.

Characteristics of Indicators

Indicators have been given scientific respectability. Examples ideal indicators:

(a) **Should be valid,** *i.e.,* they should actually measure what they are supposed to measure;

(b) **Should be reliable and objective,** *i.e.*, the answers should be the same if measured by different people in similar circumstances;
(c) **Should be sensitive;** *i.e.*, they should be sensitive to changes in the situation concerned, and;
(d) **Should be specific,** *i.e.*, they should, reflect changes only in the situation concerned.

Our understanding of health therefore cannot be in terms of a single indicators; it must be conceived in terms of a profile employing many indicators, which may be classified as:

1. Mortality indicators
2. Morbidity indicators
3. Disability rates
4. Nutritional status indicators
5. Health care delivery indicators
6. Utilization rates
7. Indicators of social and mental health
8. Environmental indicators
9. Socio-economic indicators
10. Health policy indicators
11. Indicators of quality of life

HEALTH CONDITION IN INDIA

1. Demographic Profile

A major cancern today is population explosion. The demographic profile is characterised by:

(*a*) large population base
(*b*) high fertility both in terms of birth rate and family size
(*c*) low or declining mortality.
(*d*) "young" population (about 40 per cent of the population) is below the age of 15 years.
(*e*) the proportion of illiterate population is close to 48 per cent: this explains why the decline in birth-rate has been so slow.
(*f*) dependency ratio of 0.9; that is every economically productive member has to support almost one dependent

2. Mortality Profile

During the last few decades, there has been a notable improvement in the health status of the population. The death rate has steadily declined from 10 (1994) to 5.2 (2004).

3. Morbidity Profile

Morbidity is dominated by communicable diseases. According to one estimate, about 17.2 per cent of all deaths and about 20.8 per cent of all illnesses are due to communicable diseases in India. The major problems continue to be tuberculosis, filariasis, leprosy, malaria, diarrhoeal and malnutrition. Among viral diseases smallpox was eradicated in 1980. In bacterial diseases meningococcal meningitis has shows a substantial increase. Cholera has significantly declined, but the other water-borne diseases (*e.g.*, acute diarrhoea, dysentery and enteric fever) have not abated. Half the world's tuberculosis patients are in India accounting for 14 million cases of which approximately 3.5 million are infectious cases.

HEALTH CARE

Health care is an expression of concern for fellow human beings. It is defined as a "multitude of services rendered to individuals, families or communities by the agents of the health services or professions, for the purpose of promoting, maintaining, monitoring or restoring health". Such services might be staffed, organized, administered and financed in every imaginable way, but they all have one thing in common: People are being "served", that is: diagnosed, helped, cured, educated and habilitated by health personnel.

Health Care has many characteriestics. They include:

(*i*) *appropriateness (relevance)*, *i.e.*, whether the services is needed at all in relation to essential human needs, priorities and policies;
(*ii*) *comprehensiveness*, *i.e.*, whether there is an optimum mix of preventive, curative and promotional services;
(*iii*) *adequacy*, *i.e.*, if the services is proportionate to requirement;
(*iv*) *availability*, *i.e.*, ratio between population of an administrative unit and the health

facility (*e.g.* population per centre; doctor-population ratio); and

(v) *affordability, i.e.*, the cost of health care should be within the means of the individual and the state.

CONCEPT OF DISEASE

There have been many attempts to define disease. Webster defines disease as "a condition in which body health is impaired; a departure from a state of health, an alteration of the human body interrupting the performance of vital fuctions". The Oxford English Dictionary defines discase as "a condition of the body or some part or organ of the body in which its functions are disrupted or deranged". The term " disease" literally means "without ease" (uneasiness) – disease, the opposite of ease when something is wrong with body functioning. "Illness" refers not only to the presence of a specific disease, but also to the individual's perceptions and behaviour in response to the disease, as well as the impact of the disease on the psychosocial environment. "Sickness" refers to a state of social dysfunction. Susser has suggested the following usage:-

Disease is a physiological/psychological dysfuntion;

Illness is a subjective state of the person who feels aware of not being well.

Sickness is a state of social dysfunction, *i.e.*, a role that the individual assumes when ill ("sickness role").

Natural History Of Disease

The term natural history of disease is a key concept in epidemiology. It signifies the way in which a disease evolves over time from the earliest stage of its prepathogenesis phase to its termination as recovery, disability or death, in the absence of treatment or prevention. Let us consider the events that take place in the natural history of disease using infections disease as a principal model:

1. **Prepathogenesis Phase :** This refers to the period preliminary to the onset of disease in man. The disease agent has not yet entered man, but the factors which favour its interaction with the human host are already existing in the environment. This situation is frequently referred to as "man in the midst of disease" or "man exposed to the risk of disease".
2. **Pathogenesis Phase :** The pathogonesis phase begins with the entry of the disease "agent" in the susceptible human host. The further events in the pathogenesis phase are clear cut in infectious disease, *i.e.*, the disease agent multiplies and induces tissue to a physiologic changes. The final outcome of the disease may be recovery, disability or death. The pathogenesis phase may be modified by intervention measures such as immunization and chemotherapy. In chronic diseases (*e.g.*, coronary heart disease, hypertension, cancer), the early pathogenesis phase is less dramatic, thus phase in chronic disease is refrerred to as presymptomatic phase. During the presymptomatic stage, there is no manifest disease. The pathological changes are essentially below the level of the "Clinical horizon."

Agent Factors

The "*agent*" in concept of disease is defined as a substance, living or non-living or a force, tangible or intangible, the excessive presence or relative lack of which may initiate or perpetuate a disease process.

Disease agents may be classified broadly into the following groups:

1. **Biological Agents :** These are living agents of disease, *viz*, viruses, rickettsiae, fungi, bacteria, protozoa and metazoa. These agents exhibit certain "host-related" biological properties such as:
   - ***(i) Infectivity:*** This is the ability of an infectious agent to invade and multiply (produce infection) in a host;
   - ***(ii) Pathogenecity:*** This is the ability to induce clinically apparent illness.

(iii) ***Virulence:*** This is defined as the proportion of clinical cases resulting in severe clinical manifestations (including sequelae).

2. **Nutrient Agents :** These can be proteins, fats, carbohydrate, vitamins, minerals and water.
3. **Physical Agents :** Exposure to excessive heat, cold, humidity, pressure, radiation, electricity, sound, *etc.*, may result in illness.
4. **Chemical Agents :**
   (i) ***Endogenous:*** Some of the chemicals may be produced in the body as a result of derangement of function, *e.g.*, urea (uraemia), serum bilirubin (jaundice), ketones (ketosis), uric acid (gout), Calcium Carbonate (kidney stones) *etc.*
   (ii) ***Exogenous:*** Agents arising outside of human host, *e.g.*, allergens, metals, fumes, dust, gases, insecticides, *etc.*
5. **Mechanical Agents :** Exposure to chronic friction and other mechanical forces may result in crushing, tearing, sprains, dislocations and even death.
6. **Social Agents :** It is also necessary to consider social agents of disease. These are poverty, smoking, abuse of drugs and alcohol, unhealthy lifestyles, social isolation maternal deprivation, *etc.*

Intrinsic Factors

The host factors may be classified as: *(i)* Demographic Characteristics such as age, sex, ethnicity, *(ii)* Biological characteristics such as genetic factors; biochemical levels of the blood (*e.g.*, cholesterol); blood groups and enzymes; cellular constituents of the blood; immunological factors; and physiological function of different organ systems of the body (*e.g.*, blood pressure, forced expiratory ventilation) *etc.* *(iii)* Social and economic characteristics such as socio-economic status, education, occupation, stress, marital status, housing, *etc.*

Extrinsic Factors

The study of disease is really the study of man and his environment. Hundreds of millions of people are affected by preventable diseases originating in the environment in which they live. The external or macro-environment is defined as "all that which external to the individual human host, living and non-living, and with which he is in constant interaction". This includes all of man's external surroundings such as air, water, food, housing *etc.*

CONCEPTS OF CONTROL

Disease Control

The term "disease control" describes ongoing operations aimed at reducing:

(i) the incidence of disease
(ii) the duration of disease, and consequently the risk of transmission
(iii) the effects of infection, including both the physical and psychosocial complications; and
(iv) the financial burden to the community.

DISEASE ERADICATION

Eradication literally means to "tear out by roots". Eradication of disease implies termination of all transmission of infection by extermination of the infectious agents. As the name implies, eradication is an absolute process, and not a relative goal. It is "all or none phenomenon". The word eradication and disease from the whole world.

MONITORING AND SURVEILLANCE

Monitoring

Monitoring is "the performance and analysis of routine measurements, aimed at detecting changes in the environment or health status of populations". Thus, we have monitoring of air pollution, water quality, growth and nutritional status, *etc.* It also refers to ongoing measurement of performance of a health service or a health professionals the extent to which patients comply with or adhere to advice of health professionals.

Surveillance

Surveillance is defined in many ways. According to one interpretation surveillance means to watch over with great attention, authority and often with suspicion. According to another, surveillance is defined as "the continuous scrutiny of the factors that determine the occurrence and distribution of disease and other conditions of ill-health".

MODES OF INTERVENTION

"Intervention" can be defined as any attempt to intervene or interrupt the usual sequence in the development of disease in man. This may be by the provision of treatment, education, help or social support. Five modes of intervention have been described which form a continuum corresponding to the natural history of any disease, which are as follows:—

1. Health Promotion

Health promotion is "the process of enabling people to increase control over and to improve health". The well-known interventions in this area are:

(*i*) health education
(*ii*) environmental modifications
(*iii*) nutritional interventions
(*iv*) lifestyle and behavioural changes.

2. Specific Protection

The following are some of the currently available intervention aimed at specific protection. (a) immunization (b) use of specific nutrients (c) chemoprophylaxis (d) protection against occupational hazards (e) protection against accidents (f) protection from carcinogens (g) avoidance of allergens.

3. Early Diagnosis and Treatment

A WHO Expert Committee defined early detection of health impairment as "the detection of disturbances of homoeostatic and compensatory mechanise while biochemical, morphological, and functional changes are still reversible." Thus, in order to prevent disease, the criteria of diagnosis should , if possible, be based on early biochemical, morphological and functional changes that precede the occurrence of manifest signs and symptoms. This is of particular importance in chronic disease.

4. Disability Limitation

When a patient reports late in the pathogenesis phase, the mode of intervention is disability limitation. The objective of this intervention is to prevent or halt the transition of the disease process from impairment to handicap.

5. Rehabilitation

Rehabilitation has been defined as "the combined and coordinated use of medical, social, education and vocational measures for training and retraining the individual to the highest possible level of functional ability". It includes all measures aimed at reducing the impact of disabling and handicapping conditions and enabling the disabled and handicapped to achieve social integration.

POPULATION MEDICINE

Population medicine is referred to as hygiene, public health, preventive medicine social medicine or community medicine. All these share common ground in their concern for promotion of health and prevention of disease.

Hygiene

The world "hygiene" is derived from Hygeia, the goddess of health in Greek mythology. She is represented as a beautiful woman holding in her hand a bowl from which a serpent is drinking. In Greek, mythology, the serpent testified the art of healing whose symbol is retaines even today. Hygiene is defined as "the science of health and embraces all factors which contribute to healthful living."

Public Health

The term "Public Health" came into general use around 1840. It arose from the need to protect "the public" from the spread of communicable diseases. Later it appeared in

1848 in the name of the law, the Public Health Act in England to crystallise the efforts organized by society to protect, promote and restore the people's health. Public health, in its present form, is a combination of scientific disciplines (*e.g.*, epidemiology, biostatistics, laboratory science, social sciences, demography) and skills and strategies (*e.g.*, epidemiological investigations, planning and management, interventions, surveillance, evaluation) that are directed to the maintenance & improvement of the health of the people.

OBJECTIVE QUESTIONS

1. One of the following is *not true* international classification of disease (ICD):
(*a*) It is revised once in 10 years
(*b*) It was devised by UNICEF
(*c*) The 10th revision consists of 21 major chapters
(*d*) It provides the basis for use in other health fields.
(*e*) It is accepted for National and International use.

2. The concept of social Medicine was first introduced by:
(*a*) Neumann and virchow
(*b*) Robert Gritjahn
(*c*) John Ryle
(*d*) Rene Sand
(*e*) Crew

3. Prophylactic administration of vitamin A in a child is:
(*a*) Health promotion
(*b*) Treatment
(*c*) Specific protection
(*d*) Rehabilitation

4. The restoration of body function is known as:
(*a*) Vocational rehabilitation
(*b*) Primary prevention
(*c*) Social rehabilitation
(*d*) None of these

5. *False* about primary prevention is:
(*a*) Early diagnosis and treatment
(*b*) Environmental sanitation
(*c*) Vaccination
(*d*) Health promotion

6. About community diagnosis all are *true* except:
(*a*) Virtual statistics taken
(*b*) Age and sex distribution statistics needed
(*c*) Age specific, death rate needed
(*d*) Incidence of important diseases taken

7. Administration of oral polio vaccine to the children is a measure of:
(*a*) Health promotion
(*b*) Specific protection
(*c*) Treatment
(*d*) Rehabilitation

8. Which of the following constitutes specific protection?
(*a*) Immunization
(*b*) Aviodance of allergens
(*c*) Healthy environment
(*d*) Chemoprophylaxis

9. Which of the following is tertiary level of prevention?
(*a*) Health promotion
(*b*) Specific protection
(*c*) Early diagnosis and treatment
(*d*) Disability limitation

10. Screening for carcinoma cervix is:
(*a*) Health promotion
(*b*) Specific protection
(*c*) Early diagnosis and treatment
(*d*) Disability limitation

11. Iron and folic acid supple-mentation is type of:
(*a*) Specific protection
(*b*) Health promotion
(*c*) Health education
(*d*) Primordial protection

12. The current concept of health promotion and the related activities lead to:

(a) Better treatment of a problem
(b) Critical awareness and lifestyle changes
(c) Adoption of prophylactic services
(d) Better health services usage

13. The best method of promoting healthy lifestyle in children:
(a) Primordial prevention
(b) Specific protection
(c) Secondary prevention
(d) High risk strategy

14. All are health promotion activities *except*:
(a) Better treatment of a problem
(b) Critical awareness and lifestyle changes
(c) Adoption of prophylactic services
(d) Better health services and usage

15. Primary aim of sentinel surveil-lance is:
(a) To know total number of disease patient
(b) To know trend of disease
(c) To decide mode of treatment
(d) Notification

16. Primordial prevention is applied when:
(a) Risk factors appear before disease
(b) After risk factors appear
(c) Prevalence of disease is low
(d) No disease and no risk factors

17. *False* about primary prevention is:
(a) Early diagnosis and treatment
(b) Environmental sanitation
(c) Vaccination
(d) Health promotion

18. Which type of prevention used in change of smoking habit?
(a) Primordial prevention
(b) Population (mass) strategy
(c) High risk strategy
(d) Secondary prevention

19. Tertiary level of prevention is:
(a) Health promotion
(b) Chemoprophylaxis
(c) Rehabilitation
(d) Early diagnosis and treatment

20. Sentinel surveillance is done for all *except*:
(a) HIV
(b) Diarrohea
(c) Acute flaccid paralysis
(d) Per capita income

21. A concept directed against prevention of risk factors of CAD is:
(a) Primordial prevention
(b) Secondary prevention
(c) Health education
(d) Primary prevention

22. Total morbidity is determined by:
(a) Active surveillance
(b) Passive surveillance
(c) Sentinel surveillance
(d) Annual survey

23. Pap smear is an example of:
(a) Primary level of prevention
(b) Secondary level of prevention
(c) Tertiary level of prevention
(d) None of above

24. Keeping the frequency of illness within acceptable limits is best described as disease:
(a) Control
(b) Prevention
(c) Eradication
(d) Surveillance
(e) Treatment

25. Match List I (*activities*) with List II (*levels of prevention*) and select the correct answer using the codes given below the lists:

List-I
A. Post exposure prophylaxis with rabies vaccine
B. Screening for hypertension
C. Surgical intervention for claw hand in leprosy
D. Preventing emergencey of high prevalence of obesity in the population

List-II
1. Secondary level prevention
2. Tertiary level prevention
3. Primordial prevention
4 Primary level prevention

Codes:

	(A)	(B)	(C)	(D)
(a)	4	3	2	1
(b)	4	1	2	3
(c)	2	1	3	4
(d)	1	2	4	3

26. Main purpose of sentinel surveillance is:
(*a*) To find out total number of cases
(*b*) For intervention of thera-peutics
(*c*) To depict natural history of disease
(*d*) Prevention of sentinel piles

27. Which *one* of the following is not a socio-economic indicator?
(*a*) Literacy rate
(*b*) Family size
(*c*) Housing
(*d*) Life expectancy at birth

28. The measure used to express the global burden of disease *i.e.*, how a healthy life is affected by disease, is:
(*a*) Disability-adjusted life year
(*b*) Case fatality rate
(*c*) Life expectancy
(*d*) Age-specific incidence rate

29. Most important epidemiological tool used for assessing disability in children is:
(*a*) Activities of daily living (ADL) scale
(*b*) Wing's handicaps, behaviour and skills (HBS) schedule
(*c*) Binet and Simon IQ tests
(*d*) Physical quality of life index (PQLI)

30. The burden of disease is best represented by:
(*a*) Infant mortality rate
(*b*) DALY's
(*c*) PQLI
(*d*) Case fatality

31. Lungs are enclosed in:
(*a*) Pericardium (*b*) Pleura
(*c*) Peritoneum (*d*) Perichondrium

32. Objectives of the health services include each of the following except:
(*a*) Delivery of curative care only
(*b*) Health promotion
(*c*) Prevention control, or eradication of disease
(*d*) Treatment and rehabilitation

33. PQLI includes all except:
(*a*) Per capita income
(*b*) Life expectancy at age 1 year
(*c*) Literacy
(*d*) Infant mortality

34. Shape of an eye is maintained by
(*a*) Aqueous humour (*b*) Vitreous humour
(*c*) Conjunctiva (*d*) All of these

ANSWERS

1	2	3	4	5	6	7	8	9	10
(*b*)	(*a*)	(*c*)	(*a*)	(*a*)	(*c*)	(*b*)	(*a*)	(*a*)	(*c*)
11	**12**	**13**	**14**	**15**	**16**	**17**	**18**	**19**	**20**
(*a*)	(*b*)	(*a*)	(*b*)	(*d*)	(*a*)	(*a*)	(*a*)	(*c*)	(*b*)
21	**22**	**23**	**24**	**25**	**26**	**27**	**28**	**29**	**30**
(*a*)	(*c*)	(*b*)	(*a*)	(*c*)	(*a*)	(*d*)	(*a*)	(*b*)	(*b*)
31	**32**	**33**	**34**						
(*b*)	(*a*)	(*a*)	(*b*)						

2

Communicable & Non-Communicable Diseases

Human diseases may be divide into

1. **Congenital Diseases:** Present since birth.
2. **Acquired Diseases:** Develop after birth. Acquired diseases can be grouped into:
   (a) Infections disease-caused by viruses, bacteria, protozoa, fungi and worms.
   (b) Deficiency diseases-caused by the deficiency of vitamins, minerals, carbohydrates, proteins & fat in diet.
   (c) Allergies-caused by hypersensitivity of the body like perfumes, pollen, grains etc.
   (d) Degenerative diseases-caused by mal-functioning of vital organs like heart, kidney, lungs, brain etc.

- Acquired infections diseases are communicable diseases *e.g.*, Plague, Typhoid.
- Acquired non infections disease are Non-communicable. *e.g.*, Diabetes, Night blindness, Scurvy.
- Hippocrates (B.C. 460–350) wrote detailed descriptions of disease symptoms and emphasized the need for good diet, fresh air and rest. He showed & explained that human body has self immunity power.
- Louis Pasteur and Robert Koch stated Germs theory of disease.
- Epidemology is the study which deals with the mode of transmission of diseases.
- John Snow is regarded as father of epidemology *i.e.*, the nature of the spread of communicable disease.
- Study which deals with, defence, resistant mechanism against germs called immunology.
- Edward Jenner invented small pox vaccine (1749–1823).
- Jonas Salk (1955) discovered Polio vaccine.
- Louis Pasteur in 1885 produce the first rabies vaccine. Rabbies is contagious disease which easily spread by association with infected persons *e.g.*, mumps, measles, wooping cough through cough sneezing or contact etc.
- Non-contagious diseases are spread by means of insects bites, contaminates, water and food.
- Various factors influence the infection *i.e.*, potency of organism number of organism, resistance of body and immune system.

COMMUNICABLE DISEASES

According to the nature of causative organism communicable diseases may be of following types:

1. **Bacterial Diseases:**
   1. Tuberculosis by *Mycobacterium tuberculosis.*
   2. Typhoid by *Salmonella typhi.*
   3. Leprosy by *Mycobacterium leprae.*
   4. Cholera by *Vibrio cholerae*
   5. Diptheria by *Corynebacterium diptheriae*
   6. Tetanus-by *Clostridium tetani*
   7. Plague (Gram negative) by *Yersinia pestis.*

8. Bacterial Pneumonia by *Streptococcus pneumoniae*
9. Syphilis by *Treponema pallidum*
10. Gonorrhoea by *Neisseria gonorrhoea*
11. Whooping cough - *Bordetella pertussis*

2. **Viral Diseases:** Chickenpox, Measles, Rabies, Influenza, Polio, AIDS.
3. **Protozoans Diseases:** Amoebic dysentery, balantidial dysentry, cryptosporidium diarrhoea, Giardiasis, malaria, sleeping sickness.
4. **Helminths Diseases:** Taeniasis, ascariasis schistomiasis, filariasis, ancylostomiasis.
5. **Fungal Diseases:** Due to fungal infection.

Other Classification

1. **Airborne Infection:** Disease caused by inhalation of infectious agent.
   - **Viral diseases:** chickenpox, small pox, measles, rubella (German measles mumps and influenza).
   - **Bacterial disease:** Diptheria, whooping cough (Pertusis) tuberculosis and cerebro spiral fever).
2. **Intestinal Infections:** Diseases by ingestion of infectious agent through water, food etc.
3. **Arthroprod Borne Infection:** Diseases transmitted by vectors (insects *etc.*).
4. **Surface Infections:** Disease caused by animals, bites, contact etc.

NON-COMMUNICABLE DISEASES

Non-communicable diseases (non-infectious) are (a) Deficiency diseases, (b) Degenerative diseases.

(a) Deficiency Diseases : Deficiency diseases are due to deficiency of vitamins, minerals, carbodydrates, proteins & fats, *e.g.*,

Kwashiokar - protein deficiency
Anaemia - Fe & Folic acid deficiency
Night blindness - Vit. A deficiency
Xeropthalmia - Vit. A deficiency
Beri-Beri - Vit. B_1 deficiency
Pellagra - Vit. B_3 Riboflavin deficiency
Rickets - Vit. D deficiency
Scurvy - Vit. C deficiency
Pernicious Anaemia - Vit.B_{12} deficiency
Haemorrhagic Diathesis - Vit. K

(b) Degenerative Diseases: These are associated with vital organs *e.g.* Heart, Nervous system, Lung, Kidney.

Some Common Communicable Disease

1. **Chickenpox (*Varricella*):** This is a common but mild disease found all over the world. It is highly infectious. It occurs only in human beings. The incubatim period is 2-5 weeks.
2. **Smallpox (*Variola*):** This was once a major public health problem in India. It is caused by small pox virus and used to occur at the same time with chickenpox. Vaccination against smallpox was introduced by Edward Jenner in England in 1796 and it proved to be extremely effective in preventing smallpox. World Health Organisation launched small pox eradication programme in 1967. Its transmitted through oral and nasal discharges. The incubation periods 12 days. Rashes charges to rustules finally form scales.
3. **Measles (*Rubeola*):** It is highly infectious disease occuring in children all over the world. It is severe, causes many complication and deaths particularily in very young and undernourished children. Measles is caused by RNA-virus para Myxovirus Rubeolla virus. It transmitted through the discharge from nose and throat of sick person. It has 10 days of incubation period.

   Treatment: Antibiotics are given if complications like bronchopneumonia develop. Vaccination for measles be given to every child between 9–15 months.

4. **Rubella (German Measles):** This is a disease similar to measles but caused by a different virus (rubella virus). It is spread by droplet infection and has an incubation period of 14-21 days. Period of incubation is 4-7 days. It affects children and young adults. Infected person gets the lifelong immunity.

Low fever, sore throat and cough are early symptoms. The importance of rubella is that an attack in pregnent women is serious. If a woman develops rubella in pregnency, especially during first 3 months it may cause defect in the foetus.

The only method of prevention of rubella is by active immunization with vaccine (freeze dried live). It is given to all children below 5 years age and in some countries it is given only to girls at the age of 10–14 years (before puberty).

5. **Mumps:** This is a mild virus disease found all over the world. Incubation periods 16-21 days. It spreed through the saliva of person. It cause the painful enlargment of parotid gland.

Preventions and Control: Isolation does not help. But may be necessary if an outbreak occurs in hostels of children.

6. **Diphtheria:** This is an important childhood disease and is found all over the world. It is caused by bacterium *Corynebacterium diphtherae*. The incubation period is 2-5 days. Disease appears with high fever, sore throat difficulties in breathing due to choking. Disease spreed through touching, kissing, talking, coughing and use of contaminated articles.

Treatment: Diphtheria Antitoxin is immediately given to destroy Toxin produced by *diphtheria bacilli.*

DPT Vaccine: For immunizing infants, the preparation of choice is DPT. Firstly because, the infant can be immunized simultaneously against three diseases, viz. diphtheria, pertussis and tetanus which is a great achivement. Secondly the pretussis component in DPT vaccine enhances the potency of the diphtheria toxoid.

7. **Pertusis (whooping cough):** This is another disease affecting children. It is found all over the world though in developed countries due to active immunization it has become rare. It is caused by *Bordetella pertusis*. The incubation period of this disease is 10-16 days.

8. **Cerebrospinal Fever** (Meningococal Meningitis): C.S. fever occurs all over the world. In India it is reported in sporadic and sometimes in epidemic form.

Treatment: Early treatment with penicillin, chloraphericol or with sulphadiazine may cure an attack. Carriers are given an antibiotic Rifampicix.

9. **Tuberculosis:** It is an serious disease and inspite of many advances in treatment. It is a major public health problem in India.

Treatment: For effective treatment of tuberculosis following drugs are used:

1. Streptomycin
2. I.N.H. (Isonicotinic acid hydrazide)
3. P.A.S. (Paraamino Salicylic acid)
4. Thiacetazone

DOT is effective now a days.

B.C.G Vaccination was introduced in 1927. B.C.G (*Bacillus Calmette Guerin*) is a bovine tubercle bacillus cultured in the laboratory. In India it was prepared in Madras.

10. **Poliomyelitis:** This is an old disease but at present it become a public health problem. In India the disease has become common after 1948. It is spread through intestinal discharge, contaminated food and water. It cause inflammation of nervous system and stiffess of the neck, muscles fail to work. The incubation period of disease is 7-14 day. It is caused by RNA entrovirus. There is no drugs available for polio.

Immunization: It is the only way to prevent and control poliomyelitis.

Oral polio vaccine (sabin) was prepared in 1957. It is a live vaccine. Mostly the vaccine containing all the three types is used, doses are given (in 4th, 5th and 6th month) one booster dose is given between 18–24 months.

11. **Viral Hepatitis:** Virus infection of liver is called viral hepatitis. There are many viruses which infect liver. Two are main virus A and B are found in India but viral hepatitis A is more common. Hepatis A and E are typically caused by ingestion of contaminated food or water. Hepatitis B, C and D usually occurs as a result of parental contact with infected body fluids. Hepatitis B is also transmitted by sexual contact. The symptoms of the disease is jaundice, dark urine, extreme fatigue, nausea and abdominal pain.

    Viral Hepatitis A: Viral or Hepatitis 'A' is found all over the world. It is present in endemic form. It has incubation period of 20-35 days. It cause inflammation liver and fever.

    Treatment: There is no drug treatment for infectious hepatitis. Bed rest, vitamin B complex and high carbodydrates diet are given. Fats in diet should be reduced.

12. **Cholera:** It was known in India as 'Visuchika'. It is caused by *Vibrio cholera*. It has the incubation period of 2-3 days.

    Treatment: In the treatment of cholera, the first most important thing is to maintain the water balance of the body. This is known as rehydration. The salts which must be given are sodium & potassium chlorides and bicarbonates. Rehydration may be oral or Intravenous Readymade oral rehydration solution (ORS) contains: *Sodium chloride* (3.5 g); *Potassium chloride* (2.5g); *Sodium Biocarbonate* (1.5g) and *Glucose* (20g). In cholera 500 mg tetracyline is given every 6 hours for 3 days.

13. **Diarrhoeal Diseases:** This group of diseases includes a number of acute infections caused by viruses, bacteria etc. of which diarrhoea is the main symptom. Poverty, ignorance, poor sanitation, overcrowding are also responsible for these diseases. They are transmitted through water and food. Control of these infections is similar to control of cholera. Early treatment with oral rehydration, proper nutrition and improvement of sanitation are the main preventive control measures.

14. **Food poisoning:** Diarrhoea and vomiting due to food or drink contaminated by organisms or due to chemical poisons is known food poisoning. Food poisoning may be due to bacterial or non-bacterial organisms. The *Salmonella* food poisoning is quite common. *Staphylococcal* food poisoning is due to intake of contaminated milk.

15. **Difference Between Cholera & Food Poisoning:**

Cholera	Food Poisoning
1. Occurs in endemic or epidemic form, by spread of infection.	1. Only in persons who have taken contaminated food, does not spread
2. Incubation period is few hours to 5 days.	2. Incubation period is 1–24 hours
3. Starts with diarrhoea followed by vomiting	3. Starts with vomiting followed by diarrhoea.
4. No *nausea* or *headache*	4. *Nausea* and *Headache* present
5. Watery stools, may be *rice water*.	5. Yellow coloured stools with offensive smell.
6. Severe dehydration	6. Less dehydration
7. No fever	7. Fever present

16. **Typhoid Fever:** It is found all over the world. Causative organism: *Salmonella typhi*. Incubation period 10-15 days.

    Treatment: Chloramphemicol is given in doses of 500 mlg/ 4 hourly till fever comes down and then the dose is reduced to 4 times a day for 14 days.

17. **Amoebic dysentery (Amoebiasis):** It is extremely common all over the world but more in tropical countries as in Asia and Africa. In India 10–50% persons are affected. It is a chronic disease lasting for many years. It is endemic in India. Patient passes 4–5 loose motions which contain blood and mucus and brown coloured.

18. **Arthropod Borne Infections:**
    1. *Mosquitoes:* Malaria, filariasis, yellow fever, dengue fever, virus encephalitis.
    2. *Sandflies:* Leishmaniasis (Kalaazar and oriental sore)
    3. *Rat fleas:* Plague, endemic typhus
    4. *Lice:* Epidemic typhus, relapsing fever
    5. *Ticks:* Kyasnur forest disease, relapsing fever
    6. *Mites:* Scrub typhus, scabies.

19. **Yellow Fever:** This disease is found in some parts of Africa and South America. It has never occurred in India. Yellow fever occurs in monkeys and other wild animals and from them it spreads to villages and cities becoming urban yellow fever. It is an haemorrhagic disease. The yellow fever is transmitted by *Aedes aegypti*. In most cases it cause fever, nausea, and pain. The disease is caused by RNA virus of flaviviridae family.

20. **Dengue Fever:** This disease is found in all parts of India and many parts of Asia. It is caused by four closley related virus serotypes of genus flavivirus, family flaviviridae. It is also known as backbone fever. The disease is manifest as sudden on set of serve headache, muscle and joint pains, fever and rash. Transmission is by the female *Aedes aegypti* mosquito.

    The virus is present in the blood of patients. It grows in the body of the mosquito for 8-14 days then becomes infective. Incubation period is 2 to 15 days. Control of mosquito *Aedes aegypti* is only control measures.

21. **Japanese Encephhalitis:** This is a virus disease and epidemics have been reported from Tamil Nadu, U.P., Bihar and West Bengal. Birds and animals (e.g., pigs), are reservoirs of infection. The disease is transmitted to man by a type of culex mosquito. Incubation period is 5–15 days. Fever and **encephalitis** inflammation of brain are the symptoms. Unconsciousness and death may occur in 20–40 per cent cases. There is no specific treatment for Japanese encephalitis and treatment is supportive; with assistance given for feeding, breathing or seizure control as required.

22. **Kyasnur Forest Disease:** This is virus disease found in Shimoga district of Karnataka. It mainly affects monkeys and many other animals e.g., cattle, rats, birds. The virus is transmitted to man by hard ticks which are present in forest. Incubation Period is about 8 days Persons in the age group 20–40 years are mainly attacked.

    Fever, headache and haemorrhage are the symptoms. Death occurs in about 5 per cent cases. Treatment is symptomatic. The disease is controlled by measures against hard ticks. A killed vaccine has been developed. Gloves, boots and repellents are used to prevent bites of ticks.

23. **Sandfly fever:** This is a virus disease found in some parts of Asia, Africa and S America. Some cases have been reported from India. It is transmitted by a sand fly (*Phlebotomous papatassi*) Incubation period is 3–4 days. Fever and headache are main symptoms. The disease is controlled by measure against sand flies.

24. **Malaria:** Malaria is one of the oldest diseases of mankinds. It has caused sickness and deaths for thousand of years and it is not yet completely under control.

    In 1880, Leveran discovered the malaria parasite in the blood. Ross in 1898 showed that the disease is transmitted by mosquitoes. The disease is caused by eukaryotic protists of the genus plasmodium. There are five species of plasmodium which can infect human are *P. falciparum, P. vivax, P. ovale, and P. malariae.* Symptoms of malaria include fever, shiviring, joint pain, vomiting, renal damage and convulsions.

National Malaria Control Programme: In India the National Malaria control programme was started in 1953. By 1965 the progress of NMEP was good but after that the cases of malaria started increasing every year. Therefore, a modified plan of operation was adopted by the Government of India in 1977. Now the attacks and deaths due to Malaria are lessen but it is still a big public health problem in India.

In 1958 N.M.C.P. was converted into National Malaria Eradication Programme for the following reasons:

1. It was thought that with success of NMCP eradication of malaria would be possible in about 10 years.
2. There was a possibility that if DDT was used for a long time it might reult in resistance in mosquitoes.

   The aim of NMET programme was to stop spread of malaria completely by destroying the parasites and the programme was started all over the country.

. **Filariasis:** This disease is caused by nematode. They are mostly found in tropical countries of Asia and Africa etc. This disease is also known as Wuchereriasis or Elephantiasis. The nomatode present in the lymphatic vessels and lumph nodes of man only. Man is primary host and mosquito is intermediate host of disease. The swelling and pain in the affected part (testis, breasts, hand, feet) is due to lymphatic obstruction by microfilariae. Diethyl carbamazine (Hetrazen) or MSb is the recommended drugs. The caustive agent of this disease is *Wucherea bancrofti.*

In India, Filariasis is major public health problem like malaria. U.P., Bihar, Andhra Pradesh, Tamil Nadu, Orissa, Kerala and Gujarat. Vidarbha and coastal region of Maharashtra are more affected regions.

26. **Leishmaniasis:** This is a parasitic infections caused by *Leishmania bransitiensis.* There are two types of disease in this category, they are kala azar and oriental sore. Treatment with antimony salt cures the diseases.

27. **Plague:** This disease is transmitted to man by rodents, rats. In the past it was one of the dangerous diseases and was responsible for many epidemics and death is Asia, Africa and South America. Europe also had epidemics of plague in the 14th century and was called "black death" In India epidemics occurred in 1612 and in 1896 it broke out in Mumbai and spread to the whole country. The disease exists in two forms "wild plague" in wild animals and "domestic plague" in man. This disease is caused by *Yersinia pestis.* Flea is a vector (*Xenopsylla cheopsis*) which feed on infected rodent and may bite man. Drugs used for the treatment are streptomycin, chloromycin and kanamycin. Tetracycline is given for 10 days and is quite effective in plague.

28. **Rabies:** It is a viral disease that causes acute encephalitis (inflammation of the brain) in warm-blooded animals. It is zoonotic (i.e., transmitted by animals), most commonly by a bite from an infected Rabies is almost invariably fatal if post-exposure prophylaxis is not administered prior to the onset of severe symptoms.

    The rabies virus travels to the brain by following the peripheral nerves. Once the rabies virus reaches the central nervous system and symptoms begin to show, the infection is effectively untreatable and usually fatal within days.

Early-stage symptoms of rabies are malaise, headache and fever, progressing to acute pain, violent movements, uncontrolled excitement, depression, and hydrophobia. Finally, the patient may experience periods of mania and lethargy, eventually leading to coma.

The rabies virus is the type species of the Lyssavirus genus, single stranded RNA genome.

All human cases of rabies were fatal until a vaccine was developed in 1885 by Louis Pasteur and Émile Roux. The human diploid cell rabies vaccine was started in 1967; however, a new and less expensive purified chicken embryo cell vaccine and purified vero cell rabies vaccine are now available.

29. **Tetanus:** Tetanus, also called lockjaw, is a medical condition characterized by a prolonged contraction of skeletal muscle fibers. The primary symptoms are caused by tetanospasmin, a neurotoxin produced by the Gram-positive, obligate anaerobic bacterium *Clostridium tetani*. Infection generally occurs through wound contamination and often involves a cut or deep puncture wound. Mortality rates reported vary from 40% to 78%. Administration of the antibiotic metronidazole decreases the number of bacteria but has no effect on the bacterial toxin. Passive immunization with human anti-tetanospasmin immunoglobulin or tetanus immunoglobulin is crucial.

30. **Leprosy or Hansen's disease (HD):** it is named after Norwegian physician Gerhard Armauer Hansen, is a chronic disease caused by the bacteria *Mycobacterium leprae and Mycobacterium lepromatosis*. Leprosy is primarily a granulomatous disease of the peripheral nerves and mucosa of the upper respiratory tract; skin lesions are the primary external sign. The mechanism of transmission of leprosy is prolonged close contact and transmission by nasal droplet.

MDT (multidrug therapy) for multi-bacillary leprosy consists of rifampicin, dapsone, and clofazimine taken over 12 months. Single dose MDT for single lesion leprosy consists of rifampicin, ofloxacin, and minocycline.

Lepromin test: This test is done to find out the type of disease and its future progress (prognosis).

31. **Sexually transmitted disease (STD):** It is also known as sexually transmitted infection (STI) or venereal disease (VD), is an illness that has a significant probability of transmission between humans or animals by means of human sexual behaviour, including vaginal intercourse, oral sex, and anal sex. While in the past, these illnesses have mostly been referred to as STDs or VD. Some STIs can also be transmitted via the use of infected needles childbirth or breastfeeding.

Bacterial:

- Chancroid (*Haemophilus ducreyi*)
- Chlamydia (*Chlamydia trachomatis*)
- Granuloma inguinale or (*Klebsiella granulomatis*)
- Gonorrhea (*Neisseria gonorrhoeae*)
- Syphilis (*Treponema pallidum*)

Fungal

- Tinea cruris "Jock Itch"
- Candidiasis or "yeast Infection"

Viral

- Viral hepatitis (Hepatitis B virus)-saliva, venereal fluids. Hepatitis A and Hepatitis E are transmitted via the fecal-oral route;
- Herpes simplex (Herpes simplex virus)
- HIV/ AIDS (Human Immunodeficiency Virus)- venereal fluids
- HPV (Human Papilloma Virus)-skin
- *Molluscum contagiosum* (molluscum contagiosum virus MCV).

Parasites

- Crab louse, colloquially known as "crabs" (*Phthirius pubis*)
- Scabies (*Sarcoptes scabiei*)

Protozoal

- Trichomoniasis (*Trichomonas vaginalis*)

High risk exposure cases may be treated prophylacticly using antibiotic combinations such as azithromycin, cefixime, and metronidazole.

The first three (syphilis, Gonorrahoea, Chanroid) are common all over India, but Lympho granuloma Vernerum (LGV) and Donovanosis are mainly found in South India.

32. **Acquired immune deficiency syndrome or acquired immunodeficiency syndrome (AIDS):** It is a disease of the human immune system caused by the human immunodeficiency virus (HIV). AIDS was first recognized by the U.S. Centers for Disease Control and Prevention in 1981 and its cause, HIV, identified in the early 1980s. AIDS is now a pandemic. HIV is transmitted through direct contact of a mucous membrane or the bloodstream with a bodily fluid containing HIV, such as blood, semen, vaginal fluid, preseminal fluid, and breast milk. This transmission can involve anal, vaginal or oral sex, blood transfusion, contaminated hypodermic needles, exchange between mother and baby during pregnancy, childbirth, breastfeeding or other exposure to one of the above bodily fluids. There is currently no available vaccine for HIV or cure for HIV or AIDS. The only known methods of prevention are based on avoiding exposure to the virus. HIV is an uncommon type of virus called a retrovirus, and drugs developed to disrupt the action of HIV are known as antiretrovirals or ARVs.

NON-COMMUNICABLE DISEASES

This disease donot have infections agents which make them spread from one person to another. They are caused by nonreversible pathological changes due to multiple factors. They have long and variable incubation periods. These diseases are permanent and leave residual disability. These diseases require special training of patients for treatment and rehabilitation.

The diseases considered in this group are:

1. Diabetes
2. Cancer
3. Heart diseases
4. Blindness
5. Deafness
6. Obesity
7. Asthma
8. Allergies

1. **Diabetes Mellitus:** It often simply referred to as **diabetes**—is a condition in which a person has a high blood sugar (glucose) level as a result of the body either not producing enough insulin, or because body cells do not properly respond to the insulin. If the body cells do not absorb the glucose, the glucose accumulates in the blood (hyperglycemia), leading to various potential medical complications. There are many types of diabetes, the most common of which are:
   - **Type-1 diabetes:** results from the body's failure to produce insulin, therefore injection of insulin is required.
   - **Type-2 diabetes:** results from insulin resistance, a condition in which cells fail to use insulin properly. Type-2 diabetes is uncommon.
   - **Other forms of diabetes mellitus** include congenital diabetes, which is due to genetic defects of insulin secretion, cystic fibrosis-related diabetes, steroid diabetes induced by high doses of glucocorticoids, and several forms of monogenic diabetes.

   Type-2 diabetes is determined primarily by lifestyle factors and genes.

   Diagnotic features

   - Fasting plasma glucose level at or above 7.0 mmol/L (126 mg/dL).
   - Plasma glucose at or above 11.1 mmol/L (200 mg/dL) two hours after a 75 g

oral glucose load as in a glucose tolerance test.

- Symptoms of hyperglycemia and casual plasma glucose at or above 11.1 mmol/L (200 mg/dL).
- Glycated hemoglobin (hemoglobin A1C) at or above 6.5.

Treatment: Anti-diabetic drugs treat diabetes mellitus by lowering glucose levels in the blood. With the exceptions of insulin, exenatide, and pramlintide, all are administered orally and are thus also called oral hypoglycemic agents or oral antihyperglycemic agents. In Type-I diabetic Insulin is used, which must be injected or inhaled.

2. **Cancer (malignant neoplasm):** It is a class of diseases in which a group of cells display uncontrolled growth (division beyond the normal limits), invasion (intrusion on and destruction of adjacent tissues), and sometimes metastasis (spread to other locations in the body via lymph or blood).

Cancers are classified into following general categories:

- **Carcinoma:** Malignant tumors derived from epithelial cells, including the breast, prostate, lung and colon cancer.
- **Sarcoma:** Malignant tumors derived from connective tissue, or mesenchymal cells.
- **Lymphoma and leukemia:** Malignancies derived from hematopoietic (blood-forming) cells.

Cause of cancer

Cancers are caused by abnormalities in the genetic material of the transformed cells. These abnormalities may be due to the effects of carcinogens, such as *tobacco smoke, radiation, chemicals, or infectious agents*. Other cancer-promoting genetic abnormalities may randomly occur through errors in DNA replication, or are inherited, and thus present in all cells from birth. Genetic abnormalities found in cancer typically affect two general classes of genes. Cancer-promoting oncogenes are typically activated in cancer cells, and Tumor suppressor genes are then inactivated in cancer cells, resulting in the loss of normal functions in those cells.

Symptoms of cancer

Cancer symptoms can be divided into three groups:

- **Local symptoms:** unusual lumps or swelling (tumor), hemorrhage (bleeding), pain and/or ulceration. Compression of surrounding tissues may cause symptoms such as jaundice (yellowing the eyes and skin).
- **Symptoms of metastasis (spreading):** enlarged lymph nodes, cough and hemoptysis, hepatomegaly (enlarged liver), bone pain, fracture of affected bones and neurological symptoms.
- **Systemic symptoms:** weight loss, poor appetite, fatigue and cachexia (wasting), excessive sweating (night sweats), anemia and specific paraneoplastic phenomena.

Treatment: 1. Surgry, 2. Chemotherapy by drugs, 3. Radiotherapy, 4. Symptomatic in late-stages.

SOME IMPORTANT DISEASES

TUBERCULOSIS

Tuberculosis is a specific infectious disease caused by *Mycobacterium tuberculosis*. The disease primarity affects lungs. It can also affect intestine, meninges, bones and joints lymph glands, skin and other tissues of the body. The disease is usually chronic with varying clinical manifestations.

Treatment : Treatment for TB uses antibiotics to kill the bacteria. The two antibiotics most commonly used are rifampicin and isoniazid.

- **Rifampicin** (INN) or rifampin (USAN) is a bactericidal antibiotic drug of the rifamycin group
- **Isoniazid** (Laniazid, Nydrazid), also known as isonicotinylhydrazine (INH), is the first-line antituberculosis medication in prevention and treatment.

Treatment of drug-resistant TB requires a longer time and more expensive drugs as for examples;

- **Multi-drug-resistant tuberculosis (MDR-TB)** is defined as resistance to the two most effective first-line TB drugs: rifampicin and isoniazid.
- **Extensively drug-resistant TB (XDR-TB)** is also resistant to three or more of the six classes of second-line drugs.
- **DOTS (Directly Observed Treatment Short-course)** strategy of tuberculosis treatment recommended by WHO was based on clinical trials done in the 1970s by Tuberculosis Research Centre, Chennai, India.

BCG Vaccination : Ever since Koch discovered *M. tuberculosis*, attempts have been made to prepare a prophylactic vaccine against tuberculosis. Calmette and Guerin, two French scientists began attenuating a virulent strain of *M. bovis* in 1906 with a view to develop a vaccine against tuberculosis. After 230 subcultures over a period of 13 years, they were able to evolve a strain-known as Bacillus Calmette Guerin or BCG, which was avirulent for man while retaining its capacity to induce an immune response.

BCG is the only widely used live bacterial vaccine. It consists of living bacteria derived from an attenuated bovine strain of tubercle bacilli. For vaccination, the usual strength is 0.1 mg in 0.1 ml volume.

Revised National Tuberculosis Control Programme (RNTCP)

RNTCP or the Revised National Tuberculosis Control Programme is the State-run Tuberculosis Control Initiative of the Government of India. It incorporates the principles of Directly observed treatment-Shortcourse (DOTS) - the global TB control strategy of the World Health Organization. The programme provides, free of cost, quality Anti-Tubercular drugs across the country through the numerous Primary Health Centres and the growing numbers of the private-sector DOTS-providers. DOTS strategy began as a pilot in 1993 and was launched as a national program in 1997. This programme has been declared a success and India has received accolades from the world health authorities.

District Tuberculosis Programme (DTP)

The District Tuberculosis Programme (DTP) is the backbone of the national Tuberculosis Programme. It was evolved by the National Tuberculosis Institute, Bangalore, and was accepted by the Government of India for implementation which started in 1962. The District Tuberculosis Centre (DTC) is the nucleus of the DTP.The function of the DTC is to plan, organize and implement the DTP, in the entire district, in association with general health services. There are at present 390 District Tuberculosis centres provides all services to RNTCP.

POLIOMYELITIS

Poliomyelitis is an acute viral infection caused by an RNA virus. It is primarily an infection of the human alimentary tract but the virus may infect the central nervous system in a very small percentage (about 1 per cent) of cases resulting in varying degrees of paralysis.

Environmental Factors: Polio is more likely to occur during the rainy season. Approximately 60 per cent of cases recorded in India were during June to September. The environmental sources of infection are contaminated water, food and flies. Polio virus survives for a long time in a cold environment. Overcrowding and poor sanitation provide opportunities for exposure to infection.

Prevention: Immunization is the sole effective means of preventing poliomyelitis. Both killed and live attenuated vaccines are available and both are safe and effective when used correctly. It is essential to immunize all infants by 6 months of age to protect them against polio. Two types of vaccine are used throughout the world; they are:

1. Inactivated (salk) polio vaccine (IPV)
2. Oral (sabin) polio vaccine (OPV)

1. ***Inactivated (salk) Polio Vaccine (IPV):*** First deveoped by Jonas Salk and was tested in 1952. This vaccine contains all the three types of poliovirus, inactivated by formalin. It contains 20, 2, and 4 D antigen units of types 1, 2 and 3 respectively. The primary or initial course of immunization consists of 4 inoculations. The first 3 doses are given at intervals of 1–2 months and 4th dose 6–12 months after the third dose. First dose is usually given when the infant is 6 weeks old. Additional doses are recommended prior to school entry and then every 5 years untill the age of 18. Alternatively, one or two doses of live vaccine (OPV) can be given safely as boosters after an initial course of immunization with inactivated vaccine.
2. ***Oral (sabin) Polio Vaccine (OPV) :*** Developed by Albert Sabin using attenuated poliovirus. First human trial Sabin's vaccin began in 1957. Oral polio vaccine (OPV) was described by Sabin in 1957. It contains live attenuated virus (types 1, 2 and 3) grown on primary monkey kidney cells or human diploid cell cultures. Ideally each virus type should be given separately as monovalent vaccine, but for administrative convenience, rather than efficacy, it is given as trivalent oral polio vaccine (TOPV) vaccine. The vaccine contains (i) over 3,00,000 TCID 50 of type 1 poliovirus (ii) over 1,00,000 TCID 50 of type 2 virus, and (iii) over 3,00,000 TCID 50 of type 3 virus per dose. (TCID is tissue culture infection dose).

National Immunization Schedule

The WHO programme on Immunization (EPI) and the National Immunization programme in India recommend a primary course of 3 doses of OPV at one-month intervals. Commencing the first dose when infant is 6 weeks old. OPV is given concurrently with DPT; BCG can be given simultaneously with the first dose of OPV.

Pulse Polio Immunization (PPI) Programme

It is a global initiative to eradicate poliomyelitis by the end of the year 2000 is the largest international disease control effort ever. In pursuance to the World Health Assembly Resolution of 1988, in addition to administration of routine OPV through the Universal Immunization Program, the Pulse Polio Immunization (PPI) Programme was launched in 1995-96 to cover all children below the age of 3 years. In order to accelerate the pace of polio eradication, the target age group was increased from 1996-97 to all children under the age of 5 years.

HEPATITIS

Hepatitis A (formerly known as "infection" hepatitis or epidemic jaundice) is an acute infectious disease caused by hepatitis A virus (HAV). The disease is heralded by non-specific symptoms such as fever, chills, headache, fatigue, generalised weakness and aches and pains followed by anorexia, nausea, vomiting, dark urine and jaundice.

Prevention

- Keeping away from contact with the blood and body fluids, including semen and vaginal secretions of infected persons.

- Avoid sharing personal items such as razors and toothbrushes with individuals who are infected with the hepatitis B virus.
- Use latex condoms to prevent getting infected through sexual contact.
- Vaccines protecting against Hepatitis B are available and should be seriously considered by people exposed to a high risk of infection such as those who receive blood transfusions, share needles for drug use or have multiple sex partners.

In India, it is estimated that at least 100,000 people die every year due to illnesses related to HBV infection. Realizing the dangers of Hepatitis B, the government expanded the Universal Immunization Programme (UIP) to include Hepatitis B vaccine in the year 2002.

CHOLERA

Cholera is an acute diarrhoeal disease caused by *Vibrio cholerae* O1 (classical or El Tor). It is now commonly due to the El Tor biotype. Cases range from symptomless to severe infections. The majority of infections are mild or asymptomatic. Typical cases are characterised by the sudden onset of profuse, effortless, watery diarrhoea followed by vomiting, rapid dehydration, musclular cramps and suppression of urine.

Pathogenesis : The main symptom of cholera is diarrhoea. Diarrhoea increases permeability of the intestinal epithelial cells, increased peristalsis, mucosal damage, an increase in mesenteric blood flow and failure of the "Sodium pump", *i.e.,* interference with the passage of sodium from the lumen to the plasma.

Control of Cholera : It is considered that the best way to control cholera is to implement a national programme for the control of all diarrhoeal diseases. Some of the control measures are given below:

1. **Verification of the diagnosis:** It is important to have confirmation of the outbreak as possible all cases of diarrhoea should be investigated even on the slightest suspicion. For the specific diagnosis of cholera, it is important to identify *V. cholera* O1 in the stools of the patient.
2. **Notification:** Cholera is a notifiable disease locally, nationally and internationally. Health workers at all levels (such as the community health workers and the multi-purpose workers) should be trained to identify and notify cases immediately to the local health authority.
3. **Establishment of Treatment Centres:** In the control of cholera, no time should be lost in providing treatment for the patients. To achieve this objective, it is necessary to establish easily accessible treatment facilities in the community. The mildly dehydrated patients (which account for over 90 per cent of cases) should be treated at home with oral rehydration fluid. Severly dehydrated patients, requiring intravenous fluids, should be transferred to the nearest treatment centre or hospital; if possible they should received oral rehydration on the way to the hospital or treatment centre.
4. **Rehydration Therapy:** The introduction of oral rehydration by WHO in 1971, has greatly simplified the treatment of cholera and other acute diarrhoeal diseases. The aim of oral fluid theraphy is to prevent dehydration and reduce mortality.

   Oral fluid therapy is based on the observation that glucose given orally enhances the intestinal absorption of salt and water and is capable of correcting the electrolyte and water deficit.
5. **Sanitation Measures:**

   (a) *Water Control:* As water is the most important vehicle of transmission of cholera, all steps must be taken to provide properly treated or safe water to the community for all purposes (drinking, washing and cooking).

   (b) *Excreta Disposal:* Provision of simple cheap and effective excreta disposal system (sanitary latrines) is a basic need of all human settlements. When cholera appears in a community, the need for these facilities become vital.

(c) *Food sanitation:* Since food may be an important vehicle of infection, steps should be taken to improve food sanitation, particulary sale of foods under hygienic conditions.

(d) *Disinfection:* Disinfection should be both concurrent and terminal. The most effective disinfectant for general use is a coal tar disinfectant with a Rideal-Walker (RW) Coefficient of 10 or more such as cresol.

6. **Vaccination:** Cholera vaccine is the only specific prophylactic available against cholera. The vaccine employed at present is a saline suspension of approximately 6,000 million each of classical Ogawa and Inaba serotypes of *V. cholerae* O1 per ml. So that each millilitre of the vaccine contains a total of 12,000 million vibrios.

7. **Health Education:** The most effective prophylactic measure is perhaps health education. It should be directed mainly to (a) the effectiveness and simplicity of oral rehydration therapy. (b) the benefits of early reporting for prompt treatment (c) food hygiene practices (d) handwashing after and before eating, and (e) the benefit of cooked, hot foods and safe water. Since cholera is mainly a disease of the poor and ignorant, these groups should be tackled first.

FOOD POISONING

Food poisoning is a common, usually mild, but sometimes deadly illness. Typical symptoms include nausea, vomiting, abdominal cramping, and diarrhea that occur suddenly (within 48 hours) after consuming a contaminated food or drink. Depending on the contaminant, fever and chills, bloody stools, dehydration, and nervous system damage may follow. These symptoms may affect one person or a group of people who ate the food.

Types of Food Poisoning : Food poisoning may be due to toxic chemical substances or pathogenic organisms.

(a) **Toxic chemical substances:** Food poisoning is due to adulteration or contamination with formaldehyde, melamine, 3-MCPD, cyanide, Lead poisoning, Mercury in fish, Sudan red dye, Aldicarb.

(b) **Pathogenic organisms:** Bacteria are a common cause of food poisoning.

(i) Most common bacterial food poisoning pathogens are: *Campylobacter jejuni, Clostridium perfringens,* Salmonella spp. *S. typhimurium, Escherichia coli.*

(ii) Other common bacterial food poisoning pathogens are: *Bacillus cereus; Salmonella; Listeria monocytogenes; Shigella* spp.; *Staphylococcus aureus* etc.

(iii) Exotoxins: Some food poisoning is caused by exotoxins which are excreted by the cell as the bacterium grows. e.g. *Clostridium botulinum* (causes deadly disease botulism), *Clostridium perfringens, Staphylococcus aureus* (causes intense vomiting) and *Bacillus cereus.*

(iv) Aflatoxins: It originated from *Aspergillus parasiticus* and *Aspergillus flavus.* Aflatoxin predominantly targets the liver, which will result in necrosis, cirrhosis, and carcinoma.

Salmonella Food Poisoning

An extremely common form of food poisoning. Five reasons have been given for increase of food poisining in recent years *(a)* an increase in contaiminated feeding *(b)* increase in international trade in human food *(c)* a higher incidence of salmonellosis in farm animals *(d)* wide distribution of "prepared food".

Perfringens Food Poisoning

Cl. perfringens (welchii) is the causative agent the organism has been found in faeces of humans and animals, and in soil, water and air. Incubation Period is 6 to 24 hours, with a peak from 10 to 14 hours.

Mechanism of Food Poisoning: The spores are able to survive cooking and if the cooked meat and poultry are not cooled enough, they will germinate. The organisms multiply between 30° and 50° C and produce a variety of toxins, *e.g.*, alpha toxin, theta toxin *etc*.

Clinical Symptoms: The most common symptoms are diarrhorea, abdominal cramps and little or no fever, occurring 8 to 24 hours after consumption of the food.

Bacillus cereus Food Poisoning

Bacillus cereus is a Gram-positive, facultatively aerobic sporeformer whose cells are large rods and whose spores do not swell the sporangium. The symptoms of *B. cereus* mimic those of *Clostridium perfringens* food poisoning. The onset of watery diarrhea, abdominal cramps, and pain occurs 6-15 hours after consumption of contaminated food. Nausea may accompany diarrhea, but vomiting (emesis) rarely occurs. Symptoms persist for 24 hours in most instances.

Prevention and Control

(i) *Meat inspection*: The food animals must be free from infection. This can be ensured by their examination by Veterinary staff both before and after slaughter.

(ii) *Personal hygiene*: A high standard of personal hygiene among individuals engaged in the handing, preparation and cooking of food is needed.

(iii) *Food handlers*: Those suffering from infected wounds, boils diarrhoea, dysentery, throat infection, *etc*, should be excluded from food handling.

(iv) *Food handling techniques*: The handling of ready to eat foods with bare hands should be reduced to a minimum.

(v) *Sanitary improvements*: Sanitization of all work surfaces, utensils and equipment must be ensured.

(vi) *Health education*: Food handlers should be educated in matters of clean habits and personal hygiene such as frequent and the rough hand washing.

ARTHROPOD-BORNE INFECTIONS

Dengue

Dengue viruses are arboviruses capable of infecting humans, and causing disease. These infections may be asymptomatic or may lead to (a) "classical" dengue fever or (b) dengue haemorrhagic fever without shock or (c) dengue haemorrhagic fever with shock.

(*a*) **Classical Dengue Fever:** Classical Dengue Fever or "breakbone fever" has been known in India for a very long time. It is an acute viral infection, casused by at least 4 serotypes (1, 2, 3, and 4) of dengue virus. Dengue fever can occur epidemically or endemically. Epidemics may be explosive and after start during the rainy reason when the breeding of the vector mosquitoes (*e.g. Aedes aegypti*) is genreally abundant. Temperature also plays an important role in the transmission of dengue virus by moquities. Mosquitoes kept at 26°C fail to transmit DEN-2 virus. The reservoir of infection is both man and mosquito. The transmission cycle is "Man-mosquito-Man". Aedes aegypti is the main vector. Dengue outbreaks have also been attributed to Aedes aklbopictus, Aedes polynesiensis, and several species of the Aedes scutellaris complex.

(*b*) **Dengue Haemorrhagic Fever:** Dengue Haemorrhagic Fever (DHF) is a severe from of dengue fever, caused by infection with more than one dengue virus. The severe illness is thought to be due to double infection with dengue viruses—the first infection probably sensitizes the patient, while the second appears to produce an immunological catastrophe.

DHF is transmitted by *A.aegypti*, epidemics of DHF have occurred in recent years in South East Asia (Burma,

Indonesia, Thailand and India) and western pacific (Malaysia, Philippines, singapore, Vietnam) regions of WHO. The disease is confined exclusively to children less than 15 years of age, with fatalities. Reports indicate that many adults are now being affected.

(c) **Dengue Shock Syndrome:** The clinical diagnosis is based on all the above criteria, plus Shock-manifested by rapid and weak pulse with narrowing of the pulse pressure (20 mmHg or less) or hypotension with the presence of cold. Clammy skin and restlessness.

Treatment: The management of dengue fever is symptomatic and supportive. Bed rest is advisable during the acute febrile phase. Antipyretics or sponging are required to keep the body temperature below 40°C. Aspirin should be avoided, particularly in areas where DHF is endemic, since it may be cause gestritis, bleeding and acidosis. Oral flrid and electrolyte there by is recommended for patients with excessive sweating, vomiting or diarrhoea.

In small children, five per cent dextrose in a half-strength normal saline solution (5 per cent D/1/2 NSS) is used following initial resuscitation, and 5 per cent D/1/3 NSS may be used in infants under one year of age if the serum sodium is normal. Intravenous fluid should be discontinued. When the haematocrit reading drops to around 40 per cent and vital signs are stable. A good urine flow indicates sufficient circulating renal volume.

Malaria

Malaria is a protozoal disease caused by infection with parasites of the genus Plasmosium and transmitted to man by certain species of infected female Anopheline mosquito. A typical attack comprises three distinct stages: Cold stage hot stage and sweating stage.

Malaria Control: Malaria control programmes have been defined as "an organized effort to carry out those antimalaria measures that are possible with the available resources and suitable under the prevailing epidemiological conditions, with the objective of achieving the greatest possible reduction of mortality and morbidity. National Malaria controal programme. (NMCP) was launched in India in April 1953. It was based on indoor residual spraying with DDT (1g per sq. metre in endemic areas) twice a year in endemic areas where spleen rates were over 10 per cent. The NMCP was in operation for 5 years (1953–58).

Malaria Eradication: The term "eradication" literally means "pulling out by the roots". By definition it implies an intensive short term effort for the elimination of Malaria parasites from the human population so that there is no further occurrence of Malaria even in the presence of carrier mosquitoes. In other words, Malaria eradication signifies abolition of the human reservoir of infection, and not the eradication of mosquitoes. The global programme of malaria eradication commence in 1957 under the aegis of WHO.

OBJECTIVE QUESTIONS

1. In acetone killed typhoid vaccine the immunity last for:
(a) 6 months (b) 1 year
(c) 2 years (d) 3 years

2. In salmonellosis, isolation is recommended till:
(a) 3 consecutive stool cultures are –ve
(b) Fever subsides
(c) widal reaction is –ve
(d) 72 hour after chloramphenical therapy

3. The time period is more than ______ for chronic carrier of typhoid.
(a) 3 months (b) 6 months
(c) 9 months (d) 12 months

4. Highest incidence of typhoid fever in the age group (years):
(*a*) 10–12 (*b*) 20–30
(*c*) 30–40 (*d*) 40–60

5. In typhoid, a permanent carrier is one who excretes bacilli for more than:
(*a*) 3 months (*b*) 6 months
(*c*) 1 year (*d*) 3 years

6. Only human beings are the reservoirs for:
(*a*) Pox (*b*) Influenza
(*c*) Salmonella (*d*) Rabies

7. In Salmonellosis isolation done till:
(*a*) Fever subsides
(*b*) Blood culture negative
(*c*) Spleen subsides
(*d*) Stool culture negative for three times

8. Vomiting occurs in a group of children in the night who had a meal at noon. The causative agent for food poisoning is most likely to be:
(*a*) Salmonella
(*b*) Botulism
(*c*) Staphylococcus
(*d*) Viral gastroenteritis

9. The common cause of diarrhoea in children is:
(*a*) Rota virus (*b*) Norwalk virus
(*c*) Adenovirus (*d*) Giardiasis

10. Certificate of cholera vaccination is valid after ______ days:
(*a*) 1 (*b*) 3
(*c*) 6 (*d*) 10

11. Regarding cholera vaccine all are correct except that:
(*a*) It is given at intervals of 6 months
(*b*) Long-lasting immunity
(*c*) Not useful in epidemics
(*d*) Not given orally

12. As per the latest guidelines which of the following dehydration status required ORS prescription:
(*a*) Mild dehydration
(*b*) Moderate dehydration
(*c*) Some dehydration
(*d*) Any dehydration

13. Best prophylaxis of cholera is:
(*a*) Early case detection
(*b*) Improved water sanitation
(*c*) Chemoprophylaxis
(*d*) Check spread of epidemic

14. In a cholera epidemic, the information is to be given up to level of:
(*a*) Health ministry
(*b*) DGFAMS
(*c*) Hospital
(*d*) CMO and IMO

15. Chemoprophylaxis for cholera is by administrating:
(*a*) Doxycycline 300 mg. ounce
(*b*) Metrogyl 400 mg. 3 tablets
(*c*) Vancomycin 1 mg.
(*d*) Kannamycin 500 mg.

16. The drug of choice in cholera is:
(*a*) Tetracycline (*b*) Sulphadiazine
(*c*) Ampicillin (*d*) Streptomycin

17. Osmolality of WHO ORS is (mmol):
(*a*) 240 (*b*) 270
(*c*) 800 (*d*) 330

18. Citrate is added to conventional oral rehydration solution (ORS) in order to:
(*a*) Improve sodium chloride absorption
(*b*) Correct acidosis
(*c*) Increases its shelf-life
(*d*) Improve glucose absorption

19. Oral rehydration therapy consists of the following *except*:
(*a*) Sodium chloride
(*b*) Potassim chloride
(*c*) Magnesium sulphate
(*d*) Glucose

20. The WHO formula for ORS provides in mEqIL:
(*a*) 70 of sodium (*b*) 20 of potassium
(*c*) 30 of chloride (*d*) 80 of sodabicarb

21. Oral rehydration fluid does not contain:
(*a*) Sodium chloride
(*b*) Calcium lactate
(*c*) Bicarbonate
(*d*) Glucose

22. Which is not essential in case of cholera epidemic:
(a) Weekly chlorination
(b) Notification
(c) Vaccination of individuals
(d) Treatment with ORS and tetracycline

23. The required amount of bleaching powder necessary to disinfect choleric stools is:
(a) 25 m/litre (b) 50 gm/litre
(c) 75 gm/litre (d) 100 gm/litre

24. The infectivity of a convalescent case of cholera lasts for:
(a) Less than 7 days
(b) 7 to 14 days
(c) 14 to 21 days
(d) 21 to 28 days

25. In a case control study of a suspected association between breast cancer and the contraceptive pill, all of the following are true statements *except*:
(a) The control should come from a population that has the same potential for breast cancer as the cases
(b) The control should exclude women known to be taking the pill at the time of the survey
(c) All the control needs to be healthy
(d) The attributable risk of breast cancer resulting from the pill may be directly measured.

26. Which one of the following is the longest carrier state found in the disease of cholera?
(a) 2 to 3 weeks (b) 1 to 5 years
(c) 5 to 10 years (d) Above 10 years

27. Of the total deaths, diarrhoea induced deaths among children below 5 years of age in India are:
(a) 35% to 40% (b) 25% to 30%
(c) 15% to 20% (d) 5% to 10%

28. Epidemiology of cholera in England was classified by:
(a) John Snow (b) Winslow
(c) Chadwick (d) Howard Hughes

29. *True* about eltor epidemiology are all except:
(a) Chronic carrier are common
(b) Asymptomatic mild cases common
(c) Long extraintestinal survival
(d) High secondary attack rate in families

30. *True* in Eltor cholera are E:
(a) Infections are mild and symptomatic
(b) They are resistant to polymyxin-b unit disc
(c) Chronic carriers are common
(d) Secondary attacks rate high

31. About cholera *true* is:
(a) Eltor variety rarer than classical
(b) Vaccine is essential during epidemics
(c) Antibiotic theraphy contraindicated
(d) Ganglioside receptors in the intestines

32. Cholera is a vehicle transmitted disease because:
(a) When the vehicle is controlled the epidemic subsides
(b) It is always possible to isolate the organism from the vehicle
(c) The common source of infection is not traceable
(d) The organism does not travel great distances

33. Most common cause of epidemic of infective hepatitis in India is:
(a) HAV (b) HBV
(c) HCV (d) HEV

34. Maximum maternal mortality is seen in:
(a) Hepatitis B (b) Hepatitise E
(c) Hepatitis C (d) Hepatitis

35. Best method to protect newborn from HBs Ag +ve, mother is:
(a) Isolation
(b) Stopping breastfeeding
(c) Hep B immunoglobulin
(d) Hep B-vaccine and immunoglobulin

36. *True* about viral hepatitis B is:
(a) Transmits by oral route
(b) More incubation period than viral A
(c) Different histopathologically from viral A hepotitis
(d) Can be cultured

37. Average incubation period of infectious hepatitis is:
(*a*) 7 days (*b*) 15 days
(*c*) 25 days (*d*) 50 days

38. Acute flaccid paralysis in which age group is to be reported:
(*a*) 0–5 years (*b*) 0–10 years
(*c*) 0–15 years (*d*) 0–3 years

39. All of the following feature are suggestive of asbestosis *except*:
(*a*) Occurs within five years of exposer
(*b*) The disease progress even after removal of contract
(*c*) Can lead to pleural mesothelima
(*d*) Sputum contains asbestos bodies

40. In an epidemic of poliomyelitis best to stop spread by:
(*a*) Injection of killed vaccine
(*b*) OPV drops to all children
(*c*) Isolation of the cases
(*d*) Chlorination of all the wells

41. False regarding polio vaccine:
(*a*) Helps in herd immunity
(*b*) Killed vaccine prevants paralysis
(*c*) Difficult to maintain chain
(*d*) Immunity takes a long time to develop

42. The following statements are *true* for inactivated polio vaccine *except*:
(*a*) It does not produce intestinal immunity
(*b*) It prevents paralysis
(*c*) It is contraindicated in immune deficiency disorders
(*d*) Booster doses with oral polio vaccine can be given

43. The following is *not ture* of inactivated polio vaccine:
(*a*) Induces only circulating antibodies
(*b*) Prevents both paralysis and reinfection by wild polio virus
(*c*) Does not require stringent epidemics
(*d*) Not useful in controlling epidemics

44. Least likely to diagnosed Polio is:
(*a*) Fever, malaise for 2 days
(*b*) Fever and signs of neck rigidity
(*c*) Descending symmetrical paralysis with preservation of reflexes and sensory system
(*d*) Gradual recovery of muscle function in 6 months

45. In polio transmission easy block can be applied by acting on:
(*a*) Reservoir (*b*) susceptible host
(*c*) Faecooral (*d*) Agent

46. The epidemiological trend of poliomyelitis are all *except*:
(*a*) Affects higher age groups
(*b*) Increasing in tropics
(*c*) Also cause upper limb paralysis
(*d*) Sporadic to epidemic

47. Which of the following type of polio is most common?
(*a*) Inapparent (*b*) Abortive
(*c*) Nonparalytic (*d*) Paralytic

48. *Wrong* about polio patient who had paralysis:
(*a*) Can transmit it by nasal discharge
(*b*) Subclinical infection common
(*c*) Can by given vaccine
(*d*) None of the above

49. All *true* for a polio epidemic curve in a community except:
(*a*) All cases within 7–14 days
(*b*) Orofaecal mode of transmission
(*c*) Herd immunity present
(*d*) Epidemic curve has a slow rising slope and decline

50. Number of subclinical cases for 1 paralytic polio is:
(*a*) 50 (*b*) 100
(*c*) 1,000 (*d*) 10,000

51. AIDS was first detected in India in the year:
(*a*) 1975 (*b*) 1981
(*c*) 1986 (*d*) 1991

52. All are true of BCG innoculation, except:
(*a*) Papule in 7 days
(*b*) Forms an ulcer
(*c*) Heals spontaneously
(*d*) Size of 4–8 mm in 5 weeks

53. Effectivity of BCG vaccine is:
(a) 80% (b) 60%
(c) 40% (d) Less than 40%

54. A positive Mantoux test indicates that the child:
(a) is suffering from active TB
(b) has had BCG vaccination recently
(c) has had tuberculosis infection
(d) all of the above

55. BCG is not given to patients with:
(a) Generalised eczema
(b) Infective dermatosis
(c) Hypogammaglobulin anaemia
(d) All of the above

56. In the administration of BCG vaccine, the diluent is:
(a) Glycerine (b) Glycerol
(c) Normal saline (d) Distilled water

57. The vaccine administered by subcutaneous route is:
(a) BCG (b) OPV
(c) Tetanus toxoid (d) Measles

58. The direct BCG vaccination in Inida is given up to age of:
(a) 10 years (b) 15 years
(c) 20 years (d) 25 years

59. BCG vaccine is administered to children:
(a) Intradermally (b) Subcutaneously
(c) Intramuscularly (d) Orally

60. All the following are correct regarding BCG vaccination reactions *except*:
(a) Ulceration with crust
(b) Heals within 6–19 weeks
(c) Maximum size of papule is reached at 5 weeks
(d) Suppurative lymphadenitis

61. 0.1 ml of BCG contains _____ mg. moist weight:
(a) 0.050 (b) 0.025
(c) 0.075 (d) 0.100

62. 'DOTS' indicates
(a) Long-term treatment under direct observation
(b) Short-term treatment under direct observation
(c) Short-term treatment without observation
(d) Domiciliary treatment without observation

63. Short-term antitubercular therapy is given to minimise:
(a) Resistance (b) Toxicity
(c) Relapse (d) Cost

64. To prevent emergence of resistance in TB following are done *except*:
(a) Multidrug regimen used
(b) Drug to which bacteria are sensitive is used
(c) Defaulter action
(d) Pre-treatment regular culture sensitivity

65. *True* about tuberculin test:
(a) Used for diagnosis of TB
(b) Measure incidence of disease
(c) More than 10 mm in 72 hr indicates positive test
(d) Measure immunity status

66. Tuberculin test positivity depends on:
(a) Erythema (b) Nodule formation
(c) Induration (d) Ulcerative change

67. For Mantoux test, the standard dose of tuberculin used in India is:
(a) 0.5 TU (b) 1.0 TU
(c) 5.0 TU (d) 10.0 TU

68. Tuberculin test is read after:
(a) 48 hours (b) 72 hours
(c) 96 hours (d) 24 hours

69. 'Annual infection rate' in TB is the percentage of:
(a) Persons converted from tuberculine negative to positive
(b) New cases of tuberculosis
(c) Sputum positive cases
(d) Radiological cases

70. Under the revised National Tuberculosis Control Programme, a new case is one who has never had treatment for tuberculosis or has taken anti-tubercular drugs for less than:
(a) 2 weeks (b) 4 weeks
(c) 6 weeks (d) 8 weeks

71. HIV virus can be isolated from all *except*:
(*a*) Semen (*b*) Saliva
(*c*) Blood (*d*) Skin scraping

72. A 'case' in TB is defined as:
(*a*) X-ray positive
(*b*) Culture positive
(*c*) Sputum AFB positive
(*d*) Tuberculosis positive

73. Prevalence of tuberculosis infection is measured by:
(*a*) Chest X-ray
(*b*) Sputum AFB
(*c*) Tuberculin test
(*d*) Sputum culture

74. 'Annual infection rate' in TB is the percentage of:
(*a*) Persons converted from tuberculine negative to positive
(*b*) New cases of tuberculosis
(*c*) Sputum positive cases
(*d*) Radiological cases

75. Infectious pool of tuberculosis is denoted by:
(*a*) Prevalence of sputum +ve cases
(*b*) Prevalence of X-ray +ve cases
(*c*) Clinically +ve cases
(*d*) Any of the above

76. Which is best indicator of evaluating TB and its trends in society?
(*a*) Tuberculosis conversion index
(*b*) Mortality rate
(*c*) Prevalence of infection
(*d*) New cases

77. Assessment of magnitude of TB and its trend in community is by:
(*a*) Tuberculin conversion index
(*b*) Incidence rate
(*c*) Prevalence rate
(*d*) Fatality rate

78. The drug used by health workers in the management of acute respiratory illness
(*a*) Cotrimoxazole
(*b*) Chloramphenicol
(*c*) Benzyl penicillin
(*d*) Gentamycin

79. In meningococcal meningitis:
(*a*) Fatality of typical untreated case is 10%
(*b*) Rifampicin is the drug of choice in eradicating carrier state
(*c*) Cases are the most important source of infection
(*d*) Cases start losing their infectiousness 3–4 days after starting specific anti-microbial therapy

80. The following diseases are under surveillance by WHO, *except*:
(*a*) Relapsing fever
(*b*) Plague
(*c*) Malaria
(*d*) Tuberculosis

81. In meningococcal epidemic all of the following are useful for prophylaxis except:
(*a*) Rifampicin (*b*) Sulfas
(*c*) Vaccine (*d*) Tetracycline

82. Vaccines are available against group ______ Meningococcus.
(*a*) A (*b*) B
(*c*) C (*d*) A and C

83. Which vaccine is contraindicated in pregnancy?
(*a*) Cholera vaccine
(*b*) Typhoid vaccine
(*c*) Meninggococcal vaccine
(*d*) Typhoid vaccine

84. Average incubation period for meningococcal meningitis is:
(*a*) 90 days (*b*) 25 days
(*c*) 10 days (*d*) 5 days

85. Which of the following is *true* about meaning ococcal meningitis?
(*a*) Case fatality less than 10% in untreated cases
(*b*) Cases are the main source of infection
(*c*) Rifampicin is the drug of choice
(*d*) Treatment in the first 2 days can save the life of 95% cases

86. *Not true* about carrier state of *N. gonorrhoeal* is:
(*a*) Carrier state remains for several months

(b) Organisms can be isolated from nasopharynx
(c) Affected 5–30% of cases during epidemics
(d) It is coccobacillus

87. The absolute contraindication for administration of pertussis vaccine is:
(a) Diarrhoea (b) Fever
(c) Malnutrition (d) Convulsions

88. Incubation period of pertussis is:
(a) 7–14 days (b) Less than 2 weeks
(c) 16–28 days (d) 6 weeks

89. If convulsions are present, which vaccine should not be given:
(a) DPT (b) Oral polio
(c) BCG (d) Tetanus toxoid
(e) Measles

90. Which one of the following doses in lethal flocculent units of diphtheria toxoid is incorporated in DPT vaccine?
(a) 5 (b) 15
(c) 25 (d) 35

91. Management of unimmunised contacts of diphtheria is:
(a) Antitoxins
(b) Immunoglobins and antitoxin
(c) Erythromycin
(d) Isolation

92. Treatment of choice for diphtheria carrier is:
(a) Erythromycin (b) Tetracycline
(c) Penicillin (d) DPT

93. A herd immunity of over _____ is considered necessary to prevent epidemic spread of diptheria:
(a) 50% (b) 55%
(c) 60% (d) 70%

94. Management of nonimmunised diphtheria contacted includes all *except*:
(a) Prophylactic penicillin
(b) Single dose of toxoid
(c) Daily throat examinations
(d) Throat swab culture

95. For which of the following diseases is the usual antibody source equine?
(a) Tetanus, Diphtheria
(b) Infective hepatitis
(c) Measles
(d) None of the above

96. Which one of the following combinations is of DPT vaccine?
(a) Toxoid, live and killed
(b) Toxoid, killed and toxoid
(c) Live, killed and toxoid
(d) Killed, killed and toxoid

97. One of the following is used in DPT vaccine:
(a) Magnesium sulphate
(b) Aluminium phosphate
(c) Aluminium sulphate
(d) Magnesium hydroxide

98. Bull neck in diphtheria is due to:
(a) Retropharyngeal abscess
(b) Laryngeal oedema
(c) Cellulitis
(d) Lymphadenopathy

99. The most common age group for diphtheria is:
(a) 1–2 years (b) 2–5 years
(c) 2–7 years (d) 2–9 years

100. The infectivity of a patient with diphtheria is:
(a) Till cough subsides
(b) Till patient is febrile
(c) Life-long
(d) For 15 days after infection

101. Which of the following diseases has incubation period less than one week?
(a) Tuberculosis (b) Leprosy
(c) Influenza (d) Food poisoning

102. All are features of influenza epidemic *except*:
(a) Large number of subclinical cases
(b) Long Incubation period
(c) Absence of cross immunity
(d) Sudden outburst

103. Which of the following vaccine is contraindicated in pregnancy?
(a) Rubella (b) OPV
(c) BCG (d) Hepatitis

104. True about mumps is all except:
(*a*) Incubation period 2–3 weeks
(*b*) Aseptic meningitis may be present
(*c*) Even after B/L orchitis's sterility is unusual
(*d*) Hyperamylasia falls in pancreatitis

105. Following statements is *not true* regarding mumps:
(*a*) caused by paramyxovirus
(*b*) Incubation period is less than one week
(*c*) About 31–40% of infections are clinically in apparent
(*d*) Orchitis occurs in about one in 4 males 25%

106. Incubation period for mumps is:
(*a*) 18 days (*b*) 14 days
(*c*) 10 days (*d*) 5 days

107. Which of the following diseases gives life-long immunity after an attack?
(*a*) Typhoid (*b*) Mumps
(*c*) Tetanus (*d*) Diphtheria

108. Which of the following vaccine was introduced most lately?
(*a*) Mumps (*b*) Pertusis
(*c*) Measles (*d*) Rubella

109. What is *not* usually a feature of rubella:
(*a*) Low grade fever
(*b*) Arthralgia
(*c*) Posterior auricular lymphade-nopathy
(*d*) The rash begins on the trunk

110. Vaccine contraindicated during pregnancy is:
(*a*) Rubella (*b*) OPV
(*c*) Tetanus (*d*) Influenza

111. Keratomalacia is associated with:
(*a*) Measles (*b*) Mumps
(*c*) Rubella (*d*) Diarrhoea
(*e*) Chickenpox

112. *True* about measles vaccines are:
(*a*) Given subcutaneous
(*b*) Highly efficacy
(*c*) Given below 1 year of age
(*d*) Diluent does not require for storage

113. All of the following are *true* for measles vaccine *except*:
(*a*) Fever can occur 6–10 days after vaccination
(*b*) Immunity develops 11–12 days after vaccination
(*c*) There is spread of virus from vaccine to contacts
(*d*) Single dose of vaccine gives 95% protection

114. Measles vaccine given to a contact of measles case exerts protective effect within:
(*a*) 1 day (*b*) 3 day
(*c*) 7 days (*d*) 10 days

115. Measles vaccine should be used within the following time after reconstitution:
(*a*) 1 hour (*b*) 2 hours
(*c*) 3 hours (*d*) 1/2 hour

116. In all carriers cause transmission *except*:
(*a*) Cholera (*b*) Typhoid
(*c*) Measles (*d*) Poliomyelitis

117. Carriers are *not* an important source of transmission in:
(*a*) Typhoid (*b*) Poliomyelitis
(*c*) Diphtheria (*d*) Measles

118. Carriers are *not* seen in:
(*a*) Cholera (*b*) Diphtheria
(*c*) Typhoid (*d*) Measles

119. Carriers are associated with transmission of disease in all except:
(*a*) Typhoid (*b*) Cholera
(*c*) Measles (*d*) Diphtheria

120. Following are complication of chickenpox except:
(*a*) Rey's syndrome (*b*) Meningitis
(*c*) Pneumonia (*d*) Enteritis

121. All stages of rash are seen in:
(*a*) Chickenpox (*b*) Smallpox
(*c*) Measles (*d*) Typhoid

122. *True* about chickenpox rash:
(*a*) Centrifugal (*b*) Pleomorphic
(*c*) Umbilicated (*d*) Deep seated

123. Chickenpox is characterised by all *except*:

(*a*) Live virus can be isolated from crust
(*b*) Rapid transformation of stage
(*c*) Rash is centripetal in distribution
(*d*) Lesions appear in crops usually

124. Which is *not* a complication of chickenpox?

(*a*) Pancreatitis
(*b*) Pneumonia
(*c*) Encephalitis
(*d*) Thrombocytopenia

125. Communication period of chickenpox is:

(*a*) Till last scab falls off
(*b*) 4–5 days after rash
(*c*) In the incubation period
(*d*) Only upto fill fever lasts

ANSWERS

1	2	3	4	5	6	7	8	9	10
(*d*)	(*a*)	(*d*)	(*a*)	(*c*)	(*c*)	(*d*)	(*c*)	(*a*)	(*c*)
11	**12**	**13**	**14**	**15**	**16**	**17**	**18**	**19**	**20**
(*b*)	(*d*)	(*b*)	(*a*)	(*a*)	(*a*)	(*d*)	(*c*)	(*c*)	(*b*)
21	**22**	**23**	**24**	**25**	**26**	**27**	**28**	**29**	**30**
(*b*)	(*c*)	(*d*)	(*c*)	(*d*)	(*d*)	(*c*)	(*a*)	(*d*)	(*c*)
31	**32**	**33**	**34**	**35**	**36**	**37**	**38**	**39**	**40**
(*d*)	(*a*)	(*d*)	(*b*)	(*d*)	(*b*)	(*c*)	(*c*)	(*a*)	(*b*)
41	**42**	**43**	**44**	**45**	**46**	**47**	**48**	**49**	**50**
(*d*)	(*c*)	(*b*)	(*c*)	(*d*)	(*a*)	(*a*)	(*a*)	(*d*)	(*c*)
51	**52**	**53**	**54**	**55**	**56**	**57**	**58**	**59**	**60**
(*c*)	(*a*)	(*d*)	(*d*)	(*d*)	(*c*)	(*d*)	(*c*)	(*a*)	(*d*)
61	**62**	**63**	**64**	**65**	**66**	**67**	**68**	**69**	**70**
(*c*)	(*b*)	(*a*)	(*d*)	(*c*)	(*c*)	(*b*)	(*b*)	(*a*)	(*b*)
71	**72**	**73**	**74**	**75**	**76**	**77**	**78**	**79**	**80**
(*d*)	(*c*)	(*c*)	(*a*)	(*a*)	(*a*)	(*a*)	(*a*)	(*b*)	(*d*)
81	**82**	**83**	**84**	**85**	**86**	**87**	**88**	**89**	**90**
(*c*)	(*d*)	(*c*)	(*d*)	(*d*)	(*d*)	(*d*)	(*a*)	(*a*)	(*b*)
91	**92**	**93**	**94**	**95**	**96**	**97**	**98**	**99**	**100**
(*c*)	(*a*)	(*b*)	(*a*)	(*a*)	(*d*)	(*b*)	(*d*)	(*b*)	(*d*)
101	**102**	**103**	**104**	**105**	**106**	**107**	**108**	**109**	**110**
(*d*)	(*b*)	(*a*)	(*d*)	(*b*)	(*a*)	(*b*)	(*d*)	(*d*)	(*a*)
111	**112**	**113**	**114**	**115**	**116**	**117**	**118**	**119**	**120**
(*c*)	(*d*)	(*c*)	(*c*)	(*a*)	(*c*)	(*d*)	(*d*)	(*c*)	(*d*)
121	**122**	**123**	**124**	**125**					
(*a*)	(*b*)	(*a*)	(*a*)	(*b*)					

3

Epidemiology

Epidemiology is the basic science of preventive and social medicine. Although of ancient lineage, it made only slow progress up to the start of this century. Epidemiology has evolved rapidly during the past three decades.

Definition

Epidemiology has been defined by John M. last in 1988 as "The study of the distribution and determinants of health-related states or events in specified populations, and the application of this study to the control of health problems.

Aims of Epidemiology

According to the International Epidemiological Association (IEA), epidemiology has three main aims:

(a) to describe the distribution and magnitude of health and disease problems in human populations.

(b) to identify etiological factors (risk factors) in the pathogenesis of disease; and

(c) to provide the data essential to the planning, implementation and evaluation of services for the prevention, control and treatment of disease and to the setting up of priorities among those services.

In order to fulfil these aims, three rather different classes of epidemidogical studies may be mentioned: descriptive studies, analytical studies, and experimental or intervention studies.

The ultimate aim of epidemiology is to lead to effective action:

(a) to eliminate or reduce the health problem or its consequence; and

(b) to promote the health and well-being of society as a whole.

Uses of Epidemiology

While the study of disease distribution and causation remains centred to epidemiology; the techniques of epidemiology have a wider application covering many more important areas relating not only to disease but also health and health services. In more utilitarian terms, epidemiology has been defined as "a means of learning, or asking questions and getting answers that lead to further questions. In this context, Morris has identified seven distinct uses of epidemiology, five of which extend epidemiology beyond the search for causes of disease and bring it closer to day-to-day concerns of modern medicine. These are:

1. **To Study Historically the Rise and Fall of Disease in the Population:** *Winston Churchill said:* "The farther back you look, the farther forward you can see! The first use of epidemiology relates to this aspect, that is, study of the history of disease in human population. It is well known that the health and disease pattern in a community is never constant. There are fluctuations both ever short and along periods of time.
2. **Community Diagnosis :** One of the uses of epidemiology is community diagnosis. Community diagnosis generally refers to the identification and quantification of health problems in a community in terms of mortality and morbidity rates and ratios, and identification of their correlates for the purpose of defining those individuals or

groups at risk or those in need of health care. By quantification of health problems, we lay down priorities in disease control and prevention.

3. **Planning and Evaluation** : *Planning* is essential for a rational allocation of the limited resources. For example in developing countries, too many hospitals have been built and equipped without knowledge of the particular disease problems in the community. Epidemiologic information about the distribution of health problems over time and place provides the fundamental basis for planning and developing the needed health services and for assessing the impact of these services on the people's problems.

   Evaluation is an equally important concern of epidemiology. Any measures taken to control or prevent a disease must be followed by an evaluation to find out whether the measures undertaken are effective in reducing the frequency of the disease. Evaluation of a control method such as hepatitis vaccine requires more than the demonstration of its effectiveness in reducing disease frequency.

4. **Evaluation of Individual's Risks and Chances** : One of the important tasks of epidemiologists is to make a statement about the degree of risk in a population. Besides the incidence rate and specific rates which are measures of absolute risk, the epidemiologists calculate relative risk and attributable risk for a factor related to or believed to be a cause of the disease.

5. **Syndrome Identification** : Medical syndromes are identified by observing frequently associated findings in individual patients. It is worth recalling that, although approximately 3000 so-called syndromes are described in the contemporary paediatric literature, a primary defect is known only in about 20 per cent of these. Epidemiological investigation can be used to define and refine syndromes. By observation of groups such studies have been able to correct misconceptions concerning many disease syndromes.

6. **Completing the Natural History of Disease** : Epidemiology is concerned with the entire spectrum of disease in a population. The picture of disease constructed on the basis of hospital patients is quite different from that found in the community. The epidemiologists by studying disease patterns in the coummunity in relation to agent, host and environmental factors is in a better position to fill up the gaps in the natural history of disease than the clinician. For example an outstanding contribution by epidemiology to the natural history of atheresclerosis in the recognition that one third to two thirds of all deaths due to ischaemic heart disease are sudden, is occur in less than one hour. Hospital studies could never have come to this conclusion, for most victims do not reach the hospital.

7. **Searching for causes and risk factors:** Epidemiology, by relating disease to interpopulation differences and other attributes of the population examined, tries to identify the causes of disease. The contribution of epidemiology have been many in this regard.

8. **Infection:** When an agent of an Infectious disease enters the body of man or animal and multiplies there it is called infection.

9. **Parasite:** Micro organism or plant or an animal which lives inside or outside the body of a person or animal and gets its nourishment for them.

10. **Infestation:** When a parasite establishes in or on the body it is called infestation.

    Contamination: When infectious agent is present in non living matter like soil, water *etc.* it is called contaimination.

11. **Contagious Disease:** Disease which spread by direct contact (skin, sexual *etc.*)

12. **Communicable Diseases:** All diseases which spread between man and man, man and animal and also from environment (air, water *etc.*). It includes all these due to infection, infestation or contagion.

13. **Endemic Disease:** Diseases which are present continuously in the community and never disappear (typhoid, malaria *etc.*). e.g., goitre in hill station.

14. **Epidemic Diseases:** Disease occuring in a community or in an area spreading from a common source and occuring above the expected limit (expected limit is decided by previous records), an endemic may become epidemic if too many cases occur. If the disease is not expected at all even few cases will be an epidemic. e.g., Plague in Surat 1994.

15. **Pandemic Disease:** Disease spreading quickly from one country to another or when it starts at the same time in many countries.

16. **Sporadic Disease:** When a few scattered cases of a disease occur in an area it is called sporadic.

17. **Immunity:** If a person has good resistance of the body he does not get the disease even if he is infected. This is called immunity and the person is immune.

18. **Incubation Period:** The period between the entry of an agent in the body of host and the appearance of manifestation (signs and symptoms) of disease.

19. **Infective Period:** Period in which the diseased person or animal can spread the disease to others.

20. **Cellular Immunity:** White blood cells in blood and some cells in tissues have the power to destroy germs. Some lymphocytes in the blood also stimulate production of antibodies, cellular immunity plays a very important part in protecting the body against infection. Both humoral and cellular immunity are necessary for body defence against infection.

21. **Natural (*innate*) Immunity:** This is acquired under natural condition. It is present at the time of birth and remain throughout life without any change. Man does not suffer from many diseases of animal even if he comes in contact. Similarly animals do not suffer from many disease of man (cholera, measles *etc.*). These are examples of innate immunity.

22. **Acquired Immunity:** Acquired immunity is either active or passive. When the antibodies are produced in a person's own body it is called active immunity. When they are supplied to the body from outside (from mother or an animal or any other person) it is passive immunity. Horse is usually the animal from whose blood antibodies are taken out. Passive immunity are necessary if a person does not have antibodies in his blood and if they are urgently required. Sometimes the body fails to produce antibodies due to the failure of the immune system. The liquid part of the blood (serum) contains the antibodies and this can be prepared from the blood.

23. **Immunization (Vaccination):** This is an artificial way of creating immunity in a person. This is one of the greatest achievements of modern medicine. When an antigen is introduced in the body antibodies are produced. Germs or their toxins are antigen. If they are introduced in the body artificially which is called 'Vaccination' antibodies are produced.

24. **Prevention and Control of Communicable Disease:** Common broad principles of prevention and control of communicable diseases are described here. Particular measure for each disease are described under each disease because they will be different according to nature of the disease. These principles are:

    1. Notification
    2. Isolation

3. Quarantine
4. Desinfection
5. Immunization
6. General measures
7. Health education.

25. Chemical disinfectants are solid, liquid and gases.
    1. *Solids:* Lime (CaO), Bleaching powder ($CaOCl_2$)
    2. *Liquids:* Coal Tar group, Carbonic acid (Phenol)
    3. *Gases:* Formaldehyde, Ethylene oxide

OBJECTIVE QUESTIONS

1. First step in investigation of epidemic:
   (*a*) Find the source
   (*b*) Confirm diagnosis
   (*c*) Sanitation
   (*d*) Spot map
2. In fresh bleaching powder the chlorine availability is:
   (*a*) 20% (*b*) 30%
   (*c*) 33% (*d*) 40%
3. All of the following are *false* about bleaching powder except:
   (*a*) Contains 20% available chlorine
   (*b*) 20% solution used for disinfection of faeces
   (*c*) Unstable compound on storage
   (*d*) Not used for disinfection of faces and urine
4. Sharp instruments may be sterilized with:
   (*a*) Radiation
   (*b*) Lysol
   (*c*) Hot air
   (*d*) Any of the above
5. Which of the following is most powerful chemical disinfectant?
   (*a*) Phenol
   (*b*) Lysol
   (*c*) Dettol
   (*d*) Potassium permangnate
6. For disposable items, the best method for sterilization is:
   (*a*) Dry heat
   (*b*) Incineration
   (*c*) Gamma radiation
   (*d*) Boiling heat
7. According to WHO, all the following diseases require surveillance except:
   (*a*) Chickenpox
   (*b*) Yellow fever
   (*c*) Malaria
   (*d*) Rabies
8. Chemoprophylaxis is given in all except
   (*a*) Cholera
   (*b*) Plague
   (*c*) Measles
   (*d*) Meningococcal meningitis
9. Surveillance by WHO is not done for:
   (*a*) Polio
   (*b*) Malaria
   (*c*) Viral encephalitis
   (*d*) Relapsing fever
10. The target by which primary immunization is to be completed under the Universal Immunization Programme is:
    (*a*) 1 years (*b*) 2 years
    (*c*) 3 years (*d*) 5 years
11. Vaccine which is given at earliest:
    (*a*) BCG (*b*) OPV
    (*c*) MMR (*d*) DPT
    (*e*) DT
12. Following diseases require isolation to break transmission *except*:
    (*a*) Measles (*b*) Mumps
    (*c*) Chickenpox (*d*) Tetanus
13. In control of communicable diseases, the period of quarantine in respect of a disease is determined by:
    (*a*) Incubation period
    (*b*) Infectivity period
    (*c*) Duration of illness
    (*d*) Carrier state
14. Notifiable disease is:
    (*a*) *Varicella* (*b*) Cholera
    (*c*) Malaria (*d*) Influenza
15. The following diseases are under surveillance by WHO, *except*:
    (*a*) Relapsing fever

(b) Plague
(c) Malaria
(d) Tuberculosis

16. Ideal temperature for DPT storage:
(a) Room temperature
(b) 4 to 8°C
(c) 0 to –20°C
(d) None of the above

17. Measles vaccine is kept in refrigerator in:
(a) Chilled tray
(b) Freezer
(c) Tray below the freezer
(d) Shelves in the door

18. Live attenuated vaccines are all *except*:
(a) BCG (b) Salk
(c) Sabin (d) Measles

19. Which one of the following is not a live vaccine?
(a) OPV
(b) BCG
(c) Hib vaccine
(d) Try 21a against typhoid

20. Live attenuated vaccines are:
(a) OPV
(b) Hepatitis
(c) Japanese-B-encephalitis
(d) Chickenpox

21. Killed bacterial vaccine is:
(a) BCG (b) Diphtheria
(c) Pertussis (d) Toxoid

22. Live attenuated vaccine used in man is:
(a) Influenza
(b) BCG
(c) Yellow fever
(d) Japanese-B-encephalitis

23. Live vaccines are all except:
(a) Typhoid oral (b) Measles
(c) BCG (d) Pertussis

24. Match List-I with List-II and select the correct answer using the codes given below in the lists:

List-I
A. Tuberculosis B. Measles
C. Diphtheria D. Whooping cough

List-II
1. Toxoids
2. Killed bacteria
3. Live attenuated viruses
4. Live attenuated bacteria

Codes:

	A	B	C	D
(a)	4	3	2	1
(b)	3	4	2	1
(c)	3	4	1	2
(d)	2	3	4	1

25. All are live vaccines except:
(a) Measles (b) BCG
(c) OPV (d) Hepatitis B

26. Secondary attack rate reflects:
(a) Severity
(b) Communicability
(c) Fatality
(d) Infectivity

27. Which does *not* have latent infection?
(a) Smallpox (b) Chickenpox
(c) Mumps (d) Malaria

28. Incubation period is helpful for all except:
(a) Quarantine
(b) Source identification
(c) Preventive immunization
(d) Isolation

29. The period after entry of the organism to produce maximum infection known as:
(a) Incubation period
(b) Generation time
(c) Serial interval lead
(d) Lead time

30. Which is most difficult to block spread of?
(a) Vector (b) Man to man
(c) Airborne (d) Waterborne

31. The cycle of yellow fever virus in *Aedes* is:
(a) Propagative
(b) Cyclopropagative
(c) Cyclodevelopment
(d) Any of the above

32. Vertical transmission is by:
(a) Mosquitoes (b) Direct contact
(c) Droplet (d) Placenta

33. Transovarian transmission of diseases includes:
(a) Syphilis (b) AIDS
(c) KFD (d) *Rubella*

34. Carrier state is important in following *except*:
(*a*) Measles (*b*) Polio
(*c*) Cholera (*d*) Typhoid

35. Carriers are not an important source of transmission in the following disease:
(*a*) Diphtheria (*b*) Measles
(*c*) Typhoid (*d*) Poliomyelitis

36. Healthy carriers are found in all *except*:
(*a*) Cholera (*b*) Diptheria
(*c*) Typhoid (*d*) Pertussis

37. Diseases which are imported into a country in which they do not otherwise occur is:
(*a*) Exotic
(*b*) Epizootic
(*c*) Endemic
(*d*) None of the above

38. Disease imported to a country *not* otherwise present:
(*a*) Exotic (*b*) Enzootic
(*c*) Epizootic (*d*) Endemic

39. Anthropozoonosis are all *except*:
(*a*) Guinea worm infestation
(*b*) Rabies
(*c*) Plague
(*d*) Hydatid cyst

40. The best criteria to judge association causes relationship is:
(*a*) Strength of association
(*b*) Consistency
(*c*) Chronological sequence of event
(*d*) Specificity

41. Prevalance of disease in a community can be found out by:
(*a*) case control study
(*b*) cohort study
(*c*) cross-sectional study
(*d*) analytical study

42. Evaluation of new antihypertens drug, test of significance is:
(*a*) Chi-square test
(*b*) Fischer F. test
(*c*) Paired t-test
(*d*) Pooled

43. Best indicator to determine maximum benefit to the community through preventive intervention strategies is:
(*a*) Relative risk
(*b*) Attributable risk
(*c*) Absolute risk
(*d*) Odd's ratio

44. As a Health Inspector, treatment plan of action you should use:
(*a*) Relative risk
(*b*) Attributable risk
(*c*) Population attributable risk
(*d*) Odd's ratio

45. Best method to calculate the incidence rate is:
(*a*) Case control study
(*b*) Sentinel surveillance
(*c*) Cohort study
(*d*) Cross sectional prevalance study

46. If you desire to study the incidence of diarrhoea in a community which study method would you like to opt for:
(*a*) Cross-sectional study
(*b*) Cohort study
(*c*) Case control study
(*d*) Double blind placebo study

47. All true about cohort studies *except*:
(*a*) Prospective
(*b*) Useful for rare diseases
(*c*) Necessary for incidence
(*d*) Costly

48. Case control study most characteristic is:
(*a*) Odd's ratio estimation
(*b*) Problem bias
(*c*) Yields incidence rate
(*d*) Expensive

49. When launching a study many respondents are invited some of whom fail to come. This is called:
(*a*) Respnse bias (*b*) Volunteer bias
(*c*) Selection bias (*d*) Berkesonian bias

50. Case control study is used for:
(*a*) Finding a rare cause
(*b*) Finding multiple risk factors
(*c*) Finding incidence rate
(*d*) Finding morbidity

51. Calculate the Odd's ratio:

Diseased	***Undiseased***
Positive	30 – 20
Negative	20 – 30

(*a*) 0.44 (*b*) 1.5
(*c*) 0.8 (*d*) 2.25

52. In a village of 1 lakh population among 20,000 exposed to smoking, 200 developed cancer and among 40,000 people unexposed, 40 developed cancer. The relative risk of smoking in the development of cancer is:
(*a*) 20 (*b*) 10
(*c*) 5 (*d*) 15

53. Relative risk can be obtained from:
(*a*) Case study
(*b*) Cohort study
(*c*) Case control study
(*d*) Experimental study

54. Incidence among exposed and nonexposed is called:
(*a*) Relative risk (*b*) Attributable risk
(*c*) Odd's ratio (*d*) Attack ratio

55. Weighting is:
(*a*) Normal variable
(*b*) Discrete variable
(*c*) Confounding variable
(*d*) Continuous Variable

56. All are true about case control study *except*:
(*a*) It is cheaper than other studies
(*b*) It is useful to investigate a rare disease
(*c*) Odd's ratio can be detected from it
(*d*) Relative risk can be detected from it

57. The process of 'matching' allows:
(*a*) The matched variables to be evaluated
(*b*) For selecting the case and control group with the same known confounding variables
(*c*) Matching of factors in doubt
(*d*) One to avoid focussing on variables desired

58. All of the following are true regarding case control study *except*:
(*a*) Relative risk can be calculated
(*b*) Less expensive
(*c*) Suitable for rare disease
(*d*) Backward study

59. All are true about case control studies *except*:
(*a*) It is easy to conduct
(*b*) It is cheaper
(*c*) Can measure attributable risk
(*d*) Those with disease are matched with those without

60. The most useful study in a hospital setting is:
(*a*) Cross-sectional
(*b*) Longitudinal
(*c*) Cohort
(*d*) Case control

61. Residents of three villagers with three different types of water supply were asked to participate in a study to identify cholera carriers. Because several cholera deaths had occured in the recent past, virtually everyone occurred in the time submitted to examination. The proportion of carriers was in each village who were carriers was computed and compared, this study is a:
(*a*) cross-sectional study
(*b*) case-control study
(*c*) concurrent cohort study
(*d*) non-concurrent

62. *False* about point source epidemic is:
(*a*) Children are more affected
(*b*) Rapid rise and fall
(*c*) All cases occur in one incubation period
(*d*) No secondary waves

63. *Bhopal gas tragedy* is an example of:
(*a*) Slow epidemic
(*b*) Continuous epidemic
(*c*) Point source epidemic
(*d*) Propagated epidemic

64. *Chernobyl tragedy* is an example of:
(*a*) Point source epidemic
(*b*) Propagated epidemic
(*c*) Modern epidemic
(*d*) Continuous epidemic

65. The three major types of epidemics would include all except:
(*a*) Common source epidemics
(*b*) Periodic epidemics
(*c*) Propagated epidemics
(*d*) Slow epidemics

ANSWERS

1	2	3	4	5	6	7	8	9	10
(*b*)	(*c*)	(*c*)	(*d*)	(*b*)	(*c*)	(*c*)	(*c*)	(*c*)	(*a*)
11	**12**	**13**	**14**	**15**	**16**	**17**	**18**	**19**	**20**
(*a*)	(*d*)	(*a*)	(*b*)	(*d*)	(*b*)	(*b*)	(*c*)	(*a*)	(*a*)
21	**22**	**23**	**24**	**25**	**26**	**27**	**28**	**29**	**30**
(*c*)	(*a*)	(*d*)	(*a*)	(*d*)	(*b*)	(*a*)	(*d*)	(*b*)	(*c*)
31	**32**	**33**	**34**	**35**	**36**	**37**	**38**	**39**	**40**
(*a*)	(*d*)	(*c*)	(*a*)	(*b*)	(*d*)	(*a*)	(*b*)	(*a*)	(*c*)
41	**42**	**43**	**44**	**45**	**46**	**47**	**48**	**49**	**50**
(*a*)	(*c*)	(*b*)	(*c*)	(*c*)	(*b*)	(*b*)	(*a*)	(*b*)	(*b*)
51	**52**	**53**	**54**	**55**	**56**	**57**	**58**	**59**	**60**
(*d*)	(*b*)	(*b*)	(*a*)	(*d*)	(*d*)	(*c*)	(*b*)	(*c*)	(*d*)
61	**62**	**63**	**64**	**65**					
(*a*)	(*a*)	(*c*)	(*a*)	(*b*)					

Parasitology & Entomology

Parasitology

The science that deals with the study of parasites is known as *parasitology*.

1. **Protozoa:** First animal unicellular organism with nucleus and cytoplasm. They causes diseases.
   1. Intestines—*Entamoeba histolytica, Giardia lamblia.*
   2. Mouth, vagina urethra - *Trichomonas Naginalo's.*
   3. Blood: malaria *Trypanosoma, Leishmania.*

   E. histolytica is a natural parasite with world wide distribution. It exists into two forms, vegetative or trophozoites, these forms are formed in the body.

   Cysts: Resistant from infectious form. Cysts are resistant to gastric juice get excysted in intestine and trophozoities are liberated. These trophozoites (pathogenic phase) penetrate mucosa and submucosa carried by blood to liver and sometimes to lung and brain.

   Giardia: It has trophozoite and cystic stages. It localizes in upper part of small intestine and causes pain in abdomen and diarrhoea.

   Trichomonas: *Trichomonas* (Hominis) in intestine vaginalis in vagina and urethra. Trophozoite is infective and man is the only host.

   Malaria Parasite: There are four types of malaria parasites: *Plasmodium vivax, P. falciparum, P. malaria, P. ovale* is not found in India. *P. vivax* is very common (70%).

   Leishmania: It cannot be differentiated morphologically culturally or by animal inoculation. Life cycle is completed in two hosts. Leishmania stage which alone is seen in man and leptomonad which is seen in insects or culture media. Insect is sandfly. It causes the disease kala azar.
   - *L. donovani* causes visceral leishmaniasis (Kalaazar)
   - *L. tropica* causes oriental sore.
   - *L. toroziliensis* causes mucocutaneous leishmaniasis.

2. **Hookworm:** (*Ancylostoma duodenale*) It is a blood feeding parasite, attached to small intestinal wall with hook changes occur in larvae and 3rd stage larvae are infective. Treatment consists of supportive diet iron supplement, Bephenium hydroxynaphthoate (alcopor) and Mebendazole.
3. **Round Worm:** (*Ascaris lumbricoidese*) It is a commonest of all human helminths and transmitted easily if standard of personal hygiene is very low. After piercing small intestine, via venules and lymphatics it comes to right heart and thereafter to lungs. It comes to glottis and swallowed in oesophagus and passed forward to stomach and small intestine where it matures further into adult.
4. **Thread Worm:** *(Enterobius vermicularis)*: Also called as Ring worm or oxyuris. The mode of transfer from perianal area to mouth is through fingers underneath nail, food contaminated by fingers or undergarment. Eggs once swallowed hatch in small intestines, and then enter caecum and mature. Person complains of perianal

itching (sleep may be disturbed because of this). Prevention consists of avoiding auto infection but improving personal hygiene cutting nails short, biting of nails is forbidden. Drugs effective are piperazine citrate and пprinium embonate.

5. **Filarial Worm:** Adult female live in human tissue and continuously produce elongated active microfilariae. These are picked up by certain mosquitoes (*culex* and *mansonoid*) where it grows into the infective form. Next blood meal of suck mosquito would deliever these parasites to other human host. *Wuchereria boncrafti* is most widely distributed. Next comes *Brugia malayi*, presence of large number of microfilaries in blood is a periodic phenomenon and it depends upon the biting adopted by the specific mosquito.

6. **Hydatid disease:** caused by Echinococus granulosus. Adults live in the small intestine of dogs, eggs are passed in faeces of dog. They are swallowed by men because of fonding of dog or because of close relations with dog.

   Gradually embryos develop into cysts which attain more and more diameter. In man it becomes a dead end infectious. However in case of sheep if dog eats cyst containing raw flesh or if such dead animal the life cycle can continue in the dog.

General Measures of Control and Prevention of Parasite Infection

These measures may be anyone of control of source of infection, control of transmission, control over entry into a human host *etc.* Control measures can be applied to different levels of life cycle. Application of two or more measures at one time is more beneficial than single control measure.

1. Reducing the possibility of new infections in the community (Attack *on human host*): Drug treatment for parasite, which will kill ova, eggs, which transmitted through faeces or microfilaria circulating in blood will be reduced (possibility of mosquito infestation will be reduced).
2. Attack on the host other than human beings: Attack on mosquito distribution or removal of breeding place such as Larvicide, Adulticide, Protection against bites. Control over the Dogs (killing or therapy) and rats.
3. Environmental sanitation measures:
   (i) Safe water supply and proper disposal of sewage and other waste.
   (ii) Slaughter house and meat inspection for control of hydatid, beef tape worm.
4. Protection of human host: Improved personal hygiene protective clothing and shoes hook worm and strongyloid control.
5. Food hygiene and proper cooking: Fish tape worm beef and park tape worm.

Entomology

Medical entomology includes scientific research on the behaviour, ecology, and epidemiology of arthropod disease vectors, and involves a tremendous outreach to the public, including local and state officials and other stake holders in the interest of public safety.

Vector: An insect helping in transmitting disease agent from diseased person to healthy one is called a vector.

Modes of disease transmission

(i) Mechanical: This type of transmission is mainly seen in houseflies physical contamination of mouth parts, body hairs. It occurs when it flies from faeces to food to be used by human being.

(ii) Biological transmission.

Types of hosts infection

1. *Definitive host:* The host which harbours the sexually matured forms of a disease agent is called a definitive host *e.g.*, mosquito for malaria parasite.
2. *Intermediate host:* The host harbouring sexually immature forms of the disease agent is called an intermediate host *e.g.*, man in malaria.

Important diseases and their vectors

1. **Dengue fever** - Vectors: Aedes aegypti (main vector) Aedes albopictus (minor vector) threatens -50 million people are infected by dengue annually, 25,000 die. Threatens 2.5 billion people in more than 100 countries.
2. **Malaria** - Vectors: Anopheles mosquitoes - 500 million become severely ill with malaria every year and more than 1 million die.
3. **Leishmaniasis** - Vectors: species in the genus Lutzomyia in the New World and Phlebotomus in the Old World. Two million people infected.
4. **Bubonic plague** - Principle vector: Xenopsylla cheopis At least 100 flea species can transmit plague. Re-emerging major threat several thousand human cases per year.High pathogenicity and rapid spread.
5. **Sleeping sickness** - Vector: Tsetse fly, not all species. Sleeping sickness threatens millions of people in 36 countries of sub-Saharan Africa
6. **Typhus** - Vectors: mites, fleas and body lice 16 million cases a year, resulting in 600,000 deaths annually.
7. **Wuchereria bancrofti** - most common vectors: the mosquito species: Culex, Anopheles, Mansonia, and Aedes; affects over 120 million people.
8. **Yellow Fever** - Principle vectors: Aedes simpsoni, A. africanus, and A. aegypti in Africa, species in Haemagogus genus in South America, and species in Sabethes genus in France -200,000 estimated cases of yellow fever (with 30,000 deaths) per year.
9. **Japanese encephalitis** - Several mosquito vectors, the most important being Culex tritaeniorhynchus.
10. **Chagas disease** - Vector: assassin bugs of the subfamily Triatominae. The major vectors are species in the genera Triatoma, Rhodnius, and Panstrongylus.
11. **Chikungunya** - Vectors: Aedes mosquitoes

MOSQUITOES

Four important types of mosquito are: *Anopheles*, *culex*, *Aedes* and *Mansonoids*. There are four stages of development in each mosquito. All mosquitoes breed on surface of water and egg, larva, pupa and the adult are their stages of life cycle.

Diseases Transmitted by Mosquitoes

(i) *Anopheles* - Malaria
(ii) *Culex* - Filariasis, certain viral encephalitis
(iii) *Aedes* - Dengue, chikengunya fever, yellow fever
(iv) *Mansonoids* - Filariasis

Control of Mosquitoes:

(i) Environmental control:-
a. Control of breeding places
b. Anti larval measure: using insecticides like fenthion, abate *etc.*
(ii) Anti adult measures: DDT, gammaxane
a. Biological control
b. Genetic control
c. Health education to people

HOUSEFLIES

It does not bite but transmits the disease agent mechanically from dirt to food.

Disease Transmitted by Houseflies

It takes nourishment from human excreta, respiratory tracts secretion and discharge of wounds and sputum. It exhibits equal preference to food to be consumed by man. Therefore contaminated food consumption leads to various diarrhoea and dysentry disorders, typhoid, paratyphoid, cholera and gastroenteritis. It also helps transmitting such infection as conjunctivitis, trechoma, tuberculosis *etc.*

Control of Housefly

1. Environmental control
2. Using insecticides
3. Fly papers

RAT FLEAS

Following disease is caused by rat flea

(i) Bubonic plague
(ii) Endemic typhus

Control of fleas:

(i) Insecticides
(ii) Use of repellents
(iii) Control of rats

CYCLOPS

It has a body, a tail and two pairs of antannae (one short, other long) size about 1mm just visible to naked eye.

Medical importance

Intermediate host of guinea worm (*Dracontiasis*) infestation and fish tape worm, water containing cyclops when drunk causes infection.

Control of Cyclops

1. Environmental control: Removal of steps from step wells construction of sanitary wells.
2. Physical methods
3. Chemical methods
4. Biological methods
5. Health education

DDT (Dichlorodiphenyltrichloroethane)

It is a white powder. It is practically insoluble in water. It is a contact poison, absorbed through the surfaces of legs and body. It causes the paralysis of locomotion of legs and wings.

BHC (Benzene hexachloride)

It is a white crystalline substance with musty odour. In pure form the drug is called as lindane which is a fine white odourless powder. It acts in similar way as DDT but action is much faster and can also kill by vaporisation. It is spread in a pouch of 50 mg per sq foot. Residual insecticide action can last for 3-5 months.

Malathion

Malathion and diazinon are two least toxic compounds to men. It is a clear liquid with yellowish brown colour. It has a unpleasant smell, powder from it can be given in sugar bait for housefly control.

Pyrethrum

Extract from dried heads of the flowers of Crysanthesmum plant is known as pyrethrum. *Pyrethrim* I and II are active component of pyrethrum. The compound is very unstable. It needs frequent application for controlling the insects as it has no residual action. The most important advantage of this insecticide is the 'knock down' effect on the insect immediately after spray.

SOME IMPORTANT PARASITES

1. Entamoeba histolytica

Entamoeba histolytica is a pathogenic Protozoa which causes the amoebic dysentery in man. Mainly it is found in the large intestine of man spread to the brain, liver and lungs. The disease caused by it is known as amoebiasis. It is world wide in distribution but abundantly found in tropical regions. The adult and harmful stage of Entamoeba is called trophozoite. It feeds upon debris of tissue and R.B.C.

Structure: It is microscopic acellular animalcule. Its active trophic form measures 25-30 in diameter while the smaller less active form measures 8- to 12- in diameter. It is similar to the Amoeba in structure. Generally it possesses a single pseudopodium.

Life Cycle: The life cycle to *Entamoeba histolytica* is completed in a single host so it is known as monogenetic. Transmission from one host to another takes place during encysted form through contaminated vegetables, water and food or by flies and cockroaches etc. An acute infection causes dysentry but chronic cases may pass infectious cysts in the faeces.

Reproduction: It reproduces by binary fission and encystment.

(i) *Binary fission:* In binary fission nucleus undergoes mitosis and nuclear division is followed by cell-body. In this way two daughter cells are formed which grow rapidly in size. Fully matured form penetrates the mucous lining of the intestine causing ulcers and bleeding ulcers.

(ii) *Encystment:* During encystment these are liberated into the lumen of colon from the ulcers. These are less active and become small and ulcers. These are less active and become small and rounded. They secrete a thin resistant colourless and transparent cyst wall around themselves. It contains reserve food in the form of diffused glycogen granules and 2-4 bar like chromatoid bodies. Ingested R.B.C. disappear. The cyst is protective in nature. Now nucleus divides into two and further division result into four daughter nuclei. This is known as quadrinucleated stage.

Cystic Stage: The mature tetranucleate cysts come out with the faeces of the host. The stored glycogen is used as food in this stage. These cysts are destroyed in unfavourable conditions *e.g.*, high temperature. At low temperature, these cyst can survive upto one and half months. The freshly laid cysts are green and refractile and appear as shining spheres. These cyst may easily be identified during pathological test. (Immature cyst is binucleated.

Transmission: The cysts may enter the body of new hosts through the contaminated vegetables, water and food. After reaching the intestine of host the cyst is broken down due to action of digestive juices or enzymes. The metacystic stage (only one) comes out from the cyst which gives rise to eight young Entamoebae after nuclear and cytoplasmic division. At the time of hatching four nuclei are present.

These young Entamoebae develop to change into adult trophozoites which secrete proteinous enzyme capable to dissolve the mucous membrane of intestine and ulcers are formed. In this way new infection is set and parasite causes the amoebic dysentry. They may digest the R.B.C. and blood from capillaries which is mixed with mucous causing bleeding with faeces.

Treatment: In primary infection Yeast and Enterovioform tablets are recommended with Sulphogonodine. The other medicines such as compound of Arsenic and Iodine are Neoysept, Diodoquin, Furamide *etc.* In secondary infection some percentage Arsenic and Iodine increase in compounds. Chronic and acute cases are treated with Emetin tablets, injections, *etc.*

Prevention: One should follow the principle of hygiene. Water, vegetables and food should be protected from infection.

2. Fasciola hepatica

Fasciola hepatica, commonly known as liver fluke is an endoparasite of sheep which resides in the liver and bile duct. It is world wide distributed. It causes liver rot disease in sheep.

Structure: It is flattened leaf like having somewhat oval shape. The size varies from 4-6 cms, colour of the body is slightly pinkish with brown margins.

The anterior end of the body possesses a minute circular mouth surrounded by an oral or anterior sucker. Posterior or ventral sucker lies just after the oral sucker on the ventral surface. In between the two suckers lies a genital pore, At the extreme posterior, the aperture of Laurer's canal is also developed.

Life Cycle: The liver fluke is hermaphrodite i.e. male and female reproductive organs are present in the same individual. It completes its life cycle in two hosts. The primary host is sheep or cattle while secondary host is a snail. Thus the cycle is digenetic.

Copulation: Although it is hermaphrodite but cross fertilization takes place. The cirrus of one is inserted into the opening of Laurer's canal of other. The sperms pass into the laurer's canal and finally reach to the oviduct.

Fertilization: The fertilization takes place with the help of sperms and ova in the oviduct.

Eggs: Fertilized eggs are surrounded by yolk and shell in the ootype. The shape of the egg is like a capsule having lid or operculum. The eggs pass through uterus and reach in the intestine of the host.

Cleavage: The cleavage starts in the uterus. The first cleavage is complete but unequal producing small granular propagatory cell and a large somatic cell. The somatic cell gives rise to the ectoderm of larva after division. Remaining propagatory cell divides to give rise to two types of cell:

(i) *Group of somatic cells:* These are responsible for the formation of body structure of embryo.

(ii) *Group of germ cells:* They lie in the posterior part of the larval body and responsible for the formation of new larval stage after development.

Within two weeks a ciliated larva is formed which is known as miracidium. It comes out and swims in the water.

Miracidium larva: It is conical in shape having large number of cilia all over the body. Cilia help in swimming in the water. Towards the anterior end a small apical papilla is present. In the apical region multinucleated apical gland and unicellular penetrating glands are present which open outside through the papilla.

Infection to the secondary host (Lymnaea): The larva is very active and swims freely in the water. If it finds its secondary host, the water snail, Lymnaea or Planorbis within a day, it bores, the pulmonary sac with the help of the papilla and the secretion of penetrating glands, otherwise it dies. Here cilia are lost and it develops into a new larval stage, the sporocyst.

Sporocyst: It is a sac like structure covered by cuticle. The cilia and epidermal cells are lost. Eyes spot, brain glands etc. degenerate. The subepithilial cells, muscles, and mesenchyme are as such and germ balls and protonephridia are present.

The germ balls produce daughter sporocysts which again produce third type of larva the redia.

Redia: It is an elongated sac like larva which comes out by rupturing cyst and migrates to liver or digestive gland of the snail. A small mouth is present at the anterior end. There is an aperature in the side wall near the collar which is known as birth pore.

Cercaria: It is a heart shaped larva with tail which resembles with the adult fluke in appearance. Its body is covered by thin cuticle. The rudiments of most of the adult organs are present. There is a mouth surrounded by oral sucker. Ventral sucker or posterior sucker or acetabullum is present on the ventral side. Pharynx is suctorial and intestine is bifid. Paired excretory ducts with flame cells and genital rudiments are present. Cystogenous cells is the characteristic feature of it which are responsible for the formation of cyst.

Metacercaria: It is similar to cercaria but tail and cystogenous cells are absent, Cyst is present around it. Flame cells have increased in number and excretory bladder opens out side by an aperture.

Infection to new host: Further development of metacercaria can only take place if it is swallowed by the main host, the sheep within few weeks. With the help of water plants or vegetation the cercariae reach in the intestine of sheep. The cyst is dissolved by the action of digestive juices and young fluke emerges which bores the intestinal wall. After 2 or 3 weeks they infect the liver and may enter in the bile duct for development to change into the adult forms.

3. Ascaris

Habit and Habitat: *Ascaris lumbricoides* is a common parasite found in the large intestine of man. It is world wide in distribution. The number of worms may be 500 or more in a single host.

Life Cycle: The life cycle of *Ascaris* is monogenetic *i.e.*, complete in one host only.

Copulation and Fertilization: The copulation in *Ascaris* takes place inside the host. The sperms of male which are Amoeboid are passed into the vagina of female and finally fertilize the eggs in oviduct or upper part of uterus (proximal part of uterus). The fertilized egg is surrounded by chitinous egg shell and a layer of albumen.

Infection: Embryonated or infective eggs (with 2nd stage larva) transfer through contaminated food, drinks and raw vegetables and taken by the host. The duodenal secretions stimulate the larva which comes out of egg shell. It contains nerve ring and alimentary canal.

Primary Migration of Larva: It first enters the host-intestine by penetration and reaches the liver through portal system or lymph channels. After a few days it reaches into the postcaval vein and then to the heart. From the heart through pulmonary artery, it reaches into the lung. Here it settles down in capillaries of alveoli for some time and undergoes two moultings one after the other. It increases in size measuring 1 to 2.1 mm in length. After third moulting it again starts its migration.

Secondary Migration of Larva: Larva comes into the air passages and then into the pharynx from alveoli. Here it causes coughing by irritation of the pharyngeal wall. Either it is swallowed again into the intestine with coughing or spitted out. Inside the intestine it moults for the last time (4th moulting) and assumes the adult form after development.

Economic Importance

1. Larvae cause the inflammation in the lungs. Sometimes symptoms of pneumonia, fever, anaemia eosinophilia may also appear.
2. The mature forms may cause abdominal pain, diarrhoea, headache etc, In huge quantity they may block the intestine.
3. Presence of the parasite causes abdominal pain and intestinal ulcers.
4. The parasites often cause toxic effects such as vomitting, allergies, urticaria and may cause loss of sight.

Prevention: Infection may be checked by taking preventive measures:

1. Raw vegetables, leaves, fruits and roots should be thoroughly washed and properly cooked.
2. The use of contaminated water and food should be avoided.
3. Sanitation should be proper.
4. Extra nails should be cut off from the fingers.
5. Before taking meal hands should be cleaned properly.
6. Children should not play in the dirty places.

4. Wuchereria Bancrofti (filarial worm)

Habit and Habitat: *Wuchereria bancrofti* lives in the lymphatic vessels and lymph nodes of man. The life cycle is completed in two hosts so it is a digenetic nematode. It is found in the tropical and sub-tropical countries.

Life Cycle: It is a digenetic nematode having following host:

1. Primary host-man
2. Secondary host-mosquito (Culex)

1. *Life cycle in Primary host (Man) :* The adult worm (female) gives rise to microfilariae larvae. They are surrounded by a delicate sheath. Microfilariae appear in peripheral blood circulation during night while during day they disappear. They are active and can move with and against the blood stream. Each is a colourless cylindrical form with tapering head. The body contains granules which are arranged along the central axis.
   Further development of microfilariae takes place only in the intermediate host, when they are sucked by mosquito.
2. *Life cycle in Secondary host (Mosquito):* The microfilariae are collected in the anterior part of stomach from where after casting their sheath they migrate to the thoracic muscles. Inside the muscles these increase in length. They change into thick short forms and represent first stage larvae having rudimentary canal. The second stage larvae are formed within three to six days as larvae grow rapidly, moult once and

attain a size of 212m - 325m. Metamorphosis takes place after about 102 hours. The tail is lost and development of digestive system, body cavity and genital organs takes place to change into third stage larvae measuring 1200m to 2000m in length and 15m-20m in breadth. The larvae migrate into the mouth parts of the mosquito.

Infection in Man: When the infected mosquito which is the carrier of the disease bites a man, numerous microfilariae are injected into the blood or deposited on the skin near the wound. Now larvae reach the lymphatic channels and settle down at some point and finally change into adults after metamorphosis. Near about in one year the adult form become sexually mature to reproduce new larval forms.

The parasite causes filarial fever, mental depression, headache *etc.* In case of heavy infections larval forms or adult forms block the lymph channels or vessels. Thickening of the lymphatic vessels takes place by the proliferation of endothelial cells. The lymph which cannot get back into circulatory system accumulates in the organs and causes them to swell to fantastic proportions. Generally liver, spleen, scrutum, vulva, legs and groins become greatly enlarged. This is commonly known as elephantiasis or filariasis. The disease may be eliminated by giving the compound of Antimony and Arsenic *e.g.*, Mel W, Hetrazon Msb. To control the infection preventive measures should be followed *viz.* destruction of mosquito, protection against mosquito bites *etc.*

OBJECTIVE QUESTIONS

1. The active or trophic forms of *Entamoeba histolytica* feed upon:
   (*a*) Blood
   (*b*) Food in the intestine
   (*c*) Mucosa and submucosa of colon
   (*d*) Erythrocytes, mucosa and submucosa of colon
2. In malarial infection, lysolecithin that destroys the RBCs is secreted by:
   (*a*) Spleen (*b*) WBCs
   (*c*) Liver (*d*) Plasmodium
3. If Amoeba is kept in distilled water its contractile vacuole:
   (*a*) Works slowly
   (*b*) Works faster
   (*c*) Remain as such
   (*d*) Disappear
4. Sir Ronald Ross discovered that:
   (*a*) Malaria is caused by foul air
   (*b*) Malaria is transmitted by *Anopheles*
   (*c*) Four species of *Plasmodium* cause malaria
   (*d*) Malaria is caused by protozoan
5. Cyst formation in Amoeba:
   (*a*) Occurs in adverse conditions
   (*b*) Does not occur
   (*c*) Follows sexual union
   (*d*) Preceeds sexual union
6. For prevention against amoebiasis, we should:
   (*a*) Eat more food
   (*b*) Use mosquito net
   (*c*) Drink boiled water
   (*d*) All
7. Golgi cycle is found in:
   (*a*) W.B.C. (*b*) R.B.C.
   (*c*) Liver cells (*d*) Stomach
8. Which is the locomotary organ of class suctoria:
   (*a*) Pseudopodia (*b*) Flagellum
   (*c*) Cilia (*d*) Tentacles
9. Zygote of which one is motile?
   (*a*) Hydra (*b*) Plasmodium
   (*c*) Ascaris (*d*) Pheretima
10. Quartan malaria is caused by *Plasmodium*:
    (*a*) Ovale (*b*) Falciparum
    (*c*) Malariae (*d*) Vivax

11. One of the following is Polymorphic:
(*a*) *Taenia solium* (*b*) *Trypanosoma*
(*c*) *Paramecium* (*d*) *Entamoeba*

12. In which form would you find chromatoid bodies in *Entamoeba histolytica*?
(*a*) In minuta (*b*) In mature cyst
(*c*) In trophozoite (*d*) None

13. The duration of erythrocytic cycle in *Plasmodium vivax* is:
(*a*) 48 hours (*b*) 24 hours
(*c*) Irregular (*d*) 72 hours

14. The infection stage of malarial parasite for human is
(*a*) Sporozoite (*b*) Leishmania
(*c*) Trypanosoma (*d*) Plasmodium

15. Paramecium contains:
(*a*) Two micronuclei
(*b*) One or more micronuclei
(*c*) Two macronuclei
(*d*) One micro and more macronuclei

16. Plasmodium vivax belongs to the class:
(*a*) Telesporea (*b*) Sarcodina
(*c*) Mastigophora (*d*) Ciliata

17. Malaria is an "Insect borne disease", was established by:
(*a*) Laveran (*b*) Golgi
(*c*) Sir Ronald Ross (*d*) Grassi

18. Reduction division of gametocytes in Plasmodium takes place:
(*a*) In the blood of man
(*b*) In the stomach of mosquito
(*c*) In the haemocoel of mosquito
(*d*) None of the above

19. Which of the following is a matching pair of the vector and the disease?
(*a*) Anopheles-malaria
(*b*) House fly - Yellow fever
(*c*) Body louse - Typhoid
(*d*) Sand fly - Plauge

20. The mode of nutrition in the free living Amoeba proteus is:
(*a*) Holophytic (*b*) Saprozoic
(*c*) Holozoic (*d*) Parasitic

21. Toxic malarial pigment is known as:
(*a*) Haematin (*b*) Globulin
(*c*) Proteolysin (*d*) Haemozoin

22. Infection of one of the following may reach lung, liver and brain.
(*a*) *Trypanosoma gambiense*
(*b*) *Entamoeba histolytica*
(*c*) *Plasmodium vivax*
(*d*) All the above

23. The technical name of pin worm or seat worm is
(*a*) *Trichinella* (*b*) *Ancylostoma*
(*c*) *Enterobius* (*d*) *Wuchereria*

24. Elephantiasis in man is caused by
(*a*) *Dracunculus* (Guinea worm)
(*b*) *Ancylostoma* (Hook worm)
(*c*) *Enterobius* (Pin worm)
(*d*) *Microfilairae* (Filaria worm)

25. Chenopodium oil is successfully used for expulsion of
(*a*) Tape worm (*b*) Liver fluke
(*c*) Flat worms (*d*) Round worm

26. Which one of the following has no intermediate host?
(*a*) Tape worm (*b*) Liver fluke
(*c*) Round worm (*d*) Plasmodium

27. In *Ascaris*, the 2nd moulting of larva takes place in
(*a*) Pharynx (*b*) Oesophagus
(*c*) Alveoli (*d*) Intestine

28. In *Ascaris*, the last moulting of larva takes place in
(*a*) Liver of man (*b*) Lungs of man
(*c*) Heart of man (*d*) Intestine of man

29. In Ascaris only the anterior part of the testis is functionable. Such a gonad is known as
(*a*) Monorchic (*b*) Didelphic
(*c*) Telogonia (*d*) Metagoni

30. The amphids are cuticular elevations of the ventro-lateral lips of Ascaris. These are
(*a*) Chemoreceptors (*b*) Olfactoreceptors
(*c*) Tactoreceptors (*d*) Gastoreceptors

31. Rhabditiform larva occurs in the life history of
(*a*) Round worm (*b*) Liver fluke
(*c*) Earthworm (*d*) Tape worm

32. Nematodes are called as
(*a*) Round worms
(*b*) Flat worm
(*c*) Blind worms
(*d*) Tubiculous worms

33. Ascaris lumbricoides completes its migration in man from intestine in about
(*a*) 10-14 days (*b*) 50-60 days
(*c*) 30-34 weeks (*d*) 1-2 years

34. The female Ascaris can be distinguished from the male by
(*a*) Curved posterior part
(*b*) Straight posterior part
(*c*) Pineal setae
(*d*) Shorter in size

35. Inner layer of Shelled egg of Ascaris is
(*a*) Proteinous (*b*) Lipoid
(*c*) Both (*d*) None

36. Infection of *Ascaris* is more in
(*a*) man (*b*) woman
(*c*) oldman (*d*) children

37. Cleavage in Ascaris
(*a*) Spiral & determinate
(*b*) Holoblastic
(*c*) Meroblastic
(*d*) All

38. One of the following is viviparous
(*a*) Filaria (*b*) Ascaris
(*c*) Fasciola (*d*) Taenia

39. Sense organs of Ascaris are
(*a*) Epidermal cords
(*b*) Spicules
(*c*) Papillae and amphids
(*d*) Circumcentric ring

40. Infection of *Ascaris* usually occur by
(*a*) Mosquito bite
(*b*) Tse tse fly
(*c*) Imperfectly cooked pork
(*d*) Contaminated water and vegetables

41. In *Ascaris*, the mode of formation of ova is
(*a*) Telogonic (*b*) Budding
(*c*) Hypergonic (*d*) Diphylefic

42. Elephantiasis disease is transmitted by
(*a*) Sand fly (*b*) Fruit fly
(*c*) House fly (*d*) Mosquito

43. The infective stage in the life cycle of Ascaris is
(*a*) Fertilized egg (*b*) Cyst
(*c*) Secondary larva (*d*) Tertiany larva

44. Filarial larvae are found in:
(*a*) Spleen septa of man
(*b*) Liver capsule of man
(*c*) Wall of Intestine of man
(*d*) Blood of man

45. Intermediate host of wuchereria is
(*a*) Culex (*b*) Anopheles
(*c*) House fly (*d*) Tse Tse fly

46. Parasitic *Amoeba* with single pseudopodium
(*a*) *Amoeba proteus*
(*b*) *Amoeba pilasa*
(*c*) *Amoeba verrucosa*
(*d*) *Entamoeba*

47. Euglena reproduce
(*a*) Asexually
(*b*) Sexually
(*c*) Both asexually and sexually
(*d*) Conjugation

48. Schuffmner's dots are found in life cycle of *Plasmodium* in
(*a*) R.B.C. of man
(*b*) Liver cells of man
(*c*) Gamete formation in mosquito
(*d*) All of above

49. Schizogony in *Plasmodium* takes place in
(*a*) R.B.C. of man
(*b*) Lumen of stomach of mosquito
(*c*) Liver of Man
(*d*) Liver or R.B.C. of Man

50. Asexual reproduction is most common among protozoans because:
(*a*) Sexes not well differentiated in them.
(*b*) They can multiply fast

(*c*) It has nutritional importance
(*d*) Many of them live as parasites

51. The excretion in *Entamoeba histolytica* takes place by:
(*a*) Contractile vacuoles
(*b*) General surface
(*c*) Food vacuoles
(*d*) None

52. Zygote of which one is motile?
(*a*) *Hydra*
(*b*) *Plasmodium*
(*c*) *Ascaris*
(*d*) *Pheretima*

53. Reduction division of gametocytes in Plasmodium takes place:
(*a*) In the blood of man
(*b*) In the stomach of mosquito
(*c*) In the haemocoel of mosquito
(*d*) None of the above

54. In life cycle of malarial parasite, the sporozoites are stored in
(*a*) Liver of man
(*b*) Blood of man
(*c*) Stomach of female Anopheles
(*d*) Salivary glands of female Anopheles

55. Sol & Gel theory was advocated by:
(*a*) Dobell
(*b*) Hyman
(*c*) Dellinger
(*d*) Mast & Pantin

56. "Sleeping sickness" is due to the bite of:
(*a*) Sand fly
(*b*) Tse-Tse Fly
(*c*) Bed Bug
(*d*) White fly

57. During binary fission Amoeba divides by:
(*a*) Amitotis (*b*) Mitotis
(*c*) Meiosis (*d*) None

ANSWERS

1	**2**	**3**	**4**	**5**	**6**	**7**	**8**	**9**	**10**
(*d*)	(*a*)	(*a*)	(*b*)	(*a*)	(*d*)	(*d*)	(*b*)	(*c*)	(*c*)
11	**12**	**13**	**14**	**15**	**16**	**17**	**18**	**19**	**20**
(*b*)	(*b*)	(*a*)	(*a*)	(*b*)	(*a*)	(*a*)	(*b*)	(*a*)	(*c*)
21	**22**	**23**	**24**	**25**	**26**	**27**	**28**	**29**	**30**
(*d*)	(*b*)	(*c*)	(*d*)	(*d*)	(*c*)	(*c*)	(*d*)	(*c*)	(*a*)
31	**32**	**33**	**34**	**35**	**36**	**37**	**38**	**39**	**40**
(*a*)	(*a*)	(*a*)	(*b*)	(*b*)	(*d*)	(*a*)	(*a*)	(*c*)	(*d*)
41	**42**	**43**	**44**	**45**	**46**	**47**	**48**	**49**	**50**
(a)	(d)	(c)	(d)	(a)	(d)	(a)	(a)	(d)	(b)
51	**52**	**53**	**54**	**55**	**56**	**57**			
(*b*)	(*b*)	(*d*)	(*d*)	(*d*)	(*b*)	(*b*)			

5

First Aid and Behavioural Sciences

1. **Artificial Respiration of Resuscitation:** If a person has ceased to breath then immediately place him on his back, and press the top of head backwards so as to extend the head. Pull the chin forward to make a clear airway. If patient is still not breathing, perform mouth to mouth resuscitation immediately to saves lives.

   To do this open your mouth and take a deep breath. Close the patient's nostrils with yours fingers and then seal his mouth with your lips (keeping the head held back all the time). Blow into the patient's mouth until the chest rises, then remove your mouth and watch his chest deflate. Repeat this operation as long as is necessary at normal breath rate but give the first four blows as rapidly as possible.

2. **Bleeding:** Direct pressure on an open, clean wound will usually control the bleeding. This can be done by pressure by the fingers or hand, but if readily available use a sterile dressing with an adequate pad, and bandage firmly in position. A tourniquet should never be used.

3. **Burns:** If a limb is affected, immerse the part immediately in cold water to relieve the pain. Then cover the part (including any burned clothing) with a dry sterile dressing or freshy laundered material such as tea cloth. If burns are severe, treat for shock and get medical aid as quickly as possible. Do not use ointment or oil dressings.

4. **Choking:** This is usually caused by food or some foreign body, getting into the wind pipe and can often be cured by getting the patient to bend over and then thumping with the flat of the hand between the shoulder blades. A small child can be held upside down and thumped. If this does not work tickle the back of the throat with the finger tips in an attempt to make the patient cough or vomit. If neither method succeeds get medical help at once.

5. **Electric Shock:** If the patient is still in contact with electrical equipment and you cannot switch off the electricity, do not touch him unless protected by rubber roles or rubber gloves. Apply artificial respiration and treat for burns and shock as necessary.

6. **Poisoning:** If some one is thought to have swallowed poison, send for medical help at once, even if no effect have appeared have the poison container ready to show the doctor, corrosive acid or alkaline poison such as oceosote, ammonia, caustic soda, strong carbolic and oxalic and other acids will all burns or stain the lips and mouth. Give water at once but not an emetic.

   If the poison is known to be an acid such as oxalic, nitric or sulphuric acid, rinse the mouth with an alkali such as magnesia, chalk and water, whiting and water or even plaster from the ceiling. If the poison is an alkali such as ammonia or caustic soda, give an acid drink such as vinegar or lemon juice in water. Slow pulse, pallor, sleepiness and in some cases, pin point pupils are symptoms of an overdose of narcotics such as sleeping tablets. Give emetic and try to keep patient awake. For gas poisoning, give the patient fresh air, artificial respiration and warmth and send for doctor.

7. **Shock:** Serious burns or injury always cause shock. The patient is pale, his skins cold clammy, his breathing quick and irregular and his pulse fast. He should be lying down with head low and hips and legs raised a little, keep him warm and if he is conscious, give him a warm sweet drink but no stimulants. Keep him quiet and reassure him, shock can also occur after quite minor accidents.

8. **Foreign Bodies in the Eye:** Lifting the upper eyelid over the lower will often bring the foreign body on the lower lid from which it can be removed or making the eyes water by rubbing the other eye or blowing the nose will sometimes help. If the object is clearly visible the torn and moisturised edge of a piece of soft paper can be used to remove it. Never use tweezers and never rub the injured eye. If the object appears to be embedded in the eyeball leave it for the doctor to remove.

9. **Emetics:** If the poison taken is known to be corrosive, acid or alkaline or if there is any burning or staining of the mouth an emetics is dangerous and should not be given. For other poison give two tablespoonfuls of salt or a half tablespoonsful of mustard, in a half pint of water.

Mental Health and Drug Dependence

Mental health is an important component of health of a person. It is a balanced interaction of individual personality and emotions which help him to live happily with the society.

1. **Neuroses or Psychoneuroses:** Patient is not able to react normally to life situation. These are most common forms of psychiatric illness observed in practice. These are:

   (a) Anxiety (b) Hysteria (c) Obsession (d) Depression and Phobias

2. **Mental Handicap:** Mental subnormality is an impairment of intellectual function from birth or early age.

   Broadly it has two categories:

   (i) Mild mental retardation (I.Q. 50-70) this level is below normal (I.Q. 85 to 115) the child can be benefited by special training.

   (ii) Severe mental retardation (I.Q 49 or below) they cannot lead normal life and always require supervisons, support.

   Causes of mental retardation:

   1. Down syndrome (Mongolism)
   2. Hypothyroidism (cretins)
   3. Birth injury
   4. Infections of brain

   Warning signs of poor mental health

   1. Always worrying
   2. Inability to concentrate
   3. Losing temper easily and often
   4. Loss of sleep
   5. Wide fluctuation of mood
   6. Not happy in the company of people
   7. Phobia present (fear)
   8. Aches and pains without cause

Drug Dependence

It is the state of psychological and physical dependence on a drug with tendency to increase dose of drug *e.g.*, Heroin, morphine, L.S.D. addiction means physical dependence.

Depressants: Barbiturates, Mandrax, Heroin

Stimultants: cocaine, Amphetamine

Mood elevator (Psychedelics) Hashish, charas, Ganja

Treatment of Drug Addicts

The treatment is more successful if:

1. Person is taking less dose and only one drug.
2. Newly addicted and highly motivated addict.

3. No other stress or problem is present.
4. Good family cooperation is available.

Behavioural Sciences

1. **Family:** It is basic and most universal unit of society. Family is considered as basic unit in all health programmes and role of family in health and disease as follows:
    1. Child rearing
    2. Personality formation
    3. Socialisation
    4. Care of dependents
    5. Help in facing stress in every walk of life
    6. Genetic susceptibility to disease like haemophilia, overcrowding in family to communicable disease
2. **Role of Model Social Worker:**
    1. To assist doctor.
    2. To help patient.
    3. Guiding family members how to nurse the patient.
    4. Help in securing financial assistance from social welfare agencies.
    5. Directing community for getting better health facilities
3. **Relation of Behavioural Sciences to Medicine:** Understanding of these sciences helps health workers to add more information about causes of some diseases. For scientific treatment of patient knowledge of customs, habits, level of education, economic status, relation with members of family is necessary.
4. **Personal hygiene:** Personal hygiene is the science of preserving and promoting health mainly through individual effort. Three main points are to be observed in personal hygiene.

I. *Temperature*:
1. Eating Nutrition: The diet should be adequate and balanced.
2. Personal comfort
3. Basic emotional needs
4. Clothing and shoes
5. Exercise and rest

II. Cleanliness of Body, Hair, Skin, Ears, Eyes, Nose, Teeth, Nails, Hands and feet.

Pharmacology

1. *Pharmacology* is the science which deals with sources, actions of drugs in disease and on health of living organism. A drug is defined as any substance used for diagnosis, cure or prevention of disease.
2. **Analgesics:** are drugs which decreases or eliminate pain *e.g.*, aspirin, morphine.
3. **Antiseptics and Disinfectants:** Drugs used for killing micro organisms or used to prevent growth of micro organisms on surface of body or in the environment or in articles used.
4. **Antibiotics:** Drugs are taken internally or applied locally to kill micro-organism.
5. **Anthelmintics:** They kill worm or make them loose so they do not get attached to body (piperazine, Mebendozole)
6. **Laxatives or Purgatives:** Drugs used for emptying (evacuating) bowels *e.g.*, milk of magnesia, castor oil.
7. **Expectorants:** (cough mixtures) Assist in coughing up of sputum and thereby relieve pain.
8. **Tonics:** Which are given to the patient with idea to strengthen the body and supplement deficiency of food.
9. **Forms of Drugs:** Whether drug is for internal and external use or local application. Normally used forms are:
    1. Pills, tablets, capsules, spansules (Internally).
    2. Ointment pastes, creams or jellies (externally).
    3. Liquid-mixtures (taken internally), Lotions, liniments (externally) suspension and emulsion both internally as well as externally.
    4. Injectable - powder with distilled water, liquids in ampoules and vials.
       Ampoule - usually single
       vial - single or multidose

5. Powders.
6. Enema preparation suppository per rectum.

9. Routes for administration of drugs:

Routes for Administration of Drugs

- Entral (through mouth)
  - Oral
    - Subligual
    - Swallowing tablets
- Parential (without mouth)
  - Intradermal
  - Subcutanous
  - Intra muscular
  - Intra venous
  - Intra articular

10. Major characterstic of drugs:

1. *Therapeutic effect*: This is the ability to act selectively on the part of body or disease producing agents and restore normal function.
2. *Side effects*: In addition to useful effect drug may also produce undesirable effect (oral pills cause nausea, vomitting).
3. *Allergic effect*: unexpected reaction *e.g.*, aspirin may cause asthma *etc*.

11. Habituation: There is tendency to take drug and increase dose *e.g.* smoking cigarettes psychological dependence is present.

12. Addiction: Tendency to increase dose of drug and physical and psychological dependence on effect of drug. When a person is addicted he tries to get drug by any mean and if patient does not get drug, withdrawal symptoms are produced, examples Heroin, Marphine L.S.D., Bhang, Ganja, Charas *etc*.

6

Maternal & Child Health

Maternal and Child Health

The term "maternal and child health" refers to the promotive, preventive, curative and rehabilative health care for mothers and children. It includes the sub-areas of maternal health, child health, family planning school health, handicapped children, adolescence, and health aspects of care of children in special settings such as day care.

The specific objectives of MCH are: (a) reducing of maternal, prenatal, infant and childhood mortality and morbidity; (b) promotion of reproductive health; and (c) promotion of the physical and psychologist development of the child and adolescent within the family. The ultimate objective of MCH services is life-long health.

Antenatal Care

Antenatal care is the care of the women during pregnancy. Ideally this care should being soon after conception and continue throughout pregnancy. In some countries notification of pregnancy is required to bring the mother in the preventive care cycle as early as possible.

Objectives:

The objectives of antenatal care are:

1. To promote protect and maintain the health of the mother during pregnancy.
2. To detect "high risk" cases and give them special attention.
3. To foresee complications and prevent them.
4. To remove anxiety and dread associated with delivery
5. To reduce maternal and infant mortality and morbidity.
6. To teach the mother elements of child care, nutrition, personal hygiene, and environmental sanitation.
7. To sensitise the mother to the need for family planning including advice to cases seeking medical termination of pregnancy.

Intranatal Care

Child birth is a normal physiological process, but complications may rise. Septicaemia may result from unskilled and septic manipulations, and tetanus neonatorum from the use of unsterilized instruments. The need for effective intranantal care is therefore indispensable, even if the delivery is going to be a normal one. The emphasis is on the cleanliness.

The aims of good intranatal care are:

i) thorough asepsis
ii) delivery with minimum injury to the infant and the mother.
iii) readiness to deal with complications such as prolonged labour, anterpartum haemorrhage, convulsions, malpresentations, prolapse of the cord *etc.*
iv) care of the body at delivery resuscitation, care of the cord, care of the eyes *etc.*

Postnatal Care

Care of the mother (and the newborn) after delivery is known as postnatal or post partal care. Broadly this care falls into two areas: care of the mother which is primarily the responsibility of the obstetrician and care of the newborn, which is combined responsibility of the obstetrician and paediatrician. This combined area of responsibility is also known as perinatology.

Care of the Mother "Under Five Clinic"

The objectives of postpartal care are:

1. To prevent complication of the postpartal period.
2. To provide care for the rapid restoration of the mother to optimum health.
3. To check adequency of breast feeding
4. To provide family planning services.
5. To provide basic health education to mother.

Care of Children

The section focuses on children in the age group 0-14 years. This is the most important age group in all societies, not because they constitute about 40 per cent of the total population but because there is a renewed awareness that the determinants of chronic disease in later life and health behaviour are laid down at this stage. The childhood period is also a vital period because of the so called socialization process, that is, transmission of attitudes customs and behaviour.

It is customary to divide the childhood into the following age-periods:

1. Infancy (up to 1 year of age)
   (a) Neonatal period (first 28 days of life)
   (b) Post neonatal period (28th day to 1 year)
2. Pre-school age (1-4 years)
3. School age (5-14 years)

Delivering the MCH Services

MCH (mother and child health) is not a new speciality. It is a method of delivering health care to special group in the population which is especially vulnerable to disease, disability or death. These groups (*i.e.*, chidren under the age 5 years and women in the reproductive age group (15-44 years) comprise about 31.6 per cent of the total population in India (75).

The MCH services encompass the curative, preventive and social aspects of obstetrics, paediatrics, family welfare, nutrition, child development and health education. The specific objectives of MCH are:

1. reduction of morbidity rates for mothers and children
2. promotion of reproductive health, and
3. promotion of the physical and psychological development of the child within the family.

Through concern with child development and the health education of parents and children, the ultimate objective of MCH services is life-long health.

Child Health Problems

- Low birth weight
- Malnutrition
- Behavioural Problems

Recent Trends in MCH Care

Maternal and child care was traditionally designed and provided in the form of vertical programmes with "standard" technical content based on models from a few developed countries. Applied in different socioeconomic situations, such vertical programmes have been unable to provide more than minimum coverage because of their cost, and unable to solve the priority problems of the majority of mothers and children.

These are as follows:—

1. *Integration of care:* Conventional MCH services tended to be fragmented into antenatal care, postnatal care, infant care, family planning etc.
2. *Risk approach:* A new and promising means of improving the coverage and efficiency of MCH care and family planning is the risk use of scarce resources. It is based on the early detection of mothers and children with high risk factors.
   It is also possible to assess the "degrees" of risk of each factor, by scoring according to their (a) magnitude *i.e.*, extent and severity; (b) treatability-responsiveness to treatment and control; (c) cost effect in terms of alleviating human suffering; and (d) community attitude - social concern.
3. *Manpower changes:* The special category of "maternal and child health worker" (*e.g.*, auxiliary - nurse - midwives, health visitors) at the peripheral level is gradually being phased out. A wide range of workers are now considered necessary for maternal and child health works. It includes:

(i) Professionals: Specialists

(ii) Field workers: Multipurpose workers, Health Guides, dais (traditional birth attendants), balsevikas, anganwadi, workers, extention workers, *etc.*

iii) Voluntary workers: Members of women's organizations

4. *Primary health care:* Primary health care is now recognized as a way of making essential health care available to all. It has all the elements necessary to make a positive impact on the health of mothers and children - *i.e.*, MCH care, family planning, control of infections, education about health problems and how to prevent them, and measures to ensure nutritious food- all closely related. Primary health care emphasizes family oriented care and support, and community self reliance in health matters.

MATERNAL AND CHILD HEALTH

1. **Maternal and Child Health:** MCH includes all matters pertaining to health (physical, mental, social), of women throughout reproductive cycle (15-45 years) and children of all ages from conception to adolescence. It also includes special health services needed by handicapped children.
2. **MCH Problems:** Advanced countries are having problems of mortality, congenital malformation, genetic and certain behavioural problems. In developing countries the problems are maternal mortality and morbidity, child mortality and morbidity, spacing of pregnancies, limitation of family size, preventation of communicable disease, improvement of nourishment to prevent malnutrition from prenatal period to the period of weaning. Infection of mother may cause low birth weight, abortion, puerperal sepsis. Baby may get infection with labour, delievery and weaning period. Diarrhoea respiratory infections, skin infection, tuberculosis and malaria are common ailments. Diphtheria, whooping cough tetanus, measles, polio can also occur.
3. **Antenatal care:** The basic aim is that every pregnancy should end with healthy baby and healthy mother.
   1. To promote, protect and maintain the health of the mother during pregnancy
   2. To detect complications and treat them
   3. To detect high risk cases and manage them.
4. **Prenatal advice:** Mother is most receptive at this time for advice.
   Prenatal advice for:
   1. *Diet*: Full average diet is indicated along with extra protein (20gml/day)
   2. Personal hygiene is necessary for following:
   3. Personal cleanliness daily bath, wearing of clean clothes.
5. **Child care:** Mothercraft education consists of nutrition education, childrearing, cooking, family planning education, family budgeting is taught. Fear of Pregnancy is Removed. Specific protection is given.
   1. *For anaemia*: Iron and folic acid tablets 60 mg + 500 mg from 2nd trimester. given routinely to every expectant mother.
   2. Nutritional supplements are given at MCH centres and at ICDS projects.
   3. *Tetanus*: 2 injections are given of tetanus toxoids.
   4. *Syphilis*: routine VDRL is done, if positive it is adequately treated.
   5. Rh status: If Rh negative mother and Rh positive baby.
6. **Care of New Born:** (Neonatal care)
   Immediate care:
   1. *Maintenance of respiration*: All secretion and contents from mouth and nose should be cleaned. The baby must breathe and cry. Keep the baby upside down for 1-2 minutes, use suction machine if necessary.

2. *Care of Umbical Cord*: Tie the cord when pulsation stop by two ligature and then cut it clean and dress use aseptic precautions.
3. *Care of Eyes*: Clean the eye with sterile swab and put 1%. terramycine or silvernitrate drops.
4. *Care of Skin*: Apply oil and give a bath, observe whether baby is breathless, not passing stools, persistent vomitting, convulsions report to the doctor.

7. Organisation of MCH Services:
Organisation in rural areas:
1. Primary health centre through 3 tier system of health care delivery (PHC, Subcentre and village level)
2. Private Practitioners
3. ICDS
4. Cottage hospitals
5. certain welfare centres.

8. MCH Services in Urban Areas:
Responsibility is with local bodies and provision of MCH service is at the discretion of local bodies:
Maternity hospitals are run by local bodies with full time doctor, Ayas, nurses, honorary doctors *etc*.
Some of these are run by state government, some by central government and some by voluntary agencies and local bodies.

9. Juvenile Delinquency: A delinquent child is defined as who has comitted an offence *e.g.*, theft, sexual assult, murder, burglary etc., Child means a boy less than 18 years and girls less than 16 years of age. Delinquent truly means any abnormal behaviour which results in antisocial practices. These are managed by improvement in family life, proper schooling, giving recreational facilities and child guidance cinics.

10. Laws Utilized for Welfare of Women and Children:
1. *Age of Marriage*: of a girl from 15 years raised to 18 years.
   This will improve literacy, fertility will be low and the girl will be more mature.
2. *MTP Act 1971*: Helps in maintaing health of mother and also getting rid of an unwanted child.
3. *Hindu Adoption Act of 1956*: gives women a pleasure of becoming mother by law particularly for infertile women.
4. Factory Act provides a creche for 30 working women in industry for their children upto 5 years of age.
5. *Maternity Benefit Acts*: (According ESIS, government, semi government) 90 days paid leave for delivery and 42 days leave for MTP or abortion is given so as to restore health.
6. *Suppression of Immoral Traffic Act (1956)*: Help women and girls to get rehabilitated socially from becoming prostitutes by punishing brothel keepers.

11. Laws Related to Children:
1. Children Act (1960): Provides the care, maintenance welfare, training, education and rehabilitation of delinquent children. It covers the neglected, destitute, socially handicapped, uncontrollable, victimized and delinquent children.
2. Factory Act: Children should not carry heavy load, they should not be given night shift. If at all they are to be kept as employees, their fitness should be certified by certified surgeons.

12. Infant Mortality Rate: Defined as the number of infant deaths per 1000 live births in a year. This is considered as most sensitive index of health and level of living of the people.

13. Demography: The study of population is known as Demography. Demography has been defined as the statistical study of the characteristic of human population with reference to size, growth, distribution, migration, vital statistics and the effects of all these on social and economic conditions.

14. Factors reducing birth are:
1. High divorce rate
2. Ban on remarriages of widows and divorcees.

3. High standard of living
4. Prolonged breast feeding
5. Popularity of abortion
6. Acceptance of family planning habit.

15. Factors Affecting Mortality: Reducing death rate

1. Absence of natural checks–famine, epidemics
2. Mass control of diseases–small pox, plague, cholera, malaria *etc.*
3. Advance in Medical Sciences–drugs, insecticides *etc.*
4. Better health care—Primary health centres etc.
5. National Health Programme.

16. Scope of Family Welfare:

1. *Before marriage:* Sex education, parent—craft education, Premarital and genetic counselling (advice before marriage and on genetic matters)
2. *After marriage*: Supply of contraceptives, Sterilization.
3. *Fertile couples*: MTP, screening for disease of genital tract, Parent craft and genetic counselling.
4. *Infertile couples:* Investigation and treatment of sterility, Artificial Insemination, Adoption.

17. Family Planning Methods are:

1. *Abstinence:* Means intercourse is avoided. This can not be considered as a method of contraceptives, it is difficult to bring into practice.
2. *Coitus interruptus*: In this method male partner withdraws penis so that ejaculation occurs outside the vagina. It is suspected that some get mental disturbance due to this. Failure rate is 15-20 pregnancy per 1100 women year.
3. *Rhythm method*: (Safe period) for those who will not adopt any other method of family planning because of religious or other reasons, the rhythm method is advised.

18. Cervical Cap: Widely used in Europe, also in our country in the past. It is a small bell shaped device, of rubber or metal that fits directly around cervix. A small quantity of spermicide can be applied. The cap can be kept in the position till next menses. This is better for elongated cervix. Initial examination by doctor is necessary. It should be checked before use.

19. Intrauterine Contraceptive Device: (I.U.C.D): In this method control of conception is by introducing a foreign body into uterus.

Lippe's Loop: It is made up of polyetheylene. It is monotaxic. It consists of loop itself, the inserter, plunger, the guards and threads. It is double 'S' shaped. It contains small amount of barium sulphate for gray visualisation. The loop has attached threads made up of fine neylon which protrude into vagina.

Advantages of loop:

1. No hospitalization, no complex procedure for insertion. It takes only 2 minutes for insertion.
2. It does not affect coitus.
3. It can be removed when pregnancy is desired.
4. It can be kept in place for 2-3 days.

20. Copper T : Second generation I.U.C.D. This is a small T shaped radioopaque, polyethylene device. Around its vertical arm is encircled a fine copper wire of area 200 mm from lower end of vertical arm 2 long strings project.

Sterilization: It is not necessary as it is available in sterilized pack. Copper T is introduced into uterus with the help of inserter which consists of a hollow tube and solid plunger. The copper T is straightened in the inserter and is pushed by plunger in uterine cavity with due precaution of asepsis, the thread should be in the vagina as in case of loop.

Mechanism of action: Copper from Copper T releases minute of copper which has spermicidal action and along with polyethelene T the action of implantation of fertilized ovum does not occur.

Copper T is effective for 3 years, hence should be replaced after 3 years

21. **Injectable Pills MPA:** (Medroxy Progesterone acetate) is given intramuscularly every 3 months 150 mg or 6 months 300 mg. This is safe, effective and acceptable.

    Advantages : Highly effective method for irregular patient and minimum motivation is required, it does not affect lactation. It is costly has low failure rate (less than 1/000 women year).

22. **Tubectomy:** is done by
    (*a*) abdominal route, minilap (small incision)
    (*b*) vaginal route
    (*c*) laparoscopic route

    Time of operation
    1. after delivery or abortion
    2. in between deliveries

23. **Sterilization (Male Sterlity):** This is an operation done on men and consists incutting and ligating the two ends of vas deferens that carry spermatozoa from testis. After operation fertilization of women's ova is not possible and pregnancy is prevented.

    Advantages
    1. It does not require hospitalization.
    2. Does not interfere with sexual desire or intercourse.
    3. It does not reduce the capacity for physical or mental work.

24. **Birth Control Method:** They are used when pregnancy is suspected or confirmed.
    1. Menstrual regulation
    2. Abortion (Termination of pregnancy)

25. **Medical Termination of Pregnancy Act, 1971**

    Indication of MTP
    1. *Medical:* In this continuation of pregnancy can prove dangerous to mother.
    2. *Tygemic:* Risk of baby born will be with congenital malformations (abnormal development)
    3. *Humanitarian:* Pregnancy due to rape.
    4. *Failure of contraceptives:* Methods have not been mentioned in the act therefore any method can be considered. Written consent of guardian is necessary if abortion is to be performed in a woman less than 18 years and in lunatics.

OBJECTIVE QUESTIONS

1. Breast milk compared to cow's milk has:
   (*a*) More calories
   (*b*) More fat
   (*c*) More lactose
   (*d*) More proteins
2. Milk is deficient in:
   (*a*) Ca (*b*) Vitamin A
   (*c*) Vitamin D (*d*) Fe
3. One of the following is 'biologically complete food:
   (*a*) Groundnut (*b*) Wheat
   (*c*) Soya bean (*d*) Milk
4. Protein in human milk is:
   (*a*) 1.3 gm (*b*) 2.3 gm
   (*c*) 3.3 gm (*d*) 4.5 gm
5. Highest amount of protein is seen in:
   (*a*) Soya beans
   (*b*) Groundnut
   (*c*) Bengal gram
   (*d*) Mysore Dal
6. When an abandoned child is legally accepted by a couple, it is called as:
   (*a*) Remand home placement and foster home placement
   (*b*) Remand home placement and Borstal placement
   (*c*) Adoption and foster home placement
   (*d*) Adoption and remand home placement
7. A 14 year old boy having lost his father a year ago, is caught shoplifting. The boy will be sent to:

(*a*) An orphanage
(*b*) An anganwadi
(*c*) A prison
(*d*) A remand home

8. Presence of the following substance reveals the fact of postcontamination of water:
(*a*) Chlorides (*b*) Nitrates
(*c*) Sulphates (*d*) Nitrites

9. Mental retardation is defined if IQ is below:
(*a*) 90 (*b*) 80
(*c*) 70 (*d*) 60

10. The approximate number of mentally retarded persons in India is around:
(*a*) 4-8 millions (*b*) 1-15 millions
(*c*) 15-20 millions (*d*) 20-25 millions

11. Per capita space for students in a classroom should not be less than ——— sq. feet:
(*a*) 5 (*b*) 10
(*c*) 20 (*d*) 50

12. Ideal desk recommended for a school child is:
(*a*) Minus desk (*b*) Plus desk
(*c*) Zero desk (*d*) Any of the above

13. In school health services the most important functionary should be:
(*a*) School teacher (*b*) Health worker
(*c*) Medical officer (*d*) Health assistant

14. Which country had introduced school health services for the first time?
(*a*) France
(*b*) Russia
(*c*) United States of America
(*d*) India

15. The School Health Programmes came into vogue in:
(*a*) 1946 (*b*) 1948
(*c*) 1950 (*d*) 1960

16. IMR upto:
(*a*) Less than 1 year
(*b*) Equal to 1 year
(*c*) up to 1 year
(*d*) More than 1 year

17. Commonest cause of neonatal mortality in India is:
(*a*) Diarrhoeal diseases
(*b*) Birth injuries
(*c*) Low birth weight
(*d*) Congenital anomalies

18. Postnatal (early) death rate mainly depends upon:
(*a*) Environmental factors
(*b*) Antenatal care
(*c*) Events during birth
(*d*) Events during early neonatal period

19. Which state has the lowest infant mortality rate:
(*a*) Kerala (*b*) Tamil Nadu
(*c*) West Bengal (*d*) Madhya Pradesh

20. Infantile death is taken only below:
(*a*) 7 days (*b*) 1 months
(*c*) 1 year (*d*) 2 years

21. Neonatal mortality in proportion of IMR is:
(*a*) 65-75% (*b*) 50-60%
(*c*) 35-45% (*d*) 25-35%

22. The numerator used to define neonatal death rate is:
(*a*) All infants below one year of age
(*b*) Infants between 1 to 12 months
(*c*) Infant below 1 week of age
(*d*) Infants below 28 days of age

23. Stillbirth rate includes babies dead after
(*a*) 20 weeks (*b*) 24 weeks
(*c*) 28 weeks (*d*) 32 weeks

24. Denominator of preinatal mortality is:
(*a*) Live birth
(*b*) Stillbirth
(*c*) Live and stillbirth
(*d*) Live birth minus stillbirth

25. In the calculation of IMR which is the time period considered?
(*a*) 7 days (*b*) 28 days
(*c*) Before 1 year (*d*) 1-5 years

26. The commonest cause of maternal mortality in India is:
(*a*) Anaemia (*b*) Haemorrhage
(*c*) Abortion (*d*) Sepsis

27. Most rare cause of maternal mortality is:
(*a*) Abortion (*b*) Anaemia
(*c*) Toxaemia (*d*) Haemorrhage

28. Most common indirect cause of maternal mortality in India:
(*a*) Infection (*b*) Anaemia
(*c*) Heart disease (*d*) Accidents

29. All are common causes of maternal mortality in India except:
(*a*) Anaemia (*b*) Haemorrhage
(*c*) Toxaemia (*d*) Diabetes

30. In India, all are direct causes of maternal mortality except:
(*a*) Cardiac disease (*b*) Eclampsia
(*c*) Haemorrhage (*d*) Abortion

31. Denominator of maternal mortality rate is:
(*a*) Total number of female deaths
(*b*) Total number of live births
(*c*) 1000 live births
(*d*) 1000 female deaths

32. In a population of 10,000 with birth rate 36 per 1,000 and 5 maternal deaths, the MMR is:
(*a*) 14.5 (*b*) 13.8
(*c*) 20 (*d*) 5

33. All of the following are leading obstetrical causes of maternal mortality in India except:
(*a*) Severe anaemia
(*b*) Toxaemia of pregnancy
(*c*) Vascular accidents
(*d*) Abortions

34. Emergency gland of blood is:
(*a*) Thymus (*b*) Testis
(*c*) Adrenal (*d*) Pituitary

35. All of the following are causes of postneonatal death in India except:
(*a*) Tetanus
(*b*) Respiratory infection
(*c*) Diarrhoea
(*d*) Malnutrition

36. English disease is a term used for:
(*a*) Chaga's disease
(*b*) Rheumatoid arthritis
(*c*) Chronic bronchitis
(*d*) Bronchiectasis

37. MCH care is assessed by:
(*a*) Death rate
(*b*) Birth rate
(*c*) Maternal-mortality rate
(*d*) Anemia in mother

38. Which is not true about growth chart used in India:
(*a*) There are 3 curves
(*b*) Top most curve corresponds to 50th percentile of Harvard
(*c*) Second curve corresponds to 80% of that standard
(*d*) Children with normal weight fall above the line

39. Growth is monitored by:
(*a*) Height
(*b*) Weight
(*c*) Growth chart
(*d*) Anthrabiometric measurement
(*e*) Mid-arm circumference

40. Road to health card has 2 reference points, which are:
(*a*) 30th percentile for boys and 3rd percentile for girls
(*b*) 50th percentile for boys and 3rd percentile for girls
(*c*) 50th percentile for boys and 5th percentile for girls
(*d*) 80th percentile for boys and 10th percentile for girls

41. The average birth weight in India is:
(*a*) 2.5 kg (*b*) 2.8 kg
(*c*) 3.00 kg (*d*) 3.2 kg

42. "Road to health card" line is
(*a*) 3rd percentile (*b*) 50th percentile
(*c*) 80th percentile (*d*) 97 percentile

43. Which is true about road to health card?
(*a*) 4 lines are present
(*b*) Top line rep. 50% of percentile
(*c*) Child between 1st and 2nd line is normal
(*d*) Lowest line corres to 70% of std.

44. Following is different between human and cow milk:
(*a*) Proteins and fat
(*b*) Proteins and sugar
(*c*) Proteins and lactose
(*d*) Minerals

45. A healthy mother with a healthy child should start artificial feeding by:
(*a*) 3 months (*b*) 5-6 months
(*c*) 1 year (*d*) 1-5 years

46. Perinatal mortality rate in India is:
(*a*) Late fetal death (stillbirth) + death under 1 week

(*b*) Late fetal death (stillbirth) + death under 2 weeks
(*c*) Late fetal and early neonatal death weighing over 1000 gm at birth
(*d*) Late fetal and early neonatal death weighing over 1500 gm at birth

47. Small-for-date babies are prevented by:
(*a*) Spacing of baby
(*b*) Antenatal care
(*c*) Nutritional supplement
(*d*) Immunisation

48. Low birth weight means a weight of less than:
(*a*) 2.8 kg (*b*) 2.7 kg
(*c*) 2.5 kg (*d*) 2.3 kg

49. The number of hormones secreted by anterior pituitary is:
(*a*) 3 (*b*) 4
(*c*) 6 (*d*) 8

50. The disease caused by hyposecretion of thyroxine is
(*a*) Goitre
(*b*) Cretinism
(*c*) Acromegaly
(*d*) Addision's disease

ANSWERS

1	2	3	4	5	6	7	8	9	10
(*c*)	(*d*)	(*d*)	(*a*)	(*a*)	(*c*)	(*d*)	(*b*)	(*c*)	(*c*)
11	**12**	**13**	**14**	**15**	**16**	**17**	**18**	**19**	**20**
(*b*)	(*a*)	(*a*)	(*d*)	(*d*)	(*a*)	(*c*)	(*a*)	(*a*)	(*c*)
21	**22**	**23**	**24**	**25**	**26**	**27**	**28**	**29**	**30**
(*b*)	(*d*)	(*c*)	(*a*)	(*c*)	(*b*)	(*a*)	(*d*)	(*d*)	(*a*)
31	**32**	**33**	**34**	**35**	**36**	**37**	**38**	**39**	**40**
(*b*)	(*b*)	(*c*)	(*c*)	(*a*)	(*c*)	(*c*)	(*a*)	(*c*)	(*b*)
41	**42**	**43**	**44**	**45**	**46**	**47**	**48**	**49**	**50**
(*b*)	(*b*)	(*a*)	(*c*)	(*b*)	(*a*)	(*a*)	(*c*)	(*c*)	(*b*)

7

Basic Physiology

1. **Anatomy** describes the internal structures of the different part of the body. *Physiology* describes the functions of the different structures of the body.
2. **Cell:** A cell is a unit of living matter. It has a cell membrane and the living matter called protoplasm. The protoplasm has a denser part called nucleus and a lighter part called cytoplasm. The nucleus controls the activities of the cell.
3. **Amoeboid Movement:** Some type of cells can move. They have no cell wall. They are amoeba cells, white blood cell *etc*. At first such cell puts out a projection and then the whole protoplasm flows in that direction. Such movement is called amoeboid movement.
4. **Phagocytosis:** The process of engulfing solid particles is phagocytosis. In the cells, exchange of food and gases occur by a process known as osmosis. Selective osmosis occurs frequently.
5. **Tissue:** A tissue is a group of similar type of cells bound together *i.e.*, tissue of skin, tissue of bone, tissue of muscle *etc*.
6. **Organ:** An organ is a group of tissues, which can carry out some special type of work. Heart is an organ which pumps the blood, an artery is an organ which carries blood to different parts of the body, eye is an organ of sight *etc*.
7. **System:** A system is a group of organs carrying out some special type of work.
8. **The Bony System:** The bony or the skeletal system forms the frame work of the body. There are 206 bones in our body. The bones are joined together by fibrous capsules with thickend bands called ligaments. In some cases bones are fused together and do not have any movement. The skull, sacrum, pelvis etc. are of this type.

Functions of the Bones

(i) Bones give shape and firmness to the body.

(ii) They protect the delicate organs and soft parts of the body.

(iii) They give attachment to the muscles so that the muscles contract. The bones move about the joint.

(iv) The bones manufacture red blood cells and some white blood cells.

(a) The skull consists of a large hollow cavity called the cranial cavity. In it lies the brain. Skull is fused mass of bone including the face bones. 32 teeth are fixed in the gum. A tooth has an enamel dentine and the tooth pulp. The tooth enamel is the hardest bone in the body.

(b) The spinal column consists of 33 vertebrae.

(c) Thorax is the upper portion of the trunk. It consists of a bony cage with 12 vertebrae at the back.

The Bones of the Upper Limbs are: *1.* clavicle or collar bone, *2.* scapula or shoulder blade, *3.* humerus on the bone of arm, *4.* radius and ulna or the bones of fare arm, *5.* 8 corpal bones of wrist, *6.* metacarpal bones of palm and, *7.* 14 phalanges.

The Bones of the Lower Limbs are: *1.* the hip bone, *2.* the femur or the thigh bone, *3.* tibia and fibula or the leg bones, *4.* 7 Tarsal bones of the ankle, *5.* 5 meta tarsal bone of the foot, *6.* 14 phalanges or the bones of the fingers of leg, *7.* In addition 'Patella' or the knee pan is a small flat bone in front of the knee joint. It protects the knee joint. It is a ball and socket joint.

Fracture: In fracture the bone is cracked or broken. In dislocation the capsule of the joint is torn and bone comes out of the joint.

9. The Abdomen: The abdomen is the lower part of the trunk. The diaphragm forms the roof of the abdomen.

Organs in the Abdominal Cavity are: 1. liver, 2. spleen, 3. stomach, 4. small and large intestines, 5. pancreas, 6. two kidneys, 7. urinary bladder. In females there are two ovaries and the uterus.

10. Muscular System: There are over 580 muscles in our body. The function of the muscles are: 1. They give shape to the body, 2. Muscle are attached to the bone and when such muscle contracts the bones move so that body movement is effected, 3. They protect the internal organs. All muscles act in co-ordination. Thus when the extensor muscles contract, the flexor muscles relax, or when the intestinal muscle contracts the intestinal sphincter muscle relaxes.

11. Digestive System: The digestive system starts at the cavity of mouth and ends at the anus.

At the entrance to the stomach there is a ring muscle called 'the cardiac sphincter'. It prevents food from going back to oesophagus on the other end is 'the pyloric sphincter'. It allows the food to pass to duodenum only after digestion in stomach is complete. Food remains in stomach for 2 to 3 hours.

Amylase digests carbohydrates to glucose. Trypin digests protein to peptide and amino acid. Liapase breaks up the emulsified fat to fatty acids and glycerol.

Villi are minute finger like projection from the wall of the small intestine. They are in millions. Each vilrus contains lymphatic capillaries called lacteals and the blood capillaries. The lacteals absorb fatty acid and glycerol. The blood capillaries absorb amino acid, glucose, vitamins and various salts *etc.*

The Digestive gland: The glandular systems are different types of glands. The glands of the digestive system are:

(a) Salivary gland: There are a pair of parotid gland, a pair of submaxillary gland and a pair of sublingual gland. They secrete saliva. Saliva contains "Ptyalin" which digests starch to maltose.

(b) Glands on the wall of the stomach produce Gastric juice. It contains hydrochloric acid, renin and pepsin. Hydrochloric acid curdles milk and kills some types of germs.

(c) Liver is the largest gland in the body. It is in the upper part of the abdomen on the right side. Liver manufactures bile from the broken down R.B.Cs. Hence bile is the product of excretion of R.B.Cs bile is stored in the gall bladder and passes to the duodenum through the bile duct. Bile emulsifies fat and helps digestion of fat, so bile is also a secretion. Bile duct joins pancreatic duct and open into duodenum. The functions of the liver are:

(i) It produces bile

(ii) It changes glucose to glycogen and store glycogen.

(iii) Poisonous matter in blood are changed to harmless product

(iv) It stores fat, soluble vitamin *i.e.*, A, D and K.

(d) Pancreas is situated between duodenum and spleen and is behind the stomach. It secretes.

(i) Trypsin which digests protein to peptones and amino acid.

(ii) Amylase which digests starch and other sugar to glucose

(iii) Liapase digests emulsified fat to fatty acid and glycerol. Pancreas also produces an internal secretion called insulin.

The spleen: It is on the left upper portion of the abdomen. It has no duct. It is not known if spleen produces any internal secretion or not. The spleen destroys the worn out R.B.Cs and produces W.B.Cs.

12. **Respiratory System:** The respiratory system consists of nasal passage, pharynx, larynx, trachea, bronchi and its division and subdivisions each of which finally ends in an air-sac called alveolus.

When the diaphragm contracts the air goes in the chest. It is called inspiration when diaphragm relaxes and we breathe out, it is called expiration. Inspiration and expiration is respiration.

When blood passes through capillaries the red blood cells give out CO_2 in the alveolus. This is called external respiration. In case of internal respiration the red blood cells give out O_2 to the tissue cells and take in CO_2 from the tissue cell.

Normally, a person breathes 18 times a minute. When we breathe in the oxygen is 20.95% and carbon dioxide is 0.4% and when we breathe out the oxygen becomes 16.5% and carbon dioxide increases to 4.5%

13. **Circulatory System:** The circulatory system consists of the heart, the arteries, the capillaries and the veins.

The Red Blood Cells (R.B.C.) are tiny discs of 7 microns. They contain haemoglobin which takes up oxygen from the lung alveolus and give out in the tissue cells. They take up carbon dioxide from the tissue cells and give out in the alveolus of the lung. Normally there are 5 millions R.B.Cs in one ml. of blood.

The White Blood Cells (W.B.C.) are bigger than R.B.Cs and are about 5,000 per ml. There are variety of W.B.Cs. They have nuclei and can multiply. They are also produced in the spleen and in the lymphatic glands.

The antibodies are defensive proteins in our body. They are present in as gamma globulin in blood.

The Platelets are smaller than the R.B.C. Their function is to bring about the clotting of the blood. When blood is flow from injury, the platelets break down. This causes the soluble fibrinogen in blood to become insoluble fibrin or threads. The R.B.Cs are caught up by the fibrins as the fibrin contract and then the clot is formed. The W.B.C. escape from the clot by their amoeboid movement.

14. **Heart:** The heart is hollow muscular organ on the left side of the chest. There is a complete muscular organ partitioned the heart to left and right sides. The left side has an upper chamber called left *auricle* and a lower chamber called left *ventricle.* The right side has also an upper and a lower chamber called right auricle and right ventricle respectively.

Blood Vessels: Blood vessels mean arteries, capillaries and veins.

Arteries: Arteries carry blood from the heart to the different parts of the body. Except pulmonary arteries all other arteries carry oxygenated blood. Except pulmonary vein all other vein carries the deoxygenated blood. The arteries have a thick fibrous coat, a thick muscular coat and a layer of cells forming the inner coat called endothelium. Arteries are always full of blood and produce a pressure is called diastolic pressure. Normally the diastolic pressure is about 80 mm of Hg. When the heart contracts and forces more blood into the arteries, the blood pressure increases. This is called systolic pressure. Normally the systolic pressure varies from 120 to 160 mm of Hg. If it is more, then the person has high blood pressure.

The **plasma** together with the W.B.C. is called "lymph".

The capillaries are minute veins which join together to form large veins.

Types of Circulation:

(i) The pulmonary circulation means the flow of blood from the right ventricle to pulmonary arteries-capillaries around the alveolus of the lungs-pulmonary veins and then to the left auricle.

(ii) The systemic circulation means the flow of blood from the left ventricle-Aorta-Arteries to all over the body-capillaries-veins, and then to the right auricle.

Portal Circulation: The veins of stomach, the small and large intestines, spleen and pancreas join together and form the portal vein. The blood from the portal vein and hepatic artery enters the liver. Hence the hepatic vein has the blood from the hepatic artery as well as the blood from the portal vein.

15. **The Excretory System:** The excretory system throws away the waste product from the body. The waste products are formed due to catabolic process in the body cells.

Excretory system consists of the two kidneys, the skin, the lungs and the large intestine.

Urine contains:

(a) water 96%

(b) urea uric acid *etc.*

(c) certain poisonous materials and other material that are not necessary for the body

(d) certain mineral salts that are in excess in the body or not required by the body.

Functional units of a kidneys are *Nephrons*.

The lungs remove CO_2 and water vapour. Kidneys remove waste matters like urea uric acid, salt *etc.*

16. **The Nervous System:** The nervous system consists of:

(a) The central nervous system consisting of the brain, the spinal cord and the nerves.

(b) The autonomic nervous system consisting of the sympathetic and the parasympathetic nerves.

Largest cell of human body is *Neuron.*

Largest gland of human body is *Liver.*

The brain consists of 1. cerebrum 2. cerebellum 3. Pons and 4. medulla oblongata. The medulla oblongata continues below as the spinal cord.

The medulla oblongata is the expanded upper portion of the spinal cord. At its lower ends fibres from the cerebrum cross to the other side. It regulates breathing and heart beat and controls the blood pressure and the body temperature. Injury to medulla oblongata causes instant death.

Reflex Action: The entire impulse circuit of a reflex response—

receptors → CNS → effectors

is called reflex arc. It is spontaneous without involving spinal cord.

17. **The Reproductive System:** Unlike other systems, the reproductive system of males and the females are quite different.

The Reproductive System in males consist of:

(a) The *testes* where sperms are manufactured.

(b) The *vas deferens* through which the sperms pass.

(c) The *seminal vesicle* where sperms are stored.

(d) The *ejaculatory duct*, through which the sperms are spurted out into the *urethra* and finally get discharged through the *penis.*

Reproductive System in Females: In females, the reproductive system consists of:

(a) The *two ovaries* in the lower part of the abdomen.

(b) The ovum passes through the *fallopian tube* to the *uterus.*

(c) If the ovum is fertilized by the sperm then the fertilized ovum enters the wall of the uterus and pregnancy occurs.

(*d*) Otherwise, the unfertilized ovum, together with the blood *etc.* from the wall of the uterus is thrown out through the *vaginal canal* as *menstruation.*

Ovums are discharged from any of the two ovaries after every 28 days. Hence the menstrual cycle occurs after every 28 days.

Tubectomy is the cutting of the fallopian tube. It is a permanent method of birth control in females. This operation is more difficult than *Vasectomy* in males. The ovaries also produce an internal secretion which develop the formal sexual characters.

OBJECTIVE QUESTIONS

1. Person living at high altitude will have:
(*a*) High alveolar capacity
(*b*) More erythrocytes
(*c*) Haemoglobin curve shifted toward right
(*d*) All of these

2. Carbon dioxide is carried in the blood:
(*a*) As dissolved gas
(*b*) As bicarbonates
(*c*) In combination with haemoglobin
(*d*) All of these

3. The largest quantity of air that can be expired after a maximum inspiratory effort is:
(*a*) Residual volume
(*b*) Tidal volume
(*c*) Vital capacity
(*d*) Total lung volume

4. The exchange of gases in the alveoli of the lungs takes place by:
(*a*) Osmosis
(*b*) Simple diffusion
(*c*) Passive transport
(*d*) Active transport

5. Lungs are enclosed in:
(*a*) Pericardium
(*b*) Pleura
(*c*) Peritoneum
(*d*) Perichondrium

6. Artificial respiration at the rate of 10-15 times per minute is being given to a man saved from drowing. This is because:
(*a*) Water in respiratory passage is cleared fast at this rate
(*b*) Chocking is least at this rate
(*c*) It is normal rate of respiration
(*d*) Lungs are ventilated best at this rate

7. Pasteurization of milk means that:
(*a*) All bacteria are killed
(*b*) Pathogenic bacteria are killed
(*c*) Milk is enriched with vitamins
(*d*) Milk casein is partially digested.

8. Dissociation curve is connected with:
(*a*) Oxygen
(*b*) Oxyhaemoglobin
(*c*) Carbon dioxide
(*d*) Carbonic anhydrate

9. What would happen if human body becomes acidic (low pH)?
(*a*) Oxygen carrying capacity of haemoglobin increases
(*b*) Oxygen carrying capacity of haemoglobin decreases
(*c*) RBC count increases
(*d*) RBC count decreases

10. Haemoglobin-oxygen dissociation curve is:
(*a*) Hyperbolic (*b*) Sigmoid
(*c*) Straight (*d*) Constant

11. Epithelial linning the alveoli of the frog's lung facing cavity is:
(*a*) Squamous and ciliated
(*b*) Columnar and ciliated
(*c*) Columnar and non-ciliated
(*d*) Squamous and non-ciliated.

12. Oxygen dissociation curve of haemoglobin is
(*a*) Sigmoid (*b*) Slope
(*c*) Straight line (*d*) Parabola

13. Air bladder or swim bladder in fishes is associated with
(a) Hydrostatic
(b) Sound production
(c) Gaseous exchange
(d) All of these

14. Arytenoid cartilage occurs in
(a) Nose (b) Larynx
(c) Hyoid (d) Sternum

15. Respiratory Quotient (RQ) is less than one for
(a) Banana (b) Potato
(c) Citrus fruits (d) Castor seeds

16. Oxygen carrier or the respiratory pigment in the blood of frog and other vertebrates is
(a) Haemocyanin (b) Cytochrome
(c) Haemoglobin (d) None of these

17. In an organism utilising carbohydrates as a source of energy anaerobically, RQ is likely to be
(a) 0.7 (b) 1.0
(c) 0.9 (d) Infinity

18. The state during which are respiratory centre is inhibited is termed
(a) Asphyxia (b) Chocking
(c) Anoxia (d) Suffocation

19. Which of the following are respiratory organs of scorpion?
(a) Lungs (b) Book-lungs
(c) Gills (d) Ctenidia

20. Bohr effect is related with
(a) Reduced oxygen level in haemoglobin
(b) Reduced CO_2 level in blood
(c) Reduced carbon level in lymph
(d) Oxidised phosphorus level in blood

21. Stimulation of heart during stress condition by sympathetic nerve is result of
(a) Release of acetyl choline
(b) Release of adrenalin
(c) Inhibition of acetylcholine
(d) Inhibition of adrenalin

22. Shape of an eye is maintained by
(a) Aqueous humour
(b) Vitreous humour
(c) Conjunctiva
(d) All of these

23. Eyelashes are lubricated by
(a) Ceruminous glands
(b) Meibomian glands
(c) Lacrymal glands
(d) All of these

24. Main function of semicircular canals is
(a) Perceive and transmit sound vibrations
(b) Direct the animal towards the source of sound
(c) Perceive sound vibrations
(d) Perceive the motion of head

25. Organs of Ruffini are receptors of
(a) Cold (b) Pressure
(c) Heat (d) Touch

26. Broca's area and Wernicke centre of association area of cerebrum are connected with
(a) Memory (b) Voluntary action
(c) Blind spot (d) Both (a) and (b)

27. Structure connected with vision in rabbit is
(a) Corpus callosum
(b) Corpora quadrigeuina
(c) Corpus albicans
(d) Hippocampus

28. The depression in the retina of one eye which lodges only the cones is called
(a) Blind spot (b) Fovea centralis
(c) Fenestra rotunda (d) Red nuclei

29. For sound (good) reflex actions we require intact
(a) Spinal cord
(b) Cerebellum
(c) Hypothalamus
(d) Medulla oblongata

30. Which of the following cranial nerves of man are both sensory or motor?
(a) Optic (b) Vagus
(c) Olfactory (d) Trigeminal

31. Preganglionic sympathetic fibres are
(a) Adrenergic (b) Cholinergic
(c) Synergic (d) Hypergonic

32. Atoconium is found in
(*a*) Perilymph
(*b*) Haemolymph
(*c*) Synovial fluid
(*d*) Otolith membrane

33. When the direction of nerve impulse is reversed, the condition is called
(*a*) Axo-axonic
(*b*) Axo-dendritic
(*c*) Axo-axon dendritic
(*d*) None of the above

34. Ora serrata is
(*a*) Oral cavity of protochordates
(*b*) Anterior edge of sensory part of retina
(*c*) Gland present in oral cavity of frog
(*d*) A part of utriculus of ear

35. Arbor vitae is mainly composed of
(*a*) Gray matter (*b*) Neuroglial cells
(*c*) White matter (*d*) All of these

36. Secretion of which of the following is under neuro-secretory nerve axons?
(*a*) Pineal
(*b*) Adrenal cortex
(*c*) Anterior pituitary
(*d*) Posterior pituitary

37. Sympathetic nervous in mammals arise from
(*a*) Sacral region
(*b*) Cervical region
(*c*) Thoraco-lumbar region
(*d*) 3rd, 7th, 9th 10th cranial

38. Pacinial corpuscles in the skin of mammals aries from
(*a*) Type of gland
(*b*) Pain receptors
(*c*) Naked tactilereceptors
(*d*) Encapsulated pressure receptor

39. Sensation of stomach pain is due to
(*a*) Interoreceptors (*b*) Exteroreceptors
(*c*) Proprioreceptors (*d*) Teloreceptors

40. Blood dust present in the blood plasma is known as
(*a*) Blood platelets (*b*) Chylomicrons
(*c*) Haemoconia (*d*) Chyluria

41. Cardiac cycle in man takes about
(*a*) 0.5 seconds (*b*) 1.0 seconds
(*c*) 1.2 seconds (*d*) 0.8 seconds

42. The movement of neutrophils to site of inflammation is due to
(*a*) Release of hormone
(*b*) Chemotaxis
(*c*) Activity of antigens
(*d*) Activations of antigens

43. RBCs are generally destroyed in the liver, while WBCs are destroyed in
(*a*) Plasma
(*b*) Lymph
(*c*) Inside various cells of body
(*d*) Out side the blood stream

44. With increasing distance from heart, the elasticity as well as magnitude of muscular layer of arteries would
(*a*) Decreases
(*b*) Remains constant
(*c*) Slightly decrease
(*d*) Increase

45. Pulse pressure is difference of diastole and systole and is equal to ——— mm Hg.
(*a*) 40 (*b*) 30
(*c*) 10 (*d*) 80

46. Pacemaker is implanted when one of these is defective
(*a*) SA node (*b*) AV node
(*c*) Purkinje fibres (*d*) Bundle of lines

47. Thromboplastin is secreted by
(*a*) Platelets (*b*) Lymphoaytes
(*c*) Helper T cells (*d*) Mast cells

48. Circulation of blood was discovered by
(*a*) Darwin (*b*) Harvey
(*c*) Aristotle (*d*) Pasteur

49. RBCs in mammals have no nucleus because
(*a*) It has degenerated during development
(*b*) They do not have nucleus since early
(*c*) Nucleus is harmful for RBC
(*d*) Nucleus decreases surface area.

50. Hepatic portal system starts from
(*a*) Digestive system to liver
(*b*) Kidney to liver
(*c*) Liver to heart
(*d*) Liver to Kidney

51. The number of hormones secreted by anterior pituitary is
(a) 3 (b) 4
(c) 6 (d) 8

52. The reabsorption of water in the kidneys is under the control of hormone
(a) LH (b) ADH
(c) STH (d) ACTH

53. Parathormone is secreted by
(a) Parathyroid (b) Liver
(c) Pituitary (d) Hypothalamus

54. The calcium level in blood can be increased by administration of
(a) Glucagon (b) Thyroxine
(c) Parathormone (d) Calcitonin

55. The disease caused by hyposecretion of thyroxine is
(a) Goitre (b) Cretinism
(c) Acromegaly (d) Addison's disease

56. Gigantism and acromegaly result from hyperscеretion of
(a) ADH (b) GH
(c) STH (d) None of these

57. Emergency gland of blood is
(a) Thymus (b) Testis
(c) Adrenal (d) Pituitary

58. Point out the odd one
(a) Corticotropin (b) Vasopressin
(c) Nonedrenaline (d) Prolactin

59. Receptors for protein hormones are located
(a) In cytoplasm
(b) On cell surface
(c) In nucleus
(d) On endoplasmic reticulum

60. Progesterone hormone is secreted by
(a) Corpus callosum (b) Corpus luteum
(c) Corpus albicans (d) Thymus

61. Secretin stimulates
(a) Lungs (b) Gall bladder
(c) Pancreas (d) Gastric glands

62. Parathormone induces
(a) Increase in serum calcium level
(b) Decrease in serum calcium level
(c) Increase in blood sugar level
(d) Decrease in blood sugar level

63. Which of the following is not a steroid hormone?
(a) Aldosterone (b) Androgen
(c) Estrogen (d) Thyroxine

64. Pituitary gland is under the control of
(a) Pineal gland (b) Thyroid gland
(c) Adrenal gland (d) Hypothalamus

65. Hormone responsible for urine concentration is
(a) Vasopressin (b) Pitocin
(c) Thyroxine (d) Renin

66. FSH is produced by
(a) Thyroid gland
(b) Posterior pituitary
(c) Anterior pituitary
(d) Gonads

67. Median eminence is a part of
(a) Neurohypophysis
(b) Pars inter media
(c) Adenohypophysis
(d) Pars distalis

68. At menopause, there is a rise in urinary excretion of
(a) STH (b) LTH
(c) MSH (d) FSH

69. The pituitary gland effect the urine formation through
(a) Thyroxine (b) ACTH
(c) Oxytocin (d) ADH

70. Disorders caused by hypersecretion of concerned hormones
(a) Gigantism and exophthalmic goitre
(b) Mongolism, and Cretinism
(c) Cretinism, diabetes mellitus and goitre
(d) Rickets and diabetes mellitus

71. Goitre is a pathological condition associated with
(a) Glucagon (b) Thyroxine
(c) Progesterone (d) Testosterone

72. Which disease is due to hyposecretion of an endocrine gland?
(a) Exophthalmic goitre
(b) Hypertension
(c) Gigantism
(d) Simple goitre

ANSWERS

1	2	3	4	5	6	7	8	9	10
(*d*)	(*d*)	(*c*)	(*b*)	(*b*)	(*d*)	(*a*)	(*b*)	(*b*)	(*b*)
11	**12**	**13**	**14**	**15**	**16**	**17**	**18**	**19**	**20**
(*d*)	(*a*)	(*d*)	(*b*)	(*d*)	(*c*)	(*d*)	(*c*)	(*b*)	(*a*)
21	**22**	**23**	**24**	**25**	**26**	**27**	**28**	**29**	**30**
(*b*)	(*b*)	(*d*)	(*d*)	(*c*)	(*d*)	(*b*)	(*b*)	(*a*)	(*b*)
31	**32**	**33**	**34**	**35**	**36**	**37**	**38**	**39**	**40**
(*b*)	(*b*)	(*a*)	(*b*)	(*c*)	(*d*)	(*c*)	(*d*)	(*a*)	(*b*)
41	**42**	**43**	**44**	**45**	**46**	**47**	**48**	**49**	**50**
(*d*)	(*c*)	(*b*)	(*b*)	(*d*)	(*a*)	(*a*)	(*b*)	(*d*)	(*b*)
51	**52**	**53**	**54**	**55**	**56**	**57**	**58**	**59**	**60**
(*c*)	(*b*)	(*a*)	(*c*)	(*b*)	(*b*)	(*c*)	(*c*)	(*b*)	(*b*)
61	**62**	**63**	**64**	**65**	**66**	**67**	**68**	**69**	**70**
(*c*)	(*a*)	(*d*)	(*d*)	(*a*)	(*c*)	(*a*)	(*d*)	(*d*)	(*a*)
71	**72**								
(*b*)	(*d*)								

8

Nutrition and Health

Nutrition may be defined as the science of food and its relationship to health. It is concerned primarily with the part played by nutrients in body growth, development and maintenance. The word *nutrient* or "food factor" is used for specific dietary constituents such as proteins, vitamins and minerals. *Dietetics* is the practical application of the principles of nutrition means "maintaining a nutritional status that enables us to grow well and enjoy good health". The subject of nutrition is very extensive.

CLASSIFICATION OF FOODS

There are many basis of classifying foods:

(a) Classification by origin:

1. Foods of animal origin
2. Foods of vegetable origin

(b) Classification by chemical composition:

1. Proteins
2. Fats
3. Carbohydrates
4. Vitamins
5. Minerals

(c) Classification by predominant function.

1. Body **building foods** e.g., milk, meat, poultry, fish, eggs, pulses, groundnuts, etc.
2. **Energy-** giving foods, e.g. cereals, sugars, roots and tubers, fats and oils.
3. **Protective foods**, e.g., vegetables, fruits, milk.

(d) Classification by nutritive value:

1. Cereals and millets
2. Pulses (legumes)
3. Vegetables
4. Nuts and oilseeds
5. Fruits
6. Animal foods
7. Fats and oils
8. Sugar and jaggery
9. Condiments and spices
10. Miscellaneous foods.

NUTRIENTS

Nutrients are organic and inorganic complexes contained in food. There are about 50 different nutrients which are normally supplied through the foods we eat. Each nutrient has specific functions in the body. Most natural foods contain more than one nutrient. These may be divided into:

(i) Macronutrients: These are proteins, fats and carbohydrates which are often called "proximate principles" because they form the main bulk of food. In the Indian dietary, they contribute to the total energy intake in the following proportions.

Proteins	7 to 15 per cent
Fats	10 to 30 per cent
Carbohydrates	65 to 80 per cent

(ii) Micronutrients: These are vitamins and minerals. They are called micronutrients because they are required in small amounts which may vary from a fraction of a milligram to several grams.

PROTEINS

Proteins are complex organic nitrogenous compounds. They are composed of carbon, hydrogen, oxygen, nitrogen and sulphur in varying amounts. Some proteins also contain phosphorus and iron and occasionally other elements. Proteins constitute about 20 per cent of the body weight in an adult.

Essential Amino Acids

Proteins are made up of smaller units, called amino acids. Some 24 amino acids are stated to be needed by the human body, of which 9 are called "essential" because the body cannot synthesize them in amounts corresponding to its needs, and therefore, they must be obtained from dietary proteins. Non-essential amino acids include arginine, asparaginic acid, serine, glutamic acid, proline and glycine. Both essential and non- essential amino acids are needed for synthesis of tissue proteins, the former must be supplied through diet, whereas the latter can be synthesized by the body provided other building blocks are present.

Some of the essential amino acids have important biological functions, e.g. formation of niacin from tryptophan; the action of methionine as a donor of methyl groups for the synthesis of choline, folates and nucleic acids. There is evidence the cystine and tyrosine are essential for premature babies. Now tissues cannot be formed unless all the essential amino acids (EAA) are present in the diet.

Functions: Proteins are needed by the body for *(a)* body building—this component is small component is small compared with the maintenance component, except in the very young child and infant; *(b)* repair and maintenance of body tissues; *(c)* maintenance of osmotic pressure; and *(d)* synthesis of certain substances like antibodies, plasma proteins, haemoglobin, enzymes, hormones and coagulation factors. Proteins are connected with the immune mechanism of the body.

Sources: Humans obtain protein from main dietary sources; *(a) Animal sources:* Proteins of animal origin are found in milk, meat, eggs, cheese, fish and fowl. These proteins contain all the essential amino acids (EAA) in adequate amounts. Egg proteins are considered to be the best among food proteins because of their high biological value and digestibility. They are used in nutrition studies as a "reference protein" *(b) Vegetable sources:* Vegetable proteins are found in pulses (legumes), cereals, beans, nuts, oil-seed cakes, etc. They are poor in EAA. In developing countries such as India; cereals and pulses are the main sources of dietary protein because they are cheap, easily available and consumed in bulk.

FATS

Fats are solid at 20° C they contains unsaturated fatty acid. if they are liquid at that temperature they are called oil. Fats and oils are concentrated sources of energy. They are classified as:

(a) Simple lipids, e.g., triglycerides
(b) Compound lipids, e.g. phospholipids
(c) Derived lipids, e.g., cholesterol

The human body can synthesize triglycerides and cholesterol endogenously. Most of the body fat (99 per cent) in the adipose tissue is in the form of triglycerides.

Fatty acids

Fats yield fatty acids and glycerol on hydrolysis. Fatty acids are divided into **saturated** fatty acids such as lauric palmitic and steric acids, and **unsaturated** fatty acids which are further divided into monounsaturated (e.g. oleic acid) and polyunsaturated fatty acids (e.g., linoleic acid).

The polyunsaturated fatty acids are mostly found in vegetable oils, and the saturated fatty acids mainly in animal fats.

Essential fatty acids

Essential fatty acids are those that cannot be synthesized by humans. They can be derived only from food. The most important essential fatty acid (EFA) is *linoleic acid,* which serves as a basis for the production of other essential fatty acids.

Sources: The dietary sources of fats may be classified as:

(a) *Animal fats :* The major sources of animal fats are ghee, butter, milk, cheese, eggs, and fat of meat and fish. Animal fats with few exceptions like cod liver oil and sardine oil are mostly saturated fats.

(b) *Vegetable fats :* Some plants store fat in their seeds, e.g. groundnut, mustard, sesame, coconut, etc.

(c) *Other sources :* Small quantities of fat (invisible fat) are found in most other foods such as cereals, pulses, nuts and vegetables.

Functions: Fats have always been equated with calories. They are high energy foods, providing as much as 9 kcal for every gram. Fats in the body support viscera such as heart, kidney and intestine; and fat beneath the skin provides insulation against cold.

Fats and disease:

(a) *Obesity :* A diet,, rich in fat, can pose a threat to human health by encouraging obesity.

(b) *Phrenoderma :* Deficiency of essential fatty acids in the diet is associated with rough and dry skin, a condition known as phrenoderma or "toad skin".

(c) *Coronary heart disease :* High fat intake (i.e. dietary fat representing 40 per cent or over of the energy supply and containing a high proportion of saturated fats) has been identified as a major risk factor for CHD.

(d) *Cancer :* In recent years, there has been some evidence that diets high in fat increase the risk of colon cancer and breast cancer.

CARBOHYDRATE

The major component of food is carbohydrate, which is the main source of energy, providing 4 kcals per gram. Carbohydrate is also essential for the oxidation of fats and for the synthesis of certain non-essential amino acids. There are three main sources of carbohydrate, viz, starches, sugar and cellulose. *Starch* is basic to the human diet. It is found in abundance in cereals, roots and tubers. *Sugars* comprise monosaccharides (glucose, fructose and galactose) and disaccharides (Sucrose, lactose and maltoses.) *Cellulose* which is the indigestible component of carbohydrate with scarcely any nutritive value, contributes to dietary fibre.

VITAMINS

Vitamins are a class of organic compounds categorized as essential nutrients. They are required by the body in very small amounts. They fall in the category of micronutrients. Vitamins do not yield energy but enable the body to use other nutrients. Since the body is generally unable to synthesize them (at least in sufficient amounts) they must be provided by food. A well balanced diet supplies in most instances the vitamin needs of a healthy person. Vitamins are divided into two groups : *(a)* fat soluble vitamins, viz vitamins A, D, E and K, and *(b)* water soluble vitamins, viz vitamins of the B-group and vitamin C.

Vitamin A

"Vitamin A" covers both a pre-formed vitamin, retinol and a pro-*vitamin*, beta *carotene*, some of *which is converted* to *retinol in the* intestinal *mucosa*.

Functions : Vitamin *A participates in many bodily functions* :

(a) It is indispensable for normal vision. It contributes to the production of retinal pigments which are needed for vision in dim light.

(b) It is necessary for maintaining the integrity and the normal functioning of glandular and epithelial tissue which lines intestinal, respiratory and urinary tracts as well as the skin and eyes.

(c) It supports growth especially skeletal growth.

Sources: Vitamin A is widely distributed in animal and plant foods—in animal foods as pre-formed vitamin A (retinol), and in plant foods as pro-vitamins (carotenes).

(a) *Animal foods :* Foods rich in retinol are liver, eggs, butter, cheese, whole milk, fish and meat. Fish liver oils are the richest natural sources of retinol but they are generally used as nutritional supplements rather than as food sources.

(b) *Plant foods :* The cheapest source of vitamin A is green leafy vegetables such as spinach and amaranth which are found in great abundance in nature throughout the year. The darker the green leaves, the higher its carotene content.

(c) *Fortified foods :* Foods fortified with vitamin A (e.g., Vanaspati, margarine, milk) can be an important source.

Deficiency:—

(a) *Nightblindness :* It is due to Lack of vitamin A, first causes nightblindness or inability to see in dim light. Nightblindness is due to impairment in dark adaptation.

(b) *Conjunctival xerosis :* This is the first clinical sign of vitamin A deficiency. The conjuctiva becomes dry and non- wettable instead of looking smooth and shiny.

(c) *Bitot's spots :* Bitot's spots are triangular, pearly- white or yellowish, foamy spots on the bulbar conjunctiva on either side of the cornea.

(d) *Corneal xerosis :* This stage is particularly serious. The cornea appears dull, dry and non-wettable and eventually opaque.

(e) *Keralomakia :* Liquification of cornea.

(f) Extra occular manifestations.

Treatment : Vitamin A deficiency should be treated urgently. Nearly all of the early stages of xerophthalmia can be reversed by administration of a massive dose orally on two successive days.

Vitamin D

The nutritionally important forms of Vitamin D in man are Calciferol (Vitamin D_2) and Cholecalciferol (Vitamin D_3). Calciferol may be derived by irradiation of the plant sterol, ergosterol. Cholecalciferol is the naturally occurring (preformed) vitamin D which is found in animal fats and fish liver oils. It is also derived from exposure to UV rays of the sunlight which convert the cholesterol in the skin to vitamin D.

Major advances have been made in recent years in our understanding of the metabolism of vitamin D in the body. It has been proposed that vitamin D should be regarded as kidney hormone because it does not meet the classic definition of a vitamin, that is, a substance which must be obtained by dietary means because of a lack of capacity in the human body to synthesize it. In fact vitamin D_3 is not a dietary requirement at all in conditions of adequate sunlight. It can be synthesized in the body in adequate amounts by simple exposure to sunlight even for 5 minutes per day.

Functions: The functions of vitamin D are summarised as below.

Intestine:	Promotes intestinal absorption of calcium and phosphorus
Bone:	Stimulates normal mineralization. Enhances bone resorption. Affects collagen maturation.
Kidney:	Increases tubular reabsorption of phosphate. Variable effect on reabsorption of calcium.

Daily Requirements: Pregnancy 100 mcg. Adults-2.5 mcg, Infants-5 mcg. (mcg = microgram)

Sources: Vitamin D is unique because it is derived both from sunlight and foods.

(a) **Sunlight :** Vitamin D is synthesized by the body by the action of UV rays. Dark skinned races such as Negroes also suffer from this disadvantage because black skin can filter off up to 95 per cent of UV rays. *(b)* **Foods** : Vitamin D occurs only in foods of animal origin. Liver, egg yolk, butter and cheese and some species of fish contain useful amounts.

Deficiency

1. Rickets : Vitamin D deficiency leads to *rickets,* which is usually observed in young children between the age of six months and two years. There is reduced calcification of growing bones, The disease is characterised by growth failure, bone deformity, muscular hypotonia, tetany and convulsions due to hypo- calcemia.
2. Osteomalacia : In adults, vitamin D deficiency may result in *osteomalacia* which occurs mainly in women, especially during pregnancy and lactation when requirements of vitamin D are increased.

Both rickets and osteomalacia are frequently reported in India, although they do not appear to be a problem of public health importance.

Prevention: Prevention measures include *(a)* educating parents to expose their children regularly to sunshine; *(b)* periodic dosing (prophylaxis) of young children with vitamin D.

Vitamin E (Tocoferol)

Vitamin E is the generic name for a group of closely related and naturally occurring fat soluble compounds, the tocopherols. Of these alpha-tocopherol is biologically the most potent. Vitamin E is widely distributed in foods. By far the richest sources are vegetable oils, cotton -seed, sunflower seed, egg yolk and butter. Foods rich in polyunsaturated fatty acids are also rich in vitamin E.

Vitamin K

Vitamin K occurs in at-least two major forms- Vitamin K_1 and Vitamin K_2. Vitamin K_1 is found mainly in fresh green vegetables particularly dark green ones, and in some fruits. Vitamin K_2 is synthesized by the intestinal bacteria, which usually provide an adequate supply in man. Long term administration of antibiotic doses for more than a week may temporarily suppress the normal intestinal flora, (a source of vitamin K_2) and may cause a deficiency of vitamin K. Vitamin K is stored in the liver.

The role of vitamin K is to stimulate the production and/or the release of certain coagulation factors. In vitamin K deficiency, the prothrombin content of blood is markedly decreased and the blood clotting time is considerably prolonged.

Thiamine

Thiamine (Vitamin B_1) is a water-soluble vitamin. It is essential for the utilization of carbohydrates. In thiamine deficiency, there is accumulation of pyruvic and lactic acids in the tissues and body fluids.

Sources: Thiamine occurs in all natural foods, although in small amounts. Important sources are: whole grain cereals, wheat, gram, yeast, pulses, oilseeds and nuts, especially groundnut.

Deficiency: The two principal deficiency diseases are beriberi and Wernick's encephalopathy.

Prevention: Beriberi can be eliminated by educating people to eat well balanced, mixed diets containing thiamine-rich foods (e.g., paraboiled and undermilled rice).

Riboflavin

Riboflavin (Vitamin B_2) is a member of the B-group vitamins. It has a fundamental role in cellular oxidation. It is a co-factor in a number of enzymes involved in energy metabolism.

Sources: Its richest natural sources are milk, eggs, liver, kidney and green leafy vegetables. Meat and fish contain small amounts.

Deficiency: Deficiency of riboflavin, or ariboflavinosis is widespread in India particularly in populations where rice is the staple. The most common lesion associated with riboflavin deficiency is angular stomatitis, which occurs frequently in malnourished children and its prevalence is used as an index of the state of nutrition in the children.

Niacin

Niacin or nicotinic acid is essential for the metabolism of carbohydrate, fat and protein. It is also essential for the normal functioning of the skin, intestinal and nervous systems.

Sources: Foods rich in niacin and/or tryptophan are liver, kidney, meat, poultry, fish, legumes and ground nut.

Deficiency: Niacin deficiency results in pellagra.

Disease characterised by : (*i*) Diarrhoea, (*ii*) Dermitis, (*iii*) Dementia.

Prevention: Pellagra is preventable disease. A good mixed diet containing milk and/ or meat is universally regarded as an essential part of prevention and treatment.

Vitamin B_6

Pyridoxine (vitamin B_6) exists in three forms : pyridoxine, pyridoxal and pyridoxamine. It plays an important role in the metabolism of amino acids, fats, and carbohydrate. It is widely distributed in foods, e.g. milk, liver, meat, egg yolk, fish, whole grain cereals, legumes and vegetables.

Pantothenic Acid

There is a long standing evidence for a relation between pantothenic acid and adrenal cortical function.

Folate

The recommended name is folate, alternative name is folacin and the usual pharmaceutical preparation is folic acid.

Folic acid occurs in food in two forms : Free folates and bound folates. It is also needed for the normal development of blood cells in the marrow.

Sources: The name comes from the latin folia (=leaf) but foods such as liver, meat, dairy products, eggs, milk, fruits and cereals are as good dietary sources as leafy vegetables.

Deficiency: Folate deficiency may occur simply from a poor diet. Its deficiency is common in pregnancy and lactation.

Vitamin B_{12}

Its normal requirement in adult-1 mcg, pregnant.-1.5 mcg, and infants-2 mcg.

Vitamin B_{12} is complex organometallic compound with a cobalt atom. The preparation which is therapeutically used is cyanocobalamine. Vitamin B_{12} cooperates with folate in the synthesis of DNA , so deficiency of either leads to megaloblastosis. Vitamin B_{12} has a separate biochemical role, unrelated to folate, in synthesis of fatty acids in myelin.

Sources: Good sources are liver, kidney, meat, fish, milk and cheese. Vitamin B_{12} is not found in foods of vegetable origin. It is also synthesized by bacteria in colon.

Deficiency: Vitamin B_{12} deficiency is associated with megaloblastic anaemia (pernicious anaemia), demyelinating neurological lesions in the spinal cord and infertility (in animal species). Dietary deficiency of B_{12} may arise in subjects who are strict vegetarians and eat no animal products At the present time, there is little evidenc that vitamin B_{12} deficiency anaemia represen an important public health problem.

Vitamin C

Vitamin C (ascorbic acid) is a water sol vitamin. It is the most sensitive to heat.] monkey and guinea pig are perhaps the only species known to require vitamin C in their diet.

Functions: Vitamin C plays an important role in tissue oxidation. It is needed for the formation of collagen, which accounts for 25 per cent of total body protein. Collagen provides a supporting matrix for the blood vessels and connective tissue and for bones and cartilage. It inhibits nitrosamine formation by the intestinal mucosa. Other claims such as prevention of common cold and protection against infections are not substantiated.

Sources: The main dietary sources of vitamin C are fresh fruits and green leafy vegetables. Traces of vitamin C occur in fresh meat and fish but scarcely any in cereals. Germinating pulses contain good amounts. Roots and tubers contain small amounts. Amla or the Indian gooseberry is one of the richest sources of vitamin C both in the fresh as well as in the dry condition.

Deficiency: Deficiency of vitamin C results in scurvy.

MINERALS

More that 50 chemical elements are found in the human body, which are required for growth, repair and regulation of vital body functions. These can be divided into three major groups: *(a) Major minerals:* These include calcium, phosphorus, sodium, potassium and magnesium. *(b) Trace elements:* These are elements required by the body in quantities of less than a few milligrams per day e.g. iron, iodine, fluorine, zinc, copper, cobalt, chromium, manganese, molybdenum, selenium, nickel, tin, silicon and vanadium. Many more have been added to the list in the last few years. *(c) Trace contaminants with no known function:* These include lead, mercury, barium, boron and aluminium.

Calcium

Calcium is a major mineral element of the body. It constitutes 1.5 -2 per cent of the body weight of an adult human. An average adult body contains about 1200g of calcium of which over 98 per cent is found in the bones.

Functions: Ionized calcium in the plasma has many vital functions including formation of bones and teeth, coagulation of blood, contraction of muscles, cardiac action, milk production, relay of electrical and chemical messages that arrive at a cell's surface membrane to the biochemical machinery within the cell, keeping the membranes of cells intact and in the metabolism of enzymes and hormones.

Sources: The best sources of calcium are milk and milk products, eggs and fish. The cheapest dietary sources are green leafy vegetables, cereals and millets.

Deficiency: No clear-cut disease due to calcium deficiency has ever been observed, even under conditions of low intake. It has been detectable abnormalities. An intermediate stage of "latent iron deficiency" that is, iron stores are exhausted, but anaemia has not occurred as yet.

Phosphorus

Phosphorus is essential for the formation of bones and teeth. It plays an important roles in all metabolisms. An adult human body contains about 400-700 g of phosphorus as phosphates, most of this occurs in bones and teeth.

Sodium

Sodium is found in all body fluids. The adult human body contains about 100g of sodium ion. Sodium occurs in many foods, and is also added to food during cooking in the form of sodium chloride. Sodium is lost from the body through urine and sweat; that which is passed out in urine is regulated by the kidney but that which is lost by sweating is not controlled. Depletion of sodium chloride causes muscular cramps.

Potassium

The adult human body contains about 250 g of potassium. Potassium occurs widely in foodstuffs, so there is little likelihood of its deficiency. The daily requirement of potassium has not been determined accurately.

Magnesium

Magnesium is a constituent of bones, and is present in all body cells. Human adult body contains about 25g of magnesium of which about half is found in the skeleton. The principal clinical features attributed to magnesium deficiency are irritability, tetany, hyperreflexia and occasionally hyporeflexia.

Iron

Iron is of great importance in human nutrition. The adult human body contains between 3-4 g of iron, of which about 60-70 per cent present in the blood (Hb iron) as circulating iron, and the rest (1 to 1.5 g) as storage iron. Each gram of haemoglobin contains about 3.34 mg of iron.

Functions: Iron is necessary for many functions in the body including formation of haemoglobin, brain development and function, regulation of body temperature, muscle activity, and catecholamine metabolism. Lack of iron directly affects the immune system; it diminishes the number of T cells and the production of antibodies. Besides haemoglobin, iron is a component of myoglobin, the cytochromes catalase and certain enzyme systems. Iron is essential for binding oxygen to the blood cells. The central function of iron is "oxygen transport" and cell respiration.

Fluorine

Fluorine is the most abundant element in nature. Being so highly reactive, it is never found in its elemental gaseous form, but only in combined form. About 98 per cent of the fluoride in the body is found in bones and teeth. Fluorine is essential for the normal mineralization of bones and formation of dental enamel.

Sources: The principal sources of fluorine available to man are *(a) Drinking water* : The major source of fluorine to man is drinking water. In most parts of India, the fluoride content of drinking water is about 0.5 mg/L, but in fluorosis-endemic areas, it may be as high as 3 to 12 mg/L *(b) Foods* : Fluorides occur in traces in many foods, but some foods such as sea fish, cheese and tea are reported to rich in fluorides.

Deficiency/ Excess: Fluorine is often called a two edged sword. Prolonged ingestion of fluorides through drinking water in excess of the daily requirement is associated with dental and skeletal fluorosis; and inadequate intake with dental caries. The use of fluoride is recognized as the most effective means available for the prevention of dental caries.

Other Trace Elements

Zinc

Zinc is a component of many enzymes. It is active in the metabolism of glucosides and proteins, and is required for the synthesis of insulin by the pancreas and for the immunity function.

Copper

The amount of copper in an adult body is estimated to between 100-150 mg. Copper is widely distributed in nature. Even poor diets provide enough copper for human needs. Deficiency or excess of this element is very rare. Hypocupremia occurs in patients with nephrosis, Wilson's disease and protein- energy malnutrition and in infants fed for long periods exclusively on cow's milk. Neutropenia is the best documented abnormality of copper deficiency.

Cobalt

The only established function of cobalt in the human is as a part of the vitamin B_{12} molecule, which must be ingested preformed. It is suggested that cobalt may be necessary for the first stage of hormone production. i.e. capture of iodine by the gland. Cobalt may interact with iodine and affect its utilization.

Chromium

Total body content of chromium is small, less then 6 mg. Current interest in chromium is based on the occurrence of unusual glucose tolerance curves that are responsive to chromium. Thus there is suggestive evidence that chromium plays a role in relation to carbohydrate and insulin function.

NUTRITIONAL REQUIREMENTS

The science of human nutrition is mainly concerned with defining the nutritional requirements for the promotion, protection and maintenance of health in all groups of the population. Such knowledge is necessary in order to assess the nutritional adequacy of diets for growth of infants, children and adolescents, and for maintenance of health in adults of both sexes and during pregnancy and lactation in women. In this context, a variety of terms have been used to define the amount of nutrients needed by the body such as : *optimum requirements, minimum requirements, recommended intakes or allowances, and safe level of intake,* Of these, the term "recommended daily intake" or allowance (RDA) has been widely accepted.

RECOMMENDED DAILY ALLOWANCE (RDA)

The term "recommended daily intake" is defined as the amounts of nutrient sufficient for the maintenance of health in nearly all people. They are reference standards of nutritional intakes. For all nutrients, except energy, estimates of allowances are based on the defined "minimum requirement" plus a safety margin, often generous, for individual variation and stresses of everyday life. In some cases, this has entailed adding to the observed mean, twice the standard deviation of the distribution of minimum requirement for the subjects measured. This value will more than meet the requirement of 97.5 per cent of population. In fact for many individuals this level will be in excess of their needs. It is considered that such excessive consumption of nutrients is not injurious to health. It is important to emphasize that the recommended intake of nutrients represents does not apply to sick people. The recommended intake of nutrients represents value judgements based on the existing knowledge of nutritional sciences; these will be elaborated in this section.

The recommendation is estimated to meet the requirement of practically all healthy people. The recommendation is for the intake over several days.

1. ENERGY

Energy is a prime requisite for body function and growth. When a world's intake of food falls below a standard reference, growth slows, and if low levels of intake persist, adult stature will be reduced. Similarly, if adults fail to meet their food requirements they lose weight. This may lead to reduced ability to work, less resistant to infection. This underlines the need for an adequate intake of food which is the source of all energy.

Energy requirements :

Broadly, the total energy requirement of an individual is made up of three components:

(a) energy required for basal metabolism. This is about 1 kcal/ hour for every kg of body weight for an adult;

(b) energy required for daily activities such as walking, sitting, standing, dressing, climbing stairs, etc; and

(c) energy expenditure for occupational work. This is further classified as light work (an office clerk), moderate work and heavy work (manual physical labour).

The first component is nearly the same for all individuals. It is the latter two components that vary depending upon the types of activities. Procedures for calculating total energy expenditure are given in the WHO Expert Committee Report on Energy and protein Requirements.

Factors affecting energy requirement:

Energy requirements vary from one person to another depending upon inter-related variables acting in a complex way, such as age, sex, working condition, body composition, physical activity, physiological state etc. All these factors lead to differences in food intake.

Energy requirements have been laid down by various expert groups of FAO and WHO. It has becomes customary for countries to lay down their own standards. Thus there are British standards, American standards, Canadian standards, etc.

2. PROTEIN

Protein requirements vary from individual to individual. Apart from age, sex and other physiological variables, factors like infection worm infestation, emotional disturbances and stress situations can affect a person's protein requirement.

Protein: (i) Essential Amino Acids, (ii) Non-essential Amino Acids.

Assessment of Protein

(a) **Protein Quality:** The quality of a protein is assessed by comparison to the "reference protein" which is usually egg protein. Two methods of assessment of protein quality need mention :

(i) ***Amino acid score:*** It is a measure of the concentration of each essential amino acid in the test protein expressed as a percentage of that amino acid in the reference protein.

Amino acid score =

$$\frac{\text{No. of mg of one amino acid per g of protein}}{\text{No. of mg of the same amino acid per g of egg protein}} \times 100$$

The amino acid (or chemical) score is somewhere between 50 and 60 for starches, and 70 and 80 for animal foods.

(ii) ***Net protein utilization (NPU):*** It is a product of digestibility coefficient and biological value divided by 100. The NPU gives a more complete expression of protein quality than the amino acid score. It is a biological method that requires special laboratory facilities.

$$\text{NPU} = \frac{\text{Nitrogen retained by the body}}{\text{Nitrogen intake}} \times 100$$

In calculating protein quality, 1 gram of protein is assumed to be equivalent to 6.25 g of N.

The protein requirement varies with the NPU of dietary protein. If the NPU is low, the protein requirement is high and vice versa.

(b) **Protein Quantity:** The protein content of many Indian foods has been determined and published in food composition tables. One way of evaluating foods as source of protein is to determine what per cent of their energy value is supplied by their protein content. This is know as Protein -Energy Ratio (PE ratio or percentage).

$$\text{PE per cent} = \frac{\text{Energy from protein}}{\text{Total energy in diet}} \times 100$$

This concept is useful because in many population groups adequate diet is not consumed to meet energy needs, resulting in energy deficits.

Dietary intakes: It is customary to express requirement in terms of grams per kg of body weight. This principle applies to all age groups, although absolute additions in units of grams of protein per day are made for pregnancy and lactation.

3. FAT

The daily requirement of fat is not known with certainty. During infancy, fats contribute to a little over 50 per cent of the total energy intake. This scales down to about 20 per cent in adulthood. The requirement of essential fatty acids ranges from 3 per cent energy intake to 5.7 per cent of energy intake in young children.

4. CARBOHYDRATE

The recommended intake of carbohydrate in balanced diets is between 50 to 70 per cent of total energy intake.

BALANCED DIET

A diet may be defined as the kinds of food on which a person or group lives. A balanced diet is defined as one which contains a variety of foods in such quantities and proportions that the need for energy, amino acids, vitamins, minerals, fats, carbohydrate and other nutrients is adequately met for maintaining health, vitality and general well- being and also makes a small provision for extra nutrients to withstand short duration of leanness. A balanced diet has become an accepted means to safeguard a population from nutritional deficiencies.

In constructing balanced diet, the following principles should be borne in mind; *(a)* First and foremost, the daily requirement of protein should be met. This amounts to 15-20 per cent of the daily energy intake. *(b)* Next comes the fat requirement, which should be limited to 20-30 per cent of the daily energy intake *(c)* Carbohydrates rich in natural fibre should constitute the remaining food energy. The requirements of micronutrients should be met.

The dietary pattern varies widely in different parts of the world. It is generally developed on the basis of kinds of food produced (or imported) depending upon the climatic conditions of the region, economic capacity, religion, customs, taboos, tastes and habits of the people.

DIETARY GOALS

All countries should develop a national nutrition and food policy setting out "dietary goals" for achievement. The dietary goals ("prudent diet") recommended by the various Expert Committees of WHO are as below:

- *(a)* dietary Ist should be limited to approximately 20-30 per cent of total daily intake;
- *(b)* saturated fats should contribute no more than 10 per cent of the total energy intake; unsaturated vegetable oils should be substituted for the remaining fat requirement;
- *(c)* excessive consumption of refined carbohydrate should be avoided; some amount of carbohydrate rich in natural fibre should be taken;
- *(d)* sources rich in energy such as fats and alcohol should be restricted;
- *(e)* salt intake should be reduced to an average of not more than 5 g per day; (salt intake is more in tropical countries. In India it averages 15 g per day);
- *(f)* protein should account for approximately 15-20% of the daily intake;
- *(g)* junk foods such as colas, ketchups and other foods that supply empty calories should be reduced.

There may be conditions under which the above recommendations for daily food intake do not apply. For example, diet should be adapted to the special needs of growth, pregnancy, lactation, physical activity, and medical disorders (e.g., diabetes).

NUTRITIONAL PROBLEMS IN PUBLIC HEALTH

There are many nutritional problems which affect vast segments of our population. The major ones which deserve special mention are highlighted:

1. Low birth weight

Low birth weight (i.e., birth weight less than 2500g) is a major public health problem in many developing countries. About 30 per cent of babies born in India are LBW as compared to 4 per cent in some developed countries. In countries where the proportion of LBW is high the majority are suffering from foetal growth retardation. In countries where the proportion of LBW infants is low, most of them are pre-term. Although we do not know all the causes of LBW, maternal malnutrition and anaemia appear to be significant risk factors in its occurrence. Among the other causes of LBW are hard physical labour during pregnancy, and illnesses especially infections. Short maternal stature, very young age, high parity, smoking, close birth intervals are all associated factors. All these factors are interrelated.

The proportion of infants born with LBW has been selected as one of the nutritional indicators for monitoring progress towards Health for All by the year 2000. The goal of the National Health Policy is to reduce the incidence of LBW infants to about 10 per cent by the year 2000.

2. Protein Energy Malnutrition (PEM)

Protein energy malnutrition (PEM) has been identified as a major health and nutrition problem in India. It occurs particularly in weaklings and children in the first years of life. It is not only an important cause of childhood morbidity and mortality, but leads also to permanent impairment of physical and possibly, of mental growth of those who survive. The current concept of PEM is that its clinical forms - Kwashiorkor and Marasmus - are two different clinical pictures at opposite poles of a single continuum.

The incidence of PEM in India in preschool age children is 1-2 per cent. The great majority of cases of PEM, nearly 80 per cent, are the "intermediate" ones, that is the mild and moderate cases which frequently go unrecognized. The problem exists in all the States and that nutritional marasmus is more frequent than kwashiorkor.

Early Detection of PEM

The first indicator of PEM is under -weight for age. The most practical method to detect this, which can be employed even by field health workers, is to maintain growth charts. These charts indicate at a glance whether the child is gaining or losing weight.

Preventive Measures: There is no simple solution to the problem of PEM. Many types of actions are necessary. The following is adapted from the 8th FAO/WHO Expert Committee on Nutrition for the prevention of PEM in the community:

(a) Health Promotion:

1. Measures directed to pregnant and lactating women (education, distribution of supplements)
2. Promotion of breast feeding.
3. Development of low cost weaning foods: the child should be made to eat more food at frequent intervals.
4. Measures to improve family diet
5. Nutrition education- Promotion of correct feeding practices.

(b) Specific Protection

1. The child's diet must contain protein and energy rich foods. Milk, eggs, fresh fruits should be given if possible.
2. Immunization
3. Food fortification

(c) Early Diagnosis and Treatment:

1. Periodic surveillance
2. Early diagnosis of any lag in growth
3. Early diagnosis and treatment of infections and diarrhoea.
4. Development of programmes for early rehydration of children with diarrhoea.
5. Development of supplementary feeding programmes during epidemics.

(d) Rehabilitation :

1. Nutritional rehabilitation services
2. Hospital treatment
3. Follow- up care

3. Xerophthalmia

Xerophthalmia (dry eye) refers to all the ocular manifestations of vitamin A deficiency in man. It is the most widespread and serious nutritional disorder leading to blindness particularly in South- East Asia.

Xerophthalmia is most common in children aged 1-3 years, and is often related to weaning. The younger the child, the more severe the disease. It is often associated with PEM. Mortality is often high in this age group. The victims belong to the poorest families. Associated risk factors include ignorance, faulty feeding practices and infection paticularly diarrhoea and measles which often precipitate xerophthalmia. In some countries, "epidemics" of xerophthalmia have occurred in association with food donation programmes involving skimmed milk, which is totally devoid of vitamin A.

The States badly affected are the southern and eastern States of India notably Andhra, Tamii Nadu, Karnataka, Bihar and West Bengal. These are predominantly rice-eating States and rice is devoid of carotene. The North Indian States have relatively few cases of xerophthalmia.

Prevention and control: Prevention and control of xerophthalmia must be an integral part of primary health care. An overall strategy can be defined according to WHO in terms of short-term, medium-term and long-term action.

(a) Short-term action: A short-term preventive approach that has already demonstrated its efficacy is the administration of large doses of vitamin A orally, in recommended does to vulnerable groups, on a periodic basis. This can be organized quickly and with a minimum of infrastructure.

(b) Medium-term action: An approach widely used to promote regular and adequate intake of vitamin A is fortification of certain foods with vitamin A. Addition of vitamin A to *dalda* in India is a typical example. Many other foods have also been considered for vitamin A fortification, viz. sugar, salt, tea, margarine and dried skimmed milk. Fortifying an appropriate food with vitamin A is a complex process. The greatest challenge to successful fortification programmes is choosing a food that is likely to be consumed in sufficient quantities by groups at risk.

(c) Long-term action: These are measures aimed at reduction or elimination of factors contributing to ocular disease, e.g. persuading people in general , and mothers in particular, to consume generously dark green leafy vegetables or other vitamin A rich foods, promotion of breast feeding for as long as possible, improvements in environmental health such as ensuring safe and adequate water supply and construction and maintenance of pit latrines.

4. Nutritional Anaemia

Nutritional anaemia is a disease syndrome caused by malnutrition in its widest sense. It has defined by WHO as "a condition in which the haemoglobin content of blood is lower than normal as a result of a deficiency of one or more essential nutrients, regardless of the cause of such deficiency." Anaemia is established if the haemoglobin is below the cut- off points recommended by WHO. By far the most frequent cause of nutritional anaemia is iron deficiency, and frequently folate or vitamin B_{12}.

THE NUTRITIONAL PROBLEM IN INDIA

Iron deficiency anaemia is a major nutrition problem in India and many other developing countries. In addition, many have iron deficiency without anaemia. The incidence of anaemia is highest among women and young children, varying between 60 to 70 per cent. Recent surveys indicate that in rural India anaemia is much more widespread than hitherto believed, even among men.

Iron deficiency can arise either due to inadequate intake or poor bioavailability of dietary iron or due to excessive losses of iron from the body. Although most habitual diets contain seemingly adequate amounts of iron, only a small amount (less than 5 per cent) is absorbed. This poor bioavailability is considered to a major reason for the widespread iron deficiency. Women lose a considerable amount of iron especially during menstruation. Some of the other factors leading to anaemia are malaria and hookworm infestations. In addition mothers who have born children at close intervals become anaemic due to the additional demands of the rapid pregnancies and the loss of blood in each delivery.

In some areas of India, it has been shown that folate deficiency anaemia affects 25 to 50 per cent of pregnant women attending hospital clinics. Present evidence suggests that a high prevalence of folate deficiency anaemia in pregnancy is a universal phenomenon and is associated unnecessarily with economically underprivileged.

Detrimental effects : The detrimental effects of anaemia can be seen in three important areas. *(a) Pregnancy :* Anaemia increases the risk of maternal and foetal mortality and morbidity. *(b) Infection :* Anaemia can be caused or aggravated by parasitic diseases, e.g. malaria, intestinal parasites. *(c) Work capacity :* Anaemia (even when mild) causes a significant impairment of maximal work capacity.

5. Goitre

The magnitude of the problem in India is far greater than what had been estimated in 1960s, when it was estimated that about 9 million persons were affected by goitre.

Goitre control: There are four essential components of national goitre control programme. These are iodized salt or oil, monitoring and surveillance, manpower training and mass communication.

Iodized Salt: The iodization of salt is now the most widely used prophylactic public health measure against endemic goitre. In India the level of iodization is fixed under the Prevention of Food Adulteration (PFA) Act and is not less than 30 ppm at the production point and not less than 15 ppm of iodine at the consumer level.

SELECTED NUTRITIONAL DISEASES

1. Cardiovascular disease

It is now generally agreed that diet governs many situations favouring the on set of "heart disease", particularly coronary heart disease (CHD). Of all the factors associated with CHD (e.g. plasma cholesterol, high blood pressure, cigarette smoking, lack of physical activity) plasma cholesterol has a very high statistical significance with the incidence of CHD. The risk of CHD appears to increase as the plasma cholesterol concentration rises.

The *lipid hypothesis*- although debated for more than 30 years- has not, in the opinion of some researchers, yet been proven. For instance, data from the Framingham Heart Study did not find significant association between dietary lipids and the risk of CHD within populations. This has been cited as evidence against diet- hear hypothesis. However, various other studies have supported the role of elevated blood levels of cholesterol and low density lipoproteins (LDL) in the development of atherosclerosis. Geographical studies have shown that there is no population in whom CHD is common that does not have a relatively high mean level of plasma total cholesterol (TC) in adults.

Cholesterol : Cholesterol occurs in all foods of animal origin. Part of it is synthesized in the body. The plasma cholesterol is determined by *(a)* the amount absorbed from food *(b)* the amount synthesized in the body *(c)* the rate of catabolism and excretion in the bile *(d)* intestinal reabsorption of bile acids, and *(e)* the equilibrium between plasma and tissues. The extent to which cholesterol intake influences total cholesterol levels is highly variable.

Fatty acids: In populations where the plasma cholesterol is high, there is also generally high consumption of saturated fats. Clinical studies on selected volunteers under well-defined conditions have clearly demonstrated that a high intake of saturated fatty acids over several weeks or months causes an increase in plasma cholesterol.

Polyunsaturated fatty acids (e.g. Linoleic and arachidonic acids) have an additional role, that is, to inhibit aggregation and thus prevent thrombus formation. Recent research indicates that arachidonic acid metabolises in the vascular endothelium to form two important metabolism namely prostacyclin and thromboxane.

It has been shown that cholesterol in blood can be reduced by controlling the amount and type of fat in the diet.

Carbohydrate: Coronary heart disease rates are lowest in population eating high carbohydrate diets. Support for the hypothesis that consumption of complex carbohydrates may decrease the risk of CHD comes from historical trends of food consumption patterns and mortality rates in India, It is generally recognized that such mortality rates were quite low until about 1920.

Salt: There are good and consistent correlations between dietary sodium intake and the incidence of hypertension. Thus the highest incidence of hypertension is found in north Japan where the sodium intake is above 400 mmol/day, while primitive societies ingesting less than 60 mmol/day have virtually no hypertension. Susceptible individuals in primitive populations who change from low to high intake of sodium have been found to develop hypertension.

2. Diabetes

In a diabetic, there is impaired metabolism of glucose in the body, which leads to excess of glucose in blood and urine. Insulin helps in checking and maintaining the level of glucose in blood. Insulin deficiency leads to accelerated utilization of energy reserves from fat stores. The fatty acids are oxidized by liver to ketone bodies. Excess of ketone bodies leads to their accumulation in urine. This condition is known as ketoacidosis and can result in diabetic coma. Due to insulin deficiency excess of fatty acids are converted to triglycerides. In diabetes these accumulate in the blood. Insulin is also important for synthesis of proteins and deficiency of insulin leads to muscle wasting.

It has been suggested that deficiencies of trace elements such as chromium, copper and zinc may play a role in the pathogenesis of diabetes mellitus, but clinical evidence is lacking.

Malnutrition-related diabetes mellitus has recently attracted attention. Protein deficiency may be involved in the pathogenesis of some forms of diabetes. Excessive consumption of alcohol can increase the risk of diabetes by damaging the pancreas and liver and by promoting obesity.

3. Obesity

In richer countries and in some developing countries, obesity is a health problem. The connection between severe obesity and premature death from diabetes, hypertension and CHD is well established. The basic cause of obesity is overnutrition. A diet containing more energy than needed may lead to prolonged post- prandial hyperlipidaemia and to deposition to triglycerides in adipose tissue resulting in obesity.

It is known that a relative insulin resistance takes place in obesity in peripheral tissues, mainly adipose tissues, while the insulin secretion is normal or increased. The demonstrated reduction in the sensitivity to insulin of the large adipocyte can be attributed to the decreased affinity of the insulin receptors or to a reduction in their number in the cell membrane, Through a feedback mechanism the insulin secretion is stepped up, thus leading to a state of hyperinsulinism.

From a practical point of view all hypotheses concerning the genesis of obesity could be put down to over-nutrition, to a hyper-energy food intake. This is a sound basis for preventive and therapeutic recommendations.

4. Cancer

It is postulated that 80 per cent of cancers may be due to environmental factors, and it is possible that some dietatic factors may be involved. Existing knowledge is reviewed briefly as below:

***(a)* Dietary fat:** Population surveys have shown a strong positive correlation between cancer colon and dietary intake of fat. It has been suggested that the high fat intake accounts for the high incidence of colon cancer in Western communities. Dietary fat is believed to increase the secretion of bile acids in the bowl which are then metabolised by bacterial flora into carcinogens or co-carcinogens.

A positive correlation between per capita consumption of dietary fat and breast cancer rates has also been noted. A reduction in dietary fat may alter the risk of breast cancer, perhaps by increasing oestrogen production or prolactin release.

***(b)* Dietary fibre:** Several studies indicate that the risk of colon cancer is inversely related to the consumption of dietary fibre, which may protect against intestinal carcinogens or precursors by dilutional or other effects. Although the available epidemiological data are not entirely consistent, the weight of evidence generally supports the hypothesis that fibre protects against colon cancer.

(c) **Micronutrients :** Micronutrients may also have a protective influence, since cancers of the lung and several other sites have been associated with a low intake of vitamin A. The risk of stomach cancer has been related to a deficiency of vitamin C, which may act by inhibiting the formation of carcinogenic nitrosamines in the stomach. Trace elements (e.g. selenium) have also been implicated in the aetiology of cancer.

(d) **Food additives and contaminants :** Food additives and contaminants (e.g. preservatives, artificial colours, artificial sweeteners, pesticides, flavours, anti oxidants) have always been under suspicion as possible carcinogens in their long- term effects. It is thought in some quarters that nitrosamines are responsible for certain types of gastric carcinoma.

(e) **Alcohol:** Heavy drinking increases the risk of liver cancer. It is estimated that alcohol contributes to about 3 per cent of all cancer deaths. Some recent studies have suggested that beer consumption may be related to cancer rectum, but the association has not been confirmed.

The above review, indicates that in recent years, much evidence has accumulated to indicate that nutrition has an influence on cancer incidence and mortality. There is in this field a remarkable dearth of facts and an abundance of speculation.

HYGIENE

Pasteurization

Pasteurization is a preventive measure of public health importance and corresponds in all respects to the modern principles of supplying safe milk. Pasteurization kills nearly 90 per cent of the bacteria in milk including the more heat-resistant tubercle bacillus and the Q fever organisms. But it will not kill thermoduric bacteria nor the bacterial spores. Therefore, despite pasteurization, with subsequent rise in temperature, the bacteria are bound to multiply. In order to check the growth of microorganisms, pasteurized milk is rapidly cooled to 4 deg C. It should be kept cold until it reaches the consumer. Hygienically produced pasteurized milk has a keeping quality of not more than 8 to 12 hours at 18 deg C.

Meat Hygiene

The term "meat" includes various tissues of animal origin. The diseases which may be transmitted by eating unwholesome meat are:

1. Tape Worm Infestations: *Tinea solium, T, saginata, Trichinella spiralis and Fasciola hepatica,*
2. Bacterial Infections: Anthrax, actinomycosis, tuberculosis and food poisoning.

Meat Inspection : Animals intended for slaughter are subjected to proper antemortem and postmortem inspection by qualified veterinary staff. The principal causes of antemortem rejection of animals are emaciation, exhaustion pregnancy, sheep- pox, foot-rot, actinomycosis, brucellosis, febrile conditions, diarrhoea and other diseases of an infectious nature rendering meat unfit for human consumption. The main causes of the postmortem rejection are cysticercus bovis, liver fluke, abscesses, sarcocystis, hydatidosis septicaemia, parasitic and nodular infections of liver and lungs, tuberculosis, cysticercus cellulose, etc.

Slaughter houses : Slaughter houses are the places where animals, whose flesh is intended for human consumption are killed. The hygiene of the slaughter house is of paramount importance to prevent the contamination of meat during the process of dressing. The following minimum standards for slaughter houses have been suggested under the Model public Health Act (1955) in India.

1. *Location :* Preferably away from residential areas.
2. *Structure :* Floors and walls upto 3 feet should be impervious and easy to clean.
3. *Disposal of wastes :* Blood, offal, etc. should not be discharged into public sewers but should be collected separately.

4. *Water supply :* Should be independent, adequate and continuous.
5. *Examination of animals :* Antemortem and postmortem examination to be arranged. Animals or meat found unfit for human consumption should be destroyed or denatured.
6. *Storage of meat :* Meat should be stored in fly- proof and rat- proof rooms; for overnight storage, the temperature of the room shall be maintained below 5 deg C.
7. *Transportation of meat :* Meat shall be transported in fly- proof covered vans.
8. *Miscellaneous :* Animals other than those to be slaughtered should no be allowed inside the shed.

Fruits and Vegetables

Fruits and vegetables constitute another important source for the spread of pathogenic organisms, protozoans and helminths. These infections are a serious menace to public health where sewage used for growing vegetables. The vegetables which are consume raw in the form of salads pose a problem in food sanitation. People should be educated to wash the vegetables before eating them raw. Vegetables which are cooked are free from this danger.

Sanitation of Eating Places : Sanitation of eating establishments is a challenging problem to food sanitation. The following minimum standards have been suggested for Restaurants and Eating Houses in India under the Model Public Health Act (1955).

1. *Location :* Shall not be near any accumulation of filth or open drain, stable, manure pit and other sources of nuisances.
2. *Floors :* To be higher than the adjoining land, made with impervious material and easy to keep clean.
3. *Rooms : (a)* Rooms where meals are served shall not be less than 100 sq. feet and shall provide accommodation for a persons *(b)* Walls up to 3 feet should be smooths, corners to rounded; should be impervious and easily washable *(c)* Lighting a ventilation- ample natural lighting facilities aided by artificial light with good circulation of air are necessary
4. *Kitchen : (a)* Floor space minimum 60 sq. ft *(b)* Window opening to be 25 per cent floor area. *(c)* Floor to be impervious smooth, easy to keep clean and non-slippery *(d)* Doors and windows to be rat proof, fly proof and the self closing type *(e)* Ventilators 2 per cent of the floor area.

FOODBORNE DISEASES

The term "foodborne disease" is defined as "A disease, usually either infectious or toxic in nature, caused by agents that enter the body through the ingestion of food." With the increase in urbanization, industrialization, tourism and mass catering systems, foodborne diseases are on the increase throughout the world. Foodborne diseases may be classified as:

A. Foodborne Intoxications

1. Due to naturally occurring toxins in some foods
   (a) Lathyrism (beta oxalyl amino-alanine)
   (b) Endemic ascitis (Pyrrolozidine alkaloids)
2. Due to toxins produced by certain bacteria
   (a) Botulism
   (b) Staphyloccus poisons
3. Due to toxins produced by some fungi
   (a) Aflatoxin
   (b) Ergot
   (c) Fusarium toxins
4. Foodborne chemical poisoning
   (a) Heavy metals, e.g., mercury (usually in fish), cadmium (in certain shellfish) and lead (in canned food)
   (b) Oils, petroleum derivatives and solvents (e.g.. Trycresyn phosphate or TCP)
   (c) Migrant chemicals from package materials
   (d) Asbestos
   (e) Pesticide residues (DDT, BHC)

B. Foodborne infections

Group Examples of illness in each group

1. Bacterial diseases: Typhoid fever, paratyphoid fever, Salmonellosis,

Staphylococcal intoxication, *Cl. perfringens* illness, Botulism, *B. cereus* Food poisoning, *E. coli* diarrhoea. Non - cholera vibrio illness, *V. parahaemolyticus* infection, Streptococcal infection, Shigellosis Brucellosis

2. Viral diseases: Viral hepatitis, Gastroenteritis
3. Parasites: Taeniasis Hydatidosis, Trichinosis, Ascariasis, Amoebiasis, Oxyuriasis.

FOOD TOXICANTS

1. ***Neurolathyrism :*** The cause of neurolathyrism is a toxin, Beta oxalyl amino alanine (BOAA) which is found in the seeds of the pulse, *L. sativus* (Khesari dal). Neurolathyrism is a public health problem in certain parts of the country where this pulse is eaten.
2. ***Aflatoxins :*** Aflatoxins are a group of mycotoxins produced by certain fungi, *Aspergillus flavus* and *A. parasiticus.* These fungi infest foodgrains such as groundnut, maize, parboiled rice, sorghum, wheat, rice, cotton seed and tapioca under conditions of improper storage, and produce aflatoxins of which B_1 and G_1 are the most potent hepatotoxins, in addition to being carcinogenic.

   Control and preventive Measures: A crucial factor in the prevention of fungal contamination of foodgrains is to ensure their proper storage after drying. Moisture content should be kept below 10 per cent. If the food is contaminated, it must not be consumed. It is also essential to educate the local population on the health hazards of consuming contaminated foodgrains.
3. ***Ergot:*** Unlike Aspergillus, ergot is not a storage fungus, but a field fungus. Foodgrains such as bajra, rye, sorghum, and wheat have a tendency to get infested during the flowering stages by the ergot fungus, *Claviceps fusiformis (Claviceps purpurea).* Fungus grows as a blackish mass and the seeds become black and irregular and are harvested along with food grains. Consumption of ergot infested grain leads to ergotism. Sporadic outbreaks of ergot poisoning in human population have been reported from time to time in areas where bajra is consumed as a staple. The symptoms are acute but rarely fatal and include nausea, repeated vomiting, giddiness and drowsiness extending sometimes for periods up to 24 to 48 hours after the ingestion of ergoty grain. Ergot-infested grains can be easily removed by floating them in 20 per cent salt water. They can also be removed by handpicking or air floatation. The upper safe limit for the ergot alkaloids has been estimated to be 0.05 mg per 100 grams of the food material.
4. ***Epidemic Dropsy :*** The symptoms of epidemic dropsy consist of sudden, non-inflammatory, bilateral swelling of legs, often associated with diarrhoea. Dyspnoea, cardiac failure and death may follow. Some patients may develop glaucoma. The disease may occur at all ages except breast-fed infants.

   The contamination of mustard or other oils with argemone oil may be accidental or deliberate. Seeds of *Argemone mexicana* (prickly poppy) closely resemble mustard seeds. The plant grows wild in India. It has prickly leaves and bright yellow flowers. Crops of mustard are gathered during March, and during this period, the seeds of argemone also mature and are likely to be harvested along with mustard seeds. Sometimes unscrupulous dealers mix argemone oil with mustard or other oils.

   The accidental contamination of mustard seeds can be prevented at the source by removing the argemone weeds growing among oil-seed crops. Unscrupulous dealers may be dealt with by the strict enforcement of the Prevention of Food Adulteration Act.

Food Fortification

Fortification of food is a public health measure aimed at reinforcing the usual dietary intake of nutrients with additional supplies to prevent/ control some nutritional disorders. WHO has defined "food fortification" as "the process whereby nutrients are added to foods (in relatively small quantities) to maintain or improve the quality of the diet of a group, a community, or a population."

Programmes of demonstrated effectiveness of fortification of food or water are: fluoridation of water as a preventive of dental caries: iodization of salt for combating the problem of endemic goitre, and food fortification (e.g., vansapathi, milk) with vitamins A and D. Recently, technology has been developed for the twin fortification of salt with iodine and iron.

In order to qualify as suitable for fortification, the vehicle and the nutrient must fulfill certain criteria:

(a) the vehicle fortified must be consumed consistently as part of the regular daily diet by the relevant sections of the population or total population;

(b) the amount of nutrient added must provide an effective supplement for low consumers of the vehicle, without contributing a hazardous excess to high consumers;

(c) the addition of the nutrient should not cause it to undergo any noticeable change in taste, smell, appearance, or consistency; and

(d) the cost of fortification must not raise the price of the food beyond the reach of the population in greatest need.

Finally, an adequate of surveillance and control is indispensable for the effectiveness of food fortification. Food fortification is a long-term measure for mitigating specific problems of malnutrition in the community.

Adulteration of foods: Adulteration of foods is an age-old problem. It consists of a large number of practices, e.g., mixing, substitution, concealing the quality, putting up decomposed foods for sale, misbranding or giving false labels and addition of toxicants. Adulteration results in two disadvantages for the consumer : first, he is paying more money for a foodstuff of lower quality; secondly, some forms of adulteration are injurious to health, even resulting in death, as for example, adulteration of mustard oil with argemone oil causing epidemic dropsy or adulteration of edible oils with trycresyn phosphate (TCP) resulting in paralysis and death.

Food adulteration practices vary from one part of the country to another, and from time to time. Our knowledge about the current practices of food adulteration is by no means complete.

Prevention of Food Adulteration Act, 1954

Enacted by the Indian Parliament in 1954, with the objective of ensuring pure and wholesome food to the consumers and to protect them from fradulent and deceptive trade practices, the Prevention of Food Adulteration (PFA) Act was amended in 1964, 1976 and lately in 1986 to make the Act more stringent.

Rules are framed which are revised from time to time by an expert body called the "Central Committee for Foods standards" which is constituted by the Central Government under the provisions of the Act. Any food that does not conform to the minimum standards is said to be adulterated. Although it is a Central Act, its implementation is largely carried out by the State Governments and local bodies in their respective areas. However, the Centre plays a vital role in proper coordination, monitoring and surveillance of the programme throughout the country. A chain of food laboratories and four regional appellate Central Food Laboratories (Calcutta, Mysore, Ghaziabad and Pune) whose report is considered to be final have been established.

Training being an important component of the programme for prevention of food adulteration, the Directorate General of Health Services organises in-service training programme for different functionaries responsible for implementation of the PFA Act. Food inspectors, analysts and the senior officers concerned with the implementation of the Act in States are provided training.

9

Health Education & Programmes in India

Health Education is a process that informs, motivates and helps people to adopt and maintain healthy practices and lifestyles, advocates environmental changes as needed to facilitate this goal and conducts professional training and research to the same end".

Objectives of Health Education

Under the above definition, the three main objectives of health education are :

(a) *Informing people:* For thousands of years, disease and death have been accepted as normal phenomenon. Therefore, it become necessary to educate the peoples about the necessity of health.

(b) *Motivating people:* The second objective is more important than the first. Simply telling peope about health is not enough. They must be motivated to change their habits and ways of living, since many present day problems of community health require alteration of human behaviour or changes in the health practices which are deterimental to health.

(c) *Guiding into action:* Under the above definition, health education can and should be conducted by a variety of health, education and communication personnel, in a variety of settings, starting with the physician. People need help to adopt and maintain healthy practices and life-styles, which may be totally new to them. Governments have a major responsibility to provide the necessary infrastructure of health services.

Content of Health Education

Health education is as wide as community health. In practice, the content of health education may be divided into 8 main divisions:

1. *Human Biology:* Much of the teaching pertaining to human biology is done in schools.
2. *Nutrition:* The aim of health education in nutrition is to guide people to choose optimum and balanced diets which contain nutrients necessary for energy, growth, and repair — but not to teach the familiar jargon of calories and the biochemistry of nutrients. Education is given on the nutritive value of foods. High price of foods is not always poof of its high nutitional contents.
3. *Hygiene:* This has two aspects-personal and environmental. The aim of personal hygiene is to promote standards of personal cleanliness within the setting of the conditions where people live. *Personal Hygiene* includes bathing, clothing, washing hands and toilet; care of feet, nails and teeth; spitting, coughing, sneezing, personal appearance and inculcation of clean habits in the young. Training in personal hygiene should begin at a very early age and must be carried through school age. *Environmental Hygiene* has two aspects-domestic and community. Domestic hygiene comprises that of the home, use of soap, need for fresh air, light and ventilation; hygienic storage of foods; hygienic disposal of wastes, need to avoid pests, rats, mice and insects.

4. *Family Health Care:* Family health is traditionally centred round mother and child health care. However, the focus has expanded to embrace concern for the family as a unit. Currently family health care programmes embrace human growth.
5. *Control of Communicable and Non-Communicable Diseases:* There is a wide range of specific communicable and non-communicable diseases needing health education activity, to mention a few-malaria, sexually transmitted diseases, trachoma, leprosy, tuberculosis, malnutrition, cardio-vascular diseases, drug addiction, alcoholism, accidents etc.
6. *Mental Health:* Mental health problems occur everywhere. They become more prominent when major killer diseases are brought under control. There is a tendency to an increase in the prevalence of mental diseases.
7. *Prevention of Accidents:* Accidents are a feature of the complexity of modern life in the developed countries, they are taking an increasing toll of life and limb.
8. *Use of Health Services:* One of the declared aims of health education is to inform the public about the health services that are available in the community, and how to use them. They should not be misused or abused.

Table : Health Education and Propaganda

Education	*Propaganda or Publicity*
1. Knowledge and skills actively acquired	— Knowledge instilled in the minds of people
2. Makes people think for themselves	— Prevents or discourages thinking by ready made slogans
3. Disciplines primitive desires	— Arouses and stimulates primitive desires
4. Develops reflective behaviour. Train people to use judgements before acting	— Develops reflective behaviour; aims at impulsive actions
5. Appeals to reason	— Appeals to emotion
6. Develops individuality, personality and self-expression	— Develops a standard pattern of attitudes and behaviours according to the mould used
7. Knowledge acquired through self-reliant activity	— Knowledge is spoonfed and passively received
8. The process is behaviour centred aims at developing favourable attitudes and habits and skills	— The process is information centred-no change of attitude or behaviour designed.

Principles of Health Education

Before we come to the practice of health education, we must know the principles involved. Health education brings together the art and science of medicine, and the principles and practice of general education. The link is to be found in the school and behavioural sciences—sociology, psychology. It is possible to abstract certain principles of learning and use them in health education.

1. *Interest:* It is a psychological principle that people are unlikely to listen to those things which are not to their interest. It is salutary to remind ourselves that health teaching should relate to the interests of the people. The public is not interested in health slogans such as "Take care of your health" or "be healthy". A health education programme of this kind would be as useless as asking people to "be healthy", as a nutrition programme asking people to "eat good food".
2. *Participation:* It is a keyword in health education. Participation is based on the psychological principle of active learning; it is better than passive learning. Group

discussion, panel discussion workshop all provide opportunities for active learning. Personal involvement is more likely to lead to personal acceptance.

3. *Known to Unknown*: In health education work, we proceed from the known to the unknown *i.e.*, start where the people are and with what they understand and then proceed to new knowledge. We use the existing knowledge of the people as pegs on which to hang new knowledge. In this way systematic knowledge is built up. New Knowledge will bring about a new, enlarged understanding which can give rise to an insight into the problem.
4. *Comprehension:* In health education we must know the level of understanding, education and literacy of people to whom the teaching is directed. One barrier to communication is using words which cannot be understood. A doctor asked the diabetic to cut down starchy foods. A doctor prescribed medicine in the familiar jargon "one teaspoonful three times a day"; the patient, a village woman, has never seen a teaspoon, and could not follow the doctor's directions. In health education, we should always communicate in the language people understand, and never use words which are strange and new to the people.
5. *Reinforcement:* Few people can learn all that is new in a single contact. Repetition at intervals is extremely useful. It assists comprehension and understanding. Every health compaign needs reinforcement; we may call it a "booster dose".

Barriers of Communication

These can be:

1. Physiological – difficulties in hearing, expression
2. Psychological – emotional disturbances, neurosis
3. Environmental – noise, invisibility congestion
4. Cultural – levels of knowledge and understanding, customs, beliefs, religion, attitudes

The barriers should be identified and removed for achieving effective communication.

Administration and Organisation

Governments have a responsibility for assisting and guiding the health education of the general public. For this purpose, the Central Health Education Bureau was established in Ministry of Health in 1956 at Delhi with the assistance of the Technical Co-operation Mission of the United States. The Central Health Education Bureau consists of training, media research, and evaluation divisions in addition to an administrative section. The functions of the Bureau are:

(1) to interpret the services of the central Ministry of Health so as to win the support for the maximum use of its various services;
(2) to procure and publish educational material for distribution throughout the country;
(3) to help Central Health Services, and voluntary organisations and State Health Ministries requesting technical assistance;
(4) to promote and coordinate health education work in the country, particularly by initiating and conducting specialized research, studies, and the effective use of education by health workers throughout the country.

HEALTH CARE OF THE COMMUNITY

Since health is influenced by a number of factors such as adequate food, housing, basic sanitation, healthy lifestyles, protection against environmental hazards and communicable diseases, the frontiers of health extend beyond the narrow limits of medical care. It is thus clear that "health care" implies more than "medical care". The term "medical care" is not synonymous "health care". It refers chiefly to those personal services that are provided directly by physicians or rendered as the result of physicians's instructions. It ranges from domiciliary care to resident hospital care. Medical care is a subset of health care system.

Health care is a public right, and it is the responsiblity of governments to provide this care to all people in equal measure. These principles have been recognized by nearly all governments of the world and enshrined in their respective constitutions. In India, health care is completely a governmental function.

Levels of Health Care

It is customary to describe health care services at 3 levels, *viz.*, primary, secondary and tertiary care levels. These levels represents different types of care involving varying degrees of complexity.

1. *Primary care level:* It is the first level of contact of individuals, the family and community with the national health system, where "primary health care". ("essential" health care) is provided. As a level of care, it is close to the people, where most of their health problems can be dealt with and resolved. It is at this level that health care will be most effective within the context to the areas's needs and limitations. In the Indian context, primary health care is provided by the complex of primary health centres and their subcentres through the agency of multipurpose health workers, village health guides and trained dais.
2. *Secondary care level*: The next higher level of care is the secondary (intermediate) health care level. At this level more complex problems are dealt with. In India, this kind of care is generally provided in district hospitals and community health centres which also serve as the first referral level.
3. *Tertiary Care Level:* The tertiary level is a more specialized required specific facilities and attention of highly specialized health workers. This care is provided by the regional or central level institutions, *e.g.*, Medical College, Hospitals, All India Institutes, Regional Hospitals, Specialized Hospitals and other Apex Institutions.

Elements of Primary Health Care

Although specific services provided will vary in different countries and communities, the Alma-Ata Declartion has outlined 8 essential components of primary health care.

1. education concerning prevailing health problems and the methods of preventing and controlling them;
2. promotion of food supply and proper nutrition;
3. an adequate supply of safe water and basic sanitation;
4. maternal and child health care, including family planning;
5. immunization against major infections diseases;
6. prevention and control of locally endemic diseases;
7. appropriate treatment of common diseases and injuries; and
8. provision of essential drugs.

Principles of Primary Health Care:

1. *Equitable distribution:* The first key principle in the primary health care strategy is equity or equitable distribution of health services, *i.e.*, health services must be shared equally by all people irrespective of their ability to pay, and all (rich or poor, urban or rural) must have access to health services. At present, health services are mainly concentrated in the major towns and cities resulting in inequality of care to the people in rural areas. The worst hit are the needy and vulnerable groups of the population in rural areas and urban slums.
2. *Community Participation:* Not with standing the overall responsibility of the Central and State Governments, the involvement of individuals, families, and communities in promotion of their own health and welfare, is an essential ingredient of primary health care.
3. *Intersectoral coordination:* There is an increasing realization of the fact that the components of primary health care cannot be provided by the health sector alone. The declaration of Alma-Ata states that "primary health care involves in addition to the health sector, all related sectors and

aspects of national community development, food, industry, education, housing, public works, communication and others sectors".

4. *Appropriate technology:* Appropriate technology has been defined as "technology that is scientifically sound, adaptable to local needs, and acceptable to those who apply it and those for whom it is used, and that can be maintained by the people themselves in keeping with the principle of self reliance with the resources the community and country can afford.

Health Status and Health Problems

An assesment of the health status and health problems is the first requisite for any planned effort to develop health care services. This is also known as Community Diagnosis. The data required for analysing the health situation and for defining the health problems comprise the following:

1. Morbidity and Mortality statistics.
2. Demographic conditions of the population.
3. Environmental conditions which have a bearing on health.
4. Socio-economic factors which have a direct effect on health.
5. Cultural background, attitudes, beliefs, and practices which affect health.
6. Medical and health services available.
7. Other services available.

An analysis of the health situation in the light of the above data will bring out the health problems and health needs of the community. These problems are then ranked according to priority or urgency for allocation of resources.

Health Problems

The Health problems of India may be conveniently grouped under the following heads:

1. Communicable disease problems
2. Nutritional problems
3. Environmental sanitation problems
4. Medical care problems
5. Population problems

PRIMARY HEALTH CARE IN INDIA

In 1977, the Government of India launched a Rural Health Scheme, based on the principle of "Placing people's health in people's hands" It is a three tier system of health care delivery in rural areas based on the recommendation of the Shrivastava Committee in 1975. Close on the heels of these recommendation an International conference at Alma-Ata in 1978, set the goal of an acceptable level of health care approach. As a signatory to the Alma-Ata Declacation, the Government of India is committed to achieving the goal of Health for All through primary health care approach which seeks to provide universal comprehensive health care at a cost which is affordable.

Keeping in view, the WHO goal of "Health for All" evolved a National Health Policy based on primary health care approach. It was approved by Parliament in 1983. The National Health Policy has laid down a plan of action for reorienting and shaping the existing rural health infra-structure with specific goals to be achieved by 1985, 1990 and 1995 within the framework of the sixth (1980-85) and seventh (1985-90) Five Year Plans and the new 20 point programme. Steps are already under way to implement the National Health Policy objectives towards achieving Health for All. These are described below:

1. Village Level

One of the basic tenets of primary health care is universal coverage and equitable distribution of health resources. That is, health care must penetrate into the farthest reaches of rural areas, and that everyone should have access to it. To implement this policy at the village level, the following schemes are in operation:

(a) Village Health Guides Scheme
(b) Training of Local Dais
(c) ICDS Scheme

(a) ***Village Health Guides:*** A Village Health Guides is a person with an aptitude for social service and is not a full time government functionary. The Village

Health Guides Scheme was intoduced on 2nd October 1977 with the idea of securing people's participation in the care of their own health. The scheme was launched in all states except Kerela, Karnataka, Tamil Nadu, Arunachal Pradesh and Jammu and Kashmir which had alternative systems (*e.g.*, Mini-health centres in Tamil Nadu) of providing health services at the village level.

The guidelines for their selection are:

(a) they should be permanent residents of the local community, preferable women;

(b) they should be able to read and write, having minimum formal education at least up to the VI standard;

(c) they should be acceptable to all sections of the community and;

(d) they should be able to spare at least 2 to 3 hours every day for community health work.

(b) *Local Dais:* Most deliveries in rural areas are still handled by untrained dais who are often the only people immediately available to women during the preinatal period. An extensive programme has been under taken, under the Rural Health Scheme, to train all categories of local dais (traditional birth attendants) in the country to improve their knowledge in the elementary concepts of maternal and child health and sterilization, besides obstetric skillls. The training is for 30 working days.

(c) *Anganwadi Worker:* Angan literally means a courtyard. Under the ICDS (Integrated Child Development Services) scheme, there is an anganwadi worker for a population of 1000. There are about 100 such workwes in each ICDS project. As of date over 5320 ICDS blocks are functioning in the country. The anganwadi worker is selected from the community she is expected to serve. She undergoes training in various aspects of health, nutrition, and child development for 4 months. She is a part-time worker and is paid an honorarium of Rs 200–250 per month for the services rendered, which include health check-up, immunization, supplementary nutrition, health education, non-formal pre-school education and referral services.

2. Sub-Centre Level

The sup-centre is the peripheral outpost of the existing health delivery system in rural areas. They are being established on the basis of one sub-centre for every 5000 population in general and one for every 3000 population in hilly, tribal and backward areas. As on 30th June 1996, 132730 sub-centres were established in the country; the total requirement is estimated to be 1.38 Lakh.

3. Primary Health Centre Level

The concept of primary health centre is not new to India. The Bhore committee in 1946 gave the concept of a primary health centre as a basic health unit, to provide, as close to the people as possible, an integrated curative and preventive health care to the rural population with emphasis on preventive and promotive aspects of health care.

The National Health Plan (1983) proposed reorganization of primary health centres on the basis of one PHC for every 30,000 rural population in the plains, and one PHC for every 20,000 population in hilly, tribal and backward areas for more effective coverage.

Functions of the PHC

The functions of the primary health center in India cover all the 8 "essential" elements of primary health care as outlined in the Atma-Ata declaration. They are:

1. Medical care
2. MCH including family planning
3. Safe water supply and basic sanitation
4. Prevention and control of locally endemic diseases
5. Collection and reporting of vital statistics

6. Education about health
7. National Health Programmes
8. Referral services

4. Community Health Centres

As on 30th June 2002, 5299 community health centres were establisted by upgrading the primary health centres, Each community health centre covering a population of 80,000 to 1.20 lakh (one in each community development block) with 30 beds and specialists in surgery, medicine, obstetrics and gynaecology, and paediatrics with x-ray and laboratory facilities. For strengthening preventive and promotive aspects of health care, a new non-medical post called **community health officer** has been created at each community health centre. The community health officer is selected from amongst the supervisory category of staff at the PHC and district level with minimum of 7 years experience in rural health programmes. Some states have not accepted this scheme and have opted for a second medical officer.

Voluntary Health Agencies

The voluntary health agencies occupy an important place in community health programmes. "A voluntary health agency may be defined as an organisation that is administered by an autonomous board which holds meetings, collects funds for its support chiefly from private sources and expends money, whether with or without paid workers, in conducting a programme directed primarily to furthering the public health by providing health services or health education, or by advancing research or legislation for health, or by a combination of these activities". The one country where voluntary health agencies have developed and flourished to an enormous extent is the United States.

Functions

The types of service rendered by voluntary health agencies have been classified as:

(a) *Supplementing the Work of Government Agencies:* It is well known that government agencies cannot provide complete service because they operate under financial and statutory restrictions. The voluntary health agencies can help strengthen the work of government agencies by lending personal, or by contributing funds for special equipment, supplies or services.

(b) *Pioneering:* The voluntary health agencies are in a position to explore ways and means of doing new things. Research is one formof pioneering. When the efforts succeed and bear fruit, the government agencies can step in and take over the project for the benefit of the larger numbers.The family planning programme in India is an example of pioneering by the volutary agencies which first spearheaded the movement, in the face of much opposition. When the importance of family planning was realised, the government accepted family planning as a national policy.

(c) *Education:* There is unlimited scope for health education in India. The government agencies cannot cope with the problem, unless it is supplemented by voluntary effort on the part of the people.

(d) *Demonstration:* By putting up demonstrations and experimental projects, the voluntary health agencies have advanced the cause of public health. The demonstrations of bore hole latrines by the Rockefeller Foundation to solve the problem of hookworm in India is a case in point. The bore-hole latrine and its modifications have since become an essential part of the environmental sanitation programme in India.

(e) *Guiding the Work of Government Agencies:* By setting a good example the voluntary health agencies can always guide and criticise the work of government agencies.

(f) *Advancing Health Legislation:* The voluntary agencies can also mobilise public opinion and advance legislation on health matters for the benefit of the whole community.

VOLUNTATY HEALTH AGENCIES IN INDIA

1. Indian Red Cross Society

The Indian Red Cross Society was established in 1920. It has a network of over 400 branches all over India. It has been executing programmes for the promotion of health, prevention of disease and mitigation of suffering among the people. Its activities are:

(a) *Relief Work:* When disaster strikes any part of the country in the shape of earthquakes, floods, drought, epidemics, *etc*, the Red Cross Society immediately mobilises all its resources and goes to the rescue of the affected people.

(b) *Milk and Medical Supplies:* A number of hospitals, dispensaries, maternity and child welfare centres, schools and orphanges receive assistance from the society every year. The assistance given consists mainly of milk powder, medicines, vitamins and other supplies.

(c) *Armed Forces:* The care of the sick and the wounded among the members of the forces is one of the primary obligations of the Red cross. The society runs a well-equipped hospital, "the Red cross Home" in Bangalore-the only one of its kind in India and the Far East-for permanently disabled ex-serviceman.

(d) *Maternal and Child Welfare Services:* There are a large number of maternity and child welfare centres all over India, either directly administered by or are affiliated to the Red cross. There is a bureau of maternity and child welfare, which provides technical advice and financial aid to schemes for establishing model maternity and child welfare centres.

(e) *Family Planning:* Several states in India are running family planning clinics under the auspices of the Indian Red Cross.

(f) *Blood Bank and First Aid:* Some of the state branches have started blood banks. The St. John Ambulance Association in India which is part of the Red Cross has trained several lakh men and women in first aid, home nursing and allied subjects.

2. Hind Kusht Nivaran Sangh

The Hind Kusht Nivaran Sangh was founded in 1950 with its headquarters in New Delhi. Its precursor was the Indian Council of the British Empire Leprosy Relief Association (B.E.L.R.A.) which was dissolved in 1950. The programme of work of the sangh includes rendering of financial assistance to various leprosy homes and clinics, health education through publications and posters, training of medical workers and physiotherapists, conducting All-India Leprasy workers Conferences and publication of 'Leprosy in India', a quarterly journal. The sangh has branches all over India and works in close cooperation with the Government and other voluntary agencies.

3. Indian Council for Child Welfare

Indian council for child welfare was established in 1952. It is affiliated with the International Union for Child Welfare. Since its formation, the I.C.C.W. has built up a network of state councils and district councils all over the country. The services of I.C.C.W. are devoted to secure for India's children those opportunities and facilities, by law and other means which are necessary to enable them to develop physically, mentally, morally, spiritually and socially in a healthy and normal manner and in conditions of freedom and dignity.

4. Tuberculosis Association of India

The Tuberculosis Association of India was formed in 1939. It has branches in all the states in India. The activities of this Association comprise organising a T.B. seal compaign every year to raise funds, training of doctors, health visitors and social workers in antituberculosis work, promotion of health edvcation and promotion of consultations and conferences. The following institutions are under the management of the Association: The New Delhi Tuberculosis Centre, the Lady Linlithgow Sanatorium at Kasauli, The King Edward VII sanatorium at Dharampur and the Tuberculosis Hospital at Mehrauli.

5. Bharat Sevak Samaj

The Bharat Sevak Samaj which is a non-political and non-official organisation was formed in 1952. One of the prime objectives of the Bharat Sevak Samaj (B.S.S) is to help people to achieve health by their own actions and efforts. The B.S.S. has branches in all the states and in nearly all the districts. Improvement of sanitation in villages is one of the important activities of the B.S.S.

6. Central Social Welfare Board

The Central Social Welfare Board is an autonomous organisation under the general administrative control of the ministry of Education. It was set up by the Government of India in August 1953. The functions of the Board are:

(1) Surveying the needs and requirements of voluntary welfare organisations in the country

(2) promoting and setting up of social welfare organisations on a voluntary basis

(3) rendering of financial aid to deserving existing organisations and institutions. The Board inintiated, in 1968, "Family and child Welfare services" in rural areas for the welfare of women and children.The activities of these projects comprise teaching of craft, social education, literacy classes, maternity aid for women, distribution of milk, balwadis, and organisation of play centres for children. Then Board has also started a scheme of Industrial Cooperatives to help the lower-middle class women in Urban areas supplement their family income by doing paid work.

7. The Kasturba Memorial Fund

Created in commemoration of Kasturba Gandhi, after her death in 1944, the Fund was raised with the main object of improving the lot of women, especially in the villages, through gram-sevikas. The trust has nearly a crore of rupees and is actively engaged in various welfare projects in the country.

8. Family Planning Association of India

The Family Planning Association was formed in 1949 with its headquarters at Mumbai. It has done pioneering work in propagating family planning in India. The Association has branches all over the Country. These branches are running family planning clinics with grants-in-aid from the government. The association has trained serveral hundred doctors, health visitors and social workers. One of the activities of the Headquarters is to answer enquiries on family planning by correspondance or by personal interviews.

9. All India Women's Conference

It is the only women's voluntary welfare organisation in the country. Estabilished in 1926, it has now branches all over the country. Most of the branches are running M.C.H. cilinics, Medical centres, and adult education centres, milk centres and family planning clinics.

10. The All-India Relief Society

The All-India Relief society was established in 1946 with a view to coordinate different institutions working for the blind. It organises eye relief camps and other measures for the relief of the blind.

11. Professional Bodies

The Indian Medical Association, All India Licentiates Association, All India Dental Association, The Trained Nurses Association of India are all voluntary agencies of men and women who are qualified in their respective specialities and possess registerable qualifications. These professional bodies conduct annual conferences, publish journals, arrange scientific sessions and exhibitions, foster research, set up standards of professional education and organise refief camps during periods of natural calamities.

12. International agencies

The Rockefeller Foundation, Ford Foundation and CARE (Cooperative for American Relief Everywhere) are examples of voluntary international health agencies.

Vital Statistics and Elementary Statistics

1. Vital Statistics means data collected from vital events and compilation of data. Vital events are birth, death, marriage, divorce and adoption.
2. **Health Statistics:** Data derived from sickness events in a community or items of services provided *i.e.,* it includes—
   (a) *State of health*—Morbidity, Mortality.
   (b) *Factor affecting health*: Nutrition, housing, social, economic and environmental factors.
   (c) *Services:* Preventive, curative, rehabilitory.
3. **Sources of Vital Statistics:**
   1. Census
   2. Registration of birth, death and marriage
   3. National sample survey.

   The Census: The census is defined as the total process of collecting, compiling and publishing demographic, economic and social data pertaining to a specified time to all persons in a country.
4. **Uses of Vital Statistics:**
   1. For planning various activities related to health.
   2. For evaluation of planned activity.
   3. To know geographical distribution and health trends.
   4. For comparison of various indicators from one country with another.
   5. Research in community health problems.
5. **Classifications of Death:** Death should be classified according to the International Classification of Diseases (ICD). This classification is revised by the WHO approximately every 10 years. The latest revision being the Ninth Revision which has come into force on 1st January 1979.

   The new revision is intended to be much more useful than the previous ones. It includes recommendation concerning maternal and prenatal morbidity and mortality and a proposed form of certificate of cause of prenatal death.

HEALTH PROGRAMMES

1. National Health Programme

Bhore committee's report in 1946 revealed important National problem of health. After independance the Government of India started health services in the country for people. This was very difficult work considering India is a big country. People are ignorant, mainly rural population. The work has to be done slowly due to limited resources.

Disease also spreads fast from one state to another by trade and commerce by pilgrimage. Considering certain problems requiring help from both centre as well as state, Central Government has role of planning, guiding, funding and co-ordinating National Health programmes. This is very necessary for having uniform action of control all over the country state Government has to implement these programmes.

These programmes are not static. New programmes are added like National cancer control programmes, National AIDS control programme and old ones like National Small pox Eradication Programme was deleted after its purpose was served. The trained manpower of this programme is utilized for new programme of E.P.I. *the programmes are*:

1. Control of communicable diseases Malaria, diarrhoea, tuberculosis, leprosy, filariasis, trachoma, AIDS
2. Environmental: sanitation water supply, excreta disposal, refuse disposal, minimum needs programme.
3. Nutrition: Goitre, supplementary feeding, nutrition education, Anaemia, Xeropthalmia
4. Population control (Family planning)
5. Rural health
6. Non-communicable diseases (cancer, diabetes), Blindness
7. Comprehensive (minimum need programme, Twenty point programme)

(a) National programmes for communicable diseases

1. Expanded programme on Immunisation converted to universal Immunisation Programme
2. National Malaria Eradication Programme
3. National filaria control programme
4. National Tuberculosis control programme
5. National leprosy Eradication Programme
6. Diarrhoeal Diseases control programme
7. STD control programme
8. Guinea worm eradication Programme
9. National AIDS control programme

(b) Environmental Sanitation

National water supply and Sanitation Programme

(c) Comprehensive Development

1. Minimum needs Programme
2. 20 points programme

(d) National Family Welfare Programme

(e) National Programme on Nutrition

1. Applied nutritional Anemia Prophylaxis Programme
2. Mid day meal programme
3. Special nutrition programme
4. ICDS
5. National Goitre control programme, renamed as Iodine Deficiency Disorders Programme

(f) Non-communicable diseases

(i) National cancer control programme
(ii) National diabetes control programme

2. National Malaria Control Programme

In the 1950 malaria was the India's biggest Health Problems. In order to fight this disease nation wide Malaria control programme was launched in 1953. Results of this programme were spactacular. Cases of malaria were decreases from 7.5 crores in 1952 to 2 million in 1958. Encouraged by these results and there was fear of insect vectors might develop resistance. The programmc was upgraded to National Malaria Eradication Programme is implemented in 1958.

In the control programme, strategy was insecticidal spray (D.D.T.) to kill anophele mosquitoes and thereby breaking chain of transmission of disease. Antimalarial drugs were given at low or no cost and larval control measures were introduced.

National Malaria Eradication Programme was to be carried out in 4 phases:-

(i) Preparatory phase
(ii) Attack phase
(iii) Consolidation phase
(iv) Maintenance phase

3. National Tuberculosis Control Programme, National Tuberculosis Programme (NTP), District Tuberculosis Programme (DTP)

National Tuberculosis programme started in 1962 with long term objective to reduce tuberculosis in the community to the level when it is not a public health problem.

The national Tuberculosis Institute Banglore serves as apex institute for this programme. Tuberculosis research centre at Chennai carries out various clinical trials to find out most suitable regimen of antitubercular drugs. National Tuberculosis institute also helps to solve problem at district tuberculosis centres. There are 17 tuberculosis training and demostration centres are functioning in the country to undertake training of medical and paramedical personnel.

4. National Leprosy Eradication Programme (NLCP), 1955

The National leprosy control programme was launched in 1955 as a programme with assistance from central government with following activities:

1. Early detection of cases
2. Domiciliary treatment with DDS

With strong political will the programme was redesignated as National Leprosy Eradication

Programme. The activities of this programme are:

1. Early detection of cases by population survey. School survey, contact examination and voluntary referral
2. Short term multidrug therapy.
3. Health education
4. Rehabilitation activities
5. National Leprosy Control Plan changed to National Leprosy Eradication Programme on 1983.

5. MDR (Multi Drug Therapy)

In absence of specific protection of leprosy by a vaccine the policy of leprosy control was based on chemotherapy. Initially with dapsone but due to use of single drug, resistance of organism of leprosy was noted.

Hence new strategy with multiple drug is adopted.

Objectives of MDR are:

(a) Break chain of transmission by making patient free from bacteria

(b) To cure the patient

(c) To prevent drug resistance

Advantages of MDR are:

(a) Duration of treatment reduced

(b) Better patient's co-operation

(c) Cost effective

(d) Decreased work load to health worker.

6. STD Control Programme

The programme is operated on a regional basis with regional STD teaching cum Training centres establishment at Delhi, Chennai, Hyderabad, Calcutta and Nagpur. At these centres reference laboratories and Regional Survey cum mobile STDs centres are established. They are actively engaged in training and orientation programmes of the medical and para medical personnel, conducting short orientation courses for laboratory technicians. They also carryout inter laboratory evaluation of VDRL and research related to epidemiological profile and laboratory diagnosis particularly in the backward and tribal areas of the country.

7. AIDS Control Programme

The Government of India in 1985 constituted a task force to look into this problem. An AIDS cell was established in the DGHS, New Delhi to coordinate all activities pertaining to AIDS in the country.

National Policy is as:

1. Establishment of surveillance centre to cover the whole country.
2. Identification of high risk groups and their screening *i.e.*, pregnant women, prostitutes, blood donors, homosexual and drug addict.
3. Specific guidelines for management of detected cases and their follow up.
4. Formulating guidelines for blood banks, blood donors dialysis units.
5. IEC activities by mass media research.

8. National Cancer Control

At present 150 general hospitals offer facilities for cancer treatment by surgery, radiotherapy and chemotherapy. Teletheraphy cobalt unit for treatment of cancer is available in 54 medical colleges and 45 other medical institutions. At centre, there is cancer control Board headed by Minister of family welfare. 15 states and union territories have set up state cancer control board. There are 10 regional cancer centres.

Activities of Regional Cancer Centres:

1. Surveys
2. Diagnosis, Treatment and follow up
3. Training of personnel both medical and para-medical
4. Mass examination, health education and industrial hygiene
5. Research fundamental applied.

National Cancer Control Project:

Started by government of India and works for:

1. Control of tobacco related cancers using primary prevention
2. Early diagnosis and treatment of cervical and oral cancer.

3. Research evaluation and provision of more therapeutic facilities.

9. National Goitre Control Programme:

Also known as Iodine Deficiency Disorder control programme. The Government of India launched National Goitre Control Programme in 1952 which had following activities:

1. Survey of areas where goitre is detected
2. Production and supply of iodized salt to the endemic areas to control goitre.
3. Re-survey after 5 years to know impact of the programme.

Main strategy was iodization of salt and distribution of the salt to area of endemic goitre region. It is estimated that presently 40-50 million have goitre. 2.2 million severely mentally retarded, 6.6 million suffer from mild neurological deficit. All states and 4 out of 7 union territories showing endemic goitre.

10. Integrated Child Development Services

The ICDS programme is a (Maternal and Child health) Programme. It is more than a nutrition programme and aims at total development of the child. Only the nutritional component of ICDS is described initially. It consists of growth monitoring supplementary nutrition and nutrition education. The supplementary nutrition is given for 300 days a year on the spot feeding as far as possible. All beneficiaries receive daily ration of 300 kilocalories and 8 to 10 g protein. Severely malnourished children and pregnant women receive daily supplementary nutrition providing 600 kcal and 18-20 g protein.

The cost of supplementary nutrition is as follows:

Supplementary Nutrition	Cost
Moderately malnourished children (6 months to 72 months)	75 paise per child per day
Severely malnourished children (6 months to 72 months)	125 paise per child per day
Pregnant and nursing mother	105 paise per beneficiary per day

11. National Immunization Schedule (Revised)

Beneficiaries	*Age*	*Vaccine*	*No. of doses*	*Route of administration*
Infants	6 weeks to 9 months	DPT	3	Intra muscular
		Polio	3	Oral
		BCG	1	Intra dermal
	9 to 12 months	Measles		Subcutaneous
Children	16 to 24 months	DPT	1	Intra-muscular
		Polio	1	oral
	5 to 6 years	DT	1	Intra muscular
		Typhoid	2	Subcutaneous
	10 years	Tetanus toxoid	1	Intramuscular
		Typhoid		Sub cutaneous
	16 years	Tetanus toxoid	1	Sub cutaneous
		Typhoid	1	
Pregnant women	16-36 weeks	Tetanus toxoid	1	Intra-muscular

OBJECTIVE QUESTIONS

1. Problem village is all except:
   (a) Where no water source in a distance of 1.6 km from community
   (b) Water is more than depth of 15m
   (c) There is excess on Na^+, K^+, F^- salts
   (d) Risks of guinea worm infection
2. Cancer control programme was launched in:
   (a) 1976 (b) 1986
   (c) 1970 (d) 1992
3. The national Diabetes control Programme in India includes all the following activities, except:
   (a) Primary prevention of diabetes through genetic testing and genetic counselling
   (b) Identification of high-risk subjects at an early stage, with appropriate health education
   (c) Early diagnosis and manage-ment of cases
   (d) Prevention, arrest or slowing of metabolic and cardio-vascular complications of the disease
4. In community Needs Assessments approach as part of the Reproductive and Child Health Programme, the target for various health activities are set at the level of:
   (a) Community
   (b) Sub-centre
   (c) Primary health centre
   (d) District
5. The "safe motherhood schemes" (CSSM) major thrust area is:
   (a) Promotion of reproductive health
   (b) Elimination of maternal morbidity
   (c) Fertility regulation
   (d) To provide essential prenatal, natal and postnatal services
6. In the reproductive and child health (RCH) programme the main addition over and above the child survival and safe motherhood programme is:
   (a) Care of reproductive tract infection
   (b) Essential newborn care
   (c) First referral unit
   (d) At-risk
7. Under reproductive and Child Health Programme, following two indicators are used:
   (a) Life expectancy at age 1 and MMR
   (b) Crude birth rate and IMR
   (c) Crude death rate and IMR
   (d) CDR and CBR
8. If you desire to study the incidence of diarrhoea in a community which study method would you like to opt for:
   (a) Cross-sectional study
   (b) Cohort study
   (c) Case control study
   (d) Double blind placebo study
9. Healthy carriers are found in all *except:*
   (a) Cholera (b) Diptheria
   (c) Typhoid (d) Pertussis
10. In the National Goiter Control Programme, iodine is supplied:
    (a) In drinking water
    (b) In salt as iodine
    (c) In salt as iodate
    (d) As IM injectioin of iodised oil
11. When launching a study many respondents are invited some of whom fail to come. This is called:
    (a) Respnse bias (b) Volunteer bias
    (c) Selection bias (d) Berkesonian bas
12. Under the National Programme for Prevention of Blindness, Vitamin A is to be given to:
    (a) All children between the ages of 1 to 5 years at 6 monthly intervals
    (b) Children with history of night blindness
    (c) Children with severe protein energy malnutrition
    (d) Children with Bitot spots
13. Under the national TB programme, for a PHC to be called a PHI-R, requisite is:

(a) Microscopy
(b) Microscopy plus radiology
(c) Radiology
(d) Specialities of doctors

14. Consider the following statements:
The Revised National Tuberculosis Control Programme has a strategy base that reflects in:
1. Accountability of system
2. Increasing case detection
3. Ensuring DOTS based drugs for every patient

Which of these statements is/are correct?
(a) 1 and 2 (b) 2 and 3
(c) 3 only (d) 1, 2 and 3

15. Main aim of tuberculosis treatment is
(a) Radiological cure
(b) Contact tracing
(c) Bacteriological cure
(d) To prevent complication

16. Goal of national tuberculosis control programme (NTCP) is:
(a) To eradicate TB
(b) To decrease the transmission of TB
(c) To treat all sputum +ve patients
(d) To decrease the incidence of TB to such a low level that it is no longer a major public health problem
(e) BCG vaccination of all infants

17. False about DOTS is:
(a) Continuation phase drugs are given in a multiblister pack
(b) Medication is to be taken in presence of a health worker
(c) Biweekly dosage and DOT at time
(d) Improves compliance

18. District TB control programme is mainly concerned with:
(a) Finding out new cases
(b) Finding out resistant cases
(c) Detecting cases and treatment
(d) All of the above

19. The screening method of choice in prevalance of leprosy is 1 in 1000 is
(a) Contact survey (b) Group survey
(c) Mass survey (d) Any of the above

20. Under the National Leprosy Eradication Programme mass surveys are undertaken when the prevalence of leprosy is
(a) 1/1000 (b) 3/1000
(c) 5/1000 (d) 10/1000

21. India has entered which phase of demographic cycle:
(a) High stationary
(b) Low stationary
(c) Early expanding
(d) Late expanding

22. High prevalance zone for leprosy has cases per 1,000 population as:
(a) 1-2 (b) 2-5
(c) 5-10 (d) 10-20

23. Which of the following is/are used as operational indicator in antileprosy activity?
(a) Incidence
(b) Incidence and prevalence
(c) Relapse rate and case detection ratio
(d) Incidence and case detection ratio

24. The multidrug regimen under the national leprosy eradication programme (NLEP) for the treatment of all multi-bacillary leprosy would include:
(a) Clofazimine thiacetazone and dapsone
(b) Clofazimine rifampicin and dapsone
(c) Ethionamide, rifampicin and dapsone
(d) Propionamide, rifampicin and dapsone

25. In leprosy control programme, indicator of efficacy of early diagnosis case is:
(a) Disability rate among newly used
(b) Lepromin +ve% among used
(c) Ratio of, multi/pauci bacillary cases
(d) All of the above

26. The screening method of choice in prevalence of leprosy is 1 in 1000 is:
(a) Contact survey
(b) Group survey
(c) Mass survey
(d) Any of the above

27. Longest incubation period, among the following is of:
(a) Malaria (b) Hepatitis
(c) Leprosy (d) Filaria

28. In the national leprosy eradication programme (NLEP), mass surgery are done if the prevalance is:
(a) 1/1000 (b) 2/2,000
(c) 6/1000 (d) 10/1,000

29. Which of the following is not monitored in malaria surveillance now:
(a) ABER
(b) Infant parasite rate
(c) Annual parasite incidence
(d) Slide positivity rate

30. National programmes are now organised for the following in India except:
(a) Filariasis (b) Leprosy
(c) Smallpox (d) Trachoma

31. The objective of minimum needs programme does not include:
(a) One PHC for 30,000 population
(b) Link-mid-day meal programme to sanitation
(c) Integration of health, water and sanitation
(d) Urban area given priority

32. Under NMEP the minimum annual blood examination rate should be:
(a) 10% (b) 12%
(c) 14% (d) 18%

33. Modified programme for National Malaria Eradication Programme is based on:
(a) API
(b) ABER
(c) Infant parasite rate
(d) Spleen rate

34. In NMEP, the recommendation for area API-2 are A/E:
(a) Presumptive treatment
(b) DDT spraying fortwiced in a year
(c) Epidemiological investigation of all cases
(d) Follow-up every case for one year and monthly blood & mears

35. Which is not true of malaria eradication programme (MEP):
(a) started in 1953
(b) modified plan started in 1970
(c) incidence was 2 million cases in 1958
(d) incidence decreased to 50,000 in 1961

36. Incidence among exposed and nonexposed is called:
(a) Relative risk (b) Attributable risk
(c) Odd's ratio (d) Attack ratio

37. Under NMEP, the function of fever depot treatment is:
(a) Diagnosis of cases + spraying
(b) collection of slides + treatment of fever
(c) Treatment fever cases only
(d) Treatment + slide collection + spraying

38. Under NMEP, the minimum annual blood examination rate should be:
(a) 10% (b) 12%
(c) 14% (d) 18%

39. All of the following statements about National Malaria Control Programme are true except:
(a) Number of slides examined should amount to atleast 10% of the population under surveillance in a year
(b) Annual parasite incidence based on active and passive surveillance and cases confir-med by blood examination
(c) Annual blood examination rate is calculated from the number of slides examined per 100 cases of fever
(d) The slide positivity rate provides information on the trend of malaria transmission

40. Under NMEP, for areas with API more than 2 the vector is refractory to DDT, the new recommendation is:
(a) HCH-1 round/year
(b) HCH-2 rounds/year
(c) HCH-3 rounds/year
(d) Malathione-2 rounds/year

41. Under the National Malaria Eradication programme, radical treatment for P.vivax malaria is given for:
(a) 1 days (b) 5 days
(c) 7 days (d) 14 days

42. Under NMEP for areas with API more than 2 and vector refractory to DDT, the recommendations is:
(a) Malathion-3 rounds/year
(b) HCH-1 round/year
(c) HCH-2 rounds/year
(d) HCH-3 rounds/year

43. Health education is:
(*a*) Health promotion
(*b*) Health distortion
(*c*) Thorough public health
(*d*) Not prevalent

44. In the process of health education of community the most important step is:
(*a*) Contact to doctors
(*b*) Community discussion
(*c*) Announces to community by loudspeaker
(*d*) Knowing to local needs

45. Following are used in planning of health education *except*:
(*a*) cover felt needs
(*b*) using simple words
(*c*) catchy slogans
(*d*) Ensuring participation

46. WHO constitution was made in:
(*a*) 1947 (*b*) 1950
(*c*) 1952 (*d*) 1956

47. In health education programme a group of 10 people are speaking on a topic of common interest called as:
(*a*) Workshop
(*b*) Panel discussion
(*c*) Group discussion
(*d*) Symposium

48. *Not* a feature of mass media education:
(*a*) Deals with local problem of communication
(*b*) Easily understandable
(*c*) wide approachable
(*d*) Rapid

49. The Bhore Committee was set up in:
(*a*) 1943 (*b*) 1946
(*c*) 1947 (*d*) 1952

50. PHC was introduced as a result of ——— report:
(*a*) Bhore Committee
(*b*) Kartar Singh
(*c*) Mudaliar
(*d*) Planning Commission

51. All are *true* about Mudaliar committee *except*:
(*a*) To improve the quality of health care
(*b*) Strengthening of district hospital
(*c*) Consolidation of advances made in the first two five-year plan
(*d*) Each primary centre covers a population of 80,000

52. Which one of the following was not recommended by the Mudaliar services
(*a*) Strengthening the district hospital with specialist services
(*b*) Each primary health centre to serve 8000 population
(*c*) Constitution of all India Health services
(*d*) Integration of medical and health services

53. Match *List-I (Health Planning Committees)* with *List-II (Main Recommendations/ Important Results)* and select the correct answer using the codes given below the lists:

List-I
A. Shrivastava Committee
B. Chadah Committee
C. Kartar Singh Committee
D. Jungal Wallah Committee

List-II
1. Malaria workers to look after FP work also.
2. Integration of services from the highest to the lowest level.
3. Led to creation of health guides.
4. Led to creation of multipurpose worker.

Codes:

	A	B	C	D
(*a*)	3	4	1	2
(*b*)	3	1	4	2
(*c*)	2	1	4	3
(*d*)	2	4	1	3

54. Recommendation of Shrivastava committee was:
(*a*) Abolition of private practive
(*b*) Creation of multipurpose health workers
(*c*) Creation of PHO
(*d*) All of the above

55. Panchayat Raj means:
(*a*) Local health care centre
(*b*) Community health care centre
(*c*) Primary health care
(*d*) Local self rule government

56. The community development programme is meant:
(*a*) To bring about a special and economic change in village life through the effort of the villagers themselves
(*b*) To arrange welfare programmes for women and children
(*c*) To improve agriculture product through better manure and seeds
(*d*) To plan development pro-gramme in a village high population of 60 and 80 thousand

57. Drinking water is best made free of cyclops by:
(*a*) Filtration
(*b*) Boiling
(*c*) Chlorination
(*d*) None of the above

58. Diethyl toluamide is an effective:
(*a*) Larvicidal
(*b*) Agent against pupal of anopheles
(*c*) Repellent
(*d*) Space spray
(*e*) None of the above

59. Match *List-I (Vectors)* with *List-II (Diseases transmitted)* and select the correct answer using the code given below the lists:

List-I
A. *Culex* mosquito
B. Sand fly
C. *Aedes* mosquito
D. Head louse

List-II
1. Relapsing fever
2. Yellow fever
3. Japanese encephalitis
4. Kala-azar

Codes:

	A	B	C	D
(*a*)	3	1	2	4
(*b*)	4	1	3	2
(*c*)	2	4	3	1
(*d*)	4	3	2	1

60. Which of the following disease is found in India?
(*a*) Westnile fever
(*b*) Murray valley encephalitis
(*c*) Yellow fever
(*d*) Colorado tick fever

61. *Aedes* is vector for all except:
(*a*) Dengue
(*b*) Yellow fever
(*c*) Encephalitis
(*d*) Hemorrhagic fever

62. Which is *not* transmitted by culex?
(*a*) Dengue (*b*) Filaria
(*c*) Viral arthritis (*d*) Westnile fever

63. Diseases spread by mosquito are:
(*a*) Malaria
(*b*) Toxoplasmosis
(*c*) Histoplasma
(*d*) Sleeping sickness

64. *Culex* mosquito can transmit:
(*a*) Malaria (*b*) Kala-azar
(*c*) Dengue fever (*d*) None of the above

65. "Nuisance mosquito" is:
(*a*) *Anopheles* (*b*) *Culex*
(*c*) *Ades* (*d*) Tse-tse fly

66. The maximum permissible level of occupational exposure to radiation is —— — per year:
(*a*) 5 rem (*b*) 2 rem
(*c*) 10 rem (*d*) 50 rem

67. Rat flea transmits all the following *except*:
(*a*) Plague (*b*) Salmonellosis
(*c*) *H. Dimunita* (*d*) Murine fever

68. Which of the following is *not* an arthropod-borne infection in India?
(*a*) Japanese B encephalitis
(*b*) KDF
(*c*) Dengue
(*d*) Tanapox virus

69. The vector of Kyasanus Forest diseases is:
(*a*) *Anopheles* mosquito
(*b*) *Culex* mosquito

(*c*) Flea
(*d*) Tick

70. Trench fever is transmitted by:
(*a*) Flea
(*b*) Louse
(*c*) Tick mosquito
(*d*) None of the above

71. Hard tick transmits:
(*a*) Oroyo fever (*b*) Oriental sore
(*c*) Leishmanials (*d*) Tick typhus

72. For proper functioning, an oxidation pond requires:
(*a*) Algae, sunlight and ferns
(*b*) Algae, scavenging bacteria and sunlight
(*c*) Algae, saprophytic bacteria and sunlight
(*d*) Algae, human pathogenic bacteria and sunlight

73. *True* about septic tank is:
(*a*) Disinfectants should be used periodically
(*b*) Anaerobic digestion takes place inside and aerobic digestion takes place out side
(*c*) Minimum capacity of the tank is 100 gallons
(*d*) A retention period of 24 hours is insufficient

74. An inexpensive and efficient method of sewage disposal for a small community is:
(*a*) River outfall
(*b*) Oxidation pond
(*c*) Trickling filter
(*d*) Activated sludge

75. Trickling filter is used in:
(*a*) Primary treatment of sewage
(*b*) Secondary treatment of sewage
(*c*) Sewage effluent treatment
(*d*) Sewage farming treatment

76. Biological oxygen demand denotes contamination with:
(*a*) Bacteria (coliforms)
(*b*) Organic matter
(*c*) Nitrates
(*d*) Algac

77. Oxygen demand calculated in water is for evaluating its:
(*a*) Biological Value (BOD)
(*b*) Organic nature
(*c*) Stand by time
(*d*) *E. coli* ratio

78. Strength of sewage is expressed in terms of:
(*a*) Biological oxygen demand
(*b*) Chemical oxygen demand
(*c*) Suspended solids
(*d*) *E. coli* count

79. Anaerobic digestion of sludge is seen in:
(*a*) Aquaprivy
(*b*) Effluent
(*c*) Septic tank
(*d*) All of the above

80. Septic tank decomposition takes place by:
(*a*) Anaerobic (*b*) Aerobic
(*c*) Both (*d*) None

81. Which of the following is not a sanitary latrine?
(*a*) Aquaprivy
(*b*) Bore hole
(*c*) RCA type
(*d*) Service latrine

82. Accepted depth of water in water-seal latrine should not be more than ——— cm.
(*a*) 2.5 (*b*) 4.0
(*c*) 5.0 (*d*) 2.5

83. Which is the latrine of choice for camps?
(*a*) Aquaprivy
(*b*) Trench hole
(*c*) Pit latrine
(*d*) Chemical

84. Pit latrine has depth of ——— feet:
(*a*) 2-4 (*b*) 4-6
(*c*) 6-10 (*d*) 10-12

85. Sanitation barrier is:
(*a*) Segregation of faeces
(*b*) Control of flies
(*c*) Excreta disposal
(*d*) Proper water supply

86. Soakage pit is used for hygenic disposal of:
(*a*) Garbage (*b*) Rubbish
(*c*) Sewage (*d*) Sludge

87. The disposal of night soil and refuge is by:
(*a*) Chemical sterilization
(*b*) Burning
(*c*) Composting
(*d*) Any of the above

88. Controlled tipping is a method of disposal of:
(*a*) Sewage
(*b*) Human excreta
(*c*) Sullage
(*d*) Rufuse

89. Red Cross was founded by:
(*a*) Hippocrates
(*b*) Henry Durant
(*c*) Galen
(*d*) Madam curie

90. Kata thermometer is used to measure:
(*a*) Maximum temperature
(*b*) Minimum temperature
(*c*) Radiant heat
(*d*) Cooling power of air

91. A rupture of ear drum may actually occur at a decibel level above:
(*a*) 40 (*b*) 80
(*c*) 120 (*d*) 160

ANSWERS

1	**2**	**3**	**4**	**5**	**6**	**7**	**8**	**9**	**10**
(*c*)	(*a*)	(*a*)	(*d*)	(*d*)	(*a*)	(*a*)	(*b*)	(*d*)	(*b*)
11	**12**	**13**	**14**	**15**	**16**	**17**	**18**	**19**	**20**
(*b*)	(*a*)	(*b*)	(*b*)	(*c*)	(*d*)	(*d*)	(*c*)	(*b*)	(*d*)
21	**22**	**23**	**24**	**25**	**26**	**27**	**28**	**29**	**30**
(*d*)	(*d*)	(*d*)	(*b*)	(*a*)	(*b*)	(*c*)	(*d*)	(*b*)	(*c*)
31	**32**	**33**	**34**	**35**	**36**	**37**	**38**	**39**	**40**
(*d*)	(*a*)	(*a*)	(*c*)	(*b*)	(*a*)	(*b*)	(*a*)	(*c*)	(*c*)
41	**42**	**43**	**44**	**45**	**46**	**47**	**48**	**49**	**50**
(*b*)	(*d*)	(*a*)	(*d*)	(*c*)	(*a*)	(*c*)	(*a*)	(*a*)	(*b*)
51	**52**	**53**	**54**	**55**	**56**	**157**	**58**	**59**	**60**
(*d*)	(*b*)	(*a*)	(*b*)	(*d*)	(*a*)	(*a*)	(*c*)	(*d*)	(*a*)
61	**62**	**63**	**64**	**65**	**66**	**67**	**68**	**69**	**70**
(*c*)	(*a*)	(*a*)	(*d*)	(*b*)	(*a*)	(*b*)	(*d*)	(*d*)	(*b*)
71	**72**	**73**	**74**	**75**	**76**	**77**	**78**	**79**	**80**
(*d*)	(*c*)	(*b*)	(*b*)	(*b*)	(*b*)	(*b*)	(*a*)	(*c*)	(*a*)
81	**82**	**83**	**84**	**85**	**86**	**87**	**88**	**89**	**90**
(*a*)	(*d*)	(*d*)	(*d*)	(*a*)	(*c*)	(*c*)	(*d*)	(*b*)	(*d*)
91									
(*d*)									

MULTIPLE CHOICE QUESTIONS*

1. Sinoatrial node is located in which part of the heart?
   A. Right atrium B. Right ventricle
   C. Left atrium D. Left ventricle
2. Powerhouse of the human cell is:
   A. Nucleus B. Golgi bodies
   C. Mitochondria D. Ribosome
3. Transformation of one type of cell into another type is called:
   A. Hyperplasia B. Metaplasia
   C. Dysplasia D. Anaplasia
4. The number of thoracic vertebrae in human being is:
   A. 5 B. 7
   C. 9 D. 12
5. Blood groups were first discovered by:
   A. Robert Koch
   B. Karl Landsteiner
   C. Paul Ehrlich
   D. Anton von Leuwenhock
6. Normal platelet count in human being is:
   A. 25000-50000 B. 50000-100000
   C. 10000-400000 D. 400000-600000
7. "Haversian canals" are found is:
   A. Bone B. Brain
   C. Lung D. Kidney
8. Most frequently fractured carpal bone is:
   A. Lunate B. Pisiform
   C. Scaphoid D. Hamate
9. Which of the following extraocular muscles is not supplied by third cranial nerve?
   A. Superior oblique B. Inferior oblique
   C. Superior rectus D. Inferior rectus
10. Out of the following which hormone is secreted by the posterior pituitary gland?
    A. Growth Hormone B. Prolactin
    C. ACTH D. ADH
11. McBurney's point is located in which of the following quadrant of abdomen?
    A. Left upper B. Left lower
    C. Right upper D. Right lower
12. If the phenotypes of the parents is B and AB, which of the following blood groups is not possible in offsprings?
    A. A B. B
    C. AB D. O
13. Under normal circumstances the volume of inspired air is:
    A. 200 ml B. 300 ml
    C. 400 ml D. 500 ml
14. Eating behaviour is controlled by:
    A. Hypothalamus B. Adrenal glands
    C. Pancreas D. Thyroid
15. The junction through which neurons communicate with one another is:
    A. Dendrite B. Axon
    C. Synapse D. Node of Ranvier
16. A gland which can be classified as an endocrine and an exocrine gland is:
    A. Thyroid B. Thymus
    C. Pancreas D. Pituitary
17. Which of the following sphincter does not prevent reflux of material?
    A. Lower oesophageal sphincter
    B. Gastroduodenal sphincter
    C. Ileocolonic sphincter
    D. Internal anal sphincter
18. Active transport of substance from blood into the nephrone is called:
    A. Filtration
    B. Tubular-secretion
    C. Tubular-reabsorption
    D. Osmosis
19. Heat regulating centre is located in:
    A. Thalamus

*Asked in Various Nursing Recruitment Exam.

B. Hypothalamus
C. Medulla oblongata
D. Cerebrum

20. The smallest bone of human body is:
A. Stapes B. Phallanges
C. Metacarpals D. Xiphisternum

21. Taste buds for sensing bitterness are located on which part of the tongue:
A. Anterior part of the tongue
B. Posterior part of the tongue
C. Lateral part of the tongue
D. Under surface of the tongue

22. The difference between systolic pressure and diastolic pressure is:
A. Blood pressure B. Pulse pressure
C. Apical pressure D. Lateral pressure

23. The function of fallopian tube is:
A. Secretion of oestrogen and progesterone
B. Passage way for foetus
C. Occurrence of fertilization
D. Developing foetus

24. Ovulation is defined as:
A. Maturation of graffian follicles
B. Repture of graffian follicles
C. Seepage of blood through vagina
D. Facilitate their maturation during emryonic development

25. The artery which supply blood to head and neck is:
A. Coronary artery B. Carotid artery
C. Mesenteric artery D. Intracostal artery

26. A nerve which helps in the process of smelling is:
A. Optic nerve B. Occulomotor nerve
C. Olfactory nerve D. Facial nerve

27. Normal respiration of healthy person is:
A. 5-10/min B. 10-15/min
C. 15-20/min D. 20-30/min

28. Enzyme which helps in digestion of fat is:
A. Amylase B. Lipase
C. Enterokinase D. Trypsin

29. Kidney is situated in:
A. abdominal cavity B. pelvic cavity
C. thoracic cavity D. dorsal cavity

30. Appendix is situated in:
A. Left hypochondrium
B. Right hypochondrium
C. Left iliac fossa
D. Right iliac fossa

31. Fertilization process completed in:
A. ovary B. uterus
C. cervix D. fallopian tube

32. Largest gland of the human body is:
A. Pancreas B. Liver
C. Skin D. Ovary

33. Exchange of gases in internal respiration takes place:
A. Between heart and lungs
B. Between lungs and environment
C. Between blood vessels and tissues
D. All of the above

34. Most abundant ion in extracellular fluid is:
A. Sodium B. Potassium
C. Calcium D. Magnesium

35. Smallest form of vein is known as:
A. Venule B. Vena cava
C. Vein D. Sinus

36. Vaginal canal normally has:
A. An acid environment
B. An alkaline environment
C. A neutral environment
D. An environment difficult to determine

37. Total number of bones in human is about:
A. 206 B. 180
C. 306 D. 400

38. In human body glycogen is mainly stored in:
A. Thyroid gland B. Liver
C. Kidney D. Intestine

39. In human body pituitary gland is situated in:
A. Brain B. Neck
C. Kidney D. Abdomen

40. Total number of vertebrae in human, are:
A. 7 B. 12
C. 33 D. 28

41. Total number of chambers in human heart is:
A. 4 B. 1
C. 2 D. 3

42. The only artery which supplies deoxygenated blood:
A. Pulmonary artery B. Hepatic artery
C. Gastric artery D. Renal artery

43. In following which structure is also known as pacemaker of heart?
A. SA node B. AV node
C. Bundle of His D. Mitral valve

44. In following which is both exocrine and endocrine gland?
A. Pituitary gland B. Adrenal gland
C. Pancreas D. Thyroid gland

45. Total number of muscles in human body are:
A. 200 B. 300
C. 400 D. 639

46. % of O_2 in inspired air is:
A. 78% B. 21%
C. 16% D. 52%

47. Cardiac muscles are
A. Voluntary and striated
B. Involuntary and non-striated
C. Voluntary and non-striated
D. Involuntary and striated

48. In which body cavity kidney is situated?
A. Abdominal cavity
B. Pelvic cavity
C. Thoracic cavity
D. Mediastenum

49. Total number of intercostal muscles are:
A. 7 pairs B. 11 pairs
C. 12 pairs D. 24 pairs

50. In following which is a both endocrine and exocrine gland?
A. Pituitary B. Thyroid
C. Pancreas D. Adrenal

51. In following which is the most abundant cation in extracellular fluid?
A. Na^+ B. K^+
C. Ca^{++} D. Chloride

52. The blood vessel which connect the artery and vein
A. Venule B. Arteriole
C. Capillary D. Sinus

53. Concentration of oxygen in expired air is about:
A. 0% B. 21%
C. 16% D. 4%

54. Thermophilic bacteria grow at following minimum temperature:
A. 20°C B. 35°C
C. 55°C D. 85°C

55. Sterilization of endoscope is done:
A. By autoclaving
B. By U.V. rays
C. By 2% Phenol
D. By 2% gluteraldehyde

56. Pathogen means:
A. Micro-organism which causes disease
B. Organism which are found in animals
C. Organism which are beneficial for us
D. Organism which are found in plants

57. Widal test is performed:
A. To identify the typhoid fever
B. To identify the AIDS
C. To identify the cause of diarrhoea
D. To identify the cause of dysentery

58. Asepsis means:
A. Freedom from infection
B. Freedom from anxiety
C. Freedom from noise
D. Freedom from pain

59. Stain used to identify Acid-Fast Bacilli is:
A. Lieshman B. Ziel-Nielsen
C. Giemsa D. Wright's

60. Benedict's test in a urine sample is done for the detection of:
A. Acetone B. Glucose
C. Bile Salt D. Bile Pigment

61. For effective sterilization, steam in an autoclave should be at a pressure of 15 pounds per square inch for 30 minutes and at a temperature of:
A. 100°C B. 110°C
C. 121°C D. 131°C

62. "Klebs loeffler bacillus" is the name of which of the following bacteria?
A. Clostridium tetani
B. Hemophilus influenzae
C. Corynebacterium diphtheriae
D. Lactobacillus

63. Which of the following is not a species of plasmodium parasite?
A. Plasmodium ovale
B. Plasmodium maxicana
C. Plasmodium malariae
D. Plasmodium vivax

64. Life cycle of malarial parasite was first described by:
A. Ronald Ross B. Robert Koch
C. Louis Pasteur D. Banting and Best

65. HIV virus, belongs to which of the following groups?
A. Flavivirus B. Retrovirus
C. Rhabdovirus D. Hepadnavirus

66. Which infecting serotype of dengue virus is most dangerous?
A. Type-1 B. Type-2
C. Type-3 D. Type-4

67. The most often cells from blood infected by HIV is:
A. CD_4 (Helper) T. Lymphocyte
B. B. Lymphocyte
C. CD_3 (Supressor) T. Lymphocyte
D. Polymorph

68. The Causative organism of tuberculosis is:
A. Micrococci
B. Mycobacterium tubercle bacilli
C. Steptococci bacilli
D. Meningococci

69. Urine sample for culture is collected from:
A. First urine B. Last urine
C. Midstream urine D. Both A and B

70. The following factors influence microbial growth except:
A. Temperature B. Moisture
C. Darkness D. Disinfection

71. Immunity means:
A. Antibodies & antigen reactions
B. Transfer of maternal antibodies across the placenta
C. Level of resistance of a person to a particular disease
D. Acquired immunity by immunization

72. Trichomonal infection is caused by:
A. Protozoa B. Fungus
C. Yeast D. Bacteria

73. Which of the following is the father of microbiology?
A. Louis Pasteur
B. Robert Koch
C. Antony von Leuvanhok
D. Landsteiner

74. In following which is not sterilized by antiseptic solution:
A. Suction catheter B. Rectal tube
C. Scissor D. NG tube

75. In following which is a vector borne disease:
A. Diptheria B. Dengue
C. Tetanus D. Measles

76. Which of the following is recommended along with intravenous administration of quinine sulphate for treatment of malaria?
A. Hydrocortisone B. Multivitamin
C. Glucose D. Calcium gluconate

77. Which out of the following drugs should be given first in a patient of acute myocardial infarction?
A. Statin
B. Calcium channel blocker
C. Aspirin
D. ACE inhibitor

78. Which of the following medicines is useful for reducing raised intracranial pressure?
A. I.V. Mannitol B. I.V. Phenytoin
C. I.V. Diazepam D. I.V. Nitroglycerine

79. Which of the following medicines is useful in the treatment of organophosphorus poisoning?
A. Neostigmine
B. Atropine
C. Megnesium sulphate
D. D-Penicillamine

80. During haemodialysis, which of the following drug is used to prevent blood clotting?
A. Aspirin B. Warfarin
C. Heparin D. Protomine

81. Which of the following is the antidote for a patient with overdose of heparin?

A. Protamine sulphate
B. Vitamin-K
C. Atropine sulphate
D. Physostigmine

82. Analgesics are given:
A. To relieve pain
B. Go give rest
C. To induce sleep
D. To destroy pathogenic microorganisms

83. Paracetamol medicine/drug is
A. Antipyretic B. Antitussive
C. Antiasthemetic D. Antiemetic

84. In following which is a side effect of streptomycin?
A. 8th cranial nerve damage
B. Damage to growing cartilage
C. Bone marrow depression
D. Diarrhoea

85. Morphine is contraindicated in:
A. Angina B. Bronchial asthma
C. Pancreatitis D. M.I.

86. In following which medicine is used to treat allergic condition:
A. Citrizine
B. Dexona
C. Chlorphenariamine
D. All of the above

87. Pseudoephidrine is a:
A. Antimanic B. Decongestant
C. Anticoagulant D. Antiemetic

88. 1 teaspoonful medicine is equal to:
A. 2 ml B. 3 ml
C. 5 ml D. 10 ml

89. Which drug may cause 'Gray-baby syndrome'?
A. Chloramphenicol B. Gentamycin
C. Penicillin D. Tetracycline

90. In following which drug control the progress of AIDS:
A. Ampicillin B. Zidouudine
C. Streptomycin D. Dexona

91. What is the effect of adrenalin?
A. Increase heart rate B. Vasoconstriction
C. Vasodilation D. Both A and B

92. The medicine given during acute anaphylatic reaction is:
A. Atropine B. Aminophylline
C. Deriphylline D. Adrenalin

93. Digoxin is not given when heart rate:
A. Below 60 B. Below 70
C. Below 80 D. Below 90

94. In following which analgesic is given is old age:
A. Aspirin B. Morphine
C. Diclofenic sodium D. Ampicillin

95. In a 75 year old patient who had undergone hip replacement surgery, which size of canula is used for I.V. Infusion:
A. 16 No. B. 18 No.
C. 20 No. D. 22 No.

96. Florence nightingale was born in which country?
A. England B. Germany
C. Italy D. France

97. "HOSPICE" is the treatment concept for:
A. Terminally ill cancer patients
B. Cardiac patients
C. Psychiatric patients
D. All of the above

98. In which of the following positions, patient is not lying down?
A. Trendelenburg B. Sim's
C. Fowler's D. Rose

99. There are how many deciliters in one litre?
A. 1 B. 10
C. 100 D. 1000

100. Which of the following formula is correct for conversion of centigrade to Fahrenheit temperature?
A. $F = (c(9/5)) + 32$
B. $F = (c + (9/5)) + 32$
C. $F = (c - (9/5)) + 32$
D. $F = (c(9/5)) + 32$

101. When a drug is to be given at bed time, which of the following coded instruction is used?
A. ac B. hs
C. od D. sos

102. The process of assessing patients who come to emergency department and determining the management priorities is called:

A. Mirage B. Lavage
C. Triage D. Collage

103. Method of administering a drug by topical friction over skin is called:

A. Instillation B. Inunction
C. Insertion D. Insufflation

104. "Lund and Browder chart" is used for which of the following conditions?

A. Head injury B. Acute abdomen
C. Burns D. Bone injury

105. While measuring blood pressure in upper arm, the chest piece of stethoscope is placed over which of the following arteries?

A. Axillary B. Brachial
C. Radial D. Ulnar

106. Above what body temperature, the term "Hyperpyrexia" is used?

A. 101°F B. 103°F
C. 105°F D. 107°F

107. Infusion of 1000 ml of normal saline over 12 hrs. require how many drops per minute when the drop factor is 15 drops/minute?

A. 15 drops/minute B. 17 drops/minute
C. 21drops/minute D. 23 drops/minute

108. 7.5 mg of morphine sulphate I/M start from an ampule of 10 mg is to be administered how many ml of this drug is to be administered in correct dose?

A. 0.5 ml B. 0.75 ml
C. 0.85 ml D. 1.5 ml

109. While pouring the liquid medicine from a bottle into an ounce glass, the label of the bottle is held.

A. Against the hand B. Right hand
C. Left side D. Any side

110. Insulin is injected in to:

A. Intradermal B. Subcutaneous
C. Intrathecal D. Intramuscular

111. Before administering the medicine to a patient, a nurse checks the prescription:

A. Two times B. Three times
C. One time D. Four times

112. The tube feeding should be delayed if the amount of gastric content (residual) exceeds:

A. 20 ml B. 25 ml
C. 30 ml D. 50 ml

113. Nursing intervention designed to decrease the risk of infection in a patient with an indewelling catheter include:

A. Cleanse area around meatus
B. Empty catheter drainage bag at least daily
C. Change catheter tubing and bag every 48 hrs.
D. Maintain intake of 1200-1500 ml everyday

114. While lifting a patient, a nurse bends on her

A. Hips and back B. Hips and knees
C. Back and knees D. Back only

115. To give fowler's position to a patient, the head end of the bed is raised to:

A. 35° angle B. 15° angle
C. 60° angle D. 45° angle

116. Wound dressing is done by using:

A. Septic technique
B. Medical asepsis
C. Surgical asepsis
D. Medical and surgical asepsis

117. Tonicity of ringer lactate solution is:

A. Isotonic B. Normotonic
C. Hypotonic D. Hypertonic

118. An informed consent is obtained from a preoperative patient to prevent:

A. Complication B. Infection
C. Any fall D. Legal implications

119. Cynaosis is caused in case of:

A. Lack of water B. Lack of blood
C. Lack of oxygen D. Lack of glucose

120. To maintain normal breathing pattern, which position is beneficial:

A. Sim's position B. Knee-chest position
C. Fowler's D. Dorsal

121. Intra osseous injection is given in:

A. Vein B. Bone Marrow
C. Spinal cavity D. Muscles

122. Full form of CPR is:

A. Cardio Pulmonary Resuscitation
B. Cardio Pulmonary Relapse

C. Cardio Pulmonary Restriction
D. Chronic Pulmonary Relapse

123. Anorexia means:
A. Loss of appetite
B. Absence of respiration
C. Loss of sensation
D. Absence of pulse

124. In following which solution is used for cleaning of thermometer?
A. Alcohol B. Tap water
C. Boiled water D. ORS

125. Normal respiration rate in neonate:
A. 40-60 breaths/min
B. 80-160 breaths/min
C. 16-20 breaths/min
D. 20-30 breaths/min

126. Presence of blood in stool is known as:
A. Lochia B. Melana
C. Haematemesis D. Haemoptysis

127. Term anorexia means:
A. Increase appetite
B. Decrease appetite
C. Difficulty in swallowing
D. Difficulty in chewing

128. For effective sterilization temperature in an autoclave should be:
A. 100°C B. 121°C
C. 110°C D. 9°C

129. For giving enema, the height of the enema cane from anus should be:
A. 30 cm. B. 18 cm.
C. 45 cm. D. 90 cm.

130. In an adult normal body temperature:
A. 36°C B. 37°C
C. 37.2°C D. 36.8°C

131. At which angle intradermal injection is given?
A. 90° B. 45°
C. 30° D. 15°

132. Purgative enema is given:
A. To provide nutrition
B. To destroy helminth
C. To improve peristalsis
D. To provide anesthesia

133. Abbreviation S.O.S. means:
A. Give immediate
B. Give whenever necessary
C. At bed time
D. Give twice a day

134. Knee-chest position is also known as:
A. Fowler's position
B. Lithotomy position
C. Genupectorial
D. Left lateral position

135. Enema is given in:
A. Lithotomy position
B. Side-lying position
C. Supine position
D. Knee-chest position

136. In following which is a contraindication for taking oral temperature
A. Children below 10 years
B. Psychiatric patients
C. Surgery of mouth
D. All of the above

137. While giving enema height of enema cane from anus should be:
A. 6 inch B. 9 inch
C. 12 inch D. 18 inch

138. During giving enema if the patient complains for abdominal cramps than nurse should:
A. Stop giving enema
B. Continue giving enema
C. Slow the rate of enema
D. Administer analgesic

139. For nasogastric intubation length of NG tube should be measured from:
A. Nose to the sternum
B. Nose to the umbilicus
C. Nose to the tragus of the ear plus nose to the sternum
D. Nose to the tragus plus nose to the umbilicus

140. Sharp instrument should not be sterilized by:
A. Autoclaving B. Boiling
C. Hot air oven D. Antiseptic solution

141. Amount of medicine can be injected into gluteal muscle is:

A. Upto 2 ml B. Upto 5 ml
C. Upto 10 ml D. Upto 7 ml

142. RL is a:
A. Hypertonic solution
B. Hypotonic solution
C. Isotonic solution
D. None of these

143. Concentration of $KMnO_4$ solution used for oral hygiene is:
A. 1 : 1000 B. 1 : 5000
C. 1 : 100 D. 1 : 100000

144. If air bubbles appear during chest drainage than:
A. It shows air leakage
B. It shows water leakage
C. It is a normal condition
D. It indicates air embolism

145. Endoscopic catheters are sterilized by:
A. Autoclaving B. Hot air oven
C. 2% gluteraldehye D. Boiling

146. Intradermal injection is given at:
A. 15° angle B. 30° angle
C. 45° angle D. 90° angle

147. What is mandatory before glucose tolerance test?
A. NBM 8-10 hours prior to test
B. Rich carbohydrate diet from 2-3 days before test
C. Stop the giving medication
D. No need to change anything

148. During ABG analysis blood is collected from
A. Artery
B. Vein
C. Capillary
D. It can be taken from any site

149. Tissue reaction is highest with which of the following suturing materials:
A. Plain catgut B. Chromic catgut
C. Nylon D. Vicryl

150. "Tetany" can be produced by which of the following electrolyte disturbance?
A. Hypocalcemia B. Hypermagnesemia
C. Hypercalcemia D. Hyponatremia

151. Which of the following ions is most abudant in extracellular fluid?
A. Sodium B. Potassium
C. Chloride D. Bicarbonate

152. "Mask like facies" is a typical feature of:
A. Tetanus B. Hypothyroidism
C. Parkinson disease D. Down syndrome

153. Majority of cases of mother to child (vertical) transmission of HIV-1 occur during:
A. Antepartum period
B. Intrapartum period
C. Post partum period
D. Breast feeding

154. Guillian Barre syndrome is a disease of which of the following?
A. Brain B. Spinal cord
C. Peripheral nerve D. All of the above

155. Which of the following is not a parameter for "Glasgow coma scale":
A. Eye opening B. Pupillary response
C. Verbal response D. Motor response

156. "Rice water stool" is a typical finding in cases of:
A. Cholera B. Typhoid
C. Ulcerative colitis D. Amoebiasis

157. Which out of the following drugs should be given first, in a patient of acute myocardial infarction?
A. Statin
B. Calcium channel blocker
C. Aspirin
D. ACE inhibitor

158. What concentration of NaCl in intravenous fluid is termed "isotonic"?
A. 0.25% B. 0.45%
C. 0.75% D. 0.90%

159. How much blood is drawn from a donor when one unit of blood is donated?
A. 100 ml B. 200 ml
C. 300 ml D. 400 ml

160. In case of hypothyroidism, which of the following is increased?
A. T_3 B. T_4
C. TSH D. All of the above

161. During haemodialysis, which of the following drug is used to prevent blood clotting?

A. Aspirin B. Warfarin
C. Heparin D. Protamine

162. Preferably, lumbar puncture (LP) is done at which of the following site?
A. $T_{12} - L_1$ B. $L_1 - L_2$
C. $L_2 - L_3$ D. $L_3 - L_4$

163. A major priority of nursing care of a child suspected of having meningitis is to:
A. Check the temperature and give the cold sponging
B. Isolate the child immediately
C. Administer the antibiotic as soon as it is ordered
D. Restrain the child to prevent accidents

164. The child's apical pulse is always checked before administering digoxin, the drug is not given if the pulso rate is:
A. Below 90 to 110 beats/minute
B. Above 90 to 110 beats/minute
C. Less than 60 beats/minute
D. More than 150 beats/minute

165. During the oedematous phase of nephrotic syndrome an important nursing intervention is to:
A. Provide meticulous skin care
B. Encourage fluid intake
C. Encourage moderate activity
D. Weight the child every alternate day

166. Initial nursing assessment of an infant suffering with acute diarrhoea and dehydration reveals:
A. Skin turgor
B. Low hematocrit
C. Bulging fontanelle
D. Weight gain

167. The most likely side effect of external radiation to the neck for cancer of larynx is:
A. Constipation B. Dyspnea
C. Sore throat D. Diarrhoea

168. When the respiratory rate of a 12 months old child is 35 breaths/minute, the most appropriate nursing action is:
A. Notify the physician
B. Administer oxygen
C. Reassess respiratory rate in 15 minutes
D. Document the findings

169. A nursing intervention in thrombophlebitis would be contraindicated:
A. Maintaining strict bed rest
B. Turning the patient from side-to-side
C. Applying warm packs to the affected leg
D. Massaging the affected leg

170. The most common accurate way to determine the need for oxygen in a patient with COPD by:
A. Observing the skin colour
B. Noting changes in the vital signs
C. Asking how the patient feels
D. Blood gas analysis

171. A patient is scheduled for ileostomy to treat ulcerative colitis. This is done to:
A. Prevent possible perforation from colitis
B. Decrease liquid feces
C. Control the order from diarrhoea
D. Prevent intestinal obstruction

172. Following an injury the nurse should assess for fat embolism:
A. During 1st 24 hours
B. During 1st 48 hours
C. History of chronic respiratory disease
D. Patient on skeletal traction

173. A patient with acute pancreatitis has NG tube for low intermittent suction to prevent:
A. Chronic distortion
B. Gastric reflux
C. Pancreatic stimulation
D. Peristalsis

174. Cystitis is the inflammation of:
A. Gall bladder B. Urinary bladder
C. Cyst D. Liver

175. Hydrophobia is a sign observed in a patient with:
A. Ant bite B. Dog bite
C. Snake bite D. Mosquito bite

176. Platelet count decreases in:
A. Malaria B. Filaria
C. Dengue D. Typhoid

177. A patient with cardiovascular disorder had a diminished gag reflex, the nurse will:
A. Instill artificial tears

B. Maintain side lying position
C. Offer small sips of clear fluids
D. Test cranial nerves III, IV, VI

178. Which protective items a nurse require to provide colostomy care to the patient with nosocomial infection?
A. Gloves and goggles
B. Gloves and a gown
C. Gloves, gown and shoes protector
D. Gloves, gown and goggles

179. Eye padding is applied on unconscious patients to prevent:
A. Dryness of eye B. Blinking of eyes
C. Corneal ulcer D. Eye movement

180. Addison's disease is caused by insufficiency of hormone:
A. Thyroid hormone
B. Parathyroid hormone
C. Corticosteroid hormone
D. Insulin

181. Hepatitis-A is caused:
A. Due to infected blood transfusion
B. Due to use of contaminated water
C. Due to addiction of drug
D. Due to dialysis

182. Stages of malaria fever includes all except:
A. Cold stage B. Hot stage
C. Fever stage D. Sweating stage

183. Top priority treatment of ventricular fibrilation includes:
A. ECG monitoring B. Proper positioning
C. CPR D. Catheterization

184. Cretinism occurs due to:
A. Hypothyroidism B. Hyperthyroidism
C. Aldosteronism D. Hyperpituitarism

185. Tetany occurs due to:
A. Hypernatremia B. Hyponatremia
C. Hypocalcemia D. Hypercalcemia

186. During Diabetes insipidus specific gravity of urine:
A. Decrease
B. Increase
C. First increases then decreases
D. No effect on specific gravity

187. In following which disease occur due to deficiency of thiamine?
A. Beri-Beri B. Pellagra
C. Anaemia D. Scurvy

188. The instrument used for measuring blood pressure is known as:
A. Thermometer
B. Sphigmomanometer
C. Proctoscope
D. Sim's speculum

189. By ECG which organ is examined?
A. Kidney B. Heart
C. Brain D. Liver

190. Main complication of appendicitis is:
A. Perforation B. Piles
C. Jaundice D. Cirrhosis of liver

191. What do you mean by gastrectomy?
A. Artificial incision in the stomach
B. Removal of stomach
C. Anastomosis of the stomach with duodenum
D. Widening of pyloric sphincter

192. To prevent legal implications, what should be done by a nurse during pre-operative period?
A. Provide psychological support
B. Obtain written consent
C. Provide comprehensive nursing care
D. Explain the patient and his relatives about post-operative complications

193. In head injury, mannitol is given to:
A. Prevent seizures
B. Decrease ICP
C. Maintain body temperature
D. Treat headache

194. What do you mean by cyanosis?
A. Yellowish colouration of skin
B. Blue colouration of skin
C. Increase respiration rate
D. Loss of appetite

195. Concentration of xylocaine which is used for spinal anaesthesia is:
A. 5% B. 10%
C. 2% D. 1%

196. Clinical manifestations of anaemia include except:
A. Low Hb level B. Fatigue
C. Hyperactivity D. Lassitude

197. Priority basis management of a unconscious patient include:
A. I.V. therapy
B. I.V. mannitol
C. Clearance of airway
D. Cardiac compression

198. Appendicitis is characterized by
A. Pain at umbilical region
B. Pain at pelvic region
C. Bile containing vomitus
D. Pain at McBurney point

199. Commonest cause of liver cirrhosis is:
A. Infection B. Analgesics
C. Alcohol D. Caffine

200. During Lumbar puncture which position is given to a patient?
A. Supine position
B. Side-lying 'C' shaped position
C. Lithotomy position
D. Fowler's position

201. In oligurea volume of urine is:
A. Less than 100 ml B. Less than 400 ml
C. Less than 800 ml D. Absence of urine

202. Tracheostomy is performed:
A. Between 2nd and 3rd tracheal ring
B. Between 4th and 5th tracheal ring
C. Between 6th and 7th tracheal ring
D. At the level of 1st tracheal ring

203. Management of cardiac arrest include except:
A. Massive I.V. infusion
B. O_2 therapy
C. Clearance of airway
D. Cardiac compression

204. Assessment of a unconscious patient is done by:
A. Apgar score
B. Glasgow Coma Scale
C. Partograph
D. Kurning's sign

205. During head injury what is the cause of increase in body temperature?
A. Pons injury
B. Hypothalamus injury
C. Cerebellum injury
D. Medulla injury

206. What is the cause of hypovolemic shock?
A. Burn B. Severe dehydration
C. Haemorrhage D. All of the above

207. What is the cause of anaemia in chronic renal failure?
A. Decreased erythropoetin
B. Haemolysis
C. Production of immature RBCs
D. Inappropriate renal functioning

208. In following which is not a cause of hypokalemia?
A. Vomitting
B. Potassium wasting diuretics
C. Aldosteronism
D. Renal failure

209. Which of the following drug is used to lower Intracranial pressure (I.C.P)?
A. I.V. Mannitol B. Furesemide
C. Corticosteroid D. All of the above

210. Cleft-palate is ideally repaired at
A. Between 6 months and 18 months
B. Between 6 weeks and 8 weeks
C. Between 6 years and 8 years
D. Ist week of birth

211. Ideal time for cleft lip repair is
A. First week of birth
B. Between 3 months and 6 months
C. Between 3 weeks and 6 weeks
D. Between 6 months and 18 months

212. Which of the following factor is responsible for formation of gall-bladder stone?
A. Hypercholesterolemia
B. Stasis of bile acid
C. Infection
D. All of the above

213. Commonest cause of obstructive jaundice is:
A. Chronic cholecystitis
B. Carcinoma of liver

C. Calculi (stone) in common bile duct
D. Cirrhosis of liver

214. Charcot layden crystals in sputum are seen in:
A. Tuberculosis B. Bronchial asthma
C. Pneumonia D. Pneumoconiosis

215. Which of the following is a cause of acute Pancreatitis?
A. Alcohol ingestion B. Gall-stones
C. Hypercalcemia D. All of the above

216. In the following which is the best indication for testicular biopsy in a man is:
A. Azoospermia B. Oligospermia
C. Polyspermia D. None of the above

217. Splenomegaly occurs in all except:
A. Malaria
B. Kala Azar
C. Haemolytic anaemia
D. Aplastic anaemia

218. Which of the following is the most common Cancer (Both in male and female) in India is:
A. Cancer-oral cavity
B. Lung cancer
C. Breast cancer
D. Cancer-esophagus

219. Most common cancer in male in India is:
A. Lung cancer B. Cancer-larynx
C. Cancer-oral cavity D. Colon-cancer

220. In India most common cancer in female is:
A. Carcinoma-breast
B. Carcinoma-cervix
C. Cancer-oral cavity
D. Cancer urinary bladder

221. Management for inhaled foreign body in an infant's trachea is:
A. Laryngoscopy B. Tracheostomy
C. Bronchoscopy D. Steroid therapy

222. For blood donation, screening of blood should be ruled out for following disease:
A. HIV B. Syphilis
C. Hepatitis B D. All of the above

223. In cataract surgery, spectacles are advised:
A. 6 weeks after operation
B. 12 weeks after operation
C. 16 weeks after operation
D. 21 weeks after operation

224. Following investigation should not be performed in a patient suspected of brain tumour:
A. CT scan B. MRI
C. X-ray skull D. Lumbar puncture

225. Most useful test for diagnosis of Diabetes Mellitus is:
A. Urine sugar
B. Glycated Hb
C. Glucose tolerance test (GTT)
D. None of these

226. Commonest cause of small intestine obstruction is:
A. Volvulus and intussusception
B. Malignant tumours
C. Adhesions secondary to previous pelvic surgery
D. Trauma

227. When Atropine is given as pre-anaesthetic drug, it has all of the following effects except:
A. It minimise the secretions
B. It prevent bradycardia
C. It cause bronchoconstriction
D. It prevent hypotension

228. Which of the following complication may occur after massive blood transfusion (after transfusion of several units of blood):
A. Metabolic acidosis
B. Respiratory acidosis
C. Metabolic alkalosis
D. Metabolic acidosis

229. Metabolic alkalosis is the usual result of massive blood transfusion. This occurs because of:
A. The citrate present as sodium citrate in anticoagulant solution, quickly metabolized to sodium bi carbonate
B. The stored blood have an acid pH (6.3)
C. The stored blood have an alkaline pH (7.8)
D. The stored blood contains bicarbonate in anticoagulant solution

230. Mother has blood group AB and father has B. Which blood group is not likely to occur in children?
A. Blood group-A B. Blood group-B
C. Blood group-AB D. Blood group-O

231. Chlamydia may cause:
A. Trachoma
B. Salpingitis and non-gonococcal urethritis
C. Conjunctivitis
D. All of the above

232. First of all fluid loss occurs from
A. Intracellular B. Intravascular
C. Extravascular D. None of the above

233. Most common malignancy in childhood is
A. Brain tumours B. Wilm's tumours
C. Leukemias D. Prostate cancer

234. In the following which is the treatment of choice in Aphakia?
A. Intraocular lens B. Contact lens
C. Spectacles D. Laser therapy

235. Treatment of choice for angle closure Glaucoma is:
A. Surgical (Laser irodotomy)
B. Medical (eg. Timolol)
C. Trabeculoplasty
D. None of the above

236. Treatment of choice for open angle Glaucoma is:
A. Surgical (Laser irodotomy)
B. Medical (eg. Timolol)
C. Trabeculoplasty
D. None of the above

237. Brain metastasis most commonly arise from:
A. Liver B. Lung
C. Breast D. Prostate

238. Sites involved in Psoriasis include:
A. Skin surface like scalp, knees and elbows
B. Nails
C. Joints
D. All of the above

239. For aspirating gastric content the Ryle's tube is inserted upto:
A. 100 cm B. 50 cm
C. 120 cm D. 150 cm

240. Which of the following is the most common complication of long-term use of topical steroids?
A. Cataract B. Glaucoma
C. Conjunctivitis D. Ptosis

241. Which of the following is the most common complication of systemic steroid therapy?
A. Cataract B. Glaucoma
C. Conjunctivitis D. Uveitis

242. Osteoporosis is not seen in which of the following condition?
A. Hyperthyroidism
B. Hyperparathyroidism
C. Long-term steroid therapy
D. Hypoparathyroidism

243. Characteristic features of Anorexia Nervosa include the following except:
A. Predominantly seen in women
B. Loss of weight
C. ↓ sed vital signs (temperature, pulse and B.P.)
D. Excessive (Binge) eating

244. Which of the following is not a clinical feature of Anorexia Nervosa?
A. Increased body weight
B. Amenorrhoea in female
C. Hirsutism
D. Very less eating by the patient

245. Painless gross haematuria is the most common clinical feature of:
A. Wilm's tumour
B. Polycystic kidney disease
C. Carcinoma-Urinary bladder
D. Nephrotic syndrome

246. Immediate management to restore B.P. and peripheral circulation in a patient with multiple fracture and fluid loss would be:
A. Blood transfusion
B. Ringer lactate (RL) infusion
C. Normal saline (NS) infusion
D. Dextran infusion

247. Hypoglycemia is not the feature of the following condition:
A. Addison's disease
B. Hepatocellular failure
C. Acromegaly
D. Glucose-6 Phosphatase defect

248. In the following which site is used for central venous catheterization?
A. Femoral vein

B. Subclavian vein
C. Internal juglar vein
D. All of the above

249. Transfusion of 1 unit fresh and whole blood in an average size adult, haemoglobin will raised upto:
A. 1 gm% B. 0.5 gm%
C. 5 gm% D. 2.5 gm%

250. In Glasgow Coma Scale of a conscious person, what will be the total score?
A. 5 B. 8
C. 10 D. 15

251. Emboli due to DVT (Deep vein thrombosis) goes to:
A. Brain B. Lung
C. Liver D. Spleen

252. Which of the following infection is not transmitted through blood transfusion?
A. Cytomegalo virus (CMV)
B. Hepatitis B virus
C. Dengue virus
D. Hepatitis C virus

253. A patient develops respiratory distress while inserting a central venous catheter. The nurse understand that the most likely cause is
A. Pleural effusion B. Pneumothorax
C. Bronchitis D. Emphysema

254. A patient with Nephrotic syndrome is on long-term corticosteroid therapy. Nurse understand that the patient may not develop following complication
A. Hyperglycemia
B. Psychiatric disturbance
C. Hypertrophy muscles
D. Peptic ulcer

255. A patient is on ventilator. His ABG analysis shows-pH 7.5, ↓P_4CO_2 and normal P_4O_2. The nurse understand that the diagnosis of patient is
A. Respiratory acidosis
B. Respiratory alkalosis
C. Metabolic acidosis
D. Metabolic alkalosis

256. A case of blunt trauma following road-traffic accident is brought to the emergency department in the condition of shock. I.V. fluids are infused but patient is not responding. The nurse would expect that the next step in management will be:
A. Blood transfusion
B. Immediate laparotomy
C. Albumin transfusion
D. Abdominal compression

257. A patient of road-traffic accident is brought in emergency department. He presents hypotension (↓sed B.P.), tachycardia, pallor and restlessness. Most likely ruptured organ is:
A. Mesentry B. Spleen
C. Kidney D. Urinary bladder

258. The word 'Psychology' was first used by:
A. Watson B. Rudolf Geockle
C. Sigmend Freud D. Allport

259. The word 'Psychology' is derived from words:
A. Psyche and logos B. Psyche and logus
C. Psycho and logos D. Psycho and logus

260. Psychology is defined as:
A. Study of soul
B. Study of mental diseases
C. Scientific study of behaviour and mental processes
D. Study of mechanism of brain functioning

261. Which of the following is a branch of Psychology?
A. Developmental psychology
B. Abnormal psychology
C. Clinical psychology
D. All of these

262. The branch of psychology which is related with diagnosis and treatment of mental disease:
A. Educational psychology
B. Comparative psychology
C. Clinical psychology
D. Applied psychology

263. Importance of Psychology is in:
A. the field of education
B. the field of guidance and counselling

C. the field of industry and business management
D. All of these

264. The study of psychology is of great importance to a student nurse, as:
A. Psychology will help her to understand herself and other people
B. Psychology will help her to understand human relationships and in rapport formation
C. Psychology will help her to shaping attitude and behaviour of a patient
D. All of the above

265. Which of the following method is used in Psychology?
A. Introspective method
B. Observational method
C. Clinical and case study method
D. All of the above

266. Simplest form (method) of thinking is:
A. Abstract thinking
B. Logical thinking
C. Creative thinking
D. Perceptual thinking

267. In psychoanalytic method the main focus is on:
A. Conscious mind B. Unconscious mind
C. Mind D. Behaviour

268. We can tolerate frustration because of the function of:
A. Id B. Ego
C. Superego D. Oedipus complex

269. Acquisition of skills is known as:
A. Cognitive learning
B. Affective learning
C. Learning by conditioned reflex
D. Psychomotor learning

270. A state of a person resulting when the satisfaction of the motivated behaviour become difficult or impossible, in known as:
A. Conflict B. Frustration
C. Emotion D. Problem-solving

271. What do you mean by learning?
A. Acquisition of skill
B. Acquisition of knowledge
C. Modification of behaviour which result from practice and experience
D. Any change in behaviour

272. 'Classical conditioning' theory of learning was proposed by:
A. Thorndike B. Ivan Pavlov
C. Watson D. Ernold

273. Which of the following is a positive emotion:
A. Anger B. Affection
C. Jealous D. Hear

274. When Pavlov did his experiment with dog, the sound of bell was the:
A. Conditioned response
B. Unconditioned response
C. Conditioned stimulus
D. Unconditioned stimulus

275. Which of the following is not a type of intelligence?
A. Concrete intelligence
B. Abstract intelligence
C. Mental intelligence
D. Social intelligence

276. Characteristics of a genius child is:
A. Interest in abstract thinking
B. Ability of attention
C. High level of intelligence (I.Q. more than 130)
D. All of the above

277. Habits are:
A. Acquired B. Inborn
C. Both A and B D. None of the above

278. In the Maslow's need hierarchy model which of the following need is kept above the safety needs?
A. Self actualization need
B. Belonging need or need to be loved
C. Esteem needs
D. Physiological needs

279. The term I.Q. (Intelligent Quotient) was introduced by:
A. Terman B. Allport
C. William Stern D. Watson

280. To compute I.Q. which formula is used:

A. $IQ = \frac{MA}{CA} \times 100$ B. $IQ = \frac{CA}{MA} \times 100$

C. $IQ = \frac{CA}{MA} \div 100$ D. $IQ = \frac{MA}{CA} + 100$

281. According to Terman's I.Q. formula, a normal individual has:

A. Mental age < chronological age
B. Mental age > chronological age
C. Mental age = chronological age
D. None of the above

282. The ability of a person to develop something new which was not in existence, is known as:

A. Achievement B. Aptitude
C. Attitude D. Creativity

283. Which test is important for selection of a person in a specific job?

A. Achievement test B. Aptitude test
C. Intelligence test D. Attitude test

284. Which of the following test predict a person's ability in a specific area or field?

A. Intelligence test B. Personality test
C. Aptitude test D. Achievement test

285. Which test determine the person's level of knowledge in the given area?

A. Aptitude test B. Achievement test
C. Personality test D. Memory test

286. The first test developed to measure intelligence was designed by:

A. William Stern
B. Wechsler
C. Binet and Simon
D. Terman and R.B. Cattel

287. The process of adjustment is

A. Dynamic B. Stable
C. Both A and B D. None of the above

288. Subsystem of personality which play important role to satisfy hour biological needs through right way and show the right way to behave:

A. Id B. Superego
C. Igo ideal D. Igo

289. Which of the following is the correct way to make learning effective?

A. To provide motivation
B. To give incentive
C. To give punishment
D. Used new teaching method

290. When a person do a lot of hard work without relaxation between work, he will got:

A. Motivation B. Frustration
C. Depression D. Pressure

291. Which part of the brain play important role in maintaining the state of homeostasis?

A. Hypothalamus B. Thalamus
C. Cerebellums D. Spinal cord

292. When a person get stress in the office, after reaching home he beat his wife and children to release his tension, he is using the following defense mechanism:

A. Rationalization B. Repression
C. Displacement D. Projection

293. Regression means:

A. To behave in a balanced manner
B. To interrupt in thinking process
C. To behave in a mature way
D. Revert to childish level of behaviour

294. In which defence mechanism, we make excuse giving a reason different from the real one for what we are doing:

A. Projection B. Rationalization
C. Displacement D. Reaction formation

295. In which defence mechanism, a person channelise his strong and socially unacceptable drive or urge into a form that is socially acceptable:

A. Identification B. Intellectualization
C. Sublimation B. Conversion

296. A person who has aggressive feelings may not be able to express these in society but can become a boxer. This is an example of:

A. Suppression B. Sublimation
C. Conversion D. Repression

297. In which defence mechanism, an emotional conflict is expressed by a physical illness or physical symptom without any organic cause?

A. Sublimation B. Conversion
C. Compensation D. Suppression

298. Emotion is:
A. A complex feeling state
B. Conscious stirred up state of a person
C. Subjective feeling state involving physiological arousal accompanied by characteristic behaviour
D. All of the above

299. Theory of cognitive development was proposed by:
A. Guilford B. Jean Piaget
C. Binet D. Terman

300. Perception is:
A. Sensation and interpretation
B. Sensation and language
C. Sensation and memory
D. Sensation and images

301. Psycho-analytical theory of personality development was introduced by:
A. Karl Jung B. Sigmund Freud
C. Guilford D. Harman Rosarch

302. "Personality may be defined as the most characteristic integration of an individual's structure, modes of behaviour, interests, attitudes, capacities, abilities and aptitude". This definition is given by:
A. Gordon Allport B. Freud
C. N.L. Munn D. Erikson

303. Which of the following is the characteristic of personality?
A. Personality is unique and specific
B. It is the product of heredity and environment
C. Personality includes all the behaviour pattern that is cognitive, conative and affective domains
D. All of the above

304. Who classified personality as extrovert and introvert?
A. Gordon Allport B. Karl G. Jung
C. Watson D. Bruner

305. Psychosocial theory of personality development was developed by
A. H. Erikson B. Sigmund Freud
C. Carl Roger D. Jean Piaget

306. All of the following are subjective method of personality assessment except one:
A. Autobiography
B. Questionnaire
C. Rating scale
D. Personality inventory

307. Which of the following is the objective technique of personality assessment?
A. Biography B. Rating scale
C. Sociometry D. All of the above

308. Development of human being is influenced by:
A. Parents and teachers
B. Psychosocial and cultural factors
C. Parents and relatives
D. Heredity and environment

309. Which of the following biological factor is the most important in determining one's Personality?
A. Nervous system B. Endocrine glands
C. Height and weight D. Body structure

310. Meaning of motivation is:
A. Excitement
B. External excitement
C. Internal excitement
D. None of the above

311. In which of the following personality assessment test, a person is given a picture and asked him to make a story about the picture:
A. Questionnaire method
B. Rating scale
C. Projective test
D. Interview method

312. The word personality is derived from the greek word 'persona' which means:
A. Drama B. Mask
C. Cloth D. Face

313. Which of the following is a characteristic of learning:
A. Learning is a process of modification of behaviour
B. Learning is a purposeful and goal-directed process
C. Learning is a self active process which takes place in a social set-up or environment
D. All of the above

314. Trial and error theory of learning was given by:
A. Ivan Pavlov B. Thorndike
C. Skinner D. Kohler

315. According to Thorndike which is the law of learning:
A. Law of readiness
B. Law of exercise or practice
C. Law of effect
D. All of the above

316. If a child's mental age is equal to chronological age his I.Q. will be:
A. 90 B. 100
C. 80 D. 115

317. A person's need of belongingness is called as:
A. Physical need
B. Achievement motive
C. Affiliation motive
D. Power motive

318. Which of the following statement is true?
A. According to Freud sex-instinct arise in puberty
B. 'Id' is concerned with 'reality principle'
C. Psychoanalysis is both theory of personality and treatment therapy of mental illnesses
D. Defense mechanisms are used only by person who are psychologically unhealthy

319. World's first psychology laboratory was established by:
A. Francis Galton B. Wilhelm Wundt
C. Alfred Adler D. William McDougall

320. Which of the following statement is correct about modern psychology?
A. Psychology is the science of mind
B. Psychology is the science of soul
C. Psychology is the science of consciousness
D. Psychology is the science of behaviour

321. "Psychology is the positive science of behaviour". This definition of psychology is given by:
A. William McDougall
B. R.S. Woodworth
C. C.E. Skinner
D. N.L. Munn

322. Which of the following is not a primary motive?
A. Hunger motive
B. Thirst motive
C. Affiliation motive
D. Sex motive

323. Which of the following is a secondary motive?
A. Achievement motive
B. Aggressiveness motive
C. Affiliation motive
D. All of the above

324. Which of the following is the characteristic of motivated behaviour?
A. Motivated behaviour is goal directed
B. Motivated behaviour is selective in nature
C. Motivated behaviour is energized and evocated
D. All of the above

325. A child is considered as mentally retarded when I.Q. is:
A. 100 B. Below 70
C. Below 25 D. 80-90

326. Which of the following factor affect the learning process?
A. Motivation
B. Age, sex, intellectual capabilities and level of aspiration of learner
C. Nature of learning material, learning method and environment
D. All of the above

327. Thinking is also known as:
A. Memory B. Motivation
C. Cognition D. Attention

328. In following which sentence is true regarding thinking?
A. It is a cognitive activity
B. It is goal directed and problem-solving behaviour
C. Images, concepts, symbols and languages are used as instruments of thinking.
D. All are correct

329. Which of the following is not a type of thinking?
A. Perceptual thinking (concrete thinking)
B. Conceptual thinking (abstract thinking)
C. Positive thinking
D. Problem-solving thinking

330. Which of the following steps are involved in scientific method of problem-solving?
A. Recognizing and defining the problem
B. Collecting relevant data and formulation of hypothesis
C. Putting into practice the course of action and draw conclusions/results
D. All of the above

331. What is true about emotion?
A. Emotion is a type of feeling
B. Emotion is a psycho-physiological process
C. Emotion is a complex process
D. All of the above statements are true

332. Mentally retarded child has:
A. Lack of abstract thinking
B. Inadequate adjustment
C. Lack of creativity
D. All of the above

333. Alfred Binet is associated with:
A. Personality testing
B. Intelligence testing
C. Aptitude testing
D. Value testing

334. Emotion can be expressed through which of the following?
A. Language B. Gesture
C. Facial expression D. All of the above

335. The cognitive changes during old age mostly affect which of the following aspects?
A. Emotion B. Memory
C. Sentiment D. Intelligence

336. The basic emotional task for toddler is:
A. Trust B. Industry
C. Identification D. Independence

337. The stage of growth and development basically concerned with role identification is the:
A. Oral stage B. Genital stage
C. Oedipus stage D. Latency stage

338. The client with antisocial personality disorder:
A. Suffer from a great deal of anxiety
B. Is generally unable to postpone gratification
C. Rapidlly learns by experience and punishment
D. Has a great sense of responsibility towards others

339. Mentally healthy individual can be defined as those who:
A. Have insight into their own problems
B. Are able to meat their own basic needs
C. Are not exhibiting pathological symptoms
D. Are free from both physical and emotional problems

340. The best place for a students to study effectively is where?
A. It is a little noisy
B. It is quiet
C. There are distractions
D. It is poorly ventilated

341. The laws of effective learning are except the:
A. Law of readiness
B. Law of exercise or practise
C. Law of effect
D. Law of adjustment

342. Emotion effects our body and mind if it:
A. Recurs and remains for a long time
B. Occurs and disappears
C. Recurs and disappears
D. Recurs and remains for short time

343. The part of mind that distinguish right from wrong and act as censor of behaviour is called:
A. Ego B. Id
C. Libido D. Superego

344. Exclusion of unwanted or unpleasant experiences, emotions or ideas from conscious awareness is:
A. Denial B. Repression
C. Regression D. Projection

345. Individual difference in interest ability and capacity in a specific field is measured by applying one of the following test:
A. Attitude test
B. Aptitude test
C. Intelligence quotient test
D. Mental ability test

346. Thinking is a mental process that deals with:
A. Thoughts and ideas
B. Motives and movements
C. Action and reactions
D. Feelings and emotions

347. Significant components of personality as described by sigmond freud are:
A. Conscious preconscious & subconscious
B. Id, ego and superego
C. Dream Interpretation
D. Defence mechanism

348. When a person retreat or revert to an infantile or childish level of behaviour is called:
A. Suppersion B. Repression
C. Regression D. Sublimation

349. The relationship that is of extreme importance in the formation of the personality is the:
A. Peer B. Sibling
C. Parent child D. Heterosexual

350. The emotional experience in childhood becomes traumatic when:
A. Parents are harse and restrictive
B. The superego has not been internalised
C. The child is unable to verbalise own feeling
D. The ego is overwhelmed by anxiety it cannot handle

351. All behaviour can be said to be:
A. A response to stimulus
B. A conditioned response
C. An intellectual response
D. An emotional response

352. Intellectual quotient (IQ) tells about:
A. Intellectual maturity
B. Mental age in relation to chronological age
C. Academic achievement
D. Mental growth

353. Who was the founder of Experimental psychology?
A. William James B. William Wundt
C. Wolfgang Kohler D. Sigmund Freud

354. A gifted child has an I.Q. test of:
A. >120 B. >100
C. >130 D. <115

355. A mentally retarded child has an I.Q. test of:
A. < 80 B. 80 and above
C. 70 or below D. < 90

356. Defence mechanism or mental mechanism is a reaction to:
A. Frustration B. Motivation
C. Drive D. Emotion

357. Which type of conflict takes place when a person is forced to select between two negative goals?
A. Approach–Approach Conflict
B. Approach–Avoidance Conflict
C. Avoidance–Avoidance Conflict
D. Multiple Approach–Avoidance Conflict

358. What do you mean by ethics in nursing?
A. Procedures carried out by a nurse
B. Rules for correct behaviour
C. Job responsibilities of a nurse
D. Characteristics of a good nurse

359. Characteristics of a profession includes:
A. A profession constantly enlarges its body of knowledge
B. A profession makes its own policies and controls its own activities
C. A profession offers services which are related to human and social welfere
D. All of the above

360. Criteria of a profession include except
A. A profession should be intellectual
B. It should be self governing
C. In a profession there is no place for higher education
D. A profession should be service-oriented

361. Nursing is considered as a profession because:
A. In this a nurse earns money
B. It is based on science and art
C. It provide comprehensive health services
D. Nursing fulfils all the criteria of a profession

362. Qualities of a nurse include except
A. Caring attitude B. Honesty
C. Talkative D. Well balanced life

363. A ideal nurse should be poise. Here word poise means:
A. Silent
B. Knowledgeable
C. Control of emotions
D. Self confident

364. Motivation means:
A. Refusing to do something
B. Wanting to do something

C. Changing one's mind about doing something
D. To do work completely finish

365. In following which sentence is false?
A. Code of ethics tell us that what is right and what is wrong
B. A code of ethics is a strict set of rules
C. Code of ethics tells the members what kind of conduct is expected of them as they practice
D. All of the above

366. Use of code of ethics in nursing profession includes:
A. It guides professional behaviour
B. It prevent a nurse from practising below the standard set by the code
C. It can be used to protect a nurse who is falsely accused of doing something wrong
D. All of the above

367. The first code of ethics in nursing profession was adopted in:
A. 1948 B. 1953
C. 1965 D. 1978

368. The most recent revision of code of ethics in nursing was took place in:
A. 1953 B. 1973
C. 1985 D. 1992

369. The code of ethics in nursing was adopted and published by the:
A. Indian Nursing Council
B. Rajasthan Nursing Council
C. World Health Organization
D. International Council of Nurses

370. Code of ethics for a nurse includes except:
A. The primary responsibility of a nurse is to provide care to those people who require it
B. A nurse maintains a co-operative relationship with co-workers
C. A nurse is not responsible for maintaining highest standard of nursing care
D. The nurse shares with other citizens the responsibility for initiating and supporting action to meet the health needs of the public

371. As per code of ethics in nursing profession what is the responsibility of a nurse towards his profession:
A. She should provide nursing care and earn money
B. She should know all the nursing procedures
C. She should try to maintain highest standard of nursing profession
D. She should provide nursing care to people without taking money

372. Code of ethics in nursing profession tells about:
A. What is right and what is wrong
B. What kind of conduct is expected of nursing personnel as they practice
C. What is the responsibilities of a nurse
D. All of the above

373. In following which is not a fundamental responsibility of a nurse?
A. To promote health
B. To prevent illness
C. To alleviate suffering
D. None of the above

374. A professional nurse must provide nursing care
A. First to rich people then poor
B. First to males then females
C. First to people of political background and then general public
D. To all needy people without any discrimination

375. What do you mean by legal responsibilities in nursing practice?
A. The way in which you are obligated to obey the law in professional activities
B. The responsibilities of a nurse towards his patient, society and profession
C. The responsibilities of a patient towards his nurse and treating doctor
D. The responsibility of a nurse to perform various nursing procedures

376. In following which authority provides guidance to legal responsibility for nursing practice?
A. Central government acts
B. State government acts
C. International code for nurses subscribed by the TNAI
D. All of the above

377. In following which national legislation is directly related to nursing practice?
A. The government service conduct rules
B. The Indian nursing council act
C. Law based upon the English pattern
D. The state service conduct rules

378. The laws given for nursing profession includes except:
A. Records must be treated as confidential unless the practitioner is called upon to give evidence in court
B. A practitioner must give personal attention to his cases
C. Only private nurses have right to sue for fees
D. Unregistered practitioners may be allowed to hold appointments in public hospitals

379. A written law which has been formally passed by the government, is called as:
A. Bill B. Act
C. Decision D. Code of ethics

380. The criteria which must be fulfilled by legal document, includes:
A. It should be written accurately
B. It should be signed and dated by the person who has prepared the document
C. These can be used in court cases when evidence is needed
D. All of the above

381. An agreement bond is of legal value if that fulfils following criteria except:
A. If it is written accurately
B. If it is complete
C. If it is signed by both employee and employer
D. If it is a verbal contract

382. An agreement bond which is signed and dated by both employee and employer may be legally valuable:
A. For employee only
B. For employer only
C. For both employee and employer
D. Sometimes for employee and always for employer

383. An agreement between two parties to do certain things together, is termed as:
A. Act B. Bill
C. Contract D. Legal document

384. A written statement of what a person wants to do with his property and possessions after death:
A. Act B. Agreement bond
C. Will D. Bill

385. A failure in professional duty, practice or skill that leads to injury or harm to the patient, is termed as:
A. Malpractice B. Negligence
C. Crime D. Misunderstanding

386. The legal document which is signed by both employee and employer at the time of joining, and has legal value for both, is termed as:
A. Act B. Licence
C. Agreement bond D. All of the above

387. A written permission given by a recognised authority to do a specific thing, is termed as:
A. Contract B. Licence
C. Act D. Agreement bond

388. Indian red cross society was established in:
A. 1925 B. 1920
C. 1948 D. 1932

389. Who is the president of Indian red cross society?
A. President of India
B. Home minister of India
C. Prime minister of India
D. Vice-president of India

390. What is the meaning of trends in nursing?
A. Professional qualification required for a nurse
B. Job responsibility of a professional nurse
C. Movement in a particular direction in nursing field
D. Code of ethics in nursing profession

391. Current aim in nursing education includes:
A. All school of nursing now attached to a medical college should be upgraded to the B.Sc. level
B. Nursing personnel must have authority in the selection of students
C. Nursing schools should have independent budget
D. All of the above

392. In India basic B.Sc. nursing programme was started in:
A. 1946 B. 1953
C. 1962 D. 1966

393. In India post basic B.Sc. nursing programme was started in:
A. 1961 B. 1963
C. 1946 D. 1975

394. In India first of all post basic B.Sc. nursing programme was started at:
A. Delhi university
B. Baba Faridkot university
C. Kerala university
D. RUHS, Jaipur

395. In India first at all M.Sc. nursing was started in:
A. 1946 B. 1959
C. 1966 D. 1972

396. What is the full form of TNAI?
A. Training in Nursing at All India level
B. Trained Nurses of All India
C. Trained Nurses Association of India
D. Training in Nurses at International level

397. TNAI was established in:
A. 1905 B. 1922
C. 1937 D. 1945

398. Activity of TNAI includes:
A. It gives scholarship for nurses who wish to go on for advanced study either in the country or abroad
B. Publication of nursing journal of India
C. It promotes the development of courses in higher education for nurses
D. All of the above

399. Student Nurses Association was organised in:
A. 1905 B. 1920
C. 1922 D. 1934

400. Functions of student nurse's association include except:
A. To help student nurses in learning how the professional organisation serves to uphold the dignity of nursing profession
B. To encourage both professional and recreational meetings and sports in nursing profession
C. To increase the nursing students social contacts and general knowledge
D. Publication of Indian nursing yearbook

401. The president of SNA may be:
A. A nursing student
B. A professional nurse
C. A professional nurse as well as TNAI member
D. All of the above

402. The national headquarter of student nurse's association is situated in:
A. Jaipur B. New Delhi
C. Mumbai D. Chennai

403. International Council of Nurses was established in:
A. 1920 B. 1905
C. 1922 D. 1899

404. The headquarter of International Council of Nurses located in:
A. New Delhi B. Geneva
C. New York D. London

405. The activity of Internation Council of Nurses includes:
A. Publication of nursing journal of India
B. Publication of Indian nursing yearbook
C. Publication of code of ethics for nurses
A. All of the above

406. Which organization publishes the International nursing review?
A. TNAI B. INC
C. ICN D. WHO

407. The nursing journal of India is publised:
A. Monthly B. Yearly
C. Quarterly D. Weekly

408. The Indian Nursing Council was established in:
A. 1922 B. 1939
C. 1947 D. 1949

409. From which year INC started to provide for registration of foreign nurses?
A. 1948 B. 1957
C. 1975 D. 1982

410. After registration in one state nursing council, the condition of mutual recognition by the other state nurse's registration council is termed as:

A. Code of ethics B. Reciprocity
C. Uniformity D. Red crescent

411. Activities of INC include except:
A. Registration of nursing students after completion of course
B. To decide rules and regulations for establishing new college of nursing
C. Maintain uniform standards in nursing education in all over India
D. Provide reciprocity in nursing registration throughout the country

412. What is the full form of UNICEF?
A. United Nursing Indian Child Emergency Function
B. Ultimate Nursing International Child Emergency Fund
C. United Nation's International Children's Emergency Fund
D. Unique Nation's International Children's Emergency Fund

413. UNICEF was established in:
A. 1920 B. 1946
C. 1952 D. 1948

414. WHO was established in:
A. 1945 B. 1947
C. 1948 D. 1943

415. The target "health for all by 2000 A.D." was declared by:
A. WHO B. UNICEF
C. Red Cross Society D. TNAI

416. The organization which is responsible for registration of nursing personnel:
A. INAI
B. INC
C. State Nurse's Council
D. International Council of Nurse's

417. What is the full form of RNRM?
A. Recognised Nurse Recognised Midwife
B. Recognised Nurse Recognised Mother
C. Registered Nurse Registered Midwife
D. Registration in Nurse and Registration in Midwife

418. The organisation which represents largest number of professional nurses in India?
A. ICN B. TNAI
C. UNICEF D. SNA

419. In India, in which year LHV course was started?
A. 1918 B. 1945
C. 1948 D. 1967

420. Activity of red cross society includes:
A. Relief work during disaster
B. Maternal and child welfare services
C. Provision of blood banks and first aid services
D. All of the above

421. The health agency which renders financial assistance to various leprosy homes and clinics:
A. Hind Kusht Nivaran Sangh
B. Bharat Sevak Samaj
C. TB Association of India
D. The Kasturba Memorial Fund

422. The TB association of India was establised in:
A. 1920 B. 1922
C. 1939 D. 1952

423. The voluntary health agency which is mainly related to improve the status of women:
A. Indian Red Cross Society
B. Bharat Sevak Samaj
C. The Kasturba Memorial Fund
D. WHO

424. The Kasturba Memorial Fund was estabilished in:
A. 1922 B. 1939
C. 1944 D. 1946

425. In following which is the only women's voluntary welfare organisation in the country:
A. The Kasturba Memorial Fund
B. All India Women's Conference
C. Bharat Sevak Samaj
D. TNAI

426. Bharat Sevak Samaj was formed in:
A. 1952 B. 1962
C. 1948 D. 1975

427. WHO was established on:
A. 14th April, 1948 B. 7th April, 1948
C. 7th April, 1945 D. 7th April, 1947

428. Headquarter of WHO is located in:
A. New Delhi B. New York
C. London D. Geneva

429. Activities of World Health Organization include except:
A. Registration of medical and nursing staff
B. Development of comprehensive health services
C. To provide MCH services
D. Promotion of environmental health

430. What is the full form of UNDP?
A. United Nation's Development Programme
B. Unique Nursing Developmental Programme
C. United Nation Developmental Project
D. United Nurse's Development Project

431. The food and agriculture organisation was establised in:
A. 1945 B. 1948
C. 1957 D. 1963

432. The Colombo plan was drawn up for cooperative economonic development in:
A. All word
B. Asia
C. India
D. South and South East India

433. The number of regional members in Colombo plan, are:
A. 10 B. 20
C. 6 D. 14

434. The health agency mainly assisting the national TB control programme in India:
A. The Colombo plan
B. SIDA
C. USAID
D. ILO

435. In following which is the Swedish International Agency?
A. USAID B. SIDA
C. DANIDA D. ILO

436. The health agency which is providing assistance for the development of services under national blindness control programme:
A. USAID B. SIDA
C. DANIDA D. Colombo plan

437. CARE was established in:
A. 1945 B. 1948
C. 1952 D. 1954

438. What is the full form of CARE?
A. Cooperative for Assistance and Relief Everywhere
B. Cooperative Authority for Resting Everywhere
C. Clinical Assistance and Relief Everywhere
D. Co-ordinated Assistance for Relief Everywhere

439. On going on the job instructions that is given to enhance the worker's performance in their present job is known as:
A. Job responsibility
B. Job induction
C. In service-education
D. None of the above

440. Any extension of opportunities for study and training to any person following their completion of or withdrawal from full time school or college is known as:
A. In service education
B. Job induction
C. Continuing education
D. Job-orientation

441. The structure that establishes connection between the mother and foetus during intra uterine life is:
A. Placenta B. Umbilical cord
C. Uterus D. Vagina

442. Interstitial implantation of fertilized ovum is completed on:
A. 5th day B. 11th day
C. 20th day D. 2nd day

443. At term the weight of placenta is about:
A. 100 gm B. 300 gm
C. 500 gm D. 1000 gm

444. At term the part of the placenta that is of foetal origin, is about:
A. 1/5th B. 1/4th
C. 4/5th D. 1/2nd

445. Volume of blood in mature placenta is about:
A. 500 ml B. 150 ml
C. 1000 ml D. 50 ml

446. During intra uterine life rate of fetal blood flow through the placenta is about:
A. 400 ml /min
B. 2000 ml/min
C. 200 ml/min
D. 1000 ml/min

447. The functions of placenta are:
A. Transmission of nutrients between the mother and foetus
B. Produces the hormones necessary to maintain the pregnancy
C. Barrier functions
D. All of the above

448. The enzyme that is elaborated in the placenta and essential for the synthesis of arachidonic acid is:
A. Diamine oxidase
B. Oxytocinase
C. Phospholipase A_2
D. Methargine

449. In following which statement is not true regarding amniotic fluid?
A. At term it measures about 600-800 ml
B. It is alkaline in nature
C. Specific gravity is about 1.010
D. Near term its colour is golden

450. In normal condition colour of amniotic fluid at term is:
A. Pale straw colour
B. Golden
C. Greenish yellow
D. Dark coloured

451. During Rh incompatibility colour of amniotic fluid is:
A. Pale straw colour
B. Golden
C. Greenish yellow
D. Dark coloured

452. During post maturity colour of amniotic fluid is:
A. Pale straw colour
B. Golden
C. Greenish yellow
D. Dark coloured

453. The organic compounds present in amniotic fluid:
A. Protein
B. Lipid and glucose
C. Urea and creatinine
D. All of the above

454. The function of amniotic fluid during pregnancy is:
A. It acts as a shock absorber
B. Maintains an even temperature
C. Allows free movement of the foetus
D. All of the above

455. The function of amniotic fluid during labour is:
A. It helps dilatation of cervix
B. It flushes the birth canal during labour
C. During uterine contraction, it prevents marked interference with placental circulation
D. All of the above

456. pH of vagina during pregnancy:
A. Acidic
B. Basic
C. Neutral
D. Sometime acidic and sometime basic

457. Which is not a true statement?
A. During pregnancy there is enlargement of the body of uterus
B. Weight of uterus at term is about 200-800 gms
C. In multiparae at term the position of uterus is commonly anteverted
D. The shape of the uterus becomes spherical beyond 36th weeks

458. The weight of uterus at term is about:
A. 200-300 gm
B. 900-1000 gm
C. 2-3 kg
D. 400-500 gm

459. Braxtons hicks contractions are:
A. Uterine contraction in pregnancy
B. Cardiac contraction in pregnancy
C. Uterine contraction during puberty
D. The uterine contraction that occur after delivery of baby

460. Which statement is not true?
A. Braxton-hicks contraction are found during pregnancy
B. In abdominal pregnancy braxton hicks contraction are more frequent
C. Braxton-hicks contractions can be felt by bimanual examination
D. During term uterine contraction become frequent with increase in intensity

461. The physiological changes in breast that take place during pregnancy are:

A. Increase in size of breast
B. Nipples becomes, erectile and larger
C. Increased vascularity
D. All of the above

462. The sebaceous glands which remain non-dominant in non-pregnant state become hypertrophied during pregnancy, these are known as:
A. Secondary areola
B. Montegomery's tubercles
C. Braxton-hicks contractions
D. Axillary tail

463. In following which is an important sign of pregnancy?
A. Increase in the size of breast
B. Larger, erectile and deeply pigmerded nipples
C. Squeezing of secretions of the breast who has never lacteted
D. All of the above

464. During +2 station, position of foetal head is:
A. Below ischeal spine
B. Above ischeal spine
C. Behind ischeal spine
D. Just above of pelvic inlet

465. Which is the most common and ideal pelvis?
A. Android B. Gynaecoid
C. Platy pelloid D. Anthropoid

466. The slight depressed markes predominantly found in the abdominal wall below the umblicus during pregnancy is termed as:
A. Chloasma gravidarum
B. Linea nigra
C. Striae gravidraum
D. Montegomery's tubercles

467. The total weight gain during the course of a single tone pregnancy in the healthy woman is about:
A. 5 kg B. 6 kg
C. 3 kg D. 11 kg

468. Total increment in blood volume during pregnancy is about:
A. 100 ml B. 2000 ml
C. 1500 ml D. 500 ml

469. In following which statement is true?
A. During pregnancy total protein level increases
B. During pregnancy plasma protein concentration increases
C. During pregnancy albumin level increase
D. During pregnancy globulin level slightly reduces

470. In following which statement is false?
A. During fetal development notocord develops on day 14-21 post conception
B. During fetal development external genitatia develop on weeks 8-12 post conception
C. During fetal development all major structure are formed by 6-8 weeks post conception
D. Both the testicles descend into the scrotum by 28 weeks post conception

471. In following which sentence is false?
A. During pregnancy cardiac output increases
B. During pregnancy stroke volume increases
C. During pregnancy Heart rate decreases
D. During pregnancy venous pressure increases

472. During fetal development both the testicles descend into the scrotum by:
A. 20 weeks B. 28 weeks
C. 32 weeks D. 40 weeks

473. During pregnancy physiological changes occur in which organ?
A. Uterus B. Breast
C. Vagina D. All of the above

474. Under the influence of which hormone graffian follicle develop?
A. Oestrogen B. Progesterone
C. FSH D. L.H.

475. The hormones which is necessary for the continued activity of folicle stimulating hormone?
A. Progesterone B. Oestrogen
C. L.H. D. Thyroxin

476. During pregnancy the structure that acts as power house of hormone production is:
A. Corpus luteum B. Placenta
C. Uterus D. Breast

477. Early pregnancy in human being is maintained by:
A. Placenta B. Corpus luteum
C. Breast D. Graafian follicles

478. The major biological function of hCG is:
A. Maintenance of corpus luteum till 6 weeks of pregnancy
B. Stimulates maternal thyroid
C. Increase in the size of breast
D. Hypertrophy of vagina

479. Functions of human chorionic gonadotrophin is:
A. Maintenance of corpus luteum till 6 weeks of pregnancy
B. It stimulates leydig cells of the male foetus to produce testosterone
C. Excretion of milk
D. Both A and B

480. Human chorionic gonadotrophin hormone is secreted by:
A. Corpus luteum
B. Syncytiotrophoblast of the placenta
C. Graffian follicles
D. Endometrium

481. The half life of hCG is about:
A. 10 days B. 24 hours
C. 24 days D. 10 minutes

482. The values of hCG in blood and urine reach at maximum between:
A. 10-30 days of pregnancy
B. 60-70 days of pregnancy
C. 4-5 months of pregnancy
D. 4-5 days of pregnancy

483. In following which hormone is not secreted by placenta?
A. hCG
B. Human placental lactogen
C. Pregnancy specific B-1 glycoprotein
D. Testosterone

484. Oestrial is first detectable at:
A. 4th day of pregnancy
B. On very first day of pregnancy
C. 2 months of pregnancy
D. 5 months of pregnancy

485. During pregnancy the hormone that sensitizes the myometrium to oxytocin and prostaglandins.
A. Oestrogen B. Progesterone
C. hCG D. Testosterone

486. The hormone that ripens the cervix:
A. Oestrogen B. Progesterone
C. hCG D. Testosterone

487. Which of the following sentence is true regarding pregnancy?
A. Blood volume decreases
B. Cardiac output increases
C. Plasma volume decreases
D. All of the above

488. During pregnancy hypertrophy and proliferation of the ducts of breast are achieved by:
A. Oestrogen B. Progesterone
C. hCG D. Testosterone

489. The breast is the modification of:
A. Sebaceous gland B. Sweat gland
C. Thyroid gland D. Pituitary gland

490. The time period of pregnancy defined as first trimester of pregnancy is:
A. First 12 weeks B. 5-6 weeks
C. 13-28 weeks C. 29-40 weeks

491. The time period of pregnancy defined as second trimester of pregnancy is:
A. First 12 weeks B. 5-6 weeks
C. 13-28 weeks C. 29-40 weeks

492. The time period of pregnancy defined as third trimester of pregnancy:
A. 29-40 weeks B. 20-32 weeks
C. 20-36 weeks D. 36-40 weeks

493. Duration of pregnancy in human being is:
A. 10 lunar month
B. 9 calander month +7 days
C. 280 days
D. All are right

494. Gestational age is calculated from:
A. First day of first menstrual period
B. Last day of first menstrual period
C. First day of the last menstrual period
D. 14th day of the last menstrual period

495. In following which is not a subjective symptom of pregnancy during first trimester?
A. Amenorrhea
B. Morning sickness
C. Quickening
D. Frequency of micturition

496. Frequency of micturition is an important symptom of pregnancy durng first trimester. It is occurred due to:
A. Resting of the enlarged uterus on the bladder
B. Congestion of bladder mucosa
C. Change in maternal osmoregulation
D. All of the above

497. Cervical changes that take place during pregnancy are except:
A. Cervix becomes soft
B. Cervix feels like the lips of the mouth
C. Bluish discolouration of the cervix
D. Cervix feel like the tip of nose

498. Size of the uterus by 12th week of pregnancy is:
A. Like hen's egg B. Like cricket ball
C. Like a fetal head D. Like football

499. Dusky hue of the vestibule and anterior vaginal wall during pregnancy is known as:
A. Jacquemier's sign B. Osiander's sign
C. Goodell's sign D. Hegar's sign

500. Total number of antenatal visit by a pregnant lady should be at least:
A. 2 B. 3
C. 1 D. 5

501. Softening of the cervix during pregnancy is termed as:
A. Jacquemier's sign B. Osiander's sign
C. Goodell's sign D. Hegar's sign

502. In following which is not a pregnancy sign?
A. Chadwick's sign B. Brudzinski's sign
C. Hegar's sign D. Goodell's sign

503. Urine containing hCG is an important sign of:
A. Meningitis B. Acute renal future
C. Pregnancy D. Renal tumour

504. In following which is not a pregnancy test?
A. ELISA test
B. Benedict's test
C. Radio immunoassay
D. Fluoroimmunoassy

505. In following which sentence is not true regarding pregnancy test?
A. Diagnosis of pregnancy by detecting hCG in maternal serum can be made by 48-96 hours after conception
B. The pregnancy test is not reliable after 12 weeks
C. hCG can be estimated on IInd day of missed period
D. hCG level is highest in urine upto 60-70 days after gestation

506. By USG intra decidual gestation sac is identified by as early as:
A. 10-15 days of gestation
B. 29-35 days of gestation
C. 3-4 months of gestation
D. 10-12 weeks of gestation

507. The important feature of second trimester of pregnancy:
A. Amenorrhea B. Quickening
C. Vomitting D. Anorexia

508. Perception of active fetal movement by the pregnant mother at about 18-20 weeks of gestation is termed as:
A. Montegomery's tubericle
B. Quickening
C. Goodell sign
D. Braxton-hicks contraction

509. Braxton hicks contraction are first time felt during:
A. Ist trimester
B. IInd trimester
C. IIIrd trimester
D. Post operative period

510. At the 16th week of gestation the height of the uterus is:
A. Midway between the umbilicus and symphysis pubis
B. At the level of umbilicus
C. At the junction of the lower third and upper two-third of the distance between the ensiform cartilage and umbilicus
D. At the level of ensiform cartilage

511. Fundal height at 24th week of gestation is about:
A. Midway between the umbilicus and symphysis pubis
B. At the level of umbilicus
C. At the junction of the lower third and upper two-third of the distance between the ensiform cartilage and umbilicus
D. At the level of ensiform cartilage

512. Fundal height at 36th week of gestation is about:
A. Midway between the umbilicus and symphysis pubis
B. At the level of umbilicus
C. At the junction of the lower third and upper two-third of the distance between the ensiform cartilage and umbilicus
D. At the level of ensiform cartilage

513. Fetal parts can be palpated first time during:
A. First trimester
B. IInd trimester (at 20th week)
C. Third trimester
D. Just after conception

514. In following which is not a symptom of second trimester of pregnancy?
A. Quickening
B. Fundal height at ensiform cartilages
C. Montegomery's tubercle
D. Detection of fetal heart sound

515. After 36th week of gestation the fundal height comes to 32 weeks level. It occures because of:
A. Fetus becomes short
B. Reduction in amount of amniotic fluid
C. Size of uterus decreased
D. Engagement of the presenting part

516. Fundal height at 32 weeks and 40 weeks of gestation are equal then how will you assess the gestational age if it is 32 weeks or 40 weeks.
A. If fetal part can be palpated then, it of 32 weeks otherwise 40 weeks
B. If braxton hies contraction are less than it is of 32 weeks otherwise 40 weeks
C. If Goodell's sign is present then it is of 32 weeks otherwise 40 weeks
D. If the head is floating it is of 32 weeks and if head is engaged then it is of 40th weeks of pregnancy

517. Relation of the long axis of the fetus to the long axis of the centralised uterus is known as:
A. Lie
B. Presentation
C. Attitude
D. Position of the foetus

518. The part of the growing foetus which occupies the lower pole of the uterus is called as:
A. Lie
B. Presentation of the foetus
C. Attitude of the foetus
D. Position of the foetus

519. The relation of the various parts of the foetus to one another is called as:
A. Lie
B. Presentation of the foetus
C. Attitude of the foetus
D. Position of the foetus

520. Relation of the denominator to the various quadrants of the maternal pelvis is termed as:
A. Lie
B. Presentation of the foetus
C. Attitude of the foetus
D. Position of the foetus

521. The commonest lie of human foetus is:
A. Longitudinal B. Transverse
C. Oblique D. Unstable

522. Commonest presentation of the human foetus is:
A. Cephalic B. Podalic
C. Shoulder D. Transverse

523. Universal attitude of human foetus is:
A. Extended
B. Flexion
C. Sometime extended sometime flexed
D. High extended

524. The suture that separate the occipital bone and the two parietal bone is:
A. Lambdoid suture B. Frontal suture
C. Coronal suture D. Sagittal suture

525. Which statement is false?
A. Sagital suture is also known as longitudinal suture

B. Sagital suture lies between two parietal bones
C. The coronal suture lies between parietal and occipital bones
D. Frontal suture lies between two frontal bones

526. The sutures that formed anterior fontanelle are:
A. Sagital suture anteriorly, and lambdoid suture on either side
B. Frontal anteriorly, posteriorly lambdoid and coronal on either side
C. Frontal anteriorly and lambdoid suture on either side
D. Frontal anteriorly, sagital posteriorly and coronal suture on either side

527. In human being posterior fontanelle is formed by junction of following suture:
A. Sagital suture anteriorly, and lambdoid suture on either side
B. Frontal anteriorly, posteriorly lambdoid and coronal on either side
C. Frontal anteriorly and lambdoid suture on either side
D. Frontal anteriorly, sagital posteriorly and coronal suture on either side

528. Suboccipito-bregmatic diameter of human fetal skull is about:
A. 9.5 cm B. 10 cm
C. 11.5 cm D. 14 cm

529. Suboccipito frontal diameter of human fetal skull is about:
A. 9.5 cm B. 10 cm
C. 11.5 cm D. 14 cm

530. In human fetal skull occipito frontal diameter is about:
A. 9.5 cm B. 10 cm
C. 11.5 cm D. 14 cm

531. In human fetal skull mento vertical diameter is about:
A. 9.5 cm B. 10 cm
C. 11.5 cm D. 14 cm

532. In human fetal skull distance between the centre of the bregma to the nape of neck, is termed as:
A. Suboccipito bregmatic
B. Submento bregmatic
C. Suboccipito frontal
D. Mento vertical

533. In human fetal skull distance between the centre of the bregma to the junction of floor of the mouth and neck, is termed as:
A. Suboccipito bregmatic
B. Submento bregmatic
C. Suboccipito frontal
D. Mento vertical

534. In human fetal skull highest diameter is:
A. Suboccipito bregmatic
B. Submento bregmatic
C. Suboccipito frontal
D. Mento vertical

535. In human fetal skull distance between the highest point of the sagital suture to the mid point of the chin, is termed as:
A. Suboccipito bregmatic
B. Submento bregmatic
C. Suboccipito frontal
D. Mento vertical

536. Alteration in the shape of fetal head while coming through the resistance birth passage during labour is termed as:
A. Moulding B. Caput succedaneum
C. Station D. Presentation

537. First of all fetal heart-sound can be assessed:
A. Between 2-3 weeks
B. Between 8-10 weeks
C. Between 10-12 weeks
D. Between 16-18 weeks

538. Parts of true pelvis are:
A. Inlet, brim and outlet
B. Inlet, brim and cavity
C. Inlet, outlet and cavity
D. Inlet, outlet and underlet

539. In following which statement is not true?
A. Female pelvis is formed by four bones two innominate, one sacrum and one coccyx
B. The false pelvis is formed by the iliac portions of the innominate bones
C. In the erect position the female, pelvis is tilted forward
D. None of them

540. Angle of inclination in human female is:
A. 55° B. 45°
D. 90° D. 75°

541. In which year LHV course was started?
A. 1918 B. 1975
C. 1946 D. 1953

542. Objective of nursing education includes:
A. To prepare nurses who will provide qualitative nursing care in the hospital and community
B. To prepare nurses who will be able to work as an important member of health team
C. To provide opportunities for full development of the personality of each nurse
D. All of the above

543. Four years B.Sc. nursing programme was started in:
A. 1953 B. 1946
C. 1962 D. 1973

544. In following which training is not conducted in school of nursing?
A. Multipurpose health worker female training
B. Female health supervisor training
C. GNM
D. B.Sc. nursing

545. Duration of ANM course is:
A. 12 months B. 18 months
C. 6 months D. 24 months

546. At present ANM is also known as:
A. Female nurse
B. Female health worker
C. LHV
D. PHN

547. Duration of ANM training was reduced from 24 months to 18 months in:
A. 1962 B. 1975
C. 1977 D. 1982

548. In Rajasthan how many rupees are paid to a ANM student during course as stipend?
A. ₹ 300/month B. ₹ 500/month
C. ₹ 1000/month D. ₹ 800/month

549. The basic entrance qualification for GNM course is:
A. Xth pass
B. XIIth pass in science
C. XIIth pass in any branch
D. Graduation

550. First of all basic B.Sc. nursing programme was started at:
A. RAK college of nursing Delhi
B. PGI Chandigarh
C. CML Vellore
D. Both A and C

551. In which year post basic B.Sc. (N) programme was started?
A. 1962 B. 1946
C. 1963 D. 1975

552. The basic entrance qualification for post basic B.Sc. (N) course is:
A. XIIth pass B. Graduation
C. GNM D. B.Sc.

553. In which year Indira Gandhi National Open University (IGNOU) started distance education in post basic nursing:
A. 1975 B. 1992
C. 1962 D. 1994

554. Duration of distance education in post basic nursing by IGNOU is
A. 2 years B. 3 years
C. 4 years D. None of these

555. During ANM course total instructional hours for vocational training are:
A. 1000 hours B. 1200 hours
C. 1350 hours D. 1600 hours

556. A candidate shall be eligible for admission to the GNM examination if:
A. She has attended at least 80% of theory classes and has completed at least 12 months of the course
B. She has attended at least 75% of theory classes, 75% of clinical experience and has completed at least 11 months of the course
C. Candidate has completed at least 12 months of course
D. Candidate has attended at least 70% of theory classes and 80% of clinical experience

557. In following which sentence is false?
A. If a student fails in one paper of GNM, then he will sit for a supplementary exam
B. If a student fails in two papers of GNM exam, he may be promoted to next year
C. Passing in practical exam is compulsory for promotion to the next year
D. If a student fails in two papers, he shall repeat the whole year

558. Eligibility for admission in post certificate B.Sc. nursing programme is except:
A. GNM pass
B. Have minimum 5 years experience after GNM
C. Medically fit
D. Registered nurse registered midwife

559. Eligibility criteria for admission in M.Sc. nursing programme includes except:
A. B.Sc. nursing pass
B. Medically fit
C. At least 2 years experience after B.Sc. nursing
D. RNRM

560. Eligibility criteria for Ph.D. nursing is:
A. M.Sc. nursing pass
B. At least M.Phil in nursing
C. M.Sc. nursing with more than 55% of aggregate marks
D. M.Sc. nursing with more than 60% of aggregate marks

561. For a regular student duration of Ph.D. in nursing is:
A. 3 years B. 4 years
C. 5 years D. None of these

562. All the learning activities which are planned and guided by the school, wheather they are carried out in groups or individually, inside and outside the school, known as:
A. Lesson plan B. Curriculum
C. Demonstration D. Supervision

563. In following which is not included in four-C's of curriculum planning?
A. Classification B. Continuous
C. Comprehensive D. Concrete

564. In following which sentence is false regarding curriculum planning:
A. Teaching programme should be prepare jointly by faculty
B. Provision should be made for its continuous revision
C. It should be comprehensive
D. Abstract consideration is sufficient for drawing up a programme

565. Nature of curriculum includes except:
A. It is oriented to life situations
B. It is dependent on the philosophy and objectives of the respective educational programme
C. It is prepared by traditional authority
D. It is rigid and does not accept any changes

566. A tool in the hands of artist (teacher) to mould his material (the pupil) in accordance with his ideas in his studio (school), is termed as:
A. Curriculum B. Research
C. Administration D. Demonstration

567. Aim of curriculum includes:
A. To equip the learners through bringing the desirable behavioural changes in them
B. To help the learners to cope life situations realistically
C. Help in development of health personnel at all levels
D. All of the above

568. The curriculum which is planned for a large group and prepared by groups outside the education institution is termed as:
A. Societal curriculum
B. Institutional curriculum
C. Instructional curriculum
D. Distributional curriculum

569. The curriculum planned day-by-day and week-by-week by a particular teacher for a particular group of students:
A. Societal curriculum
B. Institutional curriculum
C. Instructional curriculum
D. Distributional curriculum

570. Factor influences curriculum planning is:
A. Study projects

B. Environment within education takes place
C. Local governing body rulings
D. All of the above

571. In following which is not a principle of curriculum?
A. Principle of forward looking
B. Creativity
C. It should be institution centred
D. Principle of individual difference

572. Principles of curriculum include except:
A. Principle of leisure
B. Principle of linking with life
C. Principle of conservation
D. Principle of rigidity

573. According to Torres and Stanton stages of curriculum are except:
A. Directive B. Creative
C. Formative D. Evaluative

574. According to Torres and Stanton, which order to stages of curriculum is correct:
A. Directive functional formative evaluative
B. Directive formative functional evaluative
C. Formative directive constructive evaluative
D. Formative functional directive evaluative

575. The stage of curriculum which lays foundations for all other stages:
A. Directive B. Formative
C. Functional D. Evaluative

576. The stage of curriculum in which overall design of the curriculum take place?
A. Directive B. Formative
C. Functional D. Evaluative

577. The step of curriculum which includes formulation of philosophy and objectives of educational programme?
A. Assessment B. Planning
C. Development D. Implementation

578. The step of curriculum in which committee for curriculum preparation is constituted?
A. Assessment B. Planning
C. Development D. Implementation

579. The curriculum in which subject matter is planned with the co-operation of the learner?
A. Subject centred
B. Student centred
C. Institution centred
D. Experience curriculum

580. Training in post certificate B.Sc. (Nursing) after competition of GNM is an example of:
A. Correlated curriculum
B. Integrated curriculum
C. Fused curriculum
D. Both B and C

581. Overall plan of rotation of all students in a particular educational institution, showing the placement of the students in both theory and practical area, is termed as:
A. Clinical rotation plan
B. Master rotation plan
C. Curriculum
D. Lesson plan

582. Principles of master rotation plan include except:
A. Plan should be made according with the curriculum
B. During preparing it past experiences should be kept in mind
C. It should be prepared in advance for maximum 6 months
D. Rotate each student through each learning experience

583. Plan of rotation of students in different classes of specific nursing fields is termed as:
A. Clinical rotation plan
B. Master rotation plan
C. Lesson plan
D. Ward plan

584. Factor to be considered in planning clinical rotation plan:
A. Objective of the course
B. No. of students in each class
C. No. and size of departments
D. All of the above

585. The development of an educational plan for a specific course of study comprising of several short subject course and each course with many interrelated units, known as:
A. Curriculum B. Course planning
C. Unit planning D. Lesson planning

586. Characteristic of good unit planning includes:
A. Its aim should be clear and well defined
B. A good unit provides place for beginning and ending
C. It should be comprehensive
D. All of the above

587. The blue print of what a teacher is going to teach in the classroom is known as:
A. Unit plan B. Course plan
C. Lesson plan D. Master rotation plan

588. The pre-requisites for good lesson planning include except:
A. Teacher must have mastery over his subject
B. Participation of learners should be avoided
C. Student's educational background should be kept in mind
D. There should be variety and novelty in type of presentation

589. For effective presentation of a lesson, following are the essential things except:
A. Use appropriate teaching aids systematically
B. Introduction of the lesson should be interesting
C. During presentation move in a mechanical manner in the class
D. Pay individual attention to the pupils where needed

590. Principles in planning clinical rotation plan include except:
A. Planning must be correlated with the learning needs of the students
B. Duration of experience in each clinical block must be different
C. The clinical area chosen for learning must be in ideal set up
D. A copy of plan should be sent to the nursing superintendent

591. The devices by which teacher helps the students to clarify accurate concepts through utilization of more than one sensory channel:
A. Lesson plan B. Teaching aids
C. Unit plan D. Curriculum

592. In following which is not a projected teaching aid?
A. O.H.P.
B. Slide with slide projectors
C. Television
D. Bulletin board

593. Examples of non-projected teaching aids are except:
A. Models B. Specimen
C. Flash cards D. Laptop

594. Non-projected teaching aids are also known as:
A. Graphic aids B. Entertaining aids
C. Visual aids D. Audio aids

595. Principles of audio-visual aids include except:
A. Audio-visual material should be available whenever they are needed
B. Audio-visual material should be located in a place where users have easy accessibility
C. Audio-visual materials such as an educational film may be used as an entertainment
D. Audio-visual education programme should be flexible

596. The audio-visual aids require electricity for operation include except:
A. O.H.P. B. Television
C. Laptop D. Specimen

597. Most commonly used teaching method is:
A. Discussion B. Lecture
C. Demonstration D. Róle-play

598. In following which sentence is false?
A. Audio-visual aids are essential for all instructional programme
B. Audio-visual aids are not substitute of books and teachers
C. Audio-visual aids enable the students to learn fast
D. Audio-visual aids promotes understanding

599. In following which is a audio teaching aid?
A. Models B. Cartoons
C. Radio D. Flash cards

600. Characteristic of a good teaching aid includs:
A. Accurate in every aspect
B. Purposeful

C. According to mental level of the students
D. All of the above

601. In following which teaching aid is a substitute for real things?
A. Chart B. Model
C. Flesh card D. Television

602. Examples of three dimensional teaching aids include except:
A. Models B. Posters
C. Puppets D. Specimen

603. The method by which a student can get clinical experience include except:
A. Classroom study
B. Laboratory experiences
C. Supervised nursing care practice
D. Internship

604. One of most important purpose of clinical teaching includes:
A. To develop communication skills
B. To learn managerial skills
C. To help in integration of theoretical knowledge into practice
D. To learn various skills in giving health education

605. In following which is a both audio and visual teaching aid?
A. Specimen B. Computer
C. O.H.P. D. Bulletin-board

606. Bulletin board is an example of:
A. Audio teaching aid
B. Visual teaching aid
C. Audio-visual aid
D. Projected teaching aid

607. Qualities of a good clinical instructor include except:
A. He may be an expert in bedside nursing or not
B. He should have good communication skills
C. He should have adequate theoretical knowledge
D. He should have ability to implement the knowledge into practice

608. During nursing round total number of staff member in the group excluding group leader should not be more than:
A. 2 B. 4
C. 5 D. 8

609. Brief account of any incident that has been occurred, termed as:
A. Audit B. Anecdotal
C. Checklist D. Evaluation

610. The orderly and logical course of action taken to accomplish a particular educational goal through an environment in which students can have opportunities to achieve decided goals known as:
A. Clinical teaching method
B. Curriculum
C. Health education
D. Supervision

611. Regarding lecture method of teaching, which sentence is incorrect?
A. It is most commonly used method
B. In this both teacher and audience are equally active
C. The lecture can be made more effective by using audio-visual aids
D. For its effectivity teacher should have mastery in his subject

612. For effective teaching by lecture method, maximum number of students in the classroom should not be more than:
A. 10-12 B. 30-40
C. 70-80 D. 100-110

613. For effective teaching duration of one lecture should not be more than:
A. 8-10 min B. 15-20 min
C. 25-30 min D. 60-70 min

614. The teaching which is presented in a dramatical way known as:
A. Demonstration B. Role-play
C. Symposium D. Lecture

615. In following which teaching method will be most effecting for educating illiterate villagers
A. Lecture B. Symposium
C. Conference D. Role-play

616. The teaching method in which educator shows the various steps of doing procedure in systematic way in front of learners:

A. Lecture B. Demonstration
C. Panel discussion D. Symposium

617. No. of experts in panal discussion are:
A. 1-2 B. 2-4
C. 4-6 D. 8-10

618. No. of experts in symposium are:
A. 1-2 B. 2-3
C. 3-5 D. 7-8

619. Exchanging of ideas knowledge or meaning among individuals through the medium of a sign of one kind, termed as:
A. Supérvision B. Communication
C. Evaluation D. Administration

620. Essential elements of communication includes except:
A. Source
B. Message
C. Communication barriers
D. Sender

621. During lecture method of teaching, who is the sender of communication?
A. Teacher B. Audience
C. Blackboard D. Classroom

622. The informations, feelings or ideas that are transferred from sender to receiver is known as:
A. Channel B. Feed back
C. Message D. Barrier

623. In communication process which is also known as decoder:
A. Channel B. Message
C. Sender D. Receiver

624. In following which sentence is correct?
A. Two way communication is faster than one way
B. One way communication is more accurate than two way
C. Non-verbal communication is more close to truth than verbal
D. All of the above

625. The communication done through website is an example of:
A. Phychological communication
B. Non-verbal communication
C. Mechanical communication
D. None of the above

626. The type of communication in which the message is passed from one person to another like a chain is known as:
A. Interpersonal B. Serial
C. Two way D. Mechanical

627. Communication through facial expressions, gestures or body movements is an example of:
A. Verbal communication
B. Non-verbal communication
C. Mechanical communication
D. One way communication

628. Barriers in effective communication include except:
A. Language difference
B. Anger
C. Motivation
D. Different in culture

629. The process of determining to what extent the educational objectives are being realised?
A. Evaluation B. Supervision
C. Discussion D. Guidance

630. Characteristic of a good evaluation includes:
A. It should be comprehensive
B. Valid
C. It should be relevance
D. All of the above

631. In following which is not a evaluation tool?
A. Anecdotal records B. Checklist
C. Interview D. Demonstration

632. Rating scale is a:
A. Lecture method
B. Supervision method
C. Evaluation tool
D. Element of communication

633. A brief description of an observed behaviour that appears significantly for evaluation purposes:
A. Checklist B. Interview
C. Demonstration D. Anecdotal records

634. In following which is a disadvantage of anecdotal record?
A. Supplements and validates of other structured instruments

B. Use of formative feedback
C. Economical
D. Subjectivity

635. In a GNM school as per INC norms student tutor ratio should be:
A. 1 : 5 B. 1 : 10
C. 1 : 20 D. 1 : 15

636. For starting GNM school minimum intake of students per year should be:
A. 20 B. 30
C. 50 D. 10

637. What is the full form of ANM?
A. Academic Nursing Midwife
B. Amazing Nursing Midwife
C. Auxiliary Nurse Midwife
D. Auxiliary Nobel Midwife

638. Age limit for admission in GNM school is
A. 15-45 years B. 17-35 years
C. 17-33 years D. 17-45 years

639. Minimum qualification required for admission in GNM school is:
A. XIIth pass with 60%
B. XIIth pass with minimum 50%
C. XIIth pass with 70%
D. XIIth pass with minimum 40%

640. In following which audio-visual aid can be used to educate big no. of learners?
A. Blackboard B. Flashcard
C. Computer D. Specimen

641. Features of picnic type of personality are:
A. Fat, round, happy, very social
B. Thin body built, tall, social lacking emotions
C. Muscular built, strong body, very active, aggressive and success oriented
D. All of the above

642. Features of asthenic type of personality are:
A. Fat, round, happy, very social
B. Thin body built, tall, social lacking emotions
C. Muscular built, strong body, very active, aggressive and success oriented
D. All of the above

643. Features of atheletic personality are:
A. Fat, round, happy, very social
B. Thin body built, tall, social lacking emotions
C. Muscular built, strong body, very active, aggressive and success oriented
D. All of the above

644. Type of personality in which an individual has alternating periods of elation and depression is:
A. Cyclothymic B. Hypomanic
C. Melancholic D. Paranoid

645. Type of personality in which individual is outgoing, cheerful and full of energy is:
A. Cyclothymic B. Hypomanic
C. Melancholic D. Paranoid

646. Type of personality in which individual feel helplessness, hopelessness and always blaming themselves:
A. Cyclothymic B. Hypomanic
C. Melancholic D. Paranoid

647. Personality disorder in which an individual suspects that other people will harm him, is:
A. Cyclothymic B. Hypomanic
C. Melancholic D. Paranoid

648. In following which is not a disturbance of consiousness:
A. Stupor B. Hallucination
C. Confusion D. Coma

649. Delirium is a disorder of:
A. Consciousness B. Perception
D. Memory D. Thought

650. Illusion is a disorder of:
A. Consciousness B. Perception
D. Memory D. Thought

651. Hallucination is a disorder of:
A. Consciousness B. Perception
C. Memory D. Thought

652. Circumstantiality is the disorder of:
A. Consciousness B. Perception
C. Memory D. Thought

653. Perseveration is the disorder of:
A. Consciousness B. Perception
C. Memory D. Thought

654. Amnesia is a disorder of:
A. Consciousness B. Perception
C. Memory D. Thought

655. Hallucination is a disorder of:
A. Digestive disorder
B. Mental disorder
C. Neurological disorder
D. Obstertric disorder

656. Disorder of consiousness in which patient remains motionless and mute, is:
A. Confusion
B. Clouding of consiousness
C. Hallucination
D. Stupor

657. The term which is also used to describe cataplexy is:
A. Mannerism B. Cerea flexibility
C. Waxy flexibility D. Both B and C

658. Disorder of motor activity in which the person constantly maintains a position without any movement is:
A. Mannerism B. Cataplexy
C. Verbigeration D. Negativism

659. A disorder of motor activity in which an individual repeatedly touches the neck or lifts the shoulder while taking, is known as:
A. Mannerism B. Cataplexy
C. Verbigeration D. Negativism

660. A disorder of motor activity in which there is frequently repetition of words or sentences, is known as:
A. Mannerism B. Cataplexy
C. Verbigeration D. Negativism

661. A mental disorder in which an individual is aware of the stimuli but he tries to oppose these stimuli actively or passively, is known as:
A. Mannerism B. Cataplexy
C. Verbigeration D. Negativism

662. A mental disorder characterized by stereotype speech is:
A. Mannerism B. Cataplexy
C. Verbigeration D. Negativism

663. A mental disorder characterized by stereotype movement is:
A. Mannerism B. Cataplexy
C. Verbigeration D. Negativism

664. In following which is not a disorder of motor activity:
A. Mannerism B. Compulsion
C. Automatism D. Delusion

665. In following which is a thought disorder?
A. Mannerism B. Compulsion
C. Automatism D. Delusion

666. A mental disorder characterized by repeatedly performing an act which is unreasonable, is called as:
A. Mannerism B. Compulsion
C. Automatism D. Delusion

667. Perception of a stimulus in the absence of an actual stimulus is known as:
A. Illusion B. Hallucination
C. Verbigeration D. Mannerism

668. Misinterpretation of sense impression is termed as:
A. Illusion B. Hallucination
C. Verbigeration D. Mannerism

669. Hallucination is defined as:
A. Perception of stimulus in the presence of an actual stimulus
B. Perception of a stimulus in the absence of an actual stimulus
C. Mistaken or misinterpretation of sense impression
D. Disorientation of time, place and person

670. A mental disorder in which a person hears the noises such as some body is knocking at the door in the absence of actual stimulus. The person is suffering from:
A. Auditory illusion
B. Auditory hallucination
C. Tactile illusion
D. Tactile hallucination

671. A mental disorder in which a person feels that lice are crawling on his arm. But in actually there are no lice on his skin, the person is suffering from
A. Auditory illusion
B. Auditory hallucination

C. Tactile illusion
D. Tactile hallucination

672. In following which is not a thought disorder?
A. Perseveration B. Verbigeration
C. Circumstantiality D. Tangentiality

673. A mental disorder characterized by persistent repetition of an idea is known as:
A. Perseveration B. Verbigeration
C. Circumstantiality D. Tangentiality

674. A mental disorder in which patient finally reaches his objective but only after many unneccessary or trival details, is termed as:
A. Perseveration B. Verbigeration
C. Circumstantiality D. Tangentiality

675. A mental disorder in which patient begins to respond to a question, follows a series of related topics but never reaches the goal, is known as:
A. Perseveration B. Verbigeration
C. Circumstantiality D. Tangentiality

676. Delusion is defined as:
A. A false fixed belief, unrelated with person's intelligence
B. A disorder in which patient is over conscious about his bodily health
C. Irrational fear of a specific type of stimulus or situation
D. Misinterpretation of stimulus

677. Mental disorder hypochondriasis is defined as:
A. A false fixed belief, unrelated with person's intelligence
B. A disorder in which patient is over conscious about his bodily health
C. Irrational fear of a specific type of stimulus or situation
D. Misinterpretation of stimulus

678. Mental disorder phobia is defined as:
A. A false fixed belief, unrelated with person's intelligence
B. A disorder in which patient is over conscious about his bodily health
C. Irrational fear of a specific type of stimulus or situation
D. Misinterpretation of stimulus

679. The type of delusion most commonly seen is manic patients is:
A. Delusion of persecution
B. Delusion of grandeur
C. Nihilistic delusions
D. Delusion of guilt

680. A disorder of thought content in which patient falsely believes that he is a prime minister or he believes that he is very rich, this type of disorder is known as:
A. Delusion of persecution
B. Delusion of grandeur
C. Nihilistic delusions
D. Delusion of guilt

681. Which type of delusional disorder commonly found in parahoid shizophrenia is:
A. Delusion of persecution
B. Delusionof grandeur
C. Nihilistic delusions
D. Delusion of guilt

682. A disorder of thought content in which patient has a false belief that members of his family are trying to kill him, is:
A. Delusion of persecution
B. Delusion of grandeur
C. Nihilistic delusions
D. Delusion of guilt

683. A mental disorder in which patient becomes self critical and believes that is he a criminal, is known as:
A. Delusion of persecution
B. Delusion of grandeur
C. Nihilistic delusions
D. Delusion of guilt

684. "Delusion of negation" is also known as:
A. Delusion of persecution
B. Delusion of grandeur
C. Nihilistic delusions
D. Delusion of guilt

685. A disorder of thought control in which the patient does not accept the existence of the world around him, is known as:
A. Delusion of persecution
B. Delusion of grandeur
C. Nihilistic delusions
D. Delusion of guilt

686. Librium is a:
A. Antimanic drug
B. Antidepressant drug
C. Antiparkinson drug
D. Tranquilizer drug

687. A false belief in which patient thinks that he is being talked about by other people, is known as:
A. Delusion of reference
B. Delusion of guilt
C. Delusion of grandeur
D. Delusion of self accusation

688. Irrational pathological fear of high places, is termed as:
A. Agrophobia B. Acrophobia
C. Algophobia D. Xenophobia

689. Irrational pathological fear of open places is termed as:
A. Agrophobia B. Acrophobia
C. Algophobia D. Xenophobia

690. Irrational pathological fear of pain, is known as:
A. Agrophobia B. Acrophobia
C. Algophobia D. Xenophobia

691. Irrational pathological fear of strangers is termed as:
A. Agrophobia B. Acrophobia
C. Algophobia D. Xenophobia

692. Hydrophobia is defined as:
A. Irrational fear of closed places
B. Irrational pathological fear of water
C. Irrational pathological fear of animals
D. Irrational pathological fear of open spaces

693. Affect disorder in which patient has a constant sense of pleasant feeling and is optimistic termed as:
A. Depression B. Exaltation
C. Grief D. Euphoria

694. Zoophobia is defined as:
A. Irrational fear of closed places
B. Irrational pathological fear of water
C. Irrational pathological fear of animals
D. Irrational pathological fear of open spaces

695. Claustrophobia is defined as:
A. Irrational fear of closed places
B. Irrational pathological fear of water
C. Irrational pathological fear of animals
D. Irrational pathological fear of open spaces

696. A pleasurable affect disorder in which person has symptoms of grandiosity, is:
A. Elation B. Exaltation
C. Grief D. Euphoria

697. In following which is not a pleasurable affect disorder:
A. Elation B. Exaltation
C. Grief D. Euphoria

698. In following which is an unpleasurable affect disorder?
A. Exaltation B. Ecstasy
C. Depression D. All of these

699. A psychiatric disorder in which patient remains quiet, restrained, unhappy and pessimistic is:
A. Elation B. Hallucination
C. Depression D. Delusion

700. An unpleasurable reaction to an imagined danger, is termed as:
A. Fear B. Anxiety
C. Apathy D. Ambivalence

701. An unpleasurable reaction to a real or threatened situation is termed as:
A. Fear B. Anxiety
C. Apathy D. Ambivalence

702. A psychiatric disorder in which patient shows inadequate responses to those experiences that give rise to pleasure or pain is termed as:
A. Fear B. Anxiety
C. Apathy D. Ambivalence

703. A psychiatric disorder in which the patient has two opposite feelings towards the same thing at a same time is known as:
A. Echolalia B. Ambivalence
C. Perseveration D. Illusion

704. In following which is not an affect disorder?
A. Elation B. Depression
C. Hallucination D. Grief

705. Excessive retention of memories is termed as:
A. Amnesia B. Hypermnesia
C. Paramnesia D. Anaemia

706. In following which is not a memory disorder?
A. Amnesia B. Hypermnesia
C. Paramnesia D. Anaemia

707. Partially or completely absence of memory is known as:
A. Amnesia B. Hypermnesia
C. Paramnesia D. Anaemia

708. False recollection of memory in which the patient talks about those events which never took place, is termed as:
A. Amnesia B. Hypermnesia
C. Paramnesia D. Anaemia

709. Type of amnesia in which patient is unable to recall past events, is known as:
A. Retrograde amnesia
B. Anterograde amnesia
C. Circumscribed amnesia
D. Paramnesia

710. Type of amnesia in which patient is unable to recall the recent events, is known as:
A. Retrograde amnesia
B. Anterograde amnesia
C. Circumscribed amnesia
D. Paramnesia

711. Following are the examples of psychotrophic drugs except:
A. Risperidone B. Lithium
C. Deriphylline D. Imipramine

712. The psychiatric disorder in which a new situation is incorrectly treated as a repetition of a previous memory, as known as:
A. Insight B. Delusion
C. Dejavu D. Amnesia

713. In following which is a disorder of attention?
A. Amnesia B. Paramnesia
C. Distractibility D. Delusion

714. A psychiatric patient is able to understand his symptoms, now we can say that:
A. Insight is completely present in the patient
B. Insight is completely absent in the patient
C. Insight is partially present in the patient
D. The patient has no psychiatric problem

715. In following which is not a thought disorder?
A. Hypochondria B. Flight of ideas
C. Tangantiality D. Amnesia

716. In following which is the commonest organic disorder?
A. Dementia
B. Delerium
C. Organic Amnestic Syndrome
D. Organic Hallucination

717. Clinical features of delerium includes:
A. Clouding of Consciousness
B. Disorientation
C. Visual Hallucination
D. All of these

718. In following which statement is true?
A. Onset of dementia is acute while onset of delerium is insidious
B. During dementia sleep wake cycle is grossly disturbed while during delerium it is normal
C. Attention and concentration during delerium grossly disturbed while during dementia normal
D. All of these

719. Organic cause of mental disorder includes:
A. Hypo or hyper functions of endocrinal glands
B. Head injury
C. Sub arachnoid haemorhage and haematoma
D. All of these

720. In following which is the major indication of ECT?
A. Severe depression with suicidal risk
B. Severe mania
C. Phobia
D. Hysteria

721. The condition characterized by symptoms which develop on total or partial withdrawal of drug usually after prolonged use, is known as:
A. Acute intoxication
B. Withdrawal state
C. Dependence syndrome
D. Schizophrenia

722. The condition in which the use of a substance takes on a much higher priority than other behaviours, is termed as:
A. Acute intoxication
B. Withdrawal state
C. Dependence syndrome
D. Schizophrenia

723. Etiological factor of substance use disorder is:
A. Family history of substance use disorder
B. Poor impulse control
C. Peer pressure
D. All of these

724. Gastro intestinal complication which may occur due to alcohol dependence is?
A. Cirrhosis of liver B. Gastritis
C. Pancreatitis D. All of these

725. The complication that may occur due to chronic use of alcohol is:
A. Rum fits
B. Peripheral neuropathy
C. Wernicke korsakoff psychosis
D. All of these

726. Term dipsomania means:
A. Manic conditions
B. Compulsive drinking
C. Increased PMA, talkative
D. A condition characterised by alternating manic and depressive attacks

727. During Wernicke's encephalopathy there is defeciency of:
A. Thiamine B. Riboflavin
C. Vitamin-D D. Vitamin-E

728. In following which is not a withdrawal symptom of alcohol?
A. Delerium tremens
B. Rum fits
C. Cirrhosis of liver
C. Alcoholic hallucination

729. Most severe withdrawal syndrome of alcohol is:
A. Delerium tremens
B. Rum fits
C. Cirrhosis of liver
D. Alcoholic hallucinosis

730. The alcohol sensitizing drug that is used for the treatment of alcoholism is:
A. Phenobarbitone B. Disalfiram
C. Carbamezapine D. Haloperidol

731. The disease characterised by 4 A's of Bleuler is:
A. MDP B. OCD
C. Schizophrenia D. Delirium

732. In following which is not included in the 4 A's of schizophrenia?
A. Ambivalence
B. Autism
C. Anxiety
D. Association disorder

733. 4 A's of schizophrenia are:
A. Anxiety, ambivalence, autism, affect disturbances
B. Amnesia, anxiety, autism, and affect disturbance
C. Amnesia, anxiety, autism and ambivalence
D. Autism, ambivalence, affect disturbance, and associate disturbance

734. Clinical features of schizophrenia include:
A. Hallucination
B. Autistic thinking
C. Delusion of persecution
D. All of these

735. A patient uses newly formed words whose explaination cannot be understood, the patient is suffering from:
A. Delusion B. Neologism
C. Hallucination D. Amnesia

736. No speech production is termed as:
A. Poverty of ideation
B. Mutism
C. Poverty of speech
D. Echolalia

737. A patient has adequate speech amount but content provides little information, the patient is suffering from:
A. Povety of ideation
B. Mutism
C. Poverty of speech
D. Echolalia

738. A patient has disinhibited behaviour, poor self care and hygiene, markedly impaired social and occupational functioning and extreme social withdrawal, the patient is suffering from
A. Catatomic schizophrenia
B. Hebephrenic schizophrenia
C. Residual schizophrenia
D. Paranoid schizophrenia

739. Reduced speech productions is termed as:
A. Poverty of ideation
B. Mustism
C. Poverty of speech
D. Echolalia

740. The schizophrenia that is characterised by marked disturbance of motor behaviour is:
A. Catatonic schizophrenia
B. Hebephrenic schizophrenia
C. Residual schizophrenia
D. Paranoid schizophrenia

741. Immunity means:
A. Disease resistance capacity
B. Disease producing capacity
C. Treatment of disease
D. None of the above

742. Humoral immunity comes from:
A. Bone marrow derived lymphocytes
B. Thymus derived lymphocytes
C. RBC
D. Platelets

743. Cellular immunity comes from:
A. Bone marrow derived lymphocytes
B. Thymus derived lymphocytes
C. RBC
D. Platelets

744. The humoral immunity is based on:
A. Production of antigen
B. Production of antibodies
C. Formation of vaccines
D. All of the above

745. In following which is not a bacterial borne communicable disease?
A. Diphtheria B. Cholera
C. Measles D. Typhoid fever

746. In following which is a viral disease?
A. Diphtheria B. Cholera
C. Typhoid D. Yellow fever

747. In following which is not a virus borne communicable disease?
A. Polio B. Measles
C. Tetanus D. AIDS

748. Components of ORS are except:
A. Sodium chloride
B. Sodium citrate
C. Sodium carbonate
D. Potassium chloride

749. In India, MPW scheme was started on the recommendation of:
A. Bhore's Committee
B. Kartar Singh Committee
C. Srivastav Committee
D. Mudaliar Committee

750. In following which is not a communicable disease?
A. TB B. CVA
C. Pertusis D. Measles

751. AIDS is:
A. Bacterial disease
B. Viral disease
C. Fungal disease
D. Protozoal disease

752. In following which is a viral disease?
A. Diphtheria B. Plague
C. Chicken pox D. Typhoid fever

753. Community health nurse provides following type of health services:
A. Preventive
B. Promotive
C. Curative and rehabilitative
D. All of the above

754. Which activity considered as health promotional activity?
A. Effective public participation
B. Focusing on people at risk of specific disease
C. IEC (Information, education and communication) activity
D. All of the above

755. According to holistic concept health is considered as:
A. absence of disease
B. proper physical health
C. sound body, sound mind, sound family and sound environment
D. good interpersonal relationships

756. A person has been immunized with TT 8 years ago. Now he is injured in an accident then:

A. There is no need to administer TT
B. Give two doses of TT at the interval of one month
C. Administer single dose of TT
D. Double dose of TT should be given immediately

757. Infectious stage of plasmodium is:
A. Trophozoite B. Sporozoite
C. Merozoite D. Cryptozoite

758. Hygiene aspect of health maintenance include:
A. Personal hygiene
B. Domestic hygiene
C. Enviromnental hygiene
D. All of the above

759. In following which is a communicable disease?
A. MI B. CVA
C. Leprosy D. Peptic ulcer

760. In which of the following situation it is preferable to insert IUCD?
A. After MTP
B. Emergency postcoital
C. Six weeks after delivery
D. All of the above

761. Cholera is a:
A. Bacterial disease B. Viral disease
C. Protozoal disease D. Fungal disease

762. Causative organism of measles is:
A. Varicella zoster virus
B. Variola virus
C. Myxovirus
D. HIV

763. Infant mortality is expressed in terms of:
A. Per 1,000 B. Per 10,000
C. Per 1,00,000 D. Per 10,00,000

764. Which of the following steps are included in community health nursing process?
A. Collection of facts and data
B. Assessment and planning
C. Intervention and evaluation
D. All of the above

765. Causative organism of chicken pox is:
A. Varicella zoster virus
B. Paramyxo virus
C. Herpes simplex virus
D. Variola virus

766. Leishmaniasis is group of:
A. Bacterial disease B. Viral disease
C. Protozoal disease D. Fungal disease

767. Causative organism of small pox is:
A. Varicella zoster virus
B. Variola virus
C. Myxo virus
D. Cytomegalo virus

768. Clinical features of chicken pox includes:
A. Skin rashes B. Fever
C. Pain in back D. All of the above

769. Rashes of chicken pox first appears on:
A. Trunk B. Face
C. Arm D. Legs

770. Yellow fever is a:
A. Bacterial disease B. viral disease
C. Fungal disease D. Protozoal diease

771. Scrub typhus is transmitted by:
A. Mite B. Rat
C. Tick D. Louce

772. Characteristics of rashes of chicken pox are:
A. Rash is symmetrical
B. Evolution is rapid
C. Rash are pleomorphism
D. All of the above

773. Rash of chicken pox are pleomorphism. Here word pleomorphism means:
A. Rashes occur on all body at one time
B. Rashes disappear at one time from all body
C. All stages of rash may be seen simultaneously at one time at one area
D. All of the above

774. Which of the following day falls on 31st may?
A. World Population Day
B. Anti-tobacco Day
C. World Health Day
D. World Environmental Day

775. Which of the following day falls on 11th July?
A. World Population Day
B. U.N.O. Day
C. World Food Day
D. National Science Day

776. Chlorine tablets required to disinfect the water:
A. 1 tablet (0.5 gm) to 15 litres of water

B. 1 tablet (0.5 gm) to 20 litres of water
C. 1 tablet (0.5 gm) to 10 litres of water
D. 1 tablet (0.5 gm) to 8 litres of water

777. Health promotion and specific protection, are method of:
A. Premordial prevention
B. Primary prevention
C. Secondary prevention
D. Tertiary prevention

778. World was declared small pox free by WHO on:
A. April, 1977 B. May 8, 1980
C. July, 1987 D. May, 1982

779. India was declared small pox free in:
A. April 1977 B. May 8, 1980
C. July 1987 D. May 1982

780. In following which disease has been completely eradicated from world?
A. Polio B. Diphtheria
C. Small pox D. HIV

781. Primary prevention of TB includes:
A. DOTs B. BCG vaccine
C. Blood transfusion D. MDT

782. In which stage of bacterial growth, bacteria grow rapidly?
A. Predominant B. Log-phase
C. Mitosis D. Ionic

783. Active immunisation following exposure is given most commonly for:
A. Polio B. Cholera
C. Rabies D. Plague

784. Rash of measles first occur on:
A. Trunk B. Face
C. Hands D. Legs

785. Disease rubella is also known as:
A. Rubeolla B. German measles
C. Pertusis D. Hepatitis

786. Measles is a disease of mainly:
A. Childhood B. Adult age
C. Old age D. All of the above

787. During measles rashes occur in:
A. Prodromal stage
B. Eruptive stage
C. Post measles stage
D. All of the above

788. Primary prevention includes all except:
A. Health education
B. Health promotion
C. Specific protection
D. Early diagnosis and treatment

789. Rash of rubella first occur on:
A. Face B. Abdomen
C. Trunk D. Legs

790. Other name of whooping cough is:
A. Rubella B. German measles
C. Pertusis D. Pneumonia

791. The disease characterized by enlargement and tenderness of parotid gland is:
A. Measles B. Mumps
C. Rubella D. Chicken pox

792. Pertusis is a:
A. Bacterial disease B. Viral disease
C. Protozoal disease D. Fungal disease

793. The disease characterized by lymphadenopathy is:
A. Measles B. Mumps
C. Rubella D. Chicken pox

794. Blood sample from a patient with malaria should be collected:
A. At the peak of fever
B. After taking meal
C. When fever is just started
D. When temperature is normal

795. Sleeping sickness is transmitted by:
A. Tsetse fly
B. Phlebotomine sandfly
C. Female anopheles mosquito
D. Coxiella burnettii

796. Diphtheria is a:
A. Bacterial disease B. Viral disease
C. Protozoal disease D. Fungal disease

797. Diphtheria is caused by:
A. Corynebacterium diphtheriae
B. Clostridium tetani
C. Bordetella pertusis
D. Mycobacterium tuberculosis

798. Q fever is caused by:
A. Coxiella burnettii
B. Leishmania donovani
C. Taenia saginata
D. Taenia solium

799. Diphtheriae mainly affects:
A. Respiratory system
B. Cardiovascular system
C. Neurological system
D. Reproductive system

800. Pertusis is mainly disease of:
A. Childhood B. Adulthood
C. Old age D. All of the above

801. Schick test is done to identify:
A. Tuberculosis B. Diphtheria
C. Polio D. Mumps

802. Schick test is an:
A. Intradermal test B. Intramuscular test
C. IV test D. Subcutaneous test

803. In Schick test reaction is considered as positive when:
A. No reaction of any kind on either arm after administeration of shick test toxin
B. When test arm shows red flush of 10-50 mm diameter within 24-36 hours after administeration of shick test toxin
C. Both of these
D. None of these

804. The recommended level of fluoride in drinking water is-
A. 0.5 - 0.8 mg/L B. 0.8 - 1.2 mg/L
C. 0.1 - 0.5 mg/L D. 1.2 - 2.5 mg/L

805. Tetanus is a:
A. Bacterial disease B. Viral disese
C. Fungal disease D. Protozoal disease

806. Causative organism of tetanus is:
A. Vibrio cholera B. Salmonella typhi
C. Mosquito D. Clostridium tetani

807. In following which match is incorrect
A. DPT vaccine → IM route
B. BCG vaccine → ID route
C. Measles vaccine → IM route
D. Hepatitis-B vaccine → IM route

808. Commonest cause of infant mortality rate (IMR) in India is:
A. Prematurity
B. Diarrhoea
C. Congenital malformation
D. Respiratory infection

809. Tuberculosis is caused by
A. Mycobacterium leprae
B. Mycobacterium tuberculosis
C. Clostridium tetani
D. Corynebacterium diphtheriae

810. Tuberculosis is the diseae of:
A. Childhood B. Infancy
C. Old age D. It affects all ages

811. Most impotant type of tuberculosis is:
A. Pulmonary TB B. Bone TB
C. Intestine TB D. Skin TB

812. Mantoux test is an:
A. Intradermal test B. Intramuscular
C. IV test D. Subcutaneous test

813. Tuberculin test was discussed by:
A. Jackson B. Van Pirquet
C. Aristotle D. Khurana

814. During mantoux test amount of PPD inserted in forearm is:
A. 2 ml B. 1 ml
C. 0.1 ml D. 0.5 ml

815. During mantoux test PPD is inserted in:
A. Arm B. Forearm
C. Thigh D. Buttocks

816. Mantoux test is considered as positive when:
A. Diameter of induration and erythema is exceeding 10 mm
B. Diameter of induration and erythema is less than 5 mm
C. Diameter of induration and erythema is between 6-9 mm
D. All of the above

817. Mantoux test is considered negative when:
A. Diameter of induration and erythema is exceeding 10 mm
B. Diameter of induration and erythema is less than 5 mm

C. Diameter of induration and erythema is between 6-9 mm
D. All of the above

818. Mantoux test is considered doubtful when:
A. Diameter of induration and erythema is exceeding 10 mm
B. Diameter of induration and erythema is less than 5 mm
C. Diameter of induration and erythema is between 6-9 mm
D. All of the above

819. Tuberculosis is mainly transmitted by:
A. Droplet infection
B. Infected blood
C. Polluted water
D. Contaminated food

820. Investigation done for TB are:
A. Sputum examination
B. Chest X-ray
C. Tuberculin test
D. All of the above

821. In DOTs diagnosis of TB is made on the basis of report of:
A. MRI and sonography
B. Chest X-ray and sputum examination
C. Skull X-ray and sputum examination
D. Blood and urine examination

822. MDT is given to treat:
A. Polio B. TB
C. Leprosy D. AIDS

823. Leprosy is a:
A. Bacterial disease B. Viral disease
C. Fungal disease D. Protozoal disease

824. DOTs is given to treat:
A. Polio B. TB
C. Leprosy D. AIDS

825. Bactericidal drug given to treat TB is:
A. Ethambutol B. Thioacetazone
C. Paracetamol D. Rifampicin

826. Bactericidal drug given to treat TB is:
A. Rifampicin B. INH
C. Streptomycin D. All of the above

827. In DOTs:
A. All the drugs during intensive phase of treatment are given under direct supervision of health worker
B. Diagnosis of TB is made on the basis of chest X-ray and sputum exam report
C. Medicines are given to treat TB
D. All of the above

828. In DOTs, patient are grouped in how many categories?
A. 1 B. 2
C. 3 D. 4

829. The patients that come in category Ist of DOTs are:
A. New sputum smear positive cases
B. Relapse cases
C. Sputum smear negative but not seriously ill patients
D. All of the above

830. According to Central Birth and Death Registration Act, 1969, the event of death should be registered in:
A. 3 days B. 7 days
C. 14 days D. 21 days

831. The patients that come in category IIIrd of DOTs are:
A. New sputum smear positive cases
B. Relapse cases
C. Sputum smear negative but not seriously ill patients
D. All of the above

832. The patients that come in category I of DOTs exclude:
A. New sputum smear positive
B. Seriously ill sputum smear negative
C. Seriously ill extra pulmonary
D. Sputum smear positive failure cases

833. Disability limitation and rehabilitation are:
A. Premordial prevention
B. Primary prevention
C. Secondary prevention
D. Tertiary prevention

834. The patients that come in category II of DOTs are exclude:

A. Relapse cases
B. Failure of treatment cases
C. Extra pulmonary seriously ill
D. Default treatment

835. The patients that come in category I of DOTs are:
A. Relapse cases
B. Failure of treatment cases
C. Extra pulmonary seriously ill
D. Default of treatment

836. Treatment given during intensive phase of category I of DOTs is:
A. 2 $(HRZE)_3$
B. 2 $(HRZES)_3$ + 1$(HRZE)_3$
C. 2 $(HRZ)_3$
D. 4 $(HR)_3$

837. Screening of a woman above 35 years for carcinoma cervix by using the pap's smear, is a method of
A. Primary prevention
B. Secondary prevention
C. Specific protection
D. Tertiary prevention

838. Treatment given during intensive phase of category III of DOTs is:
A. 2 $(HRZE)_3$
B. 2 $(HRZES)_3$ + 1$(HRZE)_3$
C. 2 $(HRZ)_3$
D. 4 $(HR)_3$

839. WHO Oral Rehydration Solution includes following except:
A. NaCl B. KCl
C. Sodium citrate D. Sodium carbonate

840. The category of TB patient in which streptomycin is given:
A. Category I B. Category II
C. Category III D. All category

841. In following which statement is false?
A. At birth the uterine body and the cervix ratio is about 1 : 2
B. When menarche occurs the ratio between uterine body and the cervix becomes 1 : 1
C. After menarche the ratio becomes 2 : 1
D. After menopause the ratio remains 3 : 1

842. After menopause, a woman becomes more prone to development of osteoporosis because:
A. Fall in oestrogen level
B. Increase in oestrogen level
C. Fall in LH level
D. Fall in FSH level

843. In a postmenopausal female, which is the principle hormone used in hormonal replacement therapy?
A. Progesterone B. Oestrogen
C. FSH D. LH

844. What do you mean by delayed menopause?
A. When menopause fails to occur beyond 45 years of age
B. When menopause fails to occur beyond 40 years of age
C. When menopause fails to occur beyond 50 years of age
D. When menopause fails to occur beyond 55 years of age

845. Causative organism of syphilis is:
A. Chlamydia trachomatis
B. Treponema pallidum
C. Pox virus
D. Haemophilus ducreyi

846. Causative organism of chancroid is:
A. Chlamydia trachomatis
B. Treponema pallidum
C. Pox virus
D. Haemophilus ducreyi

847. Infection of the fallopian tube is called is:
A. Appendicitis B. Bartholinitis
C. Salpingitis D. Endometritis

848. Painful menstruation is termed as:
A. Menorrhage B. Dysmenorrhea
C. Amenorrhea D. Menopause

849. In following which is not a cause of primary dysmenorrhea?
A. Narrowing of the cervical canal
B. Uterine hypoplasia
C. Increased vasopressin release
D. Decreased production of prostaglandins

850. Primary dysmenorrhea is mainly found in:
A. Adolescent girl

B. Pregnant women
C. Females above 35 years
D. Females above 45 years

851. Physical changes occur during puberty include
A. Breast development
B. Growth of pubic and axillary hair
C. Menstruation
D. All of the above

852. The first menstruation in a female is called as:
A. Menarche B. Menopause
C. Dysmenorrhoae D. Amenorrhoea

853. In a female, at which age menarche occurs?
A. 10 years B. 13 years
C. 16 years D. 20 years

854. Which hormone plays an important role in marked proliferation of fat around the breast?
A. Oestrogen B. Progesterone
C. FSH D. Testosterone

855. Starting of menstrual cycle before the age of ten years is termed as:
A. Postcocious B. Precocious
C. Amenorrhoea D. Dysmenorrhoea

856. Permanent cessation of menstruation is termed as:
A. Menarche B. Dysmenorrhoea
C. Amenorrhoea D. Menopause

857. Endocrinological changes occur during menopause include except
A. Fall in serum oestradiol level
B. Fall in FSH level
C. Increase in LH level
D. Increase level of androgens

858. After menopause increased facial hair growth and change in voice occurs due to
A. Fall in FSH level
B. Increase in LH level
C. Increase androgen level
D. Decrease androgen level

859. After puberty obese patients have less chances of occurrence of osteoporosis, because of:
A. Fall in FSH level
B. Fall in LH level
C. Conversion of more androgens into oestrogen
D. Conversion of more oestrogen into androgen

860. In a female, changes occur after menopause include
A. Uterus becomes smaller
B. The vagina become narrower
C. Ovaries shrink in size
D. All of the above

861. State of abnormal uterine bleeding without any clinically detectable organic pelvic pathology, is known as:
A. Menorrhagia
B. Polymenorrhoea
C. Dysfunctional uterine bleeding
D. Dysmenorrhoea

862. In following which hormonal therapy is used for the management of DUB?
A. Contraceptive pills
B. Norethisterone acetate
C. 17 alpha ethinyl testosterone
D. All of the above

863. Following are the indications of endometrial resection in a female with DUB except:
A. Female who is over 35
B. Female who has completed her family
C. Female who does not has any significant endometrial pathology such as cancer
D. Female who is newly married

864. Treatment of premenstrual syndrome includes:
A. Minor tranquiliser
B. Use of antidepressants
C. Pyridoxine
D. All of the above

865. Causative organism responsible for moniliasis, is:
A. Candida albicans
B. Tinea cruris
C. Staphylococcus aureus
D. Gonococci

866. In following which is the most common cause of vaginitis in the childbearing period?
A. Trichomoniasis B. Moniliasis
C. Atropic vagina D. Streptococci

867. Vaginal trichomoniasis is more harmful when?
A. pH of vagina ranges between 1-2
B. pH of vagina ranges between 3-4
C. pH of vagina ranges between 6-7
D. No effect of changes in pH

868. Inflammation of vagina in postmenopausal women is called as
A. Toxic shock syndrome
B. Senile vaginitis
C. Clamydial vaginitis
D. Chronic vaginitis

869. Postmenopausal yellowish or blood stained vaginal discharge, soreness in the vulva and pruritus vulvae are the manifestations of
A. Menopause
B. Toxic shock syndrome
C. Atypical menorrhagia
D. Sanile vaginitis

870. What is the common cause of senile vaginitis?
A. Increase FSH level
B. Oestrogen deficiency
C. Malnutrition
D. Androgen deficiency

871. Cyclic bleeding at normal intervals but either excessive in amount or duration is termed as:
A. Menorrhagia B. Epimenorrhoea
C. Metrorrhagia D. Dysmenorrhoea

872. Cyclic bleeding in which cycle is reduced to 21 days or less is termed as:
A. Menorrhagia B. Epimenorrhoea
C. Metrorrhagia D. Dysmenorrhoea

873. Polymenorrhoea is also termed as:
A. Menorrhagia B. Epimenorrhoea
C. Metrorrhagia D. Dysmenorrhoea

874. Irregular, acyclic bleeding from the uterus is termed as:
A. Menorrhagia B. Epimenorrhoea
C. Metrorrhagia D. Dysmenorrhoea

875. When the menstrual bleeding is scanty and lasts for less than 2 days, is termed as:
A. Oligomenorrhoea B. Amenorrhoea
C. Hypomenorrhoea D. Dysmenorrhoea

876. Absence of menstrual cycle in a female during reproductive period is termed as:
A. Amenorrhoea B. Epimenorrhoea
C. Hypomenorrhoea D. Dysmenorrhoea

877. In following which a common cause of menorrhagia?
A. Fibroid uterus
B. Adenomyosis
C. Dysfunctional uterine bleeding
D. All of the above

878. The condition in which bleeding is so irregular and excessive that the menses cannot be identified, is known as:
A. Menorrhagia B. Metrorrhagia
C. Hypermenorrhoea D. Menometrorrhagia

879. In following which is not a cause of hypomenorrhoea?
A. Endometrial tuberculosis
B. Uterine polyp
C. Uterine synechiae
D. Malnutrition

880. What is the full form of DUB?
A. Direct Uterine Bleeding
B. Direct Uterine Blood Vessels
C. Dysfunctional Uterine Bleeding
D. Dysfunctional Uterine Blood Vessels

881. Following tests are done to identify HIV infection except:
A. ELISA
B. Western-Blot
C. Polymerase chain reaction
D. Widal test

882. In following which is not a characteristic feature of gonococcal salpingitis?
A. It is sexually transmitted
B. It is always bilateral infection
C. Infection occurs usually during and following menstruation
D. Infection occurs following abortion and childbirth

883. In following which is a characteristic feature of pyogenic salpingitis?
A. It is sexually transmitted
B. It is always bilateral infection
C. Infection occurs usually during and following menstruation
D. Infection occurs following abortion and childbirth

884. Collection of mucus into the fallopian tube is called as:
A. Salpingitis B. Hydrosalpinx
C. Fallotubitis D. Hydrofallo

885. Inflammation of ovary is termed as:
A. Oophoritis B. Hydrocoele
C. Salpingitis D. Oophorectomy

886. Most commonly used and effective treatment of vaginal trichomoniasis, is:
A. Cefixine
B. Use of oral contraceptives
C. Metronidazole
D. Gentamycin

887. The condition in which whole organ turns backwards in relation to the long axis of the birth canal, termed as?
A. Retroversion of uterus
B. Anteversion of uterus
C. Prolapse of uterus
D. Anteflexion of uterus

888. Normal position of uterus in pelvic cavity is:
A. Retroverted and retroflexed
B. Retroverted and anteflexed
C. Anteverted and retroflexed
D. Anteverted and anteflexed

889. The structure wkich provides support to the uterus includes?
A. Round ligament
B. Broad ligament
C. Cervico-vaginal junction
D. All of the above

890. Etiological factors responsible for genital prolapse include following except:
A. Postmenopausal atrophy
B. Increased intra abdominal pressure
C. Decreased weight of the uterus
D. Congenital weakness of the supporting structures

891. In a female possibility for occurring acute endometritis is more:
A. After menopause
B. After menarchae
C. After abortion or childbirth
D. During childhood

892. Pelvic inflammatory disease is more common in following females except:
A. Menstruating teenagers
B. Having multiple sexual partners
C. Absence of contraceptive pill use
D. Pregnant women

893. In following which statement is false?
A. PID is uncommon in women who are not menstruating
B. PID is more common in women who are using intra uterine devices
C. PID is more common in women who are taking oral contraceptives
D. PID is less common in women having monogamous partner who had vasectomy

894. Clinical manifestation of pelvic inflammatory disease include:
A. Lower abdominal pain
B. Fever
C. Irregular and excessive vaginal bleeding
D. All of the above

895. In following which is the most reliable aid to diagnose pelvic inflammatory disease?
A. Laparoscopy B. Sonography
C. Culdocentesis D. Blood examination

896. In following which is not a sexually transmitted disease?
A. Chancroid B. Syphilis
C. Fibroid uterus D. AIDS

897. Sexually transmitted disease lymphogranuloma venereum is caused by
A. Traponema Pallidum
B. Chlamydia Trachómatis
C. Haemophilus Ducreyi
D. Haemophilus Vaginalis

898. Who discovered human immunodeficiency virus?
A. Pasteur and Friedmann
B. Robert Hook
C. Watson
B. Barre Sinoussi

899. In following which statement is false?
A. Transmission of HIV from male to female is high
B. Breast feeding may also a cause of transmission of HIV
C. The vertical transmission to the newborn of the infected mothers is aobut 14-25%

D. Transmission of HIV from female to male is high

900. After HIV infection, there is immunodeficiency mainly due to
A. Decrease number of CD-4 T-Lymphocytes
B. Increase number of CD-4 T-Lymphocytes
C. Decrease number of RBC
D. Increase number of RBC

901. Which is the common chromosomal abnormality in azoospermic male?
A. Down's Syndrome
B. Turner Syndrome
C. Klinefelter's Syndrome
D. Kartagener Syndrome

902. Testicular failure due to gonadotrophin deficiency is termed as:
A. Klinefelter's Syndrome
B. Kallmann's Syndrome
C. Kartagener Syndrome
D. Young's Syndrome

903. Fault in male that may cause infertility includes:
A. Mumps orchitis
B. Raised scrotal temperature
C. Undescended testes
D. All of the above

904. In following which factor is not responsible for infertility?
A. Luteal phase defect
B. Acute retroverted uterus
C. Anteverted uterus
D. Vaginal atresia

905. pH of normal semen is
A. 3.5-4.5 B. 5.5-6.5
C. 7.2-7.8 D. 8.5-9.3

906. Normal sperm concentration in semen is about:
A. 5 million/ml or more
B. 10 million/ml or more
C. 20 million/ml or more
D. 30 million/ml or more

907. Failure of formation of semen is known as:
A. Aspermia B. Azoospermia
C. Asthenospermia D. Tetratozoospermia

908. The condition in which there is no spermatozoa in the semen, is termed as?
A. Aspermia B. Azoospermia
C. Asthenospermia D. Tetratozoospermia

909. Reduction in the viability of sperms is known as:
A. Aspermia B. Azoospermia
C. Asthenospermia D. Tetratozoospermia

910. The presence of high number of malformed spermatozoa in the semen is known as:
A. Aspermia B. Azoospermia
C. Asthenospermia D. Tetratozoospermia

911. In following which is the most important acquired predisposing factor in genital prolapse?
A. Vaginal delivery with consequent injury to the supporting structures
B. Congenital weakness of the supporting structures
C. Undernutrition
D. Increased weight of the uterus

912. Degree of uterine prolapse in which the external of protrudes outside the vaginal introitus but the uterine body still remains inside the uterus?
A. Ist degree B. IInd degree
C. IIIrd degree D. IVth degree

913. The type of uterine prolapse in which the uterine body descends to lie outside the introitus?
A. Ist degree B. IInd degree
C. IIIrd degree D. IVth degree

914. Clinical manifestation of genital prolapse includes:
A. Difficulty in passing urine
B. Backache
C. Difficulty in passing stool
D. All of the above

915. When a female moves about, she feels that something is coming down per vaginum. The female is suffering from:
A. DUB
B. Genital prolapse
C. Recto vaginal fistula
D. Cervical cancer

916. In how many cases of total infertility, males are responsible?

A. 8-10% of total cases
B. 20-25% of total cases
C. 30-40% of total cases
D. 50-60% of total cases

917. In kartagener syndrome:
A. Excessively production of sperms
B. There is loss of ciliary function and sperm motility
C. Ability of sperms to penetrate ovum increases
D. Ability of vaginal canal to receive sperms increases

918. Congenital factor related to male that is responsible for infertility includes:
A. Undescended testes
B. Hypospadias
C. Kartagener syndrome
D. All of the above

919. A male with hypospadias disease is:
A. Unable to produce sperms
B. Unable to deposit sperms in vagina
C. Unable to pass urine
D. Unable to deposit sperms high in vagina

920. The condition that raise the scrotal temperature includes:
A. Varicocele B. Big hydrocele
C. Filariasis D. All of the above

921. In following which is the classic symptom of uterine fibroid?
A. Menorrhagia
B. Pain in lower abdomen
C. Dysmenorrhoea
D. Purulent vaginal discharge

922. In following which is the life threatening complication of fibroids?
A. Persistent menorrhagia leading to anaemia
B. Severe infection leading to peritonitis
C. Sarcoma
D. All of the above

923. Following changes are seen in fibroid uterus except:
A. Increased surface area of the endometrium
B. Interference with normal uterine contractility
C. Endometrial hypoplasia
D. Pelvic congestion

924. In fibroid uterus, which condition may cause infertility?
A. Elongation of the uterine cavity
B. Dilatation of the endometrial venous plexus
C. Fibroid uterus prevents rhythmic uterine contraction during intercourse
D. All of the above

925. What is the meaning of endometriosis?
A. Inflammation of endometrium
B. Enlarged endometrium
C. Presence of functioing endometrium in sites other than uterine mucosa
D. Carcinoma of endometrium

926. Common site of endometriosis is:
A. Ovary
B. Pouch of douglas
C. Abdominal scar following hysteroctomy
D. All of the above

927. In following which is not a symptom of endometriosis?
A. Dysmenorrhoea B. Hypomenorrhoea
C. Dyspareunia D. Pelvic pain

928. Drug used for treating endometriosis includes:
A. Combined estrogen and progestogen oral pill
B. Danazol
C. GnRH analogues
D. All of the above

929. In stage II cervical cancer:
A. Carcinoma strictly confined to the cervix
B. The carcinoma extends beyond the cervix but has not extended to the pelvic wall
C. The carcinoma has extended beyond the true pelvis
D. The carcinoma has extended beyond the true pelvis

930. Staging of cervical cancer is primarily based on:
A. Severity of symptoms
B. Age of female
C. Clinical examination
D. All of the above

931. Absence of fructose content in the seminal fluid suggests:
A. Absence of one testes
B. Congential absence of prostate gland
C. Absence of testosterone hormone
D. Congenital absence of seminal vesicle

932. In following which medicine is used to treat infertility due to presence of antisperm antibodies?
A. GnRH therapy
B. Dexamethasone
C. Doxycycline
D. Clomiphene citrate

933. In a female with infertility, which drug is used in induction of ovulation?
A. Clomiphene citrate
B. FSH
C. GnRH
D. All of the above

934. In following which is the common treatment of luteal phase defect?
A. Progesterone therapy
B. Oestrogen therapy
C. Antibiotics
D. Dexamethasone

935. Following are the indications of intrauterine insemination except:
A. Cervical stenosis
B. Hypospadias
C. Asthenospermia
D. Recurrent abortions

936. Amount of washed and concentrated sperm that is injected within the uterine cavity during-artificial insemination:
A. 1 ml
B. 2 ml
C. 0.3 ml
D. 0.1 ml

937. At which stage of fertilized ova, is transferred into the uterine cavity during in vitro fertilization?
A. 1-2 cell stage
B. 2-4 cell stage
C. 4-8 cell stage
D. 16-24 cell stage

938. Health hazard of assisted reproductive technology includes?
A. Multiple pregnancy
B. Ectopic pregnancy
C. Psychological stress
D. All of the above

939. In following which is the commonest benign solid tumour in female?
A. Fibroid uterus
B. Vaginal cyst
C. Cervical cyst
D. Cervical cancer

940. Fibroid uterus is more common in:
A. Nulliparous women
B. Postmenopausal women
C. Multiparity
D. After 35 years of age

ANSWERS

1	2	3	4	5	6	7	8	9	10
A	C	B	D	B	C	A	C	A	D
11	**12**	**13**	**14**	**15**	**16**	**17**	**18**	**19**	**20**
D	D	D	A	C	C	D	B	B	A
21	**22**	**23**	**24**	**25**	**26**	**27**	**28**	**29**	**30**
B	B	C	B	B	C	C	B	A	D
31	**32**	**33**	**34**	**35**	**36**	**37**	**38**	**39**	**40**
D	B	C	A	A	A	A	B	A	C
41	**42**	**43**	**44**	**45**	**46**	**47**	**48**	**49**	**50**
A	A	A	C	D	B	D	A	B	C
51	**52**	**53**	**54**	**55**	**56**	**57**	**58**	**59**	**60**
A	C	C	C	D	A	A	A	B	B
61	**62**	**63**	**64**	**65**	**66**	**67**	**68**	**69**	**70**
C	C	B	A	B	B	A	B	C	C

71	**72**	**73**	**74**	**75**	**76**	**77**	**78**	**79**	**80**
C	A	A	C	B	C	C	A	B	C
81	**82**	**83**	**84**	**85**	**86**	**87**	**88**	**89**	**90**
A	A	A	A	B	D	B	C	A	B
91	**92**	**93**	**94**	**95**	**96**	**97**	**98**	**99**	**100**
D	D	A	C	B	C	A	C	B	A
101	**102**	**103**	**104**	**105**	**106**	**107**	**108**	**109**	**110**
B	C	B	C	B	C	C	B	A	B
111	**112**	**113**	**114**	**115**	**116**	**117**	**118**	**119**	**120**
B	D	A	B	D	C	A	D	C	C
121	**122**	**123**	**124**	**125**	**126**	**127**	**128**	**129**	**130**
B	A	A	A	A	B	B	B	C	B
131	**132**	**133**	**134**	**135**	**136**	**137**	**138**	**139**	**140**
D	C	B	C	B	D	D	A	C	B
141	**142**	**143**	**144**	**145**	**146**	**147**	**148**	**149**	**150**
B	C	B	A	C	A	B	A	A	A
151	**152**	**153**	**154**	**155**	**156**	**157**	**158**	**159**	**160**
A	C	B	C	B	A	C	D	D	C
161	**162**	**163**	**164**	**165**	**166**	**167**	**168**	**169**	**170**
C	D	B	A	A	A	C	D	A	D
171	**172**	**173**	**174**	**175**	**176**	**177**	**178**	**179**	**180**
A	A	C	B	B	C	B	D	C	C
181	**182**	**183**	**184**	**185**	**186**	**187**	**188**	**189**	**190**
B	C	C	A	C	A	A	B	B	A
191	**192**	**193**	**194**	**195**	**196**	**197**	**198**	**199**	**200**
B	B	B	B	A	C	C	D	C	B
201	**202**	**203**	**204**	**205**	**206**	**207**	**208**	**209**	**210**
B	A	A	B	B	D	A	D	D	A
211	**212**	**213**	**214**	**215**	**216**	**217**	**218**	**219**	**220**
B	D	C	B	D	A	D	A	C	B
221	**222**	**223**	**224**	**225**	**226**	**227**	**228**	**229**	**230**
C	D	A	D	C	C	C	C	A	D
231	**232**	**233**	**234**	**235**	**236**	**237**	**238**	**239**	**240**
D	B	C	A	A	B	B	D	B	B
241	**242**	**243**	**244**	**245**	**246**	**247**	**248**	**249**	**250**
A	D	D	A	C	B	C	D	A	D
251	**252**	**253**	**254**	**255**	**256**	**257**	**258**	**259**	**260**
B	C	B	C	B	B	B	B	A	C
261	**262**	**263**	**264**	**265**	**266**	**267**	**268**	**269**	**270**
D	C	D	D	D	D	B	B	D	B
271	**272**	**273**	**274**	**275**	**276**	**277**	**278**	**279**	**280**
C	B	B	C	C	D	A	B	C	A
281	**282**	**283**	**284**	**285**	**286**	**287**	**288**	**289**	**290**
C	D	B	C	B	C	A	D	A	D
291	**292**	**293**	**294**	**295**	**296**	**297**	**298**	**299**	**300**
A	C	D	B	C	B	B	D	B	A

301	302	303	304	305	306	307	308	309	310
B	C	D	B	A	C	D	D	D	C
311	312	313	314	315	316	317	318	319	320
C	B	D	B	D	B	C	C	B	D
321	322	323	324	325	326	327	328	329	330
A	C	D	D	B	D	C	D	C	D
331	332	333	334	335	336	337	338	339	340
D	D	B	D	B	D	B	B	B	B
341	342	343	344	345	346	347	348	349	350
D	A	D	B	B	A	B	C	C	A
351	352	353	354	355	356	357	358	359	360
A	B	B	C	C	A	C	B	D	C
361	362	363	364	365	366	367	368	369	370
D	C	C	C	B	D	B	B	D	C
371	372	373	374	375	376	377	378	379	380
C	D	D	D	A	D	B	D	B	D
381	382	383	384	385	386	387	388	389	390
D	C	C	C	A	C	B	B	A	C
391	392	393	394	395	396	397	398	399	400
D	A	B	C	B	C	A	D	B	D
401	402	403	404	405	406	407	408	409	410
C	B	D	B	C	C	C	D	B	B
411	412	413	414	415	416	417	418	419	420
A	C	B	C	A	C	C	B	A	D
421	422	423	424	425	426	427	428	429	430
A	C	C	C	B	A	B	D	A	A
431	432	433	434	435	436	437	438	439	440
A	D	B	B	B	C	A	A	C	C
441	442	443	444	445	446	447	448	449	450
A	B	C	C	A	A	D	C	D	A
451	452	453	454	455	456	457	458	459	460
B	C	D	D	D	A	B	B	A	B
461	462	463	464	465	466	467	468	469	470
D	B	C	A	B	C	D	C	A	D
471	472	473	474	475	476	477	478	479	480
C	D	D	C	B	B	B	A	D	B
481	482	483	484	485	486	487	488	489	490
B	B	D	C	A	A	B	A	B	A
491	492	493	494	495	496	497	498	499	500
C	A	D	C	C	D	D	C	A	B
501	502	503	504	505	506	507	508	509	510
C	B	C	B	A	B	B	B	B	A
511	512	513	514	515	516	517	518	519	520
B	D	B	B	D	D	A	B	C	D
521	522	523	524	525	526	527	528	529	530
A	A	B	A	C	D	A	A	B	C

531	532	533	534	535	536	537	538	539	540
D	A	B	D	D	A	B	C	D	A
541	542	543	544	545	546	547	548	549	550
A	D	B	D	B	B	C	B	C	A
551	552	553	554	555	556	557	558	559	560
C	C	D	B	C	B	B	B	C	C
561	562	563	564	565	566	567	568	569	570
A	B	A	D	D	A	D	A	C	D
571	572	573	574	575	576	577	578	579	580
C	D	B	B	A	B	B	B	B	D
581	582	583	584	585	586	587	588	589	590
B	C	A	D	B	D	C	B	C	B
591	592	593	594	595	596	597	598	599	600
B	D	D	A	C	D	B	A	C	D
601	602	603	604	605	606	607	608	609	610
B	B	A	C	B	B	A	C	B	A
611	612	613	614	615	616	617	618	619	620
B	B	C	B	D	B	C	C	B	C
621	622	623	624	625	626	627	628	629	630
A	C	D	C	C	B	B	C	A	D
631	632	633	634	635	636	637	638	639	640
D	C	D	D	B	A	C	B	D	C
641	642	643	644	645	646	647	648	649	650
A	B	C	A	B	C	D	B	A	B
651	652	653	654	655	656	657	658	659	660
B	D	D	C	B	D	D	B	A	C
661	662	663	664	665	666	667	668	669	670
D	C	A	D	D	B	B	A	B	B
671	672	673	674	675	676	677	678	679	680
D	B	A	C	D	A	B	C	B	B
681	682	683	684	685	686	687	688	689	690
A	A	D	C	C	D	A	B	A	C
691	692	693	694	695	696	697	698	699	700
D	B	D	C	A	B	C	C	C	B
701	702	703	704	705	706	707	708	709	710
A	C	B	C	B	D	A	C	A	B
711	712	713	714	715	716	717	718	719	720
C	C	C	A	D	B	D	C	D	A
721	722	723	724	725	726	727	728	729	730
B	C	D	D	D	B	A	C	A	B
731	732	733	734	735	736	737	738	739	740
C	C	D	D	B	B	A	B	C	A
741	742	743	744	745	746	747	748	749	750
A	A	B	B	C	D	C	C	B	B
751	752	753	754	755	756	757	758	759	760
B	C	D	D	C	C	B	D	C	D

761	762	763	764	765	766	767	768	769	770
A	C	A	D	A	C	B	D	A	B
771	772	773	774	775	776	777	778	779	780
A	D	C	B	A	B	B	B	A	C
781	782	783	784	785	786	787	788	789	790
B	B	C	B	B	A	B	D	A	C
791	792	793	794	795	796	797	798	799	800
B	A	C	A	A	A	A	A	A	A
801	802	803	804	805	806	807	808	809	810
B	A	B	A	A	D	C	A	B	D
811	812	813	814	815	816	817	818	819	820
A	A	B	C	B	A	B	C	A	D
821	822	823	824	825	826	827	828	829	830
B	C	A	B	D	D	D	C	A	B
831	832	833	834	835	836	837	838	839	840
C	D	D	C	C	A	B	C	D	B
841	842	843	844	845	846	847	848	849	850
D	A	B	D	B	D	C	B	D	A
851	852	853	854	855	856	857	858	859	860
D	A	B	A	B	D	B	C	C	D
861	862	863	864	865	866	867	868	869	870
C	D	D	D	A	A	C	B	D	B
871	872	873	874	875	876	877	878	879	880
A	B	B	C	C	A	D	D	B	C
881	882	883	884	885	886	887	888	889	890
D	D	D	B	A	C	A	D	D	C
891	892	893	894	895	896	897	898	899	900
C	D	C	D	A	C	B	D	D	A
901	902	903	904	905	906	907	908	909	910
C	B	D	C	C	C	A	B	C	D
911	912	913	914	915	916	917	918	919	920
A	B	C	D	B	C	B	D	D	D
921	922	923	924	925	926	927	928	929	930
A	D	C	D	C	D	B	D	B	C
931	932	933	934	935	936	937	938	939	940
D	B	D	A	D	C	C	D	A	A

YOUR SPACE

GENERAL AWARENESS

1. OUR INDIA

INDIA : AT A GLANCE

Population (2011)	:	1,21,08,54,977
Capital	:	New Delhi
Area	:	32,87,263 sq km
Geographic Location	:	Between 8°4' and 37°6' north latitudes
	:	Between 68°7' and 97°25' east longitudes
Coastline Length	:	7,516.6 km including the coastline of Lakshadweep, Andaman & Nicobar Islands.
Number of States	:	28
Number of Union Territories	:	8
Major Languages	:	22
National Anthem	:	Jana Gana Mana
National Currency	:	Rupee (₹)
National Animal	:	Tiger
National Aquatic Animal	:	Dolphin
National Bird	:	Peacock
National River	:	Ganga
Characteristics of Indian	:	Socialist, Secular, Democratic, Republic
Legislature	:	Bicameral Legislature at the Centre
	:	Uni/Bicameral Legislatures in States
Executive	:	President, Vice-President and Council of Ministers at the Centre Governor and Council of Ministers in States
Judiciary	:	Independent from Executive with Supreme Court at the apex of the hierarchy
Total Road Length	:	6.32 million kilometres (March 2022)

India: States & Union Territories

States/Union Territories	Capital	Area in (Sq. Km.)	Language
Andhra Pradesh	Amaravati	1,60,229	Telugu
Arunachal Pradesh	Itanagar	83,743	Nyishi, Dafla, Miji, Wancho etc.
Assam	Dispur	78,438	Assamese
Bihar	Patna	94,163	Hindi, Maithili
Chhattisgarh	Raipur	136,034	Hindi
Goa	Panji	3,702	Marathi and Konkani
Gujarat	Gandhinagar	1,96,024	Gujarati
Haryana	Chandigarh	44,212	Hindi
Himachal Pradesh	Shimla	55,673	Hindi and Pahari
Jharkhand	Ranchi	79,714	Hindi, Santhali
Karnataka	Bengaluru	1,91,791	Kannada
Kerala	Thiruvananthapuram	38,863	Malayalam
Madhya Pradesh	Bhopal	308,000	Hindi
Maharashtra	Mumbai	307,713	Marathi
Manipur	Imphal	22,327	Manipuri
Meghalaya	Shillong	22,429	Khasi, Garo and English
Mizoram	Aizawl	21,081	Mizo and English
Nagaland	Kohima	16,579	Sema, English
Odisha	Bhubaneswar	155,707	Odiya
Punjab	Chandigarh	50,362	Punjabi
Rajasthan	Jaipur	3,42,239	Hindi and Rajasthani
Sikkim	Gangtok	7,096	Bhutia, Nepali, Lepcha and Limbu
Tamil Nadu	Chennai	1,30,058	Tamil
Telangana	Hyderabad	1,14,840	Telugu, Urdu
Tripura	Agartala	10,491	Bengali, Kakborak, Manipuri
Uttar Pradesh	Lucknow	2,40,928	Hindi and Urdu
Uttarakhand	Dehradun	53,484	Hindi
West Bengal	Kolkata	88,752	Bengali
Andaman & Nicobar Island	Port Blair	8,249	Bengali, Hindi, Nicobarese, Tamil, Telugu, and Malayalam
Chandigarh	Chandigarh	114	Hindi, Punjabi
Dadara and Nagar Haveli and Daman and Diu	Daman	603	Gujarati and Hindi
Delhi	Delhi	1483	Hindi, Punjabi and Urdu
Lakshadweep	Kavaratti	32	Malayalam
Puducherry	Puducherry	492	Tamil, Telugu, Malayalam, English and French
Jammu & Kashmir	Srinagar (Summer) Jammu (Winter)	2,22,236*	Kashmiri, Urdu, Dogri
Ladakh	Leh	—	Ladakhi

* Including areas of Ladakh and illegally occupied

POPULATION

Second Largest Nation : In terms of the size of population, India is the second largest country in the world, next only to China. China tops the list with 1341.0 million people. India's population constitutes nearly 17.5 per cent of the total world population while her geographical area is only 2.42 per cent of the world area. With such a huge population to support on so small an area, the country finds herself in great difficulty in making any significant dent on its poverty and economic backwardness. India's national income, which is barely 2 per cent of the total global income, clearly shows the tremendous strain of population on her economy.

2011 Census Highlights

Population of India–Total Indian population is 17.5% of total world population	:	1,21,08,54,977 (Male: 62,32,70,258; Female: 58,75,84,719)
Decadal Growth (2001-2011)	:	17.7 per cent (Males: 17.1 per cent; Females: 18.3 per cent)
Hightest Decadal Growth (State-wise)	:	Meghalaya (27.9 per cent)
Lowest Decadal Growth (State-wise)	:	Nagaland (–0.6 per cent)
Most populous State	:	Uttar Pradesh (16.51 per cent of National Population)
Density of population	:	382 persons per sq. km.
Most densly populated State	:	Bihar : 1106 per sq. km
Sex Ratio	:	943 females per 1000 males
Total Literacy Rate	:	73% (Males – 80.9%), (Females – 64.6%)
Highest Literacy (State-wise)	:	Kerala (94%)
Lowest Literacy (State-wise)	:	Bihar (61.8)

OTHER DETAILS

(a) Population of India

1951	36,10,88,090	1961	43,92,34,771
1971	54,81,59,652	1981	68,33,29,097
1991	84,64,21,039	2001	102,87,37,436
2011	1,21,08,54,977		

(b) Density of Population (Persons per square kilometre)

1951	113	1961	138
1971	177	1981	216
1991	267	2001	324
2011	382		

(c) Annual Compound Rate of Growth

1941-1951	1.25 per cent	1951-1961	1.96 per cent
1961-1971	2.22 per cent	1971-1981	2.20 per cent
1981-1991	2.14 per cent	1991-2001	1.95 per cent
2001-2011	1.64 per cent		

2011 CENSUS OF INDIA : POPULATION DISTRIBUTION, POPULATION DENSITY AND LITERACY RATE

S. No.	State/ Union Territories*	Population 2011			Population Density (per sq. km.)	Literacy Rate 2011		
		Persons	Males	Females	2011	Persons	Males	Females
	INDIA	**1,21,08,54,977**	**62,32,70,258**	**58,75,34,719**	**382**	**73.0**	**80.9**	**64.6**
1.	Jammu and Kashmir	1,25,41,302	66,40,662	59,00,640	124	67.2	76.8	56.4
2.	Himachal Pradesh	68,64,602	34,81,873	33,82,729	123	82.8	89.5	75.9
3.	Punjab	2,77,43,338	1,46,39,465	1,31,03,873	551	75.8	80.4	70.7
4.	Chandigarh	10,55,450	5,80,663	4,74,787	9,258	86.0	90.0	81.2
5.	Uttarakhand	1,00,86,292	51,37,773	49,48,519	189	78.8	87.4	70.0
6.	Haryana	2,53,51,462	1,34,94,734	1,18,56,728	573	75.6	84.1	65.9
7.	Delhi	1,67,87,941	89,87,326	78,00,615	11,320	86.2	90.9	80.8
8.	Rajasthan	6,85,48,437	3,55,50,997	3,29,97,440	200	66.1	79.2	52.1
9.	Uttar Pradesh	19,98,12,341	10,44,80,510	9,53,31,831	829	67.7	77.3	57.2
10.	Bihar	10,40,99,452	5,42,78,157	4,98,21,295	1,106	61.8	71.2	51.5
11.	Sikkim	6,10,577	3,23,070	2,87,507	86	81.4	86.6	75.6
12.	Arunachal Pradesh	13,83,727	7,13,912	6,69,815	17	65.4	72.6	57.7
13.	Nagaland	19,78,502	10,24,649	9,53,853	119	79.6	82.8	76.1
14.	Manipur	28,55,794	14,38,586	14,17,208	115	79.2	86.1	72.4
15.	Mizoram	10,97,206	5,55,339	5,41,867	52	91.3	93.3	89.3
16.	Tripura	36,73,917	18,74,376	17,99,541	350	87.2	91.5	82.7
17.	Meghalya	29,66,889	14,91,832	14,75,057	132	74.4	76.0	72.9
18.	Assam	3,12,05,576	1,59,39,443	1,52,66,133	398	72.2	77.8	66.3
19.	West Bengal	9,12,76,115	4,68,09,027	4,44,67,088	1,028	76.3	81.7	70.5
20.	Jharkhand	3,29,88,134	1,69,30,315	1,60,57,819	414	66.4	76.8	55.4
21.	Odisha	4,19,74,218	2,12,12,136	2,07,62,082	270	72.9	81.6	64.0
22.	Chhattisgarh	2,55,45,198	1,28,32,895	1,27,12,303	189	70.3	80.3	60.2
23.	Madhya Pradesh	7,26,26,809	3,76,12,306	3,50,14,503	236	69.3	78.7	59.2
24.	Gujarat	6,04,39,692	3,14,91,260	2,89,48,432	308	78.0	85.8	69.7
25.	Daman and Diu	2,43,247	1,50,301	92,946	2,191	87.1	91.5	79.5
26.	Dadra & Nagar Haweli	3,43,709	1,93,760	1,49,949	700	76.2	85.2	64.3
27.	Maharashtra	11,23,74,333	5,82,43,056	5,41,31,277	365	82.3	88.4	75.9
28.	Andhra Pradesh	4,93,86,799	2,47,38,068	2,46,48,731	308	67.4	74.8	60.0
29.	Karnataka	6,10,95,297	3,09,66,657	3,01,28,640	319	75.4	82.5	68.1
30.	Goa	14,58,545	7,39,140	7,19,405	394	88.7	92.6	84.7
31.	Lakshadweep	64,473	33,123	31,350	2,149	91.8	95.6	87.9
32.	Kerala	3,34,06,061	1,60,27,412	1,73,78,649	860	94.0	96.1	92.1
33.	Tamil Nadu	7,21,47,030	3,61,37,975	3,60,09,055	555	80.1	86.8	73.4
34.	Puducherry	12,47,953	6,12,511	6,35,442	2,547	85.8	91.3	80.7
35.	Andaman & Nicobar Island	3,80,581	2,02,871	1,77,710	46	86.6	90.3	82.4
36.	Telangana	3,51,93,978	17,704,078	17,489,900	308	66.5	75.0	57.9

* * * * *

2. NATIONAL SYMBOLS

State Emblem: The State Emblem of India is an adaptation from the Sarnath Lion Capital of Ashoka. It was adopted by the Government of India on January 26, 1950. In the adapted form, only three lions are visible, the fourth being hidden from the view. The wheel (Dharma Chakra) appears in relief in the centre of the abacus with a bull on the right and a horse on the left. The bell-shaped lotus has been omitted. The words "Satyameva Jayate" meaning "Truth alone triumphs" are inscribed below the Emblem in Devanagari script.

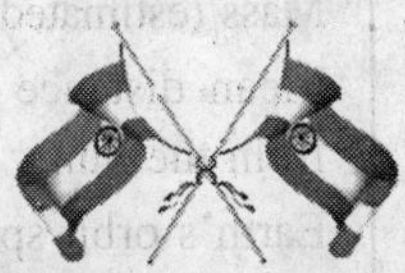

National Flag: The National Flag of India is a horizontal tricolour of deep saffron (Kesari), white and dark green in equal proportion. In the centre of the white band there is a wheel in navy blue colour. It has 24 spokes. The ratio of the length and the breadth of the flag is 3 : 2. Its design was adopted by the Constituent Assembly of India on July 22, 1947.

National Anthem: Rabindranath Tagore's song 'Jana-gana-mana' was adopted by the Constituent Assembly as the National Anthem of India on January 24, 1950.

Jana-gan-mana-adhinayaka jaya he,
Bharata-bhagya-vidhata
Punjab-Sindh-Gujarat-Maratha-Dravida-Utkala-Banga
Vindhya-Himachala-Yamuna-Ganga Uchhala-jaladhi-taranga.
Tava subha name jage, Tava subha asisa mange,
Gahe tava jaya gatha.
Jana-gana-mangala-dayak, jaya he Bharata bhagya vidhata,
Jaya he, jaya he, jaya he, Jaya jaya jaya, jaya he.

National Song: Bankim Chandra Chatterji's 'Vande Mataram' which was a source of inspiration to the people in their struggle for freedom, has been adopted as National Song. It has an equal status with the National Anthem.

Vande Mataram

Sujalam, suphalam, malayaja-shitalam,
Shasya shyamalam, Mataram
Shubhrajyotsna,pulkita yaminim,
Phulla kusumita drumadalashobhinim,
Subhasinim sumadhura—bhashinim,
Sukhadam, Varadam, Mataram.

National Bird and Animal of India: Peacock and Tiger; **National Aquatic Animal:** Dolphin; **National Flower:** Lotus; **National Calendar:** It was adopted on March 22, 1957. It has 365 days in the year and the first month of the year is Chaitra.

Months of the National Calendar

(1) Chaitra, (2) Vaishakha, (3) Jaishtha, (4) Ashadha, (5) Shravan, (6) Bhadra, (7) Ashvina, (8) Kartika, (9) Marga-Shirsha, (10) Pausha, (11) Magha, (12) Phalguna.

* * * * *

3. THE UNIVERSE

The Solar System: Some Facts

Number of Planets: 8—Mercury, Venus, Earth, Mars, Jupiter, Saturn, Uranus and Neptune.

Largest most

Massive planet	Jupiter
Brightest planet	Venus
Brightest star	Sirius
Fastest orbiting planet	Mercury
Longest (Synodic) day	Mercury
Planet with largest moon	Jupiter
Greatest average density	Jupiter
Tallest mountain	Mars
Strongest magnetic fields	Jupiter
Most circular orbit	Venus
Shortest (synodic) day	Jupiter
Hottest planet	Venus
No moons	Mercury, Venus
Planet with moon with most eccentric orbit	Neptune
Lowest average density	Saturn
Greatest amount of liquid on the surface	Earth

The Earth: Facts and Data

Composition of the Earth: Aluminium (0.4%), Sulphur (2.7%), Silicon (13%), Oxygen (28%), Calcium (1.2%), Nickel (2.7%), Magnesium (17%), Iron (35%)

Surface area	510100500 sq km
Land Surface (29.1%)	148950800 sq km
Ocean Surface (70.9%)	361149700 sq km
Type of water	97% salt, 3% fresh
Total area of water	382672000 sq km
Equatorial diameter	12753 km
Equatorial Circumference	40066 km
Polar Circumference	39992 km
Polar diameter	12710 km
Equatorial radius	6376 km
Polar radius	6335 km
Mass (estimated weight)	594×10^{19} metric tons
Mean distance from the Sun	149407000 km
Earth's orbit speed (around sun)	107320 kmph
Period of Revolution (round the sun)	365 days 5 hrs 48 min. 45.51 seconds
Time of Rotation (on its axis)	23 hrs 56 min. 4.09 seconds
Inclination of the axis (to the plane of the eclipitc)	23º27'

Solar Statistics

Distance from the Earth	149.8 million km
Absolute Visual Magnitude	4.75
Diameter Core	13,84,000 km
Temperature	15000000 K
Photosphere Temperature	5770 K

Rotation as seen from the Earth (at the equator)	:	25.38 days
Rotation as seen from the Earth (near the poles)	:	33 days
Chemical Composition	:	Hydrogen 71% Helium 26.5% Other elements 2.5%
Age	:	About 4.5 billion years
Expected lifetime of a normal star	:	About 10 billion years

Oceans of the World

Pacific	16,62,41,000 sq km
Atlantic	8,65,57,000 sq km
Indian	7,34,27,000 sq km
Arctic	94,85,000 sq km

Longest Rivers

Name	*Country/ Continent*	*Length in Kilometres*
Nile	Africa	6650
Amazon	S. America	6437
Mississippi-Missouri	USA	6020
Yangtze-Kiang	China	5494
Ob-Irtysh	Russia	5410
Lena	Russia	4400
Hwang Ho	China	4344
Niger	Africa	4180
St. Lawrence	Canada (USA)	4023
Murray-Darling	Australia	3780
Volga	Russia	3690
Indus	Asia	2900
Danube	Europe	2850
Orinoco	S. America	2575

Major Riverside Cities

City	*River*	*Country*
Alexandria	Nile	Egypt
Amsterdam	Amsel	Netherland
Ankara	Kizil	Turkey
Baghdad	Tigris	Iraq
Bangkok	Menam	Thailand
Belgrade	Danube	Yugoslavia
Berlin	Spree	Germany
Budapest	Danube	Hungary
Cairo	Nile	Egypt
Chittagong	Karnaphuli	Bangladesh
Karachi	Indus	Pakistan
Khartoum	Blue & White Nile	Sudan
Lahore	Ravi	Pakistan
Lisbon	Tagus	Portugal
Liverpool	Mersey	England
London	Thames	England
Moscow New	Moskva	Russia
Orleans	Mississipi	USA
New York	Hudson	USA
Paris	Seine	France
Yangon	Irawadi	Myanmar
Rome	Tiber	Italy

Major Gulfs of the World

Names	*Areas (Sq. Km.)*
Gulf of Mexico	15,44,000
Gulf of Hudson	12,33,000
Arabian Gulf	2,38,000
Gulf of St. Lawrence	2,37,000
Gulf of California	1,62,000
English Channel	89,900

Major Mountain Ranges of the World

Range	*Location*	*Length (km)*
Andes	South America	7,200
Himalayas-Karakoram-Hindukush	South Central Asia	5,000
Rockies	North America	4,800

Range	Location	Length (km)
Great Dividing Range	East Australia	3,600
Atlas	North West Africa	1,930
Western Ghats	Western India	1,610
Caucasus	Europe	1,200
Alaska	USA	1,130
Alps	Europe	1,050

Largest Deserts of the World

Subtropical

Sahara, North Africa	94,00,000 sq. km.
Kalahari, Southern Africa	9,00,000 sq. km.
Thar, India/Pakistan	2,00,000 sq. km.
Great Sandy, Australia	4,00,000 sq. km.

Cool Coastal

Atacama, Chile S.A.	1,40,000 sq. km

Cool Winter

Gobi, China	13,00,000 sq. km.
Colorado, Western USA (also called the painted desert)	3,37,000 sq. km.

Atmosphere

Composition of Gases in Atmosphere

Nitrogen	78.03%
Oxygen	20.99%
Argon	0.93%
Carbon dioxide	0.03%
Hydrogen	0.01%
Neon	0.0018%
Helium	0.0005%
Crypton	0.0001%
Xenon	0.000,005%
Ozone	0.000,0001%

World Important Local Winds

Chinoon: A warm day wind frequently experienced on the eastern side of the Rocky Mountains.

Fohn: A warm dry wind descending a mountain, as on the north side of the Alps.

Haboob: A sand storm or a dust storm in north and north-east Sudan near Khartoum.

Bagrrio: It is the tropical cyclone of the Philippine Island.

Loo: A hot wind which blows in summer season in Indian sub-continent.

Papasago: A cold northerly wind sometimes felt on the Mexico plateau.

Bora: It is the name given to the cold dry wind experienced particularly in winter along the eastern coast of the Atlantic Ocean and in northern Italy.

Black Toller: A hot dust wind which blows in the vast plain of North America.

Principal Mountain Peaks of the World

Mountains	Height in Metres	Range	Date of First Ascent
1. Mount Everest	8,848	Himalayas	May 29, 1953
2. K-2 (Godwin Austen)	8,611	Karakoram	July 31, 1954
3. Kanchenjunga	8,597	Himalayas	May 25, 1955
4. Lhotse	8,511	Himalayas	May 18, 1956
5. Makalu I	8,481	Himalayas	May 15, 1955
6. Dhaulagiri I	8,167	Himalayas	May 13, 1960
7. Mansalu I	8,156	Himalayas	May 9, 1956
8. Chollyo	8,153	Himalayas	Oct. 19, 1954
9. Nanga Parbat	8,124	Himalayas	July 3, 1953
10. Annapurna I	8,091	Himalayas	June 3, 1950

Mountains	Height in Metres	Range	Date of First Ascent
11. Gasherbrum I	8,068	Karakoram	July 5, 1958
12. Broad Peak I	8,047	Karakoram	June 9, 1957
13. Gasherbrum II	8,034	Karakoram	July 7, 1956
14. Shisha Pangma (Gosainthan)	8,014	Himalayas	May 2, 1964
15. Gasherbrum III	7,952	Karakoram	Aug. 11, 1975

Types of World Agriculture

Viticulture: The cultivation of the vine for production of grapes and wine.
Pisciculture: The breeding, rearing and transplantation of fish by artificial means.
Sericulture: The raising of silk worms for the production of raw silk.
Horticulture: To grow flower front, vegetables on small plots.

Apiculture: Bee keeping on a commercial scale for the sale of honey.
Floriculture: The cultivation of flowers or flowering plants.
Mariculture: Sea farming, or the cultivation of marine plants and animals for commercial purposes.
Olericulture: The cultivation of vegetables and kitchen herbs.

Famous Straits of the World

Strait	Between	Country
Malacca Strait	Andaman Sea and South China Sea	Indonesia
Palk Strait	Mannar and Bay of Bengal	India-Sri Lanka
Magellan Strait	Pacific and South Atlantic Ocean	Chile
Dover Strait	English Channel and North Sea	England-France
Berring Strait	Berring Sea and Chukasi Sea	Alaska-Russia
Sugaroo Strait	Japan Sea and Pacific Ocean	Japan
Sunda Strait	Java and Indian Ocean	Indonesia
Gibralter Strait	Mediterranean Sea and Atlantic Ocean	Spain
Harmuj Strait	Persia and Bay of Oman	Oman-Iran
Hudson Strait	Bay of Hudson and Atlantic Ocean	Canada

World's Famous Official Documents

White Paper: India; **Orange Book:** Netherlands; **Yellow Book:** France; **Green Book:** Italy and Iran; **White Book:** Portugal, China and Germany; **Grey Book:** Japan and Belgium.

Famous Newspapers of the World

Newspaper	Place of Publishing	Language
Daily News	New York (America)	English
Guardian	London (Britain)	English
Pravada	Moscow (Russia)	Russian
Al-Ahram	Cairo (Egypt)	Arabic
Merdeca	Jakarta (Indonesia)	Indonesian
Times	London (Britain)	English
People's Daily	Beijing (China)	Chinese
New Statesman	Britain	English
Daily Mirror	Britain	English
Hindu, Hindustan Times, Times of India, Tribune, Statesman, Indian Express, Economic Times	India	English
Hindustan, Nav Bharat Times, Rashtriya Sahara, Dainik Jagaran, Punjab Kesari	India	Hindi

Important Boundary Lines

Boundary Line	Countries
Hindenberg Line	Germany-Poland
Maginot Line	France and Germany
Mannerhein Line	Russia-Finland
Mc Mahon Line	India and China
Order Niesse Line	Germany-Poland
Radcliff Line	India-Pakistan
Seigfrid Line	Germany-France
Durand Line	Pakistan and Afghanistan
17th Parallel	The line which defined the boundary between North Vietnam and South Vietnam before the two were united.
38th Parallel	North Korea and South Korea
49th Parallel	U.S.A. and Canada

Areawise 10 Big and Small Countries

10 Big Countries

S. No.	Country	Sq. km (Total Portion) sq. km)
1.	Russia (Europe-Asia)	1,70,75,000
2.	Canada (N. America)	99,76,186
3.	China (Asia)	95,96,960
4.	U.S.A. (N. America)	93,72,614
5.	Brazil (S. America)	85,11,965
6.	Australia (S. Pacific)	76,82,300
7.	India (Asia)	32,87,263
8.	Argentina (S. America)	27,76,654
9.	Kazakhstan (Europe-Asia)	27,17,300
10.	Algeria (Africa)	23,81,741

10 Small Countries

S. No.	Country	Area (Sq. km)
1.	Vatican City (Europe)	0.44
2.	Monaco (Europe)	1.95
3.	Nauru (Southern Pacific)	21.00
4.	Tuvalu	26.00
5.	San Marino (Europe)	62.00
6.	Liechtenstein (Europe)	160.00
7.	Marshall Island (Central Pacific)	181.00
8.	St. Kitts and Nevis (Eastern Caribbean)	269.00
9.	Maldives	298.00
10.	Malta	316.00

Populationwise 10 Big and Small Countries

10 Big Countries

S. No.	Country	Population (2021) (In million)
1.	China (Asia)	1397.89
2.	India (Asia)	1339.00
3.	U.S.A. (North America)	334.99
4.	Indonesia (Asia)	275.12
5.	Pakistan (Asia)	238.18
6.	Nigeria (Africa)	219.46
7.	Brazil (South America)	213.44
8.	Bangladesh (Asia)	164.09
9.	Russia (Europe-Asia)	142.32
10.	Japan (Asia)	124.68

10 Small Countries

S. No.	Country	Population (2021)
1.	Vatican City (Europe)	1000
2.	Tuvalu	11,448
3.	Palau (Western Pacific)	21,613
4.	Monaco (Europe)	31,223
5.	San Marino (Europe)	34,467
6.	Liechstein (Europe)	39,425
7.	American Samoa	44,273
8.	Northern Mariana Islands	49,551
9.	St. Kitts and Nevis (Eastern Caribbean)	54,149
10.	Marshall Island (Central Pacific)	78,831

Signals/Signs and Meaning

Signal/Sign	Meaning
Red Triangle	Family Planning
Red Cross	Medical Help
Red Light	Danger, 'Stop' for the movement of vehicles
Green Light	Go
Olive Branch	Peace
White Pigeon or Dove	Peace
Black Strip on Arm	(i) Opposition (ii) Sorrow
Black Flag	Opposition
Red Flag	(i) Danger (ii) Revolution
White Flag	Treaty or Surrender
Yellow Flag	Vehicles with patients of contagious diseases
Two Bones across with a Skull	Danger of electricity
Half mast flown Flag	National mourning
Lotus	Sign of civilization and culture
Wheel (Chakra)	Sign of Progress
A blind folded woman with scale in hand	Sign of Justice
Reversed flown	National calamity flag

National Emblems of Important Countries

Country	National Emblem
America	Golden Rod
Australia	Kangaroo
Ireland	Shamrock
Italy	White Lily
Israel	Candelabrum
Iran	Rose
Canada	White Lily
Great Britain	Rose
Chile	Candor and Huemul
Germany	Corn Flower
Japan	Chrysanthemum
Zimbabwe	Zimbabwe Bird
Denmark	Beach
Turkey	Crescent and Star
The Netherlands	Lion
New Zealand	Kiwi, Fern Southern Cross
Norway	Lion
Nepal	Kukri
Pakistan	Crescent
Poland	Eagle
France	Lily
Belgium	Lion
Bangladesh	Water Lily
Mongolia	The Soyombo
Russia	Double headed eagle
Lebanon	Cedar Tree
Sudan	Secretary Bird
Syria	Eagle
India	Lioned Capital

Region wise Population

Region	Population (2021)	World Share (in percentage)
Asia	4,584,249,616	59.1%
Africa	1,375,397,882	17.4%
Europe	747,142,309	9.8%
Latin America and the Caribbean	651,321,069	8.4%
Northern America	373,076,833	4.8%
Oceania	41,663,096	0.5%

International Date Line

It roughly corresponds to 180°E or W meridian of longitude which falls on the opposite side of the Greenwich meridian and the date changes by one day (i.e. 24 hours), as this line is crossed. On crossing this line from east to west a day is added, and a day is subtracted on crossing it from west to east.

* * * * *

4. UNITED NATIONS ORGANISATION

- **Origin:** UN Charter was signed by 50 members on June 26, 1945. It officially came into existence on October 24, 1945.
- **UN Charter:** The Charter is the Constitution of the UNO and contains its aims and objectives and rules and regulations for its functioning.
- **Aims and Objectives:** They are security, welfare and human rights.
- **Headquarters:** New York.
- **Flag:** The flag is light blue in colour, and emblazoned in white, in its centre is the UN symbol—a polar map of world embraced by twin olive branches open at the top.
- **Official Languages:** The official languages of the UN are: English, French, Chinese, Russian, Arabic and Spanish. However, working languages are English & French only.

Secretary General of the U.N.O.

Name	*Country*	*Tenure*
Trygve Lie	Norway	(1946-53)
Dog Hammarsk-joeld	Sweden	(1953-61)
U. Thant	Myanmar	(1961-71)
Kurt Waldheim	Austria	(1972-81)
Javier Perez de Cuellar	Peru	(1982-91)
Dr. Boutros Ghali	Egypt	(1992-96)
Kofi Annan	Ghana	(1997-2006)
Ban Ki-moon	South Korea	(2007-2016)
Antonio Guterres	Portugal	(2017-----)

- **Main Organs of the UNO:** There are six main organs:
  1. General Assembly
  2. Security Council
  3. Economic and Social Council
  4. Trusteeship Council
  5. International Court of Justice, and (6) Secretariat.

1. **General Assembly:** It consists of representative of all members of the UN. Each member country has only one vote. It meets once a year and passes UN Budget.
2. **Security Council:** It is the Executive body of the UN and is mainly responsible for maintaining international peace and security. It has 15 members, 5 of which (USA, UK, France, Russia and China) are permanent members. The 10 non-permanent members are elected by General Assembly for two-year term and are not eligible for immediate re-election.
3. **Economic and Social Council:** It has 54 members elected by General Assembly.
4. **Trusteeship Council:** It looks after interest of the people in areas not yet independent and leads them towards self-government.
5. **International Court of Justice:** It has 15 judges, no two of whom may be nationals of the same state. They are elected by General Assembly and Security Council for a term of 9 years. The Court elects its President and Vice-President for a 3-year term.
6. **Secretariat:** It is the Secretariat of the UN and is headed by the Secretary General.

Years Observed by United Nations Organisation

1967 : International Tourism Year
1968 : Human Rights Year
1970 : International Education Year
1972 : International Book Year
1973 : Copernicus Year
1974 : World Population Year
1975 : International Women's Year

1979: International Year of the Child
1981: International Year of Disabled
1983: World Communication Year
1985: International Youth Year
1986: International Year of Peace
1987: International Year of Shelter for the Homeless
1990: International Literacy Year
1992: International Space Year
1993: International Year for World's Indigenous People
1994: International Year of Family
1995: International Year of Tolerance
1996: International Year for Eradication of Poverty
1998: Human Rights Year
1999: Year of Older Persons
2000: Year of the Culture of Peace
2001: International Year of Volunteer
2002: International Year of Eco-tourism
2003: International Year of Fresh Water
2004: International Rice Year
2005: International Year of Sports and Physical Education
2006: International Year of Deserts & Desertification
2008: International Year of Potato
2009: International Year of Astronomy
2010: International Year of Bio-diversity
2011: International Year of Forest
2012: International Year of Cooperatives
2013: International Year of Water Cooperation
2014: International Year of Family Farming
2015: International Year of Soil
2016: International Year of Pulses
2017: International Year of Sustainable Tourism for Development
2019: International Year of Indigenous Languages
2020: International year of Plant Health
2021: International year of Peace and Trust
2022: International year of Artisanal Fisheries and Aquaculture
2023: International year of Millets

- **Present Membership:** At present 193 countries are members of the UNO. South Sudan is the latest entrant to this world organisation.

Famous International Organisations, Headquarters and Year of Establishment

International Organisations	*Headquarters*	*Year of Establishment*
United Nations Organisations (U.N.O.)	New York	1945
International Monetary Fund (I.M.F.)	Washington	1945
World Health Organisation (W.H.O.)	Geneva	1948
Food & Agricultural Organisation (FAO)	Rome	1945
International Labour Organisation (ILO)	Geneva	1919
UNESCO	Paris	1946
International Court of Justice	The Hague	1945
Universal Postal Union (UPU)	Berne	1874
International Civil Aviation Organisation (ICAO)	Montreal	1947
UNIDO	Vienna	1966
International Atomic Energy Agency (IAEA)	Vienna	1957
International Finance Corporation (IFC)	Washington	1956
United Nations Development Programme (UNDP)	New York	1965
UNICEF	New York	1946
International Maritime Organisation (IMO)	London	1948
World Meteorological Organisation (WMO)	Geneva	1950
International Telecommunication Union (ITU)	Geneva	1865

International Organisations	*Headquarters*	*Year of Establishment*
Arab League	Cairo	1945
Commonwealth of Nations	London	1931
World Trade Organisation (WTO)	Geneva	1995
International Development Association (IDA)	Washington D.C.	1960
International Bank for Reconstruction and Development (IBRD)	Washington D.C.	1944
World Intellectual Property Organisation (WIPO)	Geneva	1967
Organisation of Islamic Conference (OIC)	Jeddah (Saudi Arabia)	1969
Red Cross	Geneva	1863
Interpol	Lyons	1923
Asian Development Bank (ADB)	Manila	1966
North Atlantic Treaty Organisation (NATO)	Brussels	1949
Association of South East Asian Nations (ASEAN)	Jakarta	1967
South Asian Association for Regional Cooperation (SAARC)	Kathmandu	1985
Asia-Pacific Economic Cooperation (APEC)	Singapore	1989
Organisation for Economic Cooperation and Development (OECD)	Paris	1961
Organisation of Petroleum Exporting Countries (OPEC)	Vienna	1960
Commonwealth of Independent States (CIS)	Minsk, Belarus	1991
International Olympic Committee (IOC)	Switzerland	1894
European Union (EU)	Brussels	Changed form of EEC Established in 1958
Amnesty International (AI)	London	1961
Shanghai Cooperation Organisation (SCO)	Beijing	2001

* * * * *

5. INDIAN CONSTITUTION & POLITY

INDIAN CONSTITUTION

India, as a sovereign state, has its own Constitution. The Indian Constitution has undergone a lengthy process over the years before its formal compositions. In fact, a number of legal developments contributed a lot in this direction. These developments, now acknowledged as the process of the constitutional development, are quite significant and these developments paved the way for the creation of an ideal constitution by a Constituent Assembly following a rigorous exercise.

CONSTITUENT ASSEMBLY

In accordance with the recommendation of the Cabinet Mission, which consisted of Lord Pethick-Lawrence, Sir Stafford Cripps and A.V. Alexander and which visited India in March 1946, the Constituent Assembly of India was elected by the Provincial Assemblies in July 1946. It had 389 members in all, including 93 representatives of Indian Princely States.

The important Committees of the Constituent Assembly were:

(*a*) **Union Powers Committee:** It had 9 members. Shri Jawaharlal Nehru was its Chairman;

(*b*) **Committee on Fundamental Rights and Minorities:** It had 54 members. Sardar Vallabhbhai Patel was its Chairman;

(*c*) **Steering Committee:** It had 3 members. Dr. K.M. Munshi (Chairman); Shri Gopalswamy Ayyangar and Shri Bishwanath Das;

(*d*) **Provincial Constitution Committee:** 25 members. Sardar Patel as Chairman;

(*e*) **Committee on Union Constitution:** 15 members. Pandit Nehru as Chairman.

The first session of the Assembly was held in New Delhi on December 9, 1946. It was attended by 207 members. Sachchidanand Sinha, as the oldest member of the Constituent Assembly, was elected provisional chairman of the session. However on December 11, 1946, Dr. Rajendra Prasad was elected as the Permanent Chairman of the Constituent Assembly.

THE LONG JOURNEY

- Demand for a Constituent Assembly composed of the people of India officially asserted by the Congress for the first time in 1935.
- Cripps' proposals of 1942 accepted this demand.
- The election for Indian Constituent Assembly held in 1946 according to the Cabinet Mission plan.
- First meeting of the Constituent Assembly for undivided India held on December 9, 1946.
- On 26 July, 1947, separate Constituent Assembly for Pakistan created.
- The sovereign Constituent Assembly for the Dominion of India (*i.e.,* excluding Pakistan) met for the first time on 14 August, 1947.
- Members of the Constituent Assembly indirectly elected.
- The electoral college consisted of members of the Provincial Legislative Assemblies (Lower Houses only).

- Each Province and each Indian State or group of States allotted seats in the Constituent Assembly proportional to their respective population (roughly in the ratio of one to a million).
- In all, provinces to elect 292 members and Indian states 93.
- Principle of Communal Electorate valid for election to the Constituent Assembly (Muslims, Sikhs, General).
- Method of election—proportional representation with single transferable vote.
- As the result of partition, membership of the CA reduced to 299.
- Constitution of India declared passed on 26th November, 1949.
- On 26th November, 1949, 284 members appended their signature to the Constitution.
- Drafting Committee of the Constituent Assembly chaired by Dr. Ambedkar.
- The Constitution underwent three readings before finalisation.
- Provisions relating to citizenship, elections, provisional parliament, temporary and transitional provisions came into effect on November 26, 1949.
- The Date of Commencement of Indian Constitution fixed for 26th January 1950.

Indian Constitution is a comprehensive document and it is the lengthiest written Constitution in the World.

The Preamble of the Constitution: "We the people of India, having solemnly resolved to Constitute India into a Sovereign, Socialist, Secular Democratic Republic and to secure to all its citizen."

Justice: Social, economic and political.

Liberty: Of thought, expression, belief, faith and worship.

Equality: Of status and of opportunity, and to promote among them all.

Fraternity: Assuring the dignity of the individual and the unity and integrity of the nation. In our Constituent Assembly, this twenty-sixth day of November, 1949, do hereby adopt, enact and give to ourselves this constitution."

SCHEDULES TO THE CONSTITUTION

The Constitution of India originally contained only eight schedules. Presently there are 12 schedules in the constitution.

First Schedule: It consists the list of the States and Union territories. ***Second Schedule:*** This Schedule is related to salary and allowances of the President, Governors, Speaker, Supreme Court and High Court Judges etc. ***Third Schedule:*** Contains forms of oath and affirmation. ***Fourth Schedule:*** Contains allocation of seats to each State and Union territory in the Council of States. ***Fifth Schedule:*** Provides for administration and control of scheduled areas and scheduled tribes. ***Sixth Schedule:*** Provides for administration of Tribal Areas in Assam, Meghalaya and Mizoram. ***Seventh Schedule:*** Distribution of powers and functions between the centre and state governments under three lists. ***Eighth Schedule:*** The languages recognised by Parliament. ***Ninth Schedule:*** It contains laws passed by the Union or States which cannot be taken to courts. ***Tenth Schedule:*** Provisions as to disqualification on the ground of political defection. ***Eleventh Schedule:*** Provisions regarding powers, authority etc. of Panchayati Raj institutions. ***Twelfth Schedule:*** Provisions regarding powers, authority etc. of Municipalities etc.

Foreign Sources of Indian Constitution

Foreign Sources	*Subject*
Britain	Parliamentary system, collective responsibilities of Cabinet
America	Fundamental right, Citizenship, Independent Judiciary, Judicial review
Canada	Division of powers
Ireland	Directive principles
Germany	Emergency provisions
Russia	Fundamental duties
Australia	Concurrent list

THE SUPREME COURT

The Supreme Court of India consists of the Chief Justice and other Judges whose number is prescribed by the Parliament from time to time. In 1950 there was a Chief Justice and there were 7 Judges. But the number of Judges continued increasing as per the need. The Supreme Court, at present, consists of the Chief Justice and 33 Judges.

The Chief Justice and other Judges of the Supreme Court are appointed by the President of India. For appointing the Chief Justice of India, the other Judges of the Supreme or High Courts may be consulted. Usually, the senior-most Judge in the Supreme Court is appointed as the Chief Justice. For the appointment of other Judges of the Supreme Court, the Chief Justice has to be consulted. Usually, the Chief Justice himself consults a collegium of the four senior-most Judges, and all of them need to agree for any candidate to be recommended for the appointment of a judge.

A person can be appointed as a Judge of the Supreme Court only if he/she:

I. is a citizen of India;

II. must have been at least a Judge of a High Court or of two or more such Courts in succession for at least five years; or

III. must have been an advocate of a High Court or of two or more such Courts in succession for at least ten years; or

IV. is, in the opinion of the President, a distinguished jurist.

Judges of the Supreme Court hold office till they attain the age of 65 years. But they may be removed from office by an order of the President, passed after an address by each House of Parliament supported by a special majority on the ground of proved misbehaviour or incapacity.

The Jurisdiction and Powers of the Supreme Court

The Supreme Court of India is a powerful judiciary. The Constitution of India has defined its jurisdiction and powers in detail, it has Original. Appellate and Advisory Jurisdictions Besides these jurisdictions, it has a few other important functions.

(*i*) **Original Jurisdiction:** The Supreme Court alone has the authority to hear directly certain cases. These are:

(*a*) Disputes between the Union government and one or more State governments,

(*b*) Disputes between two or more States,

(*c*) Disputes between the Government of India and one or more States on the one side and one or more States on the other side.

(*ii*) **Appellate Jurisdiction:** The power of a superior or higher court to hear and decide appeals against the judgment of the lower court is called appellate jurisdiction. The Supreme Court is a court of appeal for constitutional, civil and criminal cases. It can hear appeals against the judgments of the High Courts. It also has the power to review its own judgment. It may in its own discretion grant special lease to appeal against any judgment or order delivered or passed by any court or tribunal within the territory of India.

Moreover, an Appeal may come to the Supreme Court in any criminal case, if the High Court certifies that the case is fit for appeal to the Supreme Court. The special appellate power has become a handy weapon in the hands of the Court to review the decisions pertaining to elections and Labour and Industrial Tribunals.

(*iii*) **Advisory Jurisdiction:** The Supreme Court has a special advisory jurisdiction in matters which may specifically be referred to it by the President of India. If at any time, it appears to the President that a question of law or fact has arisen or is likely to arise, which is of such public importance that it is urgent to obtain the opinion of the Supreme Court on it, he/she may refer it to the Supreme Court. The Supreme Court may, after such hearing as it thinks fit, report to the President its opinion thereon. The report or the opinion of the Supreme Court is of course, not binding on the President. Similarly, there is no compulsion for the Court to give its advice.

(*iv*) **Judicial Review:** The Supreme Court of India has the power to examine the validity of laws or executive orders. The Supreme Court has the powers to interpret the Constitution, and through this it has assumed the power of judicial review.

(*v*) **Guardian of the Constitution:** As the interpreter of the Constitution, the Supreme Court has the power to protect and defend the Constitution. If the Court finds that any law or executive order is against the Constitution, the same can be declared unconstitutional or invalid. Similarly the Supreme Court also acts as the custodian and protector of Fundamental Rights.

PARLIAMENT

Parliament is the national legislature of the Indian Union. It consists of two Houses known as the Council of States or the Rajya Sabha and the House of People or Lok Sabha. The President is an integal part of Parliament.

Rajya Sabha

The Rajya Sabha is the Upper House of the Parliament and it is constituted of representatives from the States or the Constituent units of the Indian Union. It is a permanent body, one third of its members retiring after every two years. Its maximum strength is 250. Out of these, twelve members are nominated by the President from well-known personalities in the realm of Science, Art, Literature and Social Service. Rest of 238 representatives of the States and Union Territories are elected. Rajya Sabha at present consists of 245 members.

Lok Sabha

The Lok Sabha whose life is five years, is the Lower House of Parliament and comprises of members directly elected by the people. The House of the people (Lok Sabha) at present consists of 543 members directly elected from the states and Union Territories. Two members were nominated from the Anglo-Indian Community by the President, but by the 104th amendment of the constitution this provision have been abolished. The House of the People shall continue for five years (unless sooner dissolved) from the date of its meeting and no longer and the expiry of the said period of 5 years shall operate as dissolution of the House.

Parliamentary Committees

There are several Parliamentary Committees to assist the Parliament in its deliberations. These are appointed or elected by the respective Houses of Lok Sabha and Rajya Sabha on a motion made or are nominated by their presiding officers, i.e., the Speaker of Lok Sabha and the Chairman of Rajya Sabha respectively. Broadly, Parliamentary Committees are of two kinds–standing committees and ad-hoc committees. Among the Standing Committees, three are financial Committees:

(*i*) Public Account Committee;

(*ii*) Estimate Committee;

(*iii*) Public undertaking Committee.

Ad-hoc Committees are appointed as the need arises and cease to exist when the work is over.

Speaker of Lok Sabha

Speaker is elected by the Lok Sabha from among its members. The Speaker will have the final power to maintain order within the House of the People and to interpret its rules of procedure. Speaker decides whether a bill is a money bill or a non-money bill.

Table of Precedence

1. President
2. Vice-President
3. Prime Minister
4. Governors of States within their respective states
5. Former Presidents

5A. Deputy Prime Minister

6. Chief Justice of India, Speaker of Lok Sabha
7. Cabinet Ministers of the Union, Chief Ministers of States within their respective States, Deputy Chairman NITI Aayog

   Leaders of opposition in Rajya Sabha and Lok Sabha

7A. Holders of the Bharat Ratna Decoration

8. Ambassadors Extraordinary and Plenipotentiary and High Commissioners of Commonwealth Countries accredited to India
   Chief Ministers of States outside their respective States
9. Judges of the Supreme Court
10. Deputy Chairman Rajya Sabha, Deputy Chief Minister of States
    Deputy Speaker Lok Sabha, Members of the NITI Aayog, Minister of State of the Union and Other Minister in the Ministry of Defence.

PRESIDENT

The President is the Constitutional head of the Republic of India. He is more or less the titular head of the executive. Really speaking, he is the constitutional head but not the real executive. The real power is vested in the hands of the Council of Ministers.

Qualifications

(*i*) Indian citizen,
(*ii*) age not less than 35 years,
(*iii*) should have qualification for election to Lok Sabha,
(*iv*) should not hold any office of profit,
(*v*) should not be a Member of Parliament or State Legislature.

Powers

The Constitution has vested the President with the following powers:

(*i*) **Executive powers:** executive authority is exercised in his name. He is the supreme commander of armed forces and declares war and makes peace. He appoints all important executive officials, like Prime Minister, Governors etc.;

(*ii*) **Legislative Powers:** The President is a part of the Parliament; he summons and prorogues both the Houses jointly and separately; he nominates 12 members in Rajya Sabha. His assent to the bills is essential; money bills are introduced with his recommendation;

(*iii*) **Financial Powers:** He acts as a custodian of Contingency Fund; appoints Finance Commission;

(*iv*) **Judicial powers:** He appoints Chief Justice and other judges of the Supreme Court—he can seek the advice of the Chief Justice on any matter of public importance; he can grant pardon and reprieve, commute or suspend sentence; he is not answerable before any court;

(*v*) **Diplomatic powers:** He enjoys the right to represent India in international sphere; he has power to receive and send envoys, conclude international treaties etc.;

(*vi*) **Emergency Powers:** He enjoys extensive powers, dealing with three types of emergencies:

(*a*) emergency due to war or external aggression or internal rebellion;

(*b*) emergency due to the failure of constitutional machinery in the state; and

(*c*) emergency due to financial instability.

During emergencies, the President assumes extraordinary powers. The position of the President has been finally determined by 42nd Amendment. It has made it obligatory on the part of the President to act on the advice of the Council of Ministers.

Term and Emolument

The President holds the office for a period of five years. He is eligible for re-election. He draws a fix salary per month with various allowances. He is also entitled to rent free official residence called Rashtrapati Bhawan.

VICE-PRESIDENT

The Vice-President is elected by the elected members of the both Houses of the Parliament. A candidate for the office of Vice-President should be:

(*i*) above 35 years of age;
(*ii*) citizen of India;

(*iii*) eligible for election as a member of Rajya Sabha;

(*iv*) should not hold any office of profit;

(*v*) should not be a member of parliament; and

(*vi*) should not be of unsound mind.

Vice-President holds office for 5 years and can be removed from office earlier through a resolution passed by a two-third majority of Rajya Sabha agreed to by the Lok Sabha.

The Presiding Officer

Vice-President is the ex-officio chairman of Rajya Sabha and presides over the sessions of the Upper House. He performs all the duties of the President when the office of the President falls vacant due to the death, resignation or absence of the President. He draws a fix salary per month in his capacity of being the Chairman of the Rajya Sabha.

COUNCIL OF MINISTERS AND PRIME MINISTER

The Constitution of India provides for a parliamentary system of government under which the President is only a constitutional ruler and the real power is exercised by the Council of Ministers, headed by the Prime Minister. The members of the Council of Ministers hold office during the pleasure of the President but actually they stay in office as long as they enjoy the confidence of the majority in the Lok Sabha. As per the Constitution, the Council of Ministers is only an advisory body to assist the President but in reality, it enjoys extensive powers. Constitutionally, the executive authority has been vested in the President but in reality, these powers are exercised by the Prime Minister and the Council of Ministers.

PRIME MINISTER

The Prime Minister is the leader of the majority party in the Parliament and the President cannot exercise his discretion in the appointment of the Prime Minister. He stays in office till the majority of the members of Lok Sabha has confidence in him. He occupies an important position in relation to the Council of Ministers. He recommends the names of the persons to be included in the Council of Ministers. He allocates portfolios among them and can ask any minister to tender resignation. He can drop a minister while reshuffling the ministry. He coordinates the administration of various departments. He is the chief link between the President and the Council. He is the leader of the majority party and so, he has a great influence on the Parliament and the party. The Prime Minister enjoys such extensive powers as have been described as the virtual ruler of the country.

FUNDAMENTAL RIGHTS

Following fundamental rights are enjoyed by every Indian citizen, irrespective of caste, colour, creed and sex:

1. **Right to Equality:** No special privileges, no distinction on grounds of religion, caste, creed and sex.
2. **Right to Freedom:** The right to freedom of expression and speech, the right to choose one's own profession, the right to reside in any part of the Indian Union.
3. **Right to Freedom to Religion:** Except when it is in the interest of public order, morality, health or other conditions, everybody has the right to profess, practice and propagate his religion freely.
4. **Cultural and Educational Rights:** The Constitution provides that every community can run its own institutions to preserve its own culture and language.
5. **Right against Exploitation:** Traffic in human beings and forced labour and the employment of children under 14 years in factories or mines, are punishable offences.
6. **Rights to Constitutional Remedies:** When a citizen finds that any of his fundamental rights has been encroached upon, he can move the Supreme Court, which has been empowered to safeguard the fundamental rights of a citizen (Article 32).

Jurisdiction and Seat of High Courts

Name	Year	Territorial Jurisdiction	Seat
Allahabad	1866	Uttar Pradesh	Prayagraj (Bench at Lucknow)
Andhra Pradesh	2019	Andhra Pradesh	Amaravati
Bombay	1862	Maharashtra, Goa, Dadar and Nagar Haveli and Daman and Diu	Mumbai (Benches at Nagpur, Panaji and Aurangabad)
Calcutta	1862	West Bengal and Andaman & Nicobar Islands	Kolkata (Circuit Bench at Port Blair and Jalpaiguri)
Chhattisgarh	2000	Chhattisgarh	Bilaspur
Delhi	1966	Delhi	Delhi
Guwahati	1948	Assam, Nagaland, Mizoram and Arunachal Pradesh	Guwahati (Benches at Kohima, Aizawl and Itanagar)
Gujarat	1960	Gujarat	Ahmedabad
Himachal Pradesh	1971	Himachal Pradesh	Shimla
Jammu & Kashmir and Ladakh	1928	Jammu & Kashmir, Ladakh	Srinagar and Jammu
Jharkhand	2000	Jharkhand	Ranchi
Karnataka	1884	Karnataka	Bengaluru (Circuit Benches at Dharwar and Gulbarga)
Kerala	1958	Kerala & Lakshadweep Islands	Kochi
Madhya Pradesh	1956	Madhya Pradesh	Jabalpur (Benches at Gwalior and Indore)
Madras	1862	Tamil Nadu & Puducherry	Chennai (Bench at Madurai)
Orissa	1948	Odisha	Cuttack
Patna	1916	Bihar	Patna
Punjab and Haryana	1966	Punjab, Haryana and Chandigarh	Chandigarh
Rajasthan	1949	Rajasthan	Jodhpur (Bench at Jaipur)
Sikkim	1975	Sikkim	Gangtok
Uttarakhand	2000	Uttarakhand	Nainital
Tripura	2013	Tripura	Agartala
Meghalaya	2013	Meghalaya	Shillong
Manipur	2013	Manipur	Imphal
Telangana	2019	Telangana	Hyderabad

FUNDAMENTAL DUTIES

The fundamental duties for the Indian citizens have been incorporated in the Constitution through the Constitution (42nd) Amendment Act, 1976. These duties are:

(*i*) to abide by the Constitution and respect its ideals and institutions, the National Flag and the National Anthem;

(*ii*) to cherish and follow the noble deeds which inspired our national struggle for freedom;

(*iii*) to uphold and protect the sovereignty, unity and integrity of India;

(*iv*) to defend the country and render national service when called upon to do so;

(*v*) to promote harmony and the spirit of common brotherhood amongst all the people transcending religious, regional or sectional diversities and to renounce practices derogatory to the dignity of women;

(*vi*) to value and preserve the rich heritage of our composite culture;

(*vii*) to protect and improve natural environment including forests, lakes, rivers and wildlife, and to have compassion for living creatures;

(*viii*) to develop the scientific temper, humanism and the spirit of inquiry and reform;

(*ix*) to safeguard public property and to abjure violence;

(*x*) to strive towards excellence in all spheres of individual and collective activity so that the nation constantly rises to higher levels of endeavour and achievement.

(*xi*) who is parent or guardian to provide opportunities for education to his child or, as the case may be, ward between age of six and fourteen years.

DIRECTIVE PRINCIPLES OF STATE POLICY

The Directive Principles of State Policy are contained in Article 36 to 51 in Part IV of the constitutions. Directive principles are not enforceable through courts. Main aim of Directive principles is to provide social and economic base of a genuine democracy.

Some Important Directive Principles:

- Provisions for adequate means of livelihood for all citizens (Art. 39).
- Right to work (Art. 41).
- Right to human condition of work and maternity relief (Art. 42).
- Right to a living wage and condition of work ensuring decent standard of life of worker (Art. 43).
- Common Civil Code (Art. 44).
- Prohibit consumption of liquor (Art. 47).
- Prevent slaughter of useful cattle (Art. 48).
- Organise Panchayati Raj (Art. 40).
- Separate the judiciary from the executive (Art. 50).
- Protect and maintain places of historic monuments (Art. 49).
- International peace (Art. 51).

Voting Age: The voting age in the election to the Lok Sabha and State Legislative Assemblies has been reduced from 21 to 18 years by the Constitution (61st) Amendment Act, 1989.

GOVERNOR

The Governor is appointed by the President and holds office during the pleasure of the President. Apart from the power to appoint the council of ministers, if the governor finds that the government of state cannot be carried on in accordance with the provisions of the constitution (Art. 356), he may send his report to the President who may assume to himself the functions of the government of the state. (This is popularly known as 'President's Rule').

THE ATTORNEY GENERAL OF INDIA

The Attorney General of India is the first law officer of the Government of India. Though he is not a member of cabinet he has the right to speak in the

House of Parliament, but he has no right to vote. The Attorney General of India shall be appointed by the President and shall hold office during his pleasure.

His duty shall be to give advice on such legal matter from time to time as may be referred to him by the President.

COMPTROLLER & AUDITOR GENERAL OF INDIA (CAG)

The Comptroller and Auditor General of India is guardian of the public purse and it is his duty to see that not a *paisa* is spent out of consolidated fund of India or of a state without the authority of the appropriate legislature. He is appointed by President of India.

Status

- Appointed by the President.
- A person with long administrative experience & knowledge of accounts is appointed.
- Holds office for 6 yrs or till 65 yrs of age.
- The President can remove him only on the recommendation of the 2 houses of Parliament (as in case of judge of Supreme Court).

UNION PUBLIC SERVICE COMMISSION (U.P.S.C.)

The UPSC has one chairman and nine members. The members as well as the chairman are appointed by the President. Roughly, one half of the members of UPSC should be persons who have held important offices under the central or the state government for at least 10 years. They retire after 6 years. The chairman or a member of the UPSC can be removed from the office by the President but after referring the case to the supreme Court, which, after holding enquiry, recommends for the same. The functions of the UPSC are:

(*i*) to conduct examination for appointment to the services of the Union;

(*ii*) to advise the government on the methods of recruitment; and

(*iii*) to advise the government on disciplinary method affecting a person who is serving under the government of India.

INTER-STATE COUNCILS

Article 263 provides for inter-state councils. The power of the President to set up Inter-State Councils not only for advising upon disputes but also for investigating and discussing subjects in which some or all of the states, or the Union and one or more of the states have common interest.

STAFF SELECTION COMMISSION

The Union Government has constituted the Staff Selection Commission for recruitment to non-technical Group C and some of Group B posts in the central departments and in subordinate offices. The administrative Reforms Commission had recommended the setting up of such a Commission.

* * * * *

6. PLANNING IN INDIA

The need for planning was felt in India even before independence. A National Planning Committee was set up by the Indian National Congress as early as 1938. The Planning Commission was set up in 1950. It is an advisory body engaged in the task of meaningful national planning. The main objectives of India's Economic Planning are as follows : (*i*) securing an increase in National Income; (*ii*) achieving a planned rate of investment within a given period to bring the actual investment as a proportion of national income to a higher level; (*iii*) reducing inequality in the distribution of income and wealth; (*iv*) providing additional employment; (*v*) adopting measures to increase agricultural production, manufacturing capacity for producers and a favourable balance of payments.

Five Year Plans in India

Plans	Period	Investment (₹ Crore)	Objectives
First Plan	April 1, 1951–March 31, 1956	1,960	Priority to agriculture, electricity and irrigation.
Second Plan	April 1, 1956–March 31, 1961	4,672	Development of basic and heavy industries.
Third Plan	April 1, 1961–March 31, 1966	8,577	Long term development of India's economy.
Annual Plan	April 1, 1966–March 31, 1967	2,137	
Annual Plan	April 1, 1967–March 31, 1968	2,205	
Annual Plan	April 1, 1968–March 31, 1969	2,283	
Fourth Plan	April 1, 1969–March 31, 1974	15,779	Enlarge the income of rural population and supply of goods of mass consumption.
Fifth Plan	April 1, 1974–March 31, 1979	39,426	Attain increased self reliance and employment avenues.
Annual Plan	April 1, 1979–March 31, 1980	12,176	
Sixth Plan	April 1, 1980–March 31, 1985	1,09,292	Removal of unemployment
Seventh Plan	April 1, 1985–March 31, 1990	2,18,730	Food work and productivity were the basic priorities.
Eighth Plan	April, 1992–March 31, 1997	4,95,670	Raising employment
Ninth Plan	April 1, 1997–March 31, 2002	9,41,041	Agriculture and rural development
Tenth Plan	April 1, 2002–March 31, 2007	14,91,610	Growth rate 7.8 percent per annum.
Eleventh Plan	April 1, 2007–March 31, 2012	36,44,718	Literacy, Employment, Rural development & Transport development.
Twelfth Plan	April 1, 2012–March 31, 2017	43,30,000	Long term development of India's economy.

INDIA'S AMBITIOUS 15-YEAR VISION PLAN

Niti Aayog has come forward with a draft 15-year vision plan to catapult the country's economy to more than three times as compared to the present day. The new plan is set to replace the centralised five-year plans the country has been following for decades.

The new plan is accompanied by shorter sub-plans—a seven-year strategy for 2017-24, and a three-year 'Action Agenda' from 2017-18 to 2019-20. No less than 300 specific action points covering a wide range of sectors have been drawn up as part of the 15 year vision.

The salient features of 15-year vision plan are:

- India aims to more than triple the size of its economy in 15 years with gross domestic product (GDP) expected to rise to ₹ 469 lakh crores from ₹ 137 lakh crore in 2015-16. Per capita GDP is expected to rise by three times to ₹ 3,14,667 in 2015-2016.
- NITI Aayog plans to work closely with staes to boost infrastructure and services, including regions that require special attention. The gov-ernment made a big push for Goods and Services Tax (GST), urging the state governments to speed up the legislation of state GST bills.
- India's urban population is expected to increase by 22 crores by 2031. The plan is likely to lay emphasis on urban development, taking a note from China's elaborate long-term development agenda.
- The plan envisages a central body for overseeing the implemention of sustainable development goals. Specific goals will cover clean water, removing hunger, climate efforts, responsible consumption, clean energy, quality educaiton, reduced inequality and gender equality, among others.
- The NITI Aayog will work as a "collaborative federal body whose strength is in its ideas, rather than in administrative or financial control."

NITI AAYOG

The National Institution for Transforming India, also called NITI Aayog, was formed via a resolution of the Union Cabinet on January 1, 2015. NITI Aayog is the premier policy 'Think Tank' of the Government of India, providing both directional and policy inputs. While designing strategic and long term policies and programmes for the Government of India, NITI Aayog also provides relevant technical advice to the Centre and States. At the core of NITI Aayog's creation are two hubs - *Team India Hub* and the *Knowledge and Innovation Hub*. The Team India Hub leads the engagement of states with the Central government, while the Knowledge and Innovation Hub builds NITI's think-tank capabilities. These hubs reflect the two key tasks of the Aayog.

FINANCE COMMISSION

Article 280 of the Constitution provides for the appointment of a finance commission every five year. President appoints chairman and members of this commission. Finance commission are to recommend to President the basis for the distribution of the net proceeds of taxes between the centre and the states and the principles which should govern the grants-in-aid to be given to the states out of the consolidated funds of India.

NATIONAL DEVELOPMENT COUNCIL

The National Development Council, set-up in 1952, consists of representatives of the Central Government as well as the State governments. It is the supreme body insofar as planning is concerned and it determines policies, issues guidelines, reviews working of the plan and finally approves the plan. The Council consists of the Prime Minister (Chairman), all Union Cabinet Ministers, Chief Ministers of all States and Union Territories and the Vice Chairman and members of the NITI Aayog. For matters relating to Plans and planning, the Union Minister of Planning is responsible to the Parliament.

RESERVE BANK OF INDIA

It is the Central Bank of the country. The Reserve Bank of India was established in 1935 with a capital of ₹ 5 crore. This capital of ₹ 5 crore was divided into 5 lakh equity shares of ₹ 100 each. In the beginning the ownership of almost all the share capital was with the non-government shareholders. In order to prevent the centralisation of the equity shares in the hands of a few people, **the Reserve Bank of India was nationalised on January 1, 1949.**

Establishment Years of Major Financial Institutions of India

Institution	Year
• Imperial Bank of India	1921
• Reserve Bank of India (Nationalisation of RBI took place on January 1, 1949)	April 1, 1935
• Industrial Finance Corporation of India	1948
• State Bank of India	July 1, 1955
• Unit Trust of India	Feb. 1, 1964
• Bifurcation of UTI (UTI-I & UTI-II)	Feb. 2003
• IDBI	July 1964
• NABARD	July 12, 1982
• IRBI (Now it has been renamed a IIBIL since March 6, 1997)	March 20, 1985
• SIDBI	1990
• EXIM Bank	January 1, 1982
• National Housing Bank	July 1988
• Life Insurance Corporation (LIC)	September 1956
• General Insurance Corporation (GIC)	November 1972
• Regional Rural Banks	Oct. 2, 1975
• Technology Development & Information Co. of India Ltd.	1989
• Infrastructure Leasing & Financial Services Ltd.	1988
• Housing Development Finance Corporation Ltd. (HDFC)	1977

* * * * *

7. GENERAL SCIENCE

INVENTIONS AND DISCOVERIES

Important Inventions

Name of Invention	*Inventor*	*Nationality*	*Year*
Aeroplane	Orville & Wilbur Wright	U.S.A.	1903
Ball-Point Pen	John J. Loud	U.S.A.	1888
Barometer	Evangelista Torricelli	Italy	1644
Bicycle	Kirkpatrick Macmillan	Britain	1839-40
Bifocal Lens	Benjamin Franklin	U.S.A.	1780
Car (Petrol)	Karl Benz	Germany	1888
Celluloid	Alexander Parkes	Britain	1861
Cinema	Nicolas & Jean Lumiere	France	1895
Clock (mechanical)	I-Hsing & Liang Ling-Tsan	China	725
Diesel Engine	Rudolf Diesel	Germany	1895
Dynamo	Hypolite Pixii	France	1832
Electric Lamp	Thomas Alva Edison	U.S.A.	1879
Electric Motor (DC)	Zenobe Gramme	Belgium	1873
Electric Motor (AC)	Nikola Tesla	U.S.A.	1888
Electro-magnet	William Sturgeon	Britain	1824
Electronic Computer	Dr. Alan M. Turing	Britain	1943
Film (moving outlines)	Louis Prince	France	1885
Film (musical sound)	Dr. Le de Forest	U.S.A.	1923
Fountain Pen	Lewis E. Waterman	U.S.A.	1884
Gramophone	Thomas Alva Edison	U.S.A.	1878
Helicopter	Etienne Oehmichen	France	1924
Jet Engine	Sir Frank Whittle	Britain	1937
Laser	Charles H. Townes	U.S.A.	1960
Lift (Mechanical)	Elisha G. Otis	U.S.A.	1852
Locomotive	Richard Trevithick	Britain	1804
Machine Gun	James Puckle	Britain	1718
Microphone	Alexander Graham Bell	U.S.A.	1876
Microscope	Z. Janssen	Netherlands	1590
Motor Cycle	G. Daimler	Germany	1885
Photography (on film)	John Carbutt	U.S.A.	1888
Printing Press	Johann Gutenberg	Germany	c.1455
Razor (safety)	King C. Gillette	U.S.A.	1895
Refrigerator	James Harrison & Alexander Catlin	U.S.A.	1850

Name of Invention	Inventor	Nationality	Year
Safety Pin	Walter Hunt	U.S.A.	1849
Sewing machine	Barthelemy Thimmonnier	France	1829
Ship (steam)	J.C. Perier	France	1775
Ship (turbine)	Hon. Sir C. Parsons	Britain	1894
Skyscraper	W. Le Baron Jenny	U.S.A.	1882
Slide Rule	William Oughtred	Britain	1621
Steam Engine (condenser)	James Watt	Britain	1765
Steel Production	Henry Bessemer	Britain	1855
Steel (stainless)	Harry Brearley	Britain	1913
Submarine	David Bushnell	U.S.A.	1776
Tank	Sir Ernest Swinton	Britain	1914
Telegraph	M. Lammond	France	1787
Telegraph Code	Samuel F.B. Morse	U.S.A.	1837
Telephone (perfected)	Alexander Graham Bell	U.S.A.	1876
Television (mechanical)	John Logie Baird	Britain	1926
Television (electronic)	P.T. Farnsworth	U.S.A.	1927
Thermometer	Galileo Galilei	Italy	1593
Transformer	Michael Faraday	Britain	1831
Transistor	Bardeen, Shockley & Brattain	U.S.A.	1948
Washing Machine (elec.)	Hurley Machine Co.	U.S.A.	1907
Zip-Fastener	W.L. Judson	U.S.A.	1891

Important Discoveries

Discovery	Discoverer	Nationality	Year
Aluminium	Hans Christian Oerstedt	Denmark	1827
Atomic number	Henry Moseley	England	1913
Atomic structure of matter	John Dalton	England	1803
Chlorine	C.W. Scheele	Sweden	1774
Electromagnetic induction	Michael Faraday	England	1831
Electromagnetic waves	Heinrich Hertz	Germany	1886
Electromagnetism	Hans Christian Oersted	Denmark	1920
Electron	Sir Joseph Thomson	England	1897
General theory of relativity	Albert Einstein	Switzerland	1915
Hydrogen	Henry Cavendish	England	1766
Law of electric conduction	Georg Ohm	Germany	1827
Law of electromagnetism	Andre Ampere	France	1826
Law of falling bodies	Galileo	Italy	1590
Laws of gravitation & motion	Isaac Newton	England	1687
Laws of planetary motion	Johannes Kepler	Germany	1609-19
Magnesium	Sir Humphry Davy	England	1808
Neptune (Planet)	Johann Galle	Germany	1846
Neutron	James Chadwick	England	1932
Nickel	Axel Cronstedt	Sweden	1751
Nitrogen	Daniel Rutherford	England	1772

Discovery	Discoverer	Nationality	Year
Oxygen	Joseph Priestly C.W. Scheele	England Sweden	1772
Ozone	Christian Schonbein	Germany	1839
Pluto (Planet)	Clyde Tombaugh	U.S.A	1930
Plutonium	G.T. Seaborg	U.S.A	1940
Proton	Ernest Rutherford	England	1919
Quantum Theory	Max Planck	Germany	1900
Radioactivity	Antoine Bacquerel	France	1896
Radium	Pierre & Marie Curie	France	1898
Silicon	Jons Berzelius	Sweden	1824
Special theory of relativity	Albert Einstein	Switzerland	1905
Sun as centre of solar system	Copernicus	Poland	1543
Uranium	Martin Klaproth	Germany	1789
Uranus (Planet)	William Herschel	England	1781
X-rays	Wilhelm Roentgen	Germany	1895

Geographical Explorations/Discoveries

Place	Explorer/Discoverer	Nationality	Year
America	Christopher Columbus	Italy	1492
Hawaii Islands (Sandwich Islands)	Captain James Cook	England	1778
Newfoundland	John Cabot	England	1497
New Zealand	Abel Janszoon Tasman	Holland	1642
North Pole	Robert Peary	USA	1909
Sea Route to India (via Cape of Good Hope)	Vasco da Gama	Portugal	1498
South Pole	Roald Amundsen	Norway	1911

Scientific Instruments

Name of Instrument	Used for
Altimeter	measuring altitude
Ammeter	measuring strength of an electric current
Anemometer	measuring the velocity of wind
Audiometer	measuring level of hearing
Barometer	measuring atmospheric pressure
Callipers	measuring the internal and external diameters of tubes
Calorimeter	measuring quantity of heat
Compass	finding out direction
Dynamo	converting mechanical energy into electrical energy
Eudiometer	measuring volume changes during chemical reactions between gases
Galvanometer	detecting and determining the strength of small electric currents
Hydrometer	measuring specific gravity of a liquid
Hygrometer	measuring the humidity in the atmosphere
Lactometer	measuring the purity of milk
Manometer	measuring the gaseous pressure
Micrometer	measuring minute distances, angles, etc.

Name of Instrument	Used for
Microscope	seeing magnified view of very small objects
Periscope	with the help of this instrument an observer in a submarine can see what is going on the surface of the sea
Photometer	measuring intensity of light from distant stars
Pyrometer	measuring high temperatures
Radar	detecting and finding the presence and location of moving objects like aircraft, missile, etc.
Radiometer	measuring the emission of radiant energy
Rain Gauge	measuring the amount of rainfall
Seismograph	measuring and recording the intensity and origin of earthquake shocks
Sextant	measuring altitude and angular distances between two objects or heavenly bodies
Spectrometer	measuring the refractive indices
Spherometer	measuring the curvature of spherical objects/surface
Sphygmomanometer	measuring blood pressure
Stethoscope	ascertaining the condition of heart and lungs by listening to their function
Stroboscope	viewing objects that are moving rapidly with a periodic motion as if they were at rest
Tachometer	measuring the rate of revolution or angular speed of a revolving shaft
Telescope	viewing magnified images of distant objects
Theodolite	measuring the horizontal and vertical angles
Thermocouple	measuring the temperature inside furnaces and jet engines
Thermometer	measuring human body temperature
Thermostat	regulating constant temperature
Ultrasonoscope	measuring utrasonic sounds
Viscometer	measuring the viscosity of a fluid
Voltmeter	measuring potential difference between two points.

Diseases and the Parts of Body they Affect

Disease	Part of body affected
AIDS	Immune system of body
Arthritis	Inflammation of joints
Asthma	Lungs
Cataract	Eyes
Conjunctivitis	Eyes
Diabetes	Pancreas
Diphtheria	Throat
Glaucoma	Eyes
Eczema	Skin
Goitre	Front of the neck (due to enlargement cf thyroid gland)
Gout	Joints of bone

Disease	Part of body affected
Jaundice	Liver
Meningitis	Brain or spinal cord
Pleurisy	Pleura (inflammation of)
Polio	motor neurons
Pneumonia	Lungs
Pyorrhoea	Sockets of teeth
Tuberculosis	Lungs
Typhoid	Intestine
Malaria	Spleen
Leukaemia	Blood
Rickets	Bones

8. SPACE RESEARCH

First in Space

First creator of rules regarding space research	—	Isaac Newton
First artificial satellite launched in space	—	Sputnik-1 (1957)
First living being sent in space	—	Louika (a dog)
Firstever manned spacecraft	—	Vostok-I
First man in space	—	Yuri Gagarin, U.S.S.R. (1961)
First woman in space	—	Valentina Tereshkova, U.S.S.R. (June 1963)
First man who moved in space out of the spacecraft	—	Alexi Livonov, U.S.S.R. (June 1965)
First person to land on moon	—	Neil Armstrong, America (21st July, 1969)
First fourwheeled carriage without human being on moon	—	Leunokhev-I, U.S.S.R. (1970)
First space lab in orbit	—	Skylab (America, 1973)
First space shuttle	—	Columbia (America, 1981)
First Indian (man) in space	—	Squadron leader—Rakesh Sharma (13th April, 1984)
First Indian (Woman) in space	—	Kalpana Chawla (19th Nov., 1997)
First American woman in space	—	Sailyride (1983)
First spacecraft on Mars	—	Pathfinder (6 July, 1997)
First woman who lead spacecraft	—	Allin Collis (America)
First spacecraft without man	—	Shenzoo, China (20th Nov. 1999)

Indian Space Programme : At a Glance

Satellite	*Date*	*Type*	*Launch Vehicle*	*Result*
Aryabhatta	19-04-75	Scientific	Cosmos	successful
Bhaskara I	07-06-79	Geosurvey	Cosmos	successful
Rohini	10-08-79	Geosurvey	S.L.V.3	unsuccessful
Rohini D-1	18-07-80	Geosurvey	S.L.V.3	successful
Rohini	31-05-81	Scientific	S.L.V.3	successful
Apple	19-06-81	Communication	Ariane	successful
Bhaskara II	20-11-81	Geosurvey	Cosonos	successful
INSAT-1A	10-04-82	Multipurpose	Delta	unsuccessful
Rohini	17-04-83	Scientific	S.L.V.3	successful
INSAT-1B	30-08-83	Multipurpose	Space Shuttle	successful
SROSS I	24-03-87	Technical	ASLV-D1	unsuccessful
IRS-1A	17-03-88	Remote sensing	Vostok	successful
INSAT-1D	12-06-90	Multipurpose	Delta	successful

Satellite	Date	Type	Launch Vehicle	Result
IRS-1B	29-08-91	Remote sensing	Vostok	successful
IRS-P3	20-03-96	Remote sensing	PSLV-D3	successful
IRS-ID	29-09-97	Remote sensing	PSLV	successful
G-SAT-1	18-04-2001	Multipurpose	GSLV-D	successful
INSAT-3C	24-01-2002	Communication	Ariane-4	successful
CARTOSAT-1 & HAMSAT	05-05-2005	Maping and Communication	PSLV-C6	successful
CARTOSAT-2	10-01-2007	Communication	PSLV-C7	successful
INSAT-4CR	02-09-2007	Communication	GSLV-F04	successful
CARTOSAT-2A	28-04-2008	Communication	PSLV-C9	successful
Chandrayaan-I	22-10-2008	Maping and Scientific	PSLV-C11	successful
Oceansat-2	24-09-2009	Remote Sensing	PSLV-C14	successful
CARTOSAT-2B	12-07-2010	Communication	PSLV-C15	successful
Megha-Tropiques	12-10-2011	Maping and Scientific	PSLV-C18	successful
RISAT-1	26-04-2012	Remote Sensing	PSLV-C19	successful
Spot-6	09-09-2012	Remote Sensing	PSLV-C21	successful
SARAL	25-02-2013	Scientific	PSLV-C20	successful
GSAT-7	30-08-2013	Defence	Ariane-5	successful
MOM	5-11-2013	Mapping	PSLV-C25	successful
GSAT-14	05-01-2014	Communication	GSLV-D5	successful
IRNSS-1B	04-04-2014	Mapping and Scientific	PSLV-C24	successful
Spot-7	30-06-2014	Remote Sensing	PSLV-C23	successful
GSAT-16	07-12-2014	Communication	Ariane-5	successful
IRNSS-1D	28-03-2015	Mapping and Scientific	PSLV-C27	successful
GSAT-6	27-08-2015	Communication	GSLV-D6	successful
Astrosat	28-09-2015	Mapping and Scientific	PSLV-C30	successful
GSAT-15	11-11-2015	Communication	Ariane-5	successful
TELEOS-1 & others	16-12-2015	Mapping and Scientific	PSLV-C29	successful
IRNSS-1E	20-01-2016	Mapping and Scientific	PSLV-C31	successful
IRNSS-1F	10-03-2016	Mapping and Scientific	PSLV-C32	successful
IRNSS-1G	28-04-2016	Mapping and Scientific	PSLV-C33	successful
CARTOSAT-2 & others	22-06-2016	Mapping and Scientific	PSLV-C34	successful
INSAT-3DR	08-09-2016	Meteorology	GSLV-F05	successful
SCATSAT-1 & others	26-09-2016	Multipurpose	PSLV-C35	successful
CARTOSAT-2 & 103	15-02-2017	Multipurpose	PSLV-C37	successful
GSAT-9	06-05-2017	Communications	GSLVMK-II	successful
GSAT-19	05-06-2017	Communications	GSLVMK-III-DI	successful
CARTOSAT-2E	23-06-2017	Earth Sciences	PSLV-C38	successful
GSAT-17	29-06-2017	Communications	Ariane-5 ECA	successful
GSAT-7A	19-12-2018	Military Satellite	GSLV-MKII-F11	successful
KalamSAT-V2	23-01-2019	Student Satellite	PSLV-C44	successful
Chandrayaan-2	22-07-2019	Lunar Exploration	GSLV-MKIII MO1	—
Cartosat-3	27-11-2019	Earth Imaging Satellite	PSLV-C47	successful
GSAT-30	17-01-2020	Communication	Ariane-5	successful
E0S-01	07-11-2020	Earth Observation	PSLV-C49	successful
Amezonia & 19 others	28-02-2021	Communication	PSLV-C51	successful
E0S-04	14-02-2022	Radar Imaging	PSLV-C52	successful
TelEOS-02 and LUMILITE-4	22-04-2023	Multipurpose	PSLV-C55	successful
Chandrayaan-3	14-07-2023	Lunar Exploration	LVM3M4	successful
Aditya-L1	02-09-2023	Solar Energy Observation	PSLV-C57	successful

✸ ✸ ✸ ✸ ✸

9. INDIAN HISTORY

Famous Sites of Indus Valley Civilization

Name of Site	Year of Excavation	River/ Sea coast	Discoverer
Harappa (Montgomery–Pakistan)	1921	Ravi River	Dayaram Sahney
Mohanjodaro (Larkana–Pakistan)	1922	Indus River	Rakhal Das Banerjee
Chanhudaro (Sindh–Pakistan)	1931	Indus River	N.G. Mazumdar
Alamgir pur (Meerut – U.P.)	1952-55	Hindan River	Yagyadatta Sharma
Ropar (Punjab)	1953	Sutlej River	Yagyadatta Sharma
Rangpur (Kathiabar–Gujarat)	1953	Bhabar River	Madho Swaroop Vatsa, Rang Nath Rao
Kotdigi (Sindh–Pakistan)	1953	Indus River	Fazal Ahmed Khan
Lothal (Ahmedabad–Gujarat)	1954	Bhogwa River	Rang Nath Rao
Kalibanga (Ganganagar–Rajasthan)	1961	Ghaggar	Brajwasi Lal
Surkotara (Kutch–Gujarat)	1967	Ghaggar River	Ravindra Singh Vishta
Banawali (Hissar–Haryana)	1973	Ghaggar River	Ravindra Singh Vishta
Balakote	1979	Arabian Sea	George F. Dales
Dhaulavira (Gujarat)	1963-68	—	J.P. Joshi
	1990-91	—	Dr. R.S. Vishta

Wellknown Quotations

"Swarajya is My Birthright"	— Bal Gangadhar Tilak
"Give me blood, I shall give you freedom"	— Netajee Subhash Chandra Bose
"Inqalab Zindabad"	— Bhagat Singh
Saare Jahan Se Achcha, Hindustan Hamara"	— Dr. Mohammed Iqbal
"Dilli Chalo"	— Subhash Chandra Bose
"Sarfaroshi ki tamanna, Ab Hamare Dil Mein Hai."	-- Ram Prasad Bismil
"I am socialist by nature".	— Jawahar Lal Nehru
"Go to Vedas"	— Swami Dayanand
"Aaram Haram Hai"	— Jawahar Lal Nehru
"Jai Jawan, Jai Kisan"	— Lal Bahadur Shastri
"Jai Jawan, Jai Kisan, Jai Vigyan"	— Atal Bihari Vajpayee
"Speak less, work more"	— Sanjay Gandhi
"Vijayee Vishwa Tiranga Pyara"	— Shyam Lal Gupta

"Quit India"	— Mahatma Gandhi
"Hindi, Hindu, Hindustan"	— Bhartendu Harishchandra
"Purna Swarajya"	— Jawahar Lal Nehru
"Every lathi blow inflicted on my body will prove a nail in British coffin"	— Lala Lajpat Rai
"Jai Hind"	— Subhash Chandra Bose
"Do or die"	— Mahatma Gandhi
"Who lives if India dies"	— Jawahar Lal Nehru
"Vande Mataram"	— Bankim Chandra Chatterjee
"Jana Gana Mana Adhinayaka Jai Hai"	—Rabindranath Tagore
"Hate sin, not the sinner."	— Mahatma Gandhi
"Service of the people is the service of God"	— Swami Vivekananda
"Truth and non-violence are my God."	— Mahatma Gandhi

Battles and Wars in India

War	Year	Result
Battle of Kalinga	(261 B.C.)	Ashoka defeated the king of Kalinga
Second battle of Tarain	(1192 A.D.)	Muhammad Gori defeated Prithviraj Chauhan
First battle of Panipat	(1526 A.D.)	Babar defeated Ibrahim Lodi
Battle of Khanwa	(1527 A.D.)	Babar defeated Rana Sanga
Battle of Chausa	(1539 A.D.)	Shershah Suri defeated Humayun and became ruler of Delhi
Second Battle of Panipat	(1556 A.D.)	Akbar defeated Hemu
Battle of Talikota	(1565 A.D.)	Allied forces of Bijapur, Bidar, Golkunda and Ahamadnagar defeated the King of Vijay Nagar
Battle of Haldighati	(1576 A.D.)	Some historian say that this battle was indecisive but some say that Rana Pratap was defeated by Akbar.
Battle of Palasey	(1757 A.D.)	British forces defeated Nawab of Bengal Sirajudoulla
Battle of Wandiwash	(1760 A.D.)	British forces defeated the French
Third battle of Panipat	(1761 A.D.)	Maratha were defeated by Ahmad Shah Abadəli
Battle of Buxar	(1764 A.D.)	British forces defeated the combined forces of Mir Quasim, Shah Alam Mughal empire and Awadh's Nawab
Third Anglo-Maratha War	(1792 A.D.)	Maratha were conclusively defeated
Fourth Anglo-Mysore War	(1799 A.D.)	Tipu Sultan died fighting the British forces
Second Anglo-Sikh War	(1848 A.D.)	British forces annexed Punjab from Sikh rulers
Indo-China War	(1962 A.D.)	China attacked India unilaterally and annexed some area
Indo-Pak War	(1965 A.D.)	Pakistan attacked India but had to suffer severe setbacks
Indo-Pak War	(1971 A.D.)	Pak declared war against India.

*****

10. WORLD GEOGRAPHY

Earth: The earth constitutes land, water and air. Land is made up of rocks and soil. It is distributed in continents and islands. The water found in oceans, seas, lakes, etc. occupies about 2/3 of the earth's surface. The earth is surrounded by a cover of air, called atmosphere, which extends up to several hundred kilometres above its surface.

Shape: In ancient times people believed that the earth was flat in shape. Greek philosopher Pythagoras (6th century BC) was the first person to declare that the earth was round. After careful measurement, the scientists have found that the earth is slightly oblate (flattened at poles) and not exactly round.

Motions: The earth has two motions: *(i) Rotation:* Earth makes a complete round on its axis once each 24 hours (more exactly 23 hours, 56 minutes and 4.09 seconds). It causes days and night on the earth. *(ii) Revolution:* The earth makes a complete round of the Sun in one year. This revolution of earth produces alternate seasons.

Some Facts: **(1)** Equal Day and Night — March 21 and September 23. **(2)** Longest Day — June 21. **(3)** Shortest Day — December 22. **(4)** The sunlight takes eight minutes in travelling from the Sun to the Earth. **(5)** Average speed of the earth in orbit ---- 66,600 miles (107,220 km) per hour. **(6)** Earth's equatorial diameter is about 7926 miles (12,756 km). **(7)** Water (oceans, seas, lakes and rivers) occupies nearly 75 per cent of the surface of the earth. **(8)** Earth's average distance from the Moon — 2,38,857 miles (3,84,400 km). **(9)** Earth's average distance from the Sun — 93 million miles (149.4 million km).

Greenwich Time: It is the local time of the Greenwich observatory in London on 0° meridian. Greenwich time is international standard time.

International Date Line: Half way round the earth from the Greenwich is International Date Line on 180° longitude. It runs down mid-Pacific. It is one day earlier on the east of this line than it is on the west of the line. When it is Monday east of the line, it is Tuesday west of the line.

Zones: On the basis of temperature and distribution of solar heat on the surface of the earth, the earth has been divided into five zones: (1) Torrid Zone, (2) North Temperate Zone, (3) South Temperate Zone, (4) Arctic Zone, and (5) Antarctic Zone.

Continents: Large land masses forming large geographical divisions are called continents. There are seven continents: (1) Asia (29.5%), (2) Africa (20%), (3) Europe (6.5%), (4) North America (16.3%), (5) South America (11.8%), (6) Australia (5.2%), and (7) Antarctica (9.6%).

Highest Mountain Peaks: (1) Everest (Asia-8848 metres), (2) Aconcagua (South America-6960 metres), (3) Mckinley (North America-6194 metres), (4) Kilimanjaro (Africa-5895 metres), (5) Elbrus (Europe-5642 metres), (6) Vinson Massif (Antarctica-5140 metres), (7) Kosciusko (Australia-2228 metres).

Largest Oceans: (1) Pacific Ocean (The largest, covers almost 1/3 of the earth's total area, and the deepest about 6.8 miles at Mariana Trench in western Pacific); (2) Atlantic Ocean, and (3) Indian Ocean. Other seas and gulfs are — the Mediterranean Sea, South China Sea, Bering Sea, Caribbean Sea, East China Sea, Sea of Japan, North Sea, Baltic Sea, Hudson Bay and Gulf of Mexico.

Longest Rivers: (1) Nile (6650 km-Africa), (2) Amazon (6570 km-South America), (3) Mississippi-Missouri (5970 km-North America), (4) Yangtze Kiang (5470 km-Asia), (5) Ob Irtysh (5150 km-Europe), (6) Congo (4666 km-Africa).

Highest Waterfalls: (1) Angel (807 m-Venezuela), (2) Mongefossen (774 m-Norway), (3) Kukenaam (610 m-Venezuela), (4) Ribbon (491 m-USA), (5) King George VI (487 m-Guyana), (6) Upper Yosemite (435 m-USA).

Great Deserts: (1) Sahara (94 lakh sq km-North Africa), (2) Libyan (11.65 lakh sq km-North Africa), (3) Australian (16 lakh sq km-Australia), (4) Gobi (13 lakh sq km-Mongolia), (5) Great Victoria (6,47,000 sq km-Australia), (6) Syrian (5,20,000 sq km Arabia), (7) Arabian (23,30,000 sq km Arabia).

Largest Islands: (1) Greenland (21,75,600 sq km) (2) New Guinea (7,77,000 sq km), (3) Borneo (7,25,545 sq km), (4) Malagasy (5,90,000 sq km), (5) Baffin Island (4,76,070 sq km).

Major Producers of Crops, Minerals and Industrial goods

Coal	China, USA, India, Australia, Indonesia, Russia
Cocoa	Cote d'Ivaire, Ghana, Indonesia, Nigeria
Coffee	Brazil, Vietnam, Columbia, Indonesia
Copper	Chile, Peru, China, USA
Cotton	China, India, USA, Pakistan, Brazil
Gold	China, Australia, Russia, USA, Canada
Grapes	China, Italy, USA, France, Spain
Iron ore	Australia, Brazil, China, India
Jute	India, Bangladesh, China
Manganese	South Africa, China, Australia
Petroleum	Russia, Saudi Arabia, USA, Iraq
Rice	China, India, Indonesia, Bangladesh
Rubber	Thailand, Indonesia, Malaysia, Vietnam, India
Silk	China, India, Uzbekistan, Thailand
Silver	Mexico, Peru, China, Chili
Steel	China, Japan, India, USA
Tea	China, India, Kenya, Sri Lanka
Wheat	China, India, USA, France, Russia
Diamond	Russia, Australia, Congo, Botswana
Tobacco	China, Brazil, India, USA, Indonesia

The Highest, Biggest and Longest in the World

Airport	*Largest*	King Fahd International Airport, Dammon (Saudi Arabia)
Animal	*Tallest*	Giraffe (Average height 6.09 m)
	Largest & Heaviest	Blue Whale (190 tonnes)
	Longest recorded	Boot lace Worm (55 m)
	Fastest	Cheetah (Approximately 100 km/hr)
Bay	*With max. shore line*	Hudson Bay (Canada: 12268 km)
	With maximum area	Bay of Bengal (India: 217 million hc)
Building	*Tallest*	Burj Khalifa in Dubai (818 meter)
Canal	*Big ship (longest)*	Suez Canal (160 km) Busiest Kiel Canal (North Sea)
Church	*Largest*	Basilica of St. Peter (Vatican City Rome–Area 23000 sq. m.
Continent	*biggest*	Asia (31,845,872 km^2)
	Smallest	Australia Mainland (Area 76,17,930 km^2)

Country,	*Largest in Population*	China (over 139.7 crore)
	Largest in Area	Russia (17,098,242 sq. km)
	With largest electorate	India (over 90 crores)
	Smallest independent	State of Vatican City (0.44 km^2)
Delta	*Largest*	Sundarban's Ganga-Brahmaputra delta (1,05,000 sq. km)
Epic	*Longest*	Mahabharata
Film	*Most Oscars*	Ben Hur (11 Oscars—1959); Titanic (11 Oscars—1998); The Lord of Rings : The Return of the King (11 Oscars—2003).
Island	*Biggest*	Greenland (now known as Kalaatdlit Nunaat–2,175,600 sq km)
Lake	*Largest*	Caspian Sea (Azerbaijan, Russia, Iran border: 37.18 lakh km^2)
	Deepest	Baikal (Siberia)
	Largest (fresh water)	Superior Lake (USA—Canada border: 82,350 km^2)
Mountain	*Highest peak*	Mt. Everest (8848 m; Nepal)
	Highest range	Himalayas, Asia (upto 4200 m)
	Greatest mountain range	Himalaya-Karakoram (96 out of 109 peaks over 7315 m are here)
Ocean	*Largest and Deepest*	The Pacific (Area: 166,240,000 km^2; Depth: 10,924 m)
Planet	*Biggest*	Jupiter (equatorial diameter 142984 km)
	Brightest, hottest and nearest to Earth	Venus
	Nearest to Sun	Mercury
Plateau	*Highest*	Tibetan Plateau (Central Asia: 4900 m)
Platform	*Longest (rail)*	Shri Siddharoodha Swamiji Railway Station, Hubballi, Karnataka (India)
Religion	*Oldest*	Hinduism
Religion	*Largest*	Christianity
Rivers	*Longest*	(i) Nile (6650 km) (ii) Amazon (6437 km)
Sea	*Largest*	South China Sea (2,974,600 sq. km)
	Largest (inland)	Mediterranean
Star	*Brightest*	Sirius A (also called Dog Star)
Swimming course	*Longest recognised*	English Channel
Tunnel	*Longest (railway)*	Gotthard Base Rail Tunnel (Switzerland; 57.1 km)
	Largest (road)	Laerdal, Norway (24.51 km)
Wall	*Longest*	Great Wall of China (main length 3460 km; branches length 2860 km)
Waterfall	*Highest*	Salto-Angcl (in Venezuela on a branch of river Carrao, 807 m.)

Capital & Currencies

Country	Capital	Currency
✶ Afghanistan	Kabul	Afghani
✶ Albania	Tirana	Lek
✶ Algeria	Algiers	Dinar
✶ Angola	Luanda	New Kwanza
✶ Argentina	Buenos Aires	Peso
✶ Armenia	Yeravan	Dram
✶ Australia	Canberra	Dollar
✶ Austria	Vienna	Euro
✶ Azerbaijan	Baku	Manat
✶ Bahrain	Manama	Dinar
✶ Bangladesh	Dhaka	Taka
✶ Barbados	Bridgetown	Dollar
✶ Belarus	Minsk	Ruble
✶ Belgium	Brussels	Euro
✶ Benin	Porto Novo	Franc
✶ Bhutan	Thimphu	Ngultrum[1]
✶ Bolivia	La paz	Dollar
✶ Botswana	Gaborone	Pula
✶ Brazil	Brasilia	Real
✶ Bosnia Herzegovina	Sarajevo	Dinar
✶ Bulgaria	Sofia	Lev
✶ Cambodia	Phnom-Penh	Riel
✶ Canada	Ottawa	Dollar
✶ Chile	Santiago	Peso
✶ China	Beijing	Yuan
✶ Colombia	Bogota	Peso
✶ Congo	Brazzaville	Franc
✶ Croatia	Zagreb	Kuna
✶ Cuba	Havana	Peso
✶ Cyprus	Nicosia	Euro
✶ Czech Republic	Prague	Koruna
✶ Denmark	Copenhagen	Krone
✶ Ecuador	Quito	Sucre
✶ Egypt	Cairo	Pound
✶ Estonia	Tallinn	Euro
✶ Ethiopia	Addis Ababa	Birr
✶ Fiji	Suva	Dollar
✶ Finland	Helsinki	Euro
✶ France	Paris	Euro
✶ Georgia	Tbilisi	Lari
✶ Germany	Berlin	Euro
✶ Ghana	Accra	Cedi
✶ Greece	Athens	Euro
✶ Guatemala	Guatemala City	Quetzal

Country	Capital	Currency
✶ Guyana	George Town	Dollar
✶ Hungary	Budapest	Forint
✶ Iceland	Reykjavik	Krona
✶ India	New Delhi	Rupee
✶ Indonesia	Jakarta	Rupiah
✶ Iran	Teheran	Rial
✶ Iraq	Baghdad	Dinar
✶ Ireland	Dublin	Euro
✶ Israel	Jerusalem	Shekel
✶ Italy	Rome	Euro
✶ Jamaica	Kingston	Dollar
✶ Japan	Tokyo	Yen
✶ Jordan	Amman	Dinar
✶ Kazakhstan	Akmola	Tenge
✶ Kenya	Nairobi	Shilling
✶ Korea (S)	Seoul	Won
✶ Korea (N)	Pyongyang	Won
✶ Kyrgyzstan	Bishkek	Som
✶ Kuwait	Kuwait City	Dinar
✶ Laos	Vientiane	Kip
✶ Latvia	Riga	Euro
✶ Lebanon	Beirut	Pound
✶ Liberia	Monrovia	Dollar
✶ Libya	Tripoli	Dinar
✶ Lithuania	Vilnius	Litas
✶ Luxembourg	Luxembourg	Euro
✶ Macedonia	Skopje	Dinar
✶ Malawi	Lilongwe	Kwacha
✶ Malaysia	Kuala Lumpur	Ringgit
✶ Maldives	Male	Rufiyaa
✶ Mali	Bamako	Franc
✶ Mauritius	Port Louis	Rupee
✶ Mexico	Mexico City	Peso
✶ Moldavia	Chisinau	Leu
✶ Mongolia	Ulan Bator	Tugrik
✶ Morocco	Rabat	Dirham
✶ Mozambique	Maputo	Metical
✶ Myanmar	Nay Pyi Taw	Kyat
✶ Namibia	Winohoek	Dollar
✶ Nepal	Kathmandu	Rupee
✶ Netherlands	Amsterdam	Euro
✶ New Zealand	Wellington	Dollar
✶ Nigeria	Abuja	Naira
✶ Norway	Oslo	Krone
✶ Oman	Muscat	Rial
✶ Pakistan	Islamabad	Rupee

Country	Capital	Currency
∗ Panama	Panama City	Balboa
∗ Peru	Lima	New Sole
∗ Philippines	Manila	Peso
∗ Poland	Warsaw	Zloty
∗ Portugal	Lisbon	Euro
∗ Qatar	Doha	Riyal
∗ Romania	Bucharest	Leu
∗ Russia	Moscow	Ruble
∗ Saudi Arabia	Riyadh	Rial
∗ Senegal	Dakar	Franc
∗ Slovakia	Bratislava	Euro
∗ Spain	Madrid	Euro
∗ Sri Lanka	Colombo	Rupee
∗ Sudan	Khartoum	Dinar
∗ Suriname	Paramaribo	Guilder
∗ Sweden	Stockholm	Krona
∗ Switzerland	Berne	Swiss Francs
∗ Syria	Damascus	Pound
∗ South Africa	Capetown (Legislative) Pretoria *(Administrative)*	Rand
∗ Tadzhikistan	Dushanbe	Ruble
∗ Taiwan	Taipei	Dollar
∗ Tanzania	Dodoma	Shilling
∗ Thailand	Bangkok	Baht
∗ Tunisia	Tunis	Dinar
∗ Turkiye	Ankara	Lira
∗ Turkmania	Ashikabad	Manat
∗ Uganda	Kampala	Shilling
∗ Ukraine	Kiev	Hyrvnia
∗ United Arab Emirates	Abu Dhabi	Dirham
∗ U.K.	London	Pound Sterling
∗ U.S.A.	Washington	Dollar
∗ Uruguay	Montevideo	Peso
∗ Uzbekistan	Tashkent	Som
∗ Venezuela	Caracas	Bolivar
∗ Vietnam	Hanoi	Dong
∗ Yemen	Sana'a	Rial
∗ Zimbabwe	Harare	Dollar
∗ Congo (Zaire)	Kinshasa	Zaire
∗ Zambia	Lusaka	Kwacha

First in the World

First Chinese visitor to India	Fahien
First foreign invader of India	Alexander, the Great (Greek)
First person to climb Mt. Everest	Tenzing Norgay (India) and Edmund Hillary (New Zealand) (1953)
First atom bomb dropped at	Hiroshima (Japan)
First man in the space	Yuri Gagarin (former USSR)
First woman in the space	Valentina Tereshkova (former USSR)
First person to walk in the space	Alexei Leonov (former USSR)
First person to land on the moon	Neil Armstrong (USA)
First and the only woman to have climbed Mt. Everest twice	Santosh Yadav (Indian; May 12, 1992; May 10, 1993)
First person on Mt. Everest without oxygen	Phu Dorjee (Indian; May 9, 1984)
First person to climb Mt. Everest twice	Nawang Gombu
First President of the USA	George Washington
First woman Prime Minister	Sirimavo Bandaranaike (Sri Lanka)
First person to swim across English Channel	Mathew Webb
First woman to swim across English Channel	Gertrude Caroline Ederle
First woman to climb Mt. Everest	Junko Tabei (Japan)
First woman to climb Mt. Everest alone and without oxygen supplies	Alison Hargreaves (Briton: May 13, 1995)

First Aeroplane to fly around the world without refuelling	Voyager (Dec. 1986)
First test-tube Baby	Louise Brown (UK; 1978)
First all-talking Film	Jaz Singer (1927)
First Secretary-General of the UN	Trygve Lie (Norway: 1946-53)
First woman President of the UN General Assembly	Vijayalakshmi Pandit (India: 1953)
First woman to reach North Pole	Ann Bancroft (1986)
First person to reach North Pole	Robert Peary
First person to reach South Pole	Amundsen (1911)
First woman to command Spacecraft in space	Ellin Collins

Popular Names

Popular Name	*Real Name*
Badshah Khan	Abdul Ghaffar Khan
Bapu, Father of Nation	M.K. Gandhi
Bard of Avon	William Shakespeare
Chachaji *or* Panditji	Jawaharlal Nehru
Desert Fox	Gen. Rommel (Germany)
Desh Bandhu	C.R. Das
Father of English Poetry	Geoffrey Chaucer
Fuhrer	Adolf Hitler
Grand Old Man of India	Dadabhai Naoroji
Grand Old Man of Britain	W.E. Gladstone
Gurudev	Rabindra Nath Tagore
Guruji	M.S. Golwalkar
Grand Commoner	Pitt, the younger
Iron Man of India	Sardar Patel
Lady with the Lamp	Florence Nightingale
Lal, Bal, Pal	Lala Lajpat Rai, Bal Gangadhar Tilak, Bipin Chandra Pal
Li-Kwan	Pearl Buck
Little Corporal *or* Man of Destiny	Napoleon Bonaparte
Lokmanya	Bal Gangadhar Tilak
Lok Nayak	Jayaprakash Narain
Mahamana	Pt. Madan Mohan Malaviya
Maid of Orleans	Joan of Arc
Maiden Queen	Queen Elizabeth I
Man of Blood and Iron	Prince Bismark
Netaji	Subhash Chandra Bose
Nightingale of India	Sarojini Naidu
Priyadarshini	Indira Gandhi
Punjab Kesari	Lala Lajpat Rai
Wizard of the North	Walter Scott

Geographical Surnames

Geographical Surname	*Real Name*
Bengal's Sorrow	Damodar River
Blue Mountains	Nilgiri Hills
China's Sorrow	Hwang-Ho
City of Palaces	Kolkata
City of Skyscrapers *or* Empire City	New York
City of Dreaming Spires	Oxford
Cockpit of Europe	Belgium
Dark Continent	Africa
Emerald Isle	Ireland
Eternal City	Rome
Forbidden City	Lhasa (Tibet)
Gateway of India	Mumbai
Gate of Tears	Strait of Bab-el-mandab
Gift of the Nile	Egypt
Granite City	Aberdeen (Scotland)
Hermit Kingdom	Korea
Holy Land	Jerusalem (Palestine)
Island of Pearls	Bahrain (Persian Gulf)
Island of Cloves	Zanzibar
Key to the Mediterranean	Gibraltar
Land of Five Rivers	Punjab
Land of Golden Pagoda	Myanmar (Burma)
Land of Kangaroo	Australia
Land of Maple Leaf/Lillies	Canada
Land of Midnight Sun	Norway
Land of Morning Calm	Korea
Land of the Rising Sun	Japan
Land of Thousand Lakes	Finland
Land of Thunderbolt	Bhutan
Land of the White Elephants	Thailand
Manchester of the Orient	Osaka (Japan)
Pearl of the Antilles *or* Sugar Bowl of the World	Cuba
Pink City	Jaipur
Playground of Europe	Switzerland
Queen of the Adriatic	Venice (Italy)
Roof of the World	Pamirs
Sick Man of Europe	Turkey
Venice of the North	Stockholm (Sweden)
Windy City	Chicago
Whiteman's Grave	Guinea Coast of Africa
World's Loneliest Island	Tristan de Cunha

Countries'/Cities' Names—Old and New

Old Name	New Name
Abyssinia	Ethiopia
Basutoland	Lesotho
Bechuanaland	Botswana
British Honduras	Belize
Burma	Myanmar
Ceylon	Sri Lanka
Zaire	Congo
Constantinople	Istanbul
Dahomey	Benin
Dutch East Indies	Indonesia
East Pakistan	Bangladesh
Formosa	Taiwan
Gold Coast	Ghana

Old Name	New Name
Leningrad	St. Petersburg
Leopoldville	Kinshasa
Mesopotamia	Iraq
North Rhodesia	Zambia
Nyasaland	Malawi
Peking	Beijing
Persia	Iran
Rangoon	Yangon
Salisbury	Harare
Siam	Thailand
South West Africa	Namibia
Southern Rhodesia	Zimbabwe

IMPORTANT RESIDENCES

• **Buckingham Palace (London):** King/Queen of Britain • **10, Downing Street (London):** Prime Minister, Britain • **Elysee Palace (Paris):** President, France • **Rashtrapati Bhawan (New Delhi):** President, India • **White House (Washington):** President, USA • **Vatican (Rome):** Pope

Important towns situated on the River Banks

Town	River
Agra	Yamuna
Ahmedabad	Sabarmati
Prayagraj	Confluence of the Ganga and the Yamuna
Ayodhya	Saryu
Baghdad	Tigris
Berlin	Spree
Cairo	Nile
Kolkata	Hooghly
Cuttack	Mahanadi
Delhi	Yamuna
Dibrugarh	Brahmaputra
Dublin	Liffey
Hardwar	Ganga
Hyderabad	Musi
Jabalpur	Narbada
Kanpur	Ganga

Town	River
Karachi	Indus
Lahore	Ravi
Leh	Indus
London	Thames
Lucknow	Gomati
Nasik	Godavari
New York	Hudson
Paris	Seine
Patna	Ganga
Rome	Tiber
Srinagar	Jhelum
Surat	Tapti
Sydney	Murray-Darling
Varanasi	Ganga
Vienna	Danube
Washington	Potamac
Yangon	Irawadi

Books and Authors

FOREIGN

Book	Author
Aesop's Fables	Aesop
Adventure of Robinson Crusoe	Daniel Defoe
Adventures of Sherlok Holmes	Arthur Conan Doyle
Alice in Wonderland	Lewis Carrol
Apple Cart	G.B. Shaw
Arabian Nights	Sir Richard Burton
As You Like It	William Shakespeare
A Tale of Two Cities	Charles Dickens
A Tale of Two Gardens	Octavio Paz
A Thousand Suns	Dominique Lapierre
August Coup	Mikhail S. Gorbachev
Ben Hur	Lewis Wallace
Candida	G.B. Shaw
Das Kapital	Karl Marx
David Copperfield	Charles Dickens
Divine Comedy	A. Dante
Doctor's Dilemma	G.B. Shaw
Famished Road	Ben Okri
Freedom From Fear	Aung San Suu Kyi
Gulistan Bostan	Sheikh Saadi
Gulliver's Travels	Jonathan Swift
Hamlet	William Shakespeare
Iliad	Homer
Inferno	A. Dante
In Memoriam	Lord Tennyson
Ivanhoe	Walter Scott
Julius Caesar	William Shakespeare
Lady Chatterley's Lover	D.H. Lawrence
Lajja	Taslima Nasreen
Les Miserable	Victor Hugo
Leviathan	Thomas Hobbes
Lolita	V. Nobokov
Lycidas	John Milton
Mein Kampf	Adolf Hitler
Merchant of Venice	William Shakespeare
Midnight's Children	Salman Rushdie
Moor's Last Sigh	Salman Rushdie
Mother	Maxim Gorky
Mother India	Katherine Mayo
Nana	Emile Zola
Ninteen Eighty Four	George Orwell
Odyssey	Homer
Origin of Species	Charles Darwin
Othello	William Shakespeare
Paradise Lost	John Milton
Paradise Regained	John Milton
Path to Power	Margaret Thatcher
Pickwick Papers	Charles Dickens
Pride and Prejudice	Jane Austen
Razor's Edge	Somerset Maugham
Republic	Plato
Romeo and Juliet	William Shakespeare
Round the World in Eighty Days	Jules Verne
Rubaiyat-i-Omar Khayyam	Edward Fitzgerald (Translator)
Shape of Things to Come	H.G. Wells
The Satanic Verses	Salman Rushdie
The Social Contract	Rousseau
The Tempest	William Shakespeare
Time Machine	H.G. Wells
Tom Sawyer	Mark Twain
Treasure Island	R.L. Stevenson
Twelfth Night	William Shakespeare
Uncle Tom's Cabin	H.B. Stowe
Unto This Last	John Ruskin
Utopia	Thomas More
Universe Around Us	James Jeans
Vicar of Wakefield	Oliver Goldsmith
War and Peace	Leo Tolstoy
Wealth of Nations	Adam Smith
Wonder That was India	A.L. Basham
Wuthering Heights	Emily Bronte

INDIAN

Book	Author
Abhigyan Shakuntalam	Kalidas
Ain-i-Akbari	Abul Fazal
Anand Math	Bankim Chandra Chatterjee

Book	Author
Arthashastra	Kautilya
A Suitable Boy	Vikram Seth
Bhagwat Gita	Ved Vyas
Chidambara	Sumitranandan Pant
Devdas	Sarat Chandra Chatterjee
Diwan-i-Ghalib	Mirza Ghalib
Discovery of India	Jawaharlal Nehru
Essays on Gita	Aurobindo Ghosh
Eternal India	Indira Gandhi
Faces of Everest	Major H.P.S. Ahluwalia
Ganadevata	Tarashankar Bandopadhyaya
Geet Govind	Jaya Dev
Geetanjali	R.N. Tagore
Glimpses of World History	Jawaharlal Nehru
Godaan	Prem Chand
Gul-e-Nagma	Firaq Gorakhpuri
Gunahon ka Devta	Dharmveer Bharti
Harsh Charita	Bana Bhatta
Hindu View of Life	S. Radhakrishnan
Idols	Sunil Gavaskar
India Divided	Dr. Rajendra Prasad
The Judgement	Kuldip Nayyar
Juhi ki Kali	Surya Kant Tripathi 'Nirala'
Justice of Peace ke Aansu	Janardan Prasad Singh
Chand ka Munh Terha Hai	Muktibodh
Kapalkundala	Bankim Chandra Chatterjee
Kadambari	Bana Bhatta
Kagaz Te Kanwas	Amrita Pritam
Kamayani	Jai Shankar Prasad
Kitni Nawon	S.H. Vatsyayan
Kumar Sambhav	Kalidas
Mahabharata	Ved Vyas

Book	Author
Malgudi Days	R.K. Narayan
Manvini Bhavai	Pannalal Patel
Mati Matal	Gopi Nath Mohanty
Meghdoot	Kalidas
Meri Ekyavan Kavitain	Atal Bihari Vajpayee
Meri Sansadiya Yatra	Atal Bihari Vajpayee
Mritunjaya	B.K. Bhattacharya
Mudrarakshasa	Vishakhadatta
My Experiments with Truth	M.K. Gandhi
My Own Boswell	M. Hidayatullah
My Presidential Years	R. Venkataraman
Nisheeth	Uma Shankar Joshi
'No, Sir'	P.G. Mavlankar
One Day Wonders	Sunil Gavaskar
Panchtantra	Vishnu Sharma
Passage to England	Nirad C. Chaudhuri
Prison Diary	Jaya Prakash Narayan
Raghuvansha	Kalidas
Rajtarangini	Kalhana
Ramayana	Balmiki
Ramcharit Manas	Tulsidas
Rukh Te Rishi	Harbhajan Singh
Satyarth Prakash	Swami Dayanand
Sur Sagar	Surdas
The Guide	R.K. Narayan
The Insider	P.V. Narasimharao
The Post Office — *Dak Ghar*	Rabindra Nath Tagore
The God of Small Things	Arundhati Roy
Urvashi	Ram Dhari Singh 'Dinkar'
Yama	Mahadevi Verma
My Country : My Life (Autobiography)	L.K. Advani
The Test of My Life	Yuvraj Singh
Twenty Years in a Decade	Shah Rukh Khan

IMPORTANT BOOKS WRITTEN IN JAIL

Book	Author
My Experiments with Truth	Mahatma Gandhi
Glimpses of World History Discovery of India	Jawaharlal Nehru
Gita Rahasya	Lokmanya Bal Gangadhar Tilak

Book	Author
Pilgrim's Progress	John Bunyan
Bible (in German language)	Martin Luther
Les Miserables	Victor Hugo
Long Walk to Freedom	Nelson Mandela

11. FIRST IN INDIA

First in India

Nobel Prize for Literature (1913)	Rabindra Nath Tagore
Nobel Prize for Physics (1929)	C.V. Raman
Nobel Prize for Peace (1979)	Mother Teresa
Nobel Prize for Economics (1998)	Amartya Sen
Special Oscar award winner (1992)	Satyajit Ray
First and the last Indian Governor-General of free India	C. Rajagopalachari
Woman Governor of the State	Smt. Sarojini Naidu
Indian Chief of the Army Staff	General K.M. Cariappa
Woman Chief Minister of a State	Smt. Sucheta Kripalani
Woman President of United Nations General Assembly (1954)	Smt. Vijaylakshmi Pandit
President of International Court of Justice	Dr. Nagendra Singh
Woman to swim across the English Channel	Ms. Aarti Saha
Miss Universe	Miss Sushmita Sen
Miss World	Reita Faria
Indian to swim across the English Channel	Mihir Sen
Field Marshal	S.H.F.J. Manekshaw
Indian recipient of Victoria Cross	Khudadad Khan
Indian to conquer Mt. Everest	Sherpa Tenzing, May 29, 1953
Indian male cosmonaut (1984)	Rakesh Sharma
Indian female cosmonaut	Kalpana Chawla (19 Nov., 1997)
Woman to climb Mt. Everest	Miss Bachendri Pal, May 23, 1984
Woman to get Olympic Medal	Karnam Malleswari
Indian to address the UN General Assembly in Hindi	Atal Bihari Vajpayee
Newspaper	Bengal Gazette, Jan 27, 1780
Postage Stamp issued	In 1852
Telegraph line laid	In 1851, Kolkata; Diamond Harbour
Railways run	April 16, 1853; Bombay-Thana
Electric Train run	1925: Bombay-Kurla
Atomic Power Station	Tarapore (Maharashtra)
Passenger-cum-cargo ship made in India	Harshavardhan
Satellite	Aryabhatta (1975)
Rocket	Rohini (1967)
Atomic Reactor	Apsara (1956)
Climb Everest without oxygen	Phu Dorjee (1987)
First film (movie)	Raja Harishchandra (1913)
First film (talkie)	Alam Ara (1931)
Metro Railway	Kolkata Metro Railway

Test-tube baby, scientifically documented	Born on August 6, 1986 at K.E.M. Hospital, Mumbai
TV Centre	At Delhi
Indian to get an Oscar	Bhanu Athaiya
Woman pilot in IAF	Ms Harita Kaur Deol
Cellular Phone	Kolkata, August 1, 1995
Women president of Indian National Congress	Smt. Annie Besant
President of Indian National Congress	W.C. Banerjee (1885)
Indian who passed in I.C.S. Examination	Satendra Nath Tagore
Woman chief justice of High Court	Lila Saith (Himachal Pradesh)
Woman Foreign Secretary	Chokila Iyyar

First Important Officials of India

The Governor-General of free India	Lord Mountbatten
President	Dr. Rajendra Prasad
President (Female)	Pratibha Patil
Vice-President	Dr. S. Radhakrishnan
Prime Minister	Jawahar Lal Nehru
Prime Minister (Female)	Indira Gandhi
Deputy Prime Minister	Sardar Vallabhbhai Patel
Chief Justice	Harilal J. Kania
First Female Judge in Supreme Court	Smt. Meera Sahib Fatima Bibi
Speaker, Lok Sabha	Ganesh Vasudeo Mawlankar
Woman Speaker of Lok Sabha	Meira Kumar
Chief Election Commissioner	Sukumar Sen
Commander-in-Chief	General Sir Roy Bucher
Chief of Army Staff	General Maharaj Rajendra Sinhji
Chief of Air Staff	Air Marshal Sir Thomas Elmhirst
Chief of Naval Staff	Vice Admiral Ramdas Katari
Chief of Defence Staff (CDS)	General Bipin Rawat
Female Minister	Raj Kumari Amrit Kaur (Health Minister)
Female Governor	Sarojini Naidu (U.P.)
Female Chief Minister	Sucheta Kripalani (U.P. 1963)
Finance Commissioner	K.C. Niyogi
Leader of Opposition in Lok Sabha (Recognised)	Y.V. Chavan (Congress)
Leader of Opposition in Rajya Sabha (Recognised)	Kamalapati Tripathi (Congress)

Highest, Biggest, Largest & Longest in India

Award for Gallantry, highest	Param Vir Chakra
Award, highest civilian	Bharat Ratna
Bank, with largest number of branches	State Bank of India
Road Bridge, Longest	Bhupen Hazarika Setu, Across Lohit River (9.15 km)
Cattle fair, largest	Sonepur (Bihar)
Cellular Phone, First	Kolkata, August 1, 1995
City, Most Populous	Mumbai
Corridor, Longest	Rameshwaram Temple corridor (4,000 ft.)
Desert, Largest	Thar (Rajasthan)
Dam, Longest	Hirakud Dam (Odisha)

Delta, Largest	Sunderban's Delta
Dome, Largest	Gol Gumbaj (Bijapur)
Dam, Highest	Tihri Dam 261 m. (855 ft.)
Gateway, Highest	Buland Darwaja at Fatehpur Sikri (176 ft.)
Lake, Largest (Fresh water)	Wular Lake (Kashmir)
Literacy, Highest	Kerala (94%)
Museum, Largest	Indian Museum (Kolkata)
Mosque, Biggest	Jama Masjid (Delhi)
Peak, Highest	K-2 (Pak-Occupied Kashmir)
Platform, Longest	Shree Siddharoodha Swamiji Railway Station Hubballi, Karnataka (1507 m. long)
Railway Bridge, Longest	Vembanad Bridge, Kerala (4.6 km)
River, Longest	The Ganges (2525 Km)
Rainfall, Highest (annual mean)	Mowsynram near Cherrapunji (1178 cm)
Road, Longest	Grand Trunk Road (1,500 miles)
Road-Rail Longest Bridge	Bogibeel bridge, Assam (4.94 km)
State, (Largest population)	Uttar Pradesh
State, Largest (in area)	Rajasthan
State, with maximum forest cover	Madhya Pradesh
State, with maximum density of population	Bihar
Tunnel, Longest (Road)	Dr. Shyama Prasad Mukherjee Tunnel (9.28 kms, J & K)
Tunnel, Longest (Railway)	Pir Panjal Tunnel (Between Banihal and Qazigund stations in J&K) (11.21 km long)
Tower, Highest	Qutub Minar (Delhi, 72.5 m.)
Waterfall, Highest	Kunchikal Waterfall (Karnataka: 455 m.)
Zoo, Largest	Zoological Gardens (Kolkata)

Table of Precedence

1. President
2. Vice-President
3. Prime Minister
4. Governors of States within their respective states
5. Former Presidents

5A. Deputy Prime Minister

6. Chief Justice of India, Speaker of Lok Sabha
7. Cabinet Ministers of the Union, Chief Ministers of States within their respective States, Deputy Chairman NITI Aayog, Former Prime Ministers. Leaders of opposition in Rajya Sabha and Lok Sabha

7A. Holders of the Bharat Ratna Decoration

8. Ambassadors Extraordinary and Plenipotentiary and High Commissioners of Commonwealth Countries accredited to India, Chief Ministers of States outside their respective States, Governors of States outside their respective states.
9. Judges of the Supreme Court

9A. Chairperson Union Public Service Commission, Chief Election Commissioner, Comptroller & Auditor-General of India.

10. Deputy Chairman Rajya Sabha, Deputy Chief Minister of States, Deputy Speaker Lok Sabha, Members of the NITI Aayog, Minister of State of the Union and Other Minister in the Ministry of Defence.

✻ ✻ ✻ ✻ ✻

12. CULTURAL ACTIVITIES

AKADEMIES

There are three akademies for promotion of creative art.

1. **Lalit Kala Akademi, New Delhi:** Established in 1954, the Lalit Kala Akademi strives for the popularisation of Indian art within the country and in various countries of the world through exhibitions, publications, workshops and camps. Every three year it organises the Triennale India, an international exhibition. It publishes research papers on Indian arts. Besides organising seminars, it honours eminent artists. The Akademi has set up regional centres called Rashtriya Lalit Kala Kendras at Lucknow, Kolkata, Chennai and Bhubaneswar and a small office at Mumbai.
2. **Sangeet Natak Akademi, New Delhi:** The Sangeet Natak Akademi, set-up in 1953, aims at the promotion and development of dance, drama and music. It holds seminars and festivals, presents awards to the eminent artists and extends financial assistance to traditional teachers and scholarships to students. It also operates a scheme of exchange of troupes.
3. **Sahitya Akademi, New Delhi:** The Sahitya Akademi, established in 1954, has the main functions of development of Indian letters, setting up high literary standards, translation of literary works of one Indian language into other Indian languages, publication of books on history of literature and criticism, bibliographies and reference books. The Akademy has regional offices at Mumbai, Kolkata, Bengaluru and Chennai.
4. **National School of Drama:** It is one of the top theatre training institutes in the world and only one of its kind in India. It was set up in 1959 under Sangeet Natak Akademi but was later made autonomous organisation in 1975.

SCULPTURE

Archaeological Survey of India, set up in 1861, is responsible for preservation and maintenance of sculptures and historical monuments and manages a number of archaeological museums.

National Archives of India, established in 1891, it is the official custodian of all non-current records of permanent value of the Government of India and its predecessor bodies.

MUSEUMS

They are repositories of the cultural heritage and conserve and preserve historical technical and other materials against decay and transmit them to posterity as records of history.

MUSIC

Main Schools of Classical Music: There are two main schools of classical music, namely, the Hindustani and the Carnatic. The Hindustani school of classical music is in vogue in north-western India, eastern India and northern parts of the South India.

Musical Instruments: They are: Tabla, Mridangam, Pakhawaj, Chandai, Dholak, Veena, Sitar, Sarod, Gootuvadhyam, Sarangi, Flute, Nadaswaram, Shehnai, Shringi and Turahi.

DANCE

India has a very rich tradition of tribal, folk and classical dances.

Classical Dance

Dance	State	Famous Artists
Bharat Natyam	Tamil Nadu	Yamini Krishnamurthy, Rukmini Devi Arundale, Swapna Sundari, Sonal Mansingh, Vaijanti Mala, Mrinalini Sarabhai, Chandralekha, Indraní, Ram Gopal, Bal Saraswati
Kathakali	Kerala	Gopinath, K.K. Nayar, Kunju-Kurup, T.K. Chandu
Kuchipudi	Andhra Pradesh	Sapna Sundari, Raja Reddy, Shobha Nayar, Radha Reddy, Vedantam Satyanarayan, Vimpanti Chinna Satyam.
Kathak	North India	Birju Maharaj, Gopi Krishna, Shambhu Maharaj, Sitara Devi, Vishnu Sharma, Durga Lal, Shobhana Narayan
Odissi	Odisha	Kelucharan Mahapatra, Indrani Rehman, Madhavi Mudgal, Protima Bedi, Samyukta Panigrahi, Sonal Mansingh, Debudas
Manipuri	Manipur	Uday Shankar, Bipin Singh, Suryamukhi, Darohra Jhaveri

Famous Folk-Dance

State/(UT)	Folk Dance
Andhra Pradesh	Dandari, Banjara
Assam	Bihu, Keli Gopal, Sataria
Bihar	Chhau, Magahi, Durga dance
W. Bengal	Kirtan, Kalatri, Asweabadh, Brita, Kalidance
Chhattisgarh	Saila, Karama, Bhagoria
Gujarat	Garba, Rasalila, Tippani, Dandia,
Haryana	Damyal, Lahoor
Himachal Pradesh	Dussehra dance, Hikat, Notio
Jammu & Kashmir	Dumhal
Jharkhand	Jhau, Ghumakudia, Jadur, Sarhul, Soharai, Karama, Vaima, Loojhari, Jat-Jatin, Vidayat
Karnataka	Yakshagan, Dolu Kunitha
Kerala	Mohini Attam, Padayuni
Madhya Pradesh	Lota Nritya, Jawara
Maharashtra	Tamasha, Dahi Handi, Gof, Deepak Dindi
Manipur	Dhol Cholam
Meghalaya	Nongakarem
Nagaland	Bamboo dance
Odisha	Chhau, Maya Shabari, Dalachai
Punjab	Gidda, Bhangra, Panihari
Rajasthan	Thumar, Kathaputali, Tera Tali
Tamil Nadu	Terukalathu, Kabalatam, Kargam, Pulivesham
Tripura	Hazagiri
Uttar Pradesh	Rasalila, Nautanki, Thali, Dhurang, Jhumela, Huraka, Bol.
Uttarakhand	Kajari, Karan
Goa	Dhode Modini

Musical Instruments and Artists

Musical Instrument	*Artists*	*Musical Instrument*	*Artists*
Flute	Hari Prasad Chaurasia, Panna Lal Ghosh, T.R. Mahalingam, N. Ramani, Vijaya Raghava Rao	Sitar	Pandit Ravishankar, Vilayat Khan
		Santur	Shiv Kumar Sharma
		Rudraveena	Zia Mohiuddin Dagar
Tabla	Allah Rakha, Gudai Maharaj, Latif Khan, Zakir Hussain	Pakhawaj	Govind Rao, Anokhe Lal, Kanthi Maharaj
		Mridanga	Palghat R. Raghu, U.S. Burman
Violin	Lalgudi Jayaraman, L. Subramaniam, M.S. Gopal Krishnan, S. Subrahmaniam, V.G. Jog, N. Rajan	Harmonium	Purushottam Walawakar, M. Dhaulpuri
		Guitar	Pt. Vishnu Mohan Bhatt, Brij Bhushan Kalra
Shehnai	Bismilla Khan, Imrat Khan Ali Akbar	Ghatam	T.H. Vinayakaram
Sarod	Khan, Amjad Ali Khan, Alauddin Khan, Saren Rani, Brij Narayan	Janjira	V. Nagarajan
		Symphony	Jubin Mehta

Major Wild Life Sanctuary in India

India is rich in flora and fauna. However, due to increasing population and industrial and commercial activities, there has been acute pressure on forests. The Government has taken several steps to check the sharp fall in the number of these species. Among the measures are declaration of certain habitats as national parks and sanctuaries. 106 national parks and 567 sanctuaries have been established till January 2023, important ones being given below:

Assam: Kaziranga National Park (know for one-horn Rhinoceroses); Manas Sanctuary.
Jharkhand: Hazaribagh National Park; Betla Tiger Reserve Palamau.
Gujarat: Valvadar National Park, Bhavnagar; Marine National Park, Gir Forests.
Himachal Pradesh: Rohla National Park; Motichur Sanctuary.
Jammu & Kashmir: Dachigam Sanctuary.
Karnataka: Bandipur National Park; Bannargheta National Park, Bangalore; Nagorhole National Park, Coorg; Ranganthitto Bird Sanctuary.
Kerala: Eravikulam Rajmallay National Park, Idduki; Periyar Game Sanctuary.
Madhya Pradesh: Kanha National Park; Bandhavgarh National Park, Shahdol; Shivpuri National Park.
Maharashtra: Taloba National Park, Chandrapur; Panch National Park, Nagpur; Borivali National Park, Mumbai; Nawagaon National Park, Bandara; Melghat National Park.
Manipur: Keibul Lamjao National Park.
Odisha: Simlipal, Tiger Sanctuary.
Rajasthan: Sariska Sanctuary; Ghana Bird Sanctuary, Ranthambhor Sanctuary.
Sikkim: Khangchandzenda National Park, Gangtok.
Tamil Nadu: Vedanthangal Bird Sanctuary; Guindy National Park, Chennai; Mudumalai Sanctuary; Kalakad-Munden Thurai Reserve.
Uttar Pradesh: Chandraprabha Sanctuary; Dudhwa National Park, Lakhimpur.
West Bengal: Jaldapara Sanctuary; Sunderbans.
Uttarakhand: Corbett National Park; Nainital.

* * * * *

13. AWARDS

NATIONAL AWARDS

1. Bharat Ratna: This is India's highest civilian award. It is given for exceptional work on art, literature, science and recognition of public service of the highest order. Government servants are not eligible for it. The table shows the recipients of the award:

Bharat Ratna Award Winners:

1.	Dr. S. Radhakrishnan	1954
2.	C. Rajagopalachari	1954
3.	Dr. C.V. Raman	1954
4.	Dr. Bhagwan Das	1955
5.	Dr. M. Visvesvaraya	1955
6.	Jawahar Lal Nehru	1955
7.	Govind Ballabh Pant	1957
8.	Dr. D.K. Karve	1958
9.	Dr. Bidhan Chandra Roy	1961
10.	Purushottam Das Tandon	1961
11.	Dr. Rajendra Prasad	1962
12.	Dr. Zakir Hussain	1963
13.	Dr. Pandurang Vaman Kane	1963
14.	Lal Bahadur Shastri	1966
15.	Indira Gandhi	1971
16.	V.V. Giri	1975
17.	K. Kamraj	1976
18.	Mother Teresa	1980
19.	Acharya Vinoba Bhave	1983
20.	Khan Abdul Ghaffar Khan	1987
21.	M.G. Ramachandran	1988
22.	Dr. B.R. Ambedkar	1990
23.	Dr. Nelson R. Mandela	1990
24.	Rajiv Gandhi	1991
25.	Sardar Vallabhbhai Patel	1991
26.	Morarji R. Desai	1991
27.	Maulana Abul Kalam Azad	1992
28.	Jehangir Ratanji Dadabhai Tata	1992
29.	Satyajit Roy	1992
30.	Shri Gulzari Lal Nanda	1997
31.	Mrs. Aruna Asaf Ali	1997
32.	Dr. A.P.J. Abdul Kalam	1998
33.	M.S. Subbalakshmi	1998
34.	C. Subramaniam	1998
35.	Jaya Prakash Narayan	1999
36.	Prof. Amartya Sen	1999
37.	Pt. Ravi Shankar	1999
38.	Gopinath Bardoloi	1999
39.	Lata Mangeshkar	2001
40.	Bismillah Khan	2001
41.	Bhimsen Joshi	2008
42.	C.N.R. Rao	2014
43.	Sachin Tendulakar	2014
44.	Pt. Madan Mohan Malaviya	2015
45.	Atal Bihari Vajpayee	2015
46.	Pranab Mukherjee	2019
47.	Bhupen Hazarika	2019
48.	Nanaji Deshmukh	2019

2. Padma Vibhushan: The **Padma Vibhushan** is the second-highest civilian award of the Republic of India, preceded by Bharat Ratna and followed by Padma Bhushan. Instituted on 2 January 1954, the award is given for "exceptional and distinguished service", without distinction of race, occupation, position, or sex. The award criteria include "service in any field including service rendered by Government servants" including doctors and scientists, but excludes those working with the public sector undertakings.

During 1 May and 15 September of every year, the recommendations for the award are submitted to the Padma Awards Committee, constituted by the Prime Minister of India. The recommendations are received from all the state and the union territory governments, the Ministries of the Government of India, the Bharat Ratna and previous Padma Vibhushan award recipients, the Institutes of Excellence, the Ministers, the Chief Ministers and the Governors of State, and the Members of Parliament including private individuals. The committee later submits their recommendations to the Prime Minister and the President of India for the further approval. The award recipients are announced on Republic Day.

3. **Padma Bhushan:** The **Padma Bhushan** is the third-highest civilian award in the Republic of India, after the Bharat Ratna and the Padma Vibhushan, but coming before the Padma Shri. It is announced on the occasion of Republic Day of India every year. It is conferred by the President of India at a function held at Rashtrapati Bhavan sometime around March or April. The award was established on 2 January 1954 by the president of India. It is awarded to recognize distinguished service of a high order to the nation, in any field.
4. **Padma Shri: Padma Shri** (also Padmashree) is the fourth highest civilian award in the Republic of India, after the Bharat Ratna, the Padma Vibhushan and the Padma Bhushan. Awarded by the Government of India, it is announced every year on India's Republic Day.

Padma Awards were instituted in 1954 to be awarded to citizens of India in recognition of their distinguished contribution in various spheres of activity including the Arts, Education, Industry, Literature, Science, Sports, Medicine, Social Service and Public Affairs. It has also been awarded to some distinguished individuals who were not citizens of India but did contribute in various ways to India.

The selection criteria have been criticized in some quarters with the claim that many highly deserving artists have been left out in order to favor certain individuals.

On its obverse, the words "Padma", meaning lotus in Sanskrit, and "Shri", a Sanskrit-derived honorific equivalent to 'Mr.' or 'Ms.', appear in Devanagari above and below a lotus flower. The geometrical pattern on either side is in burnished bronze. All embossing is in white gold.

GALLANTRY AWARDS

1. **Param Vir Chakra:** The highest award for bravery or some daring and pre-eminent act of valour or self-sacrifice in the presence of the enemy, whether on land, at sea or in the air.
2. **Mahavir Chakra:** It is the second highest decoration and is awarded for acts of conspicuous gallantry in the presence of the enemy, whether on land, at sea or in the air.
3. **Vir Chakra:** It is the third in order of awards given for acts of gallantry in the presence of enemy, whether on land, at sea or in the air.
4. **Ashok Chakra:** This medal is awarded for the most conspicuous bravery or some daring or pre-eminent act of valour or self-sacrifice on land, at sea or in the air but not in the presence of enemy.
5. **Vishishta Sewa Medal:** It is awarded to personnel of all the three Services in class I, II and III in recognition of distinguished service of the "most exceptional" and "exceptional" and a "high" order respectively. Prefixes *Parma* and *Ati* are added before first two categories of medals respectively.
6. **Jeewan Raksha Padak:** Awarded for meritorious acts or a series of acts of a human nature displayed in saving life from drowning, fire and rescue operations in mines etc.

National Sports Awards

1. **Major Dhyan Chand Khel Ratna Award:** The scheme was launched in the year 1991-92 with the objective of honouring sportspersons to enhance their general status and to give them greater dignity and place of honour in society. Under this scheme, an amount of ₹ 25 lakh is

given as award for the most spectacular and outstanding performance by a sportsperson over a period of four years immediately preceding the year in which award is to be given.

2. **Dronacharya Award:** Dronacharya Award is an award presented by ministry of youth Affairs and Sports, Government of India for excellence in sports coaching. The Dronacharya (Lifetime) awardees gets ₹ 15 lakh and Dronacharya (Regular) awardees gets ₹ 10 lakh a bronze statuette of Dronacharya and scroll of honour. The award was instituted in 1985.

3. **Arjuna Award:** The Arjuna Awards are given by the ministry of youth Affairs and sports, government of India to recognize outstanding achievement in National sports. Instituted in 1961 the award carries a cash prize of 15,00,000 a bronze statue of Arjuna and a scroll.

4. **Dhyanchand Award:** Dhyanchand Award is India's highest award for lifetime achievement in sports and games, given by the ministry of youth Affairs and sports, government of India. The award is named after the legendary Indian hockey — player Dhyanchand. The award is initiated in 2002. The award carries a cash prize of ₹ 10,00,000 a plaque and a scroll of honour.

5. **Maulana Abul Kalam Azad Trophy:** This trophy was instituted in 1956-57. The top overall performing university in the inter-university tournaments is given the Maulana Abul Kalam Azad (MAKA) Trophy, which is a rolling trophy. A small replica of the MAKA Trophy is also awarded for retention by the university. In addition, the university also gets a cash prize of ₹ 15 lakh. The second and third best universities also receive cash awards amounting to ₹ 5 lakh and ₹ 3 lakh respectively.

Other Awards

1. **Jnanpith Award:** Awarded to outstanding authors of creative literature in any of the Indian languages recognised by the Constitution of India. It was sponsored by the Bharatiya Jnanpith a culturo-literary society founded in 1944 by Shanti Prasad Jain, an eminent industrialist.

2. **Sahitya Akademi Award:** It is awarded for outstanding literary works and comprises a cash prize of ₹ 1,00,000 in each of the 22 languages mentioned in the Eighth schedule of the Constitution that it supports and a copper plaque.

3. **Saraswati Samman:** The award is given by K.K. Birla Foundation to an outstanding author for his literary work in any Indian language mentioned in the Eighth Schedule of the Constitution and published during the last 10 years. The award carries a cash prize of ₹ 15 lakh.

4. **Dada Saheb Phalke Award:** The prestigious Dada Saheb Phalke Award is given to the persons for outstanding contribution to the growth and development of Indian cinema. First presented in 1969, the award was introduced by the government of India to commemorate Dadasaheb Phalke's contribution to Indian Cinema Phalke, who is popularly known as and often regarded as a the Father of Indian Cinema was an Indian film-maker who directed India's first-length feature film, Raja Harishchandra.

   The first recipient of the award was actress Devika Rani, who was honoured at the 17th National film Awards.

5. **Indira Gandhi Award:** The award has been instituted for promoting national integration and understanding amongst the religious groups, communities and ethnic groups of India and consists of ₹ 5 lakh and a citation.

6. **Gujar Mal Modi Award:** The award carries ₹ 2.01 lakh as cash prize, apart from a silver shield and a scroll and is given to the best scientist of the year who makes an outstanding contribution to research resulting in new innovative technology.

7. **Rajiv Gandhi National Sadbhavana Award:** Instituted in 1992 to mark the golden jubilee of the Quit India Movement, the award carries a cash prize of ₹ 10 lakh and a citation.

8. Vachaspati Puraskar: K.K. Birla Foundation's prestigious Vachaspati Puraskar carries a cash award of ₹ 1,50,000 for outstanding Sanskrit works published during the last ten years.

9. Bhartendu Harishchandra Awards: The Bhartendu Harishchandra Awards were instituted in 1983, by the Ministry of Information and Broadcasting for original Hindi writing on any subject in mass communications like journalism, publication, advertising, broadcasting films, etc.

10. Kabir Samman: The award is conferred annually on a person of literature of very high order on the basis of his or her superb creativity and consistent commitment to the most recent and latest trends of literary creation in any of the Indian languages. The award carries ₹ 3 lakh and a letter of citation.

INTERNATIONAL AWARDS

1. Nobel Prizes: The most prestigious award in the world is supported by the Nobel Foundation of US. This award was set up in 1900 under the will to Alfred Bernhard Nobel (1833-96). Alfred Nobel was an unmarried, Swedish scientist and chemical engineer who discovered Nitroglycerin ($C_3H_5N_3O_9$) and its use in the manufacture of dynamite in 1966. The interest accrued on the fortune left by him is divided annually among the persons who have made outstanding contribution in science, literature, peace and economics. Swedes found out about the prizes only after his death in 1896. When they read his will in which he had donated the annual income from his fortune to support the awards. In his will he ordered that 'the most worthy shall receive the prize, whether he is Scandinavian or not. This led to his criticism as being unpatriotic for not reserving the prizes only for Swedes. Even his relatives, in a futile bid, contested the will for three years.

Nobel Foundation's Prize Awarding Bodies

(*i*) The Royal Swedish Academy of Sciences, awards the Nobel prize in Physics and Chemistry.

(*ii*) The Nobel Assembly of Karolinska Chirugical Institute. Sweden, awards the Nobel Prize in Medicine and Physiology.

(*iii*) The Swedish Academy awards the Prize in Literature.

(*iv*) The Committee of the Norwegian Parliament awards the Prize for Peace.

(*v*) The Bank of Sweden awards the Nobel Prize in Economics.

2. Ramon Magsaysay Award: The Raman Magsaysay Award, named after a Philippines President, who died in an air crash in 1957, is given annually to Asian nationals or institutions who have made worthy contributions to public service, community leadership, journalism, literature and the creative arts and international understanding. It carries a gold medal, a certificate and US$ 50,000. It is awarded on August 31, every year.

3. Pulitzer Prize: Instituted in 1970 and named after the US publisher Joseph Pulitzer (1847-1911). It is conferred annually in the United States for accomplishment in journalism, literature and music under the management to the Pulitzer Prize Board at Columbia University. Each winner receives a gold medal as well as a cash award of $ 15,000.

4. Man Booker Prize: Instituted in 1968, it is the highest literary award set up by the Booker Company and the British Publishers Association along the lines of the Pultizer Prize, of USA, worth £ 20,000 (1992). The Booker Prize has only been shared in 1974 and 1992. Since 2002, it has been known as the **'Man Booker Prize'**, reflecting the sponsorship by an investment company, the Man Group plc. The winner receives £ 50,000 and both the winner and the shorlisted authors are guaranteed a world wide readership plus a dramatic increase in book sales.

Indian Recipients of Man Booker Prize

Years	Winners	Book's Names
1997	Arundhati Roy	The God of Small Things
2006	Kiran Desai	The Inheritance of Loss
2008	Aravind Adiga	The White Tiger

5. **Right Livelihood Award:** Instituted in 1980, by Jakob Von Uexkull, a Swedish-German writer and philatetic expert after selling his stamp collection. This award is known as the 'Alternative Nobel Prize'. The Pro-ecology Right Livelihood Society, based in Britain's Isle of Man, but with a staff in Stockholm, awards this prize annually for practical and exemplary solutions to real problems of today. Earlier, India received this coveted award in 1987 for the 'Chipko' movement. The prize amounts 1 million Swedish Kronor.

6. **UNESCO International Literacy Prizes:** One of UNESCO's main missions is to recognize education as a human right. The organization has placed special emphasis on the education of women, because they comprise majority with low or no literacy skills. Girls make up the majority of the children without access to primary schooling.

   Each award includes prize money of $ 15,000. The prize giving ceremony take place each year during a special ceremony on International Literacy Day, September 8.

7. **UNESCO'S Asia-Pacific Heritage Awards:** UNESCO'S Asia-Pacific Heritage Awards for Culture Heritage Conservation recognise the efforts and contributions of individuals and organisations within the private sector, including private-public partnerships, who have successfully restored and conserved structures and buildings of heritage value in the Asia-Pacific region.

8. **Oscar Awards:** The annual Oscar presentation has been held since 1929. After three-quarters of a century of recognizing excellence in cinema achievement, the annual presentation of the Oscars has become the Academy of Motion Picture Arts and Sciences' most famous activity.

9. **Kalinga Award:** The award given for popularisation of science is an international award conferred annually by the United Nations Educational, Scientific and Cultural Organisation (UNESCO) to a person with a distinguished career of service in the interpretation of science and research to the public. The award was instituted in 1952 at the initiative of Mr Biju Patnaik the founder of the Kalinga Foundation Trust in Odisha.

   The winner of Kalinga prize receives the sum of $ 40,000 and a UNESCO Albert Einstein Silver Medal. The recipient is also awarded the Ruchi Ram Sahni chair, introduced by Government of India in 2001 to mark the 50th anniversary of Kalinga Prize.

10. **United Nations Population Award:** This award is given annually to individuals and institutions for their outstanding work in the field of population and in the improvement of health and welfare of individuals. Each winner carries a certificate, gold medal and monetary prize.

11. **Grammy Award:** The Grammy Foundation was established in 1989 to cultivate an awareness, appreciation and advancement of the contribution of recorded music American culture from the and technical legends of the past to the still unimagined musical breakthroughs of the future generations of the music professionals. The Grammy Foundation works in partnership with its founder, the Recording Academy, to bring national attention to important issues such as the value and impact of music and arts education and the urgency of preserving our rich cultural legacy.

12. **Mahatma Gandhi Peace Prize:** This award, which carries an amount of ₹ 1 crore and a citation, was instituted by the Government of India in 1994, during the 125th birth anniversary celebrations of Mahatma Gandhi. The first person to receive this award in 1995, was Dr. Julius K. Nyerere, former President of Tanzania. The 1996 award was given to Dr. Ahangame Tudor Ariyaratne, the founder President of *Sarvodaya Shramdan* movement in Sri Lanka. In 1997, the award was given to Gerhard Fischer (Germany). In 1998, the award was given to Ramakrishna Mission in

recognition of its contribution towards social, economic and political transformation through nonviolence.

Baba Amte, a Gandhian and a noted social worker, was selected for the coveted Gandhi Peace Prize for 1999 in recognition of this exemplary work for treatment and rehabilitation of leprosy patients and his concept of *Shramik Vidyapeeth.*

The liberator of South Africa and Nobel Laureate Nelson Mandela and Grameen Bank of Bangladesh were to jointly share the prestigious International Gandhi Peace Prize 2000. ***2001:*** Irish Civil rights activist Mr John Hume; ***2002:*** Bharatiya Vidya Bhavan. ***2003:*** Former Czech President Vaclav Havel; ***2004:*** Red Cross; ***2005:*** Archbishop Desmond Tutu (South Africa); ***2013:*** Eminent Gandhian and environmentalist Chandi Prasad Bhatt; ***2014:*** Indian Space Research Organisation (ISRO); ***2015:*** Vivekananda Kendra, Kanya Kumari; ***2016:*** Akshaya Patra Foundation and Sulabh International; ***2017:*** Ekal Abhiyan Trust; ***2018:*** Yohei Sasakawa; ***2020:*** Sheikh Mujibur Rahman (Bangladesh's Father of the Nation). ***2021:*** Gita Press Gorakhpur.

13. **Jawaharlal Nehru Award for International Understanding:** The Government of India instituted the Jawaharlal Nehru Award for International Understanding in 1965 as a tribute to the memory of the late Prime Minister for his lifelong dedication to the cause of world peace and international understanding. The award, which is given away annually to an eminent person for outstanding contribution towards the promotion of international understanding, goodwill and friendship among the people of the world, carries an amount of ₹ 25 lakh (convertible into foreign currency) and a citation. The award is administered by the Indian Council for Cultural Relations and is made by a seven-member independent jury which includes the Vice-President and the Chief Justice of India.

Highest Honours of Some Countries

Country	*Highest Honour*	*Country*	*Highest Honour*
India	Bharat Ratna	Britain	Member of British Empire, Victoria Cross
Pakistan	Nishan-e-Pakistan		
Kuwait	Mubarak-Al-kabir Medal	Japan	Order of Moulovenice Sun
Saudi Arabia	Shah Abdul Aziz Medal	Denmark	Order of Diana Brog
Argentina	The Order of Sona Martin	France	Legend of Honour
Nicaragua	Augusto-Caesar Sandino Order	America	Presidential Medal of Freedom
Vietnam	The order of the Golden Star	Germany	Pore Lee Merit Iron Cross
Hungary	The Order of Banner	The Netherlands	Netherlands Lion

*****

14. SPORTS

Important Cups & Trophies

International

• *American Cup*	: Yacht Racing	• *Walker Cup*	: Golf
• *Ashes*	: Cricket	• *Westchester Cup*	: Polo
• *Benson and Hedges*	: Cricket	• *Wightman Cup*	: Lawn Tennis
• *Canada Cup*	: Golf	• *World Cup*	: Cricket
• *Colombo Cup*	: Football	• *World Cup*	: Hockey
• *Corbitton Cup*	: Table Tennis (Women)	• *Reliance Cup*	: Cricket
• *Davis Cup*	: Lawn Tennis	• *Rothman's Trophy*	: Cricket
• *Derby*	: Horse Race	• *William's Cup*	: Basketball
• *Grand National*	: Horse Streple Chase Race	• *European Champions Cup*	: Football
• *Jules Rimet Trophy*	: World Soccer Cup	• *Eisenhower Cup*	: Golf
• *King's Cup*	: Air Races	• *Essande Champions Cup*	: Hockey
• *Merdeka Cup*	: Football	• *Rene Frank Trophy*	: Hockey
• *Ryder Cup*	: Golf	• *Grand Prix*	: Table Tennis
• *Swaythling Cup*	: Table Tennis (Men)	• *Edgbaston Cup*	: Lawn Tennis
• *Thomas Cup*	: Badminton	• *Grand Prix*	: Lawn Tennis
• *Uber Cup*	: Badminton (Women)	• *World Cup*	: Weightlifting
• *U. Thant Cup*	: Tennis		

National

• *Agarwal Cup*	: Badminton	• *C.K. Naidu Trophy*	: Cricket
• *Agha Khan Cup*	: Hockey	• *Chakola Gold Trophy*	: Football
• *All India Women's Guru Nanak Championship*	: Hockey	• *Divan Cup*	: Badminton
• *Bandodkar Trophy*	: Football	• *Deodhar Trophy*	: Cricket
• *Bangalore Blues Challenge Cup*	: Basketball	• *Duleep Trophy*	: Cricket
• *Barna-Bellack Cup*	: Table Tennis	• *D.C.M. Cup*	: Football
• *Beighton Cup*	: Hockey	• *Durand Cup*	: Football
• *Bombay Gold Cup*	: Hockey	• *Dhyan Chand Trophy*	: Hockey
• *Burdwan Trophy*	: Weightlifting	• *Dr. B.C. Roy Trophy*	: Football (Junior)
• *Charminar Trophy*	: Atheletics	• *Ezra Cup*	: Polo
• *Chadha Cup*	: Badminton	• *F.A. Cup*	: Football
		• *G.D. Birla Trophy*	: Cricket
		• *Ghulam Ahmed Trophy*	: Cricket
		• *Gurmeet Trophy*	: Hockey

- *Guru Nanak Cup* : Hockey
- *Gyanvati Devi Trophy* : Hockey
- *Holkar Trophy* : Bridge
- *Irani Trophy* : Cricket
- *I.F.A. Shield* : Football
- *Indira Gold Cup* : Hockey
- *Jawaharlal Challenge* : Air Racing
- *Jaswant Singh Trophy* : Best Services Sportsman
- *Kuppuswamy Naidu Trophy* : Hockey
- *Lady Rattan Tata Trophy* : Hockey
- *MCC Trophy* : Hockey
- *Moinuddaula Gold Cup* : Cricket
- *Murugappa Gold Cup* : Hockey
- *Modi Gold Cup* : Hockey
- *Narang Cup* : Badminton
- *Nehru Trophy* : Hockey
- *Nixan Gold Cup* : Football
- *Obaidullah Gold Cup* : Hockey
- *Prithi Singh Cup* : Polo
- *Rani Jhansi Trophy* : Cricket
- *Ranji Trophy* : Cricket
- *Rangaswami Cup* : Hockey
- *Ranjit Singh Gold Cup* : Hockey
- *Rajendra Prasad Cup* : Tennis
- *Ramanujan Trophy* : Table Tennis
- *Rene Frank Trophy* : Hockey
- *Radha Mohan Cup* : Polo
- *Raghbir Singh Memorial* : Football
- *Rohinton Baria Trophy* : Cricket
- *Rovers Cup* : Football
- *Sanjay Gold Cup* : Football
- *Santosh Trophy* : Football
- *Sir Ashutosh Mukherjee* : Football
- *Subroto Cup* : Football
- *Scindia Gold Cup* : Hockey
- *Sahni Trophy* : Hockey
- *Sheesh Mahal Trophy* : Cricket
- *Todd Memorial Trophy* : Football
- *Tommy Eman Gold Cup* : Hockey
- *Vittal Trophy* : Football
- *Vizzy Trophy* : Cricket
- *Vijay Merchant Trophy* : Cricket
- *Wellington Trophy* : Rowing
- *Wills Trophy* : Cricket

Sports Measurements

- *Badminton Courts:* 44 ft. by 20 ft. (doubles) 44 ft. by 17 ft. (singles)
- *Boxing Ring:* 12 ft. by 28 ft. Sq.
- *Cricket Pitch:* 22 yards (distance)
- *Derby Course:* 1½ miles. (2.4 km)
- *Football Field:*
  (a) Length : 100 – 120 yards.
  [Breadth: 50 – 56 yards.
  (b) Rugby : 100 yards by 75 yards
- *Hockey Ground:* 100 yards by 55 to 60 yards
- *Lawn Tennis Court:* 78 ft. by 36 ft. (double), 78 ft. by 28 ft. (single)
- *Marathon Race:* 26 miles, 385 yards
- *Polo Ground:* 300 yards by 200 yards (if boarded)
- *Golf:* Hole 4½ inches in diameter.

Sports Terms

- **Badminton:** Mixed doubles; Deuce; Drop; Smash; Let; Foot work; Setting.
- **Base Ball:** Pitcher; Put out, Strike; Home; Bunt.
- **Billiards:** Cue; Jigger; Pot; Break; In Baulk; In Off; Cannons.
- **Boxing:** Upper cut; Round; Punch; Bout; Knock down; Hitting below the belt; Ring.
- **Bridge:** Finesse; Dummy; Revoke; Grand Slam; Little Slam; No Trump; Rubber.
- **Chess:** Bishop, Gambit; Checkmate; Stalemate.
- **Cricket:** L.B.W. *(leg before wicket)*; Creases, Popping-creases; Stumped; Bye; Leg-Bye; Googly; Hattrick; Maiden over; Drive; Bowling; Duck; Follow-on; No ball; Leg Break; Silly point; Cover point; Hit-wicket; Late-cut; Slip; Off-spinner; In-swing.

- **Football:** Off Side; Block; Drop-kick; Penalty-kick (or *goal kick*); Corner-kick; Free-kick; Dribble; Thrown-in; Foul.
- **Golf:** Boggy; Foursome; Stymic; Tee; Put; Hole; Niblic; Caddie; Links; The green; Bunker.
- **Hockey:** Carried; Short Corner; Bully; Sticks; Off side; Roll in; Striking Circle; Under-cutting; Dribble.
- **Horse racing:** Jockey; Punter.
- **Polo:** Bunker; Chukker; Mallet.
- **Tennis:** Back hand drive; Volley; Smash; Half-volley; Deuce; Service; Let; Grand Slam.

Name of Playing Compound of Different Games

Name of Compound	*Related Sports*	*Name of Compound*	*Related Sports*
Court	Lawn Tennis, Badminton, Netball, Hand ball, Volleyball, Squash, Kho-Kho, Kabaddi	Pool	Swimming
		Alley	Bowling
		Mat	Judo, Karate II
		Arena	Horse Riding
Diamond	Baseball	Vellodrum	Cycling
Ring	Boxing, Skating, Wrestling, Circus, Riding display	Field	Polo, Football, Hockey
		Track	Athletics
Course	Golf	Pitch	Cricket, Rugby
Board	Table Tennis	Rink	Ice Hockey

National Sports and Games of Some Countries

Australia	Cricket	Spain	Bull Fighting
Canada	Ice Hockey	USA	Baseball
England	Cricket and Rugby Football	China	Table Tennis
Japan	Ju-Jitsu	Malaysia	Badminton
Russia	Chess	Pakistan	Hockey
Scotland	Rugby Football		

Number of Players in Some Games/Sports

Sports	*No. of Players*	*Sports*	*No. of Players*
Badminton	1 or 2	Lacrosse	12
Baseball	9	Netball	7
Basketball	5	Polo Rugby	4
Billiards (Snooker)	1	Football (Rugby)	15
Boxing	1	Table	1 or
Bridge	2	Tennis	2
Chess	1	Lawn	1 or
Cricket	11	Tennis	2
Croquest	13 or 15	Volleyball	6
Football (Soccer)	11	Water Polo	7
Hockey	11		

OLYMPIC GAMES

First of all these games were held by the Greeks in 776 B.C. on Mount Olympus in honour of the Greek God Zeus. In this way, the history of Olympic Games is about twenty eight hundred years old. These games continued to be held every four years until 394 A.D. When these games were stopped by a royal order of the emperor of Rome. The modern Olympic Games which started in Athens in 1896, are the result of the devotion and dedication of a French educator Baron Pierre de Coubertin and the first Olympic meet in the modern series was held in 1896 in Athens, the Capital of Greece. Since then, they are being held every four years except for breaks during world wars. The Olympic flag is white in colour with five coloured rings, each ring symbolic of a continent. Summer as well as winter Olympics are held in the same year.

Olympic Games (Venues & Dates)

Year	Venue	Organising	Participating Countries	Year	Venue	Organising	Participating Countries
1896	Athens	6–15 April	13	1956	Melbourne	22nd November to 8th December	71
1900	Paris	20th May to 28th Oct.	22	1960	Rome	25th Aug. to 11th Sept.	83
1904	St. Louis	1st July to 23rd Nov.	13	1964	Tokyo	10th to 24th October	93
1908	London	27th April to 31st Oct.	22	1968	Mexico City	12th to 27th October	112
1912	Stockholm	5th May to 22nd July	28	1972	Munich	26th August to 10 Sept.	122
1916	Berlin	Cancelled due to World War	—	1976	Montreal	17th July to 1st Sept.	88
1920	Antwerp	20th April to 12th Sept.	29	1980	Moscow	19th July to 3rd Aug.	81
1924	Paris	4th May to 27th July	44	1984	Los Angeles	28th July to 12th Aug.	140
1928	Amsterdam	17th May to 12 Aug.	46	1988	Seoul	17th Sept. to 2nd Oct.	160
1932	Los Angeles	30th July to 14th Aug.	47	1992	Barcelona	25th July to 9th Aug.	170
1936	Berlin	1st May to 16th Aug.	49	1996	Atlanta	19th July to 4th Aug.	197
1940	Tokyo (Helsinki)	Cancelled due to Wold War	—	2000	Sydney	15th Sept. to 1st Oct.	199
1944	London	Cancelled due to World War	—	2004	Athens	14th to 29th August	202
1948	London	29th July to 14th Aug.	59	2008	Beijing	8th to 24th August	204
1952	Helsinki	19th July to 3rd Aug.	69	2012	London	27th July to 12 August	204
				2016	Rio de Janeiro	5th August to 21 Aug.	207
				2020	Tokyo	23rd July to 08 Aug. 2021	206

Note: Games not held in 1916, 1940, and 1944.

ASIAN GAMES

After the Second World War, most of the Asian Countries gained independence. On the lines of Olympic Games, Asian Games were planned every four years. India hosted the first Asian Games in 1951.

Asian Games: An Overview

Year	Venues	Participating Countries	No. of Games	First Position	Year	Venues	Participating Countries	No. of Games	First Position
1951	New Delhi	11	6	Japan	1986	Seoul	34	25	China
1954	Manila	18	7	Japan	1994	Hiroshima	42	34	China
1958	Tokyo	20	13	Japan	1998	Bangkok	41	36	China
1962	Jakarta	16	13	Japan	2002	Busan	44	38	China
1966	Bangkok	18	14	Japan	2006	Doha	46	43	China
1970	Bangkok	18	13	Japan	2010	Guangzhou	45	42	China
1974	Teheran	25	16	Japan	2014	Incheon	45	36	China
1978	Bangkok	25	19	Japan	2018	Jakarta	45	40	China
1982	New Delhi	33	21	China	2022	Hangzhou (Held in 2023)	45	40	China
1990	Beijing	37	27	China					

COMMONWEALTH GAMES

The Commonwealth Games are held every four years, in the year in which Asian Games are held. All the Commonwealth Countries (former colonies of Britain) can take part in it. The first Commonwealth Games were held in 1930 at Hamilton (Canada).

Venues of Commonwealth Games

Venues	Year	Countries/ Associations	Sports	Venues	Year	Countries/ Associations	Sports
Hamilton, (Canada)	1930	11	6	Brisbane, (Australia)	1982	47	10
London, (U.K.)	1934	16	6	Edinburgh, (U.K.)	1986	26	10
Sydney, (Australia)	1938	15	7	Auckland, (New Zealand)	1990	55	10
Auckland, (New Zealand)	1950	12	7	Victoria, (Canada)	1994	64	
Vancouver, (Canada)	1954	24	9	Kuala Lumpur, (Malaysia)	1998	70	16
Cardiff, (U.K.)	1958	35	9	Manchester, (U.K.)	2002	72	17
Perth, (Australia)	1962	35	9	Melbourne, (Australia)	2006	71	16
Jamaica, (West Indies)	1966	34	9	Delhi, (India)	2010	71	17
Edinburgh, (U.K.)	1970	42	9	Glasgow, (Scotland)	2014	71	17
Christchurch, (New Zealand)	1974	39	9	Gold Coast (Aus.)	2018	71	19
Edmonton, (Canada)	1978	48	10	Birmingham (UK)	2022	72	20

World Cup Football

Year	Winner	Runners-Up	Year	Winner	Runners-Up
1930	Uruguay	Argentina	1982	Italy	W. Germany
1934	Italy	Czechoslovakia	1986	Argentina	W. Germany
1938	Italy	Hungary	1990	W. Germany	Argentina
1950	Uruguay	Brazil	1994	Brazil	Italy
1954	West Germany	Hungary	1998	France	Brazil
1958	Brazil	Sweden	2002	Brazil	Germany
1962	Brazil	Czechoslovakia	2006	Italy	France
1966	England	West Germany	2010	Spain	Netherlands
1970	Brazil	Italy	2014	Germany	Argentina
1974	W. Germany	Poland	2018	France	Croatia
1978	Argentina	Holland	2022	Argentina	France

World Cup Cricket

Year	Venue	Winner/Runner	Year	Venue	Winner/Runner
1975	U.K.	West Indies beat Australia	2003	South Africa	Australia beat India
1979	U.K.	West Indies beat England	2007	West Indies	Australia beat Sri Lanka
1983	U.K.	India beat West Indies	2011	India, Sri Lanka, Bangladesh	India beat Sri Lanka
1987	India & Pakistan	Australia beat England	2015	Australia, New Zealand	Australia beat New Zealand
1992	Australia	Pakistan beat England	2019	England	England beat New Zealand
1996	India, Pakistan & Sri Lanka	Sri Lanka beat Australia	2023	India	Australia beat India
1999	U.K.	Australia beat Pakistan			

*****

MULTIPLE CHOICE QUESTIONS

GENERAL AWARENESS

1. The part of the Sun, which is visible during eclipses only, is known as
A. photosphere
B. chromosphere
C. corona
D. all the parts are visible with naked eye

2. Sphygmomanometer is used for
A. measuring the brain pulse of a patient
B. measuring the systolic and diastolic blood pressures of man
C. measuring the amount of blood in a human body
D. measuring the haemoglobin count in a human body

3. The most abundant gas in air is
A. nitrogen B. hydrogen
C. oxygen D. ozone

4. The most commonly found acid in nature is
A. hydrochloric acid B. sulphuric acid
C. lactic acid D. acetic acid

5. This bomb is used to destroy living beings but would not damage the buildings and other property
A. napalm bomb B. neutron bomb
C. hydrogen bomb D. None of the above

6. Electrical energy is measured in terms of units which are also termed as
A. KW B. KWH
C. WH D. KVAR

7. In cold countries, the radiator water of cars is mixed with glycerol. This is done to
A. increase the specific heat of water
B. reduce the freezing point of water
C. improve the engine efficiency
D. glycerol is not added in radiator water

8. If the Richter scale shows a value of 7.2, then the seismograph indicates
A. an earthquake of low intensity
B. an earthquake of very high intensity
C. an earthquake of moderate intensity
D. either A or C

9. The theory of origin of species is based primarily on
A. the process of biological evolution
B. the process of natural selection
C. the evolution of life from the oceans
D. the evolution of man from apes

10. Common coal used in our households is
A. Anthracite B. Bituminous coal
C. Lignite D. All of the above

11. Some recent findings on moon, which point out towards the possibility of settlement of man on moon, include
A. nil atmospheric gases
B. ice reserves on the poles
C. micro-organisms
D. None of the above

12. Viagra is a medicine for
A. treatment of AIDS
B. treatment of female fertility
C. treatment of male impotency
D. treatment of Lukaemia

13. Rickets is a disease which is caused by the deficiency of
A. Vitamin A B. Riboflavin
C. Vitamin C D. Vitamin D

14. When a ship enters waters of the sea from a river, then its level
A. rises as the sea water is saline and hence bouyancy force is more
B. decreases as ocean is a large mass of water
C. remains the same as water is the same for the river and the sea
D. None of the above

15. The major constituent of pearl is
A. calcium carbonate
B. calcium oxide and ammonium chloride
C. organic mass
D. calcium carbonate and silica

16. A healthy person needs ..... calories per day.
A. 2200 B. 2400
C. 2500 D. 1800

17. The value of one (marine) Naut is
A. 1951 metre per hour
B. 1852 metre per hour
C. 2305 metre per hour
D. 1860 metre per hour

18. Acid and base combine to form
A. salt and nitrogen
B. nitrogen and oxygen
C. salt and water
D. acid and alkali

19. Cellulose could be obtained from
A. wood and cotton B. silk and cotton
C. paper and silk D. wood and silk

20. ELISA test is done for the detection of
A. cancer B. AIDS
C. diabetes D. None of the above

21. Triple Antigen, prevents
A. small pox, malaria, whooping cough
B. tetanus, diphtheria, small pox
C. whooping cough, tetanus, polio
D. diphtheria, tetanus, whooping cough

22. A freely falling body
A. would fall towards the surface of the earth
B. would have no weight
C. would have one half of its original weight
D. None of the above

23. If the motor neurons of the spinal cord of a child are damaged, then he would develop the following disease.
A. Rickets B. Polio
C. Diphtheria D. Jaundice

24. Which one of the following is not a part of the balanced diet?
A. Vitamins B. Carbohydrate
C. Proteins D. Alcohol

25. Which statement is not correct in connection with human physiology?
A. The length of the small intestine is 7 metres and its diameter is 2.5 cm.
B. There are 639 muscles in a human body
C. An infant breathes 45 times per minute whereas a six year old child breathes 25 times per minute
D. The weight of the adult human brain is nearly 700 gms

26. The bottles of beer are not kept in the deep freezer because
A. beer is an alcohol which could burst under conditions of low temperature
B. alcohol could damage the deep freezer due to its corrosive action if the bottles break accidently
C. water content in beer gets converted into ice which expends (after change of state from water to ice) and this could lead to bursting of beer bottles
D. the low temperature could degrade the beer and hence, it may not good remain for consumption

27. Rocket works on the basis of
A. principle of conservation of momentum
B. principle of relativity
C. principle of conservation of mass
D. principle of conservation of energy

28. Which one of the following groups is more closely related from the viewpoint of taxonomy?
A. silverfish, starfish, cuttlefish
B. earthworm, seahorse, hookworm
C. housefly, dragonfly, butterfly
D. None of the above

29. Red blood corpuscles are produced in
A. liver B. spleen
C. bone marrow D. kidneys

30. The disease for which the first oral drug has been developed for treatment.
A. Cancer B. Pneumonid
C. Small pox D. Plauge

31. E-comm is a short form of
A. Engineering Commercial
B. Electronic Commercial
C. Electronic Commerce
D. None of the above

32. High AC voltages are used for transmitting electric power because
A. at high voltages, current is low and hence, losses are low

B. the transmission of power is quicker
C. the high voltages a consumé lesser materials for transmission
D. None of the above

33. There is a hole in the boat through which, water is seeping into the boat. Just before the boat capsizes
A. water level would decrease
B. water level would increase
C. water level would remain the same
D. None of the above

34. During which month, the rate of rotation of the earth on its axis is the fastest?
A. December
B. May
C. the rate of rotation is fixed
D. It is fastest when the earth is closest to the Sun.

35. The time taken by the Sun rays to reach the earth is
A. 9 minutes B. 10 minutes
C. 7 minutes D. 8 minutes

36. The outer planets are
A. Moon, Earth, Mercury, Venus
B. Jupiter, Saturn, Uranus, Earth, Mars
C. Jupiter, Uranus, Saturn, Neptune
D. None of the above

37. According to the astrophysicists
A. the universe is mobile and expanding
B. the universe is heading for a collision with another universe
C. the universe is stationary
D. the doomsday of universe is near due to the formation of many new black holes

38. Which is popular as the White City?
A. New York B. Belgrade
C. Bangalore D. Bab-el-mandab

39. The national currency of Haiti is
A. Rupiah B. Gourde
C. Quetzal D. Dong

40. Which one is not a news agency of India?
A. UNI
B. PTI
C. Hindustan Samachar
D. Reuters

41. The abundant element of the earth's atmosphere is:
A. Oxygen B. nitrogen
C. hydrogen D. CO_2

42. The first talking movie of India was ..... and the first silent movie of India was .....
A. Aan, Aawara
B. Raja Harish Chandra, Alamara
C. Alamara, Raja Harish Chandra
D. Purana Mandir, Raja Harish Chandra

43. Hair becomes grey because
A. rays of the Sun force it to become grey
B. the quantity of melanin is reduced in human body with growing age
C. there is a lack of vitamins in the body due to growing age
D. None of the above

44. Salaries of Supreme Court judges are drawn from:
A. Law Ministry Grants
B. Consolidated Fund of India
C. Home Ministry Grants
D. Parliamentary Grants

45. The term "Paper-gold" is associated with
A. deficit budgeting
B. loans from the World Bank
C. Special Drawing Rights (SDRs) from the IMF
D. None of the above

46. TRAI refers to
A. Terresteral Remote Sensing Authority of India
B. Telecommunication Research Authority of India
C. Transport Regulatory Authority of India
D. Telecom Regulatory Authority of India

47. NSDL is an organisation in India which
A. provides security to depositors
B. accepts deposits from recognised bodies
C. provides data security for on-line computer systems
D. None of the above

48. The enzyme pepsin converts
A. proteins into peptones
B. fats to amino acids
C. carbohydrates to sugars
D. proteins to amino acids

49. Who among the following is not a winner of the PVC?
A. Bana Singh

B. Nirmal Jeet Singh Sekhon
C. Somnath Sharma
D. Shanti Swaroop Rana

50. Which one of the following pairs is not correct?
A. Narmada – Betul district
B. Krishna – near Mahabaleshwar
C. Chambal – near Mhow
D. Godavari – Nashik district

51. The Japanese art of flower arrangement is known as
A. Bonsai B. Ongami
C. Ikebota D. None of the above

52. The meaning of the Latin word *Vive Rex* is
A. Long live the king!
B. Let the Nation Live
C. A middle course
D. Nothing wrong here

53. The permanent station of India in Antarctica is known as
A. *Vikalp*
B. Antarctica India Station
C. *Maitri*
D. *Dakshin Yamunotri*

54. A man dies due to electrocution because
A. electric current passes through his body to earth which leads to sudden contraction and expansion of muscles (including heart muscles) and this, alongwith development of heat in the body, leads to heart failure.
B. there is no resistance offered by the body
C. the body allows the current to flow through the blood which cannot circulate any longer
D. None of the above

55. "Blue Dwarfs" are
A. members of the Russian circus
B. warriors of Mongolia
C. young stars of the universe
D. naval officers in the high seas

56. What is a fly leaf?
A. thin paper sheet for making packaging material
B. a blank page at the beginning or end of a book
C. a marker in a book
D. a sheet of paper next to the main title of the book

57. Who is associated with the theory of inheritance of acquired characters?
A. Spencer B. Mandeleev
C. Lamarck D. All of the above

58. Ligaments and tendons in the body are made up of
A. skeletal tissue B. muscular tissue
C. connective tissue D. epithelial tissue

59. A cell membrane is
A. completely permeable
B. impermeable
C. semi-permeable
D. None of the above

60. The tenure of the non-permanent members of the UN Security Council is
A. one year
B. three years
C. two years
D. there is no fixed tenure

61. Why proper earthing is necessary?
A. It reduces the consumption of electricity
B. It allows the current to flow through the earth wire and into the earth, thus protecting the person
C. It allows the appliance to operate efficiently
D. None of the above

62. Which one of the following items has not been included in the minimum needs programme?
A. unemployment allowance
B. rural water supply
C. rural electrification
D. adult education

63. This is not the principle organ of digestion and absorption in the human body.
A. small intestine B. stomach
C. large intestine D. Both A and B

64. Which are the two stars which appear as morning stars in the Eastern sky and evening stars in the Western sky?
A. Jupiter and Mars
B. Mars and Venus
C. Saturn and Mercury
D. Mercury and Venus

65. Which planet rotates on its axis from East to West?
A. Mercury B. Jupiter
C. Earth D. Venus

66. The chemical compound present in the stone of human kidney is
A. calcium phosphate B. calcium carbonate
C. silica D. calcium oxalate

67. Which one of the following diseases would be caused by bacterial infection?
A. tetanus B. rabies
C. cancer D. malaria

68. India On-line Limited is
A. an advertising agency
B. a reservation office
C. an information service
D. an internet services provider

69. CTBT is related to
A. economic sanctions imposed by the USA on India
B. the codename of Pokharan-II blasts
C. the nuclear test ban treaty which India is being forced to adhere to
D. codename of Pakistani nuclear arsenal

70. The disagreement between Lok Sabha and Rajya Sabha is solved by:
A. setting up Joint Select Committee
B. dissolving Lok Sabha
C. setting up adjudication committee
D. calling a joint session

71. The national anthem was written by ..... and was translated into English by .....
A. Bankim Chandra Chatterji, Aurobindo Ghosh
B. Rabindra Nath Tagore, Aurobindo Ghosh
C. Bankim Chandra Chatterji, Rabindra Nath Tagore
D. the national anthem was originally written in English and was translated later

72. The tear in human body is a solution of :
A. Sodium hydroxide and sodium chloride
B. Calcium bicarbonate and sodium chloride
C. Magnesium bicarbonate and sodium hydroxide
D. Sodium bicarbonate and Magnesium chloride

73. The drug seroxat is
A. a new medicine for treating the lepers.
B. a new medicine developed by British scientists and is used for the treatment of shyness and social phobia
C. is anti-AIDS therapy developed by France
D. is an antacid developed in India under guidance of WHO

74. What is "Bermuda Triangle" sometimes referred to as the "Grakeyard of ships", located?
A. in the South Pacific ocean
B. in the North Atlantic ocean
C. in the Indian ocean
D. in the Arctic ocean

75. The theory propounded by Nobel laurate Professor Amartya Sen–is commonly known as
A. The Famine Economics
B. The Theory of Economic Divide
C. The Amartya Sen Shift
D. The Amartya Sen Divide

76. Which is known as the Electronics City of India?
A. Tumkoor B. Secunderabad
C. Bhopal D. None of the above

77. The main objective behind the creation of concept of *Navratnas* in the public sector was
A. to increase the control of the PSUs over economy
B. to boost local manufacturing and exports in the core sectors
C. to improve the functional autonomy
D. to improve their image and efficiency by giving them high status

78. The North American seaport on the Pacific side is
A. Baltimore B. Boston
C. New York D. Seattle

79. The old name of Harare was
A. Sam B. Rhodesia
C. Salisbury D. Batavia

80. The famous Prince of Wales Museum is located in
A. Mumbai B. Kolkata
C. Vadodara D. Bangalore

81. Who invented Atom Bomb (Uranium Fission)?
A. A W Haffmann B. Otto Hahn
C. A Einstein D. None of the above

82. The first ever woman to go into space was
A. Kalpana Chawla
B. Valentina Tereshkova
C. Mary Pierce
D. None of the above

83. The highest mountain peak in India is
A. K-2 B. Everest
C. Kanchanjunga D. Makalu-I

84. The "Garden City" of England is
A. Portsmouth B. Manchester
C. Kent D. Warwickshire

85. *Habeas Corpus* is.
A. an order of the International Court of Justice
B. a type of writ issued by a High Court or Supreme Court against illegal detention of a person.
C. the petition of a lawyer in the Supreme Court on behalf of his client for bail against the orders of any other court in India
D. None of the above

86. If impeachment motion is passed by the American Senate against the US President, he would have to
A. leave office and all his assets created by him during Presidency
B. leave office, lose his pensions, security cover and all those benefits that are accorded to a retired US President
C. jailed for five years and will not get any benefits.
D. retire honourably with all his benefits, compensations, assets and pensions remaining intact

87. Who appoints the non-permanent members of the UN Security Council?
A. the permanent members
B. the General Assembly
C. the International Court of Justice
D. None of the above

88. The Preamble of the Constitution was amended by:
A. 1st amendment B. 26th amendment
C. 42nd amendment D. 44th amendment

89. The only President to be elected twice is:
A. S. Radhakrishnan B. V.V. Giri
C. Rajendra Prasad D. N.S. Reddy

90. The official airline of Australia is
A. SIA B. Lufthansa
C. Modiluft D. None of the above

91. Which one of the following types of coal contains a higher percentage of carbon than the rest?
A. Bituminous Coal B. Lignite
C. Anthracite D. Peat

92. Ten Commandments were revealed by God to:
A. Abraham B. Moses
C. Jesus D. Peter

93. Kalinga in older days, is now known as:
A. Odisha B. Kohima
C. Karnataka D. Maharashtra

94. Bihu festival is celebrated in:
A. Gujarat B. Assam
C. Bihar D. West Bengal

95. Milk is an example of
A. gel B. emulsion
C. suspension D. mixture

96. The President can dissolve the Lok Sabha before expiry of its term, on the advice of:
A. Prime Minister
B. Speaker
C. Vice-President
D. Election Commissioner

97. In a landmark judgement, the Allahabad High Court ruled that
A. Capital Sentence is not to be imposed upon the rapists
B. pension is the fundamental right of the government employees
C. the Supreme Court should not be bothered for cases of financial compensation
D. None of the above

98. Tughlaq dynasty occupied Delhi throne after decline of:
A. Suri dynasty B. Slave dynasty
C. Lodhi dynasty D. Khilji dynasty

99. Governors of states are:
A. appointed by Chief Ministers
B. appointed by the President
C. elected by members of Legislative Assembly
D. elected by people

100. The partition of Bengal was carried out by:
A. Lord Curzon B. Lord Minto
C. Lord Canning D. Lord Ripon

101. The Air Force Day falls on
A. October 10 B. October 9
C. September 5 D. October 8

102. MAD stands for
A. Most Active Disease
B. Mica Aluminium Duo
C. Mutually Assured Death
D. Mutually Assured Destruction

103. "Disguised Unemployment" means
A. more persons employed for a job that only a few could accomplish
B. people without any technical jobs
C. woman without jobs in rural areas
D. employment of children in factories

104. In India, an active volcano is situated at
A. Lakshadweep
B. Chhotanagpur Plateau
C. Andaman and Nicobar
D. Malawa Plateau

105. The first country to establish trade relationships with India was
A. England B. France
C. Holland D. Portugal

106. Which has the highest share of electrical power generation in India?
A. thermal power
B. nuclear power
C. hydro-power
D. naphtha-based and gas-based power

107. The great ocean liner, known to be the best and luxurious during her times, sank in the year
A. 1902 B. 1912
C. 1908 D. 1889

108. Who among the following is known as the Indian Napoleon?
A. Chandra Gupta Maurya
B. Bindusar
C. Samudra Gupta
D. Harshvardhana

109. Time gap between two sessions of Parliament cannot exceed:
A. 3 months B. 6 months
C. 1 year D. no fixed gap

110. In which state, Panchayati Raj was introduced for the first time?
A. Bihar B. Punjab
C. Rajasthan D. Andhra Pradesh

111. Which one is not a national duty?
A. Respect the Constitution
B. Respect the President
C. Defend the country
D. Protect natural environment

112. Treaty of Seringapatam was signed between:
A. Tipu Sultan and Nawab of Hyderabad
B. Tipu Sultan and English
C. Tipu Sultan & Rani of Jhansi
D. Tipu Sultan and French

113. NHRC stands for
A. National Hydro Research Committee
B. National Handicapped Rahabilitation Council
C. National Human Rights Commission
D. None of the above

114. "Water water everywhere but not a drop to drink" who stated these lines in a poem?
A. John Milton
B. Samuel Taylor Coleridge
C. Lord Byron
D. P.B. Shelley

115. Rabindranath Tagore gave up his knighthood after:
A. Jallianwala Bagh Tragedy
B. Introduction of separate electorates
C. Bengal faminine
D. Bengal Partition

116. Which country is known as the land of golden wool?
A. India B. Turkey
C. Australia D. Myanmar

117. BIFR stands for
A. Bilateral and International Foreign Regulation
B. Board of Industrial Financial Resurrection

C. Board of Industrial and Financial Reconstruction
D. None of the above

118. Pinaca is a
A. drug for curing AIDS
B. multi-barrel rocket system
C. fighter aircraft developed by HAL
D. codename of the nuclear test operation carried out on May 11, 1998

119. Vice-President is ex-officio:
A. Member of Rajya Sabha
B. Chairman of Rajya Sabha
C. Member of Lok Sabha
D. Speaker of Lok Sabha

120. Vitamin C is not available in this food in sufficiently large quantities.
A. lemon B. tomato
C. cod liver oil D. fresh fruits

121. This book was not written in a jail
A. *Glimpses of World History* – J L Nehru
B. *The Bible* (German) – Martin Luther
C. *Les Miserables* – Victor Hugo
D. *Yama* – Mahadevi Verma

122. Who among the following can be removed from office through impeachment by Parliament?
A. Speaker of Lok Sabha
B. Prime Minister
C. President of India
D. Vice-President of India

123. The following is not the function of the liver.
A. to store excesssive sugar in the form of glycogen
B. the produce an antidote for neutralising poison
C. to manufacture red blood corpuscles
D. to purify the blood through bile

124. A fascist is a person whose views are extremely
A. left-winged B. rational
C. right-winged D. liberal

125. The famous mathematician and a professor of Astronomy designed this building in London
A. Westminister Abbey
B. St Paul's Cathedral
C. Stock Exchange
D. Tower of London

126. Which one of the following sounds cannot be heard by a human ear?
A. 30,000 vibrations per second
B. 10,000 vibrations per second
C. 1,000 vibrations per second
D. 300 vibrations per second

127. A weather balloon may not be inflated completely on the ground because
A. it cannot withstand the atmospheric pressure if inflated fully
B. if the balloon is inflated fully on ground, fuel consumption would be higher
C. the air inside the balloon expands as it rises and hence, the balloon could get burst
D. None of the above

128. Which one of the following vitamins is stored in the liver?
A. Vitamin C
B. Vitamin B_{12}
C. Vitamin A
D. Vitamin K and Vitamin A

129. All of the following are plant products except
A. silk B. cork
C. hemp D. linen

130. Which one of the following organs in the human body is known as "Adam's Apple"?
A. thyroid B. liver
C. thymus D. adrenal

131. Insecticides or medicines could be harmful
A. to the insects and weeds as they kill them instantaneously upon consumption
B. to the habitat as the environment could become polluted due to excessive usage of chemicals in our crop management processes
C. to the human beings and animals who consume the food adulterated by the insecticides and weedicides
D. to the transporters and movers of the crops who could inhale noxious fumes of insecticides and weedicides

132. Name the assassin of John Lennon
A. Art Buchwald
B. Lee Oswald
C. Mark David Chapman
D. None of the above

133. Which one of the following is not a sprinter?
A. Marion Jones
B. Florence Griffith Joyner
C. Ben Johnson
D. Susie O' Neill

134. Which of the following is called the "Gateway to the Pacific"?
A. Suez Canal B. Bering Sea
C. Panama Canal D. Gulf of Alaska

135. Which one of the following statements is true regarding the treaty on banning the land-mines?
A. the USA does not want to sign the CTBT
B. the treaty was kept open for signatures in Ottawa in December, 1997.
C. India has already signed it
D. A and B are true

136. Similipal Tiger reserve is situated in:
A. Madhya Pradesh B. Uttarakhand
C. Maharashtra D. Odisha

137. The famous Gandhian, who was also known as the "Frontier Gandhi," is
A. Liaqat Ali Khan
B. Yusuf Khan
C. Khan Abdul Ghaffar Khan
D. Abdul Wali Khan

138. Which one of the following is an alloy?
A. copper B. lanthanum
C. bronze D. uranium

139. World Environment Day is celebrated on
A. June 4 B. June 5
C. June 7 D. March 5

140. This country is the largest producer of cotton in the world.
A. India B. China
C. Egypt D. the USA

141. The quorum required to the Rajya Sabha is:
A. 100 B. 35
C. 25 D. 30

142. The temples of Khajuraho were built by
A. Chalukyas B. Pallavas
C. Rashtrakutas D. Chandelas

143. National Remote Sensing Agency (NRSA) is located at:
A. Hyderabad
B. Bengaluru
C. Thiruvananthapuram
D. Gadanki, near Tirupati

144. The clones for .... and .... have been developed.
A. man, cow B. crow, sheep
C. rat, cat D. sheep, rat

145. AWWA stands for
A. All Women Welfare Association
B. Army Wives Welfare Association
C. Airport Weather and Welfare Authority
D. None of the above

146. The popular book *The Gift of Time* by Jonathan Schell, deals with
A. the lewid affair of Bill Clinton and Monica Lewinsky
B. the elimination of nuclear weapons from the world
C. Indo-US relationships
D. the deteriorating environment in industrial America

147. How can a person move on a hard icy surface?
A. he should use roller skates
B. he should hop, sneeze, jump and step in the direction which is opposite to the direction of his required movement
C. he should hop, sneeze, jump and step in the direction in which the movement is required
D. he should skid on his knees and hands

148. The first conference of Non-Aligned Movement was held at:
A. The Hague
B. Moscow
C. Great Britain
D. Belgrade

149. Who is regarded as the founder of the scientific socialism?
A. Rousseau B. Karl Marx
C. Engles D. Lenin

150. Pyroclastics are
A. non-toxic gases
B. lava flows
C. fragments of hot rock and spattering lava
D. pollutant chemicals from a leather factory

151. Which one of the following is not a sedimentary rock?
A. slate B. limestone
C. clay D. sandstone

152. Oketa is
A. used to define human-induced climatic changes
B. used to describe increasing drought periods of high magnitudes
C. a unit to describe the prevailing cloudiness
D. None of the above

153. The following state produces the maximum quantities (85 percent) of raw silk in India
A. Kerala B. Jammu & Kashmir
C. Karnataka D. Tamil Nadu

154. Salal Hydro Electric Project is situated on the river
A. Beas B. Jhelum
C. Chenab D. Sutlej

155. Which is the largest island sea in the world?
A. Caribbean Sea B. Mediterranean Sea
C. Red Sea D. Beaufort Sea

156. What is the name of the bell used at the Lloyds in London?
A. The Great Bell B. The Charmer
C. The Tower Bell D. Lutine

157. What are "The Hagiographs?"
A. These are the poems written by Lord Byron
B. These are the holy writings of Jewish scriptures
C. These are the geographical lines representing same rainfall levels
D. None of the above

158. Which one of the following forms would provide the lowest protection?
A. Patent B. Trademark
C. Copyright D. Logo

159. The twenty-fifth State of India is
A. Goa B. Nagaland
C. Mizoram D. Delhi

160. What does the 17th Parallel line separate?
A. South and North America
B. North and South Korea
C. South and North Yemen
D. South and North Vietnam

161. Operation Flood-II, the prestigious milk products revolution of India, was initiated on
A. October 1, 1979 B. October 2, 1979
C. January 26, 1979 D. October 2, 1978

162. After World War I, the peace treaty was signed in:
A. Geneva B. Versailles
C. Paris D. Venice

163. Potassium chloride is given to the patient for
A. curing his bleeding gums
B. reducing his cholestrol level
C. reducing his blood pressure
D. alleviating his arthiritis pain

164. What is notation?
A. It is another word for "Mutually Assured Destruction".
B. It is the Latin deformation of the phrase "to swim"
C. It is a term used to denote the growth of illeterate masses
D. None of the above

165. The hideout of Adolf Hitler in the mountains was
A. Stuttgart B. Heidelberg
C. Berchtesgaden D. Both A and C

166. Who stated, "Where wealth accumulates decay?"
A. J M Keynes B. Adam Smith
C. Frederic Engels D. Oliver Goldsmith

167. Who was the national leader who wrote History of India on the walls of the Andaman Cellular Jail?
A. Ambedkar B. Vir Savarkar
C. Nandlal Bose D. Jyotiba Phule

168. The USA does not possess the following space shuttle
A. Columbia B. Atlantis
C. Challenger D. Discovery

169. The term "White Elephant" is used to denote
A. very bright and white item
B. very costly and expensive item
C. an item or a head that is very costly to maintain
D. an item or a head that is a part of the national economic budget of a country

170. Kolar Gold Mines are in this state.
A. Karnataka B. Bihar
C. Odisha D. Madhya Pradesh

171. Which is the morning star?
A. Pluto B. Venus
C. Neptune D. None of the above

172. Which one of the following is not an alkali?
A. sodium hydroxide
B. calcium carbonate
C. magnesium hydroxide
D. sodium sulphate

173. Polar ice is melting due to greenhouse effect. This would lead to
A. more melting of the polar glaciers and hence, subsequent submerging of land areas of earth
B. increasing temperatures on polar caps
C. reduction in temperature of ocean waters and rise in temperature of the Arctic circle waters as well as those of the Antartic circle waters
D. no impact

174. *India 2020* is a book written by
A. Trilok Gurtu
B. Khushwant Singh
C. P Chidambaram
D. A P J Abdul Kalaam

175. The Panama Canal connects:
A. The Pacific and Atlantic Oceans
B. The Pacific and Arctic Oceans
C. The Atlantic and Arctic Oceans
D. The Atlantic and Indian Oceans

176. The following are single cell structures
A. Paramaecium B. Amoebia
C. Both A and B D. None of A or B

177. 'The Last Supper' was painted by:
A. Picasso B. Francis Bacon
C. Michaelangelo D. Raphael

178. The plants, which can resist high temperatures, are known as
A. thermophilic B. thermophobic
C. thermoduric D. Both A and B

179. Which one of the following vaccines is used for controlling tuberculosis among the cattle?
A. Cell Culture Vaccine
B. Goat Tissue Adapted Vaccine
C. Adjuvant Vaccine
D. BCG Vaccine

180. Which one of the following chemicals is carcinogenic if inhaled?
A. carbon dioxide
B. suspended particulate matter
C. lead oxide
D. sulphur dioxide

181. What is a "Tenurial System?"
A. It is a system that identifies the ownership of land and the relationship of the land owner with the actual cultivator
B. It identities the land size and the *modus-operandi* of its usage
C. It identifies the ownership of the land
D. None of the above

182. Pulses are deficient in
A. methionine B. lysine
C. leusine D. iso-leusine

183. Which types of roses are grown in India for industrial applications?
A. R Centripetala and Bushra Rose
B. R Damascena Var Bifera
C. Rosa Damascena
D. A, B and C

184. Why sprinkler irrigation is preferred over other methods of irrigation?
A. It is a cheap method and does not require canal-digging and canal maintenance
B. It uses water effectively and water resolves are optimally utilised
C. It does not require well-digging measures which are costly
D. It supplies water only to those fields where the same is required

185. The size of clay particles is
A. greater than 0.2 mm
B. 0.02 mm – 0.2 mm
C. 0.002 mm – 0.02 mm
D. less than 0.002 mm

186. Which one of the following plants is of great medicinal value?
A. Ranwolfia Serpentiana
B. Thea Sinesis
C. Coffea Robusta
D. Ficus Religiosa

187. Biological control agents of soil borne plant pathogens act by
A. rapidly repleting nutrients and thereby, causing starvation and death of the pathogen

B. secreting toxic metabolitics
C. direct parastism or predation on the pathogens
D. All of the above

188. Nearly 80 percent of sugarcane in India is planted during
A. July – December B. May – August
C. June – August D. December – April

189. Soluble salt content of soil is determined by measuring its
A. pH Value
B. organic matter content
C. Sulphur content
D. electrical conductivity

190. Operation Flood is related to ..... whereas development of fisheries is related to .....
A. white revolution, black revolution
B. white revolution, blue revolution
C. green revolution, blue revolution
D. blue revolution, green revolution

191. An upper air wind system with very high velocities in certain parts of the atmosphere is called
A. Cyclone B. Anticyclone
C. Jet stream D. Tsunami

192. "Mixed Farming" refers to
A. farming by traditional and modern methods
B. agriculture and dairy farming clubbed together
C. farming without synthetic fertilisers but with traditional manure
D. farming with synthetic fertilisers and with traditional manure

193. The main constituent of *Gobar Gas* is
A. butane B. carbon monoxide
C. methane D. octane

194. Speed of sound waves is maximum in
A. solids B. liquids
C. gases D. vacuum

195. When a body gets positively charged, it actually
A. gains electrons
B. loses electrons
C. becomes a donor of ions
D. becomes a receptor of ions

196. Which type of nerves carries impulses from the sense organs in response to the stimulus?
A. sensory B. motor
C. secretory D. None of the above

197. Which gas does not pollute air (for human and animal consumption)?
A. carbon monoxide B. nitrogen dioxide
C. sulphur dioxide D. carbon dioxide

198. The human brain sends and receives signals as
A. electrical impulses B. chemical impulses
C. motor movements D. either A or B

199. "Foot and Mouth" disease attacks
A. cattle B. pigs and cattle
C. sheep and pigs D. cattle, sheep and pigs

200. While returning to earth, the spacecraft has a total communication blackout. The reason is
A. during the re-entry period, the density of the plasma generated by the intense functional heat is so high that the operational frequencies used for communication become much lesser than the plasma cut-off frequency, thus resulting in a total blackout
B. the electromagnetic waves present in the space above the earth temporarily over-power the communication system of the aircraft, thus completely crippling its operation and transmission
C. the force of gravity counters the radiowaves emitted by the aircraft
D. None of the above

ANSWERS

1	2	3	4	5	6	7	8	9	10
C	B	A	D	B	B	B	B	B	A
11	**12**	**13**	**14**	**15**	**16**	**17**	**18**	**19**	**20**
B	C	D	A	A	C	B	C	A	B

21	22	23	24	25	26	27	28	29	30
D	B	B	D	D	C	A	C	C	C
31	**32**	**33**	**34**	**35**	**36**	**37**	**38**	**39**	**40**
C	A	A	C	D	C	A	B	B	D
41	**42**	**43**	**44**	**45**	**46**	**47**	**48**	**49**	**50**
B	C	B	B	C	D	A	A	D	A
51	**52**	**53**	**54**	**55**	**56**	**57**	**58**	**59**	**60**
D	A	C	A	C	B	C	A	C	C
61	**62**	**63**	**64**	**65**	**66**	**67**	**68**	**69**	**70**
B	A	C	B	D	D	A	C	C	D
71	**72**	**73**	**74**	**75**	**76**	**77**	**78**	**79**	**80**
B	B	B	B	C	D	C	D	C	A
81	**82**	**83**	**84**	**85**	**86**	**87**	**88**	**89**	**90**
B	B	A	C	B	B	B	C	C	D
91	**92**	**93**	**94**	**95**	**96**	**97**	**98**	**99**	**100**
C	B	A	B	B	A	B	D	B	A
101	**102**	**103**	**104**	**105**	**106**	**107**	**108**	**109**	**110**
D	D	A	C	D	A	B	C	B	C
111	**112**	**113**	**114**	**115**	**116**	**117**	**118**	**119**	**120**
B	B	C	B	A	C	C	B	B	C
121	**122**	**123**	**124**	**125**	**126**	**127**	**128**	**129**	**130**
D	C	D	C	B	A	C	C	A	A
131	**132**	**133**	**134**	**135**	**136**	**137**	**138**	**139**	**140**
C	C	D	C	D	D	C	C	B	B
141	**142**	**143**	**144**	**145**	**146**	**147**	**148**	**149**	**150**
C	D	A	D	B	B	B	D	B	C
151	**152**	**153**	**154**	**155**	**156**	**157**	**158**	**159**	**160**
A	C	C	C	B	D	B	A	A	D
161	**162**	**163**	**164**	**165**	**166**	**167**	**168**	**169**	**170**
B	B	C	B	C	D	B	C	C	A
171	**172**	**173**	**174**	**175**	**176**	**177**	**178**	**179**	**180**
B	D	A	D	A	C	C	C	D	C
181	**182**	**183**	**184**	**185**	**186**	**187**	**188**	**189**	**190**
A	A	D	B	D	A	D	D	D	B
191	**192**	**193**	**194**	**195**	**196**	**197**	**198**	**199**	**200**
C	B	C	A	B	A	D	B	D	A

SPORTS

1. The first winning stroke in Lawn Tennis gives the player:
A. 2 points B. 1 point
C. 10 points D. 15 points

2. Which of the following game is played for stipulated period of 70 minutes?
A. Hockey B. Football
C. Rugby D. Basketball

3. 'Merdeka cup' is associated with:
A. Golf
B. Football
C. Squash
D. Hockey

4. Arjuna Award has been instituted for outstanding contribution in the field of
A. Social Service

B. Games and Sports
C. Literature
D. Art and Music

5. Murugappa Gold Cup is associated with:
A. Football B. Polo
C. Hockey D. Bridge

6. Jimmy Connors and Geoff Boycott are related with following games respectively:
A. Tennis, Football B. Tennis, Cricket
C. Chess, Cricket D. Football, Hockey

7. The winner of the Golden Boot Award at the World Cup Soccer tournament organised in Yokohama was .... and he scored ...... goals.
A. Zinedine Zidane, four
B. Davor Suker, six
C. Ronaldo, eight
D. None of the above

8. Number of players in a team of Water polo is:
A. 7 B. 5
C. 9 D. 11

9. The term 'Steeple Chase' is associated with which of the following games
A. Polo B. Tennis
C. Horse Racing D. Cricket

10. Who is known as Father of India's "White Revolution" and "Operation Flood"?
A. Dr. Verghese Kurien
B. J.B. Kripalani
C. Baba Amte
D. Har Gobind Khorana

11. The first Olympic games were revived by ..... in 1896 at Athens
A. Lord Welsley
B. Queen Elizabeth-I
C. Baron Piere de Cubertin
D. None of the above

12. The national game of the USA is
A. swimming B. baseball
C. athletics D. None of the above

13. Jules Rimmet Cup is associated with
A. hockey B. archery
C. football D. table tennis

14. The approximate weight of a cricket ball is
A. 5.25 Oz B. 6.30 Oz
C. 7.20 Oz D. 8.25 Oz

15. The number of players on each side in a basketball match is
A. 10 B. 6
C. 5 D. 8

16. The first woman in the history of US open Championship to have played 100 matches, is:
A. Martina Navaratilova
B. Chris Evert
C. Steffi Graf
D. Helena Sukova

17. Swaythling Cup is associated with
A. World Table Tennis Tournament (men)
B. World Table Tennis Tournament (university)
C. World Table Tennis tournament (women)
D. World Hockey Tournament (university)

18. Which one of the following is not a cricket - playing nation?
A. West Indies B. Zimbabwe
C. Kenya D. Columbia

19. The first recipient of *Rajiv Gandhi Khel Ratna Award* (Now Major Dhyan Chand Khel Ratna Award) (1991-92) was
A. Geet Sethi B. N Kunjurani Devi
C. V Anand D. P K Garg

20. The first Olympic Games were held at Olympia (Greece) in the year:
A. 300 BC B. 776 BC
C. 500 BC D. 394 AD

21. Which of the following is the National Game of Spain?
A. Bull fighting B. Baseball
C. Rugby D. Golf

22. 'Ashes' is the name of a series between ..... and ..... and it relates to .....
A. Pakistan, Australia, Hockey
B. India, England, Cricket
C. England, Australia, Cricket
D. New Zealand, Australia, Cricket

23. The term "Butterfly Stroke" is associated with
A. Kabaddi B. Wrestling
C. Polo D. Swimming

24. Neeraj Chopra is associated with which sports?
A. Javelin Throw B. Tennis
C. Hockey D. Football

25. 'Gambit' is a term normally associated with
A. Bridge B. Chess
C. Billiards D. Polo

26. 'Bunker' and 'Chukker' are the two terms associated with
A. Polo B. Rowing
C. Bungey Jumping D. Ice Hockey

27. A Lawn Tennis court measures
A. 78 feet by 28 feet
B. 79 feet by 29 feet
C. 76 feet by 26 feet
D. 70 feet by 24 feet

28. Who scored the fastest timing (in case of an under-13 swimmer) for crossing the English Channel?
A. Arati Saha
B. Uday Shenoy
C. Rihen Mehta
D. Rupali Ramdas Ropal

29. Which one of the following has been entrusted with the responsibility of training coaches in various disciplines of sports?
A. Tata Football Academy
B. Ministry of Human Resource Development
C. Netaji Subhash Institute of Sports
D. Lakshmibai National College of Physical Education

30. The term 'Tee' is associated with which of the following sports?
A. Table Tennis
B. Polo
C. Golf
D. Judo

31. 'Deodhar Trophy' is associated with which of the following games?
A. Hockey B. Cricket
C. Football D. Basketball

32. Who was the first deaf & dumb swimmer in the world to swim 30 km Gibralter strait?
A. Des Renford
B. Mihir Sen
C. Arti Pradhan
D. Taranath Shenoy

33. The height of the net in the centre of the tennis court is
A. 3 feet, 5 inches B. 3 feet, 2 inches
C. 2 feet, 8 inches D. 2 feet, 6 inches

34. 'Canon' is a sports term associated with the following game.
A. Billiards B. Volleyball
C. Shot-Put D. Table Tennis

35. The Himalayan Mountaineering Institute is located in
A. Leh B. Darjeeling
C. Kohima D. Dispur

36. The diameter of a golf hole is
A. 4.36 inches B. 4.50 inches
C. 5.63 inches D. 4.75 inches

37. The total distance of a Marathon Race is ..... miles and ..... yards.
A. 29, 388 B. 26, 380
C. 26, 385 D. 25, 372

38. The first woman, who won six gold medals in a single Olympics tournament, was
A. Evelyn Ashford
B. Florence Griffth Joyner
C. Kristin Otto
D. Susi Susanti

39. In which year on account of a decree issued by Roman Emperor the Olympic Games were ceased to be played?
A. 350 AD B. 394 AD
C. 300 BC D. 384 AD

40. Putney (UK) is a place most frequently associated with
A. swimming B. horse racing
C. boat rowing D. polo

41. Rafael Nadal is associated with which sports?
A. Tennis B. Badminton
C. Cricket D. None of the above

42. The term 'Finesse' is normally associated with this game.
A. Chess B. Bridge
C. Snooker D. Rowing

43. The following trophy is not associated with cricket.
A. Ranji Trophy
B. Rohintan Baria Trophy
C. Singer-Akai-Nidahas Trophy
D. Lady Rattan Tata Trophy

44. Tonya Harding is a controversial athlete and has been associated with the following game.
A. Rowing B. Table Tennis
C. Figure Skating D. Boxing

45. When and where the first Asian Games were held?
A. 1955, Seoul B. 1951, New Delhi
C. 1954, Manila D. 1970, Bangkok

46. Who among the following won Gold medal in Tokyo Olympics 2020?
A. Pradeep Verma
B. Mangal Singh
C. Neeraj Chopra
D. P.V. Sindhu

47. What is the measurement of a Golf Hole?
A. 3½ inch in diameter
B. 4½ inch in diameter
C. 7½ centimeter in diameter
D. 10 inch in diameter

48. The term 'Diamond' is associated with the game of:
A. Baseball B. Bridge
C. Basketball D. Billiards

49. K Sasikaran is well known as a
A. table tennis player B. swimmer
C. chess player D. football player

50. Who won men's single at the Australian Open 2023?
A. Novak Djokovic
B. Roger Federer
C. Stanislas Wawrinka
D. Alexander Zverev

ANSWERS

1	2	3	4	5	6	7	8	9	10
D	A	B	B	C	B	C	A	C	A
11	**12**	**13**	**14**	**15**	**16**	**17**	**18**	**19**	**20**
C	B	C	A	C	B	A	D	C	B
21	**22**	**23**	**24**	**25**	**26**	**27**	**28**	**29**	**30**
A	C	D	A	B	A	A	D	C	C
31	**32**	**33**	**34**	**35**	**36**	**37**	**38**	**39**	**40**
B	D	B	A	B	B	C	C	B	C
41	**42**	**43**	**44**	**45**	**46**	**47**	**48**	**49**	**50**
A	B	D	C	B	C	B	A	C	A

HONOURS AND AWARDS

1. In which of the following years 'Nobel Prizes' were instituted?
A. 1910 B. 1905
C. 1901 D. 1911

2. The writer who refused the Nobel Prize for Literature was:
A. Winston Churchill
B. Prem Chand
C. Jean Paul Sartre
D. None of the above

3. Which country awards the Noble Prize?
A. USA B. India
C. Russia D. Sweden

4. In which of the following years Arjuna Awards were instituted
A. 1951 B. 1971
C. 1961 D. 1965

5. National Awards for Popularising Science was instituted in the year
A. 1981 B. 1985
C. 1987 D. 1988

6. The Government of which state has instituted the 'Tansen Samman'?
A. Madhya Pradesh B. Uttar Pradesh
C. Gujarat D. Maharashtra

7. The Lifetime Achievement Award, instituted by DRDO, has been awarded to an eminent nuclear scientist. His name is
A. Dr A P J Abdul Kalam
B. Mr B D Nagchowdhary
C. Mr George Fernandes
D. Mr Mulayam Singh Yadav

8. Who returned the award of 'Sir' given by the British government in protest against the "Jallianwala Bagh Massacre" on April 13, 1919?
A. Prem Chand
B. Thomas Roe
C. Rabindra Nath Tagore
D. Dada Bhai Nauroji

9. Nobel Prize is not awarded in the following disciplines
A. Chemistry and Physics
B. Literature and Peace
C. Economics and Medicine
D. Geography and Space Research

10. In which year Nehru Award for International Understanding instituted
A. 1965 B. 1969
C. 1974 D. 1964

11. Which of the following Indians was awarded Legion D award, the highest civilian awards of France
A. Jawahar Lal Nehru B. Satyajit Ray
C. Mother Teresa D. Shahrukh Khan

12. 'Pulitzer' prizes are awarded to Americans for excellence in
A. Films B. Journalism
C. Medicine D. Social Work

13. C.V. Raman received Nobel Prize in the year
A. 1934 B. 1931
C. 1932 D. 1930

14. Saraswati Samman is awarded by
A. Government of India
B. Sahitya Academy
C. K.K. Birla Foundation
D. Lalit Kala Akademi

15. On which day every year National Awards for Teachers are announced?
A. August 15 B. September 5
C. November 19 D. November 14

16. The National Award given to the distinguished sportsmen/women in India is known as
A. Dronacharya Award
B. Param Vir Chakra
C. Arjun Award
D. Nehru Award

17. The prestigious Ramon Magsaysay Award was instituted in the memory of Mr Ramon Magsaysay who was
A. the Secretary – General of UN
B. the Commander of NATO in Europe
C. the President of the Philippines
D. the President of Cambodia

18. The Kalinga Prize is awarded by UNESCO but it was founded by an Indian. His name is
A. Biju Patnaik B. Sharad Pawar
C. C V Raman D. Piloo Modi

19. Who was the first Indian to receive the World Food Prize?
A. Dr. Verghese Kurien
B. Dr. Amrita Patel
C. Dr. M.S. Swaminathan
D. None of these

20. Jesse Owens Global award is given in the field of:
A. Literature B. Sports
C. Science D. Journalism

21. Nobel Alfred Bernhard after whom Nobel Prizes are given was:
A. Engineer B. Doctor
C. Chemist D. Pilot

22. Grammy Awards are given in the field of
A. painting B. architecture
C. music D. rock dance

23. The highest civilian award of India is
A. *Padma Vibhushan* B. *Padma Shri*
C. *Bharat Ratna* D. *Param Vir Chakra*

24. The highest military award of India is
A. Shaurya Chakra
B. Param Vishisht Sewa Medal
C. Param Vir Chakra
D. Kirti Chakra

25. The first ever B R Ambedkar National Award was given to
A. Baba Amte
B. T Shiv Shankar Pillai
C. International Red Cross
D. National Institute for Social Work and Social Sciences

26. 'Victory Medal' is awarded in:
A. UK B. USA
C. Russia D. France

27. Which one of the following is not a Shram Award

A. Shram Bhushan B. Shram Dev

C. Shram Devi D. Shram Vir

28. Dr Shanti Swaroop Bhatnagar Awards are given in any field of science by

A. Indian Council of Applied Economic Research

B. Defence Research and Development Organisation

C. National Institute for Social Work and Social Sciences

D. Tata Institute of Fundamental Research

29. Who is winner of the Miss Universe-2022 contest?

A. Nadia Ferreira

B. R' Bonney Gabriel

C. Lalela Mswane

D. Toni-Ann Singh

30. First Miss World Competition was established by 'Miss World Incorporation' in the year

A. 1941 B. 1950

C. 1951 D. 1957

31. The size of an Olympic medal is ..... mm and thickness is ..... mm.

A. 50, 2.5 B. 60, 3.0

C. 60.5, 3.5 D. 55.2, 2.5

32. "Dhanwantari Award" is given in the field of

A. swimming B. Bharata Natyam

C. cinema D. medicine

33. Nobel Prizes are not given for which of the following fields?

A. Physics B. Chemistry

C. Music D. Peace

34. Which is the second Highest Civilian award in India?

A. Padam Vibushan B. Padam Shri

C. Bharat Ratna D. Ashok Chakra

35. Abel Prize is associated with:

A. Mathematics B. Film

C. Music D. Writing

36. The second highest gallantry award in India is:

A. Padam Bhushan B. Vir Chakra

C. Mahavir Chakra D. Ashok Chakra

37. 'Mubarak-Al-Kabir' medal is the highest honour of

A. Kuwait B. Iran

C. Afghanistan D. Iraq

38. Bharatendu Harish Chandra awards are given annually for:

A. best local self administration

B. showing kindness and generosity of unusual kind

C. promoting original writing in Hindi

D. None of the above

39. Who won the Man Booker Prize 2022 for 'The Seven Moons of Maali Almeida'?

A. Shehan Karunatilaka

B. Subhash Khot

C. Maryam Mirzakhani

D. Arthur Avila

40. Who has been selected for the prestigious Jnanpith award for the year 2021?

A. Alok Puranik

B. Damodar Mauzo

C. Mrinal Pandey

D. Vishwanath Tiwari

41. Name the women sportsperson, who became the first Indian women to hold an honorary rank of Lieutenant Colonel in the countrys's defence forces.

A. Krishna Punia B. Saina Nehwal

C. Sania Mirza D. MC Mary Kom

42. Oscar award is related to

A. books

B. politics

C. European Community

D. films

43. Miss World award 2021 has been won by whom?

A. Karolina Bielawska

B. Manya Singh

C. Olivia Yace

D. Shree Saini

44. Out of the Gallantry awards — PVSM, AVSM and VSM — the most exceptional medal is

A. PVSM

B. AVSM

C. VSM

D. All have equal recognition status

45. *Jeewan Raksha Padak* is awarded for
A. bravery in the battle front
B. fine display of vocal music skills
C. saving the life of human beings
D. None of the above

46. Who is not eligible for Bharat Ratna?
A. A government official
B. A sportsperson
C. A film actress
D. A Prime Minister

47. Jamnalal Bajaj award is given in the field of
I. Social Work
II. Fine Arts
III. Application of Science and Technology
IV. Literature
A. I and II B. I, II and III
C. II and IV D. I and III

48. In which year Indira Gandhi Peace Prize was instituted?
A. 1985 B. 1984
C. 1986 D. 1987

49. Borlaug Award was instituted for recognising outstanding contribution in the field of:
A. Ecology B. Medicine
C. Agriculture D. Journalism

50. Except Dr. Nelson Mandela, who is the other non-Indian so far honoured with Bharat Ratna
A. Dr. Julius Nyerere
B. Helen Hint
C. Hideki Yuka
D. Khan Abdul Ghaffar Khan

ANSWERS

1	2	3	4	5	6	7	8	9	10
C	C	D	C	C	A	B	C	D	D
11	**12**	**13**	**14**	**15**	**16**	**17**	**18**	**19**	**20**
B	B	D	C	B	C	C	A	C	B
21	**22**	**23**	**24**	**25**	**26**	**27**	**28**	**29**	**30**
C	C	C	C	D	B	B	C	B	C
31	**32**	**33**	**34**	**35**	**36**	**37**	**38**	**39**	**40**
B	D	C	A	A	C	A	C	A	B
41	**42**	**43**	**44**	**45**	**46**	**47**	**48**	**49**	**50**
D	D	A	A	C	A	D	C	C	D

BOOKS AND AUTHORS

1. The book "*The Insider*" is written by
A. Madhav Rao Scindia
B. Nana Patekar
C. Shobha De
D. P V Narasimha Rao

2. *India Wins Freedom* was written by
A. Dadabhai Nauroji
B. Ashfaqulla Khan
C. Sarojini Naidu
D. Maulana Abul Kalam Azad

3. *A Tale of Two Cities* is, in fact, the story of two famous cities. Those cities are
A. Paris and New York
B. London and New York
C. London and Paris
D. Stockholm and New York

4. *Ben Hur* was penned by
A. Lewis Wallace
B. Lord Byron
C. William Shakespeare
D. None of the above

5. *Panchatantra* was written by
A. R K Narayan B. R K Laxman
C. Vishnu Sharma D. None of the above

6. Arundhati Roy has been awarded the prestigious

A. Booker's Prize – 1997
B. Jnanpeeth Award – 1997
C. Sahitya Akademi Award – 1998
D. None of the above

7. Who wrote *Odyssey?*
A. George Orwell B. Homer
C. Dom Moraes D. None of the above

8. Which one of the following was not written by Shakespeare?
A. *As You Like It*
B. *Mcbeth*
C. *Hamlet*
D. *A Farewell to Arms*

9. Lewis Carol wrote a masterpiece. What is its name?
A. *Don Quixote*
B. *Alice in Wonderland*
C. *Adventures of Robinson Crusoe*
D. *Great Expectations*

10. The *Tamil Ramayana* is the work of
A. Tulsidas B. Jayangondar
C. Kambar D. Veda Vyas

11. In *Shrimad Bhagwat Geeta,* Lord Krishna teaches his disciple Arjuna to
A. rise to the occasion and fight with his near and dear ones
B. withdraw from the battlefield
C. do his duty and not to expect anything in return
D. attack the enemy in a planned and meticulous approach

12. Who wrote *Origin of Species?*
A. Charles Darwin
B. Alexander Flaming
C. G.B. Shaw
D. D.H. Lawrence

13. The poet and the well-known friend of Prithvi Raj Chauhan, who wrote *Prithvi Raj Raso,* was
A. Harisena B. Vishnu Datt
C. Chand Bardai D. None of the above

14. The first book was printed in India in the year 1561. Its name was
A. *The spiritual Compendium of the Christian Life*
B. *Aain-e-Akbari*
C. *Babur Nama*
D. *Ram Charit Manas*

15. The famous book *Runs and Ruins* was written by
A. Sir Donald Bradman
B. Sunil Gavaskar
C. Kapil Dev
D. Richard Hadlee

16. Adam Smith wrote the following famous book
A. The Wreck
B. Dr Zhivago
C. The Wealth of Nations
D. Tarzan of the Apes

17. H G Wells is known as a
A. poet
B. science-fiction writer
C. thriller-fiction writer
D. essay writer and critic

18. Tukaram wrote his devotional songs in this language
A. Urdu B. Gujarati
C. Hindi D. Marathi

19. Our ancient scholars and writers used this language for their social, religious and political books and works
A. Tamil
B. Sanskrit
C. Urdu
D. Hindi *(Devanagari)*

20. *Gora* is the hero of a book written by Rabindra Nath Tagore. What is the name of the book?
A. *Geetanjali* B. *Patanjali*
C. *Gora* D. *Twelfth Night*

21. Shylock is
A. the villain *in A Pound of Flesh* by William Shakespeare
B. an old Jew who is a famous hero of the Israeli nation
C. the hero of *Miranda,* written by William Shakespeare
D. the comic character of *Alice In the Wonderland* by Lewis Caroll

22. The following was a famous Hindi author and story-writer

A. Shobha De B. Aruna Asaf Ali
C. Mahadevi Verma D. Amrita Pritam

23. *Mudrarakshasa* was composed by
A. Vishakhadatta B. Bhavabhuti
C. Sivananda D. Jayadeva

24. *Razor's Edge* was written by
A. Toni Morrison
B. Saul Bellow
C. W Somerset Maugham
D. None of the above

25. *Sakharam Binder* is a famous play written by
A. Anil Barve B. Vijay Tendulkar
C. V S Naipaul D. Tasleema Nasreen

26. The major work of Sir Isaac Newton is
A. *Principia*
B. *Heritage*
C. *Human knowledge*
D. *I Dare*

27. The hero of *The Jungle Book,* written by Rudyard Kipling, is
A. the lion
B. Mowghuli
C. the father of Mowghuli
D. there is no hero

28. Who stated, "Peace hath her victories, no less renowned than war?"
A. Alfred Lord Tennyson
B. William Shakespeare
C. John Milton
D. None of the above

29. Macawber is a character who was created by
A. Thomas Hardy B. P G Wodehouse
C. Charles Dickens D. J W Von Goethe

30. *Pride and Prejudice* was written by
A. Anton Chekhov B. Maxim Gorky
C. Jane Austen D. Anthony West

31. *In the Afternoon Time* is the English translation of the autobiography of the famous poet, Harivansh Rai Bachchan. The autobiography was translated into English by
A. Vikram Seth B. Dr Rupert Snell
C. William Faulkner D. P D Tandon

32. Who is the author of the book *The Celestine Vision?*
A. Paul Hockins B. Salman Rushdie
C. Joseph Conrad D. James Redfield

33. The author of the famous book *Blue Mountain Revisited* is
A. Charles Kingsley
B. Virginia Woolf
C. Arthur Koestler
D. Peter Topkins

34. Homer was the great poet of the following language
A. Italian B. Greek
C. Arabic D. French

35. Hard Choices is a famous book written by :
A. Hillary Clinton
B. Barack Obama
C. Narendra Modi
D. Imran Khan

36. *Godaan* was written by Munshi Prem Chand and it depicts
A. the methodology for taking adequate care of the cows
B. exploitation of simple rural folk by the rich landlords of rural India
C. the mutiny of 1857 in which, Indians refused to bite the *Kartoos* made with cow beef
D. None of the above

37. Manu wrote a book during ancient times in which, he divided the Aryan society into four distinct classes. What was the name of the book?
A. *Arthashastra*
B. *Manusmriti*
C. *Moti Mahal*
D. *My Truth*

38. R. Venkataraman wrote *My Presidential Years.* What was the main theme of the book?
A. It described the aristocratic procedures being followed in the *Rashtrapati Bhawan* during his tenure as President
B. It described the power equations and ploys in the centre and in the states during his term
C. It described how he felt caged while he was President due to a load of procedures and formalities
D. It explained the machinations of the political party which was in power during his tenure as President

39. The hero of the play cried in the end, "Et Tu, Brute!" and died. Which is the play and who is the author?

A. The Wealth of Nations — Adam Smith
B. Mein Kempf — Adolf Hitler
C. Julius Caesar — William Shakespeare
D. None of the above

40. Don Veto Corleone was the undisputed king of the underworld in this novel. This masterpiece was also converted into a film in which Al Pacino played the role of the Don. What is the name of the novel and that of the author?

A. *A Farewell to Arms* — E Hemingway
B. *The Godfather* — Mario Puzo
C. *From Here to Eternity* — James Jones
D. *Dialogue with Death* — Arthur Koestler

41. *Gypsy Camp Vanishes Into the Blue* was a famous blockbuster movie made by the erstwhile USSR. The original story was written by a famous author. His name is

A. Leo Tolstoy
B. Anton Chekhov
C. Maxim Gorky
D. Leon Uris

42. The total number of *Puranas* written during the Vedic age is

A. 22 B. 9
C. 18 D. 25

43. Who wrote Monsoon Memories?

A. Jo Nesbo B. Ratna
C. Renita D'Silva D. Amartya Sen

44. W B Yeats won the Nobel Prize for literature in 1923 and Samuel Backet won the same prize in 1969. Both were Irish. The third Irish to have won the Nobel Prize for literature (1995) was

A. Alison Hargreaves
B. Bobby Sands
C. Paul Crutzen
D. Seamus Heaney

45. According to *The Ramayana,* who received the last teaching lessons from the knowledgeable Ravana while he was on his death-bed?

A. Rama B. Sugreeva
C. Laxmana D. Both A and C

46. He was a German but he saved many a Jew from the cruel hands of the Nazis. A movie was made on this theme which won the coveted Oscar Prize. The book and the author are

A. *Operation Shylock* — Philip Roth
B. *Schindler's List* — Thomas Keneally
C. *The Rescue* — Joseph Conrad
D. *The Slave* — Isaac Bashevis Singer

47. He was the favourite assistant of Sherlock Holmes, the famous character created by Arthur Conan Doyle. His name is

A. Zhivago
B. Watson
C. Hawkins
D. Hector

48. He was a former member of British Parliament. He has written many hit fiction novels. One of his novels is

A. Shall We Tell the President?
B. The Rape of the Lock
C. Snow Country
D. Small Land

49. He wrote *Sharmili*, *Gaylord* and *Kati Patang*. His novels were written in Hindi and some of them have been converted into films also. His name is

A. Gita Mehta
B. B N Mullick
C. Nirad C Chaudhary
D. Gulshan Nanda

50. 'The Lives of Others' is written by..........

A. Neel Mukherjee
B. Charu Singh
C. R.D. Pradhan
D. Shivani Lohia

ANSWERS

1	2	3	4	5	6	7	8	9	10
D	D	C	A	C	A	B	D	B	C

11	12	13	14	15	16	17	18	19	20
C	A	C	A	B	C	B	D	B	C
21	22	23	24	25	26	27	28	29	30
A	C	A	C	B	A	B	C	C	C
31	32	33	34	35	36	37	38	39	40
B	D	D	B	A	B	B	C	C	B
41	42	43	44	45	46	47	48	49	50
C	C	C	D	C	B	B	A	D	A

ECONOMY, BUSINESS AND COMMERCE

1. Who is the Chairman of Island Development Authority?
A. President
B. Prime Minister
C. Finance Minister
D. Minister of Environment

2. World Economic Situation and Prospects Report is associated with:
A. IMF B. World Bank
C. United Nations D. WTO

3. The economies of the Oriental countries depend upon the growth or decline of
A. the American economy
B. the Japanese economy
C. the Korean economy
D. the Thai economy

4. The difference between the monetary policy and the fiscal policy is
A. fiscal policy tries to control aggregate demand through budgetary means whereas monetary policy controls the same through the quantity of money and the rate of interest
B. monetary policy is related to the money supply whereas the fiscal policy is related to the rate of interest
C. monetary policy is automatic whereas the fiscal policy is discretionary
D. both the policies are similar and have similar objectives

5. Which one of the following is a *Navratna* Company?
A. Delhi Vidyut Board
B. National Textiles Corporation
C. Mahanagar Telephone Nigam Ltd
D. Electronics Corporation of India Ltd

6. Which country holds the dubious distinction of becoming the biggest user of anti-dumping duty (ADD) since the Uruguay Round?
A. China B. Japan
C. US D. India

7. Find the odd city with the viewpoint of Indian Railways
A. Chittaranjan B. Chennai
C. Kapurthala D. Trombay

8. Which company released the slogan "Redefining the value of Rupee?"
A. Toshiba B. Samsung
C. Akai D. Panasonic

9. 'Shishu', 'Tarun' and 'Kishore' named enterprises are associated with:
A. SBI
B. IDBI
C. MUDRA Bank
D. NABARD

10. The major field of research of the Nobel laureate, Amartya Sen, is
A. mixed economy
B. welfare economics
C. the Amartya Sen Shift
D. capitalistic economy

11. GST has been implemented in:
A. 2014 B. 2015
C. 2016 D. 2017

12. Which one of the following is not a chief characteristic of FEMA?
A. Current account transactions are permitted unless there are RBI restrictions
B. Capital accounts transactions are permitted unless there are RBI transactions

C. Treatment for violations is harsh and is deemed to be a congnisable and non-bailable offence
D. Enforcement Directorate can arrest the accused in case of violations

13. The current market trends are
A. recession oriented
B. inflation oriented
C. recession oriented with inflation
D. boom oriented

14. Which of the following is not helpful in controlling money supply?
A. CRR
B. Bank Rate
C. Free Market Policy
D. Change in margin requirement

15. This company does not deal in consumer durables?
A. Samsung B. Akai
C. Godrej D. Nestle

16. Find the odd one out.
A. Lintas B. HTA
C. Contract D. LML

17. E-com does not require?
A. Internet connectivity
B. Technological inputs
C. Negotiations through E-mail
D. Knowledge about entertainment groups

18. Which one of the following is not an infrastructure related project?
A. Narmada Valley Project
B. North-South and East-West Corridors
C. Software exports
D. Railway modernisation

19. When the stock markets crash, then
A. stocks sell at lower prices than anticipated
B. scrips sell at higher prices than anticipated
C. the sellers are not very keen to sell in anticipation of sudden rise in values of stocks
D. None of the above

20. What is 'Dumping?'
A. It is the term given by the economists to excavation and digging activities of the MNCs that deal in earth moving equipment
B. It is the sale of the products and services by foreign nations and firms at very low prices so that they could find firm markets in India
C. It is the excessive supply of fast moving consumer goods by a developed country to an under-developed country
D. It is a series of measures taken by Government of India to facilitate international trade

21. Varishtha Pension Bima Yojna has been launched by
A. National Insurance Co.
B. LIC of India
C. Oriental Insurance Co.
D. United India Insurance Co.

22. Which company is the manufacturer of the product brand name 'Spectra?'
A. Telco B. Kinetic
C. LML D. None of the above

23. Who wrote the General Theory of Employment, Interest and Money?
A. Kaldor B. Marx
C. Keynes D. Marshall

24. Which one of the following is not an electronics products manufacturer?
A. Samsung B. Matsushita
C. Motorola D. Ford

25. World Economic Situation and Prospects Report is associated with—
A. IMF
B. World Bank
C. United Nations
D. WTO

26. What is the base year of newly introduced Consumer Price Index (CPI)?
A. 2000 B. 2004
C. 2012 D. 2011

27. The spirit of JIT is to
A. produce that much which could be sold and acquire that much of material inputs that could justify the sales
B. produce less but buy still lesser
C. collect orders from the markets and then produce
D. keep your inventory levels just equal to the market demand for the products

28. 'New Silk Route' is a rail route which links China with the European country—

A. France B. Germany
C. Italy D. Japan

29. Who among the following was first among the European nations to trade with India?

A. Britain B. Spain
C. Portugal D. France

30. GTX Extra is a brand name associated with

A. MRF B. HP
C. IOL D. Castrol

31. In India, the first bank of limited liability managed Indians and founded in 1881 was

A. Hindustan Commercial Bank
B. Oudh Commercial Bank
C. Punjab and Sind Bank
D. Bank of India

32. In the new millennium, the industries related to.....would be facing maximum growth rates?

A. manufacturing
B. FMCGs
C. information technology
D. consumer non-durables

33. Which one of the following items is not exported from India?

A. gold ornaments B. leather items
C. software products D. nuclear weapons

34. The stock value index of the registered companies of a stock exchange is known as

A. Nikkei B. Dow-Jones
C. Sensex D. None of the above

35. India has her only OTCEI in

A. Kolkata B. Indore
C. Mumbai D. New Delhi

36. Estimates of National Income in India are prepared by

A. Ministry of Finance
B. NITI Aayog
C. Reserve Bank of India
D. Central Statistical Organisation

37. If the Rupee becomes stronger vis-a-vis the US Dollar, then

A. exports would rise
B. imports would remain stagnant
C. exports would decline
D. None of the above

38. Which of the following is a subsidiary of RBI?

A. SIDBI
B. NABARD
C. National Housing Bank
D. All of the above

39. Which one of the following is not a core operation of L & T group?

A. Electricals
B. Construction Machinery
C. Shipping
D. Cement

40. The famous breakfast cereal Kellogg was started as .... during its early days of inception.

A. medicine
B. diet for patients in a nursing home
C. breakfast food for some top businessmen of the USA
D. diet enriching ingredient for the school-going children in Europe

41. Who observed, "as the population increases, the economic means of supporting that population do not grow in the same proportion?"

A. Goldsmith B. Malthus
C. Frederic Engels D. Adam Smith

42. The eminent Nobel Laureate–Amartya Sen is known for his research in

A. welfare economics
B. draughts and famines
C. poverty elimination
D. free market system of economy

43. Index 'Residex' is associated with:

A. Share Prices
B. Mutual Fund Prices
C. Land Prices
D. Price Inflation Index

44. The new industrial policy of India was announced in

A. 1996 B. 1991
C. 1997 D. 1998

45. If supply of onions is reduced, then

A. the demand would rise and the prices of the existing stocks would jump up
B. the demand would rise but prices would remain unaffected

C. the demand would fall as the users would avoid taking onions because of the fear of a sharp price rise
D. None of the above

46. How could the government break the vicious cycle of poverty among the poor masses?
A. By providing them with money
B. By providing them with opportunities of employment and entreprenenrship
C. By educating them about family planning
D. By getting loans for them from global financial agencies

47. WTO is dedicated to
A. liberal trade terms between the member nations
B. removal of all the trade protection procedures by all the member nations
C. agreements on patents of agricultural commodities like rice etc.
D. None of the above

48. Under which clause of Income Tax Act, taxpayer gets tax rebate on the premium paid for health insurance?
A. 80A B. 80C
C. 80D D. 80G

49. The basic objective of SIDBI is to
A. give more loans for infrastructure development to the corporate sector
B. grant loans to agricultural farmers for export of their commodities
C. solve the financial problems of small scale industries
D. assist IDBI and ICICI in the process of national industrial development

50. The major function of the Food Corporation of India is:
A. to control the demand side of foodgrains
B. to distribute high yielding variety seeds
C. to check the fluctuation in foodgrain price by controlling supply
D. to extend credit to farmers

ANSWERS

1	2	3	4	5	6	7	8	9	10
B	B	B	A	C	D	D	C	C	B
11	**12**	**13**	**14**	**15**	**16**	**17**	**18**	**19**	**20**
D	D	C	C	D	D	D	C	A	B
21	**22**	**23**	**24**	**25**	**26**	**27**	**28**	**29**	**30**
B	D	C	D	B	C	A	B	C	D
31	**32**	**33**	**34**	**35**	**36**	**37**	**38**	**39**	**40**
B	C	D	C	C	D	C	C	C	B
41	**42**	**43**	**44**	**45**	**46**	**47**	**48**	**49**	**50**
B	A	C	B	A	B	A	C	C	C

BANKING AND FINANCE

1. Which one of the following services is not provided by the mobile banking service?
A. Checking of balance of an account
B. Requesting for an accounts statement
C. Enquiring details of the fixed deposit
D. Asking for share prices of all the stocks at the BSE

2. Scheduled bank is that bank which is:
A. Nationalised
B. Not-nationalised
C. Based at foreign country
D. Included in the Second Schedule of R.B.I.

3. Grameen Bank and Micro Credit are asociated with:
A. Manmohan Singh B. Bill Gates
C. Md. Yunus D. Aung San Su Ki

4. ICICI Bank, prior to commencing its operations as a bank was a/an:
A. Market research group
B. Industrial finance corporation

C. Small-time player in consumer durables
D. Conduct for RRBs

5. If there is a capital flight from India:
A. Exchange rate of rupee will fall
B. Share prices will rise
C. Interest rate will fall
D. Exchange rate of rupee will rise

6. The headquarters of standard Chartered Bank are located at:
A. New York B. Hawai
C. London D. New Delhi

7. Currency notes of ₹ 2 denomination and above are liabilities of
A. Government of India
B. Reserve Bank of India
C. State Bank of India
D. All of the above

8. India's first floating ATM has been launched in Kerala by
A. Canara Bank
B. Corporation Bank
C. HDFC Bank
D. State Bank of India

9. Which are the three international credit card companies?
A. Amex, Citibank, Master
B. Master, Amex, HSBC
C. Amex, Master, Visa
D. Visa, Citibank, Standard Chartered

10. Name the first bank in India to start using PKI (Public Key Infrastructure) based digital signatures for electronic fund transfer.
A. Bank of Punjab
B. Punjab National Bank
C. Canara Bank
D. Bank of Baroda

11. Federal Reserves is the Central Bank of...
A. Britain B. U.S.A.
C. Japan D. Canada

12. Capital market means
A. Mutual funds B. Money market
C. Direct taxes D. Securities market

13. The World Bank has given a go-ahead to India on the Baglihar Hydro-electric Project being build on the river:
A. Jhelum B. Sutlej
C. Chenab D. Beas

14. Which state has maximum branches of public sector commercial banks?
A. U.P. B. Maharashtra
C. Karnataka D. Gujarat

15. The "Adhoc Treasury Bill System" of meeting budget deficit in India was replaced by 'Ways and Means Advances System' which has come into force on:
A. March 31, 1997 B. April 1, 1996
C. April 1, 1997 D. None of these

16. Plastic money relates to:
A. Plastic currency B. Paper currency
C. ATM cards D. Credit cards

17. What is the minimum period for which banks may accept term deposits, according to RBI guidelines?
A. 15 days B. 30 days
C. 46 days D. 91 days

18. In the context of stock market, the abbreviation IPO stands for
A. Immediate Payment Order
B. Internal Policy Obligation
C. External Policy Obligation
D. Initial Public Offering

19. The Reserve Bank of India (RBI) keeps on modifying various rates/ratios to keep the flow of liquidity in the market in a balanced situation. Which of the following rates/ratios/indexes is not directly controlled by the RBI?
A. Cash Reserve Ratio (CRR)
B. Bank Rate
C. Repo Rate
D. Wholesale Price Index (WPI)

20. Which bank launched the first international credit card in India?
A. Hong Kong Bank B. Citibank
C. SBI D. Deutsche Bank

21. What is near money?
A. Money that is banked in nearby banks
B. Assets that are easily convertible into cash
C. Money held in local currency
D. Money that can be recalled easily

22. What is fiat money?
A. Money not backed by gold or any other valuable goods
B. Money issued by a government fiat
C. Money used to buy worthless assets
D. Assets that are easily convertible into cash

23. Which bank introduced the first Automatic Teller Machine (ATM) in India?
A. State Bank of India
B. Citibank
C. Bank of America
D. Hong Kong Bank

24. Bank of Rajasthan, belongs to which business family of India?
A. Hindujas B. Singhanias
C. Bangurs D. Modis

25. Which company launched the first electronic cash card in India?
A. Kotak Mahindra B. SBI
C. Bank of Baroda D. Escorts Finance

26. Where is the foreign exchange of India deposited?
A. Reserve Bank of India
B. State Bank of India
C. Both (A) and (B)
D. Union Finance Ministry

27. The apex institution in the field of industrial development banking in India is:
A. IFCI B. ICICI
C. LIC D. IDBI

28. Banking Sector will fall under which of the following sectors?
A. Agricultural Sector B. Service Sector
C. Manufacturing Sector D. Industrial Sector

29. Which of the following types of borrowings from the IMF has the softest servicing conditions?
A. Second Tranch Loan B. SAF
C. ESAF D. Oil facility

30. If the cash-reserve ratio is lowered by the Central Bank, what will be its effect on credit creation?
A. It will decrease credit creation
B. It will not decrease credit creation
C. It will increase credit creation
D. It will not change credit creation

31. "Conditionality" of an I.M.F. loan to a member country stands for:
A. Schedule of disbursement of loan instalments
B. Interest and repayment terms of the loan
C. The policy steps which the borrower country must take
D. An assessment of the credit-worthiness of the borrower

32. Credit is a:
A. Stock concept B. Flow concept
C. A stock-flow concept D. None of these

33. The IBRD aims at:
A. Promoting international monetary co-operation
B. Helping in reconstruction and development of economics
C. Helping children all over the world
D. Promoting the peaceful uses of atomic energy

34. People's Bank of India was founded in the year:
A. 1910 B. 1911
C. 1901 D. 1920

35. The RBI was established in the year:
A. 1935 B. 1936
C. 1940 D. 1945

36. Blank cheque is:
A. Without date
B. A cheque which has been signed and dated but in which the amount payable has not been filled in
C. Without signatures
D. None of the above

37. The United Commercial Bank was started by the Birlas in the year:
A. 1948 B. 1943
C. 1949 D. 1950

38. Financial Investment is:
A. Any investment
B. Investment which cannot be traded
C. Any investment which can be traded, such as shares, certificates of deposit, etc
D. None of the above

39. A Joint Account is:
A. A firm account
B. A bank account owned jointly by two or more people
C. A shop account
D. None of the above

40. The Foreign Investments Board was set up in the year:
A. 1960 B. 1968
C. 1969 D. 1970

41. The SBI floated its first Mutual Fund in the year:
A. 1987 B. 1988
C. 1989 D. 1990

42. Loan Shark is:
A. A person who lends money at a very high interest rate
B. Lending money at lower rates
C. Lending money without interest
D. None of the above

43. The IDBI started its operations in year:
A. 1964 B. 1965
C. 1966 D. 1967

44. Banking Companies Act was passed in the year:
A. 1947 B. 1948
C. 1949 D. 1950

45. Bearer Cheque is a cheque that is payable to:
A. A person whosoever present it to the banker
B. Only to the account person
C. Only to the account holder
D. None of the above

46. The Imperial Bank was converted to State Bank of India in the year:
A. 1950 B. 1955
C. 1956 D. 1957

47. The Unit Trust of India was launched in the year:
A. 1964 B. 1965
C. 1966 D. 1967

48. Treasury Bills are:
A. Taxes
B. Marketable financial bills of the central government
C. Acts
D. None of the above

49. CACS (Capital Adequacy, Asset Quality, Compliance and Systems) is a rating model used by RBI. This system is used by RBI to rate:
A. State run banks outside India
B. Foreign banks operating in India
C. Private banks in India
D. Co-operative banks

50. Name of the first Indian financial institution to be listed on the New York Stock Exchange (NYSE).
A. IFCI B. UTI
C. ICICI D. IDBI

ANSWERS

1	2	3	4	5	6	7	8	9	10
D	D	C	B	A	C	B	D	C	A
11	**12**	**13**	**14**	**15**	**16**	**17**	**18**	**19**	**20**
B	D	C	A	C	D	B	D	D	A
21	**22**	**23**	**24**	**25**	**26**	**27**	**28**	**29**	**30**
B	A	D	C	D	A	D	B	C	C
31	**32**	**33**	**34**	**35**	**36**	**37**	**38**	**39**	**40**
C	C	B	C	A	B	B	C	B	B
41	**42**	**43**	**44**	**45**	**46**	**47**	**48**	**49**	**50**
A	A	A	B	A	B	A	B	B	C

*****